Seniors' Housing and Care Facilities

Development, Business, and Operations

Third Edition, Volume I

Paul A. Gordon

Urban Land Institute

About ULI–the Urban Land Institute

ULI–the Urban Land Institute is a nonprofit education and research institute that is supported and directed by its members. Its mission is to provide responsible leadership in the use of land in order to enhance the total environment.

ULI sponsors educational programs and forums to encourage an open international exchange of ideas and sharing of experience; initiates research that anticipates emerging land use trends and issues and proposes creative solutions based on this research; provides advisory services; and publishes a wide variety of materials to disseminate information on land use and development.

Established in 1936, the Institute today has more than 14,000 members and associates from more than 50 countries representing the entire spectrum of the land use and development disciplines. They include developers, builders, property owners, investors, architects, public officials, planners, real estate brokers, appraisers, attorneys, engineers, financiers, academics, students, and librarians. ULI members contribute to higher standards of land use by sharing their knowledge and experience. The Institute has long been recognized as one of America's most respected and widely quoted sources of objective information on urban planning, growth, and development.

Richard M. Rosan
President

Project Staff

Rachelle L. Levitt
Senior Vice President, Policy and Practice

Gayle Berens
Vice President, Real Estate Development Practice
Project Director

Lloyd W. Bookout
Vice President, Programs
Project Director

Nancy H. Stewart
Director, Book Program

Carol E. Soble
Manuscript Editor

Eileen Hughes
Case Studies Editor

Helene Y. Redmond, HYR Graphics
Book Design/Layout
Volume I

Joanne Nanez
Design/Layout
Volume II, CD-ROM

Meg Batdorff
Cover Design

Diann Stanley-Austin
Associate Director of Publishing Operations

Maria-Rose Cain
Word Processor

About the Author

Paul A. Gordon is a partner with the San Francisco law firm of Hanson, Bridgett, Marcus, Vlahos & Rudy, where he has represented more than 200 companies involved with seniors' housing or long-term care since 1975. He is on the executive board of the American Seniors Housing Association and has served as chair of the Housing for the Elderly Committee of the American Bar Association's Real Property section, and as chair of the Legal Committee of the American Association of Homes and Services for the Aging. Gordon frequently addresses audiences at national conferences sponsored by universities, trade associations, and professional organizations, and has written, or been interviewed for, numerous magazine and newspaper articles around the country.

Recommended bibliographic listing:

Gordon, Paul A. *Seniors' Housing and Care Facilities: Development, Business, and Operations.*
Washington, D.C.: ULI–the Urban Land Institute, 1998.

ULI Catalog Number: S45
International Standard Book Number: 0-87420-820-3
Library of Congress Catalog Card Number: 98-87160

Preface

Ten years have passed since the original version of this book was first published under the title *Developing Retirement Facilities*. In that time, much has changed and much has remained the same.

The surge in development of congregate housing in the late 1980s has been replaced today by a boom in the construction of assisted-living facilities, but the prospect of overbuilding looms as large now as it did then. Regulation of seniors' housing and long-term care facilities has grown dramatically as evidenced by implementation of the OBRA 1987 standards and enforcement remedies for nursing facilities, adoption of the Americans with Disabilities Act and the Fair Housing Amendments Act, and the proliferation of state licensure laws governing assisted-living and continuing-care retirement communities. A myriad of court cases and administrative rulings affecting zoning, taxation, tax exemption, discrimination, and operations have shaped the ways in which communities are structured, developed, and managed. As government-supported financing dries up, private lenders are embracing the product with enthusiasm. Although the federal government has failed repeatedly to find a comprehensive solution for the funding of long-term care and housing for America's older population, private enterprise and charitable organizations have risen to the challenge by creating an array of innovative, attractive alternatives available on a private pay basis.

Nevertheless, most of the fundamental considerations and choices facing an organization involved in the planning, development, or operation of seniors' housing and care facilities have not changed over the years. The unique amalgam of housing, services, and care offered by this industry continues to require that those who approach it primarily from a real estate or health care perspective rethink many of their basic assumptions.

This book is designed to help those who are new to the field—as well as those very familiar with it—to understand and appreciate its complexities and to offer solutions to the problems they are most likely to encounter. This ULI edition represents a comprehensive revision of earlier versions and offers many features not previously available. Annual updating and the addition of many new documents has almost tripled the size of the book since 1988. By converting Volume II from a book format to a CD-ROM, this edition makes the documents and forms more manageable and accessible. Several case studies prepared under the guidance of ULI staff are an added bonus.

Many of the partners and associates at my law firm deserve credit for making this book possible, but Stephen Taber and Pamela Kaufmann require special mention for their diligent research, writing, and updating year after year.

Paul A. Gordon

In memory of my parents.

Contents
Volume I

Part II: Project Planning and Implementation   57

Chapter 8: Rentals **137**

Part IV: Tax-Exempt Operation   145

Chapter 9: Federal Tax Exemption **147**

Part V: Multiparty Ventures 201

Part VII: Regulation of Seniors' Housing and Care Facilities

327

Part IX: Operations   511

Part X: Case Studies   521

Table of Illustrations

Contents
Volume II: The CD-ROM

Chapter 6: Protective Provisions

Part II: Sample Documents

Chapter 7: Corporate Documents

Chapter 8: Development, Joint Venture, Lease Agreements

The Fountains at The Albemarle; Tarboro, North Carolina.

Part I
Elderly Markets and Development Responses

Sequoias/Portola Valley; Portola Valley, California.

1 American Elderly Profile

§1.1 Seniors' Housing Fever (Again)

Real estate developers, large and small, are falling all over each other as they scramble to get into this market. Only a few seem to really know what they are doing.

Anonymous lender
1987

The term "wei-ji" has become one of my favorite expressions lately for reasons that many in our industry can appreciate. Its Chinese definition combines the Mandarin character for "danger" with the character for "opportunity." I believe this succinctly captures the current business atmosphere.

James Eden, Marriott Corporation
December 1991

The development craze in assisted living may be the equivalent of the independent-living feeding frenzy of ten years ago.... Multifamily developers who enter this booming market without a basic understanding of what makes it different from other multifamily housing could be in for a day of reckoning.

Mark Ragsdale, TRI Financial
December 1996

In the latter half of the 1980s, the development of seniors' housing communities emerged suddenly as one of the most sought-after real estate investments. What engendered this surge of interest was the recognition of factors that had been evolving for many years. These included the greatly increasing numbers of elderly people in the United States and their growing wealth, the spiraling proportion of the population consisting of the very old and their soaring demand for health care, and the arrival of seniors as a consumer force with which the business world must reckon. Industries of all kinds prepared to do business with the aging population.[1]

Crystal ball gazers were quick to join the fracas. A 1985 study estimated that approximately 1 million to 1.3 million people over age 75 could afford the relatively costly life-care services then being enjoyed by only about 200,000.[2] It was predicted that by the year 2000, approximately 1 million new nursing beds, 812,000 new conventional retirement facility units, and 116,000 new continuing-care units would be needed to meet this demand.[3] One observer expected that $33 billion would be raised between 1985 and 1990 alone to develop more than 1,800 retirement communities with a care component.[4] Another expected 4,400 life-care and congregate developments to be created by 1995, resulting in a $46 billion industry.[5]

To be sure, there was a surge of activity. The number of retirement housing units owned or managed by respondents to one nationwide survey was reported to have increased by a healthy, but sober, 15 percent in 1987[6] and 13 percent in 1988.[7] According to another informal survey, architectural design projects for retirement housing increased by more than 39 percent from 1986 to 1987, with an increase in total retirement facility billings for architects of more than 98 percent during the same period.[8] Incredibly, 80 percent of all continuing-care projects are said to have been built between 1985 and 1988, even though the concept has been around for at least 30 years.[9]

Interest in the seniors' housing market remained high as the industry entered the 1990s. In a survey of 1,500 real estate firms nationwide, prepared by the now-defunct Laventhol & Horwath, more than 73 percent of residential developers stated a desire to create some form of seniors' housing during the following five years.[10] A similar survey of lenders revealed that more than 50 percent of financial institutions were willing to increase their involvement in the field, and an additional 30 percent expected their level of involvement to remain the same.[11]

In the early 1990s, enthusiasm quickly soured. HUD suspended and then terminated its Retirement Service Center program amid the scent of scandal. Empty congregate rental projects became the targets of vulture funds. Savings and loans and other lenders, many facing financial failure due to reckless lending practices, retreated from the marketplace. Large nursing home chains began to sell off major portions of their holdings. Some major retirement facility developers went into bankruptcy or were restructured. The housing resale slump of the early 1990s hampered sales, even for upscale projects already under construction. Danger—and opportunity—loomed large on the horizon.

In a short time, however, activity in retirement housing began to reemerge. The results of a 1993 nationwide survey showed an increase in retirement housing units of 12.7 percent since the 1992 survey.[12] One assessment of commercial real estate opportunities for the 1990s continued to place housing for the elderly and nursing homes ahead of low-income housing and recreational properties as the only areas of increased need in a climate of reduced overall demand.[13] Continuing-care communities were expected to double by the year 2000,[14] but they grew

even faster than predicted. In 1991, the American Association of Homes and Services for the Aging (AAHSA) estimated that the number of continuing-care retirement communities in operation was 700. By 1995, however, AAHSA estimated that this number had increased to 1,300.[15] All the demographic factors of senior population growth, length of retirement, wealth, and need for care continued to point to major growth in the industry. An unquantifiable but real phenomenon was increasing consumer awareness and acceptance of the product.[16]

By the mid-1990s, assisted living became the facility type nominated by investors and developers to lead the charge into the next millennium. It was projected that revenues of assisted-living facilities would increase from $12.5 billion in 1990 to $30 billion by 2000.[17] From 1991 to 1996, the number of publicly traded long-term-care companies was said to quadruple to nearly 40.[18] And a record number of applications for continuing-care retirement communities was reported in California.[19] The elderly market was identified as "the most immediately promising market niche today."[20] Overall, the industry is expected to grow from $86 billion in 1996 to $126 billion in 2005 and to $490 billion in 2030.[21]

The burgeoning masses of the nation's elderly are still there, and their numbers and needs are growing dramatically (*Modern Maturity* magazine boasted an astonishing 1992 circulation of over 22 million). Developers who are having trouble filling office buildings, selling condominium units, or finding another good shopping center site (or a retailer who can pay the rent) are driven to explore new territories and markets. Hospitals and other health providers, still stinging from cuts and restrictions in government reimbursement programs, are looking for ways to diversify their portfolios and to find more customers who can pay their charges in full. Insurance companies are actively pursuing long-term health care markets. Nonprofit groups and others already well established in the field are developing new projects and reassessing old policies to keep up with or ahead of the newcomers. Hoteliers, universities, pension funds . . . all are interested and active. Even the government is looking for less costly residential alternatives to the medical-model approach to elder care.

However, seniors' housing and care facilities are neither simple nor homogeneous products. A thorough understanding of the ranges of options available and their business and legal implications is necessary for developers, lenders, market analysts, lawyers, financial advisers, managers, marketing specialists, and others connected with the project. Eventually, seniors, with the help of their advisers, will gain a complete comprehension of these matters, for they may be embarking on one of the most important transitions of their lives. Public awareness of the importance of careful selection among retirement community options is also heightened by the increasing interest of the press in the industry (see, e.g., §2.4(g)). The project development team needs to know what it is doing, what options are not being pursued, and why.

To meet the needs of the elderly, those entering the seniors' housing field may have to create specialized programs and packages, beyond mere housing, that combine elements of the amenities and services of a hotel, the care available at a nursing facility, the social and recreational activities of a private club, the benefits of insurance coverage, and the shops, bank, post office, religious facilities, and other conveniences of a small town. The presence of many of these elements, and the way in which they are structured financially and legally, can have a profound impact on facility financing, income and taxation of income, marketability, control over operations, exposure to liability, government regulation, obligations to residents, and other factors that can spell success or failure for any project.

Similarly, lenders, lawyers, financial and marketing advisers, architects, and others involved in the development process should have a comprehensive knowledge extending beyond the particular project at hand. Often, the hybrid character of many seniors' properties can create discomfort among lenders and others familiar with more conventional real estate developments. While a healthy dose of caution is prudent in any undertaking as complex and expensive as seniors' properties, a blanket, reflexive reaction against sophisticated or innovative retirement projects may result in a triumph of simplicity over success and peace of mind instead of a piece of the market. Whether a complicated or straightforward program is chosen, it should be selected because a full spectrum of alternative structures has been considered, and the needs and wants of the consumer

identified and targeted. It is therefore important first to know something about who the elderly are.

§1.2 The Numbers of Older People

The number of people age 65 and over in the United States is increasing at a dramatic rate (about 6,000 turn 65 each day).[22] Bureau of the Census figures indicate that the number of Americans in that category increased from 19.9 million in 1970 to 31.5 million in 1990 and will increase to 39.3 million in 2010 and to 65.6 million in 2030. In the same time span, they will have grown from 9.8 percent of the total population to nearly 22 percent.[23] In 1995, the number of Americans age 65 and over equaled 33.5 million. From 1990 to 1995, the number of such people increased by 7 percent, compared with a 5 percent increase in the under-65 population.[24] Some observers have noted the increasing evidence of national interest in older people in all aspects of our culture, which will culminate with the maturation of the baby boom generation (the "pig in the python") early in the next century.[25] The National Institute on Aging and the University of Southern California have determined that there will be 86.8 million Americans age 65 and older and 23.5 million age 85 and older by 2040.[26] The figure for those 65 and older is nearly 20 million higher than, and for those 85 and older nearly double, the usual projections cited by the Bureau of the Census.

The aging of America is due not only to more people reaching maturity, but also to their remaining there longer. The old are getting older and staying healthier so that four- and even five-generation families are becoming more commonplace (see §1.3).[27] Especially in the upper age groups, most of the elderly are women. These facts about the ways in which the elderly are multiplying may have a significant bearing on how developers respond, or at least should respond, to this explosive growth.

It is the sheer numbers of people who can be categorized as elderly that constitute the major impetus for the surge in the development of retirement housing. However, several other factors point to the need for additional development of seniors' communities and for the development of particular types or styles of facilities to suit the needs of the consumer.

Figure 1.1 **Projected Growth in Population, by Age Group: 1980–2050**

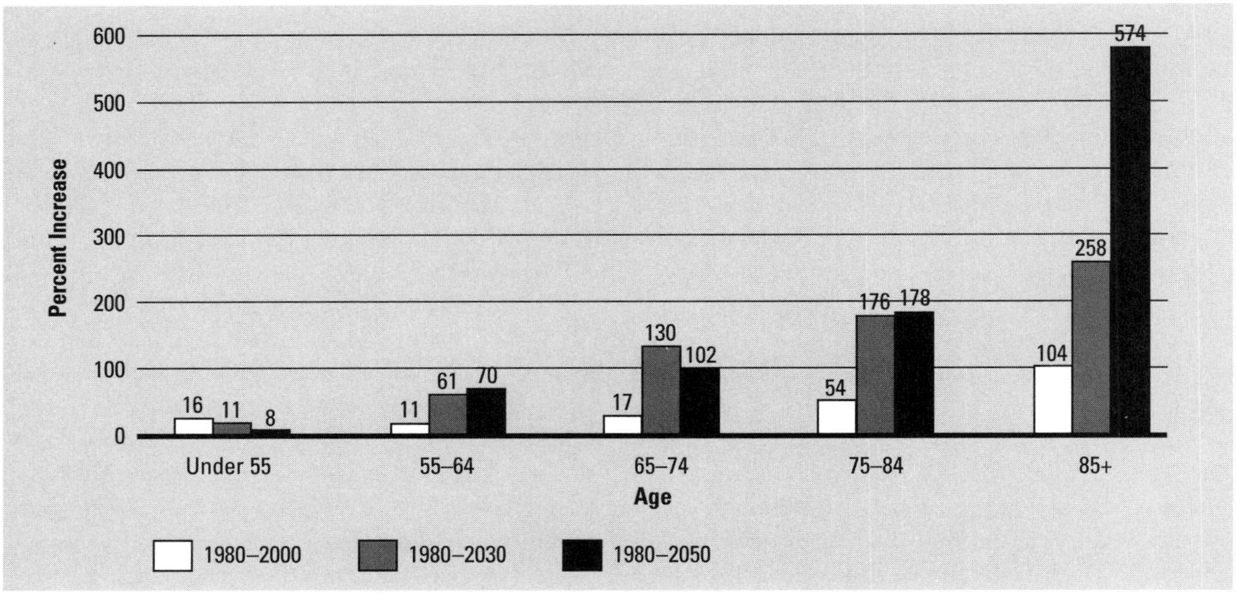

Source: Bureau of the Census, "Projections of the Population of the United States, by Age, Sex, and Race: 1988 to 2080," by Gregory Spencer, *Current Population Reports,* Series P–25, No. 1018, January 1989.

§1.3 Ages and Lifestyles of the Elderly

Because of the great strides made in this century in extending the life spans and life quality of Americans, the elderly can no longer be lumped together as a uniform group. When Prussia's Bismarck decreed in the 19th century that citizens over age 65 would receive state pensions, the average life expectancy was so low that the promise amounted to little more than a political stratagem. Since 1900, when the average age at death was 49 years, life spans have climbed by 50 percent to an average of about 75 years.[28] This leap in longevity is probably unparalleled in our evolution.

Remarkable advances in medical science, and perhaps the increasing health consciousness of the population, have helped make the fastest-growing age group in the country, for both men and women, the 85-and-over population.[29] In 1980, there were about 25.5 million people over the age of 65, 2.2 million of whom (8.6 percent) were over 85. By 2050, approximately 68.5 million will be over 65, and about

15.2 million of these (22 percent) will be over 85.[30] While the fast-growing over-65 population will more than double, the number of persons over the age of 85 is expected to multiply by nearly seven times. Figure 1.1 shows the growth of the 85+ population compared with other age groups. Since 1960, the life expectancy of an 85-year-old person has increased by 24 percent. That figure is expected to increase by another 44 percent by 2040.[31] Other studies yield comparable results. From 1980 to 1990, the 85+ population increased by almost 38 percent. In 1990, one in 35 Americans was 80 years old or older; by 2050, it is expected that one in 12 Americans will be 80 years old or older.[32] Statistics from the Agency for Health Policy and Research reveal that the number of seniors age 85 and older will increase by 42 percent between 1990 and 2000 and will double between 1990 and 2020.[33]

These oldest of the old consist overwhelmingly of women. In a federal government study of nursing and related care (personal care) facilities, it was found that the approximate ratio of resident women to men varied according to age as follows:

Under 65 years	1 to 1
65–74 years	1.5 to 1
75–84 years	3 to 1
85 and over	4 to 1[34]

Women outlive men, and as a consequence, older women often live alone. In 1980, about three out of five women over 65 were single, divorced, or widowed compared with slightly over one out of four men in the same age group.[35] At the same time, female life expectancy at age 65 was 18.7 years, whereas males could expect to live only about 14.3 more years.[36] In 1995, the ratio of older women to older men (over 65) was 145 to 100. This ratio increased with age. For people age 85 and older, there were 257 women to every 100 men.[37] Elderly men and women also tend to develop different types of diseases. Elderly women tend to develop long-term chronic disabling diseases, and elderly men tend to develop short-term fatal diseases.[38]

Of course, age frequently has a bearing on functional ability. For ease of reference, some commentators have divided seniors into the following subcategories based on their levels of independence and energy:

Go-Go
Slow-Go
No-Go[39]

These generalizations do not necessarily correlate directly with age, however. Some of the very old (e.g., George Burns and Bob Hope) still have been considered Go-Gos while some 65-year-olds unfortunately have become No-Gos due to disease or disability.

Other approaches link age broadly with general functional independence as follows:[40]

"Empty nesters" (preretirement)	55–64	Active
Young-old	65–74	Independent
Old	75–83	Semi-independent
Very old	84+	Dependent

More recently, some commentators have taken the position that the elderly are as diverse and resistant to stereotyping as any other group in society.

Despite the prolonged life spans of persons over age 65, older people continue to retire from employment long before they are forced to do so by reason of functional impairment. In 1950, 46 percent of men over 65 were still in the workforce, but by 1989 *only 17 percent* were in the labor force.[41] The average male is expected to spend around 20 percent of his lifetime in retirement.[42] This truly amazing trend toward early retirement reflects not only a desire but also a growing ability among older people to change lifestyles late in life.

Figure 1.2 Percentage of Persons Needing Assistance with Everyday Activities, by Age Group: 1986

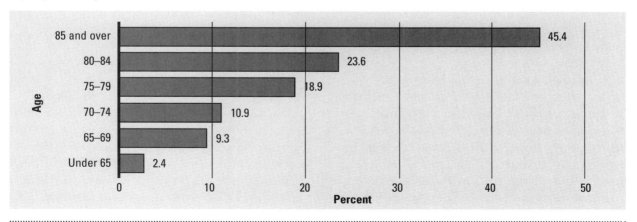

Source: Bureau of the Census, "The Need for Personal Assistance with Everyday Activities: Recipients and Caregivers," *Current Population Reports,* Series P–70, No. 19, Table B, 1990.

The age and functional ability of a given segment of the senior population often dictate the particular type of seniors' property in which they live and the types of services they want or need. One survey reports that although only 9.9 percent of the 65-through-69 age group had difficulty with one or more daily living activities, such functional limitations existed in nearly 20 percent of those between the ages of 75 and 79 and in more than 56 percent of those 85 and over.[43] Figure 1.2 shows, for various age groups, the percentage of elderly persons who need assistance with activities of daily living. One study indicated that 34 percent of elderly women and 22 percent of elderly men were functionally dependent.[44] On the other hand, the younger old—age 50 to 65—have been credited with buying more warm-up suits per capita than any other age category.[45] This younger, and probably more affluent, group has been affectionately labeled Grumpies (Gray-Haired Urban Mature Professionals). (See §1.6 for further discussion of the need for care.)

The character of retirement facilities can vary widely—from retirement subdivisions or apartments offering essentially only age-restricted housing, to nursing homes, where the housing element is incidental to health care (see §2.2). One mid-1980s estimate placed the average entry age for residents at the various types of seniors' communities as follows:

Retirement village	58
Congregate housing	62
Life care/continuing care	77
Nursing facility	83[46]

However, a national survey of over 71,000 retirement housing units published in 1993 indicated a significant similarity in the characteristics of residents of congregate housing, assisted-living facilities, and continuing-care retirement communities, including an average age for all three models of about 82 years. Some of the possible reasons for this increased similarity are that facilities have increased their supportive services, minimizing resident turnover; seniors' housing development has increased as an alternative to more institutional living environments for elderly persons who do not require skilled-nursing care; and disability laws such as the Fair Housing Amendments Act of 1988 and the Americans with Disabilities Act have increased the housing rights of disabled individuals so that facilities cannot screen residents to the same extent as before.[47] Whatever the average age at admission or after several years of operation, it is a sure bet that residents will "age in place" and that their need for services and care will increase.

Much of the focus of this book is on the middle ranges of the spectrum of independent living to totally dependent care. It is in this increasingly vast middle ground where combinations of independent housing, convenience services, assisted living, or health care may exist in a single community.

§1.4 Where the Aging Live

The elderly reflect society in general, with all its diversity and many of its shared attributes. Accordingly, more than half of all Americans age 65 or older live in the otherwise populous states of California, New York, Florida, Pennsylvania, Texas, Illinois, Ohio, Michigan, and New Jersey.[48] In 1990, California had 3.1 million residents age 65 or older, the largest number in the United States. However, Florida had the largest proportion of elderly residents, at 18 percent.[49] On the other hand, the highest concentrations of elderly often appear in many of the less-populated states (such as in the Midwest), where seniors remain after younger people have left (see Figure 1.3).[50] Growth of the elderly in the recent past has occurred mostly in the West and Southeast (see Figure 1.4), where it is projected to grow over the next decade or more (see Figures 1.5 and 1.6). California's over-65 population is expected to increase by 52 percent from 1989 to 2010.[51] In the past decade, for the first time, more elderly live in suburbs than in major cities.[52]

While there are many seniors in the Sunbelt states, such as Florida, Arizona, and California, most industry sources seem to agree that the retirement housing market is nationwide. In fact, some elderly countermigration from the Sunbelt to states of origin has been noted.[53] Fewer than one in ten of all retired persons is reported to move more than 200 miles from the area where he or she lived before retirement.[54] In continuing-care facilities, the primary market area, from which 60 to 75 percent of the

Figure 1.3 **People 65+ as Percentage of Total Population: 1995**

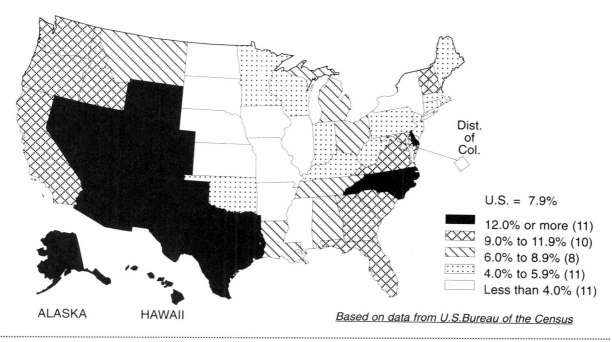

Dist. of Col.

U.S. = 7.9%

- ⬛ 12.0% or more (11)
- ▨ 9.0% to 11.9% (10)
- ▧ 6.0% to 8.9% (8)
- ⦙ 4.0% to 5.9% (11)
- ☐ Less than 4.0% (11)

ALASKA   HAWAII

Based on data from U.S.Bureau of the Census

Source: American Association of Retired Persons, U.S. Administration on Aging, *"A Profile of Older Americans,"* 1996.

Figure 1.4 **Percent Increase in Population 65+: 1990–1995**

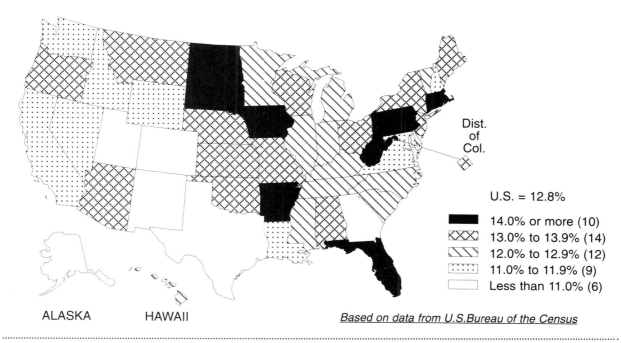

Dist. of Col.

U.S. = 12.8%

- ⬛ 14.0% or more (10)
- ▨ 13.0% to 13.9% (14)
- ▧ 12.0% to 12.9% (12)
- ⦙ 11.0% to 11.9% (9)
- ☐ Less than 11.0% (6)

ALASKA   HAWAII

Based on data from U.S.Bureau of the Census

Source: American Association of Retired Persons, U.S. Administration on Aging, *"A Profile of Older Americans,"* 1996.

Figure 1.5 **Percent Change in Population 65 Years and Over, by State: 1990–2010**

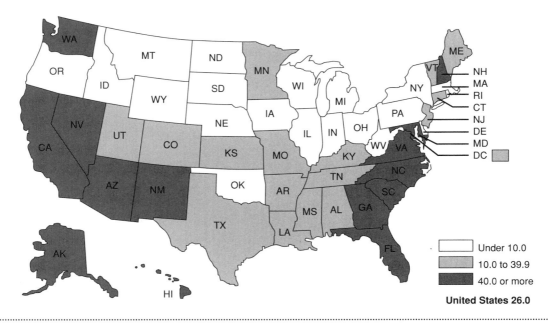

☐	Under 10.0
▨	10.0 to 39.9
■	40.0 or more

United States 26.0

Source: Bureau of the Census, 1990 from 1990 Census of Population and Housing, Summary Tape File 1A; "Projections of the Population of the United States, by Age, Sex, and Race: 1989 to 2010," *Current Population Reports,* Series P–25, No. 1053, 1990.

Figure 1.6 **Percent Change in Population 85 Years and Over, by State: 1990–2010**

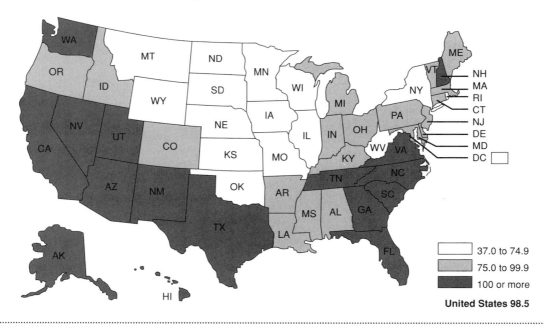

☐	37.0 to 74.9
▨	75.0 to 99.9
■	100 or more

United States 98.5

Source: Bureau of the Census, 1990 from 1990 Census of Population and Housing, Summary Tape File 1A; "Projections of the Population of the United States, by Age, Sex, and Race: 1989 to 2010," *Current Population Reports,* Series P–25, No. 1053, 1990.

residents are expected to be drawn, may have a radius of only 25 to 50 miles.[55] In some urban areas, an even smaller radius may be applicable. For the most part, therefore, retirement communities must appeal to people who already live in the vicinity of a facility.

The vast majority of the elderly remain in their own homes rather than make a planned transition to a seniors' community.[56] However, many hold out for so long in their homes that when they are forced to move to a supportive environment, the transition can be abrupt and traumatic (see §1.6). While only about 5 percent of the elderly live in nursing facilities, an estimated 43 percent of those age 65 in 1990 will use a nursing home sometime in their remaining years.[57] Nearly half of older Americans have lived in their current residences for longer than 20 years, and only 21 percent living in single-family homes have moved in the past ten years.[58] Even among people age 85 and over, a remarkable 54.3 percent continue to live in their own homes.[59] A 1992 survey by the American Association of Retired Persons (AARP) indicated that the percentage of individuals 55 years of age and older who prefer never to leave their current home increased from 78 percent in 1986 to 85 percent in 1992.[60]

A consumer survey by the Joint Center for Housing Studies reported that about 20 percent of households over the age of 55 move from their homes during a five-year-period, which is about half the rate of younger homeowners. Only 5 percent of that age group said that they planned to move during the next five years, but of those over age 65, only 1 percent had such plans.[61] Nevertheless, in one 1988 survey, seniors were found to be the leading consumers of multiunit attached housing.[62]

One study indicated that only about 5 percent of respondents lived in a planned retirement community, but 27 percent lived in a neighborhood or building where a majority of the people are 60 or older (a "NORC," or naturally occurring retirement community).[63] Interestingly, 32 percent of the respondents indicated they would consider a move to an apartment providing meals, housekeeping, transportation, and activities . . . nearly double the rate of interest in the second most popular alternative living arrangement (moving in with a relative).[64]

§1.5 Senior Wealth and Homeownership

By many standards, the older population of the United States is one of the wealthiest segments of our society. In the mid-1980s, it was noted that about 70 percent of the net worth of all American households ($7 trillion) was controlled by people over 50, and they were spending more and saving less than ever before.[65] The elderly are doing increasingly well when compared with the rest of the populace (see Figure 1.7). In 1985, households with heads age 65 or older constituted only 8 percent of the $25,000-and-over income bracket, but that share was expected to increase to 16 percent by 1995, 29 percent by 2005, and 34 percent by 2015.[66] One survey found that 38 percent of families headed by a person at least 65 years of age earned incomes of over $35,000.[67] And the median net worth of the general populace including the elderly ($35,752) is less than half that of elderly households alone $73,471).[68] In fact, more than 25 percent of elderly households are estimated to have a net worth between $100,000 and $250,000.[69] More than 14 percent had net worths in excess of $250,000.[70] Although once considered an economically disadvantaged group, the elderly have been declared to have achieved, on the whole, financial parity with the rest of the population.[71]

Americans age 65 and over also had a slightly lower percentage of the poor among their numbers in 1995 (10.5 percent) than those under 65 (11.4 percent).[72] While the elderly make up 21 percent of the nation's households, they represent about 30 percent of those receiving government housing subsidies and Medicaid payments.[73] Indeed, many large pockets of poverty exist among the elderly. Poverty statistics from 1995 indicate that although the elderly in general compared favorably with others, minority group elderly fared poorly.[74]

Group	Percent at Poverty Level
All ages 18–64	11.4
All 65 and over	10.5
Blacks 65 and over	25
Hispanics 65 and over	24
Whites 65 and over	9

Figure 1.7 **Median Net Worth, by Age Group: 1988**

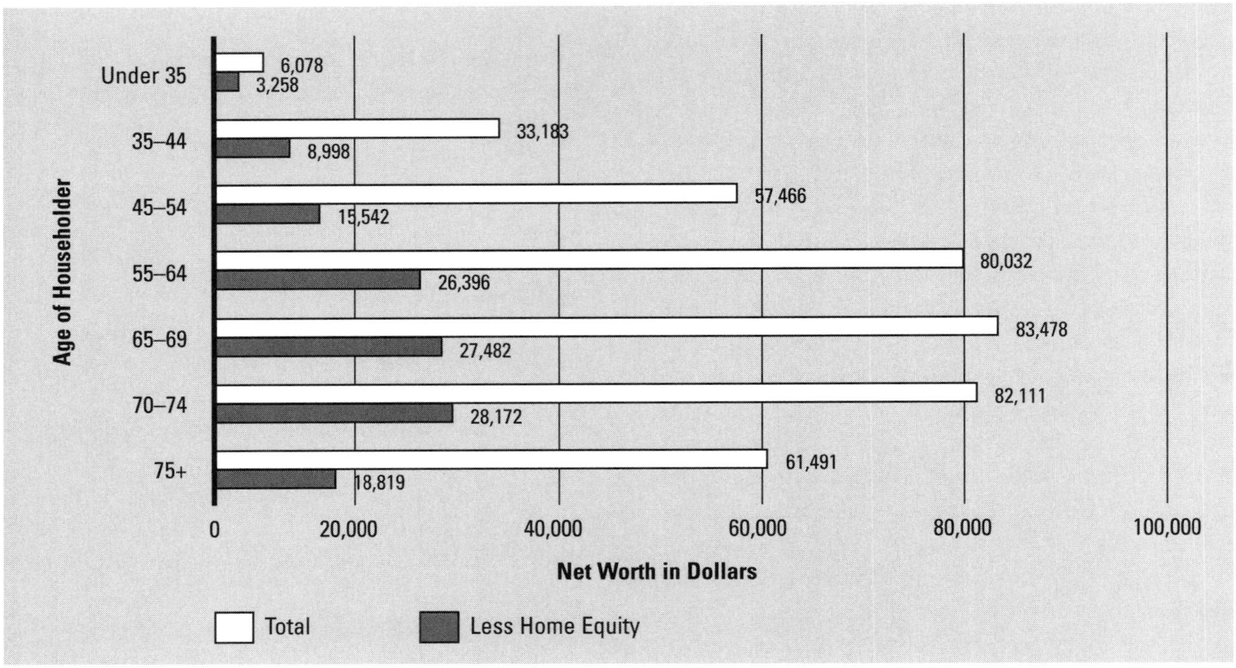

Bar chart showing median net worth (Total and Less Home Equity) by age of householder:

Age of Householder	Total	Less Home Equity
Under 35	6,078	3,258
35–44	33,183	8,998
45–54	57,466	15,542
55–64	80,032	26,396
65–69	83,478	27,482
70–74	82,111	28,172
75+	61,491	18,819

Net Worth in Dollars (axis: 0, 20,000, 40,000, 60,000, 80,000, 100,000)

Source: Bureau of the Census, "Household Wealth and Asset Ownership, 1988," *Current Population Reports,* Series P–70, No. 22, December 1990.

Women, who make up the bulk of the very old population (see §1.3), bear a disproportionate share of the burden of poverty. Though constituting 59.1 percent of the total elderly population, women represented 71.1 percent of the elderly poor.[75] This phenomenon is probably because women generally outlive men and, as single persons, have fewer sources of income.[76] Statistics from 1989 show that while 11.4 percent of all elderly are poor, 14 percent of elderly women, 18.5 percent of people age 85 and over, 30.8 percent of elderly blacks, and 60.6 percent of elderly black women living alone are poor.[77]

Perhaps even more significant than cash income is the increasing hold that the elderly population has on this country's assets. Close to 80 percent of the deposits in banks and savings and loan institutions belong to people age 55 or older.[78] Indeed, much of the income of senior citizens is generated from assets as opposed to earnings. However, earnings rates can swing wildly, as experienced by many whose mature 8 or 9 percent certificates of deposit could be renewed in the early 1990s at only about half the interest rate. According to one nationwide survey, elderly income comes from the following sources:

Source	Percent
Social Security	38
Assets	25
Earnings	17
Pensions	18
Other	3[79]

In addition, the elderly, perhaps more than any other segment of the population, have benefited from the dramatic upswing in real estate values that took place during the double-digit inflation years of the 1970s and the real estate boom years of the 1980s. Though in the meantime there has been some stabilization or even decline in value, for many seniors, their homes have undergone astonishing appreciation in value over the past 30 or more years of ownership. When they sell their homes to move into a seniors' community or some other form of group-living arrangement, release of the locked-up equity, $500,000 of which is tax free (see §7.1(d)(1)), may make their often-modest incomes pale by comparison.

The sale by a retired person of his or her principal residence creates perhaps the greatest single financial investment opportunity in that person's lifetime. Approximately 79 percent of elderly households own their own homes compared with 63 percent of under-65 households.[80] In 1993, the median value of older Americans' homes was $76,200, and about 81 percent were owned free of any mortgage.[81] Even among the elderly poor, 65 percent are homeowners, and 22 percent have over $50,000 in net home equity.[82] According to one estimate, the value of locked-up home equity controlled by people over 65 is approximately $700 billion.[83] In most instances, there is no other time in life when so much asset value can be liquidated and be available for future investment or use.[84]

There are doubtless many entrepreneurs and others in the marketplace who want the opportunity to assist retired persons in deciding how to dispose of the wealth they have accumulated over a lifetime, and investment in a retirement community and lifestyle can be one of the most important and attractive options facing the elderly person. One imaginative observer, describing the "old rush" that has possessed many in and out of the real estate development field, mused:

> Like Europeans stumbling across the New World, mass marketers are belatedly realizing that "mature" households—the vogue terms for households headed by people over 50—control a disproportionate share of the nation's buying power and most of its wealth, and are becoming more prone than ever to spend their formidable resources.[85]

Some developers eager to mine the wealth of the elderly are expecting a return on investment of 20 percent or more, largely from providing services to residents.[86] Because of the potential for unscrupulous, or well-meaning but incompetent, developers to get their hands on these large amounts of dollars without giving full value in return, a rapidly growing number of states have adopted statutes that extensively regulate seniors' housing transactions in which large sums of money are received from elderly persons in exchange for promises to provide housing, services, and health care in the future (see Chapter 21 for a detailed discussion of these laws).

§1.6 The Need for Services, Care, and Financial Security

Popular misconceptions about the elderly include that they are poor, frail, sick, or bordering on mental incompetence. While older people certainly have a greater need for care than other population segments,[87] the aging in fact comprise a cross section of the entire spectrum of American life and culture. Therefore, a given retirement housing model cannot serve and satisfy all needs, and there is a market for projects ranging from pure independent housing with extensive recreational amenities to intensive custodial and health care. Nevertheless, many elderly are moving through a phase in their lives that gives them some common desires and needs. In general, these common needs point to the provision of varying levels of services and activities beyond mere housing.[88]

Because many older people have retired from their employment, with children long since grown and out of the household, most have a good deal of unoccupied time, and retirement communities may serve as a focal point for social and recreational activities. As a further consequence of retirement, elderly persons often live on fixed incomes earned from financial holdings, pensions, annuities, or other investments. Accordingly, retirees often look for a stable living situation with predictable or controlled costs for future contingencies. To some, housekeeping, dining, and other similar services may be a convenience that adds to the enjoyment of retirement living. For others, such services may be necessary because of physical limitations caused by advancing age.

Not all seniors need health care or personal care, but all face the growing possibility that an illness or disability will deplete their assets and disrupt their lives. As noted, only about 5 percent of the elderly live in nursing facilities. However, 23 percent of those over age 85 live in one, along with 6 percent of those age 75 to 84, and only 1 percent of those age 65 to 74.[89] Nearly 50 percent of people age 75 or older have significant limitations with respect to walking, climbing, or bending (see also §1.3).[90]

According to one study,[91] the elderly have the following needs for daily assistance ("assisted living" or "personal care") or nursing care:

Age Group	Need for Nursing Care (percent)	Need for Daily Assistance (percent)
65-74	1	6.7
75-84	7	15.7
85 and over	20	39.3

It has been estimated that the needs of the elderly for assistance with "activities of daily living" (ADLs) (physical maintenance or functioning such as bathing, dressing, eating, transferring from a bed or chair, or using the toilet) and for assistance with "instrumental activities of daily living" (IADLs) (social or household functioning such as housework, preparing meals, money management, shopping, or telephone use) is as follows:[92]

Age Group	Activities of Daily Living (percent)	Instrumental Activities of Daily Living (percent)
65-74	17	21
75-84	28	33
85 and over	49	55

Of residents in nursing homes, 63 percent suffer from disorientation or memory impairment, and 47 percent from senile dementia or chronic organic brain syndrome.[93] Half the population age 85 and over develops Alzheimer's disease or some form of dementia.[94]

It has been reported that seniors between the ages of 65 and 69 have a 5 percent chance of entering a nursing facility within the next five years and a 43 percent chance of entering such a facility in their lifetimes.[95]

In a nationwide random survey of the elderly's preferences for seniors' housing services, approximately 50 percent believed that they must have access to nursing home care, even though more than 80 percent of those with incomes over $25,000 believed they were presently in excellent health.[96] Sixty-six percent of survey respondents indicated they felt a retirement facility with a nurse on call

24 hours per day was a "must," and 47 percent stated they would want health services delivered in their residences.[97]

It has been estimated that elderly nursing home use and expenditures will grow dramatically in the next 30 years:[98]

	1986–1990	2001–2005	2016–2020
Average 65 and older nursing home population (in millions)	2.285	3.272	4.021
Total expenditures (in billions of 1987 dollars)	32.982	60.901	98.117

Similarly, the need for new long-term-care beds is predicted to be as follows (in thousands of beds):[99]

	2000	2005	2010	2015	2020
Nursing home/ board and care	278	305	304	154	155
Assisted-living facilities	132	150	94	141	75

The absence of services, personal assistance, and health care can also create problems of transition for retirement housing operators. Retirement communities built according to the Sun City model, which have few or no personal services to supplement housing, may face major obstacles when their populations age and begin to need or want more assistance with daily tasks or require health care.[100] Both facility owners and residents may unwittingly conspire in a scenario where a resident who "ages in place" deteriorates to a crisis point (see below). In addition, a housing development with a population of increasingly dependent people eventually may find itself operating illegally as an unlicensed assisted-living facility (see §20.4). Even if the facility faces up to the problem of dependent residents, it may be difficult to place residents in care facilities or forcibly to transfer those who resist. In recent times, some seniors' housing facilities offering services, but not assisted living or health care, have had difficulty attracting residents (see §2.4(g)). Some experts believe that continuing-care facilities, which bring in residents while they are independent and then provide varying levels of services and care as needed, offer an ideal model for elderly housing in that they can serve all the person's progressive needs in a single setting.[101]

One of the greatest wild cards in the future of a retired person is the potential cost of health care. Although government programs such as Medicare and Medicaid provide a safety net for certain types of catastrophic medical needs (see discussion in §26.1), the expenses associated with medical care remain one of the greatest threats to an elderly person's long-term financial security. On average, nursing home care costs in 1985 ranged from $20,000 to $25,000 per year.[102] Nonetheless, costs can vary widely depending on location; for example, nursing care could cost well over $100 per day in certain parts of the country. In the 1990s, the average is more on the order of $30,000 per year.[103] Older people may sometimes require months or even years of sustained nursing care, virtually none of which is covered by the Medicare program. To lessen the resident's risk of financial adversity, seniors' facilities can offer health plans, insurance programs, or the availability of health care on a fixed-cost basis or for a prepayment or some other more predictable method of payment (see Chapters 21 and 27 for a full discussion of financial security plans).

In 1994, the Public Policy Institute of the American Association of Retired Persons and the Health Policy Center of the Urban Institute produced a report regarding health care costs for older Americans. This report includes the following findings:

■ Americans over age 65 are expected to spend four times more out of pocket for health care costs than those who are under age 65.
■ Out-of-pocket health care costs for Americans over age 65 increased by an average 112 percent between 1987 and 1994.
■ Out-of-pocket health care costs for Americans over age 65 were projected to consume 23 percent of their household incomes in 1994.[104]

Although many elderly people do not wish to face the prospect of dependence, a long-term illness, or the possibility of debilitating frailty or mental impairment, all people share a substantial risk that such an affliction will befall them. Many seniors in single-family homes—often widows or widowers living alone—will hold out against advancing disability until a crisis takes place, such as the well-known and widely ridiculed "I've fallen and I can't get up!" scenario depicted in a television commercial for an

emergency call system. An all-too-typical pattern at that point is that the older person's children must hurriedly find a nursing home, which is sometimes many miles from the person's residence, where they can place their dependent parent. Often, these decisions made in haste do not result in the best placement for the elderly person.

Sometimes, the nursing facility is geared toward a type of patient who is in need of a more intense and sustained level of medical care than that required by the older person. In 1977, the Congressional Budget Office determined that inappropriately high levels of care were being received by 10 to 20 percent of skilled-nursing patients and 20 to 40 percent of intermediate-care patients.[105] More recent estimates concluded that between 10 and 30 percent of nursing home patients are there because they could not obtain adequate outpatient services.[106] The growth of the assisted-living industry in the 1990s can in part be attributed to such findings.

The nursing facility can be cold and institutional in character and may look more like a hospital than a place to live. Because of bed shortages, available facilities may be too far away to make visiting convenient for relatives. Facilities with immediate vacancies also may offer less desirable services and amenities or even suffer from quality-of-care problems when compared with projects that have waiting lists. Nursing shortages and other scarce resources may cause facilities to shun "heavy-care" (e.g., intravenous therapy) patients in lieu of easier-to-care-for residents. It is difficult enough for the elderly person to cope suddenly with the physical and emotional burdens of dependence, but to have to endure at the same time a move away from home, family, and friends into an unfamiliar environment inhabited by strangers seems, and is, an unnecessary torment.

A seniors' community that integrates housing, personal care, health care, and assistance with activities that may be difficult for a feeble person to perform can accommodate a person in the transition from independent to dependent status without giving rise to the trauma that so often accompanies a move from a private residence to a nursing facility. However, a well-planned facility designed to take a person through this transition must emphasize the independent aspects of the program to encourage a positive outlook among residents and an atmosphere that attracts new prospects.[107] One commentator[108] observed that elderly consumers feel the same about having long-term nursing facilities in retirement homes as about having airbags in automobiles: The consumer would prefer that such amenities be kept out of sight, but when needed, they should pop into place instantly.

Seniors' facilities can offer a broad array of amenities, services, and payment mechanisms in varying combinations. While some properties may not serve all the needs of the older person, all are designed to respond to the common interests and desires of a particular segment of the elderly population to whom they are marketed. They key in developing seniors' facilities is, first, to identify the market segment to which the program will be directed and, second, to create a package of physical facilities, services, and payment structures to attract and satisfy the needs of the consumer.

Notes

1. *See, e.g.,* Hartman, C., "Gearing up for Business in the '90s: Helping Companies Sell to an Aging Population," *Inc.,* June 1988 (cover story), 58.

2. ICF, Inc., "Private Financing of Long Term Care: Current Methods and Services," Phase I Final Report, U.S. Department of Health and Human Resources (1985), 74.

3. American Association of Homes for the Aging, *Market and Economic Feasibility Studies—Guidelines for Continuing Care Retirement Facilities,* 2, citing *Healthcare Financial Management,* V. 4 (Apr. 1984).

4. Harney, K., "Facilities for the Elderly Booming," *Washington Post,* Mar. 9, 1985, quoting Aaron Rose, then of Laventhol & Horwath.

5. Lublin, J., "Costly Retirement-Home Market Booms, Raising Concern for Aged," *Wall Street Journal,* Oct. 22, 1986, 35. *See also* Graham, J., "Demand Should Foster Rapid Growth in Retirement Center Industry," *Modern Healthcare,* Apr. 24, 1987.

6. Thomas, M., "Retirement Housing Industry Burgeoning," *Contemporary Long Term Care,* July 1988, 27.

7. Thomas, M., "Retirement Housing Industry Entering Consolidation Phase," *Contemporary Long Term Care,* July 1989, 65.

8. "LTC Business Booming for Architectural Firms," *Contemporary Long Term Care,* June 1988, 86.

9. *See* "Capital Crunch Restrains CCRC Development," *Modern Health Care,* May 20, 1991, 92, reporting on an American Association of Homes for the Aging survey.

10. Gamzon, M., "State of the Seniors Housing Industry: Insights for the 90's," *Multi-Housing News,* May 1990.

11. *Ibid.*

12. "The Top 50 Retirement Housing Communities," *Contemporary Long Term Care,* June 1993, 35.

13. Lachman, M., "Outlook for U.S. Commercial Real Estate in the 90s," *The Guarantor,* Jan./Feb. 1991, 3. *See also,* Gamzon, M., "Profit Potential for Senior Housing Points Up Both Near and Long Term," *National Real Estate Investor,* Feb. 1992, 86.

14. "Before You Settle on a Retirement Community," *Business Week,* May 20, 1991, 150.

15. Pallarito, K., "CCRC Industry Growth Steady," *Modern Healthcare,* May 22, 1995, 78.

16. Eden, J., "Retirement Communities Offer Something for Everyone," *Spectrum,* Dec. 1991, 28. *See also,* Neuman, E., "Golden Years without a Care," *Insight,* Jan. 13, 1992, regarding the increasing popularity of CCRCs.

17. Prins, R., "'Seniors Housing' by Whatever Name, It's Big Business," *Real Estate Forum,* Sept. 1994, 52.

18. Johnson, B., "Seniors Housing Comes of Age at NIC '96," *National Real Estate Investor,* Dec. 1996.

19. Brass, K., "California Builders Find a New Market," *New York Times,* Sept. 10, 1995, 30.

20. Michaux, R., and J. Kempner, "Apartments Taking on a Growth Mode," *Urban Land,* Nov. 1995, 33. *See also,* Hoffman, C., "Seniors Housing Hits Its Prime," *Real Estate Forum,* Aug. 1997, 52.

21. *Senior Housing and Care Report,* Apr. 28, 1997, quoting a National Investment Conference/Price Waterhouse study.

22. *See* Gamzon, note 13 *above.* Elderly growth is even greater in countries such as Japan (three times the U.S. rate). Japan is rapidly developing senior centers and encouraging development of facilities in other countries for Japanese elderly's use. *See* "Elderly Japanese May Be Encouraged to Retire Abroad," *San Francisco Chronicle* (UPI), Aug. 8, 1986; "Japan Is Turning Gray Fast," *San Francisco Examiner,* Sept. 14, 1986, A-16; "Japan to Export Seniors," *San Francisco Examiner,* Oct. 26, 1986, A-23.

23. *Aging America: Trends and Projections,* 1991 ed., U.S. Senate Special Committee on Aging, Table 1-2; *See also, generally,* Warner, "Demographics and Housing," *Housing for a Maturing Population,* Urban Land Institute, 1983.

24. American Association of Retired Persons and Administration on Aging, *A Profile of Older Americans,* 1996.

25. *See* Dychtwald, K., ed., *Wellness and Health Promotion for the Elderly.* (Rockville, MD: Aspen Publications, 1986), 1–17. *See also,* Schless, D., "Seniors Explosion Hasn't Yet Begun," *National Real Estate Investor,* Sept. 1991.

26. *Older Americans Report,* Oct. 21, 1988, 415.

27. *See* Otten, A., "The Oldest Old," *Wall Street Journal,* Jul. 30, 1984.

28. *Ibid.*

29. *Ibid. See also Aging America,* note 23 *above,* at 10–13.

30. *Aging America,* note 23 *above,* Table 1–2; and *see generally Older American Report,* June 26, 1987, 6; and "Who's Taking Care of Our Parents?" *Newsweek,* May 6, 1985, 61.

31. Holbrook, A., and W. Quinley, "Personal Care Facilities: Opportunity for Future Development," *NASLI News,* Dec. 1987, 5.

32. Taeuber, C., "65 Plus in America," *Current Population Reports Series,* Bureau of the Census, 23, 178 [hereafter Taeuber]. 17.

33. Prins, R., "'Seniors Housing' By Whatever Name, It's Big Business," *Real Estate Forum,* Sept. 1994, 53.

34. Sirrocco, A., "An Overview of the 1982 National Master Facility Inventory Survey of Nursing and Related Care Homes," *Advancedata,* National Center for Health Statistics, Sept. 20, 1985.

35. Feldblum, C., "Home Health Care for the Elderly: Programs, Problems, and Potentials," *Harvard Journal on Legislation,* 22:193 (1985).

36. *Ibid.*

37. American Association of Retired Persons and Administration on Aging, *A Profile of Older Americans,* 1996.

38. Taeuber at 23, 178.

39. Attributed to Herb Shore, Dallas Home for Jewish Aged.

40. This is a composite of mid-1980s approaches used by such commentators as Gerald Glaser, then of Oxford Development, and James Sherman, then of Laventhol & Horwath.

41. *Aging America,* note 23 *above,* at 94.

42. *Aging America: Trends and Projections,* 1985–86 ed., U.S. Senate Special Committee on Aging, at 71.

43. *See Aging America,* note 23 *above,* at 154.

44. Taeuber at 23, 178.

45. Petre, P., "Marketers Mine for Gold in the Old," *Fortune,* Mar. 31, 1986, 70.

46. *See* Allen, Grubb, & Ellis, *Investor Outlook,* 6, No. 2 (2d quarter 1986), 4. Note, however, that opinions vary considerably on this topic. *See* Todd, L., "Rental Retirement Housing," *The Stanger Report,* Sept. 1986, 2, indicating that rental units attract more older persons than continuing care, and *The Senior Living Industry 1986,* Laventhol & Horwath, showing an average age of 79 years for both rental and entrance fee facilities.

47. "The State of the Seniors Housing Industry," American Seniors Housing Association and Coopers & Lybrand, 1993; *Seniors Housing Update,* American Seniors Housing Association, June 1993.

48. *See Aging America,* note 23 *above,* at 27.

49. Taeuber at 23, 178.

50. *Id.* at 35.

51. *Id.* at 31.

52. *Id.* at 34.

53. *Id.* at 35.

54. *See* Allen, note 46 *above.*

55. *Market and Economic Feasibility Studies,* note 3 *above.*

56. *See* Allen, note 46 *above.*

57. *Aging America,* note 23 *above,* at 97.

58. "Joint Forum on Elderly Housing Options," Subcommittee on Housing and Consumer Interests of the Select Committee on Aging, House of Representatives, and the Federal Council on Aging, Comm. Pub. No. 100–651 (Washington, DC: 1988), 26.

59. *Ibid.*

60. Dobkin, L., "The World of Retirement Housing according to AARP: Opportunities and Obstacles," *The Spectrum,* Jan. 1993, 20.

61. Apgar, W., Jr., "Home Sweet Home to Stay," *Mortgage Banking,* Sept. 1987, 70, 74.

62. *Multi-Housing News,* Oct. 1988, 59.

63. "Understanding Senior Housing for the 1990s," American Association of Retired Persons (Washington, DC: 1990), 22.

64. *Id.* at 39.

65. *See* Petre, note 45 *above.*

66. Calculated in 1980 dollars and not including income from assets, such as interest or dividends. *See* ICF, Inc., note 2 *above,* at 78.

67. *A Profile of Older Americans,* American Association of Retired Persons and Administration on Aging, U.S. Department of Health and Human Services (1996).

68. *Aging America* note 23 *above,* at 71.

69. *Aging America,* note 23 *above,* at Table 2–13; *see also* "Insurance for the Twilight Years: Life Care Takes the Uncertainty Out of Retirement," *Time,* Apr. 6, 1987, 53.

70. *Aging America,* note 23 *above.* One review of net worth among the elderly noted that the oldest householders control more wealth than those in the highest-income age group. Longino, C., Jr., and W. Crown, "Older Americans: Rich or Poor?" *American Demographics,* Aug. 1991, 48.

71. *See* Seaberry, J., "CEA Says Aged Have Attained Economic Parity," *Washington Post,* Feb. 6, 1985, citing President's Council of Economic Advisers Annual Report. Note, however, that elderly cash income is substantially less than that of nonelderly persons and that some observers argue that, even taking noncash resources into account, elderly persons are economically disadvantaged as a group.

72. *A Profile of Older Americans,* note 67 *above.*

73. *See* Seaberry, note 71 *above.*

74. *A Profile of Older Americans,* note 67 *above.*

75. *See* Seaberry, note 71 *above.*

76. Average cash income for elderly couples in 1980 was $16,600, but for elderly single persons was only $8,500. *See* ICF, Inc., note 2 *above,* at 54.

77. *Aging America,* note 23 *above,* Chart 2-11.

78. *See* Allen, note 46 *above.*

79. *Aging America,* note 23 *above,* Chart 2-14.

80. "Progress in the Housing of Older Persons," American Association of Retired Persons, 1997, 10.

81. *A Profile of Older Americans,* note 67 *above.*

82. Jacobs and Weissart, "Long Term Care Financing and Delivery Systems," Conference Proceedings, Health Care Financing Administration (Washington, DC: 1984), 83, cited in O'Shaughnessy, Price, and Griffith, "Financing and Delivery of Long-Term Care Services for the Elderly," Congressional Research Service, Feb. 24, 1987, 69.

83. U.S. Department of Health and Human Services, "Catastrophic Illness Expenses," Report to the President, Nov. 1986, cited by O'Shaughnessy et al., note 82 *above.*

84. A Bureau of the Census 1990 statistical brief ("Housing Arrangements of the Elderly," *Bureau of the Census Statistical Brief,* SB-2-90, Jan. 1990.) on housing arrangements of the elderly[71] (over 65) indicated the following:
- The elderly comprise approximately one-fourth of the nation's homeowners compared with one-sixth of all renters.
- Seventy-five percent of the elderly owned the home in which they lived.
- Elderly owners spent only half as much for housing as did their younger counterparts.
- More than one-fourth of the elderly renters spent at least half of their income on housing.
- Women living alone make up more than one-third of elderly households.

- Most elderly owners have lived in their homes for more than 17 years; 40 percent bought their units before 1960; most have no mortgage.
- About half of elderly owners paid less than $20,000 for their homes, whereas 40 percent of younger owners paid at least $40,000; by 1987, the value of properties owned by the elderly had increased to a median of $59,000.

85. *See* Petre, note 45 *above.*

86. *See,* Swallow, W., "Elderly Seen as Giant New Market," *Washington Post,* Sept. 15, 1984.

87. People over 65 comprise 12 percent of the population but account for 36 percent of total personal health care expenditures. *A Profile of Older Americans,* note 67 *above.*

88. For a general discussion of the growth of the elderly population and its need for care, *see* "Grays on the Go," *Time,* Feb. 22, 1988, 66.

89. *Aging America,* note 23 *above,* 162; and "Who's Taking Care of Our Parents?" *Newsweek,* May 6, 1985, 61.

90. Feldblum, note 35 *above,* citing U.S. General Accounting Office, Report No. PAD–80–12, Nov. 26, 1979.

91. *See* Holbrook and Quinley, note 31 *above,* 17.

92. Kenan, M., "Changing Needs for Long-Term: A Chart Book," (Washington, DC: American Association of Retired Persons, 1989). *See also* data in §1.3.

93. *Id.* at 75.

94. *Senior Housing & Care Report,* Jan. 27, 1996.

95. "Caring for the Elderly: Public/Private Sector Responsibilities Point Way to Future Trends," *Federation of American Health Systems Review,* Jan./Feb. 1988, 28. *See also Aging America,* note 23 *above,* at 97.

96. Dwight, M., "Affluent Elderly Want to Live Where Quality Care's Readily Available," *Modern Healthcare,* Apr. 26, 1985.

97. *Ibid.*

98. Rivlin, A., and J. Wiener, *Caring for the Disabled Elderly: Who Will Pay?* (Washington, DC: The Brookings Institution, 1988), 41–42.

99. Fisher Center for Real Estate and Urban Economics, as presented by R. Mollica, *National Investment Conference for Senior Living,* Oct. 12, 1995.

100. Mariano, A., "As Old Grow Older, Housing Needs Change," *Washington Post,* Sept. 15, 1984.

101. *Ibid.*

102. Doty, Liu, and J. Wiener, "An Overview of Long Term Care," *Health Care Financing Review,* 6, No. 3 (Spring 1985), 74.

103. "Before You Settle on a Retirement Community," note 14 *above,* at 151.

104. "Coming Up Short: Increasing Out-of-Pocket Health Spending by Older Americans," American Association of Retired Persons Public Policy Institute and Health Policy Center of the Urban Institute, Apr. 19, 1994. *See also* U.S. Department of Health and Human Services, "Infrastructure of Home and Community Based Services for the Functionally Impaired Elderly," which comprehensively inventories and profiles the programs administered by each state for long-term- and community-based care for the elderly, 1994.

105. Feldblum, note 35 *above,* referencing Baltay, M., "Long-Term Care for the Elderly and Disabled," Congressional Budget Office, 1977.

106. *See* "Special Report: The Future of Medicare," *New England Journal of Medicine,* 314, No. 11 (Mar. 13, 1986), 725, citing Morris, R., and P. Youket, "The Long Term Care Issues: Identifying the Problems and Potential Solutions," in *Reforming the Long Term Care System,* Callahan, J., and S. Wallack, eds. (Lexington, MA: Lexington Books, 1981), 11–28.

107. Of course, it can be beneficial to have dependent and independent residents commingle in various group activities, as this fosters a sense of community.

108. Gerald Glaser, Oxford Development Enterprises, Inc.

The Terraces of Los Gatos; Los Gatos, California.

2 The Evolution of Seniors' Housing and Care Facilities

§2.1 The Essence of a Seniors' Community

The numerous housing options[1] available to elderly persons can be grouped as follows:[2]

- **Independent Elderly**
  Homeownership
  Rental housing
  Condominiums or cooperatives
  Mobile homes
  Age-restricted housing communities
- **Semi-Independent Elderly**
  Living with family
  House sharing with another senior
  Residential hotels
  Congregate housing
  Life-care or continuing-care communities
- **Dependent Elderly**
  Board and care
  Assisted-living facilities
  Nursing homes

This list, though detailed, is probably too much of a generalization. For example, life-care or continuing-care facilities usually house people spanning the full range from independence to dependence. Congregate housing facilities may offer meals and services to independent elderly while board-and-care homes offer, in addition, personal assistance for the semi-independent and dependent.

People in the business surely will disagree about what a seniors' community is or should be. Yet, it seems clear that certain forms of elderly housing, such as a self-owned or shared home or an apartment, condominium, or hotel room standing alone, do not deserve the title. Groups of single-family homes, apartments, or condominiums in which seniors live, by accident[3] or design, are not qualitatively different by reason of their numbers, without something more. That something else is services and amenities specially designed for the center's older inhabitants.

Accordingly, this book emphasizes properties that offer some form of specialized elderly services and amenities in addition to housing. Age-restricted housing, or even large residential communities designed for retirees, face many of the issues discussed in this book (e.g., taxes, zoning, discrimination), but they do not raise the even wider array of business and legal issues that is present in a service-oriented facility. Nevertheless, service-oriented facilities can use all the devices of housing development to serve the elderly, from condominiums to rentals, and from multifamily high-rises, to single-family residential communities, to mobile home parks.

On the other hand, some facilities, such as hospitals, which may offer extensive services to the elderly and provide food and shelter as well, likewise should not be grouped with seniors' communities. It is not just the short-term stay usually associated with a hospital that puts it outside the bounds of the seniors' community definition, but also the extreme dominance of the medical services element over the housing component. Many communities have, in addition to a service element, the characteristic that they serve at least some people who are not totally dependent and who have voluntarily chosen the placement as their home. Accordingly, this book does not deal extensively with higher-acuity health facility operations such as acute and subacute care but rather focuses on long-term "custodial" models such as assisted-living and nursing.

Narrowing the focus so that "pure" housing and "pure" health facilities are treated in passing still leaves a great deal to discuss because seniors' communities can include independent housing, health care for the dependent, and every gradation of services in between. In fact, it is the tension among the housing, care, and services components of seniors' communities that makes their operation and regulation unique and sometimes presents a tightrope walk for developers and operators seeking to combine these disparate elements in a single setting.[4]

§2.2 The Four Businesses of Full-Service Seniors' Communities

Seniors' communities can consist of one or more of essentially four businesses: housing, convenience services, health care or assisted living, and insurance. These markedly different businesses may converge to provide in a single community all the basic needs of the older person. Facility developers must draw on resources from each field and bring them together in an integrated product.

An individual facility may provide all or only some mix of these four basic components. Those that provide all elements are sometimes referred to as "continuing-care," "life-care," or "multilevel" facilities, but these terms may have different meanings and implications, both legally and in the marketplace, depending on the jurisdiction or the local terminology of choice. Because many of the newer providers of these services do not necessarily fit the traditional model of continuing-care or life-care facilities, the term "full-service retirement community" is used here as a generic description for those facilities providing all four elements described below. Those that provide fewer than all four elements may be called assisted-living facilities, congregate housing, nursing homes, or simply seniors' housing. Figure 2.4 describes how service components fit into traditional types of seniors' communities.

(a) Housing

Retirement housing is more than simply housing in which elderly people live. While it may take on many physical attributes of family housing, such as high-rise construction, planned communities of single-family residences, or campus-type environments of multiunit low-rise dwellings with common-use recreation centers, elderly housing in addition caters to the particular physical and emotional needs and desires of its clientele.[5]

Everyone involved in development of a facility should be aware of certain basic guidelines and rules of thumb regarding design criteria for elderly housing. As with other types of real estate, location is of paramount importance. The property should be close to shopping, transportation, health care, and other community services and amenities. Figure 2.1 summarizes the accessibility needs of individuals over 55 years of age according to nationwide surveys conducted by the American Association of Retired Persons during 1989 and 1992. Facilities should be planned by taking into account the physical needs or potential physical needs of the elderly market segment for which the facility is being built. In addition to curb appeal, interior design is of great importance so that buildings are functional but retain home-like qualities.

If units are designed to accommodate residents both when they are independent and later when they may need personal assistance, certain design features can be incorporated into every residence. These may include features such as skid-proof floors, elevated switches and electrical outlets that do not require the user to bend or crouch, grab bars (when needed) at bathtubs and toilets, doors wide enough to accommodate wheelchairs, emergency call buttons, and similar conveniences. In addition, living

Figure 2.1 **Accessibility Needs: 1992**

Resource	Percent of Respondents Believing It Necessary to Have Nearby Access
Grocery store	62
Pharmacy/drugstore	56
Physician's office	55
Hospital	55
Public transportation	42
Children/grandchildren	40
Cultural resources	39
Senior citizen center	27
Recreational facilities	25

Source: Adapted from Dobkin, L., "The World of Retirement Housing According to AARP: Opportunities and Obstacles," *The Spectrum,* Jan. 1993, 18.

quarters that are at ground level or can be reached by elevator are generally preferable to those that may require a resident to climb stairs. Design considerations for the elderly may also include special sound-proofing measures, extra lighting without glare, avoidance of certain colors, automatic doors, particular corridor dimensions, specially positioned sinks and mirrors, care in the selection of chair designs, and numerous factors related to the visual, auditory, ambulatory, and other impairments that may accompany old age (see Figure 2.2).[6]

It is a common experience that larger units tend to be preferred by the elderly over smaller units. Some developers are finding that it is difficult to sell studio units, whereas there is significant demand for one- and two-bedroom units.[7] Residents wish to use their own furnishings and frequently desire large amounts of space to store the possessions they have accumulated over a lifetime. Often, residents wish to be able to accommodate overnight guests, such as visiting family members. Even though a facility may provide one or more meals in a common dining area, at least rudimentary kitchen facilities in the unit are desirable to enable the resident to prepare simple meals such as breakfast or lunch and to promote an atmosphere of independence and self-direction rather than one of dependence and institutionalization. In addition, retirement centers should be designed to

provide for security, recreational facilities, gardening areas, group meeting rooms, arts and crafts rooms, cable television, and other amenities that will promote a homelike, community atmosphere.

Security is especially important. Of respondents to one national survey of the elderly, 38 percent indicated they were somewhat concerned about future security from crime while 29 percent were very concerned. Of those living in seniors' housing, 78 percent currently felt very secure compared with only 55 percent in mixed-age settings.[8]

Where a retirement community includes a health care center or assisted-living wing, the conventional wisdom is that such facilities should be separated from high-visibility areas such as entranceways, lobbies, and common dining areas and instead should be equipped with separate dining facilities and located in a place where it is convenient for other residents to visit their friends in need of health services or personal care.[9] Entrance areas and highly visible portions of the building should be devoted to activity centers, shops, attractive dining facilities, or other areas that will promote a sense of independent living, luxury, or homelike qualities.

The housing element of a seniors' community may be offered to the resident on a rental basis, as a life lease, as a membership privilege, or on an ownership basis, among others. Provision of services or care as part of the same arrangement can have an impact on the form of property interest the developer transfers to residents. Generally, where it is expected that care or services are to be available to residents for extended periods, facility operators may want to retain control over the disposition of property and avoid transfer of an unrestricted fee interest (see §7.1(c)).

(b) Convenience Services

Services are that aspect of seniors' housing that most distinguishes it from any other form of housing. The types of services offered by many such communities may be likened to those provided in the hotel or hospitality industries. They may include restaurants or group dining facilities, weekly or other periodic housekeeping and flat laundry services, game rooms, fitness centers, tennis, golf and pool facilities, barber shops and beauty salons, on-site banks, convenience

Figure 2.2 **Preferred Retirement Center Amenities (One Viewpoint)**

Interiors

The affluent elderly make up a very small percentage of the market. If the project is designed to attract them it should be luxurious and loaded with recreational amenities. The wealthy buy downsized versions of their former homes. Units of 2,000 to 2,500 square feet sell well and two bedrooms are a must.

The majority of the market is middle income. This is what they want:

- Privacy within the living unit is essential whether it is a for-sale or for-rent unit. The ability to have an area to oneself is very important to older couples. The privacy issue extends to the congregate living format where the number one issue is a private toilet area (shared baths are acceptable). Even common areas both indoors and out ought to provide for some measure of privacy while also maximizing the opportunity for residents to meet face-to-face. This issue may explain why efficiency units are far less popular than one bedroom plans and why nursing homes are so disliked by the overwhelming majority of people.
- Security inside and outside the living unit. An emergency call system and smoke alarms are virtually essential.
- A liberal use of natural light in the individual living units and in all common areas. All corridors, lobbies, etc. ought to offer views to the outside.
- Careful attention to artificial light levels. As people age they need access to more light.
- Low cost occupancy features such as:
  - Cross ventilation in all rooms rather than air conditioning except in those climates where air conditioning is an absolute must.

- Individually controlled heating. The aged vary greatly in how they perceive heat and cold.
- Well-insulated structures to keep fuel costs down and assist in noise control.
- Liberal use of stained woodwork rather than high maintenance painted surfaces.
- Large areas of unbroken wall space to make furniture placement easy. An open space plan that also maximizes ease of movement with or without a wheelchair is usually very successful. Small, walled-in areas should be avoided.
- Very careful attention to avoiding barriers such as high door steps, multiple living levels, uneven walking surfaces, thick carpet (which is very hard to walk on as people get older), hard to open doors (use lever handles) and difficult to operate plumbing fixtures.
- Unobtrusive safety features such as large bathrooms, seats in all showers, non-slip floors, wide doors and halls sell well. Grab rails and railings do not sell and, in fact, are a hindrance to sales or rentals for the pre-retired or first generation elderly. Installing the bracing for them is a good idea, but it doesn't sell or rent many units. Electrical outlets and plugs that are accessible without bending over also help the unit to sell or rent.
- *Storage space.* It is almost impossible to provide too much closet or display space. The elderly have a lot of prized possessions. Built-in bookcases are very popular.
- *Flexibility.* The ability to adjust shelving, closet rod and even bath and kitchen counter heights is a saleable feature that adds very little cost to a project.
- *Kitchens.* A kitchen is a powerful amenity. In all product types except nursing homes, compact kitchens with at

---

stores and gift shops, concierge or activity director services, local minibus transportation, and a host of other programs and features (see Figure 2.3). In addition to the quality of the physical surroundings, it is the extent and scope of these services and amenities that differentiate luxury facilities from those directed to the lower- and middle-income population. The top of the line in luxury retirement facilities can be modeled after a resort or cruise ship lifestyle. Such facilities are helping change the image

of seniors' centers as desirable places to live, rather than refuges of last resort, for those who can afford such amenities.

One survey showed that food service, social programs, common rooms, housekeeping, laundry, transportation, and an on-call attendant ranked high in terms of the number of facilities offering them.[10] Allowance of pets, security services, swimming pools, libraries, guest rooms, and beauty shops were less frequently encountered.[11]

Figure 2.2 **(continued)**

least thirty inches of counter space useable while seated and which are visible to the dining and living room area are the most popular. You can avoid installing most kitchen gadgets including, in many cases, dishwashers as many of the elderly have few dishes to wash and quite a few don't want the expense of operating one. Top-mounted freezers should be avoided. All appliances should have front-mounted, easy-to-read dials and gauges. In projects without kitchens, the residents respond well to a snack bar or to some area where they can buy snacks whenever they feel like it.

- Laundry facilities should be located on the main living level, not in a basement.
- *Mail.* Provide easy access to mail delivery areas. Large graphics on housing units and mailboxes make it easy for residents to identify their units and mail slots.
- Elevators are wanted in any multi-story project but you can get by without them in two-story projects. Elevators must be large enough for wheelchairs and must have slow-operating doors.
- *Bathrooms.* Most people want only one bathroom, however, the affluent elderly will want at least two. Separating the toilet area from the tub or shower is very desirable. Bathrooms should have wide doors and be large enough to allow a wheelchair to maneuver. Mirrors should start at 40-inch level and there should be a dressing table and basin that allow a seated person to use them. Showers are more desired than bathtubs.
- Entry doors which are recessed to give protection against weather and to give a sense of "ownership," even in a high-rise project, are popular. Peepholes at two levels, one accessible to a seated person, are appreciated. All entries must be well lit.

- *Bedrooms.* One bedroom units are the most popular, no bedroom units are least popular. Bedrooms ought to be large enough to allow a wheelchair to move around the bed.
- *Unit size.* Median size is 600 to 650 square feet. The trend is toward a larger size. Typical unit sizes are:
  - *Efficiency:*
    Median—415; Range—325 to 450
  - *1 bedroom:*
    Median—600; Range—520 to 740
  - *2 bedroom:*
    Median—900; Range—750 to 1000
- *Housing Preference.* The single-family residence is number one. Duplexes sell and rent well and cluster housing with buildings up to four units are very saleable or rentable. Least desired housing is multistory, especially high-rise.

Those projects that feature a health care facility generally have one of about 21,000 square feet; the size range is 13,000 to 30,000 feet. The facility is typically a 60-bed center divided into a short-term stay area and a long-term care area.

Activity centers such as are found in congregate and life care facilities average 30,000 square feet; the range is 15,000 to 50,000 square feet. An allocation of 125 feet per resident is a good rule of thumb.

Exteriors

Site sizes range from one to two acres for a small, in-town congregate project to hundreds or thousands of acres for a destination retirement village. The median lot size for an

Continued →

Payment for these services is often included in a monthly fee charged to the resident. That fee also covers rent or supplements the entrance fee or purchase price of the residential unit. Many developers are finding that, if financially feasible, it is desirable to make many of the services available on an à la carte basis to enable individual residents to customize a service package that meets their individual wants and needs. Often, however, economies of scale and the developer's capital investment in particular por-

tions of the facility require that all residents purchase certain basic services, for example, a minimum of one meal per day to cover the cost of kitchen and dining room construction and staffing. However, making use of certain services a mandatory condition of occupancy can create regulatory problems or even give rise to antitrust issues (see §22.6(d)).

Convenience services should be carefully distinguished from care, which usually involves hands-on personal assistance and is usually a licensable activity.

Figure 2.2 **(continued)**

in-city lifecare project is six acres; those located in rural areas have a median size of 29 acres.

Density, the number of units per acre, varies widely. It ranges from 6.5 units per acre for rural projects to up to 50 units per acre for metropolitan developments. High density projects are, of course, generally the most profitable. It is possible to design pleasant environments at 35 to 50 units per acre but it can't be done without using a mid-rise or high-rise format. High-rises are the least popular with elderly residents.

Project size varies from 50 to 200 units; a 150-unit project seems most manageable. Absorption time ranges between 18 and 24 months. Rental or sale of four to six units per month is normal.

It is not necessary to provide a lot of parking especially as the entry age of the customer group increases. Even in congregate projects that appeal to the 65+ segment, a parking ratio of one space for every three units is satisfactory. Most projects that have tried one parking space for every four units have found they are eventually short of parking. Vehicle access to entries is quite important; covered access is desirable, but not essential. All walkways leading to the parking area should be smooth surfaces without any steps.

Because the elderly are either on limited budgets or have better things to do with their time, it is wise to provide low-maintenance exteriors. Brick construction or stucco finishes are good; stained, rather than painted, exterior wood trim is excellent.

A small yard or access to a garden plot will help to sell or rent the unit. The cluster format lends itself to small backyards.

Open areas that are accessible but offer some areas for privacy are very popular. Golf courses are very much overdone. Few people play golf and those who do so seldom play championship golf. Courses are valuable as open spaces and will be used for walking if paths are provided. In many cases, however, projects could succeed without a golf course if the money normally spent on this amenity was put into the living units and interior common areas. A number of surveys designed to uncover what the elderly really want have shown that golf courses are never ranked among the first ten most desired features. Indoor swimming pools usually rank ahead of golf courses and even they are well down on the list. A lot more people play cards, listen to concerts, dance and socialize than play golf.

When judging the overall desirability of a project don't be taken in by the scope of the outdoor common areas. The best designed common areas won't make up for a lack of adequate size or privacy in the living units.

The old are not very different from the young in their housing needs. There are enough differences to justify developing projects especially for the elderly, but few plans will succeed if they are designed merely to serve the old.

Source: Reprinted with permission from Allen, John B., "Housing for the Elderly," *Investor Outlook,* Vol. 6, No. 2, Grubb & Ellis, Second Quarter 1986.

Gray areas can exist when services that may be a convenience to some persons amount to a necessity to others who are dependent (e.g., beauty salon versus assistance with grooming). In such circumstances, it is important to consider the possible licensing implications of facility activities and resident mix (see §20.4(b)).

(c) Health Care or Assisted Living

A sharp dividing line exists between many communities that offer only the two elements of housing and convenience services and those that venture into the business of providing residents with health care or related forms of care and physical assistance. As for-profit developers entered the industry in the late 1980s, there was considerable debate regarding the desirability of offering health care services in a seniors' housing community. Some older people prefer to postpone thinking about and planning for the probability of their eventually needing assistance. Historically, however, many facilities developed largely by nonprofit providers were created precisely for the purpose of providing needed care. The reasons for the debate within the industry may not have been so much a lack of consumer interest in or need for these services as it was a reluctance of many real estate developers to venture into a field that was so

Figure 2.3 Typical Continuing-Care Services and Features

Included General Services
- Meals
- Activities director
- Apartment cleaning
- Apartment maintenance
- Carports/garages
- Flat linens supplied
- Flat linens laundered
- Guest accommodations
- Kitchen appliances
- Personal laundry facilities
- Prescribed diet
- Scheduled transportation by facility
- Storage (outside living unit)
- Telephone service (generally local only)
- Tray service when ordered by physician
- Utilities

Health-Related Services
- Annual or routine physical examination
- Community's physician (services of)
- Dental care
- Emergency call system
- Home health care (in apartment)
- Hospitalization in acute care hospital
- Illness or accident away from facility
- Occupational therapy
- Optician
- Physical therapy
- Podiatry
- Prescription drugs
- Recreational therapy
- Referred specialists
- Resident's own physician
- Social services
- Therapy for psychiatric disorders
- Treatment for preexisting condition

Special Features
- Bank (sometimes a check-cashing service)
- Barber shop (may be part of a beauty salon)
- Beauty salon
- Cable TV
- Chapel
- Coffee shop
- Crafts areas
- Exercise program
- Financial aid available
- Fireplaces
- Garden plots
- Greenhouse
- Hiking/walking trails
- Library
- Master TV antenna
- Pharmacy
- Private dining room (for small parties)
- Religious/vesper services
- Residents' association
- Sauna/spa/whirlpool
- Security gate/system (many communities have security guards)
- Store/gift shop
- Swimming pool (outdoor)
- Woodworking shop

Source: Reprinted with permission from Raper, Ann Trueblood, *National Continuing Care Directory,* American Association of Homes for the Aging, American Association of Retired Persons, 1984.

foreign to them (see §11.1(a)). It now seems that there is a general acknowledgment of the long-term importance of offering care, or access to care, in most facilities.

Facilities that offer only health care in a program that does not include housing for, or services to, less dependent residents in the form of health care facilities, nursing facilities, intermediate-care facilities, convalescent hospitals, or similar titles are considered by some to be institutional in character and separate from the retirement community industry. Seniors' communities usually offer health care as a supple-

ment to housing and services in a homelike environment. However, because of their residential character, freestanding assisted-living facilities are generally considered a part of the seniors' housing industry even though they may cater primarily to the care needs of residents. The lines between the "medical model" of health care facilities and the residential model of retirement facilities are blurring due to innovations in the marketplace. Unfortunately, laws and regulations often tend to classify these hybrid projects as either housing or health care facilities and fail to recognize the full dimensions of their activities.

Seniors' communities with health care or assisted-living services offer them in a wide variety of ways and combinations. Conceptually speaking, facilities identify and provide these services at various points along a "continuum of care," which may range from minimal assistance with daily tasks for residents who are slightly enfeebled, to long-term, 24-hour skilled-nursing care for those with chronic debilitating conditions, to acute hospitalization for the seriously ill.

"Assisted living"[12] may include helping residents with activities such as bathing, grooming, dressing, transferring from bed to a walker or wheelchair, and related tasks. Assistance with activities such as letter writing, shopping, maintaining a checkbook, and similar activities that do not involve care of the body may not by itself rise to the level of licensable care in most states (see §20.4(b)). The presence of care and the type and level of care offered by a facility will have a significant impact on the types of regulations imposed on the facility operator and can often have an impact on the construction standards and physical plant amenities required by law as well as on the numbers and types of staff required to operate the facility.

Unlike the concept of assisted living, which may vary widely from state to state, nursing facility services are more broadly and consistently recognized across the country as a level of care that requires the availability of trained nursing personnel on a full-time basis. The federal government and all states have extensive regulatory or licensing requirements that apply to such facilities (see §20.3). Seniors' communities may offer nursing services in a unit attached or adjacent to the residential portion of the facility and usually require a resident to give up his or her residential unit whenever the facility's medical director determines that a permanent transfer to nursing services is required (see Volume II, Chapter 4, concerning alternative transfer options for resident agreements). Seniors' centers may also have transfer arrangements with local nursing facilities under different ownership and operation.

Home health care is another type of care that can be delivered to retirement facility residents. It typically consists of nursing care and/or assisted-living or homemaker services (see the Medicare definition in §20.5). Usually, when an elderly person contracts for delivery of home health services in his or her private residence, the home does not become a licensable facility. On the other hand, substantial use of home health by a significant number of dependent elderly in a multiunit housing project could be viewed by state inspectors as circumstances warranting licensure of the facility, especially if the facility helps arrange or provide the service (see §20.4(b)).

Few seniors' communities in the nation offer general acute care hospital services on site. However, many ensure that hospital services are available by making special arrangements with nearby facilities and may even pay for some or all of the expenses related to the hospitalization as part of the retirement community's overall fee structure. For the most part, communities that agree to cover the costs of health care services rendered in-house or at another facility as part of a prepaid or fixed-fee arrangement are entering into a fourth business, that of insurance or provision for residents' financial security.

(d) Insurance

Because most retired persons live on fixed incomes, they are concerned about preserving their lifestyles for the rest of their days. They may wish to minimize the risk that a catastrophic event, such as a sudden, serious illness or a long and gradual one, will force them to become dependent on government aid, to move to undesirable housing, or to become a burden on their families. Medicare coverage for nursing care is minimal, and a person must become impoverished to qualify for Medicaid benefits (see §26.3). Consequently, many retirement communities have established financial mechanisms akin to insurance programs to help ensure that the costs of living for the remainder of a person's lifetime will be predictable and stable.

One method of ensuring stability in terms of health care or assisted-living costs is to require residents, upon admission to a community, to pay a large, lump-sum entrance fee, which is then invested by the operator and reserved for payment of future health care costs and other needs of the resident. In return for the entrance fee, the community guarantees coverage for the costs of certain of the resident's health care needs in the future. Other providers may charge a smaller entrance fee and use the proceeds to reduce rather than fully cover the increased costs when a resident moves from an apartment to nursing or other care facilities. The money to pay entrance fees is often available because the resident has sold his or her home just before moving into the seniors' property. This method of self-insurance traditionally has been prevalent among not-for-profit continuing-care facilities. It subjects the community to regulatory oversight in most states (see Chapter 21).

More recently, some communities have turned to commercial insurance carriers to provide residents with group long-term-care insurance coverage, similar to employer group medical policies. These policies typically cover the difference between the monthly costs of residential and nursing accommodations at the community, or they may offer a defined daily benefit payment for nursing stays. Enrollment may be mandatory for all occupants of the particular seniors' community, with a fixed monthly premium collected by the community as part of its monthly fee. The offer of long-term-care insurance generally does not subject the retirement community to state regulation because the third-party carrier is already heavily regulated.

§2.3 Traditional Seniors' Community Models

(a) Overview

Centers for the elderly have evolved along two separate paths, with housing as the genesis of one and health and custodial care as the source of the other. With time, these two branches have intertwined so much that many seniors' communities currently are thought of as places that are neither pure housing nor pure care but rather a little of each, with a lot of added services and amenities that form the middle ground. Accordingly, freestanding nursing facilities, where there is no independent housing, and age-restricted housing, where there is no service or care element, are distinctly different from the hybrid communities that are the focus of this book. Nevertheless, this book deals extensively with issues that affect pure nursing and retirement housing projects as well as hybrid models.

Over the years, many different models of seniors' housing and care facilities have evolved that incor-

porate some mix of housing, convenience services, care, or insurance. Principally, these fall into three basic patterns: congregate housing, assisted living,[13] and continuing care or life care. However, even these traditional points of departure are rapidly becoming arbitrary stereotypes that do not always fit marketplace realities.

Figure 2.4 places the traditional retirement community models of congregate housing, assisted living, and continuing care plus age-restricted housing and skilled-nursing facilities along a spectrum of basic amenity/service types: housing, convenience services, assisted living, and health care.[14] These service/amenity types can be loosely associated with independence or dependence of the facility's elderly residents. While communities may offer several of the service/amenity types, only one or two features may characterize the community, with other attributes incidental to the primary features. For example, nursing facilities are characterized principally as health care providers. Housing is provided, but not to independent residents and more as a necessary incident of full-time health care rather than as a primary objective. On the other hand, independent housing and some provision for health care or assisted-living care are more coequal attributes of a continuing-care community.

With more and more developers with a diversity of backgrounds and experience entering this growing field, one can expect to see distinctions fade between the traditional types of seniors' community products as new products evolve from various combinations of physical facilities, services, delivery systems, and payment mechanisms. With that, we will probably also see a whole new lexicon develop to help us describe what is going on. For example, one industry commentator has defined a retirement community as "a residential setting having one or more full-time staff and providing at least one meal per day in a congregate space for residents who are of retirement age."[15] That commentator then divided retirement communities into the following six categories:

- Adult Independent-Living Community: Level I—Offers no health care and few services; primarily housing.
- Adult Independent-Living Community: Level II—Provides some form of health care such as a

Figure 2.4 **Typical Seniors' Community Models**

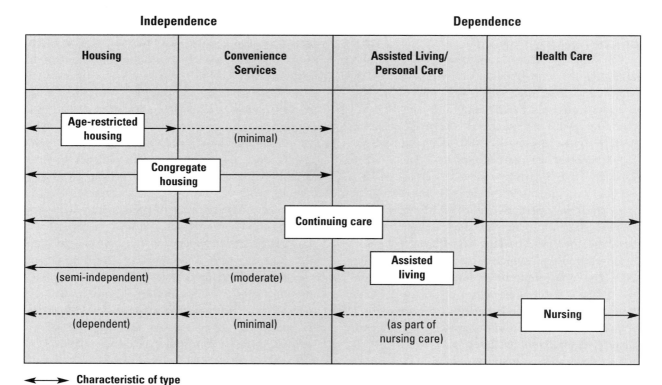

Independence — Dependence

Housing	Convenience Services	Assisted Living/ Personal Care	Health Care
Age-restricted housing	(minimal)		
Congregate housing			
Continuing care			
(semi-independent)	(moderate)	Assisted living	
(dependent)	(minimal)	(as part of nursing care)	Nursing

◄——► Characteristic of type
◄----► Incidental feature

nurse on duty for emergencies or home health services but does not have a separate health facility.

■ Adult Independent-Living Community: Level III— Offers the health care component in a separately constructed area of the building or community and consists of assisted living or nursing care.

■ Adult Independent-Living Community: Level IV— Offers a full continuum of care, including assisted living and nursing.

■ Adult Assisted-Living Community: Level I—Consists of a freestanding community that is not a component of an independent-living community and that offers assisted living.

■ Adult Assisted-Living Community: Level II—Serves residents in need of a heavier level of assistance consistently on a daily basis.

In some respects, the seniors' facility field has emerged from a stage where ice cream making was many years ago: There were just a few available flavors, selected by the manufacturer. As the elderly population grows, becomes more affluent, and discovers itself to be a powerful segment of the consumer public that can generate innovation and demand variety and custom-tailored quality in the marketplace, we can expect to see rapid diversification and creativity of the type that took vanilla, chocolate, and strawberry to 31 flavors, and ice cream to frozen yogurt, gelato, and sorbet.

(b) Congregate Housing

Congregate housing was defined, in its formative years, as:

An assisted independent group living environment that offers the elderly who are functionally impaired or socially deprived, but otherwise in good health, the residential accommodations and supporting services they need to maintain or return to a semi-independent lifestyle and prevent premature or unnecessary institutionalization as they grow older.[16]

However, today congregate housing has come to mean more universally a multiunit housing facility that provides, often to independent elderly, a rental program that includes supportive services (predominantly meals), but generally not the personal assistance or health care needed by the functionally impaired. Unlike assisted living, it generally does not require institutional licensure and is made up of self-contained, single-family occupancy units.[17] It is often referred to as "independent living," especially when part of a community with multiple levels of care.

Congregate housing is a concept that was fostered largely by the 1978 passage of the Congregate Housing Services Act,[18] which provides funding for meals and other services to be provided in low-income or otherwise federally subsidized housing (see §22.4(c)). During the 1980s, the congregate housing concept was greatly expanded in the marketplace to include market-rate multiunit facilities that offer meals, housekeeping, laundry, transportation, recreational programs, and other convenience services in settings that can range from modest to luxurious.[19] Another impetus for the development of such facilities was the now-defunct Section 221(d)(4) HUD mortgage insurance program for Retirement Services Centers, which was designed to cover the gap between independent housing and nursing homes.[20]

Although one often hears reference to congregate "care" facilities, this is sometimes a misnomer in that, technically, care of the type that is usually licensed by state regulatory agencies (e.g., nursing or assisted living) is not commonly offered in such facilities, although the facility may assist residents in obtaining access to care in the community. Due in part to the confusing terminology associated with assisted-living facilities (see below), some writers have equated congregate facilities with life-care endowment programs.[21] Although congregate living is an element of life care and other retirement housing options, standing alone it constitutes a distinct product type. While care is not routinely offered in most congregate housing, a growing percentage of operators do provide or arrange for some level of care (possibly through existing employees or home

health agencies). Liability to provide care, or to intervene and summon help, may exist whether or not the operator voluntarily assumes such responsibility (see Chapter 29).

Congregate housing facilities traditionally do not exact any lump-sum payment or entrance fee from residents but rather are made available on a monthly rental basis. The parties are in the relationship of landlord and tenant. Both the nonprofit and for-profit sectors are well represented in the field of congregate housing.

(c) Assisted Living/Board and Care

Facilities where residents need assistance with daily activities, such as bathing, grooming, and dressing, but are otherwise independent and not in need of full-time nursing care have been variously described as assisted-living, residential-care, board-and-care, personal-care, congregate-care, or sheltered-living facilities, among numerous other names.[22] The House Select Committee on Aging estimated, in 1981, that there were 100,000 boarding homes in the country (five times the number of nursing facilities), that they served 1 million people, and that they generated $12 billion to $20 billion of revenue per year.[23] It has been more recently estimated that there are nationally approximately 300,000 unlicensed boarding homes (with room and meals) and about 30,000 licensed board-and-care facilities that include supportive services.[24] Taken together, these facilities are housing between 500,000 and 1.5 million people.[25] A 1983 study of licensing programs found that of 458,500 identified board-and-care beds, about 324,000 were occupied by elderly or handicapped adults.[26] The remainder were for mentally retarded or developmentally disabled persons.[27] To some extent, the recent emergence of the term "assisted living" as the label of choice has occurred to distinguish larger, more modern projects from the negative connotation often associated with board-and-care projects. In 1991, the newly formed Assisted Living Federation of America (ALFA) estimated that 30,000 to 40,000 assisted-living facilities, either freestanding or combined with other residential options such as independent living or nursing, housed 1 million people.[28]

Such facilities have been broadly defined in proposed model legislation to include any "publicly or privately operated residence that provides personal assistance, lodging, and meals to two (2) or more adults who are unrelated to the licensee or administrator."[29] The kind of assistance that may be received by residents in such facilities, on an as-needed basis, includes help with walking; bathing, shaving, brushing teeth, combing hair; dressing; eating; getting in and out of bed; laundry; cleaning room; managing money; shopping; using public transportation; writing letters; making telephone calls; obtaining appointments; self-administration of medication; recreational and leisure activities; and other similar activities.[30] In addition, facility staff monitor residents' activities on the premises and are generally aware of their whereabouts when outside of the facility.[31]

Despite the broad definition in the model legislation, most states look to physical care such as personal hygiene assistance or administration of medications as the activities that trigger licensure, rather than services such as laundry and transportation. Assisted-living facilities also should be distinguished from facilities such as congregate housing that may offer housekeeping, recreational programs, or similar services as a mere convenience for truly independent residents. Assisted living involves somewhat dependent people who, because of physical or mental infirmity, require assistance with one or more essential daily tasks, especially matters of personal physical care.

The Housing and Community Development Act of 1992 added assisted-living facilities to the types of facilities that are eligible to receive mortgage insurance under Section 232 of the National Housing Act. In doing so, it defined an *assisted-living facility* as:

> a public facility, proprietary facility, or facility of a private nonprofit corporation that—,
>
> (A) is licensed and regulated by the State (or if there is no State law providing for such licensing and regulation by the State, by the municipality or other political subdivision in which the facility is located);
>
> (B) makes available to residents supportive services to assist the residents in carrying out activities of daily living . . .; and
>
> (C) provides separate dwelling units for residents each of which may contain a full kitchen and bathroom, and which includes common rooms or other facilities

appropriate for the provision of supportive services to the residents of the facility.[32]

Assisted-living facilities are also markedly different from nursing facilities, where patients need to have full-time, licensed nursing care or supervision available to them. Assisted-living residents are usually ambulatory and largely independent in that they often may be able to leave the premises (perhaps in groups, with or without supervision). They may have no mental impairment whatsoever but simply need some physical help to get up and about or to perform household tasks.

Board-and-care homes, some of which housed mentally handicapped, developmentally disabled, and other nonelderly dependent groups, were the subject of considerable criticism in the 1970s in response to serious problems of fraud and abuse and a series of deadly fires in elderly facilities.[33] To address these problems, Congress passed the Keys Amendment,[34] requiring states to enact minimum standards for facilities serving a significant number of recipients of federal Supplemental Security Income (SSI) payments.[35] Interestingly, Section 232 of the National Housing Act treats board-and-care homes as different types of facilities than assisted-living facilities. Under Section 232, a board-and-care home is defined as "any residential facility providing room, board, and continuous protective oversight that is regulated by a state pursuant to the provisions of Section 1616(e) of the Social Security Act."[36]

Assisted living is a particularly attractive alternative to a nursing home placement for an elderly person who needs assistance and wants a homelike environment but neither needs full-time nursing care nor wants the more institutional, medical-model surroundings of many nursing facilities. Unfortunately, assisted living has not received the kind of government financial support (Medicare and Medicaid) that health care facilities have enjoyed, and therefore many facilities rely on residents' rather meager SSI payments as a funding source.[37] However, a few private insurance companies such as Aetna Life & Casualty do cover assisted living. Moreover, it is estimated that assisted living can be at least 30 percent less expensive than nursing home care.[38] Many facilities have been run as small mom-and-pop operations. Poor reimbursement may be a principal reason for both the extent of the inferior quality historically surrounding many board-and-care facilities and the high rate of placements in nursing facilities among people requiring a lower level of care.

As the number of elderly who can pay their own way grows and government looks for less expensive and medically intensive ways to care for the elderly, we are seeing a significant rise in the development of high-quality assisted-living facilities as an alternative to nursing care. Recently, in fact, assisted-living facilities have become a distinctly recognized and fast-growing segment of the retirement facility market, as witnessed by the formation of ALFA (see §2.4(g) regarding assisted living as a trend). The following characteristics are typical of many assisted-living facilities:

- Average entry age of residents is about 80 years.
- The projects are need-driven, therefore requiring expenditure of fewer dollars for marketing.
- Facilities tend to have fewer living units than independent retirement facilities.
- Between 40 and 70 percent of the units are double occupancy (inhabited by unrelated adults).
- Average costs are $35 to $45 per day.
- Facilities maintain a minimum of ten and as many as 30 full-time staff per 100 residents.[39]

Assisted-living facilities—estimated in 1995 to be between 30,000 and 40,000 in number, serving between 600,000 and 1 million residents, and earning $10 to $12 billion in revenues—were expected to double in revenues in the next four to five years.[40] According to a 1996 survey by Capital Valuation Group, based on data from 120 freestanding assisted-living development projects throughout the United States, the average freestanding assisted-living project costs $6.4 million to develop and is expected to generate $2.3 million in annual revenues and yield a 37 percent profit on operations.[41] Based on statistics showing occupancy rates above 90 percent and average returns on investments at about 17 percent, some industry analysts report that money to finance the construction of assisted-living facilities has been pouring into the market in the mid-1990s from real estate investment trusts (REITs).[42] Many are concerned that the assisted-living market may become oversaturated as did the congregate housing field in the late 1980s.

(d) Continuing-Care Retirement Communities

In the late 19th century, retirement homes operated by church groups, fraternal organizations, and social welfare organizations sprang up in the United States as a means of caring for those who had served as missionaries, were abandoned by their families or had no families, or who were too poor to care for themselves.[43] In some cases, the elderly would be asked to turn over whatever meager assets they had to the nonprofit organization operating the facility and, in return, would be assured of a place to live, a square meal, and care, when needed, for the rest of their lives. Such facilities came to be known as life-care facilities.

Life-care facilities have evolved over the past hundred years into what are now perhaps more appropriately called continuing-care retirement communities or "CCRCs."[44] A decade ago, the continuing-care industry was estimated to be at least $4 billion strong.[45] The industry continues to be dominated by nonprofit church and fraternal groups, although for-profit developers have entered the field in increasing numbers (see §2.4(a)). In 1981, 97 percent of continuing-care communities studied nationwide had nonprofit owners or sponsors.[46] In 1984, the number of continuing-care facilities was said to have doubled in ten years, and it was expected to at least double again in the next ten years.[47] In 1986, the expectation was that the number of facilities would triple in ten years.[48] By 1991, it was estimated that there were about 700 CCRCs nationwide, serving nearly 250,000 people at an average age of 82, and the number of facilities was again expected to double in the next ten years.[49] Many facilities have waiting lists of five to eight years, especially for larger units.

CCRCs follow the life-care model in that they are designed to offer food, shelter, convenience services, personal assistance, and often medical care, to the extent needed by a resident, for the rest of his or her life. However, instead of transferring all their assets, residents usually pay a substantial entrance fee, sometimes called an endowment or founder's fee, and are charged a monthly fee averaging $1,500, subject to adjustment to cover fluctuations in the cost of operating the facility. More recently, refundable entrance fees, condominium or cooperative CCRCs, and other innovations have evolved (see Part Three). Deposits on entrance fees are sometimes collected before facility construction as a financing vehicle or to ensure sufficient demand for the project.

CCRC facility operators historically have retained ownership of the premises and granted residents the right to occupy a residential unit for life or some other long-term period. If for life, the interest transferred may be considered a life lease, except that the right of occupancy is personal to the resident and may not be sublet or transferred in any fashion. A generally accepted rule of thumb for determining whether the term of the arrangement is considered to be continuing care is whether the promise to provide residents with care and services is for more than one year (see Chapter 21). Equity arrangements can involve a sale of the entire premises to resident-owners or a sale of only the residential units and the retention of dining, health care, and other service facilities by the developer-manager (see Chapter 7).

Continuing-care facilities usually accept as residents only those who are healthy and capable of independent living. The facilities provide convenience services, assisted-living care, and health care, as needed, as the resident moves along the continuum of care from the status of complete independence to greater dependence and possibly long-term illness. Sometimes, health care or personal care is provided without any significant increase in monthly fees. Recently, facilities offering a broad range of services and assistance along the continuum of care have used alternative payment mechanisms, such as an entrance fee with fee-for-service payments for care and conveniences on an à la carte basis or straight rental payments for shelter, food, and services. Though nontraditional in format, the facilities are also considered to be CCRCs.[50]

Continuing-care facility contracts have been categorized according to the following classifications based on the extent of included health care services:

- Type A—"Extensive" services including unlimited long-term care offered without any substantial increase in monthly fees over apartment rates.
- Type B—"Modified" arrangement where a specified allocation of nursing care is available without any substantial fee increase, or a discounted fee is available.
- Type C—"Fee-for-service" arrangement for long-term nursing care, resulting in substantial additional expense on transfer from the apartment unit.
- Type D—A month-to-month contract arrangement.

For Type A projects, the median one-bedroom entrance fee was reported in 1991 as $58,637 plus $871 per month; for Type B projects, $42,259 and $721 per month; and for Type C, $34,743 plus $583 per month.[51] For luxurious projects, entrance fees can be $250,000 or more. Of course, refundable fee programs, memberships, and equity projects may be considerably more expensive and in some areas climb to $500,000 or even $1 million. Fees vary greatly depending on location, unit size and luxury, the extent of prepaid services, the refund policy of the home, and similar factors. Although eligible for tax exemption (see §9.3), these facilities often cater to middle- and upper-income elderly who can afford the expense of extensive service programs.[52] Public awareness of the varieties of CCRCs continues to grow.[53]

Two major surveys of continuing-care retirement communities were prepared jointly by the American Association of Homes for the Aging and Ernst & Young in 1987 and 1989.[54] A comprehensive database was developed from responses to nationwide surveys of the entire "suspected" universe of CCRCs. Among the topics covered were different contract types, geographic location and regional trends, building styles, sizes of units, services provided, entrance fee and monthly fee amounts, numbers of units, resident ages and other characteristics, waiting periods, turnover rates of units, nursing use, operating expenses for various types of facilities, and many other statistics, tables, and charts. The survey questions and organization vary somewhat between the 1987 and 1989 versions.

Among the more interesting findings of the 1987 and 1989 studies are the following:

- CCRCs with fee-for-service nursing contracts tended to be smaller and older and have a higher proportion of nursing beds to independent-living units (average 108 to 129), whereas CCRCs with all-inclusive health care contracts were larger and had a higher proportion of independent-living units (151 nursing to 236 independent living on the average) [1987].

- The median entrance fee for facilities ranged from $32,800 for a studio to $68,250 for a two-bedroom unit [1989].
- Approximately 73 percent of the facilities used a declining refund-of-entrance-fee plan and about 19 percent charged a fully or partially refundable fee. However, among the facilities opened or under construction since 1985, 79 percent employed a fully or partially refundable fee option [1989].
- Approximately 75 percent of the residents are women and 75 percent are not married [1989].
- Nearly 30 percent of the facilities had waiting lists of one to five years for a one-bedroom apartment, and 35 percent required a one- to five-year wait for a two-bedroom unit [1987].
- Turnover of residential units averaged about 13 percent. Depending on the age of the facility, death was the cause of 4.2 to 4.8 percent of attrition, permanent transfers accounted for 5.6 to 8.8 percent, and resident moveouts ranged from 0.7 to 2 percent [1987].

Another major survey of CCRCs was published by the American Association of Homes for the Aging and Ernst & Young in 1993.[55] The data reveal the following:

- The percentage of CCRCs with fee-for-service nursing agreements decreased to 28 percent in 1990 from 38 percent in 1988. The percentage of CCRCs with all-inclusive health care contracts increased to 43 percent in 1990 from 36 percent in 1988.
- The origin of incoming CCRC residents was reported to be 30.4 percent from less than five miles away from the facility, 36.7 percent from six to 25 miles away from the facility, 17.4 percent from 26 to 100 miles away from the facility, and 15.5 percent from 101 or more miles away from the facility.
- The total number of units in CCRCs ranges from 69 to 2,107; the average is 319. Of these total units, CCRCs have an average of 200 independent-living units, 44 assisted-living or personal-care units or beds, and 91 nursing-care beds.
- In entrance fee CCRCs, 27 percent of residents choose a nonrefundable entrance fee, 57 percent choose an entrance fee with a refund that declines to zero over a period of time, and 16 percent choose a refundable entrance fee.
- On average, residents enter independent-living units at 78.8 years of age, assisted living or personal care at 83.7 years of age, and nursing care at 84.2 years of age.
- Approximately 89 percent of CCRCs holding Certificates of Need are not required by the Certificate of Need to restrict admission to CCRC contract holders and thus are permitted to serve constituents, the community, and residents.
- Approximately 98 percent of CCRCs are sponsored by nonprofit organizations.

A study of "emerging CCRCs" in operation five years or less was released in 1994 by Herbert Sims & Co. and AAHSA.[56] It reported average entrance fees of $145,886 and average monthly fees of $1,495; unit ratios of 3.2 independent-living units for each nursing unit and of 6.6 independent-living units for each assisted-living unit; extensive (Type A) services offered by 77 percent of those studied, with only 10 percent offering modified (Type B) and 13 percent fee-for-service (Type C) programs; and nonrefundable entrance fees offered by 47 percent of facilities, but with a majority of facilities offering multiple refund options, including a 90 to 100 percent refund from 52 percent of surveyed facilities.

According to data compiled by the American Association of Homes and Services for the Aging from *The Consumers' Directory of Continuing Care Retirement Communities, 1994–1995,*

- the average entry fees for CCRCs range from $59,010 to $85,868 for one-bedroom units and from $88,541 to $120,898 for two-bedroom units;
- the average monthly fees range from $1,046 to $1,399 for one-bedroom units and $1,249 to $1,622 for two-bedroom units; and
- extensive agreements are offered by 38 percent, modified agreements by 34 percent, and fee-for-service agreements by 41 percent. Fifteen percent do not charge an entrance fee; they charge only monthly fees and provide nursing care at monthly rates. The percentage offering condominium or cooperative arrangements is 6 percent.[57]

(e) Related Facilities

(1) Planned Residential Communities

Planned residential communities for seniors have been popularized since the late 1950s by such developments as Sun City, Arizona, and Leisure World in Laguna Hills, California. Sometimes called retirement communities or retirement villages, these projects essentially provide only a housing component and, perhaps, a modicum of common area recreational facilities and services such as grounds maintenance. Except for age restrictions applicable to residents of such communities, the projects are essentially pure real estate developments that do not raise as many of the unusual business, taxation, management, regulatory, and legal questions involved in the development of a seniors' community that offers extensive services or care. Nevertheless, many of the issues discussed in this book such as taxation, sales and use restrictions, age and other forms of discrimination, zoning, finance, admissions and transfer problems, and aging in place are applicable to these projects.

Generally, planned residential communities consist of single-family residences, duplexes, or condominium or apartment units, which are sold or leased to residents. While they may charge monthly association fees, the communities generally use the fees for purposes such as maintenance of common areas and facilities and not for provision of meals, convenience services, or care.

Although not designed to offer extensive services, personal assistance, or health care to their residents, some planned residential communities are finding that it may be necessary or advantageous to construct care facilities on the premises or nearby as their populations age in place. If the increasing age and dependence of such a population is ignored, significant problems can arise in dealing with transfers of residents out of the community or caring for them on site.[58]

Retirement communities developed as a part of a larger planned residential community have been identified as a new trend in the marketplace.[59] Typical master-planned community retirees are said to be between 60 and 65 years old, a majority pay in cash when buying homes, and they are more geographically mobile than other residents. Master-planned communities appealing to retirees are age-restricted and have at least one recreational amenity such as a golf course or community center. Active adult retirement communities also create spin-off land uses such as congregate, assisted-living, continuing-care, and skilled-nursing projects. Between 70 and 90 percent of the residents in congregate-care and nursing facilities located near the Sun City or Leisure World projects are reported to originate from within the nearby retirement community. For each 1,000 units in the active retirement community, 200 to 300 congregate units, including 100 to 150 assisted-living and/or nursing units, are said to be supportable.

(2) Nursing Homes

Facilities in which elderly people receive or have available to them round-the-clock nursing care are generally referred to as nursing facilities, nursing homes, or convalescent hospitals. While these facilities provide many of the elements of shelter, food services, and health care that are present in the retirement communities discussed above, nursing homes are essentially health care facilities that are based on a medical model and do not provide the homelike environment that typifies a seniors' housing community. Moreover, such facilities are not available to healthy persons who desire retirement living in a group setting but are not in need of constant health care or personal attention. Most states recognize this distinction and separately group nursing facilities with hospitals and other health care facilities in their licensing laws and regulations, whereas retirement communities, if regulated at all, are regulated by such government entities as departments of aging, real estate, social services, or even insurance.

The need for and cost of nursing care is great and is growing rapidly (see §1.6). Nevertheless, nursing facilities have been the prevalent choice for placement of many dependent elderly who are not in need of the constant nursing attention such facilities are designed to provide. Moreover, the institutional character of many such facilities is considered by some observers to be detrimental to many elderly persons who would adjust better to a more homelike setting. Many providers of nursing care are expanding into the residential-care field and offering assisted living, congregate housing, or other levels of service below nursing. In addition, continuing-care facilities often offer nursing on site or by special arrangement with a neighboring facility. Therefore, while a nursing facility, standing alone, is not the focal point of this book, nursing issues such as health care use (see §1.6), licensing regulations (see §20.3), health care finance (see Chapters 26 and 27), and business, tax, and reimbursement issues (e.g., see §§9.6, 13.2, and 23.2) are discussed in detail.

(3) Other Elderly Housing

Numerous other types of facilities that restrict admission to elderly persons exist in communities across the United States. They may not provide any significant measure of services designed to cater to the particular needs of independent or semidependent elderly persons. Examples of such facilities include adults-only apartments or condominium units or rent-assisted or other low-income housing. However, even low-income, federally subsidized housing may include congregate services, such as meals, or service coordinators (see, generally, Chapters 14 and 22). In addition, an estimated 76,000 elderly live in urban residence hotels that rent rooms to urban elderly persons on a monthly or longer-term basis.[60] As the populations of these essentially pure housing projects age, the facilities can become excellent candidates for conversion into more traditional retirement programs through the addition of services or arrangement for care, on or off the premises.

§2.4 Trends in Seniors' Housing Development

(a) New Participants in the Marketplace

In the past, retirement homes were almost exclusively the province of the nonprofit sector or of small family-run concerns. Since the mid-1980s, the interest of for-profit real estate developers in the seniors' housing field is in part a response to the demographics of the elderly population and its expected rapid growth. In addition, many real estate developers found it difficult to achieve a large measure of success in types of real estate developments that had historically been lucrative, such as shopping centers, condominiums, and high-rise office buildings. Whatever their motivations, for-profit en-

tities have made a concerted effort over the past decade to capture a substantial segment of the seniors' housing marketplace, particularly service-oriented facilities.

One can look to any of the four businesses that make up the retirement facility industry—housing, hospitality, health, and insurance—and find a major for-profit group that has actively pursued the development or financing of new facilities. There is expanded interest not only from those real estate developers who have extensive experience in the development of housing but also from those experienced in providing hospitalization and convenience services, including operators of hotel chains. Major hospital chains and insurance companies as well have expressed an interest and are taking steps toward significant involvement in the retirement facility field. Well-known corporate names such as Marriott, Hyatt, Aetna, Prudential, Avon, and Sears have ventured into (and some have backed out of) the field in recent years. For example, in 1995, Marriott's Senior Living Services subsidiary achieved $179 million in sales, whereas Marriott International realized sales of about $9 billion. In 1996, Marriott merged with one of its biggest competitors, Forum Group, Inc., which owned 42 seniors' housing facilities. As a result, Marriott now has more than 14,500 retirement community units or nursing home beds and is considered the second-largest developer and manager of such facilities in the United States.[61]

Although nonprofit facilities continue to dominate the field, it was reported in 1987 that 8,113 for-profit units were then under construction compared with 4,899 nonprofit retirement facility units.[62] Another survey from the late 1980s reported that 71 percent of new construction in the industry was attributable to for-profit developers.[63] A nationwide organization of largely for-profit retirement facility developers, service providers, and consultants, the National Association of Senior Living Industries (NASLI) was formed in 1985. In comparison, the nonprofit provider organization, the American Association of Homes and Services for the Aging (AAHSA), was founded more than 25 years ago. More recently, in 1991–1992, the American Seniors Housing Association (ASHA) and the Assisted Living Federation of America (ALFA) both emerged.

Figure 2.5 **Health Care Systems Operating Continuing-Care Retirement Communities**

Type of Health Care System	Number Responded to Survey	Number of CCRCs		Independent-Living Beds		Assisted-Living Beds		Nursing Home Beds	
		1995	1994	1995	1994	1995	1994	1995	1994
Catholic	22	65	67	6,073	6,172	1,964	1,790	2,403	2,236
Other Religious Sponsorship	13	119	115	15,125	13,933	2,852	2,767	8,398	8,109
Secular Not-for-Profit	21	119	114	16,135	14,960	1,792	1,477	5,967	5,691
For-Profit	18	182	179	14,652	17,689	6,976	6,011	4,879	4,084
Total	74	485	475	51,985	52,754	13,584	12,045	21,647	20,120

Survey data show changes in unit types within continuing-care retirement communities.

Source: Pallarito, K., "Assisted Living Leads Growth," *Modern Healthcare,* May 20, 1996.

Expanded interest has been witnessed not only in the for-profit sector but also among nonprofit institutions. Most notable are hospitals, which have been suffering under increasingly strict limitations on government reimbursement for health care services. The emergence in the Medicare program of such cost-saving devices as diagnosis-related groups (DRGs) has forced hospitals to look to other sources of revenue to help diversify and balance their financial pictures. In 1987, 79 community hospitals closed in the United States, constituting the highest number of hospital closings ever recorded.[64] The closings were attributed primarily to inadequate Medicare payments.[65] Consolidations, mergers, and closings in the hospital industry are continuing at an accelerated pace as we approach the year 2000.

Development of seniors' housing and care facilities is a natural next step for hospitals; many have explored the possibility,[66] and some are getting into the business. Many can develop seniors' facilities on available land adjacent to the hospital site and can furnish health care, dining, housekeeping, and other services from a central location at the hospital itself. However, hospitals should be cautioned that the location may not be attractive to the healthy elderly and that the institutional character of dining, housekeeping, and other services provided by hospitals in their own facilities is likely to be inappropriate in a retirement facility, where homestyle qualities are expected.

In the mid-1980s, the number of centers owned or leased by multihospital systems was reportedly up by more than 20 percent in a year, with an 87 percent increase in hospital-managed units.[67] Nursing home chains reported an 8.5 percent increase in retirement facility operations.[68] However, many nursing home chains had mixed success in the field, and many hospitals were slow to get beyond the initial inquiry stages.[69] One reason offered for hospitals' delayed involvement in the seniors' housing business was that their first priority was to build nursing homes for acute patients waiting to be discharged to long-term care.[70] However, a 1992 survey indicated that the number of CCRCs owned and managed by health care systems increased by 16 percent in 1991.[71] A 1994 survey of 96 health care systems indicated a 6 percent increase in CCRCs owned or operated by health care systems since 1992. This survey also revealed a 10 percent increase in CCRCs owned or managed by secular not-for-profit health care systems, an 8.5 percent increase in CCRCs owned or managed by for-profit systems, a 5 percent increase in CCRCs owned or managed by Catholic health care systems, and a 4 percent increase in the number of CCRCs owned or managed by other religious facilities.[72]

Modern Healthcare's 1996 Multiunit Providers Survey indicated that although there was minuscule growth in the number of CCRCs owned or managed by hospital systems and nursing home chains, the number of assisted-living beds operated by CCRCs had risen by 12.8 percent, for a total of 13,584. The survey also showed that, within CCRCs, the number of independent-living units dipped slightly, whereas the number of nursing home beds serving CCRC residents rose by 7.6 percent (see Figure 2.5).

Hospital and nursing home operators seem well suited to the development and operation of seniors' housing and care communities and should prove successful in the long run, provided that they recognize the importance of the housing, convenience services, and financial security elements of the business.

(b) New Business Structures and Partnerships

Over the last decade, the newfound interest of real estate developers, the hospitality industry, and other for-profit enterprises in the seniors' housing industry has brought about changes in the complexion of the industry.

For example, nonprofit organizations have dominated the CCRC industry. Historically, nonprofit organizations, and particularly church groups, also have been engaged in the operation of health care facilities such as hospitals and nursing homes. It was a logical transition for them to move into the provision of health care in homes for the aging. Many real estate developers, on the other hand, have experience almost exclusively in the development of housing and are not generally familiar with the health care business or with the provision of basic services such as meals and housekeeping, which routinely go along with the provision of health care in facilities. Nevertheless, real estate developers may recognize consumer desires and needs for the provision of health care in a retirement facility and may be looking for ways to provide the full panoply of services available at many of the existing nonprofit centers— without being required to learn the new business of health and hospitality services.

A natural consequence of the desire of real estate developers to provide services not normally associated with the real estate business is the development of joint ventures or contractual relationships with management companies or health care service providers or the purchase of long-term-care insurance to cover the risk of future health care costs. These and other methods help the real estate developer provide the full spectrum of services by tapping the resources and expertise of existing companies already in the health care, service, or financial security businesses (see Chapter 11 regarding joint ventures). Some developers who have avoided the pro-

vision of care and extensive services due to their lack of familiarity with regulatory and management implications have found a shortage of consumer demand for their products (see §§2.4 (g) and (h)).

Tax laws and the desire to create new products that will be competitive with those offered by charitable organizations have also led to the development of different ownership and operational structures, including refundable entrance fees, membership clubs, and condominium and cooperative care facilities (discussed in §§2.4 (c) to (f) and more fully in Part III). Other new kinds of facility ownerships and structures also have emerged, including for-profit life-care projects, rental retirement projects with a full continuum of care, and more freestanding assisted-living facilities.[73]

Initially, the influx of eager developers into the elderly marketplace raised some controversy. Nonprofit providers expressed concern that many of the flood of new, profit-oriented developers would not remain interested in keeping long-term commitments to residents and might sell off their facilities once they depreciated, or they would overbuild and be forced to turn over unprofitable projects.[74] For-profit developers countered that many of the major retirement facility failures have been those of nonprofit operators, who, due to misguided altruism, inexperience, incompetence, or even criminally fraudulent business practices, have caused some older people to be displaced or lose money (see §5.2).

To some extent, these exchanges between the for-profit and nonprofit sectors are a byproduct of competitive pressures; mistakes have been made in both camps. On the other hand, nonprofit senior-care facilities have over the years repeatedly had to distinguish themselves before the public, the press, and lawmakers from the predominantly for-profit nursing homes where allegations of poor care seem to be regularly raised. Ironically, though, in many areas these for-profit nursing facilities are largely responsible for caring for poor Medicaid patients while many nonprofits cater to a greater proportion of private-pay patients who can afford a better standard of care. In the seniors' housing facility field, however, both groups still seem to be competing most vigorously for the more affluent market segment despite calls for expansion into the moderate-income market.

Most thoughtful observers recognize that quality of care and commitment to service of the elderly is not the exclusive domain of either group and that nonprofits and for-profits have much to offer the public and each other. Still, latent stereotypes and prejudices may have to be overcome to pursue a successful joint venture. Increasingly, there seems to be a recognition that for-profit developers and operators are here to stay and that their common interests with nonprofits outweigh many of the differences.

(c) Resident Ownership versus Rental

The debate continues regarding whether rental or resident ownership is the best approach in general or for a given project. Until recently, most service-oriented retirement housing has been offered in a rental format, even where facilities and services are contracted for on a life-time or other long-term basis. Despite the existence of large retirement subdivision developments where residents own their own homes, most congregate housing, assisted-living, continuing-care, and HUD-financed seniors' housing has been made available on the basis that the premises are not owned by the resident but are essentially leased, whether the term is on a month-to-month basis, renewable annually, or for life. For example, a survey of developers indicated that rental retirement projects, aimed mainly at younger (age 75 to 79) seniors, surpassed ownership models by a three-to-one margin in the mid-1980s.[75] Another report showed that while 70 percent of respondents to one retirement housing survey offered rental units, entry fees plus monthly fees were offered by more than 38 percent, life care by more than 23 percent, and equity ownership by more than 11 percent.[76]

In the 1990s, a definite boom in the development of condominium and cooperative retirement facilities with full services and health care has been visible.[77] Studies have shown that elderly persons overwhelmingly prefer homeownership to rentals or other arrangements.[78] Ownership also makes residents eligible to defer or exclude taxable gain on the sale of their previous residence (see §§7.1, 7.2). Moreover, the Tax Reform Act of 1986 created some serious impediments to investment in rental housing, which may hasten the trend (see §8.2). Nevertheless, tax considerations may not predominate when compared with countervailing issues that affect control of operations, especially in facilities with substantial services.

An interesting example of the phenomenon of increased ownership in facilities with services is the development of continuing-care-style communities that are sold to residents as condominiums or cooperatives. Health care and service packages can be made available through the residents' association, which can contract for services with a management company. Unfortunately, homeowners' associations are not well suited to management of complex operations that may affect members' health and welfare in ways well beyond the usual housing and maintenance issues that face most such groups. However, operations-oriented developers may retain control over services via retention of ownership or easements covering service facilities (see Chapter 7). While there are many advantages to ownership, especially tax advantages to the consumer (see §7.1(d)(1)), the concerns of the developer/operator about maintaining control over the facility vis-à-vis the homeowners will probably result in the continued pre-eminence of the rental format over true ownership in service-oriented seniors' housing. Nevertheless, the proportion of retirement communities with an ownership structure or a related equity factor such as a membership, stock ownership, or refundable fee system will certainly continue to grow.

(d) Terminable versus Continuing Contracts

Another major dichotomy in approaches is between traditional monthly rentals or annual leases and life-care or continuing-care structures where (sometimes after an initial probation period) residents cannot be evicted except for cause.[79] Because continuing-care promises are more complex and are generally accompanied by substantial entrance fees or endowment payments, sales can require more consumer education. In markets where there is little familiarity with a particular breed of retirement community, developers may face exceptional challenges in educating buyers. One consultant[80] tells the story of a developer who had created beautiful models of proposed continuing-care units but was having difficulty closing any but a few sales. When asked why they were not buying the units, prospects responded that they could not assess whether they would be getting their money's worth. The nearest continuing-care facilities were in a neighboring state. After the development of brochures comparing the project with other continuing-care facilities led to little added success, the developer, to improve sales, eventually had to charter a bus to take prospects across state lines to visit the other communities. Continuing-care arrangements, while arguably better for consumers, also can be intimidating to many lenders, who prefer a simple rental to an actuarially encumbered life-time arrangement.

In the opinion of one experienced marketing consultant, rental retirement facilities have the following advantages and disadvantages when compared with a traditional entrance fee model:[81]

- **Rental Advantages**
  - No major lump-sum cost commitment is required.
  - Resident controls investment of the proceeds of sale of home.
  - If dissatisfied with the facility, resident can leave without a significant financial loss.
  - Resident's children are generally more receptive.
  - Less education of the prospect may be required.
- **Rental Disadvantages**
  - Resident perceives that the facility has only a short-term commitment to them.
  - Any price increases are likely to have a greater impact than in an entrance fee structure.
  - Rental can be perceived as low income or lesser quality.
  - Age group responding is typically older.[82]

From a financing perspective, rentals and traditional endowment projects may have some of the following attributes and problems:[83]

- **Rentals**
  - Less than full occupancy can jeopardize meeting of debt service.
  - Renters are more subject to rent increases to pay for construction debt due to interest fluctuations, vacancies, or other factors.
  - Residents are subject to displacement as a result of foreclosure action.

- **"Endowment" or Life-Time Contract**
  - Contract helps control fluctuations in monthly fees.
  - Contract helps retire construction debt, making residence more secure.
  - Public bond issues can greatly increase project costs.
  - Repayment of bonds can be dependent on turnover and resale of units many years after the facility opens.
  - The resident's position is always secondary to that of the bondholders.

However, consumer preferences may be guided not so much by the financial arrangement as by product image. In a survey by the American Association of Retired Persons, about half the respondents reported that they would consider living in a continuing-care facility. About the same number would consider moving into congregate housing. Yet only 26 percent would consider a cooperative, and only 17 percent a board-and-care home.[84]

Continuing care is an attractive but not a simple product. Experienced developers estimate that the creation of a life-care facility can require an average four to five years: a year of planning before marketing, another year to reach the 50 to 60 percent presales level often required for financing, 18 months of construction, and six months or more to move in residents.[85] Marketing costs can easily reach $4,000 to $6,000 per unit in a continuing-care facility, whereas in rental projects, such fees may be about half that amount.[86]

Despite the complexities of continuing care, it attracted much attention during the retirement housing boom of the past decade. This is due in part to the growing ranks of the very old and the probabilities of their eventual need for care in a financially secure environment on a long-term basis (see §§1.3, 1.6). Because of the simplicity of straight rentals and many developers' and consumers' familiarity with the rental concept, rentals will probably continue to hold a substantial proportion of the over-65 market. The assisted-living boom of the mid-1990s is almost entirely grounded on a rental product. However, the proportionate share of continuing-care facilities should continue to rise, especially in areas where there is already some consumer awareness of the arrangement and its benefits. Some commentators have charged that continuing-care facilities have failed to satisfy the desires of senior citizens by attracting only slightly more than 1 percent of the current age- and income-qualified senior market.[87] On the other hand, other observers consider continuing-care retirement communities to constitute a major means of financing long-term care, which will eventually grow to serve more than 18 percent of the elderly age 76 and older:[88]

Period	Number of Elderly in CCRCs (millions)	Percent of Elderly Population
1986–1990	0.339	3.21
2001–2005	2.044	11.66
2016–2020	3.607	18.24

The availability of long-term-care insurance may result in a blurring of the distinctions between traditional continuing-care facilities, which require an entrance fee, and rental facilities, which may provide financial security for long-term care by means of a monthly premium payment.[89]

(e) Diversification and Unbundling of Services

Service packages in seniors' housing facilities traditionally have been provided on more or less an all-or-nothing basis. A definite trend over the past decade has been the unbundling of services (i.e., making them optional). A corollary tendency is toward the proliferation of services and service options. To some extent, the trends moderate each other, as facilities that offer it all tend to break up packages, and those adding services where there were previously none do so in small packaged options.

Continuing-care facilities primarily have offered comprehensive service packages for a single monthly fee, with relatively few service options available on an à la carte basis and little opportunity to receive credit for services available in the facility but not used by the resident. The more recent tendency in these facilities is to provide more optional and fewer mandatory services. On the other hand, many facilities that historically favored the congregate housing model made available relatively few convenience services other than meals. In part, this latter fact was

due to the low- and moderate-income, federally financed roots of the congregate housing market. Now, these facilities are going uptown and upscale and are offering more services, both à la carte and as a part of monthly fees. With ever-increasing competition, the range of service options between the all-included and the nothing-included extremes rapidly has been filled. Rather than moving in one direction or the other, the industry appears to have filled in the middle ground.

Examples of the unbundling of services abound. Types of optional services typically seen are extra meals, guest rooms, special diets, valet parking, cable television, health insurance, extra housekeeping, dry cleaning, errand services, catering, beauty parlor services, and private-duty nursing, among others.

With respect to health care, whereas traditional continuing-care facilities have provided all needed health care, including hospitalizations, for the rest of a resident's life, many facilities are now limiting the scope and volume of health care services that will be available in return for an entrance fee, regular monthly fee, or other form of prepayment or predictable payment. Instead of full care, the facility may offer a limited number of skilled-nursing days per year, or over the lifetime of the resident, without any additional charge. But if the resident requires additional nursing services, hospitalization, or other health care or personal services not included in the prepaid or periodically paid program, he or she will be charged for such additional care on a fee-for-service basis. Some alternatives to full health care guarantees have been categorized as follows:[90]

- Percentage Guarantee—The resident pays a percentage of the fee-for-service charges, with the facility paying the balance.
- Per Day Guarantee—The retirement community pays an established dollar amount per day and the resident pays the rest.
- Cumulative Day Guarantee—The facility covers all charges up to a certain number of days per year and the resident is responsible for all extra days.
- Cumulative Dollar Guarantee—The community pays for care up to a dollar limit per year, a lifetime limit, some percentage of the entrance fee, or a similar dollar amount.

See Volume II, §3.5, for examples of some of these provisions in resident agreements.

The trend toward more services and more service options should continue as seniors' housing developers seek to fashion custom products that will help distinguish their projects from others and from existing facilities in their areas. As consumers become more educated to the various types of available service programs and competition increases and choices expand, many will demand the ability to select from a menu of services and amenities rather than being required to enroll in and pay for a complete service package that may contain elements they do not want or need. However, the pure à la carte approach can be costly, as anyone who has eaten at a fine French restaurant can attest. The elderly will want more services, but if economies of scale require mandatory participation, many will be willing to participate only in limited mandatory programs.

A good example is meals. Three meals per day included as part of a monthly fee structure is becoming more and more rare. People want to have the option to fix their own breakfast or to go out to lunch or dinner with a friend or spouse without suffering an economic penalty. Therefore, facilities may offer one included meal per day, at the resident's choice, with additional meals available for an extra charge, or a choice between single- and multiple-meal plans. This is more of a Chinese menu approach, combining a set package with a pure à la carte option. It is representative of the probable model for many seniors' housing community programs to be developed in coming years.

(f) New Payment Mechanisms

One change that will have the greatest impact on the business structure, marketing, and legal implications of any project is the development of new payment mechanisms for seniors' housing occupancy and services. This trend is largely the product of increased competition and the influx of real estate developers and other for-profit entities into the business. For example, real estate developers who wish to provide residents with some measure of security or predictability regarding the costs of future health care but are unwilling to bear the risk themselves have turned to the insurance industry for products that will pro-

vide financial security at a fixed monthly rate and on a noncancellable, life-time basis. The insurance industry has responded, and custom-tailored insurance products designed to accommodate the needs of an individual seniors' community have been created to bridge the gap between developers familiar primarily with real estate and the perceived eventual need of the consumer for health care and financial security (see §27.2(c)(2)).

Another concept that has grown substantially in recent years is the refundable entrance fee for continuing-care facilities. Historically, about 90 percent of continuing-care facilities refunded some portion of the entrance fee upon a resident's voluntary withdrawal from the community.[91] However, such refunds traditionally were limited to those who left the facility within the first few years of residence, in which case the entrance fee would be amortized to the facility owner at the rate of 1 or 2 percent per month of residence and the balance refunded. Moreover, in the early 1980s, only about half of existing CCRCs were reported to refund any portion of the entrance fee upon the death of the resident.[92] Therefore, if a resident died very shortly after admission, a substantial entrance fee could be lost in exchange for very little in terms of services actually received (see §21.6(c) for a discussion of the actuarial rationale for this system).

In the late 1980s, many providers experimented with the concept of a refundable entrance fee, whereby the entrance fee or some fixed percentage of it is fully refunded to the resident or the resident's estate upon the termination of occupancy of the seniors' housing unit, without regard to the duration of residence or the reason for contract termination. Since then, as much as 40 percent of new CCRC projects have been developed as refundable fee projects (see §6.2). This method of financing naturally requires a higher entrance fee upon admission to the facility, and the facility operator retains the income generated by the entrance fee for the period that the resident occupies the premises. A rule of thumb is that the refundable entrance fee is of necessity 25 to 50 percent higher than a nonrefundable entrance fee in order to achieve economic equivalence. Nevertheless, many elderly people find the refundable entrance fee desirable because it is perceived not to result in a disinheritance of one's heirs and provides an opportunity for the resident to recoup some of his or her initial payments in the event of a decision to terminate occupancy after the first few years of residence. Variations on the refundable entrance fee concept have included the sale of memberships, similar to country club memberships, or cooperative or condominium interests, as a means to give the resident an opportunity to receive a return on investment through resale of the interest once occupancy is relinquished. In addition, some developers have offered residents corporate stock, which can be redeemed at cost when the buyer leaves the facility.[93]

It has been suggested that refundable entrance fee or membership types of structures, in effect, act as private investment bonds, which can replace interim public bond financing.[94] Such a system puts the resident in a primary position as creditor in the event of a failure and may reduce bond counsel costs.[95] But such fee structures may raise special securities registration issues (see Chapter 24). In addition, refundable fees or arrangements where the developer promises to repurchase resident memberships, cooperative shares, or other interests may be subject to reserve requirements to ensure that there is an ability to make good on the promise (see §21.5).

Some facilities applying "unbundling of services" thinking to their fee structures have offered residents the option of selecting a refundable or nonrefundable program. In one example, residents were able to choose between a $67,125 fee, 94 percent of which is refundable upon death or withdrawal, and a $44,750 fee, where 18 percent of it becomes nonrefundable per year of residence, and all is lost upon death. The developer reported that most prospects selected the higher, refundable fee.[96] In another case, however, where the entrance fee was the same for both the refundable and nonrefundable option, but where the refundable fee carried a higher monthly charge, most residents chose the nonrefundable plan.[97] One researcher contends that when given the choice of higher refundable entrance fees or lower nonrefundable fees, the nonrefundable fees are selected by only about one-third of prospective residents.[98]

Refundable fees are not without some controversy, however. One industry spokesperson warned, "Whoever picks a refundable entrance fee is betting

he'll die early."[99] In addition, imputed interest taxation issues may accompany a resident's refundable fee payment (see §6.2(b)). Nevertheless, a significant segment of the seniors' market will be willing to pay a premium to insure its investments against the possibility of death or a change of heart before reaching actuarially calculated life expectancies. While it may be more economical in the long run to choose a nonrefundable fee structure, refundable fees, promises to repurchase resident stock or memberships, and related plans have continued to grow in number.

(g) Consumerism, Choice, and Assisted Living

Consumers are becoming better educated about the seniors' housing marketplace. The proliferation of new product types and options and the media attention given generally to the industry have resulted in critical analysis of, and comparison shopping among, available projects based on cost, services, fee options, tax consequences, health coverage, and other factors affecting value and security. At the same time, government is acting to protect consumers through increased industry regulation and antidiscrimination laws (see Chapters 20–23). Private consumer groups also are assisting the public in evaluating facilities.[100]

For example, in 1990, the National Consumers League published an updated consumer guide to life-care communities covering topics such as the potential for fraud and mismanagement, the types of services and amenities offered, and a checklist for consumers considering a life-care community (see Figure 2.6).

The notion that "if you build it, they will come" is no longer operative. The seniors' housing industry has seen overbuilding, especially of congregate housing projects in certain areas. These projects are usually rentals and do not provide the assisted-living or health care services available at other types of facilities. There also were a number of sales of retirement housing and nursing home companies and properties in the late 1980s.[101]

Many developers are finding that the retirement community market is largely "need-driven" and that the availability of on-site care is a marketing plus. Accordingly, there has been an increased interest in

Figure 2.6 **CCRC Consumer Checklist**

Housing

- What is the size of the unit?
- Are home maintenance and repairs provided? At any extra cost?
- Are any housekeeping services provided? At any extra cost?
- Are gardening and grounds services provided? At any extra cost?
- Is there special housing for married couples?
- Are the residences furnished?
- Can you bring your own furnishings?
- What is done with your personal property in the event that you move elsewhere within the life-care community?
- How does the monthly fee compare to the cost of renting a comparable unit in the same vicinity?
- What are your rights as a tenant under an occupancy license?
- Can you be removed from your residence against your will? Under what circumstances?
- How long is the residence maintained in your absence (such as an indefinite stay in the nursing facility)? At any extra cost?
- What are the tenants' rights under state contract law in a life-care arrangement? What state agency regulates the law?

Health Care

- Is the community's health facility on the premises?
- Is the health facility approved by Medicare or Medicaid? If not, who has inspected and licensed the facility?
- Is each resident required or recommended to carry private supplementary insurance or Medigap?
- Does the community accept Medicaid payment?
- Exactly what medical services are provided as part of the community's health plan?
- Is the nursing unit licensed as a skilled-nursing facility?
- Does the community's plan equal or exceed medical coverage offered by Medicare and private health insurance?
- Do residents have to pay deductibles or coinsurance?
- How are the community's physicians selected?
- Is each resident given the option to continue with his or her family physician? At any extra cost?

- Does the community health plan provide free coverage of routine checkups? prescriptions? medical appliances? eyeglasses? dental care? psychiatric care? podiatry? care by specialists?
- Does the community health plan provide tray service, special diet, and home care when necessary? At any extra cost?
- Does the community health center meet state standards as a skilled-nursing facility?
- What is the ratio of nursing staff to patients?
- Is there a nursing staff and physician on call at the community 24 hours?
- Does the community offer private rooms to patients in the nursing facility?
- Who decides—management, the resident, or the physician—if and when a resident must enter the nursing facility?

Finances

- What is the entrance (or founder's) fee?
- Under what circumstances, if any, can it be refunded?
- Is the entrance fee subject to IRS taxation as an "interest-free loan"? How much will this increase the cost of living in the community?
- What are the monthly fees?
- How are they calculated?
- What percentage of your payments will be used toward medical care? (This percentage is the only portion of your expenditures that may be listed as deductible on income tax returns.)
- Under what conditions, if any, would the monthly fee be subject to change? Are these changes tied to predictable factors, such as the Consumer Price Index?
- What expenses are expected to be covered by the resident?
- What organization or person actually owns the community?
- Is the community a proprietary (for-profit) or nonprofit organization?
- Is the community sponsored or affiliated with a larger organization (religious or otherwise)?
- What are the legal, financial, and/or moral responsibilities of the sponsor to the life-care community?
- Is the community financially independent?

Continued →

Figure 2.6 **(continued)**

- What are the community's financial reserves?
- Are the entrance fees held in reserve funds or used to meet current operating costs?
- For life-care communities presently under construction, what percentage of the entry fees, if any, are being held in escrow or reserve funds?
- What percentage covers construction expenses?
- If a new facility, how many units were sold before construction began?
- How are monthly fees and residency status affected by changes in marital status (widowhood or remarriage)?

Contracts

- What are the community's admissions policies?
- Who serves on the community's board of directors?
- What are their credentials?
- Do residents have any redress if or when the community sponsor changes?
- How long a grace period is allowed for your decision whether or not to enter the community?
- What are the provisions of the contract? How binding is it?
- Is any balance of your investment reimbursed to you or your family in the event of your withdrawal or death?
- Are funeral services provided? At any extra cost?
- Are you provided with a choice in location of burial?
- Are there any stipulations on having guests in the community?
- What is the community policy regarding residents who encounter financial difficulty in meeting monthly fees?

Community and Social Services

- What part do residents have in formulating the community's policies and services?
- What recreation and activities are provided? At any extra cost?
- Are any transportation services provided? At any extra cost?
- Does the community provide any social workers or counseling services? At any extra cost?
- Are there facilities on the premises for religious observance? For what denominations?
- Are there any rebates for facilities not used by a resident?
- Do residents have any voice in menu planning?
- Are there arrangements for activities outside the community?

development of assisted-living facilities and other facilities, such as continuing care, that offer assistance to residents in need of such services, and in ownership models that provide more financial security.[102] The homelike environment of assisted living is also more desirable to consumers than the institutional nursing facility. Of the respondents to the State of Seniors Housing 1994 survey (conducted by the American Seniors Housing Association and Coopers & Lybrand) that planned to develop new seniors' housing during the next year,

- Forty-two percent planned to develop standalone assisted-living facilities.
- Just over 21 percent planned to develop either congregate housing with assisted-living or Alzheimer's specialty care facilities.
- Fifteen percent planned to develop CCRCs.
- Nearly 13 percent planned to develop active adult retirement communities.[103]

By 1996, the survey reported that assisted living accounted for 54 percent of all seniors' housing construction for the year.

A nationwide boom in the construction of assisted-living facilities was first identified in 1989 and 1990, particularly among for-profit companies,[104] and has continued strongly through the decade. Approximately 210,000 residents, many of them female and over the age of 80, were estimated to be receiving assisted-living services in specially designed facilities or as part of a continuing-care community[105] (see §2.3(c)). In the meantime, the growth has been dramatic. The market is so active that, from 1995 to 1997, at least a dozen companies specializing in assisted living went public.[106] Some of the attractions to developers of assisted-living projects and their residents have been that

- residents pay monthly charges, unlike nursing facilities, where the operator must rely on Medicaid funding;
- assisted-living services are less heavily regulated than skilled nursing and often not subject to Certificate of Need laws; however, this factor may lead to overbuilding;
- labor costs may be as much as 50 percent less than labor costs in a nursing home, and employees are easier to find;

- assisted-living facility rates are only 70 to 75 percent of those charged at intermediate-care facilities; and
- the presence of assisted-living services may help attract residents to a community because of their increasing concern about the ability to care for themselves.

Nursing home chains have been reported to be most interested in assisted-living services.[107] Assisted-living units, often in 30- to 60-unit projects, are built next to nursing homes, which act as a "feeder" source for patients who are discharged but unable to live safely at home. Some providers are also converting independent-living retirement center wings to assisted living. The average length of stay in assisted-living units is reportedly approximately two to two and one-half years compared with a six- to nine-month stay at a nursing facility. Monthly rates can range between $900 and $1,350, and land, development, and furnishing costs can equal $50,000 per unit. There is significant concern that assisted living can be overbuilt and that putting the nursing home population into the less-regulated assisted-living environment can lead to significant liability problems (see Chapter 29).

Some observers have detected a trend toward the development of smaller projects.[108] The results of the State of Seniors Housing 1994 survey confirmed such a trend. Respondents to the survey planned to build projects of the following sizes in the next year:

Size of Project (in units)	Percent of Respondents
25–50	22.6
50–100	39.3
100–150	23.8
150–250	8.3
Over 250	6.0[109]

In addition, many observers believe that the industry is concentrating too heavily on the upper-income market and is not serving middle-income consumers. Some developers are beginning to change their focus and to develop projects that are affordable to middle-income seniors.[110]

The 1980s taught newcomers to the industry as well as established providers that consumers want options, services, security, and affordability. Prospects will no longer simply entrust themselves to a non-profit organization without comparison shopping. They will not fall for architecture and creature comforts without consideration of their future need for care. They do not have unlimited wealth and want plenty of value for their money. To be sure, consumers will want a variety of retirement products as diverse as are they and their circumstances. Although assisted living is the current hot product, developers and operators must continually assess consumer needs and wants carefully and target their product parameters accordingly to be successful as we enter the next century.

(h) State-of-the-Industry Surveys

From 1988 through 1995, an annual State of the Seniors Housing Industry survey was conducted by Senior Housing Investment Advisors of Newton, Massachusetts. The survey polled developers, managers, marketers, and financial, legal, and other experts in the field. A snapshot view of the collective annual fads, fears, hopes, and plans of those polled is summarized for each of those years. "The State of Seniors Housing 1996," published by the American Seniors Housing Association (ASHA), surveyed 40,000 units of congregate, assisted-living, and continuing-care properties.

(1) 1988

The 1988 survey of 25 industry experts revealed a number of interesting observations about the status and predicted future of the seniors' housing field.[111] The following are representative of the conclusions drawn by the panel:

- Projects have been oriented to consumers age 75 and older on the basis of need. Greater efforts will be made to attract the younger, more demand-driven market segment.
- There has been a great expansion recently in rental congregate housing, but the supply of vacant conventional rentals and changes in the tax laws warrant close inspection of such projects in certain markets. In general, product offerings must be differentiated to increase absorption in areas characterized by overbuilding.

- The trend toward ownership housing, such as condominiums and cooperatives, will increase due in part to tax reform and the increasing desire of seniors to retain control over their investments.
- Life-care and continuing-care models will continue to be successful and will be enhanced by long-term-care insurance and innovative financial packages such as pay-as-you-go health care programs and refundable entrance fees.
- Freestanding assisted-living/personal-care facilities should increase substantially.
- Larger projects exceeding 150 units will continue to dominate, but there will be a growing trend toward building smaller, more affordable facilities. This will require exploration of innovative financing techniques, operating cost controls, reevaluation of design and amenity assumptions, and spreading developer fees over long-term operations.
- Health care providers and nonprofit organizations will become increasingly involved in the industry.
- National companies will continue to move cautiously into the industry.
- Lenders will require greater education about the industry.
- Public subsidies for seniors' housing will be limited by the deficit reduction concerns of the federal government.

(2) 1989

The 1989 survey[112] identified the following trends and issues, among others:

- a need to develop more affordable products;
- continued difficulty obtaining financing;
- the need for sound management and well-crafted residence agreements;
- an emphasis on service quality and à la carte options;
- an increase in condominiums, cooperatives, and refundable fee models;
- an increase in assisted-living units and facilities; and
- a decline in the need for more rental, congregate housing projects.

(3) 1990

The 1990 State of the Seniors Housing Industry Report[113] took a longer-term view than earlier surveys. Among the conclusions were the following:

- a move toward intergenerational mixed-use communities;
- a trend toward smaller projects with less glamorous public areas and a focus on living spaces;
- an increasing reliance on consumer financing (e.g., via condominiums and cooperatives) in view of the near collapse of the savings and loan industry and cuts in government programs;
- a deemphasis on biomedical care, with greater reliance on "low-tech" health maintenance and preventive programs;
- increased consumer awareness and participation in land use planning processes affecting seniors' housing development;
- increased consumer protection regulations, particularly affecting continuing-care and assisted-living communities; and
- recognition of the aging-in-place phenomenon and a departure from standalone rental projects without provision for health-related services.

(4) 1991

In 1991, limited financing and increased regulation were focal points for the following observations:

- Overbuilding and a credit crunch make financing the critical issue, with hope for a rebound in the economy.
- Existing projects in difficulty should be "repositioned" and larger projects developed in phases.
- Lenders require higher equity and debt service coverages.
- Management and marketing experience are more important, with an emphasis on a "caring" philosophy.
- Increased state regulation of CCRCs, extensive new antidiscrimination laws, strict new nursing facility regulations, and proposed federal regulation of assisted-living facilities will make the industry increasingly more complicated.
- Focused marketing, with an emphasis on affordability, must replace a reliance on broad-based demographics.

(5) 1992

The 1992 report[114] recognized the industry's current sense of uncertainty and emphasized the following "back-to-basics" approach:

- Lenders are viewing the industry as a service industry and look for operating experience.
- Need-oriented communities, recognizing the need for care, present better opportunities for developers.
- Alliances between for-profit and nonprofit groups, while feasible and desirable, have been slow to develop.
- Acquisition and conversion of failed or marginal housing projects and the addition of assisted-living or other care components are the current strategies.
- Industrywide standards and performance data are needed to attract financing.

(6) 1993

The following indicates that the 1993 survey struck a more optimistic note than in earlier years:[115]

- Seniors' housing and assisted living are expected to be favored by national health care reform efforts as a consequence of increasingly high costs of Medicaid-funded nursing care.
- Lenders appear to have a renewed interest in retirement communities, particularly assisted-living facilities.
- Pressure on hospitals to "download" patients to nursing facilities for subacute care will also drive low-acuity nursing patients into residential models of care.
- Affordability remains a key concern as the nation's economy shows modest signs of recovery.
- Residential-care providers fear that excessive regulation may be a consequence of the re-direction of federal funds from medical models of care.

(7) 1994

The 1994 industry survey was made in the context of a national debate about health care reform, which included concerns about integration of health care delivery systems and control of costs. Among the observations of the 20 industry experts surveyed were the following:[116]

- State or federal funding of assisted living is likely, and with it will come regulation.
- Affiliations and joint ventures, managed care, wellness programs, care delivery "without walls" to the general public, and use of insurance products are all innovative ways in which seniors' housing providers can fit into the "integrated" long-term-care system.
- Seniors' housing providers are becoming more cost-conscious and providing better value; consumers are becoming better educated and more receptive to the product; and occupancy levels are increasing.
- There is a resurgence of interest among lenders, particularly for acquisitions and refinancings and, to a lesser degree, for new construction. Wall Street investment houses, insurance companies, and pension funds appear to be most active.

(8) 1995

The 1995 survey identified the following trends:[117]

- Assisted-living regulation and disability discrimination remain the most significant regulatory issues.
- While demand for retirement housing continues to outpace supply, there is concern that new assisted-living projects may be approaching a level of overabundance.
- Excessive regulation is hampering growth in the continuing-care field.
- It is becoming increasingly difficult to develop affordable seniors' housing due to funding cutbacks.
- Developers and lenders are better informed and are making fewer mistakes than in past years.
- Managed care and community-based services represent new challenges for seniors' housing and long-term-care providers.

(9) 1996–1997

Respondents to ASHA's survey, conducted in 1996 and published in 1997, revealed the following facts about the industry:[118]

- The median level of occupancy for all seniors' housing property types is a healthy 96 percent.
- Median return on investment is 15.2 percent for assisted living, 14.6 percent for CCRCs, and 11.1 percent for congregate housing.

- Average lengths of stay are 115 months for CCRCs, 40 months for congregate properties, and 24 months for assisted living.
- The median number of units per property is 77 for assisted living, 148 for congregate, and 351 for continuing care.
- For-profit companies own 93.6 percent of all assisted-living, 83.9 percent of congregate, and 45.2 percent of the continuing-care properties that responded; the rest are not-for-profit.

Notes

1. For a general discussion of elderly housing options, *see* Hancock, J., ed., *Housing the Elderly* (New Brunswick, NJ: Center for Urban Policy Research, 1987).

2. Adapted from Elrod, L., "Housing Alternatives for the Elderly," *Journal of Family Law,* 18 (1979–1980), 723.

3. These are sometimes referred to as "naturally occurring retirement communities" or "NORCs."

4. Throughout this book, the terms "seniors' housing" and "retirement communities or facilities" or some combination of that terminology are used more or less interchangeably.

5. For discussions of various facility models and architectural and amenities options, see, generally, *Professional Builder,* Sept. 1985 and Apr. 1986.

6. Testimony of Jack L. Bowersox, House Committee on Aging, May 22, 1984.

7. A comprehensive study of retirement communities conducted in 1993 by the American Seniors Housing Association and Coopers & Lybrand showed that of the 71,000 units represented, assisted-living facilities historically contain the highest number of studio and one-bedroom units while, since 1980, CCRCs and congregate housing communities have reduced the number of smaller units and built more two-bedroom accommodations. "The State of Seniors Housing 1993," American Seniors Housing Association and Coopers & Lybrand, 1993, 16–17.

8. "Understanding Senior Housing for the 1990s," American Association of Retired Persons, 50–53.

9. *But see* handicap discrimination issues that must be considered when determining policies concerning levels of care, access to facilities and services, etc. *See* §23.3.

10. Jeck, A., and J. Carlson, "Retirement Housing: Exploring the Gray Area of Housing's Gray Market," *Real Estate Finance,* Winter 1986.

11. *Id.* Note, however, that such amenities may be very popular where they are installed. *See* "Continuing Care Retirement Communities: An Industry in Action," American Association of Homes for the Aging, Ernst & Whinney (Washington, DC: 1987), 20. One industry pundit (Maria Dwight of Gerontological Services, Inc.) wryly notes that consumers are becoming more demanding, so that an activities program can no longer consist of "making Easter baskets out of tongue depressors."

12. There are many other names for this level of care, depending on state or local usage. *See* §20.4.

13. Also known as personal care, board and care, and by other names. *See* §20.4.

14. Financial security is not considered in the analysis represented in Figure 2.4 in that it reflects a payment system usually associated with continuing care but potentially applicable to any facility type.

15. Seip, D., "The Retirement Housing Industry Plainly Defined," *Contemporary Long Term Care,* Nov. 1987, 31.

16. *See* Elrod, note 2 *above,* quoting the 1976 National Conference on Congregate Housing for Older People.

17. *See* Thompson, M., and W. Donahue, *Planning and Implementing Management of Congregate Housing for Older People* (Washington, DC: International Center for Social Gerontology, 1980), 5–6.

18. 42 U.S.C. §1437e (1978).

19. *See generally* Chellis, R., J. Seagle, and B. Seagle, eds., *Congregate Housing for Older People* (Lexington, MA: Lexington Books, 1982).

20. *See* discussion in §14.2(d)(1).

21. Caulfield, L., and J. Carlucci, "The Adult Congregate Living Facility—A Comparison and Critical Discussion of Assistance-Oriented Facilities and an Alternative Concept for the Marketplace," *The Real Estate Appraiser and Analyst* (Fall 1985), 43.

22. *See* §20.4.

23. House Select Committee on Aging, "Fraud and Abuse in Boarding Homes," June 25, 1981.

24. *See* Newcomer, R., and R. Stone, "Board and Care Housing: Expansion and Improvement Needed," *Generations* (Summer 1985), 38.

25. *Ibid.*

26. *Ibid.*

27. *Ibid.*

28. "Fact Sheet," Assisted Living Facilities Association of America, Oct. 8, 1991.

29. Beyer, Bulkley, and Hopkins, "A Model Act Regulating Board and Care Homes: Guidelines for States," *Mental and Physical Disability Law Reporter* 8 (Mar.–Apr. 1984) 157, defining "Board and Care Home."

30. *Id.* at 159.

31. *Ibid.*

32. Pub. L. No. 102–550, 12 U.S.C. §1715(b)(6).

33. *See* House Select Committee on Aging, "Fraud and Abuse in Boarding Homes," June 25, 1981.

34. Pub. L. 94–566, §505(d)(1976).

35. *See* "State Laws and Programs Serving Elderly Persons and Disabled Adults" (excerpting an American Bar Association Commission study), *Mental Disability Law Reporter,* 7 (Mar.–Apr. 1983) 158, for a comprehensive survey of individual state board-and-care licensing laws. *See also* §26.1(d)(1), regarding the SSI program.

36. 12 U.S.C. §1715w(a)(5).

37. *See* Newcomer and Stone, note 24, at 39.

38. Diesenhouse, S., "Housing the Elderly Who Do Not Require Nursing Home Care," *The New York Times,* Jan. 3, 1993, 3–12.

39. Seip, D., "Specializing in Assisted Living Facilities," *Contemporary Long Term Care,* Sept. 1987, 34.

40. Wood, M., "Seniors Housing, The Unconventional Real Estate Investment," *Real Estate Forum,* Sept. 1995, 73.

41. Pallarito, K., "Assisted Living Leads Growth," *Modern Healthcare,* May 20, 1996.

42. *See* "A Mature Housing Market: Growing Business of Not-Quite-Nursing-Home Care," Business Day Section, *New York Times,* Apr. 10, 1996. *But see also* Sullivan, J., "Ducking the Hazards," *Contemporary Long Term Care,* Sept. 1996, 38, regarding pitfalls for developers and operators of assisted living.

43. A brief history of CCRCs is discussed in Winkelvoss, H., and A. Powell, *Continuing Care Retirement Communities—An Empirical, Financial and Legal Analysis* (Philadelphia Pension Research Council, Wharton School, University of Pennsylvania; Richard D. Irwin, 1984), 6–11. A general discussion of life-care facilities is also contained in "Sizing Up Life Care," *Changing Times,* May 1987, 65. *See also* Wilcox, M., "Not a Place to Sit and Watch the Traffic," *Kiplinger's Personal Finance Magazine,* June 1996, 63. For a review of CCRC management issues, *see* Somers, A., and N. Spears, *The Continuing Care Retirement Community: A Significant Option for Long-Term Care?* (New York: Springer Publishing Co., 1992).

44. There is some confusion over the distinctions of meaning and usage between the terms *life care* and *continuing care.* Sometimes *life care* is used to distinguish the archaic fully prepaid programs from those that charge monthly fees in addition to an entrance fee. Others may use *life care* to refer to contracts that promise care and residence for life and reserve *continuing care* as a more generic term covering contracts of any duration where a person can receive varying levels of health care or per-

sonal care along a continuum of benefits. At least one study has referred to *life care* facilities as those that offer care, when needed, without an increase in the regular monthly charge for residence, as distinguished from *continuing care,* where the facility merely arranges for health services to be available at fee for service rates. *See* ICF, Inc., "Private Financing of Long Term Care: Current Methods and Resources," Phase I Final Report, U.S. Department of Health and Human Services, 1985, 36. This latter definition has also been called a "Type A" or extensive continuing-care contract. In this book, the term continuing care is used generically to refer to contracts offering long-term care and residence, usually with some form of prepayment for, or priority access to, health benefits. *See also* the statutory definitions set forth in Part VII.

45. Fairchild, T., "Profit or Nonprofit Retirement Housing: Is There a Difference?" *Aging Network News,* July 1986, 6.

46. Raper, A., ed., *National Continuing Care Directory* (Washington, DC: American Association of Homes for the Aging/American Association of Retired Persons, 1984), 11.

47. *Id.* at 5.

48. "What's Putting New Life into 'Life Care' Communities," *Business Week,* Mar. 3, 1986, 108.

49. "Before You Settle on a Retirement Community," *Business Week,* May 20, 1991, 150. For more about CCRC numbers estimates, *see generally* "Insurance for the Twilight Years: Life Care Takes the Uncertainty Out of Retirement," *Time,* Apr. 6, 1987, 53; Mariano, A., "As Old Grow Older, Housing Needs Change," *Washington Post,* Sept. 15, 1984; and Rosenblatt and Peterson, "Life Care: Insurance Against Age," *Los Angeles Times,* Aug. 5, 1986, 6.

50. However, some commentators have advised that an essential element of continuing care is that some form of below-cost or prepaid health care be included (Raper, note 46 *above,* at 4, and Winkelvoss and Powell, note 43 *above,* at 23). Under that definition, for example, facilities that charge full fee-for-service rates for nursing care but give priority health center admission status to independent-living residents would not be considered continuing care, contrary to some state statutes, such as California Health and Safety Code §§1770 *et seq.*

51. "Before You Settle on a Retirement Community," *Business Week,* May 20, 1991, 150–151.

52. An exhaustive empirical study of continuing-care retirement communities, their fees, services, amenities, resident mixes, and other characteristics, together with an analysis of actuarial projection methodologies, pricing theory, budgeting, and general accounting and financial considerations, appears in Winkelvoss and Powell, note 43

above. See also Clark L., Jr., "A Dandy Retirement, If You Can Pay," *The Wall Street Journal,* May 25, 1994, A–16.

53. *See, e.g.,* Walbert, L., "Money & Worth," *Lear's,* Oct. 1993, 22, discussing alternative service package types and fee options.

54. *Continuing Care Retirement Communities: An Industry in Action* (Washington, DC: American Association of Homes for the Aging and Ernst & Young, 1987, 1989).

55. *Continuing Care Retirement Communities: An Industry in Action* (Washington, DC: American Association of Homes for the Aging and Ernst & Young, 1993).

56. The organization changed its name to American Association of Homes *and Services* for the Aging.

57. American Association of Homes & Services for the Aging, *Currents,* Vol. 10, No. 7, July 1995, D.

58. *See* "Who's Taking Care of Our Parents," *Newsweek,* May 6, 1985, for a discussion of health care needs at Sun City 25 years after its opening.

59. Kaufman, G., and M. Waite, "Retirement Communities as a Profitable Land Use in Large Planned Communities," *Investment Properties International,* Mar.–Apr. 1990, 29, *See also,* "A Dare in the Desert: 5,500 Retirement Homes," *Business Week,* Dec. 9, 1991, 94.

60. Elrod, note 2 *above,* referencing HUD, *How Well Are We Housed, The Elderly,* 1979.

61. Marriott has cited projections that, thanks to the baby boom, there will be 8 million Americans 85 and older by 2030 and 15 million by 2050. DiGiacomo, R., "Marriott Enters Retirement," *Multifamily Executive,* Aug. 1996.

62. Jaffe, R., "Graying of America Assures Future for Retirement Housing," *Real Estate Forum,* Aug. 1987, 49.

63. Thomas, M., "Retirement Housing Industry Burgeoning," *Contemporary Long Term Care,* July 1988, 27. *See also* Lewin, T., "How Needs, and Market, for Care Have Changed," *New York Times,* Dec. 2, 1990, 24.

64. *Older Americans Report,* Apr. 1, 1988, 138.

65. *Ibid.*

66. *See* §11.2(a).

67. Dine, D., "Demand for Retirement Housing Accommodates Industry Growth," *Modern Healthcare,* June 3, 1988, 56.

68. *Ibid.*

69. *See* Seip, D., "Retirement Communities: What to Expect During 1988," *Contemporary Long Term Care,* Jan. 1988, 25. *See also* Dannenfeldt, D., "Hospitals Wary about Retirement Ventures," *Modern Healthcare,* Oct. 20, 1989, 44.

70. "Capital Crunch Restrains CCRC Development," *Modern Health Care,* May 20, 1991, 92.

71. Pallarito, K., "Opportunities Await in Retiree Communities," *Modern Healthcare,* May 18, 1992, 96 (reporting the results of *Modern Healthcare's* 1992 Multiunit Providers Survey).

72. Pallarito, K., "CCRCs See Slow Growth, Challenges in HMO Care," *Modern Healthcare,* May 23, 1994, 76 (reporting the results of *Modern Healthcare's* 1994 Multiunit Providers Survey).

73. *See* Seip, D., "1987: An Insider's Perspective on the Retirement Industry," *Contemporary Long Term Care,* Dec. 1987, 48, 49.

74. *See, e.g.,* "What's Putting New Life Into 'Life Care' Communities," *Business Week,* Mar. 3, 1986, 108, quoting Sheldon Goldberg, executive vice president, American Association of Homes for the Aging.

75. "1988 Seniors Housing Audit," *Multi-Housing News,* Sept. 1988, 14.

76. Thomas, note 63 *above.* Obviously, some respondents offered more than one option.

77. *See* "Retiring with Equity in a Full-Health-Care Facility," *New York Times,* Aug. 12, 1990.

78. *See* Adams, E., "Meeting the Varied Market for the Graying of America," *Professional Builder,* Apr. 1986, 68.

79. *See generally* Carlson, J., "What the Experts Are Saying: New Developments in Retirement Housing," *Retirement Housing Report,* Sept. 1986, 16, for a discussion of rental versus life-care trends.

80. Remarks of James Sherman, then of Laventhol & Horwath, at Sandy & Babcock seminar on "Proprietary Lifecare," San Francisco, July 19, 1985.

81. Linda Todd, senior national vice president, National Retirement Consultants, Inc., Fort Lauderdale, FL. Retirement rental rates average about $1,050 per month for a single-person, one-bedroom unit. "Rental Retirement Housing," *The Stanger Report,* Sept. 1986, 2.

82. *But see* Allen, §1.3, indicating congregate-care residents are younger than life-care residents.

83. *See* Caulfield and Carlucci, note 21 *above.* Note that this comparison assumes bond financing for the endowment project, but not for the rental.

84. *See* Dobkin, L., "AARP Releases Nationwide Housing Survey of Older Consumers," *Aging Network News,* June 1987, 5.

85. Remarks of Dr. James Smith, Retirement Centers of America, Inc., at Sandy & Babcock seminar on "Proprietary Lifecare," San Francisco, July 19, 1985.

86. *See* note 80 *above. But see* Howell, J., "Learning from Mistakes," National Association of Senior Living Industries 1987 Conference Proceedings, 29.

87. Kunerth, A., "The Impact of Long-Term Care Insurance on the Marketing of Senior Living Facilities: Part III–A Model CCRC," *Retirement Housing Report,* Feb. 1988, 9.

88. Rivlin, A., and J. Wiener, *Caring for the Disabled Elderly: Who Will Pay?* (Washington, DC: The Brookings Institution, 1988), 92.

89. *See* Kunerth, A., "LTC Group Insurance: The Catalyst in Blending CCRCs, Rental Projects," *Contemporary Long Term Care,* Mar. 1988, 67.

90. *See* Winkelvoss, H., and A. Powell, "Retirement Communities: Assessing the Liability of Alternative Health Care Guarantees," *The Journal of Long Term Care Administration,* Winter 1981, 9.

91. Raper, note 46 *above*, at 11.

92. Winkelvoss and Powell, note 43 *above*, at 42.

93. *See* note 74 *above,* referencing Life Care Communities Corp.'s Court at Palm-Aire, Pompano Beach, FL. *See also* "A New Kind of Retirement Home," *Nation's Business,* Jan. 1986, 77.

94. Caulfield and Carlucci, note 21 *above*.

95. *Ibid.*

96. *Ibid.,* referencing Mediplex Group, Inc.'s, Laurel Lake Retirement Community, Hudson, OH.

97. Remarks of David Wildgen, of Charter House, Rochester, MN, at National Real Estate Development Center Conference, May 16–17, 1985.

98. Chellis, R., and S. Meister, "Resident Payment Mechanisms: Five Models of Retirement Communities," *Retirement Housing Report,* May 1988, 10.

99. *See* note 74 *above,* quoting Lloyd W. Lewis, Kendal-Crosslands, Kennett Square, PA.

100. A February 1990 *Consumer Reports* article discusses in depth the characteristics of successful and failed life-care facilities. *See also* Fairbanks, J., "Lifetime Care Contracts: Are Senior Citizens Putting All Their Eggs in One Basket?" *Probate and Property,* Mar.–Apr. 1990, for a checklist for analyzing continuing-care retirement community contracts. The checklist covers the following topics: solvency and expertise of the provider, disclosure requirements, assurances of long-term solvency, licensure requirements, entrance fees, cancellation and refunds, monthly fees, living units, nonhealth services, health care services and coverage, level-of-care changes, resident rights and control, involuntary termination, miscellaneous other rights, proxy decision making.

101. Thomas, M., note 63 *above.*

102. *See* Nemes, J., "Retirement Centers Grow Despite Fewer Providers," *Modern Healthcare,* June 2, 1989, 50.

103. "Survey Finds Health Occupancy Acquisition Activity, Rising Rents," *Units,* July–Aug. 1995, 35–41.

104. "Assisted Living Interests Still Growing," *Modern Healthcare's Elder Care Business,* Apr. 30, 1990, 16.

105. *Ibid.*

106. Hoffman, C., "Seniors Housing Hits Its Prime," *Real Estate Forum,* Aug. 1997, 52.

107. Bowe, J., "Chains Take on Retirement Housing," *Contemporary Long Term Care,* May 1990, 46.

108. Seip, D., "1988 in Review: A Year of Refinement," *Contemporary Long Term Care,* Dec. 1988; Doyle, M., "Retirement Housing: Bigger Isn't Always Better," *Hospitals,* Mar. 20, 1989.

109. "Survey Finds Health Occupancy, Acquisition Activity, Rising Rents," *Units,* July–Aug. 1995, 35–41.

110. Gjullin, E., and R. Miller, "An Untapped Senior Housing Market Segment," *Retirement Housing Report,* Mar. 1989; "Marriott Tells Plans to Build 150 Retirement Communities," *Modern Healthcare,* Aug. 4, 1989, 41. *See also* "Growth Slows, But Continues," *Contemporary Long Term Care,* June 1990, 53, which reports a trend toward more units per facility.

111. *Seniors' Housing: A State of the Industry Report,* Senior Housing Investment Advisors, Inc., and *Multi-Housing News,* 1988.

112. Gamzon, J., "28 Seniors Housing Experts Identify Affordable Solutions," *Multi-Housing News,* May 1989, 9.

113. Gamzon, M., "State of the Seniors Housing Industry: Insights for the 90's," *Multi-Housing News,* May 1990.

114. Gamzon, M., "What Lies Down the Road for Retirement Housing," *Contemporary Long Term Care,* June 1992, 38.

115. Gamzon, M., "Assisted Living Reigns," *Contemporary Long Term Care,* June 1993, 31.

116. Gamzon, M., "Buyers, Capital Sources Warm Up to Senior Housing," *Contemporary Long Term Care,* June 1994, 46.

117. Gamzon, M., "Senior Housing Comes of Age," *Contemporary Long Term Care,* June 1995, 46.

118. "The State of Seniors Housing 1996," American Seniors Housing Association (Washington, DC: 1997).

Bentley Village; Naples, Florida.

Part II
Project Planning and Implementation

Unlike a typical multifamily housing development, retirement projects are special-use facilities that require early coordination of several disciplines, such as real estate planning and development; finance; financial forecasting; law, tax, and regulatory expertise; health care services; management of operations; marketing; insurance; architecture; construction; and other fields. It is important to spend time early in the development process giving balanced consideration to all the major issues and not to proceed too far with some parts of the project while letting others fall behind schedule.

Sometimes, developers can be too aggressive or impatient in their pursuit of certain aspects of the project with which they are most comfortable, such as development of the physical plant. Before the marketing of any project, and certainly before commencing construction of any new structure, a developer must seriously consider, study, and resolve several additional issues that will determine the overall character of the project and that may make the difference between its success or failure. It is necessary to address important factors such as the size, characteristics, and preferences of the targeted market segment; details of the service package; tax and legal implications of business structures or resident payment mechanisms; or regulatory matters such as facility licensing. If developers fail to pursue such topics concurrently with the routine real estate issues, they may find themselves in the embarrassing position of having to revise substantially their service package or business structure late in the development process—after having made public representations about the type of project planned.

Successful development depends in large part on assembling the right group of team members, establishing a comprehensive and well-integrated schedule of tasks, and obtaining appropriate review of each successive phase of the development from concept to reality.[1]

Sunlake Terrace; Las Vegas, Nevada.

3 Development Team Functions

§3.1 In General

The components of any successful seniors' housing development include a team of people from various disciplines who must work in concert to produce a balanced, cohesive product. Often, many of these team members are consultants hired by a developer or sponsoring organization to give advice or produce a study or design. Experienced retirement community developers and operators often employ some or all of the team members on a full-time, in-house basis. In either event, regular communication among those performing the different functions described below is important and, in some instances, can be critical to project success.

Although a few of the functions referred to in this chapter may be performed by the same person or entity, each function is discrete and calls for both special expertise in retirement facility development and a concentration of staff resources to ensure maximum efficiency and effectiveness. The functions described usually do not involve a single task but rather a series of analyses, recommendations, and tangible products that become increasingly detailed as project development proceeds.

§3.2 Project Coordination

Project coordination is an obvious but critical function. Depending on the type of ownership and operation of the intended project, the coordinator may be an executive officer of a nonprofit sponsoring organization, a real estate developer, a hired "clerk of the works" type of consultant, or some other representative of the moving force or forces behind the project.

Whatever the facility format, it is important for the coordinator to represent adequately the interests of the project owner and operator, especially when these are multiple parties engaged in some form of joint venture. The coordinator should have experience in supervising the development of a real estate project and in working with consultants from a broad array of other disciplines, such as finance, law, architecture, construction, health care, and personal services management. Retirement community operations experience is a plus. A coordinator must have the ability to develop a realistic timetable for the accomplishment of all the required tasks; to assign the necessary tasks to other team members and ensure follow-through; to keep all development activities, including financing, directed toward a clearly envisioned goal that is shared by all involved in the process; and to be flexible enough to revise initial plans and overcome obstacles as the project evolves.

§3.3 Market Feasibility Study

One of the most important steps in the development of almost every seniors' housing community is the preparation of a market feasibility study.[2] Unless the developer is already acquainted with and experienced in the development of retirement communities, an outside consulting firm with substantial experience and a good reputation in the retirement community industry should be retained to conduct a thorough study. The consultant performing the market feasibility study should not necessarily be the one performing the financial feasibility study.[3]

The need for a thorough market study increases as facilities become more specialized and complex.[4] Although familiarity with different types of products may vary from one community to another, in general, continuing-care facilities and other retirement centers that offer substantial service or health care packages may be more difficult to market and fill than simple rental housing. Therefore, the importance of a detailed market study, including consumer response to the specific project proposal, is heightened.[5]

The market study should identify the numbers of elderly persons within the various communities with sites that are candidates for development as well as the surrounding primary and secondary market areas from which prospective residents might be drawn. Age subgroupings should be separately evaluated, as the circumstances, desires, and numbers of potential buyers may vary with age. The incomes of such age groups by locality should be included. If possible, some effort should be made to determine the general availability of illiquid assets of the elderly in each locale, for example, by reference to housing values in the particular area. The present residential, marital, religious, and other personal circumstances of elderly households should be referenced if possible. Groups that contain large numbers of elderly persons, such as social, religious, civic, and health care organizations, as well as other constituencies of affinity groups (e.g., retired teachers or military officers), should be identified and described.

A good market study cannot be limited to demographics, however. A comprehensive report should include specific information about the types of services and amenities desired and the forms of ownership or interest in real property preferred by the potential market. Questionnaires, telephone interviews, or face-to-face focus groups may be used to determine whether prospective residents are interested in facilities that provide medical care, dining, or other services; whether respondents prefer to own, lease, or rent their units; what size units are preferred and what prices prospects can afford; whether they would be willing to pay an entrance fee or a fixed monthly insurance premium to cover the costs of unknown future health care liabilities; whether they would accept a high-rise structure as opposed to a low-rise multiunit or detached campus setting; and other preferences. The process of gathering this type of information also serves as a valuable premarketing exercise that can identify many prospective residents. One observer suggests that it is more important to look to the competition than to rely on the opinions of senior citizens in focus groups. For example, because retirement facility prospects are likely to know little about the industry and may still be oriented toward single-family residences, they may tend to oversize residential units.[6]

The market study should also examine all the other facilities within the market area. Many developers find that a large share of their target population comes from a relatively small area, within a radius of approximately 25 miles of the site.[7] All other facilities within the region should be identified, whether or not they are the type that the developer intends to construct. The types of services offered at such facilities should be analyzed, along with entrance fee rates or prices of units, monthly fees, sizes of the units, available services, occupancy levels, and length of waiting lists, if any. When possible, some effort should be made to determine the level of success experienced by existing or planned facilities in the area in filling up their projects and over what period of time. The study should identify a "penetration rate" that indicates the expected percentage of age- and income-qualified people in the area who can be expected to purchase a retirement facility product. Rates of 2 to 3 percent are common, although in some areas where retirement facilities are more widespread, projects have achieved significantly higher rates.[8] A study should also consider site issues such as topography, access to transportation and services, parking, zoning, and socioeconomic or prestige characteristics.

Fill rates or "absorption" should also be predicted. The absorption rate is defined as the number of months it will take for a project to reach a stable occupancy level, beginning with the month when the project first enters the marketplace. It has been stated that the absorption rate is the most important element to be determined when performing market and financial feasibility studies because miscalculation of the absorption rate can jeopardize the financial feasibility of the project.[9] One study has concluded that on average, the larger the facility, the longer it takes to reach a stabilized occupancy.[10] However, absorption correlates more strongly with facility location than with size. The study provides many helpful statistical tables regarding resident absorption, including the following:

Average Number of Months after Opening to Achieve Stabilized Occupancy

Facility Type	Average Time to Reach Stabilization (months)	Facilities Not Stabilized
Congregate (n = 47)	23	9
Assisted Living (n = 67)	13	11
CCRC (n = 12)	29	5

Size of the Property Compared with the Length of Time to Reach Stabilization (assisted-living facilities)

Average Size of Property	Time to Reach Stabilization (months)
Fewer than 35 beds (n = 30)	5.3
35 to 60 beds (n = 13)	9.6
61 to 85 beds (n = 10)	13.9
More than 85 beds (n = 23)	20.9

(n = number of facilities)

A 1995 survey conducted by the Harvard School of Public Health and Lou Harris and Associates found that while 20 percent of Americans over age 50 are at risk for needing long-term-care services during the next 12 months, the at-risk population is extremely uninformed about the alternatives to nursing care that might exist in the community:

Type of Facility/Service	Percent of At-Risk Population Unfamiliar with Options
Respite care	83
Continuing care	68
Alzheimer's facilities	63
Congregate-living facilities	59
Assisted-living facilities	47

§3.4 Financial Feasibility Forecasting

The financial feasibility of any product is inextricably linked to the ability to market the product.[11] In conjunction with the market analyst and management consultant,[12] the developer should create an initial marketing plan that estimates, on a quarterly or even month-by-month basis, the expected number of sales of units in the project. It is generally accepted in the industry that rental projects are marketed faster than endowment or continuing-care plans that require an entrance fee; therefore, a more precise analysis of the projected marketing strategy, together with a conservative time line for filling the project, is especially important in the latter cases. The financial feasibility study should include income and expense projections for the project during the development process and resident fill-up period. Many observers believe that it is during this phase of the project's life that the greatest risk of failure exists, particularly in the field of continuing care.[13]

The financial feasibility study should, of course, also examine the projected income and normal expenses of operation once the facility has reached a stable level of occupancy, for example, 90 percent. Depending on facility type, a period of five to 20 years after fill-up should be forecasted.[14] Suggested sale prices, entrance fees, or rental rates for each type or size of unit should be determined, perhaps with the presentation of alternative pricing structures and their effect on the bottom line.[15] Projections should include a worst-case scenario showing the financial impact of a lower-than-expected rent-up. Of course, such an analysis requires a thorough understanding of the details of the proposed service package, necessary construction elements, staffing requirements, and other costly matters that may require architectural, legal, and marketing consultation.

For projects where the facility operator charges an entrance fee but retains ownership of the residential units or is otherwise dependent on income from resale of units,[16] income projections should include expected frequency of resales of the units. This projection should be based on actuarial assumptions, plus experience concerning turnover in similar facilities. In a mature continuing-care facility, unit releases may be expected to reach approximately 8 percent per year.[17] However, it may take as long as 12 to 15 years for a new facility to reach maturity.[18] Apartment turnovers in rental facilities responding to one survey ranged from 8.6 to 14.7 percent per year, depending on facility age.[19] Of course, all these rules of thumb are based largely on traditional models, and assumptions may have to be modified for projects appealing to different age levels or with different entry criteria or health maintenance programs. However, the 1992 NASLI study on absorption rates of retirement facilities indicated that nonrental projects have higher absorption rates than rental projects. The same study also indicated that nonprofit projects perform better than for-profit projects; projects that offer a continuum of care perform better than projects with only congregate services; projects with formal sponsorship perform better than those without formal sponsorship; and projects using outside marketing firms perform better than those that attempt to use internal marketing.

A financial feasibility study should also take into account reserves required for debt service, future personal care or health care obligations (if any), building maintenance and replacement, working capital, and any reserves that may be required by state law. Of course, the numbers should take into account other factors such as inflation, construction contingencies, consultant fees, and all other projected or reasonably possible expenditures.

It is not necessary for the developer to have project financing in place in order to determine the initial financial feasibility of a project. It is, of course, advantageous to secure a financing commitment at the earliest possible stage, if financing is in place, the cost of servicing any debt should be factored into the feasibility study. Most likely, however, lenders will not be willing to look seriously at any project unless the developer can present a comprehensive development plan that includes a detailed market feasibility study, financial feasibility study, and general plan for the physical design and service package to be offered at the facility. Therefore, the typical financial feasibility study must be based on various assumptions as to the cost of financing through identified or hypothetical sources.

A financial feasibility study can often be performed by an experienced facility developer and operator in consultation with the market analyst and any management consultant, especially in projects that do not offer an insurance type of product or that, for other reasons, require actuarial study. However, many consultants in the marketplace specialize in preparing financial feasibility reports, and they may have special expertise, particularly in fields such as continuing care, where state laws may require specific types of financial analyses and submission of those studies to the applicable state agency for review.

It should be noted that financial feasibility and market feasibility study are different disciplines, and the respective studies serve different purposes. While there may be some consultants who perform both functions well, the developer should be prepared to evaluate carefully the consultant's expertise and experience in each arena.

§3.5 Legal Consultation

Two of the most frequently overlooked steps in the early stages of project development are a detailed review of the legal and regulatory implications of various business plan and product development alternatives and preparation of a proposed residence agreement. There are many legal matters with which the developer must become intimately familiar during the formative stages of the development plan.[20] These include issues such as the tax implications (for developer, operator, and resident), or implications for tax-exempt status, of various business and facility ownership structures and the tax and legal advantages or disadvantages of sole ownership, joint ventures, lease transactions, or contractual relationships with other entities that may own or operate the facility.

In addition, the types of services offered at the proposed facility may determine whether, and to what extent, the facility, or portions thereof, must be licensed and regulated by state agencies. These legal consequences may have profound effects on the structure and cost of the service package, its marketing, the ability to obtain financing, tax exemption for financing, government loans or loan guarantees, construction standards, and even construction schedules. Of course, attorneys can also be of assistance in zoning and land use planning issues, obtaining financing, preparing and reviewing contracts, and other matters that are common in the development of any form of housing. Figure 3.1 provides examples of the types of legal documents that may be included in developing a retirement facility (see also Volume II: The CD-ROM for sample forms of key documents).

A most important aspect of early legal consultation is the development of a proposed residence agreement, which may be in the form of conditions, covenants, and restrictions on the sale of real property, a lease or rental agreement, a continuing-care contract, a membership agreement, a nursing facility admission contract, or another document or combination of documents that spells out the respective rights and obligations of the facility owner or operator and the resident.

Preparation of a residence agreement early in the planning stages of a project can serve several functions, especially in facilities that are service-intensive.

- It will force the developer to focus on the details of the methodology by which the resident will be expected to pay for the residence, or use of the residence, and the services, possibly including health care, to be provided by the facility.
- It will help determine more precisely the scope and extent of the services and amenities to be provided, the nuances of which can raise issues of business structure, pricing, right of title to, or possession of, the premises, licensing, securities registration, and other matters.
- The draft can serve as a tool for use in focus group discussions or other marketing activities.
- It can serve as the framework for the final document to be signed by residents and, if applicable, be submitted to state agencies for preliminary licensing review and approval.

- It may bring to light potential operational difficulties or needs that must be explored by management and marketing consultants. Often, for example, subtleties of contractual language can result in wide-ranging differences in the extent of state regulation, and it is in the preparation of the residence agreement that a balance is struck between the considerations of pleasing the consumer, operational practicality, financial feasibility, regulatory burden, and ease of marketing.

§3.6 Experienced Architectural and Construction Services

Architectural consultation is an obvious prerequisite to the development and marketing of any housing facility. With the elderly, more than with many other groups, architectural services must deliver more than external "curb appeal."[21] A sensitivity to the particular unit sizes, physical amenities, and interior design characteristics favored by retirement community residents is essential.[22] In addition, the development process may entail many unique rules and public approvals not present in other forms of housing, and land use planning consultation may be essential (see zoning discussion in §25.1).

Nevertheless, developers sometimes employ those architectural consultants with whom they are most familiar, without regard to whether the architects have experience in designing seniors' housing facilities of the type contemplated by the developer or indicated by the market feasibility study. Because retirement communities are more than housing and may include dining, recreational, assisted-living, and even health care facilities, the choice of architect, and even of construction contractor, is an important one.

For example, retirement facilities that contain areas used for the provision of health care or assisted living, or even that house CCRC residents in "independent-living" units, may be subjected by state law to construction standards or fire safety requirements that are significantly more rigorous than those required of unlicensed residential housing. Strengths and fire resistance ratings of building components, corridor and door widths, accessibility requirements, and

Figure 3.1 **Legal Documents Checklist**

Business Documents
- Articles of incorporation and bylaws
- Partnership or limited-liability company agreements
- Fictitious name filings
- Service mark filings
- Federal tax-exemption applications
- State tax-exemption applications

Property Acquisition
- Option agreement
- Sale agreement
- Ground lease
- Lease from owner to operating organization

Consultant Agreements
- Site development services (soils, toxic, environmental impact, zoning, and planning)
- Architectural and design
- Market study
- Financial feasibility services
- Attorney fee agreement
- Marketing/sales

Finance
- Construction loan agreement
- Promissory note
- Deed of trust
- Bond indenture and official statement, etc. (see §15.7(b))

License Applications
- Permit to take deposits
- Assisted-living facility license
- Nursing facility license
- Home health licensure
- Certificate of Need (if applicable)
- Continuing-care certificate of authority
- Application for subdivision approval
- Fire clearances
- Certificates of occupancy

Construction and Development
- Agreement for architectural services
- Request for bids
- Construction contracts
- Performance bond
- Payment bond

Resident Agreements
- Reservation or waiting list agreement
- Deposit agreement
- Escrow agreement
- Care and residence agreement
- Lease agreement

Condominium/Cooperative Documents
- Deed covenants, conditions, and restrictions
- Reciprocal easements
- Homeowners' association articles and bylaws
- Grant deed
- Proprietary lease agreement/share certificate
- Standard form resale and purchase agreement

Health Care/Resident Financial Documents
- Health/financial questionnaire for residents
- Nursing facility admission agreement
- Durable power of attorney for health care
- Durable power of attorney for property
- Preferred provider agreement with local health facilities
- Home health services contract
- Medical director services contract
- Long-term-care insurance policies
- Long-term-care insurance administration agreement
- Policies and procedures for nursing, residential-care facilities
- Termination of life support policy and procedure

Management Contracts/Personnel Documents
- Master management contract
- Food service agreement
- Security services agreement
- Housekeeping/laundry services agreement
- Subleases for convenience services (such as beauty shop, bank, gift shop)
- Employment contracts for key management executives
- Personnel policies and procedures
- Pension plan

mechanical specifications relating to heating, sanitation, or emergency power are among the many special considerations that may have to be addressed (see discussion in §20.4(c)). Architects and contractors unfamiliar with these specialized construction standards might grossly underestimate the costs of construction, be required to undertake substantial research, or even substantially revise plans or completed building elements to comply with applicable laws.

§3.7 Management Expertise

It can be helpful in the early stages of the project's development to obtain the services of a person who is familiar with the actual day-to-day operation of a retirement facility of the type under contemplation for construction. Such a person, who may ultimately become the administrator of the completed facility, can be extremely valuable in the formative stages of the project. An experienced manager may have first-hand knowledge of the seniors' marketplace and of the project's competition in the particular community. The manager must also have operations experience, which can be indispensable in developing the service package that will be offered to residents, verifying marketing and other assumptions, fleshing out the details of staffing needs and other projected operational expenditures for a financial feasibility study, and advising the developer about architectural details and amenities that experience shows are preferred by elderly people. Managers may also assist later in the development process in creating policies and procedures governing residence and operations of departments, such as dining, housekeeping, social and recreational activities, and health care.

Retirement communities may also use full-service management firms to hire, train, and supervise staff, develop policy and procedure manuals, handle admissions, and operate all aspects of the facility. Compensation may be based on a flat annual fee or a percentage (often 5 percent) of the gross operating budget (see Volume II: The CD-ROM for sample management agreements). Contract management services can be particularly useful in the late development and early operation phases of a project's life, but it has been argued that residents are better served if the sponsor takes over operations after the initial fill-up.[23]

§3.8 Financing

Financing is an essential ingredient of every development but is often not as fully integrated into the process of product formulation as it should be. Often, the types of services offered at a facility, or the mechanisms used to obtain payment from residents for services or facilities, determine whether financing is available at all and, if so, from how many competitive sources.

Some lenders, for example, have serious reservations about lending to facilities offering continuing care or assuming other long-term risks that may impair their ability to repay debt; other lenders specialize in financing such facilities.[24] The availability of financing in general should therefore be incorporated into the formulation of the initial project concept. Many CCRCs or other hybrid retirement facilities have been financed through tax-exempt or taxable bonds, with credit enhancements provided by state or federal loan guarantee programs. Conventional lenders, such as banks, have tended to focus on better-known (and simpler) products such as assisted living, nursing facilities, or housing without a care component. More recently, Wall Street investment banking firms have become active in financing seniors' housing. At first, most of the money from these firms went to the refinancing or acquisition of existing facilities. However, speculation[25] that these firms would begin to finance new construction as the market stabilized has now proven accurate.

A survey of lenders conducted in 1994 found that 46 percent of respondents rated long-term-care facilities more favorably than conventional real estate investments and that 37 percent rated seniors' housing as a preferred investment.[26]

A survey entitled the State of Seniors Housing 1995, conducted jointly by the American Seniors Housing Association (ASHA) and Coopers & Lybrand, showed that although congregate-living units continue to struggle with debt service, there have been improvements in the seniors' housing industry. According to the survey, in 1993 just 43 percent of congregate units covered debt service compared with 64 percent in the 1994 survey. By contrast, 77 percent of assisted-living properties and 86 percent of CCRCs covered their debt service, up from 73 percent and 75 percent, respectively. At $28,569, CCRCs generate the highest median revenue per occupied unit, followed by assisted living at $19,456. Assisted living generates a median net profit margin of 8.7 percent, edging out CCRCs, which posted a net margin of 8.4 percent. However, according to David Schless, executive director of ASHA, lenders may remain somewhat conservative in lending money for new construction because of the industry's earlier difficulties, despite healthy profits. Capital is more available for acquisitions and refinancings. ASHA expects to see more joint venture partnerships between senior living businesses and hospitals or health care systems that are interested in new revenue streams.[27]

A lender and investor survey conducted by the National Investment Conference for the Senior Living and Long Term Care Industries and Valuation Counselors showed the following changes in lender preferences by type of project from 1994 to 1996:

Percent Chosen as First or Second Preference

Project Type	1996	1994
Active adult	5.7	22.1
Seniors' apartments, no services	16.1	41.3
Rental congregate, no health care	9.2	26
Rental congregate with assisted living	20.7	25
Entrance fee CCRC	6.9	2.9
Condominium/cooperative CCRC	1.1	2.9
Freestanding assisted living	60.9	17.3
Nursing homes	59.8	36.5
Specialty facilities	10.3	6.7
Other	5.7	5.8

Assuming that project financing is available, lenders have to be kept apprised of the progress of the development. Before issuing a loan commitment and in parallel with the statutory requirements for CCRCs in many states (see Chapter 21), many lenders require achievement of certain levels of reservation deposits from prospective residents. Lenders also want to look carefully at the precise legal rights, if any, of the residents with respect to the improvements that are used as security for the debt. This is true particularly in unconventional or unfamiliar arrangements, such as life leases or memberships or when service contracts are coupled with ownership or leasehold rights. In any case, lenders often have an interest in subordinating the contractual or other rights of residents to their own in the event of a default, and these rights may conflict with contractual obligations to residents or with regulatory requirements. Lenders' requirements must be taken into consideration when examining applicable license laws, preparing residence agreements, marketing the facility, calculating reserves, and at other relevant steps in the process. (For a thorough discussion of project financing, see Part VI.)

§3.9 Marketing/Admissions

Unlike many other types of real estate development, seniors' housing facilities tend not to be built on speculation. Instead, retirement communities are often marketed, at least in part, before and during construction. In most CCRC projects, deposits from prospective residents may be used to test market feasibility or even to assist in project financing. But even in rental projects, substantial preconstruction sales activities often take place.[28]

Although marketing may often be performed by the developer or other sponsor or may be assigned to a facility management group, it is a function that can also require unique expertise. Marketing is a role that transcends the task of filling facility vacancies; it affects product and physical plant development, pricing considerations, development of residence agreements, creation and enforcement of admissions and waiting list policies, and other considerations that precede the closing of a sale. Some have suggested that the same person or company should be in charge of both marketing and management, especially in a mature facility, so that marketing personnel cannot blame management for poor sales results or vice versa.

Some consultants specialize in retirement facility marketing as distinguished from market feasibility studies, although the advanced feasibility study functions (e.g., focus groups) and the sales process overlap. Of course, marketing is far more than advanced market feasibility study. Marketing consultants must become sensitive to the reputation, ideals, experience, and goals of the sponsor, developer, and operator, whether single or multiple entitles. Likewise, they must recognize and respond to the needs and desires of prospective residents. Most important, marketing staff must communicate their concerns and ideas and coordinate their activities with the other disciplines from early on in the development process. Finally, marketing consultants should have the requisite technical expertise to use the communications media to best advantage and to follow up personally to obtain deposits or other commitments necessary to confirm sales. Agreements with marketing consultants should cover topics such as the projected rate of facility fill-up (absorption rate), the extent to which the marketer's payment is contingent on completed sales, the number and identity of marketing staff, and a thorough description of the marketing plan.[29]

A facility's potential liability for marketing errors is more acute in recent times due to increased competition and consumerism. Potential danger areas include

- overly broad statements (especially in brochures and personal interviews) about facility services, care guarantees, financial security, nursing bed availability, activity levels of the resident population, and so on;
- lack of disclosure regarding whether persons in need of care will be required to transfer out of independent-living units;
- lack of disclosure of tax consequences of the transaction, such as imputed interest liability and absence of tax deductions;
- absence of disclaimers regarding sponsor liability, the provider's status as a fiduciary or trustee of resident payments, limits on residents' ownership interests in the corporation or facility, and use of fees for the direct benefit of the resident;
- lack of details regarding fee increases and refunds, waiting list priorities, medical eligibility criteria, and causes for transfer and termination; and
- handicap and age discrimination and impermissible questions and selection criteria (see §23.3).

Possible solutions include

- early drafting of detailed contracts and policies before marketing begins;
- coordination of sales and management personnel with attorneys who drafted agreements;
- interview checklists for sales staff, filled out for each applicant;

- written disclaimers and disclosures appended to the contract and incorporated by reference;
- routine written disclosure of basic ownership and financial information;
- discussion of issues with applicants' children or other family members;
- cross-checking of advertising, brochures, and facility policies against the contract; and
- careful drafting of admissions documents and criteria to reduce the possibility of unlawful discrimination.

Notes

1. For a comprehensive review of retirement community development issues, *see AAHA Development Manual: A Step-by-Step Guide for Trustees and Chief Executives Undertaking Development of Non-Profit Facilities for the Elderly,* American Association of Homes for the Aging, 1986. Also, for a detailed discussion of the planning process for retirement facility development, including product analysis and assessment, financial feasibility, marketing and management issues, *see* Laughlin, J., and S. Moseley, *Retirement Housing: A Step-by-Step Approach* (New York: John Wiley & Sons, 1989) and *Seniors Housing: A Development and Management Handbook* (Washington, DC: National Association of Home Builders, 1987).

2. Studies may not be indicated when, for example, a group of prospective residents is more than large enough to fill the facility.

3. Some commentators argue that the prospect of performing a financial feasibility study may bias a market analyst in favor of proceeding with a project. *See* McMullin, "Common Financial Problems Encountered by CCRCs," *Contemporary Long Term Care,* Feb. 1986, 50.

4. For a general discussion of factors affecting the feasibility of seniors' housing projects, *see* Bernstein, H., and H. Peters, "Housing for the Elderly: A Primer for Developers," *Contemporary Long Term Care,* Oct. 1987, 154.

5. *See* §5.3, regarding how feasibility studies may make inaccurate assumptions that can jeopardize the project.

6. Seip, D., "Predicting Successful Projects in Today's Retirement Industry," *Contemporary Long Term Care,* June 1988, 96, 103.

7. *See, e.g.,* Laventhol & Horwath, *The Senior Living Industry 1986,* 33, 56, which reports that nearly 80 percent of the residents in both rental and entrance fee facilities come from within a 25-mile radius of the site.

8. For a comprehensive analysis of market feasibility studies, *see* Brecht, H., *Retirement Housing Markets* (New York: John Wiley & Sons, 1991).

9. *An Analysis of Nationwide Absorption Rates: The Critical Element in the Feasibility of Senior Living Projects,* National Association for Senior Living Industries (NASLI), Mar. 1992 [hereafter NASLI Analysis].

10. Capital Valuation Group and the American Seniors Housing Association (ASHA), *Seniors Absorption Study 1990 to 1996: Insights into Development and Feasibility* (Washington, DC: 1997).

11. For a detailed analysis of financial feasibility, market feasibility, and appraisal issues, *see* Gimmy, A., and M. Boehm, *Elderly Housing: A Guide to Appraisal, Market Analysis, Development and Financing* (Chicago: American Institute of Real Estate Appraisers, 1988).

12. *See* §3.7.

13. *See* §5.3.

14. *See AAHA Development Manual: A Step-by-Step Guide for Trustees and Chief Executives Undertaking Development of Non-Profit Facilities for the Elderly,* American Association of Homes for the Aging, 1986, 31.

15. For an example of different pricing methodologies, *see* Chapters 6–8. *See also* Laventhol & Horwath, note 7 *above,* for a study of rental and entrance fee/monthly fee price ranges.

16. *E.g.,* in membership or real property sales formats where a portion of the sale price must be paid to the facility operator or developer as a transfer fee.

17. *See* Winkelvoss, H., and A. Powell, *Continuing Care Retirement Communities: An Empirical, Financial, and Legal Analysis* (Philadelphia: Pension Research Council, Wharton School, University of Pennsylvania, Richard D. Irwin, 1984), 107.

18. *See* McMullin, note 2 *above.*

19. Laventhol and Horwath, note 7 *above,* at 26–27. Interestingly, the newer facilities experienced higher turnover, which may reflect increasing frailty of new admittees rather than resident lengths of stay.

20. *See generally* Gordon, P., "What Counsel Should Know about Full Service Retirement Communities," *The Practical Real Estate Lawyer,* Mar. 1986, 7; and Steiner, J., and J. Kneen, "Senior Housing Developments Raise Legal Issues for CFOs," *Health Care Financial Management,* Dec. 1987, 70.

21. *See generally* "Building Types Study 651: Housing for the Aging," *Architectural Record,* Apr. 1988, 98.

22. *See* discussion in §2.2(a).

23. Reiss, R., "Management Contracts: Are They Worth It?" *Contemporary Long Term Care,* Mar. 1988, 52.

24. For a listing of lenders, their preferred borrower types, and loan criteria, *see* Evanson, D., and A. Mullen, *Retirement Housing Construction Finance Directory* (New York: John Wiley & Sons, 1991).

25. Zaner, L., "From Main Street to Wall Street, Seniors Housing Emerges as a Viable Real Estate Niche," *Seniors Housing* (a special supplement to *National Real Estate Investor;* 1994), 3.

26. 1994 National Investment Conference Lender & Investor Survey.

27. *See* Pallarito, K., "'Maturation' of Senior Housing Boosts Outlook for Financing," *Modern Healthcare,* Feb. 19, 1996.

28. *See* Laventhol & Horwath, note 7 *above,* at 34.

29. *See generally* Seip, D., "Challenging Absorption in Retirement Housing," *Contemporary Long Term Care,* Feb. 1988, 20.

Morningside Continuing-Care Retirement Facility; Fullerton, California.

4 Steps in the Development Process

§4.1 In General

No exact chronological process can be offered for the development of seniors' housing communities generally, but it is, to be sure, a "front-loaded" process. Many of the required tasks and inquiries are so interdependent that a casual attempt at sequencing the substantive groupings of tasks can lead to the conclusion that everything should be done simultaneously. In reality, development progress does not involve so much the movement from one type of task or discipline to another but rather is characterized by growth from a simple interplay of several disciplines to a more complex one. In other words, the members of the development team are all, to varying degrees, called on throughout the process to expand, rethink, and refine their work as the project evolves. This chapter attempts to outline, in a rough chronological format, milestones in a representative development process and to show how the talents of team members can be brought to bear on the various tasks. Figure 4.1 is a sample critical path development timetable for a multilevel retirement community project.

In addition, Figure 4.2 provides an overview of the regulatory approval process for an equity continuing-care retirement community.[1]

§4.2 Basic Concept Structuring

(a) Team Selection

Selection of the following team members should occur at the beginning of the process:

- project coordinator;
- architect/land use planner for site review and conceptual drawings;
- market feasibility consultant for basic demographic study of the area; and
- legal counsel for evaluation of business structure options, license requirements, tax consequences, zoning issues, drafting and review of documents, and so on.

(b) Site Selection

Site selection should include financial, marketing, operational, and legal considerations such as

- cost, seller financing;
- location in relation to desirable community services such as transportation, shopping, health care, and cultural and recreational activities;
- location in relation to elderly population centers and other retirement facilities that may be competitive;

Figure 4.1 **Sample Development Timetable: California Continuing Care**

Months

Step	0	1	2	3	4	5	6	7	8	9	10	11

1. Consultant agreements (feasibility study, legal, accounting, financial, architectural, construction, marketing)
   `1 ----------------------------------------------------`

2. Preparation of overall business structure
   `2 -------------------------------`

3. Creation of new legal entity and preparation of joint venture agreements (if necessary)
   `3 -----------------------------------------`

4. Obtaining tax exemption (if necessary)
   `P          S                                                      A`
   `4 --------------------------------------------------------------------`

5. Application for plan approval and site data (nursing facility)
   `P                S`
   `5 xxxxxxxxxxxxxxxxxxx`

6. Preliminary drawings and outline specifications (nursing facility)
   `P`
   `6 xxxxxxxxxx`

7. Certificate of Need (nursing facility)
   `P`
   `7 xxxxxxxxxxxxxxxxxxx`

8. State tax-exempt financing approval (if necessary)
   `P`
   `8 $$$$$$$$$$$$$$$$$$$$$$$$$$$$$$$$$$$$$$$$$$$$$$$$$$$$$$$`

9. Prelicensing application and questionnaire (assisted-living facility)
   `P          S          A`
   `9 +++++++++++++++`

10. Basic legal documents (residence agreement, deposit subscription agreement, escrow agreement)

11. Financial and occupancy projections
    `11 _____`

12. License application (nursing facility)

13. License application (assisted-living facility)

14. Permit to sell deposit subscriptions

15. Working drawings and final specifications (nursing facility)

16. Environmental impact report
    16a. Negative declaration
    `P                    S          A`
    `16a vvvvvvvvvvvvvvvvvvvvvvvvv`
    16b. Full review and certification
    `P                    S`
    `16b vvvvvvvvvvvvvvvvvvvvvvvvvvvvvvvvvvvvvvvvvvvvvvvvvv`

17. Land use permit

18. Building permit

19. Sale of deposit subscriptions

20. Selection of bond counsel

21. Bond marketing

22. Closing on bond issue

23. Construction of project

24. Release of initial deposit subscription funds from escrow

25. Occupancy permit

26. License (nursing facility) (including preparation of written policies)

27. License (assisted-living facility) (including preparation of written policies)

28. Certificate of authority

29. Signing of care agreement

30. Admission of residents

12	13	14	15	16	17	18	19	20	21	22	23	24	25	26	27

Legend
P = Preparation
S = Submission
A = Approval

xxx = Nursing facility
+++ = Assisted-living facility
ooo = Continuing care
vvv = Local land use planning
$$$ = Financing
---- = Preliminary legal work
___ = Activity or event

```
      A
xxxx
            S               A
xxxxxxxxxxxxxxxxxx
            S               A
xxxxxxxxxxxxxxxxxx
         S        A
$$$$$$$$$$$$


      P                             S
10 ooooooooooooooooooooooooooooooo


_____     S
                    P        S
                 12 xxxxxxxx
                    P         S
                 13 ++++++++
                 P              S                   A
              14 oooooooooooooooooooooooooooooooooooooo
   15 xxxxxxxxxxxxxxxxxxxxxxxxxxxxxxxxxxxxxxxxxxxxxxxxxxxxxxxxxxxxxxxxxxxxxxxxxxx     A
      P                                          S


                                                       A
vvvvvvvvvvvvvvvvvvvvvvvvvvvvvvvvvvvvvvvvvvvvvvvvvvvvvvvvv
   17 vvvvvvvvvvvvvvvvvvvvvvvvvvvvvvvvvvvvvvvvvvvvvvvvvvv  A
      P                          S                        v
                                 18. v                    A
                                 19 oooooooooooooooooooooooooooooooooooooooooooooooooooooooo
   20 $$$$$$$$
                                         21 $$$$$$$$$$$$$$$$$$$$$$$$$$$$$$$$$$$$$$$$$$$$$$$$
                                         22 $$$$$$$$
                                         23 _____
```

Figure 4.1 **(continued)**

Months

Step	28	29	30	31	32	33	34	35	36	37	38	39
1. Consultant agreements (feasibility study, legal, accounting, financial, architectural, construction, marketing)												
2. Preparation of overall business structure												
3. Creation of new legal entity and preparation of joint venture agreements (if necessary)												
4. Obtaining tax exemption (if necessary)												
5. Application for plan approval and site data (nursing facility)												
6. Preliminary drawings and outline specifications (nursing facility)												
7. Certificate of Need (nursing facility)												
8. State tax-exempt financing approval (if necessary)												
9. Prelicensing application and questionnaire (assisted-living facility)												
10. Basic legal documents (residence agreement, deposit subscription agreement, escrow agreement)												
11. Financial and occupancy projections												
12. License application (nursing facility)												
13. License application (assisted-living facility)												
14. Permit to sell deposit subscriptions												
15. Working drawings and final specifications (nursing facility)												
16. Environmental impact report												
16a. Negative declaration												
16b. Full review and certification												
17. Land use permit												
18. Building permit												
19. Sale of deposit subscriptions	ooooooooooooooooooooooooooooooo											
20. Selection of bond counsel												
21. Bond marketing	$$$$$$$$$$$$$$$$$$$$$$$$$$$$$											
22. Closing on bond issue												
23. Construction of project												
24. Release of initial deposit subscription funds from escrow						24 $\overset{A}{\underset{o}{}}$							
25. Occupancy permit												
26. License (nursing facility) (including preparation of written policies)								26 $\overset{P}{}$ xxxxxxxxxxxxxxxxxxxxxxxxxxxxxxxxxxxxxxxxxx					
27. License (assisted-living facility) (including preparation of written policies)								27 $\overset{P}{}$ ++++++++++++++++++++++++++++++++++++					
28. Certificate of authority												
29. Signing of care agreement												
30. Admission of residents												

Months

40	41	42	43	44	45	46	47	48	49	50	51	52	53	54	55

Legend

P = Preparation
S = Submission
A = Approval

xxx = Nursing facility
+++ = Assisted-living facility
ooo = Continuing care
vvv = Local land use planning
$$$ = Financing
---- = Preliminary legal work
___ = Activity or event

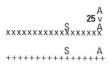

```
                        A
                     25 v
                  S     A
xxxxxxxxxxxxxxxxxxxxxx
                  S     A
+++++++++++++++++++
               P  S  A
             28 oooooo
             28 _____
             30 _____
```

- ability to retain an option on land pending initial project concept development;
- topography, especially if a campus-style setting is desired;
- zoning status and community atmosphere and attitudes toward multiunit development or presence of a health facility;
- Certificate of Need availability in the local health facility planning area; and
- location of potential joint venture partners and elderly constituency groups.

(c) Formulation of Basic Concept

All team members should share ideas concerning

- basic architectural format, for example, high-rise, single-family campus development;
- basic service concept, for example, meals, housekeeping, laundry, social programs, transportation, health care, insurance product;
- basic fee arrangements, for example, rental, entrance fee, purchase;
- basic resident interest, for example, condominium owner, monthly lessee, life lessee, cooperative owner, membership;
- basic structure of owner and operator, for example, for-profit, nonprofit, lease to operator, hire management company, joint venture, and so on; and
- basic legal and regulatory implications of the concept on licensing, marketing, scheduling, construction, costs, finance, taxation, and so on.

§4.3 Concept Testing and Refinement

(a) Additional Team Members

Refinement of the basic concept may require input from additional sources, including the following:

- a financial feasibility consultant to cost out preferred options;
- a marketing consultant to test and refine elements of the service package;
- a manager to point out operational difficulties and solutions; and

- a financial consultant or broker to survey availability of funding.

(b) Financial Modeling

Different variations of the basic options under consideration should be subjected to financial analysis and projection, taking the following into account:

- different pricing options, for example, all prepaid, prepaid plus à la carte, all fee-for-service, refundable versus nonrefundable fees, unit purchases;
- balancing pricing levels, for example, size of entrance fee versus liberality of refund, lower costs of mandatory services versus higher-priced optional programs;
- assessment of actuarial factors affecting future service liabilities and unit turnover, unit resales, and transfer fees;
- rent-up delays and effect on initial cash flows (monthly sales, income and expenditures projection);
- need for reserves for debt service, plant replacement, future health care obligations, other contingencies;
- state laws imposing financial disclosure or security requirements such as liens, reserves, or bonding;
- probable requirements of lenders;
- review of the competition's practices and level of success;
- costs of long-term-care insurance or health plan enrollment, self-insured or commercially purchased;
- costs of special licensing requirements or elevated construction standards;
- other usual costs such as construction, interest, insurance, consultant and legal fees, permits, staffing requirements, food and other supplies, and so on.

(c) Premarketing

Before attempting to sell a fully defined product, it can be important to communicate with prospective residents and other interested parties.

- Identify senior constituency or affinity groups.
- Survey preferences by questionnaire and selected interview regarding services and amenities, fee structures, unit sizes, and so on.

Figure 4.2 **Overview of Continuing-Care and Real Estate Process**

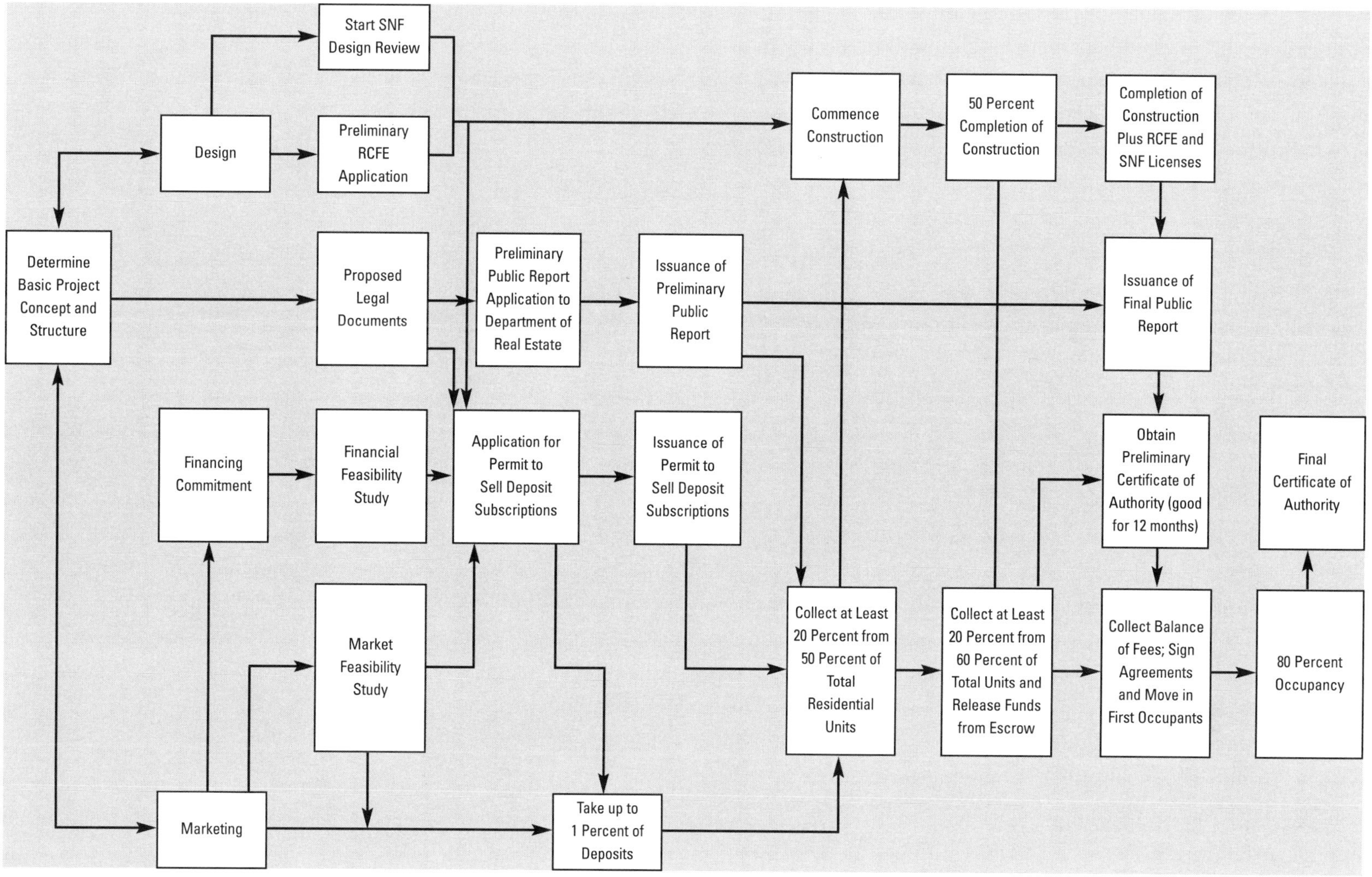

RCFE = Residential-care facility for the elderly

SNF = Skilled-nursing facility

Source: Equity CCRC, California.

- Survey attitudes about the sponsor, project, residents' ability to pay, self-image as to physical and social needs, and so on.
- Establish relationships that will be useful in public approvals and sales.
- Possibly approach local land use planning officials and neighborhood groups to test early reactions.
- Keep lists of all inquiries and prospects.
- Sell the sponsor and the basic concept.

(d) Exploration of Financing

A financing commitment should be sought early in the development process. The availability of construction financing and permanent financing depends on the type of project. The following sources should be reviewed:

- HUD loans or loan guarantees;
- state loan guarantees for health care facility development;
- tax-exempt bond financing (often through municipal government);
- banks and other conventional lenders;
- syndications;
- pension funds; and
- resident funding through deposits toward entrance fees or sales of condominium interests, cooperative shares, or memberships.

(e) Defining the Product

The project will require further adjustments, but by now a product should be identified for implementation. Product identification requires the following:

- final determination of all owner/operator identities and relationships, including joint venture partners;
- completion of proposed site plan, architectural design, unit sizes and mix;
- drafting of a proposed resident agreement, with input from legal, marketing, management, and financial consultants, to cover fees, services, resident transfer policies, and so on;
- development of marketing materials to be submitted for legal review to ensure consistency with fair housing laws and the proposed resident agreement and to ensure sufficient flexibility to accommodate moderate adjustments;

- determination of how and by whom each basic service is to be provided, for example, in-house, by third-party contract, on or off site, by a joint venture partner, and so on; include consideration of HMOs, insurance, and health facility transfer arrangements for health care services;
- identification of all government approvals and legal steps necessary to implement the plan; check for licensing, zoning, securities offerings, subdivision approval, Certificate of Need, fire clearances, and so on, and meet with appropriate officials;
- identification of all remaining team members and responsibilities; and
- development of a realistic (i.e., conservative) timetable showing each task and its place in the overall development process.

§4.4 Initial Implementation

Once the product concept has been sufficiently refined, it is time to go public and begin implementation on several fronts. The priority and timing of the various steps may differ widely among projects based on the duration of government review processes, the resolution of identified problems, prerequisites demanded by lenders or the law, marketing strategies, and other considerations.

(a) Site-Related Tasks

- Commence the formal local land use planning, zoning, environmental impact (often time consuming), subdivision mapping approval processes.
- Finalize working drawings and specifications.
- Put project out to bid for construction.
- Fund construction financing.
- Commence construction only after zoning, financing, sufficient presales or other market response, preliminary license approvals, contract reviews, and other essentials are in place.

(b) Legal and Management Tasks

In general, management and legal team members should work together to carry out the following initial steps in the implementation process:

- Complete sponsors' required organizational documents, for example, new corporations or partnerships, joint venture agreements, leases, tax-exemption applications, private letter ruling requests.
- During marketing phase, review questions about resident agreement and modify if necessary.
- Prepare or review contracts pertaining to construction, management, food service, housekeeping, finance, and so on.
- Prepare or review third-party agreements concerning provision of health care, such as transfer agreements, health insurance policies, managed-care agreements, contracts with medical director, home health agencies, and so on.
- Create and review policies and procedures for on-site health and personal-care facilities.
- Create and review admissions and waiting list policies, with marketing input.
- Review issues concerning resident financial or medical qualifications, private-pay agreements, resident trusts, powers of attorney, handicap and age discrimination issues.
- Prepare deposit agreements and other presales documentation.
- Review insurance needs of the facility, including general liability, directors' and officers', professional malpractice, employee bonding.

(c) Marketing

- Make draft of resident agreement and marketing materials available to prospects.
- Assemble an admissions review team, with marketing and legal help, to establish age, health, and financial criteria for acceptance and to develop waiting list procedures.

- Begin intensive marketing, including taking of deposits on sales or entrance fee structures (check for licensing prerequisites).

§4.5 Later Development and Project Opening

Project opening generally involves completing the details associated with each ongoing element of the project, with a heightened emphasis on close coordination and timing.

- Review and adjust budget and pricing assumptions in light of sales experience.
- Complete construction.
- Obtain certification for occupancy from local government.
- Obtain site inspections and certifications required for licensure of health or care facilities.
- Execute contracts with management company and other vendors.
- Hire other necessary personnel.
- Collect final deposits from residents and execute residence agreements, powers of attorney, and trust agreements, if any.
- Coordinate move-in of residents.

Note

1. For a good summary of design, marketing, and financing considerations for the development of seniors' housing, *see* Porter, D., et al., *Housing for Seniors: Developing Successful Projects* (Washington, DC: Urban Land Institute, 1995).

The Fountains of Lake Pointe Woods; Sarasota, Florida.

5 Avoiding Financial Pitfalls

§5.1 In General

Although the vast majority of seniors' housing communities operate successfully, financial failures have captured the widespread attention of the press.[1] Lifecare or continuing-care communities, in particular, seem to have attracted the most attention, although it is not clear that they have any higher proportion of failures than other types of retirement housing, such as rental units, condominiums, or cooperatives.

Some commentators believe that the most spectacular failures of continuing-care communities may not fairly represent the risks actually present in the industry:

> Like the crash of a jumbo jet, the failure of a lifecare community attracts attention from the press and is brought glaringly into public scrutiny. Although statistics are not readily available to prove it, troubled facilities and failures in the lifecare industry may not occur with any greater frequency than in other segments of the real estate industry.[2]

On the other hand, tangible evidence suggests that a substantial number of retirement community projects end in failure. Of the estimated $5 billion worth of tax-exempt retirement center and nursing home bonds marketed in the 1980s, more than $1 billion worth went into default.[3] Similarly, one study of 109 continuing-care communities reported that 64 had a negative net worth, a negative net income, or both.[4]

One reason, of course, for the notoriety of CCRC failures is that residents or prospective residents typically make large lump-sum payments to community developers or operators as a condition of admission. Advance deposits or entrance fees used to help develop or operate projects that eventually fail can often involve a substantial portion of the elderly resident's life savings. Where continuing-care entrance fees are protected under state laws by escrow provisions or reserve requirements, residents may not be at risk, although bondholders often become the victims of a default.

In rental projects, by contrast, developers and commercial lenders rather than tenants and bondholders tend to bear the brunt of the financial risk that a project will fail. Moreover, the limited term of the lease reduces resident expectations. As a more conventional form of real estate, rental projects tend to draw less attention than housing in general when they fail. The usual presence of actuarial pricing considerations, future medical liabilities, higher intensities of services, and the slower sales experiences of continuing-care facilities may help explain why the continuing-care feature is a common element in many well-publicized defaults. As noncontinuing-care facility programs become more complex—involving more extensive services and unusual payment mechanisms—and public and government concern about transfers of persons in need of medical care grows more acute, other types of retirement facilities may account for a more representative share of the problems brought to public attention. Chapter 29 and Volume I discuss various types of development and operational liabilities.

§5.2 Examples of Serious Financial Difficulties

Probably the largest group of continuing-care communities to file for bankruptcy was the Pacific Homes Corporation, which operated and now—after reorganization—continues to operate several facilities located primarily in California.[5] Many of the homes' older life-care contracts required payment only of an initial accommodation fee, or an assignment of the resident's assets, without monthly fees or other additional fees in return for life-time residence and services. Later contracts required payment of entrance fees plus a fixed monthly fee. Without the ability to adjust fees to keep up with inflation and meet rising operational costs and due to the use of capital funds for "capital expansion, speculative investment, and financing of operating losses,"[6] Pacific Homes soon needed to expand its facilities in order to sell new contracts and bring in new accommodation fees to cover obligations under earlier contracts.[7] From 1969 to 1976, Pacific Homes's deficit grew from $17 million to $27 million; in 1977, the corporation filed for bankruptcy.[8]

At least six lawsuits claiming damages in excess of $600 million resulted from the bankruptcy and related financial difficulties,[9] including suits alleging that the United Methodist Church was an alter ego of Pacific Homes and was therefore liable for its contract obligations[10] and that the state of California wrongfully failed to revoke Pacific Homes's life-care license for failure to meet state-mandated reserve requirements.[11] Ultimately, Methodist Church groups contributed $21 million to settle the litigation, creditors have been repaid, and resident contracts have been renegotiated to permit operation on a fiscally sound basis.[12]

Another series of serious financial problems plagued homes operated by Reverend Jimmy Ballard and/or Reverend Kenneth Berg. In one case, Ballard was convicted in 1981 of securities fraud in connection with the sale of bonds for a proposed life-care facility. Undisclosed to offerees was the fact that the bonds were to be encumbered by a debt from one of Ballard's previously failed life-care projects.[13] In 1984, Berg was also convicted of securities fraud in connection with loans solicited from residents of the same troubled project.[14] In another massive, 1,900-unit retirement community once operated by Berg, a lender paid $13 million to plaintiffs, $1 million to the facility, and $500,000 to the plaintiffs' lawyers and forgave a $48.3 million mortgage on the facility to settle litigation over financial problems in the development of the project.[15] In all, Berg was involved with about 40 projects.[16] (See also *Ross v. Bank South*,[17] in which the circuit court found sufficient evidence of fraud to order a trial to determine whether those involved in the financing of a retirement facility with revenue bonds should be held liable for marketing bonds that were allegedly "unmarketable" due to the facility's insufficient projected revenues.)

The conscientious developer should easily be able to avoid the problems of securities fraud and overly restrictive pricing structures. However, most other cases of financial failure appear to involve individual facilities that cannot attract a sufficient number of residents to make the project financially feasible but that are nevertheless financed and developed. Examples include a bond default involving an attempted conversion of Florida apartments into a continuing-care project, allegedly with only 11 percent of the units presold[18]; a 300-unit Philadelphia-area facility that had completed only 16 sales when construction was completed in 1982[19]; and a 300-unit seniors' rental facility in California, for which only one apartment had been rented a year after the scheduled completion of construction.[20] While these individual failures do not always attract the type of national media attention generated by the bankruptcy of a chain of occupied facilities or the filing of criminal indictments, they probably constitute the pattern most representative of the real dangers to well-meaning developers of seniors' housing communities.

Other notable financial problems in the field have included HUD's Retirement Service Center program (see §14.2(d)(1)) and the Chapter 11 bankruptcy reorganization of the Forum Group (eventually acquired by Marriott).

§5.3 Causes of Failures

In the absence of a precise formula for success, commentators on the seniors' housing industry have attempted to identify and address factors that account for the financial failures of some communities.[21] A preliminary survey conducted by the American Association of Homes for the Aging[22] identified 70 facilities as having experienced financial difficulty. The following reasons were offered:

Reason	Number of Facilities
Poor marketing/inadequate presales	23
Poor or inexperienced management	12
Poor financial planning	11
Fraud	3

Failure to fill up a new facility immediately upon completion is surely one of the greatest causes of financial failure. It is important to study a project's market feasibility before securing financing or undertaking construction,[23] but there is no substitute, especially in entrance fee projects, for actual presales of units with receipt and deposit into escrow of a substantial portion of the expected fee. Feasibility studies can make certain assumptions that later turn out not to be matched by actual consumer behavior. For example, studies may be overly optimistic about the percentage penetration of the age- and income-qualified marketplace that can be achieved.[24] Of course, percentages of market penetration may vary widely depending on factors such as consumer familiarity with the type of product and the reputation of comparable facilities in the area. Studies may also make imprecise assumptions about the age group likely to be attracted to the facility,[25] about the ability to obtain licensure for health care facilities,[26] or about other factors critical to sales and financial success. Feasibility studies are important but require testing throughout the development process by identifying and maintaining contact with prospects and, if possible, by securing binding financial commitments from them. Many CCRC statutes, for example, provide for a financial penalty for prospective residents who withdraw during facility construction (see §21.6(c)).

Financial planning and management problems can sometimes strike facilities years after the onset of operations, but their roots are frequently traceable to the initial development plan. Pricing structures should be sufficiently flexible to cover fluctuations in operating costs, allow for adjustable periodic charges rather than only entrance fees, or permit periodic fees with dollar or percentage caps on increases. Nonetheless, the ability to adjust fees is not enough. A common postopening problem is that monthly fees must be raised substantially because of unanticipated costs or pricing that, for marketing or other reasons, was set at an unrealistically low level. If reserves for substantial health care costs, plant replacement, entrance fee refund obligations, or other liabilities are not funded from the outset, even a mature retirement community may find residents unable to absorb the increased costs occasioned by a sudden hike in monthly charges. Accordingly, it is important for the initial financial feasibility studies to consider long-term obligations and establish a funding mechanism for them from entrance fees, monthly fees, or both.

In addition, where entrance fees are the primary source of financing, financial feasibility studies should contain an actuarial component that conservatively predicts the rate of unit turnover. The unexpected longevity of residents in a facility that relies on future entrance fee income from unit turnovers can spell financial disaster.[27] The often-quoted lament of the retirement facility administrator is, "I have two ladies who are 100 years old . . . and they're killing me!"

Other problems causing financial difficulties have included high mortgage interest rates that make it difficult for prospective residents to sell their homes[28]; the loss of a nonprofit home's property tax exemption[29]; use of too great a portion of financing for purposes other than construction[30]; and the collection of deposits from prospective residents that are too small to ensure that the prospects will move in to the facility when it is ready for occupancy. Other causes of facility bankruptcy include construction costs that escalate out of control and excessive underwriting and related fees.[31]

In addition, the following problems are causes of facility failure:

■ a smaller-than-anticipated market because of the high average entry ages of retirement community residents and the large percentage of people who are not income-qualified;

- the relatively small percentage of the elderly population that will ever need nursing home care;
- the extremely local sensitivity of each elderly market;
- the slow pace of sales;
- the high cost of marketing;
- failure to retain program and design flexibility to meet actual market demands;
- failure to put a professional team together early in the development process;
- an overemphasis on demographics without a feel for the "pulse" of the market area;
- construction of small units that become obsolete due to demand for larger units; and
- poor location.[32]

While the Federal Trade Commission identified several problems in its investigation of fraud in one corporation's sale of continuing-care contracts, well-intentioned developers of any retirement facility should take heed of the following points made by the FTC:[33]

- use of entrance fees to cover construction costs but not future increases in health care costs for the facility's maturing population;
- exploitation of the mortgage lender's reputation to assure consumers of the project's financial soundness;
- representations that monthly fee increases will be limited by a factor other than actual operating costs;
- use of reserves principally for lender's debt service requirements while consumers believed future health liabilities were covered;
- falsely implying a religious affiliation and a corresponding legal and moral obligation of some other organization for facility debts;
- failure to escrow resident presales deposits for refund in the event of project failure during development, thereby resulting in dissipation of deposits for development costs; and
- use of entrance fees, monthly fees, or reserves from one project to fund expenses or cover losses at other, unrelated projects.

(See also §14.2 regarding failure of HUD's Section 221(d)(4) Retirement Service Center program, §17.7(c) regarding financial risk factors, and Figure 17.1 for financial rating guidelines for CCRCs.)

While careful planning can avert the problems associated with failed or financially troubled retirement facilities, new entrants into the marketplace in particular should study the failures as well as the successes of others and work with a development team with a proven record of long-term success.

§5.4 Developments That May Reduce Some Risks

While certainly neither a panacea nor a substitute for careful market and financial feasibility work and the other planning steps discussed earlier, four trends over the past decade may help to diminish the risk of failure in some retirement community projects: the growing availability of long-term-care insurance, more widespread state legislation and industry self-regulation, the movement toward resident equity structures, and stricter CCRC accounting standards.

Long-term-care insurance has become more readily available and offers more comprehensive coverage than was historically the case.[34] Taking the actuarial forecasting responsibilities out of the hands of individual (and possibly inexperienced) facility developers and spreading the risk pool beyond the inhabitants of a single self-insured facility can reduce the dangers of inaccurate predictions of future health care liabilities. In addition, commercial insurers can avail themselves of economies of scale and make long-term, noncancelable coverage available on a monthly premium basis rather than relying on a lump-sum entrance fee model that exposes more of the resident's assets to risk at the more vulnerable early stages of operation.

Since the late 1980s, many states have adopted legislation dealing with continuing care or other prepaid or long-term promises of care.[35] While stringent regulation is no guarantee that financial failures will not occur,[36] legal requirements such as financial disclosures and projections, escrows of resident deposits, minimum reserves, and presales thresholds should reduce the incidence of financial difficulty.

In the past, facility failures have posed serious problems for the seniors' housing industry. Some continuing-care facility operators claimed that it took longer than desired to fill facilities because, in part, of the adverse publicity associated with some retirement communities that had gone bankrupt.[37] In response, some providers spent as much as $1 million to $2 million per project in preconstruction costs to ensure preenrollment of 50 to 60 percent of the facility's units and thereby reduce the risk of failure.[38] In addition, the CCRC industry established an Accreditation Commission to help self-regulate and set standards for the field.

The development of more resident equity models for retirement facilities may also have the effect of preserving more of the resident's investment in the event of a failure. Theoretically at least, structures using condominium, cooperative, membership, or even refundable entrance fee structures, if backed by a security interest, retain for the resident some legal interest in the assets of the facility or the provider. Of course, if the project is financially unsound, the security of the resident's ownership interest may be largely cosmetic in that construction lenders or other creditors usually have first priority in the event of foreclosure. Further, the project may have diminished in value if it needs to be converted to some use other than the planned retirement facility. Once initial lenders are paid off, however, resident equity can provide a degree of long-term financial security.

Finally, accounting guidelines established in 1990 by the American Institute of Certified Public Accountants for continuing-care facilities require, first, reporting as a liability the extent to which the projected cost of care exceeds the present value of entrance fees and monthly fees for residents' lifetimes and, second, calculation of life expectancies and future care liabilities on a resident-by-resident basis.[39] These rules are expected to result in a more realistic view of a facility's financial condition and may help flag a potential financial problem while it is still correctable and before it escalates out of control.

Notes

1. *See, e.g.,* Rudnitsky and Konrad, "Trouble in the Elysian Fields," *Forbes,* Aug. 29, 1983, 58; Topolnicki, D., "The Broken Promise of Life-Care Communities," *Money,* Apr. 1985, 150; and other articles cited below. *See also* Cole-

man, B., "Life Care Pacts Create Woes for Some People," *AARP News Bulletin,* Apr. 1988.

2. Curran, S., and S. Brecht, "A Perspective on Risks for Lifecare Projects," *Real Estate Finance Journal,* Summer 1985, 64.

3. Schifrin, M., "An Expensive Free Lunch," *Forbes,* Jan. 25, 1988, 34. *See also* "Tax Exempt Bonds: Retirement Center Bonds Were Risky and Benefited Moderate-Income Elderly," U.S. General Accounting Office, Mar. 1991. However, bond defaults for 1991 were reported to be at about 25 percent of the rate in the mid-1980s. Bond Investors' Association Study reported in *NASLI News,* June 1992.

4. Ruchlin, H., "Continuing Care Retirement Communities: An Analysis of Financial Viability and Health Care Coverage," *The Gerontologist,* Apr. 1988, 156.

5. For more detailed discussions of the Pacific Homes cases, see "Continuing-Care Communities for the Elderly: Potential Pitfalls and Proposed Regulation," 128 *U. Pa. L. Rev.* 900 (1980); "Continuing Care Communities: A Promise Falling Short," 8 *George Mason Univ. L. Rev.* 47 (1985); *Matthews v. State of California,* 104 Cal. App. 3d 424, 163 Cal. Rptr. 741 (1980); *Barr v. United Methodist Church,* 90 Cal. App. 3d 259, 153 Cal. Rptr. 322 (1979), *cert. denied,* 444 U.S. 973 (1979), *reh'g. denied,* 444 U.S. 1049 (1980); *General Council, etc., of the United Methodist Church v. Superior Court,* 439 U.S. 1355 (1978); *In re Pacific Homes Corp.,* 1 Bankr. 574 (C.D. Cal. 1979); Senate Special Committee on Aging, Life Care Communities: Promises and Problems, S. Hrg. 98–276, 98th Cong., 1st Sess. (1983).

6. *See* Comment, *George Mason Univ. L. Rev.,* note 5 *above.*

7. *Id.,* citing Bankruptcy Trustee's report, Oct. 15, 1979.

8. *Ibid.*

9. United Methodist Communications News Release, Oct. 1979.

10. *See Barr v. United Methodist Church,* note 5 *above.*

11. *Matthews v. State of California,* note 5 *above.*

12. Conversation with Mort Swales, president, Pacific Homes Foundation.

13. *See* Topolnicki, note 1 *above.*

14. *Ibid.*

15. *See* John Knox Village (Lee's Summit, Missouri) news release, Dec. 11, 1985; *In re Christian Services International,* 102 F.T.C. 1338 (1983); Comment, *George Mason Univ. L. Rev.,* note 5 *above,* at 53–55.

16. Rudnitsky and Konrad, note 1 *above.*

17. 837 F.2d 980 (11th Cir. 1988). *But see Ross v. Bank South,* 885 F.2d 723 (11th Cir. 1989), *cert. denied,* 495 U.S. 905 (1990), in which the court of appeals, rehearing the

case *en banc,* held that there was insufficient evidence that the bonds were "unmarketable" and thus upheld judgment in favor of the defendants without a trial.

18. *See* Moore, "Major Southern Firms Swept into Bond Default Litigation Net," *Legal Times,* Oct. 14, 1985.

19. *See* Henriques and Holton, "Of Faith Misplaced: How Investors Lost Millions on Fiddler's Woods," *Philadelphia Inquirer* (copy on file with author).

20. *See* Pyle, "Bank Sues over Maple Village Bonds," *Fresno Bee,* July 18, 1986, B-1.

21. *See generally* Wade, E., and D. McMullin, "Lessons to Learn in Retirement Living," *Contemporary Long Term Care,* Oct. 1985, 21; McMullin, "Common Financial Problems Encountered by CCRCs," *Contemporary Long Term Care,* Feb. 1986, 50.

22. Draft memorandum, May 15, 1986.

23. *See* §3.3.

24. *See, e.g.,* allegations reported in *Philadelphia Inquirer,* note 19 *above.*

25. *See, e.g.,* the allegation that the 79-to-82 age group, rather than the predicted 55-year-and-older segment, should have been targeted in one project. *Fresno Bee,* note 20 *above.*

26. *See* allegations reported in *Legal Times,* note 18 *above.*

27. *See, e.g.,* Swallow, W., "Agreement Near to Resolve Life-Care Homes' Bankruptcy," *Washington Post,* Oct. 13, 1984.

28. *See, e.g.,* "Shaky Lifecare Center Put Up for Sale," *Modern Healthcare,* Nov. 1980, 54.

29. *See, e.g.,* Smith, "Baptist Homes in Bankruptcy," *Detroit News,* Mar. 19, 1977.

30. *See* discussion in Rudnitsky and Konrad, note 1 *above.*

31. *See* Schifrin, note 3 *above.*

32. Los, J., "Straight Talk about Retirement Housing," *Contemporary Long Term Care,* Sept. 1987, 120. *See also* Zeisel, J., and K. Sloan, "Troubled Senior Housing Projects," paper presented to the American Society on Aging/American Association of Retired Persons Conference, Mar. 1991, which identified six causes of failure: overbuilding, low value, overborrowing, insufficient and depleted financial reserves, poor marketing, and financial and operational mismanagement. *See also* Struve, K., "Turning Around Troubled Senior Housing and Health Care Projects," *Commercial Lending Review,* Spring 1992, 8, which asserts that most financial failures of seniors' housing and health care projects are rooted in one of the following four areas: a marketing plan with outdated projections and assumptions, an ineffective marketing team, inexperienced management and administration personnel, and facilities that are out of line with the needs of the marketplace.

33. *See* statement of Patricia P. Bailey, Hearing, Senate Special Committee on Aging, note 5 *above,* at 54–59.

34. *See* discussion in Part VIII.

35. *See* Chapter 21.

36. For example, the Pacific Homes bankruptcy took place despite California's relatively strict legislation.

37. Graham, J., "Retirement Centers Increasing Numbers in Effort to Accommodate Affluent Elderly," *Modern Healthcare,* June 5, 1987, 112.

38. *Ibid.*

39. *See* Forster, W., and E. Orfanon, "Life Care Facilities Will Struggle with Proposed Auditing Rules," *Contemporary Long Term Care,* Oct. 1988, 42. For a complete discussion of the AICPA guidelines, see §17.7(b).

Vista Del Rio; Albuquerque, New Mexico.

Part III

....

Fee and Occupancy Options

The business operations of the project and the tax liabilities of both operator and resident are inextricably linked to how the resident pays the operator for the shelter, food, medical care, and other services that may be made available at a retirement community and the type of real property or other interest acquired by the resident.

Most seniors' housing types, such as congregate housing, assisted living, and HUD housing, operate on a rental basis. Continuing-care retirement communities have traditionally relied on entrance fees and, more recently, ownership structures. However, the fee and occupancy options discussed in this part need not be limited to particular service packages.

Historically, nonprofit operators controlled the care-oriented segment of the retirement community industry, especially projects offering endowment or entrance fee programs or continuing care. For many years, these facilities had special concerns relating to maintenance of their tax-exempt status (see Part IV), but their structures have generally followed a traditional "nonrefundable" entrance fee pattern. The more recent growth of for-profit involvement in the retirement housing field is largely responsible for raising several new business, tax, and legal issues and spurring some creative structural solutions.

Several business and tax concerns have helped shape the new options that have emerged over the past decade. Relevant tax considerations may include the taxability of fees paid by residents to the facility owner or operator, the deductibility to the resident of all or some part of the fees, the ability of the resident to defer or avoid recognition of gain on the sale of a previous residence, and the characterization of payments as below-market loans resulting in imputed interest. Business considerations can range from the developer's or operator's profit opportunity, to operational control and ability to assemble desired services or amenities, to product attractiveness in the marketplace. The basic legal structure of the provider/resident relationship is of at least as much significance as architectural and operational expertise in determining how the project will sell and function. The legal structure should be one of the first decisions made in the development process after carefully considering the numerous alternatives that may be available.[1]

Several of the business and tax issues discussed in this part pertain to more than one of the fee structures discussed below. However, the issues may be addressed in detail in the context of only one structure (e.g., at-risk rules discussed in the rental section apply to all real estate). This part should therefore be read as a whole to appreciate fully the interplay of the various issues and options. The table on page 90 summarizes the various advantages and disadvantages of several business structures discussed in this part from both the developer's and residents' points of view.

Business Structure Comparisons

	I Nonrefundable Entrance Fee	II Refundable Entrance Fee	III Membership	IV Condominium/ Cooperative	V Rental with Long-Term-Care Insurance
A. Resident Concerns					
1. Housing security	High	High	High	Highest	Low
2. Service security	High	High	High	Depends on structure transportable	Low, unless insurance
3. Return of payments	No	Yes	Possible gain, risk of loss	Possible gain, risk of loss	No
4. Investment flexibility	Slight	No	No	No	Yes
5. Initial cost	Moderate	High	High	Highest	Lower
6. Capital gain sheltered	No	No	No	Yes	No
7. Imputed interest	No	Yes	No	No	No
8. Initial medical deduction	Yes	Possible	No	No	No
B. Developer Concerns					
1. Initial income tax	Substantial	Not to extent refundable	No, nonprofit operator	Only to extent exceeds cost basis	Insubstantial
2. Long-term financing	From residents	From residents	From residents	From residents	From third party
3. Need for consumer education	Highest	High	High	Lower	Lowest
4. Management control	High	High	High	Depends on structure	Highest
5. Continuing-care regulation	Probable	Probable	Probable	Probable	Doubtful

Business Structure Comparisons (continued)

Notes:

A. Resident Concerns
   1. Housing security: resident's subjective sense that housing will be available for as long as needed.
   2. Service security: resident's subjective sense that services, including care, will be stable, available, affordable.
   3. Return of payments: entrance fees will be refundable or possible return on investment in the event of voluntary termination or upon death.
   4. Investment flexibility: substantial opportunity to invest home sale proceeds in ventures other than retirement community.
   5. Initial cost: relative size of initial payment required for move-in.
   6. Gain on resale eligible for capital gains exclusion of up to $500,000 for joint filers.
   7. Imputed interest: payments to operator likely to be treated as loans on which interest income, if not paid, will be imputed.
   8. Initial medical deduction: fee may be partly deductible to the extent it is a prepayment for health care services.

B. Developer Concerns
   1. Initial income tax: unless provider is tax-exempt, it will be subject to income tax on initial entrance fee or purchase prices.
   2. Long-term financing: source of funds to take out short-term or construction financing.
   3. Need for consumer education: lack of familiarity with product or difficulty accepting or understanding concept.
   4. Management control: ability of developer or operator to retain control over operations.
   5. Continuing-care regulation: assuming availability of care, is the arrangement of sufficient duration to trigger continuing-care regulation?

Morningside Continuing-Care Retirement Community; Fullerton, California.

6 Entrance Fee Models

§6.1 "Nonrefundable" Entrance Fees

(a) Marketing and Business Issues

The traditional entrance fee format requires the resident to pay the facility upon admission a substantial sum of money in addition to monthly fees. One of the principal purposes of obtaining a relatively large entrance fee at the inception of the project is to help fund construction costs or rapidly retire the construction debt and, possibly, to set aside reserves for future medical care or other variable expenditures that may not be covered by routine monthly fees.

Usually, continuing-care facilities collect substantial entrance fees in return for a long-term or lifetime promise of care and residence. Traditionally, most entrance fees paid to such facilities are not refundable either to the resident upon withdrawal from the facility or to the estate upon death.

A common exception to nonrefundability occurs in the event of a resident's voluntary withdrawal from the community or termination for cause during the first five or six years of residence, in which case a pro rata portion of the fee based on a declining amortization schedule of 1 to 2 percent per month is refunded ("declining refund"). However, when the resident dies, even during the first years or months after taking up residence, the continuing-care contract may be deemed to have been fully performed such that the resident's estate often receives no re-fund of the entrance fee or any portion of it (see examples of contract provisions in Volume II, Chapter 5). In contrast, a truly refundable fee is paid whenever the resident leaves the facility regardless of the reason. As of 1987, approximately 76 percent of continuing-care retirement communities had a declining refund or nonrefundable entrance fee plan.[2]

A 1991 survey of CCRCs conducted by the American Association of Homes for the Aging and Ernst & Young revealed that approximately 30 percent offer a nonrefundable entrance fee option and approximately 58 percent a declining refundable entrance fee option. The survey also found that the declining refundable entrance fee is the most popular option among residents; approximately 57 percent of residents choose a declining refundable entrance fee option, 27 percent select a nonrefundable entrance fee option, and 16 percent elect a refundable entrance fee option.[3]

Concern about the fairness of nonrefundable entrance fees has given rise to modified fee structures that permit some form of refund in the event of an early death or withdrawal (see discussion in §§2.4(f) and 21.6(c)). Retention of the entrance fees of residents who die before reaching their life expectancy is economically justifiable in the self-insurance scenario of a typical continuing-care facility because the funds retained from the deceased are needed to defray the costs of caring for those who will exceed the average life span. Nevertheless, in individual cases where many tens of thousands of dollars may have to be paid for a few days or months of residence and daily services actually received, many observers lose sight of the insurance dimensions of the transaction and find the payment unconscionable (see §21.6(c)).

The seeming unfairness inherent in some of the more extreme fact situations in part has led to more liberal partial refunds in the event of a death very early after taking up residence and has spawned the development of entrance fees that are refundable, in whole or in part, whenever the contract terminates —whether by voluntary cancellation, forcible discharge, or reason of death. However, the principal impetus behind the move away from nonrefundable fees has probably been the potentially drastic tax consequences of nonrefundable fee systems on the emerging for-profit sector of the retirement industry.

(b) Fees as Taxable Income

(1) Treatment as Prepaid Rent or Service Fees

For a for-profit seniors' housing community that follows the traditional nonrefundable entrance fee format, the Internal Revenue Service is likely to treat the entrance fee or a substantial portion of it as prepaid rent or a prepaid service fee, which would be characterized as income in the year of receipt. Unless the developer sells the resident an interest in the real property, the money received from the resident cannot be offset by the developer's cost basis in the project and may be taxable in its entirety.

Assuming that virtually all the entrance fees from initial sales are received during the first year or two of operation, the financial impact of taxation on that income may significantly affect the developer's ability to pay down construction costs. Passing the additional costs to the consumer in the form of higher entrance fees or increased monthly fees would put the for-profit facility operator at a competitive disadvantage with similarly situated nonprofit entities that do not pay tax on entrance fees. In large luxury projects, the amount of entrance fees that could be subjected to income taxation during facility fill-up might equal tens of millions of dollars.

Under Treasury Regulation §1.61–8, gross income includes rents received or accrued for the occupancy of real property and specifically includes "advance rentals, which must be included in income for the year of receipt regardless of the period covered or the method of accounting employed by the taxpayer."[4]

(2) Recognition of Income on an Actuarial Basis

In 1967, the U.S. Tax Court ruled in *Wide Acres Rest Home* that a nonrefundable stock transfer made by an elderly person upon admission to a rest home in return for a promise of life-time care should be included as income in the year of receipt.[5] The home, an accrual basis taxpayer, argued that the payment did not constitute advance rentals under Regulation §1.61–8 (presumably, the payment was characterized as a service fee) and was not earned in the first year but would instead be received as income over the resident's lifetime. The court responded that the regulatory reference to advance rentals was only an example of reportable prepaid income and that the home's access to and use of the stock was unrestricted, compelling treatment of the stock as income when received. Similarly, where there was neither a restriction on the use of advance payments received for services to be rendered in the future nor any provision for refund, the payments were deemed taxable income when received.[6]

In general, prepayments for future services or rent are treated as income in the year of receipt, even for accrual basis taxpayers.[7] Revenue Procedure 71–21[8] sets forth some exceptions that permit accrual basis taxpayers providing services to defer income until the requisite service is performed, but only until the end of the following year. More interesting for retirement facilities is the Revenue Procedure provision that permits deferral of income when received pursuant to an agreement requiring the taxpayer to perform contingent services:

> (a) *On a statistical basis if adequate data are available to the taxpayer;* (b) on a straight-line ratable basis over the time period of the agreement if it is not unreasonable to anticipate at the end of the taxable year of receipt that a substantially ratable portion of the services will be performed in the next succeeding taxable year; or (c) by the use of any other basis that, in the opinion of the Commissioner, results in a clear reflection of income.[9] [Emphasis added.]

It can be argued that certain obligations of a continuing-care facility are contingent upon the resident's need for health services, the payment of monthly fees, and so on, and that actuarial statistics can be used to calculate the appropriate reflection of income. When required, however, retirement facility prepayments are almost universally a condition of occupancy and could be characterized as prepaid rent, which is expressly excluded from the benefits of the Revenue Procedure.[10] For example, HUD payments are ineligible for deferral of recognition as income,[11] but payments for the occupancy of rooms where "significant services" are rendered to the occupant are not considered rent and may be eligible for deferral under Revenue Procedure 71-21.[12]

One problem with the application of this entire analysis to lump-sum retirement facility payments is that although the actuarial statistics standard for deferral of income does not appear on its face to be limited in scope or time, the intent of the Revenue Procedure in general is to permit accrual basis taxpayers to defer income for no more than one year.[13] However, one Revenue Ruling considered the application of Revenue Procedure 71-21 to a deferral of retirement facility entrance fees over the resident's life.

In Revenue Ruling 73-549,[14] the Internal Revenue Service considered whether an accrual basis retirement community offering life-time contracts could defer recognition of lump-sum entrance fees based on the resident's actuarially determined life expectancy. The financial arrangement was unusual in that the facility issued two *separate* contracts to residents. The first guaranteed life-time use of an apartment and various common dining, recreational, medical, laundry, and other facilities in return for the entrance fee. The second covered the provision of all the services delivered in those facilities in return for a monthly fee. Interestingly, the IRS cited Revenue Procedure 71-21 and found that recognition of the entrance fee income could not be deferred because the first contract had no service component; therefore, the payment took the form of rent. By implication, it can be argued that a lump-sum payment under a single contract combining lodging and substantial services could be eligible for income deferral on an actuarial basis under Revenue Procedure 71-21.

Still, it does not appear that recognition of entrance fees as income can be spread over the resident's life simply by characterizing the contract as providing services. General Counsel Memorandum (GCM) 37019 briefly discussed Revenue Ruling 73-549 in the context of a retirement facility transaction acknowledged to be a service contract that did not require the payment of rent. The general counsel did not find any significance in the distinction between prepaid rent and prepaid service fees:

> In any event, whether the entrance fees are for rent or for rent and services, will make no difference in the determination of when the fee is taxable to the Corporation. In both cases such determination depends on when payment is received. (See Rev. Rul. 60-85, 1960-1 C.B. 181, modified by Rev. Rul. 71-299, 1971-2 C.B. 218.)

Thus, as in the *Wide Acres Rest Home* case, the analysis of whether entrance fees are earned as income should turn on whether the home's access to the fees is unrestricted when received or restricted based on resident life expectancy or some other extended period.

(3) Declining Refund Arrangements

In 1992, the IRS National Office determined that entry fees charged by a retirement community, which are refundable on a declining basis if the tenant terminates the tenancy before a certain number of years, are also fully includable in the retirement community's gross income in the year of receipt. The fact that the amount of the refund declines with the tenant's occupancy of the unit suggested to the IRS that the fee is an advance or prepayment for services. The National Office also rejected characterization of the entry fee as a security deposit.[15]

Nonetheless, the U.S. Tax Court rejected the IRS's reasoning in *Highland Farms Inc. v. Commissioner.*[16] In that case, the court held that entry fees received by an accrual basis corporation operating a continuing-care retirement community did not constitute prepaid rent or advance payments for services that had to be reported in the year of receipt. In accordance with Statement of Position 90-8 of the American Institute of Certified Public Accountants (AICPA), the taxpayer reported as income only that portion of the entry fees that became nonrefundable or nonforfeitable during the tax year. The IRS contended that the entire advance payment was includable in income as prepaid rent when received by the taxpayer. However, the court ruled that because the refunds were within the residents' rather than the taxpayer's control, the refundable portions were not advance payments for services; thus, the taxpayer needed only to include the nonforfeitable amounts in income each year.

This case is a major breakthrough for retirement communities concerned with the taxation of entrance fee income. By spreading income over a refund amortization period of up to eight years, the provider can defer taxation, avoid the imputed interest rules that complicate longer refund arrangements (see §6.2(b)), and offer the consumer some recovery of fees in the event of early contract termination.

(4) Security Deposits

It is generally recognized that when parties intend a payment to be held as security for the future performance of the payor, there is sufficient restriction on the payee's use of the deposit that it need not be characterized as income when received. Thus, security deposits received by a developer of residential rental property were not properly treated as income in the year of receipt.[17] Likewise, one year's advance rent received from a tenant on delivery of the lease was not income where the intent was that the rent would be held as security for the lessee's performance, that interest was to accrue, that the balance was to be applied to last year's rent, and that all was to be accounted for by the lessor to the lessee.[18]

On the other hand, where the landlord's access to the resident's deposit is insufficiently restricted or the landlord is not strictly bound to refund it, the money is likely to be treated as prepaid rent. For example, deposits were treated as rent when they were refundable only in the event of destruction of the property,[19] they were to be applied to the last month's rent but were commingled with the taxpayer's general funds,[20] or the landlord had unrestricted use of the money pending occurrence of a limited refund contingency.[21] The IRS has established detailed guidelines for reporting tenant security deposit trust account transactions.[22]

If structured as security deposits, entrance fees most likely could not be used to retire construction debt or to cover ongoing operational expenses. On the other hand, if entrance fees are set at amounts designed to fund reserves for future contingencies such as resident health care, plant replacement or improvement, refunds to residents or their estates,

an endowment for residents who run out of funds, or other future obligations, it can be argued that they should not be received into income when initially paid to the facility. Of course, it would be important to earmark such entrance fees or portions of fees for specific future uses and to deposit them to segregated, restricted accounts. At least one ruling, however, considered funds held in a replacement and operating reserve by a low-income apartment manager as taxable gross income even though their distribution was subject to approval by the state housing authority.[23] The court determined that the taxpayer had a "reasonable expectation" of receipt of the funds, which constituted a fixed right to the funds sufficient to justify characterization as income. Deposits that are refundable to a resident on demand may not, however, be taxable on receipt (see §6.2(a)(2)).

(5) Trusts

One possible solution to the problem of receiving entrance fees as ordinary income over a short period is to establish a mechanism whereby the payments are distributed from the resident to the facility operator over a longer time. Nonetheless, the developer may find it valuable to have all entrance fee monies available at the outset of facility operation for purposes such as retirement of the construction debt. Another advantage of entrance fees paid in a lump sum at the time of admission is that the funds usually are readily available. Most likely, the resident has just sold his or her previous residence and has liquidated a substantial amount of equity. It is desirable from the developer's point of view to tap those funds before they are depleted. On the other hand, the developer may not want to tie up the funds in the manner of a security deposit arrangement but instead prefer to receive periodic distributions for retirement of debt and operating expenses.

One method for preserving entrance fee monies without realizing substantial taxable income in the first year is to establish a trust. The resident can pay the entrance fees to the trust in a lump sum at the time of admission. The trust then pays out the funds to the facility in increments over a period of several years. As an alternative, the facility can borrow some or all of the trust corpus. The designation of a trustee can give added confidence to both the resident and the facility owner that funds will be available when needed for payment to the retirement community or for refund to the resident. In general, funds placed in trust for services to be performed over several years are not income when transferred to the trust.[24] However, compensation paid into a trust for eventual distribution to a beneficiary may be deemed constructively received and taxable in the year of deposit when the right to payment is irrevocable and not subject to any contingency.[25]

GCM 37019 extensively examined the use of a trust as a device for avoiding taxation of retirement facility entrance fees. There, an accrual method life-care retirement facility required payment by residents of an entrance fee into an irrevocable trust, the income and principal of which were to accrue to the benefit of the corporate facility owner. A percentage of the trust corpus was to be paid to the corporation each month. The undistributed balance of the trust for each resident would be refundable to the resident or his or her estate only in the event of contract termination or death during the first ten years. The trustee bank had general powers of management and control of the trust, but an advisory committee appointed by the corporation had authority to remove the trustee as well as to give advice about investments and other matters. In addition, the trustee was to have no liability for mismanagement of the trust corpus.

The general counsel's analysis first recited that income is taxable when received,[26] except that an accrual method taxpayer may elect to include income upon the earliest of performance of the required service, payment becoming due, or payment being made.[27] Moreover, income is deemed constructively received when it is set aside for the taxpayer to draw on without substantial limitation or restrictions.[28] The question, the general counsel determined, is whether the payment into the trust is to be considered a payment directly or constructively to the corporation.

After discussing several cases, the memorandum concluded that the corporation's dominion and control over the trust corpus—through the advisory committee's ability to terminate the trustee—and the limitation imposed on the trustee's liability eclipsed the fact that the corporation did not have actual possession or ownership of the entrance fee payments. For example, the corporation could in effect require the trustee, under penalty of removal, to invest funds in the exact manner the corporation would if the latter had actual title to and possession of the trust corpus. Thus, the corporation was found to have constructively received the entrance fees when paid to the trust.

This conclusion does not mean that a trust for retirement facility entrance fees will always result in a finding that the payments are constructively received by the facility (see, for example, Private Letter Ruling 8326113 discussed in §6.1(b)(6)). For example, when setting up a trust for receipt of entrance fees, the facility operator must give the trustee the usual powers of dominion and control over the trust corpus plus the concomitant responsibility for losses or mismanagement. If the trustee is to be subject to removal for cause, perhaps that decision could be the responsibility of a committee comprised of residents or others not controlled by the retirement facility owner. In any case, it appears that if the concerns of GCM 37019 are met, an entrance fee trust with periodic payments to the facility operator/beneficiary, conditioned on continued performance of services and furnishing of lodging for the residents/grantors, can be used effectively to secure residents' payments without the facility immediately receiving taxable income on the entire amount set aside.

Even with the integrity of the trust recognized, some additional tax issues related to trust income still remain. A trust is itself a taxable entity, and income earned by it is subject to taxation. However, if income from the trust corpus is distributed to trust beneficiaries, the trust is treated as a conduit, with the beneficiaries taxed instead of the trust.[29] In the event the grantor of the trust has retained substantial powers over the trust or a reversionary interest in the principal, the grantor rather than the trust could be treated as the owner and be taxed (presumably at a higher rate) on the trust income.[30] Before the Tax Reform Act of 1986,[31] the major exception to this rule applied to Clifford Trusts, in which a grantor with a reversionary interest could avoid taxation on trust income if the trust was irrevocable for at least ten years. This longstanding rule has now been repealed such that a reversionary interest or other substantial control over the corpus generally results in taxation of income to the grantor.[32]

Retirement communities may wish to have trust income distributed to the operator, which normally leads to taxation of income to the operator. However, if the entrance fee paid into the trust is refundable to the resident/grantor upon death or withdrawal from the facility, the income, even if distributed to the operator, is likely to be taxed to the resident when earned by the trust. In that scenario, there may be reason to pay the interest or other income to the resident. If the funds are borrowed from the trust, of course, income earned by the borrower thereafter is taxable to it.

(6) Trust with Loan

In one private letter ruling,[33] the IRS examined in detail whether lump-sum payments into a trust by "life-tenant" retirement community admittees would be treated as prepaid rents in circumstances where the trust later loaned the trust funds to the corporate facility owner. There, the elderly applicant was required to pay an initial lump-sum rental amount into a grantor trust, along with monthly rent and a monthly service fee, in return for life-time residence and services. However, the monthly rent obligation ceased after 15 years, and thereafter the resident could remain for life rent-free. The initial rent was not refundable after the first six months of residency but was to be used presumably to prepay or offset the rental costs of those who stopped paying rent after 15 years. When the resident took occupancy, the trust was to loan a defined amount per resident to the facility.

The corporation agreed to repay the loan in equal monthly payments over 14 years at 9 percent interest, with a final balloon payment. The facility would further execute a negotiable promissory note payable to the trust and secured by a mortgage on the facility property, thereby giving the trust a first lien subordinate only to construction loans on the project. The loan proceeds paid to the facility were to be escrowed and used primarily for payment of construction debt as well as for repayment of loans for residents who terminated early and for administrative and other expenses. The trustee could make distributions of interest to residents, most of whom had their distribution applied automatically to monthly rent payments. Tenant interests in the trust could be sold, transferred, or assigned at the tenant's elec-

tion. If a tenant elected to terminate the agreement, the corporation would not be relieved of its obligation to repay the loan from the trust. The trust in Letter Ruling 8326113 was assumed by the parties to be a grantor trust that would result in taxation of the grantor for income earned by the trust.[34]

The IRS noted that gross income includes advance rentals but, distinguishing Revenue Ruling 73–549,[35] found that the trust/loan arrangement amounted to a loan to the corporation rather than prepaid rent. Importantly, the IRS noted that the corporation did not have unrestricted enjoyment of the funds but was required to pay off its construction loan. In addition, however, the ruling emphasized that unlike a rental situation, the resident will receive repayment of the principal plus interest. And if the resident transfers the interest in the trust to a third party, the corporation's repayment of the loan will benefit the third party. The ruling concluded, "A tenant will not, therefore, receive an apartment unit and other facilities for a deposit of a defined amount."

It is unclear whether transferability of the tenant's trust interest is a necessary or even properly significant factor in avoiding treatment as prepaid rent of amounts received by a retirement facility as a loan from a trust. If the right to payments from the trust is sufficiently restricted and loans are properly secured and subject to definite repayment schedules, the transaction should not result in taxation of entrance fees in the year of payment as prepaid rent or service fees.

An example of a trust fund entrance fee arrangement is one in which the resident is required to deposit one-half of the entrance fee in Trust A and the other half in Trust B. Trust A is distributed to the facility operator at the rate of 20 percent per year. Each year, the facility operator recognizes 20 percent of Trust A (10 percent of the total entrance fee) as taxable income. The resident earns interest on the undistributed portion of the Trust A deposits. The facility operator borrows in its entirety the half of the entrance fee deposited into Trust B immediately after deposit. In order not to burden the resident or trust with tax on imputed interest,[36] the developer pays interest annually at the federal borrowing rate on the funds borrowed from Trust B. The borrowed proceeds of Trust B should not be treated as taxable income to the facility operator and will be repaid to the resident on withdrawal from the facility or upon death.

(c) Resident Tax Considerations

(1) Medical Deductions

From the resident's perspective, one of the advantages of a nonrefundable entrance fee is that to the extent that a portion of the entrance fee is a prepayment for future health care, the resident will be eligible for a medical expense deduction. Medical expenses incurred in any given year are deductible only to the extent that they exceed 7.5 percent of the taxpayer's adjusted gross income.[37] It is difficult to meet the test for deductibility of medical expenses in any given year, absent a catastrophic injury or long-term illness, and the prepayment of medical expenses by means of an entrance fee creates a unique opportunity to incur a deductible expense that exceeds the threshold required by the Internal Revenue Code. Several IRS rulings expand on the availability of the deduction.

Revenue Ruling 75–302[38] allowed a medical deduction in the year paid by the resident for that portion (about 30 percent) of a lump-sum life-care fee that the retirement facility could demonstrate from experience was allocated to the provision of medical care, medicine, and hospitalization. The facility issued a separate statement to residents showing their medical expenses. The IRS noted that the fee was refundable to the resident under certain circumstances (perhaps early withdrawal) and that, in the event of a later refund, such amounts would have to be reported as income. Most likely, a fee that is intended to be refundable upon contract termination does not qualify as a deductible expense. The IRS will treat it as a loan rather than as a prepayment (see discussion of loans in §6.2(a)(1)).

In a later ruling, the IRS approved a medical deduction for residents of a new life-care facility with no experience as to the cost of medical services; the facility used the financial information of a comparable retirement home to estimate its costs.[39] The IRS concluded that a portion of residents' fees was deductible because it was "made in order to secure medical services despite the fact that the medical services were not to be performed until a future time if at all."

In Revenue Ruling 93–72,[40] the IRS clarified that Revenue Rulings 75–302 and 76–481 should not be interpreted to allow a current deduction of payments for future medical care (including medical insurance) that extends substantially beyond the close of the taxable year if the future care is not purchased in connection with obtaining "life-time care" as described in those rulings. Thus, the IRS clearly evidenced its intent to preserve the prepaid medical expense deduction for residents of continuing-care or life-care communities.[41]

In addition to physician and hospital care, nursing and personal care may be considered a deductible medical expense.[42] Assistance with dressing, bathing, grooming, and other daily living activities qualifies for a medical deduction. However, some attendant services such as household help do not qualify, and an allocation must be made where one person performs such multiple functions.[43] Portions of the entrance fee used for the construction of health care or personal-care units in a retirement facility may not be deducted.[44]

In one private letter ruling, portions of nonrefundable resident fee payments to a retirement community offering as-needed nursing care could be deducted, where the calculation excluded construction debt service and to the extent that insurance did not cover such payments.[45] Another ruling further clarified that medical expenses include staff costs; medications and supplies; pro rata shares of housekeeping, maintenance, utility, administrative, and marketing costs; interest on indebtedness; real estate taxes; insurance; and depreciation of the nursing facility and that these costs could be allocated among residents in order to place them on an equal footing with each other, taking into account variances in the cost of accommodations.[46]

In addition to entrance fees, monthly fees may be deducted to the extent they can be shown to equal the retirement home's cost of providing medical care, medicines, or hospitalization.[47] In a pair of companion private letter rulings,[48] the Internal Revenue Service ruled that residents of the independent-living and assisted-living portions of a retirement facility offering nursing care, assisted living, and independent living for an entrance fee and monthly service fee were each entitled to deduct the portion of the entrance fee and monthly fee representing unreimbursed medical expenses. In that case, residents were guaranteed only ten free days of nursing care per year of residency, with any additional days charged at 90 percent of the regular rate.

The retirement community operator should keep records demonstrating what proportion of entrance and monthly fees is allocated to health services or health care reserves. The operator should make these records available to residents for preparation of their tax returns. Generally, because of the 7.5 percent-of-income threshold that must be met before any deduction is permitted, residents benefit to the extent that a facility allocates most of the deductible medical expense costs to entrance fees[49] rather than to monthly fees.

(2) Appreciation in Home Value

One of the traditional benefits of owning one's principal residence has been the ability for persons 55 and older, under Internal Revenue Code Section 1034, to defer recognition of gain on the sale of the residence as taxable income if, within two years before or after the sale, the resident purchases another qualifying residence.[50] A significant issue for seniors' housing communities has been whether the communities qualify as residences that, when entered, permitted the buyer to carry over or defer recognition of any gain from the sale of a previous residence. This was an especially important consideration for entrance fee facilities that tended to rely on the resident's sale of a previous residence as the funding source for initial fee payments. The amounts subject to taxation have been significant for elderly persons whose mortgage-free homes may have undergone exponential rises in value over several decades of ownership. With enactment of the Taxpayer Relief Act of 1997 (P.L. 105–34), however, Congress changed the rule so that now up to $500,000 of gain (for joint filers) is excluded whether or not it is reinvested in a qualifying "principal residence." Currently, therefore, the question of whether a retirement community qualifies as a "principal residence" is relevant to determine if appreciation in *its* value is eligible for the capital gain exclusion, and not whether proceeds from the sale of a previous residence can be reinvested in the seniors' facility without recognition of capital gains.

In 1960, the Internal Revenue Service determined in Revenue Ruling 60–135[51] that a retirement facil-

ity furnishing a resident with living quarters and life-time services such as meals, personal care, and medical care did not qualify as a residence for purposes of exercising the Section 1034 carryover privilege. There, the resident paid a lump-sum fee for living quarters plus a deposit in a life-care assurance fund that, together with monthly fees, covered the facility's service component. The resident did not acquire any proprietary interest in the facility or any other asset as a result of the transaction.

Citing Revenue Ruling 55–37,[52] the Internal Revenue Service noted that Section 1034 does not apply to circumstances where the proceeds of the sale of the previous home are reinvested in a residence in which the taxpayer has no legal interest. Moreover, unlike cooperatives,[53] there is no specific provision granting the benefits of Section 1034 to such retirement facilities. The IRS found that "[s]uch acquisition represents future support to the taxpayer rather than a purchase of an interest in the real property of a retirement home."[54]

Another problem not discussed in the revenue ruling but nevertheless apparent is that application of Section 1034 to nonrefundable retirement facility entrance fees would have resulted in the U.S. Treasury's inability ever to tax the gain from the sale of the previous residence. If proceeds of a sale are reinvested in a home owned by the taxpayer, the home remains an asset of the taxpayer or of his estate, which will be subject to a final sale resulting in eventual recognition of taxable income. With the nonrefundable fee, however, no interest (real property or otherwise) is left to sell, resulting in no gain and no opportunity for taxation. Even where there is a transferable interest, such as a membership, the IRS disallowed the capital gain rollover because the interest is not equivalent to ownership of the real property.[55]

All the above factors have pointed to some advantages for resident ownership of seniors' housing units (including condominiums and cooperatives).[56]

§6.2 Refundable Entrance Fees

A refundable entrance fee is one taken by the facility operator at the time of the resident's admission and returned in its entirety or either in some specified portion to the resident whenever he or she leaves the facility or to the resident's estate in the event of death. A truly refundable fee should be distinguished from a "declining refund" arrangement, as discussed in §6.1. While a refundable entrance fee does not confer the benefits of an equity interest, it gives a resident the opportunity to recoup some of his or her investment in the event of an early withdrawal from the facility and preserves some of the resident's estate for the benefit of heirs. Approximately 20 percent of all continuing-care retirement communities and 40 percent of those opened or under construction since 1984 employ fully or partially refundable entrance fee plans.[57]

(a) Taxation of the Provider

(1) Treatment as a Loan

At least one reason for the emergence of the refundable entrance fee in the late 1980s was the growing interest of for-profit developers in the retirement community industry in general and in continuing-care facilities in particular. Refundable entrance fees may well solve an income tax problem experienced by proprietary facilities that receive entrance fees in that the proceeds of the refundable entrance fee should be treated as a loan rather than as taxable income. Traditional tax-exempt providers do not face this problem.

The U.S. Supreme Court, considering what constitutes income under Internal Revenue Code Section 61, wrote that income is received "[w]hen a taxpayer acquires earnings without the consensual recognition, express or implied, of an obligation to repay and without restriction as to their disposition."[58] Although it seems elementary that a payment is not income to the payee if there is either an obligation to repay (a loan) or sufficient restriction on its use (e.g., a deposit), courts have carefully scrutinized the details of loans from lessees to lessors and have sometimes recharacterized the payments as prepaid rent.

In *Blue Flame Gas Co.,*[59] where a corporation leased its assets to its sole shareholder and received a loan from the lessee, the U.S. Tax Court found that the alleged loan constituted a payment of advance rent. The court noted that the loaned amount and the aggregate rent due under the lease were identical, that the payment dates for each loan and lease

installment payment were identical, and that no payments actually changed hands but were represented by offsets recorded in the parties' books of account. Despite the existence of a promissory note, the loan was noninterest-bearing and unsecured and was an express condition of the lease transaction, prompting the court to call the transactions interdependent.[60]

United States v. W. B. Williams[61] treated payment on a loan as prepaid rent, even though the lessee's loan had no specified repayment date, no promissory note had been executed, and payments on the loan were to be made by the lessor out of yearly lease payments made by the lessee. In addition, the taxpayer made no attempt to seek a loan apart from the lease, and the amount loaned was directly related to annual rental payments. Although the lessor/borrower was obligated to pay interest on amounts due, the Fifth Circuit Court termed the charge "compensation for advance rent." By contrast, in *Illinois Power Co. v. Commissioner,*[62] the Seventh Circuit Court distinguished *United States v. Williams* and found that "[t]he underlying principle is that the taxpayer is allowed to exclude from his income money received under an unequivocal contractual, statutory, or regulatory duty to repay it."

In Technical Advice Memorandum 9307007, the IRS National Office determined that one-third of a purported loan by residents of an independent-living facility to the facility's builder/operator was actually an advance payment of rent, where the purported loan was evidenced by a noninterest-bearing negotiable promissory note, the note incorporated the terms of the occupancy agreement, and, under the occupancy agreement, the principal amount of the note was reduced each year for the first three years and the reduction deemed an additional residence and care fee. Under such circumstances, the IRS concluded that the payment by the residents to the operator of the one-third portion of the note and the right to occupy the unit were interdependent and that the economic substance of the arrangement more closely resembled a prepaid contract to rent property.

Loans from residents to retirement facilities as a condition of admission certainly raise some of the issues addressed in the recharacterization cases discussed above. For example, the loan and resident agreement are generally interdependent, and the loans and lease payments are one and the same. Unlike a conventional loan, interest may not be paid and the date when payment is due may not be predictable.

Nonetheless, the facts of the recharacterization cases also raise serious questions about whether there was an unequivocal intention and an enforceable obligation on the borrower's part to repay the amounts not taken into income. If retirement facility operators oblige themselves to repay loaned amounts upon the occurrence of some inescapable future event, such as death or contract termination, and then secure that obligation, the unequivocality of the repayment obligation should be the controlling factor.

Two revenue rulings involving refundable fees taken by swim clubs highlight the definiteness of the refund obligation as the determinative factor. The first[63] ruling treated membership fees as loans because they were to be refunded five years after the pool was constructed. The second ruling, however,[64] treated membership fees as ordinary income because they were to be refunded only on a declining balance basis if the member moved out of the area within five years of joining. Distinguishing its earlier ruling in which the club had a "continuing obligation of refund," the IRS found the declining refund arrangement to be "contingent" and the club's repayment liability "not fixed."

Despite the dissimilarities between refundable entrance fees and conventional loans, the fees should not be considered income in a properly structured transaction where the repayment obligation is definite.[65]

(2) Deposits

The U.S. Supreme Court has held that a refundable deposit will not be treated as taxable income to the recipient if it meets certain characteristics that distinguish a loan from an advance payment.[66] In that case, a utility company required certain customers to make deposits to it to ensure payment of future fees for services. The customer could obtain a refund of the deposit, with 3 percent interest, by giving notice to terminate service. The Court noted that because of the company's obligation to refund the deposits with interest on demand from the customer, the payment was similar to a loan and therefore not income to the company. The Court found

that the deposit was not like an advance payment in that the customer made no commitment to continue to purchase the service and retained the option to terminate at any time.

The Court rejected the Internal Revenue Service commissioner's argument that the deposits should be considered the company's income because the company did not place them in escrow or segregate them from its other funds. Instead, the decision looked at whether the use of the funds was "unconstrained" and found no guarantee that the company would keep the money; the utility would have to return the money on demand from the customer. By contrast, with an advance payment, the customer has no right to request a return of the monies on deposit. The Court determined that the lender, at the time the loan falls due for repayment, can decide to apply the money owed toward the purchase of goods or services from the borrower rather than to accept repayment in cash. Finally, the Court noted that the heavily regulated environment in which a utility operates was helpful in reaching its conclusion.[67]

This opinion is especially helpful for seniors' housing facilities that receive deposits or loans from residents as security for the payment of future fees or for the purposes of generating interest income to be applied toward periodic fees. If such fees meet the test of the Supreme Court case discussed above, the deposit or principal amount of the loan should not be considered taxable income to the facility. Therefore, deposits need not be segregated in individual accounts for each resident; the deposit or principal amount of the loan must be refundable to the resident on notice of the resident's desire to terminate the services; the resident may agree to apply some part of the deposit toward the payment of periodic service charges; and a regulated environment, such as the continuing-care industry, may be helpful in supporting the conclusion that the arrangement should not be recharacterized as an advance payment.[68]

(b) Resident Tax on Imputed Interest

(1) Below-Market Loans Generally; Reporting

One of the most significant concerns regarding the refundable entrance fee structure stems from the Deficit Reduction Act of 1984.[69] The act subjects below-market loans to imputed taxable interest to the lender to the extent that the borrower pays no interest or pays interest at a rate less than the short-term federal rate. The secretary of the U.S. Treasury periodically determines this rate based on average yields of outstanding obligations of the U.S. government.[70]

If the imputed interest rules are applied to retirement community fees, the Internal Revenue Service would pretend that the resident had received taxable interest income at the federal borrowing rate on the entire refundable portion of any entrance fee paid to the facility for each year that the loan exists. Because such lenders may be required to pay tax on income never actually received, the act can pose serious problems for elderly residents, many of whom on fixed incomes.

Depending on circumstances, it should be noted at the outset that there is significant variation and some uncertainty in the application of the imputed interest rules to retirement facility entrance fees. The House–Senate Conference Committee Report accompanying the original 1984 tax act notes that "advances to continuing-care facilities by residents of such facilities prior to June 6, 1984, are not subject to the provision." The report then goes on to say that "no inference is intended regarding the application of the provision to advances to continuing care facilities made after that date."[71]

However, the 1985 tax act amendments specifically exempt loans made to "qualified continuing care facilities" before to the effective date of the act (October 11, 1985) and create a limited exemption for such loans made after that date.[72] The amendments seem to imply application of the act to refundable entrance fees. To date, the IRS has not yet issued final regulations, and the issue is not completely resolved.[73]

The conference agreement to the 1985 amendments to the act clarifies that the act also was not intended to apply to continuing-care entrance fees whereby, for consumer protection purposes, refunds are available only during initial occupancy periods or on a declining basis for the first several years of residence:

> In addition, the conferees understand that a payment to a continuing care facility pursuant to a continuing care contract frequently is wholly or partially refundable for a relatively brief period (e.g., six months)

essentially for consumer protection purposes pursuant to State law or regulations. The conferees also understand that payments to a continuing care facility are often refundable on a declining pro rata basis over a somewhat longer period (often up to eight years). The conferees understand that such payments would ordinarily be treated as advance payment of fees and not as loans under present law.[74]

Proposed regulations state that where refundable deposits are not to be treated for tax purposes as a prepayment or an advance payment,[75] the amount transferred will be treated as a loan for purposes of the below-market loan rules.[76] Deposits that are "custodial in nature" or "held in trust for the benefit of the transferor" will not be treated as loans if the transferee is not entitled to the beneficial enjoyment of the amount deposited, including interest, unless received as security for the transferor's obligation.[77]

For transactions that are subject to the below-market loan rules, the resident (lender) must attach a statement to his or her income tax return reporting all interest imputed by reason of the below-market loan. The borrower must file 1099 forms recording the amount of imputed interest "paid" to the resident as well as a statement attesting to any interest expense deduction claimed as a result of the transaction. The statement must identify the parties involved, the character and amount of the income imputed to the lender, and the mathematical assumptions used for computing the interest.[78]

(2) Demand Loans versus Term Loans

The Internal Revenue Code defines a below-market loan according to whether it is a demand loan or a term loan. For demand loans, which are payable in full on demand of the lender, the loan is below market if the interest rate is less than the "applicable federal rate," which is the short-term rate under Section 1274(d).[79] All other loans are term loans, which are deemed below market if the loan amount exceeds the present value of all payments due under the loan as determined by applying a discount value equal to the short-term federal rate.[80] Imputed interest for a demand loan is calculated annually for as long as the loan remains outstanding,[81] whereas the entire excess of the term loan over the present value of repayments due is subject to imputed interest in the year the loan is made.[82]

It is unknown whether refundable retirement community entrance fees, if covered by the act, would be categorized as demand or term loans. Even though many of the newer forms of refundable fees generally are refundable in full[83] and a refund may be "demanded" at the option of the resident/lender, the resident must give up the right to live in and receive services at the facility as a condition of repayment. Thus, more than a mere demand is required to obtain repayment; accordingly, refundable fees may well be characterized as term loans. The proposed regulations under the imputed interest rules clarify that a term loan is one in which the loan agreement "specifies an ascertainable period of time during which the loan is to be outstanding."[84] If a period may be determined actuarially, the loan will be treated as a term loan under the proposed regulations.[85] Therefore, a loan to a continuing-care facility that is intended to be refunded upon the death of the resident could be treated as a term loan because the life expectancy of the resident can be determined actuarially.

However, the situation is complicated because the entrance fee may also be refundable if the resident leaves the facility voluntarily, which gives the transaction more of the characteristics of a demand loan. Offering some clarification is the regulation stating that if the benefits of the interest arrangements of a term loan are not transferable by the borrower and are conditioned on the future performance of substantial services by the borrower, the loan will be treated as a demand loan.[86] It appears that this latter provision supersedes the others and turns what would ordinarily be a term loan into a demand loan where the rendition of services is a condition of the loan. For example, in Private Letter Ruling 9252015, the IRS determined that a bond that residents of a retirement community were required to purchase constituted a demand loan, where the bond was nontransferable, nonamortizing, and noninterest-bearing and where the operator was obligated to repay the face amount of the bond, less a deferred fee of 5 percent, in the event of termination of the residency agreement.

(3) Significant Effect Loans

The law further divides below-market loans into the following categories: gift loans, compensation-related loans,[87] corporation-shareholder loans, tax avoidance loans, and other below-market loans.[88] A later amendment added the category of loans to "qualified continuing-care facilities"[89] (see discussion in §6.2(b)(4) concerning a limited exemption for loans to such facilities). The following discussion pertains to loans to retirement facilities that do not fit the definition of a "qualified continuing-care facility" (see also §6.2(b)(5)).

The category that best describes retirement community transactions is that of "other below-market loans," which includes loans not fitting the other categories, where the interest arrangements of the loan "have a *significant effect* on any federal tax liability of the lender or borrower."[90] The legislative history provides an example of a below-market loan fitting the "other" or "significant effect" category:

> The interest arrangement of a below-market loan has an effect on the tax liability of the borrower or the lender if, among other things, it results in the conversion of a non-deductible expense into the equivalent of a deductible expense. *For example, if a member of a club makes a non-interest bearing refundable deposit to the club in lieu of part or all of his or her membership fee, the member is paying the fee with money that has not been included in his income* (i.e., the investment income from the proceeds of the deposit), and has, in effect, converted the fee into the equivalent of a deductible expense.[91] [Emphasis added.]

The country club example is generally analogous to a retirement facility's refundable entrance fee. However, the U.S. Treasury must take into account several factors that may result in a determination that entrance fees do not constitute below-market loans:

> The conferees anticipate that in determining whether an effect is significant, the Treasury will consider all the facts and circumstances including (1) whether items of income and deduction generated by the loan offset each other, (2) the amount of such items, (3) the cost to the taxpayer of complying with the provision, and (4) any nontax reasons for deciding to structure the transaction as a below-market loan rather than a loan with interest at a rate equal to or greater than the applicable federal rate and a payment by the lender to the borrower.[92]

For the following reasons, application of these criteria to retirement community transactions may warrant a finding by the Treasury Department that the transactions should not be considered below-market loans.

- To the extent that entrance fees or the unrecovered interest thereon covers prepaid medical services (beyond the statutory threshold), there would be a tax deduction to offset some or all of the taxable interest income.
- On average, the magnitude of entrance fees across the nation is relatively small (about $45,000 per lifetime).[93]
- Most elderly residents are on fixed incomes and may have difficulty paying tax on interest never received.
- Payments are usually made to charitable, tax-exempt facilities operating at the lowest feasible cost.
- Continuing-care residents who paid entrance fees have historically been denied the opportunity to defer or exclude the recognition of gain on the proceeds of the sales of their previous residences while other similarly situated seniors who reinvested in a new residence owned in fee simple or in a cooperative have avoided taxation on those same proceeds for the rest of their lives. (This was remedied by Congress in 1997; see §6.1(c)(2)).
- For fiscal[94] and humanitarian reasons, government should create tax incentives for private long-term-care self-insurance programs and senior-living communities at least equal to incentives for the purchase of increasingly expensive homes with no services.

Despite these considerations, the IRS has *proposed* to treat continuing-care loans as significant effect loans but has never finally adopted a regulation (see §6.2(b)(5)). Although it can be argued that the imputed interest rules should not apply to certain retirement community fees, developers and operators should seriously consider the potential impact of the rules and advise residents with refundable fees to seek tax advice. They should also avoid touting the financial or tax benefits of the refundable entrance fee feature because the imputed interest rules apply to below-market loans made for tax-avoidance purposes (see §6.2(b)(6)).

(4) Exemption for Loans to Qualified Continuing-Care Facilities

The 1985 amendments to the 1984 tax act exempted from the imputed interest rules the first $90,000 of entrance fees loaned to a "qualified continuing care facility for each year in which the lender or lender's spouse has attained 65 years of age."[95] In determining the cap on the exemption, the law requires aggregation of all outstanding loans from the lender and spouse to any qualified continuing-care facility. The dollar amount of the exemption has been adjusted annually since 1986 based on increases in the Consumer Price Index. The exemption amounts follow:

Year	Amount
Before 1987	$90,000
1987	$92,200
1988	$94,800
1989	$98,800
1990	$103,500
1991	$108,600
1992	$114,100
1993	$117,500
1994	$121,100
1995	$124,300
1996	$127,800
1997	$131,300
1998	$134,800[96]

To qualify for exemption, the facility must permit the individual resident or spouse to use the facility for life. The resident(s) must first reside in an independent-living unit with outside facilities available for provision of "meals and other personal care"[97] but not require "long-term nursing care." After entering the independent-living unit, the occupant must be provided, when needed, with "long-term and skilled nursing care." The facility may not charge residents substantially more if they need "personal care services or long-term and skilled nursing care." Finally, the borrower must own or operate substantially all the facilities used to provide the services stipulated by the continuing-care contract. Conventional nursing homes are not considered continuing-care facilities.

The exemption from imputed interest rules is thus available primarily to traditionally styled Type A continuing-care communities that provide health and assisted-living services, when needed, as part of a fixed or regular fee that is actuarially determined at the time of admission (subject to adjustment). Long-term promises of priority access to facilities on the basis of the then-current fee-for-service, when the service is delivered in the future, do not qualify. In addition, residential facilities using other vendors of care services are ineligible except in cases of common ownership or operation.

The statute's references to "meals and other personal care" and "long-term and skilled-nursing care" seem a bit out of step with the jargon used in the trade and in state licensure laws.[98] In any event, facilities that offer both licensed assisted living and skilled nursing to supplement independent residences should be eligible for the exemption. However, facilities with unlicensed convenience services that supplement independent living as well as arrangements for skilled-nursing care, with common ownership or operation, arguably need not offer licensed assisted living to qualify for exemption.[99]

A private letter ruling[100] may provide some clarification of the qualified continuing-care facility exemption under Section 7872(g)(4) of the Internal Revenue Code. In that ruling, the IRS made the following determinations:

- Substantially all the facilities were owned or operated by the borrower, which directly owned the independent-living and assisted-living components of the retirement community, and by an entity that owned a 99 percent general partnership interest in the borrower-operated health center component of the community.
- The facility did not charge residents "substantially more" for personal care or long-term care if residents who participated in the mandatory group insurance program paid an additional 5 percent in monthly fees to move from independent living to assisted living and an additional 20 percent in monthly fees to move from assisted living to the health center, for a total monthly fee increase of approximately 25 percent.
- An enrollment level of 81 percent was sufficient to meet the requirement that "substantially all" the residents of the community be covered by continuing-care contracts.
- Despite the fact that the health center component was a traditional nursing home, the community

was not operated as a traditional nursing facility because the independent-living, assisted-living, and health center components together provided an overall plan for independent living.

Based on these factors, the IRS concluded that the community was a qualified continuing-care facility for purposes of Section 7872(g)(4).

(5) Loans to Nonqualified Continuing-Care Facilities

There is a great deal of confusion regarding whether the application of imputed interest rules to "qualified continuing care facilities"[101] necessarily implies that all *nonqualified* continuing-care facilities will likewise be subject to the below-market loan rules. In a Notice of Proposed Rulemaking filed August 15, 1985,[102] the IRS characterized "loans to institutions providing meals, lodging, and/or medical services (e.g., continuing care facilities) in lieu of fees for such services" as examples of "significant effect loans" or "other below-market loans" under Section 7872(c)(1)(E).[103] However, the IRS decided at that time not to propose regulations treating significant effect transactions and declared that no transaction will be treated as a significant effect loan until the date that future regulations are published in proposed form.[104] No such regulations have been published to date. When Congress that same year amended the statute to add Section 7872(c)(1)(F), "loans to *qualified* continuing care facilities" become a new category of below-market loan. A strict reading of the statute leads to a conclusion that loans to retirement facilities that do not meet the test of a qualified continuing-care facility as set forth in Section 7872(g) will be subject to the "other" or "significant effect" rules when the IRS promulgates regulations. In the meantime, such facilities are not subject to the below-market loan rules.[105] The ruling produces the counterintuitive result that nonqualified continuing-care retirement communities will receive, at least in the short term, more advantageous treatment than qualified continuing-care retirement communities, which are subject to a cap on their exemption.

While the IRS apparently does not now require the reporting of below-market loan interest income, it is uncertain whether the regulations, once adopted, will be prospective only or require retroactive payment of taxes. However, an IRS representative from the National Office has hinted that the regulations will be prospective with respect to imputing interest on below-market loans but that loans outstanding when the regulations are promulgated may become subject to the below-market loan provisions of Section 7872. The representative stated that it was possible that outstanding loans to nonqualified continuing-care facilities would be "grandfathered" and exempted from the provisions in Section 7872.[106]

(6) Tax-Avoidance Loans

Two private letter rulings (8622017 and 8638052) found that below-market loans to a charity to support the financing of low-income housing were not made with the purpose of avoiding income tax and were not subject to the imputed interest rules. However, the IRS has recharacterized a loan that otherwise would have been exempt as a compensation-related loan of under $10,000[107] as a tax-avoidance loan, subject to the imputed interest rules. The seller of a product required purchasers to make a one-time refundable payment to the seller. The cost of the product to the buyer was equivalent to the foregone interest on the amount deposited with the seller. The seller's sales literature showed how the "real cost" of its product was less than that of a competitor's product purchased with after-tax dollars because of the loan arrangement. The IRS determined that, because avoidance of federal tax on interest income was a principal factor in the sale or purchase, the exemption normally available for compensation-related loans under $10,000 would not be available (*see* Technical Advice Memoranda 8831004, 8952001, and 9131003; the IRS found that refundable deposits constituted tax-avoidance loans where the borrower advertised the tax savings aspect of the deposit scheme). The IRS has indicated informally that it will also apply the tax-avoidance rules where a facility advertises that the refundable deposit arrangement will result in a reduction in fees-for-services or facilities (see §6.2(b)(5)).

Retirement facilities should avoid advertising the tax advantages or comparative cost savings of a refundable entrance fee and instead emphasize features such as the preservation of home sales proceeds and the ability to leave the facility without loss of principal.

(7) The Gift Loan Exemption

The U.S. Treasury's 1986 announcement of a proposed exemption for loans of up to $250,000 to nonprofit organizations raised hopes among nonprofit retirement facility operators for a broader exemption from the imputed interest rules.[108] Applied to refundable entrance fees, the exemption would mean that if the borrower were a tax-exempt organization, the first $250,000 loaned interest-free as a refundable entrance fee would not be characterized as a below-market loan. Shortly after the initial announcement, however, the U.S. Treasury amended the proposed rule to its original intention that only *gift* loans of up to $250,000 were to be exempted.[109]

This provision, as amended, clearly does not apply to those refundable entrance fees paid as a quid pro quo for admission to a retirement facility. Such fees are not likely to be characterized as gifts. (See §9.13, concerning deductible contributions to tax-exempt retirement facilities.) Presumably, a truly charitably motivated interest-free loan of up to $250,000 to a nonprofit retirement facility would be eligible for exemption.

(8) Coping with the Imputed Interest Rules

The possibility that imputed interest rules may be applied to refundable entrance fees has led facility operators to address the problem in advance of the issuance of clarifying regulations. Some facilities have structured their transactions so that they pay residents interest at the relatively modest federal rate. Most, however, pay no interest and simply leave the matter to the resident taxpayer and the Internal Revenue Service. In such cases, it is prudent to warn residents about the problem and to advise them to engage tax counsel. In any case, the requirement that a resident pay tax on interest income he or she never received (at least not in cash) may create more of a marketing problem than the dollars warrant.

One alternative may be for the facility not to pay interest but rather to agree to pay any tax on imputed interest for which the resident may be obligated. This approach makes sense because the applicability of the rules is uncertain, and it is less costly for the facility to pay the tax on imputed interest income rather than the interest itself.

Pending adoption of the significant effect regulations, however, it is probably safe for everyone except "qualified continuing-care facilities" not to file 1099 forms unless interest payments actually are made. Essentially, the entire refundable fee segment of the industry has been in a "wait and see" mode since 1984. Some "qualified" facilities have intentionally restructured to become "nonqualified" and now enjoy the current moratorium on the enforcement of such arrangements. The American Association of Homes and Services for the Aging has developed a flowchart (see Figure 6.1) that should help continuing-care facilities determine whether the imputed interest rules apply to their entrance fees.

(c) Securing the Refund

Among the nontax business considerations surrounding refundable fees are the necessarily higher initial cost of the fees,[110] the financial benefits to the resident or the resident's estate in the event of an early death or withdrawal versus a long-term stay,[111] and the ability of the provider to make refunds when due.[112] One way for a resident to be reasonably assured that the facility will have the substantial refund on hand when repayment is due is for the facility to set aside a reserve for that purpose. At least one state has adopted a refund reserve requirement based on the actuarial life expectancies of residents.[113] Major corporate parents of a few retirement facilities, for example, may have sufficient assets to give reasonably reliable corporate guarantees that refund obligations of the subsidiary facility will be paid from the parent's funds whenever they become due. Some other facilities have secured the promise to make refund payments with mortgages or trust deeds on the facility itself.[114] Of course, the problems with reliance on the building as security include the probable lien priority of construction lenders or others, the problems inherent in an individual resident undertaking a foreclosure and collection action against an operating retirement community, and the eventual deterioration of the building asset. Refunds may also be made from fees received from the next resident to occupy a vacated unit. However, if the refund is contingent on a resale, the transaction may be recharacterized from a loan to a sale, thus avoiding some of the problems of loans but resurrecting tax problems for the provider.

While these problems of the presence and reliability of security for the debt are inherent in any loan transaction, lenders usually are institutional enterprises with sufficient resources and expertise to evaluate thoroughly the individual borrower. Here, however, though retirement facility applicants are often sophisticated and have professional advisers, they are not well equipped as a group to evaluate the financial strength of the retirement facility borrower. This fact may lead to more legislation dealing with reserve requirements or may strengthen the impetus in the private sector to establish strict, objective, and credible financial rating or accreditation systems for entrance fee retirement communities.

Notes

1. For a general discussion of entrance fee taxation problems, *see* Gordon, P., "Taxation of Lump Sum Admission Fees," *Retirement Housing Report,* Aug. 1990.

2. "Continuing Care Retirement Communities: An Industry in Action," American Association of Homes for the Aging and Ernst & Whinney, 1987, 17.

3. American Association of Homes for the Aging and Ernst & Young, *Continuing Care Retirement Communities: An Industry in Action,* 1993. *See* §2.3(d) for more results from this survey.

4. Treas. Reg. §1.61–8(b).

5. *Wide Acres Rest Home,* 26 T.C.M. 391 (1967).

6. *Beaver v. Comm'r.,* 55 T.C. 85 (1970).

7. *See M.E. Schlude v. Comm'r.,* 372 U.S. 128 (1963), 63–1 USTC 9284; and CCH, *Standard Federal Tax Reports* 21,005.703 (1992).

8. 1971–2 C.B. 549.

9. Rev. Proc. 71–21, §3.06.

10. *Id.* at §3.08.

11. *BJR Corp. v. Comm'r.,* 67 T.C. 111 (1976).

12. Note 9 *above,* at §3.08.

13. *Id.* at §1.

14. 1973–2 C.B. 17.

15. TAM 9246006. Technical advice memoranda, issued by the IRS National Office, are initiated primarily by the IRS in the course of its audit activities. In contrast, private letter rulings are initiated at the request of taxpayers. Neither type of ruling may be used or cited as precedent. I.R.C. §6110(j)(3).

16. 106 T.C. 237 (1996).

17. Priv. Ltr. Rul. 7852009.

18. *Clinton Hotel Realty Corp. v. Comm'r.*, 128 F.2d 968 (5th Cir. 1942).

19. *Hirsch Improvement Co. v. Comm'r.*, 143 F.2d 912 (2d Cir., 1944), *cert. den.*, 323 U.S. 750.

20. *Shaucet*, T.C.M. 1957-133.

21. *Detroit Consolidated Theatres, Inc. v. Comm'r.*, 133 F.2d 200 (6th Cir., 1942).

22. Rev. Rul. 77-260, 1977-2 C.B. 466.

23. *Stendig v. United States*, 843 F.2d 163 (4th Cir. 1988).

24. *Harrison v. Comm'r.*, 62 T.C. 524 (1974). *See also Meile v. Comm'r.*, 72 T.C. 284 (1979).

25. *E.T. Sproull v. Comm'r.*, 16 T.C. 244 (1951), *aff'd.*, 194 F.2d 541 (6th Cir. 1952).

26. I.R.C. §451(a).

27. *Citing* Treas. Reg. §1.451-1(a), Rev. Rul. 74-607, 1974-2 C.B. 149, and *Schlude*, note 7 *above.*

28. G.C.M. 37019, *citing* Treas. Reg. §1.451-2(a).

29. *See* I.R.C. §§643, 651, 661, CCH *Standard Federal Tax Reporter*, 24,834.05 (1992).

30. *See, e.g.*, I.R.C. §676.

31. P.L. 99-514.

32. I.R.C. §§673-675, CCH, note 29 *above*, at 25,115.

33. Priv. Ltr. Rul. 8326113.

34. *See* text accompanying notes 29 and 32.

35. *See* discussion in §6.1(b)(2).

36. *See* discussion in §6.2(b).

37. I.R.C. §213(a).

38. 1975-2 C.B. 86. *See also* Priv. Ltr. Ruls. 8641037, 8651027, 8748026.

39. Rev. Rul. 76-481, 1976-2 C.B. 82. *See also* Priv. Ltr. Rul. 8221134.

40. 1993-34 I.R.B.

41. This revenue ruling will not apply to sums paid before October 14, 1993, or to sums paid on or after October 14, 1993, if paid pursuant to a binding contract entered into before that date.

42. Treas. Reg. §1.213-1(e)(1)(ii); Priv. Ltr. Rul. 8502009.

43. Rev. Rul. 76-106, 76-1 C.B. 71.

44. Rev. Ruls. 76-481, 1976-2 C.B. 82; 68-525, 1968-2 C.B. 112.

45. Priv. Ltr. Rul. 8502309.

46. Priv. Ltr. Rul. 8630005.

47. Rev. Rul. 67-185, 1967-1 C.B. 70.

48. Priv. Ltr. Ruls. 8930023, 8930024.

49. Assuming entrance fees are greater than one year's worth of monthly fees.

50. This rule is also discussed in §§7.1(d)(1), 7.2(b)(2), and 7.3(c)(2).

51. 1960-1 C.B. 298.

52. 1955-1 C.B. 347.

53. *See* §7.2(b)(2).

54. Rev. Rul. 60-135; *id.*

55. *See* discussion at §7.3(c)(2).

56. *See* §7.1(d).

57. "Continuing Care Retirement Communities: An Industry in Action," note 3 *above*, 17-18.

58. *James v. United States*, 366 U.S. 213, 253 (1961).

59. 54 T.C. 584 (1970).

60. Likewise, where an accrual basis taxpayer received an advance payment from its lessee, the U.S. Tax Court determined—although the taxpayer contended that the payment was intended as a construction loan—that the payment constituted prepaid rent because the funds were not earmarked but were commingled with general corporate funds, no promissory notes were executed, and no interest was charged. *Harold Bell Co.*, T.C.M. 1955-103, Dec. 20, 1976.

61. 395 F.2d 508 (5th Cir. 1968), 68-1 USTC 9394.

62. 792 F.2d 683, 689 (7th Cir. 1986).

63. Rev. Rul. 58-17, 1958-1 C.B. 11.

64. Rev. Rul. 66-347, 1966-2 C.B. 196.

65. *See also* the discussion of a loan from a trust in §6.1(b)(6).

66. *Commissioner v. Indianapolis Power*, 493 U.S. 203, 110 S. Ct. 589, 107 L. Ed.2d 591 (1990).

67. Likewise, in *Oak Industries v. Commissioner*, 96 T.C. 559 (1991), the U.S. Tax Court held that the operator of a subscription television service was not required to include in income security deposits paid by subscribers in connection with their use of signal decoders because the service was obligated to refund the entire deposit when the subscriber met the terms of the subscription agreement. *See also* TAM 9735002 (refundable country club membership deposits as loans).

68. However, in a private letter ruling, the IRS distinguished the payments described in *Indianapolis Power* from entry fees paid to a retirement community. Priv. Ltr. Rul. 9246006. In that ruling, the IRS rejected the argument that *entry fees* charged to tenants and refundable on a declining basis over a period of years were security deposits. Where the fees were not linked to the tenant's perfor-

mance under a contract, but rather to the duration of occupancy, the entry fees could not be deemed security deposits.

69. P.L. 98–369, Section 172, 98 Stat. 494, amended by P.L. 99–121.

70. I.R.C. §1274(d).

71. H.R. Rep. 98–861, 1984–3 C.B.V. 2, 278.

72. *See* P.L. 99–121, §204(a)(2). Qualified continuing-care facility is defined in I.R.C. §7872(g). *See* §6.2(b)(4) for discussion.

73. *See* the discussion regarding "significant effect" loans in §6.2(b)(3).

74. *U.S. Code Cong. & Admin. News,* 99th Cong., 1st Sess., V. 2, 451–452.

75. *See* §6.1(b)(1).

76. Proposed Treas. Reg. §1.7872–2(b)(1)(i).

77. Proposed Treas. Reg. §1.7872–2(b)(1)(iii).

78. *See* 1985–2 C.B. 827–828.

79. I.R.C. §§7872(e)(1)(A), (f)(2)(B), (f)(5).

80. I.R.C. §§7872(e)(1)(B), (f)(1), (f)(2)(A), (f)(6).

81. I.R.C. §7872(a)(1).

82. I.R.C. §7872(b).

83. For example, if a $100,000 fee is 90 percent refundable, the loan amount is only $90,000 and thus the *loan* would be refundable in full.

84. Proposed Treas. Reg. §1.7872–10(a)(2).

85. *Ibid.*

86. Proposed Treas. Reg. §1.7872–10(a)(5).

87. Proposed Treas. Reg. §1.7872–4(b)(4) specifically provides that a loan to a continuing-care community will *not* be treated as a compensation-related loan.

88. I.R.C. §7872(c)(1).

89. I.R.C. §7872(c)(1)(F).

90. I.R.C. §7872(c)(1)(E).

91. 1984–3 C.B.V.2, 273–274.

92. *Id.* at 274.

93. *See* §2.3(d).

94. *See, e.g.,* "Private Financing of Long Term Care: Current Methods and Resources," ICF, Inc., Phase I, 1985, 6, submitted to U.S. Department of Health and Human Services, which suggests that the government could reduce federal health care expenditures by encouraging private financing of life-care and other long-term-care insurance programs.

95. *See* P.L. 99–121, 99 Stat. 511–513 (1985), I.R.C. §7872(g). A bill was introduced in Congress in 1987 to repeal the $90,000 exemption from imputed interest rules for continuing-care retirement communities. However, seniors' housing interest groups were able to preserve the exemption. *See AAHA Provider News,* Jan. 8, 1988.

96. Rev. Rul. 97–57, I.R.B. 1997–52.

97. I.R.C. §7872(g)(3)(B)(i)(I). Note that meals are generally not considered personal care under state licensing laws. It is unclear, therefore, if licensed assisted living or personal care must be available while the resident is residing in the independent-living unit.

98. A principal question is whether qualified facilities *must* provide licensed personal care (now generally called "assisted living" in the industry). It is not entirely clear from the statute whether licensed assisted living must be available to residents of independent-living units because the statute equates personal care with the generally unlicensed service of providing meals and because residents in need of licensed personal care generally are not considered independent. When the resident can no longer remain independent, the law requires provision of long-term care, if needed, *in addition to* skilled-nursing care. Long-term care is a generic term that usually includes skilled-nursing care. It is thus unclear whether the law uses the words long-term care as a euphemism for licensed assisted-living services, whether it refers to other licensed long-term care, such as intermediate care, or whether the reference is simply to services that generally are unlicensed, such as meals, housekeeping, and laundry.

99. But see Senate Finance Committee Report to P.L. 99–121, which discusses in detail the need for care and services to prolong the ability of residents to maintain their independence.

100. Priv. Ltr. Rul. 9252015.

101. *See* §6.2(b)(4).

102. 1985–2 C.B. 812.

103. *Id.* at 813.

104. *Id.* at 814. *See also* TAM 9735002.

105. Technical Advice Memorandum 9521001, May 26, 1995.

106. Gallagher, R., "The Current Status of the Imputed Interest Rules," *American Association of Homes for the Aging Technical Assistance Brief,* 1992. *See also* Kaufmann, P., "Phantom Income of the Elderly: The IRS Clarifies the Application of the Imputed Interest Rules to Refundable Entrance Fees Paid to Retirement Communities," *California Tax Lawyer,* Fall 1995, 21–26.

107. Priv. Ltr. Rul. 8952001.

108. *Fed. Reg.* 25032, July 10, 1986.

109. *51 Fed. Reg.* 28553, Aug. 8, 1986.

110. *See* §2.4(f).

111. *See* §§2.4(f) and 21.6(c).

112. *See* §21.5.

113. *See* §21.5.

114. *See* trust/loan arrangement discussed in §6.1(b)(5). Priv. Ltr. Rul. 8326113.

Highland Village; Issaquah, Washington.

Ownership Models

7 Ownership Models

§7.1 Condominium Ownership

(a) In General

The central characteristic of condominiums is that their owners have fee simple interests in their residential units and share with other owners an undivided interest in the land and other common areas of the project, such as hallways, entrance areas, and recreational facilities. Residents enjoy all the practical and tax advantages of homeownership and leave the burdens of maintenance and repair of the facilities to the homeowners' association.

On the other hand, the association's bylaws, together with deed restrictions or covenants, require the payment of dues and adherence to procedural rules of operation and likely limit the individual owner's ability to alter or improve the unit or to sell it to a buyer of the owner's choice. For retirement communities, the issues of management control over both operations and resales of individual units present the greatest challenges to long-term and harmonious functioning of the project as originally intended. Although full-service retirement communities that permit residents to accumulate equity are not commonplace, they have generally been successful.[1]

Condominiums are typically financed by short-term construction loans, with each unit owner obtaining longer-term financing on an individual basis. While some HUD mortgage insurance programs are available for condominiums, they are of limited usefulness.[2] Condominiums also may be subject to federal and state securities registration laws or specific state statutes requiring detailed filings and disclosures.[3]

(b) Business Issues

(1) Marketing

Homeownership is a cherished American opportunity, especially among seniors, many of whom have been homeowners for most of their lives. Most mature adults are familiar with the concept of condominium ownership such that the condominium probably does not require the degree of consumer education necessary for many other entrance fee or membership formats.[4]

Providing the resident with ownership of the housing unit creates several advantages for both developer and resident. From the for-profit developer's point of view, sale of a unit permits the developer to receive a large amount of cash, similar to the receipt of an entrance fee. Unlike the case of nonrefundable entrance fees, however, the developer need not report the entire sales proceeds as income but may offset the cost basis expended in development of the facility. Residents receive the tax benefits of homeownership, including the ability to deduct both real estate taxes and mortgage interest and to exclude up to $500,000 of gain, per couple, upon sale of the condominium unit (see §7.1(d)).

While condominiums may be familiar to consumers and their sale easier than some other forms of occupancy, seniors' housing facilities with services create special problems of control (discussed below) that are not present in conventional developments and that should be of considerable importance to the astute purchaser.[5]

(2) Homeowner Management Concerns

For a developer or management company, sale of the entire premises to condominium homeowners can result in a loss of control over the character and day-to-day operations of a retirement community. If homeowners are able to resell their units without restriction or to exercise complete control over service management, they can compromise the facility concept as originally envisioned by the developer. Moreover, developers interested in operation of the community could become powerless to maintain cohesiveness and clear direction.

Deed conditions, covenants, and restrictions (CC&Rs) may be effective in maintaining the character of a facility by, for example, controlling sales only to persons over a certain age who both meet specific financial and health status standards set forth by the homeowners' association and pass review by a committee of the association. Conflicts of interest may develop, however, when those who control the homeowners' association have to make decisions about matters such as the liability of the association to care for residents who have extraordinarily high medical expenses or other problems that may have a financial or highly personal impact on association members and even the association directors themselves. The businesslike detachment of nonowner management with control over service facilities can help avoid the discord often evident in homeowners' associations. The importance of objective, professional management is only amplified in a facility that offers extensive personal and health care services. An alternative, discussed below, is for the "declarant" of the covenants (e.g., the developer) to retain powers over the services.[6]

Several examples of resident-controlled condominiums or other resident equity projects operating with a continuing-care or congregate housing format have emerged in the past decade. Such facilities may have a health care center, dining room, and other areas owned in common by the homeowners and controlled by the homeowners' association. The association can then hire a management company to staff and operate the facilities. The homeowners' association is responsible for developing facility policies and procedures, overseeing admission to the facility, and hiring and firing management.[7] For those concerned with the long-term success of the project, however, it may be a mistake simply to turn over unbridled control to the homeowners' association. If state law permits, developers should seriously consider retaining ownership or other substantial control over operations and service areas.

(3) Lost Resale Opportunity/Transfer Fees

From the facility developer's point of view, it may be more desirable to retain ownership of the residential units than to offer them for sale. Not only does retention of ownership alleviate concerns about control, as discussed below, but the facility developer who elects to continue with community operations also maintains a continuing financial benefit from the project that goes beyond management fees. For example, a mature continuing-care facility can experience, on average, complete turnover of population about once every 14 years. With some form of substantial entrance payment, the operator in effect enjoys the opportunity to "sell" a residential unit again after it is vacated. It is upon the resale of the unit, many years after the facility has been constructed and the costs of development substantially paid, that the developer/operator can expect to generate significant income over expenditures. On the other hand, a similar result can be obtained from a for-sale project by imposing a transfer fee on resales of residents' interests. A typical transfer fee may be 10 to 20 percent of the original purchase price, plus one-third to three-quarters of any appreciation. A transfer fee is likely to be treated as a real property interest retained by the developer.[8]

In some respects, the resident also benefits from the operator's ability to resell the unit or to collect a transfer fee. The continued interest of the developer in keeping the project marketable should result in maintenance of high-quality services and attractive facilities. In addition, to the extent that the developer may look forward to profit from the resale of units many years after construction, initial entrance fees

Figure 7.1 **Typical Condominium Structure**

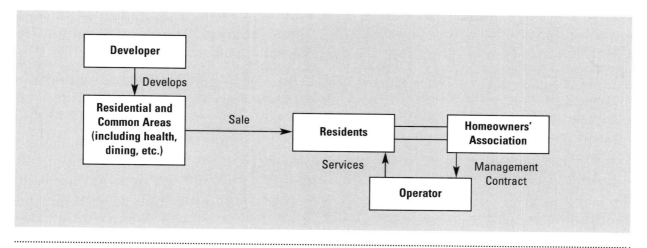

or purchase prices can be reduced to encourage initial fill-up of the new project. These opportunities are lost when the facility is sold as condominiums or as some other form of fee simple ownership unless substantial transfer fees, based on a percentage of appreciation value, can be worked into the transaction (see §7.3(c)(3)).

(c) Developer Control Issues

(1) Maintaining Management Control

Although the character of the condominium and its operations can be controlled by conditions, covenants, and restrictions contained in the deeds and by association bylaws and rules, homeowners' associations historically have earned a well-deserved reputation for engendering discord and even lawsuits over relatively simple matters of maintenance of the premises. At least in theory, all homeowners' association governing board members may unwittingly harbor conflicts of interest that pit their personal welfare against that of the community at large. In a seniors' housing facility, where services require more intensive day-to-day management oversight and decisions may have to be made about serious personal matters such as medical care benefits or the ability to remain in the residential unit with one's spouse, the homeowners' association may not be as well positioned to make important management deci-

sions as an operator who maintains ownership of the facility.

In general, condominium developers establish the overall character of a property through its physical design and the creation of deed restrictions and homeowners' association bylaws. Pending the sale of a majority of the units, the developer usually controls the homeowners' association and thus facility management. Eventually, however, association voting rights devolve to the individual unit owners, and the extent to which the developer or any operator can retain control over or ensure perpetuation of the intended character of the community becomes an issue for all concerned. Figure 7.1 illustrates a typical condominium model wherein homeowners control both residential and common service areas as well as management. Figure 7.2 and the accompanying text provide an alternative arrangement.

Every state has some form of condominium law[9] that, whether interpreted by regulation or case law, may place specific restrictions on the ability of a developer to maintain control over management of the facility after its transfer to the association.[10] For example, in California, homeowners' associations are prohibited, with limited exceptions, from entering into contracts for goods or services for a term longer than one year unless a majority of the voting power of the association residing in members other than the developer approves the transaction.[11] Similarly, in Florida, where a developer had procured a management contract with the association while it was under the developer's control, the association was able to cancel the contract once it acquired 75 percent of the units from the developer, irrespective of whether the contract was fair and reasonable and without regard to whether the contract had been breached.[12]

Interestingly, however, at least one Florida case has held that where the promoters, before selling units to individual purchasers, had the association enter into a 25-year management contract with them, the purchasers were deemed to have affirmed the existence of the long-term contract upon the sale of the units. Thus, the contract was found to be enforceable.[13] Moreover, with the advent of condominium continuing-care facilities in California, regulatory restrictions on developer management of condominiums have yielded to continuing-care regulations, which require the licensed operator to retain controls normally reserved to the homeowners' association (e.g., building maintenance).[14]

Other attempts to limit developer management contracts have been based on general concepts of fairness and policies against self-dealing. For the most part, such attacks have been unavailing.[15] Thus, individual state statutes must be reviewed to determine the extent of restrictions on homeowners' association management contracts with developer/promoters, bearing in mind that the statutes may be preempted or modified by continuing-care or facility licensure laws.[16]

(2) Requiring Owners to Purchase Services

An alternative or additional method of retaining control over the service and amenity components of a seniors' condominium project is for the developer or operator to own service areas such as dining, recreational, and health care facilities and/or to include deed covenants requiring payment for such amenities or common services. Another option may be for the developer/operator to retain easements or long-term leases over such essential service areas, although state statutory and case law may dictate different strategies.

One Illinois case,[17] for example, upheld a covenant that required condominium owners to pay annual dues to an adjacent sports facility owned by the developer. The court rejected arguments that the deed restriction was unconscionable and a restraint on alienation and did not run with the land. Instead, the court upheld the sports club's lien against the condominium unit owner for unpaid dues on the grounds that the covenant was part of the original deed and known to the purchasers and the club was part of the same complex of buildings.[18] However, where a developer executed a lease of recreational space to himself on behalf of the homeowners' association before the association was officially formed and without subsequently obtaining the association's ratification, the association was not bound to honor it.[19] In addition, statutes requiring recreational leases or management contracts to be fair and reasonable, if entered into before unit owners control the association, can preclude long-term leases to the promoter.[20]

For facilities interested in providing mandatory long-term-care insurance, some precedent exists for mandatory insurance assessments against condominium owners.[21] However, where the mandatory services, amenities, or facilities are not a usual and integral part of a condominium project, the transaction may be viewed as an arrangement involving the tying of two products for sale and thus in violation of federal antitrust or state unfair competition laws.[22] Generally, unlawful tying arrangements occur when a seller with market control over one product conditions the sale of that product on the purchase of another product. Therefore, while leases of common areas or assessments for property insurance or maintenance might more readily be considered part of a single condominium product, assessments for dining or medical facilities and services may be considered a separate product unlawfully tied to the condominium purchase. Potential plaintiffs may include the residents themselves as well as competitors such as health care providers in the tied product business.

In an effort to overturn long-term management contracts or leases,[23] condominium unit owners have successfully turned to antitrust theories to initiate legal actions against developers. When, however, approval of a long-term lease with the developer for garage space was made a condition of initial purchase of the units before formation of the condominium association, at least one court viewed the transaction as the sale of a single product and merely a limitation on the estate purchased.[24]

Although no clear pattern emerges from the cases and specific state laws may yield different results, some potential condominium retirement facility arrangements appear less vulnerable to challenge than others. Of course, making payment for facilities and services optional is the most legally secure alternative. If developers retain ownership of adjacent or on-site properties where dining, recreational, or medical facilities are available but use of the facilities is not mandatory, the mere convenience of their location could be sufficient to make them economically successful. If mandatory resident support of the facilities is desired, it seems safer to include such requirements in deed restrictions rather than resorting to leases or other contracts between the developer and the homeowners' association. Mandatory services and amenities should be integrated as much as possible into the project to create a unified product resistant to claims of tying arrangements. This can mean more than merely physical integration. For example, if the financial arrangements are such that a fixed, overall fee covers dining, availability of different levels of health care facilities, housekeeping, recreational programs, and other services, the transaction is more likely to be treated as a single comprehensive program rather than as a series of separately priced but tied products. In addition, blanket state licensure of the entire program (e.g., as a continuing-care facility) can give weight to the single-product concept.

(3) Restricting Resales

A fundamental requirement for any retirement condominium is the ability to restrict occupancy to elderly people. Where health care or other substantial services are included, it may also be necessary to establish financial and health criteria for occupancy. Unlike entrance fee, rental, or even cooperative formats, the individual-unit ownership characteristic of condominiums raises special questions about the developer's ability to place limits on the owner's freedom to use or sell his or her own property.

While federal and state laws generally prohibit age discrimination in the sale or rental of housing, the same laws recognize exceptions for seniors' housing in response to the perceived special needs of the elderly to live together among their own age group.[25] Where special services catering to the elderly are part of a project's overall program, the ability to restrict resales on the basis of age, health, and other relevant factors is enhanced.

The courts have upheld deed restrictions that provided for a residential association's right of first refusal to ensure "a community of congenial residents."[26] On the other hand, the courts have determined that the arbitrary refusal to consent to a transfer without provision for compensation of the unit owner is an unreasonable restraint on alienation.[27] Rights of first refusal exercisable by condominium associations have raised issues concerning violation of the rule against perpetuities.[28] And the courts have upheld a statute that created a rebuttable presumption of unconscionability for any covenant or bylaw provision giving the association a right of first refusal.[29]

Covenants that limit residence to members of or those sympathetic to a particular religious or philosophical sect have been found to be unenforceable.[30] Federal law also prohibits discrimination in the sale of homes on the basis of race, color, religion, sex, or national origin.[31] Nonetheless, the courts have upheld deed covenants permitting the developer or its successors or assigns to enforce restrictions on the sale or use of the property even when the developer no longer owns units in the project.[32] Covenants requiring owner occupancy and forbidding the leasing of units have also been found to be reasonable where the purposes were to discourage the artificial price inflation caused by property rental and sales to speculators and to preserve low- and moderate-income housing opportunities.[33]

In general, seniors' housing facilities should be able to enforce deed covenants that restrict resales to persons meeting age, health, and financial criteria reasonably related to some required or fundamental component of the service program offered at the community.[34] If the developer or homeowners' association seeks to place restrictions on resales without objective standards based on program features, a right of first refusal may present a legitimate vehicle to accomplish that end.[35] However, state laws and court opinions must be reviewed to identify any particular limitations that may be applicable.

Figure 7.2 **Sample Condominium with Services Structure**

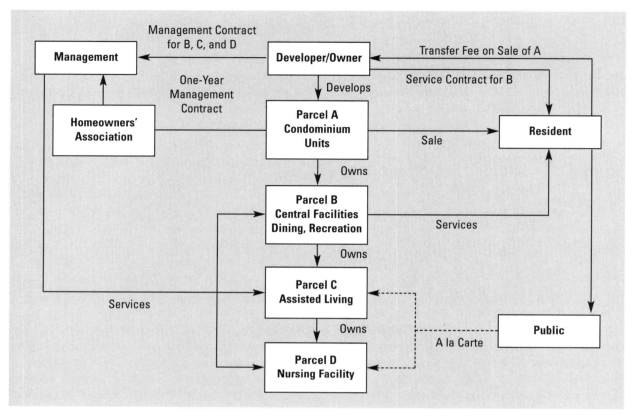

Notes:

1. Resident Features
   a. Resident purchases Parcel A unit.
   b. Homeowners' association for Parcel A is in charge of maintenance of Parcel A only; initially, management will have a one-year maintenance contract, subject to homeowner ratification, extension.
   c. Deed covenants require purchase of Parcel B services as condition of ownership; resident must enter into service agreement; violation of service agreement is grounds for a lien against the unit for unpaid fees and, if necessary, forced sale of the Parcel A unit.
   d. Parcels C and D are open to the public on the site on an à la carte basis, but residents are not required to purchase services there; if resident moves to Parcel C or D, he or she may retain unit A and pay fees; Parcel A residents receive a reduction of fees in the amount of variable costs for absences of more than 30 days.
   e. Upon resale, buyer must be determined to be qualified according to age, income, and health by developer or its designee. Developer will actively market the project and maintain a listing of qualified prospective buyers.
   f. A percentage of the gross resale price must be paid to developer as a transfer fee for sales brokerage and admission screening services.

2. Owner/Management Features
   a. Developer sells Parcel A to residents; retains ownership of Parcels B, C, and D.
   b. Management is under contract with developer to provide management services to Parcels B, C, and D. Parcel B services will conform to the service agreement between developer and the residents.
   c. Developer will perform brokerage/admission screening services and collect transfer fee directly.
   d. Continuing-care licensure may be avoidable because Parcel C and D services are not covered by the service agreement and are available to the resident as a member of the general public.

(4) Multiparcel Condominium Example; Retained Easements; Leaseholds

Figure 7.2 illustrates one method of providing residents with the advantages of homeownership without depriving the facility developer or operator of the control necessary to manage the facility properly. The project is developed as multiple independent parcels, one consisting of all the residential units and one or more others consisting of all the service areas such as dining, recreational facilities, nursing, assisted living, maintenance, and housekeeping. The residential units only are transferred to the homeowners while the developer retains ownership of the service areas. In the alternative, the developer may wish to sell or lease the service areas to an operating organization or sell the service areas to the homeowners but retain an easement for operation of the service program.

Although the homeowners' association will have control over the residential units, including common areas such as connecting hallways, the vast majority of the service components essential to a successful retirement facility will not be subject to homeowners' association control because the operator either owns or retains an easement in those areas. Therefore, the owner can retain control over the overall character of the facility and avoid the problems inherent in putting residents in charge of their own service programs (see §7.1(c)(1)).[36]

One problem with the multiparcel model for a for-profit developer is that retention of ownership of the service parcels reduces the extent to which the cost basis of construction of facilities may be offset against sales income. If the developer seeks to cover the costs of both residential and service areas with proceeds from the sale of the residential areas alone and does not sell the service areas, it cannot use the cost basis of the service areas to reduce taxable income (see Figure 7.3). One alternative is to sell the service parcel to a for-profit operating organization, but this arrangement merely shifts the problem to another organization. A preferred arrangement is to sell the entire project to a tax-exempt operator to enable the developer to recover its full cost basis.

If it is not practical to sell the service areas, the retained area can be reduced in size and cost to minimize the basis problem, with control maintained by identifying and retaining only the most crucial service areas (e.g., nursing and kitchen, but not library and recreation areas).

Another alternative is for the operator to retain an easement or leasehold in the service areas after selling the entire project to the homeowners. While this arrangement solves the tax basis recovery problem,[37] it results in an interest that is less than fee simple and may be more easily challenged. Easements, which may "run with the land" (pass to successive owners indefinitely), provide more security than leases, which, while specifically enforceable, are unenforceable if breached. Management contracts, which do not have the "possessory" character of a lease, are not specifically enforceable; therefore, money damages may be the only remedy. These basic legal distinctions are important to the extent that the developer/operator desires long-term operational control.[38] Figure 7.4 provides a comparison of the characteristics of the various methods of controlling services.

(5) Leasehold Condominiums

A further variation on the retirement condominium structure outlined in Figure 7.2 is the leasehold condominium, as illustrated in Figure 7.5. In it, the developer retains ownership of both the residential and service areas and leases the entire project to a management company or service provider.[39] The operating organization then sells transferable leasehold condominium interests in the residential units only. One reason for such a structure may be the owner's or developer's desire to retain title to the ground and, possibly, the improvements due to restrictions in the original grant (e.g., university lands) or for tax reasons (e.g., building depreciation). For a discussion of other features of Figure 7.5, such as the lease/loan transactions and transfer fee payments, see the text accompanying Figure 12.1, §12.3.

One issue of concern with the leasehold condominium structure is whether the residents will be eligible to exclude recognition of capital gain from the sales of their homes. Although Congress drastically altered the rules in 1997 by establishing a $500,000 per couple capital gains exemption for the sale of a principal residence (see §7.1(d)(1)), the case law regarding capital gains from home sales was established in the context of the former Section 1034 capital gain rollover privilege. In *Boesel v. Commissioner*,[40] the U.S. Tax Court rejected the taxpayers' attempt

Figure 7.3 **Cost Basis Recovery Problem: Two-Parcel Model**

1. Problem

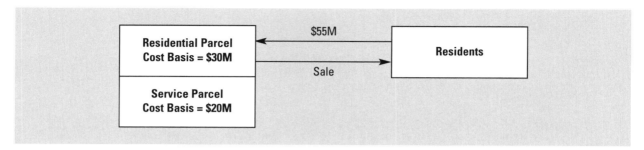

a. Developer sells only the residential parcel but collects cost of developing both parcels plus 10 percent profit ($55M). Developer retains the service parcel for reasons of control.

b. Developer can offset only the cost of the residential parcel ($30M), not the service parcel basis ($20M), and is taxed on the difference ($25M).

c. One remedy is to reduce the size and cost of the retained service parcel.

2. Alternative 1

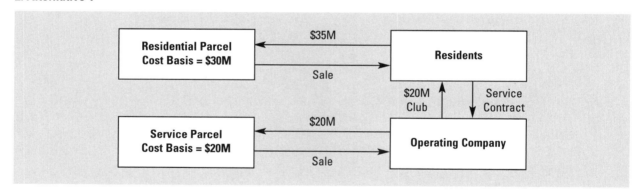

a. Developer sells residential units for $35M and sells service parcel to an operating company for $20M. Control and long-term revenues are maintained through real estate covenant and contractual arrangements.

b. Developer can offset full $50M cost basis, resulting in tax on only $5M profit.

c. Operator sells club memberships or collects entrance fees from residents ($20M); however, unless the operator is tax-exempt, fees will be taxable and the service parcel purchase price will not be a deductible expense.

d. Operating company is unlikely to be eligible for tax exemption if it has no control over the residential property.

e. Resident's Section 1034 capital gain carryover is reduced to extent home equity is reinvested in the service club membership or fee.

Figure 7.3 (continued)

3. Alternative 2

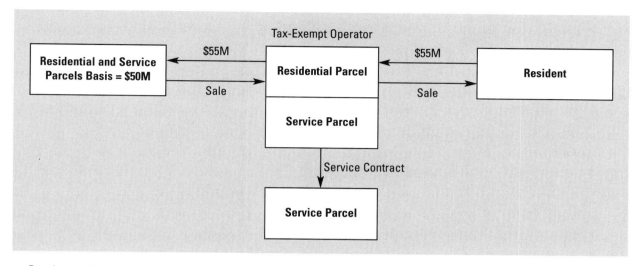

a. Developer sells both parcels to an exempt operator; developer offsets entire cost basis against sales income; taxed on $5M profit; developer's control and income stream maintained through sale agreement, deed of trust, and deed covenants.

b. Exempt operator sells residential units to residents, retains ownership of service parcel, and contracts with manager of its choice.

c. Residents have full Section 1034 carryover privilege.

Figure 7.4 **Operator Control of Condominium Service Areas**

	I **Separate Service Parcel**	II **Retained Easement**	III **Long-Term Lease**	IV **Management Contract**
1. Cost Basis Recovery	No, unless sell to exempt operator	Yes	Yes	Yes
2. Security of Interest	Fee simple	Runs with land; unauthorized uses can be enjoined, but right not extinguished except by abandonment	Contract right, unenforceable if breached	Contract right, unenforceable if breached
3. Remedies	Quiet title	Injunction	Specific performance	Damages only; no specific performance

Figure 7.5 **Leasehold Condominium Structure (Two-Parcel)**

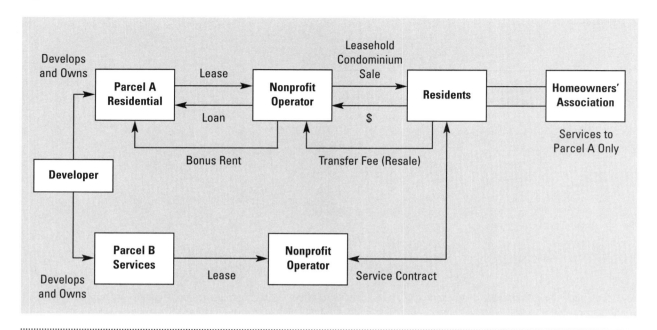

to capitalize the value of future lease payments under a 73-year ground lease. In response to the taxpayers' argument that their leasehold was the economic equivalent of ownership in fee simple, the court held that Section 1034 provided an "unequivocal mandate" that nonrecognition of gain be permitted only to the extent that a taxpayer holds title in fee simple to the property occupied as his or her principal residence. The court, however, acknowledged in a footnote that there may be "equivalent forms of ownership" qualifying for the benefit.[41]

That only a "fee simple" interest will qualify for a capital gains exemption seems unduly harsh and contrary to the actual practice of the IRS and the marketplace. It apparently has been common for homeowners to take Section 1034 benefits for the entire purchase price of a home, even though the underlying land may be subject to a long-term (e.g., 99-year) lease. Moreover, there are acknowledged exceptions to the "rule" that fee simple ownership has been required to qualify for the Section 1034 carry-over. For example, in Revenue Ruling 84–43,[42] the IRS ruled that a life estate was a sufficient interest to qualify as a "principal residence" under Section 121.[43] In addition, Section 1034 specifically included coop-

eratives, where residents own shares in the cooperative association rather than fee simple interests in the underlying real property and where the association is permitted by Section 216(b)(1)(B) to own *or* lease the building.

Furthermore, for tax purposes, the IRS has often viewed long-term lease arrangements as tantamount to an ownership interest. In Private Letter Ruling 8946079, cooperative members were deemed entitled to deduct their proportionate shares of real estate taxes and interest deductible to the cooperative corporation where the cooperative held title to the residential buildings but leased the land for a term of 150 years. The IRS determined that the transactions pertaining to both the building and land constituted a sale of property for federal tax purposes because the cooperative paid only a nominal amount of rent to the landowner and enjoyed the entire worth of the buildings, whose useful life was shorter than the lease term.[44]

Revenue Ruling 72–266[45] also sheds some light on the definition of a principal residence with an underlying ground lease. There, the taxpayer's new residence was situated on leased land with a remaining term of 50 years. The lease did not provide for

Figure 7.6 **Ground Lease Condominium Example**

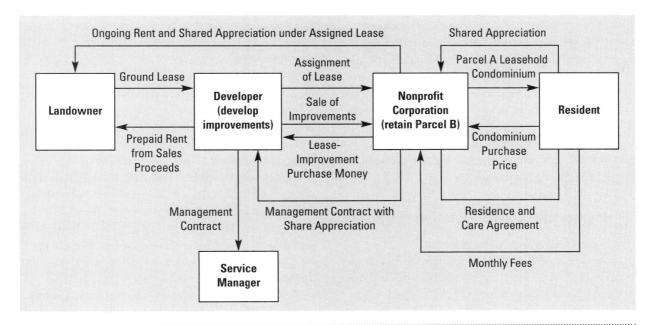

renewal upon expiration and did not contain an option to purchase the land. In the taxpayer's attempt to roll over gain from the sale of his previous principal residence, he added to the cost of the home the present value of the future lease payments. Although tax regulations provide that the cost of purchasing a new residence may include an indebtedness, the IRS ruled that in this case that the taxpayer did not purchase the property to which the future lease payments related; therefore, he acquired no equity in it. The present value of future lease payments thus could not be included in the purchase price of the new residence for purposes of applying the nonrecognition provisions of Section 1034 to the gain realized from the sale of the taxpayer's previous residence. Therefore, in a leasehold condominium structure, it is possible that any capital gain exclusion privilege would be applied to amounts attributable to purchase of the condominium unit, but not to amounts paid to fund ground lease payments. Figure 7.6 illustrates a ground-lease condominium in which the developer sells its interest to a nonprofit corporation to recover its cost basis.

But Private Letter Ruling 9026033 treated a 99-year lease, renewable indefinitely for $1 per renewal, as a sale for purposes of deducting mortgage interest and property taxes, partly because the rental price approximated the price at which the property could be purchased.

As a practical matter, the $500,000 per couple exclusion makes the ability to treat a retirement community as a principal residence less significant. Rather than rolling over gain from the previous home sale, the resident can simply exclude gain. The ability to exclude gain upon sale of the retirement community residence depends on the nature of the acquired interest.

Another concern pertaining to leasehold arrangements is cost basis recovery (see §7.1(c)(4)). If a developer leases the project over the long term to an operating organization, it cannot deduct its cost basis from prepaid rental payments. Moreover, if the developer builds on leased land, it cannot deduct its cost basis upon transfer to a resident or operating organization unless it completely disposes of its leasehold interest by sale or assignment (as opposed to subletting).[46] (But see Revenue Ruling 70–607,[47] which finds that an apartment building sold subject to a 75-year ground lease is a sale whereby owners could remove the building and receive condemnation proceeds.)

State law may also help determine whether a long-term lease or other non–fee simple interest will be sufficient to qualify the property as a principal residence. State property tax laws in particular may be helpful in establishing that long-term lessees are treated as owners. Most important, however, the resident's interest in the underlying leasehold should be transferable and follow as closely as possible the attributes and formalities of a conveyable ownership interest.[48]

Unfortunately, the IRS has announced that it will give no advance rulings regarding the qualification of property as a principal residence.[49]

(d) Homeowner and Association Tax Issues

(1) Resident Ownership Tax Advantages

In many areas of the country where elderly homeowners have seen phenomenal rises in home sales prices and a correspondingly high exposure to taxable capital gains on sale, the tax benefits of an equity retirement community historically have had profound marketing implications when compared with entrance fee, membership, or rental communities.

Because a condominium structure allows the resident to obtain a real property interest in the retirement facility unit, he or she may enjoy several tax advantages that attach to the ownership of real property used as a principal residence. Before 1997, to the extent any gain was received from the sale of a principal residence occupied before entering the retirement facility, recognition of the profit as taxable income was deferred to the extent that it was reinvested within two years in another principal residence in which the taxpayer had an ownership interest.[50]

One of the advantages of using the Section 1034 carryover of gain on the sale of a principal residence was that the resident's appreciated home equity could pass through to the homeowner's estate without the recognition of taxable capital gain. For a couple, up to $1.2 million of assets could be passed through the estate tax-free.[51] In 1997, however, Congress greatly liberalized homeowners' tax privileges by creating a $500,000 per couple ($250,000 per individual) capital gains exclusion for the sale of a primary residence under Internal Revenue Code Section 121.[52] The exclusion may be exercised once every two years as of May 7, 1997. The 1997 act superseded the former rule that permitted persons over age 55 to exercise a one-time life-time exclusion from income of $125,000 on capital gains from the sale of a principal residence.[53]

Ownership structures offered comparatively greater tax advantages than entrance fee or rental models before the Tax Reform Act of 1997, when the Section 1034 rollover and $125,000 exclusion had to be used instead of the $500,000 exemption. Nonetheless, increases in an equity project's value will be eligible for capital gain exclusions. And, as a perquisite of ownership, residents may deduct real estate taxes and mortgage interest.[54] Membership fees and dues are not likely to be deductible.[55] Finally, assisted-living or nursing facilities that are not sold as condominiums may not be eligible for a capital gains exclusion because they may not qualify as principal residences.

For spouses co-owning retirement facility property as community property or in joint tenancy, another federal tax benefit is a stepped-up tax basis in the property upon the death of the first spouse.[56] Many states also provide property tax rollover benefits for elderly homeowners moving from one principal residence to another.

(2) Homeowners' Association Tax Exemption

The Internal Revenue Code's Section 528 creates an exemption from taxation for homeowners' associations, including a "condominium management association."[57] The association qualifies if it is organized and operated to provide for the acquisition, construction, management, maintenance, and care of association property; at least 60 percent of its gross income consists of dues, fees, or assessments from owners of residential units; at least 90 percent of its expenditures are for the acquisition, construction, management, maintenance, and care of association property; no part of the net earnings inure to the benefit of any private individual; and the association files an election form with the Internal Revenue Service for each taxable year.[58] Significantly, regulations require that 85 percent of the total project square footage be used by individuals for residential purposes.[59] Income from sources other than membership dues, fees, and assessments is taxable at the rate of 30 percent.[60]

In addition, several IRS rulings deal with the question of whether a condominium homeowners' association is eligible for income tax exemption as a social welfare organization under Section 501(c)(4). In Revenue Ruling 72-102,[61] a nonprofit homeowners' association organized to preserve the appearance of a housing development and to maintain streets, sidewalks, and common areas for the use of residents was deemed exempt from taxation under Section 501(c)(4). The IRS found that all homeowners would benefit from the association's activities, that the organization was primarily engaged in promoting the common good and general welfare of the people of the community, and that the association operated primarily for the purpose of bringing about civic betterment and social improvements. The IRS noted that a subdivision or housing development may constitute a "community" and stated:

> By administering and enforcing covenants, and owning and maintaining certain non-residential, non-commercial properties of the type normally owned and maintained by municipal governments, this organization is serving the common good and the general welfare of the people of the entire development.

Despite Revenue Ruling 72-102, the IRS found in Revenue Ruling 74-17[62] that an association formed by unit owners of a condominium housing project to provide for management, maintenance, and care of the common areas of the project was not eligible for exemption under Section 501(c)(4) on the grounds that condominium unit owners' maintenance and care of commonly owned areas amounts to provision of private benefits for the unit owners and not promotion of social welfare.

Similarly, in Revenue Ruling 74-99,[63] the IRS found that a homeowners' association is eligible for Section 501(c)(4) treatment only if it serves a "community" that bears a "reasonably recognizable relationship to an area ordinarily identified as a governmental subdivision or a unit or district thereof." Moreover, the association must not be involved in exterior maintenance of private units but needs to have responsibility for the types of nonresidential, noncommercial properties such as streets, parks, and sidewalks that are normally owned and maintained by municipal government.

Revenue Ruling 80-63[64] offered further clarification of the scope of the Section 501(c)(4) exemption for homeowners' associations. The ruling asserted that a "community" need not embrace some minimum area or certain number of homeowners but could include projects with areas and facilities available for the use and enjoyment of the general public rather than merely for members of the association.

The IRS has also considered the eligibility of a homeowners' association for Section 501(c)(7) status, which is the basis for a tax exemption of clubs organized for pleasure, recreation, and other non-profitable purposes.[65] The exemption applies only where substantially all of the club's activities are for such purposes and where no part of the net earnings of the club inure to the benefit of any private shareholder. Generally, the exemption extends to clubs that are supported solely by membership fees, dues, and assessments.[66] Furthermore, a club engaged in business, such as making its facilities available to the general public or selling real estate or other products, is not entitled to the Section 501(c)(7) exemption. Solicitation of public patronage of its facilities constitutes prima facie evidence that the club is engaging in business and thus is not operated exclusively for pleasure, recreation, or social purposes.[67]

For example, in Revenue Ruling 64-118,[68] the IRS found that an organization whose primary activity was to rent a chapter house to a fraternity composed of students might, under proper circumstances, be exempt from taxes under Section 501(c)(7). Likewise, in Revenue Ruling 69-281,[69] the IRS held that a social club providing exclusive and automatic membership to homeowners in a housing development might qualify for a Section 501(c)(7) exemption if the club operated exclusively for the pleasure and recreation of its established membership by providing recreational facilities that afforded opportunities for fellowship and commingling. In Revenue Ruling 75-494,[70] however, the IRS denied Section 501(c)(7) status to a club that provided social and recreational facilities to members limited to homeowners of a housing development, where the club owned and maintained residential streets that were not part of its social facilities, administered and enforced covenants to preserve the architecture and appearance of the housing development, and provided the housing development in which its members lived with fire and police protection and trash collection service. The IRS reasoned that under such circumstances, the club was not operated exclusively for pleasure, recreation, and other nonprofitable purposes. Once the services went beyond merely maintaining social facilities and extended to residential areas, they were no longer exclusively in furtherance of pleasure and recreation.

Because an equity retirement community involves the sale and maintenance of real estate and often the furnishing of services to residents that are not purely social, the homeowners' association probably is not eligible for the Section 501(c)(7) exemption.

While it may be difficult for a homeowners' association to qualify for tax exemption, even a taxable association may employ strategies designed to minimize or eliminate taxes.

(3) Taxation of a Homeowners' Association

If the homeowners' association does not qualify for exemption under Sections 501(c)(4), 501(c)(7), or 528, it is likely that the association will be treated as a taxable entity. However, to the extent that income to the homeowners' association is derived from fees and assessments to homeowners that are then used to offset the expenses of operating the condominium project, no taxable income should remain after payment of the business expenses of operation.

If the homeowners' association collects excess assessments from homeowners, at least one revenue ruling holds that such excess assessments are not taxable income so long as they are held in reserve until the next taxable year and applied against that year's assessments for managing, operating, maintaining, and replacing the common elements of the condominium property.[71] In addition, to the extent that a homeowners' association levies a special assessment that is specifically earmarked and segregated for certain capital improvements, such payments qualify as contributions to the capital of the association and are not taxable as income.[72]

(4) Tax-Exempt Operating Organization

In the event that a seniors' condominium is structured so that a tax-exempt organization owns or controls and operates service facilities that form a part of the project, it is important to take care that control of the residential units is not lost to third

parties. IRS General Counsel Memorandum 39487 (discussed in detail in §9.3(b)(3)) found that where individual condominium units had been purchased by residents subject to mortgages held by third-party banks, the nonprofit facility operator could not meet the requirement of Revenue Ruling 72–124 that it provide housing. Simply put, the operator could not control ownership of a residence in the event of a default on the loan and subsequent foreclosure. One solution would be for the nonprofit operator to permit no encumbrances on the units other than as security for a debt owing to the exempt organization itself. Another response may be to control the use and disposition of residents' units so comprehensively, through deed covenants, that the charitable objective of controlling and securing the inventory of specialized housing for the elderly is ensured.

Another IRS concern is that the very fact of resident ownership, coupled with the opportunity to profit upon resale of the unit, may create a private benefit that is inconsistent with tax exemption for the developer/operator of the project. Nevertheless, the IRS has granted an exemption to the developer/operator of both condominium and cooperative continuing-care projects on the condition that the operator impose a ceiling on resale prices charged by residents, reserve the right to repurchase units to ensure their affordability, and agree to monitor and regularly report the unit resale prices to the IRS (see §9.3(b)(3)).

If tax-exempt financing is sought, the residents' ownership of condominium units may prove an insurmountable obstacle unless a separately owned service parcel is carved out for the exempt operator.

§7.2 Cooperatives

(a) Cooperative/Condominium Differences

Cooperatives are a form of multiunit ownership that may be suitable for retirement communities. In most respects, cooperatives are similar to condominiums in that residents have the right to occupy specific units and use common areas; a governing body administers general services, such as maintenance and repairs, and residents share the associated expenses; residents' interests are transferable; and tax deductions related to the pro rata costs of real estate ownership are available to individual occupants. Like condominiums, cooperatives may be subject to federal and state securities registration requirements or specific state disclosure requirements.[73] Most of the discussion pertaining to condominiums on subjects such as management controls (see §7.1(c)(1)), recovery of cost basis (see §7.1(c)(4)), availability of the capital gain rollover and exemption privileges (see §7.1(d)(1)), multiparcel and leasehold structures (see §7.1(c)(4) and (c)(5)), transfer fee considerations (see §§7.1(b)(3) and 7.1(c)(3)), and eligibility for tax exemption (see §7.1(d)(2)) is applicable as well to cooperatives.

Unlike condominiums, however, where each resident can be the fee simple owner of the individual residential unit and an undivided portion of the common areas, cooperatives generally are corporations that own the entire project and sell transferable memberships or shares to tenant-stockholders. The memberships or shares are coupled with "proprietary leases" that entitle tenant-stockholders to occupy residential units and use the common areas. Several practical differences between cooperative and condominium development and operations result from this basic difference in structure.

Because cooperative residents' ownership interest is in a corporation or association rather than in real estate, cooperatives tend to have more control flexibility than many condominiums. The cooperative's board of directors can more easily control who is admitted to residence in the building. Further, the board is not subject to the rules prohibiting unreasonable restraints on alienation (conditions upon transfer) of real property interests.[74] Because co-op residents generally have a leasehold interest in their units, association rights of first refusal over the transfer of co-op shares are not likely to be subject to the rule against perpetuities.[75]

In addition, blanket mortgage financing is more readily available to cooperatives, which have a single owner, than to condominiums, which have numerous owners, each of whom may be required to obtain separate financing.[76] This advantage can be of special importance when contemplating conversion of an existing rental apartment facility or other structure into a resident ownership structure. Specifically, the cooperative may assume any existing mortgages that carry a sufficiently low interest rate.[77] On the other hand, in the event of a default in payments by an individual resident, the cooperative must absorb any financial loss, whereas condominium owners bear only individual responsibility.[78] A cooperative may not allocate shares to nonresidential units such as professional offices[79]; therefore, the service areas of a cooperative retirement facility should probably be part of the common area or separated from the cooperative regime.

Another possible advantage of a cooperative is that Internal Revenue Code Section 216(b)(1)(B) specifically permits a building to be leased and still qualify for treatment as a principal residence (see §7.2(c)(5)), presumably resulting in a qualification for the $500,000 per couple gain exclusion (see §7.1(d)(1)). On the other hand, cooperatives are subject to a restriction on income under Section 216(b) (see below).

The ultimate choice between a cooperative and condominium most likely depends on what format is most familiar to prospective residents and what facilities are already in the marketplace.

(b) Tax Benefits for Cooperative Members

(1) Tax and Interest Deduction Pass-Through; General Limitations

A tenant-stockholder of a cooperative housing corporation may deduct real estate taxes and interest on indebtedness incurred in the acquisition, construction, alteration, rehabilitation, or maintenance of the land or building to the extent of the tenant's proportionate share of the cooperative's expense.[80] Before the adoption of the Tax Reform Act of 1986, shareholders' pro rata deductions could be based only on the percentage of the total stock they owned, irrespective of unit size. Now, any basis reasonably reflecting the corporation's cost for the stockholder's unit may be used.[81]

The Internal Revenue Code's Section 216(b) defines a "cooperative housing corporation" as a corporation having only one class of stock outstanding; each of the stockholders of which is entitled, solely by reason of ownership of stock in the corporation, to occupy for dwelling purposes a house or an apartment in a building owned or leased by such corporation; no stockholder of which is entitled to receive any distribution that is not out of earnings and profits of the corporation, except on a complete or partial liquidation of the corporation; and 80 percent or more of the gross income of which, for the taxable year in which the taxes and interest for which the deduction is sought are paid or incurred, is derived from tenant-stockholders.

Although members of a cooperative nonstock apartment corporation who acquired "perpetual use and equity contracts" or proprietary leases were eligible to qualify as tenant-stockholders,[82] a life-care retirement community that provides residents with life leases in exchange for an entrance fee would not qualify as a cooperative.[83] The IRS found the life-care project to be distinguishable because residents did not have a right to a pro rata distribution of assets upon liquidation of the corporation and no right to participate in the election of the board of directors. Moreover, the life-care residents' interests were not transferable.

In determining what constitutes income derived from tenant-stockholders for purposes of meeting the test for 80 percent of gross income, Revenue Ruling 68–387[84] makes it clear that while fees charged to tenants for diverse items such as maid services and recreational facilities will be treated as income derived from tenant-stockholders, income from commercial leases or from operations other than residential housing for the tenant-shareholders will not qualify. (For a discussion of what constitutes income versus a capital contribution, see §7.2(b)(4).)

Not all cooperative interests meeting the Section 216(b) definition qualify for real estate tax benefits. In Revenue Ruling 62–177,[85] the cooperative leased a parcel of land in an existing apartment building for a period of 70 years. Although the estimated useful life of the building and improvements was substantially shorter than the term of the lease, the Internal Revenue Service held that because the lessor was benefiting from the building and improvements through rental payments, the cooperative lessee was not entitled to sole enjoyment of the entire worth of the building and improvements and was not entitled to deduct real estate taxes. Accordingly, the co-op's residents also were not entitled to deduct taxes.

Revenue Ruling 62–178[86] dealt with similar facts, except that the cooperative lessee was directly liable on the loan procured to finance the construction of the building and the lessor received no rental income from the building. In that ruling, the lessee enjoyed the entire worth of the building while the obligation to pay tax was that of the lessee and not the landlord. Consequently, the tenant-stockholders were entitled to the deduction. On the other hand, co-op members could not deduct taxes levied on recreational facilities owned and operated by an organization other than the cooperative.[87] See also §7.1(c)(5) regarding the eligibility of equity interests subject to a leasehold for treatment as a principal residence for tax purposes.

In summary, the eligibility for homeownership tax benefits of a cooperative subject to a lease likely depends on the duration of the lease, whether the lease pertains only to the land or to the improvements as well, who is obligated to pay taxes, who is entitled to insurance or condemnation proceeds, who is responsible for construction debt, and related matters.

(2) $500,000 Capital Gain Exclusion

Because a co-op qualifies as a "principal residence," another resident tax advantage of cooperative membership is the ability to exclude up to $500,000 per couple of capital gain on sale of the membership. IRS regulations indicate that "[p]roperty used by the taxpayer as his principal residence may include a houseboat, a house trailer, or stock held by a tenant-stockholder in a cooperative housing corporation."[88] Several revenue rulings have upheld principal residence treatment for the ownership of stock in cooperative housing.[89] In Revenue Ruling 60–76,[90] for example, the IRS noted that where the co-op owner was obligated under the terms of the lease to pay his or her proportionate share of principal and interest payments on the lease and where his or her stock interest was pledged as security on the note, the transaction was identical to a purchase of real property subject to an indebtedness, and the cost of the new residence would include debt-financed portions of the purchase price. A membership in a nonstock cooperative association may also qualify.[91]

As with condominiums, the right to exclude capital gain from the sale of a cooperative may be lost if a resident must sell the co-op share upon transfer to an assisted-living or nursing facility, unless the care facility is itself eligible for treatment as a principal residence. Unlike condominiums, however, Section 216(b) requires co-op interests to be in a "house or apartment," and care facilities are unlikely to qualify because they normally do not include cooking facilities.[92] (See also §§7.1(c)(5) and 7.2(b)(1) concerning leasehold cooperative interests.)

The former one-time exclusion of $125,000 of gain from the sale of a principal residence for persons over age 55 (now a $500,000 per couple per sale exclusion)[93] also applies to cooperative shares.[94]

(c) Taxation of the Cooperative Housing Corporation

(1) Eligibility for Tax Exemption

The law relating to the eligibility of a cooperative housing corporation for exemption from taxation as a social welfare organization under Section 501(c)(4) of the Internal Revenue Code parallels that relating to condominiums (see §7.1(d)(2)). *Commissioner v. Lake Forest, Inc.*,[95] denied a cooperative housing corporation exemption under Section 501(c)(4) because its activities were deemed to be of the nature of an economic and private undertaking. In addition, cooperative housing associations are not eligible for exemption under Section 528 (see discussion in §7.1(d)(2)) because co-op members are not the actual owners of units, residences, or lots in the subdivided real property.[96]

In General Counsel Memorandum 37464,[97] the IRS found that a cooperative association formed to enable its low-income members to purchase decent housing otherwise unavailable to them did not qualify as a charitable organization under Section 501(c)(3) because it served the private interests of its members rather than the public interest. The general counsel noted that members built up equity over the years in the form of membership interests, which the organization had the option to purchase at current book value. The opinion noted that the cooperative would qualify for a charitable exemption if the low-income families to which it provided housing had no relationship to the organization or its controllers. The opinion concluded, however, that the basic function of a cooperative is to provide some form of economic benefit to its members and that this objective is inherently incompatible with the requirement that Section 501(c)(3) organizations must be devoted to a public purpose.

Despite the IRS's view that cooperatives and, presumably, condominiums exist for the purpose of enriching members, it may still be possible for an organization that develops and operates a cooperative or condominium to be tax-exempt if it complies with a separate basis for exemption such as that noted in Revenue Ruling 72–124. For example, the IRS has granted tax exemption to a developer and operator of a cooperative continuing-care retirement community. In addition to complying with the requirements of Revenue Ruling 72–124 (see §9.3), the developer/operator imposed on the homeowners several controls intended to eliminate or minimize any private benefit to them arising from their ownership of cooperative interests in the project. Such controls included monitoring and reporting annually to the IRS the resale prices of cooperative memberships, imposing a ceiling on owners' profits upon resale of their memberships, and reserving the right to repurchase memberships if resale prices increased at a rate that jeopardized the affordability of memberships in the association.[98]

(2) Tax Treatment of Nonexempt Cooperative Associations

The initial payments made by tenants to a cooperative housing association in exchange for stock are likely to be treated as paid-in capital rather than income.[99] In addition, funds set aside by the cooperative as an earmarked reserve for purposes such as the remodeling or replacement of facilities are considered capital contributions.[100] If, however, such reserves accumulate for operating expenses and are not returned to cooperative members as "patronage dividends," they are treated as income.[101]

Transfer fees collected by a cooperative association when a stockholder resold stock to a third party were considered to be income rather than capital contributions because the payment received by the association was not in exchange for the sale of stock from the association.[102] Similarly, revenues generated by a cooperative association from real estate brokerage services rendered to tenant-stockholders in connection with the transfer of the apartment units is income to the association.[103] As a membership organization within the meaning of Section 277 of the Internal Revenue Code, a cooperative housing corporation can take deductions attributable to furnishing goods and services to members, but only to the extent that it derives income from members.[104]

§7.3 Memberships

(a) Business Considerations Generally

In recent years, some retirement communities have been developed with a membership format similar to that offered by health clubs or country clubs.[105] Rather than sell an interest in the real property of the retirement community, as is the practice of condominium developers, a membership format community sells an intangible personal property membership to residents while the facility operator or developer retains ownership of the apartment unit or other real property. Unlike the case of a cooperative, however, the resident has no equity interest in the entity that owns the project. Instead, membership confers only a transferable right or license to use facilities and receive services.

When a resident dies or decides to leave the facility, the membership may be sold to a new resident who meets the age, financial, health status, and other prerequisites of admission to the facility. The selling member may reap a profit or suffer a loss upon the sale of the membership. The facility developer may be entitled to a transfer fee that includes a share of any appreciation in the value of the membership upon its resale. This arrangement gives both resident and developer an economic incentive to ensure appreciation in the value of the membership, which, in turn, should promote proper management and upkeep of the facilities and cooperation in maintaining a desirable place to live.

One of the advantages of the membership format is that, like the refundable entrance fee concept, it gives the resident an opportunity to recover some or all of his or her original investment in the retirement community. Although there is no equity interest in real property, as in a condominium, there is equity in the membership itself as well as an opportunity to make a profit on resale. On the other hand, the resident stands to lose money if the facility is a failure or, if for other reasons, the value of the membership declines. The opportunity for profit and the risk of loss inherent in the membership structure may raise particular questions about whether the transaction constitutes a security under federal or state laws.[106]

A decided disadvantage, when compared with other equity interests, is that the IRS has determined that the membership format is ineligible for the former Section 1034 carryover of gain available to condominiums and cooperatives; therefore, the current $500,000 capital gain exclusion is also unavailable (see §7.3(c)(2)). However, a membership community does not have to deal with the complex problems of control facing communities with homeowners' associations (see §§7.1(c), 7.2(a)). For further discussion of memberships and major legal provisions, see Volume II, §3.4.

(b) Taxation of Sales Proceeds

Several cases have considered whether membership fees should be treated as income or a capital contribution to the organization receiving them. In *Washington Athletic Club v. United States*,[107] a membership athletic club charged substantial initial fees plus monthly fees to members in return for a membership that could be terminated only by voluntary resignation, vote of the board of governors, or nonpayment of dues. No refund was available at termination of membership except in the event of dissolution of the club. Memberships could be transferred under limited circumstances upon payment of a transfer fee to the club. The club established a capital improvement fund and characterized membership fees deposited into it as capital contributions exempt from taxation. The court rejected the club's position, finding that the motivation of members was not to make a capital contribution but rather to pay a fee that was a condition of entitlement to use the club's facilities.[108] The court found that, due to the absence of significant refund rights, there could be no significant, long-term investment motive.[109] Moreover, it distinguished cooperative cases wherein shareholders' payments are considered capital contributions because they amortize the cooperative's mortgage payments and increase shareholders' equity.[110]

Although retirement community memberships that can be resold by residents for a profit have some of the characteristics of a capital investment, it is doubtful that membership purchase prices will be treated as capital contributions instead of income.[111] Most likely, the resident's primary goal of membership is to receive services and use the facilities of the retirement community rather than to profit from its resale. While the same may be said of stock cooperative housing associations, co-op shareholders have an equity interest in the real property owner, voting rights and management control, and special opportunities to take pro rata deductions for real estate taxes and mortgage interest, which are distinguishable from the license type of interest typically extended to a club member.

Treatment of membership fees as income poses a problem for the proprietary facility operator in the form of a substantial tax obligation for fees received during the initial sellout of the project. Assuming that the membership sale does not involve the sale of an interest in the real property of the retirement facility, the developer/owner will not be able to offset its cost basis in the property against membership fee income, which may therefore be taxable in full. As a result, membership structures generally have been used by nonprofit entities or in for-profit/nonprofit joint ventures (see §12.3).

One variation on the membership format is the sale of nonvoting corporate stock in the seniors' housing corporation. If eligible for treatment as a capital contribution, the receipt of proceeds from the sale of such stock would not create a taxable income problem for the proprietary developer; as a result, the use of a nonprofit joint venture partner may not be necessary.

(c) Resident Tax Considerations

(1) Imputed Interest

While the membership format offers, from the consumer's perspective, some of the advantages of the refundable entrance fee, it should not be subject to the imputed interest concerns that may accompany refundable fees. Because the transaction can be characterized as a sale, it should be distinguishable from loan transactions, even though the resident has an opportunity to recoup all the money originally expended as a condition of admission to the development. One key to preserving the characterization of the transaction as a sale rather than a loan is to ensure that the developer or operator has no obligation to repurchase the unit from the resident who wishes to sell a membership. If the facility owner or operator assumes such an obligation, its position appears indistinguishable from that of a borrower obligated to repay a loan on the hap-

pening of a condition, such as the lender's death or withdrawal from the facility. (For the distinctions between loans and other transactions such as sales or prepaid service fees, see §6.2(a).)

(2) Principal Residence Treatment

As a transaction involving intangible personal property, the membership format does not offer the resident the tax benefits inherent in the purchase of a real property interest in the retirement community, such as the Section 121 capital gain exclusion on sale of a principal residence.

Memberships that can be resold by the resident or his or her estate straddle the middle ground between conventional nonrefundable entrance fee arrangements, which have been found ineligible for principal residence treatment,[112] and real property ownership interests eligible for the carrying over of gain.[113] In Private Letter Ruling 8837022, however, the IRS denied a request for capital gain carryover treatment under former Section 1034 for proceeds of membership sales. Although analogous to a cooperative, which provides express authority for Section 1034 treatment of a stock or membership purchase, the IRS found no express authority for a membership interest permitting deviation from the standard principle that the taxpayer must acquire an ownership interest in the new principal residence in order to take advantage of the section. Therefore, a membership interest also is likely to be ineligible for the $500,000 capital gains exclusion available for ownership interests.

(3) Taxation of Transfer Fees

If a membership or other equity type of structure involves the payment of a transfer fee by the selling resident out of the proceeds of sale, an issue arises as to whether that portion of the gain is subject to income tax to the seller before it is paid to the seniors' housing operator. Normally, commissions paid for the sale of real estate are offset against the selling price and reduce the profit on the sale.[114] Similarly, commissions on the sale of securities are offset against the sale price.[115] However, the situation can also be compared with a shared-appreciation mortgage, in which a lender loans money to a homeowner at a below-market interest rate in exchange for a percentage of the appreciation in the value of the property during the term of the loan. In such a case, the percentage of appreciation paid to the lender is likely to be treated first as income to the homeowner because value was received in the form of a reduced interest rate on the loan.[116] However, the homeowner may also have an interest expense deduction under Internal Revenue Code Section 163.

§7.4 Life Estates

Granting a resident a life estate in a unit owned by the developer/operator may confer some of the real property advantages enjoyed by condominium and cooperative owners. For example, a life estate has been held to be eligible for the former $125,000 capital gain exemption normally reserved for fee simple owners.[117] Presumably, this bodes well for application of the new $500,000 exclusion (see §7.1(d)(1)).

In a series of revenue rulings, however, the Internal Revenue Service suggested that to take advantage of the former Section 1034 capital gain rollover privilege, the taxpayer must have a legal interest in the property sold or acquired if such property is to be considered an eligible residence. Thus, for example, a new home to which a taxpayer's daughter had title was not a "residence" to the taxpayer.[118] The IRS, referring to the predecessor of Section 1034 (Section 112), noted that the purpose of the section:

> Is to defer recognition of all or a part of the gain realized on the sale of the "old residence" to a future taxable event. This is accomplished under Section [1034(c)] by deducting from the basis of the "new residence" the nonrecognized gain realized from the sale of the "old residence," and using this adjusted basis in computing taxable gain, if any, upon the subsequent sale or exchange of the "new residence."

In that ruling, the taxpayer had reinvested the proceeds of the sale from the old home in a home in which she had no legal interest but to which her daughter held title. Thus, in a subsequent sale, her daughter rather than she would be taxed on any gain realized from the sale of the new residence. Therefore, if Section 1034 were applicable, the mother would never pay tax.

In the case of a life estate, there is no interest left to sell at the end of the first resident's lifetime,

and the Section 1034 carryover thus would become a total exemption. That fact alone casts some doubt on the ability of seniors' housing community owners/operators to confer homeowner tax benefits on residents through a grant of successive life estates. Under the new Tax Act of 1997, however, the rollover concept is abolished and a blanket exclusion enacted that is more compatible with a life estate. Nevertheless, life estates are similar to and likely to be treated much as life-care contract arrangements (see §6.1(c)(2)). For further discussion of life estates, see Volume II, §2.2(b).

Notes

1. For a discussion of the success of equity continuing-care communities, *see* Goldman, J., "Condominium and Coop CCRCs: How are they doing?," *Spectrum,* Sept.–Oct. 1996, 25.

2. *See* Warren, Gorham, & Lamont, *Housing & Development Reporter,* 20:0029.

3. *See* discussion in §24 and Rohan and Reskin, *Condominium Law & Practice* (New York: Bender, 1987 [looseleaf, published annually]), Ch. 10, §3.05.

4. For a general discussion of the advantages and disadvantages of condominium retirement facilities, *see* Gordon, P., "Taking a Closer Look at Continuing Care Condos and Co-Ops," *Retirement Housing Report,* Feb. 1990; and Wood, S., "A Warming Trend: Climate Right for Condo/Coop Development," *Contemporary Long Term Care,* July 1990, 48. *See also* discussion in §§2.4(c) and (d).

5. Developers that attempt to characterize the conveyance of condominiums as something other than a sale will likely not succeed. In *Highland Farms, Inc. v. Commissioner,* 106 T.C. 12 (1996), the U.S. Tax Court held that a retirement community's conveyance of cluster homes and condominiums with an option to repurchase were sales, not financing, arrangements. Under state law, the characterization of the conveyance was determined by the parties' intention. A key factor in gleaning the parties' intention in this case was the characterization of the transaction as a sale in the transfer documents. The developer had made no oral or written representations that the transactions were loans or mortgages, and the senior citizens benefited from characterization of the transaction as a sale, as they would otherwise have lost their tax deductions for mortgage interest and real estate taxes.

6. Carefully drafted restrictions may be the developer's best means of controlling the project since courts may

be inclined to pay such restrictions great deference. For example, the California Supreme Court has held that CC&R restrictions are enforceable unless the challenger can show that the restrictions are unreasonable because they are arbitrary; violate a fundamental public policy; bear no rational relationship to the protection, preservation, operation, or purpose of the property; or impose burdens that are disproportionate to the restrictions' benefits. *Nahrstedt v. Lakeside Village Condominium Ass'n.*, 8 Cal. 4th 361 (1994). The court noted in this decision that trial courts do not have "unbridled license to question the wisdom of the restriction." *Id.* at 389. Thus, at least in California, CC&Rs enjoy a presumption of reasonableness.

7. Residents of condominium projects and other common-interest developments will also enjoy a relatively unrestricted right of free speech at the community, including the posting of signs advocating political candidates or opposing governmental decisions. In *City of Ladue v. Gilleo,* 114 S. Ct. 2038 (1994).

8. A transfer fee right is likely to be considered a "profit a prendre." *See Restatement of Property,* 1st, §450. If the right vests at the time of the first sale, it should not violate the rule against perpetuities, even though it binds successive owners. *See* Restatement §399, comment a.

9. Rohan and Reskin, note 3 *above,* Part II.

10. *See, generally,* Rohan and Reskin, note 3 *above.*

11. 10 Cal. Code of Regs. §2792.21(b)(1).

12. *Tri-Properties, Inc. v. Moonspinner Condominium Ass'n., Inc.,* 447 So. 2d 965 (Fla. Dist. Ct. App. 1984), *review denied,* 455 So. 2d 1033 (Fla. 1984).

13. *Point East Management Corp v. Point East One Condominium Corp.,* 282 So. 2d 628, 284 So. 2d 233 (Fla. 1973), *cert. den.,* 415 U.S. 921 (1974). *See also Plaza del Prado Condominium Assoc. v. Del Prado Management Co.,* 298 So. 2d 544 (Fla. 1974).

14. *See* Cal. Health and Safety Code §1775(b).

15. *See* Annot. "Self-Dealing By Condominium Developers," 73 *A.L.R.* 3d 613, §3.

16. The Federal Condominium and Cooperative Abuse Relief Act of 1980 (P.L. 96–399, §601; 15 U.S.C. §§3601–3616) also restricts operation, maintenance, or management contracts of more than three years as well as unconscionable leases benefiting developers or their affiliates entered into in *conversion* of projects from rentals to condominium or cooperative units, where the developer at the time had control of the owners' association. Although the act creates judicial relief for alleged violations, actions respecting unconscionable leases had to be brought before October 9, 1984; accordingly, the law has little impact at this time.

The developer of a condominium project may also find itself subject to an enhanced fiduciary standard, at least as long as the developer controls the board of directors of the homeowners' association. For example, in California, a court of appeal held that the failure of a developer-controlled board of directors of a homeowners' association to provide adequate funding for replacement of capital assets constituted a breach of its fiduciary duty. *Raven's Cove Townhomes, Inc. v. Knuppe Development Co.,* 114 Cal. App. 3d 783 (1981).

17. *Stream Sports Club, Ltd. v. Richmond,* 99 Ill. 2d 182, 457 N.E.2d 1226 (1983).

18. *See also Point East Management Corp. v. Point East One Condominium Corp.,* note 13 *above.*

19. *Berman v. Gurwicz,* 189 N.J. Super. 89, 458 A.2d 1311 (1981), *aff'd.,* 189 N.J. Super. 49, 458 A.2d 1289 (1983), *cert. den.,* 94 N.J. 549, 468 A.2d 197 (1983).

20. *See, e.g., Point East One Condominium Corp. v. Point East Developers, Inc.,* 348 So. 2d 32 (1977) (99-year lease); Fla. Stat. Ann. §711.66(5)(e).

21. *Sun-Air Estates Unit 1 v. Manzari,* 137 Ariz. 130, 669 P.2d 108 (1983) (blanket policy on condominium unit).

22. See discussion of antitrust arguments against mandatory meals in HUD-subsidized projects in §22.6(d).

23. *See, e.g., Mission Hills Condominium Ass'n. v. Corley,* 570 F. Supp. 453 (N.D. Ill. 1983); *Miller v. Granados,* 529 F.2d 393 (5th Cir. 1976); *Imperial Point Colonnades Condominiums, Inc. v. Mangurian,* 549 F.2d 1029 (5th Cir. 1977), *reh'g. denied,* 552 F.2d 369 (5th Cir.), *cert. denied,* 434 U.S. 859 (1977).

24. *Johnson v. Nationwide Industries, Inc.,* 450 F. Supp. 948 (N.D. Ill. 1978), *aff'd.,* 715 F.2d 1233 (7th Cir. 1983).

25. *See, e.g.,* 42 U.S.C. §3607(b), *O'Conner v. Village Green Owner's Ass'n.,* 33 Cal. 3d 790, 191 Cal. Rptr. 320 (1983), and discussion in §23.2.

26. *Chianese v. Culley,* 397 F. Supp. 1344, 1346 (S.D. Fla. 1975).

27. *Aquarian Foundation, Inc. v. Sholom House, Inc.,* 448 So. 2d 1166 (Fla. App. 1984).

28. *See Cambridge Co. v. East Slope Investment Corp.,* 672 P.2d 211 (Colo. App. 1983), *rev'd.,* 700 P.2d 537 (Colo. 1985), in which the Colorado Supreme Court upheld such a right of first refusal even though it technically violated the rule against perpetuities. Some states have by statute exempted condominium rights of first refusal from application of the rule against perpetuities. *See* Rohan and Reskin, note 3 *above,* §10.03(2).

29. *Berkley Condominium Ass'n. v. Berkley Condominium Residence, Inc.,* 185 N.J. Super. 313, 448 A.2d 510 (1982).

30. *See, e.g., Taormina Theosophical Community, Inc. v. Silver,* 140 Cal. App. 3d 964, 190 Cal. Rptr. 38 (1983); *State v. Celmer,* 80 N.J. 405, 404 A.2d 1 (1979) *cert. denied,* 444 U.S. 951 (1979); "The Rule of Law in Residential Associations," 99 *Harvard L. Rev.,* 472 (1985).

31. *See* 42 U.S.C. §§3601–3631. Note, however, that there are some exceptions for religious organizations. See §23.4.

32. *B.C.E. Development, Inc. v. Smith,* 215 Cal. App. 3d 1142 (1989).

33. *City of Oceanside v. McKenna,* 215 Cal. App. 3d 1420 (1989).

34. For a general discussion of restraints on alienation in a condominium, see DiLorenzo, V., "Restraints on Alienation in a Condominium Context: An Evaluation and Theory for Decision-making," *Real Property, Probate and Trust Journal,* 24:402, Fall 1989. The article concludes that rights of first refusal, consent requirements based on objective determinations, and consent requirements that may be based on subjective determinations all should be permitted. Only absolute prohibitions on alienation should be unlawful.

35. *See generally* Annot., "Validity, Construction, and Application of Statutes, or of Condominium Association's Bylaws or Regulations, Restricting Sale, Transfer, or Lease of Condominium Units," 17 *A.L.R.* 4th 1247.

36. *See Caughlin Homeowners Ass'n. v. Caughlin Club,* 849 P.2d 310 (Nev. 1993), in which a homeowners' association's attempt to modify covenants pertaining to the developer's adjacent commercial property was unenforceable.

37. Note, however, that the retained interest may have some residual value that may need to be allocated against cost basis recovery. *See Urbanek v. U.S.,* 52 A.F.T.R. 2d 83-5231, 83-1 USTC ¶ 9389, *aff'd.,* 731 F.2d 870 (Fed. Cir. 1984). However, this value should be far less than a retained fee simple interest.

38. Although easements theoretically offer superior control to leases and contracts, they are also a more abstract interest and therefore more difficult to describe concretely in the declaration of covenants, conditions, and restrictions or other documents. This fact may present a marketing setback to developers, who will have difficulty describing the easement interest to prospective residents. In addition, title companies may refuse to insure title to easements unless they are appurtenant to another real estate interest. *See Restatement (First) of Property* §450 *et seq.* (1992).

39. One motivation for this structure is to bring in a joint venture partner, for example, a nonprofit operating organization. *See* §12.3, Figure 12.1 and accompanying text.

40. 65 T.C. 378 (1975).

41. 1988-1 C.B. 75. Similarly, the IRS in Revenue Ruling 88-29 ruled that the sale of rights in a rent-controlled apartment by a 60-year-old man who had lived there for 25 years did not qualify for the (former) one-time $125,000 exclusion of gain from the sale of a residence under Section 121 of the Internal Revenue Code because the lease interest did not qualify as an ownership interest in a principal residence. However, the IRS noted that the lessee could not acquire any equity in the property, that the landlord could repossess the property for his personal use or for its substantial alteration, and that there was no right to sublet or transfer the lease by gift or sale. On the other hand, a leasehold condominium can be structured to give the unit owner essentially the same privileges as a fee simple condominium owner, including transferability, a share in appreciation, and a right of life-time occupancy provided covenants and rules of occupancy are followed.

42. 1984-1 C.B. 27.

43. The service employed the same definition of "principal residence" under Sections 121 and 1034.

44. *See also* Private Letter Ruling 8949036, which recites the rule set forth in Revenue Rulings 62-177 and 62-178 that a lessee may deduct real estate taxes under Sections 164 and 216 of the Internal Revenue Code even though legal title is vested in the lessor, provided that the lessor receives no substantial rental income attributable to the building and the useful life of the building is substantially shorter than the term of the lease.

45. 1972-1 C.B. 227.

46. *See generally* BNA Tax Management Portfolio, 47-4th, A-42-A-44 (1989).

47. 1970-2 C.B. 9.

48. For a discussion of a leasehold condominium project, *see* "CCRC's Lease-Hold Condo Status Offers Tax Savings for Buyers," *Multi-Housing News,* Mar. 1989, 31.

49. Rev. Proc. 89-3, 89-1 C.B. 761.

50. Former I.R.C. §1034. *See also* Rev. Ruls. 64-31, 1964-1 C.B. 300 and 85-132, 1985-2 C.B. 182 regarding eligibility of condominiums for Section 1034 treatment. *But see* §7.1(c)(5) regarding issues concerning leasehold condominiums and cooperatives.

51. I.R.C. §§2001, 2010.

52. The Taxpayer Relief Act of 1997 P.L. 105-34.

53. Former I.R.C. §121. Lesser ownership interests, such as life estates, are also eligible. Rev. Rul. 84-43, 1984-1 C.B. 27.

54. I.R.C. §§163, 164; Rev. Rul. 64-31, 1964-1 C.B. 300.

55. I.R.C. §262.

56. *See* I.R.C. §1014.

57. *See* I.R.C. §528(c)(2); Treas. Reg. §1.528-4(c).

58. I.R.C. §528(c)(1)(A)–(E). The IRS allowed a homeowners' association to revoke its election to be treated as a tax-exempt organization and to file the normal corporate return for the previous tax years, when the association's accountants never informed the association that it could file the corporate return and when the association acted in good faith. Priv. Ltr. Rul. 9315020.

59. Treas. Reg. §1.528-4(b).

60. I.R.C. §§528(b), (d).

61. 1972-1 C.B. 49.

62. 1974-1 C.B. 130.

63. 1974-1 C.B. 131.

64. 1980-1 C.B. 116.

65. I.R.C. §501(c)(7).

66. Treas. Reg. §1.501(c)(7)-1(a).

67. Treas. Reg. §1.501(c)(7)-1(b).

68. 1964-1 C.B. 182.

69. 1969-1 C.B. 155.

70. 1975-2 C.B. 214.

71. Rev. Rul. 70-604, 1970-2 C.B. 9.

72. Rev. Ruls. 74-563, 1974-2 C.B. 38; 75-370, 1975-2 C.B. 25; 75-371, 1975-2 C.B. 52.

73. *See* discussion in Chapter 24.

74. *See, e.g.,* Kazlow and Schrager, "Cooperative, Condominium Ownership Compared," *The National Law Journal,* June 16, 1980, 19, and discussion, §7.1(c)(3).

75. *See* Rohan and Reskin, note 3 *above,* at §10.03(2).

76. Kazlow and Schrager, note 73 *above.*

77. *Id.,* discussing New York law requiring existing blanket mortgages to be paid off in a condominium conversion.

78. *See generally Housing & Development Reporter,* note 2 *above,* at 20:0028.

79. *See* Priv. Ltr. Rul. 9035075.

80. I.R.C. §216(a).

81. I.R.C. §216(b)(3)(B).

82. Rev. Rul. 55-316, 1955-1 C.B. 312.

83. Priv. Ltr. Rul. 8517006.

84. 1968-2 C.B. 112.

85. 1962-2 C.B. 89.

86. 1962-2 C.B. 91.

87. Rev. Rul. 69-76, 1969-1 C.B. 56.

88. Treas. Reg. §1.1034-1(c)(3)(i). Before the Tax Act of 1997, many capital gain issues for "principal residences" were decided in the context of former Section 1034.

89. *See, e.g.,* Rev. Ruls. 85-132, 1985-2 C.B. 182; 64-31, 1964-1 C.B. 300; 60-76, 1960-1 C.B. 296.

90. 1960-1 C.B. 296.

91. Rev. Rul. 55-316, 1955-1 C.B. 312; Priv. Ltr. Rul. 8034068.

92. *See* Rev. Ruls. 74-241, 1974-1 C.B. 68; 85-147, 1985-2 C.B. 86.

93. I.R.C. §121.

94. *See* Treas. Reg. §1.121-3(a).

95. 305 F.2d 814 (4th Cir. 1962).

96. *See* Treas. Reg. §1.528-1(a).

97. Mar. 20, 1978.

98. Application of Pacific Lifecare, granted June 22, 1993. *See* discussion in §§7.2(d) and 9.3.

99. *Eckstein v. United States,* 452 F.2d 1036 (Ct. Cl. 1971).

100. *Concord Village, Inc.,* 65 T.C. 142, 157 (1975).

101. *Ibid.*

102. *Id.* at 162.

103. Rev. Rul. 79-137, 1979-1 C.B. 118. *But see* Priv. Ltr. Rul. 9039011 where insurance premium payments collected by the cooperative and then remitted to the insurance carrier were not deemed income to the cooperative.

104. Rev. Rul. 90-36, 1990-1 C.B. 59.

105. For a review of membership legal issues, see Gordon, P., J. Goldman, and P. Kaufmann, "Membership Formats for Retirement Facilities," *The Spectrum,* Nov. 1990, 19.

106. *See* discussion in Chapter 24.

107. 614 F.2d 670 (9th Cir. 1980).

108. *Id.* at 675.

109. *Ibid.*

110. *Id.* at 676, citing *Lake Forest, Inc.,* 36 T.C. 510 (1961), *rev'd., other grounds,* 305 F.2d 814 (4th Cir. 1962); and *Eckstein v. U.S.,* 452 F.2d 1036, 1048 (Ct. Cl. 1971). In *Eckstein,* it was noted that cooperatives are viewed as pass-through organizations by the IRS, allowing shareholders to deduct mortgage interest expenses and property taxes.

111. *See,* e.g., *Affiliated Government Employees' Dist. Co. v. Commissioner,* 322 F.2d 872 (9th Cir. 1963), *cert. den.,* 376 U.S. 950; *Oakland Hills Country Club,* 74 T.C. 35 (1980).

112. *See* §6.1(c)(2).

113. *See* §§7.1(d)(1) and 7.2(b)(2).

114. *Hunt v. Commissioner,* 47 B.T.A. 829 (1942).

115. Treas. Reg. §1.263(a)-2(e).

116. *See* Rev. Rul. 83-51, 1983-1 C.B. 48.

117. Rev. Rul. 84-43, 1984-1 C.B. 27.

118. Rev. Rul. 55-37, 1955-1 C.B. 347.

Eastern Park Apartments; San Francisco, California.

8 Rentals

§8.1 Business Issues

Rental retirement facilities have the advantages of being easy to understand and market in comparison with entrance fee structures, requiring relatively small commitments of consumer capital compared with entrance fee or equity models, being relatively easy for the consumer to leave without penalty, having fewer problems of owner flexibility and control concerning program content or transferability of units, generally not being subject to continuing-care laws or securities registration, and having HUD financing or loan insurance programs more readily available to them. A major advantage of rental facilities is that residents may choose to invest their accumulated home equity or other assets in whatever manner they choose rather than spending a large sum as an entrance fee or for purchase of an equity interest in the retirement community. Despite the absence of tax advantages available to condominium and cooperative structures, a rental arrangement still may be more profitable to the resident if the proceeds of the sale of a previous residence are sheltered from capital gains tax and placed in an investment whose return is expected to be substantially higher than the appreciation potential of an equity interest in the retirement facility.

Among the disadvantages of a rental facility are the absence of a long-term commitment by either party, which could result in, first, the unavailability of shelter and health care or other services when most needed by the elderly resident and, second, greater fluctuations in occupancy levels for the owner; the inability of the developer to tap the home equity of seniors as they sell their single-family residences; and the unavailability of resident tax benefits, such as real property tax and mortgage interest deductions, carryover of gain on the sale of a principal residence, and deductions for prepaid medical expenses. For a comparison of the advantages and disadvantages of rental and other business structures, see table on page 90.

By definition inherent in a rental structure, the absence of a long-term service commitment to the resident can be mitigated somewhat by the offer of long-term-care insurance as a benefit of facility residence. Premiums for the insurance can be paid as a supplemental monthly charge, and the insurance might be made transportable in the event that the resident leaves the rental facility. Coverage might be available at reduced rates due to the availability of group marketing to facility residents (see §27.2 generally regarding long-term-care insurance).

There are also ways in which a developer might preserve the home equity of residents for future use as rental payments. For example, a resident might place a lump sum of money into a trust that is used to make rental payments out of principal and income. It is important to note, however, that such a trust may be considered a "grantor trust" in the event that the resident has the right to have the principal refunded when he or she leaves the facility (see discussion in §6.1(b)(5)).

A word of caution is in order concerning the form or duration of rental agreements and their impact on licensing issues. Most continuing-care statutes regulate care that is promised for more than a year (see §21.1). Many rental agreements in facilities offering assisted living or health care may inadvertently fall within the "more-than-one-year" criterion of a continuing-care statute if the resident has the option to renew the agreement for a period greater than one year or the agreement renews automatically absent the presence of good cause for the operator to terminate the contract. To avoid a contract of more than a year and its possible regulatory consequences, a contract should be renewable beyond 12 months only at the discretion of the provider.

The passage of the Tax Reform Act of 1986 eliminated the once-favorable tax treatment given to rental housing investment. Nevertheless, rental retirement housing is considered by some to offer excellent investment potential.[1] Rental housing for low-income tenants may also be eligible for tax credits (see §19.8) and various forms of federal financing (see Chapter 14).

§8.2 Treatment of Investors under the Tax Reform Act of 1986

(a) Passive Loss Rules

Residential rental housing was one of the enterprises most dramatically affected by the Tax Reform Act of 1986.[2] Under the act, losses incurred by individuals, certain closely held corporations, and certain personal service corporations from "passive activities," which consist of any business in which the taxpayer "does not materially participate," may be deducted only to the extent income is received from other passive activities.[3] Thus, except for one circumstance described below, such losses cannot be offset against income from wages, investment portfolios, or active businesses but instead must be carried into future years until they can be offset against passive income. Passive activities expressly include "any rental activity,"[4] which is further defined as activities "where payments are principally for the use of tangible property."[5]

A limited exemption from the passive loss rules applies only to persons who "actively" or "materially" participate in rental real estate activities. As originally enacted, the law provided that if such persons had an adjusted gross income of $100,000 or less, they could offset nonpassive income with up to $25,000 of tax deductions or credits from such active real estate interests.[6] However, the $25,000 exemption was reduced by 50 percent of every dollar of the taxpayer's adjusted gross income over $100,000 so that a person earning $150,000 or more receives no exemption.[7] If the taxpayer sought exemption as a tax credit for certain low-income housing projects,[8] the phaseout did not commence until the taxpayer's income exceeded $200,000.

Congress liberalized the passive loss rules with passage of the Revenue Reconciliation Act of 1993, enacted as part of the Omnibus Budget Reconciliation Act of 1993.[9] Effective for taxable years beginning January 1, 1994, and later, the new law removed the $25,000 limit on deductions by taxpayers who materially participate in rental real estate activities, provided they devote more than half their personal services (and more than 750 hours) in the taxable year to real property trades or businesses in which they materially participate. Personal services performed as an employee are not included in this calculation unless the employee owns more than a 5 percent interest in the employer. A closely held C corporation meets the material participation standard if more than 50 percent of its gross receipts for the taxable year are derived from real property trades or businesses in which it materially participates.[10] The reform was funded, in part, by increasing the depreciation period for nonresidential real property from 31.5 to 39 years.[11] The new law generally affects property placed in service after May 12, 1993 (see §8.3 regarding other 1993 tax reforms affecting real estate investments).

The passive loss rules raise some fundamental issues when applied to the seniors' housing field. If, for example, rental retirement facilities offer a sufficiently high proportion of services, can they avoid the rules altogether on the grounds that payments are not "principally for tangible property" but rather for services? Or does service component income need to be separated from rental income? The Senate report for the 1986 act notes that certain short-term rental activities with heavy user turnover and a significant service component (e.g., a hotel) should not be covered by the passive loss rules.[12] The report also mentions, as another factor indicating an activity that should not be treated as a rental activity, circumstances where "the expenses of day-to-day operations are not insignificant in relation to rents produced by the property, or in relation to the amount of depreciation and the cost of carrying the rental property."[13] Rental retirement facilities generally do not meet the short-term occupancy criterion that would exempt hotels, but they may qualify for the alternative exemption if daily operating expenses (e.g., staffing costs, food and medical supplies) are significant when compared with depreciation, debt service, taxes, insurance, and other costs related to pure real property ownership.

In addition, where "extraordinary personal services" are provided by or on behalf of the owner of the property in connection with making the property available for use by customers, the activity is not considered a rental activity without regard to the average period of customer use.[14] Extraordinary personal services are those:

> . . . [p]rovided in connection with making property available for use by customers only if the services provided in connection with the uses of the property are performed by individuals, and the use by customers of the property is incidental to their receipt of such services. For example, the use by patients of a hospital's boarding facilities generally is incidental to their receipt of the personal services provided by the hospital's medical and nursing staff. Similarly, the use by students of a boarding school's dormitories generally is incidental to their receipt of the personal services provided by the school's teaching staff.

In Technical Advice Memorandum 9247003, the IRS applied the rules regarding extraordinary personal services to retirement centers and found that their management constitutes trade or business undertakings and not rental activities for purposes of the passive activity rules. In the memorandum, each retirement center was owned by a separate limited partnership in which several of the management company's employees were general partners. In exchange for a monthly fee, each retirement center provided residents with three mandatory meals per day, tray service to the resident's apartment, weekly maid service, weekly laundry service, personal laundry facilities, all utilities, on- and off-site recreational activities, transportation services, an emergency intercom system in each apartment, and half-kitchens. The monthly fees were more than twice the cost of renting a luxury apartment in the same area. Based on these facts, the IRS National Office concluded that the gross income attributable to operation of the retirement centers represented amounts paid principally for services provided rather than for the use of tangible property. Thus, under Section 1.469–1T(e)(3)(i) of the Temporary Regulations, the activity constituted a trade or business.

This Technical Advice Memorandum bodes well for full-service retirement communities. Where a retirement community can demonstrate that more than half of its monthly fee income is attributable to services provided to residents, it should be able to establish that operation of the retirement community is an active trade or business, not a passive rental activity.

Even if the project is *not* characterized as rental property (generally deemed passive), investors still must materially participate in the retirement facility activity to avoid general application of the passive loss rules.[15] In other words, the taxpayer's involvement must be regular, continuous, and substantial.[16]

The temporary regulations define "material participation" of an individual to include the following:

- participation of more than 500 hours during the taxable year;
- where the individual's participation constitutes substantially all of the participation in the activity of all individuals involved during the year;
- more than 100 hours of activity, with no other individual participating to a greater degree;
- a significant participation activity (at least 100 hours and other requirements), with the individual's aggregate participation in all significant participation activities exceeding 500 hours;
- the individual's material participation in the activity for any five of the previous ten years;
- a personal service activity (such as health or another trade or business in which capital is not a material income-producing factor), with the individual materially participating in the activity for any three years preceding the taxable year; or

- individual participation on a regular, continuous, and substantial basis based on all the facts and circumstances.[17]

Limited partners can be considered to participate materially only if they meet the 500-hour test, the five-of-the-past-ten-years test, or the three-year personal service activity test.[18]

It is important to note that the passive activity loss rules applied specifically to rental real estate activities impose a higher "material participation" standard by requiring the taxpayer to devote more than 750 hours and more than one-half of his or her personal services to real property activities in which he or she materially participates.[19]

Regulations pertaining to the aggregation of passive and nonpassive activities were adopted in 1994.[20] The highlights of these regulations include the following:

- Whether activities may be treated as a single activity for purposes of the passive activity loss rules depends on the relevant facts and circumstances. Facts and circumstances accorded the greatest weight include similarities and differences in types of businesses, the extent of common control, the extent of common ownership, geographic location, and interdependencies between activities.[21]
- A rental activity may not be grouped with a nonrental trade or business unless the activities constitute an appropriate economic unit and the rental activities are insubstantial in relationship to the trade or business, the trade or business is insubstantial in relationship to the rental activity, or each owner of the trade or business has the same proportionate ownership interest in the rental activity, in which event the portion of the rental activity that involves the rental of items of property for use in the trade or business activity may be grouped with the trade or business activity.[22]
- An activity involving the rental of real property and an activity involving the rental of personal property may not be treated as a single activity unless the personal property is provided in connection with the real property or vice versa.[23]
- The IRS may regroup a taxpayer's activities if a principal purpose of the grouping of activities

(or failure to group) is to circumvent the passive activity loss rules.[24] These regulations generally apply to tax years ending after May 10, 1992.[25]

In 1995, the IRS issued final regulations under Section 469(c)(7) that interpret the material participation rules.[26] These regulations made the following clarifications:

- If the taxpayer elects to treat all interests in rental real estate as a single activity and at least one of the interests is held as a limited-partnership interest, the combined activity will be deemed a limited-partnership interest for purposes of determining material participation. This restriction will not apply if the taxpayer's limited-partnership interests provide less than 10 percent of the gross rental income from all of the taxpayer's rental real estate interests.
- A taxpayer may change his or her election to treat all rental real estate interests as a single activity in future tax years if there is a material change in facts and circumstances. The fact that an aggregation election may be less advantageous to the taxpayer is not in itself a material change.
- Interests in rental real estate as a rule cannot be combined with other trades or businesses in a single activity (for example, a taxpayer may not combine rental real estate, construction, and development activities). Thus, only the taxpayer's rental real estate activities may be used to determine whether the taxpayer materially participated in rental real estate activities.
- If a taxpayer holds at least a 50 percent interest in the capital, profits, or losses of a pass-through entity in a taxable year, each rental real estate interest held by the entity will be deemed a separate interest of the taxpayer irrespective of the entity's grouping of activities. The taxpayer may, however, elect to treat all his or her rental real estate interests as one activity.
- Management activity will be taken into account for purposes of the material participation test for rental real estate only to the extent that the work is performed in connection with the taxpayer's own real property.

The regulations are effective for tax years beginning after 1994 and for elections made with returns filed after 1995.[27]

In 1994, the Internal Revenue Service issued a *Market Segment Specialization Program Guide for Passive Activity Losses.* This 200-page guide instructs IRS personnel in how to spot potential passive activity loss issues and focuses on "problem areas" such as net leases and work performed as an investor under the material participation test. Because it is based on the tax law as it existed before the Revenue Reconciliation Act of 1993 and generally does not reflect the material participation rules described in this section, the guide is of limited utility.[28]

In 1996, the IRS revised the *Market Segment Specialization Program Guide* to reflect changes in Internal Revenue Code Section 469 and the regulations promulgated through June 1995. Among other things, the guide recites audit techniques to be used to challenge a taxpayer's self-characterization as a real estate professional. Although the guide cannot be cited as precedent, it provides valuable insight into the IRS's thinking and auditors' likely enforcement focus and is likely to set the industry standard.[29]

(b) At-Risk Rules

At-risk rules limit the amount an individual or closely held corporation can deduct for a particular activity in any tax year to the amount of the taxpayer's risk for that activity.[30] Before the Tax Reform Act of 1986, real property was exempt from the at-risk rules,[31] permitting real estate limited partners to take deductions in amounts greater than the total of their investment at risk in the enterprise. The 1986 act eliminated the real estate exemption but added a new rule that should neutralize the impact of the law for most conventionally financed facilities.[32]

Under the current code, the taxpayer's share of qualified nonrecourse financing for a project is considered at risk. Eligible financing is that which is borrowed with respect to holding real property, made by a qualified person such as a bank or savings and loan, or made or insured by a government entity, for which no person is individually liable and which is not convertible.[33]

For retirement communities with conventional nonrecourse loans, inclusion of the loaned amount as an amount at risk permits the investor to take a pro rata share deduction up to the project value, even though the community was built or purchased with borrowed funds. However, if the property is seller-financed or financed directly by residential deposits and entrance fees, it is unlikely that the nonrecourse financing exception applies.[34]

(c) Conclusion

The passive loss and at-risk rules certainly pose some serious impediments to those seeking to use limited-partnership syndications as tax shelters for investors' employment income or portfolio interest or dividends. The rules should, however, cause little concern if investors have other passive investment income against which to offset losses, the project does not generate significant losses but is entered into for economic value, or investors participate in project operations. Moreover, corporate investors are unaffected. Retirement communities should be well suited to attracting investors seeking value rather than tax shelter.

§8.3 Real Estate Reforms under the Revenue Reconciliation Act of 1993

The Revenue Reconciliation Act of 1993[35] introduced a number of reforms intended to stimulate real estate investment by both tax-exempt organizations and proprietary developers. These reforms include the following:

- liberalization of the passive activity loss rules to enable material participants in rental real estate activities to treat an unlimited portion of their rental real estate losses as nonpassive (see §8.2(a))[36];
- reinstatement and extension of the low-income housing tax credit (see §19.8)[37];
- relaxation of the definition of real estate investment trusts (REITs) to enable more pension trusts to qualify and enjoy REITs' favorable tax treatment[38];
- reinstatement and extension of the qualified mortgage bond program, which allows local governments to issue qualified mortgage bonds to finance the purchase, rehabilitation, or improve-

ment of single-family, owner-occupied residences within the issuer's jurisdiction[39];

- reinstatement and extension of the mortgage credit certificate program, under which local governments may issue, in lieu of qualified mortgage bonds, mortgage credit certificates that entitle homebuyers to tax credits equal to a percentage of the interest paid on their mortgage loans[40]; and
- an opportunity to defer recognition of income from the discharge of qualified real property business indebtedness.[41]

These reforms are funded in part by increasing the depreciation period for nonresidential real property from 31.5 years to 39 years for purposes of calculating the depreciation deduction.[42] This change, one of the few disincentives to real estate investment contained in the 1993 act, should not adversely affect retirement facilities that already qualify as residential real property. It is important to note, however, that certain service areas within retirement facilities may be deemed nonresidential real property.

The act also contains several specific incentives for tax-exempt entities to invest in or dispose of real property. These include relaxation of the following rules governing unrelated business taxable income (UBTI) (for a general discussion of UBTI, see §9.12):

- liberalization of the "dealer UBTI rule" to allow exempt organizations to exclude from UBTI gains and losses from the disposition of real property acquired from financially troubled financial institutions[43];
- clarification that loan commitment fees, gains, and losses from the lapse or termination of real estate options and gains and losses from the forfeiture of good faith deposits are all exempt from UBTI[44];
- elimination of the rule that treated all income from publicly traded partnerships as UBTI rather than considering the underlying character of the partnership income[45];
- relaxation of the rule that prohibited title-holding companies under Section 501(c)(2) or Section 501(c)(25) of the code from receiving any UBTI[46]; and
- relaxation of the UBTI rules affecting debt-financed real property investments by certain title-holding companies and pension and profit-sharing plans.[47]

By stimulating investment in and disposal of real property by proprietary developers and tax-exempt retirement facility operators, the 1993 act has helped ameliorate some of the negative effects of the Tax Reform Act of 1986 on real estate activities.

Notes

1. *See, e.g.,* Smith, "Syndication Topics: Rental Retirement Housing," 16 *Real Estate Rev.* 4 (Winter 1987), 10.

2. H.R. 3838, P.L. 99–514.

3. *See generally* I.R.C. §469. Regulations specify the manner in which "personal service corporations" and "closely held corporations" will be evaluated for purposes of determining if they materially participate in the activity for a given tax year. *See* Treas. Reg. §1.469–1T(g).

4. I.R.C. §469(c)(2).

5. I.R.C. §469(j)(8).

6. I.R.C. §469(i).

7. I.R.C. §469(i)(3)(A).

8. *See* discussion below.

9. H.R. 2264, Pub. L. No. 103–66, 107 Stat. 312.

10. I.R.C. §469(c)(7).

11. I.R.C. §168.

12. *See A Complete Guide to the Tax Reform Act of 1986* (Englewood Cliffs, NJ: Prentice-Hall, 1986), 4075.

13. *Ibid.*

14. Treas. Reg. §§1.469–1T(e)(3)(ii)(C), (e)(3)(v).

15. I.R.C. §469(c)(1).

16. I.R.C. §469(h)(1).

17. Treas. Reg. §§1.469–5T(a), (c), (d).

18. *See* Treas. Reg. §1.469–5T(e)(2). Note that the IRS has adopted final regulations for some of the passive activity rules. *See* 57 *Fed. Reg.* 20747, May 15, 1992.

19. I.R.C. §469(c)(7).

20. 59 *Fed. Reg.* 50485, Oct. 4, 1994.

21. Treas. Reg. §1.469–4(c)(2).

22. Treas. Reg. §1.469–4(d)(1).

23. Treas. Reg. §1.469–4(d)(2).

24. Treas. Reg. §1.469–4(f)(1).

25. Treas. Reg. §1.469–11(a)(1).

26. 60 *Fed. Reg.* 66496, Dec. 22, 1995.

27. 60 *Fed. Reg.* 66496, Dec. 22, 1995.

28. "Passive Activity Audit Guide Issued by IRS," *RIA Special Report,* May 5, 1994.

29. "Revised Audit Guide Reveals IRS Stance on PALs," *RIA Federal Tax Weekly Alert,* June 6, 1996.

30. I.R.C. §465(a)(1).

31. Former I.R.C. §465(c)(3)(D).

32. *See* Holtz and Brecht, "Tax Reform Will Hit Retirement Housing," *Retirement Housing Rep.* 1, No. 1, Sept. 1986, 12–15.

33. I.R.C. §465(b)(6).

34. *See generally* Holtz and Brecht, note 32 *above.*

35. H.R. 2264, Pub. L. No. 103–66, 107 Stat. 312.

36. RRA §13143; I.R.C. §469(c)(7).

37. RRA §13142; I.R.C. §42.

38. RRA §13149; I.R.C. §856(h).

39. RRA §13141; I.R.C. §25.

40. RRA §13149; I.R.C. §143.

41. RRA §13150; I.R.C. §§108, 1017.

42. RRA §13151; I.R.C. §168.

43. RRA §13147; I.R.C. §512(b).

44. RRA §13148; I.R.C. §512(b).

45. RRA §14145; I.R.C. §512.

46. RRA §14146; I.R.C. §§501(c)(2) and (c)(25).

47. RRA §13144; I.R.C. §514.

Pacific Regent–La Jolla; San Diego, California.

Part IV
Tax-Exempt Operation

The Cypress; Hilton Head Island, South Carolina.

9 Federal Tax Exemption

§9.1 In General

(a) Historical Background

Over the years, tax-exempt organizations have been responsible for developing a major share of the nation's retirement housing, especially in the heavily service-oriented sector (see §2.3). These facilities are largely owned by or affiliated with religious or fraternal organizations that qualify for exemption as public charities under Section 501(c)(3) of the Internal Revenue Code. Often, these organizations engage in a wide variety of activities that are charitable in nature and recognized as tax-exempt activities, such as furnishing health care in hospitals or nursing facilities. Generally speaking, however, the mere fact that such a tax-exempt organization may own and operate housing for the elderly does not make the ownership and operation of that housing a tax-exempt activity; therefore, income may be subject to taxation.

Historically, merely providing market-rate elderly housing, without care and services, has not been considered a tax-exempt activity, even if the owner or operator is already a tax-exempt charitable organization. While a tax exemption may be available when such housing is offered on a charitable basis or at below-market rates (see discussion in §9.4), not-for-profit operation of market-rate housing for the elderly does not in and of itself justify a tax exemption. Even seniors' housing composed of low- and moderate-income units is not necessarily eligible for tax exemption. Yet, if a developer follows certain guidelines set forth by the Internal Revenue Service, even a luxury facility for the elderly may qualify for exemption from income tax under Section 501(c)(3) of the code.

(b) Challenges to Exempt Organizations

For the past decade, Congress has expressed concern about the expansion of activities of tax-exempt, nonprofit organizations into areas traditionally the province of proprietary businesses.[1] Some of Congress's concerns include the following:

- the lack of established criteria defining what activities are "substantially related" to a charitable purpose;
- the lack of stringent standards for determining whether a subsidiary of a tax-exempt organization is a controlled organization;
- the exemption for passive investment income of Section 501(c)(4) social welfare organizations where the income is not expended for charitable purposes; and
- the shifting of deductions to a taxable entity in a taxable/tax-exempt partnership.[2]

Criticisms of exempt organizations have focused on the high volume of organization revenues, the increasing pressure on the federal budget, and the participation of exempt organizations in business activities in which tax-paying companies also are engaged.[3]

IRS scrutiny of tax-exempt hospitals has been particularly intense. In November 1991, the IRS chief counsel issued a general counsel memorandum in which the IRS concluded that certain hospital-physician joint ventures would result in per se private inurement. The memorandum also conditioned preservation of the hospital's tax exemption on compliance with the Medicare/Medicaid Fraud and Abuse Law and other federal laws[4] (see §12.1(b)(2)(G) for further discussion of the memorandum). In addition, in April 1992, the IRS released its new hospital audit guidelines, which were approximately ten times longer than the predecessor guidelines.[5] The guidelines instructed IRS auditors to condition continued exemption on compliance with federal laws, including the Medicare/Medicaid Fraud and Abuse Law and the COBRA antidumping laws.[6] In 1995, the IRS also issued a proposed revenue ruling that describes situations in which a hospital's physician recruitment practices might result in revocation of the hospital's tax exemption.[7] Moreover, the IRS listed physician recruitment activities and certain HMO activities among its 1995 priorities for tax regulations and other administrative guidance.[8]

For two reasons, such IRS scrutiny is relevant to retirement communities; first, these facilities may also recruit health providers and, second, CCRCs essentially function as HMOs for the elderly. In some states, the department of insurance governs retirement communities; in other states, retirement communities may even be expressly exempt from HMO laws (see §21.2). Furthermore, the IRS has frequently applied to tax-exempt homes for the aging several of the same legal principles that it has applied to exempt health care organizations.

In addition, health care reform bills proposed in 1994 by the House Ways and Means and Senate Finance committees would have required nonprofit health care facilities, as a condition of their tax exemption, to admit applicants without regard to whether they are covered by Medicaid or any other government insurance program.[9] Nonprofit health care facilities would have included nursing facilities. If either reform bill had passed with this provision intact or a comparable reform bill passes in the fu-

ture, facilities that fail to comply with this "first-come-first-served" rule could lose their federal exemptions or become subject to intermediate sanctions.[10]

Furthermore, Section 501(c)(4) social welfare organizations have come under increased scrutiny. For example, the U.S. Senate has conducted hearings challenging the tax exemption of the American Association of Retired Persons, which has engaged in significant amounts of lobbying. Moreover, the Senate voted in 1995 in favor of an amendment that would make Section 501(c)(4) organizations involved in lobbying ineligible for federal grants, awards, contracts, and loans.[11] Two bills that would have required hospitals to provide charity care as a condition of their tax exemption died with the retirements of their sponsors.[12]

One outgrowth of IRS concern over the expanded activities of exempt organizations has been the adoption of intermediate sanctions such as fines against tax-exempt organizations that violate the conditions of their Section 501(c)(3) status (see §9.15). Previously, revocation of exempt status was the only sanction available against public charities that violated the terms of their exemption. Because of the severity of the sanction of revocation, the IRS had been hesitant to employ it, particularly with respect to health care organizations.

At the same time, states have grown increasingly strict in granting tax exemption even to facilities that qualify under federal standards (see generally, Chapter 10). The culmination of these restrictive tests is Utah's requirement that exemption must be based on an annual finding that the organization's "gift to the community" (which may consist of a numeric calculation of below-cost or free services) exceeds the value of its property tax exemption (see §10.2). A survey by the American Association of Homes and Services for the Aging revealed that facilities for the aging in over half the states have had or expect to have their tax-exempt status challenged. Challenges by tax assessors have focused on nursing homes, CCRCs, housing providers, and assisted-living facilities.[13]

§9.2 Basic Tests for Tax Exemption

While Section 501(c) of the Internal Revenue Code sets forth numerous specific exemptions for various types of organizations, Section 501(c)(3), which deals generally with charitable organizations, is most relevant for those contemplating development of a seniors' housing facility. That section provides a basis for exemption for:

> Corporations, and any community chest, fund, or foundation, *organized and operated exclusively* for religious, *charitable,* scientific, testing for public safety, literary, or educational purposes, or to foster national or international amateur sports competition (but only if no part of its activities involve the provision of athletic facilities or equipment), or for the prevention of cruelty to children or animals, *no part of the net earnings of which inures to the benefit of any private shareholder or individual,* no substantial part of the activities of which is carrying on propaganda, or otherwise attempting, to influence legislation (except as otherwise provided in subsection (h)), and which does not participate in, or intervene in (including the publishing or distributing of statements), any political campaign on behalf of (or in opposition to) any candidate for public office. [Emphasis added.][14]

This section was amended to clarify that the organization shall not participate or intervene in any political campaign on behalf of *or in opposition to* any candidate for public office (Pub. L. No. 100–203, §10711(a)(2)).

(a) Organizational Test

To qualify as an exempt charitable organization under Section 501(c)(3), a corporation must be both organized and operated exclusively for a charitable purpose. The regulations explain that, to meet the organizational test, the corporate articles must limit the purposes of the organization to one or more exempt, charitable purposes and not empower it to engage, except to an insubstantial extent, in activities that do not further an exempt purpose.[15] The term *charitable* is used in its generally accepted legal sense and may include:

> [R]elief of the poor and distressed or of the underprivileged; *advancement of religion;* advancement of education or science; erection or maintenance of public buildings, monuments, or works; *lessening of the burdens of Government;* and *promotion of social welfare* by organizations designed to accomplish any of the above purposes, or (i) *to lessen neighborhood tensions;*

(ii) *to eliminate prejudice and discrimination;* (iii) to defend human and civil rights secured by law; or (iv) *to combat community deterioration* and juvenile delinquency. [Treas. Reg. §1.501(c)(3)–1(d)(2); emphasis added.]

As discussed more fully in the following sections, retirement communities may fit under one or more of the examples of charity, but beyond the matter of charitable purposes, the organization must be structured so that it is not expressly empowered to participate in any political campaign for a candidate or to devote more than an insubstantial part of its activities to attempting to influence legislation.[16] Finally, the organization's assets must be dedicated to an exempt purpose so that on dissolution, for example, the assets would go to another Section 501(c)(3) exempt organization or the government.[17]

(b) Operational Test

The first principal aspect of the operational test requires that the exempt organization engage primarily in activities that will accomplish the exempt purposes, provided that no more than an *insubstantial* portion of the activities can be other than in furtherance of the exempt purpose.[18] This apparently confusing test seems even less intelligible in light of the statute's requirement that operations must be *exclusively* for charitable purposes. However, it is important to note that the code looks to the exclusivity of the charitable *purpose* and not to whether the organization's *activities* are exclusively charitable.[19] Therefore, under the statutory language, it is possible for an organization with a purely charitable purpose to engage in activities that, standing alone, are not charitable endeavors but that are performed by the exempt organization solely to further its charitable purpose. The regulations further expand on this distinction by requiring only a primary devotion to charitable *activities,* although an all but insubstantial part of the total activities must further charitable *purposes.* This distinction may be of significance in analyses of retirement projects containing mixed uses such as low- and moderate-income units (see §9.5).

The second principal aspect of the operational test is called the "private inurement" test, which requires that no part of the *net* earnings of the organization benefit private shareholders or individuals.[20]

This requirement can have particular significance for retirement facility joint ventures or contract relationships involving taxable and nonprofit entities (see §§12.1(b), 12.1(d)). It may also be relevant in equity retirement facilities where residents can profit from the resale of their units; however, such profits do not usually derive from the earnings of the exempt operating organization (see §9.3(a)(3)). The tax-exempt status of a retirement facility is not jeopardized by the presence of residents on the board of directors, provided that they neither control nor dominate the board.[21]

In 1996, the president signed legislation authorizing a new IRS enforcement remedy against Sections 501(c)(3) and 501(c)(4) organizations that violate the private inurement proscription. The new law authorizes a two-tiered excise tax on all "excess benefit transactions" with "disqualified persons" (that is, persons in a position to exercise substantial influence over the organization's affairs, their family members, and entities, 35 percent or more of which are controlled by a disqualified person). The first-tier tax, payable by the disqualified person, is 25 percent of the excess benefit; the second-tier tax is 200 percent if the problem is not corrected within the taxable period. In addition, officers and directors who knowingly participate in an excess benefit transaction can be liable for up to $10,000 per transaction. The law affects all transactions entered into on or after September 14, 1995.[22]

§9.3 Home for the Aging Tax Exemption

(a) Revenue Ruling 72–124

In 1972, the Internal Revenue Service issued a landmark revenue ruling for the seniors' housing industry. Revenue Ruling 72–124[23] considered the application for exemption of a church-sponsored home providing housing and medical care for persons over age 65. Rather than serving poor persons, the home admitted only those who were able to pay the entrance fees and monthly fees charged by the facility. However, the facility used net earnings to provide services and set aside a limited amount as reserves for expansion or unforeseen expenses. Most impor-

tant, the home had a policy of maintaining in residence any person who subsequently became unable to pay the monthly charges.

The IRS distinguished earlier rulings that had based exemptions on below-cost charitable services[24] and concluded that the elderly experienced forms of nonfinancial distress that could be alleviated by means other than providing free or below-cost services. Citing the Older Americans Act of 1965,[25] the ruling declared that, if unmet, seniors' needs for housing, physical and mental health care, civic, cultural, and recreational activities, and an overall environment conducive to dignity and independence were also causes of elderly distress. The ruling concluded that a home for the aging qualifies for charitable tax-exempt status if it operates in a manner designed to satisfy three primary needs of retired persons: housing, health care, and financial security.

(1) Housing Element

Under Revenue Ruling 72–124, residential facilities must be specially designed for the elderly and meet some combination of their physical, emotional, recreational, social, religious, and similar needs. Revenue Ruling 79–18[26] later interpreted this standard to have been met when apartment units were constructed with fire-resistant materials and equipped with amenities such as indoor and outdoor recreation areas, skid-resistant floors, ramps, grab bars, wide doorways, 24-hour emergency call systems, and similar features. Presumably, a structure designed for general public use could not qualify under the ruling without some remodeling or special accommodation for the needs of the elderly.

The housing element of a retirement community clearly is provided when the owner or operator of a continuing-care facility makes a residence available to elderly persons on a rental or life-lease basis, as was the case in the home for the aging considered in Revenue Ruling 72–124. However, a facility in which residents purchase their units in fee simple may need to impose special restrictions in order to meet the housing element of the IRS's three-pronged test. The concern is that by turning ownership of the housing over to a resident, the facility developer and operator are arguably no longer providing the housing when that resident at some later date resells the unit to another person. Moreover, an IRS general counsel's memorandum has concluded that a facility selling condominium units in a life-care facility did not meet the financial security requirement of Revenue Ruling 72–124. Nonetheless, concern over the exempt organization's retaining control over the inventory of housing can be addressed by restrictive covenants and other limits on resident ownership (see §9.3(b)(3)).

Another situation that may pose a problem in meeting the housing test arises when the resident more clearly provides his or her own housing. For example, if a developer establishes a mobile home park for the elderly, with health care and other services available on the premises, but residents supply their own mobile home units on land leased from the developer and can remove them to another location, it is questionable whether the arrangement would meet the provision of the housing requirement of Revenue Ruling 72–124. Similarly, if a management company goes into an existing seniors' housing development, where residents already own their own homes, and begins to offer health care and service programs to those residents without controlling the housing, it is doubtful that the arrangement would meet the housing test.

In most circumstances, however, the housing element is probably the most easily satisfied of the three tests set forth in Revenue Ruling 72–124.

(2) Health Care Element

The second prong of Revenue Ruling 72–124 requires a retirement facility to provide directly "some form of health care, or in the alternative, maintain some continuing arrangement with other organizations, facilities, or health personnel, designed to maintain the physical, and if necessary, mental well-being of its residents." Many retirement communities directly provide skilled nursing or other health care to residents in facilities owned and operated by the same organization supplying the housing. However, it is sufficient for the facility to help its residents gain access to health care in the surrounding community by means of ongoing transfer agreements or other preferred relationships with hospitals or other related health care facilities already in the community. It also appears that an arrangement with a health maintenance organization or other form of prepaid plan for health care would qualify.

In Revenue Ruling 79–18, a seniors' housing facility's provision of 24-hour nonmedical emergency aid and referral as well as transportation for medical examinations and treatment were enough to satisfy the test. Some facilities that specifically exclude provision of mental health care from coverage under their health plans may run afoul of the literal language of Revenue Ruling 72–124 (see contract examples in Volume II, Chapter 2).

An unanswered question in the interpretation of Revenue Ruling 72–124 concerns application of the health care test to long-term-care insurance or other forms of health insurance.[27] If, for example, a facility operator obtains a group insurance policy with special provisions, coverages, and premiums geared to the particular needs of the individual retirement facility's population and arranges for premium payments as a part of the regular monthly fee, that developer truly is assisting the resident population in obtaining health care in a way that a mere health facility transfer agreement could not. Although an insurance policy is not an arrangement with a direct provider of health services, the insurer often has arrangements with preferred providers of health services. Thus, establishment of a group health insurance policy should qualify as a "continuous arrangement . . . designed to maintain the physical and . . . mental well-being of the residents." While the specific facts of Revenue Ruling 72–124 and its progeny have not dealt with the question of long-term-care insurance or the provision of similar benefits, the IRS should consider such services as satisfying the health care element of the home for the aging exemption in that the services can respond to the specific health care needs of the elderly at least as well as other methods already approved by the IRS.

(3) Financial Security Test

To qualify for the home for the aging tax exemption, a facility must provide for the financial security needs of its elderly residents. A facility may meet the financial security test by instituting a policy that permits residents to remain at the facility even though they may run out of funds and operating the facility at the lowest feasible cost.

(A) No-Eviction Policy. The first aspect of the financial security test of Revenue Ruling 72–124 requires facilities to put in place a policy that permits residents who exhaust their funds or otherwise become unable to pay their charges to remain at the facility.[28] The policy may be activated by drawing on reserve funds, contributions, federal or state assistance payments, or other sources. Revenue Ruling 79–18 slightly amplifies the financial security requirement by approving a plan that would retain residents unable to pay, but only to the extent the facility is able to do so. A facility need not place itself in financial jeopardy to adhere to its no-eviction policy.[29] The no-eviction policy may be informal and need not be set forth in the resident contract.[30] Of course, those who are able but refuse to pay or to abide by reasonable rules governing residence should be subject to eviction without jeopardizing the facility's exempt status.

One exception to the no-eviction policy standard of Revenue Ruling 72–124 is for "an organization that is *required* by reason of federal or state conditions imposed with respect to the terms of its financing agreements to devote its facilities to housing *only aged persons of low or moderate income* not exceeding specified levels *and* to recover operating costs from such residents." [Emphasis added.] Revenue Ruling 72–124 then cites Section 236 of the National Housing Act[31] as an example of a financing program with such requirements. Unfortunately, Section 236 financing is unavailable today, and other federal housing programs for the elderly currently in vogue, such as Sections 221(d) and 232, do not limit admissions solely to low- and moderate-income elderly persons. The exception is probably still applicable to Section 202/Section 8 elderly housing projects, for which limited federal funds are still available (see §14.4).

(B) Operation at Lowest Feasible Cost. Revenue Ruling 72–124 requires a facility to operate at the lowest feasible cost but does not prohibit the facility operator from generating excess income over expenditures. In fact, facilities are permitted to set aside reserve funds for the payment of indebtedness, for subsidization of residents unable to pay, for future contingencies and expenditures, and for expansion or improvement of the services or facility.[32] Operation at the lowest feasible cost does not preclude the creation of "lavish" facilities (see G.C.M. 37101, §9.3(a)(4)).

One situation that may create problems in meeting the lowest feasible cost test can occur when a charitable organization in another business, such as the operation of a hospital, establishes a retirement community as an expected profit center for the hospital. For example, a nonprofit hospital looking to expand its revenue base may desire to set up a nonprofit subsidiary to operate a seniors' housing community on land adjacent to the hospital. Normally, a nonprofit subsidiary could donate any net income to the nonprofit parent without jeopardizing the subsidiary's exempt status. If, however, a retirement facility corporation exempt from taxation pursuant to Revenue Ruling 72–124 were simply to make an unrestricted gift of surplus funds to a parent hospital corporation, the corporation's action would arguably run afoul of the criterion for operation at lowest feasible cost. Nonetheless, the seniors' community could use surplus funds to improve services to its residents and perhaps even to expand the hospital's health services or facilities that are devoted to the residents of the seniors' community. In at least one case, the IRS has apparently ignored the lowest feasible cost test and, after the setting aside of reasonable reserves, permitted net revenues to be distributed for the organization's related low-income housing activities.[33]

In situations where the resident receives an interest that can be resold at market value, the IRS has questioned whether the facilities are made available at the lowest feasible cost. For example, in the case of a condominium, cooperative, or membership arrangement wherein a resident is entitled to resell his or her interest at an appreciated market price, it can be argued that the purchaser is paying more than the lowest feasible cost. However, any money received by the selling resident goes to reduce his or her costs of gaining access to the facility's accommodations and services; furthermore, the purchasing resident will eventually have the same opportunity. Moreover, to the extent that the tax-exempt operating organization shares in a portion of the appreciation in value (through transfer fees), the proceeds can be applied to reduce operating expenses and the monthly fees charged to other residents. Finally, the tax savings to a resident from an equity purchase reduces the cost of admission (see §§7.1, 7.2). Overall, therefore, the system is designed to reduce the ultimate costs to the consumer without profit to any third party.

In at least one case, the IRS National Office indicated concern regarding the private benefit to resident-owners arising from their ability to realize gain from the resale of equity interests in a retirement community that otherwise complied with Revenue Ruling 72–124. Eventually, the IRS granted an exemption on the condition that residents' gains on unit resales be limited in accordance with an inflation-based index, that resale prices be monitored by the operator and reported annually to the IRS, and that the operator reserve the right to repurchase units to maintain affordability.[34]

Revenue Ruling 72–124 provides further that if there is doubt that the facility operates at the lowest feasible cost, the fact that it makes some units available at less than its usual charges for persons of more limited means constitutes additional evidence of meeting the test. The amount of entrance fees or monthly fees charged to residents is not per se determinative of whether the facility meets the lowest feasible cost test (see Revenue Ruling 64–231,[35] which provides that, for purposes of determining if a retirement facility's fees are below cost, entrance fees are to be amortized over the expected life of each resident; see, too, Private Letter Ruling 9225041, in which a retirement community requiring residents to surrender assets or fund a trust in an actuarially determined amount was found to qualify for exemption).

(4) Community Affordability

Although Revenue Ruling 72–124 is silent on the point, Revenue Ruling 79–18 mentions the setting of fees at a level within the financial reach of a significant segment of the community's elderly population. In addition, an IRS General Counsel Memorandum (GCM 37101, April 26, 1977) concluded that a facility may be lavish and populated by residents who are "better-off financially" if fees are set at a level permitting a significant portion of the elderly community to avail itself of the facility.

The community affordability standard has not been consistently identified as a part of the test of charitability set out in Revenue Ruling 72–124, although it has been referenced in Private Letter Rulings (e.g., 8722082 and 9214031) and discussed in more detail in Private Letter Ruling 9001036. There, the IRS followed Revenue Ruling 72–124 and determined that the tax-exempt status of a corporation that previously had developed only low-income housing would not be jeopardized by the development of a residential rental project for the elderly. The project consisted of independent-living units, assisted-living units, and skilled-nursing facilities with special physical features for the elderly. There was no entrance fee or endowment fee, and a significant percentage of the elderly in the project's community would be financially able to qualify for residency. The board had adopted a policy of maintaining in residence persons who subsequently become unable to pay the regular charges and of supporting other charitable activities through income generated in excess of the project's cost.

Importantly, the ruling states that the requirement that the organization's facilities be reasonably available to elderly members of the community is "implicit in Revenue Ruling 72–124"; therefore, a facility serving only an insignificant portion of the community's elderly may not be classified as a charity (for more on this test, see §9.3(b)(1)).

(b) Implementing Revenue Ruling 72–124

Revenue Ruling 72–124, particularly its no-eviction policy, seems so restrictive that it is easy to conclude that only traditional charities with a substantial base of endowments or public contributions can as a practical matter qualify for the exemption and embark on development of a facility. On the contrary, many such facilities are self-starting and self-sustaining and may eventually generate enough revenue to fund development of additional projects.

(1) Luxury Projects

Many nonprofit facilities that qualify for the home for the aging exemption can be and are structured as luxury seniors' communities. Nothing in Revenue Ruling 72–124 requires that nonprofit tax-exempt facilities be made available to elderly residents at below-market rates or that low- or middle-income residents be targeted to occupy the facility. Provided that such facilities meet the housing, health care, and financial security needs of the elderly residents they serve, tax-exempt retirement facilities may cater to middle- and upper-income clientele and provide the finest of services and accommodations. Facilities can even make some services available to the general public without treatment of the income as unrelated business taxable income.[36] Nonetheless, fees must be set at an affordable level for the particular community to be served by the facility (see §9.3(a)(4)). IRS General Counsel Memorandum 37101 states that "if the fees charged are so high that the facility is not reasonably available to the elderly in the community because *only an insignificant portion* of that group can afford to avail itself of the facility," then the benefit to the community is insufficient to warrant a tax exemption.

Affordability should be measured on the basis of community standards, which may reflect great asset wealth on the part of the elderly, particularly in areas where home values have risen dramatically over the past few decades (see §1.5). In other contexts, 8.3 to 20 percent of an activity or expenditure has been found to be significant for tax exemption purposes (see §9.12). In the retirement facility context, the IRS has found that a facility was affordable to a significant segment of the community when over one-half the population in the surrounding community could afford the facility's monthly service charges.[37] In another unpublished ruling, the IRS determined that a retirement facility was affordable to a significant segment of the surrounding community when over 38 percent of elderly persons in the facility's market area could afford the community's monthly fees.[38]

In establishing an affordable pricing structure, developers often gear entrance fees or purchase prices to the high equity values of prospective residents' homes and thus keep monthly fees low and in line with prospective residents' relatively more modest incomes. Tax savings inherent in certain equity structures or in prepaid medical plans should also figure into an affordability analysis.

In addition, programs that guarantee long-term health care by requiring well-to-do residents to set aside their assets and income for that purpose, rather than spend them on other things, can be said to be eligible for exemption because they relieve the "burden of government" to cover health care for elderly or indigent persons under the Medicare and Medicaid programs (see §§9.2(a), 26.1, 27.3).

While operation at lowest feasible cost and community affordability standards go hand-in-hand, fee structures that require higher upfront payments

(e.g., equity purchase or refundable fee) but result in possible tax benefits on admission and refunds on termination can satisfy both tests (see §§9.3(b)(3) and (4)). A facility providing residents with an interest that can be resold at market value may also raise an affordability issue. The exempt organization may need to retain the power to limit resale prices or exercise a repurchase option if prices rise to a level that is unaffordable to a significant segment of the population.

(2) Financial and Health Screening

For seniors' housing facilities that are tax-exempt and yet operate on a market-rate basis, a significant concern is whether residents will run out of funds, thus obligating the operator to provide for their food, shelter, and medical care for life without compensation. A further concern is that a person who is suffering or likely to suffer from a protracted, serious illness shortly after admission to the facility will substantially deplete reserves. To help reduce the risk of such large financial drains on the facility's operations, most providers require applicants to undergo a thorough financial and health status screening before their acceptance as residents. Financial screenings typically require a listing of all assets as well as a statement of retirement income. Usually, a review of tax returns is warranted. Many communities across the country, including nursing facilities, also have sought to obtain the agreement of an elderly person's family to guarantee payment of the charges incurred in caring for the relative residing in the facility. Indeed, elderly persons under consideration for admission are often closer to financial dependency than their sons or daughters. In those cases, the children are usually willing to execute a payment guarantee, although such activity can amount to criminal conduct if used with Medicaid patients and therefore must be handled with extreme caution (see §23.5(b)(2)).

In addition to a health questionnaire completed by the prospective resident, most facilities require a physical examination and report from the applicant's physician. However, health or functional ability questions must be carefully drafted or limited to avoid unlawful disability discrimination (see §23.3).

While these measures do not eliminate the risk of resident insolvency or illness, they help screen for the worst-case applicants. Most resident agreements provide that any misstatement in the financial or health questionnaire is grounds for automatic termination of the contract and dismissal (see Volume II, Chapter 5, for forms of such contract provisions). In reality, many facilities qualifying for federal exemption are able to prescreen residents sufficiently such that the volume of uncompensated residence and care given to residents is often inadequate to satisfy the stricter real property tax exemption standards imposed by many states (see generally Chapter 10).

(3) Maintaining Control over the Premises

Generally, those communities meeting the no-eviction test of Revenue Ruling 72–124 are continuing-care facilities, which are designed to care for all residents for life. They rely on entrance fees to help fund reserves for those who become unable to pay fees. However, monthly rental facilities may also be structured to meet the no-eviction criterion if rents are set high enough to create a reserve or reserves are available from contributions or are set aside from borrowed funds.[39] In both cases, the facility does not relinquish title to or control over the property to be occupied by the resident.

However, the IRS found in at least one case that retirement housing units offered to residents on a fee simple ownership basis could not qualify for exemption under Revenue Ruling 72–124. A 1986 General Counsel Memorandum[40] analyzed the requirements of Revenue Ruling 72–124 in connection with a life-care facility wherein residents purchased residential units as condominiums but were also required to purchase a full program of life-time medical care, meals, housekeeping, recreational and social programs, and related life-care services for an initial payment plus a monthly fee. Membership in the program was limited to those who met the nonprofit operator's admissions criteria while the organization retained a right of first refusal respecting any proposed resale of a unit. The organization had a policy of maintaining in residence those who became financially unable to pay ongoing charges. Sales of some of the units were financed by loans from third-party lenders, secured by mortgages on the units.

The IRS general counsel observed that when the housing was sold to residents, the endowment and monthly fees paid to the nonprofit operator for life-

time services could not guarantee the resident a continued right to housing. If the resident were to default on a loan secured by the condominium, the nonprofit operator would be powerless to prevent foreclosure and keep the resident in the community. Therefore, the general counsel concluded that the no-eviction criterion of the financial security test articulated in Revenue Ruling 72–124 could not be met.

A further issue raised by the IRS was that a fee simple sale would conflict with the community accessibility requirement[41] on the grounds that once the organization sold a unit, it lost control over pricing of the unit upon resale by the resident. The general counsel's concern, however, was not that the resale price might rise but rather that the organization could lose control over access to the community.

General Counsel Memorandum 39487 does not seem to pose insurmountable difficulties for a facility seeking to sell units to residents and still qualify for the home for the aging exemption. The concerns raised in the GCM could be met by leaving in the hands of the nonprofit organization control over facility access and any encumbrances on the resident's title. Thus, for example, deed covenants and restrictions could require cash-only sales or permit financing only by the organization or a controlled entity. In addition, all buyers of units could be required to be prequalified for residence by the organization (see generally §§7.1 and 7.2). Moreover, if a facility is affordable to a significant segment of the community when it is built, price increases on resales of units are likely to reflect real estate fluctuations in the community at large and not result in a loss of community access.

Nevertheless, in one exemption ruling, the IRS has conditioned the tax exemption of the operator of a retirement community operated as a stock cooperative on provisions intended to ensure the affordability of the project to future residents.[42] In addition, project documents prohibited independent third-party financing so that the resident could not be evicted by an unrelated third party. This ruling bodes well for facilities that offer equity interests in the form of memberships or condominiums, provided that operators are willing to impose certain limitations on resales and refinancing.

Similarly, the IRS in 1995 recognized the ability of a tax-exempt charitable organization to operate a condominium continuing-care retirement community, where the organization retained a right of first refusal to repurchase units when resale prices exceeded increases in the cost of living as measured by the Consumer Price Index and where the organization maintained a fund to exercise the right.[43]

(4) Endowment Funds; Resident Equity; and Refundable Fees

Many nonprofit communities establish endowment funds geared primarily to solicitation of contributions from residents. Most residents of retirement facilities feel that they are part of a community of friends and neighbors with whom they share a strong attachment. A property with such an atmosphere is a natural object of bequests in residents' wills. Such endowment funds may be used to care for those who run out of funds or to improve or expand facilities and services in the retirement community. The availability of endowment funds makes it easier to comply with the no-eviction requirement of Revenue Ruling 72–124. While facilities must exercise caution to prevent violation of the Medicaid fraud and abuse statute and related state laws (see §23.5(b)), relatives of residents may also be good prospects for contributions to an endowment fund (see also §9.13 regarding the tax deductibility of contributions).

Another method of creating standby reserves (in excess of those prudently reserved from entrance fees or monthly fees) is to require residents in a condominium, cooperative, or membership project to pledge their equity to cover their costs of care should a decline in their income make it impossible for them to continue paying monthly fees. In a refundable entrance fee project, the refund amount can also be spent down before the facility operator bears the cost of care of an indigent resident.

Private Letter Ruling 8722082 (March 3, 1987) deemed operation of a retirement facility a charitable activity under Section 501(c)(3) when the facility made units available for an initial occupancy fee, 75 percent of which would be returned to the resident or his or her estate after the unit was vacated. Financial statements submitted by the home indicated that the fee structure would allow the community to operate on an at-cost basis with a small reserve.

Of course, the home also met the other criteria of Revenue Ruling 72–124, such as financially assisting residents who ran out of funds and providing arrangements for medical help when needed.

(5) Charity Services

Many facilities comply with Revenue Ruling 72–124 by providing free or below-cost services to a substantial number of residents within the facility. Facilities that serve the middle- and upper-income population, however, tend to require all residents to pay market-rate fees, except in the rare case when a resident runs out of funds. These facilities have found it prudent, however, to engage in certain charitable services that may be directed to the outside community. An example is Meals on Wheels provided to the elderly urban poor from a facility's kitchens. Such services delivered in connection with a market-rate luxury facility may also be helpful in preserving tax-exemption benefits under state laws.

(6) Transfer to Related Facilities

As already noted, a facility's required policy of retaining in residence residents who run out of funds need not be absolute, but it must be enforced to the extent of the financial ability of the sponsor. One interesting application of this exception is discussed in IRS Private Letter Ruling 8117221. There, the organization planned to maintain in their apartments residents who could not continue to afford monthly fees, but only for so long as contingency funds and public contributions permitted. When funds ran out, the facility operator planned to transfer the nonpaying residents to the organization's adjacent nursing facility; in no event, would the operator turn out the nonpaying residents from that facility. The IRS found that the plan qualified for exemption by constituting a sufficient commitment to keep in residence those who became unable to pay.

By transferring a destitute resident to a controlled nursing facility, the exempt organization can at least take advantage of Medicaid reimbursement, which is not available for residence in an apartment.[44] Of course, the placement should be medically appropriate and not motivated solely by financial considerations, as was implied in the facts of Letter Ruling 8117221.

§9.4 Homes Operated at less Than Cost

When Revenue Ruling 72–124 was issued, it departed from precedential rulings that limited the privilege of tax-exempt status to retirement homes providing services at substantially below actual cost. Yet, the earlier rulings continue to represent an alternative route to exemption. For example, Revenue Ruling 61–72[45] considered whether a facility that did *not* provide free care and did *not* reduce the charges of those who became unable to pay could qualify for exemption. The organization offered its residents care and assistance as well as food and shelter and sought to serve elderly persons without the financial means to care for themselves adequately. It screened applicants to determine that they would be able to pay the charges but set charges at a level that resulted in operational expenses 35 percent higher than resident revenue. Gifts and contributions made up the difference.

Relying on rulings relating to hospital services, the Internal Revenue Service determined that free services are not necessary and that the organization is making a gift to a charitable class when it is dedicated to and does furnish care and housing to the aging who would otherwise be unable to provide it for themselves without hardship; it renders such services to all or a reasonable proportion of the residents below cost, to the extent it is financially able; and the services are of a type that minister to the needs and relief of distress of the aged.[46]

Three years later, in Revenue Ruling 64–231,[47] the IRS considered an argument that retirement home entrance or membership fees should not be considered in determining whether fees are set below cost. The rationale advanced by the home was that the entrance fee constitutes a capital contribution as distinguished from the costs of care. The IRS noted, however, that the payments were prerequisites to obtaining services at the facility, gave no ownership interest to residents, and were partially refundable in the event of contract cancellation. Therefore, they could not be considered a capital contribution but must be included in the determination of whether services were rendered at a level below actual cost.

In calculating the relationship of fees to costs, entrance fees are to be amortized over the actuarial life expectancy of each resident by using annuity tables appearing in federal regulations.

These rulings leave open the question of whether the capital contribution distinction can have validity under appropriate circumstances. For example, it seems possible that an arrangement involving the fee simple sale of a housing unit plus the provision of below-cost services could qualify for exemption under Revenue Rulings 61–72 and 64–231. This is of particular interest because of the IRS's difficulty with the concept of a fee simple sale qualifying for exemption under the more modern home for the aging criteria of Revenue Ruling 72–124 (see §9.3(b)(3)).

Private Letter Ruling 9009038 deemed operation of a seniors' lodging facility consistent with the charitable purposes of a tax-exempt organization when it provided housing, food, clothing, social support programs, and necessary medical services to indigent and homeless elderly persons free of charge.

§9.5 Low- and Moderate-Income Housing

While the provision of low- and moderate-income housing for the elderly is commonly thought of as a tax-exempt charitable activity, the availability of a broad exemption for such projects is unclear, and relevant IRS pronouncements do not disclose a single, unifying path to tax exemption. Low-income housing is not automatically charitable. When a low-income project gave admission preferences to employees of a particular proprietary organization, the IRS denied the exemption on the basis that the housing served a private rather than public interest.[48] It should be noted that low- and moderate-income housing units are not necessarily or commonly offered at below-cost rates. Nor are residents who run out of funds and fail to pay rent usually permitted to stay. Low- and moderate-income housing is therefore analyzed with the assumption that it does not meet the criteria set forth in Revenue Ruling 72–124 (see §9.3) or 61–72 (see §9.4).

(a) Revenue Ruling 70–585

Revenue Ruling 70–585[49] sets the tone for considering the tax-exempt status of low- and moderate-income housing projects. In it, the Internal Revenue Service reviews the Treasury Regulation[50] that defines *charitable* to include relief of the poor and distressed or of the underprivileged and the promotion of social welfare by organizations designed to lessen neighborhood tensions, eliminate prejudice and discrimination, or combat community deterioration. The Ruling then sets forth four illustrative scenarios and examines the charitability of each circumstance as follows:

- In the first example, an organization sells new and renovated homes to *low*-income families who qualify for loans under a federal housing program. The organization also provides financial aid to those unable to assemble the downpayment. The organization seeking exemption is funded through federal loans and public contributions.
- The second hypothetical case involves the sale of new units to *low- and moderate*-income persons, with preference given to racial and ethnic minority groups previously located in ghetto areas.
- The third case concerns an organization planning to rehabilitate a deteriorated area and rent apartment units at cost to *low- and moderate*-income families, with preference given to those already living in the area.
- The last example involves the rental of housing at cost to *moderate*-income families in a community with a shortage of affordable housing. Federal and state funds as well as public contributions finance the project.

According to the ruling, the first three situations result in a tax exemption because, respectively, they relieve the burdens of the low-income poor, help eliminate prejudice and discrimination and lessen neighborhood tensions, and combat community deterioration. It is not clear from the ruling whether moderate-income facilities meeting the social welfare test of the regulation must, for example, rent at cost or duplicate other factors set forth in the examples. The fourth project is not eligible for exemption because, even by serving moderate-income persons in need, it does not cater to the poor or serve the specific types of community social welfare purposes articulated in the regulation.

What is clear from Revenue Ruling 70–585 is that the fact that the organization qualifies for federal or state funding for housing programs does not make the activity tax-exempt; what constitutes service to the low-income (poor and distressed) population is to be determined on an individual case basis; moderate-income housing is charitable if combined with low-income housing *and* if a social welfare purpose such as elimination of neighborhood tension, prejudice, or community deterioration is met; and not-for-profit provision of needed moderate-income housing that may be otherwise unavailable through private sector initiative is not a charitable activity.

Thus, by studying the feasibility of housing rehabilitation, a demonstration program designed to aid low-income families living in deteriorating neighborhoods was deemed to serve a charitable purpose.[51] Similarly, provision of interest-free loans to low-income homeowners for the purpose of rehabilitation of a deteriorated neighborhood is charitable[52] (but see Revenue Ruling 77–3,[53] which held that an organization leasing housing to a city *at cost* for temporary free occupancy by displaced victims of fire did not engage in a charitable activity).

(b) Safe Harbor

In 1996, the IRS issued a revenue procedure for organizations seeking Section 501(c)(3) status as low-income housing providers.[54] The procedure does not change the exemption standards but simply expedites the application process by offering a safe harbor for low-income housing providers and condensing into one document relevant information on existing standards.

Under the safe harbor, an organization must establish that for each housing project, at least 75 percent of the units are occupied by residents who qualify as "low income" as defined by HUD. Although the low-income limit established by HUD is generally 80 percent of the area's median income, HUD may establish different limits based on conditions such as high housing costs. In addition, at least 20 percent of the units must be occupied by very-low-income residents (generally 50 percent of the area's median income), *or* at least 40 percent must be occupied by residents at or below 120 percent of the very-low-income limit (typically, 60 percent of the area's median income). Up to 25 percent of the units may be provided at market rates to tenants whose income exceeds the low-income limit. Local adjustment to all these items is permissible to reflect housing cost variations and family size. The limits mirror the occupancy restrictions contained in the laws governing low-income housing tax credits (see §19.8).

Residents who originally meet the income test can continue to be counted toward the income requirement, provided that their income does not exceed 140 percent of the applicable safe harbor income limit. Once a resident's income exceeds this limit, the organization has satisfied the safe harbor, provided that it rents the next comparable nonqualifying unit to a tenant who meets the same income limit.

The low-income occupancy requirement may be satisfied within a reasonable startup period for new construction and within one year or any longer period permitted by an applicable government program (for example, HUD) for existing projects that are acquired. Several other requirements apply. For example, the housing project must ensure affordability to low-income residents through the adoption of rent restrictions or other means. For home-ownership programs, the affordability criterion is ordinarily satisfied by the adoption of a mortgage policy that complies with government-imposed mortgage limits or otherwise makes the cost of purchasing a home affordable to low- and very-low-income residents. If a project consists of more than one building, the buildings must be situated on the same campus. If an organization might be eligible for tax exemption under either the low-income housing rules or another applicable revenue ruling, it cannot use a combination of low-income and elderly or disabled tenants to meet the 75 percent test.

To permit greater program flexibility, the revenue procedure states that an organization that fails to meet the safe harbor guidelines may still qualify for tax exemption by showing facts and circumstances, including the following that support such a determination:

- Substantially more than 40 percent of the residents have incomes at or below 60 percent of the area's median income.

- There is limited deviation from the safe harbor percentages.
- Rent and mortgage limits ensure the affordability of the project to very-low-income and low-income residents.
- The project participates in a government program designed to provide affordable housing.
- The project provides additional social services that are affordable to poor residents.
- The housing is operated through a community-based board of directors, particularly if the selection process demonstrates that community groups have input into the organization's operation.[55]
- An existing Section 501(c)(3) organization with at least five years' experience in providing low-income housing controls the project.
- The project accepts residents with unusual burdens, such as high medical costs, whose financial condition is similar to that of low-income residents notwithstanding the fact that their income is greater than that of low-income residents.
- The project participates in a program to provide families that otherwise could not afford to buy decent and safe housing with an opportunity to own a home.
- The covenants and restrictions running with the land include affordability covenants.

Furthermore, even if it does not satisfy the numeric standards for relief of the poor and distressed, an organization may qualify for exemption under Section 501(c)(3) by providing housing in a manner that accomplishes any of the purposes recognized under Section 501(c)(3), including, without limitation, combating community deterioration, lessening the burdens of government, eliminating discrimination, reducing neighborhood tensions, and relieving distresses of the elderly or physically handicapped. (This aspect of the revenue procedure merely restates grounds for exemption already recognized under Revenue Rulings 70-585, 85-1, 85-2, 68-17, 68-655, 72-124, 79-18, and 79-19 and other rulings.)[56]

Finally, an organization that satisfies the requirements of this revenue procedure might still fail to qualify for Section 501(c)(3) status if the organization promotes the private interests of individuals with a financial stake in the project. Therefore, the IRS carefully scrutinizes the involvement of any private developer or a management company to prevent impermissible private inurement or private benefit from property sales, development fees, or management contracts.

The IRS projects that as a result of the safe harbor procedure, the average processing time for low-income housing organizations' applications for exemption will be reduced from one year to 45 days. The service reports that it receives roughly 1,000 applications per year from housing organizations.[57]

(c) Hybrid Projects

Revenue Ruling 70–585 presents a major problem for the hybrid low- and moderate-income elderly housing projects typically encountered in the marketplace. Often, facilities with HUD insurance programs such as Section 202 (see §22.4(a)) or those seeking to qualify for the low-income housing tax credit (see §8.3) reserve only 20 to 40 percent of their units for low-income occupancy. The remainder may be rented at market rates for moderate-income or even higher-income use. Unless such projects meet the safe harbor, are part of a community redevelopment plan, or can demonstrate aggressive minority group outreach, Revenue Ruling 70–585 on its face appears to be an obstacle to tax exemption.

(1) Elderly Distress

An argument can be made that the moderate-income elderly, though not poor, are "distressed" and accordingly fit the language of the regulation defining charitable activities. Revenue Ruling 70–585 dealt with moderate-income housing in general, not projects for the elderly. Indeed, that the nonpoor elderly may be "distressed" is a basis for the home for the aging tax exemption.[58] Unfortunately, the applicable revenue rulings set out the precise kinds of distress to which the elderly are susceptible and the specific steps that must be taken to relieve that distress, such as the arrangement for health care, operation at lowest feasible cost, and retention in residence of those who run out of funds.[59] The requirement of Revenue Ruling 72–124 that a facility retain in residence those unable to pay does not apply to facilities required to serve only low- and moderate-income elderly pursuant to federal financing restrictions, although this exception is of limited use.[60] The

elderly-as-distressed argument is therefore of little comfort for low- and moderate-income projects that do not independently meet the criteria of Revenue Ruling 72–124.

It is no surprise, therefore, that in *American Science Foundation v. Commissioner*[61] a corporation established to sponsor "cooperative, active retirement homes," to "demonstrate model and advanced concepts in urban living, to promote improvements in the quality of life and health of the occupants of such projects," and to "drastically reduce the cost of housing" was denied tax-exempt status. The court noted that there was no minimum age requirement for admission and no procedure for dealing with those who may become unable to maintain their financial commitment to the cooperative. The petitioner was found to have failed to distinguish the proposed housing cooperative from any other commercially developed cooperative.

(2) Low-Income Presence; Low-Income Purpose

Though difficult, it is still possible under Revenue Ruling 70–585 that the presence of a low-income component in a project could trigger an exemption even though the project also contains moderate-income units. Letter rulings granting exemption to combined low- and moderate-income housing projects do not appear to rely on the presence of the low-income housing component as a basis for exemption. In Letter Ruling 7823072, for example, where the project was designed for 25 percent low-income, 55 percent moderate-income elderly or handicapped, and 20 percent moderate-income families, the IRS found a charitable purpose but focused almost exclusively on the fact that the project was undertaken by a redevelopment authority to "combat community deterioration."[62] The existence of a substantial low-income component or of a senior/handicapped setaside for the majority of units did not ostensibly enter into the government's analysis. However, less than half the units in that example were intended for low-income occupancy.

It is theoretically possible that a project making less than all its units available for low-income residents can qualify for tax exemption on the basis of relief of the poor without independently meeting one of the social welfare tests, the home for the aging exemption, or some other separate basis for exemption. The fact that Section 501(c)(3) requires the organization seeking exemption to pursue a charitable purpose "exclusively" does not necessarily mean that all its activities must be charitable. As discussed in §9.2(b), it is possible to engage in a hybrid exempt and nonexempt activity that is exclusively charitable in its ultimate purpose. The regulations[63] merely require the organization's *primary activity* to be charitable, provided that all but an insubstantial portion of the total activities serves the charitable purpose. Therefore, a housing project with more than 50 percent low-income units arguably could qualify for exemption if it can demonstrate that the exclusive purpose of providing the other, non-low-income units is charitable; that is, the market-rate units are economically necessary to support the development and ongoing provision of the low-income units. It is possible but more difficult to apply this reasoning to projects with a majority of moderate-income or other noncharitable units, where the sole purpose of the units is to make possible the provision of a lesser proportion of low-income facilities.

In Private Letter Ruling 8801067 (October 19, 1987), the IRS considered the tax-exempt status of a rental housing project for the elderly, handicapped, poor, and qualified minorities. The enterprise would acquire and rehabilitate housing for such individuals at monthly rents sufficient only to pay debt service plus costs incurred in maintaining the property. Individual rents would be based on tenants' ability to pay, and elderly and handicapped persons would be maintained even if they became unable to pay rent. Residents would include "low-income individuals" (income less than 80 percent of the area median) and "very-low-income individuals" (less than 50 percent of area median income).

Citing Revenue Ruling 70–585, the IRS found that the activity would not jeopardize the organization's tax-exempt status. Although some housing might be provided to moderate-income residents, the primary purpose of the housing was to aid low-income persons. In addition, the project was formed to promote racial integration in housing. The ruling also considered that charges were to be maintained at the lowest feasible cost and that special adaptations for the needs of handicapped and elderly were provided. The ruling warned, however, that the program must continue to comply with situation three of Revenue Ruling 70–585 (combating community deterioration) and that rentals to moderate-income persons in excess of those reasonably necessary to fulfill the conditions in the revenue ruling would constitute an unrelated trade or business.

§9.6 Health Facilities and Health Insurance

(a) Health Facilities

Despite no specific reference to it in the Internal Revenue Code or Treasury Regulations, the promotion of health has come to be recognized as a charitable purpose under Section 501(c)(3).[64] Most of the legal authority for this exemption has evolved in the context of hospitals.

As was the case with retirement communities, early Internal Revenue Service rulings required that exempt hospitals furnish free or below-cost care.[65] This position changed in 1969, when it was recognized that promotion of health, even for private-pay or insured patients, was inherently charitable, provided that care was available to the community at large through, for example, an emergency room open to all.[66] Of course, exempt health care facilities must serve a public purpose and cannot benefit private interests.[67]

Even hospitals without emergency rooms have been found to be exempt when they had a community board of directors, an open medical staff policy, patients who pay their bills with the aid of government programs such as Medicare and Medicaid, and the application of surplus funds to the improvement of facilities, care, education, and research.[68] "Integrated delivery systems" combining hospital and physician services and "joint operating agreements" between hospitals and clinics likewise have been granted tax exemption.[69]

Health care facilities have come under a great deal of pressure to require greater levels of uncompensated care or care to indigent persons in order to maintain their tax-exempt status. A 1990 General Accounting Office report[70] concluded that many nonprofit hospitals are not doing their fair share of providing uncompensated care, that many hospitals' potential tax liability exceeds the level of uncompensated care they provide, and that the strategic goals of some tax-exempt hospitals do not focus on the health needs of the poor or underserved members of the community. The GAO recommended that Congress consider revising the criteria for tax exemption by directly linking exemption to free care to the poor, efforts to improve the health status of underserved portions of the community, or a certain level of care provided to Medicaid patients. For a discussion of maintenance of exempt status in the context of health care joint ventures, see §12.2.

Not only hospitals are entitled to exemption. In 1972, the Internal Revenue Service ruled that a home health organization providing professional nursing and therapeutic services primarily to elderly persons in their homes, pursuant to a physician-prescribed course of treatment, promotes health and is eligible for exemption.[71] Skilled-nursing facilities also appear to be routinely granted exemptions.[72] Assisted living has also recently been recognized as an exempt activity.[73] In addition, the delivery of physical therapy, occupational therapy, speech therapy, injury prevention, and pediatric and adult daycare services by a nursing facility has been deemed consistent with the facility's exempt purposes.[74]

Likewise, a health care organization did not jeopardize its tax-exempt status by providing home health aide and homemaker services. The IRS deemed personal care, housekeeping, and meal preparation for the elderly, sick, and handicapped an "inherent part" of the organization's health care program necessary to promote its patients' health.[75] Similarly, the operation of a guest facility for outpatients, visitors of patients, and other patrons by a corporation related to a tax-exempt hospital did not endanger the hospital's exemption because the guest facility encouraged patient visits, which promoted patient recovery.[76]

Furthermore, when a tax-exempt health care system consisted of two entities operating as acute care hospitals and two housing facilities serving the elderly and disabled, an extended-care facility operator that merged into the parent corporation of its affiliated health care system did not jeopardize the parent's tax-exempt status. The parent had proposed a merger with one of the entities originally operating as an acute care hospital and extended-care facility, but financial difficulties caused that entity to sell its hospital to a tax-exempt organization and lease its extended-care facility to a for-profit organization. As part of the merger, the parent organization assumed all obligations under the lease with the for-profit organization. The IRS ruled that the transfer of assets to the parent did not affect the parent's tax exemption because its role in the health care system furnished an independent basis for its exemption.[77]

Similarly, several community hospitals' reorganization of several home health care entities did not adversely affect their tax-exempt status or generate unrelated business taxable income where the reorganization of services would enhance resource allocation; maximize third-party reimbursement under Medicare, Medicaid, and private insurance programs; facilitate regulatory compliance; and provide organizational flexibility.[78]

(b) Insurance

Prepaid health plans generally have been treated as Section 501(c)(4) social welfare organizations rather than as charitable organizations because of the preferential treatment given to members (a private inurement problem) and because the prepayment is viewed as a form of insurance, which is a noncharitable activity.[79] The U.S. Tax Court has ruled that a health maintenance organization can be exempt from tax under circumstances where it provided care facilities directly, carried on research, and made services available to those unable to pay and where the class of members was large enough to constitute a community.[80] There, the court found that while the *activity* of providing insurance was commercial and nonexempt, the organization's purpose of promoting health was charitable.[81]

The Tax Reform Act of 1986 has made it clear, however, that entities otherwise qualifying under Sections 501(c)(3) and 501(c)(4) will be denied tax exemption if any substantial part of their activities consists of providing "commercial insurance."[82] Although the prohibited activity does not include "incidental health insurance provided by a health maintenance organization of a kind customarily provided by such organizations,"[83] the congressional committee reports[84] make clear that only those HMOs providing services to their own members—with their own employees in their own facilities (the Kaiser model)—will remain eligible for exemption. Those engaged primarily in insurance for health services rendered by others (Blue Cross model) will be taxable.[85] Therefore, a Section 501(c)(3) organization, benefiting its members and the public and offering special programs for the elderly, would risk loss of its exemption by providing group term health insurance to its members if it could not show that the organization's exempt purpose was served.[86] However, if a retirement facility designed to address seniors' health needs arranges for group insurance, the activity should be consistent with the facility's charitable purposes (see also §9.7 regarding church group health plans).

(c) Application to Seniors' Housing

Promotion of health is a concept that may be of limited usefulness in obtaining an exemption for a retirement facility. Many facilities, while arguably designed to promote the general health of their residents, primarily offer independent housing and are not licensed in their entirety, if at all, as health facilities. This class of facility is probably preemptively covered by the criteria of Revenue Ruling 72–124 and related rulings (see §§9.3 and 9.4).

It may be possible, however, to obtain an exemption on the basis of health promotion for facilities that are primarily dependent-care oriented, such as assisted-living facilities. While these facilities technically are not health facilities under most state license laws, they are at least primarily directed toward the provision of care rather than housing. In Letter Ruling 8506116, the Internal Revenue Service found a "long-term care facility for the elderly" to be eligible for exemption. Although it reviewed the criteria for a home for the aging exemption under Revenue Ruling 72–124 (housing, health care, and financial security), the IRS also noted that the organization would operate exclusively for the "charitable purpose of promotion of health." It is important to note also that personal-care or assisted-living costs are eligible for the medical expense tax deduction (see §6.1(c)).

Whether or not the housing aspect of a retirement community can be subsumed under the banner of an overall charitable purpose of health promotion, the concept presents opportunities for facility developers. Where housing facilities are to be combined with health services, it may be possible to

establish a separate organization for the health care provider and obtain an exemption for it on its own merit. Thus, the residents of nonexempt, independent seniors' housing offered at market rates could be served by an exempt home health agency, health maintenance organization, or nearby nursing facility.

The exempt health promotion purpose of a given facility may also be used to justify otherwise nonexempt activities, such as the provision of housing. For example, Revenue Ruling 81–28[87] found that the provision of free, temporary, modest housing for relatives of patients in neighboring hospitals and nursing facilities served a charitable promotion of health purpose in that visitation of patients had therapeutic value. Similarly, condominium units provided on a temporary basis to patients of a medical clinic who had to travel considerable distances to receive treatment were not unrelated to the organization's exempt health purposes.[88] While neither of the referenced rulings permits permanent housing as an adjunct to a health promotion purpose, a plausible argument can be made that retirement housing can, for example, serve the health promotion purposes of an adjacent sponsoring hospital.[89]

§9.7 Religious Organizations

Religious as well as charitable organizations are eligible for tax exemption under Section 501(c)(3). Churches are included among the groups to which a contribution may qualify for a charitable deduction.[90] It is clear, however, that the exemption is not limited to the house of worship itself but may also include entities such as schools owned by religious groups.[91]

To qualify as an integrated auxiliary of a church, the IRS formerly required an organization to show that its principal activity is "exclusively religious."[92] In 1995, the IRS and the Treasury Department abandoned the "exclusively religious" test for integrated church auxiliaries in response to court rulings questioning whether it was within the IRS's discretion to assess the religious nature of a church's activities.[93] New regulations define an *integrated church auxiliary* as a tax-exempt organization that is affiliated with the church (i.e., is controlled by the church or shares common religious bonds and convictions) and is "internally supported."[94] An organization will be deemed "internally supported" *unless* it offers admissions, goods, services, or facilities for sale, other than on an incidental basis, to the general public for a substantial portion of the cost *and* normally receives more than 50 percent of its support from a combination of government sources, public solicitation of contributions, and receipts from the sale of admissions, goods, performance of services, or furnishing of facilities and activities that are not an unrelated trade or businesses.[95] Therefore, a retirement facility that is exempt under Section 501(c)(3) and affiliated with a church will not be deemed internally supported and thus not an integrated auxiliary if it offers its services to the general public and normally receives more than 50 percent of its support from the performance of those services and public and private contributions.[96] If the organization has an independent basis for exemption, it may not qualify as an integrated auxiliary. Accordingly, a charitable home for the aging, even though it limits admissions to members of the church, is not a religious organization entitled to a separate home for the aging exemption.[97] Examples of integrated church auxiliaries include men's or women's organizations and mission societies.[98]

In addition, the IRS ruled that a tax-exempt organization providing residential and health services to elderly members belonging to or sympathetic with a particular church did not need to file the annual information return (Form 990) because the organization was affiliated with the church (under Rev. Proc. 86–23) and satisfied the internal support test.[99]

Churches are subject to the same types of limitations as other charities regarding unrelated activities. For example, the tax-exempt status of a church that operated, among other things, a health insurance program was revoked because of the church's substantial commercial activities.[100] On the other hand, the courts found that a church that spent more than 20 percent of its disbursements on a medical plan for church members was serving a sufficiently religious purpose.[101]

Under the former "exclusively religious" test, all but the most unusual retirement communities probably would be disqualified. For example, a mountain lodge operated for religious retreats was found not to be engaged in an exclusively religious activity be-

cause its religious activities were optional and not regularly scheduled and typical recreation activities were available.[102] Rent-free housing for retired missionaries in financial need was found exempt, but probably on the basis of its charitable rather than religious nature.[103] Under the new test, however, it appears that any facility not open to the general public (e.g., by restricting admission to members of the religion) can qualify.

It should be noted here that retirement facilities affiliated with major church groups may qualify for inclusion under a group exemption by means of a listing in the church's national directory of related organizations.[104] Application is made to the church group for listing, not to the Internal Revenue Service. Upon listing, the organization is automatically deemed exempt pursuant to the church's blanket ruling. While this may be a convenience for the applicant organization, it does not provide retirement facilities with carte blanche to engage in otherwise nonexempt activities in the name of a church. Further, it is incumbent on the organization to demonstrate to the listing church the basis for qualification as an exempt organization.

§9.8 Government Facilities

The IRS treated a home for war veterans created by a state legislature as an exempt organization that was an integral part of the state government.[105]

§9.9 Exempt Services

Several activities benefiting the elderly but not involving the furnishing of housing or health care facilities also have been deemed charitable. (Health services such as home health and prepaid health plans have already been discussed in §9.6). For example, Revenue Ruling 76–244[106] found a Meals on Wheels service designed to provide meals at cost to elderly persons in their homes to be tax-exempt and charitable. Although it charged a fee, the organization used volunteers for deliveries and reduced the charge or continued free service to those who could not afford the usual charge. Interestingly, the ruling did not focus exclusively on the financial relief afforded to those unable to pay but rather took an expansive approach and considered in general the nonfinancial distress of the elderly. Although similar to the analysis of Revenue Ruling 72–124 (see §9.3), this ruling infers that the nonfinancial distress of the elderly may be relieved without providing housing and health care, as Revenue Ruling 72–124 dictates.

A seniors' center that maintains a seniors' recreation center and provides referral and counseling services regarding health, housing, finances, education, and employment is exempt if there is no membership requirement as a prerequisite to use of the facilities and services.[107]

Exemption was also granted to a publicly supported rural rest home that for a nominal charge admitted elderly poor from nearby metropolitan areas for two-week stays; services included food and recreation programs.[108]

Revenue Ruling 77–246[109] held that the provision of transportation services to the elderly and handicapped is an exempt activity. The ruling referred to the elderly as a "charitable class." In contrast, a nonprofit corporation formed to create and administer group self-insurance for charitable organizations providing transportation services to the elderly was not exempt because it provided commercial-type insurance under Internal Revenue Code Section 501(m).[110]

There are definite limits on what services the IRS will consider charitable. Revenue Ruling 70–535[111] held, rather summarily, that a nonprofit's mere fee-based management of low- and moderate-income housing owned by tax-exempt nonprofit organizations does not sufficiently amount to promotion of the common good and general community welfare to qualify the organization for exemption as a Section 501(c)(4) social welfare organization. The IRS found that the organization's primary activity was the carrying on of a business with the general public in a manner similar to for-profit organizations. This finding is consistent with rulings in other fields where nonprofit management or consulting services to unrelated exempt organizations have been deemed not to be exempt activities.[112] However, an organization controlled by exempt organizations and providing below-cost services to them was eligible for exemption.[113] In addition, the provision of management services to a retirement community has been

recognized as exempt, where the services were provided to a related organization.[114] Likewise, the provision of coordination, long-range planning, and policy making for a group of organizations, including a retirement community operator, was exempt because such services were provided only to the related organizations.[115]

In *Senior Citizens Stores, Inc. v. United States,*[116] an organization that was engaged in retail sales on a nonprofit basis and that used proceeds of sales to provide training, jobs, and recreational activities to seniors was found to be ineligible for exemption because a substantial portion of its activities did not further its exempt purpose.

While no clear pattern emerges from the authorities, some activities that do not meet elderly housing needs can qualify for tax exemption. However, they should be able to demonstrate recognized charitable characteristics such as health promotion or include free or below-cost services, as did the Meals on Wheels program in Revenue Ruling 76–244. In addition, they should not be too similar to businesses normally operated for profit.

In the seniors' housing context, it may therefore be possible to reduce program costs by structuring or working with nonprofit service organizations that cater to residents of a nonexempt housing facility. (For a full discussion of for-profit and nonprofit ventures and relationships, see Part V.)

§9.10 Homeowners' Associations

Since the mid-1980s, some service-oriented retirement communities have been structured as condominiums, cooperatives, or subdivision units in which the homeowners' association acts, through employed or contracted-for management, as the provider of services to the residents. According to Internal Revenue Code Section 528, certain income of a qualifying homeowners' association is exempt from taxation if the association so elects; however, only condominium or residential real estate management associations are eligible.[117]

"Exempt function income" (i.e., that portion exempt from tax) includes amounts received as dues or assessments from owners of the condominium units or other real property.[118] To be exempt, however, at least 60 percent of income must derive from dues, fees, or assessments from owners[119] while at least 90 percent of the annual expenditures of the organization must go to the "acquisition, construction, management, maintenance, and care of association property."[120] The regulation provides examples of such expenditures, including upkeep and repair of streets, signage, recreation areas, and hallways; hiring security and management personnel; legal and accounting fees; property insurance; and property taxes.[121] It therefore appears that homeowners' associations that spend more than 10 percent of their expenditures for nonproperty-related services to residents, such as meals, housekeeping, and health care, will be subject to taxation of income received as dues or assessments.

Nevertheless, it appears possible to use both a tax-exempt homeowners' association to provide property-oriented services and a nonprofit organization to provide other exempt services, such as health care or low-cost meals or recreation programs, through individual contracts with resident owners (see §§9.6 and 9.8). See §§7.1(d) and 7.2(b) regarding details about the taxation of condominium and cooperative homeowners' associations.

§9.11 Avoidance of Private Foundation Status

Tax-exempt seniors' housing facilities should be structured to avoid classification as private foundations because contributions to private foundations generally are tax deductible to the donor to a lesser degree than contributions to public charities. Private foundations are also subject to an excise tax on investment income, must file more complex reports than other exempt organizations,[122] and are subject to a battery of taxes for certain proscribed activities. Internal Revenue Code Section 509(a) sets forth the tests for avoiding the private foundation classification and defines three relevant categories of public charities as follows:

- Type 1—a religious, charitable, or otherwise exempt organization normally receiving a substantial part of its support (other than income from an activity constituting the basis of its ex-

emption) from a government source or from contributions from the general public.[123]
- Type 2—an organization normally receiving more than one-third of its annual support from a combination of gifts, grants, contributions, or membership fees *and* gross receipts from admissions, sales, performance of services, or furnishing of facilities in an activity that is not an unrelated trade or business, but not including receipts from any one person or entity to the extent they exceed the greater of $5,000 or 1 percent of the organization's annual support; and normally receiving one-third or less of its annual support from gross investment income (e.g., interest, dividends, rents) and the excess of unrelated business taxable income over the tax on such income.[124]
- Type 3—an organization operated exclusively for the benefit of, or to function for, and that is controlled, operated, or supervised by one or more Type 1 or Type 2 organizations.[125]

The first category—Section 509(a)(1)—is not a likely vehicle for most retirement facilities. The test for avoiding classification as a foundation may be met by showing that at least one-third of the organization's total support comes from public contributions or government sources[126] or that at least 10 percent is from such sources, that an ongoing solicitation program is in operation, and that other facts and circumstances exist.[127] Although membership fees are included in the computation of public support,[128] exempt function income is not.[129] In *The Home for Aged Men v. United States*,[130] a federal district court found that entrance fees required to be paid to a life-care type of retirement facility as a prerequisite to admission are funds derived from running the business of caring for the aging and are therefore exempt function income rather than membership fees. Therefore, such fees were not counted as public support, and the organization was characterized a private foundation. Most retirement facilities that rely primarily on resident fees for their income will likely face a similar fate under this analysis.[131]

In *Trustees for the Home for Aged Women v. United States*,[132] a retirement facility that did not charge a periodic fee but required residents to assign all their property to the home on admission sought the reversal of a determination that it was a private foundation subject to excise tax. The home argued that investment income received from property transferred by residents should be considered indirect public support because it was generated by the home's endowment fund, all of which was originally donated by the public. Thus, the home would arguably meet the one-third public support test. The court, however, rejected the facility's contention, holding that indirect public support refers simply to contributions from other organizations that are themselves publicly supported.

The home also attempted to meet the "facts and circumstances test" of Treasury Regulation §1.170A–9(e)3 but was found not to meet the requirements that it maintain a continuous and bona fide program for solicitation of funds from the general public. It simply maintained its tax-exempt status and encouraged attorneys to mention to their clients possible bequests to the home.

The second type of public charity—Section 509(a)(2)—can rely on contributions as well as on gross receipts from admissions, sales, performance of services, or furnishing of facilities to meet its one-third test. Therefore, entrance fees, monthly fees, sale prices of condominiums or memberships, and related receipts from furnishing or operating an exempt facility count toward qualification. Medicare and Medicaid income in connection with the exempt activity should also count as gross receipts that are credited toward meeting the one-third test.[133] However, income from any single source does not qualify to the extent that it is in excess of the greater of $5,000 or 1 percent of the organization's total support. As a practical matter, construction of larger facilities—for example, 100 units or more—can ensure that no resident contributes more than 1 percent of total income, although smaller facilities may also qualify.

The third category—Section 509(a)(3) support organization—can be of use when an existing Type 1 or Type 2 organization such as a hospital spins off a controlled organization to operate the retirement facility. The supporting organization need not independently meet the public support criteria of the other two categories if it is operated, controlled, or supervised by the supported organization (parent-subsidiary model); shares common supervision or control with the qualifying public charity (brother-sister model); or is operated in connection with the public charity in that it takes over a function of the charity or pays 85 percent or more of its income to the organization, which must be sufficient to ensure a significant voice in the charity's investments, and the charity is responsive to the supporting organization.[134]

For an example of a retirement facility employing all three types of public charity status, see Letter Ruling 8506116, where a long-term-care facility for the elderly (X) transferred all its fund-raising activities to one related organization (Y) and all its investment income-producing activities to another (Z). The government found that X was a Type 2 entity, which could qualify on the basis of its exempt operations income, Y a Type 1 entity supported by the public, and Z a Type 3 support organization.

§9.12 Unrelated Business Taxable Income

(a) Unrelated Trades or Businesses

An exempt organization can be subject to payment of tax on income from a trade or business that is not substantially related to the exercise of its charitable or other exempt purpose.[135] The regulations explain that the unrelated trade or business must be regularly carried on[136] and generally involve the generation of income from the sale of goods or performance of services.[137] In addition, if unrelated activities become too substantial a portion of the organization's overall activities, they can jeopardize the tax-exempt status of the entity (see §9.2(b)).

The "substantiality" of an organization's nonexempt activities is a question of fact. Ten percent of an organization's *expenditures* has been found to be insubstantial while 20 percent has been found to be more than insubstantial.[138] On the other hand, the IRS has determined that an organization devoting 8.3 percent of its *time* to an unrelated activity was engaged in substantial unrelated activities.[139]

In Revenue Ruling 81–61,[140] the IRS considered whether the operation, at market-rate fees, of beauty and barber shops for older people by a nonresidential senior citizen center was an exemption-related activity. The activity was deemed to be related to the exempt purpose, which included ministration to elderly persons' social, recreational, physical, and health needs. Moreover, the activity was conveniently located for those who might suffer from an impaired ability to travel and met the psychological and health needs of area elderly by serving their grooming needs. Similarly, a retirement home's provision of an information and referral system and of community-care management for nonresident older persons in the surrounding area was deemed related to the home's exempt purpose.[141] Likewise, the IRS has ruled that physical therapy, occupational therapy, speech therapy, injury prevention, and pediatric and adult daycare services were related to the exempt purposes of the owner and operator of a skilled-nursing facility.[142]

A nonprofit organization that operated a retirement facility was found not to generate unrelated business taxable income when it implemented a fee-for-service plan. In that ruling, traditional residents were required to assign all of their income and assets to the home, but participants in the fee-for-service plan were not required to make such assignment, provided that they made a fixed deposit on entry and paid a daily fee. Fee residents who could no longer afford the fee-for-service plan were then admitted as traditional residents. The IRS found that a reasonable proportion of the residents still received services below cost because 75 percent of the home's residents would be traditional residents after the fee-for-service plan was implemented. Furthermore, the IRS found that this plan furthered the facility's exempt purposes because fees received from residents were used for their care.[143]

In another ruling, a nonprofit organization that owned and operated a nursing home but amended its charter to offer continuing care, assisted living, and congregate senior housing could develop and sell condominium units and rent apartments without triggering unrelated business taxable income.[144] The nonprofit persuaded the IRS that the organization could protect its exempt function by maintaining two funds. The first fund financed the exempt organization's right of first refusal to maintain condominium resale prices within cost-of-living increases (see discussion in §9.4). The second fund maintained tenants who became unable to pay their rents.[145]

In a companion ruling to Revenue Ruling 81–61,[146] however, the government held that a senior citizen

center's sale of heavy-duty appliances to seniors was not related to any exempt purpose because, unlike hairstyling, appliance purchases need not be conducted in person and are a sporadic rather than ongoing need. Thus, the organization did not relieve any significant form of elderly distress by selling appliances. In addition, the IRS has ruled that a social club's sale of homesite lots on the club's land to raise funds constituted an unrelated business.[147] In *United States v. American Bar Endowment*,[148] a tax-exempt organization also was found subject to unrelated business income from offering group insurance to its members. The activity was deemed to constitute a separate trade or business.[149]

To avoid tax on income, activities should directly serve the object of the exempt purpose—the residents—rather than simply line the coffers of the organization, even if the income is ultimately dedicated solely to the benefit of the aging.[150] However, elderly residents need not be the exclusive users. In the nonprofit hospital context, for example, gift shops, cafeterias, and parking lots, while not patronized exclusively by patients, were deemed exemption-related activities.[151] The theory was that facilities fostering patient visitation by relatives and friends contributed to patients' well-being and that staff use of such facilities enabled the institution to accomplish its exempt purposes more efficiently. Similar logic can be applied to retirement facility restaurants, recreation centers, transportation, or other amenities open to visitors or even the public on a limited basis. Likewise, a long series of IRS pronouncements has established that hospitals' construction of adjacent medical office buildings does not result in unrelated business income because these buildings serve the organization's exempt purposes by encouraging physicians to locate nearby and refer patients.[152]

It is conceivable to stretch the relatedness point so that, for example, a nonprofit hospital could argue that its adjacent retirement facility, which otherwise would not qualify for exemption, serves the *hospital's* exempt purpose on the grounds that it establishes a potential new patient base, attracts physicians, and promotes cost-efficient sharing of services. Unfortunately, there is little, if any, direct authority for such a proposition. In Letter Ruling 7733070, a residential retirement center to be built and operated by a hospital near its medical complex was found not to generate unrelated business income, but the Internal Revenue Service recited criteria and qualifying facts, including continuing service for those who became unable to pay, sufficient to gain a home for the aging exemption under Revenue Ruling 72–124 or 79–18 (see §9.3(a)). Although there are occasional unpublished decisions where exemption has been granted for seniors' housing facilities without strict compliance with precedent or as an apparent bootstrapping from an existing exempt activity, it appears that retirement centers generally have been so comprehensively discussed in IRS rulings as to warrant independent analysis of their exempt purposes.

The IRS frequently issues letter rulings reviewing corporate reorganizations involving establishment of retirement communities to determine whether unrelated business taxable income is generated as a result of the reorganization.[153] For example, the reorganization and transfer of land, services, and other assets by a seniors' housing community and related health care and services organizations did not alter their exempt status.[154] The IRS announced that, effective February 1990, it would no longer issue "comfort letter" rulings where there is clear published authority that disposes of the subject in a private letter ruling request.[155] Several UBTI rules were liberalized with the passage of the Revenue Reconciliation Act of 1993 (see §8.3 for a summary of these reforms).

(b) Dividend, Interest, or Rental Income

Dividend and interest income is "passive" and thus not considered income from an unrelated trade or business subject to tax.[156] Rental income from real property generally is also excluded from the definition of unrelated business taxable income.[157] Payments for the use or occupancy of rooms or space where services are also rendered to the occupant, such as "apartment houses furnishing hotel services," do *not* constitute income from rental property.[158] While maid service would disqualify property from the rental income exemption, services such as furnishing utilities, cleaning of public areas, and trash collection are not considered disqualifying services "to the occupant."[159] Therefore, seniors' housing or land on which the housing is to be built may be leased by a tax-exempt property owner to another person or entity that operates the facility for profit or for some other purpose unrelated to the owner's exemption, without taxation of rental income or jeopardy to the lessor's exempt status. When, however, the exempt organization furnishes services to occupants in an operation unrelated to its exempt purposes, the income will not be eligible for the rental income exemption and will be taxable.

Even if it otherwise meets the rental income definition, a payment will be subject to inclusion as unrelated business income when the amount of the rent is based on income or profits derived from the leased property, unless such payment is a fixed percentage of receipts or sales[160] or includes substantial personal property.[161] Therefore, a nonprofit's rental income from property used in an unrelated business can be a fixed rate or a percentage of gross revenues, but not a share of profits or net revenues.

Except in limited circumstances, the rental income exemption generally does not apply to income received from debt-financed property, as discussed in §9.12(c).

(c) Debt-Financed Property

Income from debt-financed property is subject to taxation as unrelated business income.[162] Debt-financed property is that which is held to produce income and for which there was an acquisition indebtedness outstanding at any time during the taxable year.[163] The principal exception is for property, substantially all of the use of which is related to the organization's charitable or other exempt purpose.[164] The primary purpose of taxing debt-financed property income is to prevent use of a nonprofit as a strawman buyer/lessor to fund a bootstrap property sale from future operating income, generated by a lessee related to the seller,[165] where the nonprofit's use of the property is unrelated to its exempt purpose.

Most retirement facility rulings dealing with debt-financed property have concerned property to be used as the site for the facility itself. Therefore, if the retirement facility is eligible for exemption, operating income derived from it is related to the exempt purpose and not subject to taxation, even though the acquisition may have been debt-financed.[166]

In Notice 90–41,[167] the IRS set forth certain conditions under which a partnership holding debt-financed real property will be able to provide reasonable preferred returns and guaranteed payments for tax-exempt organization partners without the income being treated as unrelated business taxable income. In addition, certain educational organizations, pension and profit-sharing plans, and title-holding companies enjoy a limited exception from UBTI for income generated by debt-financed real property, provided they meet several criteria (Internal Revenue Code Section 514(c)(9)). These criteria were liberalized by the Revenue Reconciliation Act of 1993, H.R. 2264, Section 13144, effective for property acquired on or after January 1, 1994.[168]

§9.13 Deduction of Payments to Exempt Facilities

Contributions to charitable organizations generally are deductible to the donor for purposes of calculating income subject to taxation.[169] Early on, though, the IRS held that no part of a founder's fee paid by a taxpayer to a nonprofit home in return for life care in the home was deductible.[170] In 1962, however, the Eighth Circuit Court of Appeals, in *Wardwell v. Commissioner,* determined that a "room endowment" paid to a tax-exempt home for the aging on the day before the taxpayer moved into the facility was deductible.[171] The home solicited endowments of $5,000 per room and generally permitted the donor to occupy the room or designate its occupant. The Internal Revenue Service had argued successfully before the U.S. Tax Court that the payment was made with the motive and expectation of securing occupancy in the home, was a quid pro quo arrangement, and was not the result of a detached charitable intention. The Eighth Circuit reversed, finding that the taxpayer's motive on the date the *payment* was made was not relevant but that her intention on the date the gift was made was relevant. Although the payment in this case had been made before moving in, it had been pledged in writing after the taxpayer's application for residence had been approved by the home. The court concluded that a legally binding pledge was made regardless of any expectation about admission.

The IRS criticized the *Wardwell* ruling in Revenue Ruling 72–506,[172] where it denied the deduction for a "sustainer's gift" payment solicited by a retirement facility from all applicants who were "financially able" and where the requested amount varied according to the size of each unit. The service found the "gift" to have been made with an "expectation of benefits." It also disagreed with *Wardwell* in that the case could be interpreted to preclude denial of the deduction unless the donor had a legal right to (versus an expectation of) admission in return for the payment.

The Seventh Circuit followed the reasoning of the IRS in *Sedam v. United States,*[173] in which payments made with the intent to induce admission to a facility did not constitute a gift, even though there was no legal obligation to make the payment.[174] In *Dowell v. United States,*[175] however, the Tenth Circuit found a charitable gift where the sponsorship gift was solicited during the process of application for a residence but after acceptance to the facility had been granted.[176]

The IRS permitted a deduction by retirement community residents of contributions made to build a pedestrian bridge on the premises, even though the donors might use and benefit from the improvement.[177] The service noted that the contribution was voluntary, did not reduce residents' obligation to pay fees, and resulted in only an incidental benefit to them.

Tax-exempt seniors' housing facilities generally may solicit contributions from applicants for admission or from their relatives but should be extremely cautious about the circumstances described in §23.5(b)(2) concerning Medicaid fraud and abuse. In addition, facilities should not represent to applicants for admission that payments made to the home are tax deductible, especially when solicited or paid before acceptance at the facility, as the IRS has consistently taken a negative view of such payments. Of course, solicitation of existing residents does not present the types of tax deductibility problems addressed above. If a facility is concerned that applicants will be dissuaded from making truly voluntary contributions because of the uncertainty of the contributions' deductibility, it may wish to devise a carefully crafted solicitation program along the lines of the *Wardwell* and *Dowell* criteria, taking no pledges or payments before acceptance for admission and making no guarantees of any quid pro quo. One might even seek a blanket Internal Revenue Service letter ruling, although the IRS may feel compelled to analyze the individual facts of each contribution to determine the taxpayer's donative intent. (For a review of the deductibility of a portion of entrance fees or monthly fees as a medical expense, see §6.1(c)(1).)

Tax-exempt operators may use a charitable remainder trust as a vehicle for obtaining donations and, at the same time, create income for a resident during his or her lifetime. Under Internal Revenue Code Section 664 and the regulations promulgated thereunder, a person establishing a $100,000 trust for a single beneficiary (assuming a 10 percent interest rate) may deduct the following amounts in the initial year the trust is created, based on the trustor's age and the yield of the trust:[178]

	Payout Rate		
Age	5%	7%	9%
50	$31,500	$21,500	$15,400
55	$37,400	$26,900	$20,200
60	$43,800	$33,100	$25,700
65	$50,600	$40,000	$32,300
70	$57,700	$47,500	$39,700
75	$64,900	$55,600	$48,100

Moreover, a charitable remainder trust can be used to avoid capital gains tax on the sale of a home. The trust is tax-exempt and therefore is not subject to capital gains tax when it sells real property in the trust. A resident thus may deposit all or a portion of his or her principal residence into the charitable remainder trust, have the trust sell the property, and use the proceeds to generate income that the resident can use to help defray the cost of monthly fees.[179] The need for such machinations is greatly reduced by the $500,000 per couple capital gain exclusion for sale of a principal residence passed in 1997 (see §6.1(c)(2)).

It is important that deposits into a charitable remainder trust are not made mandatory by the retirement community; otherwise, they are likely to be treated as a quid pro quo rather than a truly voluntary contribution, thus jeopardizing the resident's tax deduction.

In a related matter, the IRS in Private Letter Ruling 8851030 denied a gift tax charitable deduction under Section 2522(a) when a person contributed money to a charitable organization pursuant to an agreement requiring the organization to purchase a bond with the funds and use the bond interest to fund an annuity for the donors. The IRS noted that Section 2522(c)(2) prohibits the deduction when the donor retains an interest in the transferred property. The ruling noted, however, that the deduction would be available if the agreement had provided that the annuity would be paid out of the general funds of the charity rather than from interest earned on the bond.

§9.14 Reporting and Technical Requirements

Since the mid-1980s, Congress and the IRS have imposed several disclosure and related requirements on tax-exempt organizations. Legislation signed into law in 1987 contained a number of significant provisions as follows:

- Any fundraising solicitation by or on behalf of any Section 501(c) organization that is not eligible to receive contributions deductible as charitable contributions must include an express statement that contributions or gifts to it are not deductible. Failure to make the required disclosure can result in a penalty of $1,000 per day.[180]
- Exempt organization tax returns must be made available for public inspection for a period of three years at the organization's principal office and certain regional offices[181] (see also §9.15).
- Applications for tax exemption must be made available for public inspection[182] (see also §9.15).
- A Section 501(c) organization that offers to sell or solicits money for information or a routine service that could be readily obtained by an individual from an agency of the federal government free of charge or for a nominal charge must disclose that fact in a conspicuous manner.[183]
- A Section 501(c)(3) organization must disclose in its annual return information regarding direct or indirect transfers to, and other direct or indirect relationships with, other organizations described in Section 501(c) or in Section 527, unless the other organization is a Section 501(c)(3) organization.[184]

- User fees are required of any organization seeking an IRS determination of exempt status or a private letter ruling.[185]

The types of political activities in which a Section 501(c)(3) organization can be involved are also restricted. In 1990, the IRS released regulations describing three distinct forms of lobbying: direct lobbying, grass-roots lobbying, and nonlobbying advocacy. Organizations that seek protection under a "lobbying safe harbor" can elect to file IRS Form 5768, an election to make expenditures to influence legislation. Excise taxes apply to expenditures in excess of specified lobbying limits.[186] In late 1995, the IRS issued final regulations imposing excise taxes on Section 501(c)(3) organizations that improperly involve themselves in political activities.[187]

Beginning in 1989, the Form 990 annual return was revised to require tax categorization of all sources of revenue, a written narrative of the relationship of activities to exempt purpose, disclosures about taxable subsidiaries or joint venture entities in which there is 50 percent or more ownership, and expanded disclosure of benefits paid to directors, officers, and trustees.

Effective in 1992, Form 990 also asks for information regarding the compensation of any officer, director, trustee, or key employee who received from the organization *and all related organizations* aggregate compensation of more than $100,000 during the taxable year if more than $10,000 was provided by a related organization. Based on its coordinated examination program, the IRS believes that exempt organizations have been hiding compensation paid to officers and directors through their subsidiaries. The 1992 Form 990 also requires charities not electing to file Form 5768 to report lobbying expenditures and requires all charities to identify programming expenses as either "fundraising" or "educational" costs where one programming expense has dual purposes.[188] Furthermore, in 1993, the IRS issued special instructions for district-level IRS determination specialists to use in processing the tax exemption applications of organizations that intend to issue tax-exempt bonds[189] (see Volume: II, §10.5, for a copy of the instructions).

Effective in 1994, all donations to charities valued at $250 or more, whether in the form of cash or other property, must be substantiated with a receipt, and all charities that provide a good or service in exchange for a gift in excess of $75 must inform the donor in writing of the value of the good or service and the deductible portion of the gift.[190] More recently published proposed and temporary regulations provide further guidance regarding substantiation of charitable contributions of $250 or more, quid pro quo gifts, and contributions made by payroll deductions.[191] Final regulations designed to eliminate confusion arising from these rules were promulgated late in 1995 and 1996[192] and include, among other things, detailed instructions for substantiating contributions made by payroll deductions.[193]

§9.15 Intermediate Sanctions

In 1996, Congress enacted legislation granting the IRS an enforcement remedy short of revocation of an organization's tax-exempt status. The new law permits the IRS to impose "an excise tax" on each "excess benefit transaction" entered into between a Section 501(c)(3) or Section 501(c)(4) organization and a disqualified person. A "disqualified person" is any person who is in a position to exercise substantial influence over the organization's affairs, a member of his or her family, or an entity at least 35 percent of which is controlled by the disqualified person. An "excess benefit transaction" is one in which the economic benefit provided to or for the use of the disqualified person exceeds the value of the consideration received by the organization.

If the IRS finds that an excess benefit transaction has occurred, it will levy against the disqualified person a tax equal to 25 percent of the excess benefit. If the excess benefit is not "corrected" within the tax period, the IRS will impose an additional tax on the disqualified person equal to 200 percent of the excess benefit. "Correction" includes not only disgorging the excess benefit but also making the organization whole, even if that includes repaying interest or appreciation to it.

The law creates a safe harbor in the form of a rebuttable presumption of reasonableness if the compensation was approved by an independent board after reviewing appropriate comparability data and adequately documenting the basis for its determination that the compensation was reasonable. However, this presumption can be rebutted by evidence that the data used by the board to justify the compensation were not genuinely comparable because the positions or actual responsibilities were not comparable.

The new intermediate sanction is expected to change significantly the manner in which tax-exempt organizations do business, because it can be implemented much more readily than the single, draconian sanction of revocation of an organization's exempt status.[194] The law is also significant because it permits the imposition on the "foundation manager" (which may include an officer, director, trustee, or anyone with similar powers) of an excise tax if the manager participated in a transaction knowing that it was an excess benefit transaction. The tax is equal to 10 percent of the excess benefit up to $10,000. These sobering excise tax provisions are intended to help promote compliance from both within and outside the exempt organization.[195]

The 1996 act also enhances certain reporting obligations of Section 501(c)(3) and Section 501(c)(4) organizations, including a requirement that they make available to the public upon request *copies* of their annual information returns (Form 990), tax exemption applications (Form 1023), and related rulings. Previously, the organizations were required simply to make such documents *available* for public inspection during regular business hours. The new law also requires exempt organizations to disclose on their Form 990 any taxes paid by the organization during the tax year relating to excess benefit transactions, excess expenditures to influence legislation, and certain other lobbying and political expenditures.[196]

Notes

1. Hearing on Unrelated Business Income Tax on Exempt Organizations before the Subcommittee on Oversight of the House Committee on Ways and Means, 100th Cong., First Sess. (1987).

2. Bromley, R., and M. Clark, "Congress Looks at Overhaul of Unrelated Business Income Tax," *Hospital Law,* Oct. 1987.

3. Tax-exempt organizations have annual revenues estimated at $300 billion. *AAHA Provider News,* Jan. 22,

1988, 4. Between 1982 and 1984, however, federal spending in areas served by human service nonprofit groups decreased by $42 billion. *Ibid.* Members of the U.S. Chamber of Commerce and the Council of Small Business have raised allegations particularly about unfair competition with private industry on the part of tax-exempt organizations. Tax-exempt health care organizations especially have been criticized. Bromley and Clark, note 2 *above.* During congressional hearings held in early 1988, it was estimated that if income-earning activities of tax-exempt organizations were subject to federal tax, $5 billion a year in additional revenues would be raised. "Tax Exemptions Still Threatened," *AAHA Provider News,* May 27, 1988. Among the options considered were to change the "substantially related" test to a "directly related" test and to separate each income-producing activity of an organization and determine whether, standing alone, it should be tax exempt. *Ibid.* While these proposals were not enacted, new limitations on tax-exempt bonds for retirement facilities have become law in recent years and a 1991 General Accounting Office (GAO) report further criticizing retirement facility exempt bonds has been issued (see §15.2). A 1990 GAO report critical of exempt hospitals' level of free or below-cost care (see §9.6), together with legislation proposed in 1991 to impose conditions on hospital tax exemptions, puts increased pressure on retirement facilities to comply strictly with existing criteria for exemption. See Rajecki, R., "Aiming at Not-for-Profits: Congress Looks for Justification of Tax Exemptions," *Contemporary Long Term Care,* Aug. 1991, 36, and "Lawmakers, IRS Question Nonprofits' Tax-Free Status," *AAHA Provider News,* Mar. 1991, both discussing the Hospital Charity Care Act (H.R. 790: Roybal, and H.R. 1374: Donnelly).

4. Gen. Couns. Mem. 39862, Nov. 22, 1991.

5. "Internal Revenue Service Audit Guidelines for Hospitals," contained in *Manual Transmittal 7 (10) 69–38 for Exempt Organizations Guidelines Handbook,* Mar. 27, 1992.

6. They also invited auditors to request technical advice memoranda from the National Office regarding questions that arose during audits. *Id.* About one-half to two-thirds of such cases are expected to result in such requests. Of the 34 hospitals already audited under the new audit guidelines, the IRS expects one hospital to have its exemption revoked based on the hospital's acquisition of a physician's practice for a price equal to four times its fair market value. *See* "One Hospital Likely to Face Revocation as Result of Audits, IRS Official Says," *Bureau of National Affairs Health Law Reporter,* May 6, 1993. By summer 1995, the IRS reported that 46 hospital audits were open and that health care organizations continued to be the

service's highest priority, consuming 34 percent of the resources of the service's coordinated examination program. Of the 13 health care institution audits and three college and university audits that had closed as of that date, the average examination time was approximately 27 months and the average assessment in 1995 was $750,000. *See* "Exempt Healthcare Guidance Is in the Works, Says IRS's Sullivan," *The Exempt Organization Tax Review,* July 1995, 18–19.

7. *See* Announcement 95–25, 1995–14 I.R.B. 11; Kaufmann, P., and M. Curry, "IRS Proposed Guidelines Allow for Reasonable Physician Recruitment Incentives," *The Journal of Taxation,* Sept. 1995, 162–167.

8. *See* "Expect More Guidance for Health Care Entities, IRS and Treasury Officials Say," *BNA Daily Tax Report,* Apr. 25, 1995, G–2.

9. Health Reform Consensus Act of 1994, H.R. 3955; Health Security Act [of 1994], S. 1757.

10. Opponents of this rule also voiced the following fears: nursing facilities would not be able to maintain a percentage of beds for Medicaid or other charitable care; facilities not currently participating in Medicare or Medicaid might be compelled to do so to maintain their exemptions; Alzheimer's units might be eliminated as they were filled with non–Alzheimer's residents; and/or patients more appropriately cared for in subacute units might be retained in nursing beds at a great cost to the Medicare and Medicaid programs. *See* "Nursing Facilities Still Threatened By 'First-Come-First-Served' Rule," *American Association of Homes and Services for the Aging Health Reform Update,* July 22, 1994. There was also concern that the first-come-first-served rule might preclude policies giving priority access to patients' spouses, patients temporarily transferred to a hospital for acute care, continuing-care retirement community residents (to be admitted to the on-site nursing facility), or employees or volunteers at the nursing facility. *Id.*

11. *See* "Senate Votes to Make 501(c)(4) Groups That Lobby Ineligible for Federal Grants," *BNA Taxation, Budget and Accounting,* July 25, 1995, G–6-G–7.

12. *Id.; see* Roybal Bill (H.R. 1374); Donnelly Bill (H.R. 790).

13. "Tax-Exemption Threats Target Nonprofits in Several States," *AAHSA Provider News,* Apr. 1995.

14. This section was amended to clarify that the organization shall not participate or intervene in any political campaign on behalf of *or in opposition to* any candidate for public office. Pub. L. No. 100–203, §10711(a)(2).

15. Treas. Reg. §1.501(c)(3)–1(b)(1).

16. Treas. Reg. §1.501(c)(3)–1(b)(3). Final regulations regarding limits on lobbying expenditures by tax-exempt public charities were issued in 1990. 55 *Fed. Reg.* 35,579, 1990.

17. Treas. Reg. §1.501(c)(3)–1(b)(4).

18. Treas. Reg. §1.501(c)(3)–1(c)(1).

19. *See* Hopkins, B., *The Law of Tax-Exempt Organizations,* 4th ed. (New York: John Wiley & Sons, 1983), 201– 208, for a good discussion of this distinction.

20. Treas. Reg. §1.501(c)(3)–1(c)(2).

21. Letter from Gene E. Godley, assistant secretary, Department of Treasury to Hon. William S. Cohen, Nov. 22, 1977.

22. Taxpayer Bill of Rights 2, §1311(a), adding I.R.C. §4958. (See §9.15).

23. 1972–1 C.B. 145.

24. *See* §9.4.

25. 42 U.S.C. §3001.

26. 1979–1 C.B. 194.

27. *See* §27.2, for a discussion of long-term-care insurance.

28. *See also* Priv. Ltr. Rul. 8022085. Note that private letter rulings are not to be relied on as precedent.

29. *See* Priv. Ltr. Rul. 8405083.

30. Rev. Rul. 72–124.

31. 2 U.S.C. §1715z–1.

32. *See* Rev. Ruls. 72–124, 79–18. However, *see Onderdonk v. Presbyterian Homes of New Jersey,* 85 N.J. 171, 425 A.2d 1057 (1981), which held that a life-care provider could not base residents' fee increases on expenses incurred in the defendants' other operations.

33. Priv. Ltr. Rul. 9001036.

34. Application of Pacific LifeCare Corporation, granted June 22, 1993 (see §9.3(b)(3)).

35. Rev. Rul. 76–408, 1976–2 C.B. 145.

36. Priv. Ltr. Rul. 8030105.

37. Priv. Ltr. Rul. 9318048.

38. Application of Pacific LifeCare, note 34 *above.*

39. *See, e.g.,* Priv. Ltr. Rul. 9001036, which concerns a rare rental facility that met the Rev. Rul. 72–124 criteria, discussed in §9.3(a)(4).

40. G.C.M. 39487, Mar. 21, 1986.

41. *See* §9.3(a)(4).

42. Application of Pacific LifeCare Corporation, granted June 22, 1993 (see §9.3(b)(1)).

43. Priv. Ltr. Rul. 9540067.

44. *See* §26.1(c) for a general discussion of Medicaid coverage.

45. 1961–1 C.B. 188.

46. *See also* Priv. Ltr. Rul. 7916068.

47. 1964–2 C.B. 139.

48. Rev. Rul. 72-147, 1972–1 C.B. 147.

49. 1970–2 C.B. 115.

50. Treas. Reg. §1.501(c)(3)–1(d)(2).

51. Rev. Rul. 68-17, 1968–1 C.B. 247. *See also* Priv. Ltr. Rul. 8101009 and G.C.M. 33671.

52. Rev. Rul. 76-408, 1976–2 C.B. 408.

53. 1977–1 C.B. 140.

54. Rev. Proc. 96-32, 1996–20 I.R.B. 14, May 13, 1996, *superseding* Notice 93–1.

55. In 1994, a representative of the IRS clarified that resident councils should not jeopardize the low-income housing provider's exemption if residents are initially selected based on "more restrictive charitable criteria." That is, once residents are identified as members of a charitable class, they will not lose this status merely by convening as a resident council. The IRS representative also distinguished limited-equity cooperatives from other cooperatives in which members' equity shares resemble stock (and private interests are thus presumably promoted). However, the IRS representative stated that limited-equity cooperatives might *not* be tax-exempt if members have a right to receive appreciation tied to the Consumer Price Index "because it looks like participation in the profit or loss of the organization." *See* "IRS to Ease Stance on Exemption for Low-Income Housing Groups," *The Exempt Organization Tax Review,* July 1994, 5. This position contrasts with an IRS ruling approving the tax exemption of a co-operative-model retirement facility in which resident-owners were entitled to retain a share of the appreciation in their equity interests, subject to a ceiling based on the Consumer Price Index (see §7.2(d)).

56. In addition, the IRS ruled that the purchase of housing stock from the Resolution Trust Corporation to provide and maintain low- and moderate-income housing was not inconsistent with the organization's exempt status, assuming that the organization could demonstrate it provided relief of the poor and distressed, as applied in Revenue Ruling 70-585, by reference to all of the facts and circumstances or by use of the safe harbor. Priv. Ltr. Rul. 9311034.

57. *Id. See also* "IRS Issues Guidance to Expedite Charitable Housing Tax-Exemptions," *BNA Daily Tax Report,* May 2, 1995; "Practitioners Praise New and Improved Safe Harbor for Low-Income Housing," *The Exempt Organization Tax Review,* June 1995, 1173–1174.

58. *See* Rev. Ruls. 72-124 and 79-18; *see also* §9.3(a).

59. *See* G.C.M. 39487, Mar. 21, 1986, which confirms that the housing, health care, and financial security tests must be met to relieve elderly distress.

60. *See* §9.3(a)(3).

61. CCH Dec. 34,504, T.C.M. 1986-556, 1986 WL 21764.

62. *See also* Priv. Ltr. Rul. 8101009, which similarly uses the community deterioration rationale for exempting a 20 percent low-income housing project.

63. Treas. Reg. §1.501(c)(3)–1(c)(1).

64. *See also Restatement Second of Trusts,* §372, which states that "a trust for the promotion of health is charitable."

65. Rev. Rul. 56-185, 1956–1 C.B. 202.

66. Rev. Rul. 69-545, 1969–2 C.B. 117.

67. *Universal Church of Jesus Christ, Inc. v. Commissioner,* 55 T.C.M. (CCH) 144 (1988).

68. Rev. Rul. 83-157, 1983–2 C.B. 94.

69. The IRS has granted tax exemptions to two "integrated delivery systems" that combined hospitals' and physicians' services in a medical practice foundation setting. *In re Friendly Hills Medical Practice Foundation* (Jan. 29, 1993); *In re Facey Medical Foundation* (Mar. 31, 1993). In both decisions, the organizations' tax exemption was contingent on the hospitals' compliance with Revenue Ruling 69-545, provision of charity care, treatment of emergency room patients regardless of their ability to pay, nondiscrimination against Medicaid and Medicare beneficiaries, and other requirements. *Id.* These two decisions are considered significant because they essentially create a "safe harbor" for other integrated delivery systems seeking tax exemptions. They also reveal the IRS's heightened scrutiny of hospitals and hospital systems, which may in the future carry over to long-term-care or residential-care facilities seeking tax exemption.

The *Friendly Hills* ruling was criticized by a report to Congress that inquired whether the private benefit to the physicians stemming from the sale of their facilities was more than incidental to the public benefit resulting from the sale. The report suggested considering a temporary moratorium on granting Section 501(c)(3) rulings in the health care context and otherwise urged congressional review of current law in this area. *See* "Tax Aspects of Healthcare Report: The Tax Treatment of Healthcare Providers," *Congressional Research Service Report for Congress,* 1994 WL 546254, Apr. 25, 1994.

Similarly, the IRS has approved a joint operating agreement among four previously unrelated tax-exempt hospitals and their affiliated health care facilities. Under the agreement, a new entity was created to provide various corporate and administrative services to the network facilities, including financial, information processing, human resource management, risk management, and legal and other services. The IRS concluded that the joint operating agreement did not trigger unrelated taxable income because the services were performed as an integral part of the organizations' exempt charitable activities by enhancing quality and efficiency of health care and patient access to services. Priv. Ltr. Rul. 9609012, Nov. 22, 1995. Likewise, in Priv. Ltr. Rul. 9623011, the IRS ruled that a joint operating agreement by two nonprofit hospital systems did not jeopardize the tax-exempt status of either system's revenue bonds. These rulings are significant because the IRS's historic stance has been to regard as an unrelated trade or business the provision of administrative and related services to unrelated Section 501(c)(3) organizations.

The IRS also approved a tax exemption for a medical clinic converted from for-profit to nonprofit status when a tax-exempt hospital controlled the clinic's governing board and physicians were limited to 20 percent of the board composition. The IRS stated that the hospital retained such close supervision and control over the organization that the medical clinic functioned as an integral part of the hospital. IRS Advance Letter Ruling, October 3, 1995, issued to Marietta Health Care Physicians.

70. "Nonprofit Hospitals: Better Standards Needed for Tax Exemption," General Accounting Office, May 1990. *See also* Simpson, J., and S. Strum, "How Good a Samaritan? Federal Income Tax Exemption for Charitable Hospitals Reconsidered," *Univ. of Puget Sound L. Rev.,* Spring 1991.

71. Rev. Rul. 72–209, 1972–1 C.B. 148. *See also* Priv. Ltr. Ruls. 8427078, 8510068, 8534089. In Priv. Ltr. Rul. 9210032, an organization providing nursing services to residents of a continuing-care retirement community was found to be exempt.

72. *See, e.g.,* Priv. Ltr. Ruls. 8616095, 7948104.

73. Priv. Ltr. Rul. 9735047.

74. Priv. Ltr. Rul. 9241055.

75. Tech. Adv. Mem. 9405004.

76. Priv. Ltr. Rul. 9404029.

77. Priv. Ltr. Rul. 9501037.

78. Priv. Ltr. Rul. 9501040.

79. *See* Hopkins, note 19 *above,* at 94.

80. *Sound Health Association v. Comm'r.,* 71 T.C. 158 (1978).

81. *Id.* at 189. In contrast, the Third Circuit has ruled that a health maintenance organization (HMO) did not meet the community benefit standard under Section 501(c)(3) where it served only its paying subscribers, a class of members too small to constitute a community. *Geisinger Health Plan v. Commissioner,* 985 F.2d 1210 (3d Cir. 1993), *aff'd.,* 30 F.3d 494 (3d Cir. 1994). On remand, the U.S. Tax Court ruled that the HMO was likewise not entitled to tax-exempt status as an "integral part" of a larger health organization.

100 T.C. 394 (1993). The tax court held that the HMO failed to meet the integral-part test because it provided services to parties who were not patients of the related tax-exempt organizations of which the HMO claimed it was an integral part. *Id.* The IRS is currently developing guidance to address how much point-of-service or "commercial-type" insurance activity a nonprofit HMO may engage in without running afoul of the commercial-type insurance provisions of Section 501(m). *See* "Exempt Healthcare Guidance Is in the Works, Says IRS's Sullivan," *The Exempt Organization Tax Review,* July 1995, 18–19.

82. I.R.C. §501(m).

83. I.R.C. §501(m)(3)(B).

84. *Standard Federal Tax Reports,* (CCH), at ¶¶37,022–37,023 (1987).

85. *Ibid.*

86. G.C.M. 39735, June 6, 1988.

87. 1981–1 C.B. 328.

88. Priv. Ltr. Rul. 8427105.

89. *See, e.g.,* the discussion of construction of medical office buildings as exempt activities of hospitals (§12.1(b)(2)).

90. I.R.C. §170(b)(1)(A)(i).

91. *See St. Martin Evangelical Lutheran Church v. South Dakota,* 451 U.S. 772, 101 S. Ct. 2142 (1981).

92. Treas. Reg. §1.6033–2(g)(5).

93. 60 *Fed. Reg.* 65,550, 65,551, 1995.

94. Treas. Reg. §1.6033–2(h)(1), (2), 1996.

95. Treas. Reg. §1.6033–2(h)(4), 1996.

96. Treas. Reg. §1.6033–2(h)(7), ex. 2 (1996). *See also* Treas. Reg. §1.6033–2(h)(2)(i), which provides that an organization is affiliated with a church if it is covered by the church's group exemption letter.

97. Treas. Reg. §§1.6033–2(g)(5)(ii), (iv) (Ex. 4).

98. Treas. Reg. §1.6033–2(g)(5)(iv).

99. Priv. Ltr. Rul. 99619024.

100. *Universal Church of Jesus Christ, Inc.,* 55 TCM 143 (1988).

101. *Bethel Conservative Mennonite Church v. Comm'r.,* 746 F.2d 388 (7th Cir. 1984), *overruling* 80 T.C. 352.

102. *Schoger Foundation,* 76 T.C. 380 (1981).

103. Priv. Ltr. Rul. 7718008.

104. *See* Rev. Proc. 80–27, 1980–1 C.B. 677.

105. Priv. Ltr. Rul. 8835034.

106. 1976–1 C.B. 155.

107. Rev. Rul. 75–198, 1975–1 C.B. 157.

108. Rev. Rul. 75–385, 1975–2 C.B. 205.

109. 1977–2 C.B. 190.

110. *Paratransit Insurance Corp. v. Commissioner,* 102 T.C. 745 (1994). *See also Nonprofits' Insurance Alliance of California v. United States,* 32 Fed. Cl. 277 (Cl. Ct. 1994).

111. 1970–2 C.B. 117.

112. Rev. Rul. 72–369, 1972–2 C.B. 245; *B.S.W. Group v. Comm'r,* 70 T.C. 352 (1978).

113. Rev. Rul. 71–529, 1971–2 C.B. 234.

114. Priv. Ltr. Rul. 9318048.

115. *Id.*

116. 602 F.2d 711 (5th Cir. 1979).

117. I.R.C. §528(c)(1).

118. I.R.C. §528(d)(3).

119. I.R.C. §528(c)(1)(B).

120. I.R.C. §528(c)(1)(C).

121. Treas. Reg. §1.528–6(c).

122. *See generally* I.R.C. §§170 and 4940 *et seq.*

123. I.R.C. §§509(a)(1), 170(b)(1)(A)(vi).

124. I.R.C. §509(a)(2).

125. I.R.C. §509(a)(3).

126. Treas. Reg. §1.170A–9(e)(2).

127. Treas. Reg. §1.170A–9(e)(3).

128. Treas. Reg. §1.170A–9(e)(7)(iii).

129. Treas. Reg. 1.170A–9(e)(7)(a).

130. CCH, 80–2 U.S.T.C. 9711 (N.D.Va. 1980).

131. *See also Williams Home, Inc. v. U.S.,* 540 F. Supp. 310 (W.D.Va., 1982).

132. 86–1 USTC 9290 (D. Mass. 1986).

133. *See* Rev. Rul. 83–153, 1983–2 C.B. 48.

134. *See* Treas. Reg. §1.509(a)–4.

135. I.R.C. §§511–514. For a detailed summary of unrelated business income taxation of exempt care providers, see Mancino, D., "The Unrelated Business Income Taxation of Nonprofit Hospitals," *The Exempt Organization Review,* Mar. 1991, 35.

136. Treas. Reg. §1.513–1(a).

137. Treas. Reg. §1.513–1(b).

138. *World Family Corp. v. Comm'r,* 81 T.C. 958 (1983).

139. G.C.M. 39735, June 6, 1988.

140. 1981–1 C.B. 355.

141. Priv. Ltr. Rul. 9107030.

142. Priv. Ltr. Rul. 9241055.

143. Priv. Ltr. Rul. 9307027.

144. Priv. Ltr. Rul. 9540067.

145. Similarly, the reorganization of a health system, including a tax-exempt nursing facility, to permit the provision of life care did not generate unrelated business taxable income because the proposed reorganization actually helped the entities achieve their tax-exempt purposes. Priv. Ltr. Rul. 9615031. Likewise, the reorganization of an exempt public foundation into a system of affiliated organizations that provided housing and health care to the elderly did not generate unrelated business income for any of the entities. Priv. Ltr. Rul. 9608006 (see also §9.6, regarding the "integral-part" concept applied by the IRS to administrative services organizations formed under joint operating agreements between health care providers).

146. Rev. Rul. 81–62, 1981–1 C.B. 355.

147. Tech. Adv. Mem. 9307004.

148. 477 U.S. 105, 106 S. Ct. 2426, 91 L. Ed. 2d 89 (1986).

149. Note also that Section 501(m) of the Internal Revenue Code provides that a Section 501(c)(3) or (c)(4) exempt organization may not substantially engage in the provision of commercial-type insurance and that any income generated thereby will be subject to the unrelated business income tax. Exceptions are made for below-cost policies, incidental health insurance from an HMO, church casualty insurance, and church employee benefits. I.R.C. §501(m)(3). (See also §9.7 for church-insurance cases.)

150. *See, e.g.,* Rev. Rul. 55–449, 1955–2 C.B. 599, which found that a church group's sale of housing to raise revenue was an unrelated activity.

151. *See* Rev. Ruls. 69–267, 69–268, 69–269, 1969–1 C.B. 160.

152. *See, e.g.,* Priv. Ltr. Ruls. 8134021, 8201072, 8301003, 8312129, 9315021, 9438039.

153. *See, e.g.,* Priv. Ltr. Ruls. 9729018 through 9729022, 9714004, 8927061, 8925069, 8922065, 8920055, 8912042, 8850054, 8845020, 8837053, 8836060, 8832016, 8830038, 8821062, 8818041, 8817051, 8808082, 8807049, 8807007, 8752008, 8715058.

154. Priv. Ltr. Ruls. 8941006, 8941007, 8941012, 8941015, 8941061, 8941073, 8941082, 8941083. *See also* Priv. Ltr. Ruls. 9114031 and 9318048 (continuing-care facility), 9014050 (hospital-related housing and long-term care), 9235056, 9234042, 9213027, 9220053, 9542043, 9552021 (retirement facility), 9608006 (facilities providing various levels of care to the elderly), 9615031 (life-care community, skilled-nursing facility, and adult daycare program), and 9617053 (community-based medical and support services to the frail elderly and an acute care hospital).

155. Rev. Proc. 89–34 (1989–20 I.R.B. 145) and 89–51 (1989–36 I.R.B. 19); *see also Federal Tax Coordinator,* Aug. 17, 1989, 245, regarding the implementation date and other proposals such as "no-action letters" and increased user fees.

156. *See* I.R.C. §512(b)(1).

157. I.R.C. §512(b)(c)(A)(i).

158. Treas. Reg. §1.512(b)-1(c)(5).

159. *Ibid.*

160. I.R.C. §512(b)(3)(B)(ii).

161. Treas. Reg. §1.512(b)-1(c)(2)(iii)(a).

162. I.R.C. §§512(b)(4), 514(a)(1).

163. I.R.C. §514(b)(1).

164. I.R.C. §512(b)(1)(A)(i).

165. For example, A sells income-producing property to B (a nonprofit) for a small downpayment. B leases to C, which is related to A, for a rent based on a share of operating profits. B pays off the debt to A out of rents from C. C gets a rent deduction. A generates more after-tax income (capital gains) than if it had continued to operate the property and take ordinary income. B eventually acquires the property for virtually no investment. *See* Hopkins, note 19 *above,* at 682ff, and *Commissioner v. Brown,* 380 U.S. 563 (1965).

166. *See, e.g.,* Priv. Ltr. Ruls. 8025132, 8117221.

167. 1990-26 I.R.B. 7.

168. An updated version of Publication 598 *(Tax on Unrelated Business Income of Exempt Organizations,* revised February 1995) is available from the IRS. The publication explains, among other things, the treatment of acquisition indebtedness under the UBTI rules. Announcement 95-38, 1995-20 I.R.B. 21.

169. I.R.C. §170.

170. Rev. Ruls. 54-430, 1954-2 C.B. 101; 58-303, 1958-1 C.B. 61.

171. 301 F.2d 632 (8th Cir. 1962).

172. 1972-2 C.B. 106.

173. 518 F.2d 242 (7th Cir. 1975).

174. *See also* Priv. Ltr. Rul. 9423001, in which the IRS found that payments to a retirement community to reserve units were not donations when the payments guaranteed the payor the unit of his preference, allowed him to customize his unit, gave his surviving spouse the right to continue occupying his unit at single-occupant rates, and were fully refundable if the payor died or withdrew from the contract before moving into the community.

175. 553 F.2d 1233 (10th Cir. 1977). However, *see Klappenback v. Comm'r,* 52 T.C.M. 437 (1986), in which the U.S. Tax Court distinguishes *Dowell* and rules against the taxpayer.

176. *See also* 34 *A.L.R.* Fed. 840 for a general survey of cases.

177. Priv. Ltr. Rul. 9141011. However, see *Ohnmeiss v. Comm'r,* T.C. Memo 1991-594, in which a charitable contribution deduction was denied when a worker at a religious community turned her salary over to the organization but received housing and other necessities of life in return.

178. See I.R.C. §664 and Treas. Reg. §1.1664-4A(d)(5), Table E.

179. *See* Rev. Proc. 89-20 for model language for a charitable remainder unitrust. *See* Rev. Proc. 89-21 for an example of a charitable remainder annuity trust. Other charitable remainder trust models approved by the IRS appear at Rev. Proc. 90-30, 90-31, 90-32, and 90-33.

180. I.R.C. §6113.

181. I.R.C. §6104(e).

182. *Ibid.*

183. I.R.C. §6711.

184. I.R.C. §6033(b)(9).

185. Revenue Act of 1987, §10511. For a general discussion of the revised procedures for application for tax exemption, *see* Rev. Proc. 90-27, 1990-1 C.B. 514.

186. Treas. Reg. §1.501(h)-1 *et seq.* For an explanation of these special lobbying rules, *see* Colvin, G., "A Guide to the New IRS Rules on Lobbying by Charities," presented to the Tax-Exempt Organizations Committee of the Taxation Section of the State Bar of California, Oct. 4, 1991.

187. 60 *Fed. Reg.* 62,209.

188. IRS Form 990 (1992), Parts II, V.

189. Advance copy of *Internal Revenue Manual Supplement* (providing instructions for Internal Revenue Service personnel who process exemption applications submitted by charitable organizations that finance facilities with proceeds of tax-exempt bond financing), Feb. 16, 1993.

190. Revenue Reconciliation Act of 1993, §§13172-13173, I.R.C. §§170, 6115, 6714. Because of difficulties taxpayers experienced in obtaining the required acknowledgments, the IRS announced that it would extend the time by which taxpayers who made charitable contributions in 1994 would be required to provide substantiation of their contributions. Notice 95-15, 1995-15 I.R.B. 22. Reporting the deductible portion of gifts to charities was encouraged but not mandated under a voluntary compliance program described in IRS Publication 1391, issued in 1988. Token benefits (such as key chains and note cards) need not be considered in making such valuation. *See* Rev. Rul. 67-246, 1967-2 C.B. 104 and Rev. Proc. 90-12, I.R.B. 1990-8 for guidance to charities in valuing benefits offered

in exchange for charitable contributions, including token benefits.

191. Temp. Reg. §1.170A–13T.

192. 60 *Fed. Reg.* 53126, Oct. 12, 1995; additional regulations were released Dec. 6, 1996.

193. Treas. Reg. §1.170A(13)(f)(11)(i).

194. The impact is expected to be particularly pronounced on health care organizations that have historically paid a premium to attract physicians.

195. Taxpayer Bill of Rights 2, §1311 *et seq.,* adding I.R.C. §4958.

196. *Id.*

Hunt Community Continuing-Care Retirement Facility; Nashua, New Hampshire.

10 State Tax Exemption

§10.1 In General

In 1986, approximately 16 states were reported to have enacted statutes specifically addressing the availability of a tax exemption for homes for the aging.[1] About 20 states had laws dealing with state tax exemptions for nonprofit-owned, low-income, or federally subsidized housing projects.[2] Today, 45 states have statutory or case law specifically addressing taxation of seniors' housing communities. In addition, virtually every state has a general law exempting from state taxes those activities deemed charitable in nature.

One must look principally to case law in the various states to determine how the general and specific statutory pronouncements have been interpreted in the context of different types of retirement facilities.[3] If an exemption is available, it can result in avoidance not only of state income taxes but also, more important, of local ad valorem real property taxes.

In general, a housing facility's exemption from federal income tax is no guarantee of state tax exemption. To the contrary, most states have developed much stricter standards for retirement projects than the IRS. Thus, for example, while the federal government exempts self-supporting, often luxury, elderly projects that follow the standards of Revenue Ruling 72–124 (provision of housing, health, and financial security), most states that have considered the question deny tax exemption where the owner charges residents fees sufficient to meet operating expenses. As at the federal level, state governments have become increasingly strict in granting tax exemptions to nonprofit organizations.[4] As of 1988, several states —including Arizona, Colorado, Connecticut, Illinois, Indiana, Kansas, Kentucky, Minnesota, Missouri, New York, Oregon, Pennsylvania, South Dakota, West Virginia, and Wisconsin—had considered changing the rules for tax exemption for nonprofit charitable organizations[5] (see also §9.1(b) regarding federal tax exemption). In 1994, more than half the state legislatures considered bills to restrict the availability of property tax exemptions to homes for the aging. Although most bills failed, New Hampshire, New Jersey, Pennsylvania, and Utah did pass such statutes. Many states whose legislation failed are reintroducing such bills, and new states are challenging such exemptions.[6]

Some states will not challenge a nonprofit entity's tax exemption if the facility provider agrees to pay a fee in lieu of property taxes in an amount equal to a percentage of its gross revenues or of the property taxes that the facility would pay if it were not tax-exempt. Other states allow facilities to donate services in lieu of taxes in an amount equal to a proportion of their gross revenues or the property taxes that they would pay if they were taxable.

To avoid a loss of their tax-exempt status, homes for the aging may need to demonstrate their "social responsibility." They should document charitable (that is, unreimbursed) care and community services and measure community need for (and, if appropriate, provide) services such as blood pressure screening, health checks, and child care. The American Association of Homes and Services for the Aging also recommends establishing coalitions between long-term-care providers and other nonprofit organizations to forestall the introduction of legislation in this arena.[7]

§10.2 Survey of State Laws and Cases

A survey of selected contemporary case law and statutes from 45 states that have considered tax exemptions for homes for the aging follows:[8]

(a) Alaska

Alaska statute allows an ad valorem tax exemption for multipurpose seniors' centers developed and operated by nonprofit corporations.[9] A multipurpose seniors' center is a facility where persons 60 or older are provided with services and activities suited to their particular needs.[10]

(b) Arkansas

Arkansas provides for a kind of partial tax exemption in some instances: housing owned and operated by a nonprofit corporation or association for occupancy or use by elderly people, the construction of which is financed by the federal government, shall be valued, for purposes of assessment of property tax, on the basis of the equity owned in the housing by the nonprofit corporation or association.[11]

(c) Arizona

Arizona statute provides for a property tax exemption for residential apartment house facilities that are designed to serve the handicapped or elderly and where the operating expenses are substantially subsidized by either federal, state, or local governments or by nonprofit organizations.[12] In addition, Arizona statute provides for a property tax exemp-

tion for apartment house facilities that are designed to serve the handicapped or persons over 62 years of age, when such a facility is not used or held for profit and is located adjacent to property exempted from property taxes as a not-for-profit facility providing health-related services to the handicapped or persons over 62 years of age and such facility is operated by the same persons or associations as the adjacent property.[13] Consequently, senior citizen apartments that were owned and operated by a hospital to provide low-rent housing and medical care for aging persons and that were not designed to make a profit constituted a charitable institution for the purposes of a property tax exemption.[14]

(d) California

California Revenue and Taxation Code Section 214(f) provides an exemption for elderly housing owned and operated by an entity exempt from federal income tax pursuant to Section 501(c)(3) and that:

- was financed by the federal government through one of several specified HUD programs; or
- offers care or special services designed to meet the particular needs of the elderly; or
- provides housing and related facilities for low- and moderate-income elderly or handicapped families.

The second provision was added by amendment in 1984 to provide specifically that non–HUD facilities offering services specially tailored to meet the needs of the elderly be exempted from real property tax.[15]

Before that amendment, several cases in the courts sought interpretation of the earlier version of the statute. The courts had determined that the mere provision of housing to the elderly at market rates would not qualify for the tax exemption, even though the facility owner was a nonprofit corporation.[16] The courts had also made clear that, in situations involving nonprofit continuing-care facilities, the provision of personal care to the elderly would make even a market-rate, upper-income facility eligible for property tax exemption.[17] The very liberal amendment to Revenue and Taxation Code Section 214(f) now makes it possible for facilities to qualify for the exemption even if they do not necessarily provide care but offer some specialized service program for their elderly residents. It remains to be seen in California what types of specialized services will be required to meet the test of the amended statute.

In addition, California provides an exemption from sales and use tax for meals served to and consumed by residents of a health facility, community-care facility, residential-care facility, any house supplying board and room for a flat monthly rate and serving as a principal residence exclusively for persons 62 years of age or older and for any housing that primarily serves older persons and is financed by a state or federal program.[18]

(e) Colorado

Colorado statute provides an exemption for homes for people age 62 years and over whose income is up to 150 percent of the limits for low-income public housing[19] as well as for charity-run health care facilities.[20] Accordingly, a nursing home for elderly persons is exempt from tax where all residents need nursing care and those unable to pay are not charged or receive a reduced rate.[21]

(f) Connecticut

Connecticut statute exempts property of a Connecticut corporation that is organized exclusively for charitable purposes.[22] Exemption was denied in the case of a church's housing project for the elderly because the church failed to prove that the project was not self-supporting and that admission of residents to the project would make it less likely that the residents would become burdens on society.[23] Relevant to these determinations were the facts that the residents had paid an initial fee of $73,000 and a monthly maintenance fee of $350 and that there were no income or wealth restrictions on applicants.

However, a congregate-living facility for elderly people was allowed a tax exemption based primarily on the fact that the facility did not require a downpayment for the unit occupied, even though residents were charged an average monthly payment of $1,273 for the room or suite they occupied.[24] Also taken into consideration was the fact that the facility had a policy that once a resident was admitted, if he or she became unable to meet the standard fee and any other charges for reasons that were beyond the res-

ident's control, then the facility would take such steps as were necessary to maintain that person in the residence.

(g) Delaware

Delaware statute exempts land and improvements held by a church, religious society, charitable corporation, or nonprofit organization devoted to the housing of elderly persons, provided that the entire property is operated on a nonprofit basis and no less than 75 percent of the dwelling units are rented and occupied by elderly persons. Elderly persons are defined as persons age 62 or over. However, a facility that is granted a tax exemption must pay a special assessment in lieu of taxes in an amount not less than 10 percent of the gross rentals derived from the project, less the cost of utilities and the cost of providing special social services to the elderly residing in the project.[25]

A nonprofit corporation operating an apartment house for the elderly and handicapped was allowed an exemption even though the corporation's charter could be amended to eliminate its nonprofit and charitable activities and the corporation leased several apartments to tenants under 62 years of age. The rents set for the apartments were lower than rents generally charged for ordinary apartments. Residents who could not afford to pay an increase in rent were permitted to remain at the previous rate. There was no discrimination of any nature in the selection of tenants and no evidence that the apartments were held as an investment.[26]

(h) Florida

Florida statute bases tax exemption on the renter relief section of the state constitution and not on a general notion of charitability. The statute exempts homes for the aging under the following circumstances: the applicant must be a nonprofit corporation that has qualified as an exempt charitable organization under Section 501(c)(3) of the Internal Revenue Code; at least 75 percent of the occupants must be over age 62 or totally and permanently disabled; those portions of the home for the aging that are devoted exclusively to the rendering of nursing or medical services are exempt from ad valorem taxation; and, after removing the assessed value exempt from ad valorem taxation, homes for the aging are exempt only to the extent that residency in the facility is restricted to persons who are permanent residents of the state and are either persons who have gross incomes of not more than $7,200 per year and are 62 years of age or older or couples, one of whom is 62 years of age or older, having a combined gross income of not more than $8,000 per year.[27] The nonprofit corporation will not be denied tax exemption if, for tax purposes, the property is leased to a Florida limited partnership, the sole general partner of which is the nonprofit corporation, and the facility was in existence or under construction before April 1, 1995.[28]

Under Florida law, a facility that was the equivalent of a high-priced condominium providing luxury living did not qualify for tax-exempt status as fulfilling a charitable purpose, even though its use was limited to older persons and it was operated by a licensed nonprofit organization.[29] In a nursing facility case, exemption from ad valorem taxes was upheld for the entire facility, even though only one-third of the patients were private-pay.[30] The court found it inappropriate to look at the income levels of patients rather than at the overall charitable objectives of the corporation. In addition, Florida provides an exemption from sales and use tax for nonprofit corporations that are exempt from federal income tax under Section 501(c)(3) and that operate either homes for the aging under Fla. Stat. §196.1975 or licensed nursing homes and hospices.[31]

(i) Hawaii

Hawaii statute provides an exemption for nursing homes and federally subsidized housing for seniors.[32] However, a church-run retirement facility that accepted only reasonably healthy persons and required all residents to pay established charges was also entitled to an exemption since the primary purpose of such charges was to further the residence's objectives of providing housing and services for elderly persons and not to produce income.[33]

(j) Idaho

The Idaho general exemption for charitable institutions provides in part an exemption for property belonging to any fraternal, benevolent, or charitable corporation or society used exclusively for the purposes for which such corporation or society is formed.[34] Therefore, to be granted an exemption, the organization must prove, first, that it is a charitable organization and, second, that the claimed exempt property is used exclusively for charitable purposes.[35]

A religious nonprofit community for the elderly consisting of skilled-nursing facilities and independent-living apartments was allowed a partial exemption only for the skilled-nursing facilities. The independent-living apartments were denied a tax exemption primarily because the residents were required to pay an initial founder's fee and a monthly maintenance fee (or no initial fee but an elevated monthly fee). In addition, no person who was unable to pay the founder's fee was ever admitted to the apartments. When one resident was unable to pay the monthly fee, she was referred to the county welfare director. Finally, the independent-living apartments were provided at the same or comparable rate as housing available in the private sector or commercial retirement centers.[36]

In addition, an Idaho seniors' housing community with residential units and an intermediate-care facility was found not to be a charitable institution eligible for exemption from Idaho real property tax because the $25,000 entrance fee and monthly fees charged to residents were sufficient to cover current operating expenses and to retire the home's debt.[37] To qualify for tax exemption as a charitable institution under Idaho Code §63–105C, the institution must provide a "general public benefit" by directly donating to the general public or by "fulfill[ing] a need which the government might otherwise be required to fill." The Supreme Court of Idaho held that a facility providing low-income housing to senior citizens (persons 62 years of age or older) and disabled persons did not qualify for tax exemption because the facility was supported only by federal tax dollars and rent payments from residents rather than by private donations. That is, the facility did not fulfill a government need because it was "not created to lessen the burden on government" but instead derived almost all of its support from federal funding.[38]

(k) Illinois

Illinois statute exempts "old people's homes," homes for the aging, facilities for the developmentally disabled, and nonprofit organizations that provide services or facilities related to the goals of educational, social, and physical development, provided that certain requirements are satisfied. First, the organization must be exempt pursuant to the Internal Revenue Code. Second, either the applicant's bylaws must provide for a waiver or reduction of any fees based on the individual's ability to pay, or the home or facility must be qualified, built, or financed under Section 202 of the National Housing Act of 1959.[39]

In Illinois, to receive an exemption, the organization must show, among other things, that funds are derived mainly from private and public charity and that charity is dispensed to all who need it and apply.[40] In one case, an exemption was denied when applicants for residence were required to pay a substantial founder's fee, 85 to 97 percent of total facility funding came from residents' fees, and the facility was not required to accept applicants or maintain residents who could not pay the required fees, even though approximately 5 percent of the residents were accepted or maintained despite their inability to pay the fees.[41] In Illinois, "all facts are to be construed and all debatable questions are to be resolved in favor of taxation."[42]

In another case, a religious nonprofit organization ran a facility for the care of elderly people. It consisted of an intermediate-care section and an independent-living section. The organization charged a fee in the form of a life-lease payment plus a no-interest loan. The intermediate-care portion received an exemption because it accepted applicants who needed care regardless of ability to pay, eliminated the application fee, assisted residents who became unable to pay monthly fees, and did not base room assignment on ability to pay. The independent-living portion of the facility was not granted an exemption, however, because it limited residence to members of the faith and friends who were able to pay the admission fee. While there had been evidence of some subsidies, there was no corporate commitment to pay the established fees.[43] Similarly, a life-care community was found ineligible for occupation and use tax exemptions because it failed to provide charity

to all who needed it and did not derive its funds mainly from charity.[44]

(l) Indiana

Indiana statute allows an exemption to the owner of a residential facility for the aging upon a showing that the owner is a licensed, not-for-profit Indiana corporation.[45] Nevertheless, a licensed, not-for-profit corporation that owns and operates housing projects for low-income elderly residents and that does not qualify for exemption as a licensed residential facility for the aging is not precluded from claiming exemption under a statute exempting property owned, occupied, and used for educational, literary, scientific, religious, or charitable purposes.[46] In addition, two retirement homes for the aging were found to be operated exclusively for charitable purposes and thus exempt from gross income tax under Ind. Code Ann. §6-2.1-3-20 even though the residents of the retirement homes were charged a fee for the services and amenities provided. The court found that the benefits provided were "beyond mere shelter, food, and assistance to the aged" and that financial adjustments were made to accommodate residents who could not afford the rent.[47]

(m) Iowa

Iowa has recognized tax exemption for seniors' properties that generate only enough income to stay in operation, do not discriminate against persons unable to pay, and provide some gratuitous or partly gratuitous care.[48] In addition, in a case where residents paid rent sufficient to cover operating costs, but construction costs and some staff services were donated, exemption was granted.[49] Property tax exemption similarly was granted to an intermediate-care facility because of both the facility's admissions policy, which did not discriminate between private-pay and Title XIX patients, and the fact that the Title XIX payments did not fully cover the per diem costs of covered patients. However, the same case upheld a denial of the exemption to the residential-care portion of the facility.[50] Another case granted exemption to the operator of a nonprofit community for elderly people even though there was a fitness requirement for applicants, residents were charged fees, contributions came largely from residents and were a small percentage of the operating budget, and the income of the community slightly exceeded its expenses for the year in question.[51] Where, however, a nonprofit home provided no concessions on rent to those unable to pay, there was no basis for tax exemption.[52]

A continuing-care retirement community was not granted an exemption from property tax under Iowa Code §427.1(9) for a portion of its facility even though the rest of its facility was tax-exempt.[53] The retirement community provided several cottages for elderly persons who were able to live and function independently as well as several buildings of housing units for elderly persons who needed direct care. The Iowa Supreme Court found that the cottages were not used for a charitable purpose and thus were not tax-exempt because only persons able to pay the entrance fees were accepted into the cottages and the housing and care provided to occupants benefited persons who were capable of paying for them.

Similarly, the Iowa Supreme Court denied tax-exempt status to a low-income housing provider that was unable to demonstrate a charitable purpose under the Care Initiatives criteria.[54] Among other deficiencies, the provider presented no evidence that it leased units to persons who could not pay the subsidized rental fee or waived rent for lessees who became unable to pay. Although the residence at issue had a policy designating one rent-free apartment for abused women, the court concluded that one rent-free apartment out of 37 total apartments did not qualify the entire property as charitable.

In an action to determine which property tax rate should apply (there was no question of tax-exempt status), a multistory building occupied by older adults was determined to be commercial (and so subject to a higher rate) despite its organization as a cooperative. Residents had insufficient ownership control over the building to classify it as residential: entry and monthly fees went to the nonprofit corporation that organized the cooperative, maintained the building, provided services to residents, and included the building in its financial statements and long-term debt structure.[55]

(n) Kansas

Kansas statute exempts nonprofit hospitals and adult-care homes operated by nonprofit organizations when charges to the residents produce an aggregate amount that is less than the actual operation cost of the home. Factors to be taken into consideration include reasonable depreciation and interest on indebtedness, acquisition costs, interest and other expenses of financing acquisition costs, lease expenses and costs of services provided by a parent corporation at its cost, contributions that are deductible under the Kansas income tax act, and all intangible property, including monies, notes, and other evidences of debt and the income therefrom, belonging exclusively to such a corporation and used exclusively for the purposes of the adult-care homes. Limitations on the charges to residents are not applicable when the property is either actually and exclusively used for housing for elderly and handicapped persons with limited or lower income or exclusively used for cooperative housing for persons with limited or low income. Tax-deductible contributions to a nonprofit corporation dedicated to providing housing and associated services to the elderly should not be included in revenues when determining whether "charges to residents" produce an amount less than the actual operation cost.[56]

In *Congregational Homes, Inc. v. Shawnee County,* No. 93–CV–1222 (Sept. 6, 1994), a continuing-care retirement community with entrance fees and monthly fees producing revenues that amounted to less than the actual cost of operations was found eligible for property tax exemption under Kansas law. An apartment complex operated by a nonprofit corporation for low-income elderly residents was granted an exemption even though four of the residence's tenants had income that exceeded HUD guidelines for subsidization and four other apartments were rented to handicapped individuals who were not elderly.[57]

(o) Maine

Maine statute provides an exemption for property owned and occupied or used solely by "benevolent and charitable" institutions for their own purposes. "Benevolent and charitable" institutions include nonprofit nursing homes, with nonprofit defined the same way as under Section 501 of the Internal Revenue Code.[58] Accordingly, a project operated for low-income, elderly, or handicapped persons was found to be a "benevolent and charitable" institution, although the residents of the project paid a portion of the rent and could be evicted if they failed to pay the nominal fees.[59] In *City of Lewiston v. Marcotte Congregate Housing, Inc.*,[60] the Supreme Judicial Court of Maine emphasized the requirement that an institution be operated solely for charitable purposes in order to qualify for tax exemption. The court held that a multiple-use building that included a congregate-care facility, among other types of facilities, did not qualify for tax exemption because 18 percent of the building was not used for charitable purposes.

(p) Maryland

Maryland has granted tax exemption for continuing-care facilities for the aging and for property owned by a facility and used either to provide nursing care, domiciliary care, or comprehensive care or to deliver exclusively nonprofit services and activities to residents.[61] Maryland statute also specifically exempts nonprofit housing for senior citizens.[62] In addition, Maryland provides a property tax exemption for property owned by a nonprofit hospital or a nonprofit housing corporation.[63]

Property eligible for the domiciliary care exemption includes the portion of land reasonably allocable to the provision of administration, activities, or services but does not include independent-living units. In one facility providing independent-living apartments, domiciliary care, and a health center, all as part of a continuing-care program, a real property tax exemption was denied for the apartment units but retained for the care facilities.[64] Apartment residents were charged entrance fees and had to meet health criteria before admission. While there was a policy to care for those who ran out of funds, no apartment resident had ever invoked the provision. However, such a facility should now be able to qualify under the continuing-care facility exemption.

A nonprofit housing property tax exemption was denied to a facility for the elderly and handicapped that, in addition to operating and maintaining the property, performed only minimal other services,

mostly for tenants. The provision of nonprofit housing alone was not sufficient to entitle the organization to the exemption; rather, the organization must also "promote the general welfare of the people of the state." No private donations supported the operation of the building, and federal government subsidies could not be considered "donations" for the support of a property for which a charitable exemption was claimed.[65]

(q) Michigan

Michigan statute provides an exemption for housing occupied or used solely by elderly or handicapped families if the units are financed pursuant to the HUD Section 202 program.[66] However, facilities that probably would have qualified for federal exemption under Revenue Ruling 72–124 were found not to be exempt from state tax where residents had to pay substantial entrance fees and pass health and financial examinations; moreover, residents enjoyed above-average accommodations.[67] Two homes for the elderly were found not to qualify as charitable facilities and thus were not eligible for tax exemption because residents of the homes were chosen on the basis of their good health and ability to pay the monthly charge, were not provided with any fee waivers, and received only the benefits for which they paid.[68] Even a facility that provided elderly housing and moved residents to an adjacent nursing unit if they became unable to pay was not exempt, contrary to the federal position in Letter Ruling 8117221 (see §9.3(b)(6)).[69]

Nonetheless, the Michigan Tax Tribunal allowed an exemption from ad valorem tax for an office building owned by a nonprofit corporation on land adjacent to a HUD Section 236 elderly and handicapped facility, where the office building was used to provide essential services to the project.[70] A religious home for the elderly was also deemed exempt when room, board, and care were offered free of charge on an unlimited basis.[71]

(r) Minnesota

The Minnesota Supreme Court has listed several factors bearing on whether a facility qualifies as a purely public charity entitled to an exemption. Those factors include whether the stated purpose of the undertaking is to be helpful to others without the immediate expectation of material reward; whether the entity involved is supported by donations and gifts in whole or in part; whether the recipients of the charity are required to pay for the assistance received in whole or in part; whether the income received from gifts, donations, and charges to users produces a profit; whether the beneficiaries are restricted; and whether dividends or assets upon dissolution are available to private interests.[72]

In addition, homes are denied an exemption as purely public charities when three conditions apply: residents are required to submit financial statements showing their ability to pay entrance fees and monthly charges, residents are required to undergo physical examinations, and only one person had been accepted for residency when it appeared he could not meet the monthly payments for at least three-fourths of his lifetime.[73] In another Minnesota case, a nonprofit home providing seniors' housing and health care was denied an exemption when it charged a $17,000 refundable "warrant," provided only a month-to-month lease, and did not have any policy regarding persons unable to afford the warrant.[74]

(s) Mississippi

In *Hattiesburg Area Senior Services, Inc. & Wesley Manor Retirement Community v. Lamar County*,[75] a continuing-care retirement community founded by a church organization was denied property tax exemption because the facility was used by residents and not exclusively for the charitable society's activities, fees covered all operating expenses, and the application process was designed to produce residents capable of paying the fees.

(t) Missouri

Missouri allows an exemption from ad valorem tax when real and personal property are used exclusively for purely charitable purposes and not held for private profit.[76] This does not include real property that is not actually used or occupied for the organization's activities but rather real property that is held or used as an investment, even if the income

or rentals received from that property are used wholly for a charitable purpose.

The Missouri Supreme Court has devised a three-pronged test to determine whether use of property is charitable: the property must be owned and operated on a not-for-profit basis, earnings from operations must be directed toward the charitable objective, and the property must benefit society generally as well as the persons directly served.[77]

Under this test, a Missouri retirement home with residential- and medical-care facilities was denied a charitable exemption on the grounds that it required a substantial initial endowment by its residents with an equal amount of additional assets remaining in reserve, charged a substantial monthly fee, and retained discretion in determining whether the fee should be waived, thereby effectively denying its services to a large percentage of the elderly based on finances.[78] Similarly, a life-care facility was not entitled to a tax exemption because the facility effectively screened out low-income residents through the application process despite the facility's contractual obligation to support those residents who became financially dependent while living at the facility.[79]

On the other hand, a facility that operated on a not-for-profit basis, received significant subsidies both from HUD and private charity, and was designed to meet the physical, social, and psychological needs of the elderly was held to benefit society and lessen the likelihood of burdens on the government, thereby qualifying for a charitable exemption.[80]

One entrance fee life-care community received different treatment for its nursing facility than for its residential units. The skilled-nursing facility was granted an exemption because that portion of the community had never denied admission based on inability to pay for services. However, the apartment portion was denied the exemption and classified as commercial property because the entrance fee structure did not conform to the statutory scheme whereby only condominiums, cooperatives, and buildings with four or fewer dwelling units are deemed residential.[81]

(u) Montana

Montana statute provides a property tax exemption for institutions that are directly used for purely pub-

lic charitable purposes, specifically including property owned and used by nonprofit organizations
operating facilities for care of the retired, aging, or
chronically ill. Property leased from a federal, state,
or local government entity by a nonprofit organization and similarly used is also exempt from property
tax. An institution of purely public charity means an
organization that qualifies as a tax-exempt organization for federal tax purposes under Internal
Revenue Code Section 501(c)(3) and accomplishes
its activities through absolute gratuity or grants.[82]

(v) Nebraska

Even though a Nebraska home charged residents
who could afford fees, it was deemed tax-exempt
when ability to pay was not a condition of admission and no patient had ever been removed from
the home for inability to pay.[83] However, a facility
simply operating at cost from rents did not qualify.[84] On the ground that its primary purpose was
the furnishing of low-rent housing, an apartment
complex for the elderly that included an adjacent
nursing home was also denied an exemption.[85]

(w) Nevada

Nevada statute allows an exemption for property
used exclusively for housing and related facilities
for elderly or handicapped persons if the property
is owned and operated by a nonprofit corporation
and is at least partially financed by a loan under
the National Housing Act.[86]

(x) New Hampshire

New Hampshire statute allows an exemption for
nonprofit community housing and community health
care facilities for elderly and disabled persons.[87]
Apartment units in a housing project operated by a
charitable corporation for low-income elderly and
handicapped individuals were held exempt from
taxation even though the apartments were not open
to all senior citizens. The project was subsidized by
HUD, and the tenants living in the project were required to pay 25 percent of their income as rent to
defray operating expenses.[88] In addition, a home
for the aging operated by a nonprofit corporation

was held exempt as a charitable entity when, based
on the terms of its charter and the fact that it had
provided low-cost care for the elderly exclusively
for 55 years, the corporation had an enforceable
obligation to provide charitable services.[89]

(y) New Jersey

In addition to a tax exemption for general charitable
purposes, New Jersey statute specifically exempts
buildings used for "hospital purposes," including nursing homes, residential health care facilities, assisted-
living residences, similar facilities that provide medical, nursing, or personal care services to the elderly,
and portions of continuing-care retirement communities that are reasonably allocable as health care
facilities for the elderly.[90]

Under New Jersey's statutory requirement that
property be "actually and exclusively used" for "religious or charitable purposes"[91] to qualify for state
tax exemption, a retirement community failed to
qualify because it did not obligate itself to care for
residents who became either unable to meet their
monthly charges or unmanageable because of illness.
Also cited as grounds for the failure to qualify were
the community's substantial admittance fee ($25,000),
monthly charges ($205 to $365), and a policy of
refunding only part of the admittance fee when a
resident's agreement had to be terminated for reasons other than death.[92] In two other cases, a nursing and retirement facility failed to qualify its parent
organization for a state tax exemption because the
facility was a consistent profit earner whose patients
and residents bore the costs of operation[93] while a
nonprofit corporation formed to construct and operate senior citizen apartments for persons of low
and moderate income failed to qualify because residents were required to offer substantial security for
rental payment ($15,000 refundable deposit and
sponsorship by a person who could guarantee that
the rent would be paid), pay substantially all operating expenses, and leave the premises if they no
longer could pay rent.[94]

(z) New Mexico

A nursing home operated by a nonprofit corporation was exempt from property tax when the sub-

stantial and primary use was for charitable purposes and residents were largely aging, ill, and indigent.[95]

(aa) New York

In New York, a retirement home was found exempt when it provided residential care, 90 percent of the residents received government benefits, and voluntary contributions were required to meet a financial deficit.[96] The fact that a home, in good faith, paid more for its property than it was worth did not disqualify it from exemption.[97] However, property used as a retirement community for "middle-income" elderly did not qualify for a tax exemption.[98]

(bb) North Carolina

North Carolina law provides that property may qualify for a tax exemption if it is owned by a "home for the aged, sick, or infirm," which is defined as a self-contained community designed for elderly residents that operates a skilled-nursing facility, intermediate-care facility, or home for the aging; includes residential dwelling units, recreational facilities, and service facilities; is owned, operated, and managed by a religious or fraternal organization or by a nonprofit corporation whose board of directors was elected by a religious or fraternal organization; and maintains an active program to generate funds for the subsidization of financially needy residents.[99] One facility was deemed to have satisfied the last criterion by establishing and actively soliciting contributions to an endowment fund to assist the indigent.[100]

Before enactment of the exemption statute, a non-profit corporation that owned and operated a self-contained community complex for the elderly was not allowed an exemption if prospective residents had to undergo an application process that included financial screening, had to demonstrate financial ability to support themselves for a reasonable time after admission, and had to pay a substantial "life-occupancy" fee on admission and a monthly "service fee." In addition, the corporation neither received nor relied on donations from outside sources for the operation of its programs.[101]

In *Southminster, Inc. v. Justus*,[102] the court granted a sales and use tax exemption for an entrance fee retirement community—complete with a health care center—targeted to the affluent elderly but with an endowment fund for residents who run out of assets. The court rejected the state's argument that the facility's residents were not "legitimate subjects of charity" and found that the meaning of "charitable" is "sufficiently broad to include aid and assistance provided for the elderly and infirm without regard to individual poverty."

(cc) North Dakota

North Dakota statute provides for an ad valorem tax exemption for general charitable purposes.[103] The Supreme Court of North Dakota has ruled that even though a nonprofit operator of a home for the aging and infirm charged fees to its residents, earned a profit, and never had provided free care, the operator's property was entitled to a charitable tax exemption because the profit earned was directly and entirely related to the institution's charitable use and was reinvested in the upkeep and expansion of the home instead of inuring to a private individual.[104] Nevertheless, the court also has ruled that merely providing a multiunit residential facility for the elderly where applicants are required to "function independently" is not enough to qualify an organization for a charitable tax exemption. Rather, the organization must provide care to elderly persons who have a demonstrated need for it.[105]

(dd) Ohio

Ohio statute allows an exemption for general charitable purposes and specifically includes property owned and used by nonprofit organizations exclusively as a home for the aged, though not independent-living facilities.[106] A home for the aged is a place of residence for the aged that is either a nursing home, rest home, adult-care facility, or assisted-living facility and that meets the following standards: owned and operated not for profit; open to the public without regard to race, color, or national origin; does not pay unreasonably high compensation for services rendered, interest on debts incurred, or purchase price for land, buildings, equipment, supplies, or other goods; and provides services for the life of each resident without regard to his or her ability to continue payment for the full cost of the services.[107] This standard replaces the former requirement that no more than 95 percent of the operating expenses at the facility be paid for by or on behalf of the resident and that certain services be made available at or below reasonable cost for the life of each resident without regard to his or her ability to continue payment to cover the services' full cost.[108] To be entitled to a real property tax exemption for a home for the aged, an applicant for the exemption must have received a license to operate the facility by the tax lien date of the year for which the exemption is sought.[109]

A congregate housing facility providing below-market-rate shelter, food, and minimal care was not eligible for exemption because it provided primarily building maintenance services rather than personal care. Furthermore, residents essentially had to be independent, and no permanent medical facilities existed.[110]

One case underscores the strict view of charitability followed in Ohio. Although residents of a facility for the elderly and handicapped received HUD rental assistance if the contract rent exceeded 30 percent of their incomes, the appellate court denied tax exemption on the grounds that residents paid part of their rent and received elective services not funded by the provider. The court followed precedent that furnishing of low-cost housing at or below market prices is not exclusively charitable where residents pay some or all the rent.[111]

In *Board of Education v. Limbach*,[112] the Ohio Supreme Court reversed the Ohio Tax Commissioner and Board of Tax Appeals and found that a continuing-care retirement community could not qualify as a "hospital facility" because of its "residential living quarters" and therefore was not entitled to a real property tax exemption. The court required a split listing of exempt (nursing) and nonexempt (residential) quarters.[113]

(ee) Oklahoma

Oklahoma statute provides that all property of any institution organized as a nonprofit or charitable institution under Oklahoma law shall be exempt from ad valorem taxation, provided that the net income from such property is used exclusively within the state for charitable purposes and none of the income

benefits any private stockholder. The facilities of the institution must also be available to anyone regardless of ability to pay.[114]

An Oklahoma residential community center for the elderly that collected rent from its residents was exempt when rent receipts were an inconsequential revenue source as compared with the operational costs of the facility and when charitable donations provided nearly all the funds for operating and maintaining the facility.[115] A not-for-profit corporation that was created to promote the charitable purpose of health care also was exempted from the ad valorem tax pursuant to the statute.[116]

(ff) Oregon

Oregon statute provides an exemption for incorporated literary, benevolent, charitable, and scientific institutions. State or federally financed property that is exclusively occupied by and used in the operation of nonprofit homes for the elderly and that provides permanent housing, recreational and social facilities, and care for the elderly is entitled to a state tax exemption.[117] However, a home for the aging is not exempt when it fails to treat residents alike without regard to ability to pay and does not have a charitable trust fund.[118] A nonprofit corporation organized as a nursing home has been held to be entitled to a tax exemption.[119]

(gg) Pennsylvania

In addition to a tax exemption for general charitable purposes, Pennsylvania statute specifically exempts organizations providing residential housing services when the organizations receive subsidies for at least 95 percent of their units from a low-income federal housing program. Any surplus from such assistance must be used for charitable purposes within the organization.[120]

An exemption was denied to a retirement community that charged substantial admission and monthly fees, financially screened applicants, had the right to require a resident to vacate for nonpayment of fees, and had only once provided a subsidy to a resident.[121] In a case with similar facts, an exemption was denied because, although the home alleged it had a policy not to terminate residence of those unable to pay, it could point to no instance where a person had become unable to pay.[122] Seniors' housing adjacent to an exempt home also was not considered a charitable use when the admission fee was calculated to meet the cost of residence, the facility required financial and physical screenings, and no substantial financial subsidy or benefit was available if a move to the exempt home was required due to financial or health reasons.[123] In addition, an exemption was denied to a housing project for elderly and handicapped residents because the entire funding for the project, apart from rents paid by residents, was derived from the federal government; thus, the project was not a "purely public charity" within the meaning of the statute.[124] Furthermore, cottages founded by a private charity that provided housing for the elderly were deemed not to be "purely public charity" because they consistently realized a substantial profit.[125]

However, an apartment complex for the elderly was exempt when it was founded and maintained by a private charity, residents did not pay the full cost of care, admission was not based on any financial test, and private charity subsidized operations.[126] Notwithstanding the fact that there were no indigent residents who received government support, a nursing home was exempt when it provided shelter and care for many residents who could not pay the cost of care, bore one-third of the cost of care for half its residents, served residents who were only partially covered by Medicaid, earned no private profit, and was founded in part by a large contribution from a charitable organization.[127]

(hh) Rhode Island

Rhode Island statute allows an exemption for property held exclusively for the aid or support of the aging poor or for a hospital for the sick or disabled.[128]

(ii) South Carolina

South Carolina statute allows an exemption for all property of nonprofit housing corporations devoted exclusively to providing below-cost housing for either the aging or the handicapped, as authorized by Section 202 of the Housing Act of 1959 and reg-

ulated by regulations that appear in the *Federal Register,* 24 C.F.R. Part 885.[129]

(jj) South Dakota

South Dakota statute permits an exemption for property owned and used primarily for health care and related purposes and may include congregate housing. Congregate housing is deemed health care-related if it is an assisted-, independent-, or group-living environment that offers residential accommodations and supporting services primarily for the elderly and is operated by a licensed health care facility.[130]

A provider of congregate housing was entitled to an exemption when apartment units were located next to and associated with a tax-exempt nursing home. The apartments provided residential accommodations and supporting services and admitted all applicants consistent with the facility's ability to provide required medical services.[131]

(kk) Tennessee

Tennessee statute provides exemption from ad valorem and personalty taxes for property of not-for-profit corporations whose projects are financed by a grant under Section 515(b) or 521 of the Housing Act of 1949 or by a loan made, insured, or guaranteed by a branch, department, or agency of the U.S. government under Sections 8, 202, 221, 231, or 236 of the National Housing Act and provided that certain additional requirements are met (e.g., a volunteer board).[132] A nonprofit corporation providing housing for the elderly and handicapped met the qualifications of the statute and was granted an exemption from ad valorem taxes without having to meet an additional test of "charitability."[133] However, a nonprofit retirement community promising life care was denied a charitable tax exemption because it required substantial entrance fees from residents, only once had subsidized a resident, and judged applications for admission on the basis of financial ability as well as moral character and physical condition.[134]

(ll) Texas

In Texas, statutory exemptions exist for elderly facilities providing housing, health care, and other services and for medical care facilities, provided that services in both cases are provided without regard to ability to pay.[135]

Thus, a home that subsidized certain residents from a charitable fund was exempt, even though residents were generally charged fees and in some years the facility realized a profit.[136] Likewise, a nursing home that charged fees but did not refuse admission or continued occupancy to the indigent was held to be exempt.[137] The Texas Court of Appeals has held that a nonprofit religious organization operating a retirement center with housing, social, health, and educational programs, without regard to the residents' ability to pay, is entitled to exempt status.[138]

However, when a facility was designed only for those paying with private funds or public welfare monies and the corporation accumulated large sums over the years, exemption was denied.[139] And when an entrance fee facility sought to fill one-third of its units with residents in need of charity but was unsuccessful in doing so except for a very small percentage, exemption was denied.[140]

(mm) Utah

The Utah Supreme Court, interpreting the Utah statute that provides for a tax exemption for any property dedicated to charitable or religious purposes, has enunciated several factors that must be weighed in determining whether a particular institution is using its property exclusively for charitable purposes. These factors include whether the stated purpose of the entity is to provide a significant service to others without immediate expectation of material reward; whether the entity is supported, and to what extent, by donations and gifts; whether recipients are required to pay in whole or in part for the assistance received; whether the income received from all sources produces a profit; whether recipients are restricted; and whether some form of financial benefit is available to private interests.[141]

A later case explained that for property to qualify as a "charitable use" for purposes of exemption, there must be a public benefit or contribution to the common good or the public welfare. Furthermore, it is necessary that there be an element of a gift to the community. Accordingly, an apartment building for needy, elderly, and handicapped families and indi-

viduals was exempt when none of the residents would have been able to live in comparable housing anywhere else in the county for the amount that each resident paid at the apartment. The apartment building provided "a gift to the community" in that the corporation owning the building made substantial contributions of both money and services for management of the building and there was a substantial imbalance in the exchange between the management corporation and the tenants. The case explains that an organization may be exempt even though some charges are made to recipients of its services to help cover operating expenses as long as the charges are not commensurate with the benefits provided.[142]

The Utah State Tax Commission has more recently established very strict standards under which a charitable nonprofit hospital or nursing home may receive a property tax exemption. These standards were adopted in 1990 following the guidelines set forth in *Intermountain Health Care* and are as follows: The institution must establish that it is organized on a nonprofit basis to provide hospital or nursing home care, promote health care, or provide health-related assistance to the general public; that none of its net earnings and no donations inure to the benefit of private individuals; that it admits and treats members of the public without regard to race, religion, or gender; that hospital or nursing service is based on the clinical judgment of the physician and not on the patient's ability to pay; and that indigent persons who require generally available hospital or nursing home services receive those services for no charge or for a reduced charge in accordance with their ability to pay; that the institution's policies integrate and reflect the public interest; and that its total gift to the community exceeds on an annual basis its property tax liability for that year. Calculation of the value of the "gift" can include unreimbursed indigent care (but not usual discounts), donated volunteer hours, monetary donations, and community education and services.[143]

(nn) Vermont

Vermont statute grants a property tax exemption for property used for charitable purposes to the extent that the property is not used for private profit.[144] Tax exemption was denied to a nonprofit nursing home that provided long-term care to a hospital's patients and others on the hospital's property. The nursing home was not a "home" or "hospital" as defined by Vt. Stat. Ann. §3832(6) and was found not to be directly connected to the hospital because it accepted patients from other places. Because Vt. Stat. Ann. §3832(7) provides an exception to the property tax exemption in Vt. Stat. Ann. §3832(6) for "property used primarily for health . . . purposes," the nursing home was not exempt from the tax.[145]

(oo) Virginia

Tax-exempt status in Virginia may be achieved by two means: classification under Virginia statutes, according to which the organization must be conducted exclusively as a charity and the property used exclusively for charitable purposes; or specific designation by a three-quarter vote of the general assembly. The Supreme Court of Virginia ruled that a corporation was not entitled to exemption by classification when its housing and health care facility for the elderly levied an initial founder's fee and monthly charges in exchange for housing and nursing home care for life, and when the median net worth of residents was $110,000 after payment of the founder's fee, even though 20 of the residents had virtually no assets and 56 of the 339 apartments were specially designed for handicapped persons.[146]

(pp) Washington

Washington statute allows an exemption for nonprofit homes for the aging if the benefit of the exemption inures to the home and at least 50 percent of the occupied dwelling units are occupied by eligible residents and the home is subsidized under a U.S. Department of Housing and Urban Development program.[147]

An exemption also exists in statute for homes for the aging that meet the general provisions for exemptions for nonprofit corporations.[148] However, for a facility where almost all the income was derived from resident rents and government rent subsidies, exemption was denied because it was not shown that the organization was supported "in whole or in part by public donations or private charity."[149] For-profit nursing homes were not eligible for the "patient services" exemption from business and occupation taxes provided in Wash. Rev. Code §82.04.4289.[150]

(qq) West Virginia

West Virginia's general charitable purposes exemption includes nonprofit hospitals and nonprofit homes for the aged, friendless, or infirm.[151]

(rr) Wisconsin

Wisconsin provides a statutory state tax exemption for "benevolent" nursing homes and retirement homes for the aged.[152] A nursing home that admitted patients without regard to their ability to pay and that operated at a financial loss was therefore found to be exempt.[153] However, an organization need not operate at a loss to be benevolent, provided that there is no private inurement of net revenues.[154]

(ss) Wyoming

Wyoming statute grants a property tax exemption for "property used by a secret, benevolent and charitable society or association and senior citizens centers to the extent it is not used for private profit nor primarily for commercial purposes by the society, association or center, or lessee thereof."[155]

Notes

1. Sweterlitsch, M., "State Tax Exemptions: Homes for the Aging," Sept. 1986 (unpublished survey on file with Community Health and Nursing Services, Columbus, OH, and the author).

2. *Ibid.*

3. A detailed review of case law regarding state tax exemption for homes for the aging and for nursing homes appears at 34 A.L.R. 5th 529 (1195), 37 *A.L.R.* 3d 565 (1971), and 45 *A.L.R.* 3d 610 (1972).

4. Mayer, D., "Challenges to Non-Profits' Tax Exemption on the Rise," *Health Week,* Feb. 1, 1988, 1.

5. Gallagher, J., "The Nonprofit Tax Climate in the Fifty States," *Association Management,* Feb. 1988, 29, 32.

6. "Tax-Exemption Threats Target Nonprofits in Several States," *AAHSA Provider News,* Apr. 1995.

7. *Id.*

8. States having general charitable exemption pronouncements not specifically dealing with some form of retirement community are not addressed.

9. Alaska Stat. §47.60.080.

10. Alaska Stat. §47.60.030.

11. Ark. Stat. Ann. §26-26-1206 (1994).

12. Ariz. Rev. Stat. Ann. §42-271(13) (1986).

13. Ariz. Rev. Stat. Ann. §42-271(A)(11), (12) (Michie 1994).

14. *Memorial Hospital v. Sparks,* 453 P.2d 989 (1969).

15. Stats. 1984, c. 1102, at 22, §1.

16. *Martin Luther Homes v. County of Los Angeles,* 12 Cal. App. 3d 205, 90 Cal. Rptr. 524 (1970).

17. *John Tennant Memorial Homes v. City of Pacific Grove,* 27 Cal. App. 3d 372, 382-85, 103 Cal. Rptr. 215 (1972).

18. Cal. Rev. & Tax Code §6363.6 (West 1995).

19. Colo. Rev. Stat. §39-3-112(2), (3)(a)(II)(A). This exemption applies only if the property is owned by a non-profit corporation, by a limited partnership with a non-profit general partner formed to take advantage of federal low-income housing tax credits, or by a limited partnership, so long as each general partner of the limited partnership is a for-profit corporation with 75 percent or more of its outstanding voting stock owned by one or more non-profit corporations and with at least 75 percent of the members of its board of directors elected by one or more nonprofit corporations. Colo. Rev. Stat. 39-3-112(3)(c).

20. *Id.* at 39-3-108 (1990).

21. *Stanbro v. Baptist Home Assoc.,* 475 P.2d 23 (1970).

22. Conn. Gen. Stat. §12-81 (7) (1958).

23. *United Church of Christ v. Town of West Hartford,* 539 A.2d 573 (1988).

24. *Bannon v. Wise,* 586 A.2d 639 (Conn. App. Ct. 1990), *aff'd.,* 586 A.2d 596 (Conn. 1991).

25. Del. Rev. Code Ann. title 9, §§8151-8156 (Michie 1989 and Supp. 1990).

26. *Electra Arms Apartments and Medical Center Foundation, Inc. v. City of Wilmington,* 254 A.2d 244 (1969). The corporation was exempt from city taxation under Section 8103, the general charitable purpose exemption, and the court found it unnecessary to consider exemption under Sections 8151-8156, which specifically provide for the exemption from taxation of nonprofit housing for the elderly.

27. *Note:* The Florida Supreme Court declared the resident income test of Section 196.1975(4) unconstitutional when the statute was based on charitability in the Florida constitution. *Markham v. Evangelical Covenant Church,* 502 So. 2d 1239 (1987). However, after this case was decided, the statute was modified and is currently based on the renter relief portion of the Florida constitution rather than on charitability. These income requirements do not apply to totally and permanently disabled veterans. Fla. Stat. Ann. §196. 1975 (West Supp. 1991).

28. Fla. Stat. Ann. §196.1975(1) (West 1995).

29. *Mikos v. Plymouth Harbor, Inc.,* 316 So. 2d 627 (Fla. App. 1975). *cert. discharged,* 337 So. 2d 975 (Fla. 1976).

30. *Markham v. Broward County Nursing Home,* 540 So. 2d 940 (1989).

31. Fla. Stat. §212.08(7)(m) (1995).

32. Hawaii Rev. Stat. §§246-32(b)(2), (c)(2) (1985).

33. *Matter of Tax Appeal of Central Union Church,* 624 P.2d 1346 (Hawaii 1981).

34. Idaho Code §63-105C.

35. However, if part of a property is used for a purpose that is not directly related to charitable purposes, but that part is valued at 3 percent or less of the value of the whole property, the whole property is still exempt.

36. *Appeal of Evangelical Lutheran Good Samaritan Soc'y.,* 804 P.2d 299 (1990).

37. *Appeal of Sunny Ridge Manor, Inc.,* 675 P.2d 813 (Idaho 1984); Idaho Code §63-105C (1976) (general charitable purpose exemption only).

38. *Housing Southwest, Inc. v. Washington County,* 913 P.2d 68 (Idaho 1996).

39. Ill. Ann. Stat. ch. 35, §200/15-65 (West's Smith–Hurd 1994). *See also Henderson County Retirement Center Inc. v. Department of Revenue,* 604 N.E.2d 1003 (Ill. 1992). (Property must be "owned" by charitable organization, and right to choose when and if property may be transferred is single most significant incident of real estate ownership; organization not tax-exempt until not-for-profit lessee had control over decision to convey.)

40. *Clark v. Marian Park,* 400 N.E.2d 661 (1980); Ill. Ann. Stat. ch. 120 §500.7 (Smith–Hurd 1990) (general charitable purpose).

41. *Plymouth Place, Inc. v. Tully,* 370 N.E.2d 56 (1977). *See also Small v. Pangle,* 328 N.E.2d 285 (1975), *cert. den.,* 423 U.S. 918 (1975). (Facility not exempt as a charitable institution when all residents paid substantial monthly fees, greater source of funds was not from either public or private charity, and home had never had a resident who was unable to pay the substantial monthly charges.)

42. *Methodist Old Peoples Home v. Korzen,* 233 N.E.2d 537, 540 (1968). (Facility not exempt when home not ob-

ligated to retain residents, amount of founder's fees and monthly charges determined location of accommodation, and there were stringent health requirements for admission.)

43. *Fairview Haven v. Department of Revenue,* 506 N.E.2d 341 (1987). *See also Good Samaritan Home of Quincy v. Illinois Dep't. of Revenue,* 474 N.E.2d 1387 (1985). (Nonprofit corporation operating a nursing home and related apartment facilities for aging persons was given an exemption for the nursing home, but the apartments were held not entitled to a tax exemption because most applicants were required to pay a substantial "prepaid rent" to cover construction costs.)

44. *Wyndemere Retirement Community v. Department of Revenue,* 654 N.E.2d 608 (Ill. App. Ct.), *reh'g. denied,* 660 N.E.2d 1282 (Ill. 1995).

45. Ind. Code Ann. §6–1.1–10–18.5(2).

46. *Lincoln Hills Dev. Corp. v. Tax Comm'rs.,* 521 N.E.2d 1360 (Ind. T.C. 1988).

47. *Raintree Friends Housing, Inc. v. Indiana Department of State Revenue,* 1996 Ind. Tax LEXIS 16 (Ind. T.C. 1996).

48. *Twilight Acres v. Board of Rev. of Sac.,* 346 N.W.2d 40 (Iowa App. 1984); Iowa Code §427.1.9 (West 1990) (general charitable purpose). Iowa Code §427.1.34 (West 1990) (exempts nonprofit low-rent housing for the elderly for the term of the mortgage).

49. *Hilltop Manor v. Board of Rev. of Marion,* 346 N.W.2d 37 (1984).

50. *Bethesda Foundation v. Board of Review of Madison County,* 453 N.W.2d 224 (1990). *See also Glen Haven Homes, Inc. v. Mills County Bd. of Review,* 507 N.W.2d 179 (Iowa 1993). (A nursing home had previously challenged a determination that it was not exempt from property taxes. In the course of that action, it had stipulated to a formula, to be effective in future years, pro rating tax exemption based on the proportion of Title XIX (Medicaid) funds it received. The nursing home was precluded from relitigating its tax-exempt status in a subsequent year when it had admitted that all material facts remained unchanged from the time of previous action.)

51. *Richards v. Iowa Dep't. of Revenue,* 414 N.W.2d 344 (1987). A taxpayer was held to be entitled to judicial review of an order upholding a tax exemption for a nonprofit community for the elderly. *Richards v. Iowa Dep't. of Revenue and Finance,* 454 N.W.2d 573 (1990).

52. *Dow City Senior Housing, Inc. v. Board of Review,* 230 N.W.2d 497 (1975). *See also Atrium Village v. Board of Review,* 417 N.W.2d 70 (1987) (nursing home and retirement facility for elderly not exempt due to its strong policy against admitting applicants or retaining residents unable to pay the fees). *Care Initiatives f/k/a Mercy Health Initiatives v. Board of Review of Union County,* 500 N.W.2d 14 (Iowa 1993). (A nursing home with policies to accept all patients for admission without regard to ability to pay and with no discrimination between private-pay and Title XIX patients was denied exemption because there was no charitable contribution of money, goods, or services; virtually all control had been surrendered to a related for-profit organization; and it admitted only one "hardship" patient, who was charged more than the Title XIX rate and more than the facility's calculated average cost.) *Holy Spirit Retirement Home, Inc. v. Board of Review,* 543 N.W.2d 907 (Iowa 1995). (Apartment division added to a nursing home found not to be operated for a charitable or benevolent purpose and not tax-exempt because residents were required to be physically and financially independent, and its purpose was to provide living quarters for those who could care for themselves rather than to provide medical care to residents.)

53. *Friendship Haven, Inc. v. Webster County Board of Review,* 542 N.W.2d 837 (Iowa 1996).

54. *Partnership for Affordable Housing v. Board of Review,* 550 N.W.2d 161 (Iowa 1996).

55. *City of Newton v. Board of Review for Jasper County,* 532 N.W.2d 771 (Iowa 1995).

56. *In re Application of Presbyterian Manor, Inc.,* 830 P.2d 60 (Kan. Ct. App. 1992).

57. *Appeal of Board of County Commissioners of Johnson County,* 694 P.2d 455 (1985).

58. Me. Rev. Stat. Ann. tit. 36, §652 (1)(A) (1978).

59. *Me. AFL–CIO Housing Dev. v. Town of Madawaska,* 523 A.2d 581 (1987).

60. 673 A.2d 209 (Me. 1996).

61. Md. Tax, Property Code Ann. §7–206 (Michie 1986 and Supp. 1990).

62. Md. Tax, Property Code Ann. §7–502.

63. Md. Tax-Prop. Code Ann. §7–202.

64. *Supervisor v. Asbury Methodist Home,* 547 A.2d 190 (1988), *reversing* 529 A.2d 852 (1987).

65. *Supervisor of Assessments v. Har Sinai West Corp.,* 622 A.2d 786 (Md. 1993).

66. Mich. Comp. Laws Ann. §211.7d.

67. *Michigan Baptist Homes v. Ann Arbor,* 223 N.W.2d 324 (1974), *aff'd.,* 242 N.W.2d 749 (1976).

68. *Holland Home v. City of Grand Rapids,* 1995 Mich. T.C. LEXIS 58 (Mich. T.C. 1995).

69. *Retirement Homes of Detroit v. Sylvan Township,* 330 N.W.2d 682 (Mich. 1982).

70. *Detroit Metro. Baptist Manor, Inc. v. City of Farmington Hills,* 1991 WL 19334 (Mich. Tax Tribunal, 1991).

71. *Sisters of Mercy–Providence of Detroit, Inc.* Mich. Tax Tribunal, No. 119590 (April 26, 1991).

72. *North Star Research Inst. v. County of Hennepin,* 236 N.W.2d 754 (1975). *See also Chicago Health Serv. v. Commissioner of Revenue,* 462 N.W.2d 386 (1990). (A nonprofit hospital was denied an exemption for an outpatient clinic in part because, although patient information packets stated that patients may receive care even if they are unable to pay for it, this policy was not distinguishable from the practice of for-profit clinics of writing off uncollectible bills.) In *Community Memorial Home v. County of Douglas,* 1997 Minn. LEXIS 930, an assisted-living facility operating at a loss failed to qualify as a charity under the *North Star* standard.

73. *Petition of United Church Homes,* 195 N.W.2d 411 (1972); Minn. Stat. Ann. §272.02 (West Supp. 1987) (general charitable purpose).

74. *Chapel View, Inc. v. Hennepin County,* NO. TC-5686 (Minn. Tax Court, 4th Dist., 1988), citing *Madonna Towers v. Comm'r,* 167 N.W.2d 712 (1963) where the supreme court denied an exemption to a life-care facility with entrance fees, even though facility permitted people who ran out of funds to remain in residence.

75. 633 So. 2d 440 (Miss. 1994).

76. Mo. Ann. Stat. §137.100(5).

77. *Franciscan Tertiary Province of Missouri, Inc. v. State Tax Comm'n.,* 566 S.W.2d 213 (1978).

78. *Evangelical Ret. Homes v. State Tax Commission,* 669 S.W.2d 548 (Mo. Banc 1984); Mo. Ann. Stat. §137.100(5) (Vernon Supp. 1987) (general charitable purpose).

79. *Cape Retirement Community, Inc. v. Kuehle,* 798 S.W.2d 201 (1990).

80. *Franciscan Tertiary Prov. v. State Tax Commission,* note 77 *above. See also Pentecostal Church of God v. Hughlett,* 737 S.W.2d 728 (1987) (apartment building used as subsidized housing for elderly and handicapped tenants exempt from ad valorem taxation); *Senior Citizens Bootheel Serv., Inc. v. Dover,* 811 S.W.2d 35 (1991) (apartments with rent subsidies for qualified individuals 62 years of age or older or handicapped or disabled of any age, which were financed by an individual donation and a loan through HUD, exempt from ad valorem tax); and *Rolla Apartments/ Overall Constr. Indus., Inc. v. State Tax Comm'n.,* 797 S.W.2d 781 (1990) (a housing project for elderly and handicapped persons met the *Franciscan* three-pronged test where the facility acted under guidelines promulgated by HUD, provided activities organized for residents' individual needs, and administered a rent subsidy program that enabled occupants to have housing that would otherwise be unaffordable and unavailable).

81. *Village North, Inc. v. State Tax Comm'n. of Missouri,* 799 S.W.2d 197 (1990).

82. Mont. Ann. Code, tit. 15, ch. 6, §201(1)(e) & (o).

83. *Bethesda Foundation v. County of Saunders,* 264 N.W.2d 664 (1978); Neb. Rev. Stat. §77–202(1)(c) (1981) (general charitable purpose).

84. *Christian Retirement Homes v. Board of Equalization,* 180 N.W.2d 136 (1970).

85. *Ev. Lutheran Good Samaritan Society v. Buffalo County Bd. of Eq.,* 430 N.W.2d 502 (1988).

86. Nev. Rev. Stat. §361.086 (1989).

87. N.H. Rev. Stat. Ann. §72:23 (Equity Supp. 1992). Furthermore, N.H. Rev. Stat. Ann. §72:23 exempts by name certain nonprofit community housing for the elderly, community health care facilities, and convalescent care facilities.

88. *Senior Citizens Housing Development Corporation of Claremont v. City of Claremont,* 453 A.2d 1307 (1982).

89. *Appeal of City of Franklin,* 631 A.2d 537 (N.H. 1993).

90. N.J. Stat. Ann. 54:4-3.6 (West Supp. 1994).

91. *Ibid.*

92. *Presbyterian Homes v. Div. of Tax Appeals,* 55 N.J. 275 (1970). *See also Woodstown Borough v. Friends Home at Woodstown,* 12 N.J. Tax 197 (1992). (Failure to seek actively the admission of below-average-income or indigent patients negates charitable purpose.)

93. *Christian Research Institute v. Dover,* 5 N.J. Tax 376 (1983).

94. *St. Luke's Village v. Peapack & Gladstone Borough,* 11 N.J. Tax 76 (1990). Some New Jersey courts have narrowly interpreted N.J. Stat. Ann. 54:4-3.6 in that tax exemptions are not favored and doubts are to be resolved against the one claiming the exemption. *Intercare Health Systems, Inc. v. Cedar Grove,* 11 N.J. Tax 423 (1990), *aff'd.,* 12 N.J. Tax 273 (1991), *cert. denied,* 606 A.2d 369 (N.J. 1992). This is a case where a registered nonprofit skilled-nursing facility was denied a tax exemption as a hospital because the facility was not fully integrated into the functions of an authorized operating hospital. The appeals court also stated that a corporation must be incorporated explicitly for hospital purposes.

95. *Retirement Ranch, Inc. v. Curry Cty. Val. Protest Bd.,* 546 P.2d 1199 (1976), *cert. den.,* 89 N.M. 206 (1976); N.M. Const. art. VIII, §3 (general charitable purpose).

96. *Belle Harbor Home v. Tishelman,* 420 N.Y.S.2d 343 (1979), *aff'd.,* 441 N.Y.S.2d 413 (1981); *appeal den.,*

447 N.Y.S.2d 1025 (1981); N.Y. Real Prop. Tax Law §422 (McKinney 1984) (not-for-profit housing). *See also* Priv. Hous. Fin. §§11 *et seq.* (McKinney 1976 and Supp. 1991), which allows an exemption for limited-profit housing companies that provide dwellings for low-income aged.

97. *Marino Jeantet Residence for Seniors v. Comm'r. of Finance*, 430 N.Y.S.2d 545 (1980), *aff'd.*, 449 N.Y.S.2d 933 (1982).

98. *Greer Woodycrest Children's Services v. Fountain*, 526 N.Y.S.2d 780 (1988), *aff'd.*, 543 N.E.2d 722 (1989).

99. N.C. Gen. Stat. §105-275(32).

100. *Matter of Tax Appeal of Moravian Home*, 382 S.E.2d 772 (1989).

101. *Appeal of Chapel Hill Residential Retirement Center, Inc.*, 299 S.E.2d 782 (1983).

102. 459 S.E.2d 793 (N.C. Ct. App. 1995).

103. N.D. Cent. Code §57-02-08.8 (Smith Supp. 1989).

104. *Evangelical Lutheran Good Samaritan Society v. Board of County Commissioners*, 219 N.W.2d 900 (1974).

105. *Riverview Place v. Cass County*, 448 N.W.2d 635 (1989).

106. Ohio Rev. Code §5709.12 (Page 1986).

107. Ohio Rev. Code §5701.13 (Page 1986) as amended Ohio Legis. 30, 1993 WL 5701.13. This test was met in *Nordonia Hills Bd. of Education v. Tracy*, (Ohio Bd. of Tax Appeals, No. 96-M-848, Aug. 22, 1997).

108. *See Ohio Presbyterian Homes v. Kinney*, 459 N.E.2d 500 (Ohio 1984).

109. *Christian Benevolent Ass'n. v. Limbach*, 631 N.E.2d 1034 (Ohio 1994).

110. *S.E.M. Villa II v. Kinney*, 419 N.E.2d 879 (1981). *See also National Church Residences of Chillicothe*, 479 N.E.2d 870 (1985). (Apartments for elderly and handicapped at or below market prices to residents who pay part or all their rental costs do not constitute an exclusive use of the property for charitable purposes that will result in a tax exemption.)

111. *Good Samaritan Society v. Limbach*, No. 5-86-14, Aug. 29, 1988, reported in *Housing and Development Reporter*, Oct. 17, 1988, 499.

112. 631 N.E.2d 604 (Ohio 1994).

113. *See also Judson Retirement Community v. Limbach*, 638 N.E.2d 546 (Ohio 1994), and *Judson Retirement Community v. Tracy, Ohio, Bd. of Tax Appeals*, No. 95-T-674, June 6, 1997.

114. Okla. Stat. tit. 68, §2887 (Supp. 1992).

115. *Baptist Health Care v. Bd. of Equalization*, 750 P.2d 127 (1988).

116. *William K. Warren Medical Research Center Inc. v. Paynes County Board of Equalization*, 905 P.2d 824 (Okla. Ct. App. 1994).

117. Or. Rev. Stat. §§307.130, 307.370 and 307.241-245 (1989).

118. *Oregon Methodist Home v. Horn*, 360 P.2d 293 (Or. 1961). *See also Friendsview Manor v. State Tax Comm'n.*, 420 P.2d 77 (Or. 1967) and *Rigas Maja, Inc. v. Department of Revenue*, 12 Or. Tax 471 (1993). (Adult foster care facility for Latvians that charged close to market rates was exempt when facility's rates did not vary with level of care, facility did not discriminate against non-Latvians, and substantial volunteer labor was used to provide services.)

119. *Mercy Health Promotion, Inc. v. Department of Revenue*, 795 P.2d 1082 (1990). In a rental agreement between two exempt organizations, the exempt property owner may charge rent sufficient only to recover its costs of repairs, maintenance, amortization, and upkeep. Or. Rev. Stat. §307.166(1).

120. Pa. Stat. Ann. tit. 72, §5020-204(a)(3) (Purdon Supp. 1992).

121. *In re Marple Newtown School District*, 453 A.2d 68 (Pa. 1982). *See also Lutheran Home at Topton v. Board of Assessment*, 515 A.2d 59 (Pa. 1986), *appeal denied*, 529 A.2d 1084 (Pa. 1987); *In re Appeal of Capital Extended Care*, 609 A.2d 896 (Pa. Commw. Ct. 1992).

122. In Re Eastern Dist. Conference, 455 A.2d 1274 (1983).

123. *Lutheran Home v. Board of Assessment*, 293 A.2d 888 (Pa. Cmwlth. 1972), *appeal den.*, 515 Pa. 589 (1987); *appeal den.*, 515 Pa. 611 (1987).

124. *G.D.L. Plaza Corporation v. Council Rock School Dist.*, 526 A.2d 1173 (1987). *See also Advanced Living, Inc. v. Montgomery County Board of Assessment Appeals*, 537 A.2d 948 (1988).

125. *Appeal of Lutheran Social Services, East Region*, 539 A.2d 895 (1988).

126. *Ibid.*

127. *St. Margaret Seneca Place v. Board of Property Assessment*, 640 A.2d 380 (Pa. 1994).

128. R.I. Gen. Laws §44-3-3 (Michie 1980 and Supp. 1990).

129. S.C. Code §12-37-220.A (Lawyers Co-op. Supp. 1992).

130. S.D. Cod. Laws §10-4-9.3 (Michie 1989).

131. *United Retirement Center v. Brookings County Bd. of Equalization*, No. 90-1166 (Brookings Co., 3d Cir., Nov. 26, 1990).

132. Tenn. Stat. §67-5-207 (1992). However, certain tax-exempt federally financed projects for the elderly with more than 12 units will be required to make payments in lieu of taxes for certain facilities provided by public entities. Ch. 399, Laws 1991 (H.B. 568).

133. *Heritage Acres, Ltd. v. Reece* (Tenn. Ct. App., 6/30/89).

134. *Christian Home for the Aged v. Tennessee Assessment Appeals Comm.*, 790 S.W.2d 288 (1990).

135. Tex. Tax Code 11.18(d) (Vernon Supp. 1991).

136. *Needville Ind. School Dist. v. S.P.J.S.T. Rest Home*, 566 S.W.2d 40 (1978).

137. *City of McAllen v. Evangelical Lutheran*, 518 S.W.2d 557 (1975), *aff'd.*, 530 S.W.2d 806 (1976).

138. *El Paso Cent. Appr. Dist. v. Ev. Lutheran*, 762 S.W.2d 207 (1988). *See also First Baptist/Amarillo Found. v. Potter County Appraisal Dist.*, 813 S.W.2d 192 (Tex. App. 1991). (A nonprofit organization operating an independent-living and nursing center for the elderly was denied a tax exemption where residents were required to pay an entrance fee and a monthly service charge.)

139. *Challenge Homes, Inc. v. County of Lubbock*, 474 S.W.2d 746 (1971).

140. *Air Force Village v. Northside Ind. School Dist.*, 561 S.W.2d 905 (1978). *See also Baptist Memorial Geriatric Center v. Tom Green County Appraisal District*, 851 S.W.2d 938 (Tex. 1993). (Residential complex did not provide services without regard to residents' ability to pay where, among other things, the complex had never advertised its services as being available to the community regardless of financial status and all units rented for the same rate.)

141. *Utah County v. Intermountain Health Care, Inc.*, 709 P.2d 265 (1985). The Utah Supreme Court emphasized that each case must be decided on its own facts and that, generally, taxation is the rule and exemption is the exception. Those factors were discussed in relation to a nonprofit hospital.

142. *Yorgason v. County Board of Equalization*, 714 P.2d 653 (1986).

143. "Nonprofit Hospital and Nursing Home Charitable Property Tax Exemption Standards," Utah State Tax Commission, Aug. 22, 1990. These standards were upheld by the Utah Supreme Court in *Howell v. County Board of Cache County*, 881 P.2d 880 (Utah 1994).

144. Vt. Stat. Ann. tit. 32, §§3802(4), 3832(6).

145. *Central Vermont Hospital, Inc. v. Town of Berlin*, 672 A.2d 474 (Vt. 1995).

146. *Westminster-Canterbury of Hampton Roads v. City of Virginia Beach*, 385 S.E.2d 561 (1989).

147. Wash. Rev. Code §84.36.041(1) (West Supp. 1990). In addition, Washington statute provides that if the home does not meet the requirements of subsection (1) because fewer than 50 percent of the occupied dwelling units are occupied by eligible residents, the home for the aging is still eligible for a partial exemption. Wash. Rev. Code §84.36.041(3). Seventy-five percent of the total amount financed for reconstruction, acquisition, or rehabilitation of a home must be financed by tax-exempt bonds. Wash. Rev. Code §84.36.041(2).

148. Wash. Rev. Code §§84.36.040(4), 84.36.805 (West Supp. 1987). There are new criteria for nonprofit organizations. Among other factors, an organization must be organized and conducted for nonsectarian purposes and, in most cases, the services of such organizations must be directed to persons of all ages. Wash. Legis. 79 (1993) (Westlaw) 84.36 RCW (1) and (5) (amending Wash. Rev. Code §§84.36.800 and 84.36.805).

149. *Yakima First Baptist Homes v. Gray*, 510 P.2d 243 (1973).

150. *In re Sehome Park Care Center, Inc.*, 903 P.2d 443 (Wash. 1995).

151. W.Va. Code Ann. §11-3-9 (Michie Supp. 1990).

152. Wisc. Stat. Ann. §70.11(4) (West Supp. 1986).

153. *Family Hospital Nursing Home v. City of Milwaukee*, 254 N.W.2d 268 (1977).

154. *St. John's Lutheran Church v. City of Bloomer*, 347 N.W.2d 619 (1984).

155. Wyo. Stat. §39-1-201 (1977).

Classic Residence by Hyatt; Teaneck, New Jersey.

Part V
Multiparty Ventures

Service-oriented seniors' housing communities historically have been owned and operated primarily by nonprofit organizations. The influx of for-profit real estate developers into the retirement housing market in the late 1980s, together with the desire of many hospitals and health care institutions to expand into areas of service that are not completely dependent on reimbursement from government health programs, has caused a heightened interest in the pursuit of joint ventures in the development of seniors' facilities. Because the retirement business can involve a combination of several traditionally separate disciplines, such as housing development, hospitality services, delivery of health care, and provision of health insurance, it can make sense for parties from different businesses to join together in the development of a single project.

In this part, the terms "partner" and "joint venture" are used loosely to refer to multiparty relationships and can include equity pooling in a corporation, partnership, or a limited-liability company or simply involve contractual arrangements such as leases or management contracts. Volume II: The CD-ROM sets forth in detail several contractual and equity-contribution arrangements. In any case, it is important to consider the interplay of the respective venturers' abilities, needs, and goals as well as the possible tax and other regulatory implications of various relationship options.

Although ventures can include two or more parties of any type, this part concentrates on ventures between nonprofit and for-profit entities because they are a likely type of venture in this field and thus give rise to the most significant business and legal concerns.

The Fountains at Franklin; Southfield, Michigan.

Courtesy of Fountains Affiliated Companies; Tucson, Arizona

11 Multiparty Relationships

§11.1 What Others Have to Offer

The potential partners who may be available as a resource for the development of a seniors' housing and care project are legion and may include existing owners/operators of for-profit or nonprofit facilities, hospitals, nursing or assisted-living operators, real estate developers, church groups, fraternal or civic organizations, retired persons' affinity groups such as teachers', alumni, or military officers' associations, insurance carriers or health maintenance organizations, hotel operators, physician groups, food service operators, or any others either engaged in some service needed for retirement community development or operation or otherwise involved with elderly constituencies.

(a) Expertise, Staffing, and Resources

Most potential joint venture partners have some area of expertise that is attractive to the other partner and therefore may fill a void in that partner's background. Most commonly, real estate developers seeking to develop and sustain an ongoing interest in a seniors' facility with services can use the operational expertise, staff, or other resources of a management company, health care provider, operator of an existing facility, or other person or entity familiar with management of food services, hospitality services, recreation programs, health care, or the other services and amenities to be offered by the facility.

Of course, established facility operators have the most comprehensive and extensive experience. They are likely to have strong convictions about appropriate operating techniques and are probably less willing than other potential partners to share control over operations. While many hospitals or other health care facilities may have significant experience in creating medical model projects, they may have little involvement in the development of residential housing and may have a tendency toward creating the institutional environment that an experienced developer of housing would knowingly avoid. Nonetheless, their familiarity with health facility licensing and operations and complex matters such as government reimbursement programs may be invaluable to a partner untutored in such issues. Similarly, those involved in the insurance industry, the delivery of prepaid health services, or the provision of continuing care are likely to have background in the actuarial and risk-pooling considerations necessary to the success of a prepaid or endowment type of facility. A large share of a facility's day-to-day operations concerns food service, housekeeping, social-recreation programs, transportation, and related hospitality activities with which hotel operators have considerable experience. Although their entry into the marketplace is more recent than others, hotel operators seem particularly well suited to operating service-intensive facilities, provided that planning for health care contingencies receives adequate attention.

Real estate developers can offer much more to a venture than their obvious expertise in overseeing construction. Developers often have valuable experience and knowledge in obtaining financing, marketing real estate, dealing with local zoning and planning agencies, designing structures and amenities that are attractive to consumers, and working with leases, restrictions on sales, homeowners' association documentation, and the related accoutrements of conventional real estate transactions. One concern in entering into an equity joint venture with a developer relates to the developer's long-term interest and involvement in operations. Many developers are accustomed to selling their projects after construction or when fully depreciated and therefore pay little attention to sustaining project feasibility during operations.

(b) Constituency

Many potential joint venture partners, such as community hospitals, established operators of existing retirement facilities, or church, fraternal, or civic groups, may well have a constituency or at least a following within a given community that can form the core of the prospective resident population of the planned community. The marketing advantage of involving, for example, a retired military officers' group, a church or religious group, or a respected hospital or university as a partner in a retirement project can be significant. Especially in service-intensive facilities, where residents may be planning to spend the remaining years of their lives, the reputation, trustworthiness, and sense of security imparted by such an affiliation is of great importance. In addition, prospective residents may have a greater assurance that the other residents, with whom they may be living on an intimate basis for many years, will share common values and outlooks.

Usually, affinity groups are formed as nonprofit, tax-exempt organizations. In most cases, the benevolent motivations of the group warrant the residents' trust. Affiliation with such an affinity group is, however, no substitute for a sound financial plan, a high-quality product, and expert management. Some of the most dramatic retirement facility failures have

involved situations where residents placed their faith in affinity groups or individuals who were proceeding without a sound business plan (see §5.2).

(c) Tax Advantages

Joint ventures between for-profit and nonprofit entities can provide certain tax advantages for the project and its residents. Real estate developers faced with problems of substantial income taxation of entrance fees, for example, may work with a nonprofit organization as the operator and recipient of entrance fees on a tax-free basis and still make a profit through property leasing, development fees, or management activities. Facilities owned and operated by nonprofit organizations may also be eligible for local or state property tax exemption. In addition, tax-exempt financing may be available to nonprofit facilities. All these tax savings can enhance a project's feasibility, marketability, and ability to generate higher cash flows from operations.

(d) Capital, Land, or Other Assets

Developers may have access to conventional sources of financing and enjoy relationships with lenders generally unknown to church groups or smaller health care institutions. On the other hand, nonprofit organizations generally can turn to a wider range of tax-exempt bond financing options under the law (see §15.2). Many hospitals, church groups, or universities may own excess land that has been donated to them but that has yet to undergo development. In addition, health care providers may own underused facilities that could provide nursing care or other services to an adjacent residential complex. Similarly, real estate developers may have completed apartment or condominium units that are not selling or that need to be converted to a more marketable use.

§11.2 Partner Goals and Approaches

(a) Hospitals

A major reason for hospitals' increasing interest in the retirement housing market is the pressure directed against the traditional hospital function of providing acute inpatient care in a large, institutional setting. The Medicare system, which provides for much of the revenue of most acute care hospitals, has shifted away from the reimbursement-of-cost approach, which for many years was the hallmark of the program. Rather than paying whatever hospitals charge for services delivered to patients, Medicare now specifies the precise duration and scope of services it pays for in the hospital setting by dividing virtually all possible hospital procedures into diagnosis-related groups (DRGs) (see §13.2). In addition, some state Medicaid programs have begun to contract selectively with only the most efficient hospitals, which results in a loss of Medicaid revenues to those hospitals that were not fortunate enough to obtain Medicaid contracts.

DRGs have greatly reduced the ability of hospitals to keep their beds filled for long occupancy periods. They also encourage hospitals to discharge patients sooner than in past years, possibly before medically indicated.[1] As a consequence, many hospitals are interested in positioning themselves at the receiving end of that transfer and therefore are expanding into the construction of nursing or assisted-living facilities at an increasingly rapid rate (see also the discussion of managed care in §27.4).

Moreover, overhead costs involved in maintaining large institutional hospital centers, which include increasingly expensive high-technology diagnostic equipment, operating rooms, and other costly support facilities, add up to hospital charges that exceed most people's means such that hospitals have become less cost-efficient places to treat all but the most extreme illnesses or injuries. These pressures have led hospitals to diversify and enter markets that are less cost-intensive and less dependent on government programs; these markets include outpatient clinics; ambulatory surgery centers; skilled-nursing facilities; freestanding pharmacies, laboratories, or diagnostic centers; and, within the seniors' market, seniors' housing, assisted-living, and continuing-care facilities.

According to one survey conducted in 1985, approximately 30 percent of hospitals with 400 or more beds were found to be in some phase of pursuing the development of a continuing-care retirement community.[2] One study showed that 15 percent of hospitals responding in 1988 owned, leased, or managed one or more retirement facilities.[3] Another survey reported that the number of multiunit hospital systems owning or leasing retirement communities rose by 59 percent from 1987 to 1988.[4] While a 1990 survey indicated that the number of retirement centers operated by hospital and nursing home chains rose only slightly in 1989 (13 percent), a 1992 survey reported a surge in the growth of hospital-sponsored retirement communities.[5] A 1994 survey reported a 6 percent increase from the previous year in the number of CCRCs owned or operated by health care systems.[6]

Many hospitals interested in developing seniors' housing or care want to do so within their own communities and at a location that can maximize the benefits to the hospital and make the best use of hospital resources. Sometimes hospitals own land adjacent to the acute care facility that may be available for development. The retirement facility can serve, to some extent, as a feeder of inpatients to the hospital while facility residents may use the outpatient services, pharmacy, physical therapy, or other services available at the hospital. Hospitals may also benefit from retirement housing as a source of bequests or volunteers. If nursing facilities are constructed, they may serve as a place for some hospital inpatient transferees to convalesce.

To an extent, hospital staff and facilities may be used on a shared basis to assist in the operation of retirement community services and amenities. The hospital can benefit as well by achieving maximum use of its resources and realizing economies of scale in areas such as dining, housekeeping, laundry, pharmacy, shared purchasing, and use of nursing, administrative, and other staff (see discussion of employment issues in §13.4). Developers in joint ventures with hospitals should, however, be vigilant to ensure that services and amenities such as dining, housekeeping, and interior design do not succumb to the often-institutional character typified by many hospitals. The developer should strive for homelike qualities and, if necessary, bring in a third party to manage critical services such as dining, especially in upscale, market-rate properties.

One of the most frequent frustrations voiced by developers in their dealings with hospitals relates to the slow-moving, bureaucratic structure that characterizes many hospitals. Whereas developers tend to want to move quickly, hospitals often spend a good deal of time carefully weighing alternatives. Much of this deliberateness has to do with the complex structure and politics of most hospitals. The board of trustees is usually composed of civic and health care leaders who may be most concerned with community image and services. The medical staff of physicians is motivated by interests that span the hospital, the physicians' patients, and the doctors' own professions and prestige. The business-oriented administration, which is employed by the board of trustees, is in many respects also answerable to the physicians, who are ultimately responsible for bringing patients into the hospital. Finally, the several committees with jurisdiction over hospital departments, medical disciplines, and business functions further compound the complexity of the hospital structure.

Because of their byzantine, often politically charged structure, hospitals usually move slowly and consider the impact of any proposed venture on diverse issues such as profitability, effect on government reimbursement, maintenance of tax-exempt status, impact of bond indenture restrictions, community image, effect on physician referral patterns, and competing uses for the hospital's money, land, or other resources, which could be allocated to constructing physician office buildings or freestanding clinics, remodeling or equipping existing facilities, developing health maintenance organizations or home health agencies, and other options. In general, hospitals want substantial controls over projects that bear their name as owner, sponsor, or operator.

According to one major developer of hospital-owned retirement communities, the following factors, issues, and strategies are of special importance to hospitals involved in the industry:

Advantages
- The hospital can point to its reputation and credibility.
- The hospital can develop and finance the project at lower cost.
- Unique resources such as land in an ideal location, shared services, capital, and personnel make the hospital a logical operator.

Risks
- To attract residents, hospitals must understand that successful retirement communities need to "create a want" rather than merely fulfill a need.
- Hospitals are sensitive to maintaining a favorable debt-to-equity ratio and may have to be wary of continuing-care programs that may downgrade the institution's debt rating.

Some Solutions
- Hospitals must recognize that the retirement community business is a different business that requires experienced management.
- Building smaller projects may help overcome the problem of reliably predicting the parallel development of competitive facilities in the same market area.
- Use of long-term-care insurance through a self-insured continuing-care program may help avoid the problem of jeopardizing a hospital's financial rating.
- Use of nonrecourse financing once a project reaches break-even occupancy can improve the hospital's debt capacity.[7]

In 1991, the following factors were identified as creating an impetus for hospitals and nursing home operators to diversify into independent and assisted-living facilities:

- Health care costs nationally have risen to $2 billion per day.
- Average hospital lengths of stay and patient days are declining.
- The over-65 population in most markets is 13 percent of the total population and more than 50 percent of hospital patient days.
- Outpatient services are becoming more diverse and complex.
- Reimbursement programs are more complicated and less generous.
- Many facilities have excess or underused land or other resources.[8]

(See also §2.4 regarding growth among health care industry sponsors of retirement centers.)

(b) Religiously Affiliated Organizations

Religiously affiliated organizations cover a broad spectrum, from the very unsophisticated to extremely well-managed businesses. Most, however, have something in common: a constituency group and a sense of mission to serve that one group or elderly people generally.

In the main, individual congregations should be distinguished from larger, organized religious groups such as a church conference or diocese or a church-sponsored corporation experienced in developing and operating retirement communities. Often, an individual congregation is loosely structured and composed principally of volunteers. Although individual board members may have expertise in one or more relevant areas, the organization as a whole often cannot be relied on to take the lead in developing or operating a given facility. If there is any one danger in smaller groups' developing or operating retirement centers, it is that good intentions in the absence of sufficient business acumen, experience, or organization can lead to financial and operational weakness. Therefore, small groups need to rely heavily on the leadership of an experienced developer or management company involved in formulating the facility's service program. Of course, even with the benefits of a constituency group, careful market and financial feasibility analyses or firm presales are essential.

On the other hand, regional divisions of major church groups or religiously sponsored retirement facility corporations or hospitals tend to rely on professional business management that is sophisticated in matters of finance, construction, and operations. Those religiously sponsored organizations already in the seniors' housing business have invaluable experience in both marketing and day-to-day operations. Most religiously oriented sponsors have a keen interest in operating a project that is financially sound and not heavily dependent on donations to meet operational expenses. Even so, such organizations have an ethical desire as well as an obligation under the terms of their federal income tax exemptions to keep operational charges, however luxurious the facilities, reasonably related to the costs of providing services (see §9.3). On balance, these sponsors have demonstrated the ability to operate as success-ful growth businesses and still serve their charitable purposes. In working with for-profit organizations, they are concerned that their partners remain committed for the long term to providing high-quality services to elderly residents. Accordingly, they are unlikely to overreach in their pursuit of a return on investment.

Although religious groups often have specific congregations or groups of adherents within a community that may form the basis of a seniors' residential market, most such groups do not limit admissions to persons who are members of the particular denomination. Quite the contrary, most market to all seniors regardless of religious preference. From the consumer's perspective, the signs of religious affiliation generally are limited to the name of the organization and perhaps a chapel where services are regularly held. In some facilities, however, a religious or cultural atmosphere may be more pervasive, including regular religious services and observance of religious holidays, dietary practices, and other traditions.[9]

Religiously affiliated organizations have dominated much of the retirement and health care industries, yet they are not islands without the desire to branch out or the need for resources to do so. They are obvious candidates for consideration as joint venture partners.

(c) For-Profit Developers

For-profit real estate developers are, of course, interested in profit, but it is a mistake to think that profit is their only goal. Most successful developers realize that they must produce the best possible product for the segment of the marketplace they have targeted in order to maintain the type of reputation necessary for sustained success in housing development. It is not uncommon to find a developer's mother residing in the retirement community her child created.

The need for developers to make a lasting commitment to the ongoing quality of their product is especially crucial in seniors' projects. Aging-in-place residents often require increasingly intensive health and service programs in addition to mere shelter. Developers may seek a joint venture partner to help ensure that appropriate programs are formulated and can be operated on an essentially permanent basis.

On the whole, developers have a tendency to move much more rapidly than other types of sponsors and may have a greater inclination than others to proceed precipitously with the marketing and development of a project's physical facilities and amenities before adequately considering regulatory requirements or the details and consequences of service packages. Of course, larger institutional developers and the more sophisticated of the smaller development partnerships moderate their instincts to proceed at breakneck speed by undertaking a meticulous study of options. In areas such as continuing care, in which many for-profit developers are relative newcomers, many developers have shown a remarkable ability to learn the system and make aggressive strides through determined hard work. In particular, for-profit companies have dominated the recent surge in assisted-living development.

Developer strengths include an ability to move boldly and decisively, quickly and tirelessly in pursuit of a project. Development companies are often lean organizations with few of the bureaucratic burdens of committees or other structures. Smaller developers especially have a strong sense of entrepreneurial independence and an innate desire to avoid regulation. They use creative means to streamline the development process, reduce costs, and improve the product, but they should proceed conservatively and cautiously to ensure compliance with applicable laws. They are strong in conventional finance and marketing abilities and usually very familiar with design, zoning laws and procedures, and all aspects of construction in their particular locale.

National or other large corporate development companies have many of the qualities of smaller developers, but they may share some of the institutional characteristics of organizations such as hospitals. Their in-house expertise in a given area of development may be so pervasive as to make them disinclined to seek outside consultation when it is advisable to gain familiarity with local land use planning policies, unusual local or state laws, peculiar local market characteristics, or other important issues that may require extensive use of regional expertise.

Generally, developers are concerned with generating and sheltering income, depreciating capital investments, deducting losses, minimizing government regulation, and efficiently producing an appealing product that will sell quickly and enhance the firm's reputation.

(d) Other Possible Partners

Several other types of candidates for coventuring a seniors' project have surfaced in the marketplace. They include those in the hotel or hospitality industry; insurance companies; universities; affinity groups such as military officers', retired teachers, or fraternal organizations; nursing home or assisted-living chains; management companies; and others that can bring a relevant field of expertise or residents to the venture. Physicians have also been suggested as likely joint venturers with hospitals in the development of life-care retirement communities.[10]

University-related retirement communities, for example, are beginning to develop for a number of reasons that benefit both the university and the resident. The university is able to put its unused land to profitable use, cement relationships with alumni, and create a pool of potential students for adult education programs; the relationship also may foster an increase in bequests made to the institution. The resident lives in a setting that may be more peaceful than the community at large, but it is nonetheless physically attractive and intellectually stimulating. Marketing of the project may also be enhanced by the built-in constituency and solid community reputation that a university may enjoy. Among the impediments to such a facility are the many competing interests vying for the resources of the university as well as the generally bureaucratic and cautious nature of university governing bodies.[11] In any joint venture, it is important to select a partner whose attributes and resources complement your own and who has compatible goals and operating style.

§11.3 Multiparty Roles and Structure

(a) Alternative Roles and Relationships and Their Impact on Development Issues

Joint ventures between nonprofit and for-profit organizations are a natural marriage of many for-profit developers' need for operational expertise, health care experience, or resident constituency groups and nonprofit hospitals' or churches' need for development or marketing expertise and capital. The form of the joint venture may, however, vary widely depending on the desires and abilities of the partners and the tax and other legal consequences of mixing taxable and tax-exempt entities.

The potential role of a joint venture partner in any retirement center project can be reduced to one or more of three basic functions: development, ownership, or operations. Whether a for-profit or nonprofit organization fulfills each of those functions can have a significant effect on, among other things, the facility's marketability, financing, and opportunity to generate profits as well as the tax treatment of income and tax status of property.

Ventures between for-profit and nonprofit entities often take one of the following typical forms:

- a limited or general partnership in which the for-profit and nonprofit businesses are cogeneral partners;
- a limited or general partnership in which the nonprofit's for-profit subsidiary is a partner with another for-profit entity;
- a lease of facilities by the for-profit developer/owner to the nonprofit operator, perhaps with a share of profits as part of the rent payment; and
- a management contract from a for-profit facility owner to a nonprofit operator or from an exempt owner to a for-profit operator, possibly with a share of profits as partial compensation.

Each of these forms can give rise to significant tax issues and other development concerns for both the for-profit and nonprofit venturer (see Chapter 12 for a discussion of tax concerns).

Figure 11.1 sets forth several possible scenarios for for-profit and nonprofit involvement (designated A through G) in a retirement facility. Its purpose is to present, as a planning guide, some alternative roles and relationships and broadly sketch several considerations inherent in each format. The notes to the figure then offer general commentary on the possible issues or consequences of each structure as they pertain to marketability, finance, taxation, and related aspects of facility development. These issues are discussed throughout this part as well as in greater

detail in Parts Three, Four, and Six (see in particular the joint venture example discussed in §12.3).

(b) Formation of New Entities

(1) Reasons for a New Entity

Rather than relying on the existence of the venture partners themselves, a joint venture may call for the formation of a new organization to develop, own, or operate a retirement facility. Reasons for forming one or more new organizations can include insulation of the joint venturers from liability, the need for a repository for the capital or equity contributions of the venturers or third-party investors, creation of an organization with specific purposes to ensure its qualification for tax exemption, avoidance of the application of venturers' collective bargaining, Employment Retirement Income Security Act (ERISA), bond indenture, or other strictures on the new venture, and reimbursement for health care services from government programs such as Medicare.

(2) Pros and Cons of Entity Form

When contemplating the formation of a new entity, venturers must consider the specific form of the entity itself. The primary options are a general or limited partnership or a for-profit or nonprofit corporation. In some circumstances, a trust, although not a business entity, may also be used for certain purposes in the business structure of a retirement facility. Many states have recently enacted legislation permitting the formation of limited-liability companies or limited-liability partnerships that combine some of the features of partnerships and corporations.

A principal advantage of a corporate format is that if the corporation is properly capitalized and observes corporate formalities (i.e., procedures for operation set forth in articles, bylaws, and state statutes), the founders and shareholders of the corporation generally remain insulated from liability, with only the corporate assets at risk. A major drawback of the corporate form is taxation of earnings at the corporate level in addition to the taxation of shareholders for earnings distributed to them. In addition, corporate formation and continued observance of formalities can make corporate operation rigid and cumbersome. On the other hand, unlike partnerships, the corpo-

Figure 11.1 **Proprietary and Nonprofit Roles and Relationships**

	A	B	C
Development	Nonprofit	For-Profit	For-Profit Sale
Ownership	Nonprofit	For-Profit	Nonprofit
Operations	Nonprofit	For-Profit	Nonprofit

	D	E	F
Development	For-Profit	For-Profit Sale	Joint
Ownership	For-Profit Lease	Nonprofit Contract	Joint
Operations	Nonprofit	For-Profit	Joint

	G
Development	For-Profit Sale
Ownership	Resident Contract
Operations	Nonprofit

Notes:

I. **Issues** (discussed below for each model A through G)
1. Marketability
2. Financing
3. Profit opportunity
4. Tax treatment of fees
5. Tax treatment of property

II. **Analysis**

    A. Nonprofit
1. Perceived trustworthiness, charitable objectives, built-in constituency
2. Additional government financing available, e.g., tax-exempt bond issue, state bond programs, HUD Section 202 grants
3. No private inurement but can generate revenues for expansion and improvements
4. a. No tax to operator for entrance fee or unit sales income
   b. Refundable fees may carry imputed interest taxable to resident

Figure 11.1 **(continued)**

    c. Resident deduction for medical expense portion of entrance fee and monthly fee

    d. Contributions deductible

  5. Exemption from property tax available in some states

B. For-Profit

1. New entrants in the market may be suspect, especially when taking large entry fees for future services unless equipped with excellent reputation and resources
2. May have other capital sources, e.g., syndication
3. Opportunity for profit from operations, resales of units, or life leases
4. a. Entry fees may be taxed as prepaid rent unless structured as a loan (imputed interest issue) or trust used
   b. Probably no effect on resident medical deduction
   c. No deductions for contributions
5. Probably subject to property tax but can depreciate

C. Developer Sale to Nonprofit

1. a. Credibility and constituency of nonprofit as owner/operator
   b. Developer need not learn health business but should not build on speculation
   c. Operator should be involved early in development
2. Flexible; can finance through either entity
3. Profit limited to development
4. Favorable tax treatment of nonprofits
5. Same as 4

D. For-Profit Owner/Lease to Nonprofit

1. Most of the marketing attributes of nonprofit ownership, provided lease is long-term
2. Nonprofit financing sources probably not available; nonprofit can loan entrance fees or sales proceeds to owner to retire debt
3. Additional profit opportunity in percentage lease
4. Can avoid income tax on entry fees by having operator receive them; percentage lease raises unrelated business income issues
5. Property probably taxable; problem with taking the accelerated cost recovery system (ACRS) deduction for tax-exempt property

E. Nonprofit Owner/For-Profit Development and Operation

1. Attributes of ultimate nonprofit control over operations
2. Flexibility to finance through developer or owner, but tax-exempt finance may be unavailable unless operation contract is limited
3. a. Can profit from development and operation
   b. For-profit must have real estate *and* operations expertise
   c. Operation contract can be terminated by owner
4. Possible tax advantages of nonprofit ownership, but mere ownership may not be an exempt activity; percentage contracts with for-profits raise a private inurement issue
5. Same as 4, plus limits on for-profit management when using tax-exempt bonds

F. Joint Undertaking (e.g., partnership)

1. Marketing attributes of both forms of ownership, but nonprofit control and limited liability are advisable unless for-profit subsidiary is formed
2. For-profit finance model, syndication opportunities
3. Profit incentive shared with nonprofit party in return for expertise in operations; limits on profit of partners advisable unless nonprofit has formed for-profit subsidiary and can take unrelated business income
4. Property and income are taxable; ACRS dilution likely
5. Same as 4

G. For-Profit Development/Resident Ownership/Nonprofit Operation

1. Ownership may have enhanced initial marketability; confidence in nonprofit services; resale market limited; problems of developer-operator control
2. Follows for-profit finance model
3. Profit on initial real estate sales but not necessarily on turnover of units
4. Fees not taxable if paid to nonprofit; exempt status may be questioned if management role only
5. Property taxed, but resident may obtain capital gain exemption, other advantages of ownership

ration's transfer of ownership interests is relatively simple through the sale of stock by shareholders.

Nonprofit corporations do not have shareholders as such but may have members who elect directors and make other important decisions. In some cases, the directors themselves may be the sole members and may be self-perpetuating (i.e., appoint their own successors). Except to the extent they receive unrelated business income, nonprofits may be exempt from taxation, but they must adhere strictly to their exempt purpose (see Part IV).

Unlike corporate shareholders, general partners are personally liable for the debts and other obligations of the partnership. Earnings, however, are not taxed at the partnership level but are taxed only once, upon distribution to partners. Management and operating protocols of partnerships are very flexible and can be informal or spelled out in detail in the partnership agreement. Transfers of partners' interests are cumbersome and may require the consent of other partners or even dissolution and reformation of the partnership (see also §19.4).

Limited partnerships offer limited partners—whose liability is often limited to the amount of their investments—some of the liability-insulating features of the corporate form. While the general partners of a limited partnership bear the same type of unlimited liability for partnership debts as partners in a general partnership, many such general partners are themselves corporations, thereby limiting their exposure to individual shareholders. Thus, assuming that adequate capitalization and other requirements are met, investor shareholders of the corporate general partner have only their corporate shares at risk—and not other personal assets—in much the same way that the limited partners' liability is limited to the amount of their investments (see also §19.5).

A limited-liability company offers a flexible legal structure that combines the advantages of limited liability enjoyed by corporate shareholders with the tax advantages of pass-through treatment enjoyed by the participants in a partnership.[12] The use of limited-liability companies is expected to become commonplace in the health care industry because such companies permit investors to manage the organization actively without risking personal liability for the organization's debts.[13]

In a 1995 private letter ruling, the IRS approved a for-profit/nonprofit health care joint venture where the joint venture agreement resulted from arm's length negotiations; the agreement provided for an allocation of all profits and losses in proportion to the parties' ownership interests; the for-profit entity would manage the limited-liability company for a fee comparable to that charged by independent third parties; and the for-profit entity agreed to submit certain major management decisions to a nonprofit subsidiary of the exempt joint venturer and not to change the business of the venture if doing so would be inconsistent with the subsidiary's tax-exempt purposes (Priv. Ltr. Rul. 9517029).

Thus, it appears that the IRS will analyze for-profit/nonprofit joint ventures in much the same manner, regardless of whether the ventures assume the form of a partnership or a limited-liability company. One can expect to see a proliferation of limited-liability companies in the health care context because of the attractive combination of partnership tax treatment and limited liability in an arena renowned for a great liability exposure.

Notes

1. *See, e.g.,* Sweeney, J., and J. D'Itri, "New Success Factors for Management under Prospective Payment," *Topics in Health Care Financing,* Spring 1985, 10.

2. Survey by Kurt Salmon Associates, Inc., of Atlanta, cited in McMullin, D., "Hospitals and CCRCs: A Growing Alternative," *Contemporary Long Term Care,* Nov. 1985, 43. *See also* "Life Care: You Must Know More Than Health Care," *Hospitals,* May 5, 1987, 98.

3. Southerland, K., "Hospitals' Plan for Long-Term Care," *Contemporary Long Term Care,* Oct. 1988, 32.

4. Nemes, J., "Retirement Centers Grow Despite Fewer Providers," *Modern Healthcare,* June 2, 1989, 50.

5. Pallarito, K., "Slowdown Signals Transition for Retirement Centers Run by Nursing Homes, Hospitals," *Modern Healthcare,* May 21, 1990, 77; Bowe, J., "New Growth Opportunity: Hospitals Expand Their Continuum of Care," *Contemporary Long Term Care,* Feb. 1992, 27.

6. Pallarito, K., "CCRCs See Slow Growth, Challenges in HMO Care," *Modern Healthcare,* May 23, 1994, 76.

7. Lanahan, M., "Hospitals as Owners of Retirement Communities," *Contemporary Long Term Care,* Apr. 1988, 87.

8. Moore, J., "Hospitals and Nursing Homes Eye Housing," *Contemporary Long Term Care,* Oct. 1991, 22.

9. *See* §23.4 for a discussion of religious discrimination in admissions.

10. Cohen, D., "Contracting Issues Regarding Life Care Retirement Communities," *The Medical Staff Counselor,* Summer 1988, 57.

11. *See* Hutchinson, W., "University-Related Retirement Communities: Advantages and Drawbacks," *Retirement Housing Report,* Oct. 1987. *See also* "A New Breed of Retirement Community," *Newsweek,* Nov. 11, 1991, 62, regarding the trend of retirement communities built on or near college campuses.

12. *See* Rev. Rul. 88-76, 1988-2 C.B. 360, and Priv. Ltr. Rul. 9147017, in which the IRS recognized the partnership status of a Wyoming limited-liability company.

13. *See* Plantner, K., "Limited Liability Companies Are Increasingly Popular," *Tax'n. for Lawyers,* Jan./Feb. 1992.

Morningside Continuing-Care Retirement Facility; Fullerton, California.

12 Tax Implications of For-Profit/Nonprofit Ventures

§12.1 Preservation of Tax-Exempt Status

(a) In General

Nonprofit hospitals, church groups, and other organizations may be eligible for exemption under Section 501(c)(3) of the Internal Revenue Code as organizations "organized and operated exclusively for . . . charitable, scientific . . . or educational purposes" (see Part IV). Tax-exempt organizations may not engage in acts that substantially benefit private persons or businesses financially. To the extent a nonprofit organization does not further the specific charitable purposes set forth in its articles of incorporation, it faces the threat of generating unrelated business income, which is taxable to the nonprofit corporation. Substantial activity in a nonexempt undertaking may even jeopardize the entire tax-exempt status of the organization (see discussion in §9.12).

The mere fact that an activity of a nonprofit corporation may result in some benefit to a private business or person does not make the activity necessarily inconsistent with the corporation's charitable purposes. Of course, all nonprofit entities, in the course of carrying out their charitable or other exempt purposes, do business with for-profit concerns as when, for example, they purchase goods or services, lease property, and deal with related matters. However, the private benefit must be incidental, insubstantial,

and not unreasonable in relation to the primary public benefit resulting from the activity.[1] In general, prices paid by nonprofits for goods or services must be reasonable so as not to result in any undue private benefit in excess of value received by the exempt organization in pursuit of its charitable goals. In recent years, tax law amendments have required Section 501(c)(3) organizations to disclose in their annual returns information regarding direct or indirect transfers to, and other direct or indirect relationships with, other noncharitable exempt organizations and political organizations. Excess benefit transactions are subject to serious penalties (see generally the discussion in §§9.14 and 9.15.)

The IRS has used nursing home and hospital examples to identify several transactions involving the use of tax-exempt bonds that may result in impermissible private benefit or private inurement and loss of the organization's tax-exempt status.[2] One IRS news release provides three examples.

- Using the proceeds of tax-exempt bonds, a charitable organization acquires a nursing home from a developer. The developer exercises control or influence over the charity and realizes a substantial profit on the sale. The developer may also have a contract to rehabilitate, manage, or operate the nursing home for an excessive fee.
- A charitable organization leases or sells a facility financed with the proceeds of tax-exempt bonds

to partnerships or other entities in which physicians or medical staff of the charitable organization have a financial interest.

- Using tax-exempt bond proceeds, a charitable organization purchases at an inflated price an unprofitable health facility from a private corporation.[3]

In addition, the IRS has issued guidelines for use by district-level IRS personnel in determining whether to grant exemptions to organizations that intend to issue tax-exempt bonds[4] (see Volume II, §10.5, for the complete text of the instructions). Under the guidelines, the applicant must complete a risk-assessment profile worksheet to determine whether he or she is likely to use bond proceeds for non-exempt purposes. If the worksheet indicates a low risk of private benefit or private inurement, the district is instructed to issue a favorable determination letter, provided that the applicant satisfies the organizational and operational tests of exemption. If, however, the assessment suggests a high risk of private benefit, the applicant is referred to the IRS National Office, which requests further information supporting the exemption. The worksheet's 25 questions include the following:

- Will a for-profit entity manage the project?
- If yes, was selection based on competitive bidding?
- If the facility will be managed by a for-profit manager, does the management contract require the manager to set rates? Hire and fire at will? Spend $5,000 or more annually without the applicant's previous consent?
- Is the manager compensated by a percentage of net profits?
- Does the management company or developer control the applicant's board of directors?[5]

Although these examples are directed to the use of tax-exempt bonds, they also illustrate the types of for-profit/nonprofit transactions that jeopardize the nonprofit's exempt status (see also the management contract restrictions discussed in §15.2).

(b) Equity Joint Ventures

(1) Pursuit of Exempt Purposes
The involvement of a nonprofit organization in the ownership or operation of a for-profit business nat-

urally raises concerns about the potential for generating unrelated business taxable income or losing the business's tax exemption (see discussion in §9.12). While these concerns may not be significant when the exempt organization is merely investing passively in the for-profit enterprise as a corporate shareholder,[6] they become more serious when the nonprofit becomes a general partner, placing its assets at risk and actively participating in the business. Although the Internal Revenue Code clearly indicates that an exempt organization may be a partner in an unrelated trade or business,[7] few statutory provisions, instances of case law, or revenue rulings have amplified the circumstances under which participation in such a business jeopardizes tax exemption, leading one commentator to call the law on this subject "cryptic."[8] However, some private letter rulings, discussed below, provide guidance on the approach likely to be taken by the IRS in such circumstances.

The IRS will analyze a nonprofit's participation or limited-partnership interest in a joint venture partnership to determine whether the activity, if carried on directly by the nonprofit, is related to the organization's exempt purposes. If that activity is not related to the exempt purposes, the nonprofit's share of the partnership revenues is subject to unrelated business income tax.[9] In fact, regulations governing partnership allocation rules specify the circumstances under which a qualified tax-exempt organization that holds debt-financed real estate in partnership with a nonqualified organization does not generate unrelated business taxable income (UBTI).[10] Essentially, to avoid UBTI, the exempt organization cannot receive a percentage share of partnership income for any taxable year that exceeds its share of partnership loss for the year in which the share of loss will be the smallest. The regulations do not apply to partnerships in which the exempt organization owns an aggregate interest of no more than 5 percent of partnership capital or profits. Both the nonprofit and for-profit partners would be subject to the new partnership antiabuse regulations issued in late 1994. These regulations are intended to identify joint ventures that do not constitute bona fide partnerships entered into for a substantial business purpose as well as partnerships in which form is elevated over substance.[11]

The IRS has found that a hospital may act as a general partner of a limited partnership owning a medical office building without jeopardizing its exempt status or receiving unrelated business income from management fees paid by the partnership. The IRS reasoned that the hospital's general-partner interest was related to its tax-exempt purpose because physicians would be attracted to the medical office building, which would help the hospital attract a better medical staff and improve patient care.[12] It can similarly be argued that the existence of a retirement community serves the tax-exempt purposes of a hospital either through the provision of health services to the elderly at the facility or by attracting residents and elderly people in general to the hospital. Thus, hospitals as well as existing providers of seniors' housing services are logical nonprofit candidates for a joint venture.

In general, the various revenue rulings discussed in Part IV set forth the tests of whether a retirement center is operating for exempt purposes. As the letter rulings below demonstrate, however, these usual tests are not dispositive of the question of whether a nonprofit entity can participate with a for-profit enterprise in a seniors' housing equity joint venture.

Of course, nonprofit venture partners should also be concerned about whether equity participation with a for-profit entity will result in a problem of private inurement. A sharing of profits does not necessarily result in a partnership.[13] In general, however, sharing net profits can lead to unrelated business taxable income for the nonprofit organization.[14] Nevertheless, the letter rulings described below have deemed that some sharing of partnership net profits with exempt organizations does not give rise to unrelated business income, even where the nonprofit clearly was a partner.[15]

(2) Letter Rulings Concerning For-Profit/Nonprofit Retirement Facility Partnerships

Several private letter rulings have considered partnerships between nonprofit and for-profit organizations in the context of seniors' housing and care facility projects.

(A) Ruling 7820058. In Letter Ruling 7820058, the IRS considered whether a nonprofit organization could maintain its tax exemption when it sought to become a general partner, along with two for-profit

interests, in a limited partnership designed to develop low-income seniors' housing in deteriorated urban renewal areas. The nonprofit would be the managing partner, with return on investment limited to 8 percent. The IRS ruled that such an arrangement would jeopardize the nonprofit's exempt status because the organization:

> Would be a direct participant in an arrangement for sharing the *net profits* of an income producing venture with private individuals and organizations of a noncharitable nature. By agreeing to serve as the general partner of the proposed housing project, [the nonprofit] would take on an obligation to further the private financial interests of the other partners. This would create a *conflict of interest* that is legally incompatible with [the nonprofit] being operated exclusively for charitable purposes. [Emphasis added.]

Despite the serious concerns about profit sharing raised by Letter Ruling 7820058, several later IRS pronouncements have concluded that some forms of for-profit and nonprofit equity partnerships are permitted and will neither affect the exempt status of the nonprofit nor result in taxable income to it. In General Counsel Memorandum 37852 (1979), the IRS's general counsel acknowledged that private benefit or inurement from the earnings of a nonprofit organization does not necessarily result merely from the organization's involvement in a joint venture or partnership with a for-profit business.

(B) Ruling 8417054. In Letter Ruling 8417054 in 1984, the IRS reviewed a request from a nonprofit organization intending to enter into a limited partnership as a cogeneral partner with a for-profit entity that was totally independent from the nonprofit organization. All dealings between the general partners were at arm's length. The nonprofit organization proposed to sell an existing retirement project operated by the nonprofit to the limited partnership at fair market value. Limited-partnership interests would then be sold to independent investors. The nonprofit organization was to participate actively in managing the project and receive a 1 percent allocation *of profit* or less in the limited partnership, plus a standard management fee pursuant to a HUD-approved management contract as well as reimbursement for expenses incurred. The limited-partnership agreement would state that the nonprofit would not be responsible for any operating losses. The project was subject to HUD mortgage insurance requirements and operated for the benefit of low- and moderate-income elderly persons. Part of the nonprofit's management duties called for ensuring that the to-be-formed for-profit facility would be operated to serve the special needs of the elderly and would comply with HUD policies and procedures.

The IRS noted that:

> An exempt organization's participation in a partnership arrangement as a general partner will not *per se* result in loss of status under Section 501(c)(3) of the Code. Each partnership arrangement must be examined closely to determine that the statutorily imposed obligations on the general partner do not conflict with the exempt organization's ability to pursue its charitable goals.

The IRS examined first whether the nonprofit organization was serving a charitable purpose, noting that *charitable* includes "relief of the poor and distressed"[16] as well as caring for the "special needs of the aged."[17] The IRS determined that the management functions of the nonprofit organization—ensuring compliance with HUD policies and procedures and implementing various tenant grievance systems and social programs—would serve the special needs of the elderly and constitute sufficient charitable activities.

The IRS then reviewed the partnership arrangement itself to determine if it "permits the exempt organization to act exclusively in furtherance of the purposes for which exemption was granted and not for the benefit of limited partners." The IRS concluded that the partnership did not, to a substantial extent, further private interests because the nonprofit organization was insulated from loss due to the HUD-insured mortgage and was protected by the partnership agreement's provision that the nonprofit would not be responsible for operating losses. The government concluded that the nonprofit's tax-exempt status would not be adversely affected and that management fees received from the partnership would not be considered unrelated business income.

Although letter rulings are not to be relied on as precedent,[18] 1984's Ruling 8417054 is indicative of the approach that the IRS takes in reviewing the tax-exemption implications of a seniors' housing joint venture partnership between for-profit and non-profit entities. Even though Ruling 7820058 seemed concerned with the sharing of net profits and the obligation of a nonprofit general partner to further the for-profit limited partners' interests, Ruling 8417054 appeared more concerned with the ongoing charitable nature of the nonprofit manager's role and the organization's insulation from liability.

(C) Ruling 8449070. In Letter Ruling 8449070, the government determined in another 1984 ruling that a nonprofit organization acting as a limited partnership's managing general partner with a 1 percent interest in profits and losses and receiving a fee of 6 percent of *gross* rentals was not jeopardizing its exempt status or receiving unrelated business income. Again, the IRS appeared concerned not with the sharing of profits so much as with the "charitable goals" of managing and maintaining the elderly housing complex and the "limited responsibility" of the nonprofit under the partnership agreement.

(D) Ruling 8425129. In yet another 1984 ruling involving seniors' housing, Letter Ruling 8425129 permitted a nonprofit organization to enter into an arrangement whereby it would act as the general partner, contributing a 20 percent share of capital and realizing a 10 percent share of profit. In addition, a for-profit management company was to be treated as a special limited partner entitled to a 10 percent share of profits in return for making a 10 percent capital contribution *and* would receive a 5 percent management fee for managing the project. In response to the IRS's concerns about the payments to the management company constituting a private benefit, the applicant convinced the IRS that the transaction was exempt by showing that the nonprofit general partner could not be removed without its consent and that the 5 percent management fee was reasonable. Here, even for-profit management appeared acceptable, provided that it was for a reasonable fee and did not disempower the nonprofit entity.

(E) Ruling 8545063. In Letter Ruling 8545063, the Internal Revenue Service considered the exempt status of a nonprofit corporation acting as the general partner in limited partnerships established to invest in low-income housing and eventually sell the properties to tenant cooperatives. Although the limited partnership was required to have a "standby general partner" that would maintain a minimum net worth in the event the nonprofit's net worth decreased, it was the nonprofit entity that was to manage the entire partnership. Importantly, however, the nonprofit's liability for partnership obligations, unlike most general partners, was to be limited to the amount of its capital investment, which equaled 10 percent of project cost. In addition, general and limited partners were to receive a return on investment of only about 4 percent per year from rental payments made after the co-ops reserved funds for capital improvements and operations expenses.

The IRS noted that the participation of a nonprofit organization in a partnership arrangement does not per se result in denial of exempt status but that if a charitable purpose is established, the partnership arrangement will be examined to determine if it "permits the exempt organization to act exclusively in furtherance of the purposes for which the exemption may be granted and not for the benefit of the limited partners."

After finding the cooperative housing purpose to be exempt as "combating community deterioration" (see §9.5), the IRS listed several factors supporting its conclusion that the joint arrangement was exempt and the income not subject to tax.

- The nonprofit made nominal contributions to capital.
- The nonprofit's liability was limited to its investment, and it had no responsibility to repay limited partners from its account.
- The nonprofit shared with the standby partner the obligations to provide additional working capital.
- The for-profit limited partners had no voice in management, and the standby general partner had no managerial control absent a severe deficit or mismanagement.
- The terms of the construction loans required leases to low- and moderate-income tenants.
- The requirements for reserves and the cap on return on investment limited the income to limited partners.

(F) Ruling 8927061. In Private Letter Ruling 8927061, the IRS ruled that the participation of a Section 501(c)(3) organization as a general partner in a limited partnership to develop a board-and-care facility did not jeopardize the organization's tax-exempt status. The nonprofit organization proposed to syndicate the project to limited-partner investors, who would be eligible for low-income housing tax credits. Noting that the exempt organization's role in the project was intended to enable it to carry out its exempt purposes, the IRS also found that development, management, and consulting fees received by the organization would not be treated as taxable income from an unrelated trade or business. The ruling relies on the fact that the project would provide affordable housing to low-income and elderly residents and combat community deterioration by operating a job training program.

(G) Ruling 9518014. In Private Letter Ruling 9518014, the Internal Revenue Service determined that a religiously affiliated hospital's participation in a partnership with a for-profit elderly care facility did not jeopardize its exempt status or generate unrelated business taxable income. In that ruling, the nonprofit entity and the developer had equal equity interests in the partnership and equally shared the partnership's profits and losses. The arrangement required the developer to manage the facility for a percentage of the gross revenues derived from it. The nonprofit, however, retained equal control over policy and decision making for the partnership. The IRS was satisfied that any private benefit to the developer resulting from the partnership was merely incidental to its exempt purposes. It stated that the hospital's exempt status would not be threatened because the elderly care facility would further the institution's charitable purposes by providing for the housing, health care, and security needs of the elderly; and at the end of the partnership's term, the nonprofit entity would have gained valuable expertise in developing and operating elderly care facilities that would be useful in establishing other such facilities in the future.

As noted, private letter rulings cannot be relied on as precedent,[19] yet the pattern of rulings relating to the role of a nonprofit general partner in a seniors' housing limited partnership indicates an IRS position that permits such transactions when the nonprofit maintains control over the charitably oriented operations and does not put its assets at unlimited risk for partnership liabilities. In other words, when the nonprofit exhibits the management and control attributes of a general partner but has limited liability more akin to that of a limited partner, the nonprofit can, at least in the circumstances discussed here, venture with for-profit investors on an equity-contributing, profit-sharing basis without jeopardizing its exempt status or generating unrelated business taxable income. The parties to any contemplated joint venture partnership between nonprofit and for-profit entities should, however, give careful consideration to obtaining a private letter ruling in advance of formation.

(H) Hospital/Physician Ventures. Although rulings related directly to retirement communities have largely concerned nonprofits in the role of general partner in a limited partnership, the IRS has reviewed several other permutations of involvement in the context of medical office buildings, in which exempt hospitals joint venture with private physicians. In general, medical office buildings have been found to promote the general exempt purposes of the nonprofit hospital by attracting physicians and their patients to use the hospital and its services. Various IRS letter rulings have approved joint ventures between exempt hospitals and physicians when the hospital's nonprofit subsidiary is a general partner in the limited partnership,[20] when the hospital itself was the general partner,[21] when the hospital's for-profit subsidiary was the general partner in a limited partnership,[22] when the hospital forms a general partnership directly with a for-profit entity,[23] and when the hospital enters into various lease relationships with the for-profit entity.[24]

General Counsel Memorandum 39862 (November 22, 1991), however, found that a hospital's joint venture with a physician group jeopardized its exempt status because the sharing of revenues from the use of existing surgical facilities was an improper sharing of *net* earnings; the private benefit to physicians amounted to private inurement and was not incidental to a charitable purpose, where no new health service had been created; and the arrangement arguably constituted an unlawful kickback in violation of Medicare and Medicaid antifraud and abuse laws. Several months after the publication of General Counsel Memorandum 39862, the IRS announced that hospitals could voluntarily enter into an agreement with the IRS to terminate prohibited revenue-stream joint ventures between hospitals and medical staffs.[25] Although this announcement specifically dealt with hospital-physician joint

ventures, the IRS indicated that "closing agreements" might be used more often in other contexts as a solution less draconian than revocation of exempt status. Nonetheless, the service has remarked that closing agreements offer neither precedential guidance nor consistent treatment of behavior and do not take the place of statutory intermediate sanction authority.[26]

(I) Limits on Private Benefit. Despite initial fears that General Counsel Memorandum 39862 prohibited all types of joint ventures, the memorandum's application is actually quite narrow. The IRS continues to approve joint ventures between taxable and tax-exempt entities if they satisfy three criteria: the activity of the joint venture or the exempt entity's participation in the venture furthers the organization's exempt purposes; the venture arrangement permits the exempt partner to operate exclusively in furtherance of its exempt purposes; and the terms of the venture adequately protect the exempt entity's financial interest and prevent nonexempt investors from deriving improper financial gain from the venture (see also Priv. Ltr. Rul. 9308034). It is important to note, however, that these criteria may not be assiduously applied when a court suspects abuse or the facts are particularly egregious.

For example, in *Housing Pioneers, Inc. v. Commissioner,*[27] the U.S. Tax Court held that a housing corporation organized to provide affordable housing for low-income and disabled persons did not qualify for tax-exempt status because the organization had become a cogeneral partner in two for-profit limited partnerships in order to take advantage of a state property tax reduction for low-income rentals. The court found that the organization's activities under the management agreements benefited the limited partnerships and their for-profit partners by providing a property tax reduction and services that allowed the partnerships to receive other tax benefits, including depreciation and low-income housing credits. The U.S. Court of Appeals for the Ninth Circuit affirmed the decision of the tax court, holding that Housing Pioneers failed to qualify as a nonprofit entity for purposes of the low-income tax credit provisions contained in Section 42(h) of the Internal Revenue Code. Given that Housing Pioneers was not a nonprofit entity under Section 42(h), the court did not discuss the relationship between that section and

Section 501(c)(3). The appeals court upheld the tax court's ruling because the joint venture had a substantial nonexempt purpose and its activities benefited private interests.[28]

(3) Drafting the Joint Venture Agreement

When reviewing joint ventures for private inurement, private benefit, and unrelated business taxable income (UBTI), the IRS also reviews the joint venture or partnership agreement. The service has found that the following features of such an agreement permit the nonprofit partner to pursue its charitable goals:

■ The agreement requires equal allocations of contributions, profits, losses, distributions, and assumptions.
■ The nonprofit entity is not required to place its assets at risk for the benefit of the venture.
■ The agreement is negotiated at arm's length.
■ The nonprofit partner's contributions to the venture are based on the fair market value of the venture's assets.
■ The nonprofit entity's influence over the partnership's executive committee is sufficient to ensure that the partnership maintains a high level of community benefit, even if the nonprofit entity is not involved in the venture's day-to-day operations.
■ The for-profit partner is precluded from controlling the nonprofit entity.[29]

These guidelines are useful in both drafting joint venture agreements between nonprofit and for-profit entities and articulating the exempt purposes to the joint venture. It is especially important to obtain an independent appraisal of the venture assets to ensure the payment of fair market value.

(c) Use of a Subsidiary Corporation

While it is possible for a nonprofit to engage directly in a partnership or other equity joint venture with a for-profit organization or individual investors, limitations imposed by financial commitments of the nonprofit entity or concerns about sharing control with profit-motivated investors may dictate a different structure. Therefore, nonprofit organizations often form a for-profit subsidiary corporation to act as the joint venture partner with the coventuring for-

profit organization. In addition, a for-profit subsidiary, although subject to taxation, creates less risk of jeopardy to the nonprofit's exempt status than a direct coventure.[30]

The IRS generally has permitted exempt organizations to perform unrelated business activities through for-profit subsidiary corporations. The government has viewed the situation as a permissible investment by the nonprofit parent—with no taxation of dividends paid to the parent and no attribution of the subsidiary's income to the parent—even though the parent and subsidiary share office space and management (but not financial accounts).[31] It is important to note, however, that if the subsidiary's corporate identity goes ignored due to undercapitalization or other defect, the IRS will likely treat dividends as interest income taxed to the parent.[32]

In General Counsel Memorandum 39326, IRS counsel opined that when the taxable subsidiary of a nonprofit exempt organization was formed for a bona fide business purpose and not as a mere agent of the parent, the parent's exemption would not be jeopardized. The analysis considered, among other things, the parent's degree of involvement in both the subsidiary's management structure and its day-to-day activities. Despite the fact that the parent owned all the stock of the subsidiary, received dividends, appointed the subsidiary's board of directors, and had the same executive director as the subsidiary, the subsidiary was found not to be a mere instrumentality of the parent.

In Private Letter Ruling 8821044, a nonprofit corporation classified as a church and presently operating residential facilities for older adults, children, or developmentally disabled persons wished to establish a for-profit subsidiary to plan, develop, market, and operate retirement centers, nursing homes, and other facilities to serve the needs of the elderly. Initially, the parent corporation would own all the shares of the subsidiary and, in the future, would always retain absolute majority control. No more than two of the five members of the subsidiary's board of directors would also be members of the parent's board, and parent board members would not be officers or employees of the subsidiary. Despite the possibility of some sharing of expertise during the startup phase of the subsidiary's operations, the two corporations would not substantially share employees in the course of their respective operations. The IRS ruled that the formation of the for-profit subsidiary, purchase of its stock, continued ownership of a controlling majority interest, and the receipt of dividends would not adversely affect the nonprofit organization's exempt status. Moreover, the subsidiary's income would not constitute unrelated business taxable income to the parent corporation. The unrelated trade or business of the for-profit subsidiary was found to be a bona fide business activity carried on in a manner wholly separate and apart from the nonprofit parent organization.

For reasons such as insulation from liability or the advantages of health care reimbursement, nonprofit parent organizations may wish to create a nonprofit subsidiary to participate in a venture. Even so, in addition to issues related to the relationship between the joint venturers, such an arrangement raises the question of whether the joint activity is itself charitable or otherwise eligible for exemption (see, generally, Part IV). Even if a subsidiary organization engaged in a nonexempt activity turns over all its profits to its tax-exempt parent, that organization will still be subject to taxation as a "feeder organization."[33] For example, laundries or other shared-service organizations controlled by tax-exempt hospitals have been found not to be eligible for exemption.[34] One exception that may be applicable in the seniors' housing context relates to organizations engaged in deriving rents, whereby the rents qualify as income exempt from unrelated business income taxation.[35] Thus, a nonprofit's subsidiary whose sole purpose is collecting rents and turning them over to the parent could still qualify for exemption.[36]

Nonetheless, most nonprofits that joint venture with for-profit entities resort to the use of for-profit subsidiaries. Formation of a for-profit subsidiary amounts to acquiescence that the joint venture activity is unrelated to the parent corporation's exempt purpose and that the income from the venture is taxable. In any event, creation of a nonprofit subsidiary is a desirable option for venturers when the benefits of the venture are not limited to tax considerations, provided that the nonprofit parent's exempt status is not jeopardized.

(d) Nonprofit Vendor Contracts

Equity joint venture relationships between for-profits and nonprofits may pose significant concerns for both parties with respect to their tax treatment, sharing of control, divisions of responsibility, disparate objectives, and related matters. While these problems can be overcome with careful planning that benefits all parties to a joint venture, it is often easier to structure a relationship that involves a simple management contract or development agreement. This section discusses issues for exempt organizations furnishing contract services.

(1) Unrelated Business Taxable Income

Nonprofit organizations that execute contracts to provide goods, facilities, or services to for-profit entities normally receive income from the for-profit organizations. Yet, a tax-exempt corporation's receipt of payments from for-profit organizations does not necessarily lead to receipt of unrelated business taxable income (UBTI). Rather than considering the source of payment, the law generally looks to the nature of the activity (see Chapter 9).

Passive investment activities generally do not result in UBTI. For example, under Internal Revenue Code Section 512(b)(1), interest received by a tax-exempt corporation as a result of a loan to a for-profit venture is exempt. Similarly, rents received by an exempt organization as the result of a lease of real or personal property to a for-profit business are exempt from unrelated business income tax unless the exempt organization provides significant services to the lessee under the rental agreement,[37] rent is based on a percentage of income or profits derived from the leased property (unless based on a fixed percentage of gross receipts or sales),[38] or substantial personal property is leased with the real property.[39] The tax-exempt organization can also receive income from the sale of real property to the venture without substantial fear of taxation.[40] The exempt organization, however, is subject to tax on rents or interest received from a for-profit entity that it controls (i.e., owns 50 percent or more of the shares).[41]

When a tax-exempt hospital and its tax-exempt subsidiary leased land to a limited partnership for the construction of a medical office building and parking lot, the IRS found that the hospital's receipt of fair market rent for the land on which the for-profit medical office building was to be constructed, plus a percentage of receipts from the parking lot, was passive income and not taxable as unrelated business income.[42] Rental income based on a percentage of the lessee's net profits rather than on gross receipts is, however, subject to tax on unrelated business income.[43]

Passive involvement on the part of the exempt entity simply may not be sufficient incentive for either party to proceed with a venture. Developers often approach nonprofit organizations because of the organizations' experience in operations and delivery of services. Nonprofits are a natural choice, especially for the delivery of health care services. With health promotion generally considered a charitable activity (see §9.6), the provision of such services under contract with a proprietary organization should not jeopardize exempt status or lead to unrelated business taxable income. In situations, however, where the nonprofit is acting as a residential retirement housing manager, mere management of elderly housing (even tax-exempt elderly housing) may not be deemed a charitable purpose and may lead to the realization of unrelated business taxable income or even loss of tax exemption if pursued to a substantial degree.[44] One solution may be for the managing nonprofit to establish an equity interest in the venture or substantial control over the housing inventory (see §9.3).

(2) Private Inurement

A major tax exemption concern for nonprofits contemplating contractual relationships with for-profit organizations is private inurement. In general, the exempt organization must receive adequate compensation for its services, for rental of its property, or for loans of its money to a for-profit organization.

Gifts or transfers of assets,[45] rentals or sales of the nonprofit's property at less than fair market value,[46] loans at below-market rates, or insufficiently secured loans have been found to result in private inurement.[47] However, a loan from a hospital to members of its medical staff to renovate a clinic furthered the hospital's exempt purposes and therefore did not jeopardize its exempt status.[48]

The IRS has upheld some arrangements that appear on the surface to be for less than full value.

For example, Private Letter Ruling 8134021 deemed that a nonprofit hospital's leasing its land to a for-profit corporation for one dollar per year did not constitute private inurement when the corporation was to develop a medical office building on the site for the hospital's benefit and the building would revert to the nonprofit at the end of a 40-year lease term. A key to the ruling was a finding that the value of the building at the end of the 40 years was more than double the fair market rental value of the land during the same period.

In general, if contract prices are negotiated at arm's length and represent fair market values when the entire transaction is viewed in context, private inurement problems should be easily avoided. Nevertheless, unusual payment arrangements involving sharing of income, deferred payments, in-kind transfers, contingent payments, and the like should be supported by appraisal or valuation data demonstrating fair market value.

(e) For-Profit Vendor Contracts

Many nonprofit organizations, such as smaller church groups or congregations, may have little or no experience in the operation of a complex business such as a retirement facility, whereas many for-profit management companies in the marketplace specialize in comprehensive retirement facility operations, food service, or health care service delivery. Nonprofits may maintain tax-exempt status for their retirement facility while contracting with a for-profit organization to manage and operate the entire facility, provided that all the prerequisites of the applicable revenue rulings are met (see Chapter 9), the nonprofit organization retains sufficient control over the operations of the facility, and compensation to the for-profit does not result in private inurement.

If a nonprofit grants the for-profit management company absolute discretion in management, a question arises as to whether the nonprofit organization retains sufficient control over the retirement property to ensure the pursuit of exclusively charitable purposes. Revenue Ruling 72–124 and successive rulings tended to focus on facilities owned and operated by a tax-exempt organization and did not deal with the issue of for-profit management of a facility owned by an exempt organization. In at least one general counsel memorandum,[49] however, a community lost its exempt status when it lost control over its no-eviction policy by permitting uncontrolled banks to hold mortgages against units sold as condominiums. Therefore, it is important for the tax-exempt owner to retain sufficient control over operations, such as through the imposition of restrictions in the for-profit manager's contract, to ensure that charitable activities are carried out.

In addition to retaining control, the exempt entity must be sure that its activities do not benefit private interests except to the extent necessary to pursue its exempt goals. Therefore, in its contractual dealings with the for-profit entity, a nonprofit cannot pay more than is reasonable when purchasing goods or services, borrowing money, or leasing property.

Although the U.S. Tax Court has held that compensation paid by a nonprofit corporation based on a percentage of its revenues resulted in private inurement,[50] such compensation is permissible when it is reasonable and negotiated at arm's length, when the income base bears some relation to the services being performed, and when the arrangement does not result in undue control over the exempt entity's activities.[51] The IRS approved as reasonable compensation the management fee—5 percent of gross rents plus 10 percent of profits (in return for an equity contribution)—paid by a nonprofit to a for-profit under the terms of a seniors' housing venture.[52]

If a nonprofit organization has obtained or wishes to obtain tax-exempt financing for a project, it must honor certain limitations imposed on service contracts with for-profit or other "nonqualified" entities. In January 1997, the Internal Revenue Service released Revenue Procedure 97–13, which significantly broadened the ability of for-profit management companies to contract with charitable organizations that have financed their facilities with tax-exempt bonds. The rules, which became effective on May 16, 1997, set forth several types of permissible contract arrangements not previously available.

The rules retain the basic preexisting requirements that management contracts must provide for reasonable compensation and that such compensation must not be based in whole or in part on a share of net profits from operation of the tax-exempt facility. The rules specify, however, that fees based on a percentage of gross revenues or a percentage of expenses (but not both), along with capitation fees or per unit of service fees, will *not* be considered to be based on a share of net profits. The rules also permit "productivity awards" based on increases or decreases in gross revenues or reductions in total expenses (but not both).

Previously, for-profit management contracts were limited to terms of five years and required the nonprofit organization to retain the right to terminate the contract without cause within three years. Under the new rules, a contract with compensation that is at least 95 percent based on a periodic fixed fee may have a term of 15 years or 80 percent of the expected useful life of the financed property, whichever is less. A contract based at least 80 percent on periodic fixed fees may have a term of ten years or 80 percent of useful life. The five-year limit with a three-year termination option applies to contracts in which at least 50 percent of the compensation is based on a periodic fixed fee or all of the compensation is based on a capitation fee or a combination of capitation and periodic fixed fees. Contracts in which all of the compensation is based on a per unit fee or a combination of per unit and periodic fees are limited to three years with a termination option at the end of the second year. Finally, management contracts based on a percentage of revenues or expenses, a per unit fee, or some combination of these must not exceed two years and must be terminable after the first year. This last contract type is available only when services are provided to third parties (e.g., radiology) or when management contracts involve a facility during a startup period of insufficient length to establish a reasonable estimate of annual gross revenues and expenses.

In all qualifying contracts, the for-profit service provider may not have any role or relationship with the exempt user that limits the exempt organization's ability to exercise its rights, including contract cancellation rights. This requirement is met if no more than 20 percent of the voting power of the exempt organization is vested in the management company or related individuals, overlapping board members do not include chief executive officers, and the entities are not otherwise considered related parties under IRS rules.

The new rules should make it easier for for-profit and nonprofit organizations to enter into longer-term management agreements and to include performance-based incentives in their arrangements. Nonetheless, failure to comply with any of the several revenue procedures could result in the borrower's bond default and the taxation of bond interest to bondholders (see also discussion in §15.2).

§12.2 Preserving For-Profit Tax Advantages

(a) ACRS after the Tax Reform Act of 1986

The accelerated cost recovery system (ACRS) permits an owner to depreciate real property, equipment, and improvements on real property such as buildings at an accelerated rate, depending on the class in which the Internal Revenue Code places the particular property. Before the Tax Reform Act of 1986, real property could be depreciated over a 19-year recovery period by using 175 percent accelerated depreciation.[53] Low-income housing could be depreciated by using a 200 percent acceleration factor.[54] For residential rental property, the excess of accelerated depreciation over the straight-line method is recaptured on its disposition, that is, treated as ordinary income.[55] For commercial property, the entire depreciation is recaptured.[56]

The Tax Reform Act of 1986 retained a modified ACRS system but required residential real property to be depreciated by using the straight-line method over a 27.5-year period. The current rules do not permit recapture of depreciation for residential or commercial property. However, the difference between the amount allowable under the modified method and the asset depreciation range (ADR) system (see §12.2(b)) is treated as a tax preference item.[57]

Before the 1986 act, low-income housing had special ACRS status as 15-year real property compared with the 19-year depreciation classification of other residential real property. The 1986 act eliminated the favored treatment of low-income housing and now treats such housing and all other residential rental structures as 27.5-year property. It subjects nonresidential real property to a 31.5-year ACRS depreciation schedule.[58] For nonresidential real property put into service after May 13, 1993, the ACRS depreciation schedule is 39 years.[59]

(b) Tax-Exempt Use Property

(1) In General

An alternative to the 27.5-year depreciation schedule is based on asset depreciation range (ADR) midpoints. Under this approach, real property depreciation is based on a straight-line method over a 40-year recovery period; no tax preference income is attributable to use of the ADR system. While application of the system is always an option for real property owners, its use in lieu of the 27.5-year ACRS system is mandatory for "tax-exempt use property" and tax-exempt, bond-financed property.[60]

Tax-exempt use property includes residential rental property that is leased to a tax-exempt entity for any period of time and nonresidential property where any one of the following circumstances applies: the lease term exceeds 20 years; any part of the property is financed by the exempt organization or a related entity using tax-exempt financing under Internal Revenue Code Section 103; the exempt entity retains an option for it or a related entity to purchase the property at a fixed or calculable price; or the property has previously been used by the tax-exempt corporation or a related entity and is then sold and leased back to the tax-exempt organization.[61] Tax-exempt use property must be depreciated over a term of 40 years or 125 percent of the lease term, whichever is greater, by using the straight-line method.[62]

Low- and moderate-income housing projects financed with tax-exempt bonds are not subject to the 40-year depreciation schedule used for other forms of tax-exempt use property but may qualify for an alternative 27.5-year schedule.[63]

A nonprofit organization cannot circumvent tax-exempt use rules simply by creating a new for-profit organization that would, for example, lease property in its stead, due to a five-year "look back" rule, which characterizes the transaction as one with the exempt parent entity.[64]

(2) Service Contracts

Another attempted method of circumventing tax-exempt use property rules has been to structure transactions as service agreements rather than as leases.[65] The IRS may, however, recharacterize the transaction as a lease based on factors such as whether

- the service recipient is in physical possession of the property;
- the service recipient controls the property;
- the service recipient has a significant economic or possessory interest in the property;
- the service provider does not bear any risk of substantially diminished receipts or substantially increased expenditures if there is nonperformance under the contract;
- the service provider does not use the property concurrently to provide significant services to entities unrelated to the service recipient; and
- the total contract price does not substantially exceed the rental value of the property for the contract period.

In the context of retirement housing, for example, a contract for more than 20 years in which a for-profit facility owner purports to deliver operational or other services to a nonprofit organization may be recharacterized as a lease when the exempt organization has possession or control of the property, pays service fees approximately equal to the property's rental value, and has no right to withhold payments or terminate the contract in the event of the for-profit's nonperformance of services. A more typical service agreement is one in which a nonprofit organization is the provider of services to a for-profit retirement facility owner and, in the course of managing the facility, takes possession or control of the premises. Such an arrangement should not be subject to recharacterization as a lease, assuming the nonprofit service provider receives reasonable payment for the services and is not in effect performing such services as some form of in-kind payment of rent to the for-profit owner.[66] A Section 501(c)(3) or 501(c)(4) organization that operates low-income housing with 80 percent or more of the units leased to low-income tenants is exempt from the service contract rules.[67]

§12.3 Example of a For-Profit/ Nonprofit Joint Venture

(a) Benefits of the Venture

One possible joint venture scenario between a for-profit developer and a nonprofit operating entity involves a lease of the premises from the developer to the nonprofit entity. In projects where entrance fees or other substantial sums are to be received by the retirement facility from residents, for-profit operators are justifiably concerned about the considerable tax consequences of receiving such fees as income.[68] Although the use of a loan of entrance fees from the resident to the facility can solve the problem of taxable income to the for-profit operator, it can also create an imputed interest problem for the resident-lender unless market-rate interest is paid to the resident.[69]

A lease arrangement between a for-profit and nonprofit entity permits the retirement community to receive entrance fee proceeds from the nonprofit organization without taxation while allowing the for-profit owner to take advantage of the accelerated depreciation deductions available to real property owners. Of course, to avoid characterization as tax-exempt use property, the lease must run for fewer than 20 years; it cannot contain a fixed or calculable price purchase option and cannot be part of a sale-leaseback transaction. Further, the project cannot be financed by tax-exempt bonds.[70] The facility will not be eligible for exemption from real property tax because the nonprofit organization has the status of lessee without any ownership interest.[71]

For some developers, depreciation and rental incomes may be sufficient economic reward and motivation for engaging in real estate transactions. Other developers, however, may want to reap the benefits and bear the responsibilities of ongoing operation of the project, although lease payments to a for-profit business based on revenues of a tax-exempt organization may raise significant concerns about private inurement.[72] Nonetheless, sharing profits as a form of lease payment may be justifiable if commercially reasonable. For example, periodic rents initially set at below-market rates may justify the later payment of a bonus to the developer once the facility has sold out and is consistently generating positive cash flows. A further potential reason for sharing net revenues from the nonprofit operation includes unusual risks taken or benefits offered by the lessor/developer in the development process, such as delivering a turnkey, sold-out project or covering tenant operating deficits pending sellout of the project.

Figure 12.1 **Sample For-Profit/Nonprofit Joint Venture**

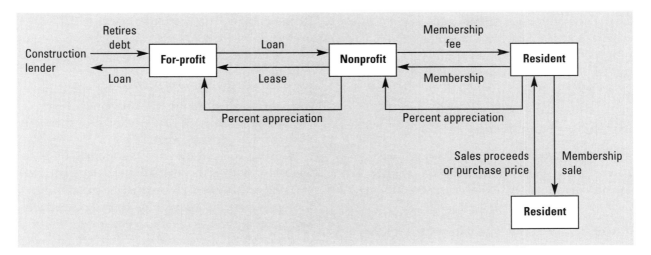

For-Profit
1. Borrows construction financing
2. Owns and develops property
3. Leases building to nonprofit
4. Borrows membership fees from nonprofit to repay construction lender

Nonprofit
1. Rents building from for-profit
2. Obtains license to operate facility and collects resident fees
3. Loans membership fee proceeds to for-profit owner
4. Collects share of appreciated membership values and pays portion as rent

In the context of a continuing-care facility, where residents may pay the nonprofit corporation substantial entrance fees at the outset of facility operations, the developer may also be interested in obtaining some use of those entrance fees to help retire construction debt. It may be possible, therefore, for the nonprofit organization to loan the developer some or all of the entrance fees received from residents. To some extent, interest on the loan received by the nonprofit may be used to fund the cost of monthly lease payments.

Figure 12.1 illustrates a structure[73] whereby a for-profit owner-developer leases a retirement facility to a nonprofit operating organization, which sells transferable memberships to residents for a substantial price. The nonprofit loans the membership sales proceeds, less amounts needed for reserves and operations, to the for-profit at market-rate interest. Whenever a resident sells a membership to another person at an appreciated value, the resident is required to turn over a portion of the appreciation to the nonprofit as a "transfer fee." Rent payable by the nonprofit

lessee includes a bonus payment consisting of a share of any appreciation received by the nonprofit from residents.

The goals and possible benefits of this structure include the following:

- The resident, nonprofit operator, and for-profit developer all benefit from sharing in the appreciated value of memberships upon resale and thus all retain a long-term interest in the success of the project.
- The development experience of the for-profit and operational experience of the nonprofit benefit the overall project.
- Lump-sum fees paid by residents reach the developer via a loan from the nonprofit for use in retiring construction debt, without taxation of the fees as income to the developer.
- As is the case with residents of refundable entrance fee communities, residents have the opportunity to recover some or all of their payments through the resale of their memberships, but they

are not subject to tax on imputed interest because the transaction is fashioned as a sale rather than as a loan.

- The nonprofit organization is able to fund at least part of its lease payment obligation from interest income received from the loan to the developer.
- The developer as owner can depreciate the property.

(b) Venture Legal Issues

Any complex structure such as this example can raise a host of legal questions related primarily to the tax consequences of the transaction. Among the issues[74] raised by the illustration are

- whether the tax-exempt status of the nonprofit organization is jeopardized because
  - the payment of bonus rent from appreciation in membership values results in private inurement or gain from the exempt organization's activities; or
  - the transaction is tantamount to an equity joint venture in which the nonprofit has significant liability exposure and insufficient operational control, or other factors exist that compromise pursuit of the nonprofit's charitable purposes; and
- whether the loan from the lessee to the lessor results in treatment of the transaction as a sale rather than as a true lease or characterization of the loan as prepaid rent.[75]

While the lease/loan structure offers many advantages for both parties, the transaction must be approached with caution. For example, to reduce the risk of its characterization as a mere instrumentality or alter ego of the for-profit,[76] the nonprofit corporation should not be controlled by the for-profit organization. Such characterization could result in loss of the organization's tax-exempt status. The transaction between the nonprofit and for-profit must be at arm's length, and lease payments and interest rates must be set at fair market values. If the nonprofit corporation is to avoid characterization as a passive agent or nominee of the for-profit entity, it should have broad functions and business purposes not solely limited to improving the tax consequences of the retirement facility transaction for the for-profit

entity.[77] If the nonprofit corporation has been created solely for the purpose of engaging in lease and loan transactions with the for-profit owner or serves no business or economic purposes other than tax avoidance for the for-profit owner, its exempt status or very existence may be ignored and the transaction subjected to taxation as a sale directly from the for-profit entity to the resident. On the other hand, where the nonprofit has significant management functions and control over its charitable activities, its separate status should be recognized.

A further concern with a for-profit/nonprofit lease and loan arrangement relates to IRS treatment of the for-profit owner of the property as the owner, so that the latter can take depreciation deductions. In addition, if the IRS views the arrangement as a sale, it could consider the loan proceeds as the sale price and thus as taxable income received by the developer.

In *Sun Oil v. Commissioner*,[78] the U.S. Third Circuit Court of Appeals pointed to several factors in a lessee-financed sale-leaseback transaction[79] that tended to jeopardize the status of the lessor as owner, including the correlation between the lessee's rental payments and the lessor's interest and principal payments on the loan; the lessee's option to purchase the property at the end of the lease term for less than fair market value; the right of the lessee to renew the lease for a cumulative term of 90 years, with reduced rental payments during the later renewal periods; the right of the lessee to terminate the lease by purchasing the property in certain situations; and the right of the lessee to receive all appreciation value of the property in the event of a taking by eminent domain. The court found in *Sun Oil* that the seller/lessee had not relinquished ownership of the property.

In another sale-leaseback case, *Frank Lyon Co. v. United States*,[80] the U.S. Supreme Court found that because, among other things, the lessor/owner financed the purchase of a building through a third-party lender and was personally liable for the debt, the lessor was the true owner even though the rental payments were equivalent to the loan payments due; the lessee had purchase options designed to return a calculable profit on the lessor's investment; and the lease term exceeded the useful life of the building.

Hilton v. Commissioner,[81] however, found that a sale-leaseback arrangement lacked economic substance when the lessee's rents and lessor's debt service were correlated, the lessee had options to renew the lease, rental payments were not tied to fair market value, and investors had made no significant investment in the property and could realize no significant gain from their participation in the transaction. Likewise, the U.S. Tax Court has construed as advance rental payments loan proceeds from a lessee when the lease and loan payments were identical, all payments were due at the same time, no money changed hands, and the loan was neither interest-bearing nor secured.[82]

A lessee-financed or leveraged lease from a for-profit to a nonprofit entity is less likely to be recharacterized as a sale or prepaid lease if the obligations of the loan and lease are severable and not contingent on each other; the financial obligations of the parties to each other under the lease and loan do not exactly offset each other and payments are actually made; the lease term is substantially less than the property's useful life; the loan bears interest and is secured; rental payments, interest, and purchase options are at fair market value and the purchase option price is not fixed or calculable at the beginning of the lease term; the lessee does not have substantial ownership rights (see discussion below); and the lessor retains some of the risks and benefits of ownership. In addition, the existence of at least initial third-party recourse financing arranged by the lessor, to be taken out by the loan of entrance fee proceeds, can aid in a determination that the lessor is the owner.

One of the incidents of ownership in a retirement facility operation may be the right to benefit from appreciation in the value of units upon resale. For reasons noted earlier, it may well be in the interest of both parties to structure the transaction so that any appreciation resulting from the resale of a unit is shared by the owner and lessee. In a service-oriented facility, sharing appreciation in value with the lessee should be justifiable on the basis that the lessee, as operator of the facility's services, contributes substantially to the appreciation in value of a given unit. To that extent, receipt of a portion of the appreciated value of that unit is not necessarily an indicator that real property ownership is being retained by the lessee, and the owner's relinquishment of a portion of the appreciation should not

eliminate the owner's ability to take advantage of ownership tax benefits.

Although sharing appreciation of unit values is a form of profit sharing, which is a characteristic of a partnership, the transaction should not be characterized as such. The central feature of a joint venture that is treated as a partnership for tax purposes is "a proprietary interest in the *net* profits of the enterprise coupled with an obligation to share its losses."[83] In this example, a portion of gross profit is divided according to contractual arrangement, the owner does not share any of the nonprofit's losses from business operations, and the lessee does not share the owner's losses, if any, as a result of a decline in real estate values.

Notes

1. *See Plumstead Theatre Society, Inc. v. Comm'r.*, 74 T.C. 1324 (1980), *aff'd.*, 675 F.2d 244 (9th Cir. 1982). *See also* Priv. Ltr. Rul. 9736039, in which the Internal Revenue Service found that a charitable low-income housing provider in a partnership with a for-profit entity retained insufficient control to pursue its charitable purposes.

2. I.R.–90-60, 1990 I.R.B. Lexis 328 (Apr. 3, 1990).

3. *See also* "IRS to Step Up Scrutiny of 501(c)(3) Firms," *Modern Healthcare's Elder Care Business,* Apr. 30, 1990, 2.

4. *Internal Revenue Manual Supplement* (providing instructions for Internal Revenue Service personnel who process exemption applications submitted by charitable organizations that finance facilities with proceeds of tax-exempt bond financing), Feb. 16, 1993.

5. *Internal Revenue Manual Supplement,* at §§4, 5.

6. *See* I.R.C. §512(b)(1).

7. *See* I.R.C. §512(c).

8. Hopkins and Beckwith, "The Federal Tax Law of Hospitals: Basic Principles and Current Developments," 24 *Duquesne L. Rev.,* 691, 718 (1986).

9. *See* I.R.C. §512(c), Rev. Ruls. 74-197, 1974-1 C.B. 143 and 79-222, 1979-2 C.B. 236; *Service Bolt and Nut Company Profit Sharing Trust v. Comm'r.,* 78 T.C. 812 (1982), *aff'd.,* 724 F.2d 519 (6th Cir. 1983).

10. Treas. Reg. §1.514(c)-2(b) *et seq.*

11. Treas. Reg. §1.701-2.

12. Priv. Ltr. Rul. 8201072, referencing Rev. Ruls. 69-464, 1969-2 C.B. 132, and 69-463, 1969-2 C.B. 131. Likewise, the IRS ruled that a proposed general partner-

ship between a for-profit operator of an acute care hospital and a supporting organization for a nonprofit tax-exempt operator of three acute care hospitals did not jeopardize the exempt organization's Section 501(c)(3) status and did not generate UBTI because the joint venture furthered the exempt entity's charitable purpose of promoting health. Specifically, the IRS found that patients of the venture hospital would enjoy access to more sophisticated medical programs, that medical staff members of the venture hospital would be able to participate in advanced cancer treatment protocols, that patients would have access to a sophisticated trauma center, and that the venture hospital would comply with the traditional criteria applied to tax-exempt hospitals. Priv. Ltr. Rul. 9308034.

Similarly, the service held that a community hospital's entry into a partnership with a for-profit entity for the purposes of expanding and operating its rehabilitation services did not jeopardize the hospital's tax exemption because the venture expanded health care services and improved the quality of care to patients. Priv. Ltr. Rul. 9352030.

13. *See* Treas. Reg. §301.7701–3(a), which describes a lease to a farmer in exchange for a share of crops as not necessarily constituting a partnership. *See also Herzberg v. U.S.,* 176 F. Supp. 440 (S.D. Ind. 1959).

14. *See* §12.1(d)(2).

15. For a good discussion of tax exemption issues surrounding a variety of for-profit/nonprofit joint venture situations, *see* Brier, B., "Special Tax Problems of Health Care Providers," *The Exempt Organization Tax Revue,* Aug.–Sept. 1989.

16. Treas. Reg. §1.501(c)(3)–1(d)(2).

17. Rev. Rul. 72–124, 1972–1 C.B. 145.

18. I.R.C. §6110(j)(3).

19. I.R.C. §6110(j)(3).

20. Priv. Ltr. Rul. 8226146.

21. Priv. Ltr. Rul. 8201072.

22. Priv. Ltr. Rul. 8243212.

23. Priv. Ltr. Rul. 8206093.

24. *See, e.g.,* Priv. Ltr. Ruls. 8134021, 8232035.

25. Ann. 92–70 1992–19 I.R.B. 89.

26. *See* "IRS Sees Need for Intermediate Sanctions for Exempt Health Organizations," *BNA Daily Tax Report,* Apr. 27, 1995, J–1.

27. T.C. Memo 1993–120, 65 T.C.M. 2191 (1993).

28. *Housing Pioneers, Inc. v. Commissioner,* 49 F.3d 1395 (9th Cir. 1995), *opinion amended,* 58 F.3d 401 (9th Cir. 1995).

29. Priv. Ltr. Rul. 9308034.

30. *See also* Priv. Ltr. Ruls. 9311034, 9349032.

31. Priv. Ltr. Ruls. 8111030, 8116121, 8303019. *See, generally,* Hopkins and Beckwith, note 8 *above,* at 736.

32. *See* I.R.C. §§482, 512(b)(13).

33. *See* I.R.C. §502.

34. *See Associated Hospital Services, Inc.,* 74 T.C. 213 (1980).

35. I.R.C. §§502(b)(1), 512(b)(3). *See, generally,* discussion in §9.12(b).

36. *See also* I.R.C. §§501(c)(2), (c)(25) regarding tax-exempt title-holding corporations and trusts.

37. Treas. Reg. §1.512(b)–1(c)(5).

38. Treas. Reg. §1.512(b)–1(c)(2)(iii)(b).

39. Treas. Reg. §1.512(b)–1(c)(2)(iii)(a).

40. *See* I.R.C. §512(b)(5).

41. I.R.C. §§512(b)(13), 368(c). In 1997, the code was amended to reduce the percentage deemed to be "controlling" from 80 to 50 percent.

42. Priv. Ltr. Rul. 8138024. *See also* Priv. Ltr. Ruls. 8232035, 8134021, 9315021.

43. *Ohio County & Independent Agricultural Societies v. Comm'r.,* 43 T.C.M. 1126, T.C.M. 1982–210.

44. *See* Rev. Rul. 70–535 and discussion in §9.9 *above.*

45. *Maynard Hospital, Inc. v. Comm'r.,* 52 T.C. 1006 (1969) *supplemental opinion,* 54 T.C. 1675 (1970).

46. *Harding Hospital, Inc. v. U.S.,* 505 F.2d 1068 (6th Cir. 1974).

47. *Lowry Hospital Ass'n. v. Comm'r.,* 66 T.C. 850 (1976).

48. Priv. Ltr. Rul. 9023091.

49. G.C.M. 39487, March 21, 1986.

50. *See, e.g., Sonora Community Hospital v. Comm'r.,* 46 T.C. 519 (1966), *aff'd.,* 397 F.2d 814 (9th Cir. 1968).

51. *University of Maryland Physicians v. Comm'r.,* 41 T.C.M. 732 (1981).

52. Priv. Ltr. Rul. 8425129.

53. I.R.C. §168(b)(2)(A) as it existed before the Tax Reform Act of 1986.

54. I.R.C. §168(b)(4)(A) as it existed before the Tax Reform Act of 1986.

55. I.R.C. §§1245(a)(5) and 1250 as they existed before the Tax Reform Act of 1986.

56. I.R.C. §1245(a).

57. The 1986 act's changes are generally effective for property placed in service after December 31, 1986. Certain exceptions were available for property acquired or constructed under a contract binding as of March 1, 1986, not subject to substantial modification, and placed in service before 1991. A contract is deemed binding only if it is

legally enforceable and does not contain a provision limiting damages for breach to less than 5 percent of the contract price. A binding contract includes a contract subject to a condition, provided neither party has control over the condition. P.L. 99–514, §203(b)(1)(A), 203(b)(2); Rep. of the Comm. of Conf. on H.R. 3838, at II–53, reprinted in 1986 *U.S.C. Cong. & Admin. News* No. 9B, at II–53. It also includes an irrevocable put, but not an option to purchase the property. Rep. of the Comm. of Conf. on H.R. 3838, at II–55, reprinted in 1986 *U.S.C. Cong. & Admin. News* No. 9B, at II–55. A disqualifying substantial modification does not include design changes made for reasons of technical or economic efficiencies that do not significantly increase project costs.

Relief from the rules is also available for certain property constructed or reconstructed by the taxpayer if the lesser of $1 million or 4 percent of the property cost was incurred or committed by March 1, 1986; significant work on the property had been commenced by that date; and the property was placed in service by January 1, 1991. Qualifying property is also eligible for this exemption if it is sold and leased back within three months of being placed in service by the buyer.

58. I.R.C. §168(c).

59. P.L. 103–66, §13,151(a).

60. I.R.C. §168(g)(1)(B), (C).

61. *See* I.R.C. §168(h)(1)(B).

62. I.R.C. §168(g)(2), (3). The restrictions of the 1986 act do not apply to exempt-bond-financed property placed in service after December 31, 1986, to the extent that the bond issue predated March 2, 1986. P.L. 99–514, §203(c). In addition, the rules do not apply to projects with binding construction contracts in place before March 1, 1986. P.L. 99–514, §203(b). However, pre–1986 law also placed similar 40-year depreciation schedules on tax-exempt use property, and the 1986 act does not represent a significant departure from earlier law. *See* I.R.C. §168(j) before amendment by the Tax Reform Act of 1986.

63. I.R.C. §§168(g)(5)(C), 142(a)(7), 142(d).

64. I.R.C. §168(h)(2)(E).

65. *See* I.R.C. §7701(e)(1).

66. *See, e.g., Federal Tax Coordinator 2d*, RIA (1993), L-8133, at 34,788A–92 to 34,789–89, *citing* S. Rep. on Pub. L. No. 98–369, at 137–141.

67. I.R.C. §7701(e)(5).

68. *See* discussion in §6.1(b).

69. *See* §6.2(b).

70. *See* §12.2(b).

71. *See* discussion in Chapter 10.

72. *See* discussion in §12.1(e).

73. This structure is presented for purposes of illustrating business considerations and legal issues that may be present in a for-profit/nonprofit coventure. It is not meant to describe any particular transaction or facility structure in the marketplace. Its presentation and the discussion do not purport to represent the position that the IRS or the courts would take respecting such a structure.

74. These issues are also discussed generally elsewhere in this book, *e.g.,* private inurement (see §§9.2(b), 12.1), equity joint ventures (see §12.1(b)), loans versus sales (see §6.2(a)).

75. One additional issue concerns whether the ability of a resident to resell a membership at market values results in disqualification for tax exemption under Revenue Ruling 72-124 on the grounds that the seller has a noncharitable profit motive or that access to the facility is not available to the purchaser at the lowest feasible cost (*see* discussion in §9.3(a)(3)(B)).

76. *See, e.g., Vaughn v. U.S.,* 740 F.2d 941 (Fed. Cir. 1984) for a discussion of agency for federal tax purposes.

77. *See generally Stringfellow v. United States,* 246 F. Supp. 474 (W.D. Wash. 1965); *Niagara County Savings Bank v. Commissioner,* 48 T.C.M. 51 (1984). *See also Commissioner v. Bollinger,* 485 U.S. 340 (1988), in which the U.S. Supreme Court ruled that a corporation that was the title holder of record of a group of apartment complexes was to be disregarded for tax purposes and that the partnerships that operated the buildings were to be considered the true owners of the properties because the corporation had been formed for the sole purpose of obtaining financing.

78. 562 F.2d 258 (3d Cir. 1977), *cert. den.,* 436 U.S. 944 (1978).

79. In a sale-leaseback transaction, the property owner sells the property and then leases it back from the buyer. The issue analogous to this example is whether the lease terms in actuality give the lessee an ownership interest in the property.

80. 435 U.S. 561 (1978).

81. 74 T.C. 305 (1980), *aff'd.,* 671 F.2d 316 (9th Cir.), *cert. den.,* 459 U.S. 907 (1982).

82. *Blue Flame Gas Co.,* 54 T.C. 584 (1970). *See also* Rev. Proc. 75-21, 1975-1 C.B. 715. Rev. Proc. 75-28, 1975-1 C.B. 752; *as modified by* Rev. Proc. 81-71, 1981-2 C.B. 731; Rev. Proc. 76-30, 1976-2 C.B. 647; Rev. Proc. 79-48, 1979-2 C.B. 529.

83. *Federal Bulk Carriers, Inc. v. Commissioner,* 66 T.C. 283, 293 (1976), *aff'd.,* 558 F.2d 128 (2d Cir. 1977).

The Terraces of Los Gatos; Los Gatos, California.

13 Other Joint Venture Considerations

§13.1 In General

Several other legal and business structure issues may arise out of seniors' housing transactions involving joint venture partners. These issues may extend to the antitrust consequences of creating a new joint venture entity or of the venture parties' dealings with the entity, Medicare reimbursement implications pertaining to one or more of the venturing parties, or the joint venture's effect on the respective parties' pension plans or collective bargaining agreements.[1] Although these are matters that may not come to light until operations are well underway, they should be considered at least in general terms during project planning and development.

§13.2 Medicare/Medicaid Issues

(a) Reimbursement

Medicare reimbursement considerations can be extremely complicated, particularly for institutional coventurers such as hospitals. Historically, Medicare has reimbursed almost all covered health care services on the basis of the provider's cost or reasonable charges, whichever is less.[2] Normally, this practice has meant, for example, that a nursing facility purchasing a service, such as laundering, from another entity would be reimbursed in accordance with Medicare

utilization for the percentage of cost of the service to the nursing facility; that cost would include a profit margin charged by the laundry service. When, however, a provider receives facilities, goods, or services from another organization related to it by common ownership or control, Medicare's related party rule limits the purchasing provider's reimbursement to the related seller's cost or the market price, whichever is less.[3] Therefore, there is little reimbursement advantage in a joint venture context for parent organizations to lease facilities or sell services or goods to a subsidiary joint venture entity (which can be reimbursed for only the seller's cost) when a sale to an unrelated provider can be reimbursed in the amount of the seller's cost plus a reasonable margin of profit or return on capital investment.[4]

The 1983 adoption of the prospective payment system (PPS) for Medicare reimbursement of inpatient hospital services has provided a strong incentive for hospitals to become involved in other activities that permit more favorable Medicare or Medicaid reimbursement. Under PPS, hospital inpatient services are not reimbursed retroactively on the basis of costs but rather according to a schedule of rates prospectively determined for each hospital discharge per diagnosis-related groups (DRGs).[5] The PPS system is designed to reduce overall expenditures by the Medicare program. Even if the related party rule could be circumvented, PPS eliminates the incentive to maximize reimbursement for inpatient services by creating multiple cost-reimbursed profit centers. The prospective payment is the total payment for the service, even if other entities supply portions of the service.[6] Thus, hospitals may be looking for joint venture opportunities involving health care services other than inpatient hospital care that are directly reimbursable by Medicare on the more favorable basis of cost. In addition, PPS will be applied to Medicare nursing services effective July 1, 1998 (see §28.12(c)).

Seniors' communities present opportunities for provision of Medicare cost-reimbursable health services such as skilled nursing,[7] home health,[8] rehabilitation,[9] and health maintenance.[10] Hospitals or other health care providers may benefit from the more favorable reimbursement principally by having an equity interest in the nursing facility or other cost-reimbursed provider.[11] In addition, if the hospital furnishes facilities, goods, or services to the cost-reimbursed provider, the buyer—including a subsidiary or controlled entity subject to the related party rule discussed above—can pay and be reimbursed for the hospital's cost of providing the services.[12] Even this cost reimbursement for the hospital's services or resources (without any profit) may be more remunerative than if the same resources were used to provide inpatient services subject to DRG limitations. Therefore, parent hospitals can indirectly use cost-based reimbursement to subsidize some of their existing in-house activities, such as laundry, dining, or pharmacy, that might be used to serve a controlled rehabilitation, nursing, or other facility or to provide services to a home health agency or health maintenance organization. Using existing in-house departments to serve outside enterprises also can promote desirable efficiencies and economies of scale.

(b) Fraud and Abuse

(1) Bed Reserve Agreements

Often, coventuring nursing facilities and hospitals contract to hold beds open or to reserve other facilities or services for use when needed by the other venture party. For example, Medicare or Medicaid reimbursement restrictions may induce hospitals to discharge patients to a lower level of care sooner than if full reimbursement were available for a longer hospital stay. Hospitals may therefore decide to enter into an arrangement with a retirement facility that

has excess bed capacity in its nursing unit whereby the facility agrees to hold beds open and available to receive transfers from the hospital on a moment's notice. Similarly, a seniors' housing facility can benefit from an arrangement with a nursing home or hospital that agrees to hold beds open or otherwise accept priority admissions, reduce fees, or favor facility residents whenever health care services are needed.

One Medicare/Medicaid issue inherent in such relationships concerns the payment received by a provider in exchange for its agreement to hold beds open or to bestow other favored treatment on the other contracting party. Medicare and Medicaid providers are prohibited by regulatory fraud and abuse provisions from charging an individual for a facility's agreement to admit the individual at a specified future date for inpatient services covered by the program.[13] In addition, there are criminal sanctions against requiring any payment from a Medicaid recipient or his or her family for covered services as a condition of admission or continued stay at the facility.[14]

Bed reserve agreements, in which, for example, a hospital agrees to pay the difference between the nursing facility's private-pay charges and the lower payment made by Medicaid for patients referred from the hospital, violate the nursing facility's provider agreement.[15] It is also a violation for the hospital to agree to provide personnel to the nursing facility whenever Medicare-covered patients referred by the hospital occupy a reserved bed.[16] The hospital may, however, pay a fee to the nursing facility for each day a bed is held open or may agree to provide personnel or services to the nursing facility without regard to whether the reserved beds are filled with Medicare patients so long as the payment of consideration for holding beds open does not depend on admission of or service to a Medicare or Medicaid patient.[17] Because the payment for reserving beds is not related to the care of patients, it is not an allowable cost to the payor, and revenue need not be offset by the payee against its reimbursable costs.[18]

(2) Referral Payments

Solicitation, offering, payment, or receipt of remuneration for referring a person for the furnishing of goods or services reimbursed by Medicare or Medicaid or for participating in or recommending a sale, lease, or order of any reimbursable item is a federal felony.[19] An exception is made for discounts or price reductions if disclosed and properly reflected in cost reports and for payments to employees for provision of covered items or services.[20]

A principal concern underlying the above prohibition appears to be that a person in a position to control or direct the delivery of federally funded goods or services might be compensated for that exercise of discretion.[21] In one case, a medical laboratory was convicted for an arrangement in which it gave shares of its corporate stock to a medical clinic and a percentage of profits to the clinic director and, in return, received permission to set up its laboratory in the clinic at no cost to the clinic or its owners and with no real administrative duties required of the clinic director.[22] The court viewed the arrangement as one clearly involving remuneration for arranging the purchase of Medicaid-reimbursable laboratory services. Even when a provider performs a service for the party making the incentive payment, criminal conduct has been found when the purpose of the payment is to induce future referrals.[23]

In 1991, the federal government published "safe harbor" regulations that outline certain activities that are not considered unlawful "remuneration" for fraud and abuse purposes.[24] The exceptions include real property or equipment leases or personal services contracts that

- are expressed in writing;
- contain a detailed description of the property, goods, or services;
- run for one year or more; and
- require fair market remuneration, not taking into account the volume or value of Medicare or Medicaid referrals otherwise generated between the parties.

For investment interests, persons in a position to refer patients or generate business or who provide services to the venture may hold no more than 40 percent of the venture. In addition, referring investors may not receive loans, special compensation, or other special benefits, among other restrictions. Further, no more than 40 percent of referrals can come from investors. Referral services must base

fees on operating costs rather than on numbers of referrals generated.

The rules also cover sales of practices, discounts, employee compensation, and group purchasing organizations. Subject to specific requirements for hospitals and Public Health Services programs, waivers of coinsurance or deductible payments owed by a beneficiary do not constitute unlawful remuneration. The rules are detailed and complicated and should be analyzed for any venture receiving Medicare or Medicaid funds.

Health care providers participating in seniors' housing coventures must be cautious in cases of expectations that the housing facility will become a source of patient or service referrals to the health facility or that the retirement home will receive referrals from the other provider. If the entity making the referral of a Medicare or Medicaid patient or reimbursable product or service has a financial interest in the referee, the parties should have a strong independent basis for the referral. If, however, the two entities are so closely related as to be considered a single entity—for example, equity partners—the danger of a violation is arguably less.[25] Generally, it is advisable to avoid exclusive transfer agreements or bonus payment arrangements.[26]

§13.3 Antitrust Issues

Any joint venture may raise antitrust or restraint-of-trade issues, including Sherman Act violations of participation in a contract, combination, or conspiracy in restraint of trade[27] or creation of a monopoly.[28] Automatic or per se violations can occur when competitors contract or otherwise join forces to fix prices or divide markets or when a party with sufficient economic power over the sale of one product or service establishes a tying arrangement that requires the buyer's purchase of a second product or service as a condition of obtaining access to the first.[29] In addition, exclusive dealing arrangements can be deemed per se violations when the arrangements have the effect of excluding a significant number of competitors from the marketplace.[30]

Another area of antitrust concern is price discrimination between purchasers in the sale of like commodities (not services) when the effect is a restraint of competition.[31] An exemption exists for sales to nonprofit institutions purchasing products for their own use in pursuit of their operations.[32]

Retirement community coventurers must carefully analyze the antitrust implications of practices or arrangements such as

- a coventurer's agreeing to make certain coventurer goods or services available to only the joint venture entity or to purchase certain goods or services exclusively from that entity (exclusive dealing problem);
- a coventurer's agreeing not to enter into other ventures or operations or to go into other territories that may compete with the other coventurer or with the joint venture entity (market division problem);
- a coventurer's requiring patients who use, for example, that coventurer's hospital services to accept a discharge to the joint venture nursing facility (tying arrangement problem);[33]
- a nonprofit hospital coventurer's using pharmaceuticals that it received at a discount for patients of a for-profit venture entity (price discrimination issue); and
- a coventurer's agreeing with the venture to set the price of a product or service they both sell when the coventurer owns 50 percent or less of the venture (price-fixing issue).

The presence of any significant market power on the part of a coventurer or the joint venture entity exacerbates the potential antitrust problems associated with any of the foregoing activities.

For those violations such as price fixing and market division that require a combination or conspiracy, at least two parties must be involved before a violation can occur. Independent joint venturers, of course, will be found to engage in such a prohibited agreement or understanding, but very closely related parties such as a parent corporation and its wholly owned subsidiary may be viewed as a single entity incapable of conspiring as a matter of law.[34] Similarly, competitors who combine as equity-contributing, risk-sharing partners in a joint venture business are treated as a single entity and may set the price that the business will charge.[35]

Published jointly by the U.S. Department of Justice and the Federal Trade Commission in 1994, guide-lines for joint purchasing arrangements among competing health providers create an antitrust safety zone for arrangements that meet the following criteria:

- The purchases account for less than 35 percent of the total sales of the purchased product or service in the relevant market.
- The cost of the products or services purchased jointly accounts for less than 20 percent of the total revenues from all products or services sold by each competing participant in the joint purchasing arrangement.

In 1996, the federal government released new guidelines for health provider networks. These guidelines establish a more relaxed "rule of reason" that permits the sharing of quality and clinical information designed to improve quality and reduce utilization without necessarily requiring risk sharing by participants. Some observers believe, however, that full financial integration and risk sharing is the safest course of action.[36] Nonetheless, health provider network arrangements still may be subject to characterization as per se violations, such as when a network contracts only on a fee-for-service basis (no risk sharing) or providers use an agent to negotiate prices jointly with payors. Existing "safety zones" remain for nonexclusive physician joint ventures limited to 30 percent of the market's practitioners and for exclusive joint ventures of up to 20 percent when substantial risk sharing takes the form of capitated or fixed, predetermined payments for services.

§13.4 Employment-Related Issues

(a) Workers as Employees

In Revenue Ruling 87–41,[37] the IRS set forth a 20-factor test to assess the degree of control held by a person contracting for services and whether, in fact, an employer/employee relationship exists between that person and the provider of services. The determination of whether the service provider is classified as an employee or an independent contractor depends on the extent to which the provider of services

- complies with the employer's instructions about the work;

- receives training from or at the direction of the employer;
- provides services that are integrated into the business;
- provides services that must be rendered personally;
- hires, supervises, and pays assistants for the employer;
- maintains a working relationship with the employer;
- must follow set hours of work;
- works full time for the employer;
- performs the work on the employer's premises;
- performs the work in the sequence set by the employer;
- must submit regular reports to the employer;
- receives payments of regular amounts at set intervals;
- receives payments for business and/or travel expenses;
- relies on the employer to furnish tools and materials;
- lacks a major investment in the facilities used on the job;
- cannot make a profit or suffer a loss from services;
- works for only one employer at a time;
- does not offer services to the general public;
- can be fired by the employer; and
- may quit work at any time without incurring liability.

These factors were distilled from cases and rulings that considered the employee/independent contractor classification issue. Unfortunately, they are merely guidelines and do not specify the precise number of factors that must be present in order to classify an individual as either an employee or contractor. The relative importance of each factor depends on the occupation at issue and the factual context.[38]

In addition, certain individuals are statutorily classified as either employees or independent contractors. For instance, under Internal Revenue Code Section 3506(a), individuals who provide companionship or household care services to children, the elderly, or the disabled are not employees of any person who places the individual with the recipient of the services for purposes of income tax withholding, Federal Insurance Contribution Act taxes, and Fed-

eral Unemployment Tax Act taxes. In a 1995 case, a federal bankruptcy court held that nurses working through a nurses' registry were independent contractors rather than employees of the registry because the factors indicating the right to control the nurses' work strongly indicated that the nurses were not employees. Therefore, the registry's owner was not liable for withholding the nurses' FICA and FUTA taxes.[39]

Private Letter Ruling 9535001 deemed that a construction-period administrator, a medical director, and the members of a utilization review committee were employees of a nursing facility. Despite independent contractor language in the various individuals' employment agreements, the determination hinged on, among other things, integration of the individuals' services into the facility's business, duties established by the facility, furnishing of tools and space, and payment by the hour, week, or month.

In general, individuals performing nursing and home care services, including the charting of medication taken by the patient and the performance of other duties as instructed, were considered to be employees for tax purposes because the taxpayer exercised a sufficient degree of control and direction over the nurses' duties.[40]

In Private Letter Ruling 8915023, the IRS determined that a salaried person caring for residents in a board-and-care facility three days per week under the terms of an oral contract terminable at will was an employee rather than an independent contractor even though the facility provided no training and the worker's services were not subject to the facility's supervision. For other rulings that classified workers as employees, see Private Letter Rulings 8839073 (home health agency nurse), 8840037 (nursing facility nurse's aide), and 8845049 (private practical nurse).

(b) Employment Retirement Income Security Act (ERISA)

The principal employment-related issue in a joint venture is whether the venture results in creation of a separate employer or is instead a mere extension of one or both of the venture's founders.

Employee benefit plans under the Employment Retirement Income Security Act[41] must not unduly discriminate in favor of shareholders, managerial employees, or others similarly situated,[42] and top-heavy plans where officers and shareholder-employees earn more than 60 percent of the benefits must meet special tests regarding contributions and vesting.[43] When two entities are affiliated, they may be considered a single employer for purposes of aggregating top-heavy benefit calculations and reviewing discrimination.[44] The ostensible purpose of ERISA is to prevent employers from shifting higher-level employees or shareholder-employees to related or controlled entities in order to permit favored treatment or avoidance of top-heavy rules.

Common vertical control is deemed to exist when one organization (the parent) owns at least 80 percent of another (the subsidiary).[45] Horizontally, an affiliation exists when five or fewer individuals, estates, or trusts own in aggregate at least 80 percent of two or more organizations or when the smallest of each such owner's interests, taken together, exceeds 50 percent of the organizations' ownership. In addition, affiliated service groups, which can include, among other things, an entity whose principal business is performing management services for both another organization and the managed organization, are treated as a single employer.[46]

Joint venturers such as hospitals often loan employees to the joint venture retirement facility for reasons of economic efficiency and maximum use of existing resources. Such practices could, however, also be adopted to circumvent the intent of ERISA by employing only managerial or upper-level employees at the retirement home and using leased hospital employees to perform all other functions. ERISA addresses this problem by treating the leased employee as the employee of the recipient of the employee's services when the services are performed pursuant to an agreement between the service recipient and the leasing organization; the person has performed the services for the recipient or a related organization on a substantially full-time basis for at least one year; and the service is of a type historically performed by employees in the recipient's business field.[47] An exception to this rule applies to leased employees who do not constitute more than 20 percent of the recipient's nonhighly compensated workforce covered by certain pension plans that vest immediately and require an employer contribution of at least 10 percent of the employee's earnings.[48]

(c) Labor Laws

The Fair Labor Standards Act mandates minimum wage and overtime (time-and-a-half) pay requirements for work weeks of more than 40 hours.[49] Homes for care of the aging are subject to the Fair Labor Standards Act,[50] but certified nurse's assistants are excluded from minimum wage protections because they perform companionship services and are not "trained personnel."[51]

Again, the principal issue for joint ventures is whether an employee is working for one or more employers when his or her services are received by more than one of the entities involved in or resulting from the venture. Federal regulations state that a joint employment relationship requiring aggregation of work hours and wages for minimum wage and overtime calculations generally is considered to exist when arrangements among employers call for sharing or interchanging employees; one employer acts in relation to the employee in the interest of the other employer; or employers are not disassociated and can be deemed to share control over the employee by reason of the fact that one employer controls the other or both share common ownership.[52]

Similarly, for purposes of determining appropriate collective bargaining units under the National Labor Relations Act,[53] the National Labor Relations Board (NLRB) looks to factors such as centralized control of labor relations, functional interrelation of operations, and common ownership, control, or management to determine if multiple entities should be treated as a single employer.[54] If the entities are treated as a single employer, the employees of all the related businesses may be aggregated for purposes of union elections and collective bargaining.[55]

Notes

1. *See generally* Roble and Mason, "The Legal Aspects of Health Care Joint Ventures," 24 *Duquesne L. Rev.* 455 (1985).

2. *See generally* 42 C.F.R. Part 413.

3. 42 C.F.R. §413.17.

4. *See, e.g.,* 42 C.F.R. §415.157.

5. *See* 42 C.F.R. §§412.1 *et seq.*

6. 42 C.F.R. §412.50.

7. Unlike most other cost-reimbursed services under Medicare, skilled-nursing services may be limited to a maximum per diem rate, which corresponds to the per diem rate for nursing services paid by states under their Medicaid programs. The federal government must satisfy itself that the state Medicaid rate fairly reflects costs; in some cases, it may pay a higher daily rate for Medicare skilled-nursing services than does the state Medicaid program. *See Medicare and Medicaid Guide (CCH)* ¶¶6081. It should be noted that Medicare coverage for skilled-nursing care is extremely limited in scope (see discussion in §26.1(b)).

8. *See* discussion at §20.5.

9. *See* 42 C.F.R. §§485.50 *et seq.* regarding Comprehensive Outpatient Rehabilitation Facilities (CORFs).

10. *See* 42 C.F.R. §§417.530 *et seq.*

11. Skilled-nursing facilities that are distinct parts of hospitals or directly operated by them may be eligible for reimbursement on a cost basis in the same manner as other hospital services not subject to the prospective payment system. *See Medicare and Medicaid Guide* note 7 *above,* at ¶¶ 6081.

12. *See generally* Medicare Prov. Reimb. Man., Part 1, §2135, *Medicare and Medicaid Guide (CCH)* ¶¶5995.

13. 42 C.F.R. §489.22(d).

14. Social Security Act §1909(d); 42 U.S.C. §1320a–7b(d); *see* discussion in §23.5(b)(2).

15. *See* note 12 *above,* ¶¶5875B.

16. *Ibid.*

17. *Ibid.*

18. *Ibid.*

19. 42 U.S.C. §§1320a–7b(b)(1)–(2).

20. 42 U.S.C. §§1320a–7b(b)(3).

21. *See generally* Roble and Mason, note 1 *above,* at 463ff.

22. *U.S. v. Universal Trade and Industries, Inc.,* 695 F.2d 1151 (9th Cir. 1983).

23. *U.S. v. Greber,* 760 F.2d 68 (3d Cir. 1968). A federal court of appeals has held that before a person may be found guilty for illegally offering, paying, or accepting referral payments, the government must show that the person knew that the law prohibits payments to induce referrals and engaged in prohibited conduct with intent to violate this law. *The Hanlester Network v. Shalala,* 51 F.3d 1390 (9th Cir. 1995).

24. 56 *Fed. Reg.* 35,952, July 29, 1991; 42 C.F.R. §§1000.952 *et seq.*

25. *See* Roble and Mason, note 1 *above,* at 469.

26. *Ibid.*

27. Sherman Act, Section 1; 15 U.S.C. §1.

28. Sherman Act, Section 2; 15 U.S.C. §2.

29. *See generally* Roble and Mason, note 1 *above,* and discussion regarding tying arrangements in §7.1(c) and §22.6(d).

30. *See Jefferson Parish Hosp. Dist. No. 2 v. Hyde,* 466 U.S. 2 (1984), for a discussion of exclusive dealing arrangements (no violation found).

31. Robinson-Patman Act, 15 U.S.C. §§13–13b, 21a.

32. *See* 15 U.S.C. §13c and *Abbott Laboratories v. Portland Retail Druggists Ass'n.,* 425 U.S. 1 (1976).

33. An exception may exist where a unifying dimension to the arrangement, such as a continuing-care contract or comprehensive health insurance policy, makes the hospital and nursing service part of a unified, single product.

34. *Copperweld v. Independence Tube Co.,* 467 U.S. 752 (1984).

35. *See Arizona v. Maricopa County Society,* 457 U.S. 332, 356 (1982).

36. Weissenstein, E., "Providers Applaud Relaxed Guidelines," *Modern Healthcare,* Sept. 2, 1996.

37. 1987–1 C.B. 296.

38. "Proper Classification of Workers Still a Tough Job," 82 *Standard Federal Tax Reports Tax Focus,* No. 56, Dec. 19, 1995.

39. *In re Serino,* 190 Bankr. 778 (M.D. Pa. 1995).

40. Employee Retirement Income Security Act, I.R.C. §§401 *et seq.*

41. *See, e.g.,* I.R.C. §§105(h), 125, 401, 410, 505.

42. I.R.C. §416.

43. *See* I.R.C. §§414(b),(c), 416(c)(2).

44. I.R.C. §§414(c), 1563.

45. I.R.C. §414(m)(5).

46. I.R.C. §414(n)(2).

47. I.R.C. §414(n)(5).

48. Priv. Ltr. Rul. 8806017.

49. 29 U.S.C. §§201 *et seq.*

50. *Dole v. Odd Fellows Home,* 912 F.2d 689 (4th Cir. 1990).

51. *McCune v. Oregon Senior Services Division,* 894 F.2d 1107 (9th Cir. 1990). *See also Cox v. Acme Health Servs., Inc.,* 55 F.3d 1304 (7th Cir. 1995), in which the U.S. Court of Appeals for the Seventh Circuit concluded that a home health aide for a home health agency was performing companionship services and therefore was not entitled to overtime compensation under the FLSA. The court stated that although trained personnel, such as reg-

istered nurses, providing services for the aging and infirm are excepted from the companionship services exemption under the FLSA, the aide did not have sufficient training to fall within the "trained personnel" exception. The court held that in order for a person providing companionship services to qualify for overtime compensation under the "trained personnel" exception, the person must provide the type of services required to be performed by someone with training comparable to that of a registered or practical nurse and must have received such training.

52. 29 C.F.R. §791.2.

53. 29 U.S.C. §§151 *et seq.*

54. *See Radio & Television Broadcast Technicians Local 1264 v. Broadcast Services of Mobile, Inc.,* 380 U.S. 255, 256 (1965).

55. *See, e.g., Blumenfeld Theatres Circuit,* 240 N.L.R.B. 206, 216 (1979).

Hamilton Heights; West Hartford, Connecticut.

Part VI

Financing Seniors' Facilities

Stephen L. Taber

Stephen L. Taber is a partner at the law offices of Hanson, Bridgett, Marcus, Vlahos & Rudy, San Francisco, and specializes in the financing of seniors' housing and care facilities. He is the author of Chapters 15 through 19.

Lakeside Village; Lantana, Florida.

14 HUD Financing Programs*

§14.1 In General

Historically, the U.S. Department of Housing and Urban Development (HUD) has offered three basic types of housing finance programs: mortgage insurance, direct loans, and grants to local government bodies.[1] Yet, HUD itself as well as many of the programs discussed in this book is in disarray. The 1980s saw drastic cuts in funds for new housing commitments (an 80 percent decline over ten years).[2] More recently, HUD has undertaken significant actions that have largely eliminated the mortgage insurance and coinsurance programs for retirement facilities. In addition, direct loan programs and grant programs (see §§14.3 and 14.4) have been the target of several budget cuts of late. While many of the programs discussed in this section have been repealed or suspended or are not being funded, they are described for general informational purposes; furthermore, many existing projects were developed under the auspices of these programs. Even though HUD created a new capital advance and rental assistance program in 1991 (see §14.4(a)), funding levels continue to decline. Dramatic cuts in HUD financing programs proposed by Congress and the administration in the 1990s will likely force developers of low-income housing to look to other means for financing new

projects[3] (see Figure 14.1 for a list of relevant programs).

The applicability of HUD financing vehicles to retirement housing depends largely on the types of architectural amenities (e.g., private kitchens or common dining areas) and services packages (e.g., medical care, meal programs) that the facility intends to offer (see Chapter 22 for a detailed discussion of HUD operational requirements). In addition, the income level of residents, the area in which the development is proposed, and the facility's financial relationship with the resident (e.g., rental or entrance fee) have a bearing on the availability of government funding or loan insurance.

Beyond the several eligibility conditions imposed by HUD on the structure and operations of a facility, the federal government imposes a variety of financial requirements as conditions of receiving either direct loans or mortgage insurance for the construction of eligible seniors' facilities. Section 14.2 first discusses the detailed HUD procedures for obtaining mortgage insurance or direct loans. It then outlines some of the specific characteristics and requirements for the individual HUD mortgage insurance and secondary financing programs. Sections 14.3 and 14.4 cover, respectively, HUD's direct loan programs and the general grant programs for local development.

In addition to the financial provisions discussed in this section, HUD mortgagors and facilities are subject to a number of general operational require-

* Special thanks to Dana Wolf for assisting with the chapter on HUD financing.

Figure 14.1 **HUD Elderly Housing Finance Programs**

Program	Statute	Regulations	HUD Handbook	Other
Mortgage Insurance				
Section 221(d)(4)	12 U.S.C. §1715l		4561.1; 4560.2	Notices H–85–33, 4–41,
1. New construction and substantial rehabilitation		24 C.F.R. §221		83–58, 91–21 (HUD)
2. Retirement Service Center program (inactive)		Former 24 C.F.R. §251		
Section 223(f)	12 U.S.C. §1715n		4565.1	HUD Fact Sheet
1. Moderate rehabilitation of existing facilities		24 C.F.R. §223		
2. Retirement Service Center program (inactive)		Former 24 C.F.R. §255		
Section 232 Board-and-care homes	12 U.S.C. §1715w	24 C.F.R. §232	4600.1	Notice H86–20 (HUD); P.L. 98–181
Section 221(d)(3)	12 U.S.C. §1715l		4560.1	
1. Cooperatives		24 C.F.R. §221		
2. Retirement Service Center program (inactive)		Former 24 C.F.R. §251		
Section 213 Cooperatives	12 U.S.C. §1715e	24 C.F.R. §213	4550.1	
Section 231 New construction or rehabilitation of elderly rental housing (inactive)	12 U.S.C. §1715v	24 C.F.R. §231	4570.1	
Section 236 Interest reduction payments (inactive)	12 U.S.C. §1715z–l	24 C.F.R. §236	N/A	
Subsidy Programs				
Section 202	12 U.S.C. §1701q	24 C.F.R. §885	4571.1 REV–2	
1. Direct loans (superseded)				
2. Capital advances and rental assistance (since October 1991 revisions)		24 C.F.R. §889		
Section 8 Housing assistance payments	42 U.S.C. §1437f	24 C.F.R. §880	7420.1 REV–1	
Congregate housing program	42 U.S.C. §8001–801l	N/A	N/A	HUD Fact Sheet; P.L. 95–537; HUD Appropriations

ments (outlined in detail in Chapter 22) that apply to considerations such as the type of structure that may be built, the services that can be made available, escrows, rent controls, eviction procedures, and related topics. A project is also subject to various federal and state antidiscrimination provisions related to housing (see Chapter 23).

§14.2 Mortgage Insurance

(a) General Procedural Requirements

HUD prescribes extremely detailed application procedures for mortgage insurance under its housing finance programs. While the following sections provide a broad overview of these general procedures and some specifics for each program, developers are advised to consult the local HUD field office and the relevant HUD regulations, handbooks, and notices.[4]

HUD mortgage insurance applications involve several parties. The mortgagor (borrower) is the organization or entity that owns the property to be used as security for the mortgage insured by HUD. The sponsor is the organization or entity that initiates and promotes the development of the facility. That sponsor, if it meets HUD requirements, may qualify as the mortgagor or may set up a separate entity for the purpose of qualifying as a mortgagor. The sponsor, if different from the mortgagor, must also be a bona fide entity. Most mortgagors under HUD programs must be single-asset mortgagors; that is, they may not own more than one major asset that is the subject of a HUD mortgage.[5]

The sponsor or mortgagor is responsible for locating a source for the required mortgage funds. HUD may not recommend a specific source of mortgage funds, although its local offices may assist sponsors to the extent of providing lists of approved mortgagees (lenders) in the local area that make loans of the type and amount desired. Approved lenders include national banks, state banks, mortgage banking companies, insurance companies, savings and loan associations, and savings banks.[6]

The procedures set out below cover the three stages of processing: feasibility, conditional commitment, and firm commitment. Depending on the spon-

sor's level of experience, processing may require only one or two stages. The HUD processing procedure is as follows:

- The sponsor makes the first contact with the HUD field office regarding the development proposal; that contact may include a preapplication conference.
- The sponsor prepares an application that outlines the proposal, complete with related exhibits.
- HUD makes a feasibility analysis of the proposal.
- A feasibility conference is held. If HUD and the sponsor are in substantial agreement, a feasibility letter is prepared at the end of the conference. The field office director signs the letter and presents it to the sponsor.
- The sponsor prepares forms, exhibits, and brief specifications and pays the application fee if he or she files an application for conditional commitment.
- HUD reviews the sponsor's exhibits and issues a conditional commitment to the mortgagee.
- The sponsor's architect prepares complete architectural drawings and specifications for the project.
- The mortgagee prepares an application for a firm commitment and pays the application fee (unless already paid) as well as the commitment fee. HUD reviews the contract drawings and documents and issues the firm commitment.
- The preconstruction conference is held.
- Initial closing is held and the original credit instrument is endorsed (initial endorsement).
- The project is constructed.
- Cost certification is made.
- Final closing is held (final endorsement).[7]

(b) HUD Evaluations

The procedural stages require HUD to conduct several different analyses and evaluations (summarized below) to determine whether the project is eligible for HUD-backed mortgage insurance.[8] Other conditions cover concerns such as displacement of existing tenants in rehabilitation projects, construction in flood hazard areas, historic site concerns, and the payment of Davis-Bacon prevailing wages during construction.

(1) Architectural Analysis

The architectural review determines the acceptability of the physical improvements and provides architectural consultation essential to minimizing mortgage risk and improving housing. The scope of the analysis includes the buildings and their attachments, parking facilities and their adaptation to the site, land improvements (such as water supply, sanitary sewage systems, gas mains, and heating tunnels), and all other elements of design or construction. A site analysis is also required to alert the lender to any soil faults, drainage problems, zoning ordinances, and other possible problems affecting design.

(2) Architectural Inspection

The stated purpose of the architectural inspection is to protect the interests of the lender and HUD, evaluate the performance of the contractor and architect responsible for administration of the construction contract, ensure that construction occurs according to contract documents, and report on conformance with prevailing wage and other contractual requirements. The lender and HUD must have access to the property at all times and the right to inspect all work performed and materials furnished to complete the project.

(3) Cost Estimation and Processing

A further requirement is the provision and evaluation of cost estimates as a prerequisite to insurance. Estimates pertain to on-site land improvements, structures, major movable equipment, minor equipment, supplies, general overhead expenses, architect fees, carrying and financing charges, organizational and audit expenses, and a profit and risk allowance for either the builder, the sponsor, or both (where there is an identity of interest between the two).

(4) Valuation Analysis

The valuation analysis requires the development of conclusions with respect to feasibility; suitability of improvements; the extent, quality, and duration of earning capacity; and other factors related to the acceptability of insurance risk or the economic soundness of the property. The analysis must show a reasonable expectation that project income will, for the duration of the mortgage term, be adequate to maintain the property properly, pay all required project expenses, and meet debt service requirements and provide a reasonable return on the owner's equity investment.

The procedure calls for estimating annual project expenses and net income before mortgage payments, figuring the tentative mortgage amount, determining the maximum allowable rents and operating deficit, and figuring the replacement cost of the facility.

(5) Mortgage Credit Analysis

The mortgage credit analysis requires a credit investigation, a review of the amount and amortization period of the loan, a determination of estimated requirements for completion of the project, a determination of the mortgagor's ability to close the transaction, insurance of advances, a review of possible construction changes, and cost certification. Among the mortgage credit risks reviewed by HUD are the probability of the mortgagor's failure to complete construction of the project satisfactorily or to provide competent management for operation of the facility and the likelihood that income will not provide for all operating expenses, liquidation of the mortgage, and all other debts. The credit determination thus involves analysis of the character and reputation of the project sponsors, the financial capacity of the mortgagor, and the anticipated net income of the facility.

(c) Closing and Funding Procedures

Once the mortgage insurance has been approved, HUD requires a variety of documents at both the initial endorsement and final closing, including an assurance of completion by the mortgagor in the form of a performance bond, completion assurance agreement, or personal undertaking.[9] At initial endorsement, all mortgagors, other than nonprofit organizations, must set up an escrow of at least 2 percent of the face amount of the mortgage by cash, letter of credit, U.S. bearer bonds, or excess mortgage proceeds, if any.[10] The deposit is used to defray the project's initial marketing and rent-up, set up accruals for items due during the first operating year that project income is not expected to cover, and cover shortfalls in mortgage insurance premiums, taxes, interest, and other items. The lender controls disbursements from the escrow, which must be fully documented by the mortgagor. If the mortgage is not in default, the balance of the working capital escrow is generally released one year after the construction completion date. Escrows from projects in poor financial condition are held until the problems are resolved.

HUD and the lender make advances on the mortgage in three stages. The first advance, usually made at initial closing, covers the mortgagor's early expenditures (e.g., architect fees, bond fees, insurance premiums, building permits, etc.). Except in the case of an early start of construction,[11] no construction funds may be advanced at this point. Subsequent advances of the insured mortgage proceeds are based on construction progress as documented in inspections. The final balance is made at final endorsement. For each advance, a 10 percent holdback requirement provides the mortgagor and general contractor with an incentive to see that the job is completed promptly, to submit cost certification, and to reach final endorsement. After all required contractor cost certification documents are approved, the contractor (through the mortgagor) is entitled to the balance of the holdback (less certain escrows), and the balance of the mortgage proceeds is insured.[12]

(d) Specific HUD Mortgage Insurance Programs

(1) Retirement Service Centers and Section 221(d)(4)

CAUTION: The Retirement Service Center Program was terminated as of September 30, 1991. This description is provided as background for existing projects, for projects with existing commitments, and for general information about the Section 221(d)(4) program.

In the early 1980s, the U.S. Department of Housing and Urban Development established the Retirement Service Center (ReSC) housing insurance program within the Section 221(d)(4) program[13] to cover the gap between the totally independent-living arrangements of noncongregate housing for the elderly and health care-oriented nursing homes.[14] The Section 221(d)(4) program (still active) is designed to assist in financing the construction or substantial rehabilitation of rental housing for low- and moderate-income families.[15] Under this program, HUD and the Federal Housing Administration insure mortgages made by approved lenders, thereby increasing the mortgage

credit available from private lenders. The ReSC program was designed to build on the existing Section 221(d)(4) mortgage insurance program to provide meals, services, and an amenities package exceeding that normally submitted under the Section 221(d)(4) program. All mortgage insurance proposals under the ReSC program were to be processed under both the general Section 221(d)(4) and ReSC procedures.

The maximum insurable loan for a ReSC facility (generally based on Section 221(d)(4) rules) was limited to the lowest of the following: statutory dollar limits; 90 percent of the project's estimated replacement cost; 90 percent of the project's estimated value, assuming that no more than 90 percent of the net operating income would be required for debt service; or 90 percent of the lender's estimate of value before rehabilitation plus the full cost of rehabilitation for property owned by the sponsor and subject to existing financing.

Property is considered to be undergoing substantial rehabilitation if the cost of repairs exceeds the greater of the following: 15 percent of the property's value after repair or $6,500 per dwelling unit (adjusted by applicable high-cost area factor); or repairs involving the replacement of more than one major building component.

Under the ReSC procedures, nonprofit sponsors were subject to the same maximum insurable limitations as any other type of mortgagor. The term of the mortgage could run for as long as 40 years, with the interest rate negotiated by lender and mortgagor. No secondary financing was permitted. The mortgagor also could obtain an insured construction loan, with insured advances administered by the insurer.

Because HUD perceived an extremely narrow market for ReSCs (which results in slow initial rent-up) and voiced concern over limited industry experience and the small number of market comparables, it required substantial reserves in one of the following forms: an operating deficit escrow funded at 200 percent of HUD's determination of the initial operating deficit, a six-month debt service reserve, or an operating deficit escrow and a six-month debt service reserve.[16]

HUD required all rents and other receipts of the project to be deposited in the project's name in accounts fully insured by an agency of the federal government. Project funds would be used only for payment of mortgage obligations, payment of reasonable expenses necessary to the proper operation and maintenance of the project, and certain distributions of surplus cash as specified in HUD procedures.[17]

Despite all these precautions, the ReSC program registered great financial losses, and HUD spent several years attempting to terminate the program. Finally, on July 6, 1989, HUD suspended processing for Section 221(d)(4) mortgage insurance for retirement service centers. Approximately 30 percent of all HUD-approved ReSC projects were reported to be in default, resulting in $119 million in direct losses and $225 million in mortgage defaults. One regional audit revealed that HUD field offices had failed to ensure the adequacy of the projects' markets or had approved insufficiently experienced project sponsors.[18]

On November 23, 1990, HUD published a proposed rule to terminate the Section 221(d)(4) Retirement Service Center program.[19] The agency reported that the default rate for the program was 29 percent as of January 1990, with an additional 23 percent of projects determined to be financially or operationally troubled.[20] A HUD audit report released on April 6, 1990, also indicated that retirement service center loans evidenced the following underwriting deficiencies, among others:

Item	Deficiency
Rental income	Overstated on average by 73 percent
Operating costs	Understated on average by 67 percent
Unit absorption rate	Overstated on average by 62 percent
Cash flow	Overstated on average by 319 percent
Nonshelter net income	Average shortfall of 428 percent
Rejected field office determinations overturned by HUD headquarters	Overturned 62 percent

HUD announced that following the termination of the Section 221(d)(4) ReSC program, it would continue to make financing for non–ReSC elderly housing available under Sections 221(d)(3), 221(d)(4),

and 223(f), provided that insured elderly projects not make the provision of services a mandatory condition of occupancy. HUD would have to review any service charges for reasonableness. Formal dining areas and scheduled meals could not be provided (whether mandatory or voluntary). Special nonshelter spaces such as a central kitchen, multipurpose rooms, lounges, and libraries could not exceed 10 percent of the project's gross square footage for new construction.[21] Final regulations further provided that projects designed for the elderly could not have "institutional" central kitchens but that a modest common kitchen could be installed for use by tenants or Meals on Wheels. In new or substantially rehabilitated projects, however, a dining room accommodating no more than half the residents would be permissible.[22]

In March 1991, HUD announced that until a final regulation on the ReSC program is published in the *Federal Register*, processing of ReSC applications would resume with minor procedural changes.[23] Despite efforts by the National Association of Home Builders, the American Association of Homes for the Aging, and the American Association of Retired Persons to restructure the program, HUD issued terminating final regulations effective September 30, 1991.[24]

(2) Retirement Service Centers and Section 223(f)

In addition to Section 221(d)(4), HUD permitted the financing of existing structures as retirement service centers under the Section 223(f) program.[25] Section 223(f) authorizes HUD to insure mortgages in connection with the purchase or refinancing of existing multifamily projects without requiring a program of substantial rehabilitation.[26] Substantial rehabilitation projects for ReSCs also had to be insured under the Section 221(d)(4) program as outlined above. The Section 223(f) program remains active but is no longer an available vehicle for the terminated ReSC program.

No more than one major building component may be replaced in Section 223(f) projects, and the cost of repairs cannot exceed the greater of 15 percent of the property's value after repairs or $6,500 per dwelling unit (adjusted by the applicable high-cost area factor) plus equipment.

The term of the mortgage may be up to 75 percent of the estimated remaining economic life of the structure but may not exceed 35 years. The lender and mortgagor negotiate the interest rate. For acquisition loans, the mortgage amount cannot exceed the lowest of the following: statutory limits, 85 percent of the project's estimated value, or 85 percent of acquisition, repair, architectural, legal, title, and organizational costs plus discounts and the initial deposit to the reserve for replacements.

For refinancing loans, the mortgage amount cannot exceed the lower of statutory limits or the greater of 70 percent of the project's estimated value or 100 percent of costs (not to exceed 85 percent of value).

In no event can debt service exceed 85 percent of net operating income. Section 223(f) applications for ReSCs also had to meet the financial reserve, marketing, and sponsor criteria required under Section 221(d)(4), although no insurance of construction advances was available.

HUD permits a second mortgage on the property as long as it does not exceed 7.5 percent of the property's value (if an acquisition) or half the difference between the cost to refinance and the maximum mortgage amount (if a refinancing). The second mortgage may only be a promissory note approved by HUD. The note cannot be due before the maturity date of the mortgage, although it is payable from surplus cash. Nonpayment of the note cannot trigger a default on the first mortgage. The note may be recorded to protect the noteholder in the event of a sale or refinancing of the project.

As stated in its proposed rule published on November 23, 1990 (see §14.2(d)(1)), HUD intended to limit the purchase and refinancing of ReSCs under Section 223(f) to facilities currently insured by the agency and to eliminate the 70 percent-of-value criterion for refinancing loans; effective September 30, 1991, however, HUD terminated the ReSC program. For non–ReSC rehabilitation projects after that date, the common area, meals, and mandatory services restrictions of the new regulations apply (see §14.2(d)(1)).[27]

(3) Section 232 Board-and-Care Homes and Assisted-Living Facilities

The Housing and Urban-Rural Recovery Act of 1983 amended the Section 232 program[28] to permit federal mortgage insurance to help finance the construction or improvement of board-and-care homes.[29] Section 232 had previously been limited to nursing homes and intermediate-care facilities (ICFs). Board-and-care homes are known by many different names in different states, including domiciliary care, shelter care, adult congregate living, personal care, and residential care.[30] Whatever the name, this facility type provides living arrangements for individuals who cannot live independently but who do not require the more extensive care offered by ICFs or nursing homes.

To qualify for FHA financing, board-and-care homes either may be privately owned and operated for profit or owned by a private nonprofit corporation or association. A proprietary mortgagor may be a corporation, partnership, trust, individual, or any other qualified legal entity. A nonprofit mortgagor must be a nonprofit corporation or association. The law specifically requires that no part of the net earnings of the nonprofit mortgagor shall inure to the benefit of any private shareholder or individual. Public bodies wishing to sponsor a project must create a separate private nonprofit corporation or association to serve as the mortgagor.

The Housing and Community Development Act of 1992[31] expanded the availability of Section 232 mortgage insurance to the development of assisted-living facilities for the care of frail, elderly persons.[32] To be eligible under Section 232, an assisted-living facility must

- be a public facility, a proprietary facility, or a facility of a private nonprofit corporation;
- be licensed and regulated by the state, municipality, or other political subdivision as applicable;
- provide assistance to residents in carrying out activities of daily living, which include "dressing, eating, getting in or out of bed or chairs, walking, going outdoors, using the toilet, laundry, home management, preparing meals, shopping for personal items, obtaining and taking medication, managing money, using the telephone, or performing light or heavy housework"; and
- provide separate dwelling units for residents and common rooms and other facilities for providing supportive services to residents.

Assisted-living facilities obtaining mortgage insurance under Section 232 may provide home health care services such as nursing and therapy but are not required to do so.[33]

The Section 232 program for assisted-living facilities became an active program on the effective date of HUD's final regulations, i.e., December 29, 1994.[34] The regulations amended 24 C.F.R. Part 232 and define *frail, elderly persons* as those unable to perform at least three activities of daily living. The regulations also set forth construction standards, including the following, for assisted-living facilities: the facility may be one or more freestanding buildings, part of an existing building, or connected to one or more buildings; the facility may not have fewer than five residential efficiency, one-bedroom, or two-bedroom units; the facility may not contain any nursing facility or intermediate-care beds (but may contain board-and-care beds); the facility must have space for a central kitchen and dining area; and each unit in the facility may contain a full bathroom and a full kitchen or kitchenette.

The maximum mortgage amount under the Section 232 program for new construction is 90 percent of the HUD-FHA estimate of the value of the property or project, including the equipment that will be used in the operation of the project.[35] For rehabilitation of projects, the maximum mortgage amount may not exceed the lesser of either 90 percent of the HUD-FHA estimate of the value of the project, including the equipment to be used in the project's operation, or one of the following amounts:

■ for property owned by the mortgagor, 100 percent of the HUD-FHA estimate of the cost of rehabilitation;

■ for property subject to an existing mortgage, the HUD-FHA estimate of the cost of rehabilitation plus the portion of the outstanding indebtedness that does not exceed 90 percent of the HUD-FHA estimate of the fair market value of the land and improvements before rehabilitation; or

■ for property to be acquired by the mortgagor, 90 percent of the total of the HUD-FHA estimate of the cost of rehabilitation plus the lesser of the actual purchase price of the land and improvements or the HUD-FHA estimate of the fair market value of the land and improvements before rehabilitation.[36]

The Housing and Community Development Act of 1992 amended the Section 232 program to increase the loan-to-value ratio for private nonprofit mortgagors from 90 to 95 percent. In addition, the act amended the program to permit HUD to insure mortgages for a new addition to an existing project regardless of whether the existing project is undergoing rehabilitation.[37]

The maximum mortgage term for Section 232 projects is 40 years, and the mortgage must bear interest at a rate that is agreed to by the mortgagor and mortgagee. In addition to making monthly payments covering the principal, interest, and mortgage insurance premium, the mortgagor is required to include in the monthly payment an amount sufficient to provide for the payment of taxes, property insurance, special assessments (if any), and ground rents.

(4) Section 223(f) Board-and-Care Homes and Assisted-Living Facilities

Section 223(f) of the National Housing Act, as amended by the Housing and Community Development Act of 1987,[38] authorized HUD to insure mortgages for the acquisition or refinancing of an existing board-and-care home.[39] HUD also insures mortgages for the acquisition or refinancing of existing nursing and intermediate-care facilities under the Section 223(f) program. The Housing and Community Development Act of 1992[40] further amended Section 223(f) to permit HUD to insure mortgages for the acquisition or refinancing of existing assisted-living facilities. In 1988, HUD implemented the Section 223(f) program with respect to board-and-care homes[41] and, effective December 29, 1994, adopted regulations to implement the program for assisted-living facilities.[42] Before adoption of the implementing regulations, the acquisition and refinancing of board-and-care facilities under Section 223(f) was limited to facilities that carried existing HUD-insured debt. The new regulations permit refinancing of uninsured projects.

To be eligible for insurance, a project may not require substantial rehabilitation, and three years must have elapsed from the latter of the date of completion of project construction or substantial rehabilitation or the beginning of project occupancy. The project also must have a level of occupancy that will produce income sufficient to pay operating expenses, annual debt service, and a reserve fund for replacements.[43] Rehabilitation is considered substantial if its cost exceeds the greater of 15 percent of the project's value after completion of the rehabilitation or $6,500 per dwelling unit for most areas.

The insurable mortgage amount may not exceed the lowest of 85 percent of the HUD-FHA estimate of the value of the project, including major movable equipment to be used in the operation of the project and any repairs and improvement; the amount that could be amortized by 85 percent of the net project income available for payment of debt service; or the following amounts: the cost to refinance the existing indebtedness of a project to be refinanced or 85 percent of the cost of acquisition for a project to be acquired.[44] The Housing and Community Development Act of 1992 also amended the program to increase from 85 to 90 percent the loan-to-value ratio for private nonprofit mortgagors.

HUD must approve the term of the insured mortgage under Section 223(f). In no circumstances may the mortgage term be less than ten years or more than the lesser of 35 years or 75 percent of the estimated remaining economic life of the physical improvements.[45]

(5) Coinsurance Programs

CAUTION: All HUD coinsurance programs were terminated in November 1990. Some applications submitted before that date may, however, still be approved for the program.

HUD regulations previously provided for a coinsurance program for the Section 221(d)(4), 223(f), and 232 programs.[46] Under this program, the HUD-FHA mortgagee assumed approximately 20 percent of the loan loss in the case of default and no longer assumed strictly a processing role. The program was designed to increase the amount of mortgage credit available from the private market for HUD-approved projects. In return, the private coinsurer retained a portion of the mortgage insurance premiums and fees otherwise payable to HUD.

HUD had to approve participants in the coinsurance program while the coinsurer assumed all processing functions previously performed by HUD, including review of plans and specifications, cost analysis, appraisal of projects, mortgage credit review, and management review. The coinsurer could contract out the technical reviews or perform them in-house but retained full liability under the coinsurance contract. The program was designed to give

the approved lenders maximum oversight and servicing responsibility as well as autonomy.

This coinsurance program was terminated effective November 12, 1990,[47] although HUD honored any legally binding and validly issued commitments made before termination. In addition, the agency instituted a precommitment review procedure to review only those applications for which a lender had accepted a nonrefundable application fee before November 12, 1990. Before issuing any commitment on these applications, the lender had to obtain written approval from the HUD commissioner.

(6) Cooperatives—Sections 221(d)(3) and 213

Under Sections 213 and 221(d)(3), HUD insures mortgages made by private lending institutions on cooperative housing projects.[48] The cooperatives must have five or more dwelling units for occupancy by members of nonprofit cooperative ownership housing corporations. Loans under under Sections 213 and 221(d)(3) may finance the following: new construction, rehabilitation, acquisition, improvement, or repair of a project already owned as well as resale of individual memberships; construction of projects composed of individual family dwellings to be purchased by individual cooperative members with separate insured mortgages; and construction or rehabilitation of projects that the owners intend to sell to nonprofit cooperatives. Eligible applicants include nonprofit corporations or trusts organized to construct homes for members of the corporation or beneficiaries of the trust as well as qualified sponsors who intend to sell the project to a nonprofit corporation or trust.

For Section 213 management projects, the mortgage amount cannot exceed the lesser of a statutory limit or an amount equal to 98 percent of the HUD-estimated replacement cost of the project. For Section 221(d)(3) projects, the mortgage amount is 100 percent of estimated cost. If the project is to be rehabilitated, further limits apply. The term of the mortgage in these management-type cooperatives cannot exceed 40 years. Interest is paid monthly on the outstanding principal. The HUD mortgage insurance premium is 0.5 percent.

(7) Condominium Housing—Section 234

HUD insures mortgages made by private lending institutions to any person with good credit for the purchase of one-family units in multifamily housing projects.[49] HUD also insures blanket mortgages to finance the construction or rehabilitation of housing projects that the sponsor intends to sell as individual condominium units. To be eligible, a project must contain at least four dwelling units in detached, semi-detached, row, walkup, or elevator structures. Under the Section 234 program, condominium is defined as joint ownership of common areas and facilities by the separate owners of single dwelling units in the project.

(8) Low-Income Housing Preservation and Resident Homeownership Act of 1990 (LIHPRHA)

Owners of Section 236 and 22l(d)(3) projects have the right to prepay their 40-year mortgages after 20 years and convert their projects into market-rate rentals and condominiums. To prevent the displacement of low-income tenants because of such prepayment, Congress passed the Low-Income Housing Preservation and Resident Homeownership Act of 1990 (LIHPRHA), which attempts to strike a compromise between the owners' right to prepay and the public interest in preserving housing for low-income tenants.[50]

LIHPRHA permits owners to terminate low-income restrictions through prepayment only if there is an adequate supply of other low-income housing in the area and other statutory requirements are satisfied. However, LIHPRHA creates incentives for owners to extend the low-income restrictions or for other organizations to purchase the project and maintain the restrictions. HUD may offer the following incentives to owners who agree to extend their low-income restrictions:

- access to residual receipts accounts;
- an increase in allowable rents under an existing Section 8 contract;
- additional assistance under Section 8 or other assistance attached to the housing;
- an increase in the rents of current tenants in non–Section 8 units;
- financing for capital improvements under Section 201 of the Housing and Community Devel-

opment Amendments of 1978 or through insurance for a second mortgage under Section 241 of the National Housing Act;

- redirection of Section 236 interest reduction payment subsidies to a second mortgage;
- access to preservation equity in the housing through insurance for a second mortgage loan under Section 241(f) of the National Housing Act or a coinsured mortgage loan approved by HUD and the mortgagee; or
- an increase in the amount of allowable distributions up to the annual authorized return.

HUD offers the same incentives to any purchaser who agrees to maintain the low-income restrictions for the life of the project. Originally, Section 241(f) mortgage insurance could be used to cover 95 percent of the cost of acquisition. The purchaser could negotiate with sellers for seller takeback financing of the other 5 percent. Thus, the purchaser of a Section 236 or 221(d)(3) project essentially could secure 100 percent financing under the LIHPRHA program as originally envisioned. Resident councils organized to acquire housing for a homeownership program, state or local agencies, and nonprofit corporations (priority purchasers) receive first priority (over for-profit organizations) to purchase a project. A priority purchaser may also receive, for each unit, a grant that may not exceed the projected fair market rent for the next ten years.

On September 3, 1992, HUD announced that $15 million in planning grants would be available for purchasers seeking to acquire housing under the LIHPRHA program. The planning grants are available only to community-based nonprofit organizations. These organizations are set up as single-purpose borrower corporations, with at least one-third of the seats on their boards of directors reserved for low-income members of the community.[51]

The 1996 HUD appropriations bill provided $624 million for LIHPRHA. By July 12, 1996, however, HUD had used all of its available 1996 funds, leaving several projects—with approved plans of action—awaiting government funding.[52] Moreover, on March 28, 1996, President Clinton signed the Housing Opportunity Program Extension Act of 1996, which restored owners' rights to prepay project mortgages, provided that owners do not raise rents for 60 days after prepayment. The act also prohibited HUD from processing preservation applications that lacked approved plans of action as of October 1, 1996.[53]

The 1997 HUD appropriations bill provided for $350 million for both LIHPRHA and the Emergency Low-Income Housing Preservation Act. The funds were to be allocated as follows: $75 million for special carve-out projects that were listed as priorities in 1996 but were not funded; $100 million in rental assistance to prevent tenant displacement in projects whose owners prepay or, if any funds remain, for sales to priority purchasers; $10 million to reimburse owners of preservation-eligible properties for the costs of preparing plans of action that were not funded before October 1, 1996; and $165 million for sales to priority purchasers. The appropriations bill also repealed Section 241(f), thus eliminating the use of Section 241(f) as an incentive under the program. Under the new law, sales are funded with capital grants, and extensions of affordability restrictions are funded with noninterest-bearing capital loans.[54]

(e) Secondary Financing

(1) Generally

Residential mortgages are commodities that can be marketed either individually or pooled with other mortgages to stand behind the sale of a mortgage security. While savings and loan associations and other institutional lenders originate mortgage loans for their own portfolios, many mortgages are created expressly to be sold on the secondary mortgage market. Indeed, a major purpose of the secondary mortgage is to enhance the liquidity of the lender. Because a lender has a limited amount of funds it can loan, it also has a finite number of mortgages that can be in effect at any given time. If it can sell its mortgages, however, a lender can generate cash to issue new mortgages.

The advent of federal agencies in the secondary mortgage market was intended to offset the often regionally variable swings in demand for mortgage loans and to keep in balance on a national level the demand for and availability of credit.[55]

(2) Federal National Mortgage Association

The Federal National Mortgage Association (FNMA), also called Fannie Mae, is the largest residential mortgage investor in the country. The corporation is chartered by Congress but is a publicly traded business with shares sold on the New York Stock Exchange.[56] Its mission is to purchase mortgages created by private and other lenders and to sell various types of mortgage-backed debt instruments, including debentures, short-term notes, mortgage-backed bonds, and master notes. Fannie Mae purchases conventional mortgages, residential second mortgages, conventional multifamily mortgages, cooperative blanket loans, and HUD-FHA insured loans, among others.

(3) Government National Mortgage Association Mortgage-Backed Securities

The Government National Mortgage Association (GNMA), also known as Ginnie Mae, is a government-owned corporation that guarantees the timely payment of principal and interest on securities issued by private lenders and backed by pools of government-underwritten residential mortgages.[57] Ginnie Mae attempts to attract nontraditional investors into the residential mortgage market by offering a high-yield, risk-free, government-guaranteed security without the servicing obligations associated with a mortgage loan portfolio. It issues securities backed by Section 221(d)(4) and 232 insured project mortgages.

Applicants must be FHA-approved mortgagees in good standing and must have a net worth that meets GNMA's minimum requirements. GNMA has guaranteed more than $519 billion in mortgage-backed securities since it began operation in 1968.

The newer GNMA II mortgage-backed securities (MBS) program, which was established in 1983, supplements the GNMA program by providing a comprehensive menu of new GNMA securities. It takes advantage of technological improvements that have occurred since GNMA's creation. The program relies on a central paying agent that makes consolidated payments to investors, offers larger, geographically dispersed multiple-issuer pools as well as custom pools, and provides for a mix of interest rates among mortgages within a pool. MBSs are privately issued, backed by pools of FHA, VA, and FMHA mortgages, and guaranteed by GNMA to assure investors of timely and accurate monthly payments. They provide for pools of single-family level-payment mortgages, graduated-payment mortgages,[58] growing-equity mortgages,[59] and manufactured housing loans.

To become an issuer, a firm must gain approval based on net worth, staffing, and experience criteria. Once approved, the issuer applies for a commitment for the guarantee of securities. The issuer originates or acquires mortgage loans and assembles them into a pool or package of mortgages. The issuer then selects the securities funding method and submits the documents to the central paying agent, which prepares and delivers securities to investors. Issuers are responsible for marketing the securities and servicing the mortgages that back them and for providing the paying agent with the monthly payments due investors. The paying agent is responsible for making consolidated payments to security holders and provides GNMA with activity and control reports.

(4) Federal Home Loan Mortgage Corporation

The Federal Home Loan Mortgage Corporation (FHLMC), commonly referred to as Freddie Mac, is a taxable, government-owned corporation created by Congress in 1970.[60] It was established as a part of the Federal Home Loan Bank system and is owned entirely by the Federal Home Loan Banks. Its original purpose was to provide a secondary market for mortgages originated by federally insured financial institutions, such as banks and savings and loans. More recently, Freddie Mac was authorized to extend its scope to include HUD-approved mortgage bankers.[61]

Freddie Mac usually resells the mortgages it purchases as guaranteed mortgage securities, which take the form of mortgage participation certificates (PCs) or collateralized mortgage obligations (CMOs). The corporation purchases first mortgages with fixed or adjustable rates and second mortgages on single- and multifamily properties. It purchases entire loans as well as fractional participations between 50 and 95 percent on one- to four-family properties.

§14.3 Direct Loans

(a) Section 202/8 Program

CAUTION: The Section 202 program was amended as of October 1, 1991. The program no longer provides loans for elderly housing. The new program is a capital advance and rental assistance program (see §14.4).

The HUD Section 202/8 program[62] previously provided loans at reduced interest rates to nonprofit sponsors for the development cost of new or substantially rehabilitated housing for the elderly or handicapped.[63] Section 202 provided 40-year loans at below-market interest rates for up to 100 percent of the total development cost of a project. Section 8 offered rental subsidies to qualifying low-income families and individuals living in approved residential facilities. With the consolidation of the application requirements of both the Section 202 and Section 8 programs, HUD deemed that projects satisfying the requirements of the Section 202 program also met the requirements for housing assistance payments under Section 8. Accordingly, the agency did not require a separate application for Section 8 assistance.

(1) Financial Requirements

The Housing and Community Development Act of 1974 amended the Section 202 program to permit construction loans and direct 40-year permanent financing to nonprofit sponsors for the construction or substantial rehabilitation of housing projects for the elderly, handicapped, or disabled. Because the Section 202 program involved direct loans, the availability of federal funding was dependent on annual appropriations by Congress. In practice, the actual level of recent HUD funding for Section 202 has been relatively low, making it difficult to secure funds even for projects deemed worthy by HUD.[64] In general, Congress required HUD to allocate 95 percent of all its funds for assisted-housing programs to very-low-income persons; however, the agency could establish different limits for different programs, provided that it met the overall target.[65]

The law also required HUD to allocate funds on a geographic basis among the ten HUD regions and further between metropolitan and nonmetropolitan areas based on a needs formula. The geographic distribution took into account the number of elderly households in each region, households lacking some or all plumbing facilities, and households with incomes below regionally adjusted poverty levels. Of the total amount of Section 202 assistance, 20 to 25 percent was allocated to nonmetropolitan areas. Moreover, approximately 15 percent of the total funding was set aside for the development of facilities specifically designed to meet the needs of the nonelderly handicapped. These restrictions further limited the availability of Section 202 funds to interested borrowers.

(2) Eligible Applicants

Only private nonprofit corporations, including incorporated nonprofit consumer cooperatives, were eligible under the regulations to apply for Section 202 loans. The program regulations and handbook defined such an applicant as the borrower. The borrower was responsible for the construction, rehabilitation, ownership, and operation of the project.

Frequently, the borrower was a local nonprofit corporation established by a national organization such as a religious group or a labor union. This organization, defined as the sponsor, did not have to be incorporated but did have to be a private nonprofit group.

When a sponsor set up a nonprofit corporation to act as the Section 202 borrower, HUD looked to the sponsor for the financial strength and experience needed to carry out the project successfully. The sponsor was expected to pledge its support to the borrower for the full 40-year term of the Section 202 loan. The relationship between the sponsor and borrower was spelled out in detail in the application.

In actuality, the law creating the Section 202 program allowed public agencies and private profit-motivated entities as well as nonprofit corporations to be project developers. However, HUD regulations and annual appropriations bills restricted the program to nonprofits.[66] The program handbook made clear that even indirect participation by public agencies or profit-motivated groups was prohibited. A profit-motivated entity could not sponsor a nonprofit borrower while a public agency could not set up an agency or instrumentality to participate in the Section 202 program.

(3) Amount and Terms of Financing

Projects under the Section 202 program could be new construction or substantial rehabilitation. They had to be designed in accordance with the appropriate HUD minimum property standards and include only units designed for elderly or handicapped persons. The total amount of the loan approved under Section 202 could not exceed the lowest of the following: the total development cost of the project as determined by the HUD field office; an amount that entailed a debt service of no more than 97 percent of anticipated net project income; or the sum of the cost of exterior land improvements, the cost of improvements not attributable to dwelling use such as game rooms, central kitchens and dining rooms, and commercial space, and a statutory amount per unit for the part of the property attributable to dwelling use.

The following additional limitations applied to rehabilitation projects:

- For property held by the borrower in fee simple, the maximum loan amount was 100 percent of the cost of rehabilitation.
- For property subject to an existing mortgage, the limit was the cost of rehabilitation plus such portion of the outstanding debt that did not exceed the fair market value of the property before rehabilitation.
- For property to be acquired and rehabilitated through Section 202 financing, the loan was limited to the cost of rehabilitation plus such portion of the purchase price that did not exceed the fair market value before rehabilitation.

The loans were made at a rate based on the average interest of all interest-bearing obligations of the United States that formed a part of the public debt, plus an amount that covered administrative costs.

(b) Section 312 Rehabilitation Loans

Under Section 312, direct federal loans finance rehabilitation of single- and multifamily residential, mixed-use, and nonresidential properties in federally aided Community Development Block Grant (CDBG) and Urban Homesteading areas certified by the local government.[67] The rehabilitation financed by these loans brings the property up to applicable local code, project, or plan standards, thus preventing unnecessary demolition of basically sound structures. In addition, the loans provide financing for both insulation and the installation of weatherization materials.

Section 312 loans may not exceed $33,500 per dwelling unit or $100,000 for nonresidential properties, although the actual amount of a loan may be less, depending on certain factors. The term of the loan may not exceed 20 years or three-fourths of the remaining economic life of the structure after rehabilitation, and loans are repayable at interest rates of 3 percent for low-income homeowners or a rate based on adjusted family income for moderate-income families.

Property owners in CDBG and Urban Homesteading areas and business tenants of such property whose leases have at least as long to run as the term of the loan are eligible for Section 312 loans. Applicants must prove that they are able to repay the loan. Low- and moderate-income applicants have priority in receiving Section 312 loans. Historically, Section 202/8 projects have used such loans.

Unfortunately, Congress has allocated no new funds to the program since 1989. As of September 30, 1989, the only loans that can be made under the program are those originated pursuant to a contract, commitment, or other obligation entered into before that date.[68]

§14.4 Grants

(a) Capital Advances and Rental Assistance under Section 202

The Cranston-Gonzalez National Affordable Housing Act[69] revised Section 202 of the Housing Act of 1959, effective October 1, 1991, and recast it from a direct loan program to a grant program. HUD intended to use Section 202 in its revamped form to increase supportive housing for the elderly.[70]

Under Section 202, HUD provides assistance to private nonprofit organizations and consumer cooperatives in the form of either capital advances or project rental assistance (see §14.3(a) regarding eligible applicants under the former Section 202 direct loan program). The organizations or cooperatives may use the funds to finance the construction, reconstruction, or rehabilitation of a structure to be used as supportive housing for the elderly; the acquisition of a structure from the (former) Resolution Trust Corporation to be used as supportive housing for the elderly; or the cost of real property acquisition, site improvement, conversion, demolition, relocation, and other necessary expenses to increase supportive housing for the elderly. All facilities receiving Section 202

assistance must be available for 40 years for occupancy by very-low-income elderly persons.

(1) Forms of Assistance

Section 202 capital advances do not bear interest and do not need to be repaid so long as housing is available for the very-low-income elderly. The amount of the advances must be calculated in accordance with development cost limits set by the secretary of HUD by market area for various types and sizes of supportive housing for the elderly. The cost limits must reflect the cost of the following: land; construction, reconstruction, or rehabilitation of supportive housing for the elderly that meets state and local housing and building codes; movables necessary to the basic operation of the housing; special features necessary to make housing accessible to the elderly; special features necessary to make the individual units meet the physical needs of elderly residents; needed congregate space; and compliance with energy-efficiency standards. If an owner's development costs are less than the amount of the capital advances received, the owner may retain either 50 percent of the savings in a special housing account if it does not add energy-efficient features or 75 percent in the housing account if it does incorporate energy-efficient features that meet statutory requirements.

Rental assistance is provided through 20-year contracts that require HUD to make monthly payments covering any costs not met from project income. The maximum annual contract amount permitted by the program is the initial annual project rentals for all units occupied by very-low-income elderly plus any initial utility allowances for the units. If necessary, the maximum may be increased to provide for reasonable project costs. On expiration, HUD must extend the rental assistance contracts for at least five years.

Very-low-income tenants living in units receiving Section 202 assistance must pay as rent the highest of 30 percent of the tenant's adjusted monthly income; 10 percent of the tenant's monthly income; or the portion of welfare assistance that is designated to meet the tenant's housing costs.

(2) Application Procedure and Selection Criteria

When funds available for capital advances are allocated, HUD must publish a Notice of Fund Availability in the *Federal Register,* indicating the amount of funds available within the HUD field office, the date the field offices will publish Invitations for Applications, the application deadlines, and any other appropriate guidance. Each field office receiving a Section 202 allocation must then publish an Invitation for Applications for Section 202 fund reservation in newspapers of general circulation and any minority newspapers serving the affected jurisdiction. The invitation must state the areas where funding is available and the amount of funding; provide copies of regulations as well as instructions and forms; specify the date, time, and place applications will be accepted; and note the deadline for receipt of applications.

The legislation specifies certain information that must be included in an application for Section 202 assistance. Each applicant must describe the proposed housing, the assistance sought, the resources expected to be made available, the category of elderly persons the housing is intended to serve, the supportive services to be provided, the manner in which such services will be provided, and the public or private sources of assistance that will fund such services; furnish certification from the public official responsible for submitting the housing strategy for the affected jurisdiction that the proposed project is consistent with that strategy; and supply any other information deemed necessary and appropriate by the HUD secretary. Notices of Fund Availability, which HUD publishes following an allocation of funding authority, set forth detailed requirements for Section 202 applications.[71]

Once applications are submitted, the HUD field office selects sponsors to receive Section 202 funds. The field office bases its decision on the following selection criteria:

- the ability of the sponsor to develop and operate the proposed housing on a long-term basis;
- the sponsor's financial capacity;
- the need for supportive housing for the elderly in the area;
- project design; and
- proposed supportive services.

(3) Funding Authorizations

Funding allocations for the first several years of the program reflect a declining federal commitment to low-income housing. For Fiscal Year (FY) 1991, Congress authorized HUD to appropriate $659 million to fund capital advances and $363 million to fund rental assistance. At least 20 percent of the allocated funds had to be made available to nonmetropolitan areas. For FY1992, HUD allocated $539 million in grants for 9,400 new units, with another $451 million for rental assistance. Administration proposals for FY1993, however, called for a reduction of over 90 percent in the number of new units (822), grant funding of $48.7 million, and rental assistance of only $54.4 million. The Housing and Community Development Act of 1992 authorized $1.31 billion for FY1993 and $1.365 billion for FY1994 for both the Section 202 and Section 811 programs (for the disabled) and allocated 70 percent of that amount to the Section 202 program. For FY1993, Congress appropriated $1.1 billion to be divided between grants and rental assistance for 8,900 new units of Section 202 housing.[72]

For FY1994, President Clinton requested $630.5 million for 4,900 units of Section 202 housing, a sharp reduction from FY1993.[73] However, the House-Senate Conference Report for the 1994 HUD appropriations bill provided funding for 9,000 new units.[74] For FY1995, President Clinton proposed $150 million in funding to support 1,156 units of Section 202 housing.[75] The final 1995 HUD appropriations provided for $1.279 billion in funding for 9,654 units of Section 202 housing.[76] The FY1996 appropriations bill signed by President Clinton on April 26, 1996 (almost seven months into the fiscal year), provided $830 million for the Section 202 program. Of that amount, $50 million had to be applied to extending the contract terms of rental assistance as opposed to constructing new units.[77] The FY1997 and 1998 appropriations bills provided $645 million for the Section 202 program, but the administration's FY1999 proposal calls for an 83 percent cut in appropriations to $159 million.[78]

(b) Urban Development Action Grants

CAUTION: The UDAG program is presently inactive.

To stimulate economic development activity in aid of local economic recovery, HUD formerly made Urban Development Action Grants (UDAGs) to cities and urban counties experiencing severe economic distress.[79] UDAGs relied on a combination of public and private investments in economic development projects. In fact, the private sector's financial commitment to the grant was a prerequisite to preliminary UDAG approval. The program required a minimum ratio of 2.5 private dollars to every action grant dollar. Generally, projects could take no more than four years for completion. No additional funding was available for a project following the execution of a grant agreement, although HUD could make additional UDAGs available to a city to support different projects during the life of the program.

Eligible applicants were cities and urban counties that met minimum criteria indicating severe economic distress and that demonstrated results in providing housing for low- and moderate-income persons and equal opportunity in housing and employment for low- and moderate-income persons and members of minority groups. HUD determined the level of economic distress experienced by cities and urban counties by taking into account a combination of characteristics such as aged housing, low per capita income change, high percentage of poverty, loss of population and jobs, unemployment, and designation as a labor surplus area. Communities that did not meet the distress criteria could qualify for UDAGs if they contained distressed areas defined as pockets of poverty. The city had to meet special eligibility criteria and plan to target the action grant assistance and benefits to the residents of the pocket area. Retirement facilities could use funds for off-site costs.

At least 25 percent of each year's appropriation had to be set aside for small communities with populations of less than 50,000, and up to 20 percent of each year's appropriation had to be used to fund projects in communities with pockets of poverty. UDAG funding was not based on entitlement; every two months, HUD reviewed all new applications it received and all applications it held over for further consideration and determined which projects were fundable. Each application had to compete against all the applications under review for the period for which funds were available. Though the regulations specified several criteria for the selection of projects for funding, the primary criterion was the comparative degree of economic distress among all applicants. The HUD central office had to make preliminary approval decisions within two months of the deadline for submission of applications.

Even though the UDAG program has received no new appropriations since 1988, it distributed $50 million between 1986 and 1988 from recaptured appropriations.[80]

(c) Community Development Block Grants

(1) Entitlement Grants (Metropolitan Cities and Urban Counties)

The Community Development Block Grant (CDBG) program provides annual grants to metropolitan cities and urban counties (entitlement communities) to implement activities that benefit low- and moderate-income persons, aid in the prevention or elimination of slums and blight, or address other community development needs that present a serious and immediate threat to the health or welfare of the community.[81] A metropolitan city is defined as a central city of a metropolitan statistical area (MSA) or a city of 50,000 or more population within an MSA. An urban county is defined as a county within an MSA that is authorized to undertake community development and housing activities and that meets certain population requirements. Grants are useful for non–FHA-eligible development costs.

After consulting with local residents, entitlement communities develop their own programs and funding priorities. Some examples of the activities that can be implemented with community development funds include the acquisition of real property, rehabilitation of residential and nonresidential properties, provision of public facilities and improvements such as water and sewer, streets, and neighborhood centers, and assistance to profit-motivated businesses to help with economic development activities. At least 70 percent of the funds must be used for activities that benefit low- and moderate-income persons over a period specified by the grantee but not exceeding three years.

Excluding the amounts provided for the UDAG program and the Secretary's Discretionary Fund, entitlement communities receive 70 percent of each year's CDBG appropriation. A statutory formula that uses several objective measures of community need, including poverty, population, housing overcrowding, age of housing, and growth lag, determines the amount of each entitlement grant. Since 1987, Congress has allocated about $3 billion to the CDBG program ($3.2 billion for 1991 and $3.4 billion for 1992).[82] The Housing and Community Development Act of 1992, however, authorized $4 billion in funding for Community Development Block Grants for 1993 and $4.168 billion for 1994.

(2) Nonentitlement Grants (States and Small Cities)

The Nonentitlement CDBG program provides grants to states and small cities to help them implement community development activities directed toward neighborhood revitalization, economic development, improved community facilities, and services. As with the entitlement grants, applicants must give maximum feasible priority to activities that will benefit low- and moderate-income families, aid in the prevention or elimination of slums and blight, or address other community development needs that present a serious and immediate threat to the health or welfare of the community. In addition, at least 70 percent of the funds must be used for activities benefiting low- and moderate-income persons over a period specified by the state but not exceeding three years. Excluding the amounts provided for the Urban Development Action Grant program and the Secretary's Discretionary Fund, 30 percent of each year's CDBG appropriation is allocated to nonentitlement areas and then allocated among the states on a formula basis.

Each state has the option to administer the block grant funds provided for its nonentitlement areas. If a state exercises the self-administration option, HUD provides the block grant funds directly to the states, which then distribute the monies as grants to eligible units of general local government. States must consult with affected citizens and local elected officials to determine their objectives and methods for distributing the funds. Funds must be made available to citizens and units of general local government throughout the state. States must report annually on how they used the funds. If a state does not exercise the self-administration option, HUD continues as administrator and awards funds competitively on the basis of selection criteria established by the department.

(d) Housing Development Grants

CAUTION: The HODAG program was repealed in October 1991.

Under the Housing Development Grant (HODAG) program, the secretary of HUD made grants to help private developers construct or substantially rehabilitate rental housing for low-income people in areas with a severe housing shortage.[83] Based on a national competition, HUD awarded the grants to cities, urban counties, and states acting on behalf of units of local government. They were useful for off-site seniors' housing improvements in rural areas. At least 20 percent of the units in projects assisted by HODAGs had to be reserved for a 20-year period for families with incomes at or below 80 percent of the median income of the area. In addition, owners could not convert the units to condominiums during the 20-year term.

Development grants could not exceed 50 percent of the total cost of construction or substantial rehabilitation of a project, less the cost of acquisition. Once projects received a notice of preliminary funding approval, they had to begin construction within 24 months. When HUD determined that construction or rehabilitation of a project had been completed and that the project had reached a certain level of occupancy, the agency would close out the project, at which point the city, urban county, or state assumed responsibility for monitoring project operations and approving rent increases.

Eligible areas were cities, urban counties, or other units of government with a population greater than 2,500 and that were determined to be experiencing severe housing shortages as defined in accordance with the statutory criteria. Other areas could apply for the HODAGs if they could demonstrate a special housing need or had a particular neighborhood preservation purpose. Selection criteria generally included extent of poverty, extent of occupancy of physically inadequate housing by low-income families, extent of housing overcrowding by low-income families, level and duration of housing vacancies, and lag between the need for and production of rental housing.

No funds for the HODAG program have been appropriated since 1987. Effective October 1, 1991, the program was repealed.[84]

(e) Rental Rehabilitation

CAUTION: The Rental Rehabilitation Program was repealed in October 1991.

The Rental Rehabilitation Program provided two types of assistance: grants to cities and states to encourage rental housing rehabilitation and rental subsidies to help low-income tenants remain in their building or relocate to other suitable housing.[85] HUD awarded grants on a formula basis to cities with 50,000 or greater population, urban counties, and states. Rental Rehabilitation grant amounts could be used for up to one-half of a project's total eligible rehabilitation costs. An average minimum rehabilitation cost of $600 per unit was a prerequisite to the receipt of funds.

Eligible activities included rehabilitation necessary to correct substandard conditions, make essential improvements, and repair major systems in danger of failure. Other rehabilitation costs were also eligible if they did not cover administrative costs and services provided or costs incurred by the grantee. Priority went to projects with units occupied by very-low-income families and projects that would offer units accessible to persons with disabilities.

After rehabilitation, low-income families had to occupy 70 to 100 percent of the units, and an equitable share of grant funds had to be used to aid large families. After-rehabilitation rents had to be market-rate rents not limited by rent controls. Grants could be used only in neighborhoods where the median family income did not exceed 80 percent of the median for the area and where rents were not likely to increase more rapidly than the rate for rent increases reasonably projected to occur in the market area.

The specific allocation for each metropolitan city, urban county, and state was based on a formula that considered three specific factors: rental units where the income of rental households was at or below the poverty level; rental units built before 1940 where the income of the household was at or below the poverty level; and rental units with at least one of four housing problems—overcrowding, high rental costs, incomplete kitchen facilities, or incomplete plumbing. The formula gave the last factor double weight. To allow a reasonable program level, the lowest amount HUD granted to each entity under the formula was $50,000 each year. Amounts under $50,000 were added to the appropriate state's formula amount for distribution to eligible units of general local government. In any state that did not elect to administer its share of Rental Rehabilitation funds, HUD awarded funds to eligible grantees through a competitive program.

The Rental Rehabilitation Program was repealed as of October 1, 1991. Grants may be made only in the case of binding commitments entered into before that date.[86]

Notes

1. *See generally Programs of HUD,* U.S. Department of Housing and Urban Development, 1989–1990.

2. *See generally* "A Decent Place to Live: The Report of the National Housing Task Force," Mar. 1988, 10.

3. Woodside, J., "Affordable Retirement Housing in a Post-HUD Era," *Spectrum,* Sept.–Oct. 1995, 34.

4. *HUD Handbook* 4561.1, which was designed for participants in the previous Section 221(d) multifamily coinsurance program (see §22.2(a)), provides one of the clearest examples of the overall HUD processing requirements.

5. *See, e.g.,* Notice H86–20 (HUD) at 3 (issued Aug. 11, 1986) (on Section 232 mortgage insurance for board-and-care homes).

6. *HUD Handbook* 4600.1, Ch. 1–6 (Section 232, board-and-care homes).

7. *Id.* at Ch. 2. Processing for new construction is known as Site Area Market Analysis (SAMA).

8. *See generally HUD Handbook* 4561.1 (Section 221(d), multifamily coinsurance).

9. *Id.* at Ch. 12.

10. For a discussion of the special escrow and operating deficit requirements for ReSC projects under Sections 221(d)(4) and 223(f), *see* §22.2.

11. Construction may not begin before the initial closing and recording of the coinsured mortgage, except under certain conditions where a construction delay could seriously jeopardize the project. *HUD Handbook* 4561.1, Ch. 7–12.

12. *Id.* at Ch 13.

13. *See* 12 U.S.C. §1715l(d)(4). For the operational requirements of this program, *see* §22.2(a).

14. *See* Notices H85–33, 84–41, 83–58 (HUD).

15. *See generally* 24 C.F.R. Part 251 (before Nov. 1990 revisions); *HUD Handbook* 4560.1.

16. The reserve requirements for ReSC projects were determined by calculating the initial operating deficit and a six-month debt service reserve amount. If the operating deficit was less than the six-month debt service reserve amount, the amount of required reserve funds would be the greater of two times the operating deficit calculation or the six-month debt service reserve amount. If the projected operating deficit equaled or exceeded the debt service reserve amount, both an operating deficit escrow and debt service reserve were required. Funds remaining in the operating deficit escrow and/or debt service reserve had to be released after sustaining occupancy had been maintained for 90 days.

17. These general HUD processing procedures were subject to a few additional requirements for ReSC projects. First, in figuring the replacement cost of the facility, both major movable equipment for congregate dining facilities and furniture in common areas had to be included. Minor movable equipment was not included. Moreover, no leasing or lease-purchase agreements were permitted for these items. Second, in calculating the debt service limitation under the valuation analysis, the cost of shelter services had to be separated from the fees and costs of nonshelter services and amenities. Only the gross income from the shelter income factor was used in calculating the debt service limitation. The intent was for HUD to process elderly proposals and determine project feasibility where a mortgage amount attributable only to shelter or realty was established and reflected an acceptable degree of risk. In addition, special market analysis was required to determine whether sufficient demand existed among ReSC's target group (fragile elderly of 70 years and up) to support the project (*see also* §22.2(a)).

18. *See Housing & Development Reporter,* July 10, 1989, 139–140.

19. 55 *Fed. Reg.* 48,863.

20. *Housing & Development Reporter,* Aug. 20, 1990, 279.

21. 55 *Fed. Reg.* 48,863.

22. 56 *Fed. Reg.* 42,798.

23. Notice H-91-21 (HUD) (Mar. 8, 1991).

24. 56 *Fed. Reg.* 42,798, Aug. 29, 1991; *see also Older Americans Report,* Sept. 13, 1991, 355.

25. 12 U.S.C. §1715n; for operational requirements of the Section 223(f) program, *see* §22.1(b).

26. 24 C.F.R. §207.32a; *HUD Handbook* 4561.1; HUD Fact Sheet.

27. 55 *Fed. Reg.* 48,863, 56 *Fed. Reg.* 42,798.

28. For operational requirements of the Section 232 program, *see* §22.3.

29. P.L. 98-181; 24 C.F.R. §232; *see also HUD Handbook* 4600.1 and Notice 86-20 (HUD).

30. *See* discussion in §20.4.

31. Pub. L. No. 102-550 (Oct. 28, 1992).

32. *See* 12 U.S.C. §1715w.

33. 12 U.S.C. §1715(b)(6).

34. 59 *Fed. Reg.* 61222, Nov. 29, 1994.

35. 24 C.F.R. §232.30.

36. 24 C.F.R. §232.32.

37. 12 U.S.C. §1715w(d).

38. Pub. L. No. 100-242 (Feb. 5, 1988).

39. 12 U.S.C. §1715n(f).

40. Pub. L. No. 102-550 (Oct. 28, 1992).

41. *See* 24 C.F.R. §232.901 *et seq.*

42. 59 *Fed. Reg.* 61222, Nov. 29, 1994 (amending 24 C.F.R. Part 232).

43. 24 C.F.R. §232.902.

44. 24 C.F.R. §232.903.

45. 24 C.F.R. §232.904.

46. Former 24 C.F.R. §§251, 255, 252 (before Nov. 1990 revisions).

47. 24 C.F.R. §§251, 255, 252 as revised.

48. 24 C.F.R. §213, *HUD Handbook* 4550.1 (§213); 24 C.F.R. Part 251, *HUD Handbook* 4560.1 (§221(d)(3)).

49. 12 U.S.C. §1715y; 24 C.F.R. §234.

50. 12 U.S.C. §17511; 24 C.F.R. Part 248.

51. "Financing Options for the Development of Affordable Housing and Assisted Living Facilities: A Resource Guide for Nonprofit Providers," American Association of Homes for the Aging, 1993, 21.

52. *Housing & Development Reporter,* May 6, 1996, 79 and July 29, 1996, 161.

53. Pub. L. No. 104-120.

54. *Housing & Development Reporter,* Oct. 7, 1996, 321, 348.

55. For a more detailed general discussion of secondary mortgages, *see Housing & Development Reporter,* 70:0011 *et seq.*

56. *See* 12 U.S.C. §1717.

57. *See* 12 U.S.C. §1721(g).

58. 24 C.F.R. §203.45.

59. 24 C.F.R. §203.47.

60. *See* 12 U.S.C. §1451.

61. *See* P.L. 95–557 (1978).

62. For operational requirements of the old Section 202/8 program, see §22.4.

63. 24 C.F.R. §§880, 885; *HUD Handbook* 4571.1 REV-2, 7420.1 REV-1.

64. For example, Section 202 loan funds for 1990 were reduced to $480 million. *Housing & Development Reporter,* Oct. 30, 1989, 432. Section 202 appropriations for 1991 were $1.3 billion for both capital grants *and* rental assistance. *Housing & Development Reporter,* Oct. 29, 1990, 501. Section 8 funds were also lowered for 1990 to $1,092 billion. *Housing & Development Reporter,* Oct. 30, 1989, 432.

65. S.825; *see AAHA Provider News,* Jan. 22, 1988.

66. *Housing & Development Reporter,* Oct. 30, 1989, 432.

67. 42 U.S.C. §1452b; 24 C.F.R. §510; *see also* discussion of CDBGs, §14.4(c).

68. 42 U.S.C. §1452b(h).

69. P.L. 101–625.

70. 12 U.S.C. §1701q; *see* 24 C.F.R. Part 891 (published at 61 *Fed. Reg.* 11956, Mar. 22, 1996); *see also HUD Handbook* 4571.3.

71. 24 C.F.R. §891.115.

72. *Aging News Alert,* Mar. 10, 1993, 9.

73. *Washington Report,* American Association of Homes for the Aging, May 6, 1993.

74. *Housing & Development Reporter,* Oct. 11, 1993, 323.

75. *Housing Bulletin,* American Association of Homes for the Aging, Feb. 10, 1994.

76. California Association of Homes and Services for the Aging, *The CAHSA Report,* Oct. 28, 1994, 6.

77. *Housing & Development Reporter,* May 6, 1996, 825.

78. *Older Americans Report,* Sept. 27, 1996, 316; Issues Brief, American Association of Homes and Services for the Aging, Mar. 1998.

79. 42 U.S.C. §§5318, 5320.

80. *Housing & Development Reporter,* Oct. 17, 1988, 476.

81. U.S.C. §§5301 *et seq.*; 24 C.F.R. §570.

82. *See* note 64, *above,* and *Housing & Development Reporter,* Oct. 14, 1991, 423.

83. Former 42 U.S.C. §1437o; 24 C.F.R. §850.

84. P.L. 101–625.

85. Former 42 U.S.C. §1437o; 24 C.F.R. §511.

86. P.L. 101–625.

Dory Inn; Hampton, New Hampshire.

Tax-Exempt Financing

15 Tax-Exempt Financing

§15.1 In General

Tax-exempt bond financing has long been an attractive option for financing public facilities. Pursuant to Section 103 of the Internal Revenue Code, private individuals and corporations are not, as a general rule, required to include in gross income for purposes of federal income tax any interest received with respect to government obligations. Consequently, an issuer can pay a lower interest rate on its obligations and yet produce after-tax earnings to bondholders equivalent to a taxable investment.

While tax-exempt financing had been used extensively for financing purely governmental facilities, it was only in the 1970s that it began to be used widely for various private activities. To comply with the terms of the exemption, public agencies issued revenue bonds and either lent the proceeds to private companies or used the proceeds themselves to construct facilities for lease to private companies. The use of tax-exempt financing was available only for public purposes, but a finding that such purposes existed was not difficult to make and ranged from the provision of health or educational services to the community by nonprofit institutions to the general economic benefits conferred on the community by for-profit businesses.

Cities, counties, and special authorities began to use tax-exempt financing as a means to compete against one another to attract new business enterprises or to retain existing businesses. Eventually,

Congress grew alarmed by the fact that a substantial amount of the nation's capital financing was being executed on a tax-exempt basis, thereby resulting in a serious revenue drain for the U.S. Treasury. Beginning in 1968 and continuing in subsequent years, Congress enacted legislation to restrict the use of tax-exempt "industrial revenue bonds," a term that Section 103(b) of the Internal Revenue Code defined to include bonds issued to finance the trade or business of a nonexempt person. The 1986 revision to the code continues to impose these restrictions, together with various additional restrictions, as described below.

While tax-exempt financing has been restricted over the years for for-profit activities, it has been retained for many types of retirement housing, both for-profit and nonprofit ventures, although with fewer limitations for nonprofit undertakings. Thus, nonprofit organizations that are exempt from taxation under Section 501(c)(3) of the Internal Revenue Code are able to finance their projects by using a government agency as a conduit—and with only a few restrictions that do not apply to the government agency itself.

§15.2 Qualified 501(c)(3) Bonds

The 1986 Internal Revenue Code includes special provisions for bonds issued on behalf of organizations described in Section 501(c)(3) of the code (called Qualified 501(c)(3) Bonds[1]) and, for the most part, treats those bonds the same as it does bonds issued for government agencies. However, Section 145 of the code, which applies to qualified bonds, imposes the following qualifications:

- All property provided by the net proceeds of the issue must be owned by a Section 501(c)(3) organization or a government unit.
- Not more than 5 percent of the net proceeds may be expended on property used in a private business, and the principal of or interest on not more than 5 percent of the security for the bonds may be secured by or derived from payments in respect to property used in a private business.
- Before 1997, no individual borrower or group of related borrowers was permitted to have outstanding at any time debt derived from Qualified 501(c)(3) Bonds (including defeased bonds that have not yet been redeemed) exceeding $150 million except that portion of any bond issue devoted to hospital purposes (not including skilled-nursing facilities).[2] In 1997, this limitation was eliminated,[3] but only prospectively. Thus, Section 501(c)(3) organizations may borrow the proceeds of 501(c)(3) bonds without limit for new projects but may not refinance existing facilities financed before 1997 if doing so would exceed the limit.

For 501(c)(3) bonds to be used, the proceeds must be applied only to operations that qualify the organization for Section 501(c)(3) status. Thus, this type of tax-exempt financing could not be used for a project that does not provide low-income housing, that does not include the elements of security set forth in Revenue Ruling 72–124, or that does not otherwise constitute a charitable activity.[4] Qualified 501(c)(3) Bonds issued after October 21, 1988, for purposes of housing development must comply with the income limits applicable to residential rental project bonds (see §15.3) unless the financed facility is within the jurisdiction of the government issuer and either the first use of the project is pursuant to the bond issue or the project is "substantially rehabilitated," as that term is used in Section 48(g) of the code.[5] An exception to this rule permits tax-exempt financing to refinance taxable financing in two cases: where a reasonable expectation that the taxable financing would be so financed (as in the case of a

taxable construction loan) and where there was no state or local program for tax-exempt financing of the property in operation when the taxable financing was originally incurred.[6]

Given the stringent requirements imposed by the 1986 amendments, limitations on the use of proceeds of Qualified 501(c)(3) Bonds for any nonexempt purpose may be problematic. The law provides that no more than 5 percent of the net proceeds of the bond issue may be used for a nonexempt purpose. Because the law deems that the costs of issuance are not an exempt purpose, that expense (capped at 2 percent; see below) must be deducted from the 5 percent; as a result, a maximum 3 percent in private business activity is permitted to be financed by the net proceeds of or to secure the bonds. The following are some general guidelines as to the treatment of typical retirement home activities as nonexempt businesses:

- In general, property made available to a private business enterprise on a preferential or exclusive basis is considered a nonexempt business. Thus, if the facility contains retail stores, a beauty parlor, or a private physician's office rented to a private person or subject to a concession agreement, that portion of the facility is considered a nonexempt business.
- A component of the housing may be considered a nonexempt business, depending on the basis of the organization's exemption. For example, if an organization's exemption is based on the provision of low-income housing and the organization develops a project with 50 percent low-income and 50 percent market-rate units, the operation of the market-rate housing may be a nonexempt business because it does not advance the charitable purpose of providing low-income housing. Given that the unrelated business component is more than 3 percent of the project, expenditure of bond proceeds on the market-rate housing component of the project could endanger the tax-exempt status of the entire bond issue. One solution calls for using tax-exempt bond proceeds only for the low-income units and financing the market-rate component with taxable financing or equity.
- Under management contracts with for-profit or unrelated nonprofit managers, the managed property

is considered a nonexempt business unless the borrower complies with certain rules promulgated by the Internal Revenue Service.[7] These rules do not apply to contracts for services that are solely incidental to the primary functions of the financed facility, such as janitorial, office equipment repair, or billing. Instead, they include the following standards:

- Compensation under a management contract must be "reasonable" for the services rendered.
- No compensation may be based, in whole or in part, on a share of net profits. A contract may, however, include a "productivity reward" based on either gross revenues or total expenses, but not both.
- The permitted term and termination provisions of the management agreement are dependent on the annual compensation arrangements as noted below.

Compensation Arrangements	Maximum Term and Termination Requirements (if any)
At least 95% based on fixed fee	The lesser of 80% of the life of the facilities and 15 years
At least 80% based on fixed fee	10 years
At least 50% based on fixed fee	5 years, terminable without cause at the end of the third year
Per unit fee	3 years, terminable without cause at the end of the second year
100% based on percentage of revenue (available only for startups)	2 years, terminable without cause at the end of the first year

- Notwithstanding the term and termination provisions above, management contracts may have an "evergreen" clause, providing for automatic renewal year to year unless one party elects to terminate.

In some instances, it is desirable for a facility to contain private business activity in excess of the limit set forth in the code, as, for example, when street-level commercial spaces would be desirable to generate income and to provide shops for the convenience of residents. In such a case, the corporation's equity contribution (which may consist of entrance fee receipts) can be allocated to the space devoted to private business activity. If the contribution is not sufficient, such space could be financed by a separate taxable loan, which is secured on a parity basis with the tax-exempt loan, or the space could be developed as a separate condominium unit pledged independently as security for a taxable loan.

The Tax Reform Act of 1986 brought about the most far-reaching changes in the Internal Revenue Code since the adoption of the 1954 code. Its effects on tax-exempt financing were so profound that some observers thought that Congress would leave the structure of tax-exempt financing alone for a while. Nonetheless, while Section 501(c)(3) borrowers emerged from the 1986 act virtually unscathed, some lingering concern suggested that the rules regarding tax-exempt borrowing by Section 501(c)(3) organizations could be too liberal. In particular, concerns focused on the use of tax-exempt money for projects that benefit persons who are not legitimate objects of charity (e.g., the wealthy) and projects that are alleged to be for-profit ventures. With tax-exempt borrowing limited for for-profit housing developments under the 1986 act,[8] some concern also focused on the possible use of contractual arrangements with a nonprofit corporation as a means whereby a for-profit entity could obtain otherwise forbidden financing. Even though the effect of these transactions on the U.S. Treasury is insignificant (as viewed by Congress),[9] these matters have been pursued largely out of a concern for "equity" and abatement of "abuses." In response to concerns about the propriety of certain 501(c)(3) bond issues, the Internal Revenue Service has taken the position that organizations newly applying for Section 501(c)(3) status must disclose their intentions, if any, of using tax-exempt bond financing and must answer certain questions regarding the uses to which the bond proceeds will be put.[10]

These questions inquire as to the existence of contracts with for-profit entities, whether the nonprofit is sponsored by an existing established nonprofit organization, how much experience the sponsoring organization has had with the business to be conducted by the new organization, and other matters designed to determine whether the new organization has a legitimate reason to exist, aside from any relationship with a nonexempt organization.

The questions are evaluated by allocating a given number of positive or negative points to each answer.

(a) The GAO Report

At the request of certain members of Congress, the IRS and the General Accounting Office initiated investigations into the use of tax-exempt financing for retirement communities. The investigations were aimed at certain supposed abuses of tax-exempt financing, particularly, charges that nominally nonprofit projects in fact have been developed for the benefit of for-profit developers. Some members of Congress were concerned that development agreements, management agreements, and "turnkey" developments have yielded profits accruing to for-profit developers and that the benefits of tax-exempt, bond-financed retirement housing go disproportionately to wealthy individuals who are not legitimate objects of public charity or tax-exempt financing.

In March 1991, the GAO issued its report[11] and concluded that "retirement center bonds were risky and benefited moderate-income elderly." Specifically, a study of 271 bond issues issued from 1980 to 1990 showed that 75 percent of the financed facilities housed residents with average incomes greater than $15,000, making the facilities affordable primarily to 27 percent of the nation's elderly. The GAO also found that the default rate for the bonds was 20 percent compared with about 1 percent for other bonds. The GAO did note, however, that tax-exempt financing made projects more affordable than if they been financed with taxable debt and that certain precautions could reduce the default rate.

As a result of the investigation, some experts expect that the IRS will increase its audits of retirement home corporations to ascertain compliance with the guidelines for tax exemption.[12] Because all borrowers of tax-exempt bond proceeds are required to covenant that the facilities will be used for Section 501(c)(3) purposes to the extent required for maintenance of tax-exempt interest on the bonds, borrowers should carefully review their activities to ensure that they meet the existing standards for Section 501(c)(3) status.

(b) Limits on Section 501(c)(3) Residential Rental Projects

The law prohibits proceeds of 501(c)(3) bonds from being used directly or indirectly to provide residential rental units except for

- residential rental units if the first use of the property is pursuant to the issue;
- residential rental units that meet the income limits for residential rental project bonds. These limits require 40 percent of the units to be affordable to persons earning not more than 50 percent of the area median income or 20 percent of the units to be affordable to persons earning not more than 60 percent of the area median income; and
- units that are acquired and substantially rehabilitated. The value of such rehabilitation must equal at least the basis of the units at the time of rehabilitation.[13]

An exception applies to certain current refundings of bonds that otherwise would not comply with the foregoing.[14] Revenue Ruling 89–24[15] provides that income limits for meeting the minimum setaside requirements for tax-exempt facility bonds must be computed by reference to limits listed by HUD according to family size.

Certain recent private letter rulings issued by the Internal Revenue Service have created confusion as to whether and in what circumstances assisted-living facilities constitute "residential rental projects" (for a more complete discussion of the issues raised, see §15.3). If an assisted-living facility does not constitute a "residential rental project," the restrictions discussed above do not apply to the acquisition of such a facility by a Section 501(c)(3) corporation.

While 501(c)(3) bonds are usually the best vehicle for use by a Section 501(c)(3) corporation, there may be reasons why such financing would not be desirable. For example, there may be a noncomplying management contract or the property may otherwise be used by a nonexempt person. In such a case, the Section 501(c)(3) corporation may elect not to use 501(c)(3) bonds but rather to take advantage of one of the other categories of tax-exempt financing (see §15.3).

§15.3 Residential Rental Projects

Section 142(d) of the Internal Revenue Code of 1986 provides that the proceeds of government bonds may be lent to for-profit or nonprofit owners to be used for "residential rental projects." To fall within the definition of "residential rental project," a facility must meet certain standards. Each unit must be self-contained in that it must have a private bath and kitchen, and each kitchen must contain a sink, a stove, and a range.[16] In a 1997 private letter ruling involving an assisted-living facility,[17] the Internal Revenue Service ruled that a unit's kitchen may include a microwave oven instead of a "range." In addition, the facility must not be a "nursing home, sanitarium or rest home."[18] Unfortunately, these terms are not terms of art and are subject to interpretation. In another 1997 private letter ruling,[19] the Internal Revenue Service ruled that an assisted-living facility was not a "residential rental project" because residents received substantial amounts of health-related services, making the project a "rest home" or "convalescent hospital." A private letter ruling is not to be relied upon as precedent, and this last ruling was driven largely by the details of the facility under consideration and the regulatory scheme of the state in which it was located. Even so, a private letter ruling gives an indication of how the IRS will deal with an issue and this last ruling indicates that the nature, extent, and government regulation of services rendered to residents of an assisted-living facility could be such as to result in the facility's no longer qualifying as a residential rental project. The IRS is expected to produce a general ruling on this issue in the near future.

To qualify for financing under Section 142(d), the issuer must elect to require the facility to meet one of the following tests:

- Twenty percent or more of the residential units are occupied by individuals whose income is 50 percent or less of area median gross income.
- Forty percent or more of the residential units are occupied by individuals whose income is 60 percent or less of area median gross income.

The qualified project period commences on the first day on which 10 percent of the units are occupied and terminates 15 years after 50 percent of the units are occupied, upon repayment of the bonds, or at termination of a federal Section 8 rental assistance contract.

Determination of median area income is made in accordance with existing HUD guidelines and is adjusted by family size. The code permits residents to qualify if their income increases during residency to up to 140 percent of the qualifying income; above that amount, the project does not cease to qualify so long as the next available unit of comparable or smaller size is made available to a qualified resident.[20]

Residential rental project bonds can be a valuable tool when 501(c)(3) bonds cannot be used, such as when the sponsor is not a Section 501(c)(3) organization, a long-term management contract with a for-profit organization is desired, the project is an unrelated trade or business of a Section 501(c)(3) organization, or access to the 4 percent low-income housing tax credit is desired. However, because interest on the bonds is includable as preference income for the alternative minimum tax, residential rental project bonds sell at a somewhat higher interest rate than 501(c)(3) bonds and should be used only when 501(c)(3) bonds are not available.

The Internal Revenue Code includes residential rental project bonds in a volume cap imposed on all private activity bonds (except 501(c)(3) bonds).[21] The cap is imposed on each state and, for each calendar year, equals the greater of $50 multiplied by the state's population or $150 million. To issue residential rental project bonds, the issuer (which must be a state or local government agency) must apply to the state agency responsible for allocating the volume cap to the project proposed to be financed.

§15.4 Limitations on All Tax-Exempt Bonds

The following limitations apply to all types of tax-exempt bonds described above:

(a) Arbitrage

The Internal Revenue Code defines an arbitrage bond as any bond that is part of an issue, any portion of the proceeds of which are reasonably expected at the time of issuance of the bond to be used directly or indirectly to acquire higher-yielding investments or to replace funds used for that purpose.[22] This type of investment is disfavored because it permits a borrower to profit at the expense of the U.S. Treasury; therefore, interest on arbitrage bonds is generally taxable.[23] Nonetheless, the code makes certain exceptions to the arbitrage bond definition, including the following:

- The code permits unlimited yield during a "reasonable temporary period until such proceeds are needed for the purpose for which [the bond] issue was issued."[24] In general, the period may not exceed three years. With respect to pooled bond issues, however, the higher yield may be retained only during a six-month period before it is loaned to the ultimate borrower. That borrower may then take advantage of the remainder of the three-year temporary period.[25]
- The code permits unlimited yield on a reasonably required reserve or replacement fund not to exceed 10 percent of the proceeds of the bond issue unless the secretary of the U.S. Treasury is satisfied that a higher amount is necessary.[26] Typically, a tax-exempt amortized bond issue has included a debt service reserve fund equal to the maximum annual debt service (principal, interest, and credit enhancement fee, if any). If interest rates return to the levels that prevailed in the early 1980s, this traditional formula will result in a debt service reserve in excess of that permitted by the code.[27]

The foregoing exceptions are subject to the requirement that excess earnings must be rebated to the federal government every five years.[28] Therefore, while the exceptions allow arbitrage gains and losses to be averaged over the five-year period, they do not permit retention of any net arbitrage profits.

(b) Relationship of Bond Maturity to Life of Assets

The Internal Revenue Code prohibits the average maturity of tax-exempt bonds from exceeding 120 percent of the average reasonably expected economic life of the facilities being financed with the net proceeds of the bond issue.[29] Land is not taken into account unless it represents 25 percent or more

of the bond issue, in which case it is treated as having a life of 30 years.[30]

(c) Public Approval Requirement

The code also requires tax-exempt bonds issued for private activities to be approved by either the electorate or the applicable representatives of the affected government unit after notice and a public hearing.[31] The hearing (called a TEFRA hearing, after the legislation that originally required it) can be held by either a hearing officer appointed by a local public governing body or a state elected official, but issuance of the bonds must be approved by the elected body or official.

(d) Restriction on Issuance Costs

Issuance costs financed by the bond issue cannot exceed 2 percent of the aggregate face amount of the issue.[32] Such costs include underwriting discounts, attorney fees, commitment fees, and other fees incidental to issuance of the bonds but exclude credit enhancement fees and prepaid interest. In practice, issuance costs may and often do exceed the 2 percent limit. In such cases, the costs must be paid from a source other than bond proceeds, such as equity or a supplemental taxable borrowing.

(e) Reimbursement of Prior Expenditures

In a typical project, a developer incurs numerous expenses before bonds are issued to finance the project. Such expenses may include architect and consultant fees, land use and permit expenses, and the cost of land acquisition. Since these expenses are legitimate, a developer may legitimately desire to be reimbursed from the proceeds of the bond issue. The Internal Revenue Service, however, has concerns about the use of tax-exempt bonds to generate unrestricted cash to borrowers and therefore has promulgated regulations setting forth limited conditions under which prior expenditures may be reimbursed from bond proceeds.[33] These regulations require the following:

- Not later than 60 days after the payment of the original expenditure, the issuer or the borrower may adopt an official intent to reimburse. An appropriate representative such as a board of directors, finance committee, or chief executive officer may adopt the intent so long as it is the party that would reasonably be expected to make such a commitment.

- The official intent must generally describe the project for which the original expenditure is paid and must state the maximum principal amount of the obligations expected to be issued for the project.

- On the date of adoption of the intent, the issuer or borrower must have a reasonable expectation that the expenditure will be reimbursed. A history of routinely adopting expressions of intent or of failing to reimburse is evidence of unreasonableness.

- Reimbursement of the original expenditure must occur not later than 18 months after the later of the date the original expenditure is paid or the date the project is placed in service or abandoned, but in no event more than three years after the original expenditure is paid.

(f) Advance Refundings

A typical fixed-rate, long-term bond issue provides call protection[34] for a specified period (e.g., ten years) and thereafter provides the right of redemption with a declining premium for a further specified period (e.g., 2 percent, declining at 1 percent per year). During the call protection period, the borrower may wish to refinance the debt in order to obtain new debt at lower interest rates, modify certain covenants or conditions in the underlying debt instruments that would otherwise require bondholder consent, or incur additional debt not otherwise permitted. Typically, refinancing occurs through an advance refunding. In an advance refunding, new bonds are issued and the proceeds are used to purchase U.S. government securities in such denominations and maturities as will discharge the old bonds at the first permissible call date or a specified later date. The securities are then placed in trust for the benefit of the old bondholders, and the existing indenture or other security instrument is thereby released, permitting the security instrument for the new bonds to be installed in its place.

The result of an advance refunding is that, for some period of time, two bond issues are outstanding where previously only one issue was outstanding such that tax-exempt interest is paid on principal representing approximately twice the borrower's capital requirement. Likewise, if the second bond issue is refunded, three issues could be outstanding. Potentially, any number of refundings could occur before the first bonds are redeemed. Out of concern about the resulting revenue loss to the U.S. Treasury, Congress in 1986 provided that tax-exempt bonds issued for government or Section 501(c)(3) organizations generally can be advance refunded only once and that all other tax-exempt bonds may not be advance refunded at all.[35] Generally, the code defines advance refunding as a transaction in which the refunding bond is issued more than 90 days before redemption of the refunded bond.[36] This definition is significant in that many debt instruments permit redemption of bonds to occur on only one of the semiannual interest payment dates. To ensure maximum flexibility, at least quarterly redemption should be permitted.

In addition, the code requires refunded bonds to be redeemed on the earliest date on which a bond may be redeemed. For bonds issued after 1985, the code provides no exception related to the premium that must be paid on that date; therefore, there is no opportunity to time the redemption to avoid paying a high premium.[37] Furthermore, an advance refunding may be undertaken only "if the issuer may realize present value debt service savings (determined without regard to administrative expenses) in connection with the issue of which the refunding bond is a part."[38] However, the conference committee report indicates that Congress did not intend to prohibit low to high refundings to avoid adverse covenants or to restructure debt, so long as they do not constitute a device to obtain a material financial advantage based on arbitrage.[39]

(g) Change in Use

In some circumstances, the use of property as proposed at the time of bond issuance becomes infeasible or undesirable and must be changed to a purpose that disqualifies the project for bond financing. For example, a developer might find it financially infeasible to rent to persons within the income levels necessary to qualify the project for residential rental project bonds, or the developer might sell the project to a for-profit owner such that the project is ineligible for residential rental project bonds.

In the case of bonds issued for residential rental property under Section 142(d) of the Internal Revenue Code, if the project no longer meets the requirements of that section (for example, because the rent limits are not observed or because the project has become a "nursing home"), interest on the bonds ceases to be tax-exempt beginning on the first day of the taxable year in which the project is disqualified and continues to be tax-exempt until the date on which the project again meets the requirements.[40] In the case of a facility financed with 501(c)(3) bonds, if the facility continues to be owned by the Section 501(c)(3) organization but is used in the trade or business of a person other than a Section 501(c)(3) organization (such as in the case of a lease or a nonqualifying management agreement), interest on the bonds remains tax-exempt, but the Section 501(c)(3) organization must treat an amount not less than fair market rent on the facility as unrelated business income on which it must pay income tax, and it may not deduct from such income the debt service on the bonds.[41]

The Internal Revenue Service has ruled that so long as the issuer and conduit borrower had the proper expectations on the date of closing, a subsequent unexpected change in use would not cause the bonds to be taxable if all callable bonds were redeemed and all other bonds were defeased before the change in use. (Private Letter Ruling 9124030 was revoked for nonsubstantive reasons by Private Letter Ruling 9227030.) The Internal Revenue Service has set forth certain conditions under which bonds can remain outstanding despite a change in use.[42]

- On the date of the bond issue, the issuer and borrower had to expect reasonably that the proceeds would be used for qualifying uses for the entire term of the bond issue.
- The change in use must occur not sooner than five years after the bond-financed facilities are placed in service.

- Any agreement that gives rise to a nonqualifying change in use must be bona fide and at "arm's length."
- At least one of the three following types of remedial action must be taken in connection with the bonds: the bonds must be redeemed or defeased; within one year after change in use, all disposition proceeds must be allocated either to an alternative qualifying use or to redeeming the bonds on their first call date; and it must be established that the changed use of the facility could have qualified for tax-exempt financing at the time the bonds were issued. An example would be 501(c)(3) bonds issued for a project that met the low-income requirements; over time, however, the use of the project changes to a non–low-income facility that qualifies under Revenue Ruling 72–124.

§15.5 Use of Bond Proceeds for Religious Purposes

Because many retirement communities are developed by organizations affiliated with religious denominations, it is important to consider the implications of the First Amendment prohibition against the establishment of religion in the context of tax-exempt financing.[43] The First Amendment does not preclude the lending of proceeds of tax-exempt bonds to religious institutions merely because they are religious, but it does preclude the use of such funds for solely religious purposes, such as the construction of a chapel used exclusively for religious services and the construction of housing occupied exclusively by members of a religious order. A multipurpose assembly facility can, however, be financed even if it is to be used, among other purposes, for religious services.

§15.6 The Issuer and Form of Tax-Exempt Bonds

As noted above, while the proceeds of tax-exempt bonds may be used to finance the activities of a nongovernmental entity, tax exemption is granted only if the bonds constitute an obligation of a state or a political subdivision of the state, such as a city, county, or special district. Thus, a public agency must be willing to act as a conduit for the transaction. As the term implies, a conduit is merely an instrumentality through which bond proceeds flow from the bond purchasers to the ultimate borrower for the sole purpose of rendering the bonds tax-exempt. The conduit has no liability for repayment of the bonds other than from the debt service payments made by the borrower and is in many cases a thoroughly disinterested party. In some cases, however, especially when a state authority is involved, the conduit imposes various requirements on the borrower and monitors its activities for both programmatic reasons and to protect its reputation or to carry out legislatively mandated policy.[44]

Occasionally, it is difficult to identify a suitable and willing conduit. Some issuers are unsophisticated but accommodating as long as there is no residual liability. More often, though, issuers are concerned about the quality of the securities they are issuing and thus impose various other obligations on borrowers, including the following:

- bond rating or credit enhancement requirements;
- restriction of unrated bonds to large denominations (e.g., minimum of $250,000 to $1 million) and prohibition against sale or resale to other than institutional investors;
- social objections, such as affirmative action requirements and restrictions on rent and tenant income;
- substantial fees; and
- actual selection of the financing team.

The following subsections list possible issuer candidates and explain factors to consider in making a selection.

(a) State Authorities

Most states have set up separate units of state government that are known as authorities. Authorities operate under legislative enabling acts that set out their power to issue bonds, limit their bonding capacity, and often specify other rules and regulations connected with their operations. State authorities are usually limited to specific purposes (e.g., health care, housing, education, pollution control) or com-

binations of purposes, and most states have established several authorities. Most appropriate to retirement homes are state housing finance authorities and state health facility finance authorities. Some states have multipurpose authorities with a broad range of financing jurisdiction. The advantages of these agencies are that they are well established, enjoy sufficient legislative authority, and often sponsor pooled programs, which can help spread the costs of smaller projects. The disadvantages are that they may impose rigid program requirements, operate under a maximum aggregate debt authorization, depend on politicized project selection processes, and require borrowers to use preselected investment bankers and other consultants.

(b) Local Authorities

State law allows many cities and counties to establish independent financing authorities. These authorities function like the state authorities but are controlled at the local level. Examples of these authorities include health facility finance authorities, housing authorities, redevelopment agencies, and joint exercise of powers authorities. Because they are less bureaucratic and more open to borrower initiative than the state authorities, local authorities have the advantage of greater flexibility. One disadvantage is that they may be overly influenced by local politics and lack sufficient legislative authority for certain types of projects.

(c) City or County Bonds

Often, cities and counties are empowered to issue revenue bonds and loan the proceeds to private borrowers to accomplish ends that benefit local residents. Authority for such bonds must be either specifically granted by the state legislature or provided pursuant to a city's charter under its constitutional home rule authority.[45] As a general rule, cities are vested with more extensive bond-issuing authority than counties. As with the foregoing options, city or county revenue bonds do not constitute a debt or obligation of the public agency but are issued entirely on the strength of the private borrower. A city or county may offer more flexibility than an authority, but smaller governments in particular may suffer from lack of experience with conduit financing. In addition, they may be overly influenced by local politics and may charge excessive fees.

(d) Certificates of Participation

A relatively new vehicle has evolved in recent years to permit a local government entity to serve as a conduit even if it does not have the authority to issue bonds. Internal Revenue Code Section 103 grants tax exemption for interest on obligations generally rather than for interest on bonds specifically; therefore, the Internal Revenue Service has found that the exemption extends as well to interest components of a public agency's obligation to make payments under a lease or a contract of sale.[46] Because public agencies, usually cities, have been given broad authority to buy and sell or lease property to achieve public purposes, they can contract to buy property from and sell it back to an owner such that the interest component of the entity's obligation under the purchase contract is exempt from taxation. The seller's right to receive these payments is assigned to a trustee; the trustee then sells participations in the right to receive the payments. These participations (called certificates of participation) are marketed in conventional bond denominations and are treated by the market as though they were bonds.

(e) 63–20 Bonds

One arrangement permits a nonprofit organization to issue tax-exempt bonds directly, without the use of a government conduit. Under Internal Revenue Service Revenue Ruling 63–20,[47] a nonprofit corporation can issue tax-exempt bonds directly for the benefit of a public agency. This form of debt, which is almost never used, is burdened with some very stringent conditions as follows:

- The public agency on whose behalf the bonds are issued must approve the transaction.
- A deed conveying the property from the nonprofit corporation to the public agency must be placed in escrow for delivery on the date on which the debt is repaid; the property may not be encumbered with other debt when conveyed.

- The public agency must be given the option to purchase the property at any time by repaying the debt.
- Once the property is conveyed to the public agency, it may not be reconveyed to the borrower for at least 90 days.[48]

Because the property may not be further encumbered beyond the term of the bonds, refinancings can be accomplished only for shorter and shorter periods as time goes on, making expansions and renewals less and less feasible. In addition, in the absence of guarantees that the public agency will not decide to acquire the property for the amount of the debt and oust the nonprofit borrower, the use of 63–20 bonds requires a great deal of trust between the nonprofit borrower and the public agency. Further, it is difficult to undo the transaction. Therefore, this method should be considered a last resort.

(f) Issuer Requirements

Issuers vary with respect to the type and characteristics of projects that can be financed. For example, an authority constituted to finance health facilities may require a retirement housing development that it finances to incorporate a health care component. In addition, jurisdictional issues may apply. Some agencies are permitted to finance projects outside their jurisdictions while others are limited to projects within their jurisdictions or, in the case of redevelopment agencies, within a project area. In 1988, Congress effectively prohibited tax-exempt financing of housing outside the issuer's jurisdiction by defining the use of bond proceeds for such purpose as an "investment" subject to arbitrage limits.[49] Some state and local legislation has mirrored the federal concern that tax-exempt bond proceeds should be used for low- and moderate-income housing. In particular, some state laws impose income limits on state and locally financed housing that differ from and are more extensive than those imposed by the Internal Revenue Code.[50] Local agencies may also impose requirements related to affirmative action in the engagement of bond counsel, investment bankers, printers, and other parties and the hiring of local residents. They may also require that preference be given to local residents for admission to the development.

§15.7 Participants and Documents in a Tax-Exempt Bond Issue

Because tax-exempt bond issues are usually carried out as conduit transactions, they are more complex and involve more parties than conventional loan transactions. This section discusses the structure of a tax-exempt bond issue, describes the parties involved in structuring and administering the issue, and notes the duties and particular considerations applicable to the parties.

(a) Structure and Participants

In a typical tax-exempt conduit financing (see Figure 15.1), a public agency issuer issues bonds for sale at a discount to an underwriter, which resells the bonds to individual bondholders at a price that usually (but not always) equals par. The underwriter's discount is its compensation for structuring the transaction and selling the bonds. The issuer then lends the bond proceeds to the borrower for development of a qualified project. The issuer assigns to a trustee its obligation to the bondholders and its rights against the borrower; thereafter, because it is only a conduit, the issuer has few if any rights or obligations. If the bonds are credit-enhanced, the credit enhancer (such as an insurance company or a bank) enters into an agreement with the borrower for the benefit of the bondholders, usually naming the issuer and the trustee as beneficiaries. The borrower then grants a security interest (such as a deed of trust) for the benefit of the credit enhancer.

The following is a list of the participants in a tax-exempt bond issue, together with a brief description of their functions:

- Borrower—The borrower is the organization that develops the project and, for that purpose, borrows the proceeds of the bond issue.
- Borrower's counsel—Legal counsel represents the borrower and is responsible for reviewing and negotiating the documents to see that they meet the borrower's needs. Borrower's counsel also drafts documents related to the borrower, such as resolutions, certificates, and various contracts, and, at closing, delivers an opinion relating to the borrower's participation in the transaction.

- Financial consultant—The financial consultant is engaged by the borrower and is responsible for analyzing the capital needs of the borrower and recommending a course of action. The role of the financial consultant may be combined with that of the underwriter, although some borrowers desire to obtain independent advice, fearing that otherwise the underwriting firm may tend to structure the transaction more to facilitate the sale of the bonds than to meet the needs of the borrower and may not explore alternatives outside the transactions with which the firm is familiar. The financial adviser may solicit competitive proposals from underwriters in order to obtain the most advantageous arrangement, but care should be taken so that the financial adviser's fee does not exceed the value of any such advantage.
- Underwriter—The underwriter is an investment banking firm that structures the transaction and agrees to purchase the bonds for resale to the ultimate purchasers. The underwriter's role is central to making the financing work in that the underwriter must coordinate the demands of the market with the needs of the borrower. The underwriter also frequently functions as the leader of the financing team, coordinating the activities of the other participants.
- Underwriter's counsel—Underwriter's counsel is an attorney who advises the underwriter with respect to the structuring of the transaction. In addition, underwriter's counsel usually drafts the official statement and the bond purchase agreement as well as any remarketing agreement, tender agent agreement, or paying agent agreement required as part of a variable-rate transaction. Underwriter's counsel is responsible for advising the underwriter with respect to compliance with securities laws, for giving an opinion with respect to exemption from registration with the Securities and Exchange Commission, and for ensuring qualification of the bonds with the securities commissioners in the various states in which it is expected that the bonds will be sold.
- Bond counsel—Bond counsel drafts the principal legal documents setting forth the form of the bonds and the terms and conditions on which they are issued. In addition, bond counsel gives an opinion for the benefit of the bondholders to

Figure 15. 1 **Example of a Summary of Proposed Terms for a Publicly Offered Tax-Exempt Bond Issue**

Principal Amount: $40,000,000

Maturity: No principal payments for first 3 years; serial bonds due May 1, 1991, through 2002; term bond due 2021, with mandatory sinking fund

Issuer: _____ Health Facilities Authority

Borrower:

Closing: Closing date to be November 25, 1987, or such other date mutually agreed to

Dated: Bonds dated November 1, 1987

Interest Rate (estimated): Serial bonds—4.5%–6.6%
Term bonds—7%

Rating: AAA Standard & Poor's
Aaa Moody's

Credit Enhancement: California Health Facility Construction Loan Insurance Program

Security: (1) First deed of trust on the project
(2) Pledge of gross revenues of the borrower

Project: Construction of a life-care facility with 300 residential units, 30 personal-care units, and a 50-bed skilled-nursing facility

Presales: 60% of the units to be sold before closing with nonrefundable deposits of not less than $10,000

Rate Covenant: Maintain rates to produce debt service coverage ratio of at least 1.10; covenant met if ratio is at least 1.0 and a report of a management consultant is obtained and followed.

Additional Debt: Additional parity debt, either by issuance of additional bonds or otherwise, may be issued if the debt service coverage ratio for the most recent fiscal year (adjusted to include the proposed debt service) is at least 1.25 or the report of a management consultant projects a debt service coverage ratio of at least 1.30 for the next three fiscal years.

Call Provisions: No call permitted before November 1, 1997; the bonds may be called at the borrower's option on any interest payment date on or after November 1, 1997, at a premium of 3%, declining 1 percent per annum until the percentage equals par.

the effect that the bonds have been legally issued and that interest on the bonds is exempt from federal income tax. Bond counsel usually orchestrates the issue and assists the underwriter in coordinating the performance by the other parties.

■ Issuer—The issuer, which is a public agency, takes those actions necessary to issue the bonds but otherwise plays a fairly passive role.

■ Issuer's counsel—Issuer's counsel reviews the documents and issues an opinion at closing. As this opinion is usually narrowly drawn and relates largely to the due existence and organization of the issuer and its approval of the transaction, the issuer's attorney usually plays a limited role.

■ Trustee—The trustee under the indenture is responsible for maintaining funds, authenticating bonds, making principal and interest payments, and, in the event of a default, protecting the interests of the bondholders through foreclosure or other remedies. The trustee is concerned that its duties are provided for in a manner with which it is comfortable and that it is indemnified with respect to the acts of other parties.

■ Trustee's counsel—Trustee's counsel advises the trustee with respect to matters of concern to it and may render an opinion at closing.

■ Credit enhancer—The credit enhancer, which may be a bank, insurance company, or other guarantor, agrees to make payments in the event of a default by the borrower. It is concerned that its obligation is set forth clearly and that the transaction as a whole is structured so as to give it adequate security before and after any default.

■ Credit enhancer's counsel—The credit enhancer's attorney drafts the principal credit enhancement documents such as the letter of credit, reimbursement agreement, or insurance contract and negotiates other documents affecting the security or obligations of the credit enhancer. The credit enhancer's counsel also gives an opinion at closing to the effect that the credit enhancer has legitimately entered into the transaction.

■ Accountants—The accountants for the borrower are asked to present audited financial statements and comfort letters, as described below. The accountants may play an important role in ascertaining the effect of the financing on the borrower's financial statements, calculating and

certifying coverage ratios for purposes of qualifying the bond issue under financial covenants, and providing general advice on accounting issues.

■ Feasibility consultants—A feasibility consultant is engaged with respect to a new or expanded facility to assure the bondholders and credit enhancers that the revenue generated by the new project will be sufficient to service the debt. The feasibility consultant's report is usually included in the closing documents and may be incorporated into the official statement or made available to prospective bondholders upon request. The feasibility study should be integrated into the structuring of the transaction rather than prepared after the business terms and nature of the facility have been determined.

■ Rating agencies—Rating agencies review the transaction and assign a rating to the bonds to indicate their assessment of the quality of the investment represented thereby. Rating agencies must approve all documents before giving their ratings; therefore, they receive copies of draft documents and comment on provisions they find unacceptable. Ratings based on the credit of a letter of credit bank or bond issuer are usually given as a matter of course because the underlying credit has already been analyzed by the rating agency. However, a rating based on the credit of a previously unrated borrower will involve meetings with, submissions to, and close governing by the rating agency.

(b) Basic Bond Documents

The issuer—a government agency such as a state or local authority or a city or county government—issues the bonds and usually evidences its determination to do so by adopting two resolutions: an inducement resolution and a final resolution. The issuer adopts the inducement resolution before the transaction is structured to let the parties know that it will look favorably on the bond issue and that the parties can expend time and money to structure the transaction. The inducement resolution also frequently contains an expression of an intent that the borrower will reimburse itself from bond proceeds for expenditures made before issuance of the bonds. Without such a resolution, reimbursement is not permitted; with such a resolution, reimbursement is permitted for certain preliminary costs and for other costs incurred beginning 60 days before adoption of the resolution. When the required documents are in substantially final form and the principal amount and other terms are substantially established, the issuer adopts the final resolution, which approves the documents and authorizes officers of the issuer to execute them.

The bonds are issued in accordance with the terms of an indenture, which is a trust agreement between the issuer and a trustee, the latter usually being a substantial bank or trust company. The indenture governs the terms of the bonds, setting forth matters such as the actual text of the bonds, the establishment of various funds to be held and administered by the trustee, restrictions on and conditions of parity debt and additional bonds, repayment and defeasance provisions, and other matters. The indenture usually does not contain particular covenants of the ultimate borrower but pledges as security the borrower's payments to the issuer.

The trustee receives the actual bonds and, once the transaction is closed, authenticates the bonds pursuant to the provisions of the indenture and delivers them to the purchaser, usually one or more investment bankers, pursuant to the terms of a purchase agreement. In recent years, it has become common for bondholders not to obtain possession of the physical bonds; rather, the bonds are held in a broker's "street name," with the actual bonds held by a depository trust company. This arrangement is provided for in the indenture.

The bond purchase agreement is an agreement among the issuer, the purchaser, and the borrower and governs the terms under which the purchaser will purchase the bonds. The agreement contains numerous terms and conditions set forth in great detail and obligates the purchaser to a multimillion dollar expenditure for securities, which the purchaser will sell in the securities markets. Understandably, the purchaser is concerned that the bonds will conform to the standards of that market. Typically, the bond purchase agreement conditions the purchaser's obligations to purchase the bonds on the following:

- the absence of adverse changes of facts on which the transaction was based;

- the borrower's issuance of a letter of representation making certain factual statements regarding the borrower and its operations; and
- the receipt of opinions of counsel, in substantially the form set forth in the purchase agreement, from counsel to borrower, counsel to issuer, counsel to underwriter, counsel to credit enhancer, and bond counsel, as described below.

In the case of counsel to the borrower, counsel opines that the borrower is duly incorporated and in good standing; that it has authorized, executed, and delivered the documents required by the transaction and that such documents are valid and binding against the borrower in accordance with their terms; that the borrower holds title to its property, which is not subject to any nonpermitted encumbrances (in many states, counsel relies on a policy of title insurance); that the transaction does not violate law, the organizational documents of the borrower, or contracts to which the borrower is a party; and that there is no litigation pending that materially affects the borrower other than that which has been disclosed.

In the case of counsel to the issuer, counsel opines that the issuer is a duly organized public agency and has authorized, executed, and delivered the transaction documents and that such documents are valid and binding against the issuer.

In the case of counsel to the underwriter (purchaser), counsel opines that the bonds are exempt from registration under federal securities laws and that the bonds comply with applicable state securities laws.

In the case of counsel to the credit enhancer, counsel opines that the credit enhancement documents have been properly executed and delivered and are enforceable against the credit enhancer.

Finally, bond counsel opines that the transaction documents have been properly entered into and are valid and enforceable and that interest on the bonds is tax-exempt under federal tax laws. Following the Tax Reform Act of 1986, bond counsel's opinion has been expanded to note certain exceptions to the general rule related to tax-exempt status in the case of the environmental superfund tax on corporations and other similar exceptions. In the case of bonds other than 501(c)(3) bonds, tax opinion is further qualified by references to the alternative minimum tax.

A comfort letter from the borrower's auditors brings down the audit to within an acceptable period before the closing (usually five days). This is often referred to as a cold comfort letter because the letter merely states that nothing has come to the attention of the auditor that indicates a substantial change since the date of the audit.

Usually the purchaser has purchased the bonds for resale in the public market. It may sell the bonds by relying entirely on its own personnel, especially if demand for the bonds is strong and the aggregate principal amount is not large. Often, however, the purchaser consists of a syndicate of investment bankers, with one serving as the manager. The manager structures the transaction and receives a fee for that service, and the other investment bankers agree, pursuant to an agreement among underwriters, to take a certain portion of the issue and to sell it by using their own retail facilities.

The purchaser is usually compensated by means of a discount. That is, if the face amount of the bonds is $10 million and the underwriters' discount is 1 percent, the issuer sells the bonds to the purchaser for $9.9 million and the purchaser sells the bonds to investors at par, retaining $100,000 as compensation for its services.

In connection with the transaction, the issuer issues an official statement, which consists of an explanation of the terms of the bond issue; the covenants to which the borrower is subject; the credit enhancement; certain facts about the issuer, the borrower, the credit enhancer, and the project to be financed; and the risks involved in the transaction. The official statement is similar to a prospectus included in a registration statement filed with respect to a public offering of securities under federal securities laws. Tax-exempt obligations, however, are exempt from the registration requirements of a prospectus. Nonetheless, because Rule 10b-5 promulgated under Section 10(b) of the Securities Act of 1934 applies to all offers or sales of securities and prohibits dissemination of inadequate, false, or misleading information to prospective investors, the official statement is the conventional means of providing disclosure in compliance with that law. Even so, in the absence of explicit federal guidelines or approval processes for compliance with Rule 10b-5, the extent and style of disclosure in any official statement is greatly influenced by what appears to be the practice of the investment banking community in recent comparable transactions.

The official statement is distributed in preliminary form before the pricing of the bonds. The preliminary version is called the red herring because of the red printing on the cover warning readers that it is subject to change. On the basis of this document, which explains the bond issue but leaves blank the interest rate and certain other key terms, the investment banker tests the market; when the banker knows on what terms it can sell the bonds, it prices them. Once the terms are established, a final official statement is prepared and disseminated. Rules of the Securities and Exchange Commission require that the final official statement be substantially identical to the preliminary, official statement except for the completion of items.[51] The borrower usually must provide a certificate to that effect.

At closing, the purchaser pays for the bonds by delivering funds to the trustee, which deposits those funds in trust accounts established under the indenture. Occasionally, funds are transferred outside the indenture, such as when prior indebtedness is paid off directly, with a receipt delivered to the trustee. The trustee uses the bond proceeds, as provided in the indenture, to repay prior indebtedness, pay the cost of issuance, pay the credit enhancement fee, and advance proceeds to the borrower.

Proceeds advanced to the borrower are advanced pursuant to an agreement between the issuer and the borrower. While this agreement is usually a loan agreement, it could be an installment purchase agreement or a lease, depending on the structure of the transaction. These latter arrangements are used when the issuer is not permitted by law to make a direct loan but is permitted to purchase and sell or lease and sublease property. In the loan agreement, the borrower obtains the funds from the loan, agrees to repay the bonds, promises to abide by certain restrictive covenants imposed pursuant to the transaction, and is subject to certain default provisions (see §18.3). In the case of a transaction involving a master indenture, the loan agreement contains few restrictive covenants, but the borrower's obligation under the loan agreement constitutes an obligation under the master indenture.

The loan agreement usually contains a cross-default provision, which provides that a default under the loan constitutes a default under the indenture and vice versa and that the borrower has ultimate responsibility for all performance under the transaction except in the case of malfeasance by one of the other parties. The reason for this provision is that the other parties (such as the issuer) are involved in the transaction for the benefit of the borrower, and, ultimately, only the borrower is responsible for the debt. Thus, the loan from the bondholders to the issuer and the loan from the issuer to the borrower are essentially collapsed into one obligation. The only exception to the rule occurs in certain HUD-financed conduit transactions in which HUD insures the loan from the issuer to the borrower and refuses to permit a default under the bond issue to affect its insured mortgage adversely.

Notes

1. I.R.C. §145.

2. I.R.C. §145(b).

3. Pub. L. 105–33.

4. For a discussion of the standards for determination that a retirement home activity is related to an organization's Section 501(c)(3) status, *see* Chapter 9.

5. P.L. 100–647, §5053(a), adding subsection (d) to I.R.C. §145.

6. I.R.C. §145(d)(3).

7. Treas. Reg. §1.141–3(b)(4) Rev. Proc. 97–13, 1997–5 I.R.B. 18.

8. *See* §15.3.

9. H. Rep. 100–795, 633.

10. Advance copy of *Internal Revenue Manual* Supplement (providing instructions for Internal Revenue Service personnel who process exemption applications submitted by charitable organizations that finance facilities with proceeds of tax-exempt bond financing), issued Feb. 16, 1993. *Internal Revenue Manual* 7668(17). *See* Volume II: The CD-ROM for the full text of the instructions.

11. General Accounting Office, Tax Exempt Bonds, Mar. 1991, GAO/GGD–91–50.

12. Larkin, H., "Feds Take Aim at Continuing Care Tax Exemption," *Hospitals,* Sept. 5, 1988, 106.

13. I.R.C. §145(d).

14. H. Rep. 100–1104, §5053(c)(3).

15. 1989–1 C.B. 24.

16. Treas. Reg. §1.103–8(b)(8)(i).

17. Priv. Ltr. Rul. 9711021.

18. Treas. Reg. §1.103–8(b)(4)(i).

19. Priv. Ltr. Rul. 9740007.

20. I.R.C. §142(d)(3).

21. I.R.C. §146.

22. I.R.C. §148(a). For detailed regulations on the arbitrage rules, *see* new Treas. Reg. §1.148 (57 *Fed. Reg.* 20971, May 18, 1992).

23. I.R.C. §103(b)(2).

24. I.R.C. §148(c)(1).

25. I.R.C. §148(c)(2).

26. I.R.C. §148(d).

27. The pre-1986 code permitted a 15 percent reserve, which was adequate for even the highest interest rates prevailing during that period.

28. I.R.C. §148(f).

29. I.R.C. §147(b).

30. *Ibid.*

31. I.R.C. §147(f).

32. I.R.C. §147(g).

33. 26 C.F.R. §1.150–2.

34. That is, a prohibition against calling the bonds for repayment; *see* §18.5.

35. I.R.C. §149(d).

36. I.R.C. §149(d).

37. I.R.C. §149(d)(3)(A).

38. I.R.C. §149(d)(3)(B)(i).

39. Tax Report Bill of 1986 (H. Rep. 3838) Statement of the Managers, pp. II–758.

40. I.R.C. §150(b)(2).

41. I.R.C. §150(b)(3).

42. Treas. Reg. §1.141–12, §1.142–2, §1.150–4.

43. Regarding the historical origin and application of the Establishment Clause, *see* Note, "Establishment Clause Analysis of Legislative and Administrative Aid to Religion," 74 *Colum. L. Rev.* 1175 (1974).

44. For example, the California Health Facilities Financing Authority imposes, pursuant to its enabling act, a "community service obligation" requiring financed facilities to

provide services to a population representative of the community served, including Medicaid patients. Cal. Gov. Code §15459.

45. Generally, municipal corporations can exercise only those powers granted in express words by either an authorizing statute or a charter. 56 *Am. Jur. 2d, Municipal Corporations,* §194.

46. *Marsh Monument Co., Inc. v. U.S.,* 301 F. Supp. 1316 (E.D. Mich. 1969).

47. 1963–1 C.B. 24.

48. Rev. Proc. 82–26, 1982–1 C.B. 476.

49. H. Rep. 100–1104, §5053(b); I.R.C. §148(b)(2)(E).

50. *E.g.,* Cal. Health and Safety Code §§33760, 33760.5, 33335, 52080, 51335.

51. Securities and Exchange Commission Rule §13(c)(2)(12).

The Woods; Little River, California.

16 Conventional Financing

§16.1 In General

Chapters 14 and 15 discussed different forms of government-assisted debt financing that involve government loans, guarantees, or bond issuance. Completely private financing is an option that should be considered for the following reasons:

- It involves no approval by a public agency.
- It may permit greater flexibility in structuring the terms and covenants.
- It may avoid certain fees and expenses.

On the other hand, where they are available and feasible for a particular project, public financing programs usually confer substantial benefits, including lower interest costs, less expensive credit enhancement, and greater access to the capital markets. The decision to use conventional financing or government assistance should be made on a case-by-case basis.

A full discussion of conventional financing (or the conventional aspects of government-assisted financing) would take more space than is available here. Therefore, the following is a brief discussion of certain aspects of conventional financing that are of particular concern to retirement home developments.

§16.2 Sources of Conventional Financing

The sources of conventional financing have traditionally consisted of banks and insurance companies, although the variety of potentially available sources is virtually limitless, including conventional business corporations, individuals, and mutual funds. Recent years have seen the development of a product called mortgage-backed securities (MBSs). MBSs allow a single borrower to use the services of an investment banker to finance a portfolio of multifamily properties on a nonrecourse basis by directly accessing the capital markets. Although currently securitized financing represents only about $37 billion out of $313 billion of debt in the multifamily market, it could represent a growing source of capital.[1]

Financial service and credit companies provide a broad spectrum of financial services, including consumer financing, commercial and industrial financing, real estate financing, specialty insurance, and asset management and leasing. One example of such a company is General Electric Capital Corporation, a $115 billion institution that provides financing to select retirement housing developers and operators. While financial service and credit companies currently focus on funding acquisitions and refinancing, they are considering entry into the financing of new retirement housing developments.

One lender that is actively pursuing the retirement housing market is the National Cooperative Bank, an institution created by Congress to provide financing to cooperatives and community-based nonprofit corporations. Through its NCB Development Corporation, the bank has become interested in the seniors' housing market and makes available predevelopment loans as well as long-term fixed-rate financing. It is investigating the establishment of a HUD coinsurance program whereby it will make financing available for a 30- to 40-year term. The bank is A rated, makes letters of credit available to secure retirement housing bonds, and may support lower-floater transactions.

A recent survey of retirement housing executives asked respondents to identify their one best source for debt financing. The executives responded as follows:

Regional/local bank	39%
Government-backed vehicles	22%
Life insurance company	7%
REITs	7%
Investment banks	6%
Pension funds	1%
Do not use debt financing	3%
Other 13%	

Source: American Seniors Housing Association, 1995 Seniors Housing Industry Executive Survey.

The survey seems to underscore the continuing importance of traditional financing sources such as bank loans and HUD financing.

A developer may approach a lender directly for a loan, especially if that developer enjoys a preexisting business relationship with the lender. Often, a developer finds that reliance on a mortgage broker or other professional is advantageous in that many lenders, particularly insurance companies, turn to a broker for their loans and the broker has contacts that are used to place debt. Frequently, larger loans are placed with a consortium of lenders that has been structured by a broker.

§16.3 Structure of the Transaction

In its simplest form, a conventional financing transaction involves a loan of money from the lender to the borrower and a promise to repay. Usually, the parties execute a document called a loan agreement if the lender is a bank or a note purchase agreement if the lender is an insurance company. The distinction between these terms is historical. Banks perceive their business as that of making loans and insurance companies as that of purchasing investments. References here to a loan agreement encompass both terms.

The loan agreement contains a recital of the nature of the transaction and attaches a form of the promissory note. It establishes the terms and conditions of the closing, including the closing date and location; responsibility for payment of expenses, representations, and warranties of the borrower; and the conditions of closing, which include opinions of counsel and certifications that the warranties and representations recited in the loan agreement remain true as of the date of closing. If the transaction uses a short-form promissory note, the loan agreement includes the terms and conditions of repayment of the note, including interest rates, restrictions on prepayment, and other such terms. The loan agreement contains restrictive covenants relating to the borrower, unless such covenants are contained in some other document such as a deed of trust.

If in the short form, the promissory note contains a basic promise to pay, the interest rate, and some additional terms, but it refers to the loan agreement with respect to the detailed terms. A long-form promissory note contains all the promises to the noteholder without reference to the loan agreement. Even with a long-form note, additional promises, especially those including the business covenants, are found in security instruments such as a deed of trust.

A loan may be a general unsecured promise to pay. This form, especially if coupled with negative covenants precluding the borrower from pledging security to anyone else, may be sufficient. Usually, however, a security arrangement that involves a pledge of an asset or stream of revenue is necessary. The most common form of security is a deed of trust or mortgage on the facility. The deed of trust pledges the facility for the benefit of the lender and restricts the borrowers by requiring maintenance and upkeep of the facility and placing limits on the property's use. In addition, it imposes other covenants on the borrower to protect the security of the lender. Other

Figure 16.1 Example of a Summary of Proposed Terms for a Privately Placed Taxable Debt Issue: $6,000,000, 10% Secured Notes Due 2010

Amount: $3,500,000

Maturity: 2010

Rate: 10%, payable monthly

Closing: January 1988

Repayment: Interest only, payable semiannually until 1990; starting January 1, 1990, equal amortized semi-annual principal and interest payments of $343,668.97

Prepayment: The secured notes are nonrefundable for life; otherwise, they are callable after year seven at a premium equal to the coupon, declining to par at maturity.

Collateral: The secured notes will be collateralized by (i) a first mortgage lien on the _____ Health Center; (ii) a second mortgage lien (junior only to an existing first mortgage lien securing no more than $1 million of debt due 1991 owing to _____, which lien will not be extended) on the _____ retirement residence; and (iii) an assignment, subject only to the prior lien, if any, of _____ as in (ii) above, of owner's fee simple interest in the land (the "premises") on which these buildings are situated together with all improvements, equipment, furniture, and fixtures owned by owner and located on the premises (the "collateral"). Lender will be named as a loss payee as its interests appear on policies insuring the collateral against such risks as customary and appropriate but in any event in an amount sufficient to prepay the secured notes in the event of a casualty.

Use of Proceeds: The proceeds will be used to refund a like amount of debt owing to former lender and to fund the expenses of this transaction.

Special Counsel:

Principal Covenants: On a consolidated basis:

(1) The annual long-term debt service coverage ratio (sum of: (i) revenues less expenses (expenses to include capitalized development expense); (ii) depreciation, amortization, and the write-off of noncash development expenses deducted as an expense; (iii) debt service deducted as an expense; and (iv) cash accommodation fees received less the amount amortized divided by debt service (interest and principal)) shall not be less than 1.25:1, and owner shall levy charges sufficient for this purpose;

Continued→

security devices, such as a pledge of personal property and a pledge of funds and accounts, may be required. In a life-care facility, a pledge of the escrowed entrance fees may be requested.

See Figure 16.1 for an example of the terms for a conventional retirement community financing.

§16.4 Securitized Loans

Securitized debt transactions, particularly for refinancing and acquisition (but not as readily for new construction), are now used to finance retirement housing. As an indication of the investment commu-

Figure 16.1 **(continued)**

Principal Covenants (continued):

(2) The current ratio (adjusted to include unbilled receivables due within 30 days and to exclude from current maturities long-term debt all but three months thereof) maintained at 1.3 to 1.0;

(3) The sum of cash, marketable securities, and the available unused portion of bank revolvers shall not be less than $1.5 million;

(4) The fund balance (total assets less total liabilities) shall not be less than $17 million plus the sum of: (i) a cumulative amount equal to 100% of excess revenues over expenses (without regard to losses); and (ii) an amount equal to the difference, from time to time, between the current value basis as acceptable by owner's independent auditor of properties and equipment and the book value of such property and equipment on an original depreciated cost basis;

(5) The ratio of total liabilities to fund balance shall not be greater than 1:1, accounting for properties and equipment using current value basis as acceptable by owner's independent auditor;

(6) No liens will be incurred except (i) those existing at 9/30/87; (ii) those incurred in the ordinary course of business other than to secure debt for money borrowed; (iii) those in connection with lender's collateral; (iv) purchase money liens on after acquired property, including improvements that lien will secure debt limited to the cost of the property and improvements and that may extend to encumber the assets to which the improvement is an integral part; and (v) extensions and renewals of the above (except for the lien in favor of _____ on the _____ retirement residence, which lien may not be extended or renewed); and

(7) Owner will maintain its status as a nonprofit public benefit corporation and will maintain its present line of business.

(8) Guarantees will be treated as debt and will be further limited to 1% of the fund balance.

(9) Restricted payments are limited to 5% of total assets.

(10) Mergers are permitted only if the survivor is a U.S. nonprofit public benefit corporation, is exempt from taxation as an organization described in Section 501(c)(3) of the Internal Revenue Code, assumes this obligation, and, on a pro forma basis, no default or event of default exists.

(11) Sale of assets, other than in the normal course of business, are limited to 5% of total assets in any one year.

---

nity's growing appetite for this product, approximately $160 million of seniors' housing securitized transactions were completed in 1990, whereas, thanks to the large RTC portfolio transactions, nearly $1 billion of seniors' housing and residential health care securitized transactions were closed in 1992. In 1993, the level dropped to $700 million as a result of the diminished RTC inventory but included a $200 million Daiwa Securities transaction covering 61 loans, 70 percent of which were rated A or better. In 1993,

Nomura Securities International, Inc., offered $167.5 million in Congregate Care Mortgage Pass-Through Certificates, Series 1993–1, which represented undivided interests in a trust fund consisting primarily of 33 conventional fixed-rate, monthly-pay balloon payment mortgage loans on congregate residences managed by Holiday Retirement Corp., the nation's largest operator of seniors' housing communities.

To date, major securitized loan financings have been limited to single-borrower entities with multiple assets that can be cross-collateralized and cross-defaulted. Loan-to-value ratios have ranged from 65 to 70 percent and debt service coverage from 1.25 to 1.45, depending on factors such as the number of properties in the portfolio, the age and quality of the properties, the consistency of portfolio net operating income, and the geographic diversification of the properties.[2]

Securitized loans are offered by "conduit lenders" that originate, underwrite, and close the loans. While retaining servicing, these lenders sell each loan to an investment banker that warehouses the loans until a pool of $150 to $250 million is formed, at which point the pool is securitized and sold.[3]

Notes

1. Greco, M., "Mortgage-backed Securities Financing Gains Popularity," *National Real Estate Investor,* Jan. 1993.

2. American Seniors Housing Association, *Seniors Housing Finance: Trends and Prospects,* 1992, p. 35.

3. "Conduit Financing: A Road Map," *Multi-Housing Newsletter,* Apr. 1993.

RiverMead Retirement Community; Peterborough, New Hampshire.

Courtesy of Tsomides Associates Architects Planners; Newton Upper Falls, Massachusetts; Photographer: Hutchins Photography; Watertown, Massachusetts

17 Ratings and Credit Enhancement

§17.1 In General

Lenders judge debt on the basis of its quality; higher-quality debt is more attractive and bears a lower interest rate than lower-quality debt. Debt can be either rated by a rating agency or unrated. The quality of debt can be judged solely on the basis of the borrower's strengths and weaknesses, or it can be enhanced by means such as insurance, a letter of credit, or a guarantee.

§17.2 Unrated Debt

Most debt does not carry the credit rating of a rating agency but rather is subject to direct evaluation by the lender or purchaser. Much unrated debt consists of private placements in which the transaction is negotiated directly with the ultimate holder, which independently evaluates the credit of the borrower. Unrated debt may also be offered publicly, in which case purchasers make their decisions based on information disclosed in an official statement, including financial statements and feasibility analyses prepared by reputable consulting firms.

With private loans, the lenders are often banks or insurance companies that have set forth well-defined underwriting criteria that they expect their borrowers to follow. Likewise, privately placed bond issues are usually sold to one or more of a small number of institutional buyers that have specific standards for transactions. Thus, the standards that the borrower is expected to meet and the business covenants that are written into the loan documents are often rigidly prescribed and not susceptible to much negotiation.[1] In most cases, however, these standards can be negotiated to fit the circumstances of individual transactions.

§17.3 Rated Debt

Most publicly offered debt is rated by prominent rating agencies that assign a rating based on standard criteria developed by the agency. The criteria include several factors such as financial performance projections, the nature of the business, strength of management, characteristics of the service area, and the terms and conditions of the debt itself. Thus, where the rating is based entirely on the borrower, the rating agency inquires into the strength of its management, the demand for its services and the potential for growth in demand, the prevalence and strength of its competitors, and numerous other factors. The rating agency also imposes strict standards on the debt itself and requires certain covenants, such as those relating to debt service coverage ratios, insurance, and establishment of reserves.

The most prominent rating agencies are Standard & Poor's and Moody's Investors Service. Until recently, neither rated debt associated with retirement communities or nursing facilities. Standard & Poor's, however, now rates retirement community debt, citing improvements in the industry such as standardization of accounting and financial reporting policies, increasing state regulation, and the movement by many operators toward contracts that reduce health care liability. To obtain a Standard & Poor's rating, a facility must be well established and demonstrate an occupancy level of 90 percent or more; engage an experienced management team and a committed and credible sponsor; and exhibit adequate financial performance (such as cash reserves equaling 50 percent of long-term debt, appropriate debt service coverage, a positive fund balance, and less than 80 percent debt to total capital). Fitch Investors Service also rates life-care facilities and imposes the conditions set forth in Figure 17.1. Standard & Poor's has announced that it has developed criteria for use in rating bonds for low-income multifamily housing projects owned by either nonprofit or for-profit entities. Factors considered in rating these bonds include debt service coverage ratios; stated support of a federal, state, or local government; projections of financial feasibility; evaluation of the property ownership and management structure; evaluation of environmental concerns; project marketability; outcome of site review; reserves; and overflow in debt service coverage. Other factors include property management teams with extensive experience and successful track records and regulatory oversight.

§17.4 Bond Insurance

Bond insurance constitutes a contract whereby one of several bond insurance companies agrees to make required payments of principal and interest in the event that a borrower defaults. Once debt is insured, purchasers generally evaluate it according to the strength of the insuring entity. Thus, debt insured by an insurance company with a rating of AAA trades at AAA interest rates, even though the borrower's rating, standing alone, might not be as favorably treated. Examples of insurers are the federal govern-

ment,[2] state agencies,[3] and private insurance organizations (such as AMBAC and MBIA).

In determining whether to purchase bond insurance, a borrower should calculate the present value cost of issuing debt based on its own credit and compare it with the present value cost of issuing the debt with bond insurance. Bond insurance should be purchased only if a savings results. Sometimes borrowers whose debt can obtain an investment-grade rating are better off purchasing bond insurance because the interest rate savings resulting from a bond insurer's rating (e.g., an A– credit can upgrade to AAA through insurance) could produce more net present value of savings than the cost of the insurance.

§17.5 Letters of Credit

An irrevocable letter of credit is a commitment on the part of a bank to advance funds to a named party upon application by that party under certain prescribed circumstances. A letter of credit can serve as a form of credit enhancement if it is purchased by the borrower in favor of the lender or the lender's trustee and is to be drawn upon in the event that the borrower defaults. Because the letter of credit is irrevocable, the bank remains committed to advance funds even if the borrower is in default and, at the time of the default, has no means of making payment. Banks enter into this type of arrangement for a fee, usually in the form of a one-time commitment or participation fee plus an additional annual fee ranging from 0.5 to 1.5 percent of the total amount payable under the letter of credit, payable by the purchaser of the letter of credit. Letters of credit are not available on a long-term basis but rather can be obtained for a maximum term of five to seven years and must be renewed from time to time, resulting in some uncertainty. For this reason, a letter of credit cannot be used with respect to long-term fixed-rate debt. A letter of credit can, however, be used for long-term variable-rate debt; if at expiration it has not been extended or replaced, the letter of credit can be drawn on for the purpose of calling the bonds.

A letter of credit is issued pursuant to the terms of a reimbursement agreement, whereby an obligor, usually the borrower or a corporation related to the

Figure 17.1 **Fitch Rating Guidelines for CCRCs**

1. *Presale:*

   A minimum number of apartment units are required to be presold, as explained below, at the time of the rating application. The presale should be evidenced by a deposit at least equal to 10% of the entrance fee. It is suggested that not more than 80% of the 10% deposit or $1000, whichever is higher, is refundable prior to the date the apartment unit is available for move-in. This requirement has been established to ensure a "valid" presale and to verify the existence of a "Market." Exceptions can be made to the above penalty refund requirements for reason of death or health or applicable state legislation.

   A. A corporation which has been in operation for 5 years or less is required to have a minimum of 60% of the entire project being financed, presold at the time of the rating application.

   B. A corporation which has been in operation for more than 5 years is required to have a minimum of 50% of the entire project being financed, presold at the time of the rating application.

   C. A multi-corporate operator or multi-facility corporation which has been in operation for 5 years or more will have a required presale established by Fitch after a review of the most recent 5 years of certified audited financial statements and related statistical information. The presale will range between 40% and 60% at the sole discretion of Fitch.

2. *Entrance Fees:*

   Entrance fees and any equity contributions should generate an amount equal to 60% of the total project costs excluding the debt service reserve fund and funded interest. This requirement can be changed upward or downward at Fitch's sole discretion depending upon the scope of the services that will be offered at the facility.

3. *Escrowed Funds:*

   A minimum percentage of the entrance fees must be escrowed and restricted for specific purposes.

   A. An organization which has been in operation for 5 years or less:

      (1) During start up and construction, a minimum of 85% of the received deposits/entrance fees are to be escrowed until the project is completed and operating. The 85% of the received deposits/entrance fees can only be used for refunds. The remaining 15% of the received deposits/entrance fees may be used for an initial working capital reserve fund.

      (2) Upon completion of the construction and commencement of operations, 80% of all the received deposits/entrance fees must be escrowed and restricted for refunds, debt service, additional working capital (to be considered a loan and repaid within 24 months), and plant, property and equipment replacement.

   B. An organization which has been in operation for 5 years or more will be required to escrow a minimum percentage of received deposits/entrance fees. The required escrow percentage will be established by Fitch after a review of the most recent 5 years of certified audited financial statements and related statistical information is considered. The range for this requirement will be between 40% and 80%. The restriction in A.(2) above will then apply.

4. *Debt Service Reserve Fund:*

   A minimum of one year's maximum annual debt service is to be funded at the time of the closing for the bond issue, or, in lieu thereof, an irrevocable Letter of Credit must be obtained from a bank or bankholding company, acceptable to Fitch and/or rated "AA" or higher by Fitch, for the full amount or for any deficit in this Fund. The Letter of Credit must remain in effect until such time the Debt Service Reserve Fund has been fully funded from other sources (i.e., equal to the maximum annual debt service requirement).

Continued→

Figure 17.1 **(continued)**

5. *Reserve Ratio:*

   Facilities which offer any type of health care guarantees of service that are not completely covered by patient/resident charges are required to produce and maintain a ratio of Total Cash Reserves (inclusive of Letters of Credit) available to Total Debt (Reserve ratio) equal to the higher of a minimum of 35% of outstanding total debt or at least 3 times the amount of the annual debt service (principal and interest). Facilities which offer any type of health care guarantees/services and completely cover such related costs through user charges or a facility which does not offer any type of health care guarantees/services could possibly have a lower minimum reserve ratio requirement determined by Fitch.

6. *Funded interest:*

   Funded Interest during construction must be equal to the anticipated interest expense during the construction period. It is favorable to have three to six months of additional interest expense also funded. Upon completion of the project, any excess Funded Interest should be transferred from the designated Funded Interest account to an appropriate debt reduction account or applied to completion of construction. The three to six additional months of funded interest requirement can be changed due to Federal, State or State agency requirements.

7. *Project Participants:*

   A. The architect, the construction company, the management company, the marketing/developer group, the feasibility consultant, and the investment banker must have prior experience in CCRC projects or related types of projects. The experience and track records of the above mentioned project participants, as well as the costs associated with the project, will be heavily scrutinized.

   B. The construction company must have a guaranteed maximum price type contract with a daily penalty clause equal to the minimum of the daily interest expenses if the construction is not completed on time.

   C. Professional management should be obtained by contractual arrangements to operate the facility. The management fees must be subordinated to debt service.

   D. Should contractual arrangements not be made with outside professional management and an individual is selected as administrator, he/she must have a successful track record of prior management responsibilities and experience at a CCRC or related types of projects. Verifying information must be made available to Fitch.

   E. Only a marketing/developer group with prior successful experience in marketing and developing CCRC's will be considered. Their fees and method of compensation will be reviewed.

   F. The feasibility consultant should be nationally recognized (regionally recognized consultants will be considered) and have prior experience with the preparation of feasibility studies of successful CCRC projects.

8. *Residency Contract:*

   Residency contract should provide for the following:

   A. Maintenance/monthly service fee increases to be made at management's sole discretion. The fee increases should not be limited in any way by the contract.

   B. Minimum entry age should be set at 62 years. If a husband and wife enter the facility at the same time, the older spouse should be at least 62 years of age.

   C. Apartment entrance fee refund provisions should not exceed a pro-rated 5-year period. Justified alternative prorated periods will be considered.

   D. A refund should not be paid until the resident's unit is resold.

   E. Resident's lien, if any, must be subordinated to lender's lien.

   F. It is not expected that the contract provide for acute care health services (hospitalization). However, consideration will be given to those contracts which do provide for acute care health services where adequate resident health insurance or participation in a Health Maintenance Organization (HMO) is required.

Continued→

Figure 17.1 **(continued)**

9. *Marketing of the Apartment Units:*

   We will review the marketing strategy and actual performance of the marketing efforts to date. Our analysis of the marketing strategy will include, but are not limited to, the review of the following components:

   A. Type of marketing techniques utilized (i.e., direct mail, television, radio, etc.).

   B. Number of sales people involved with the project.

   C. The direct sales approach developed and used.

   D. How the sales people are compensated.

   E. Number of accepted resident applications.

   F. Comparison of monthly acceptance resident applications versus monthly projections from inception to date.

   G. A review of the average age of accepted residents to date. (This is an important component since the actual average age of accepted residents will help support the turnover/attrition assumptions in the feasibility study.)

10. *Financial Screening Criteria:*

    The criteria used to screen the prospective resident's financial ability to meet his/her future needs and obligations will be reviewed. It is favorable that the prospective resident not need to rely upon the sale of his/her home to meet the entrance fee requirement. A qualifying prospective resident's initial monthly service fee should not be in excess of 50% of that prospective resident's monthly income. The screening should be done by a Board Committee *not by a developer.*

11. *Nursing/Health Care Facility:*

    A. If the residency contract includes the provision for nursing care, then this nursing care facility must be provided either as a part of the retirement community or by contractual arrangements with an affiliate offering a similar quality life style as offered at the resident's facility. Also, if it is part of the retirement community, the organization must have an *unrestricted* "Certificate of Need" (CON) from the appropriate health planning agency. Should any other type of "Certificate of Need" be issued (i.e., conditional or restrictive), such conditions or restrictions applicable to such issued "Certificate of Need" will be reviewed by Fitch as to the reasonableness of such conditions/restrictions and the acceptance of such conditions/restrictions will be made solely by Fitch.

    B. If the residency contract provides for nursing care services not covered by the monthly service fee, then the potential health care liability must be covered by an established health care fund which is adequate to cover such deficit on an on-going basis.

    C. The number of nursing beds to residency units should not ordinarily exceed a 1 to 4 ratio or 20% of the total resident population, whichever is less. Should the total nursing beds exceed this ratio, justification is required.

12. *Feasibility Study:*

    A feasibility study prepared by a nationally recognized consulting/CPA firm with experience in CCRC's is required. It is also required to submit a copy of any and all feasibility studies which were prepared in connection with the proposed project. In addition, an actuarial study should be conducted, by an organization experienced in the preparation of such studies, to provide the residents' mortality and morbidity assumptions for the feasibility study based upon the residents' characteristics gathered from a minimum of 50% of the presales. The feasibility study should present the following in addition to the usual financial, demographic, and statistical information.

    A. Market area including population characteristics for the over-age-65 groups preferably in 5 year increments with income/assets statistical ranges.

    B. A survey result of the existing presold prospective residents as to the number dependent upon sale of their homes before the entrance fee requirement can be made. In addition, we require the number of residents who do not need to sell their homes in order to pay the full entrance fee and will not satisfy the entrance fee requirement until their home is sold.

Continued→

Figure 17.1 **(continued)**

C. Resident turnover, segregated by reason for (i.e., death, health, etc.) and utilization of the nursing facility, both on a permanent and temporary basis.

D. A review of the screening criteria utilized and their opinion of its reasonableness.

E. Marketing of units as of the date of the study, by month.

F. Information regarding area competitionboth for the residential units and the nursing facility. This would include any CON's or Permits in process.

13. *Legal Provisions:*

The following should be included in all appropriate legal documents and other provisions required as necessary:

A. *Annual Reports*—We require that the name, Fitch Investors Service, Inc., be included in the appropriate legal documents to receive the annual certified financial statements *and* other information as may be reasonably requested within 120 days of year end.

B. *Rate Covenant*—We require a rate covenant of at least 110% based upon revenues available for debt service on a cash flow basis from annual operations to commence by the third full year of operation. The rate covenant should not include the entrance fee reserves in the calculation even though they are available. If debt service coverage falls below a 110% level, it then becomes mandatory to retain a consultant to make appropriate recommendations. Also, Fitch's name is to be included in this section to receive a copy of the management consultant's report.

C. *Security*—The Bonds should be secured by a revenue pledge and grant the bondholders a first mortgage lien.

D. *Maintenance of reserves at an adequate level*—This would include the entrance fee reserve fund, debt service reserve fund, health care liability fund, plant, property and equipment replacement fund, and maintenance fund.

E. *Additional Debt Test*—The Additional Debt Test should be reasonable but sufficiently restrictive to ensure that the bondholders are adequately protected. The tests should be based upon a debt service coverage test and others, as may be appropriate.

F. Allowances should be provided for completion bonds.

G. *Actuarial Update*—An Actuarial Analysis is required to update the mortality and morbidity study every 3 years until the facility reaches maturity, after which, the minimum requirement will be for every 5 years until the bonds are called or mature. The update studies must be conducted on only the residents then living in the financed project.

Source: Reproduced with permission from Fitch Investors Service, Inc.

borrower, agrees to reimburse the letter of credit bank for draws under the letter of credit. Usually, a drawing that is required to permit the trustee to purchase demand bonds is not immediately reimbursable, but if the bonds cannot be remarketed within a reasonable amount of time (e.g., 90 days), the obligation is converted to a term loan and is repayable at a specified interest rate (usually pegged to the bank's prime rate) over a fairly short period of time. Drawings for other purposes, such as those necessary to pay principal and interest or to repay the bonds upon default, are repayable immediately, thus giving the bank immediate rights since the draw-

ings are a good indication that the debt is deteriorating rapidly.

The reimbursement agreement is the vehicle whereby the letter of credit bank obtains security for its advances and imposes covenants on the borrower that are more stringent than those imposed under the principal transaction documents. It is advisable for the more stringent covenants to be placed in the reimbursement agreement rather than in the document in which the bondholders have an interest (such as the indenture or loan agreement) because it is easier to obtain waivers and consents from the bank than from several thousand bondholders. In addition, changes in the covenants may be introduced on expiration or termination of the letter of credit by substituting a new letter of credit.

The letter of credit bank usually requires security for the reimbursement obligation over and above that of the promise of the obligor. The bank usually demands the following:

- Pledge of the tendered bonds held by the trustee —If the drawing is for the purpose of repurchasing tendered bonds, the bank is entitled to acquire those bonds on the occurrence of a default, giving it the advantage of the security pledged for the benefit of bondholders.
- Deed of trust—The deed of trust usually encumbers the facility financed by the bond issue, but it may cover other property deemed necessary. The lien is usually on a parity basis with that in favor of the bondholders.
- Other security interests usually on a parity basis with bondholders—These interests may include liens on gross revenues.

§17.6 Guarantees

A guarantee can serve somewhat the same function as bond insurance in that it constitutes the promise by a third party to repay the debt; therefore, if the third party is more creditworthy than the borrower, the debt should be more attractive to the lender.

One effective type of guarantee arrangement consists of a master indenture, whereby two or more corporations agree to cross-guarantee the obligations of other parties to the master indenture. These obligations are secured on a parity basis with all other such obligations, and the holders have recourse against any member of the obligated group, not only the member that originally incurred the debt.

A master indenture typically involves a pledge of gross revenues of the obligated group (all the parties to the master indenture) and, rather than pledging a security interest in real and personal property, contains a negative pledge, whereby each party agrees not to encumber any, or at least most, of its property. The master indenture form of security offers substantial flexibility when the organizational structure of the business involves several affiliated corporations, the businesses of which are aggregated for purposes of borrowing.

Other forms of guarantee may involve the extension of credit by the manager of the financed facility (for example, for working capital) or a guarantee by the owner or parent company of the borrower.

§17.7 Underwriting Considerations

In any line of business, whether for-profit or non-profit, the likelihood of securing debt or equity financing depends on how the investor perceives the prospects of the financed enterprise. As noted in §§17.2 and 17.3, investors and/or rating agencies evaluate credit on the basis of several factors. Unfortunately, retirement homes in general and life-care facilities in particular are difficult credits to analyze, and many investors, rating agencies, and credit enhancers are not confident that adequate underwriting standards exist to evaluate their risk.

A facility that provides accommodation only or accommodations with meals and some services will be evaluated as a real estate investment, with an emphasis on the value of the facility and the local rental market. Assisted-living facilities and skilled-nursing facilities will be evaluated as businesses, with emphasis on factors such as quality of management, liquidity, and production of surplus revenue over expenses. Continuing-care or life-care facilities are evaluated as businesses, with additional concern about actuarial factors. Although CCRCs are often viewed as risky,[4] application of appropriate underwriting standards can mitigate much of the perceived risk.

The following risk factors are among those that have been identified:

- Existing facilities—When an existing successful facility is refinanced or financing is obtained for a moderate expansion of such facility, risk is minimal because the viability of the facility and its financial performance have already been ascertained. Instead of a feasibility study, in most cases the facility need only demonstrate its ability to service the new debt, given continuation of its past performance.

- Presales—The probability of a CCRC's success can be improved by a requirement of substantial presales. Provided they are accompanied by a substantial (e.g., 10 percent or higher) nonrefundable deposit, presales are an indication of market acceptance. Successful projects have achieved at least 50 percent presales, with average presales of over 70 percent. Unsuccessful projects have achieved presales below 50 percent. Presales requirements of 50 to 60 percent are common. Preleasing of a rental retirement facility is usually not required.
- Experience—Not surprisingly, successful projects were more often developed by established operators with substantial experience. The defaulted projects were often developed by organizations with no experience with retirement facilities. Successful experience in rental real estate development does not indicate the necessary expertise to develop and operate a retirement community. In such cases, engagement of an experienced manager may be required.
- Feasibility study—The assumptions that underpin the feasibility study are important. A project may look good on paper, but unrealistic projections of rapid fill-up can overstate the cash flow and debt service coverage ratios. A careful lender or credit enhancer will question these assumptions. Moreover, the existence of a "safe" number of elderly people in the service area who can afford the project does not end the inquiry. Pricing and location must be attractive enough to induce them to buy. Has the feasibility consultant completed a competent market analysis? If the feasibility consultant works from the assumptions provided by management, he or she may not be in a position to analyze the market independently. However, a responsible feasibility consultant will conduct a market study and advise the owner regarding the optimum configuration and pricing of services.
- Hard costs to total debt—Defaulted projects have tended to demonstrate a lower ratio of hard costs to total debt, with significantly higher fees paid out to developers, consultants, and investment bankers.
- Health care and charity care risk—While the actuarial risk of providing health care (in the case of full-service plans) and charity care is conventionally perceived as a major peril of loans to Section 501(c)(3) organizations, such risks have not historically resulted in defaults. When a facility provides full coverage of health care, it should maintain adequate reserves and consider carrying "stop loss" insurance coverage. When the sponsor provides health care services but charges on a fee-for-service basis, risk relates to the financial capacity of the resident. The financial capacity and charity care risk can be mitigated by appropriate resident selection criteria, resident contracts that permit revision of monthly fees to meet rising costs, and a modest reserve for charity care.
- Accommodation fee fluctuations—A startup CCRC counts on initial accommodation fees for its initial capital, funding reserves, and a portion of construction and development costs. Revenues from resales of units go to ongoing facility operations. In the case of large multifacility operators, resales revenues are fairly constant from year to year. Smaller facilities, however, are likely to experience significant year-to-year fluctuations, with the swings accentuated in inverse proportion to project size. A year with low resales could result in net income that is low enough to cause a violation of the corporation's rate covenant (see §18.3(d)), thereby leading to a loan default or, worse, the corporation's not having sufficient operating funds. A succession of two or three such years is not uncommon and could be disastrous. Therefore, the corporation could be required to maintain a resale reserve fund as part of its overall reserves, which it could draw on in lean years and replenish out of subsequent resales in excess of projected levels. Most important, proceeds of the fund could be counted in ascertaining debt service coverage ratios.

Notes

1. *See* summary of typical business covenants in Figures 15.1 and 16.1.

2. Through various FHA programs; see Chapter 14.

3. Such as the California Health Facility Construction Loan Insurance Program. Cal. Health and Safety Code §436 *et seq.*

4. Nationwide, there are approximately 700 continuing-care retirement communities. According to the GAO study (see §15.2), of the 271 bond issues totaling $2.8 billion that were issued from 1980 through July 1990, the overall estimated default rate was about 20 percent. This figure is sufficient to cause investors and insurers to consider the CCRC business risky. The question is whether it is possible to distinguish in advance the good projects from those that are likely to fail. If standards are available to evaluate projects, then investors and insurers can proceed with confidence. Fortunately, the past several years have seen the identification of risk factors and the development of standards to protect against failure (see also §5).

Town Park Towers; San Jose, California.

18 Debt Terms and Covenants

§18.1 Variable-Rate Versus Fixed-Rate Debt

Traditionally, long-term capital debt bears a fixed interest rate that is established at the time the debt is incurred. In recent years, however, a substantial market has developed for variable-rate debt. Understanding why a borrower may choose variable-rate debt requires a look at the economics of the capital markets as they have worked during the past several years. Except in unusual circumstances (such as when a long-term deflationary trend is perceived), lenders prefer short-term debt to long-term debt because it provides them with greater flexibility in avoiding adverse interest rate trends. The price they pay for this flexibility is that they cannot lock in favorable rates and must accept lower interest rates. For example, when interest on bonds is readjusted to market every 30 days and sells at 4 percent, long-term debt with an equal rating may sell at 7 percent. As a result, many borrowers find it worthwhile to explore variable-rate debt. On the other hand, if borrowers perceive that interest rates are abnormally low, they may desire to lock in low long-term rates. Furthermore, borrowers who operate facilities with fixed sources of revenue may want to avoid interest rate fluctuations that could result in high and unpredictable rates, even though variable-rate debt historically offers, on average, a lower rate than fixed-rate debt.

(a) Publicly Offered Variable-Rate Debt

Variable-rate debt is usually structured with the use of variable-rate demand bonds, although a variable-rate note to a bank or other financial institution may be used. In the case of a variable-rate note, the interest rate is established by reference to a standard, such as the bank's prime rate. In the case of demand bonds, bonds are issued bearing an interest rate that is good for a short period, such as 30 days. Every 30 days, a remarketing agent, usually an investment banking firm, establishes a new interest rate that is good for the next 30 days. The remarketing agent sets the rate at the lowest level possible that will permit the bonds to be marketable. The bondholders are notified of the rate and, on short notice, may put the bonds back to a trustee or tender agent (if the trustee is not located in New York City) and obtain repayment of the principal. If the bondholders put the bonds back, the remarketing agent is required to resell the bonds to another investor. Thus, it is essential to establish the appropriate interest rate in order to avoid giving bondholders a disincentive to hold the bonds and to ensure that the remarketing agent can remarket the bonds once they are put back.

Because the borrower is unlikely to have sufficient cash on hand to repurchase the bonds on short notice, it must provide for funds in advance to repurchase the bonds expeditiously in the event that it cannot sell them immediately. To this end, the borrower provides a liquidity facility in the form of a bank letter of credit. The trustee can draw on the letter of credit to repurchase the bonds. If the bonds are resold, the bank is repaid; if the bonds are not resold in a reasonable period, the bank either makes a term loan (on extremely unfavorable terms) or purchases the bonds directly (also on extremely unfavorable terms). Because the bondholders look to the bank to repay the bonds if they decide to sell them, the liquidity facility may also serve as credit enhancement on the bonds,[1] although in some cases a guarantor bank or a bond insurer provides the credit enhancement.

Unlike fixed-rate bonds, variable-rate bonds are not marketed to individuals and small investors. Rather, they are marketed to large institutional investors—either large corporations needing short-term investments or tax-exempt money market funds. For this reason, the bonds are usually issued in $100,000 denominations. Variable-rate debt usually has at least one conversion feature: the ability to convert to fixed-rate debt. On conversion, an interest rate is established that is sufficient to market the bonds, and the bonds are sold on a fixed-rate basis. At that time, they are converted to the more standard $5,000 denomination. Other possible conversion features include conversion to daily, weekly, monthly, and semiannual periods. Some sophisticated structures permit conversion to short- or long-term periods of any specified length in order to tailor the term of the bonds to the need of the investors. The flexibility resulting from the various conversion features permits the remarketing agent to shop the market for the most attractive interest rates that may be available.

(b) Institutional Variable-Rate Debt

The foregoing discussion involved variable-rate debt structured as a public offering, even though it may be privately placed. A different type of variable-rate debt involves long-term debt with a variable-rate of interest that can be prepaid without premium by the borrower but cannot be put by the lender. This type of arrangement, which most frequently takes the form of taxable privately placed mortgage debt, can be a fairly simple transaction involving a note and a deed of trust. Rather than being based directly on market experience, the interest rate is calculated according to an index that itself reflects market con-

ditions. Such debt is most frequently used for taxable debt, although it has occasionally been used for tax-exempt debt held by a single institution.

(c) When Variable-Rate Debt Should Be Used

Retirement home sponsors have recognized the potential volatility of variable-rate debt and thus exercise caution in its use. While it may be true that variable-rate tax-exempt debt, even during the period of highest interest rates, has not exceeded about 9 percent, the possibility of extremely high rates compared with the relative inability of most retirement homes to levy significant fee increases discourages such financing except for a minor portion of debt. The judicious use of variable-rate debt can, however, significantly lower interest expense. For example, some larger retirement housing owners use a combination of fixed- and variable-rate financing.

In fact, devices have evolved for the purpose of limiting the risk of variable-rate debt while maintaining a substantial amount of its cost savings. One such device is the purchase of an interest rate cap, whereby the borrower pays another institution, such as a bank, a given percentage for assuming the payment of interest over a given cap. Before the Tax Reform Act of 1986, it was possible to lock in a fixed-rate by means of an advance crossover defeasance. A second bond would be issued at a fixed rate and its proceeds used to purchase investment securities at maturities that would yield interest sufficient to service the debt. If the variable-rate interest rose to an unacceptable level, the securities would be liquidated to pay off the variable-rate debt, and the borrower would be obligated only under the fixed-rate debt. The 1986 tax law, however, requires prompt repayment of the old bonds with the proceeds of the new debt, thereby limiting the use of the interest rate cap.[2]

In some cases, borrowers enter into "swap" agreements whereby they swap their variable rate for a fixed rate or their fixed rate for a variable rate. The party on the other side of the transaction is a financial institution that hedges its participation in the contract. It is entirely logical to ask why the borrower does not simply obtain the rate it wants in the first place. As a practical matter, there may be reasons that a swap is desirable. One such instance involves a bond issue that cannot be defeased under the tax laws, although its interest rate can be converted under a swap agreement. In another case, a client may want the benefits of a short-term interest rate but the security of long-term credit enhancement. Such security may not be available for variable-rate transactions because letter of credit banks rarely give a commitment beyond five years. Long-term fixed-rate debt is issued and insured by a bond insurer with the interest rate swapped to variable. Another reason for a swap transaction is that the swap market is capable of offering interest rates lower than those offered by the conventional market. Thus, a borrower could, in the right circumstances, borrow with variable-rate interest and swap to fixed-rate interest and end up paying a lower interest rate than that which the borrower could have obtained by initially borrowing at a fixed rate.

§18.2 Conditions Precedent to Closing

Borrowers must meet certain conditions imposed on them before the financing transaction can be closed. Some of these conditions relate specifically to the transaction itself, such as the receipt of legal opinions and title insurance policies. Other conditions are of broader application and ensure that the borrower and the given project meet the underwriting standards applicable to the transaction.

(a) Conditions Relating to the Financing Transaction

Conditions relating to the financing transaction are largely of a technical nature and need not be explained here in detail. The partial list that follows provides some idea of the various conditions applicable to a transaction:

- Various opinions of legal counsel (see §15.6(a)).
- A policy of title insurance (usually the ALTA [American Land Title Association] mortgagor's policy) that covers the lender, the trustee for benefit of the bondholders, and the credit enhancer, as appropriate. The lender may possibly request one or more endorsements that go beyond the basic

ALTA policy terms. These endorsements, which are standard and are referred to by number, provide additional protection beyond that afforded by the basic policy. Because some lenders are prone to request endorsements whether or not they are needed, borrowers should, given the characteristics of the project, determine which endorsements are reasonably necessary to protect the lender and then negotiate to exclude the others.

- If the financing is to be closed following the commencement of construction, the title insurance policy will probably make an exception for mechanics' liens, which relate to the start of construction. The lender, however, will not want its lien to be junior to mechanics' liens and may reject the exception. If the project is properly bonded, the title company may be willing to remove the exception in consideration of an indemnification agreement provided by the borrower.
- Audited financial statements and comfort letters (see §15.6(a)).
- Financial feasibility study.
- Officer's certificates that are executed by officers on behalf of the borrower and make certain representations of fact. The certificates also may contain conclusions stated in absolute terms, which the borrower may not know absolutely. It may be possible to qualify the statements so that they are represented "to the best of such officer's knowledge." However, in recognition that the borrower has ultimate responsibility to the lender with respect to the debt, lenders usually want representations to be absolute.
- Articles of incorporation of the borrower certified by the secretary of state of the state of incorporation.
- Bylaws of the borrower certified by its secretary.
- A good standing certificate from the secretary of state to the effect that the corporation is in good standing and qualified to do business. If the project is located in a state other than the state of incorporation, it will have to provide a certificate from the secretary of state of the state in which the project is located to the effect that the borrower is in good standing as a foreign corporation qualified to do business in the state.
- A resolution of the borrower approving the trans-

action and authorizing officers of the borrower to execute appropriate documentation.

(b) Presales

In the case of a new facility or a substantial expansion, the lender is obviously concerned about the ability of the borrower to market the new units at the prices indicated in the feasibility study and within the period of time during which capitalized interest is budgeted. Given that facilities with a substantial entry fee are perceived as more difficult to market, lenders understandably desire assurance that the projected occupancy will be met. For this reason, they often require a certain number of units to be presold as a condition of closing. Beyond the presales, lenders require the receipt of substantial nonrefundable deposits to ensure that buyers will be unlikely to back out. A typical closing condition of this type requires a specified number (e.g., 60 percent) of units to be presold with nonrefundable deposits of at least a specified amount.

(c) Construction Contract

In a financing involving new construction or remodeling, it is crucial to know that the project can be built with the amount of financing available. Obviously, an unfinished project generates little revenue, and additional debt to finish a project plagued with cost overruns could be unobtainable or could jeopardize the borrower's financial condition. Therefore, a common condition of closing is that the borrower must have obtained government approval of its plans and specifications and must have entered into a construction contract with a fixed cost of construction or a guaranteed maximum price.

§18.3 Business Covenants

In any financing transaction, the borrower is required to enter into certain agreements, or covenants, designed to restrict its financial operations to assure the lender that the company will continue to operate in a financially responsible manner. Business covenants vary considerably with different types of financing transactions and are occasionally tailored to the peculiarities of the company and project in an individual transaction. Yet, there is enough common ground among the types of transactions that a discussion of covenants in general avoids much repetition that would be involved in discussing the covenants for each type of transaction.

Covenants are usually subject to at least some negotiation. The exception is the case of standards set forth in a federal or state statute[3] or an explicitly nonnegotiable requirement set down by a rating agency, credit enhancer, or lender. In general, the covenants in an unrated public offering offer the borrower the most flexibility. They are established between the borrower and the investment banker, who is interested in satisfying the borrower. The constraints in such a transaction relate to the ability to obtain buyers for the securities on the terms offered and the investment banker's concern about its own reputation.

A rated transaction is subject to covenants prescribed by the rating agency. These covenants are standard among transactions, although the rating agencies may request particular provisions related to the specifics of the transaction. Figure 18.1 sets forth the Fitch Investors Service criteria.

Structuring financial covenants for rated and unrated standalone public offerings requires the utmost care. If a covenant causes problems in the future, it usually can be amended only by obtaining consent from the holders of at least a majority of the debt, which could amount to literally thousands of people, or by defeasing or refinancing the debt, which may be costly or even prohibited by the tax laws or the debt instruments themselves. Therefore, covenants for rated and unrated public offerings are broadly written and are designed to remain appropriate for the life of the debt, even if the borrower undergoes substantial changes.

Such covenants either contain absolute requirements or prohibitions (such as those requiring maintenance of tax-exempt status or the license to operate the facility) or set forth requirements in relative terms (such as ratio tests) so that as the size of the borrower grows or inflation diminishes purchasing power, limitations are adjusted proportionately. Both types of provisions should be considered in light of the potential for changed circumstances. A requirement considered standard a few years ago called for

Figure 18.1 **Borrower's Affidavit (To Be Furnished with Each Advance)**

STATE OF _____,)

: ss.:

COUNTY OF _____)

_____, being duly sworn, deposes and says:

That affiant is the of (the _____ of _____ the "Borrower"), and has made due investigation as to matters hereinafter set forth and does hereby certify the following to induce _____ (the "Lender") to make and advance the sum of _____ ($_____) Dollars to the Borrower pursuant to the terms of a Building Loan Agreement, dated April _____, 19_____ , between the Lender and the Borrower, and Request for Advance number _____, dated _____, 19_____, between the Lender and the Borrower, and Request for Advance number _____, dated _____, 19_____, the day on which this Affidavit is sworn to be affiant, being submitted to the Lender herewith:

1. All representations and warranties contained in the Building Loan Agreement are true and accurate in all material respects as of the date hereof.

2. No event of Default exists under the Building Loan Agreement, the Note, the Mortgage, the Guaranty, or under any other security document, and no event or condition has occurred and is continuing or existing or would result from the advance about to be made which, with the lapse of time or the giving of notice, or both, would constitute such an Event of Default.

3. Construction of the Improvements has been carried on with reasonable dispatch and has not been discontinued at any time for a period of Unavoidable Delay for reasons within the control of the Borrower, the Improvements have not been damaged by fire or other casualty, and no part of the Premises has been taken by eminent domain and no proceedings or negotiations therefor are pending or threatened.

4. Construction of the Improvements is progressing in such manner so as to insure completion thereof in substantial accordance with the Plans on or before the Completion Date.

5. All funds received from the Lender previously as advances under the Building Loan Agreement have been expended or are being held in trust for the sole purpose of paying costs of construction ("Costs") previously certified to the Lender in Requests for Advances; and no part of said funds has been used, and the funds to be received pursuant to the Request for Advance submitted herewith shall not be used, for any other purpose. No item of Costs previously certified to the Lender in a Request for Advance remains unpaid as of the date of this Affidavit.

6. All of the statements and information set forth in the Request for Advance being submitted to the Lender herewith are true and correct in every material respect at the date hereof, and all Costs certified to the Lender in said Request for Advance accurately reflect the precise amounts due, or where such Costs have not yet been billed to the Borrower, the same accurately reflect the Borrower's best estimates of the amounts that will become due and owing during the period covered by said Request for Advance. All the funds to be received pursuant to said Request for Advance shall be used solely for the purposes of paying the items of cost specified therein or for reimbursing the Borrower for such items previously paid by the Borrower.

7. Nothing has occurred subsequent to the date of the Building Loan Agreement which has or may result in the creation of any lien, charge or encumbrance upon the Premises or the Improvements or any part thereof, or anything affixed to or used in connection therewith or which has or may substantially and adversely impair the ability of the Borrower to make all payments of principal and interest on the Note, the ability of the Borrower to meet its obligations under the Building Loan Agreement or to the best of its knowledge, the ability of the Guarantor to meet its obligations under the Guaranty.

Continued→

Figure 18.1 **(continued)**

8. None of the labor, materials, overhead, or other items of expense specified in the Request for Advance submitted herewith have previously been made the basis of any Request for Advance by the Borrower or of any payment by the Lender.

9. The status of construction of the Improvements is as follows:

10. The estimated aggregate cost of completing the Improvements including but not limited to labor, materials, architectural and engineering fees, management, financial and other overhead costs and expenses, does not exceed _____ dollars ($_____).

11. All conditions to the advance referred to above and to be made in accordance with the Request for Advance submitted herewith in addition to those to which reference is made in this Affidavit have been met in accordance with the terms of the Building Loan Agreement.

The capitalized terms used herein have the meaning given thereto in the Building Loan Agreement.

BORROWER

By_____

certain types of insurance to be carried or mandated a nursing facility to be qualified to receive Medicaid payments. Now, many borrowers are insisting on out provisions that, for example, allow self-insurance or no insurance if a consultant certifies that the premium for such insurance is not reasonable or permit a facility to decide not to qualify for Medicaid if the terms of reimbursement are inadequate.

It may be desirable to convert an absolute requirement to a ratio covenant so that changes over time do not distort the covenant's original intent. For example, a prohibition against incurring more than $100,000 of short-term debt could be recast by expressing the limit in terms of a given percentage of net revenue. Even ratio tests should be examined carefully. A requirement calling for satisfaction of a debt service coverage test may seem innocuous if the required ratio is well below the actual existing ratio. If, however, market or regulatory pressures 20 years from now are likely to preclude the maintenance of the ratio, an out provision should be included.[4]

Negotiations with a credit enhancer or with a lender or bond purchaser in a private placement permit greater flexibility in structuring the financial covenants because the party at risk is literally at the negotiating table. Such parties, however, usually fol-

low prescribed underwriting standards and often insist on highly restrictive covenants. They reason that because they deal with only one or a small number of parties, they have the opportunity to come back for approval in the event of a good business reason to obtain waiver of a covenant. Besides a general waiver provision, the documents sometimes contain a provision relating to waiver of specific financial covenants and require the credit enhancer or lender to agree that the waiver should "not be unreasonably withheld." The risk to the borrower of a general waiver provision is that in the event interest rates rise after the transaction is closed, the lender will have an interest in not approving a waiver either to force the borrower to get out of the covenant by paying off the debt or to require the borrower to adjust the interest rate as the price of obtaining the waiver. The borrower wants to eliminate the possibility of such an eventuality, first, by avoiding covenants that may at some future point not lend themselves to compliance and, second, by including in the loan documents requirements that the lender act reasonably, possibly in accordance with certain standards, when responding to requests for a waiver.

Covenants may take the form of straight mandates or prohibitions, such as the requirement that the borrower maintain prescribed insurance or refrain from incurring certain encumbrances. Covenants may also take the form of ratios or prescribed limits that require the maintenance of a prescribed debt service coverage ratio or a specified level of net worth. They may also take the form of an absolute mandate or prohibition coupled with a ratio or prescribed-level exception, such as a prohibition against incurring additional indebtedness, with the exception that such indebtedness may be incurred if, after its incurrence, a prescribed debt service coverage ratio is maintained. The following discusses covenants that are often contained in financing documents.

(a) Limits on Consolidations, Mergers, Sales, or Transfers

A corporation is prohibited from merging or consolidating with another corporation and from dissolving, selling, or otherwise disposing of all or substantially all of its assets unless certain conditions, including those noted below, are met.

- The surviving corporation (if other than the borrower) must agree to assume the borrower's debt obligations.
- The transaction must not result in a violation of the other covenants. In the case of a net worth covenant, for example, the resulting corporation must comply with its terms. Some merger covenants require the new corporation to be capable of incurring at least one dollar of additional indebtedness without violating a covenant. The purpose is to impose additional indebtedness tests on the merger.
- The most common financial restriction on publicly offered tax-exempt debt requires the debt service coverage ratio after the merger to be not less than a specified level. Often, the specified level is the same as that required by the rate covenant, in which case the requirement is merely a statement of the requirement of no covenant breach after the merger. On occasion, however, the ratio is set at a higher level.
- If the borrower is a nonprofit corporation, the successor corporation is required to be a nonprofit corporation with appropriate tax-exempt status. This covenant is particularly important with respect to tax-exempt bonds because the tax-exempt status of the borrower is usually the factor that results in the tax-exempt status of bond interest. Even if the debt is not tax-exempt, the condition usually requires the successor to be a tax-exempt corporation because any change in tax status would significantly change the nature of the transaction while tax-exempt status may result in exemption from property tax and other benefits that would be advantageous from the standpoint of the project.

- If the debt is tax-exempt, an opinion of bond counsel may be required to confirm that the debt will remain tax-exempt and that the borrower's obligations under the bond issue have been properly assumed.
- If the debt is insured or guaranteed or is privately placed, additional tests may be required. For example, the projected long-term debt service coverage ratio (as calculated by an independent consultant) for the next three years must be at least equal to the ratio of the borrower before the proposed transaction while the resulting corporation's net worth must at least that of the borrower.
- In some cases, a lender or credit enhancer may be so concerned about the possible effects of mergers and transfers that it will prohibit them outright or require approval on a case-by-case basis.

(b) Limitation on Encumbrances

Whether security for the debt is a mortgage or deed of trust or a pledge of gross revenues, the borrower typically is prohibited from creating or permitting any liens or encumbrances on the project (usually defined to include the complete facility financed by the proceeds of the indebtedness) and, in some cases, on certain or all of its other properties. Usually, an exception is made for certain liens and encumbrances that are defined as permitted encumbrances, which may include the following:

- various liens, easements, and other encumbrances that typically exist (e.g., mechanics' liens, liens for nondelinquent taxes, easements for utilities) and that do not in the aggregate materially affect the operation of the project;

- occasionally, any encumbrance of record disclosed in the title policy issued in connection with the transaction. Such an encumbrance is favorable to the borrower in that it grandfathers any matters already on record that the parties have not otherwise arranged to remove. It forces the parties to deal with those items that may be objectionable to the lender and eliminates the possibility of open questions of interpretation with respect to preexisting matters;
- liens resulting from the indebtedness itself;
- liens for permitted indebtedness. Often, any lien in connection with other indebtedness, which is junior to the primary indebtedness, is automatically permitted if the other indebtedness itself is permitted under the indebtedness covenant;
- purchase money deeds of trust and security interests. The borrower can acquire real or personal property for which it grants a security interest for all or a portion of the purchase price. In some instances, the amount of the lien is limited to a percentage of purchase price less than 100 percent. In addition, a limit may be imposed as to the amount of the borrower's property that may be so encumbered (e.g., 10 percent);
- nonrecourse indebtedness. The lender's remedies are limited to its lien, and the lender cannot go against the borrower or the property pledged for the principal debt;
- accounts receivable financing. Often, a corporation pledges its accounts receivable as security for short-term debt. Such a pledge requires an exception to the prohibition against liens and encumbrances because it is a form of a pledge of gross revenue. The exception is generally stated in the form of a ratio of secured debt to accounts receivable or annual operating revenue;
- leases and contracts related to the operation of the facilities. The terms of these agreements are usually limited to obligations entered into in the ordinary course of business. For example, resident contracts may constitute a form of an encumbrance covered by this exception;
- the rights of the state under any regulatory scheme. While the residents of a life-care facility usually subordinate their rights to the rights of the bondholders,[5] such subordination may be limited or supplanted by state legislation designed

to protect residents' interests; and
- additional liens and encumbrances that may be approved by the lender or credit enhancer.

(c) Limits on Indebtedness

The ability of a borrower to incur additional indebtedness, whether junior to or on parity with the principal indebtedness, is usually restricted to protect the security of the debt holders. In the case of multifacility borrowers, the lender occasionally imposes restrictions on indebtedness incurred with respect to facilities other than the one financed because of potential adverse impacts on the financed project. The following covenants are typical:

- The borrower may incur parity debt only if it meets a certain debt service coverage ratio (that is, maximum annual debt service compared with net revenue available for debt service). The ratio test is often structured in the form of two alternative tests: a comparison of historical net income available for debt service with the maximum annual debt service for both existing debt and the proposed parity debt; or a comparison— developed by a consultant—of projected net income available for debt service following completion of the new project with maximum annual debt service for both existing debt and proposed parity debt. The ratio for the former is usually less than that for the latter because the former does not depend on yet-to-be-realized revenues. The former test assumes no additional revenues from the new project but may be impossible to satisfy if the object of the borrowing is the development of additional revenue-producing capacity. The latter test yields a higher ratio but permits the borrower to count revenues from the project.
- In the calculation of maximum annual debt service, one point of negotiation is often the extent to which it is necessary to take into account the debt of other corporations that is guaranteed by the borrower. On the theory that the borrower could be liable for the payment of such debt, a conservative lender requires 100 percent of guaranteed debt to be counted. A more generous viewpoint holds that, given the possibility rather than the probability that the borrower will be

called on to pay the debt, only a fraction of the guaranteed debt should be taken into account. Thus, some covenants require debt service to be counted on only 25 percent of guaranteed debt. Another common approach is to vary the percentage of counted debt in accordance with the quality of the prime obligor under the guaranteed debt. Thus, if the prime obligor has a high debt service coverage ratio, the percentage that must be claimed by the guarantor would be small because of the reduced risk and vice versa. Finally, some lenders prohibit guarantees altogether on the theory that the borrower should not guarantee the debt of other companies but rather should devote its assets solely to its own business.

- A privately placed transaction may impose a limit on both the amount of debt and the debt service. Such a limit may be expressed, for example, in terms of a percentage of the original cost of assets, a percentage of appraised value, or other terms.
- Separate tests usually apply to short-term debt. Short-term debt, which is defined as debt not outstanding for one year and requiring that all (or all but a specified minor percentage) must be paid off for a specified period of time each year, is generally limited by some percentage of total annual revenues.

(d) Debt Service Coverage Ratios

The most typical form of ratio covenant is the debt service coverage ratio. It is the ratio of the net income available for debt service to debt service, where "net income available for debt service" is net income as shown on audited financial statements, to which is added depreciation and interest. It is commonly expressed in the rate covenant and requires the corporation to maintain rates sufficient to meet the ratio. The covenant usually includes two important exceptions: a provision for free or reduced-rate services in order to maintain the borrower's tax-exempt status, and a provision that if the required ratio is not met, a management consultant will be retained. In the case of the second exception, if the consultant's report is adopted (assuming that the board of the borrower finds it to be reasonable), the ratio requirement is waived. Yet, even if the consultant's advice is followed, documents typically provide for

a default if the ratio falls below 1.0. Maintenance of the debt service coverage ratio at specified levels can also be used as a condition to incur additional indebtedness and to dispose of property.

(e) Limitation on Disposition of Properties

The borrower is usually limited as to the disposition of properties. The covenant is stated as a general prohibition, subject to certain exceptions, which may include disposition of property in the ordinary course of business as applied to such activities as selling goods to customers; disposition of property that has become inadequate, obsolete, or unnecessary so long as the disposition occurs at fair market value; and a further exception often stated as a percentage of total property, plant, and equipment (e.g., 5 percent during any one year with an aggregate total of 15 percent).

In recent years, it has been a common practice to restructure health care corporations in such a way as to provide for a parent corporation or sister corporations that may not be subject to the indebtedness of the borrower and to require the borrower to pay over surplus cash to such other corporations. In response, lenders have required dispositions of cash to be subject to the foregoing covenants or to separate covenants. A stringent covenant applied to nonprofit corporations requires net worth to be increased each year by an amount equal to net earnings. A more liberal form of this covenant restricts dispositions to a given percentage of net worth or a specified dollar amount each year.

(f) Other Financial Covenants

While the debt service coverage ratio is most frequently associated with both property-backed and gross income-backed debt, credit enhancers and private lenders in particular often require additional covenants that take the form of ratios. The function of the ratios is to test other indicators of financial stability, security, and ability to service the debt. The most common ratios follow:

- Debt equity ratio—Usually applied in the case of debt backed by a security interest in property, the debt equity ratio provides assurance that total debt will not exceed a certain percentage (e.g., 75 percent) of the value of the property. Usually value is book value—acquisition price less depreciation. Some borrowers, especially those owning property that has appreciated considerably since acquisition, have successfully argued for substitution of appraised value for book value.

■ Liquidity ratio—A liquidity ratio, such as "days' cash on hand," assures lenders that the borrower has sufficient cash to pay its obligations as they come due. While the covenant can be useful, it can also be subject to manipulation. For example, a borrower can defer payment of its bills in order to meet the covenant but, in doing so, risks violating the trade payables covenant.

■ Trade payables covenant—This covenant prohibits extending payment of trade payables beyond a certain period (e.g., 90 percent not more than 60 days and 10 percent not more than 90 days).

■ Fill-up requirements—Startup facilities may require covenants related to fill-up and sales, such as percentage of total units sold or occupied. They may set project targets for particular dates or establish conditions to certain events, such as start of construction or release of certain security.

(g) Insurance and Condemnation

The borrower is usually subject to a general obligation to carry insurance of a type and amount customarily carried by like businesses. This obligation has the advantage of offering a degree of flexibility such that if a particular type of insurance is no longer available, the borrower need not carry it. At the same time, though, the standard is vague. Therefore, if challenged, a borrower may be hard pressed to demonstrate what insurance a like business customarily carries.

As an adjunct to the above requirement, the borrower is often required to carry certain types of insurance with certain minimum limits. These include comprehensive property insurance in an amount equal to the lesser of replacement cost or the remaining principal amount of indebtedness; public liability insurance (including, with respect to health care facilities, professional liability insurance) with specified limits; various other types of insurance, including business interruption insurance, boiler insurance,

and fidelity bonds for officers and employees who handle money; and in California, earthquake insurance. Because of the high cost of earthquake coverage and the high coinsurance provisions, borrowers often seek a waiver of this requirement.

The insurance requirement may be subject to a provision that calls for review of the borrower's insurance coverage by a recognized insurance consultant on an annual (sometimes biannual) basis. Given that insurance availability and cost can change over time, the borrower may be permitted to reduce its coverage if the insurance consultant reports that the insurance is not available at a cost that is reasonable in view of the associated risks. Finally, depending on the favorable review of the insurance consultant, the borrower can substitute self-insurance for the required insurance coverage.

(h) Disposition of Insurance and Condemnation Proceeds

Debt instruments treat in detail the disposition of insurance and condemnation proceeds. Such proceeds constitute substitute value for property that otherwise would have secured the debt or provided the means of generating revenue to service the debt. The lender or credit enhancer wants to ensure that the money is used in such a manner as to maximize the borrower's chances of servicing the debt. At the same time, the borrower wants to preserve maximum flexibility in the use of the proceeds. The following is a type of covenant usually encountered when dealing with the disposition of insurance and condemnation proceeds:

■ The most restrictive covenant provides for the proceeds paid over to the lender to be applied as the lender sees fit. In less arbitrary terms, the lender may, at its discretion, apply the proceeds either to repayment of debt or restoration of the premises. Borrowers usually reject this covenant because it gives all power to the lender. They contend that it unfairly permits the lender to change the terms of the debt in exchange for releasing the funds for needed construction. The lender argues that after the destruction or taking of the premises, conditions are changed to such an extent that the lender needs to reassess its status and decide whether repayment of debt or reconstruction makes sense.

- The covenant may give the borrower the right to choose between repayment of principal or reconstruction of the building in substantially its original value, condition, and character. While the agreement gives the lender essentially what it bargained for, the outcome may be inefficient or even absurd from the borrower's point of view. It may be that a building of the same value but different use or character would be more appropriate.

- The covenant may provide for restoration of a facility of equivalent value, thereby permitting the borrower to determine what is built. Such a covenant is certainly necessary when the debt is publicly sold and there is no lender with which to negotiate in the event that a pure replacement project is not appropriate.

- Most covenants permit a certain amount of insurance or condemnation proceeds to be paid to the borrower with no further requirements. The de minimus amount depends on the total size of the facility involved.

- To the extent that proceeds are not otherwise used, they are required to be used to pay the principal on the debt.

§18.4 Timing, Funding, and Disbursements

When obtaining capital for a project, it is necessary to reconcile the needs of the project with the demands of the capital markets. The result is often a transaction whose structure appears unnecessarily complex but that is otherwise essential if the disparate interests are to be served in a single transaction.

(a) Timing

During the course of developing a project, it is never too early to investigate financing options and to incorporate the results of the investigation into the project planning effort. Indeed, feasibility determinations must necessarily include confirmation of the cost and availability of financing as well as its terms and restrictions.

Upon confirmation of the general availability of financing on acceptable terms, project planning can proceed with development of the schematic design. The design makes it possible to determine with a fair amount of precision the economics of the project, including the cost of construction, the cost of operating the project, and the expected revenues. At this point, it is desirable to obtain a commitment for the financing because the next step, the production of working drawings, is an expensive proposition. It may even be desirable to secure some form of bridge financing to ensure completion of the design work. But closing on the financing itself usually must await completion of the working drawings and the execution of a firm construction contract as a condition of obtaining assurances that the project can be completed with the available financing.

(b) Construction Financing and Permanent Financing

In many cases (including publicly offered and tax-exempt debt), project developers secure a single loan that funds construction and remains in place thereafter. More commonly, however, conventionally financed projects rely on two loans: a construction loan and, upon construction completion, a permanent loan. The permanent loan is either in place with its proceeds deposited in escrow or committed before the commencement of construction. In both cases, the proceeds of the permanent loan pay off the construction loan. The reason for the two loan types is that each represents a distinct lending risk for which there are two different capital markets with different objectives. Lenders interested in keeping money out for a short term and at fairly high risk make construction loans. In return, they receive a high interest rate. To manage their risk, they exercise a supervisory role over the project, inspecting the work and disbursing funds only when they are satisfied that progress has been made as represented and that liens have been removed. If the project is not completed as planned, the construction loan may not be paid off with the proceeds of the permanent loan. For its part, the permanent lender desires a low-risk long-term investment. Though the interest rate on the permanent loan is lower, the lender does not bear the risk of construction but instead must bear the risk of the successful operation of the project.

(c) Lender Control of Construction

Given that the construction lender assumes significant risk with respect to completion of the project, lending documents assert various elements of control. The loan documents provide that before loan closing, the construction lender must be assured that the contractor is competent, that a valid and binding construction contract has been executed, that performance and payment bonds are in place, and that provision has been made for reasonable contingencies. During construction, the lender can be expected to inspect the site periodically, keep abreast of and exercise the right to approve changes in the plans or construction contract (or at least be assured that funds are sufficient to pay for such changes), and approve disbursement of loan proceeds. Usually, loan proceeds and such equity as may be necessary to yield the total construction cost are placed into a trust fund for disbursement by the trustee on receipt of a certificate for payment signed by the borrower and the architect.

Occasionally, the lender requires additional documentation at the time of each disbursement, including an endorsement from a title company ensuring that no unpermitted liens have been filed against the property and certificates submitted by the contractor and subcontractors releasing or partially releasing their mechanics' liens.

§18.5 Call Protection and Prepayment Premium

One crucial term of any indebtedness relates to whether the borrower is permitted to call the debt, that is, to repay the principal of the debt before its maturity and, if so, whether a premium is charged for the privilege of so doing. To ensure the equitable treatment of the borrower, the terms of long-term fixed-rate debt often place restrictions on the prepayment of the debt. In the event that market interest increases above that of the debt, the borrower realizes a savings and is therefore unlikely to prepay the debt. If, however, market interest drops below

that of the debt, the borrower has an economic incentive to prepay the debt with the proceeds of less costly debt. Such an outcome is perceived as unfair to the lender in that it locks in an interest rate favorable to the borrower but unfavorable to the lender. From the perspective of the borrower, restrictions on the right to prepay are important because even if the borrower intends to keep indebtedness outstanding for the entire term, unforeseen events—such as lower prevailing interest rates, the need for expansion or renewal, the need to revise business covenants, or the sale of the facility—may make refinancing desirable or necessary.

Call protection is a prohibition against prepayment of debt for a given period of time. In publicly offered tax-exempt, 30-year debt, call protection typically extends for a period of ten years. The final 20-year period is left unrestricted because call protection during that period does not currently buy a borrower a lower interest rate. In a privately placed transaction in which the lender has more bargaining power, the prepayment prohibition may extend for the entire term of the debt. Rather than agreeing to a prohibition against prepayment, the borrower may be permitted to prepay with a prepayment penalty, which is an amount of money in excess of the principal that must be paid in consideration of the right to prepay. The penalty is often calculated on the basis of a percentage of the principal paid such that a premium could, for example, total 10 percent of the principal. The penalty also may be expressed in terms of a combined sum; for example, principal may be repaid at 110 percent. The premium usually declines over a period of time to the point that, in the final years, it reaches 0 percent. In an example of a combined call protection and prepayment premium, no prepayment is permitted for the first ten years; a prepayment premium of 10 percent is imposed in the 11th year, declining by 1 percent a year for ten years; and no prepayment premium is imposed for the 21st through 30th years.

In the case of publicly offered tax-exempt debt, the typical prepayment premium is negligible. Usually, such debt provides for ten-year call protection and thereafter a 2 percent prepayment premium, declining by 1 percent a year. In essence, the modest prepayment premium remains in place for only two years. More complex forms of prepayment premiums sometimes attempt to measure the loss of interest and to compensate the lender accordingly.

Some transactions, especially privately placed issues, make exceptions to the absolute prepayment prohibition as noted in the following examples:

- A borrower might be permitted to make prepayments on any principal payment date equal to twice the amount of principal owing on that date.
- In the case of taxable debt, the borrower might be permitted to prepay the principal from the proceeds of tax-exempt debt.
- If all or a portion of a facility is destroyed by fire or taken by eminent domain and is not reconstructed, the borrower may prepay principal. Even in a liberal form, this provision finds acceptance in the tax-exempt market but resistance in the taxable market.
- In some cases, prepayment of principal is permitted so long as it is not for the purpose of ob-

taining a lower interest rate. This type of restriction usually involves either a straight comparison of interest rates or a formula test that the new transaction must meet, whereby the premium is adjusted depending on the rate differential.

Notes

1. *See* §17.5.

2. *See* §15.4(e).

3. For example, the California Health Facility Construction Loan Insurance Program Law mandates a community service obligation. California Health and Safety Code §436.82.

4. *See* §18.3(d).

5. *See* §21.9.

Newbury Court Retirement Community; Concord, Massachusetts.

19 Equity Financing

§19.1 In General

Capital may be obtained for a project by means of either debt or equity. Debt financing involves a loan of money by a lender to the owner. Equity financing involves raising capital through the sale of ownership interests in the project. Some of the more innovative capital structuring techniques blur the demarcation between debt and equity, as evidenced by the following:

- convertible debentures, whereby a corporation issues debt that is accompanied by an option, exercisable at the will of the creditor, to convert the debt into a specified number of shares of stock;
- preferred stock, which is an equity interest with limited voting rights and a guaranteed rate of return; and
- debt, for which a portion of interest consists of a share of net earnings and capital appreciation.

The decision as to how much equity and how much debt financing to include in a given project depends on several factors and is often dictated by the availability of capital, the condition of the financial markets, the requirements of lending programs, and the economics of the given project. The following considerations may apply to particular types of projects:

- Nonprofit projects, especially those that pursue social goals (such as housing for low-income persons) and thus are not prone to generating excess revenues, may not be able to generate sufficient amounts of revenue to service debt at levels that would attract debt capital. In some cases, however, federal tax incentives may make equity investment attractive notwithstanding little or no economic return from the project. Moreover, such projects may be able to secure government or private grants and gifts that could be invested in the project without expectation of return. Accordingly, many nonprofit projects rely on extremely high proportions of equity, if not 100 percent equity financing.
- Many debt financing programs require a certain minimum percentage of equity investment.[1] Even when a program has no formal equity requirement, lenders usually require the borrower to have some stake in the project to ensure that the latter has an incentive to manage the project properly and to provide the lender with some cushion in the event of a foreclosure. An exception is the case of certain federal loan guarantees that permit 100 percent financing (see Chapter 14).

A recent survey of retirement housing executives asked respondents to identify their one best source of equity. They replied as follows:

Internally generated capital	38%
Related-party investor	15%
Third-party investor	15%
Parent company/subsidiary	14%
Selling stock/partnership shares	11%
Venture capital	1%
Other	4%

Source: American Seniors Housing Association, 1995 Seniors Housing Industry Executive Survey.

These responses suggest that retirement housing organizations depend more on internally generated or related-party capital than on the equity capital markets.

§19.2 Owner Contribution

The simplest form of equity financing is the infusion of capital by the project owner. Whether an individual or an existing corporation, the owner may contribute capital by paying for that portion of the project that is not otherwise financed. The owner's capital may come from surplus earnings from other ventures or take the form of property already held. Examples of such equity financing follow:

- A church concludes that a portion of the parcel on which the institution is located is not needed for church purposes and thus decides to build a retirement home on the site. The land represents an equity contribution by the church.
- A hospital uses revenues from its operations to pay architectural, engineering, feasibility, and legal costs to start a retirement home project. The payment of those expenses is an equity contribution.
- A corporation that owns an existing retirement home pays a portion of the cost of expansion of the facility out of its surplus revenues.

The process of determining how much of the owner's money to invest in a project hinges on two important factors: the amount of equity that needs to be invested, and the opportunity cost of the invested equity as compared with the cost of outside financing. Thus, if the project owner can use its own capital in a manner that will give it a higher rate of return than it would have to pay for debt or equity capital in the financial markets, it would be wise to

finance a larger portion of the project. If, however, the owner cannot earn a higher rate, it may be well advised to use a higher proportion of its own capital to finance the project.

Because different parties are differently situated, their rate of return necessarily varies, notwithstanding the equilibrium otherwise created by the market. For example, a nonprofit sponsor might receive a 6 percent return on its investment in the project but could receive an 8 percent return by investing its capital elsewhere. A for-profit investor, however, may be content to contribute debt or equity capital to the project and thus receive a 6 percent return by taking advantage of tax treatment that results in a higher effective yield. The nonprofit corporation and perhaps other for-profit investors may not be able to capitalize on such tax treatment because of their individual situations.

§19.3 Corporate Stock

The issuance of stock by a corporation is the typical method for raising equity capital in the market. While the federal and state governments impose stringent regulations on activities related to stock issuance, the subject is not treated in detail here. Instead, several good treatises on the subject should be consulted for further information. Nonetheless, a general discussion provides some insight into the elements of corporate equity finance.

A corporation that is considering entry into the financial markets to raise equity capital, whether on a private or public basis, must engage in careful preparation, including the development of a business plan that projects growth of the enterprise and financial results. A private offering usually calls for approaching a limited number of prospective investors and negotiating the terms of the investment, which may include issues of control, buyout, and the nature of future offerings. Public offerings are usually structured in conjunction with an investment banking firm, which assists the corporation in developing the terms of securities that the market will accept. Often through a syndicate, investment bankers market the stock by relying on their retail capabilities.

The issuance of stock is governed by the registration and disclosure scheme set out under the

Securities Act of 1933[2] and the blue sky laws of the states in which the stock is to be offered for sale (unless otherwise exempt under the provisions of those laws). For example, a for-profit corporation issuing stock may not rely on a public agency's exemption for securities as typically applied to tax-exempt debt offerings. Nonetheless, several other exemptions from registration may be available, principally those for private offerings. In general, private offerings are those made to a limited number of persons deemed capable of both evaluating the nature of and bearing the investment risk. Such offerings must be made without general advertisement or public solicitation. Because some issuers find it difficult to determine whether they have in fact complied with the vaguely worded standards of the generic private offering exemption, the Securities and Exchange Commission (SEC) provides certain detailed "safe harbor" exemptions from registration for offerings made to institutional investors such as banks, insurance companies, investment companies, employee benefit plans, and wealthy individuals (accredited investors) or to others determined to have sufficient knowledge and experience, so long as it is reasonably believed that there will be no more than 35 of such other purchasers.[3] If the entire offering is less than $5 million, the 35 purchasers who are not accredited do not necessarily have to meet any particular requirements. The exemptions for private offering provided in the federal securities laws usually have parallel provisions in the laws of the various states. There is also a federal exemption for a stock offering that "comes to rest" in a single state; however, state law may then become a concern.

If the issue is not exempt and is therefore subject to registration with the Securities and Exchange Commission pursuant to the Securities Act of 1933, it is necessary, as a condition to the offering, to register the securities with the SEC and to disseminate a prospectus approved by the SEC to prospective investors. In addition to these conditions to the offering of stock, companies with registered stock must file annual, quarterly, and periodic reports with the SEC, disseminate some of the reports to stockholders, and make all reports available for public inspection. These same companies also are subject to the proxy rules promulgated by the SEC.

§19.4 General Partnerships

A partnership is a venture carried on between two or more persons (who may be corporations). In a partnership, two persons may contribute capital to and share the management and control of a project. Characteristic attributes of a general partnership (in contrast to a corporation) include the following:

- Limited scope—The partnership is usually established to own and operate a particular project rather than with the authority to engage in unlimited business enterprises.
- Limited duration—The partnership may have a limited term of existence, for example, a 65-year ground lease of the property from one of the partners. It may be subject to dissolution by either party on certain terms. Limited duration is a partnership characteristic taken into account in the taxation of partnerships (see below for discussion of tax treatment of partnerships).
- Liability of partners—General partners, unlike corporate stockholders, members of nonprofit corporations, and limited partners, are jointly and severally liable for the debts and obligations of the partnership.
- Management of the partnership—Unless otherwise set forth in the partnership agreement, general partners have equal rights to manage the business of the partnership. Because of the general liability feature, all the partners probably want to exercise at least some ability to manage.

The advantage of a general partnership is that the parties can pool their equity, share risk, and contribute their respective expertise and management capability. For example, a housing developer may have some capital and knowledge of how to develop and operate a housing project but know nothing about the development and operation of health facilities. Likewise, a hospital may have some capital and knowledge of how to develop and operate health facilities but know nothing about housing development. Together, the two parties command the skills, expertise, and resources essential to their undertaking. The risk associated with a general partnership comes from the fact that both partners have control over the partnership, unless one of them is given managerial rights. The partnership could be unstable and, in the event of a conflict between the parties, even ungovernable (see also §11.3(b)(2)).

§19.5 Limited Partnerships

A limited partnership is a partnership made up of at least one general partner (that is, a partner who is generally liable for the debts and obligations of the partnership and who is granted the right to control the partnership) and at least one limited partner (that is, a partner whose liability is limited to the amount of his or her investment and who does not generally have the right to control the partnership). Limited partnerships have found widespread use, especially in real estate development, because they offer some of the benefits of both a general partnership and a corporation.

Like a general partnership, a limited partnership is not taxed directly, although its partners are taxed on their share of partnership earnings. This arrangement prevents so-called double taxation, whereby corporations are taxed and their earnings are taxed again when distributed to shareholders as dividends. As with a corporation, investors are shielded from liability except to the extent of their investment. Because of the tax benefits of the limited partnership and its similarity to a corporation, a limited partnership must be careful that the Internal Revenue Service does not consider it an association and thus subject to taxation at corporate rates. A limited partnership will not be treated as an association taxable as a corporation unless the organization has more major corporate characteristics than noncorporate characteristics.[4] The four major relevant corporate characteristics are continuity of life, centralization of management, limited liability, and free transferability of interests. The U.S. Tax Court has held[5] that where only two of the four characteristics are found to exist, the organization is not deemed an association taxable as a corporation but instead is classified as a partnership.

With respect to continuity of life, the regulations[6] provide that "if the death, insanity, bankruptcy, retirement, resignation or expulsion of any member will cause a dissolution of the organization, continuity of life does not exist." To come within this provision, the partnership agreement often provides that the partnership will dissolve on the dissolution of a general partner, if a corporation, or on the death or incompetency of an individual general partner or the general partner's retirement, resignation, removal, or bankruptcy, unless the limited partners elect unanimously to continue the partnership. U.S. Treasury regulations further provide that a limited partnership organized pursuant to a state law corresponding to the Revised Uniform Limited Partnership Act is deemed to lack the corporate characteristic of continuity of life.[7]

Centralization of management and limited liability are two corporate features that are usually present in a limited partnership. However, even if the other two characteristics are missing, a partnership should still be able to avoid corporate taxation.

To avoid a finding of "free transferability of interests," partnership agreements often contain a provision requiring the consent of the general partner before any limited partner transfers a partnership interest.

Unlike a general partnership interest, which is considered to be the ownership of the business itself, limited partnership interests are considered to be securities under the Securities Act of 1933 and the Securities Exchange Act of 1934.[8] As a consequence, public offerings of limited partnership interests must be accompanied by disclosure documents and may be required to be registered with the SEC. If no exemption is available, state blue sky laws are also applicable.

With the enactment of the Tax Reform Act of 1986, restrictions on limited partnerships that had the avoidance of federal income tax as their predominant economic rationale are of less importance than in the past. To the extent, however, that such transactions continue to be developed, projects that anticipate inordinately great tax benefits must be registered, and the at-risk rules, which require investors to be at risk with respect to the capital on which they are claiming tax benefits, come into play. The overriding consideration is that tax benefits are not available for those "activities not engaged in for profit."[9] Although statutory and case law have held that a partnership must be engaged in the activity with the predominant purpose and intention of making a profit (excluding tax benefits),[10] the IRS has ruled that the construction and operation of an apartment project for low- and moderate-income housing under Section 236 of the National Housing Act is not an activity to which Section 183 of the code applies. In limiting the amount of rental that could be charged in Section 236 projects, Congress assumed that deductions of tax losses would be allowed as a means of encouraging investment in such projects.[11] This same reasoning should also apply to Section 42, which relates to low-income housing tax credits. By limiting rental rates to very low levels, Congress must have intended that credits rather than profit would provide the necessary incentive for an investment in low-income housing projects (see also §11.3(b)(2)).

§19.6 Real Estate Investment Trusts

While most real estate syndication uses the limited-partnership form of organization (see §19.5), a significant amount of syndication relies on real estate investment trusts (REITs). A REIT is a trust rather than a partnership that can be used for both equity and debt investment in real estate.

As distinguished from a limited partnership, a REIT is generally subject to federal income tax. It is not, however, subject to tax on earnings distributed to its shareholders so long as 95 percent or more of its ordinary taxable income and foreclosure property income is distributed. Furthermore, at least 75 percent of a REIT's annual gross income must be derived from passive real estate or real estate mortgage investments. An additional 20 percent must be derived from either the foregoing or dividends or interest from any source or gain from the sale or other disposition of stocks and securities.[12]

The REIT industry has expanded from $7 billion to $25 billion since the 1970s, according to the National Association of Real Estate Investment Trusts.[13] More recently, the growth of REITs has been directed toward pension funds and IRA investments. In fact, REITs often pursue specialized objectives appropriate to the aims of their investors. For example, some REITs make leveraged-equity investments in the manner of limited partnerships; other REITs focus on all-equity (unleveraged) investments; still other REITs make loans secured by mortgages or deeds of trust. The last are often characterized by provisions

that result in a current return plus a share in excess cash flow and sale proceeds of the financed project.

REITs tend to specialize in particular types of real estate; those most appropriate to retirement housing are apartment REITs and health care REITs. Heretofore, apartment REITs have performed well by focusing largely on affordable family apartments, although some are now considering investments in retirement housing. Health care REITs, which take an equity position and lease a property back to the operator, have traditionally concentrated on acute care hospitals, rehabilitation centers, psychiatric facilities, and nursing homes. In fact, the market capitalization of the eight publicly traded health care REITs totaled $3.44 billion as of mid-1994. Health care REITs tend to favor properties with the following characteristics: competitive entry barriers (such as Certificate of Need requirements), government regulation, and third-party payment for services. Although retirement housing, particularly congregate housing, lacks some of these characteristics, health care REITs can be expected to increase their investment in such real estate in the future, particularly in the case of a creditworthy manager and owner or where cross-collateralization provides sufficient comfort.

§19.7 For-Profit/Nonprofit Joint Ventures

To raise a greater amount of equity capital than they can realize on their own, many nonprofit organizations have entered into joint ventures with for-profit investors (see Part V). This approach permits the organizations to tap equity capital that would otherwise be unavailable and thereby develop projects usually under their own management and control.

The structure of such an enterprise is that of a limited partnership in which the nonprofit organization, with little equity contribution, is the general partner and the investors are limited partners, contributing capital but not sharing in project management. This type of partnership usually includes a for-profit cogeneral partner with fiduciary responsibility to the limited partners, especially regarding tax matters.

A limited partnership involving a nonprofit general partner gives rise to a potential conflict of interest in that the nonprofit organization as a general partner has a fiduciary duty to the limited partners, but, as a nonprofit organization, it has a duty to carry out the objectives of its charitable purposes. In fact, questions raised in the past have challenged whether a nonprofit can function as a general partner that could be said to benefit private investors impermissibly. Recently, however, the Internal Revenue Service found that such an arrangement is permissible if it follows the guidelines described in §12.1.

§19.8 Low-Income Housing Tax Credits

(a) Generally

The Tax Reform Act of 1986 added Section 42 to the Internal Revenue Code to create a substantial tax credit for certain low-income rental housing projects, which may include new construction, acquisition, or rehabilitation.[14]

Projects involving construction or substantial rehabilitation without the use of federal financing receive an income tax credit for each of ten years. The credit has a present value of 70 percent of the basis and is expressed as a specified percentage of the basis—approximately 9 percent—for each of the ten years.[15] To qualify for the so-called 9 percent credits, the property may be newly constructed, or it may be rehabilitated so long as the cost of rehabilitation is equal to the greater of $3,000 or 10 percent of the adjusted basis of the building.

For the construction of facilities financed with tax-exempt bonds or below-market federal loans and for the acquisition of nonrehabilitated existing buildings in service more for than ten years, the credit is the amount that, over a ten-year period, results in a present value of 30 percent of the basis. That amount is approximately 4 percent per year[16] such that the credits are conventionally referred to as 4 percent credits. A loan made to a developer of low-income housing by a city is not considered a federal subsidy, even though the city received the loan funds from a grant under HUD's Housing Development Grant Program. In such a case, the developer could take advantage of the 9 percent credit.[17]

The U.S. Treasury Department, by regulation, sets specific credit rates to reflect the 70 or 30 percent present values described above.[18] In general, the tax credit is not available with respect to any existing building unless at least ten years has elapsed between the date the taxpayer acquired the structure and the later of the date it was placed in service or underwent its most recent substantial improvement.[19] This requirement may, however, be waived with respect to certain acquisitions in connection with projects in default under certain federally assisted loans.[20] For example, such a waiver is permissible with respect to property acquired from a defaulted financial institution insured by the federal government.[21]

To qualify for the tax credit, a facility must meet the following conditions:

- At least 20 percent of the units must be occupied by persons with income of 50 percent or less of the area median income, or 40 percent of the units must be occupied by persons with 60 percent or less of the area median income.[22]
- Units counted to qualify for the credit must be rent-restricted so that the gross rent charged to each tenant is no more than 30 percent of the applicable 50 or 60 percent of the median income limit.[23]
- Qualified projects must commit to adhering to the eligibility criteria for a 15-year period, or else the credits will be recaptured.[24]
- Except for projects where at least 50 percent of the cost is financed by bonds subject to an allocation of a state's tax-exempt bond cap (see §15.3) for which an allocation was received, credits available to taxpayers in each state are limited to an aggregate sum equaling $1.25 per state resident, the unused credit of that state for the preceding calendar year, the unused credit returned to the state by a recipient, and the unused credit from other states that have not allocated the full amount available to them (allocations are based on population).[25] Amounts are allocated from states that have not used all available credit to states that have used all available credit. Because more states have made efforts to use all of the credit allocated to them, the amount of credit reallocated to other states has declined dramatically in recent years. For calendar year 1997, the states noted below

received the following allocations in accordance with the reallocation provision:[26]

Alabama	$77,659
Alaska	$11,032
California	$579,360
Colorado	$69,480
Connecticut	$59,503
Delaware	$13,176
Florida	$261,710
Georgia	$133,636
Idaho	$21,609
Illinois	$215,311
Indiana	$106,156
Iowa	$51,833
Kansas	$46,744
Maryland	$92,180
Massachusetts	$110,718
Michigan	$174,364
Minnesota	$84,656
Mississippi	$49,361
Missouri	$97,396
Nebraska	$30,024
Nevada	$29,133
New Hampshire	$21,119
New Jersey	$145,176
New York	$330,500
North Carolina	$133,090
Ohio	$203,061
Oregon	$58,230
Pennsylvania	$219,109
Rhode Island	$17,993
South Carolina	$67,227
South Dakota	$13,304
Texas	$347,638
Utah	$36,349
Vermont	$10,705
Virginia	$121,313
Washington	$100,558

For a taxpayer to be eligible for the credit, the project sponsor must apply to the designated state agency for an allocation of the state's credit limit. States must reserve at least 10 percent of their credits for projects in which nonprofit organizations materially participate.[27] No allocation is required for the 4 percent credits on projects financed by tax-exempt residential rental project bonds for which a tax-exempt bond allocation was received.

■ All projects (including those that do not require an allocation) are subject to a low-income housing commitment, which the developer enters into with the state credit allocation agency. Notwithstanding the allowable credit amount described above, the credit amount may not exceed the amount necessary to support the number of low-income housing units in the building.[28]

(b) Use of Tax Credits for Retirement Facilities

Rental retirement facilities that offer services probably can qualify for the credit if compliance is financially feasible. Although nursing homes, hospitals, hotels, and trailer parks do not qualify, related facilities can be covered if their purpose is subordinate to the provision of residential rental units.[29] Each unit, however, must have full facilities for "living, sleeping, eating, cooking, and sanitation."[30]

Meeting the tenant income and rent restriction criteria can be difficult without use of the Section 8 rent subsidy. Except for existing projects that have subsidies already in place, a Section 8 rent subsidy is difficult to obtain.[31] However, fees for services such as meals, recreational programs, or health care probably can be charged to tenants without regard to the 30 percent limit on rents, assuming that separate service fees are not considered rent.[32]

While the provision of nonhousing services (such as meals, nursing, or assisted living) to residents does not disqualify a facility for the low-income housing tax credit, fees for such services are, as a general proposition, included in rent for the purpose of the rent limitation imposed by the tax credit program (see discussion in §19.8(a)), even if the provision of such services is required by federal or state law.[33] The result is a financially infeasible assisted-living development. To avoid such a situation, the development can provide needed services on an optional basis by offering the resident the opportunity to enter into a separate fee-based contract for such services. Yet, with assisted-living facilities subject to state licensure requirements (see §20.4), state laws may prohibit or restrict an optional arrangement for services. If state laws do not permit residents in need of care to remain in a licensed facility without the provision of care, the resident could probably either enter into a care contract or obtain appropriate services from an outside provider (such as a family member or home health agency).

Notwithstanding the delivery of assisted-living services on the conditions described above, the regulations provide that if "continual or frequent nursing, medical, or psychiatric services are provided, it is presumed that the services are not optional and the building is ineligible for the credit."[34] Thus, in these cases (which include hospitals and nursing facilities), the provision of assisted-living services has the effect of rendering a facility ineligible for the credit altogether.

The regulations further provide that the following two types of services can be required without including the associated charges in the rent limitation:[35] supportive services "provided under a planned program of services designed to enable residents . . . to remain independent and avoid placement in a hospital, nursing home, or intermediate care facility . . ." and the cost of mandatory meals in any federally assisted project for the elderly (in existence on or before January 9, 1989) that is authorized by federal regulations to provide a mandatory meals program.

In Private Letter Ruling 8945036, the IRS held that a housing project for low- and moderate-income elderly persons that included a separate nursing facility could qualify for the credit, provided that the nonhousing services, if mandatory, were included in the 30 percent limit on rent.

(c) Time Limitations and Allocation Issues

As originally enacted, the Tax Reform Act of 1986 provided no credit for property placed in service after 1989. Since 1989, however, Congress extended the credit on a year-to-year basis for 1990, 1991, and 1992. With the intent either to abolish the program or make it permanent some time in 1992, Congress wrote the 1992 extension as a half-year extension with the full amount of allocation. The Omnibus Budget Reconciliation Act of 1993 (Pub. L. No. 103–66, enacted in August 1993) permanently extended the program as of June 30, 1992.

Responding to reports that substantial amounts of low-income housing credit were possibly being claimed improperly and that the IRS and state administering agencies were not adequately monitoring the tax credit program, the chair of the House Ways and Means Committee on July 5, 1995, requested the General Accounting Office to review the administration of the program and report to the committee in 1996. The study would examine issues such as whether the credit was being allocated to projects in which low-income tenants were charged full market rents; whether inappropriate amounts of the subsidy were being diverted from low-income tenants to developers and syndicators through fees or unnecessarily high rates of return on investment; what controls existed at the state level to ensure that credits were allocated as intended and that costs were reasonable; and how efficiently the IRS was administering the program. To "facilitate" the GAO review, a provision to "sunset" the program after December 31, 1997, was included in a budget bill subsequently vetoed by the president. At present, the program appears relatively safe from termination.

Given that construction generally cannot begin until financing commitments such as tax credits have been authorized, it is impractical to place a building in service in the year the credit is allocated. Accordingly, a 1988 amendment to the law provides that a building may be placed in service by the end of the second year following the year for which the credit is allocated if 10 percent of the expected basis in the project is incurred by the end of the year in which the credit is allocated.[36] Thus, for 1991 credit, if 10 percent of the basis is incurred by the end of 1991, a project placed in service by the end of 1993 can qualify for the credit. For the purpose of meeting the 10 percent test, the IRS has held that the cost of land may be counted (even though it is not eligible for inclusion in the credit basis) so long as the taxpayer has assumed the burdens and benefits of ownership.[37]

For the years 1990 and following, a procedure written into the law permits the recapture and reallocation of unused tax credit. A state may reallocate to new projects any of the previous year's credit that was either unallocated or allocated and then returned. Any of the credit still remaining is allocated to other states in the following year.[38]

(d) Use of Low-Income Housing Tax Credits

Despite its complicated rules, short authorization periods, and frequent legislative changes, the low-income housing tax credit program has led to the development of a significant niche in the capital market. The following are some common characteristics of successful projects:

- Owners are usually organized as limited partnerships. The developer or operator (sometimes a nonprofit corporation) serves as the general partner while limited-partner investors own most of the shares.

- Limited-partner investors are often large corporations that enjoy steady earnings and have the capacity to use the credits to reduce their corporate income tax within the margin between the corporate tax rate and the alternative minimum tax rate. Because of passive loss limitations, individual investors have use for only small increments of low-income housing tax credit. Some organizations syndicate tax credit projects through pooled funds and market to these investors.

- Transactions are usually structured to produce little if any return to the investor other than the tax benefits. Proceeds paid by the investors usually run around 50 cents for every dollar of credit, producing an internal rate of return of 18 to 22 percent.

- In large urban areas, the tax credit alone is not a sufficient subsidy to make a low-income housing development feasible. Additional sources of public or private subsidy are usually necessary.

- A nonprofit corporation desiring to retain the long-term affordability of its project attempts to structure the tax credit transaction in a manner that permits it to reacquire the development at the lowest possible cost so it can afford to continue operation on that basis. This is often accomplished by providing for the partnership to pay the nonprofit a development fee and/or ground rent, deferred with interest, which is then paid when the partnership sells the property following the end of the 15-year compliance period. The nonprofit is then granted an option or a right of first refusal to purchase the project at fair market value (required for tax reasons) after the compliance period. The combination of the development fee and/or ground rent, with interest, and restrictive covenants on the property can be sufficient to reduce the purchase price to a level that achieves the nonprofit's purposes. The limited partners, however, cannot be left with an obligation to the nonprofit that is greater than the project's fair market value because extinguishment of the loss would result in taxable income.

§19.9 Equity Leases

An equity lease is a means whereby it is possible to finance 100 percent of the value of a facility through the sale of the facility to a third party and a lease-back. As contrasted with a conventional lease, the lease payments are broken into two components: a fixed component and a variable component. The fixed component is usually calculated to equal at least debt service on the lessor's debt. The variable component is paid as a percentage of net revenues. The ratio between the two components may vary; the larger the variable component, the greater is the percentage of net revenues comprising variable rent.

From the operator's standpoint, a financing lease can reduce financial risk by requiring only payment of the fixed component unless the property produces net revenues. Another advantage is that the debt on the facility is not reflected on the lessee's balance sheet. The lease can be structured so that the lessee has a right of first refusal in the event that the lessor decides to sell or has an option to purchase back the facility at fair market value.

§19.10 Charitable Contributions

A method of equity financing that has been long used by nonprofit retirement home operators is that of charitable contributions, particularly by retirement home residents. For residents in their declining years, the retirement home corporation is often an obvious choice for charitable giving. Charitable giving may take one of several forms, including outright gifts, bequests in a will, and deferred giving.

§19.11 Cooperatives and Condominiums

Cooperatives and condominiums permit individual ownership of units within a retirement home (see §§7.1 and 7.2). Permanent financing of residences involves the sale of units to residents, who are directly or indirectly responsible for debt service. One advantage of cooperative and condominium ownership is that qualification for financing is based on the financial condition of the resident rather than that of an owner of the development. A second advantage is that residents may be entitled to certain tax benefits such as the principal residence interest deduction and the deferral of capital gains on the sale of a previous residence. Nonetheless, as the following notes, condominiums and cooperatives differ substantially in how they are financed:

- A condominium consists of a common ownership of the underlying ground and the sole and exclusive ownership of the air rights that the dwelling unit occupies. The resident is the sole owner of a particular space and the portion of the building contained within it. That separate unit may be purchased and sold and may be pledged as security for a loan. Condominiums are usually financed by means of a mortgage or deed of trust on each individual unit. In the event of a foreclosure, the unit itself may be foreclosed and sold.
- A cooperative consists of residents' ownership of stock in a corporation that owns the entire development. The ownership of stock gives a resident the right to occupy a particular unit in the development. The resident does not directly own real estate but rather owns an interest in a corporation that owns real estate. Therefore, the resident cannot finance the purchase of the unit by means of a mortgage or deed of trust. As a result, cooperatives are financed by means of one of two methods. In the first method, the cooperative itself may borrow the money and grant a security interest in the entire development, passing through the obligation for repayment to the residents. Each resident is potentially exposed to foreclosure if other residents fail to make their payments. In the second method,

each resident may borrow the purchase price separately and pledge shares of stock in the cooperative corporation.

Notes

1. *E.g.,* the California Health Facility Construction Loan Insurance Program requires 10 percent equity investment for nonprofits.

2. 15 U.S.C. §77a *et seq.*

3. 17 C.F.R. §230.506.

4. Treas. Reg. §301.7701-2(a)(1).

5. *Larson v. Comm'r.* 66 T.C. 159 (1976).

6. Treas. Reg. §301.7701-2(b)(1).

7. Treas. Reg. §301.7701-2.

8. *Mayer v. Oil Field Systems Corp.,* 721 F.2d 59 (2d Cir. 1983); *Goodman v. Epstein,* 582 F.2d 388 (7th Cir. 1978); *McGreghar Land Co. v. Meguiar,* 521 F.2d 822 (9th Cir. 1975).

9. I.R.C. §183.

10. *Sanderson v. Comm'r,* 50 T.C.M. 1033 (1985).

11. Rev. Rul. 79-300, 1979-2 C.B. 112.

12. For a more detailed description of REITs and the applicable tax restrictions, see Jarchow, S., *Real Estate Syndication,* §2.4 (New York: John Wiley & Sons, 1985).

13. Seip, D., "1987: An Insider's Perspective on the Retirement Industry," *Contemporary Long Term Care,* Dec. 1987, 48.

14. I.R.C. §§42(b)(1)(A), (e)(3), (f)(1).

15. I.R.C. §42(b)(2).

16. I.R.C. §§42(b)(1)(B), (i)(2). *See* Priv. Ltr. Rul. 8813006 regarding waiver of the ten-year requirement where necessary to avert an assignment of the mortgage.

17. Priv. Ltr. Rul. 8813024.

18. I.R.C. §42(b)(2)(B).

19. I.R.C. §42(d)(2).

20. I.R.C. §42(c)(6).

21. Priv. Ltr. Rul. 9322024.

22. I.R.C. §42(g)(1).

23. I.R.C. §42(g)(2).

24. I.R.C. §42(i)-(j).

25. I.R.C. §42(h)(3).

26. Rev. Proc. 97-42, I.R.B. 1997-33, July 31, 1997.

27. I.R.C. §42(h)(5).

28. I.R.C. §42(h)(6).

29. *See* Senate Report, *Standard Federal Tax Reports (CCH),* at ¶ 11,286.

30. *Ibid.*

31. *See* discussion at §22.4(b).

32. *See* discussion at §22.6(d).

33. Treas. Reg. §1.42–11.

34. Treas. Reg. §1.42–11(b)(2).

35. Treas. Reg. §1.42–11(b)(3)(ii).

36. I.R.C. §42(h)(1)(E).

37. Notice 89-1, 1989-2 I.R.B. 10.

38. I.R.C. §42(h)(3).

RiverMead Retirement Community; Peterborough, New Hampshire.

Part VII
Regulation of Seniors' Housing and Care Facilities

Seniors' housing and care communities may be regulated to varying degrees by federal, state, or local governments. Federal laws are often tied to a funding source such as a HUD grant, loan, or loan guarantee or Medicare or Medicaid payments, but they may also involve civil rights issues such as age or disability discrimination or commerce-related concerns such as securities registration or antitrust laws (see, e.g., §§20.5 and 20.6 and Chapters 22 and 24). Part V discussed antitrust laws in the context of joint venture issues. Most regulation occurs at the state level and focuses on licensure for the provision of assisted living or health care, regulation of continuing-care agreements, and control of health care planning. Even though housing subdivisions are frequently the target of state regulation, such developments generally do not have distinctive features affecting elderly housing and therefore are not discussed. To the extent that local government regulation is a factor, it is usually limited to zoning and land use planning, rent controls, and similar real property development issues.

Sunlake Terrace; Las Vegas.

Courtesy of ARV Assisted Living; Costa Mesa, California

20 Licensing of Care Programs

§20.1 In General

Facilities and organizations that offer health care or assisted living (personal care) are heavily regulated by the states. The source of most state regulation in the health care field is federal law, which imposes requirements on the states as a condition of receiving funding pursuant to the Medicare or Medicaid programs. Regulation may apply to pursuits such as construction of facilities, addition of licensed beds, purchase of substantial equipment, construction standards, staffing requirements, resident rights, reimbursement for services, transfer of residents, and other issues touching on almost every aspect of the operation of care facilities. Assisted living or personal care is generally not considered to be health care and tends to be regulated differently by each state.

§20.2 Certificate of Need

(a) Evolution of the Process

CAUTION: In the final days of the 99th Congress, the entire federal health planning law, contained at 42 U.S. Code Section 300k-1 through Section 300n-6, was repealed by Public Law 99-660, effective January 1, 1987. Nevertheless, many states still operate programs patterned after the former federal program. The following discussion of the former federal program requirements is a general guide to readers subject to state laws.

Public Law 93-641, effective as of 1975, established a system of national health planning and development designed to encourage states to control the distribution, efficiency, and costs of health care services and thereby reduce spiraling increases in federal health care expenditures.[1] States that did not comply with federal health planning requirements were subject to loss of federal funding for various health programs; as a result, by 1981, all states but Louisiana had enacted health planning programs.[2]

A chief product of federal health planning is Certificate of Need (CON) programs.[3] State health planning and development agencies administer Certificate of Need programs, which review and determine the need for certain capital expenditures for health care projects, major medical equipment purchases, and additions of institutional health services.[4] Each state developed a state plan that inventoried existing resources and evaluated its needs and long-term goals for health care. The state plan comprises health systems plans (HSPs) created by local health systems agencies (HSAs). Sponsors planning to add new institutional health services or make certain capital expenditures or purchases for health care equipment or facilities have to undergo a review and secure a Certificate of Need before undertaking the project or committing to the expenditure.

For retirement facilities in development, the principal issue has been whether a proposal for a new institutional health service or capital expenditure will exceed the statutory threshold. The secretary of the (then) U.S. Department of Health, Education, and Welfare defined institutional health to include health services offered by nursing homes, rehabilitation facilities, and other health facilities that met a minimum annual operating expenditure threshold of $306,750.[5] Federal law also specified that any obligation of a capital expenditure, by or on behalf of a health facility, of $600,000 or more during a specified 12-month period was subject to review.[6] According to federal regulation, health facilities are defined to include skilled-nursing and intermediate-care facilities.[7] However, under the former federal law, a Certificate of Need could not be required with respect to a health service offered by certain qualifying health maintenance organizations (HMOs).[8]

Federal regulations provided that a project requiring a Certificate of Need be reviewed by the HSA with regard to numerous criteria, such as the project's relation to the applicable health systems plan, the needs of the population to be served, the availability of less costly alternatives, the project's financial feasibility, and the needs of underserved groups such as low-income persons, persons with disabilities, or ethnic minorities (elderly are not specified).[9] Generally, the federally prescribed process of determining need involved a detailed application, public hearings with the right to have legal counsel and to present evidence, written findings, and the opportunity for full judicial review of any decision.[10]

Although their impact has been felt less acutely among retirement centers than in the hospital industry, state Certificate of Need laws generally have required any seniors' housing developer contemplating construction of a skilled-nursing or intermediate-care facility to show that such a facility is needed in the particular health planning area in which the project is to be located. Usually, the determination of need includes an assessment of the number of existing facilities of the same type in the area, their census or occupancy figures, and a demographic prediction of future health care needs in the locale. Facilities offering care at a level below that of skilled nursing or intermediate care—for example, assisted-living facilities—generally are not included within the Cer-

tificate of Need requirements, except in a few states. Home health agencies are, however, subject to CON review under the laws of approximately 27 states.[11]

A determination of the need for a particular facility can involve contested, trial-like hearings in which other providers opposed to the project present evidence and opinion showing why the project is not economically feasible, why it would lead to underuse of resources already in the community, or why, for other reasons, it would waste the health care resources of the particular area. Retirement communities, however, tend to be less subject to these types of arguments from competitors than freestanding health care facilities. The reason is that retirement center health services are usually offered as part of an overall residential and services program that does not offer services to the general public and thus does not directly compete with typical nursing facilities (see §20.2(c) regarding specific statutory exemptions).

(b) State Programs since Repeal of the Federal Law

Many commentators believe that the federal Certificate of Need program failed to control the costs of health care and, in fact, simply added administrative burdens to the already climbing costs of developing health care facilities.[12] With the repeal[13] of the federal program and the loss of the funding that went with it, many states repealed their own Certificate of Need laws. As of 1997, 13 states have no Certificate of Need review process: Arizona, California, Colorado, Idaho, Kansas, Minnesota, New Mexico, North Dakota, Pennsylvania, South Dakota, Texas, Utah, and Wyoming.[14] States that do have some form of health planning law generally cover activities related to the construction of hospitals, skilled-nursing facilities, and intermediate-care facilities. Several states, however, rely on broader definitions that include residential care facilities, rehabilitation facilities, or other related or accessory services. These states include Arkansas, Connecticut, Maine, Maryland, Michigan, Mississippi, Missouri, New Jersey, and Tennessee.[15]

In states that still mandate a Certificate of Need as a prerequisite to developing a facility that offers health care services or possibly assisted-living or related services, the retirement housing developer should, as a first step, determine the state's published calculation of the need for the facility in the area where construction is contemplated. The developer should then determine whether any exemptions are available for seniors' communities of the type under consideration and take immediate steps to put the appropriate state agency on notice of the intention to build so that, in the event any need for beds is shown in the state or local area plan, a competitor does not preempt the project by submitting an earlier application to fill the same need.

(c) Exemptions for Continuing-Care Retirement Communities

Some states have adopted statutory provisions that give special preferences in the application of Certificate of Need laws to continuing-care retirement communities (CCRCs). Because CCRCs with health care centers tend to have a captive market for their health care facilities, the population to be served may be considered to be the CCRC residents themselves rather than the general public. Health planning agencies may therefore look to the needs of only the retirement community rather than to those of the entire planning area. As a consequence, a health planning agency may determine that new health beds are needed for a CCRC despite the absence of need in the community at large, and it may ignore CCRC health beds in calculating the inventory of health resources for the planning area.

Coverage of health care costs is another justification for granting Certificate of Need preference to a CCRC. Coverage may take the form of a prepaid, self-insured continuing-care program or use of an HMO or long-term-care insurance policy. Because of the favored treatment that federal regulation accorded prepaid health plans and cost-efficient payment mechanisms, states may give special treatment to retirement facilities either by rule or regulation or on the basis of case-by-case review.

Eighteen states have established separate review of CCRCs in Certificate of Need proceedings: Connecticut, Delaware, Florida, Georgia, Illinois, Maine, Maryland, Massachusetts, Nevada, New Hampshire, New Jersey, New York, North Carolina, Pennsylvania, Oregon, South Carolina, Virginia, and Washington.[16]

Half the states prohibit the facility from ever allowing a member of the general public to use the nursing beds and require the beds to be used only for retirement community residents. The other half permits outsiders to use the beds during the first several years of operation until the CCRC resident population reaches a stable level of maturity and demand for nursing services. Usually, the number of exempt or specifically reviewed CCRC nursing beds must be limited to a ratio of one to every four or five resident units in the facility.[17]

§20.3 Nursing Facility Licensure

Most nursing facility licensure standards adopted by the states have their genesis in federal Medicare and Medicaid laws, which are imposed as a condition of receiving funding from the federal government.[18] States may adopt licensing statutes that incorporate federal requirements and make them applicable to all nursing facilities seeking to do business within the state irrespective of their status as a provider certified under one or both of the federal programs. In addition to skilled-nursing facilities, the federal government once regulated intermediate-care facilities (ICFs).[19] Intermediate-care facilities are essentially skilled-nursing facilities with a less intensive level of nursing services. The 1987 Omnibus Budget Reconciliation Act (see §20.3(a)), however, abandoned the distinction in the Medicaid program between skilled-nursing and intermediate-care facilities and now refers simply to nursing facilities. Medicare still retains the "skilled" nursing terminology.

All states require nursing facilities to obtain licenses from a regulatory agency as a condition of doing business. Although regulation varies from state to state, virtually all have numerous elements in common as a consequence of the federal standards. Under federal law, to be eligible for Medicare or Medicaid funding, nursing facilities generally must provide 24-hour nursing service as well as social, dietary, pharmaceutical, dental, and other services, assess residents and plan their care, require residents to be under physician supervision, maintain clinical records, guarantee resident rights, protect resident funds, meet sanitary and life safety standards, and establish a governing body and a budget, among other requirements.[20] These laws have undergone substantial revision in recent years as discussed below.

Typically, state statutes have expanded even further on the federal regulatory framework. They usually set staffing standards at a minimum ratio of daily nursing hours per patient in the facility. Basic services standards may elaborate on the performance of functions such as dining, housekeeping, laundry, dietitian services, and physical therapy. Physical plant criteria may relate to the basic requirements for sterilization facilities, water temperatures, fireproofing requirements, emergency power systems, and other similar health and safety minimums. State regulations also routinely require implementation of facility policies and standards relating to admissions and discharges, records of storage and use of medications, keeping patient care plans and nursing notes, logging physician orders and visits, documenting patient falls and other incidents, reporting grievances to an ombudsperson, and other recordkeeping requirements. More so now than in the past, many of the details left to the states appear in federal law.

(a) The Omnibus Budget Reconciliation Act of 1987

(1) Generally

On December 22, 1987, the president signed into law the Omnibus Budget Reconciliation Act of 1987 (OBRA).[21] The stated overall purpose of OBRA was to enhance the quality of life of each resident in a Medicare- or Medicaid-certified skilled-nursing facility.[22] The law attempts to achieve that goal primarily by imposing on care providers detailed resident rights provisions as well as resident assessment, nurse's aide training, and facility survey requirements. The act elevated to statute and completely rewrote the Medicare and Medicaid conditions of participation formerly contained in regulation.

Regulations implementing the 1987 OBRA were adopted in 1989.[23] In 1991 and 1992, more detail regarding the expected implementation of the act appeared as "Interpretive Guidelines." Intended for state licensing surveyors, the requirements took the form of "Final Final" regulations published on September 26, 1991, and still additional regulations published on February 5, 1992 (general amendments), and March 6, 1992 (advance directives).[24]

(2) Admissions and Discharges

(A) Payment Issues. Upon admission, a facility may not require applicants to waive their rights to Medicare or Medicaid benefits or to make assurances, either orally or in writing, that they are not eligible for or will not apply for Medicare or Medicaid benefits. In addition, a facility may not require a third party to guarantee payment as a condition of admission. A facility may, however, ask an individual with access to a resident's funds to sign a contract for payment for services out of the resident's funds.[25] Presumably, this arrangement would permit a facility to contract with a trustee of resident funds or an attorney-in-fact pursuant to a power of attorney. Further, OBRA reiterates former law by prohibiting a facility from accepting any gift, money, or other consideration as a precondition to admission of a person entitled to Medicaid benefits.[26] The facility also may not charge a resident for any item or service for which payment is made under Medicaid or Medicare; charge a resident for any item or service not requested by the resident; or require the resident to request any item or service as a condition for admission or a continued stay. Finally, the facility must inform the resident when it will impose a charge for a requested item or service and what the charge will be.[27] Solicitations of charitable, religious, or philanthropic contributions from a person unrelated to the resident or applicant is expressly allowed.[28]

(B) Resident Assessment. For each resident, the facility must provide a written plan of care that describes the medical, nursing, and psychosocial needs of the resident and how such needs will be met. The plan of care must be prepared with the participation of the resident or the resident's attending physician and a registered professional nurse. It must be developed within seven days of the initial patient assessment and reviewed and updated periodically after each subsequent patient assessment (discussed below).[29]

Each facility also must prepare a comprehensive written Preadmission Screening and Resident Review (PASARR) that assesses each resident's functional capacity. The assessment must be based on a uniform Minimum Data Set (MDS) established by the secretary of the U.S. Department of Health and Human Services. A registered professional nurse must sign and certify the assessment. The facility is to examine each resident promptly on, and in no event later than 14 days after, admission. The resident must thereafter be examined and the assessment reviewed at least quarterly and revised as needed to ensure continued accuracy. A new assessment must be conducted whenever a significant change occurs in the resident's physical or mental condition and, in any event, at least once every 12 months. OBRA provides for a civil penalty of up to $1,000 per assessment for willful and knowing certification of an assessment containing a false material statement.[30] No reassessment is required for readmission to a nursing facility after a hospital stay or for a patient who is expected to stay in the nursing facility for less than 30 days for recovery from a condition for which he or she was hospitalized.[31]

Of great concern to retirement communities are the rules relating to admissions of mentally retarded or mentally ill persons (MR/MI screening). A Medicaid nursing facility is not allowed to admit on or after January 1, 1989, any resident who is deemed mentally ill or mentally retarded unless the state determines that the individual requires a skilled-nursing level of care and that specialized services are needed for the resident's mental condition.[32] A resident deemed in need of specialized services for mental illness or mental retardation but not in need of a nursing level of services must be discharged and the specialized services provided. If the resident has lived in the facility for more than 30 months, he or she can opt to remain there, but the specialized services must be provided in any event.[33]

A person is considered to be mentally ill if he or she has "serious mental illness," as defined by the secretary of the U.S. Department of Health and Human Services in consultation with the National Institute of Mental Health,[34] and does not have a primary diagnosis of dementia, including Alzheimer's disease or a related disorder. Dementia is defined as impairment of memory and one of the following: impairment of abstract thinking, impaired judgment, other disturbances of higher cortical function, or personality change, provided that the disturbance significantly interferes with work or usual social activities or relationships with others.[35]

In addition to the problems associated with the broad definition of mental illness, the rules require a resident so diagnosed to be moved out of the Medi-

caid skilled-nursing facility; they do not permit the facility operator to bring appropriate services into the health care center. This requirement can create particular problems for continuing-care facilities that contract to provide a broad spectrum of in-house services. The purported application of these rules to all residents in a Medicaid-certified facility (not just Medicaid-eligible patients) raises enforceability questions and might constitute an unlawful impairment of the contracts by which residents are promised such services within the facility.

(3) Basic Resident Rights

Residents have specified rights set forth in the statutes as follows:[36]

(A) Free Choice. The right to choose a personal attending physician, to be fully informed in advance about care and treatment, to be fully informed in advance of any changes in care or treatment that may affect the resident's well-being, and (except with respect to a resident adjudged incompetent) to participate in planning care and treatment or changes in care and treatment.

(B) Freedom from Restraints. The right to be free from physical or mental abuse, corporal punishment, involuntary seclusions, and any physical or chemical restraints imposed for purposes of discipline or convenience and not required to treat the resident's medical symptoms.[37] Restraints may be imposed only to ensure the physical safety of the resident or other residents and only upon the written order of a physician who specifies the duration and circumstances under which the restraints are to be used (except in emergencies specified by the secretary of the U.S. Department of Health and Human Services until such an order can reasonably be obtained).

(C) Privacy. The right to privacy with regard to accommodations, medical treatment, written and telephonic communications, visits, and meetings of family and of resident groups.

(D) Confidentiality. The right to confidentiality of personal and clinical records and access to current clinical records of the resident upon request by the resident or the resident's legal representative within 24 hours (excluding hours occurring during a weekend or holiday) after making such a request.

(E) Accommodation of Needs. The right to reside and receive services with reasonable accommodation of individual needs and preferences, except where the health or safety of the individual or other residents would be endangered, and to receive notice before the room or roommate of the resident in the facility is changed.

(F) Grievances. The right to voice grievances with respect to treatment or care that is (or fails to be) furnished, without discrimination or reprisal for voicing the grievances, and the right to prompt efforts by the facility to resolve grievances the resident may have, including those with respect to the behavior of other residents.

(G) Participation in Resident and Family Groups. The right to organize and participate in resident groups in the facility and the right of the resident's family to meet in the facility with the families of other residents in the facility.

(H) Participation in Other Activities. The right to participate in social, religious, and community activities that do not interfere with the rights of other residents in the facility.

(I) Examination of Survey Results. The right to examine, upon reasonable request, the results of the most recent survey of the facility conducted by the secretary of the U.S. Department of Health and Human Services or a state and any plan of correction in effect with respect to the facility.

(J) Refusal of Certain Transfers. The right to refuse a transfer to another room within the facility if a purpose of the transfer is to relocate the resident from a portion of the facility that is a skilled-nursing facility (Medicare-certified) to a portion of the facility that is not so certified.

In addition, requirements for access to and visitation of the resident are specified in the statutes as follows:[38]

- immediate access—federal or state representatives, an ombudsperson, or personal physician;
- immediate access subject to resident right to withdraw consent—immediate family members or relatives;
- immediate access subject to patient consent and reasonable restrictions—other visitors; and
- reasonable access subject to resident refusal—those providing health, social, legal, or other services to the resident.

Residents' funds are also statutorily protected so that while a resident is not required to deposit personal funds with the facility, if funds are deposited, the facility must

- manage and account for the funds;
- deposit and pay interest on funds over $50;
- maintain separate accounting records for each resident;
- provide an accounting to the resident or the resident's estate; and
- impose no charge against the personal funds for such services.[39]

Other rights established in regulation include

- in some cases, to refuse to authorize release of records;
- to refuse to perform services for the facility;
- to have regular access to and private use of a telephone;
- to retain and use personal property and valuables;
- to share a room with one's spouse; and
- to self-administer drugs.[40]

Amendments to OBRA passed in 1990 added the Patient Self Determination Act provisions,[41] which require facilities to provide residents with written information about their rights under state law[42] to accept or refuse medical or surgical treatment and their right to formulate advance medical directives (durable powers of attorney for health care, or "living wills") and about the facility's policy regarding the implementation of such rights. The act also prohibits the facility from discriminating against a person based on whether he or she has executed an advance directive.

Resident rights must be communicated to the resident orally and in writing at the time of admission and upon reasonable request.[43]

(4) Program and Staffing Requirements

For purposes of compliance with Medicaid requirements, the distinction between nursing facilities and intermediate-care facilities no longer holds.[44] Every nursing home must have 24-hour nursing service sufficient to meet residents' needs. A registered nurse must be on duty for at least eight consecutive hours a day, seven days a week.[45] The Medicare provisions include a waiver of these requirements in the case of certain rural facilities with a full-time registered nursing staff regularly on duty at least 40 hours per week. In addition, Medicaid facilities may qualify for a waiver if they have been unable to recruit personnel and a registered nurse or physician is on call, as long as the waiver does not endanger the health and safety of the residents. Medical care of all residents must be provided under the supervision of a physician.[46] Further, any nursing facility with more than 120 beds must employ at least one full-time social worker who holds at least a bachelor's degree in social work or is otherwise qualified for the job.[47]

The law also establishes federal standards for the training of nurse's aides. Every nurse's aide must receive extensive training in nursing and residents' rights. In addition, the state must maintain a registry of all individuals who have satisfactorily completed an approved nurse's aide training program. A facility may not use a nurse's aide for more than four months unless the individual has completed a state-approved program. Amendments in 1990 required, among other things, that part-time aides receive the same training as full-time aides and that certified aides who have not provided services for 24 months complete an evaluation before resuming work.[48]

Either directly or under agreement, each nursing facility is to provide the following: nursing and specialized rehabilitative services designed to attain the "highest practicable" physical, mental, and psychosocial well-being of each resident; social services; pharmaceutical services; dietary services; an activities program directed by a qualified professional; routine and emergency dental services (for which a Medicare facility may levy an additional charge); and treatment and services required by mentally ill persons and persons with mental retardation not otherwise provided or arranged for by the state.[49]

(5) Transfers and Discharges

A facility may not transfer or discharge a resident from the facility unless

- such action is necessary for the resident's welfare;
- the transfer is appropriate due to improvement of the resident's health such that the resident no longer needs the facility's services;
- the action is necessary for the health or safety of other individuals in the facility;

- the resident has failed to pay, or have paid on his or her behalf under the Medicaid Act, for a stay at the facility; or
- the facility ceases to operate.

Reasons for all transfers or discharges need to be documented in the patient's health record. In the first two cases above, the resident's physician must document the circumstances. In the third case, another physician can document the circumstances.[50] Although the law is silent generally on transfers within a facility, it is important to note that a transfer from one certified portion of a facility to another (for example, from a Medicare bed to a Medicaid bed within the same facility) is considered a transfer between facilities that is subject to the rules.

Before a transfer or discharge from the facility, each facility must notify the resident and either a family member or the resident's legal representative of the action to be taken and the reasons therefor. The notice must describe the resident's right to appeal and contain the name, mailing address, and telephone number of the state's long-term-care ombudsperson. When a developmentally disabled or mentally ill resident is discharged, Medicaid requires the above information to be provided to the appropriate agency responsible for protection and advocacy on behalf of such individuals. The facility must give notice at least 30 days in advance of the transfer or discharge date unless the health or safety of individuals in the facility is or would be endangered, a more immediate transfer is possible due to the resident's improved health, an urgent transfer is needed because of failing health, or the resident has been in the facility for less than 30 days.[51]

Upon transfer or discharge, the facility must sufficiently prepare and orient the resident to ensure a safe and orderly transfer or discharge. If the resident of a Medicaid facility is transferred because of hospitalization or therapeutic needs, the facility must provide a family member or legal representative with information regarding bed-hold and return policies.[52]

(6) Survey and Certification Process

OBRA sets forth a survey and certification process that includes required state-sponsored educational programs and sets guidelines for the investigation of allegations concerning resident neglect, abuse, and misappropriation of resident property.[53] Each facility is subject to an annual, unannounced survey by the state. In assessing the quality of care, the state considers medical, nursing, and rehabilitative care, dietary and nutrition services, activities and social participation, the physical environment, the accuracy of written plans of care, and a review of residents' rights compliance. If a facility is found to be substandard, the state conducts an extended survey immediately after completion of the initial survey. The surveys are to be performed in accordance with a protocol developed, tested, and validated by the secretary of the U.S. Department of Health and Human Services.

OBRA also provides for validation surveys, which are to be conducted by the secretary of the U.S. Department of Health and Human Services. These are on-site surveys of a representative sample of facilities in each state within two months of the standard and extended surveys. The secretary's determination of noncompliance is binding on the state.

If a nursing home fails to meet the federal standards, OBRA provides for the application of several remedies, including the appointment of a temporary facility manager, termination of Medicare/Medicaid participation, denial of payments, imposition of civil money penalties not exceeding $10,000 per day, and, in the case of an emergency, closure of the facility and/or transfer of residents.[54]

After years of industrywide anticipation, the survey and enforcement regulations for nursing facilities under OBRA 1987 were finally adopted on November 10, 1994. The final regulations reflect substantial changes from the draft regulations published in 1992.[55]

The regulations categorize a wide array of enforcement remedies as mandatory or optional based on the nature of the regulatory violation: "directed" plans of correction, directed in-service training of staff, denial of Medicare and Medicaid payments for new resident admissions, denial of payment for all residents (federal remedy only), on-site monitoring of compliance by state personnel, civil money penalties, temporary management of the facility, termination of participation in the Medicare and Medicaid programs, and emergency facility closure or resident transfers (state remedy only). The type of remedy depends on the character of the alleged violation.

The regulations dropped the former distinction between Level A and Level B violations[56] in favor of the following scope and severity classification system that embodies 12 deficiency classifications labeled A through L.

- **Severity**
  - Immediate jeopardy to the health or safety of one or more residents
  - Actual harm to a resident, but not immediate jeopardy
  - No actual harm, but a potential for harm that is more than minimal but less than immediate jeopardy
  - No actual harm and potential for minimal harm
- **Scope**
  - Isolated incident
  - Pattern of deficiencies
  - Widespread deficiencies

Choices of remedies are divided into the following categories based on the scope and severity of the alleged deficiency:

- **Category I**
  - Scope/Severity—Isolated or pattern deficiencies that cause no actual harm and have a potential for more than minimal harm but pose no immediate jeopardy.
  - Remedies—Directed plan of correction, directed in-service training, and/or state monitoring. When the facility is not in "substantial compliance" (i.e., any deficiency poses more than minimal potential harm), any deficiency may result in a Category I remedy. No plan of correction or other remedy is called for if the incident is isolated, no actual harm occurred, and there is a potential for no greater than minimal harm.
- **Category II**
  - Scope/Severity—Widespread violations involving no actual harm, with the potential for more than minimal harm, but no immediate jeopardy; deficiencies involving actual harm but no immediate jeopardy.
  - Remedies—Denial of payments for new admissions or for all admissions and/or civil money penalties.

■ **Category III**
  ■ Scope/Severity—Immediate jeopardy regardless of scope; widespread deficiencies with actual harm but no immediate jeopardy.
  ■ Remedies—Termination (immediate-jeopardy cases only) or temporary management, plus Category II remedies for widespread, nonimmediate-jeopardy cases.

Until substantial compliance is achieved, civil money penalties may be assessed at the rate of $50 to $3,000 per violation per day for nonimmediate-jeopardy cases. For immediate-jeopardy cases, fines may range from $3,050 to $10,000 per violation per day. Fines may be charged retroactively for past conduct. Penalties may not be collected until after the provider has exercised or waived its right to appeal the deficiency to an administrative law judge. The administrative law judge must accept the evaluator's determination of the existence, scope, and severity of the alleged violation unless the provider shows that the allegation is "clearly erroneous." The evaluator's choice of remedy is not appealable. Fines are "discounted" by 35 percent if the provider waives its right to appeal. Fines, with interest, may be offset against payments due to the facility from Medicare or Medicaid. Repeat deficiencies can result in enhancement of the punitive measures taken against the facility. For example, if the same category of violation is found two years in a row, the civil money penalty in year two must be increased beyond the amount assessed in year one. The regulations state that in the event of immediate jeopardy, the Health Care Financing Administration (HCFA) or the state must immediately remove the jeopardy "through temporary management" or terminate the provider.

A finding of "substandard quality of care" results when an annual survey identifies significant (e.g., not isolated) deficiencies in any of the following areas: resident behavior and facility practices, quality of life, or quality of care.[57] Such a finding may result in notification to the state licensing board for nursing home administrators, notification to the physicians whose patients are affected, and loss of the facility's nurse's aide training program. If a finding of substandard quality of care is made in three consecutive annual surveys, nonpayment for new admissions and state monitoring are mandatory until the facility shows that it not only has corrected the deficiencies but that it can also remain in "substantial compliance" in the future.

In general, resident outcomes are the primary measure of whether a violation has occurred. When the state and HCFA disagree on whether a deficiency has occurred, the finding of noncompliance prevails. Exemplary facilities may be publicly recognized or receive incentive payments.

The survey and certification rules are considerably more complex than represented in this summary and raise questions of interpretation, internal consistency, and legality. In the summer of 1995, HCFA released its State Operations Manual (Rev. 273) and a series of questions and answers regarding interpretation of the enforcement regulations. The materials address a level of detail beyond the scope of this book. Anyone facing enforcement actions under the regulations should contact qualified legal counsel. See Figure 20.1 for a grid correlating OBRA violations with the available enforcement remedies.

(b) Transfers in Multilevel Facilities

Of particular interest to CCRCs or other multilevel seniors' facilities is OBRA's patients' rights standard that requires a resident to be transferred or discharged only for medical reasons, for the safety of the resident or others, or for nonpayment.

Often, new retirement projects with a health care unit cannot fill the health care beds with retirement home residents. Because the community is new, residents are likely to be healthy, independent, and comfortable in their residential units. Only after the resident population matures over many years is the stream of residents in need of care likely to be sufficient to keep the health center reasonably full. Therefore, it is common for facility operators, especially in the early years of operation, to make health center beds available to members of the general public, with the idea that general public nursing residents will increasingly over time need to make way for retirement community residents in need of nursing services.

Of course, the problem is that, under the federal residents' rights rules, a general public resident cannot be discharged simply to make room for another nursing resident unless, for example, there is a change

Figure 20.1 **HCFA State Operations Manual Grid for Enforcement Remedies**

Licensing of Care Programs

	Isolated	Pattern	Widespread
Immediate jeopardy to resident health or safety	**J PoC** Required: Cat. 3 Optional: Cat. 1 Optional: Cat. 2	**K PoC** Required: Cat. 3 Optional: Cat. 1 Optional: Cat. 2	**L PoC** Required: Cat. 3 Optional: Cat. 2 Optional: Cat. 1
Actual harm that is not immediate jeopardy	**G PoC** Required: Cat. 2 Optional: Cat. 1	**H PoC** Required:* Cat. 2 Optional: Cat. 1	**I PoC** Required:* Cat. 2 Optional: Cat. 1 Optional: Temporary Management
No actual harm with potential for more than minimal harm that is not immediate jeopardy	**D PoC** Required: Cat. 1 Optional: Cat. 2	**E PoC** Required:* Cat. 1 Optional: Cat. 2	**F PoC** Required:* Cat. 2 Optional: Cat. 1
No actual harm with potential for minimal harm	**A No PoC** No Remedies; Commitment to Correct Not on HCFA–2567	**B PoC**	**C PoC**

 Substandard quality of care is any deficiency in 42 CFR 483.13, Resident Behavior and Facility Practices; 42 CFR 483.15, Quality of Life; or 42 CFR 483.25, Quality of Care, that constitutes immediate jeopardy to resident health or safety, or a pattern of widespread actual harm that is not immediate jeopardy, or a widespread potential for more than minimal harm that is not immediate jeopardy, with no actual harm.

 Substantial compliance

Remedy Categories

Category 1 (Cat. 1)	*Category 2 (Cat. 2)*	*Category 3 (Cat. 3)*	*Optional:*
Directed Plan of Correction State Monitor; and/or Directed In-Service Training	Denial of Payment for New Admissions Denial of Payment for All Individuals Imposed by HCFA; and/or CMPs: $50–$3,000/day	Temporary Management Termination	CMPs $3,050–$10,000/day

Denial of payment for new admissions must be imposed when a facility is not in substantial compliance within three months after being found out of compliance.

Denial of payment and state monitoring must be imposed when a facility has been found to have provided substandard quality of care on three consecutive standard surveys.

Note: Termination may be imposed by the state or HCFA at any time when appropriate.

Following a determination of scope and severity, the state agency enters on Form HCFA–2567L the letter corresponding to the box of the grid for at least any deficiency that constitutes substandard quality of care and any deficiency that drives the choice of a required remedy category. The state agency enters this letter in the ID prefix tag column immediately below the tag number of the Form HCFA–2567L. Deficiencies falling in box A are recorded on Form A.

* This is required only when a decision is made to impose alternative remedies instead of or in addition to termination.

in the level or type of care needed by the person in the nursing facility that warrants the resident's transfer, he or she fails to pay the charges for care and the care is not covered by the Medicaid program,[58] or the resident's continued stay in the facility endangers another resident.

Facilities cannot be arbitrary or cavalier in discharging nursing residents for medical reasons, especially when a discharge to a lower level of care could result in ineligibility for government benefits. Even though the U.S. Supreme Court has held that a nursing home patient threatened with transfer does not have a constitutional right to due process notice and hearing procedures before transfer,[59] the provider must allow the patient's physician to participate in the utilization review committee's determination of the appropriateness of a transfer and must report any transfer to the relevant state agency.[60]

It can be argued that moving a nursing resident to make room for an admission from the residential side of a multilevel facility is a transfer made to protect the health and safety of another (the incoming) resident. Probably the most practical and defensible solution to the dilemma of transferring patients to make room for residents in need is to admit as patients from the general public a sufficient ratio of persons whose need for nursing care is likely to be convalescent rather than long-term in nature. For example, an experienced nursing administrator can screen entering patients and admit only those recovering from surgery, but not those suffering from degenerative diseases from which a hope of speedy recovery appears dim. In this way, it should be possible to control with reasonable accuracy the rate at which beds will become available for use by occupants of the residential facilities or for temporary refilling by another outsider.

(c) Construction Standards

Any retirement facility developer contemplating construction of any type of health care facility as part of a retirement project should carefully review state and local construction standards applicable to the particular facility. Depending on the jurisdiction, health care facilities may be required to be built to much higher construction standards than the standards imposed on purely residential structures. For example, earthquake-prone California has developed an elaborate set of hospital construction standards to ensure that its hospitals will remain standing and able to treat the injured in the event of a serious earthquake. These seismic standards apply to skilled-nursing facilities that exceed one story in height. The type of steel and concrete construction required to ensure a skilled-nursing facility's conformance to hospital seismic safety standards can be so much more expensive than, for example, conventional wood-frame construction as to be prohibitive.

Statutes or regulations that set higher construction standards for health facilities can also pose particular problems in multiple-story buildings where a health care facility is to be incorporated into the structure as one or two floors of an otherwise residential building. Depending on the location of the health care unit within such a high-rise structure, it may be necessary to build the entire structure to the stringent standards mandated for the health facility component.

Another consideration for health care facility construction is flexibility to convert structures to different uses over time. For example, facilities initially used for assisted living may be so designed that they are convertible to meet standards for later use as a skilled-nursing facility when the retirement facility population has matured and generally requires a higher level of care.

The intricacies of these types of regulations, which vary from state to state and deal with matters such as corridor widths, door size, structural strengths, fireproofing, and the like, are beyond the scope of this book. Suffice it to say that the prudent developer should inquire into these issues early in the planning process and consult with an architect or structural engineer experienced in constructing health facilities in the region where development is contemplated.

§20.4 Assisted-Living Facility Licensure

Assisted-living facilities—called by a wide variety of names such as personal care or board and care[61]— offer a level of care substantially below that required to be provided by nursing facilities. Whereas skilled-nursing facilities offer 24-hour, physician-supervised, professional nursing care, assisted-living facilities provide care for residents who may need assistance with bathing, dressing, grooming, mobility, taking of medications, or other activities of daily living (ADLs) that can be delivered by an unlicensed assistant who does not have nursing training.[62] Some promoters of the assisted-living concept distinguish it from other types of residential care by insisting on single-occupancy rooms with cooking facilities, among other features. Assisted living is viewed as more humane and cost-effective than—and thus an alternative to— "institutional" nursing care.

(a) A Patchwork of State Laws

A survey of state laws and regulations reveals a crazy quilt of approaches to the regulation of group residential facilities offering nonmedical services and care. Figure 20.2 provides a summary of each state's regulations.[63] Not only does the nomenclature vary widely from state to state, but statutes cover facilities for seniors, children, mentally and developmentally disabled persons, and drug dependents or delinquents and apply to residential and daycare formats and operations ranging from massive institutions to "mom-and-pop" programs run in the owners' personal residences. Some states have enacted statutes affording only piecemeal coverage of the various possible permutations while others prescribe as many as six separate categories of licensure tailored to the size, purpose, and clientele of each class of facility. Some states also regulate assisted living as a service (as with home health care) rather than as a facility.[64]

Licensure provisions generally include an application and screening process. State regulators inspect physical plants for conformity with construction standards, including fire safety, sanitation, and accessibility. Provisions may prescribe basic staff qualifications and levels, criminal record clearance, and bonding and require basic services such as meals, supervision and observation, planned recreation activities, assistance with personal activities, housekeeping, and so on. Patient rights may be established, including the rights to have visitors, privacy, and personal possessions, to be free from restraint or involuntary work, and to certain procedures before eviction. Record-keeping requirements can involve

patient care plans, incident reports, medications records, and accounting of patient funds. Finally, enforcement mechanisms are usually in place in the form of grievance systems, ombudspersons, injunctions, license suspension or revocation, and criminal sanctions.[65]

For operators of multilevel care facilities, a major problem with the current patchwork of laws is that, depending on the state, applicable regulations may not be well suited to the particular realities of a residential community, which, for example, may house healthy, independent senior citizens on the same premises with those in need of substantial care.

In 1993, the American Association of Retired Persons (AARP) reported the results of a 1990 nationwide survey of regulatory agencies charged with regulation of and payment for board-and-care homes.[66] The survey reconfirmed the complexity of and lack of conformity in state board-and-care regulations. Some of the interesting findings from the survey follow:

- Of the 62 licensing agencies surveyed, 60 required regular inspections. The vast majority of the agencies (45) conducted or required annual inspections; only four conducted inspections less frequently than annually.
- Although sanctions are authorized, licensing agencies rarely impose them on board-and-care homes. Authorized sanctions include corrective action plans (59 agencies), license revocation (59 agencies), provisional license (37 agencies), ban on admissions or referrals of new residents (36 agencies), and fines (33 agencies).
- State agencies vary significantly in how they define assisted living, in the types of facilities that call themselves assisted living, in whether assisted-living facilities are subject to board-and-care regulations, and in the level of agency officials' understanding of assisted living. For example, only half of the surveyed licensing agencies (31 agencies) reported that the state's definition of board and care covered assisted-living facilities.
- Only five of the 62 state licensing agencies allow licensed homes to admit bedfast residents without describing the admission as conditional. Forty-nine agencies prohibit the admission of bedfast residents.

Figure 20.2 **Assisted-Living Regulations**

Originally prepared for the American Seniors Housing Association (1997). Reprinted with permission.

	Alabama	Alaska	Arizona
1. **Classification**	Assisted-Living Facilities	Assisted-Living Homes	Supportive Residential Living Centers (pilot)
2. **Statutory/Regulatory References**	Alabama Code 22–21–20 *et seq.* Ala. Admin. Rules §§420–5–4 *et seq.*	Alaska Stat. §§47.33.005 *et seq.* Alaska Admin. Code §§75.010 *et seq.*	Ariz. Comp. Admin. R. & Regs. R9–10–1501 *et seq.*
3. **Minimum Size**	2+	3+	
4. **Mandatory Services**			
a. ADL care	Y	Y	Y
b. Transportation			
c. Laundry	Y		
d. Activities/recreation			Y
e. Arranging health-related services	Y		
f. Housekeeping	Y		Y
g. Medications management	Y		Y
h. Monitoring	Y		Y
i. Other	3+ meals/day; communications		3 meals/day and snacks
5. **Permitted Services**			
a. Assistance with medications	Y	Y	Y
b. Administer medications	By licensed nurse		By licensed nurse
c. Intermittent nursing		Y	Y
d. Other	Home health by certified agency	Skilled nursing if not disruptive	
6. **Regulated Subjects**			
a. Admission agreements	Y	Y	Y
b. Resident funds	Y	Y	
c. Care plan	Y	Y	Y
d. Medication storage	Y		Y
e. Dietary requirements	Y		Y
f. Other			
7. **Administrator**			
a. Education/examination	"Well-trained"	Sufficient education	Training program
b. Continuing education	6 hours/year		
c. Availability			40+ hours/week
d. Other (qualifications, etc.)			
8. **Staffing Levels**			
a. Staff: resident ratio	1:6		
b. Required hours			1+ awake and certified in CPR, 24 hours/day
c. Licensed			
d. Other qualifications	16 hours' training within 1st year of service		16-hour initial training 20 hours/year training
9. **Mandatory Discharge**			
a. Ongoing nursing care			Y
b. Danger to self/others			Y
c. Unable to evaluate			
d. Restraints			Y
e. Beyond capabilities	Y		
f. Other			Unable to direct self-care
10. **Physical Plant**			
a. Maximum occupancy/unit			
b. Size of unit (single occupancy)	80 square feet*		220 square feet
c. Size of unit (multiple occupancy)	130 square feet*		220 square feet
d. Toilet	1:6 beds		1 per unit
e. Bath or shower	1:8 beds		1 per unit
f. Other	Detailed	Cooking facilities: If conducted on premises, areas for food preparation; appropriate furniture, storage space, signal device, lines, and toiletries	Bathroom; lockable doors; kitchen
11. **Agency (Licensure/Authority)**	Department of Public Health, Division of Licensure and Certification	Department of Administration, Division of Senior Services	Department of Health Services, Home and Community-Based Licensure
12. **Notes**	*Larger if room contains "sitting area"		

Continued →

Figure 20.2 (continued)

	Arkansas	California	Colorado
1. Classification	Residential Long-Term-Care Facilities	Residential Health Care Facilities for the Elderly	Alternative Care Facilities (Personal Care Boarding Homes)
2. Statutory/Regulatory References	Ark. Code §§20–10–213 et seq. Rules of Licensure §§100 et seq.	Health and Safety Code §§1569.2 et seq. Cal. Code of Regs., Title 22, §§87100 et seq.	Colo. Rev. Stat. §§25–27–101; 26–4.5–133 et seq.; Regulations for Personal Care Boarding Homes (Chapter VII)
3. Minimum Size			3+
4. Mandatory Services			
a. ADL care	Y	Y	Y
b. Transportation		Y (or arrange)	Y
c. Laundry	Y	Y	Y
d. Activities/recreation	Y	Y	Y
e. Arranging health-related services	Y	Y	Y
f. Housekeeping			
g. Medications management	Y	Y	
h. Monitoring	Limited	Y	Y
i. Other	3 meals/day	3+ meals/day	3+ meals/day
5. Permitted Services			
a. Assistance with medications	Y	Y	Y
b. Administer medications			By qualified staff
c. Intermittent nursing	Y		
d. Other	Home health	Hospice; Alzheimer's; home health by separate licensee	
6. Regulated Subjects			
a. Admission agreements	Detailed	Y	Y
b. Resident funds	Y	Y	Y
c. Care plan		Y	Y
d. Medication storage	Y	Y	Y
e. Dietary requirements	Y	Y	Y
f. Other			
7. Administrator			
a. Education/examination	High school or GED and certification program	Certification program (40+ hours) and examination	Combination of education and experience
b. Continuing education		40 hours/2 years	
c. Availability	40 hours/week	Or designee 24 hours/day	
d. Other (qualifications, etc.)		More limited requirements for nursing home administrators	
8. Staffing Levels			
a. Staff: resident ratio	Variable	Variable	
b. Required hours	1+ 24 hours/day		1+ on site 24 hours/day
c. Licensed			
d. Other qualifications	Direct care: 4 hours per quarter in-service training or continuing education	10 hours' initial in-service training; 4 hours/year (ADL caregivers)	Education and/or experience for those with direct care responsibilities
9. Mandatory Discharge			
a. Ongoing nursing care	Y	Y	Y
b. Danger to self/others	Y		Y
c. Unable to evaluate	Y	Y	
d. Restraints			Y
e. Beyond capabilities	Y		Y
f. Other	Various	Bedridden; several enumerated health conditions	Bedridden; other medical reasons
10. Physical Plant			
a. Maximum occupancy/unit	2 (new)	2 (per bedroom)	2 (4 pre-1986)
b. Size of unit (single occupancy)	100 square feet		100 square feet
c. Size of unit (multiple occupancy)	80 square feet/resident		60 square feet/person
d. Toilet	1:6 residents	1:6 persons*	1:6 residents
e. Bath or shower	1:10 residents	1:10 persons**	1:6 residents
f. Other			Window
11. Agency (Licensure/Authority)	Department of Human Services, Office of Long-Term Care	Department of Social Services; Community Care Licensing Division	Department of Health, Health Facilities Division
12. Notes		75% of residents 60+ years * Persons = Residents, family, and personnel ** Persons = Residents, family, and live-in personnel	Residents' council must be established (17+-bed facilities)

Continued →

Figure 20.2 **(continued)**

	Connecticut	Delaware	Florida
1. **Classification**	Managed Residential Communities*/ Assisted-Living Agencies**	Residential (Rest) Homes Assisted-Living Agencies	Assisted-Living Facilities
2. **Statutory/Regulatory References**	Conn. Genn. Stat. §19a–490; Conn. State Agency Regs. §§19–13–D105	Delaware Code, Title 16, §§1101 *et seq.* Health and Social Services Regs. §§63.0 *et seq.*	Florida Stat. 400.401 *et seq.* Fla. Admin. Code Ch. 10A–5, §§10A–5.013 *et seq.*
3. **Minimum Size**			4+
4. **Mandatory Services**			
a. ADL care	Y	Y	Y
b. Transportation	Y	Y	Y
c. Laundry	Y	Y	
d. Activities/recreation	Y	Y	Y
e. Arranging health-related services	Y		Y
f. Housekeeping	Y	Y	
g. Medications management	Y		
h. Monitoring		Y	Y
i. Other	Security and call system, 3+ meals/day		
5. **Permitted Services**			
a. Assistance with medications	Y		Y
b. Administer medications	By licensed staff		By nurse
c. Intermittent nursing	Y	Y	Limited
d. Other	Nursing services		
6. **Regulated Subjects**			
a. Admission agreements		Y	Y
b. Resident funds		Y	Y
c. Care plan	Y	Service Agreement	Y
d. Medication storage		Limited	
e. Dietary requirements			Y
f. Other			
7. **Administrator**			
a. Education/examination	R.N. and BA + 2 years' experience***		High school or GED or equivalent
b. Continuing education			
c. Availability	Variable		12 hours/2 years
d. Other (qualifications, etc.)			Core training program
8. **Staffing Levels**			
a. Staff: resident ratio			
b. Required hours			Varies with number of residents
c. Licensed	R.N. on call or on site	.	Required to perform certain tasks
d. Other qualifications			
9. **Mandatory Discharge**			
a. Ongoing nursing care		Y	24-hour nursing supervision
b. Danger to self/others		Y	Y
c. Unable to evaluate			Y
d. Restraints			
e. Beyond capabilities		Y	
f. Other		Bedridden ≥14 days; Special transfer assistance	Bedridden > 7 days; Stage 2, 3, or 4 pressure sores
10. **Physical Plant**			
a. Maximum occupancy/unit	Shared if by choice	2	4
b. Size of unit (single occupancy)			80 square feet
c. Size of unit (multiple occupancy)			60 square feet/bed
d. Toilet	1 per unit		1:6 residents
e. Bath or shower	1 per unit	1 per unit*	1:8 residents
f. Other	Access to cooking facilities	Kitchen*	
11. **Agency (Licensure/Authority)**	Department of Public Health and Addiction Services Hospital and Medical Care Division	Department of Health and Social Services Division of Public Health, Licensing and Certification	Agency for Health Care Administration
12. **Notes**	* Unlicensed **Licensed ***Or AA/Diploma + 4 years' experience	*Or "readily accessible"	Resident association required; certain licensed individuals have a duty to report observations to physicians

Continued →

Figure 20.2 (continued)

	Georgia	Hawaii	Idaho
1. **Classification**	Personal-Care Homes	Assisted-Living Facilities*	Residential-Care Facilities
2. **Statutory/Regulatory References**	Ga. Code Ann. §§31–2–4 *et seq.*; Ga. Comp. R. & Regs. R.290–5–35–.01 *et seq.*	Hi. Admin. Rules §§11–90–1 *et seq.*	Idaho Code §§39–3301 *et seq.* Idaho Admin. Rules Title 3, Ch. 21
3. **Minimum Size**	2+		3+
4. **Mandatory Services**			
a. ADL care	Y	Y	Y
b. Transportation	Y	Y (or arrange access)	Y
c. Laundry		Y	Y
d. Activities/recreation	Y	Y	Y
e. Arranging health-related services		Y	Y
f. Housekeeping		Y	
g. Medications management	Y	Y	Y
h. Monitoring	Y	Y	Y
i. Other	3+ meals/day	3 meals/day	
5. **Permitted Services**			
a. Assistance with medications	Y	Y	Y
b. Administer medications	Y	Y	By trained staff
c. Intermittent nursing		"Routine nursing tasks"	Y
d. Other			
6. **Regulated Subjects**			
a. Admission agreements	Y	Y	Y
b. Resident funds	Y	Y	Y
c. Care plan		Y	Service agreement
d. Medication storage	Y	Y	Y
e. Dietary requirements	Y	Y	Y
f. Other			
7. **Administrator**			
a. Education/examination		ALF administration course	Administrator's license
b. Continuing education	16 hours/year	6+ hours/year	
c. Availability			Full time (20 hours/week)
d. Other (qualifications, etc.)		2 years' experience in related field	
8. **Staffing Levels**			
a. Staff: resident ratio	1:15 (waking hours); 1:25 (night)		Variable
b. Required hours	1+ 24 hours/day	Awake 24 hours	1+ staff 24 hours/day
c. Licensed		L.N.s, 7 days/week	
d. Other qualifications	Direct care staff; 16 hours/year education	6+ hours/year in-service education	16 hours/year training (personal assistance staff)
9. **Mandatory Discharge**			
a. Ongoing nursing care	Y		Y
b. Danger to self/others	Y	Y	Y
c. Unable to evaluate	Y		
d. Restraints	Y		Y
e. Beyond capabilities		Y	Y
f. Other	Bedridden		Bedfast; unable to feed self
10. **Physical Plant**			
a. Maximum occupancy/unit	4		2 (new)
b. Size of unit (single occupancy)	80 square feet	220 square feet	100 square feet
c. Size of unit (multiple occupancy)	80 square feet/resident	22 square feet	80 square feet/resident
d. Toilet	1:4 residents	1 per unit	1:6 persons*
e. Bath or shower	1:8 residents	1 per unit	1:8 persons*
f. Other	Furnishings	Kitchen; call system; wiring for telephone and television	
11. **Agency (Licensure/Authority)**	Department of Human Resources Personal Care Home Program	Department of Health Hospitals and Medical Facilities Branch	Department of Health and Welfare
12. **Notes**		*Based on December 1997 draft rules; final rules anticipated in the near future	* Includes employees

Continued →

Figure 20.2 **(continued)**

	Illinois	Indiana	Iowa
1. Classification	Sheltered-Care Facilities	Residential-Care Facilities	Assisted-Living Facilities
2. Statutory/Regulatory References	Ill. Rev. Stat. Ch. 111fi ¶4151–101 et seq.; Ill. Adm. Code Title 77 §§330.110 et seq.	Ind. Adm. Code Tit. 410, R. 16.2–1–36, 16.2–2–1 et seq. and 16.2–5–1 et seq.	Iowa Code §§135.C.1 et seq. 481 Iowa Admin. Code §§321.27. et seq.
3. Minimum Size	3+		
4. Mandatory Services			
a. ADL care	Y	Y	Y
b. Transportation			
c. Laundry	Y	Y	Y
d. Activities/recreation	Y	Y	Y
e. Arranging health-related services			Y
f. Housekeeping	Y		Y
g. Medications management	Y		Y
h. Monitoring			
i. Other	Variable meal plans	3+ meals/day	1+ meals/day
5. Permitted Services			
a. Assistance with medications	Y	Y	Y
b. Administer medications	By licensed M.D. or nurse	Y	Y
c. Intermittent nursing			
d. Other			
6. Regulated Subjects			
a. Admission agreements	Detailed		Detailed
b. Resident funds	Y	Y	Y
c. Care plan			Y
d. Medication storage	Y	Y	Y
e. Dietary requirements	Y	Y	
f. Other	Resident's council	Y	Managed-risk statement
7. Administrator			
a. Education/examination	High school or equivalent	High school	
b. Continuing education			
c. Availability			
d. Other (qualifications, etc.)			
8. Staffing Levels			
a. Staff: resident ratio			
b. Required hours	Full-time food services director	1+ on duty 24 hours/day (more if > 100 residents)	
c. Licensed		L.N. on site or on call	
d. Other qualifications		In-service training	
9. Mandatory Discharge			
a. Ongoing nursing care			Y
b. Danger to self/others	Y	Y	Y
c. Unable to evaluate			
d. Restraints			
e. Beyond capabilities			Y
f. Other		Serious mental or emotional problems	
10. Physical Plant			
a. Maximum occupancy/unit	4	5	
b. Size of unit (single occupancy)	100 square feet	100 square feet	190 square feet
c. Size of unit (multiple occupancy)	80 square feet/resident	60–80 square feet/bed	290 square feet/bed
d. Toilet	1:10*	Variable formula	1 per unit
e. Bath or shower	1:15*	Variable formula	1 per unit
f. Other	Furnishings	Detailed	Lockable doors; kitchen
11. Agency (Licensure/Authority)	Department of Public Health	Department of Health, Division of Regulations and Information Services	Department of Elder Affairs
12. Notes	* Minimum 1 for each sex on each floor housing residents		

Continued →

Figure 20.2 **(continued)**

	Kansas	Kentucky	Louisiana
1. Classification	Assisted-Living Facility*	Assisted-Living Residences	Adult Residential-Care Homes
2. Statutory/Regulatory References	Kansas Stat. Ann. 39–923 *et seq.* Admin. Regs. §§28–39–300 *et seq.*	Kentucky Rev. Stat. Ann. §§209.200 *et seq.*; 905 KAR 5:080	Louisiana Rev. Stat. 40:2151; Louisiana Admin. Code §§48:8901 *et seq.*
3. Minimum Size	6+	2+	2+
4. Mandatory Services			
a. ADL care	Y	Y	Y
b. Transportation	Y		
c. Laundry	Y		Y
d. Activities/recreation	Y		Y
e. Arranging health-related services	Y		
f. Housekeeping	Y		
g. Medications management	Y		Y
h. Monitoring			
i. Other	Facilitate residents' council		
5. Permitted Services			
a. Assistance with medications	By licensed staff	Y	Y
b. Administer medications	By licensed staff		
c. Intermittent nursing	Y		
d. Other			
6. Regulated Subjects			
a. Admission agreements	Y**	Y	Y
b. Resident funds	Y		Y
c. Care plan	Y		Y
d. Medication storage	Y		
e. Dietary requirements	Y		Y
f. Other	Negotiated service agreement		
7. Administrator			
a. Education/examination	High school or equivalent		BA or experience
b. Continuing education			
c. Availability			
d. Other (qualifications, etc.)			
8. Staffing Levels			
a. Staff: resident ratio			1:3 (budgeted)
b. Required hours			
c. Licensed			
d. Other qualifications	Direct care: 40 hours' training for providers		
9. Mandatory Discharge			
a. Ongoing nursing care	Y*		
b. Danger to self/others	Y*		
c. Unable to evaluate	Y*		
d. Restraints	Y*		
e. Beyond capabilities	Y*		
f. Other			
10. Physical Plant			
a. Maximum occupancy/unit		2 if by agreement	
b. Size of unit (single occupancy)	200 square feet		80 square feet
c. Size of unit (multiple occupancy)	200 square feet		60 square feet/resident
d. Toilet	1 per unit	1 per unit*	
e. Bath or shower	1 per unit	1 per unit*	
f. Other	Kitchen; lockable doors	Kitchenette*; lockable doors	Some sprinkler system; locking doors required
11. Agency (Licensure/Authority)	Department of Health and Environment	Cabinet for Human Resources, Division of Licensing and Regulations	Department of Social Services, Licensing Bureau
12. Notes	* Subset of adult care homes **Unless negotiated service agreement provides for special 24-hour services	*Unless home-style residence	A new category for assisted living is being developed.

Continued →

Figure 20.2 **(continued)**

	Maine	Maryland	Massachusetts
1. Classification	Assisted-Living Facilities/ Residential-Care Facilities*	Domiciliary Care Homes	Assisted-Living Residences
2. Statutory/Regulatory References	22 M.R.S. 7901–A *et seq.* and 7902**	MD Code Ann. §§708.4 *et seq.;* Code of MD Reg. 10.07.03 *et seq.*	Mass. Ann. Laws Ch. 109, §1 *et seq.*
3. Minimum Size	5+	5+	3+
4. Mandatory Services			
a. ADL care	Y	Y	Y
b. Transportation	Y		
c. Laundry	Y	Y	Y
d. Activities/recreation	Y	Y	Socialization
e. Arranging health-related services	Y		
f. Housekeeping	Y	Y	Y
g. Medications management	Y	Y	Y
h. Monitoring		Y	
i. Other		3 meals/24 hours	Up to 3 meals/day
5. Permitted Services			
a. Assistance with medications	Y	Y	Y
b. Administer medications	Y	By licensed staff	
c. Intermittent nursing	Y	Y	Y
d. Other			Home health
6. Regulated Subjects			
a. Admission agreements	Y	Y	Y
b. Resident funds	Y		
c. Care plan	Y		Y
d. Medication storage	Y		
e. Dietary requirements	Y	Y	Y
f. Other			
7. Administrator			
a. Education/examination	Training program		BA or experience
b. Continuing education	10 hours/year		6+ hours/year
c. Availability	40 hours/week if 50+ beds	24 hours (or delegate)	
d. Other (qualifications, etc.)			
8. Staffing Levels			
a. Staff: resident ratio	1:12 (7 a.m. to 3 p.m.) 1:18 (3 p.m. to 11 p.m.) 1:30 (11 p.m. to 7 a.m.)	1+ direct care workers: 12 residents (days)	
b. Required hours	≥2 awake 24 hours/day	24 hours/day	1+ 24 hours/day
c. Licensed			
d. Other qualifications	Direct care: certification course	Direct care; course work	6+ hours/year continuing education; 54+ hours' training (personal-care service providers)
9. Mandatory Discharge			
a. Ongoing nursing care		Y	Y*
b. Danger to self/others		Y	
c. Unable to evaluate			
d. Restraints			
e. Beyond capabilities			
f. Other			
10. Physical Plant			
a. Maximum occupancy/unit	2 (newer facilities)	6	2
b. Size of unit (single occupancy)	100 square feet	80 square feet	
c. Size of unit (multiple occupancy)	80 square feet/resident	60 square feet/resident	
d. Toilet	1:6 users	1:6 residents (same sex)	1/unit (new)
e. Bath or shower	1:15 users	1:12 beds	1/unit (new)
f. Other			Lockable doors; access to cooking facilities
11. Agency (Licensure/Authority)	Department of Human Services, Bureau of Medical Services, Division of Residential Care	Office on Aging, Senior Assisted Housing Division	Executive Office of Elder Affairs
12. Notes	*Level II **"Emergency Rules" effective 10/20/97		*Unless certain conditions are met

Continued →

Figure 20.2 **(continued)**

	Michigan	Minnesota	Mississippi
1. Classification	Homes for the Aged Establishments/Assisted Living	Housing with Services	Personal-Care Homes
2. Statutory/Regulatory References	MSA 14.15.20301 *et seq.* Mich. Admin. Code R 325. 1801	Minn. Stat. §§144D.01 *et seq.*; Minn. Rules §§4668.0002 *et seq.**	Miss. Code Ann. 43–11–1 Miss. Regs. §§1201.1 *et seq.*
3. Minimum Size	21+*		
4. Mandatory Services			
a. ADL care	Y	Y**	Y
b. Transportation			
c. Laundry	Y		Y
d. Activities/recreation			Y
e. Arranging health-related services			
f. Housekeeping			
g. Medications management		Y**	Y
h. Monitoring			
i. Other	3+ meals/day	Professional or delegated nursing**	3 meals/day
5. Permitted Services			
a. Assistance with medications		Y	
b. Administer medications		By trained staff	
c. Intermittent nursing		Y	
d. Other			Administration of insulin by L.N.
6. Regulated Subjects			
a. Admission agreements		Detailed	Y
b. Resident funds	Y		
c. Care plan		Y	
d. Medication storage		Y	Y
e. Dietary requirements	Y		Y
f. Other			
7. Administrator			
a. Education/examination			
b. Continuing education			
c. Availability			Full time
d. Other (qualifications, etc.)			
8. Staffing Levels			
a. Staff: resident ratio			1:10 (7:00 a.m. to 6:00 p.m.)
b. Required hours	1+ awake 24 hours/day		
c. Licensed			
d. Other qualifications		In-service training	Full-time dietary if 11+ residents
9. Mandatory Discharge			
a. Ongoing nursing care	Y		Y
b. Danger to self/others			Y
c. Unable to evaluate			Y
d. Restraints			Y
e. Beyond capabilities			Y
f. Other	Certain mental conditions		Nonambulatory; incontinent
10. Physical Plant			
a. Maximum occupancy/unit	4 (new construction)		4
b. Size of unit (single occupancy)	80 square feet (100 new)		80 square feet
c. Size of unit (multiple occupancy)	70 square feet (80 new)		80 square feet/resident
d. Toilet	1:8 beds per floor		1:6
e. Bath or shower	1:15 beds per floor		1:12
f. Other			
11. Agency (Licensure/Authority)	Department of Consumer and Industry Services Bureau of Health Systems	Department of Health, Interagency Long-Term Care Planning Committee	Department of Health, Health Facilities License and Certification Division
12. Notes	Residents must be over 60 *Up to 21 if operated as distinct part of nursing home	* Based on draft rules; over 80% of residents must be 55 or older **At least one of the above	

Continued →

Figure 20.2 **(continued)**

	Missouri	Montana	Nebraska
1. Classification	Residential-Care Facilities II	Personal-Care Facilities	Assisted-Living Facilities
2. Statutory/Regulatory References	Mo. Rev. Stat. §§198.003 *et seq.* Mo. Code of Regs. Tit. 13 §§15–10.010 *et seq.*	Mont. Code Ann. §§50–5–101; 50–5–225 *et seq.*; Mont. Admin. Rules 16.32.380; 1632.388; 16.32.901–22	Neb. Rev. Stat. §§71–2017 Neb. Admin. Regs. Tit. 175, Ch. 11
3. Minimum Size	3+	18+	4+
4. Mandatory Services			
a. ADL care	Y	Y	Y
b. Transportation		Y	
c. Laundry		Y	Y
d. Activities/recreation	Y	Y	Y
e. Arranging health-related services		Y	
f. Housekeeping	Y	Y	
g. Medications management	Y	Y	
h. Monitoring	Y	Y	
i. Other	3 meals/day	3+ meals/day	
5. Permitted Services			
a. Assistance with medications	Y	Y	Y
b. Administer medications	Y	Category B only	Y
c. Intermittent nursing		Category A: 20 days; Category B: nursing permitted for up to 5 residents	
d. Other	Dietary supervision		
6. Regulated Subjects			
a. Admission agreements		Y	Y
b. Resident funds	Y		
c. Care plan		Y	Y
d. Medication storage	Y	Y	Y
e. Dietary requirements	Y	Y	Y
f. Other			
7. Administrator			
a. Education/examination	Licensed nursing home administrator	High school or GED	
b. Continuing education		6 hours/year	
c. Availability			
d. Other (qualifications, etc.)			
8. Staffing Levels			
a. Staff: resident ratio	1:15 (day); 1:20 (evening); 1:25 (night)		
b. Required hours		1+ staff 24 hours/day	1+ staff 24 hours/day
c. Licensed			
d. Other qualifications		Preservice training (direct care staff)	
9. Mandatory Discharge			
a. Ongoing nursing care	Y	Over 20 days*	
b. Danger to self/others			
c. Unable to evaluate			
d. Restraints		Y*	
e. Beyond capabilities	Y		
f. Other	Hospitalization (45+ days)	Bedridden;* complete incontinence; unable to self-administer medications (Category A)	
10. Physical Plant			
a. Maximum occupancy/unit	4	4	3
b. Size of unit (single occupancy)	70 square feet*	100 square feet	80–100 square feet*
c. Size of unit (multiple occupancy)	70 square feet/resident*	80 square feet/bed	60–180 square feet/resident*
d. Toilet	1:6 residents	1:4 residents	1 per room (new)
e. Bath or shower	1:20 residents	1:12 residents	1:8 residents (new)
f. Other	Detailed	Detailed	Detailed
11. Agency (Licensure/Authority)	Department of Social Services, Division of Aging	Department of Public Health and Human Services, Health Facilities Division	Department of Health, Division of Licensing and Data Management
12. Notes	* Licensed pre-1987, 60 square feet	* Exceptions for up to 5 residents in Category B facilities	*New facilities must provide larger bedrooms.

Continued →

Figure 20.2 (continued)

	Nevada	New Hampshire	New Jersey
1. Classification	Residential Facilities for Groups	Residential-Care Home Facilities	Assisted-Living Residences
2. Statutory/Regulatory References	Nev. Rev. Stat. §§449.017 et seq.; Nev. Administrative Code §§449.156 et seq.	New Hampshire Revised Stat. Ann. §§151:1 et seq.	25 N.J. Reg. §§6037 et seq. N.J.A.C. 8:36–1.1 et seq.
3. Minimum Size	3+	2+	4+
4. Mandatory Services			
a. ADL care	Y	Y	Y
b. Transportation			Y
c. Laundry	Y	Y	Y
d. Activities/recreation	Y	Y	Y
e. Arranging health-related services		Y	Y
f. Housekeeping		Y	Y
g. Medications management	Y	Y	Y
h. Monitoring	Y	Y	
i. Other	Meals	3 meals/day	3 meals/day
5. Permitted Services			
a. Assistance with medications		Y	Y
b. Administer medications			By qualified staff
c. Intermittent nursing		Y	Y
d. Other			
6. Regulated Subjects			
a. Admission agreements	Y	Y	Y
b. Resident funds	Y		Y
c. Care plan		Y	Y
d. Medication storage		Y	Y
e. Dietary requirements	Y	Y	Y
f. Other	Advertising		Managed-risk agreements
7. Administrator			
a. Education/examination	High school or equivalent; examination	High school plus additional education and experience*	High school or equivalent
b. Continuing education			10 hours/year
c. Availability		Full time	2+ at all times (designee)
d. Other (qualifications, etc.)	3 years' experience		Nursing Home Administrator, eligible to take nursing home administrator examination or course work
8. Staffing Levels			
a. Staff: resident ratio			
b. Required hours	1+ awake 24 hours/day if >20 residents	1+ 24 hours/day (awake if 17+ residents)	2+ on site 24 hours/day (1+ awake)
c. Licensed			R.N. on call
d. Other qualifications			
9. Mandatory Discharge			
a. Ongoing nursing care		Y, or can contract for care	
b. Danger to self/others			
c. Unable to evaluate			
d. Restraints			
e. Beyond capabilities	Y		
f. Other	Bedfast	Nonmobile, or can contract for care	
10. Physical Plant			
a. Maximum occupancy/unit		2	
b. Size of unit (single occupancy)	80 square feet/bed	80 square feet/resident	150 square feet
c. Size of unit (multiple occupancy)	60 square feet/resident	140 square feet/resident	80 additional square feet/resident
d. Toilet	1:9 residents	1:6 residents	1 per unit
e. Bath or shower	1:6 residents	1:6 residents	1 per unit
f. Other	Sprinkler system		Kitchenette; lockable door
11. Agency (Licensure/Authority)	Division of Health, Bureau of Licensure and Certification	Department of Health and Human Services, Bureau of Health Facilities	Department of Health, Division of Health Facilities Evaluation and Licensing
12. Notes	"Financing plan" required by state	* Varies according to facility size	

Continued →

Figure 20.2 **(continued)**

	New Mexico	New York	North Carolina
1. Classification	Adult Residential Shelter Care Home	Assisted-Living Program*	Assisted-Living Residences*
2. Statutory/Regulatory References	N.M. Stat. Ann. §§24–1–1 *et seq.*; N.M. Reg. HED 90–1	N.Y. Soc. Serv. Law §§461–1 *et seq.* N.Y. Comp. Codes R. & Regs. Title 18, Ch. 2, Subpart D, §§485.1 *et seq.*	N.C. Gen. Stat. §§131D–2 *et seq.* N.C. Admin. Code Title 10, Ch. 42 §§1200 *et seq.*
3. Minimum Size	3+	5+	2+
4. Mandatory Services			
a. ADL care	Y	Y	Y
b. Transportation	Assistance in using (public)		
c. Laundry	Y		
d. Activities/recreation	Y	Y	Y
e. Arranging health-related services	Y	Y	
f. Housekeeping	Y	Y	Y
g. Medications management	Y	Y	Y
h. Monitoring	Y	Y	
i. Other	Money management; correspondence; telephone calls	Home health	1+ meal/day
5. Permitted Services			
a. Assistance with medications	Y	Y	Y
b. Administer medications	By licensed staff		
c. Intermittent nursing	Y	Y	Through licensed agencies
d. Other			
6. Regulated Subjects			
a. Admission agreements	Y	Y	Y
b. Resident funds	Y	Y	Y
c. Care plan	Y	Y**	Y
d. Medication storage	Y	Y	
e. Dietary requirements	Y	Y	
f. Other		See additional rules**	
7. Administrator			
a. Education/examination	High school or GED		High school or GED
b. Continuing education			12 hours/year
c. Availability			
d. Other (qualifications, etc.)			
8. Staffing Levels			
a. Staff: resident ratio	1:15*	Variable	Variable
b. Required hours			
c. Licensed			
d. Other qualifications	In-service training	40 hours' training (direct care) plus 3 hours/year in-service	Variable training requirements for personal-care aides
9. Mandatory Discharge			
a. Ongoing nursing care	Y	Y	Y
b. Danger to self/others		Y	
c. Unable to evaluate			
d. Restraints			
e. Beyond capabilities		Y	
f. Other	4+ nonmobile residents	Bedfast; chairfast; cognitive impairments	Various physical conditions 4+ ADLs
10. Physical Plant			
a. Maximum occupancy/unit	2	Only if by choice in "Enriched Housing"	4
b. Size of unit (single occupancy)	100 square feet	85 square feet (enriched) 100 (adult)	100 square feet**
c. Size of unit (multiple occupancy)	80 square feet	140 square feet (enriched) 160 (adult)	80 square feet**
d. Toilet	1:8	1 per unit (enriched) 1:6 (adult)	1:5 residents**
e. Bath or shower	1:8	1 per unit (enriched) 1:10 (adult)	1:10 residents**
f. Other		Call system; sprinkler (some)	
11. Agency (Licensure/Authority)	Department of Health, Division of Public Health	Department of Health, Department of Social Services,	Department of Human Resources, Division of Facility Services Office of Housing and Adult Services
12. Notes	*Fewer during sleeping hours	* Must also be licensed adult home or enriched housing program *and* **be or contract with a home health agency	*Adult care homes **Or self-contained apartments

Continued →

Figure 20.2 **(continued)**

	North Dakota	Ohio	Oklahoma
1. Classification	Basic Care Facilities	Residential-Care Facilities	Residential-Care Homes
2. Statutory/Regulatory References	N.D. Cent. Code §§23–09.3–01 *et seq.*; N.D. Administrative Code §§33–03–24.1–01 *et seq.*	Ohio Rev. Code Ann. §§3721.01 *et seq.* OAC Ann. §§5122:3–5–01 *et seq.*	63 Okla. Stat. §§1–819 *et seq.*; Okla. Admin. Regs. §§310:680–1–1 *et seq.*
3. Minimum Size	5+	3+	
4. Mandatory Services			
a. ADL care	Y	Y	Y
b. Transportation	Y	Y	
c. Laundry	Y	Or transport to laundromat	
d. Activities/recreation	Y	Y	
e. Arranging health-related services	Y	Y	
f. Housekeeping	Y		Y
g. Medications management	Y	Y	Y
h. Monitoring	Y*	Y	
i. Other	3 meals/day	Shopping; correspondence	3 meals/day
5. Permitted Services			
a. Assistance with medications	Y	Y	Y
b. Administer medications	Y	By licensed staff	By licensed or certified staff
c. Intermittent nursing	Y	Y	Implied
d. Other			
6. Regulated Subjects			
a. Admission agreements		Risk agreement	Y
b. Resident funds		Y	Y
c. Care plan	Y	Y	
d. Medication storage	Y	Y	Y
e. Dietary requirements	Y	Y	Y
f. Other			Residents' advisory council
7. Administrator			
a. Education/examination	BA and Nursing Home Administrator license or experience	Nursing Home Administrator or 100 hours' post–high school education in gerontology*	Certificate of training 50 hours
b. Continuing education	12 hours/year		16 hours/year
c. Availability		≥ 16 hours/week	1/3 of working time on site
d. Other (qualifications, etc.)		+ 2,000 hours' experience	
8. Staffing Levels			
a. Staff: resident ratio		1+ on site 24 hours/day	
b. Required hours			3/4 hour/resident/day (based on average daily census)
c. Licensed			
d. Other qualifications	Continuing education for dietary and activities staff; in-service training	Training (personal care)	Training
9. Mandatory Discharge			
a. Ongoing nursing care		Unless authorized	Y
b. Danger to self/others			Y
c. Unable to evaluate	Y		
d. Restraints			
e. Beyond capabilities	Y	Unless risk agreement is signed	Y
f. Other			Nonambulatory
10. Physical Plant			
a. Maximum occupancy/unit			
b. Size of unit (single occupancy)	100 square feet	100 square feet	80 square feet
c. Size of unit (multiple occupancy)	80 square feet/bed (double occupancy) 70 square feet/bed (3+ beds)	80 square feet/person	60 square feet/bed
d. Toilet	1:4 residents	1:8 residents	1:6 residents
e. Bath or shower	1:15 residents	1:8 residents	1:10 residents
f. Other	Window; furnishings	Sprinkler system	Window
11. Agency (Licensure/Authority)	Department of Health, Health Resources Section	Department of Health, Division of Health Facilities Regulation	Department of Health
12. Notes	*General supervision North Dakota law contains a definition of assisted living—it is not a licensure category.	A statutory scheme for assisted living was enacted and then repealed.	Proposed legislation for assisted living is being developed.

Continued →

Figure 20.2 **(continued)**

	Oregon	Pennsylvania	Rhode Island
1. Classification	Assisted Living	Personal-Care Homes	Residential-Care and Assisted-Living Facilities
2. Statutory/Regulatory References	Oregon Rev. Stat. 443.400 *et seq.* Oregon Admin. Rules §411–56–000 *et seq.*	62 Pa. Stats. §§211 *et seq.* 55 Pa. Code §§2620.1 *et seq.*	R.I. Gen. Laws §§23–17.4–1 *et seq.* Code of R.I. Rules 14–090–025
3. Minimum Size		4+	2+
4. Mandatory Services			
a. ADL care	Y	Y	Y
b. Transportation	Y	Securing transportation	
c. Laundry	Y	Y	Y
d. Activities/recreation	Y	Y	Y
e. Arranging health-related services	Y	Y	"Supportive services"
f. Housekeeping	Y	Y	Y
g. Medications management	Y	Y	Y
h. Monitoring	Y	Y	Y
i. Other	Money management; 3+ meals/day	3+ meals/day	3+ meals/day
5. Permitted Services			
a. Assistance with medications	Y	Y	Y
b. Administer medications	Y		By licensed or specially trained staff*
c. Intermittent nursing	Y		
d. Other			
6. Regulated Subjects			
a. Admission agreements		Y	
b. Resident funds	Y	Y	Y
c. Care plan	Y		
d. Medication storage	Y	Y	Y
e. Dietary requirements	Y	Y	Y
f. Other			
7. Administrator			
a. Education/examination	Required internship	High school or GED plus 40 hours' training	40 hours' course work or Nursing Home Administrator
b. Continuing education	20 hours/year	6 hours/year	16 hours/year
c. Availability		24 hours or designee	
d. Other (qualifications, etc.)			May not administer more than 3 facilities with 120 aggregate beds
8. Staffing Levels			
a. Staff: resident ratio	Variable	Variable	
b. Required hours			"Responsible adult" 24 hours/day
c. Licensed			R.N. visit once every 30 days
d. Other qualifications	Preservice training		4+ hours' training
9. Mandatory Discharge			
a. Ongoing nursing care	8+ days (unless approved by department)		
b. Danger to self/others		Y	
c. Unable to evaluate			
d. Restraints			
e. Beyond capabilities		Y	
f. Other		"Capable of self-preservation in emergency" unless facility meets stringent life safety code	
10. Physical Plant			
a. Maximum occupancy/unit		4	2
b. Size of unit (single occupancy)	220 square feet (new construction)	80 square feet	100 square feet
c. Size of unit (multiple occupancy)	220 square feet (new construction)	60 square feet/person	160 square feet (double occupancy)
d. Toilet	1/unit*	1:6 users	1:8 beds
e. Bath or shower	1/unit**	1:15 users	1:10 beds
f. Other	Kitchen; storage space; telephone jack; lockable doors	Window; furnishings	Locking doors with master key; no portable cooking facilities
11. Agency (Licensure/Authority)	Department of Human Resources, Senior and Disabled Services Division	Department of Public Welfare Department of Aging, Division of Policy	Department of Health, Facilities Regulation Division
12. Notes	*Or 1:8 **Or 1:10		*In "M" level facilities

Continued →

Figure 20.2 (continued)

	South Carolina	South Dakota	Tennessee
1. **Classification**	Community Residential-Care Facilities	Assisted-Living Center	Assisted-Care Living Facilities*
2. **Statutory/Regulatory References**	S.C. Code Ann. §§40–35–10 *et seq.* 44–7–130, 44–7–260 *et seq.*; S.C. Code Regs. 61–84	S.D. Cod. Laws Ann. §§34–12–1.1 *et seq.*; S.D. Admin. R. 44:04:01:01.01 *et seq.*	Tenn. Code Ann. 68–11–201; Tenn. Rules §§1200–8–25–.01 *et seq.*
3. **Minimum Size**	2+	5+	1+
4. **Mandatory Services**			
a. ADL care	Y	Y	Y
b. Transportation	Arranging for		
c. Laundry	Linens	Y	
d. Activities/recreation	Y	Y	Y
e. Arranging health-related services			
f. Housekeeping	Y		
g. Medications management	Y	Y	Y
h. Monitoring	Y		Y
i. Other	Money management		3 meals/day
5. **Permitted Services**			
a. Assistance with medications	Y		Y
b. Administer medications	Y	Y*	By licensed professional
c. Intermittent nursing			Y**
d. Other			
6. **Regulated Subjects**			
a. Admission agreements		Y	Y
b. Resident funds	Y		Y
c. Care plan	Y		
d. Medication storage	Y	Y	Y
e. Dietary requirements	Y	Y	Y
f. Other			
7. **Administrator**			
a. Education/examination	High school or equivalent; 12 months' experience; examination	High school or equivalent; training program	High school or GED
b. Continuing education	12 hours/year		24 hours/2 years
c. Availability	Full time during "normal working hours" (if 10+ beds)		
d. Other (qualifications, etc.)			
8. **Staffing Levels**			
a. Staff: resident ratio	1:10/building ("peak" hours); 1:44/building (night)		
b. Required hours	1+ on active duty at all times	Detailed	1+ 24 hours/day
c. Licensed			
d. Other qualifications			
9. **Mandatory Discharge**			
a. Ongoing nursing care	Y	Y	
b. Danger to self/others	Y		Y
c. Unable to evaluate	Y		Y
d. Restraints			Y
e. Beyond capabilities			
f. Other		Nonambulatory (unless call system is provided); "capable of self-preservation" (unless stringent life safety code is met); some cognitive impairments	Various health-related conditions
10. **Physical Plant**			
a. Maximum occupancy/unit	4	2	2
b. Size of unit (single occupancy)	80 square feet	120 square feet (new)	80 square feet/resident
c. Size of unit (multiple occupancy)	60 square feet/bed	200 square feet (double occupancy) (new)	80 square feet/resident
d. Toilet	1:8 residents	1:2 rooms (up to 4 beds)	1:6 persons
e. Bath or shower	1:10 beds		1:6 persons
f. Other	Detailed		Furnishings; detailed fire safety
11. **Agency (Licensure/Authority)**	Department of Health and Environmental Control	Department of Health, Division of Health Facilities Licensure	Department of Health, Division of Health and Environment
12. **Notes**	Plan for assisted living under development	* But facility must contract with R.N. for review and with R.N. or pharmacist for training	*Draft rules; will go into effect in near future **By licensed home care organization

Continued →

Figure 20.2 **(continued)**

	Texas	Utah	Vermont
1. Classification	Personal-Care Facilities	Assisted-Living Facilities	Residential-Care Homes
2. Statutory/Regulatory References	Tex. Health & Safety Code §§247.001 *et seq.*; Tex. Admin. Code §§92.1 *et seq.*	Utah Code Ann. §§26–21–1 *et seq.* Utah Admin. Code R432–15–1	Vt. Stat. Ann. Tit. 33 §§710 *et seq.*; Vermont RCH Lic. Regulations
3. Minimum Size	4+	2+	3+
4. Mandatory Services			
a. ADL care	Y	Y	Y
b. Transportation		Make arrangements	Y
c. Laundry		Y	Y
d. Activities/recreation		Y	
e. Arranging health-related services		Y	
f. Housekeeping		Y	
g. Medications management	Y	Y	Y
h. Monitoring	Y		Y
i. Other		3+ meals/day	3 meals/day
5. Permitted Services			
a. Assistance with medications	Y	Y	Y
b. Administer medications	By licensed staff	By licensed nurse	Y
c. Intermittent nursing		Y	Level III facilities only
d. Other			Intermittent home health
6. Regulated Subjects			
a. Admission agreements	Y	Y	Y
b. Resident funds	Limited	Y	Y
c. Care plan	Y	Y	
d. Medication storage	Y	Y	Y
e. Dietary requirements	Y	Y	Y
f. Other			
7. Administrator			
a. Education/examination	High school or equivalent	BA or license or AA plus 4 years' experience (large facility)	State-approved course work and additional experience
b. Continuing education	6 hours/year		
c. Availability	40 hours/week		
d. Other (qualifications, etc.)			
8. Staffing Levels			
a. Staff: resident ratio	1:15 (day); 1:20 (evening); 1:40 (night)		
b. Required hours		24 hours (direct care personnel)	1+ staff 24 hours/day
c. Licensed			
d. Other qualifications		In-service training	Direct care: 20 hours' training/year
9. Mandatory Discharge			
a. Ongoing nursing care			Y
b. Danger to self/others	Y	Y	
c. Unable to evaluate	Type A facilities		
d. Restraints			
e. Beyond capabilities	Y		Y
f. Other		Tuberculosis or other communicable diseases (under some circumstances)	
10. Physical Plant			
a. Maximum occupancy/unit	4	2	2 (new)
b. Size of unit (single occupancy)	Type A: 80 square feet Type B: 100 square feet	120 square feet*	100 square feet
c. Size of unit (multiple occupancy)	Type A: 60 square feet/bed Type B: 80 square feet/bed	200 square feet**	80 square feet/bed
d. Toilet	1:6 residents	1:4 residents	1:8 beds per floor
e. Bath or shower	1:10 residents	1:10 residents	1:8 beds per floor
f. Other	Fire alarm system; other detailed requirements	Sprinkler system required in some facilities	Window; furnishings
11. Agency (Licensure/Authority)	Department of Human Services	Department of Health, Health Facility Licensure	Agency of Human Services, Department of Aging and Disabilities
12. Notes	Medicaid waiver in place for services provided in apartment-type settings	If unit has additional living space: * 100 square feet ** 160 square feet	

Continued →

Figure 20.2 **(continued)**

	Virginia	Washington	West Virginia
1. Classification	Adult-Care Residences*	Assisted-Living/Boarding Homes*	Personal-Care Homes
2. Statutory/Regulatory References	Va. Code Ann. §§63.1–172 *et seq.* 22 VAC §§40–71–10 *et seq.*	Wash. Rev. Code §7.38 and 74.39A *et seq.*; Wash. Admin. Code §§388–110–005 *et seq.*; 246–316–010 *et seq.*	West Va. Code §§16–5C–1 *et seq.*; West Va. Admin. Rules §§64–14–1 *et seq.*
3. Minimum Size	4+		4+
4. Mandatory Services			
a. ADL care	Y	Y	Y
b. Transportation	Assistance arranging	Assistance arranging	Y
c. Laundry	Y	Y	Y
d. Activities/recreation	Y	Y	11+ hours/week
e. Arranging health-related services	Y	Y	Y
f. Housekeeping		Y	Y
g. Medications management		Y	Y
h. Monitoring			Y
i. Other	3+ meals/day	3+ meals/day; limited nursing	
5. Permitted Services			
a. Assistance with medications	Y	Y	Y
b. Administer medications	By licensed or trained staff	By licensed staff	Y
c. Intermittent nursing	Y	Y	Y
d. Other			
6. Regulated Subjects			
a. Admission agreements	Y	Y	Y
b. Resident funds	Y	Y	Y
c. Care plan	Y	Y	Y
d. Medication storage	Y		Y
e. Dietary requirements	Y	Y	Y
f. Other			
7. Administrator			
a. Education/examination	High school or GED plus 1 year post-secondary education (with some exceptions)	40-hour training course	High school or equivalent; New: AA in related field
b. Continuing education		10 hours/year	10+ hours/year
c. Availability	40 hours/week awake (or designee)	Full time	
d. Other (qualifications, etc.)	Training course within 30 days	Various combinations of education and experience	
8. Staffing Levels			
a. Staff: resident ratio			Variable
b. Required hours	1+ awake 24 hours/day		1+ 24 hours/day
c. Licensed	Employ or contract with health care professional	To provide some services	
d. Other qualifications	8+ hours/year training (direct care)	10+ hours/year training	
9. Mandatory Discharge			
a. Ongoing nursing care	Y		
b. Danger to self/others	Y	Y	
c. Unable to evaluate			
d. Restraints			
e. Beyond capabilities	Y	Y	Y
f. Other	Certain health-related conditions		
10. Physical Plant			
a. Maximum occupancy/unit	4	2 (if by choice)	4 (existing); 2 (new)
b. Size of unit (single occupancy)	100 square feet/ (new) 80 square feet (change in use)	220 square feet (new) 180 square feet (existing)	80 square feet
c. Size of unit (multiple occupancy)	80 square feet (new) 60 square feet (change in use)	220 square feet (new) 180 square feet (existing)	60 square feet (existing); 80 square feet (new)
d. Toilet	1:7 residents	1 per unit	1:5 residents
e. Bath or shower	1:10 residents	1 per unit	1:10 residents
f. Other	Window	Kitchen; lockable door	Windows; furnishings; sprinkler and fire alarm systems
11. Agency (Licensure/Authority)	Department of Social Services, Division of Health and Human Resources	Department of Social and Health Services	Department of Health and Human Resources
12. Notes	2 classifications: assisted living (summarized here) and residential living (lower level of care)	*Residential care (boarding) homes contract with state to provide assisted-living-type services (Medicaid waiver).	

Continued →

Figure 20.2 (continued)

	Wisconsin	Wyoming
1. **Classification**	Residential-Care Apartment Complex	Assisted-Living Facilities
2. **Statutory/Regulatory References**	HFS §§89.11 *et seq.* Wis. Stat. §§46.03, 50.01 *et seq.* Wis. Admin. Code Ch. HSS 3	Wyo. Stat. §§35–2–901 *et seq.*
3. **Minimum Size**	5+	
4. **Mandatory Services**		
a. ADL care	Y*	Y
b. Transportation		Y
c. Laundry	Y*	Y
d. Activities/recreation		Y
e. Arranging health-related services	Y*	Y
f. Housekeeping	Y	Y
g. Medications management	Y*	Y
h. Monitoring	Y*	Y
i. Other		Several other services
5. **Permitted Services**		
a. Assistance with medications	Y*	Y
b. Administer medications	By or supervised by nurse or M.D.	By licensed staff
c. Intermittent nursing	Y*	Y
d. Other		
6. **Regulated Subjects**		
a. Admission agreements	Y	Y
b. Resident funds		
c. Care plan		Y
d. Medication storage		
e. Dietary requirements		Detailed
f. Other	Risk agreement	
7. **Administrator**		
a. Education/examination		Examination
b. Continuing education		
c. Availability		24 hours or delegate
d. Other (qualifications, etc.)		
8. **Staffing Levels**		
a. Staff: resident ratio		
b. Required hours		1+ staff awake 24 hours (if 10+ beds)
c. Licensed		R.N., L.P.N., or C.N.A./every shift; must employ or contract with R.N.
d. Other qualifications		
9. **Mandatory Discharge**		
a. Ongoing nursing care		
b. Danger to self/others		
c. Unable to evaluate		
d. Restraints		
e. Beyond capabilities		
f. Other		Care for certain health-related conditions is prohibited
10. **Physical Plant**		
a. Maximum occupancy/unit	2 (spouse or chosen roommate)	2
b. Size of unit (single occupancy)	250+ square feet	120 square feet
c. Size of unit (multiple occupancy)	250+ square feet	80 square feet/bed
d. Toilet	Individual	1:2 residents
e. Bath or shower	Individual	1:10 residents
f. Other	Kitchen; lockable entrances	Furnishings
11. **Agency (Licensure/Authority)**	Department of Health	Wyoming Department of Health, Health Facilities
12. **Notes**	* Up to 28 hours of combined services/week	

Figure 20.2 **(continued)**

Notes:

In general—Figure 20.2 was derived principally from information contained in the statutes and regulations of each state and from conversations with the applicable regulatory authorities. "Y" indicates that there is a provision on point; a blank space indicates that there is no provision on point in the specific laws summarized here. Certain additional regulatory requirements may, however, be contained in separate code provisions that supplement the licensure scheme. Rules are generally much more complex than the figure indicates.

1. **Classification**—Term used to describe the regulated facility or service.
2. **Statutory/regulatory references**—Beginning citation to applicable laws and regulations.
3. **Minimum size**—Number of residents unrelated to the provider who, if housed and cared for, trigger the need for licensure within the given classification.
4. **Mandatory services**—Services that *must* be provided by licensee (assumes housing and meals will be provided but may specify number of meals required).
   a. **ADL care**—activities of daily living are usually defined by state regulations and ordinarily include some combination of bathing, grooming, dressing, toileting, transferring, feeding, and ambulating.
   b. **Transportation**—Transportation to medical appointments or other activities required (or assistance arranging transportation, if indicated).
   c. **Laundry**—May include linens and clothing; may include equipment accessible by residents.
   d. **Activities/recreation**—Regulations may specify types and minimum number of hours.
   e. **Arranging health-related services**—May include medical and dental care and therapeutic services.
   f. **Housekeeping**—Typically includes cleaning rooms and changing bed linens.
   g. **Medications management**—Oversight that may include distribution of and recordkeeping regarding medications (may also include items included under "Assistance with medications," below).
   h. **Monitoring**—Ongoing or regular periodic evaluations of residents' health status and functional abilities.
5. **Permitted services**—Services that *may* be provided within the limits of the license.
   a. **Assistance with medications**—Assistance that does not include actual administration of medications; may include reminders, prompting, identifying medications, opening containers, positioning residents, storage, and disposal.
   b. **Administer medications**—States define variously; may include opening containers, preparing dosages, giving to residents, observance of swallowing, preparing and injecting injectables, and charting.
   c. **Intermittent nursing**—Nursing services short of 24-hour nursing care; may include supervision and monitoring, performance of specified services, and case management.
   d. **Other**—Health-related services that may be provided directly or under contract.
6. **Regulated subjects**
   a. **Admission agreements**—Contract with residents that usually sets forth services, fees, etc.
   b. **Resident funds**—Typically provides for safeguarding of and/or account for such funds.
   c. **Care plan**—Written description of services needed by resident; periodic update may be required.
   d. **Medication storage**—Typically includes locked area, temperature, labeling, and documentation.
   e. **Dietary requirements**—Usually details varieties of foods; provision of therapeutic diets.
   f. **Other**—Other significant subjects of regulation; this list is not exhaustive. "Detailed" means numerous or complex regulatory requirements in addition to those summarized here.
7. **Administrator**—Individual with overall supervisory authority.
   a. **Education/examination**—High school, bachelor's degree, associate's degree, licensed nursing home administrator.
   b. **Continuing education**—Coursework or training related to administrator's role expressed in terms of number of hours per year or other period.
   c. **Availability**—Number of hours on site or in proximity to facility.
   d. **Other (qualifications, etc.)**—Additional training, experience, or other requirements.
8. **Staffing levels**
   a. **Staff: resident ratio**—May set only minimum levels; regulations may also require "sufficient" staff, which the licensing agency will evaluate.
   b. **Required hours**—May vary depending on hours (e.g., days and evenings) or size of facility.
   c. **Licensed**—Licensed Nurse, Registered Nurse, Licensed Practical Nurse, Licensed Vocational Nurse, Certified Nurse's Aide.
   d. **Other qualifications**—Additional training or education requirements for staff.
9. **Mandatory discharge**—Circumstances under which discharge of a resident is required by law.
   a. **Ongoing nursing care**—May be defined as daily or 24-hour/day nursing care.
   b. **Danger to self/others**—Poses an imminent threat to the health/safety of self or others.
   c. **Unable to evacuate**—In some states, this encompasses the technical definition of nonambulatory: inability to self-propel to safety in an emergency.
   d. **Restraints**—Residents requiring restraints.
   e. **Beyond capabilities**—Licensee is unable to provide needed level of care.
   f. **Other**—Regulations may specify, for example, certain health conditions.
10. **Physical plant**
    a. **Maximum occupancy/unit**—Number of residents who may share a bedroom or a self-contained apartmentlike unit.
    b, c. **Size of unit**—This ordinarily excludes closets, bathrooms, vestibules, etc.
    d. **Toilet**—Expressed in terms of number of toilets per number of residents.
    e. **Bath or shower**—Expressed in terms of number of baths/showers per number of residents.
    f. **Other**—Note: A state building code often contains additional requirements, e.g., structural requirements and fire safety.
11. **Agency (licensure/authority)**—Agency that oversees licensing or certification.
12. **Notes**—May refer to a similar or proposed scheme for assisted living; many states are planning to develop or have in draft form legislation covering new assisted-living models.

- Efforts by licensing agencies to identify unlicensed board-and-care homes are minimal.
- Many community-based services are not available to residents of board-and-care homes. A majority of the surveyed counties offered optical, routine medical, senior center, and protective/legal services but did not make available mental health care, home health care, transportation, and outreach services.

Based on the survey, AARP made the following recommendations to improve board-and-care regulations:

- States should establish staff-to-resident ratios that ensure quality of care but offer flexibility for industry innovation.
- States should guarantee annual inspections and upgrade the skills of inspection staff.
- States should grant regulators wider authority to enforce regulations, including the authority to revoke licenses and ban admissions or referrals. They should also encourage prosecutors to indict and try violators with serious or repeated deficiencies that present a threat to residents' health and safety.
- County or local agencies and state agencies should develop complementary roles to ensure the implementation and enforcement of state regulations.
- In cooperation with local agencies, states should make efforts to identify and license board-and-care homes that meet licensure criteria.
- States should promulgate regulations that require regulatory agencies both to assist unlicensed homes in obtaining licensure and to close and relocate the residents of homes refusing licensure or failing to meet standards.
- Counties should be required to offer board-and-care residents the same community services that they offer to other eligible county residents.

The American Seniors Housing Association published a 1997 summary of the assisted-living laws and regulations for all 50 states (see Figure 20.2). The following highlights the more interesting topics covered by the assisted-living laws and the number of states taking a similar approach:

Mandatory Services	States Regulating
Assistance with activities of daily living	All 50 require
Arranging health-related services	25 require, 25 do not require
Medications management	34 require
Monitoring resident health status	22 require
Permitted Services	
Assisting with medications	39 permit
Administering medications	32 permit, most require licensed staff
Intermittent nursing	25 permit, with limits
Regulated Subjects	
Admission contracts	32 regulate
Care plans	24 regulate
Staffing Levels	
Ratios	17 regulate, from 1:10 to 1:30 during days and 1:45 during nights
Hours	27 regulate, usually 1 or more awake 24 hours
Mandatory Discharge	
Ongoing nursing care	21 prohibit
Danger to self/others	22 require discharge
Physical Plant	
Maximum occupancy	33 restrict; usually 2 people
Baths and toilets	1 per unit to 1 per 20 residents
Miscellaneous	Lockable doors, kitchens, call systems, sprinklers, furniture

(b) The Subtle Boundaries of Licensure

An early step toward uniformity of licensing approaches came in 1984 with the completion of the American Bar Association/U.S. Department of Health and Human Services Model Act for state licensure of board-and-care homes. The model act defined a board-and-care home as "a publicly or privately operated residence that provides personal assistance, lodging, and meals to two (2) or more adults who are unrelated to the licensee or administrator."[67]

Personal assistance is defined to include helping with the resident's "activities of daily living," assisting with daily activities necessary to access the "supportive services"[68] required in the board-and-care plan, being aware of the resident's general whereabouts but allowing for independent travel, and monitoring resident activities while on the premises.[69]

Daily activities under the model act include bodily functions such as bathing, dressing, eating, and grooming as well as room cleaning, laundering, making appointments, and managing money. A potential problem with the model act and with some state statutes as applied to many retirement facilities is that they do not distinguish between bodily care and other services or between services provided because of the recipient's frailty or dependence and those furnished to independent persons as a convenience.

Laws should recognize that the receipt of personal services from a valet, concierge, housekeeper, hairdresser, or manicurist does not necessarily warrant licensure even when offered as part of the standard program in a group residence for the elderly. Some states deal with this problem by limiting the activities described in licensure-triggering definitions to hands-on bodily assistance such as bathing and dressing rather than extending definitions to hotel-type services such as housekeeping, laundry, or transportation, which are more likely to be mere conveniences for some residents.

Retirement community developers should become familiar with their states' particular approaches to determining what activity triggers licensure. Homes with units designed for a mix of independent and dependent residents should be especially aware of licensure parameters. States may require the licensing of all facilities in a mixed-use project, even though some units are designed strictly for independent living. In particular, such a regulatory scheme may apply if the contractual arrangement with the resident contains a promise that initially independent residents will eventually receive care when needed. Moreover, the potential for facility licensure of otherwise independent-living units can pose special problems with respect to fire safety and structural building requirements (see §20.4(d)).

While licensure of independent-living facilities may seem anathema from the viewpoint of the facility operator, many facilities with a mix of independent and personal-care units have actively sought licensure for the entire project on the ground that licensure distinguishes the facility from conventional housing and thus may constitute a basis for exemption from rent controls, property taxes, certain discrimination laws, landlord-tenant obligations, or other strictures that may not apply to licensed care facilities. From a public policy perspective, licensure of independent as well as care units can be beneficial by helping to avoid circumstances where, due to a provider's fear of licensure, residents are kept in inadequate independent facilities after having gradually deteriorated (aging in place) to a state of dependence and need.

Often, the process of aging in place can pose problems for independent-living facilities that lack licensed units equipped to provide various levels of needed care. Facility owners can face the difficult problem of being forced to transfer, or even evict, people for whom they cannot care and who may be reluctant to accept their advancing dependence. Although home health services may provide care in an unlicensed residential unit, such service delivery is a stopgap measure at best. If any significant number of residents require care, their numbers may trigger a requirement that the facility become licensed. Even if residents arrange for home care themselves without the facility owner's assistance, an out-of-control management problem may develop. For example, unsupervised personnel may solicit business from other residents, create theft and loss problems or suspicions, or deliver inadequate care, any one of which may call for management intervention (see Volume II, §§15.11–15.16, for a set of private-duty aide policies and procedures). All retirement communities in the development stage should seriously address the problems of transition from independence to the need for care and should develop a specific plan for identifying and dealing with the associated social, legal, and operational consequences.

Given the growing elderly cohort, the current lack of uniformity among state laws, and the continuing need for an alternative to nursing facility placement for those in need of assistance but not yet ready for 24-hour care, it is reasonable to project increased efforts to regulate assisted living (see §29.3 regarding liability concerns for assisted-living operators).

(c) The Prospect for Adoption of Federal Standards

The only significant federal legislation dealing with assisted-living facilities is the Keys Amendment,[70] which requires states to adopt standards for "board-and-care" facilities to deal with matters such as admission policies, safety, sanitation, and protection of civil rights, where the facilities house or are likely to house a significant number of recipients of Supplemental Security Income benefits (SSI). Most states provide an additional state supplemental payment for needy board-and-care residents above the SSI payment furnished by the federal government.[71] Unfortunately, the only sanction available for failure to conform to the Keys Amendment has been to deny SSI payments to needy facility residents. No federal enforcement mechanism is in place against states or operators of board-and-care facilities that parallels the standards imposed on health facilities as a condition of Medicare and Medicaid enrollment.[72]

Both government and private organizations have severely criticized the board-and-care system. In 1989, the U.S. General Accounting Office (GAO) prepared a report entitled "Board and Care: Insufficient Assurances That Residents' Needs Are Identified and Met." The report noted that states continue to find serious problems even in licensed board-and-care homes, including sanitation problems, physical abuse, and lack of medical care. The study found that most board-and-care residents have very low incomes and high service needs. GAO estimated that between 500,000 and 1.5 million persons lived in boarding homes at the time of the study, but it was unknown how many of these were or should have been considered to be living in facilities that should be regulated as board-and-care homes. The report also uncovered widespread confusion respecting basic issues such as the definition of board and care, the variety of licensing requirements among the various states, and how to impose sanctions on or otherwise deal with unlicensed facilities without harming residents. The report further noted that the federal government had devoted virtually no resources to ensuring that state board-and-care programs comply with the Keys Amendment. The GAO recommended that the U.S. Department of Health and Human Services conduct a comprehensive review of the states' oversight activities and report its findings and recommendations to Congress regarding the steps required both to ensure the protection of board-and-care residents and to implement changes needed to make the Keys Amendment more effective.[73]

In 1990, the Office of Inspector General, U.S. Department of Health and Human Services, conducted a study[74] of board-and-care facilities. Based on interviews of federal officials, government officials in all 50 states, and various providers and resident advocates, the study revealed that while almost all states have set forth standards governing personal-care services, fire safety, physical structure, sanitation, and licensing, matters such as residents' level-of-care needs, staff training, unlicensed facilities, complaints, and coordination among responsible agencies, providers, and consumers have received little attention. Even though states have the authority to conduct inspections and issue corrective action plans, only about one-third have taken advantage of sanctions such as penalties or prohibiting admissions of new residents to cited homes. Moreover, most states have the power to revoke or deny licenses, but less than half have actually exercised such authority.

At the time, nearly 75 percent of state respondents and more than 80 percent of surveyed providers and advocates called for a common set of national minimum standards. The inspector general's report did not recommend adoption of federal standards but rather urged the U.S. Department of Health and Human Services to provide technical assistance to the states and encourage adoption of the ABA's model act (see discussion in §20.4(b)). By the mid-1990s, the desire for federal regulation had waned considerably.

Results of a 1995 survey of seniors' housing executives conducted by the American Seniors Housing Association revealed that while 74 percent of respondents believed federal regulation of assisted-living facilities is unnecessary, 71 percent thought that it would likely occur. As of year-end 1997, the General Accounting Office was in the midst of a study of assisted-living quality and consumer protections that some observers feel may be a harbinger of federal legislation.

Many providers and provider associations are pushing for accreditation as a superior alternative to regulation, arguing that accreditation focuses on quality improvement and performance and therefore leads to customer satisfaction, facilitates rapid adjustments or corrections, and provides consistent data for comparisons between facilities. Regulations merely gauge whether a provider has instituted the proper process to meet minimum standards, whereas the goal of accreditation is to measure performance and upgrade outcomes.[75]

Several associations have joined forces to formulate an industry-specific quality assurance program intended to avoid the prescriptive regulatory system that characterizes the nursing home industry. The Assisted Living Coalition has proposed a plan with three components: a review of a facility's history and capacity to meet state minimum standards, quality monitoring and improvement of the facility's daily operations, and enforcement mechanisms.[76]

(d) Enhanced Building Standards for Assisted-Living Facilities

(1) Generally

Often, a particularly vexing problem relates to the building standards applicable to residential care facilities. Seniors' housing facilities or portions thereof that offer only residential or assisted-living services may be subject to enhanced institutional building standards usually reserved for hospitals or nursing facilities. The application of such standards can be devastating because of the substantial additional costs incurred in comparison to the costs of buildings constructed in accordance with residential standards. Depending on how a local government interprets and enforces state licensing laws and fire codes, the developer can be lured into a trap that could require substantial remodeling or reconstruction even after the project is built and apparently approved. Frequently, architects and local fire officials do not recognize that institutional standards may be applicable at the design stage of development. Indeed, the problem first surfaces when the building is completed, the facility license is applied for . . . and it is too late.

For example, facilities that are essentially residential in use and character but house persons who either may need care or live on the premises pursuant to continuing-care agreements that promise future care can be subject to construction standards

and fire safety standards that would otherwise apply only to licensed care facilities.[77] Therefore, even before building design commences, developers and architects must be certain that they understand the substance of and relationship among licensing and fire clearance requirements, which are usually the province of different agencies at different times during the development process.

(2) Uniform Building Code Requirements

The Uniform Building Code (UBC),[78] which many states have adopted, sets forth two basic occupancy classifications that are germane to the construction of facilities with residential care components.

Group I (Institutional) Occupancies—Includes hospitals, sanitariums, nursing homes with nonambulatory patients, and "similar buildings" accommodating more than five persons (division 1.1) and nursing homes for more than five ambulatory patients (division 2).[79]

Group R (Residential) Occupancies—Includes hotels and apartment houses as well as congregate residences accommodating more than ten persons (division 1) and dwellings and lodging houses or congregate residences accommodating ten persons or fewer (division 3).[80]

The code does not specify what constitutes a building occupancy that is "similar" to a "nursing home"; however, in the index to the code, the listing for "Aged, Homes for" refers the reader to the Group I occupancy classification. The definition of "congregate residence"[81] excludes nursing and includes a shelter or dormitory but not board-and-care or assisted-living facilities.

Similarly, the UBC does not define the terms "ambulatory" and "nonambulatory," although states are likely to focus on the ability of a resident to leave the premises in an emergency without the assistance of a person or a mechanical device such as a wheelchair, walker, or cane.

Group I occupancies require considerably stricter construction standards than residential uses. For example, every exit serving areas occupied or used by "bed or litter patients" must be at least 44 inches in width.[82] In addition, corridors serving any area housing one or more "nonambulatory persons" must be at least eight feet in width and must have ramps for all elevation changes in the floor corridor.[83]

Patient room doors must be readily openable from either side without the use of keys, and panic hardware is required on exit doors of areas with an occupant load of 50 or more.[84] Type I occupancies are also required to install automatic sprinkler systems that meet the requirements of the National Fire Codes.[85] Some states (e.g., California) have established a special category for residential care facilities that falls between the criteria for purely residential occupancies and the criteria for health care facilities.

(3) Application of Occupancy Categories to Retirement Facilities

State regulatory agencies generally do not consider retirement communities offering independent or assisted living to be subject to licensure as "nursing homes." Purely residential facilities are generally unlicensed, and facilities in which assisted living or personal care is available are usually licensed as board-and-care or residential care facilities. Nursing facilities are generally those in which full-time nursing care is needed by persons who are essentially totally dependent. Unfortunately, the UBC makes no provision for facilities that fall between purely residential housing and skilled-nursing care or that provide a continuum of care from total independence to traditional health care services.[86]

The greatest pitfall for a facility developer is to construct a residential building to Type R standards and to obtain fire approvals on the basis that only independent residents will be permitted to live there—all without first coordinating with state licensing authorities. The developer may find out later that the state licensing authority requires licensure not only for the adjacent care facilities but also for the independent apartment units and that the apartment building should have been built to much stricter institutional standards. The potential for licensure may be exacerbated when home health is delivered to "independent" apartment residents. Such a scenario is entirely possible in that facility licensure approvals are routinely received *after* construction is completed, and local fire officials, unaware of the licensing requirements, initially approve the structure for residential purposes and do not check for compliance with institutional standards.

Here is an example of the type of trap that may snare a developer:

- The developer builds independent apartment units to Type R standards and *obtains approval* from the local fire chief.
- The developer also builds a separate nursing facility to Type I standards for the eventual use of apartment residents.
- The developer applies for a state permit to offer continuing-care contracts as well as for state licensure of the nursing facility.
- The developer is surprised to learn that the state requires assisted-living facility licensure for the residential units as a prerequisite to obtaining continuing-care contract approval.
- The state seeks local fire chief approval for the residential units as a *licensed* facility.
- The local fire official applies Type I standards to all licensed facilities and refuses to certify units for licensure unless corridors and doors are widened and automatic sprinklers are installed.
- No license is available for existing construction, and the required structural changes are so drastic as to be economically infeasible.

Disaster can result if the developer is not aware of all licensing requirements *and* knows how the local fire authority will apply state building code standards to the necessary licensed uses *before* construction commences. Use of an architect experienced in the construction of licensed facilities in the relevant state and of legal counsel familiar with licensing requirements can help avert disaster.

(4) Proposed Uniform Fire Standards for Assisted Living

In 1985, the National Fire Protection Association (NFPA) developed its Life Safety Code for fire protection in buildings and structures, which for the first time recognized major distinctions between residential board-and-care facilities and skilled-nursing or other health care facilities. The requirements for eight-foot corridors and 44-inch doors continue to apply to nursing homes.[87] On the other hand, residential board-and-care facilities that provide "personal care services" are subject to less stringent standards depending on the ability of the particular population to evacuate the building.[88]

The evacuation capability of the residents is divided into the three following categories:

- Prompt—The evacuation capacity of the group is equivalent to that of the general population.
- Slow—The group is capable of moving to a point of safety in a timely manner, with some residents requiring staff assistance.
- Impractical—Even with staff assistance, the entire group cannot be reliably moved to a point of safety in a timely manner.[89]

For board-and-care facilities with "prompt" or "slow" occupancies, the fire safety standards require essentially the same corridor and door widths as for existing hotels or dormitories.[90] In addition, such facilities must meet minimum fire resistance ratings and, depending on building type, may be required to have automatic sprinkler systems.[91] Smoke detection systems are generally required in all corridors and common spaces.[92] Where it is impractical to evacuate a facility's population, the facility must meet the requirements for "custodial care facilities" or for nursing homes.[93]

Unfortunately, the NFPA life safety standards relating to residential board-and-care facilities, although established in 1985, have not been incorporated into the UBC, which continues to recognize no middle ground between residential and nursing facilities. Many state building codes are based on the UBC, and although some states have made modifications, the problem of unduly rigid standards for residential care facilities remains widespread. In 1992, California adopted an "R-2" residential fire safety classification for assisted-living facilities. It is based on the residential model but adds certain safety features without approaching institutional standards.

(e) The American Seniors' Housing Association Model Assisted Living Act

After a review of legislation from 12 selected states, the American Seniors Housing Association in 1994 published a Model Assisted Living Act, which was two years in the making. The model act incorporates ideas from several aging and seniors' housing organizations and covers the following topics:

- required facilities and services;
- staffing;

- physical plant requirements;
- fire safety;
- admission and transfer criteria;
- resident rights; and
- enforcement provisions.

The following are among the more interesting provisions:

- allowance for an accreditation program that meets or exceeds statutory requirements and for a pilot program that measures "resident outcomes" rather than regulatory compliance;
- a requirement for a quality assurance program;
- basic services that include furnishings, assistance with activities of daily living, housekeeping, laundry, dining, transportation, activities, and other services only to the extent needed or desired by residents;
- assistance with medications;
- overnight staffing;
- lockable resident accommodations;
- sprinklering and fire and smoke detection;
- masonry, concrete, or steel construction for buildings of more than two stories;
- "continuous" nursing care disallowed beyond 90 days unless provided by "private-duty" personnel who assume full legal responsibility for care;
- a written resident assessment and service plan with resident input;
- a requirement for a written admission agreement detailing services, fees, and transfer provisions;
- extensive resident rights; and
- in addition to state enforcement, a provision for a licensed competitor to bring an unfair business practices action against the operator of an unlicensed facility.

§20.5 Home Health Care Regulation

Home health care is a well-defined concept nationally due to its eligibility for reimbursement under the Medicare program. The Medicare conditions of participation set forth the salient features of an approved home health care program.

- It must provide part-time or intermittent skilled-nursing care plus one or more of the following:

physical, speech, or occupational therapy; medical social services; or home health aide services, which may include services such as personal care, household services essential to health, exercise, and assistance with medications.

- The program must be provided on a visiting basis to people in need of intermittent nursing care or physical, speech, or occupational therapy. Such people must be confined to or "homebound" in their homes or in a facility that is not a hospital, nursing, or rehabilitation facility.
- Services must be rendered pursuant to a plan and be provided under the supervision and direction of a physician or nurse and periodically reviewed by the physician.[94]

Services excluded from coverage are those that would not be covered as an inpatient hospital service (bed and board, nursing services, medical social services, and appliances are included), transportation to services, housekeeping, and food service or Meals on Wheels.[95] Medical supplies and durable medical equipment (DME) are expressly included.[96] A 20 percent-of-customary-charges copayment is required of the beneficiary for DME,[97] but otherwise reimbursement to the provider is based on the lesser of its costs or reasonable charges. There is no limit on the number of visits and no prior hospitalization requirement.

The Medicare homebound requirement limits reimbursable services to persons unable to leave home without the assistance of either medical devices or another person or when medically inadvisable, although recipients need not be bedridden.[98] A retirement community unit can be considered the person's home. However, if a resident of a seniors' facility needs, for example, personal assistance to be bathed, groomed, and dressed but then is able to leave the facility, the personal assistance may not be reimbursable as a Medicare home health service.

The intermittent requirement can also pose problems in the seniors' housing facility context. In an unlicensed congregate living community, the facility can use home health care services to provide intermittent care as the population ages in place. If, however, residents' need for care becomes ongoing, the facility could face the dual prospect of loss of Medicare reimbursement and the necessity for licensure

as an assisted-living or personal care facility (see §20.4(b)). Generally, an intermittent need is one that predictably requires a visit at least once every 60 days but no more than four days per week or part-time service up to seven days a week for a short time, such as two to three weeks.[99] In *Duggan v. Bowen*,[100] however, the U.S. District Court for the District of Columbia issued an injunction prohibiting the U.S. Department of Health and Human Services (HHS) from denying benefits for part-time home health care needed for more than four days per week, even if such care was provided for an indefinite period. The court found that HHS's interpretation improperly required that care be both part-time and intermittent to qualify for reimbursement.

Pursuant to a state plan "waiver" request, home- and community-based services for the elderly (excluding room-and-board costs) are also eligible for Medicaid reimbursement when it can be shown that if such services were not delivered, the individual would likely require nursing care.[101] As of November 1990, 47 states had already taken advantage of this option. Amendments from the 1990 OBRA established a new, capped Medicaid entitlement program to permit functionally disabled elderly persons to receive home- and community-based care[102] (see §26.3(c) for a detailed discussion of Medicaid waivers).

Home health is a growing segment of the continuum of care available to seniors in retirement facilities. In 1995, more than 9,000 Medicare-certified providers generated close to $15.7 billion in Medicare expenditures. From 1990 to 1996, Medicare home care expenditures rose from $3.9 billion to an estimated $18.1 billion. To curb rising costs, the federal Health Care Financing Administration (HCFA) has for a decade considered a prospective payment system to replace the current retrospective-payment-of-cost method. Prospective payment systems can take a form such as a fee schedule, diagnosis-related groupings (DRGs), or a daily rate. The 1997 federal budget requires home health companies to shift to prospective payment in 1999.

Not surprisingly, the home care reimbursement system has come under criticism over the years. A report of the Senate Committee on Aging[103] identified several problems with the home care system: numerous funding sources such as Medicare, Medicaid, Social Services Block Grants, the Older Americans Act, and various private sources; the three-week limit on Medicare coverage (intermittent requirement); increased need due to the prospective payment system of reimbursement for hospitals; the increase in Medicare denials of coverage; inconsistent Medicaid policies among the states; the number of home health providers dropping out of Medicare; problems of training and wages among home health personnel; and lack of provider standards and accountability. The principal improvement noted by the report was a loosening of the "homebound" requirement under the 1987 OBRA (see §20.3) to permit Medicare coverage if the patient can leave the home for short periods of time.

Efforts begun in 1984 to standardize the administration of home health care benefits resulted in "significant increases in denials in the area of utilization." In 1988, the Congressional Budget Office reduced its estimate of Medicare expenditures for home health services in fiscal year 1992 from $5.9 billion to $3.5 billion.[104] A survey of 59 home care companies indicated that the 1993 revenues of home care chains increased by 47 percent to $5.1 billion. Further, the respondent companies noted a 33 percent increase in their home care branches. The survey also revealed a 45.3 percent increase in the number of Medicare-certified home health agencies.[105] In 1997, a study of fraud among home care providers led the president to order a moratorium on certification of new providers.

A community care demonstration project conducted by the U.S. Department of Health and Human Services tested the hypothesis that long-term care for chronic conditions would cost less if the disabled person received care at home rather than while a permanent resident of a nursing home.[106] The hypothesis was based in part on research indicating that between 10 and 40 percent of those in nursing homes were inappropriately placed there (see also §1.6.) The study collected data from several demonstration projects spanning a period of more than ten years. It concluded that the expansion of publicly financed community care would not reduce the aggregate costs of the long-term-care system. Despite some reductions in nursing home costs for some people, the savings would be offset by the increased costs of providing community services to people who would remain at home in any event. Part of the prob-

lem lies in the challenge of identifying those at high risk of nursing home placement, thus making it difficult to effect large reductions in nursing home occupancies. Moreover, in-home service of a level deemed appropriate by demonstration project participants proved costly. The study did conclude that, in general, the quality of life for the treatment group was enhanced.

While the federal Certificate of Need laws (now repealed; see §20.2) did not extend to home health care, 27 states require new home health services to obtain Certificate of Need review.[107] In addition, 28 states have home health license laws. The Joint Commission on Accreditation of Health Care Organizations (JCAHCO) has developed accreditation standards for home health agencies, which may be used by states as a uniform standard for licensure.

Retirement communities can use home health as an interim measure for residents in need of short-term care. While reliance on home health care may forestall a move to continuous or long-term care for residents as they grow more dependent, home health cannot take the place of a plan for transition to ongoing licensed care for those who need it (see §28.7 regarding health care reform proposals that would provide new federal funding for home health services).

§20.6 Regulation of Health Maintenance Organizations

Health maintenance organizations (HMOs), or prepaid health plans, are entities that provide health care services to enrollees who, for a fixed periodic membership fee, are entitled to receive various health care services with no adjustment in fee based on the frequency, extent, or type of an individual's use of the services. The classic and familiar model of an HMO is the Kaiser health plan. Although various forms of HMOs have evolved over the years (see §27.2(c)(2) regarding "SHMOs"), they all share a basic trait: they combine the risk-pooling and set-premium characteristics of insurance with the control over service delivery enjoyed by a health care provider. A more recent twist is the development of "Medicare risk" HMOs, which contract with the Medicare program to provide services to a defined population of older persons for a fixed per capita rate.

HMOs should be distinguished from conventional insurance carriers in that insurers generally do not control the delivery of health care services but rather indemnify the insured for health care expenses in the marketplace. More recently, however, many insurers have started offering favored benefits, such as waiver of deductibles, when insureds use the services of preferred health providers with whom the carrier contracts to provide cost-efficient or discount services. The theoretical distinctions between HMOs and insurance companies fade as insurance carriers obtain more contractual control over the delivery of health care services.

Legally, HMOs are defined by the federal Health Maintenance Organization Act of 1973,[108] which established federal financial assistance for HMOs in the form of grants and loans. Importantly, the act also exempted federally assisted programs from any state laws that, among other things, required HMOs to conform to minimum capitalization and reserve requirements for insurance companies or prohibited solicitation of members through advertising.[109] Instead, the federal act established many of its own criteria for HMOs and required the organizations to provide a range of basic health services such as physician, hospital, diagnostic, home health, and preventive services.[110] In addition, the law requires eligible HMOs to enroll persons broadly representative of age, social, and income groups; not to expel or refuse to reenroll a member due to his or her health status or need for services; and to insure or make other arrangements for funding its health care contingent liabilities.[111] State laws governing HMOs not applying for federal assistance generally mimic basic federal requirements.

To participate in the Medicare program, HMOs must contract with the Health Care Finance Administration on a "risk" or a "cost" basis. Risk contracts result in advance payments to the HMO on a monthly, per capita basis for each class of enrollee, creating an incentive for the HMO to limit or restrict costly benefits and utilization levels and to employ less costly, preventive interventions. Except in rural areas, Medicare risk HMOs must have a minimum of 5,000 enrollees.[112]

One further feature of health plans is that they are based almost universally on an annualized financial model. That is, premiums and eligibility are often determined on an annual rather than a life-time actuarial basis (unlike many continuing-care communities). Elderly enrollees seeking a life-time hedge against the costs of health care may find HMOs more susceptible to substantial increases in premiums or to cancellation than either continuing-care arrangements or some of the newer, noncancelable long-term-care insurance products.

In 1997, Congress passed legislation permitting providers of health care to create Provider Sponsored Organizations (PSOs), which function much as HMOs but allow providers to share financial risk and accept capitated payments directly for services, without an HMO acting as an intermediary.

For a discussion of the impact of "managed care" on retirement communities, see §27.4.

Notes

1. *See* former 42 U.S.C. §§300k *et seq.*

2. *See generally Hospital Law Manual,* "Health Planning," Vol. IIA, 1–5 *et seq.,* Aspen Systems, 1983.

3. *See* former 42 U.S.C. §300m–6.

4. Former 42 U.S.C. §300m–6(a)(1).

5. *See* former 42 U.S.C. §300n(5), and 50 *Fed. Reg.* 14,027, 1985, raising the statutory expenditure minimum from $250,000.

6. 42 C.F.R. §123.401.

7. *Ibid.*

8. Former 42 U.S.C. §300m–6(b)(1).

9. Former 42 C.F.R. §122.412 (removed 52 *Fed. Reg.* 10094, 1987).

10. Former 42 C.F.R. §123.410 (removed 52 *Fed. Reg.* 10094, 1987).

11. "How to Establish a Home Health Agency: Some Preliminary Considerations," National Association of Home Care, 1984.

12. *See generally* Sfekas, "Can Health Planning Survive the 1980's?" *Aging Network News,* June 1986.

13. P.L. 99–660.

14. *Modern Healthcare,* August 11, 1997, 33. For a summary of state Certificate of Need provisions, *see* Fox, T., *Long-Term Care and Retirement Facilities* (New York: Bender, 1989), §9.04. *See also* "Summary of State Certificate of Need Requirements," American Association of Homes for the Aging, Dec. 1988; and Reding, R., "Certificate of Need Review of Continuing Care Retirement Communities," *Spectrum,* Apr. 1991, 34.

15. *Modern Healthcare,* note 14, *above.*

16. *Modern Healthcare,* note 14, *above.*

17. *Ibid.*

18. *See generally* 42 U.S.C. §1396r(e) (Medicaid); 42 U.S.C. §1395i-3 (Medicare).

19. *See, e.g.,* 42 C.F.R. Pt. 442, Subpt. F.

20. 42 U.S.C. §1395i-3.

21. P.L. 100–203.

22. 42 U.S.C. §1395i-3(b)(Medicare); 42 U.S.C. §1396r(b) (Medicaid).

23. *See* 54 *Fed. Reg.* 5352, Feb. 2, 1989, now in 42 C.F.R. Pt. 483.

24. Final Interpretive Guidelines, Transmittal 232 and Rev. 250 [April 1992], Medicaid State Operations Manual. *See generally* Infante, M., "The Interpretive Guidelines: Rote, Reason or Regulation," *Contemporary Long Term Care,* July 1991, 54. For later regulations, *see* 56 *Fed. Reg.* 48826, Sept. 26, 1991; 57 *Fed. Reg.* 4515, Feb. 5, 1992; 57 *Fed. Reg.* 8194, Mar. 6, 1992.

25. 42 U.S.C. §1395i-3(c)(5) (Medicare) and §1396r(c)(5) (Medicaid); 42 C.F.R. §483.12(d).

26. 42 U.S.C. §1396r(c)(5)(A)(iii) (Medicaid *only*). *See* §23.5(b)(2), regarding Medicaid fraud and abuse issues generally.

27. 42 C.F.R. §483.10(c)(8).

28. 42 U.S.C. §1396r(c)(5)(B)(iv); 42 C.F.R. §483.12(d)(6).

29. 42 U.S.C. §§1395i-3(b)(2), 1396r(b)(2); 42 C.F.R. §483.20(d).

30. 42 U.S.C. §§1395i-3(b)(3), 1396r(b)(3).

31. 42 U.S.C. §1396r(e)(7).

32. 42 U.S.C. §1396r(b)(3)(F).

33. 42 U.S.C. §1396r(e)(7)(C).

34. Final rules by the Health Care Financing Administration (HCFA) define "serious mental illness" as "a major mental disorder diagnosable under the *Diagnostic Statistical Manual of Mental Disorders,* 3rd Ed." 57 *Fed. Reg.* 56450, Nov. 30, 1992.

35. *State Medicaid Manual,* Department of Health and Human Services, May 26, 1989, §4250.1.8.2.

36. 42 U.S.C. §§1395i-3(c)(1)(A), 1396r(c)(1)(A).

37. *See* Romano, M., "Unshackling the Elderly," *Contemporary Long Term Care,* April 1994, 37, which discusses the shift away from the use of restraints by skilled-nursing facilities since the enactment of OBRA. The Health Care Financing Administration (HCFA) stated that, at most skilled-nursing facilities, the use of restraints over the previous two years was down from more than 40 percent to about 22 percent. Although OBRA standards are as stringent with regard to chemical restraints as physical restraints, according to HCFA, chemical restraints at the time were still used on approximately 32 percent of all skilled-nursing residents. *Id.*

38. 42 U.S.C. §§1395i-3(c)(3), 1396r(c)(3).

39. 42 U.S.C. §§1395i-3(c)(6), 1396r(c)(6); 42 C.F.R. §483.10(c).

40. 42 C.F.R. §483.10

41. 42 U.S.C. §1395cc(f)(1). The Health Care Financing Administration published the final regulations implementing the Patient Self Determination Act, to be effective July 27, 1995. 60 *Fed. Reg.* 33262, June 27, 1995. The regulations require facilities to document in an individual's medical record whether that individual has executed an advance directive. 42 C.F.R. §489.102(a)(2).

42. The laws that must be disclosed to residents under the Patient Self Determination Act vary depending on the state. California has taken a unique approach to providing nonemergency care to incompetent nursing facility residents. Under this law, nursing homes may treat an incompetent resident who does not have a legal representative if a physician has determined that the resident is unable to give informed consent and an interdisciplinary review team consisting of the resident's attending physician, a registered nurse with responsibility for the resident, other appropriate staff, and, where practicable, a patient representative finds the treatment to be medically appropriate. The interdisciplinary review team must take into consideration certain prescribed factors, such as the known desires of the resident and the probable impact on the resident's condition. Cal. Health & Safety Code §1418.8. A California Court of Appeal upheld the constitutionality of this law in *Rains v. Belshe,* 32 Cal. App. 4th 157 (1995).

43. 42 U.S.C. §§1395i-3(c)(1)(B), 1396r(c)(1)(B). *See* Volume II, §13.1b, for a detailed federal resident's rights notice.

44. 42 U.S.C. §1395r(a).

45. 42 U.S.C. §§1395i-3(b)(4)(C), 1396r(b)(4)(C).

46. 42 U.S.C. §§1395i-3(b)(6), 1396r(b)(6).

47. 42 U.S.C. §§1395i-3(b)(7), 1396r(b)(7).

48. 42 U.S.C. §§1395i-3(b)(5), 1396r(b)(5). Nurse's aide training program regulations are set forth at 56 *Fed. Reg.* 48880, Sept. 26, 1991.

49. 42 U.S.C. §§1395i-3(b)(4), 1396r(b)(4).

50. 42 U.S.C. §§1395i-3(c)(2), 1396r(c)(2).

51. *Ibid.*

52. 42 U.S.C. §1396r(c)(2)(D).

53. 42 U.S.C. §§1395i-3(g); 1396r(g).

54. 42 U.S.C. §§1395i-3(h); 1396r(g).

55. (57 *Fed. Reg.* 39278). They became effective on July 1, 1995.

56. Before OBRA, nursing facilities were required to conform to "conditions" that were contained in statute and to "standards" that appeared in regulation. This terminology was then abandoned, with conditions referred to as Level A Requirements and standards as Level B Requirements. The Level A and Level B distinction has now been abandoned.

57. 42 C.F.R. §§483.13, §483.15, §483.25.

58. A Medicaid provider is required to accept the government payment as payment in full for covered services, even though the usual charges may be higher; *see* §9.3(b)(4).

59. *Blum v. Yaretsky,* 457 U.S. 991, 73 L. Ed. 2d 534, 102 S. Ct. 2777 (1982).

60. *See* 42 C.F.R. §§456.336(f), 456.337.

61. Other names used in various state statutes include sheltered care, group home, boarding home for the aged, residential care, congregate living, supervised living, rest home, domiciliary care, supportive living, community residential facility, adult family home. *See Mental Disability Law Reporter,* Vol. 7, no. 2, Mar.–Apr. 1983, 158–209.

62. For a general study of assisted-living programs across the nation and their ability to provide services to the frail elderly at savings of up to 35 percent, compared with nursing facilities, *see* "Assisted Living in the United States: A New Paradigm for Residential Care for Frail Elderly Persons?" American Association of Retired Persons, 1993. *See also* §28.7(d), for a discussion of how proposals for health care reform may include assisted-living facilities.

63. *Seniors Housing State Regulatory Review,* American Seniors Housing Association, 1997. *See also* American Association of Retired Persons, "Assisted Living and Its Implications for Long-Term Care," Feb. 1995, 7–10.

64. *See* "States Explore Assisted Living Licensure," *American Association of Homes and Services for the Aging News,* Vol. 9, 1994, which discusses recent action by many states and state associations to develop rules regarding assisted-living facility licensure.

65. For a synopsis of each state's board-and-care laws, with statutory references, *see* "Summary of State Board and Care Requirements" *Legal Memo,* American Association of Homes for the Aging, Jan. 1989. *See also* American Association of Retired Persons, "The Regulation of Board and Care Homes: Results of a Survey in the Fifty States and the District of Columbia," 1993; American Health Care Association and Murtha et al., *Assisted Living: A State-by-State Summary,* 1995, for a review of the statutes and regulations applicable to assisted-living facilities in each state.

66. *See* American Association of Retired Persons, "The Regulation of Board and Care Homes: Results of a Survey in the Fifty States and the District of Columbia," State Summaries and National Summary, 1993.

67. *See Mental and Physical Disability Law Reporter,* Vol. 8, no. 2, Mar.–Apr. 1984, 157.

68. *E.g.,* medical, social, financial, legal, or transportation services. *Id.* at 160.

69. *Id.* at 159.

70. P.L. 94–566, 42 U.S.C. §1382e(e).

71. Dobkin, L., *The Board and Care System: A Regulatory Jungle* (Washington, D.C.: American Association of Retired Persons, 1989), 5. In addition to reviewing the regulatory background of board-and-care facilities on a national basis, this report focuses on the details of board-and-care law in Maryland and analyzes its strengths and weaknesses, with recommendations for improvement. For 1993, the SSI payment was $434 per month for individuals and $652 per month for couples. In 1990, 33 states provided supplemental payments to residents of board-and-care homes. "Developments in Aging: 1992," U.S. Senate Special Committee on Aging, S. Rep. 103–40, Vol. 1, Apr. 20, 1993, 237.

72. *See Mental Disability Law Reporter,* note 55 *above,* at 159.

73. In a March 9, 1989, brief prepared for the U.S. Senate Special Committee on Aging, entitled "Board and Care Homes in the United States: Failure in Public Policy," the following problems, causes, and policy options were identified:

Problems

- ▪ Homes continue to lack adequate fire escapes, cleanliness, and nutrition standards.
- ▪ Providers overuse and misuse medications and inadequately supervise the dispensing of medications.
- ▪ Many board-and-care home residents' basic personal care needs are neglected.
- ▪ Many board-and-care residents require more care than the operator is competent to provide.
- ▪ Special-care needs such as Alzheimer's disease and mental illness often remain inappropriately addressed.
- ▪ Board-and-care residents are often financially exploited.
- ▪ Some operators are clearly unqualified to care for the elderly and disabled due to poor character.

Causes of Problems

- ▪ States have failed to establish adequate licensing, inspection, and enforcement standards.
- ▪ The U.S. Department of Health and Human Services has failed to monitor state enforcement of quality standards.

- The absence of public or private insurance to reimburse personal-care services jeopardizes access to quality care for the low-income elderly and disabled.
- There is a lack of training and education among care providers.
- The Medicare and Medicaid programs have attempted to move patients into the lowest possible level of care at the earliest opportunity.
- Placement decisions are left up to providers due to the lack of case management and coordination of the long-term-care system.
- Board-and-care residents are often isolated and vulnerable, without family, friends, ombudspersons, or state regulatory oversight.

Policy Options for Reforming Board-and-Care Homes

Policy options for reforming board-and-care homes would

- include personal-care services in any long-term-care program enacted by Congress;
- add personal-care services to the list of mandatory state Medicaid services;
- specify minimum enforcement powers states must enact and use against substandard board-and-care operators under threat of loss of federal matching funds for the state Medicaid program;
- require states to establish minimum health, safety, and security standards for board-and-care operators;
- increase funding to states for inspections;
- expand resources to the long-term-care ombudsperson program;
- establish federal loan guarantees to licensed operators for upgrading facilities' physical plant; and
- direct the U.S. Department of Health and Human Services to enter into contracts to provide training and support for providers.

74. "Board and Care," Office of Inspector General, U.S. Department of Health and Human Services, Mar. 1990.

75. Coates, C., "Assisted Living Accreditation: Is It the Answer to Less Regulation and Better Care?" *Multifamily Executive,* Aug. 1996.

76. The coalition, which originally included the Alzheimer's Association, American Association of Homes and Services for the Aging (AAHSA), American Association of Retired Persons (AARP), American Seniors Housing Association (ASHA), Assisted Living Facilities Association of America (ALFAA), and the American Healthcare Association (AHCA), experienced some divisiveness. AHCA and ASHA were dismissed from the coalition when they ex-

pressed concern that the program reflected a traditional and overly prescriptive regulatory-based approach to quality that lacked the means to measure or improve upon a true quality outcome—an opinion disputed by remaining coalition members. AHCA vowed to prepare its own prototype quality initiative focusing on care outcomes and customer satisfaction. "Split Spawns Second Assisted Living Quality Initiative," *Contemporary Long Term Care,* Aug. 1996. As of the end of 1997, however, the coalition members had rejoined forces.

77. For example, it is the practice of the California Department of Social Services to require all independent-living units (residential apartments) occupied by continuing-care contract holders to be licensed as residential care facilities for the elderly, even though residents are presently capable of independent living and care is intended to be provided in other facilities specially designed for residents' occupancy as needed.

78. All references are to the 1991 code.

79. U.B.C. §1001.

80. U.B.C. §1201.

81. U.B.C. §404.

82. U.B.C. §3320(b).

83. U.B.C. §3320(c).

84. U.B.C. §3320(f).

85. NFPA Standard 13.

86. *But see* discussion of the NFPA Life Safety Code, §20.4(d)(4).

87. NFPA 101, §§12–2.3.3, 12–2.3.6.

88. *See id.,* §21–1.3.

89. *Ibid.*

90. *Id.,* §21–3.2.2.1.

91. *Id.,* §21–3.2.2.2.

92. *Id.,* §21.3.2.2.5.

93. *Id.,* §21–3.2.3.1.

94. *See* 42 C.F.R. §§484.14, 409.42–47; 42 U.S.C. §§1395f(a)(2)(C), 1395x(m),(n),(o).

95. 42 C.F.R. §409.49.

96. 42 C.F.R. §409.45(e),(f).

97. 42 C.F.R. §409.50; 42 U.S.C. §1395f(k).

98. *See* Regan, J., *Tax, Estate and Financial Planning for the Elderly* (New York: Bender, 1997); Medicare Intermediary Manual §3117.1. Proposed regulations published in 56 *Fed. Reg.* 50542, Oct. 7, 1991, would define "homebound" based on an average of ten to 16 hours per month absence from the home for reasons other than to receive medical treatment.

99. Medicare Intermediary Manual §3118.1C.

100. 691 F. Supp. 1487 (D.D.C. 1988).

101. *See* 42 U.S.C. §1396n(d). *See also* §26.3(c). Draft policy objective, American Association of Homes for the Aging, Jan. 16, 1992.

102. 42 U.S.C. §1396a(a)(10)(A)(ii)(VI). "Basic Statistics about Home Care," National Association for Home Care, Oct. 1996. Medicare denials for home care services increased, however, by 133 percent from 1984 to 1986. *See* "Hospitals Travel Some Rough Ground in LTC," *Hospitals,* Dec. 20, 1986, 70.

103. "Home Care at the Crossroads," U.S. Senate Special Committee on Aging, S. Rep. 100–102, Apr. 1988.

104. *Older Americans Report,* Feb. 12, 1988, 63.

105. Scott, L., "Home-Care Revenues Soar to $5.1 Billion via Mergers," *Modern Healthcare,* May 23, 1994, 85 (reporting results of *Modern Healthcare*'s 1994 Multi-Unit Providers Survey). *See also* Snow, C., "Home Health Heats Up," *Modern Healthcare,* August 18, 1997.

106. Kemper, P., R. Applebaum, and M. Harrigan, "Community Care Demonstrations: What Have We Learned?" *Health Care Financing Review,* Vol. 8, no. 4, Summer 1987, 87. *See also* Schwartz, R., "Home Care versus Nursing Home Costs," *Contemporary Long Term Care,* Feb. 1988, 16, for a discussion of this "longest running long-term care debate."

107. *"How to Establish a Home Health Agency: Some Preliminary Considerations,"* National Association for Home Care, Jan. 1984.

108. 42 U.S.C. §300e *et seq.; See also* regulations at 42 C.F.R. §§417.101 *et seq.* For a discussion of the growth surge among Medicare HMOs, *see* Hudson, T., "Senior Surge: Are You Ready?" *Hospitals & Health Networks,* Apr. 5, 1997.

109. 42 U.S.C. §300e-10(a).

110. 42 U.S.C. §§300e-1(1), 300e(b).

111. 42 U.S.C. §300e(c).

112. *See generally,* CCH *Medicare & Medicaid Guide,* ¶¶13,945 *et seq.*

Collier Park; Beaumont, Texas.

21 Regulation of Continuing-Care Retirement Communities

§21.1 Regulatory Definition

With a substantial increase in the number of states enacting new legislation in recent years, at least 36 states now have some form of regulation covering continuing-care retirement community (CCRC) or life-care arrangements.[1] Often, a state requires a provider or promoter to obtain a "certificate of authority" or other permit or license before entering into a continuing-care contract, collecting fees or deposits toward a contract, or even advertising or beginning construction of a facility. Generally speaking, the type of regulated activity is the promise to furnish health care or assisted living for the life of a resident or an extended period in exchange for a prepaid entrance fee, a fixed periodic fee, or both. Usually, covered "care" consists of health (e.g., nursing) or health-related services and often includes personal care or assistance with activities such as bathing, grooming, and dressing (assisted living). Some states may look to whether the promise for care is actually for life, and others to whether it is for more than a year or more than a month (as to what constitutes a promise for more than one year, see Volume II, §2.2(c)). Some cover all entrance fee arrangements regardless of duration.

Entrance fees may be subject to a minimum definition computed either as the equivalent of a year's or a certain number of months of monthly fees or according to a minimum dollar threshold (see Table 21.1 for a comparison of statutes). Usually, pure fee-for-service arrangements are not subject to continuing-care regulation unless the arrangement promises or implies that fee-for-service care will be available in the future or for an extended period of time beyond a year on a priority basis not extended to the general public. Condominium, cooperative, or membership arrangements involving promises of long-term-care access are also likely to be subject to continuing-care regulation. Some states make statutory distinctions between "continuing care" and "life care," where the contract is for life and nursing care is available on site with no substantial increase in fees over the residential accommodation.

Given several varieties of arrangements introduced into the marketplace over the last decade, jurisdictional definitions are taking on added importance (see §21.11 regarding similar regulated products or services). Whereas traditional continuing-care facilities usually involved a single organization that furnished housing, comprehensive health care, and services in a single facility for an entrance fee and a regular monthly fee, many providers are now experimenting with different organizational structures, service packages, and fee mechanisms, all of which pose a challenge to regulatory agencies.

Among the issues to be considered by government is whether regulations should cover only transactions where some entrance fee or other prepayment is involved in return for a promise of future health care or whether a statute or regulation should also cover the promise merely that fee-for-service care will be available on a priority basis in the future. Another concern is whether the allocation of entrance fees to housing rather than to health care can circumvent the triggering of the regulatory mechanism. Some argue that if residents pay a large entrance fee or purchase price in addition to a monthly fee for housing that incorporates nursing facilities on the premises, consumers will expect health care to be available on some priority basis or at a reduced rate irrespective of the express terms of the contract; therefore, continuing-care regulation is appropriate. Many statutes now specify that location of the services is irrelevant in determining the need for state certification of the arrangement.

Various approaches to definitional issues can be summarized as follows, with most states using some combination of the listed factors:

- **Types of Service**
  - Housing for the elderly, plus a minimum of nursing; health-related or personal care services (most common); nonhealth personal or supportive services; or priority access to one of the above
  - Condominiums or cooperatives with the above services
- **Type of Fee**
  - Entrance fee, which is the equivalent of one year of monthly fees; one, three, or six months; or more than $100, $5,000, or $10,000
  - Entrance fee or a periodic fee
  - Any fee or transfer
- **Term of the Contract**
  - For life
  - For a term in excess of one year
  - Any duration

The American Association of Homes and Services for the Aging (AAHSA) has adopted comprehensive guidelines for state continuing-care regulations (see Table 21.1 and the following text).[2] AAHSA's recommended CCRC definition would include all entrance fee projects, plus any rental or equity projects offering extensive (Type A) or modified (Type B) health-related services without extra charge. Rental or equity facilities with fee-for-service (Type C) care would be

called multilevel retirement communities (see also §2.4(e) regarding health plan types).

Because insurance commissioners regulate CCRCs in many states, the National Association of Insurance Commissioners (NAIC) undertook the development of a model statute for state CCRC regulation.[3] North Carolina (see Table 21.1) developed its statute in conjunction with NAIC as a possible basis for the latter's model statute. In addition, many states have adopted the idea of establishing advisory councils composed of providers, consumers, and others to assist the relevant state agency in regulating facilities. All these efforts reflect the increasing complexity and popularity of continuing-care communities and the increased scrutiny of regulators.[4]

§21.2 Applications and Disclosures

Virtually all state statutes require some form of disclosure as part of the license application or registration procedure. Disclosure may have to be made to the state regulatory agency, to residents, or to both. Most laws require submission of minimum basic information about the business entity and owners as well as submission of audited financial statements (see generally Figure 21.1). States that more thoroughly regulate CCRCs may also require submission of projected budgets, feasibility studies, marketing projections, forms of resident agreements, and advertising copy. States may require license applicants to adhere strictly to their own projections of marketing progress, construction schedules, and income and expenditures and may tie conformance with projections to the ability to release escrowed funds, admit residents, or obtain final state approval. Regulations may also require that evidence of application for appropriate facility licenses (e.g., nursing and assisted living) accompany the continuing-care license application. Sometimes, the types of information required in license applications or disclosure statements may be mandated to appear in resident contracts (see §21.6).

Specific types of provisions that may be found in CCRC disclosure or license application statutes include the following:

- **Owners and Operators**
  - Detailed basic information
  - Information about investors, trustees, officers
  - Affiliations with other entities or sponsors
  - Business history
  - Tax status
  - Criminal record clearances, bankruptcies
  - History of license activities, fines, suspensions, revocations, denials
- **Services and Fees**
  - Facility description
  - List of services included in regular fee
  - List of optional services
  - Location of services
  - All entrance fees and monthly fees
  - Criteria for changing fees, scope of services
  - History of fee increases
  - Criteria for refunds
  - Health and financial criteria for residency
  - Circumstances under which a resident may be required to vacate the unit
  - Circumstances under which a resident may remain in the unit if he or she becomes impoverished
  - Charges in the event of marriage or unit changes
  - Description of resident grievance procedure
  - Copy of resident contract
  - Copy of house rules
- **Financial and Marketing Information**
  - Financial feasibility study
  - Certified financial statements
  - Budget projections; source and application of funds
  - Actuarial projections (mortality and morbidity)
  - Startup losses and reserves
  - Description of all financing, assets pledged as collateral
  - Bonds, letters of credit
  - Financial liability of affiliated organizations
  - Market feasibility study
  - Sales projections, occupancy rates
  - Development schedule and expected completion date
  - Copies of reservation, deposit agreements
  - Copies of escrow agreements

States generally require submission of an application and approval of provider submissions before execution or performance of a continuing-care agreement. Some states require disclosure only. Often, states have a two-tiered process that requires provisional approval of initial marketing efforts, unit reservations, taking of deposits, and project development, with a final approval process upon contract execution, move-in, or project fill-up. Many states charge a nominal application fee, but California charges one-tenth of 1 percent of the facility cost and uses the funds to pay professional consultants to review the applicant's financial and market projections.

In 1980, AAHSA published its first model act and, in it, recommended limiting state regulation to a process of registration and disclosure. More recently, however, the association has recommended in its guidelines for state regulation of CCRCs a more extensive form of regulation, including filing audited financial statements, pro forma budgets with actuarial analysis, a market review and marketing schedule, state approval before the taking of substantial deposits, escrow of deposits, achievement of presales thresholds, and reserve requirements.

§21.3 Escrow of Resident Deposits

Prospective residents' payment of deposits toward entrance fees before completion of project construction has traditionally served at least two purposes. First, the deposits indicate the prospective buyer's interest in the development and secure a place on the waiting list or reserve a particular unit pending completion of development. Second, the funds often help retire construction debt or actually fund some of the facility's construction or startup operations costs. Often, developers require progress payments on entrance fee deposits as construction proceeds, with the final increment due on move-in. State license procedures may track a two-step process that requires, first, a provisional certificate or permit as a condition of collecting deposits and, second, a final certificate of authority before residents are permitted to move in or to sign continuing-care agreements.

When continuing-care facility developers collect preconstruction deposits from prospective residents, most regulated states require such deposits to be

Figure 21.1 **Continuing-Care Statute Provisions**

See notes at end for an explanation.	AAHSA Guidelines (1992)	Arizona Title 20, Ch. 8 §§20–1801 *et seq.*	Arkansas Title 23, Ch. 93 §§23–93–101 *et seq.*
1. Definition			
a. For life			Any duration
b. One year	Y	Y	Any duration
c. Entrance fee required		Y	
d. Priority admission			
e. Health/health-related services	Y	Y	Y
f. Personal care			Y
2. Application			
a. Disclosure statement	Y	Y	Y
b. Financials	Y	Y	Y
c. Financial feasibility study	Y	Y	
d. Actuarial study	Y	Y	Y
e. Market study	Y		
f. Accreditation in lieu of regulation	Y		
3. Escrow of Fees			
a. Required	Y	Y	Y
b. Basis for release			
i.Presales	100% from 75%		
ii. Funds	or letter of credit	90% of costs	
iii. Construction	Availability of unit	Completed	Availability of unit
iv. Financing	—	Commitment	
4. Additional Presales			
a. To begin development	10% from 60%		
b. For final certification	—		
5. Reserves			
a. Principal and interest	1 year	1 year	
b. Percent of deposits	—		
c. Operating costs	15% of annual		Actuarial
d. For refunds	—		
6. Bonds			
a. Surety	—		
7. Disclosure to Residents			
a. Financial report	Y	Before signing	Upon request
b. Public inspection of filings	Y		
8. Contract Terms			
a. Submit form	Y	Y	Y
b. Detailed contents	Y	Y	Y
c. Rescission period	30 days	7 days	7 days
d. Refunds in general	—		
e. Required amortization of refund	—		
f. Full refund if resident dies before occupancy	—		
9. Advertising			
a. Prior approval	No		
b. Sponsor liability	Y		
10. Resident's Right to Organize			
a. Association	—		
b. Meetings with management	—		
11. Liens			
a. For residents	Y	Y	Y
b. Subordinated to priors	Y	Y	Y
12. Agency	Unspecified	Insurance	Insurance

Continued →

Figure 21.1 **(continued)**

See notes at end for an explanation.	California Health & Safety Code §§1770 *et seq.*	Colorado Title 12, Art. 13 §§12–13–101 *et seq.*	Connecticut Title 176, Ch. 319hh §§176–520 *et seq.*
1. Definition			
a. For life	Y	Y	
b. One year	Y		Y
c. Entrance fee required		Y	$20,000+
d. Priority admission	Y		
e. Health/health-related services	Y	Y	Y
f. Personal care	Y		
2. Application			
a. Disclosure statement	Y	Y	Y
b. Financials	Y	Y	Y
c. Financial feasibility study	Y		Y
d. Actuarial study			Y
e. Market study	Y		
f. Accreditation in lieu of regulation			
3. Escrow of Fees			
a. Required	Y	Y	Y
b. Basis for release			
i. Presales	20% from 60%		
ii. Funds		90% of costs	75% of costs
iii. Construction	50%	Completed	Maximum-price contract
iv. Financing	Commitment	Commitment	Commitment
4. Additional Presales			
a. To begin development	20% from 50%		5% or $10,000 from 50%
b. For final certification	100% from 80%; alternatives		
5. Reserves			
a. Principal and interest		12 to 18 months	1 year
b. Percent of deposits			
c. Operating costs	Unfunded contract liabilities	20% of annual	1 month
d. For refunds	Y		
6. Bonds			
a. Surety	If necessary		
7. Disclosure to Residents			
a. Financial report	At signing	On request	Before signing
b. Public inspection of filings			
8. Contract Terms			
a. Submit form	Y	Y	
b. Detailed contents	Y	Y	Y
c. Rescission period	90 days	60 days	30 days
d. Refunds in general	Y	Y	
e. Required amortization of refund	All but cost	Y	
f. Full refund if resident dies before occupancy	`		Less costs
9. Advertising			
a. Prior approval	Submit only		
b. Sponsor liability	Y	Y	
10. Resident's Right to Organize			
a. Association	Y		
b. Meetings with management			
11. Liens			
a. For residents	If necessary	Y	
b. Subordinated to priors	Y	Y	
12. Agency	Social Services	Financial Services	Social Services

Continued →

Figure 21.1 **(continued)**

See notes at end for an explanation.	Delaware Title 18, Ch. 46 §§4601 *et seq.*	Florida Title XXXVII, Ch. 651 §§651.011 *et seq.*	Georgia Title 33, Ch. 45 §§33–45–1 *et seq.*
1. Definition			
a. For life		Any duration	Any duration
b. One year	Y	Any duration	Any duration
c. Entrance fee required	Y	Y	Y
d. Priority admission			
e. Health/health-related services	Y	Y	Y
f. Personal care		Y	Y
2. Application			
a. Disclosure statement	Y	Y	Y
b. Financials	Y	Y	Y
c. Financial feasibility study	Y	Y	
d. Actuarial study			
e. Market study		Y	
f. Accreditation in lieu of regulation		Y	
3. Escrow of Fees			
a. Required		Y	Y
b. Basis for release			7 days only
i. Presales		100% from 70%	
ii. Funds			
iii. Construction		Completed	
iv. Financing		Commitment	
4. Additional Presales			
a. To begin development		10% from 30% to apply for license	
b. For final certification		10% from 50%	
5. Reserves			
a. Principal and interest		1 year	
b. Percent of deposits			
c. Operating costs		30% of annual	
d. For refunds			
6. Bonds			
a. Surety			$10,000
7. Disclosure to Residents			
a. Financial report	Before signing	Posting and before signing	Before signing
b. Public inspection of filings	Y	Y	Y
8. Contract Terms			
a. Submit form	Y	Y	
b. Detailed contents		Y	Y
c. Rescission period		7 days	7 days' refundable/ 90 days' nonrefundable fee
d. Refunds in general		Y	Y
e. Required amortization of refund		Pro rata basis	Pro rata/2% maximum per month
f. Full refund if resident dies before occupancy		Y	Y
9. Advertising			
a. Prior approval		Y	
b. Sponsor liability		Y	
10. Resident's Right to Organize			
a. Association		Y	
b. Meetings with management		Quarterly	
11. Liens			
a. For residents		Preferred claim	
b. Subordinated to priors		Y	
12. Agency	Secretary of State	Insurance	Insurance

Continued →

Figure 21.1 (continued)

See notes at end for an explanation.	Idaho Title 67, Ch. 27 §§67–2750 *et seq.*	Illinois Ch. 210 §§40/1 *et seq.*	Indiana §§24–2–4–1 *et seq.*
1. Definition			
a. For life			
b. One year		Y	1 month
c. Entrance fee required	Y (6-month value)	Y	Y
d. Priority admission			
e. Health/health-related services	Y	Y	Y
f. Personal care		Y	
2. Application			
a. Disclosure statement	Y		Y
b. Financials	Y		Y
c. Financial feasibility study			
d. Actuarial study	Y		
e. Market study			
f. Accreditation in lieu of regulation			
3. Escrow of Fees			
a. Required	Y	Or letter of credit	Or security
b. Basis for release			
i. Presales		50% reserved	
ii. Funds	90% of costs		50% of costs
iii. Construction	Completed	Staggered release	
iv. Financing	Commitment	Commitment if necessary	Commitment
4. Additional Presales			
a. To begin development			
b. For final certification			
5. Reserves			
a. Principal and interest		6 months	
b. Percent of deposits			
c. Operating costs			
d. For refunds			
6. Bonds			
a. Surety	Y		
7. Disclosure to Residents			
a. Financial report	Before signing	Before signing	Before signing
b. Public inspection of filings			
8. Contract Terms			
a. Submit form	Y	Y	Y
b. Detailed contents	Y		
c. Rescission period	7 days	14 days	
d. Refunds in general			
e. Required amortization of refund			
f. Full refund if resident dies before occupancy	Less agreed costs		
9. Advertising			
a. Prior approval			
b. Sponsor liability			Y
10. Resident's Right to Organize			
a. Association			
b. Meetings with management			
11. Liens			
a. For residents			
b. Subordinated to priors			
12. Agency	Finance	Public Health	Securities

Continued →

Figure 21.1 **(continued)**

See notes at end for an explanation.	Iowa Ch. 523D §§523.D.1 *et seq.*	Kansas K.S.A §40–2231 *et seq.*	Louisiana Title 51 §§2171 *et seq.*
1. Definition			
a. For life		Not defined	Any duration
b. One year	Y	Not defined	Any duration
c. Entrance fee required	Y	Y	Y
d. Priority admission			
e. Health/health-related services	Y	Y	Y
f. Personal care	Supportive services		Y
2. Application			
a. Disclosure statement	Y	Y	Y
b. Financials	Y	Y	Y
c. Financial feasibility study	Y		Y
d. Actuarial study	Y		
e. Market study	Y		
f. Accreditation in lieu of regulation			
3. Escrow of Fees			
a. Required	Y		Or security
b. Basis for release			
i. Presales	50% reserved and		
ii. Funds	90% of costs		50% of costs
iii. Construction	or occupancy		
iv. Financing			Commitment
4. Additional Presales			
a. To begin development	10% from 50%		
b. For final certification			
5. Reserves			
a. Principal and interest			
b. Percent of deposits			
c. Operating costs			
d. For refunds			
6. Bonds			
a. Surety			
7. Disclosure to Residents			
a. Financial report	Before signing	Before signing and annually on request	On request
b. Public inspection of filings			Y
8. Contract Terms			
a. Submit form	Y	Y	Y
b. Detailed contents	Y	Y	Y
c. Rescission period	30 days from disclosure; 3 days from signing		30 days
d. Refunds in general	Y	Y	Y
e. Required amortization of refund			Pro rata
f. Full refund if resident dies before occupancy	Less agreed costs		Less agreed costs
9. Advertising			
a. Prior approval			Filing only
b. Sponsor liability	Y		Y
10. Resident's Right to Organize			
a. Association	Y		Y
b. Meetings with management			Quarterly
11. Liens			
a. For residents			
b. Subordinated to priors			
12. Agency	Insurance	Insurance	Health and Hospitals

Continued →

Figure 21.1 **(continued)**

See notes at end for an explanation.	**Maine** Title 24–A §§6201 *et seq.*	**Maryland** Art. 70B §7 *et seq.*	**Massachusetts** Title XV, Ch. 93 §76
1. Definition			
a. For life			
b. One year	Y	Y	Y
c. Entrance fee required	Any prepayment	Y	
d. Priority admission		Y	
e. Health/health-related services	Y	Y	Y
f. Personal care	Supportive services	Y	
2. Application			
a. Disclosure statement	Y	Y	Y
b. Financials	Y	Y	Y
c. Financial feasibility study	Y	Y	Y
d. Actuarial study	Y	Y	
e. Market study	If any	Y	
f. Accreditation in lieu of regulation			
3. Escrow of Fees			
a. Required	Y	Y	Disclosure to resident of reserve and escrows
b. Basis for release			
i. Presales			
ii. Funds			
iii. Construction	Complete	Availability of unit	
iv. Financing			
4. Additional Presales			
a. To begin development			
b. For final certification		10% from 65%	
5. Reserves			
a. Principal and interest	1 year		
b. Percent of deposits			
c. Operating costs	20% of annual	15% of annual operating expenses	
d. For refunds			
6. Bonds			
a. Surety	$100,000		
7. Disclosure to Residents			
a. Financial report	10 days before deposit	Two weeks before signing	Before signing
b. Public inspection of filings		Y	
8. Contract Terms			
a. Submit form	Y	Y	Y
b. Detailed contents	Y	Y	Y
c. Rescission period	1 year	Before occupancy up to 90 days	Before occupancy
d. Refunds in general	Y	Y	Y
e. Required amortization of refund	2% per month		1% per month
f. Full refund if resident dies before occupancy	Less specified costs	Y	Less costs
9. Advertising			
a. Prior approval	Y	Y	Filing only
b. Sponsor liability			Y
10. Resident's Right to Organize			
a. Association	Y	Y	
b. Meetings with management	Quarterly	Minimum annually	
11. Liens			
a. For residents			
b. Subordinated to priors			
12. Agency	Insurance	Aging	Elder Affairs

Continued →

Figure 21.1 **(continued)**

See notes at end for an explanation.	**Michigan** Title 14, Ch. 130 §§544.801 *et seq.*	**Minnesota** Ch. 80D §§80D.01 *et seq.*	**Missouri** Title XXIV, Ch. 376 §§376.900 *et seq.*
1. Definition			
a. For life			
b. One year	Y	Y	Y
c. Entrance fee required		$100	
d. Priority admission			
e. Health/health-related services	Y	Y	Y
f. Personal care	Y		
2. Application			
a. Disclosure statement	Y	Y	Y
b. Financials	Y	Y	Y
c. Financial feasibility study	Y	Y	Y
d. Actuarial study			
e. Market study			
f. Accreditation in lieu of regulation			
3. Escrow of Fees			
a. Required	Or trust account	Y	Y
b. Basis for release			
i. Presales		65% or 1/3 from 50%	
ii. Funds		90% of costs	90% of costs
iii. Construction	Availability of unit	50% and maximum-price contract	Maximum-price contract
iv. Financing		Commitment	Commitment
4. Additional Presales			
a. To begin development			
b. For final certification			
5. Reserves			
a. Principal and interest		1 year	1.5% x annual debt
b. Percent of deposits			50%
c. Operating costs			
d. For refunds			5% of moveouts per year
6. Bonds			
a. Surety	If necessary		
7. Disclosure to Residents			
a. Financial report		Before signing and annually	Before signing and annually
b. Public inspection of filings	Y		
8. Contract Terms			
a. Submit form		Y	Y
b. Detailed contents			
c. Rescission period	7 days	10 days	7 days
d. Refunds in general	Y	Y	Y
e. Required amortization of refund	Y		
f. Full refund if resident dies before occupancy	Less costs	Less costs and reasonable service charge	
9. Advertising			
a. Prior approval	Y		
b. Sponsor liability		Y	Y
10. Resident's Right to Organize			
a. Association	Y	Y	
b. Meetings with management	Board seat		Board seat
11. Liens			
a. For residents		Y	
b. Subordinated to priors		No	
12. Agency	Corporations and Securities	None, file with county recorder	Insurance

Continued →

Figure 21.1 **(continued)**

	New Hampshire Title XXXVII, Ch. 420–D	New Jersey Title 52, Ch. 27D, §§330 *et seq.*	New Mexico Ch. 24, Art. 17 §§24–17–1 *et seq.*
1. Definition			
a. For life			Y
b. One year	Y	Y	Y
c. Entrance fee required	Y	Y	
d. Priority admission			
e. Health/health-related services	Y	Y	Y
f. Personal care			
2. Application			
a. Disclosure statement	Y	Y	Y
b. Financials	Y	Y	Y
c. Financial feasibility study		Y	
d. Actuarial study			For entrance fees
e. Market study		If any	
f. Accreditation in lieu of regulation		Y	
3. Escrow of Fees			
a. Required	Or bond	Or security	Y
b. Basis for release			
i. Presales	50% of all fees and 35% of each fee	50% of all fees and 35% of each fee	
ii. Funds	or 50% of costs	and 50% of costs	
iii. Construction		and 50% of construction	Availability of unit
iv. Financing		and commitment	
4. Additional Presales			
a. To begin development			
b. For final certification			
5. Reserves			
a. Principal and interest	1 year	> of 1 year's principal and interest or 15% of operating costs	
b. Percent of deposits			
c. Operating costs	2 months	> of 1 year's principal and interest or 15% of operating costs	
d. For refunds	If necessary		
6. Bonds			
a. Surety			
7. Disclosure to Residents			
a. Financial report	Y	Before signing	7 days before signing and annually
b. Public inspection of filings			
8. Contract Terms			
a. Submit form			
b. Detailed contents	Y	Y	Y
c. Rescission period	10 days	30 days	7 days
d. Refunds in general	Y	Y	Y
e. Required amortization of refund			
f. Full refund if resident dies before occupancy	Less processing fee	Less costs	
9. Advertising			
a. Prior approval			
b. Sponsor liability			
10. Resident's Right to Organize			
a. Association	Y	Y	Y
b. Meetings with management	Quarterly	Quarterly	
11. Liens			
a. For residents	If necessary	If necessary	
b. Subordinated to priors		Y	
12. Agency	Insurance	Community Affairs	Aging

Continued →

Figure 21.1 **(continued)**

See notes at end for an explanation.	**New York** Public Health Law Art. 46 §§4600 *et seq.*	**North Carolina** Ch. 58, Art. 64 §§58–64–1 *et seq.*	**Ohio** Title I, Ch. 173 §173.13
1. Definition			
a. For life	Y		
b. One year		Y	Y
c. Entrance fee required			
d. Priority admission			
e. Health/health-related services	Y	Y	Y
f. Personal care			
2. Application			
a. Disclosure statement	Y	Y	
b. Financials	Y	Y	
c. Financial feasibility study	Y	Y	
d. Actuarial study	Y	Y	
e. Market study	Y		
f. Accreditation in lieu of regulation		Y	
3. Escrow of Fees			
a. Required	Y	Y	
b. Basis for release			
i. Presales	25% from 60%	10% from 75%	
ii. Funds	85% of costs	90% of costs	
iii. Construction	Availability of unit or maximum-price contract	Completed	
iv. Financing	Commitment	Commitment	
4. Additional Presales			
a. To begin development	10% from 50%		
b. For final certification			
5. Reserves			
a. Principal and interest	1 year		
b. Percent of deposits			
c. Operating costs	6 months' operating; 1 year's repairs	50% of annual	
d. For refunds			
6. Bonds			
a. Surety		If necessary	
7. Disclosure to Residents			
a. Financial report	Before deposit or signing	Before signing	On request
b. Public inspection of filings			
8. Contract Terms			
a. Submit form	Y	Y	
b. Detailed contents	Y	Y	
c. Rescission period	90 days	30 days	
d. Refunds in general	Y	Y	
e. Required amortization of refund	2% per month		
f. Full refund if resident dies before occupancy	Less agreed costs	Less agreed costs	
9. Advertising			
a. Prior approval			
b. Sponsor liability			
10. Resident's Right to Organize			
a. Association	Y	Y	Y
b. Meetings with management	Quarterly	Annually	Board seat/quarterly
11. Liens			
a. For residents		Y	
b. Subordinated to priors		Y	
12. Agency	Health	Insurance	Aging

Continued →

Figure 21.1 **(continued)**

See notes at end for an explanation.	Oregon Title 10, Ch. 101 §§101.010 *et seq.*	Pennsylvania Title 40, §§3201 *et seq.*	Rhode Island 23 R.I. Gen. Laws §§23–59–1 *et seq.*
1. Definition			
a. For life			
b. One year	Y	Y	Y
c. Entrance fee required	Y	Y	
d. Priority admission			
e. Health/health-related services	Y	Y	Y
f. Personal care	Y		
2. Application			
a. Disclosure statement	Y	Y	Y
b. Financials	Y	Y	Y
c. Financial feasibility study	Y	If prepared to secure financing	Y
d. Actuarial study			
e. Market study		Y	
f. Accreditation in lieu of regulation		Y	
3. Escrow of Fees			
a. Required	Y	Or security	
b. Basis for release			
i. Presales	10% from 50%	50% of all fees and 35% of each fee	
ii. Funds	50% of costs	and 50% of costs	
iii. Construction			
iv. Financing	Commitment	Commitment	
4. Additional Presales			
a. To begin development			
b. For final certification			
5. Reserves			
a. Principal and interest	1 year	1 year's principal and interest or 10% of operating costs	
b. Percent of deposits			
c. Operating costs	3 months	1 year's principal and interest or 10% of operating costs	
d. For refunds			
6. Bonds			
a. Surety			
7. Disclosure to Residents			
a. Financial report	Before signing	Before signing	3 days before signing and annually upon request
b. Public inspection of filings			
8. Contract Terms			
a. Submit form	Y	Y	Y
b. Detailed contents		Y	Y
c. Rescission period	6 months (partial refund)	7 days	7 days
d. Refunds in general	Y		
e. Required amortization of refund			
f. Full refund if resident dies before occupancy		Less agreed costs	Less agreed costs
9. Advertising			
a. Prior approval			
b. Sponsor liability			Y
10. Resident's Right to Organize			
a. Association		Y	Y
b. Meetings with management		Quarterly	Quarterly
11. Liens			
a. For residents		If necessary	
b. Subordinated to priors		Y	
12. Agency	Senior Services	Insurance	Health

Continued →

Figure 21.1 **(continued)**

See notes at end for an explanation.	**South Carolina** S.C. Code Ann. §§37–11–10 *et seq.*	**Tennessee** Tenn. Code Ann. §§4–3–1305 *et seq.*	**Texas** Title 4, Ch. 246 §§246.001 *et seq.*
1. Definition			
a. For life		Not defined	
b. One year	Y	Not defined	Y
c. Entrance fee required			3 months' rent
d. Priority admission			
e. Health/health-related services	Y	Y	Y
f. Personal care			Y
2. Application			
a. Disclosure statement	Y		Y
b. Financials	Y		Y
c. Financial feasibility study	Y		Y
d. Actuarial study	Y		For life care
e. Market study			
f. Accreditation in lieu of regulation			
3. Escrow of Fees			
a. Required	Y	If necessary	Y
b. Basis for release			
i. Presales			10% from 50%
ii. Funds	90% of costs		90% of cost
iii. Construction	Availability of unit		Maximum-price contract
iv. Financing	Commitment		Commitment
4. Additional Presales			
a. To begin development			
b. For final certification			
5. Reserves			
a. Principal and interest			1 year
b. Percent of deposits			
c. Operating costs			
d. For refunds			
6. Bonds			
a. Surety	Fixed life fee only		If necessary
7. Disclosure to Residents			
a. Financial report	Before signing		Before signing
b. Public inspection of filings			
8. Contract Terms			
a. Submit form	Y		Y
b. Detailed contents	Y		Y
c. Rescission period	30 days		7 days
d. Refunds in general	Y		Y
e. Required amortization of refund			Pro rata
f. Full refund if resident dies before occupancy			Less costs
9. Advertising			
a. Prior approval			On request
b. Sponsor liability			
10. Resident's Right to Organize			
a. Association			
b. Meetings with management	Grievance procedure		
11. Liens			
a. For residents			Y
b. Subordinated to priors			Y
12. Agency	Consumer Affairs	Commerce and Insurance	Insurance

Continued →

Regulation of Continuing-Care Retirement Communities

Figure 21.1 (continued)

See notes at end for an explanation.	Vermont Part 4, Ch. 151 §§8001 *et seq.*	Virginia Title 38.2, Ch. 49 §§4900 *et seq.*	Washington Title 70, Ch. 70.38 §§70.38.015 *et seq.*
1. Definition			
a. For life			
b. One year	Y	Y	Y
c. Entrance fee required	Y	Y	
d. Priority admission			
e. Health/health-related services	Y	Y	Y
f. Personal care	Y		Y
2. Application			
a. Disclosure statement	Y	Y	Y
b. Financials	Y	Y	Y
c. Financial feasibility study	Y		Y
d. Actuarial study	Y		Y
e. Market study	Y		Y
f. Accreditation in lieu of regulation			
3. Escrow of Fees			
a. Required	Y	Y	Y
b. Basis for release			
i. Presales	10% from 60%		50% of total fees
ii. Funds	100% of costs		
iii. Construction	Maximum-price contract	Availability of unit	Commitment
iv. Financing	Secured		
4. Additional Presales			
a. To begin development			
b. For final certification			
5. Reserves			
a. Principal and interest	> of 1 year or 15% of operating costs		
b. Percent of deposits			
c. Operating costs	> of 1 year or 15% of operating costs		
d. For refunds			
6. Bonds			
a. Surety			
7. Disclosure to Residents			
a. Financial report	Before signing	Annual	
b. Public inspection of filings	Y		
8. Contract Terms			
a. Submit form	Y	Y	Y
b. Detailed contents	Y	Y	Y
c. Rescission period	30 days	7 days	90 days
d. Refunds in general	Y		Y
e. Required amortization of refund	2% per month		
f. Full refund if resident dies before occupancy	Y	Y	Less costs
9. Advertising			
a. Prior approval	On request		
b. Sponsor liability			
10. Resident's Right to Organize			
a. Association	Y	Y	Y
b. Meetings with management	Annually	Quarterly	
11. Liens			
a. For residents	If necessary		
b. Subordinated to priors	Y		
12. Agency	Banking and Insurance	Insurance	Social and Health Services

Continued →

Figure 21.1 **(continued)**

	Wisconsin Ch. 647 §§647.01 *et seq.*
1. Definition	
a. For life	
b. One year	Y
c. Entrance fee required	$10,000 or 50% of estate
d. Priority admission	
e. Health/health-related services	Y
f. Personal care	Y
2. Application	
a. Disclosure statement	
b. Financials	Y
c. Financial feasibility study	Y
d. Actuarial study	
e. Market study	
f. Accreditation in lieu of regulation	
3. Escrow of Fees	
a. Required	
b. Basis for release	
i. Presales	
ii. Funds	
iii. Construction	
iv. Financing	
4. Additional Presales	
a. To begin development	
b. For final certification	
5. Reserves	
a. Principal and interest	
b. Percent of deposits	
c. Operating costs	
d. For refunds	
6. Bonds	
a. Surety	
7. Disclosure to Residents	
a. Financial report	On request
b. Public inspection of filings	Y
8. Contract Terms	
a. Submit form	Y
b. Detailed contents	Y
c. Rescission period	90 days
d. Refunds in general	Y
e. Required amortization of refund	Y
f. Full refund if resident dies before occupancy	Less costs
9. Advertising	
a. Prior approval	Keep on file
b. Sponsor liability	
10. Resident's Right to Organize	
a. Association	
b. Meetings with management	Grievance procedure
11. Liens	
a. For residents	
b. Subordinated to priors	
12. Agency	Insurance

Continued →

Figure 21.1 **(continued)**

Notes:

In general—Figure 21.1 was derived principally from information compiled by AAHSA. It summarizes statutory language and may not reflect regulatory or other interpretation. Rules are generally much more complex than the figure suggests. "Y" indicates a provision on point; a blank space indicates no provision on point.

1. **Definition**
   a., b. Shows required duration of contract subject to licensure. If a statute covers contracts for life or greater than one year, figure shows only "1 year" filled. If a and b both are filled, may be multiple categories of licensure.
   c. Statute applies only when there is some form of entrance fee.
   d. Priority admission to services, even if not prepaid, triggers licensure.
   e., f. Figure refers to type of activity considered to trigger licensure. Health-related services and personal care may be similar activities in some states.

2. **Application**
   a. Disclosure to residents or state of various information about provider and/or project plans.
   b. Financial statements or budgets required to be submitted to state.
   c.,d.,e. These studies are required to be submitted to state and may contain overlapping information depending on state definitions.
   f. Accreditation accepted in lieu of state review; may be subject to agency discretion.

3. **Escrows**
   a. Some escrowing of entrance fees required, at least for initial facility sellout.
   b. Factors considered in releasing money from escrow.
      1. Percentage of total entrance fee required to be on deposit from a specified percentage of total units in project.
      2. Total funds, such as construction and startup costs, required for escrow release.
      3. Construction standard required for escrow release.
      4. Financing standard required for escrow release.

4. **Additional presales (see 3.b.1 for presales required for escrow release)**
   a. Presales required to begin development or license application; expressed as percentage of entrance fees from a percentage of units.
   b. Presales required to obtain final certification; expressed as percentage of entrance fees from a percentage of units.

5. **Reserves**
   a. Required reserve of principal and interest payments or other real property expenses for facility; expressed in months of payments.
   b. Reserve calculated as percentage of deposits received from residents.
   c. Reserves measured by costs of operation.
   d. Reserves measured by entrance fee refund obligation.

6. **Bonds**
   Surety bond for contract obligations required automatically or when deemed necessary by state.

7. **Disclosure to residents**
   a. When operator's financial report must be given to residents.
   b. License statute provides specifically for public inspection of licensee's filings with state; most other states may permit inspection by reason of other general statutes.

8. **Contract terms**
   a. Contract form must be submitted to state.
   b. Statute sets forth detailed requirements for contents of contracts; for example, services offered, fees, cancellation, terminations for cause, consequences of death, and so on.
   c. Statute provides for period in which resident can rescind contract without penalty, usually measured after contract execution or commencement of occupancy.
   d. General statutory treatment of refunds to residents in event of voluntary cancellation, termination for cause, or death, often with different amounts due depending on circumstances.
   e. Statute sets forth refund schedule based on resident length of stay (usually after rescission period).
   f. Full refund required if resident dies before taking occupancy, sometimes less actual cost of care or a fixed or percentage charge.

9. **Advertising**
   a. Advertising must be submitted to state and approved or filed only. Some states have express prohibitions against false advertising; these are not noted in the figure.
   b. State requires that if sponsoring or other organization in addition to licensee is mentioned in the contract or in advertising, the other organization must accept or clarify its financial responsibility for contract obligations.

10. **Resident right to organize**
    a. Provision for resident right to organize in an association.
    b. Statute sets forth minimum meet and confer requirements between management and residents, establishes resident seat on home's board of directors, or requires establishment of grievance procedure.

11. **Liens**
    a. A statutory lien is or may be established against facility assets to secure obligations to residents.
    b. The statutory lien is recognized to be subordinate to prior recorded liens or to secured lenders (e.g., holders of mortgages).

12. **Agency**
    State agency in charge of continuing-care certification or enforcement.

placed in approved escrow accounts. State statutes then place various conditions on the release of the deposits out of escrow for use by the developer to pay down construction debt or to cover other expenses of development or operations. Some states may allow the developer to post a surety bond or letter of credit in lieu of escrowed deposits.

For previously occupied units, most states require deposits to be escrowed until the unit is available for occupancy. In addition, several states (Arkansas, Maryland, Michigan, New Mexico, New York, South Carolina, and Virginia) require deposits for newly built units to be held in escrow until the building is available for occupancy. Most of the other regulated states condition the release of escrow funds on adherence to a complex matrix of criteria, including the size and number of deposits; percentages of completion of construction; accumulation of funds from entrance fees; financing sufficient to cover a specific percentage of construction costs, equipping the building, and startup losses; existence of guaranteed maximum-price construction contracts; and/or the existence of a financing commitment. Thus, for example, Arizona, Colorado, and Idaho require a unit to be completed, a commitment for long-term financing to be secured, and entrance fees and financing proceeds to equal at least 90 percent of the costs of the building and of starting up project operations. On the other hand, Pennsylvania, New Jersey, and New Hampshire require 50 percent of total entrance fees to be secured with a minimum of 35 percent of each entrance fee and/or 50 percent of all construction and startup costs to be secured. At one extreme is Florida, which does not permit release of escrow funds until the developer can demonstrate payment in full for 70 percent of the units, completion of construction, and in-place financing. At the other end of the spectrum is Georgia, which requires only that deposits be escrowed for the first seven days.

Some states provide for a staggered release of escrow funds. For example, Illinois permits release of the first 20 percent of escrow funds when 50 percent of the units are reserved and loan commitments are in place, another 20 percent when the foundation is completed, another 20 percent when the roof is completed, and the remainder when the project is available for occupancy. Maine and North Carolina permit 25 percent of escrow monies to be pledged or released when certain presales levels are met, with the remainder released when the facility commences operations and attains a higher level of presales.

Linking the release of escrow monies to presales, financing, and construction progress—measures of the eventual success of the project—is generally acknowledged as prudent practice. In addition, progress in the construction of the facility may give prospective residents a tangible asset that can be tapped in the event of a marketing failure. Furthermore, construction has a tendency to encourage further sales.

Occasionally, even after making initial deposits toward entrance fees early in the development process, some prospective residents may later decide against making additional deposits and moving into the facility. Most states require entrance fee deposits to be refundable, although some such as Florida may permit the developer to charge a penalty for the prospective resident's withdrawal. Other states may permit the developer to withhold refunds from escrow until the particular unit is resold. Even after occupancy is commenced, most state laws require an initial trial or "rescission" period during which a resident may withdraw from the facility, with or without cause, and receive a refund of entrance fees on a pro rata basis, or less the actual cost of services actually delivered (see §§21.6(b) and 21.6(c)).

Provisions for refund of escrowed deposits should permit some penalty, such as 1 or 2 percent of the entrance fee, withholding of interest, or refund deferral until the unit is resold, so that prospective residents are motivated not to make deposits at several projects with the intention of dropping out of all but one.[5] Most project failures occur during development due to lack of enrollment, and presales should be firm so that developers and applicants for residence may proceed with confidence.

Many influential people in the continuing-care field believe that some of the more restrictive provisions contained in state law reflect sound business practices necessary to the successful development of any continuing-care facility. Accordingly, to help prevent failures and to protect the consumer and the reputation of CCRCs, some states have established in law—with the concurrence and assistance of CCRC owners and operators—business practices such as escrow of entrance fee deposits and minimum levels of presales (see next section).

AAHSA's guidelines recommend escrow of resident deposits, with release of 25 percent when a 10 percent deposit has been received for 60 percent of the independent-living units and release of the other 75 percent when payment in full has been received for 75 percent of the units. A letter of credit may be substituted for presale deposits. AAHSA also recommends assessing a 2 percent penalty against prospective residents who withdraw.

§21.4 Presales Thresholds as a Condition of Ongoing Development

Because one of the most vulnerable periods for any seniors' housing community—especially continuing-care facilities—is the initial marketing stage, many states engage in rigorous regulation of the presales process, thereby helping to protect consumers' monies and ensure a project's financial soundness.

Presales requirements often function as a condition of release of escrowed entrance fees (see §21.3). Some authorities believe that presales are so important to the success of a new CCRC that substantial presales are necessary before commencement of any construction or even before applying for project approval. For example, in Florida, 10 percent of the entrance fee for 30 percent of the units must be collected to apply for a certificate of authority. Before construction can begin, Connecticut requires 5 percent or $10,000 on deposit and New York and Iowa 10 percent for half of the units in a project. Similarly, in California, construction may not commence until 50 percent of the residential units are reserved with a 20 percent deposit on the entrance fee.

Presales requirements may also be a condition for either obtaining final state approval for the project or executing contracts with residents. For example, Florida law requires a minimum 10 percent payment for at least 50 percent of the units to obtain a certificate of authority, and Maryland requires a 10 percent downpayment for 65 percent of the units. To obtain a final certificate, California requires full payment for 80 percent of the units, or lesser amounts in the case of a business plan or collateral satisfactory to the state, although a provisional certificate is available earlier to permit the gradual move-in of residents. The apparent concern underlying such statutes is that facilities that do not reach certain optimum levels of occupancy sufficient to sustain operations may fail or convert to another use. Some states may be able to extend escrows, impose resident liens, or possibly even take over management in an effort to preserve resident deposits or facility assets for resident refunds or claims.

Although many CCRCs traditionally have been constructed with the proceeds of presales deposits, states will increasingly face situations in which facilities are financed by other means. It will become more common, for example, for CCRCs to be financed from the holdings of a major corporate developer. In addition, conversions of failed condominium projects or other existing structures into CCRCs will become more frequent. In these situations, resident presales deposits will not serve construction financing purposes so much as indicate the seriousness of a prospective buyer's interest in the project. While it makes sense to preserve resident funds in escrow if deposits are collected before admission, it may not be necessary to mandate a developer to collect resident deposits before construction or opening when the developer is risking only its own funds on the venture.

On the other hand, if presales deposits are to be a serious indication of projects' marketing success, depositors should not be able to walk away from a project without some loss. Accordingly, several states allow or even require some penalty to be assessed against depositors who withdraw during either the development period or an initial rescission period (see discussion of refunds generally in §21.6(c)).

To file an application for a certificate, AAHSA guidelines require a 10 percent deposit for 30 percent of the units, with a 2 percent withdrawal penalty. When 60 percent of the units are reserved, the application is deemed complete and a provisional certificate of authority (PCOA) can be issued. A developer cannot take deposits over $1,000, begin site preparation, or construct a model unit without first securing a PCOA.

§21.5 Reserves

A unique characteristic of many CCRCs is that they offer future health care or assisted living at a stabilized or discounted rate in exchange for some form of prepayment or predictable periodic payment. To the extent that such facilities act as self-insurers of the health care risks and needs of their resident populations, it is prudent for facilities to set aside reserves, usually out of entrance fees, for such future contingencies. Even if costs of care are funded from ongoing cash flows, reserves may be warranted to cover normal business needs such as remodeling or plant replacement or simply to cover debt service in the face of temporary cash flow variances. Many states have mandated reserve requirements by law (see also §§5.4 and 17.7(b) regarding the American Institute of Certified Public Accountants audit standards for CCRCs).

Most statutes relate reserve requirements directly to expenditures such as debt service. For example, Arizona, Minnesota, and Texas require one year's debt service reserve while Illinois requires six months' reserve. Several states require one year's debt service, plus some percentage or number of months' worth of annual operating expenses (e.g., Connecticut [one month], Florida [four months], Oregon [three months], Maine [one-fifth year], New Hampshire [two months]). Some states require either a percentage of operating expenses or a year's debt service (Pennsylvania) or the greater of the two (New Jersey, Vermont).

Other states require an actuarially based reserve for obligations not covered from other sources (e.g., Arkansas, California, Maine). In Missouri and Colorado, developers must reserve a percentage of deposits or entrance fees. Indiana has no reserve requirement but establishes a state fund for residents whose facilities are unable to make contractual refunds.

Reserve statutes generally prescribe the amount of required liquid reserves and the amount and types of investments permitted to be counted among liquid assets. Generally, CCRC laws do not prescribe what must be done with funds that are not reserved. One state court has ruled, however, that a life-care contract implied that the provider could not use fees paid by members of one facility to fund other operations but rather must base fees on services rendered to facility residents.[6]

Statutorily mandated reserve requirements should take into account the extent to which different CCRC business structures may reduce the risk inherent in a pure self-insurance type of format. For example, one facility may provide all needed health care, including hospitalizations, in return for an entrance fee and no charge beyond the regular monthly fee required for apartment residents (Type A facility). Another facility may offer only a limited number of days of nursing care per year for the regular monthly fee and may charge an additional per use fee for all services beyond that threshold (Type B facility). A third facility may guarantee access to nursing care as a benefit of residence and charge a fee for service for all care (Type C facility) but limit residents' risk by providing them with group health insurance—purchased from a third party—as part of the regular monthly fee. These three examples all carry different degrees of risk, and while significant reserves may be appropriate in the first case, no reserves may be necessary in the third case, where the facility has not assumed risk respecting future health care costs. In a condominium or cooperative facility, the homeowner's equity may be pledged as security for future costs of care.

California has also recognized that refundable entrance fees represent a distinct additional future liability for which reserves may have to be set aside. Although entrance fee refunds for residents leaving the facility normally can be paid from new entrance fees received from resale of the unit being vacated, the California statute requires a reserve based on resident life expectancies when the refund is not conditioned on resale of the unit.

AAHSA's guidelines state that reserves should include debt service and lease payments for 12 months, plus 15 percent of annual operating expenses exclusive of depreciation. Reserves must be funded by marketable securities or an irrevocable letter of credit and can be spent at a rate of no more than one-twelfth per month.

A draft report indicates that the Continuing Care Retirement Facilities Working Group of the National Association of Insurance Commissioners (NAIC) will recommend that NAIC require CCRCs to maintain the following reserves in liquid asset accounts:

■ Each CCRC shall maintain an account for debt service and redemption for all obligations that have an initial term exceeding 12 months and that are collaterized by the CCRC's property, plant, or equipment. The minimum value of this account must be either 12 months' interest plus one-twelfth of the principal amount of the original debt for obligations requiring a balloon payment or 12 months' debt service for all other obligations.

- At the end of each fiscal year, each CCRC shall establish and maintain an account for repair and replacement of property, plant, and equipment. For buildings and related fixtures and improvements, the annual increment to the account would equal one-sixtieth of the original cost adjusted for changes in the Consumer Price Index; for tangible assets with limited lives, including furniture, fixtures and equipment, the annual increment would equal one-fifteenth of the original cost adjusted for the Consumer Price Index.

- Each CCRC shall establish and maintain an account based on operating expenses that are applicable to the immediately preceding year or that are anticipated in the current year and a balance of not less than 20 percent of operating expenses for the period elected.[7]

The draft report by the NAIC working group also recommended that NAIC require any funds supporting these accounts to be invested in securities that are readily convertible to cash through a demonstrated secondary market. In addition, the report recommended that CCRCs be required to establish acceptable plans of debt retirement for construction loans and provide plans for paying or refinancing balloon payments at least 24 months before maturity. The group considered but did not recommend adoption of standards for future service obligations.

§21.6 Resident Contracts and Related Documents

Many states define the parameters of certain provisions that must appear in the contract between the resident and the CCRC operator. The primary intent of the provisions is to ensure that providers cover certain essential contract terms, specify detail concerning eventualities such as resident transfer, fee changes, and terminations, and protect the resident from loss of substantial funds in the event of an early death or an ill-considered or hastily concluded transaction. Virtually all states regulating continuing care require contract forms to be submitted to the state agency for review. In addition, operators must give residents related documents such as deposit and escrow agreements, financial disclosure forms, resident handbooks, and other documents whose provisions may be prescribed by statute (see also §21.2 regarding disclosure statements).[8]

The variety of required CCRC contract provisions found in state laws is noticeably broad.

- **Services**
  - Description of residential unit
  - All services included in the monthly fee
  - Optional services at an extra cost
  - Notice of change in scope of services
  - Whether funeral services are included (rare) (See also §21.2 for disclosure statement requirements, often required for contracts as well.)
- **Admissions and Transfers**
  - Description of admission policies
  - Health and financial admission criteria
  - Preexisting health conditions not covered by contract
  - Circumstances under which a resident who runs out of funds can remain in the facility
  - When a resident may be required to transfer out of the apartment unit
  - When a resident can return to the apartment after a stay in personal care or nursing
  - Policies regarding the effect of marriage, divorce
  - Whether a resident must have health insurance, Medicare.
  - Physician approval of transfer (rarely required)
  - Policy if a nursing bed is unavailable
- **Fees**
  - List of all entrance fees, monthly fees, optional charges, taxes, and utility costs
  - Conditions under which monthly fees can be changed, method of calculation
  - Specified notice of fee changes
  - Fee adjustments while resident is absent from the facility
  - Entrance fee adjustments on unit transfer, transfer of spouse

- Description of how entrance fees are earned by the facility
- Limit on increases in fees (e.g., costs, Consumer Price Index)
- **Terminations and Refunds**
  - Specified initial period of resident rescission and full refund
  - Refunds in the event of death or cancellation before occupancy
  - Interest paid on preoccupancy deposit refunds
  - No withdrawal of deposit during facility construction without penalty or resale of unit
  - Circumstances under which provider or resident may terminate
  - No termination without just cause
  - Specified refund amortization schedule
  - No termination for inability to pay (rare)
- **Resident Rights**
  - To form an association
  - To participate in decision making
  - To a grievance procedure
- **Owner Information**
  - Basic information
  - Existence and liability of any sponsoring or affiliated organization
- **Miscellaneous**
  - Language written in "plain English"
  - Minimum type size, some provisions in bold type
  - Prior approval of entire contract by state agency
  - Consumer warning to seek legal or financial advice
  - "Fair" contract

The discussion below explores the different regulatory approaches to contract language as well as some of the policy reasons underlying them.

(a) Disclosure of Basic Information and Policies

Most states require contract recital of basic information regarding routine and optional services and amenities and the normal and extra charges that accompany them. Increases in monthly fees often present a particular problem because of many residents' fixed income and residents' expectation to live in a CCRC for life. States therefore often require disclosure of past fee increases and the basis for future increases and require notice of such increases. Some also limit increases based on cost.

Transfers of residents to nursing or assisted living also can give rise to misunderstandings and disputes. States often require contracts to deal with the complex issues of who makes the transfer decision, what criteria are used, what fee changes are made, the use of off-campus facilities, and the circumstances governing return to the residence. These provisions are further complicated in the case of spouses who may need different levels of care.

State law may also require contracts to give residents basic rights to organize, participate in management, or submit grievances. Often contract language is subjected to statutory tests of legibility, fairness, or comprehensibility. In addition, state law may require disclosure of basic provider information and the responsibilities of related organizations.

Most states with continuing-care regulation either require the provider to furnish financial statements directly to prospective residents before contract execution or allow public inspection of financial statements and other provider information filed with the state. Those requiring the furnishing of statements to prospective residents include Arizona, California, Florida, Illinois, Indiana, Maryland, Minnesota, Missouri, and Pennsylvania. Florida, Indiana, Michigan, and Wisconsin permit public inspection.

Some states, such as Minnesota, Missouri, and Virginia, require financial statements to be updated annually and furnished to residents. Others require detailed disclosures about facility or operator operations, the history of fee increases, and related matters. One state supreme court has found that life-care contracts by their nature impose on the provider an obligation to furnish residents with meaningful financial information sufficient for them to determine if fee increases are reasonable.[9] (For more detail about financial disclosures, see §21.2 and Figure 21.1).

(b) Contract Termination

Many states have specific provisions dealing with termination of either the CCRC contract or preoccupancy deposit agreements, whether by the resident, by the facility, or by reason of death of the resident.

These statutes often further provide for certain specified refunds of preoccupancy deposits, entrance fees, and possibly of monthly fees paid to the facility operator.

Many states require care agreements to be terminable at will (with or without cause) either during a specified number of days after execution of the agreement or after initial occupancy, with a full refund to the resident of entrance fees and possibly monthly fees. In some cases, the operator may be able to retain a pro rata portion of the fees or the actual cost of care for the period. These "rescission periods" (sometimes called probationary or cooling-off periods) are intended to give the resident, and in some cases the facility, the opportunity to void the transaction in the event that either party decides that the individual made a serious mistake in taking up residence at the facility. Rescission periods mandated by statute may range from seven days to one year.

Once the rescission period has expired, some states permit the provider to dismiss the resident, after notice, only upon a showing of good cause (e.g., California, Florida, Maryland, New Jersey, New York). While inability to pay is normally just cause to terminate in most states, it is not in New Jersey and New York, thus requiring all CCRCs to meet the national standard set for tax-exempt facilities (see §9.3). Permissible causes for termination in most states include disruptive behavior, a medical condition the facility cannot treat, or creation of a danger to self or others. Most other states that address the subject at all require only that the contract set forth termination provisions.

(c) Refunds

Refunds present special problems and issues depending on when they occur. As discussed in the previous section, in the event of a termination during an initial rescission period, some states require refund of all entrance fees, less perhaps some retention based on the cost of care or a fixed percentage. In the event of a termination by the facility after such a rescission period, a few states also regulate in detail the amount of refunds and the manner in which they are given. Still other states specify the circumstances under which a prospective CCRC resident, or his or her estate, may recover deposits in the event of death

or withdrawal during the preoccupancy development period.

Some states regulate the timing and amount of refunds when a consumer cancels a preoccupancy deposit agreement. During facility development, it is important for the provider to be able to have some assurance that depositors are seriously interested. The developer may rely on deposits to meet not only marketing and financial milestones but also statutory presales thresholds. If all applicants are entitled to a full refund on demand, sales progress may prove to be a house of cards. Therefore, states such as California, Maryland, and Oregon permit a depositor to receive a refund only after another person has placed a new deposit on the reserved unit. Many other states permit a monetary penalty on withdrawal before or after occupancy (see below regarding preoccupancy death and postoccupancy terminations).

For withdrawals or terminations after commencement of occupancy, states have taken several different approaches. Some are silent on the point; others require only that the contract set forth the refund policy for the various circumstances of termination (e.g., resident cancellation, death, dismissal by the provider) as well as the relevant time periods (e.g., before or after the rescission period). Still other states, such as Florida, Maine, and Massachusetts, require entrance fees to be amortized, with the unamortized portion refunded according to a set schedule.

Michigan requires a refund of all but the cost of care after six months. Colorado requires a refund of all entrance fees in excess of the cost of care, payable on resale of the unit, except that nonprofits may use a 60-month entrance fee amortization schedule. New York provides for a cost-based refund for 90 days, followed by a 2 percent per month plus 4 percent processing fee retention thereafter. Generally, such detailed regulations vary with the time of and reason for withdrawal and establish fixed, percentage-, or cost-based caps on facility retention of entrance fees.

One of the most difficult refund situations encountered by CCRCs and residents has been that of entrance fee refunds upon the death of the resident early in the life of the continuing-care agreement. Traditional continuing-care agreements have been based on a pure self-insurance model, which relies on an actuarial assumption that each person of a given age has a predictable life expectancy. Both the economic viability of the facility and the entrance fee structure are based on the assumption that for every person who dies sooner than expected, another facility resident will exceed her or his life expectancy. Therefore, when a resident dies shortly after moving into a facility, it is important, at least in theory, to retain the person's entire entrance fee to pay the expenses for that other person who is likely to surpass the actuarial average.

While many courts have traditionally accepted the actuarial philosophy underlying insurance coverage,[10] some are growing reluctant to permit a CCRC to retain the entire entrance fee of a person who died shortly after moving into the facility when that fee may be several times the value of services actually received by the resident. The courts hold that such circumstances give essentially no value to the provider's promise—inherent in each transaction—to care for the resident for life and to assume the risk that the resident may live far beyond anyone's expectations. Once the resident has died, disgruntled heirs who were not a party to the transaction occasionally charge that the retirement community took advantage of the elderly decedent. Unfortunately, sympathetic courts are increasingly finding retention of entrance fees after an early death to be unconscionable or to constitute an unenforceable penalty or forfeiture. Courts may also look for some ambiguity in the contract in an effort to find a way to interpret the agreement against the retirement facility draftor.[11] Although the issue arises relatively infrequently, due in part to the health screenings of applicants performed by most facilities, it has received a good deal of critical attention from the courts and other observers.[12]

In a 1995 case, the Wisconsin Supreme Court held that entrance fees paid by residents of a retirement community were in fact security deposits governed by state landlord-tenant law. At issue were provisions in a residency agreement that arguably subordinated the residents' interests in a fund holding their entrance fees (which exceeded $1 million) to the interests of other secured creditors.[13] When the owner of the residence defaulted on its mortgage obligation, the trustee for those who held bonds issued to finance facility construction claimed a priority security interest in the fund. The court, however, determined that the entrance fees were security deposits, which,

under Wisconsin state law, could not be withheld from tenants (other than for standard items such as property damage) unless agreed to in a writing that is not a "form" provision of a contract. Because the residency agreements were preprinted forms, the court ruled that the subordination provisions in the residency agreements were unenforceable and that the fund should be held in a constructive trust for the residents.

Many state statutes require that, in the event of death before occupancy, the facility must make a full refund of any fees or deposits already paid (Georgia, Idaho, Iowa, Maryland, Michigan, New Hampshire, North Carolina, Rhode Island, Texas, Vermont, Wisconsin). Others require a refund less a certain percentage of the fee: Florida (4 percent); Louisiana and Minnesota (2 percent); Massachusetts (1 percent); Connecticut (formula). However, while some states have imposed overall caps on retained earnings from entrance fees, legislatures generally have not dealt specifically with concerns about the absence of refunds in the event of death after a short period of residence. One solution to the issue is for facilities to refund fees no matter when the resident dies or leaves the facility, but there are tradeoffs, such as the necessity of charging higher entrance fees and securing the ability to pay the refunds when due.

In its guidelines, AAHSA recommends that contracts set forth the facility's refund policies and procedures, but it does not prescribe the contents.

§21.7 Advertising

All states probably have some form of statute generally prohibiting false or misleading advertising. Many states, however, have specific provisions relating to the advertising of CCRCs. In some cases, these provisions may require prior review and approval of advertising materials by the state or simply require materials to be kept on file for later review. Many states also specifically deal with the issue of the liability of facility sponsors or other organizations related to the certified provider.

The case of Pacific Homes, Inc., one of the most publicized failures of a continuing-care community, points to the importance of avoiding references to entities other than the contracting parties without setting forth the extent of their responsibility for contract obligations. Pacific Homes was a nonprofit organization that operated several facilities in California, Arizona, and Hawaii and that filed in bankruptcy court for a Chapter XI reorganization in 1977. One of the principal issues in the ensuing class action lawsuit for damages was whether the United Methodist Church was in fact an alter ego of Pacific Homes and had any financial responsibility for performance of the contracts.[14] Pacific Homes, Inc., was originally established by members of what came to be known as the Pacific and Southwest Conference of the Methodist Church. Advertising materials referred to Pacific Homes's affiliation with the organization, but the conference denied any legal liability for resident agreements. The United Methodist Church argued that it was not a suable entity because it is not a hierarchical church but rather a confederation of regional conferences and national or global entities, all separately incorporated. The U.S. Supreme Court refused to prevent prosecution of the case against the church entities, and eventually church sources contributed $21 million to settle the case (see §5.2 for further discussion of this case).

As a result of the Pacific Homes case, California enacted a statute in 1978 prohibiting any developer of a facility from mentioning the name of any other organization or person in its contracts or advertising materials unless that other organization or person has first filed a written statement of financial responsibility for continuing-care agreements with the state.[15] Colorado, Florida, Indiana, and Missouri, among others, have adopted similar requirements.

In general, developers of facilities should carefully review advertising materials to make sure that representations comport with the service program that will be provided under the terms of the resident agreement. Abbreviated descriptions of contract features appearing in brochures can be characterized as misleading or viewed as modifying contract language. In addition, developers should be careful not to use phrases or terminology in advertising materials and licensure that imply a certain type of service not in the contract and that the provider does not intend to deliver. For example, developers occasionally use words such as "continuing care" or "care for life" in advertising materials when they have no intention of providing a program that would meet the

definitions and requirements of the particular state's continuing-care or life-care regulations. While the developer's use of such jargon may not be intentionally misleading, the state, a dissatisfied resident, or the operator of a competing facility may find that the use of such terms in advertising materials is misleading. Any one of the affected parties could bring an action to enjoin the advertising, change the program to comply with license standards, or seek damages.

AAHSA recommends that state legislation require licensees to explain their legal relationship with other organizations mentioned in advertising and set out the affiliates' financial obligations.

§21.8 Residents' Rights

Whether such rights are embodied in statute or regulation, some states require residents to be accorded certain rights of organization or participation in facility management or the right to a grievance process. Several states give residents the right to form a residents' association. Florida, Louisiana, New Hampshire, New Jersey, New York, Pennsylvania, Rhode Island, and Virginia further require management to meet quarterly with the organized residents. Michigan, Missouri, and Ohio, on the other hand, require one resident to be a member of the board of directors of the retirement facility. Michigan law permits the resident member of the board to have advisory status only.

There is some objection in the industry to placing residents on boards of directors, and with good reason. As directors, residents inherently face a continuous problem of conflict of interest and self-dealing that most state corporation laws recognize as a handicapping, if not prohibited, status for any corporate director. If only by attending board meetings as invited guests, residents certainly should be able to organize and refer suggestions and grievances to facility management. However, residents' voting membership on the board of directors may hamper the effective functioning of the board when it must deal with matters of resident policy or the application of policies to individuals in the community.

AAHSA's guidelines agree that while residents should have the right to organize and to meet with facility management, it may be inappropriate to require either resident appointments to the governing board or formal representation at owners' meetings.

§21.9 Resident Protection and Enforcement

Enforcement mechanisms for violation of statutes or regulations generally include typical features such as civil and criminal penalties, injunctive powers, and suspension or revocation of facility certification. CCRC statutes, however, often also include statutory protections such as escrows and reserves (discussed above) and bonds, liens, and receiverships (discussed below).

Some states have provisions dealing with the circumstances of a possible facility bankruptcy or other failure. An example is the type of provision that specifies that the rights of residents under continuing-care agreements constitute liens or preferred claims against the assets of the failed community. A preferred claim gives residents priority over general creditors but is usually subordinate to any creditor with a lien, such as a mortgage lender. Some states, including Arizona, Colorado, and Minnesota, give residents an automatic statutory lien against facility assets. Other states, such as Pennsylvania and California, impose statutory liens only if the state determines that a particular facility's financial condition warrants it. In all states but Minnesota, statutory liens may be subordinated to other prior liens, such as those of construction lenders. A few states require providers to post a bond automatically as security for CCRC contract obligations; other states require a bond to be posted in the event of financial trouble. Some statutes also permit the state or a receiver to take over management of a facility that, in its opinion, appears to be on the verge of financial collapse.

As a practical matter, preferred liens are of questionable use in protecting residents from CCRC failures. Many failures occur during facility development as a consequence of poor financial management or overly optimistic assumptions about the ability to sell the product. In these situations, assets may not be of sufficient significance to ensure that residents do not lose all or a portion of their entrance fees. In fact, in many such facility failures, it has been the

assets of a sponsoring organization, a lender, or the residents themselves that have permitted the facility to rebound and return to a financially sound status.

Even if facility assets are of any substance, they are likely to be predominantly tied up in the physical plant of the facility itself. If resident entrance fees have been used to pay off construction loans, residents may be able to tap any accrued equity in the building, but there is no guarantee that entrance fees will be used for such purposes. As a result, residents may find themselves in a second position behind a secured lender. Moreover, buildings that have been designed specifically for use as CCRCs are not readily salable for other purposes, and it may make little sense to attempt to liquidate such an asset in an effort to pay off construction lenders, residents, and other creditors in the event of a dissolution. It makes more sense for all concerned, and indeed it is more common, for a CCRC with any substantial assets to be reorganized and operated as a going business under new management and possibly after renegotiation of care agreements.

§21.10 Accreditation

The American Association of Homes and Services for the Aging has established an independent Continuing Care Accreditation Commission to develop and implement a comprehensive accreditation program for use by nonprofit and for-profit continuing-care facilities. Modeled in part after the efforts of the Joint Commission on Accreditation of Health Care Organizations, the program includes an extensive self-evaluation process in the areas of governance and administration, finance, health care, and resident protections. The process includes review by a visiting team and evaluation by an accreditation committee.

Eligibility for the accreditation process, which is estimated to take approximately eight months, is limited initially to common entrance fee models with an ongoing monthly service fee, although the program will include other financial structures as it develops. Applicants must have had one year of 90 percent occupancy and must have completed an audited fiscal year, or, if less than 90 percent occupancy, must demonstrate financial viability. The program also reviews facilities for compliance with applicable state regulation.

Accredited facilities must submit annual reports, including financial audits, and pay a fee to the commission to maintain their status. Facilities denied accreditation may appeal the denial to a committee of the commission. A few state licensing agencies have considered the accreditation process as a possible substitute for or supplement to certain state regulatory functions that might duplicate accreditation. As of March 1998, 236 facilities in 27 states had been accredited.

§21.11 Similar Regulated Industries

A retirement facility developer intending to provide some form of guaranteed access to health care or coverage of health care costs may encounter problems of jurisdictional overlap or gaps in coverage between two or more state agencies. Even in states with extensive regulation of continuing-care facilities, a given product may raise questions as to whether the financial transaction with the resident constitutes a prepaid health plan or health maintenance organization (HMO), a continuing-care arrangement, a contract of insurance, or all or none of the foregoing. The problem is exacerbated by the taking of pre-construction deposits, which may give rise to securities registration implications (see Chapter 24), and by the use of an equity (condominium or cooperative) structure, which may trigger inconsistent state regulatory requirements. The developer's legal counsel should carefully review state law to determine which state statutes may be applicable.

In states with multiple layers of regulation covering CCRCs, HMOs, and insurance companies, both the regulatory agencies and the developer find it difficult to determine which agency, if any, has jurisdiction over the arrangement. The situation is complicated by the variety of new approaches that facility developers are now exploring. Facility developers who have structured their programs to avoid a particular kind of licensure, such as continuing care, have sometimes found themselves subject to more burdensome regulation under a more general statute, such as the state's insurance code. Generally, licensure as an insurance carrier can, from the facility's

perspective, be the most onerous form of regulation because of the stringent reserve requirements that are usually applicable.

Another problem encountered in forum shopping among multiple state authorities is that certain agencies are unfamiliar with and perplexed by the hybrid of insurance, annuity, residential, and health care concepts represented by a single facility's operational plan. Trying to fashion a continuing-care facility, which may be heavily regulated, as a prepaid health plan, which may be subject to less regulation, can lead to costly delays as bureaucrats unfamiliar with life-time actuarial risks ponder the implications of a project that is foreign to them. Sometimes, therefore, it may be economically and legally prudent to accept rather than avoid the jurisdiction of an agency that is best equipped to regulate the project. One motivation for real estate developers to seek a joint venture with an insurance company, prepaid health plan, or hospital or other health care provider is that these partners are usually already familiar with many of the regulatory requirements and may already be licensed to provide the kind of services or coverage of services that the developer intends to offer facility residents.

Another reason to embrace CCRC regulation is that it may act as a "safe harbor" from inconsistent laws or regulations governing real estate sales deposits, rent controls, age discrimination laws (see §23.2), antitrust tying arrangements (see §22.6(d)), homeowners' association rights, and a myriad of other potentially applicable laws that do not bear on the health insurance nature of the transaction.

In analyzing a given retirement facility structure, regulators should find the statutory structure that most closely fits the circumstances. Providers should not be subject to multiple regulation for a single transaction between resident and retirement community. For example, if a retirement facility is offering to purchase group health insurance for its resident population through a carrier that is already licensed by the state's insurance department and the retirement facility operator is not directly engaged in the provision of health care and is not promising to provide the health care covered by the insurance carrier, the facility should not be subject to licensure as a CCRC or health plan.

Either administratively or by amendment of their statutes, states should clarify the jurisdictional parameters of insurance, continuing-care, and health plan regulations. The CCRC statutes should also contain exemptions from such regulations as well as from regulations covering securities and age and disability discrimination and from inconsistent real property laws.

Notes

1. Eighteen state laws were reviewed in the first edition of this book. Now *see* Figure 21.1 for a summary of 36 state laws and AAHSA's model statute guidelines. *See generally* "Current Status of State Regulation of Continuing Care Retirement Communities," American Association of Homes for the Aging, Aug. 1991. For a detailed narrative discussion of state regulation issues for CCRC contracts, *see* "Continuing Care Retirement Communities: Issues and State Regulation," 8 *St. Louis Public Law Review,* 245 (1989); and Stearns, L., et al., "Lessons from the Implementation of CCRC Regulation," *The Gerontologist,* Vol. 30, no. 2, 1990, 154.

2. *See* American Association of Homes for the Aging, "Guidelines for Regulation of Continuing Care Retirement Communities," 1992. Since 1992, the organization has changed its name to the American Association of Homes and Services for the Aging (AASHA).

3. *See Contemporary Long Term Care,* Aug. 1989, 12–13.

4. *See, e.g.,* Fox and Ritchie, "Watch Your Language: Regulators Scrutinize Resident Contracts and Advertising Materials," *Retirement Housing Report,* Oct. 1986, 8, regarding expansive interpretation of activities subject to life-care licensure in Pennsylvania. *See also Moravian Manors, Inc. v. Commonwealth of Pennsylvania,* 521 A.2d 524 (1987).

5. For more regarding refund requirements, *see* §21.6(c).

6. *Onderdonk v. Presbyterian Homes of NJ,* 85 N.J. 171, 425 A.2d 1057 (1981).

7. Continuing Care Retirement Facilities Working Group of the National Association of Insurance Commissioners, draft report, July 1, 1993.

8. For a discussion of key CCRC contract provisions, *see* Gordon, P., "Are Your Resident Contracts Due for a Tune-Up?" *D&O Forum,* Summer 1995.

9. *See Onderdonk,* note 6, *above.*

10. *See generally* 44 *ALR* 3d 1174.

11. *See Howe v. American Baptist Homes of the West,* 112 Cal. App. 3d 622, 169 Cal. Rptr. 418 (1980).

12. *See generally* 44 *ALR* 3d 1174, and Schact, "Protection for the Elderly Person and His Estate: Regulating and Enforcing Life-Care Contracts," 5 *Prob. L.J.* 105 (1983).

13. *M&I First National Bank v. Episcopal Homes Management, Inc.,* 195 Wis. 2d 485, 536 N.W.2d 175 (1995).

14. *See United Methodist Council v. Superior Court,* 439 U.S. 1369, 99 S. Ct. 36, 58 L. Ed. 2d 77 (1978).

15. An exemption was made for church-sponsored facilities already in existence and for affinity groups showing good cause, but these are required to state expressly in their agreements the precise scope and extent of financial responsibility of any sponsor or other organization referred to in advertising or contract materials.

Hunt Community Continuing-Care Retirement Facility; Nashua, New Hampshire.

22 HUD Operational Regulations

§22.1 In General

In addition to the financial requirements imposed by the federal government as a condition of receiving loans or loan guarantees for construction of seniors' housing (see Chapter 14), the U.S. Department of Housing and Urban Development (HUD) imposes numerous conditions on eligibility that affect the business structure and operations of a project. While some of the programs discussed in the following sections are no longer available for new project development, a description of them is included here because many facilities already in the marketplace relied on the provisions of the previously available programs.

Despite the overall cutback in federal funding for elderly housing, the federal government has, to some extent, acknowledged the desirability of combining housing and services, including care, in a single product (see §§22.2 and 22.3). Nonetheless, financial problems have caused many programs to become inactive or to be suspended.

The Housing and Community Development Act of 1992 required HUD to appoint a task force for the purpose of issuing recommendations to Congress and HUD about occupancy and management issues in public and assisted housing.[1] The Public and Assisted Housing Occupancy Task Force released its report on April 7, 1994.[2] Much of the report focused on the issue of discrimination in public housing and federally assisted housing (see §23.3(c)). The report also made recommendations regarding the application process for prospective tenants, housing management issues, evictions, provision of reasonable accommodations, and access to support services. The recommendations of the task force with respect to the improvement of access to and delivery of support services called for

- HUD to allow housing providers to fund service coordinators from operating budgets, replacement reserves, or any other sources deemed feasible;
- housing and service providers to establish and maintain a listing of state and/or local service providers for residents' use;
- housing and service providers to enter into collaborative agreements that offer residents a direct link to service providers;
- housing providers to offer orientation and education programs to residents; and
- housing providers to provide meeting space for residents' self-help groups.

§22.2 Retirement Service Centers (suspended program)

(a) Section 221(d)(4)

(1) Generally

HUD regulations formerly provided for a housing insurance program within the Section 221(d)(4) program to cover the gap between the totally indepen-dent-living arrangements of noncongregate housing for the elderly and the health care-oriented nursing home. Numerous projects developed before pro-gram termination near the end of 1991 remain in operation.

The Section 221(d)(4) program was designed to assist in financing the construction or substantial re-habilitation of rental housing for low- and moderate-income families.[3] Under this program, HUD and the FHA insured mortgages made by approved lenders to increase the mortgage credit available from private lenders.[4] The Retirement Service Center (ReSC) pro-gram was intended to build on the existing Section 221(d)(4) mortgage insurance program to provide meals, services, and an amenities package exceeding that normally covered under the mortgage insurance program.[5] ReSC facilities were developed for the frail elderly of 70 years and up who no longer desired to prepare their own meals and were willing to pay a substantial part of their income—in excess of 30 percent—for shelter, amenities, and services. There are four major differences between ReSCs and basic Section 221(d)(4) elderly housing projects.

- Prospective mortgagors must prove experience and ability to manage retirement housing.[6]
- ReSCs must use modified market and rental analysis techniques.
- ReSCs must provide a broader range of amenities and services.
- ReSCs must maintain special reserve funds.

ReSC projects consist of five or more dwelling units, which may be detached, semidetached, row-houses, or multifamily structures. Projects are on real estate held in fee simple, under a renewal lease for not less than 99 years, under a lease running at least 75 years from the date the mortgage was executed, or under a lease executed by a government agency or HUD-approved lessor for a term of not less than 50 years.[7] The property must be free and clear of all liens other than the insured HUD mortgage. New construction projects had to comply with local re-quirements and HUD minimum property standards. Rehabilitation projects had to comply with local re-quirements. All projects had to comply with appli-cable local zoning or deed restrictions.

(2) Services and Amenities

Each ReSC unit contains kitchen and bathroom facil-ities. Kitchens must have at least a small sink, refrig-erator, and a two-burner stove; no oven is required. Bathrooms in 5 to 10 percent of the project units generally are designed for handicapped eligibility. Weekly linen and housekeeping services are per-mitted as part of the services package. Amenities such as arts and crafts spaces, lounges, recreation rooms, and similar facilities are included to a greater extent than in noncongregate housing for the elderly. Reasonable charges to ReSC tenants and facilities may be made only after obtaining any lender approval required by HUD's administrative procedures.[8] No part of the project may be rented for transient or hotel purposes, and single-room occupancies (SROs) are prohibited. Commercial rentable area in any proj-ect may exceed 5 percent of the total rentable area only with HUD's approval but in no event may ex-ceed 20 percent.[9]

No medical services are permitted as part of the ReSC project itself or as part of the service package without prior approval by HUD. With approval, a small number of infirmary beds may be included. Access to a nursing home, hospital, or other medical facility may be part of an ReSC; however, any charges to ensure access are prohibited.

ReSCs offer meals to their tenants by operating a congregate dining facility. In the event of an identity of interest between the owner of the ReSC and the operator of the congregate dining facility, the pur-chase of meals by each tenant may be made a manda-tory condition of occupancy to ensure stability of demand for meals. The charges to the tenants must be sufficient to exceed the expense shown by a small safety factor or margin of proprietary return for man-aging the provision of meal services. Even if the meal service is operated by a commercial food service vendor independent of the ReSC sponsor, the spon-sor may determine that a mandatory meal require-ment will contribute to the success of the facility. However, in exchange for making meals mandatory, the commercial lease must provide the ReSC spon-sor with a right to concur with changes in service and charges for meals. Certain additional requirements apply to a commercial lease of restaurant space in an ReSC.[10] A Meals on Wheels type of approach to providing meal service can also be used in conjunction with an ReSC.

With termination of the ReSC program, the elderly housing program under Sections 221(d)(3) or (d)(4), 231, 232, or 223(f) may not provide mandatory services, formal dining rooms, or common meal services (even voluntary) (see §14.2(d)(1)).

(3) Rents and Fees

Projects may not charge a founder's fee, initial admission fee, or similar fee beyond normal security deposits associated with standard rental projects. Security deposits must be maintained in a trust account separate from all other funds in the project. The owner must comply with any state or local laws regarding investment of security deposits and the distribution of interest or other income earned thereon.[11]

The mortgagor of the property sets the charges for ReSC project accommodations, which are expected to be market-rate. No HUD subsidy of rents is provided in the form of Section 8 payments or direct loans, and there are no income limitations for tenants. As noted above, however, the mortgagor must obtain HUD approval for any charges for services or facilities. Mortgagors may also be subject to state and local rent control regulation of project rents (see discussion in §22.6(a)). In addition, mortgagors and their agents must comply with federal law and HUD-FHA regulations prohibiting discrimination on the basis of race, color, creed, or national origin. The mortgagor must likewise comply with state and local laws and ordinances prohibiting discrimination[12] (see discussion in Chapter 23).

All rents and other receipts of the project must be deposited in the project's name in accounts that are fully insured by an agency of the federal government. Project funds may be used only for payment of mortgage obligations, payment of reasonable expenses necessary to the proper operation and maintenance of the project, and certain distributions of surplus cash under HUD procedures.[13]

The ReSC program requires substantial reserves because of what HUD perceived as the extremely narrow market for ReSCs (which results in slow initial rent-up), few market comparables, and limited industry experience. In particular, ReSC projects require one of the following: an operating deficit escrow funded at 200 percent of HUD's determination of the initial operating deficit, a six-month debt service reserve, or an operating deficit escrow and a six-month debt service reserve.[14]

(4) Program Termination

The ReSC program led to great financial losses (see §14.2(d)(1)) such that HUD, in July 1989, suspended processing for Section 221(d)(4) mortgage insurance for retirement service centers.[15] Final regulations terminating the program took effect September 30, 1991.[16] Although mortgage coinsurance is still available for Section 221(d)(4) projects, the congregate services component that characterized the ReSC program is no longer available.[17]

(b) Section 223(f)

HUD continues to permit the financing of existing structures as ReSCs under the Section 223(f) program. Section 223(f) authorizes HUD to insure mortgages in connection with the purchase or refinancing of existing multifamily projects without requiring a program of substantial rehabilitation.[18] Substantial rehabilitation projects for ReSCs also had to be insured under the Section 221(d)(4) program.

Section 223(f) insurance applies to any existing rental housing of more than five units that is more than three years old. The property must consist of at least eight living units and have a remaining economic life long enough to permit at least a ten-year mortgage. The cost of repairs cannot exceed the greater of 15 percent of the property's value after repairs or $6,500 per dwelling unit (adjusted by the applicable high-cost area factor), plus equipment. No more than one major building component may be replaced, and applications must meet the financial reserve, marketing, and sponsor criteria required for ReSC financing under Section 221(d)(4).

Since the demise of the ReSC program, Section 223(f) projects have been restricted to offering limited common area amenities, no meals, and no mandatory services (see §14.2(d)(1)).

§22.3 Section 232 Board-and-Care Homes and Assisted-Living Facilities (Active)

(a) Board-and-Care Homes

The Housing and Urban-Rural Recovery Act of 1983[19] amended the Section 232 program to permit federal mortgage insurance to help finance the construction or improvement of board-and-care homes. Section 232 had previously been limited to nursing homes and intermediate-care facilities (ICFs). Board-and-care homes are known by many different names in different states, such as assisted living,[20] domiciliary care, shelter care, adult congregate living care, personal care, and residential care. Whatever its name, this facility type provides living arrangements for individuals who cannot live independently but who do not require the more extensive care offered by ICFs or nursing homes.[21] (For a full discussion of the financing aspects of Section 232 board-and-care facilities, see Chapter 14.)

Board-and-care homes may be privately owned and operated for profit; to qualify for FHA financing, however, they must be owned by a private nonprofit corporation or association. Board-and-care facilities may be freestanding structures, they may be attached to—but form an identifiable and separate portion of—an ICF or nursing home. ICF or nursing home services may not be carried out in a board-and-care home or in the board-and-care portion(s) of an ICF or nursing home. In addition, a separate entrance must be provided for a board-and-care facility where it is part of an ICF or nursing home.[22] Single-room-occupancy hotels and boarding houses providing only food and shelter are not eligible for federal mortgage insurance. HUD emphasizes that good accessibility to residential areas is important when evaluating the suitability of board-and-care home sites. Other factors include the location of family, friends, social support groups, health services, and recreation facilities. Eligible facilities must certify that the state in which the home will be located is in compliance with Section 1616(e) of the Social Security Act (Keys Amendment) (see discussion in §20.4(a)).

Facilities must contain a minimum of five bedrooms. Accommodations may be bedrooms with shared living, kitchen, and dining areas and shared bathroom facilities or efficiency and one-bedroom dwelling units. Each bedroom must accommodate no more than four persons. Congregate dining facilities must be provided for all board-and-care homes, including those with dwelling units with kitchen and dining space. Kitchen and dining space must be provided in efficiency and one-bedroom dwelling units. These units must also have a full separate bathroom. In congregate facilities, a full bathroom must be provided for at least every four residents. Dormitory or communal-type bathroom facilities are not permitted.

Interior space must also be provided for passive activities such as sitting, reading, and conversing; active pursuits such as parlor games and crafts; and communal activities such as meetings and group entertainment. A lounge for board-and-care residents must be separate from any ICF or nursing home use.

Board-and-care homes must offer three meals per day to each resident. Residents in accommodations without kitchens must take the three meals a day provided by the home. Residents whose accommodations have kitchens must take at least one meal a day provided by the home.

Board-and-care homes must also provide residents with continuous protective oversight, which involves a range of activities. Oversight services for relatively independent occupants may include awareness on the part of management staff of an occupant's condition and whereabouts and the ability to intervene in the event of a crisis. Charges may be assessed for other services that are in addition to those services included in the basic residential fee. Such services may include housekeeping, laundry, supervision of nutrition or medication, assistance with daily living—such as bathing, dressing, shopping, or eating—or 24-hour responsibility for the welfare of the resident.

No founder's fees, life-care fees, or any other similar charge is allowed in any insured proposal. Any proposal that requires the client-tenant to give or deposit money or surrender property beyond the normal security deposit and the first month's charges is ineligible.

Only 25 percent of an entire board-and-care facility may consist of independent-living units (efficiency or one-bedroom units). If the facility does include independent-living units, HUD requires a 12-month prorated debt service reserve. For example, if the facility consists of 25 percent independent-living units, the reserve must equal 25 percent of the annual debt service. Any independent-living board-and-care proposal is, according to HUD, attempting to reach the same narrow market as rental housing for the elderly.[23]

(b) Assisted-Living Facilities

The Housing and Community Development Act of 1992[24] extended the availability of mortgage insurance under Section 232 to assisted-living facilities for the care of the frail elderly.[25] Under Section 232, an assisted-living facility must be a public facility, a proprietary facility, or a facility of a private nonprofit corporation and must be licensed and regulated by the state, if there is a state law for licensing such facilities, or, if no such law exists, by the affected municipality or other political subdivision.

Section 232 assisted-living facilities must assist their residents with activities of daily living: dressing, eating, getting in and out of bed or chairs, walking, going outdoors, using the toilet, doing laundry, performing activities of home management, preparing meals, shopping, obtaining or administering medication, managing money, using the telephone, or performing housework. Facilities may also provide their residents with health care, such as nursing care and therapy, but are not required to do so.[26]

Assisted-living facilities must provide separate dwelling units for their residents and must make available common rooms and any other facilities necessary for providing supportive services to occupants. Dwelling units may not be occupied by more than one person without the residents' consent. It is unclear from the law whether a facility may designate certain units as double-occupancy units for consenting cohabitants. Under the amended law, individual dwelling units may or may not contain a full kitchen and bathroom.[27]

The Section 232 program for assisted-living facilities was implemented by the adoption of regulations that took effect December 29, 1994[28] (see §14.2).

§22.4 Section 202

(a) Section 202 Capital Advances and Rental Assistance Program

The Cranston-Gonzales National Affordable Housing Act[29] revised Section 202 of the Housing Act of 1959, effective October 1, 1991, moving it from a direct loan program to a grant program. Through the new Section 202 program, HUD intends to increase supportive housing for the elderly by providing assistance to private nonprofit organizations and consumer cooperatives in the form of capital advances or project rental assistance.[30] The funds may be used to finance the construction, reconstruction, or rehabilitation of a structure to be used as supportive housing for the elderly; the acquisition of a structure from the former Resolution Trust Corporation to be used as supportive housing for the elderly; or the cost of real property acquisition, site improvement, conversion, demolition, relocation, and other necessary expenses to increase supportive housing for the elderly. All facilities receiving Section 202 assistance must remain available for occupancy by very-low-income elderly persons for at least 40 years. (For a discussion of the financing aspects of Section 202, see Chapter 14.)

The individual units in projects built under Section 202 must be either efficiencies or one-bedroom units. A two-bedroom unit may be provided only for the resident manager of the project. In addition, all Section 202 projects must comply with the Uniform Federal Accessibility Standards and the design and construction requirements of the Fair Housing Act.[31]

The design of Section 202 projects may not be extravagant. Many amenities are not eligible for HUD funding, including individual unit balconies and decks, atriums, bowling alleys, swimming pools, saunas and jacuzzis, dishwashers, trash compactors, and washers and dryers.[32] Section 202 project facilities also may not include commercial spaces, infirmaries, nursing stations, and spaces for overnight care.[33]

The secretary of HUD must ensure that all facilities funded under Section 202 provide a range of services tailored to the specific needs of the facility. Some examples of these services include meal service adequate to meet nutritional needs, housekeeping, personal assistance, transportation services, and health-related services. The secretary may also deem other mandatory services essential for the elderly to maintain independent living.[34]

(b) The Section 202/8 Direct Loan Program (superseded)

The HUD Section 202/8 program has provided loans at reduced interest rates to nonprofit sponsors for the development cost of new or substantially rehabilitated housing for the elderly or handicapped. Section 202 provided 40-year loans at below-market interest rates for up to 100 percent of the total development costs of a project. The Section 8 program offered rental subsidies to qualifying low-income families and individuals living in approved residential facilities. With the consolidation of the application requirements of both the Section 202 and Section 8 programs, projects that met the requirements of the Section 202 program were deemed by HUD to have met the requirements for housing assistance payments under Section 8. Accordingly, a separate application for Section 8 assistance was not necessary.[35]

(1) Section 202

The Housing and Community Development Act of 1974[36] amended the Section 202 program to permit construction loans and direct 40-year permanent financing to nonprofit sponsors for the construction or substantial rehabilitation of housing projects for the elderly or disabled. Many projects with such loans are still in existence today.[37]

Given that the Section 202 program was a direct loan program, the availability of federal funding was dependent on annual appropriations by Congress. Funds were also allocated on a geographic basis among the ten HUD regions and further between metropolitan and nonmetropolitan areas based on a needs formula, thus further restricting fund availability to interested borrowers.

(A) Eligible Applicants. Although the law creating the Section 202 program permitted public agencies, for-profit entities, and nonprofit corporations to develop projects, HUD regulations and annual appropriations bills restricted the program to nonprofit borrowers.[38] In addition to the private nonprofit corporation borrower, Section 202 projects had to have a sponsor that was expected to provide the funds

required by the borrower to carry out the project. The sponsor was expected to pledge its financial and other support to the borrower over the full 40-year term of the Section 202 loan. It was largely on the basis of the sponsor's experience and arrangements with and pledge of support to the borrower that HUD selected a borrower for a Section 202 loan.[39]

Among the groups that typically qualified as Section 202 sponsors were religious organizations, minority organizations, fraternal orders, labor unions, senior citizens' groups, and consumer cooperatives.[40] While religious bodies could serve as sponsor, the borrower had to be a separate legal entity. Moreover, no religious purposes could be included in the articles of incorporation or bylaws of the borrower corporation.[41]

Projects, whether new construction or substantial rehabilitation, had to be designed in accordance with appropriate HUD minimum property standards and could include only units that were designed for elderly or handicapped persons.[42] Projects for the elderly generally were not approved for more than 200 units, thereby avoiding undue concentration of seniors' housing yet expanding the number of areas in the community in which the elderly could choose to live in housing specially designed to meet their needs.[43] Moreover, in approving sites, HUD took into account the impact of a development on fair housing and equal opportunity concerns, particularly if a project was to be located in an area of minority concentration.[44]

Finally, occupancy of housing financed under the Section 202 program was open only to elderly or handicapped families and to handicapped persons, as defined by HUD.[45] Projects were not required to be designed to serve all four groups intended to benefit from the Section 202 program (i.e., the elderly, physically disabled/mobility impaired, developmentally disabled, and chronically mentally ill) (see discussion in §23.3).

(B) Required Amenities. Proposals for projects had to contain a mix of efficiency and one-bedroom units, with at least 25 percent of the units efficiencies. Two-bedroom units were not permitted. Architectural barriers, such as steps and narrow doorways, had to be eliminated to ensure ingress and egress, livability of units, and access to all areas by all residents. Buildings were designed to meet special safety requirements, including wider corridors, nonslip flooring, grab bars, shelves, and specially placed electrical outlets. Each unit had to include a kitchenette or a kitchen, even if central dining was provided, as well as a complete bathroom.

Projects financed under the Section 202 program are not elaborate or extravagant in design or materials. Unacceptable amenities include dishwashers, individual unit trash compactors, and balconies.[46] Commercial spaces, such as beauty and barber shops, are not provided unless they are self-sustaining, provide needed services for residents, and do not exceed 5 percent of total project space.[47]

Projects were designed to include an assured range of essential services for occupants such as, among others, health, continuing education, welfare, information, recreation, homemaker, counseling, and referral services and transportation necessary to facilitate convenient access to such services and to employment opportunities and participation in religious activities. Projects had to include special spaces such as multipurpose rooms, game rooms, libraries and reading rooms, lounges and snack bars, and a central kitchen and dining facilities. These common areas normally could not exceed 10 percent of the total project space.[48] Facilities could not be set aside solely for religious purposes; however, a multipurpose room may be used for religious services and other purposes from time to time and on an equitable basis for all religious groups comprising the tenancy.[49]

Provisions for health and medical care are expected to be based primarily on the services offered in the community rather than by the project. The project could incorporate an emergency room for temporary treatment, but not for care overnight or for extended periods. The program did not allow provision for doctors, nurses, or other medical personnel, although it did permit consideration for rental of space to medical professionals.[50]

(2) Section 8 Housing Assistance Payments

Because the relatively small reduction of interest to Section 202 borrowers did not permit much reduction of rents, HUD coupled Section 202 loan assistance with a reservation of Section 8 subsidies for all Section 202 units. All projects receiving Section 202 long-term loans had to meet the requirements for, and receive the benefits of, leased housing assis-

tance payments under the Section 8 program. Reservations for Section 8 funds were set aside at the time a Section 202 reservation was made; accordingly, a separate application for Section 8 assistance was not necessary. Except for Section 202 housing for the elderly and handicapped, Section 8 is now used solely with existing housing stock rather than with new construction.[51]

Participation in the Section 8 Housing Assistance Payments Program is required for a minimum of 20 percent of the units in any Section 202 project.[52] However, in any facility with Section 8 subsidized residents, none of the units in the building can command a rent higher than the HUD ceilings regardless of whether the resident of a particular unit is a recipient of Section 8 assistance.[53]

Under the Section 8 program, a family pays 30 percent of its gross income for rent directly to the landlord. The federal government pays the rest pursuant to a Housing Assistance Payments (HAP) contract between HUD and the landlord. Eligible households are those with incomes below 80 percent of the median in their area, adjusted for family size. The HUD funds pay for adequate and reasonable use of all utilities except telephone. One problem with a Section 8 type of subsidy for elderly housing projects is that the subsidy does not cover the costs of any programs provided to tenants, including meals.[54]

HUD sets the ceilings for the maximum rents that can be charged in facilities that house Section 8 residents; Section 202 financing imposes the same limits. For projects built with Section 202 funds, the maximum rent is 115.5 percent of the fair market rent, including utilities and taking into consideration accessibility to the elderly and handicapped, structure type, and market area.[55] HUD regulations govern rent increases as well as eviction procedures.[56]

(c) Congregate Housing Services Program

The Congregate Housing Services Program (CHSP) was authorized as a demonstration project under Title IV of the Housing and Community Development Amendments of 1978[57] and was revised and expanded in 1990 under the Cranston-Gonzales National Affordable Housing Act.[58] The revised CHSP is intended to provide supportive services to selected public housing and Section 202 projects to help the frail elderly and handicapped individuals avoid premature institutionalization.[59]

Under CHSP, the secretaries of HUD and the U.S. Department of Agriculture enter into contracts with states, Indian tribes, units of local government, and local nonprofit housing sponsors to provide congregate services programs for the frail elderly, disabled, or temporarily disabled residing in eligible housing for the elderly and to promote their independence with supportive services; or to adapt the housing so as to better accommodate the physical requirements and service needs of the frail elderly, disabled, or temporarily disabled. Contracts run for five-year terms and are renewable.[60]

The cost of providing the CHSP is distributed among all the involved parties. Program funds cover 40 percent of program costs and must be supplemented with contributions from the contract recipients in an amount sufficient to cover 50 percent of program costs. The remaining 10 percent of costs must be covered by fees charged to residents. Resident fees may be waived for tenants with insufficient incomes. If the waiver causes a reduction in tenant fees to less than 10 percent of program costs, the shortfall is shared equally by the program funds and the contract recipient.[61]

CHSP may include any services that may prevent premature and unnecessary institutionalization of residents. The program must meet at least one-third of the daily nutritional needs of residents. Assistance under CHSP may also be used to retrofit or renovate individual dwelling units and congregate space. In addition, assistance may be used to employ a service coordinator (see §22.6(e)). Other examples of services that may be provided under CHSP include transportation; personal care, dressing, bathing, toileting, housekeeping, and chore assistance; nonmedical counseling; assessment of the safety of housing units; group and socialization activities; assistance with medications; case management; and personal emergency response.[62]

As stated above, the revised CHSP expanded the original program. Under the original program, funds could be used for the provision of congregate service; however, there was no mention of using funds to adapt housing to the needs of the residents. The original program also did not provide for the cost distributions above.[63] Recipients of assistance under the current program will continue to receive assistance through the term of their contract and will receive priority for assistance under the revised program.[64]

When HUD and the Farmers Home Administration published the final implementing regulations for the Congregate Housing Services Program on April 29, 1994,[65] the two agencies promulgated regulations dealing only with those provisions of the program that fund congregate services. The regulations do not address the use of congregate housing services funds for retrofitting or renovating individual units and congregate space. In fact, HUD and the Farmers Home Administration received a number of public comments expressing dissatisfaction with their failure to develop such implementing regulations. In response, the two agencies stated that they have invited comments from the public regarding implementation of the retrofit and renovation component and will use the responses to assist in drafting regulations at a later date.[66]

Plagued with funding irregularities over the years, the CHSP program has been pronounced dead in recent years.[67]

§22.5 Other Federal Housing Programs for the Elderly

(a) Section 231 Mortgage Insurance for Elderly Housing

Section 231 is a program of federal mortgage insurance to facilitate financing of the construction or rehabilitation of rental housing for the elderly or handicapped.[68] Under the program, HUD insures mortgages made by private lending institutions for the construction or rehabilitation of multifamily projects consisting of five or more units. HUD may insure up to 100 percent of project cost for nonprofit and public mortgagors and up to 90 percent for private mortgagors. All units insured under the program may be occupied by elderly (at least 62 years of age) or handicapped persons. The Section 231 program was intended to be used in conjunction with the Section 8 program (see §22.4(b)).

In terms of the availability of Section 231 insurance, statistics reveal that the program has become almost dormant. From $75 million in insured loans in FY 1979, the Section 231 program received only $2 million in appropriations in FY 1983, insuring only one project—with 85 units—nationwide.[69]

(b) Section 236 Mortgage Insurance and Interest Reduction Payments

The Section 236 program combined federal mortgage insurance with subsidized interest payments to mortgagees (lenders) to reduce the mortgagor's (owner's) monthly mortgage payment. The interest payment subsidy lowered the mortgage's effective interest rate to 1 percent. Tenants realized the benefits of the reduced interest payments in the form of lower rents. Eligible tenants were low-income families, including the elderly and the handicapped.[70]

As originally enacted, the Section 236 program was intended to stimulate housing production by making private industry the primary vehicle for providing shelter for low- and moderate-income families. Suspended during the 1973 subsidized housing moratorium, the Section 236 subsidy never saw revival as an active production program. Altogether, the program produced approximately 600,000 housing units; those units will continue to receive the mortgage subsidy until termination of their HUD contracts, which usually extend 30 to 40 years. With owner approval, several Section 236 units have been shifted to the Section 8 program.

§22.6 Regulations Generally Applicable to HUD Programs for the Elderly

(a) Rent Control

HUD regulations regarding the applicability of state and local rent control laws to government-assisted elderly housing projects depend on whether a program is classified as subsidized or unsubsidized. The principal active subsidy program is the Section 202/8 Direct Loan Program. The Section 232 Assisted Living/Board and Care Facilities (Mortgage Insurance) program is an example of an active unsubsidized program.[71]

With regard to subsidized programs, HUD regulations declare that "it is in the national interest to preempt . . . the entire field of rent regulation by local rent control boards . . . or other authority."[72] Therefore, rent increases for Section 202/8 programs must be submitted to the appropriate local office of HUD for approval. For unsubsidized projects, HUD generally does not, except under certain conditions, interfere in the regulation of rents by a rental control board or agency constituted under state or local laws. For example, HUD may preempt rent regulation for an unsubsidized project when the agency determines that the action of a rent board prevents the mortgagor from achieving a level of residential income necessary to meet the financial obligations under the mortgage such that the project is not adequately maintained and operated.[73]

When a mortgagor determines that the permitted increase in rents as prescribed by the local board will not provide a rent level necessary to maintain and operate the project adequately, the mortgagor may file an application for preemption with HUD and must notify the tenants of the application for preemption. The mortgagor must also seek whatever relief or redetermination is permitted under state and local law. The HUD regulations outline in detail the type of notice that must be given to tenants and the materials that must be submitted to HUD in support of the application for preemption.[74]

(b) Eviction Procedures

HUD regulations govern evictions only from subsidized housing projects, which for the elderly are principally units under the Section 202/8 Direct Loan Program. State and local law governs evictions from unsubsidized projects. The landlord may not terminate any tenancy in a subsidized project except for material noncompliance with the rental agreement; material failure to carry out obligations under any state landlord and tenant act; certain criminal activities that pose a threat or disturbance to others or are drug-related; or other good cause.[75] The conduct of a tenant cannot be deemed "other good cause" unless the landlord has given the tenant prior notice that the conduct constitutes a basis for termination of occupancy. Prior notice must be served on the tenant in the same manner as that provided for termination notices.

The term "material noncompliance with the rental agreement" includes one or more substantial violations of the rental agreement or repeated minor violations of the rental agreement that disrupt the livability of the project, adversely affect the health or safety of any person or the right of any tenant to the quiet enjoyment of the leased premises and related project facilities, interfere with the management of the project, or have an adverse financial effect on the project. Failure of the tenant to supply in a timely fashion all required information on income and composition of the tenant household (including required evidence of citizenship or eligible alien status) constitutes material noncompliance with the rental agreement. Nonpayment of rent or any other financial obligation due under the rental agreement, or any portion thereof, beyond any grace period permitted under state law also constitutes material noncompliance with the rental agreement. The payment of rent or any other financial obligation due under the rental agreement after the due date but within the grace period permitted under state law constitutes only a minor violation.

The regulations further specify the required contents of the termination notice to the tenant and the manner in which such notice must be served.[76] Actual eviction of the tenant pursuant to HUD regulations must be made by judicial action pursuant to state or local law. A tenant may also rely on state or local law governing procedures that provide the tenant with procedural rights in addition to those provided by HUD, except where 24 C.F.R. §246 (see discussion in §22.6(a)) preempts local rent law.

In its 1994 reports to Congress and HUD, the Public and Assisted Housing Occupancy Task Force set forth its recommendations with regard to evictions in public and assisted housing. The task force did not recommend any changes to the portions of the regulations discussed in this section but did recommend that public and assisted housing providers use alternatives to eviction when the housing provider has a reasonable expectation that the resident will comply with the lease provisions. Although the task force concluded that one alternative to eviction is the provision of support services, it noted that housing providers are not permitted to require a resident

to obtain services or treatment as a condition of initial or continued occupancy. The task force also recommended that lease violation notices, lease termination notices, and eviction notices be required to be in writing and in accessible formats that include a clear description of the violation and of any measure that the resident can take to cure the problem.[77] (For more discussion of the Public and Assisted Housing Occupancy Task Force Report, see §§22.1 and 23.3(c).)

(c) Pet Regulations

The question of pet ownership in elderly housing was one of the most hotly debated topics of HUD regulation. Section 227 of the Housing and Urban-Rural Recovery Act of 1983[78] provides that no owner or manager of federally assisted rental housing for the elderly or handicapped may prohibit or prevent a tenant from owning or having common household pets or restrict or discriminate against any person regarding admission to or occupancy of such housing because of the person's ownership of pets.[79]

In 1986, HUD issued detailed and voluminous final regulations, as directed by the statute, to establish guidelines under which owners or managers of covered housing, first, may prescribe reasonable rules governing the keeping of common household pets and, second, must consult with tenants when prescribing the rules.[80] Household pet rules must be reasonably related to a legitimate interest of the project owner, such as an interest in both providing a decent, safe, and sanitary living environment for existing and prospective tenants and protecting and preserving the physical condition of the project and the owner's financial interest in it. In addition, pet rules must be narrowly drawn to achieve the owner's legitimate interests without imposing unnecessary burdens and restrictions on pet owners. Within these regulations, project owners retain a significant amount of flexibility in formulating pet rules.

HUD regulations apply the prohibitions against discrimination on the basis of pet ownership to all *housing* projects that are designated for occupancy by elderly or handicapped tenants and that are assisted under statutory authority identified by HUD through notice. At the same time, HUD regulations exclude from the prohibition "health and care facilities" with federal mortgage insurance.[81]

More specifically, HUD's pet regulations apply to HUD-insured mortgages under Sections 221(d)(3), 221(d)(4), and 231, even though these projects may be unsubsidized. The regulations exclude mortgages insured under Section 232 for board-and-care facilities because HUD does not consider such facilities to be rental housing within the meaning of the statute. Clearly, the regulations apply to Section 202/8 direct loan projects.[82] In addition, the regulations define under what conditions a particular project is considered to be "designated for occupancy by elderly or handicapped families."

The regulations require that project owners must, at a minimum, establish rules on several important matters as follow:

- Pet owners must have their pets inoculated in accordance with state and local law.
- Project owners must prescribe sanitary standards that govern the disposal of pet waste. When a pet is determined to constitute, under state or local law, a nuisance or threat to the health and safety of the occupants of the rental housing project or other members of the community, removal of that pet may be required.
- Pets must be appropriately and effectively restrained and under the control of a responsible individual while in the common areas of the project.
- Pet owners must register their pets with project owners. Project owners may refuse to register pets if the owner reasonably determines, based on the pet owner's habits and practices, that the pet owner will be unable to keep the pet in compliance with the house rules and other lease obligations.

Project owners may require an additional, refundable pet security deposit, which may be used only to pay reasonable expenses directly attributable to the presence of the pet in the project. The deposit may be required only for cats and dogs. For tenants whose rents are subsidized by HUD, the department from time to time sets a maximum deposit; the initial deposit may be paid in installments. For unsubsidized tenants, the deposit may not exceed one

month's rent and may be paid in installments at the discretion of the project owner.

The regulations are clear that project owners may neither ban all pets from a project nor limit the total number of pets in the project, even if the ban were consistent with the wishes of the owner and a majority of the residents. In addition, the project owner may not designate "pet" and "no pet" residential areas of the project, as HUD has determined that the health threat from allergic reactions to pet in residential areas is insufficient to warrent such designation. The project owner may, however, give consideration to the "density" of pets and tenants in the project and impose reasonable limits on the number of pets per unit as well as on pet size, weight, and type. Pets that pose a health and safety threat or that are a nuisance may be removed.

The regulations further define "common household pet" and state that the owner may limit the number of "four-legged, warm-blooded" pets to one per dwelling unit. The project owner may not, however, place any quotas on overall pet occupancy. The regulations do not apply to animals that assist the handicapped. The regulations also provide detailed procedures for tenant input into the formulation of house rules, notice to tenants of the rules and rule-making procedures, and the enforcement of house pet rules.

Finally, the regulations do not preempt state and local laws designed to protect the public health and safety by establishing reasonable limits on pet ownership within their jurisdiction. The pet rules prescribed by project owners may not conflict with state or local authority; when they do, state and local law or regulation applies.[83]

(d) Mandatory Meals

In an effort to ensure adequate nutrition and encourage socialization among residents, subsidized elderly housing facilities sometimes offer congregate meal programs. To spread overhead costs and minimize the charges necessary for providing central dining, many facilities require enrollment in the meal program as a condition of admission for every resident. The federal guidelines that took effect in 1963 required the provision of mandatory meals at cost, the purchase of only one meal per day (with some exceptions), and prior HUD approval. At present, HUD deems certain mandatory services, such as meals, to be essential for the elderly to maintain independent living (see, e.g., §22.4(a)).

In the late 1980s, however, several court cases brought on behalf of residents challenged mandatory meal programs. Although plaintiffs generally had agreed to participate in meal programs to gain initial admission to their residences, they wanted to opt out of the program for reasons of convenience, affordability, special medical needs, conflict with work schedules, dissatisfaction with food quality, or similar grounds.

The first series of mandatory meals cases centered on the argument that the charge for meals, because it is a condition of occupancy, constituted rent and therefore resulted in a rental charge in excess of the 30 percent of income rent cap specified for Section 8 subsidized facilities. The federal courts generally rejected as a matter of law both this argument and a related argument to the effect that mandatory meal programs contravened congressional intent by establishing an impermissible barrier to receipt of subsidized housing.[84] At least one court, however, refused to follow the trend and held that meal charges as a component of rent presented an issue of fact that could be decided only by a trial.[85]

In a second approach to challenging mandatory meals, plaintiffs in a federal case argued that requiring the purchase of meals as a condition of renting housing constituted a tying arrangement that violated antitrust law.[86] One response to this argument is that the program of the facility as a whole, including housing, meals, housekeeping, and other services, is a single product rather than several separate products unlawfully tied together. After the plaintiffs' antitrust arguments withstood the defendants' attempts for summary dismissal, the district court ruled that the meal program, although approved by HUD, was not exempt from antitrust scrutiny and certified that question to the court of appeals and the question whether, on a stipulated set of facts, the meal program was an illegal tying arrangement.[87] In *Gonzales v. St. Margaret's House,*[88] the Second Circuit Court of Appeals, vacating the district court judgment, found that the home's meal program raised a triable issue of fact regarding the plaintiff's claim that the program constituted an illegal tying arrangement under the antitrust laws. The tying arrangement argument can pose a threat to all seniors' housing projects, whether or not HUD-financed, that offer substantial service programs as a mandatory condition of residence.[89]

A third approach to challenging mandatory meals attacked the HUD guidelines for having been developed without compliance with the public notice and hearing requirements of the federal Administrative Procedure Act. It was this attack that brought the most immediate results for complainants. In *Birkland v. Rotary Plaza,*[90] a case involving a HUD Section 236 project, the federal district court found the HUD guidelines to be improperly promulgated and ordered HUD to adopt final rules governing mandatory meals by February 1987.

In response to the federal court order, HUD promulgated regulations regarding mandatory meals (repealed in 1995 but still applicable to programs existing as of that time).[91] The regulations permitted current HUD-approved mandatory meals programs to continue but prohibited any new programs in existing or future projects after April 1, 1987. The regulations affected projects with Section 202 direct loans, Section 221(d)(3) and 221(d)(5) below-market interest rates, Section 236 interest reduction payments, and Section 8 or 101 rent subsidy projects. The rules did not apply to Section 231, 232, or 221(d)(4) programs that involve only HUD mortgage insurance in the absence of HUD rental assistance.

The final regulations reflected HUD's attempt to balance competing considerations in the mandatory meals program. Acknowledging that current programs provide nutritional and socialization benefits for facility residents, HUD permitted the continuation of such programs. Further, if such programs were required to convert to voluntary participation, project sponsors may not be able to obtain necessary sources of subsidies to fund the programs and thus might terminate them as financially infeasible. HUD saw this outcome as frustrating the reasonable expectations of project sponsors, tenants, and HUD with regard to the affected projects.[92]

For HUD-assisted projects after March 1987, HUD determined that no such reliance considerations existed. Sponsors of HUD-assisted projects who decided to offer tenants a meal service could either site their projects near a community facility with a suitable meals program or make an informed decision to include a central dining facility in their project and offer only a voluntary meals program.[93]

For existing programs as of April 1987, a project owner could grant exemptions from the mandatory meals program for the following conditions: when medical reasons necessitated a special diet; when a tenant had a paying job requiring absence from the project during mealtime; when a tenant was temporarily absent from the facility for more than one week; and when a tenant was permanently immobile or otherwise incapable of reaching the central dining facility. A project owner could also grant any tenant an exemption for dietary practices, financial reasons, or any other reasons. In addition, the final regulations required either an alternative menu that did not conflict with a tenant's religious dietary practices or an exemption from the program. Programs had to continue to be offered at cost and with the approval of HUD. All prospective project tenants also were to be given notice that participation in the meals program was a condition of occupancy in the project. Further, the regulations added the requirement that the mandatory meals program had to comply with state or local nutritional statutory standards. When no such standards existed, the project was required to submit a nutritional statement to HUD on an annual basis.[94]

As part of HUD's "regulatory reinvention initiatives," the regulations were repealed in 1995 as part of a group of regulations pertaining to "expiring programs," but with the note that ongoing programs in existence before October 11 of that year would still be subject to the old rules.[95]

(e) Service Coordinators

To help address the support needs of residents who elect to "age in place" at federally assisted housing projects, HUD has provided mechanisms for the funding of service coordinators.[96] As defined by HUD, a service coordinator is a social service staff person who is responsible for linking residents to the supportive or medical services they need to continue living independently. The specific functions of the service coordinator include providing general case management to residents; establishing linkages with agencies and service providers in the community; setting up a directory of providers; referring residents to service providers in the community; assisting outside assessment agencies or project professional assessment committees in the development of case plans; monitoring the ongoing provision of services from outside agencies; and educating project management on issues related to aging in place and service coordination. A service coordinator may not directly provide the needed support services.[97]

Funds for service coordinators may come from one of the following sources: Section 8 housing assistance payments, a grant from HUD, the project's residual receipts account, budget-based rent increases, or special rent adjustments.[98] A project owner may use these funds directly either to employ a service coordinator or to compensate a management company for providing the project with a service coordinator.

HUD requires service coordinators to have certain qualifications: two to three years' experience in social work with senior citizens and a minimum of 36 hours of training in the aging process, elder services, disability services, federal and state entitlement programs, legal liability issues, substance abuse, and mental health issues. Although not required, HUD prefers that service coordinators have either a bachelor's degree in social work or a degree in gerontology, psychology, or counseling. Persons without college degrees may work as service coordinators if they have appropriate work experience.[99]

The availability of service coordinators has had many positive effects on residents of seniors' housing facilities. Observers of the program have noted that service coordinators have been successful in "generating awareness of and use of services offered by community agencies; averting crisis by identifying and responding to residents in need; initiating supportive interactions between neighbors, including participation in tenant associations; building a sense of community; and reducing apartment turnover and damage to building property."[100]

The retention of a service coordinator may give rise to an increased legal duty on the part of the facility to monitor the needs of its residents and ensure that residents are referred to needed care. To protect itself against liability for breaching such a duty, owners and managers should make sure that both residents and service coordinators understand the responsibilities of the service coordinator. For a discussion of similar liability issues, see also §§29.1–29.3.

Notes

1. Pub. L. No. 102–550, Oct. 28, 1992.

2. Public and Assisted Housing Occupancy Task Force, "Report to Congress and the Department of Housing and Urban Development," Apr. 7, 1994.

3. For a full discussion of the financing aspects of the Section 221 program, see text in §14.2(d).

4. *See generally* 24 C.F.R. §251 (prior to Nov. 1990 revisions) for ReSC regulations; *HUD Handbook* 4560.1; and 24 C.F.R. Pt. 221 for §221(d)(4) regulations.

5. *See HUD Handbook* 4561.1, Ch. 17; Notices H85-33, 84-41, 85-58 (HUD); and May 15, 1984, HUD Memorandum of Assistant Secretary Maurice L. Barksdale.

6. HUD indicated that ReSC project applicants had to be familiar with this type of retirement housing and the special needs and expectations of the target occupancy group. HUD was also concerned that the mortgagor group be able to promote rentals effectively and handle the long rent-up periods and complex services and expenses of retirement housing. All mortgagors eligible under the Section 221(d)(4) program, which included both for-profit and nonprofit developers, could develop ReSCs. All mortgagors had to meet the requirements of and be processed under both the Section 221(d)(4) and the special ReSC procedures. *HUD Handbook* 4561.1, Ch. 17-5.

7. *HUD Handbook* 4560.2, Ch. 1-11–1-12.

8. 24 C.F.R. §251.703(c) (prior to Nov. 1990 revisions).

9. 24 C.F.R. §203(a)(5).

10. *See* May 15, 1984, HUD Memorandum, note 5 *above.*

11. Former 24 C.F.R. §704(d).

12. *See HUD Handbook* 4560.2, Ch. 1-5.

13. 24 C.F.R. §§251.704, 705 (prior to Nov. 1990 revisions).

14. The reserve requirements for ReSC projects are determined by calculating the initial operating deficit and a six-month debt service reserve. If the operating deficit is less than the six-month debt service reserve, the amount of required reserve funds will be the greater of two times the operating deficit calculation or the six-month debt service reserve. If the anticipated operating deficit equals or exceeds the debt service reserve amount, both an operating deficit escrow and debt service reserve are required. Funds remaining in the operating deficit escrow and/or debt service reserve can be released after sustaining

occupancy has been maintained for 90 days. Notice H85-33 (HUD).

15. On November 23, 1990, HUD published a proposed rule to terminate the program. In March 1991, however, HUD announced that until the *Federal Register* published a final regulation on the ReSC program, processing of ReSC applications would resume with minor procedural changes. Notice H-91-21 (HUD), Mar. 8, 1991.

16. *See* 24 C.F.R. §255.233.

17. *Ibid.*

18. *See* 24 C.F.R. §255.233 (prior to Nov. 1990 revisions).

19. P.L. 98-181.

20. Many states do not differentiate assisted-living from other residential care facilities.

21. *See* 12 U.S.C. §1715w; 24 C.F.R. Pt. 232.

22. Notice H86-20 (HUD).

23. Notice H91-21 (HUD).

24. Pub. L. No. 102-550 (Oct. 28, 1992),

25. *See* 12 U.S.C. §1715w.

26. 12 U.S.C. §1715w(b)(6).

27. 12 U.S.C. §§1715W(b)(6), 1715w(d)(4)(C).

28. 59 *Fed. Reg.* 61,222, Nov. 29, 1994 (proposing amendments to 24 C.F.R. Pt. 232).

29. P.L. 101-625.

30. P.L. 93-383.

31. 12 U.S.C. §1701q; 24 C.F.R. Pt. 891 (published at 61 *Fed. Reg.* 11,956, Mar. 22, 1996).

32. 24 C.F.R. §891.120(b).

33. 24 C.F.R. §891.120(c).

34. 24 C.F.R. §891.220.

35. 12 U.S.C. §1701q(g)(1); *HUD Handbook* 4571.1 REV.2, Ch. 1-4.

36. *See generally* 12 U.S.C. §1701q (prior to Oct. 1991 revisions); 24 C.F.R. Pt. 891, Subpt. E.

37. Department of HUD-Independent Agencies Appropriations Bill, 1987, H.R. Rep. No. 731, 99th Cong., 2nd Sess., at 9 (1986). The loans were made at a rate based on the average interest of all interest-bearing obligations of the United States that form a part of the public debt, plus an amount to cover administrative costs.

38. *See* 24 C.F.R. §891.505. The program handbook made it clear that indirect participation by public agencies or profit-motivated groups was prohibited. A profit-motivated group could not sponsor a nonprofit borrower, and a public agency could not set up an agency or instrumentality to participate in the Section 202 program. HUD was to reject "applications proposing loans to groups acting as 'fronts' for profit-motivated developers or builders, and

proposals based on syndications to profit-motivated investors." *HUD Handbook* 4571.1 REV.2, Ch. 2-7.

39. *Id.* at Ch. 2-2.

40. In contrast to the borrower, HUD expected the sponsor to have a history of interest and successful activity in housing generally or housing for the elderly or the handicapped or to have been involved in one or more other social or community activities or services that provide the background and skills that may be transferable to housing for the elderly or handicapped. A sponsor was evaluated primarily on the strength of its activities as an organization.

41. *HUD Handbook*, note 39 *above.*

42. Special consideration had to be given to such factors as location and site, architectural and design features, and the inclusion of a wide range of services and programs. Sites had to be selected to avoid steep inclines. Convenience to transportation, shopping, personal, and other services critical to the residents of the projects was also to be considered. *Id.* at Ch. 5-15, 17.

43. *Id.* at Ch. 1-5.

44. *Id.* at Ch. 4-23, 34.

45. *See id.* at Ch. 1-4.

46. *Id.* at Ch. 5-17.

47. *Id.* at Ch. 1-5(6).

48. *Id.* at Ch. 5-17.

49. *Id.* at Ch. 1-4(8).

50. *Id.* at Ch. 1-4(7).

51. *See* Housing and Urban-Rural Recovery Act of 1983, P.L. 98-181.

52. However, if the borrower proposed Section 8 assistance for fewer than 100 percent of the units, HUD had to review and approve the request before selection of the application. *HUD Handbook* 4571.1 REV.2, Ch. 1-7(b).

53. Ward, "Congregate Living Arrangements: The Financing Option," *Topics in Health Care Financing,* Spring 1984, 40.

54. *Ibid.*

55. *Id.* at 39.

56. *See generally* 24 C.F.R. §880 and discussion in §§22.6(a)-(b).

57. P.L. 95-557.

58. P.L. 101-625.

59. 42 U.S.C. §8011.

60. 42 U.S.C. §8011(b).

61. 42 U.S.C. §8011(i).

62. 42 U.S.C. §8011(d).

63. *See generally* 42 U.S.C. §§8001-8010.

64. 42 U.S.C. §8011(j)(3).

65. 59 *Fed. Reg.* 22,220, Apr. 29, 1994; 24 C.F.R. Part 700.

66. 59 *Fed. Reg.* 22,223, April 29, 1994.

67. Congress authorized $25 million for fiscal year 1991 and $26 million for fiscal year 1992 to be appropriated under the revised program. For 1991, $9.5 million was appropriated. *Housing and Development Reporter,* Oct. 29, 1990, 502. HUD then proposed to rescind this appropriation and did not seek any funding for CHSP in FY 1991. Although Congress appropriated $17.7 million for 1992, the administration has proposed to rescind $16.7 million and eliminate the program for 1993. *Housing Bulletin,* American Association of Homes for the Aging, Feb. 22, 1991, and Feb. 6, 1992. CHSP was not eliminated for 1993. Rather, the Housing and Community Development Act of 1992 reauthorized $21 million for 1993 and $21.8 million for 1994 to be appropriated under the revised program. Pub. L. No. 102-550, Oct. 28, 1992. In 1994, Congress appropriated $25 million to fund new CHSP projects. For 1995, the Clinton Administration proposed $6.3 million in appropriations to extend funding for the 53 existing CHSP projects; however, the Clinton Administration did not request any additional funding for new projects in 1995. *Housing Bulletin,* American Association of Homes for the Aging, Feb. 10, 1994. The House Appropriations Committee approved the funding proposed by the Clinton Administration. *Older Americans Report,* June 24, 1994, 211. The Senate Appropriations Committee, however, approved an appropriation of $25 million. *Older Americans Report,* July 22, 1994, 246. In 1995, the CHSP program was pronounced dead when HUD rescinded its notice of funding availability after the president signed a bill rescinding $37 million of the $38.8 million requested for the program. *Aging News Alert,* Oct. 11, 1995, 15.

68. *See generally* 12 U.S.C. §1701; 24 C.F.R. §231; *HUD Handbook* 4570.1.

69. Ward, note 53 *above,* at 34, 42.

70. *See generally* 12 U.S.C. §1701 *et seq.*; 24 C.F.R. Pt. 236.

71. *See generally* 24 C.F.R. Pt. 246.

72. 24 C.F.R. §246.21.

73. 24 C.F.R. §246.5. *See also* rental rehabilitation grants, §14.4(d).

74. *See* 24 C.F.R. §§246.6-246.12. *See also* §14.4(d).

75. 24 C.F.R. §247.3. *See also* 24 C.F.R. Parts 880, 881, 882.

76. 24 C.F.R. §247.4. *See also* 24 C.F.R. Parts 880, 881, 882.

77. Public and Assisted Housing Occupancy Task Force, "Report to Congress and the Department of Housing and Urban Development," Apr. 7, 1994, Ch. 3.

78. P.L. 98-181.

79. 12 U.S.C. §1701r-1.

80. 24 C.F.R. §§5.300 *et seq.*

81. 24 C.F.R. §5.306.

82. An interim rule published in the *Federal Register* on March 2, 1995, adds the new Section 202 capital advance and rental assistance program to the other programs to which the pet regulations apply. 60 *Fed. Reg.* 11,831, Mar. 2, 1995.

83. Numerous sections of the regulations further explicitly preserve state and local law. The exceptions, where state and local laws are not to apply, pertain principally to HUD's management and procedural responsibilities under the statute.

84. *See Aujero v. CDA Todco, Inc.,* 756 F.2d 1374 (9th Cir. 1985); *Mayoral v. Jeffco American Baptist Residences, Inc.,* 726 F.2d 1361 (10th Cir. 1984), *cert. den.,* 469 U.S. 884, 105 S. Ct. 255, 83 L. Ed. 2d 192 (1984).

85. *Gonzalez v. St. Margaret's House,* 620 F. Supp. 806 (S.D. N.Y. 1985). The court eventually ruled that mandatory meal charges did not constitute rent and that the extra rental charge did not violate the 30 percent cap on tenant's rent. *See Gonzalez v. St. Margaret's House Housing Development Fund Corporation,* 668 F. Supp. 187 (S.D. N.Y. 1987) *aff'd.* 848 F.2d 391 (2d Cir. 1988).

86. *See Johnson v. Soundview Apartments,* 585 F. Supp. 559; 588 F. Supp. 1381 (S.D. N.Y. 1984) and order filed Nov. 17, 1986, reported at 1986-2 Trade Cases, CCH *Trade Regulation Reporter,* 67,349. The case has since been settled.

87. *Ibid.*

88. 880 F.2d 1514 (2nd Cir. 1989).

89. *See* discussion concerning condominiums with services, §7.1(c)(2).

90. 643 F. Supp. 223 (N.D. Cal. 1986).

91. Former 24 C.F.R. §278.

92. 52 *Fed. Reg.* 6,301.

93. *Ibid.*

94. 24 C.F.R. §278.

95. 60 *Fed. Reg.* 47,260, Sept. 11, 1995.

96. *See* Holland J., L. Ganz, P. Higgins, and K. Antonelli, "Service Coordinators in Senior Housing: An Exploration of Their Emerging Role in Long Term Care," *Journal of Case Management,* Fall 1995, 108 [hereinafter Holland].

97. *See HUD Handbook* 4381.5 REV.2, ¶ 8.4.

98. *See* 12 U.S.C. §1701q(j)(6); 42 U.S.C. §§13631, 13632; *HUD Handbook* 4381.5 REV.2, Ch. 8; HUD Notice H 94-98; HUD Notice H 94-99 (extended by HUD Notice H 96-35).

99. *See HUD Handbook* 4381.5 REV.2, ¶ 8.4.

100. Holland, 108-109.

Friendship Heights; Chevy Chase, Maryland.

23 Discrimination

§23.1 In General

Developers and project sponsors must be careful to comply with applicable federal and state laws regarding discrimination in admissions, access to services and amenities, transfers, and facility policies in general.

Numerous antidiscrimination laws, particularly at the federal level, have been enacted or strengthened in recent years, and receipt of federal funds or benefits is no longer a prerequisite to the applicability of many of them. Activities that may trigger application of such laws can include operation of a nursing facility, sale or rental of housing or delivery of services in connection with housing, operation of a public accommodation, and being an employer as well as participating in federal programs.

The principal areas addressed by federal statute or case law that are of interest to retirement communities concern discrimination on the basis of age, disability, religion, race, national origin, and income. The following sections discuss various discrimination-related provisions of federal law. State laws typically cover the above as well as additional bases of discrimination (such as marital status or gender) and may in some instances be more restrictive than federal law.[1]

§23.2 Age

(a) Age Discrimination Act of 1975

The Age Discrimination Act of 1975 provides that no person shall, on the basis of age, be excluded from participation in, denied the benefits of, or subjected to discrimination under any program or activity receiving federal financial assistance.[2] There are, however, several statutory exceptions to this basic provision, which are outlined in detail in the regulations of the U.S. Department of Housing and Urban Development (HUD) and the U.S. Department of Health and Human Services (HHS).[3] Furthermore, there has been little action in the courts under the Age Discrimination Act as related to housing or health facilities.

It is important to note at the outset that the HUD and HHS regulations implementing the act interpret the phrase "receiving federal financial assistance" to include assistance in the form of funds or the services of federal personnel.[4] This means, for example, that all projects that proceed under HUD, involving both mortgage insurance and direct loans, must comply with the provisions of the act. Facilities constructed solely with private monies but that receive Medicare or Medicaid funds may also be subject to the provisions of the act.[5]

The statute itself contains three exceptions to the act's discrimination provisions while the regulations establish a fourth exception, all of which are discussed below. First, the act does not apply to age distinctions established under the authority of any law that provides benefits or establishes criteria for participation on the basis of age or in age-related terms.[6] This exemption must be based on age distinctions that are contained in a federal, state, or local statute or ordinance adopted by an elected, general-purpose legislative body.[7] For example, Medicare is a program whose benefits begin at a certain age by virtue of federal statute enacted by Congress; therefore, such age distinctions do not violate the act. It is also possible that admissions distinctions based on age are permissible where a state statute expressly establishes a licensure regime for facilities providing care or services to the "elderly" or to persons over a certain age. It is important to note that this provision does not provide an automatic exemption for age distinctions in regulations or in ordinances enacted by bodies that are not elected or that are special-purpose even though elected, such as commissions or housing authority boards.[8]

As for the second exception, a recipient of federal financial assistance is permitted to make age distinctions if that action reasonably takes into account age as a factor necessary to the "normal operation" or achievement of any "statutory objective" of a program or activity.[9] "Normal operation" is defined as the operation of a program or activity without significant changes that would impair its ability to meet its objectives.[10] "Statutory objectives" are those purposes expressly stated in the statute or ordinance.[11] To determine when age is a necessary factor, HUD and HHS regulations establish a strict four-part test as follows:

- Age must be used as a measure or approximation of one or more other characteristics.
- The other characteristics need to be measured or approximated in order for the normal operation of the program to continue or to achieve any statutory objective of the program.
- The other characteristics can reasonably be measured or approximated by the use of age.
- The other characteristics are impractical to measure directly on an individual basis.[12]

To qualify for the second exception, the age distinction must meet all four parts of the test. The burden of proof that the age distinction falls within the exception rests with the recipient of federal financial assistance.[13]

Given some confusion regarding the application of the four-part test, HUD provided a sample situation in the preamble to the final regulations.[14] In the example, a project providing housing for the elderly or handicapped under Section 202 refuses to accept as tenants persons over 66 years of age and does not provide services for those unable to live independently. Section 202 housing was generally designed to provide housing for those elderly or handicapped individuals capable of "independent living."[15] In determining whether the age distinction is a "factor necessary to the normal operation of a program or activity," HUD's analysis of the hypothetical situation under the four-part test concluded that

- age is used as a measure or approximation of prospective tenants' ability to live independently;
- the nonage characteristic (the ability to live independently) must be measured for normal operation of the program or activity to continue;
- the nonage characteristic cannot reasonably be measured or approximated by the use of age in that many people well over the age of 66 are capable of independent living; and
- it is not impractical to measure the ability to live independently on an individual basis.

Thus, while the project's action satisfies the first two parts of the test, it fails the second two and, as such, violates the Age Discrimination Act.[16]

The third exception in the statute is for reasonable distinctions based on criteria other than age.[17] Regulations clarify that this exception permits discrimination that may have a disproportionate effect on persons of different ages.[18] Thus, for example, reasonable distinctions based on health, while they may have a disproportionate impact on older people, should not violate the Age Discrimination Act.[19] It is important to note, however, that health distinctions raise disability discrimination issues (see §23.3).

A fourth ground for exemption appears in regulations for programs that provide "special benefits" to the elderly or children.[20] Such benefits are presumed to be necessary to the normal operation of the program and thus exempt from the act.[21] While this exception appears to have been intended to apply to benefits such as senior citizens' or children's discounts, it can arguably apply as well to seniors' facilities where the overall program is designed to benefit the elderly.

On the whole, age discrimination is an issue with potentially devastating impact on the seniors' housing industry. The Office of Civil Rights of HHS has taken the position that age-based admissions discrimination in freestanding nursing facilities violates the act. Some regional offices of the national Office of Civil Rights have extended their reach to the residential portions of continuing-care retirement communities (CCRCs) where residents receive priority access to nursing facilities. While there are many bases for arguing that the normal operation of a retirement community depends on age discrimination due to the distinctive medical, daily living, psychological, social, and spiritual needs of the elderly, it is helpful to be able to rely on a statutory framework. For example, a state licensure statute for elderly care facilities, a HUD financing program designed for the elderly, or a Medicare eligibility requirement for a facility that insures certain health costs is helpful in justifying an age requirement for facility admission.

The age issue is often mingled with and complicated by disability issues as when, for example, a young person with AIDS seeks admission to a CCRC nursing unit or a nonelderly person in a wheelchair applies for residence in a HUD Section 202 elderly housing facility. Despite some confusion about the ability of Section 202 programs to reserve occupancy only for the elderly and to exclude nonelderly handicapped persons, the HUD occupancy handbook appears to confirm that such age-specific admissions criteria continue to be acceptable. Clarification of HUD's policy, which can be found in the revisions to Chapter 2 of *HUD Handbook* 4350.3, states the following:

- Elderly families with children may not be restricted from occupancy of Section 221, 231, or 236 units. However, projects designed for the elderly may restrict occupancy of elderly units to persons age 62 or older and to families whose head or spouse is 62 years or older.
- The following documents may furnish evidence that a project was designed for the elderly: regulatory agreements, loan commitment papers, fi-

nancial documents, notice of fund availability, bid invitations, owner's management plans, and applications for funding. If these documents do not furnish sufficient evidence, owners may request the project to be approved as a facility designed for the elderly by taking into account factors such as historical data and bedroom configuration.

- Occupancy policies that exclude more than two persons per bedroom are generally deemed reasonable, but occupancy policies requiring fewer than two persons per bedroom are generally deemed unreasonable.[22]

In May 1994, HUD published rules[23] that implement the Section 8 elderly preference provisions of the Housing and Community Development Act of 1992.[24] Effective June 1994, the rules permit certain projects to give preference to applicants age 62 or older if the owner can document that the facility was originally designed and built to serve seniors. Documentation must be established by at least one "primary source" (the documents already listed above in connection with Chapter 2 of *HUD Handbook* 4350.3) or two "secondary sources," including lease records from the first two years of occupancy showing the tenant mix, evidence that services for the elderly have been provided, a high percentage of efficiency and one-bedroom units, and other relevant data.[25] Projects covered by the rules include Section 8 projects, Farmers Home Administration projects, and projects assisted under HUD's multifamily disposition program. Section 202, 221(d)(3), and 236 projects are not covered by the statute and thus are exempt from the setaside rules.[26] Section 221(d)(4) retirement service centers are also exempt (see discussion in §23.3(c)).

Projects covered by the rules that wish to give an occupancy preference to the elderly must reserve a minimum number of units for nonelderly disabled persons. The minimum setaside is the percentage of occupancy by nonelderly disabled on October 28, 1992 (the effective date of the act), or January 1, 1992, whichever figure is higher, up to a maximum of 10 percent of the project's units.[27]

Other interim rules issued by HUD clarify that

- public housing agencies (PHAs) cannot deny disabled elderly persons admission to designated elderly family projects based on their disability or deny disabled applicants admission to a project designated for disabled families based on their age;

- PHAs must provide or obtain supportive services only in connection with projects designated for occupancy by disabled families. Projects providing supportive services to elderly families are encouraged but not required to continue doing so; and

- unless a state or local law requires otherwise, service providers need not be licensed, provided that they are "qualified and experienced" in providing supportive services.[28]

In any event, minimum and maximum age criteria should be carefully examined and related to a statutory objective or a defensible and necessary program element. If possible, it is wise to use a nonage characteristic to accomplish the same purpose.

(b) Familial Status Provisions of the Fair Housing Act

The Fair Housing Act Amendments of 1988 created a new prohibition against discrimination in housing on the basis of "familial status."[29] This law was intended principally to prevent discrimination against families with children in the sale or rental of housing.[30] The familial status restrictions have, however, specifically exempted "housing for older persons."[31] Such housing is defined as housing that is

- provided under any state or federal program and determined to be specifically designed and operated to assist elderly persons; or

- intended for, and solely occupied by, persons 62 years of age or older; or

- intended and operated for occupancy by at least one person 55 years of age or older per unit.

A project is intended and operated for occupancy by at least one person 55 years or older per unit if the following minimum standards are met:

- At least 80 percent of the units are occupied by at least one person age 55 or older per unit. In 1995, Congress repealed the former requirement that a project must have "significant facilities and services" designed to meet the physical or social needs of older persons (H.R. 660). See §23.2(c)

for a discussion of the evolution and demise of the rule.[32]

- Policies and procedures are published and adhered to that demonstrate an intent by the owner or manager to provide housing for persons 55 years of age or older.[33]

An organization that does not satisfy the "policies and procedures" requirement will not be protected under this exemption. For example, in *Massaro v. Mainlands Section 1 & 2 Civic Association,*[34] a subdivision homeowners' association was ineligible for the older persons' housing exemption because it had not instituted any age-verification procedures evidencing its intent to provide housing for people age 55 or older before it took action against younger homeowners with children. The association's board of directors failed to develop a credible process for enforcing its bylaws, and the secretary of the homeowners' association testified that she did not believe that the bylaw amendment requiring residents to be 55 or older was enforceable. Moreover, the association in fact did not enforce the provision.

Persons residing in housing as of September 13, 1988, who do not meet the age requirements set forth in the statute are exempted from its coverage, provided that new occupants of the housing do meet such requirements. Unoccupied units must be reserved for people meeting the age requirements of the statute.

A blanket exemption is created for religious organizations that own or operate a dwelling for other than a commercial purpose. Such organizations may give preference to persons of the same religion provided that membership in the religion is not restricted on account of race, color, or national origin.[35] The religious organization exemption has been construed narrowly.[36]

Similarly, a private club, not open to the public, which as an incident to its primary purpose provides lodging for other than a commercial purpose, may limit rental or occupancy of the lodgings to its members or give them preference over nonmembers.[37]

The law has withstood a challenge on the basis that it violated the rights of privacy and freedom of association of older persons.[38]

Case law interpreting the familial status rules has often involved numerical occupancy restrictions.[39]

Fair Housing Council v. Ayres deals with a restriction of two persons per unit, ostensibly to prevent damage to the apartments. Plaintiffs alleged discrimination based on familial status. The court noted that HUD has held, in administrative decisions, that the business necessity defense to discrimination under the act requires a showing that a numerical occupancy restriction is a necessity of business; and that the party that allegedly engaged in discrimination bears the burden of proving that no less discriminatory alternatives were available.[40] The court, applying a least restrictive means standard, stated that the defendant did not consider a number of less restrictive alternatives that would have achieved the goal of preventing needless wear and tear on the complex, such as detailed maintenance requirements, frequent inspections, higher security deposits, and more careful tenant screening.

The U.S. Court of Appeals for the Tenth Circuit, however, reversed HUD's decision that a three-person occupancy limit in a mobile home park violated the Fair Housing Act. The park's owner presented a reasonable business justification in the form of concerns regarding demands on the sewer system and quality of life at the park.[41] In *Pfaff v. HUD,*[42] the Ninth Circuit Court of Appeals upheld a landlord's refusal to rent a home to a family of five, citing the owner's longstanding practice of renting the property only to families of four or fewer because of the home's small size. Despite this restriction, the landlord had always rented properties to families with children.

In July 1995, HUD issued interim guidance providing that if a housing provider has established maximum occupancy standards as broad as those provided in the model code published by the Building Officials and Code Administrators, HUD will not pursue an allegation that the occupancy standard constitutes discrimination on the basis of familial status. General counsel for HUD stated that the model code should provide for more objective guidance than previous standards, including specifications for bedroom configurations. Compliance with this standard will provide a "safe harbor" for housing providers.

A series of cases has dealt with the number of unrelated persons who can live together. In *Elliott v. Athens,*[43] a federal court held that an ordinance restricting the maximum number of unrelated occu-pants living in homes zoned for single families did not violate the Fair Housing Act because the ordinance was covered by a provision of the act that permitted reasonable maximum occupancy restrictions that applied equally to all applicants. The plaintiffs in the case had claimed that the ordinance was unreasonable because it had a disparate impact on the residents of a proposed group home for recovering alcoholics. The court found that the restriction as applied in the case was reasonable because the city produced evidence of a strong, legitimate interest in controlling density, traffic, and noise in a single-family residential district and preserving the district's residential character. The city demonstrated that its restriction was the only practical method of serving these interests and that other municipalities had similar restrictions.

The U.S. Supreme Court's decision in *City of Edmonds v. Oxford House,*[44] however, casts doubt on the continued validity of the *Elliott* decision. The Court concluded that ordinances restricting the number of unrelated occupants who may live in homes zoned as single-family residences were not "reasonable maximum occupancy restrictions." Only ordinances that simply cap the total number of occupants can be deemed reasonable maximum occupancy restrictions; those that attempt to define the categories of persons who might live together receive no protection under the act.

(c) Significant Facilities and Services Rule (repealed)

Note: The significant facilities and services rule was repealed by H.R. 660, signed by President Clinton on December 28, 1995.

As originally enacted, the "housing for older persons" exemption for projects with occupants age 55 and over required the existence of facilities and services specifically designed to meet the physical or social needs of older persons; if such arrangements were not practical, the exemption required that such housing was necessary to provide important housing opportunities for older persons.

Pursuant to the 1992 Housing and Community Development Act,[45] HUD in July 1994 issued a 60-page proposed rule to define "significant facilities and services especially designed to meet the physical or social needs of older persons." HUD proposed the following criteria to determine whether the facility or service is "significant:"

- the extent to which the facility or service is not customarily offered to residents of comparable housing in the relevant geographic area;
- the extent to which the facility or service can accommodate the older population of the housing facility, taking into consideration factors such as size of the facility, scope of the service offered, and number of locations at which the service is offered;
- the extent to which the facility benefits older persons, given the climate and physical setting of the facility;
- the extent to which older residents actually use the facility or service;
- the extent to which the facility or service is provided by the housing provider rather than by others; and
- whether the facility or service is not required by a law related to housing for the elderly.[46]

HUD proposed the following as relevant in determining whether a facility or service is "specifically designed to meet the physical or social needs of older persons:"

- whether the facility or service is readily accessible to and usable by elderly persons with mobility, vision, and hearing impairments;
- the extent to which the facility or service benefits the current and future health, safety, or leisure needs of the elderly population;
- whether the provider has published and adhered to policies and procedures manifesting its intent to comply with all disability discrimination laws and to make its facilities readily accessible to disabled persons even when not required by law;
- the extent to which the housing provider has taken "meaningful steps" to offer an off-site facility or service that would otherwise not be available to elderly residents of the facility; and
- the extent to which the service specifically designed to meet the physical or social needs of older persons is provided in connection with the facility.[47]

HUD's proposed rule raised significant concerns for many providers of seniors' housing because, among other things, it expanded the current scope of disability discrimination laws; tended to require housing providers to accommodate the aging-in-place needs of populations that do not have a present need; tended to force seniors' housing providers into the continuing-care or assisted-living business; greatly increased the potential costs to current seniors' housing residents; and threatened the existence of affordable seniors' housing options such as mobile home parks.[48]

In August 1995, HUD issued final rules defining "significant facilities and services." To qualify, a community would be required to make available, directly or indirectly, at least two facilities or services in at least five categories from among the following 12 categories of facilities and services, including at least two facilities in the "leisure needs" or "health/safety needs" category:

- social and recreational services provided on a regular, organized basis, such as athletic team activities, bridge or cards, exercise classes, bingo, dances, crafts classes, holiday parties, field trips, and organized travel opportunities;
- continuing education activities, including monthly presentations, consumer protection classes, regularly offered CPR and language study classes, videotapes on health care, and courses offered at local educational institutions;
- information and counseling services, such as bulletin boards for exchanges of information or services, bus schedules, seminars on aging or government benefits programs, and on-site legal services;
- homemaker services, including employee assistance with housework or yardwork, bill-paying services, pet care or pet therapy services, minor home repair services, and tool loan services;
- outside maintenance and health and safety services, such as Meals on Wheels, on-site repair service, snow shoveling and plowing, lawn care, security guards, referrals for transportation, and referrals to health care professionals;
- emergency and preventive health care programs, such as meetings about nutrition, back care, or other health care issues, monthly blood pressure checks, or periodic vision or hearing tests;

- congregate dining for at least one meal daily;
- transportation to provide access to social services;
- services to encourage and assist residents to use available facilities and services, such as providing dance instructors or lifeguards or publishing newsletters or a monthly calendar of events;
- social and recreational facilities, such as a clubhouse, library, swimming pool, communal kitchen, exercise equipment, bank, convenience store, dry cleaner, or hair salon (collectively, "leisure needs");
- an accessible physical environment, including ramps, handicapped parking, vans or buses with wheelchair lifts, accessible common areas, or at least one accessible restroom in public and common use areas (collectively, "health/safety needs"); and
- any other facility or service that is not listed above but that is designed to meet the health, safety, social, or leisure needs of persons age 55 or older and is actually available to and used by such residents.[49]

A housing provider is deemed to provide "significant facilities and services" if the facilities and services are provided on the premises by paid staff, resident volunteers, or agencies, entities, or persons other than the housing provider, or off the premises if transportation service or coordination of information and transportation resources is made available.[50]

A provider still would have been eligible for protection under this section if it could demonstrate that it was impractical to offer significant facilities and services to the elderly.[51]

All of the rules referenced above became obsolete with passage of the Housing for Older Persons Act of 1995, H.R. 660, which deleted entirely the "significant facilities and services" requirement from the 55-and-over familial status provisions. Under H.R. 660, housing for persons age 55 and over is exempt from the familial status provisions if the housing is in a facility intended and operated for occupancy of at least 80 percent of the occupied units by at least one person age 55 or over; the facility publishes and adheres to policies and procedures that demonstrate the intent required in the immediately preceding point, whether or not such procedures are set forth in writing; and the facility complies with HUD rules for verification of occupancy,

including verification by reliable surveys and affidavits. In addition, once a community has provided the necessary facilities and services, it may self-certify that it qualifies for the Fair Housing Act exception. Absent evidence to the contrary, HUD would assume that a self-certifying community qualifies as housing for persons age 55 and over.

H.R. 660 also protects from liability for monetary damages any person who reasonably relied in good faith on the application of the exemption to a particular facility. This provision protects employees and agents of a community if they believe in good faith that the community satisfies the 55-and-over housing requirements.

(d) State Laws

With seniors' housing also subject to state statutes and case law regarding discrimination in the provision of housing or services, developers should check all applicable state provisions. In one case, for example, the California Supreme Court interpreted the state's general civil rights act as prohibiting discrimination on the basis of age in all business establishments and held that a landlord's "no-children" policy violated the law.[52] While the language of the state civil rights act on its face limits its application to discrimination based on "sex, race, color, religion, ancestry, or national origin,"[53] the court held that the statute barred all types of arbitrary discrimination and that the reference to particular bases of discrimination was illustrative rather than restrictive.[54]

The California court did, however, recognize the validity of age-limited admission policies for retirement communities or housing complexes reserved for older citizens. It found that such policies were a reasonable means of establishing and preserving specialized facilities for those in need of particular services.[55] This view was later incorporated into state law by statutory amendments[56] that permit limited age discrimination "where accommodations are designed to meet the physical and social needs of senior citizens." The amendments set out in some detail the conditions under which age limitations may be implemented in seniors' housing and when nonelderly companions of seniors may reside in such housing.

In response to such legal challenges, retirement communities that offer health care services may argue that they are not subject to the discrimination provisions of housing statutes on the ground that any admissions criteria are health care-related and that housing is incidental to the provision of licensed care.[57]

Before enactment of the federal familial status laws, the Florida courts took a more expansive view of age restrictions in housing. In *White Egret Condominiums v. Franklin,*[58] the Florida Supreme Court upheld a restriction against residency by children under the age of 12 in a condominium apartment. The court found that such a policy was a reasonable means of identifying and categorizing varying desires of the population in regard to housing and that it did not violate either the 14th Amendment to the U.S. Constitution or Florida statute. The court did note, however, that age restrictions cannot be used unreasonably or arbitrarily to restrict certain classes of individuals from obtaining desirable housing. Of course, state laws or decisions that contradict the federal statutes prohibiting age or familial discrimination are superseded by the federal law and may not be relied on.

§23.3 Disability

Discrimination on the basis of handicap or functional ability is one of the thorniest issues for retirement communities due largely to the communities' hybrid nature as facilities that provide not only shelter but also extensive services, and sometimes care, in a group living environment. Discrimination issues can arise with respect to admissions, transfers, and policies governing the use of facilities or services in the retirement community. Although this section is subdivided according to the various disability discrimination laws, most claims of discrimination are brought under multiple laws; therefore, the case discussions may have more widespread relevance than their placement indicates.

(a) Fair Housing Amendments Act of 1988

(1) Prohibited Discrimination; Applicability

The Fair Housing Amendments Act of 1988 added new provisions prohibiting discrimination against persons with disabilities in the sale or rental of a dwelling or in the provision of services or facilities in connection with such a dwelling.[59] Discrimination is defined to include

- a refusal to permit, at the expense of the handicapped person, reasonable modifications of existing premises if such modifications may be necessary to afford the person full enjoyment of the premises, except that in the case of a rental unit, the landlord may condition permission for a modification on an agreement from the renter to restore the premises to its original condition, except for reasonable wear and tear;
- a refusal to make reasonable accommodations in rules, policies, practices, or services, when such accommodations may be necessary to afford the person an equal opportunity to use and enjoy a dwelling; or
- beginning in March 1991, failure to design and construct multifamily dwellings for first occupancy with the following features: public use and common use areas readily accessible to the handicapped, all doors sufficiently wide to allow passage of persons in wheelchairs, and adaptive design features, including an accessible route into and through the dwelling, light switches, electrical outlets, thermostats, and other controls positioned in accessible locations, reinforcements in bathroom walls to allow installation of grab bars, and kitchens and bathrooms designed to permit an individual in a wheelchair to maneuver about the space.

Multifamily dwellings are defined to include all buildings of four or more units containing one or more elevators and ground-floor areas in other buildings consisting of four or more units. Certain dwellings used by religious organizations or private clubs are, however, exempt (see §§23.2(b) and 23.4).

HUD has clarified that its 1991 Fair Housing Handicapped Accessibility Guidelines cover "continuing care facilities which incorporate housing, health care and other types of services" if the project includes at least one building with four or more dwelling units. To be deemed a dwelling, the facility must be used as a residence for more than a brief period of time as determined on a case-by-case basis. Factors that HUD uses to make the dwelling determination include the length of time persons stay in the project; whether there are policies in effect at the project designed and intended to encourage or discourage occupants from forming an expectation and intent to continue to occupy space at the project; and the nature of the services provided by or at the project. HUD's notice does not clarify whether the Americans with Disabilities Act, which HUD does not administer, applies to continuing-care communities.[60]

In March 1991, HUD issued final guidelines for fair housing accessibility, setting forth detailed structural parameters.[61] Among other things, the regulations require at least one accessible entrance for all buildings with elevators, regardless of terrain. Other buildings may be eligible for a site impracticability exemption. Dwelling unit door openings must be at least 32 inches wide and access routes 36 inches wide.

Federal regulations published in January 1989 broadly define handicap to include "a physical or mental impairment which substantially limits one or more major life activities; a record of having such an impairment; or being regarded as having such an impairment."[62] The regulations further specify that it is unlawful even to make an inquiry to determine whether an applicant for a dwelling, a person intending to reside in a dwelling, or any person associated with the applicant has a handicap; similarly, it is unlawful to inquire as to the nature or severity of a handicap.[63] It is, however, lawful to inquire, for example, into the "applicant's ability to meet the requirements of ownership or tenancy," provided that such inquiries are made of all applicants, whether or not they have handicaps.[64] The regulations at 24 C.F.R. §100.2(c)(2) specifically allow an inquiry to be made of all applicants "to determine whether an applicant is qualified for a dwelling available only ... to persons with a particular type of handicap."

The duty under the act to extend reasonable accommodations to disabled persons may, in some circumstances, require a landlord to waive fees generally applicable to all residents.[65] Similarly, a housing cooperative was required to provide an indoor parking space to a resident as a reasonable accommodation of her physical disability.[66] In contrast, a group daycare center was not required to provide one-on-one care when doing so would impose an undue financial burden on the center.[67] And in *United*

States v. Hillhaven, summary judgment was granted in favor of a congregate seniors' housing facility that had been accused of a Fair Housing Amendments Act violation when it placed restrictions on the time, place, and manner in which disabled residents could use motorized carts in crowded common areas of the facility.[68]

(2) "Independent-Living" and Retirement Community Admissions

Preliminary indications from HUD suggested that it may be permissible to inquire about an applicant's ability to "live independently." In *Cason v. Rochester Housing Authority,*[69] however, the U.S. District Court for the Western District of New York ruled that requiring an applicant to demonstrate the ability to live independently in order to enter public housing violates the Fair Housing Act. In that case, the admissions criteria required applicants to release confidential medical information and to submit to an evaluation by a social worker. The court concluded that application of the admissions criteria caused the housing authority to "consider handicapped applicants by a different standard than so-called able-bodied applicants." The court also found the standard of independent living to be both arbitrary and subjective and not the least restrictive means of advancing the legitimate goal of ensuring that tenants would respect the privacy rights of others. According to the court, the difference in treatment of the handicapped stemmed from "unsubstantiated prejudices and fears regarding those with mental and physical disabilities." The court therefore enjoined use of the admissions criteria (see also §23.3(c) regarding handicap discrimination in HUD-financed facilities).

In a departure from its position against use of the "independent-living" admission criterion adopted after the *Cason* case, HUD acknowledged, in the preface to a 1995 final rule[70] governing Section 8 and Section 202 projects, that a Section 202 elderly project owner's "suitability" requirements for tenants may include the tenant's "ability to live independently." HUD noted, however, that in a project that does not provide supportive services, it is "irrelevant whether the obligations of tenancy are met by the individual alone or with assistance that the individual with handicaps arranges." In other words, despite dependency on a third party to provide assistive services, the tenant may qualify for residency on the basis of the owner's suitability requirements for independent living. HUD emphasized that, absent any evidence to the contrary, a presumption would exist in favor of a disabled individual's own assessment of his or her capabilities.[71]

On the theory that disparate treatment based on health status in the delivery of health services is not housing discrimination, the Fair Housing Amendments Act arguably should not be applied to licensed care facilities such as hospitals, skilled-nursing facilities, and residential care facilities.[72] The House report to the Fair Housing Amendments Act[73] addresses discrimination against handicapped persons who are excluded from equal access to housing "because of stereotypes about their capacity to live safely and independently" and states that "[t]he right to be free from housing discrimination is essential to the goal of independent living." Therefore, the act appears to have been intended to apply to housing designed for the independent living of its inhabitants and not to facilities that, by definition and their licensing, are designed to provide health care and personal care to persons with handicaps who are dependent on the provision of such services. Unfortunately, there is no express exemption for facilities designed to care for persons with medical, functional, or mental disabilities. Moreover, the act has frequently been found to apply to care facilities[74] (see also §23.3(b) regarding facilities that may be subject to a dual Fair Housing Amendments Act/Americans with Disabilities Act analysis).[75]

For retirement communities generally, whether or not they offer a care program, any prohibition against inquiring about a person's ability to live independently is troublesome. Project operators have a legitimate interest in knowing whether an applicant for admission will be able to function safely without assistance and whether facility services, if any, can adequately serve resident needs.[76] Unfortunately, the Fair Housing Amendments Act was enacted without due consideration of the realities of retirement community operations.

To address the concerns of the *Cason* case and still function in a reasonable manner, retirement community operators should review and, if necessary, modify policies regarding admissions, use of services

and facilities, and transfers and discharges along the following lines:

- Questions about "requirements of tenancy," such as a person's physical and mental ability to live safely, not interfere with others' peaceable enjoyment of the premises, pay rent or other charges, maintain personal hygiene, not destroy property, and so on, are probably acceptable if asked equally of all.
- If, however, the person is unable to perform the types of functions described above, the facility should consider whether others such as outside social services agencies, family members, or live-in assistants can ensure the performance of these functions.
- Admission or transfer criteria directly related to regulatory safety or licensure criteria, such as certification for nonambulatory occupancy or level-of-care criteria for assisted living or nursing, are probably acceptable.
- Policies such as "no wheelchairs in the dining room" are highly questionable when the reason is aesthetics or decorum for the benefit of non-disabled residents.[77]
- Medical questionnaires or other more detailed inquiries about specific health or functional issues may be acceptable if related to specific program benefits, such as those provided in a Type A (comprehensive health coverage) continuing-care retirement community.
- Inquiries unrelated to essential or integral program elements should be eliminated.
- Reasonable accommodations (e.g., waiving the admission age requirement for a live-in aide) should be made to enable the impaired person to have equal access to and enjoyment of facilities and services.[78]

Guidance regarding Fair Housing Act restrictions on real estate advertisements[79] appears in a HUD memorandum addressing a number of prohibited bases of discrimination, including disability and concluding that:

> Real estate advertisements should not contain explicit exclusions, limitations, or other indications of discrimination based on handicap (i.e., no wheelchairs). Advertisements containing descriptions of properties (great view, fourth-floor walk up, walk-in-closets), services

or facilities (jogging trails), or neighborhoods (walk to bus-stop) do not violate the Act. Advertisements describing the conduct required of residents ("non-smoking," "sober") do not violate the Act. Advertisements containing descriptions of accessibility features are lawful (wheelchair ramp).

(3) Zoning and Fire Safety Regulations

(A) Preemption of Local Zoning Controls. Courts are split on whether the handicap amendments supersede local zoning ordinances. In *Familystyle of St. Paul v. City of St. Paul*,[80] a 1,320-foot spacing requirement for the siting of group residential facilities for the mentally handicapped was found valid under the Fair Housing Act. Although plaintiffs claimed that the statute and local zoning code limited a handicapped person's choice of where to live, the court found that the act did not preempt such a zoning ordinance and that there was a compelling governmental interest in ensuring that the mentally ill receive proper care in an appropriate setting.

The court's reasoning in *Familystyle* was repudiated in *Larkin v. Michigan Department of Social Service*,[81] in which the court declared that a spacing and notice requirement for adult foster care facilities was discriminatory on its face. The statute violated the Fair Housing Amendments Act because the defendant failed to demonstrate that the statute was warranted by the unique and specific needs and abilities of the disabled to whom the statute would apply.[82] A federal court in Michigan also determined that a city violated the Fair Housing Amendments Act when it refused to allow an adult foster care home to accommodate 12 disabled elderly residents in a single-family residential neighborhood.[83] Despite criticism by other circuits, the Eighth Circuit, which encompasses Michigan, has continued to follow the *Familystyle* decision. In *Oxford House-C v. City of St. Louis*,[84] for example, the Eighth Circuit upheld a city ordinance limiting the number of unrelated disabled residents who could live together in single-family homes. For more zoning cases, see subsections (C) and (D) below and §25.1.

The Fair Housing Act may invalidate not only zoning ordinances and land use laws but also restrictive covenants that restrict disabled persons' access to housing.[85]

(B) Fire Safety and Similar Restrictions. Several courts have struck down fire safety and similar restrictions as violative of the disability discrimination provisions of the act. For example, in *Potomac Group Home v. Montgomery County*,[86] county health department regulations that prohibited group homes from accommodating residents unable to respond properly in the event of a fire or other emergency were found to violate the Fair Housing Amendments Act on the ground that the regulations "unreasonably limited" the ability of two wheelchair-bound Alzheimer's patients to live in a "community of their choice."

Likewise, in *Alliance for the Mentally Ill v. City of Naperville*,[87] a city's requirement that a group home for mentally ill adults install automatic sprinklers and an exterior stairwell and make other significant improvements was ruled a violation of the Fair Housing Amendments Act. To pass muster under the act, the code had to make allowances for the unique abilities of the disabled residents. The court stated that the city's actions constituted a failure to make reasonable accommodations for the disabled because the desired accommodation—waiving the fire code's requirements—would enhance disabled residents' quality of life by allowing their placement in group homes most suited to treating their illnesses; and that the benefits of the requested accommodation outweighed the costs to the city.

Similarly, in *Proviso Association of Retarded Citizens v. Village of Westchester*,[88] a residential facility for developmentally disabled adults successfully challenged a village's decision to require the installation of a sprinkler system in a two-unit residence for developmentally disabled adults. Because the residents were capable of evacuating the premises quickly in response to fire alarms, a waiver of the sprinkler requirement would not undermine the fire code's stated purpose of decreasing fire-related mortalities.

The courts have invalidated other restrictions that purported to protect residents but were instead found to be a pretext for discrimination against the disabled or were poorly tailored to the safety needs of the resident population. For example, in *Marbrunak, Inc. v. City of Stow*,[89] an ordinance violated the Fair Housing Amendments Act because it imposed excessive and overly broad safety requirements on housing for the developmentally disabled without making distinctions among various types of developmental disabilities. *Bangerter v. Orem City Corp.*[90] ruled that a conditional use permit requiring 24-hour supervision of mentally retarded persons and establishment of a community advisory committee to field neighbors' complaints was not rationally related to a legitimate governmental purpose. Noting that reasonable restrictions may be imposed on housing to prevent a threat to others' health or safety or substantial property damage, the court remanded the case to the lower court to explore the public safety issue further and to determine whether the restrictions placed on the group home were sufficiently tailored to residents' needs.

(C) Invalidated Zoning Ordinances and Decisions. In addition to the safety restrictions described previously, federal courts have invalidated several other ordinances as enforced against residences for the disabled. For example, in *Turning Point, Inc. v. City of Caldwell,*[91] the Ninth Circuit struck down a city's attempt to condition its acceptance of a homeless shelter's special use permit upon fulfillment of a number of special requirements, including annual review by the city. The court concluded that the annual review requirement violated the act because the city already had sufficient power under its nuisance laws to address any perceived deficiencies in the shelter's operation.

Likewise, in *City of Edmonds v. Washington State Building Code Council,*[92] the court ruled that a zoning ordinance restricting the number of unrelated persons who could live together did not fall within the exemption from the Fair Housing Amendments Act for reasonable local, state, or federal occupancy restrictions.[93] The court held that the facially neutral ordinance could have had the effect of excluding congregate living arrangements for persons with disabilities and therefore was subject to the act's substantive standards. The U.S. Supreme Court affirmed, holding that the city zoning ordinance's definition of "family" was not a maximum-occupancy restriction exempt from scrutiny under the Fair Housing Amendments Act. The Court remanded the case to the Ninth Circuit to determine whether the city's actions were indeed discriminatory.

Similarly, in *Hovsons, Inc. v. Township of Brick,*[94] a township's refusal to approve a nursing home within an area zoned primarily for residential use was held to violate the Fair Housing Amendments Act, where the zoning ordinance already permitted a number of nonresidential, conditional uses of the land, including hospitals, churches, convents, and cemeteries.

Finally, in *Epicenter of Steubenville, Inc. v. City of Steubenville,*[95] a federal court enjoined a city from enforcing a one-year prohibition against all new adult care facilities in one neighborhood because of the prohibition's obviously discriminatory treatment of individuals with mental disabilities. The court stated that the city had acted "to halt the immigration of handicapped people into its borders, a motivation clearly prohibited by the Act."[96]

From these cases, it appears clear that federal courts will limit local governments' authority to issue use permits and grant similar privileges for legitimate, nondiscriminatory purposes.[97]

(D) Local Ordinances and Regulations That Have Withstood Challenge. Despite the large number of cases invalidating zoning ordinances under the disability provisions of the act, courts continue to recognize that some ordinances, regulations, and regulatory actions are narrowly enough circumscribed and sufficiently reasonable to be upheld.

In *Brandt v. Village of Chebanse,*[98] a village concerned about traffic congestion and drainage problems refused to grant a variance that would have allowed the plaintiff developer to build a four-unit apartment building on property zoned for single-family housing. The Seventh Circuit found that the village acted properly in view of its infrastructure concerns.

In *Erdman v. City of Fort Atkinson,*[99] a developer sought a conditional use permit to build a residential facility for elderly disabled individuals in an area zoned for single-family residences. The city properly rejected the application, which failed both to describe the developer's plans for use of the land surrounding the actual building and to account for concerns about future complications in water and sewer line planning. Likewise, a county did not discriminate under the act by denying a retirement facility operator's request to increase the size of its facility and the number of residents it served. The application failed to address adequately parking congestion resulting from the facility's capacity increase.[100]

Lawsuits challenging a state department's regulation or failure to regulate certain residential care facilities have not met with success. In *Wolford v. Lewis,*[101] a state's failure to enforce wheelchair accessibility standards in residential facilities did not violate the Fair Housing Amendments Act because the law did not create a disparity between the abled and disabled but instead between disabled persons in different living arrangements. Similarly, in *Dibble v. Brunty,*[102] a federal court dismissed with prejudice a complaint alleging that enforcement of state social services regulations and the state building code discriminated against people with disabilities and that the commissioner of the department of social services failed to make reasonable accommodations to the needs or abilities of the disabled plaintiffs by refusing to waive or modify the state's public safety provisions as enforced against owners of adult care residences housing nonambulatory residents.

(4) Lenders' Liability

Liability under the Fair Housing Amendments Act is not limited only to providers of housing but also extends to any entity that intentionally aids others in violating the act, including lenders. In *United States v. Hughes,*[103] banks were required to go to trial for allegedly discriminating against mentally ill adults on the basis of handicap. The banks had financed the purchase of a house by a third party even as a social service organization, acting on behalf of a mentally disabled group, was trying to purchase the same house for use as a group home.

Likewise, *United States v. Massachusetts Industrial Finance Agency*[104] found that the Fair Housing Amendments Act applies to conduit bond financing. An organization that sought to develop a school for the emotionally disabled could not transact business in a tax-exempt bond market without the agency's authorization.

In addition, a provider of housing that does not itself discriminate on the basis of handicap may nonetheless be liable for violating the act if its real estate agents or brokers discriminate.[105]

(b) Americans with Disabilities Act

(1) Covered Activities

On July 26, 1990, the Americans with Disabilities Act (ADA) was enacted into law.[106] The ADA encompasses four major titles covering employment, public services, telecommunications, and public accommodations and services operated by private entities.

In the arena of employment, Title I of the act extends the basic rule of the Rehabilitation Act of 1973 (making reasonable accommodations for qualified individuals with a disability) from employers with contacts with the federal government to all private employers with 15 or more employees.[107]

Most germane to retirement community developers is Title III, which deals with public accommodations. All construction designed for occupancy more than 30 months after the law's enactment date must be readily accessible unless structurally impractical.[108] The act generally provides that no individual shall be discriminated against on the basis of disability[109] in the full and equal enjoyment of the goods, services, facilities, privileges, advantages, or accommodations of any place of public accommodation by any person who owns, leases (or leases to), or operates a place of public accommodation.[110] A public accommodation includes an inn, hotel, motel, or other place of lodging as well as a senior citizens' center or other social service center. Professional offices of a health care provider, hospital, or other service establishment are also included.[111] Commentary on the regulations notes that places of a purely residential character are not covered by the act but may be covered by the Fair Housing Act because the term "places of lodging" connotes a short-term stay.[112] Residential care facilities are specifically mentioned as examples of facilities that may have to be analyzed both as housing under the Fair Housing Act and as a "social service center establishment" under the ADA.[113] On the other hand, "long-term-care facilities" and "nursing homes" are expressly covered by the ADA's regulatory "accessibility guidelines" and are required to make accessible at least 50 percent of all bedrooms, toilets, and common areas.[114]

The transportation provisions of the ADA also affect retirement communities that operate a van or shuttle service. The regulations promulgated under the ADA state that a public accommodation that provides transportation services but is not "primarily engaged" in the business of transporting people must nonetheless remove transportation barriers on existing vehicles when such removal is "readily achievable." Transportation services subject to these regulations include customer shuttle services operated by private companies and shuttle services operated between transportation terminals and places of public accommodation.[115] U.S. Department of Transportation regulations provide that private entities operating a "demand responsive" (as opposed to fixed route) system must make all vehicles with a capacity over 16 ordered after August 25, 1990, readily accessible to people with disabilities, including people in wheelchairs.[116]

(2) Covered Disabilities

The ADA covers mental and physical disabilities, including recovering substance users but not current illegal drug users.[117]

The courts have repeatedly found that health care providers who refuse to provide routine care to HIV-positive patients are in violation of the ADA despite the providers' arguments that the needed treatment was outside their areas of expertise and that providing services to HIV-positive patients would pose a direct threat to the health or safety of others. The Centers for Disease Control have recommended that health care providers use "universal precautions" with all patients.[118]

It is clear that allegations of disparate treatment of HIV-positive patients are likely to meet with a court's sympathy. Long-term-care facilities cannot refuse care to HIV-positive or AIDS patients on the theory that they are ill-equipped to meet the special needs of such patients or that such patients' HIV-positive status or AIDS presents a direct threat to the health or safety of others. Finally, such facilities may be liable for the discriminatory conduct of not only their employees but also possibly of any physicians whom they engage. For more regarding HIV and AIDS, see §23.3(d)(4).

(3) Prohibited Discrimination

It is considered discriminatory to deny participation to a handicapped person, to provide unequal benefits, or to set up different or separate benefits for handicapped persons unless such action is "necessary to provide the individual or class of individuals with a good, service, facility, privilege, advantage, or accommodation, or other opportunity that is as effective as that provided to others."[119] Services, facilities, and other benefits must be provided in the most integrated setting appropriate to the needs of the individual, and, even if separate or different programs exist, a disabled person "shall not be denied the opportunity to participate in such programs or activities that are not separate or different."[120]

Prohibited discrimination also includes

- the imposition or application of eligibility criteria that tend to screen out disabled persons unless such criteria can be shown to be necessary for the provision of the services or other amenities being offered;
- failure to make reasonable modifications in policies, practices, or procedures when such modifications are necessary to afford services and privileges to disabled persons unless the entity can demonstrate that making such modifications "would fundamentally alter the nature of such goods, services, facilities, privileges, advantages, or accommodations";
- failure to take steps to ensure that a disabled person is not denied services or amenities or is segregated from others because of the absence of auxiliary aids and services unless such steps would fundamentally alter the nature of the services or amenities or would result in an undue burden;
- failure to remove architectural and communication barriers in existing structures where such removal is readily achievable.[121] New construction designed for first occupancy after January 26, 1993, and areas of existing buildings altered after January 26, 1992, generally must be made readily accessible to people with disabilities in accordance with detailed architectural accessibility standards;[122] and
- where removal of barriers is not readily achievable, failure to make alternative methods or systems available where they are readily achievable.[123]

Case law under the ADA has yielded mixed results for facilities seeking to restrict admissions based on disability. A court found that one state violated the ADA by requiring certain residents of nursing homes to receive care in a nursing home rather than through the state's attendant care program because of a lack of funds. The court held that the plaintiff was entitled to receive care in the most integrated setting appropriate to her needs as long as the state was not required to make fundamental alterations in its program.[124]

Similarly, a federal district court in *Roe v. Housing Authority*[125] denied a city housing authority's motion to dismiss a lawsuit filed against it by a mentally ill and hearing-impaired tenant. The plaintiff, who suffered from manic depression and hearing loss, lived in a public housing facility for the elderly and/or disabled. During his residency, the plaintiff verbally threatened other residents and housing authority employees on several occasions and actually struck and injured another resident. Despite the documented instances of abusive behavior by the plaintiff, the court concluded that the housing authority was first required to attempt to accommodate him reasonably and to demonstrate that reasonable accommodation would not "eliminate or acceptably minimize" the direct threat that the plaintiff posed to other tenants.

On the other hand, in *Alexander v. Pathfinder, Inc.,* the court found that an intermediate-care facility properly discharged a mentally retarded man whose complex medical problems required a level of care the facility was unable to provide.[126] The court declared that "the ADA was never intended to prevent a facility, whose 'customers' are all disabled, from limiting the scope of the services it provides to the disabled."[127]

(4) Remedies; Exemptions

The ADA creates a private right of action for individuals[128] subjected to discrimination and empowers the U.S. attorney general to investigate and prosecute violations. Remedies include injunctive and other regulatory relief, monetary damages, and civil penalties of up to $50,000 for a first violation and up to $100,000 for any subsequent violation. Punitive damages are excluded from the remedies available in attorney general enforcement actions.[129]

The title does not apply to private clubs or others exempted from coverage under Title II of the Civil Rights Act of 1964[130] or to "religious organizations or entities controlled by religious organizations."[131]

No civil action may be brought against a business that employs 25 or fewer employees and has gross receipts of $1 million or less for the first six months after the effective date of January 26, 1992.[132] No action may be brought against a business with ten or fewer employees and $500,000 or less of gross receipts for the first 12 months after the act's effective date.[133]

(5) Insurance Justification

The ADA explicitly recognizes discrimination on the basis of insurance risk as a defense against handicap discrimination. It states that insurers, hospitals, health maintenance organizations, administrators of benefit plans, and other organizations are not prohibited from underwriting, classifying, or administering risks based on or "not inconsistent with" state law, provided they do not use such considerations as a subterfuge to evade the purposes of the act.[134] The legislative history accompanying the ADA states that the law is intended to afford insurers and employers the same opportunities they would enjoy in the absence of the law to design and administer insurance products and benefit plans in a manner consistent with basic principles of insurance risk classification. Without such a clarification, the ADA could arguably find violative of its provisions any action taken by an insurer or employer that treats disabled persons differently under an insurance or benefit plan because they represent an increased hazard of health, death, or illness.[135]

It is important to note, however, that case law under Title VII (sex discrimination) and under Section 504 of the Rehabilitation Act prohibits benefits from being broadly based on protected classifications, such as disability, even when actuarial justifications for such distinctions exist.[136] Moreover, if risk classification procedures are based on mere speculation and not sound actuarial data, a defense to violation of the ADA will not exist.[137]

Thus, retirement communities with an insurance-like health program (e.g., certain continuing-care retirement communities) may be able to deny an applicant admission to the community if the denial is justifiably based on principles of insurance risk classification. Nonetheless, the requirement to make "reasonable accommodations" may mean that the applicant must be admitted on different financial terms (e.g., by imposing more exclusions or charging higher fees based on the costs of caring for such resident) rather than denied admission outright.

(6) EEOC Guidelines

Guidelines issued by the Equal Employment Opportunity Commission (EEOC) in the context of employer-provided health insurance may be useful in helping retirement facilities determine when the ADA permits them to make disability-based distinctions in admitting residents or offering specially tailored health care plans.[138] Under the guidelines, if a health-related term of a health insurance plan is alleged to violate the ADA, the EEOC must determine whether the provision is a "disability-based distinction." If the EEOC finds such a distinction, the employer is required to prove, first, that the health insurance plan is either a bona fide insured health insurance plan that is not inconsistent with state law or a bona fide self-insured insurance plan and, second, that the disability-based distinction is not a subterfuge to evade the purposes of the ADA. The EEOC provides the following examples of what are and are not "disability-based distinctions:"[139]

Distinctions that are not disability-based include

- broad distinctions that apply to the treatment of several dissimilar conditions and that limit individuals both with and without disabilities (e.g., providing fewer benefits for eye care);
- a blanket preexisting exclusion clause that excludes from coverage conditions that predate the person's eligibility for plan benefits so long as the clause does not single out a disability, group of disabilities, or all conditions that substantially limit a major life activity;[140]
- universal limits on or exclusions from coverage (e.g., all experimental drugs, all mental conditions, or all elective surgery); and
- coverage limits on medical procedures that are not exclusively or nearly exclusively used for the treatment of a particular disability (e.g., blood transfusions or x-rays).

Distinctions that are or may be disability-based include

- a lower dollar limit on the treatment of a specific disability (e.g., an insurance plan that limits coverage of AIDS treatment to $5,000 per year but allows coverage of $100,000 per year for non–AIDS conditions);

- a blanket preexisting condition clause that excludes from coverage conditions that predate the person's eligibility for plan benefits so long as the clause singles out a particular disability (such as AIDS, deafness, or schizophrenia), a discrete group of disabilities (e.g., cancer, kidney disease, or disability generally), or all conditions that substantially limit a major life activity; and
- a plan that excludes coverage of certain preexisting conditions but not others for a specified period (this plan may be disability-based).

Under the EEOC guidelines, the employer bears the burden of proving that it offers a bona fide insurance plan and that its disability-based distinction, if any, is not a subterfuge to avoid the ADA. "Subterfuge" is defined as "disability-based disparate treatment that is not justified by the risks or costs associated with the disability." Whether an employer uses a disability-based distinction as a subterfuge is determined on a case-by-case basis.[141]

Any of the following business/insurance justifications will negate a claim that a disability-based distinction is a subterfuge:

- The distinction is justified by legitimate actuarial data or by past or anticipated experience (applying legitimate classification and underwriting principles).
- The distinction is necessary to ensure that the plan satisfies commonly accepted standards of fiscal soundness and that nondisparate treatment would result in financial insolvency.
- The distinction is necessary to prevent an "unacceptable" change in the coverage or premiums under the plan, including drastic premium increases and drastic changes in the scope of coverage.[142]

Under the public accommodations title of the ADA, it is likely that a continuing-care retirement community would be required to meet similar standards to demonstrate that any disability-based distinctions in either its admission policies or the administration of its health plan are not a subterfuge to avoid the ADA. These determinations would presumably be made on a case-by-case basis, and the facility operator would presumably bear the burden of proof. Because traditional all-inclusive "life-care" communities operate on a self-insurance model, they would not (under guidelines similar to those of the EEOC) be required to demonstrate that the plan was consistent with state law, but only that it was bona fide.

(7) Other Defenses

In addition to the insurance justification expressly described by statute, public accommodations may adopt the following defenses to charges of discrimination under the ADA:

■ The eligibility criteria that screen out disabled persons are necessary to provide the required goods, services, or accommodations.[143]

■ Modification of the facility's policies, practices, or procedures would "fundamentally alter" the nature of the goods, services, or accommodations offered by the facility.[144]

■ Providing the auxiliary aids and services that are not otherwise provided would "fundamentally alter" the nature of the goods, services, or accommodations offered by the facility.[145]

■ Removal of architectural barriers is not readily achievable, and the alternative measures already taken are readily achievable.[146]

■ The disabled person presents a direct threat to the health or safety of others.[147]

■ The facility is not required to provide its residents with personal devices (such as wheelchairs, prescription eyeglasses, or hearing aids) or to alter its inventory to include special goods designed for people with disabilities (such as Braille versions of books or special lines of clothing).[148]

The regulations implementing the ADA state that, in determining whether a disabled individual poses a direct threat to the health or safety of others and thereby can be justifiably excluded from a program, a public accommodation must "make an individualized assessment, based on reasonable judgment that relies on current medical knowledge or on the best available objective evidence, to ascertain: (1) the nature, duration and severity of the risk; (2) the probability that the potential injury will actually occur; and (3) whether reasonable modifications of policies, practices, or procedures will mitigate the risk."[149]

(c) HUD Projects

(1) Statutory and Case Law

Historically, the issue of whether seniors' housing facilities may discriminate in admissions on the basis of handicap arose most prominently in the context of projects that were constructed with the assistance of Section 202 direct loans. Despite the more recent statutory activity (Fair Housing Amendments Act of 1988 and Americans with Disabilities Act), much of the case law is based on older enactments. By statute, four groups are intended to benefit from the Section 202 program: the elderly and three subgroups of the handicapped—the "mobility impaired," the "chronically mentally ill," and the "developmentally disabled."[150] The issue in the courts has been whether a project must serve individuals from all four groups or may restrict its programs to one or some groups.

In a major victory for housing providers, a passage in the Housing and Community Development Act of 1992[151] clarified the beneficiaries issue. Under the act, owners of Section 202, 221(d)(3), and 236 HUD projects originally designed for the elderly may continue to restrict occupancy to elderly tenants under the rules, standards, and agreements that govern such housing at the time of development. Nonetheless, the act prohibits evictions of current nonelderly tenants. Owners of Section 8 elderly projects may give preference to elderly applicants, provided that they reserve units for nonelderly disabled residents based on (1) 10 percent of the total units or (2) the project's number of nonelderly disabled residents as of January 1, 1992, or as of the date of the act's enactment, whichever number is less. Near-elderly disabled persons (ages 50–61) receive preference if there is an insufficient number of nonelderly applicants with disabilities in Section 8 projects to fill the reserved units.[152]

In two early cases on point, developmentally disabled individuals sued unsuccessfully to gain admission to facilities that restricted admissions to the elderly and the mobility-impaired handicapped.[153] The courts found that restricting admission to only two of the four statutory groups did not violate Section 202.[154] For example, in *Brecker v. Queens B'nai B'rith Housing Development,* the court held that Congress precisely drafted Section 202 to permit a sponsor to provide housing for the elderly or the handicapped if the sponsor so wished; a sponsor need not serve all eligible needy groups.[155] The facility, designed for residents capable of independent living, did not offer the substantial range of services that would be required for developmentally disabled residents. Given that the Section 202 program was intended to provide both a housing and a services component, the facility clearly did not meet the needs of the developmentally disabled group. The court found that the Section 202 statute does not require a sponsor to change its program to accommodate all the groups entitled under the statute. Rather, a sponsor may target its project to a particular group.[156] A second basis for recovery sought by plaintiffs was Section 504, discussed in §23.3(d).

In *Secretary of HUD v. United Church Homes, Inc.*, HUD concluded that a facility discriminated against an applicant with cerebral palsy when, upon testing his ability to open the facility's front doors, the facility determined that he could not live independently and thus denied his application for admission. The facility claimed that the applicant never submitted a complete application or demonstrated a willingness to pay to retrofit the doors in accordance with the Fair Housing Amendments Act. In response to the facility's rejection of the applicant, the U.S. Department of Justice filed suit against United Church Homes, alleging violations of the Fair Housing Amendments Act and Section 504 of the Rehabilitation Act. The parties settled the dispute by entering into a consent decree that required United Church Homes to select applicants consistent with the Fair Housing Act and the Rehabilitation Act, begin immediately using new criteria and forms provided by the Department of Justice for tenant selection and occupancy, train employees regarding such criteria and forms, file semiannual reports with the Department of Justice indicating the number of admissions and rejections of applicants (including the reasons for rejections), maintain records of all written applications for the period of the consent decree (two and one-half years), and pay the applicant $40,000 to settle his claims against United Church Homes.[157]

HUD administrative decisions have yielded mixed results depending on the facts.[158] A HUD-assisted facility's denial of housing to a physically disabled applicant was upheld on the basis of ample evidence supporting a finding that the reason for denying the plaintiff's application was a good faith belief that the plaintiff would not be able to pay his rent and that his conduct (as documented by his arrest record), unrelated to any handicap, was likely to be disruptive to other handicapped and elderly residents.[159] In a related issue, the court also noted the lack of any case holding that violent conduct accompanied by use of alcohol, as opposed to alcoholism, constitutes an "impairment" or "handicap."

(2) HUD Regulation

In 1988, HUD adopted final rules governing nondiscrimination based on handicap in federally assisted programs and activities.[160] The rules apply to all applicants for and recipients of HUD assistance in the operation of programs, including the Section 8 program, Section 202, Community Development Block Grants, and public housing.[161] In general, the rules prohibit a program or activity that receives HUD financial assistance from discriminating solely on the basis of handicap in the provision of housing or services.[162] With respect to new construction of a multifamily housing project, a minimum of 5 percent of the total dwelling units, or at least one unit, whichever is greater, must be made accessible for persons with mobility impairments.[163] In addition, 2 percent of the units must be accessible for persons with hearing or vision impairments.[164]

With respect to existing housing programs, the rules are less specific. The general standard is that the program must be operated in such a manner that, when viewed in its entirety, it is readily accessible to and usable by individuals with handicaps.[165] The regulations note that this standard does not mean that each of the existing units must be made accessible to and usable by handicapped persons or that, under threat of undue financial or administrative burdens, the recipient must make fundamental alterations to the nature of the program.[166] Operators of existing housing programs may comply by methods such as reassignment of services to accessible buildings, assignment of aides to beneficiaries, provision of housing or related services at alternative accessible sites, alteration of existing facilities, construction of new facilities, or other methods.[167]

In its analysis of the rules, HUD has noted that a qualified handicapped person must meet the basic eligibility requirements for admission, care, or services normally provided to others in the project. For example, a handicapped person not meeting the age requirement would be ineligible for admission to an elderly housing project.[168] Moreover, a project is not required to provide supportive services such as counseling, medical, or social services that fall outside the scope of its housing program or otherwise to make accommodations that fundamentally change the nature of its program.[169] In addition, nothing in the handicap discrimination provisions requires a dwelling to be made available to an individual "whose tenancy would constitute a direct threat to the health or safety of other individuals or whose tenancy would result in substantial physical damage to the property of others."[170]

In 1993, HUD released a revised Chapter 2 of *HUD Handbook* 4350.3 entitled "Admissions, Eligibility for Assistance, Marketing and Tenant Selection."[171] The revised chapter advises owners to develop a written plan prescribing procedures for accepting applications and screening tenants in compliance with nondiscrimination laws. Selection criteria should focus on ability to pay rent on time and to meet requirements of tenancy, comments from previous property managers (e.g., disruptive behavior or violations of lease or house rules), credit references, housekeeping habits, and other items. Physical examinations, questions about handicap status (except for units designed for persons with handicaps), and mandatory services or meal requirements are all prohibited screening criteria. Interestingly, the rules note that all applicants can be asked to furnish evidence of their ability to meet the requirements of tenancy (which, presumably, may be affected by the applicant's handicap) but state that a handicapped person may meet the requirement with the assistance of others, such as personal attendants.

(3) Housing Occupancy Task Force Report

In 1994, the congressionally authorized Public and Assisted Housing Occupancy Task Force published a several-hundred-page report that reviews and makes recommendations with respect to existing standards, regulations, and guidelines governing occupancy and tenant selection policies in federally assisted housing. The report emphasizes compliance with civil rights laws and discusses the following subjects in detail: developing procedures for preselection

inquiry; prohibiting behavior that endangers the health or safety of other residents; assessing the need to provide and providing reasonable accommodation under the Fair Housing Amendments Act and Section 504 of the Rehabilitation Act of 1973; and proposing criteria for occupancy and compliance standards consistent with the reasonable accommodation requirements.[172]

Although the task force's findings are not legally binding and apply only to HUD projects, they suggest an approach to the disability discrimination laws that might be adopted by HUD, which is the agency charged with enforcing both the Fair Housing Act and Section 504. The report is therefore useful not only for operators of HUD housing but also for all providers affected by the Fair Housing Act, Section 504, or even the ADA, which relies on many of the same definitions as the Fair Housing Act and Section 504.

The task force report recites the following "eleven principles" governing admission to federally assisted housing and recommends that HUD issue guidelines incorporating these principles:

- Each individual must be judged on his or her merits without presumption of abilities based on race, color, disability, etc., recognizing that specific program requirements may limit participation by certain groups.
- When the initial application for housing is made, the provider may confirm the existence of an applicant's disability if the disability makes the applicant eligible for special housing or a special rent computation.
- Providers should require all residents to meet "performance-based" standards for occupancy of an assisted unit, as stated in the tenant obligations section of the lease.
- Providers must employ "performance and behavior" admission requirements defined by the lease, not by the resident's presumed needs or by other residents' biases. Providers may not consider an applicant's "ability to live independently."
- Screening methods should be designed to determine the likelihood that an applicant can meet the "essential requirements of tenancy" described in the lease, including the ability to pay rent and other charges under the lease in a timely manner;

care for and avoid damaging the unit and common areas, use the facilities and equipment in a reasonable way, avoid creating health or safety hazards, and report maintenance needs; avoid interference with the peaceful enjoyment of others or damage to their property; avoid engaging in criminal activity that threatens the health, safety, or peaceful enjoyment of other residents or staff and avoid engaging in drug-related criminal activity on or near the premises; and comply with all necessary and reasonable rules and program requirements of HUD and the housing provider and comply with health and safety codes.

■ The initial evaluation of an applicant must be "disability neutral" and must not seek any information beyond the minimum required to discern eligibility for special programs. The evaluation cannot be based on disability-related presumptions about the applicant's ability to meet the essential obligations of the lease.

■ If a disabled applicant cannot satisfy the requirements of tenancy because of a previous rental history, the provider must, if so requested by the applicant, consider whether any mitigating circumstances related to the disability could be verified to explain and/or overcome the problematic behavior. The provider must also make a reasonable accommodation that would allow the applicant to meet the requirements.

■ Reasonable accommodations permit a disabled applicant to meet the essential requirements of tenancy; however, they do not require reducing or waiving essential requirements. Providers and applicants must work together to identify specific accommodations that each accepts as reasonable.

■ Accommodations are not reasonable if they require fundamental alterations to the nature of the program or impose undue financial or administrative burdens on the housing provider. Likewise, providers need not make specific accommodations or physical modifications if equally effective alternatives permit full program participation.

■ If a disabled applicant who would otherwise be rejected in accordance with objective screening criteria claims that mitigating circumstances would overcome negative information obtained in screening, the provider cannot dismiss the claim but may require the applicant to verify the mitigating circumstances. If the applicant's claim of mitigating circumstances is disability-based, the provider may make inquiries about the claim, but only to the extent necessary to confirm the claim.

■ If a disabled applicant who would otherwise be rejected in accordance with objective screening criteria states that he or she could meet the requirements of tenancy with assistance that the provider is not obligated to offer, the provider may require verification that the assistance will be provided and accepted and that it will allow the applicant to comply with the lessee's essential requirements. If the assistance to be provided includes treatment, verification may include inquiries only to the degree necessary to confirm the applicant's claims regarding the disability. Lease addenda or conditional leases are not permitted; however, a resident who fails to comply with the lease is subject to enforcement of the lease, including eviction.[173]

The remainder of the task force report clarifies and provides examples of the 11 principles. It also includes guidance on a myriad of subjects, including the following:

(A) Agreeing on Reasonable Accommodation. Reasonable accommodation must be both effective (that is, allow the applicant to satisfy the requirements of tenancy) and reasonable (that is, not impose an undue burden on the provider or constitute a fundamental alteration to the requirements of tenancy). The task force suggests the following methodology to reach agreement regarding reasonable accommodation:

■ When two or more accommodations are effective from the viewpoint of the disabled person and reasonable from the viewpoint of the provider, the provider may select from among the effective accommodations.

■ Generally, the provider is in the best position to determine whether a suggested accommodation poses undue burdens or constitutes a fundamental alteration to the program.

■ Generally, the disabled person is in the best position to determine whether a suggested accommodation is effective.

■ If the provider proposes an accommodation that the applicant maintains is ineffective and is unwilling to make the accommodation that the applicant prefers, the provider should make clear that its offer remains open. If the applicant accepts the offer of accommodation but maintains that he or she needs more, the provider should not refuse to provide the accommodation. Likewise, the applicant's acceptance of the accommodation should not be deemed a waiver of his or her right to secure the preferred accommodation.

■ If the provider and the applicant cannot reach agreement, the provider might ask the applicant to propose a third-party expert to help them do so.[174]

(B) Fundamental Alterations in the Program. An accommodation is not reasonable if it would result in a fundamental alteration to the nature of the provider's program. The task force report offers the following examples of accommodations that might result in such fundamental alteration:

■ those that require substantial modifications to or elimination of essential lease provisions or program eligibility requirements based on obligations of tenancy;

■ those that require the provider to add supportive services (e.g., counseling, medical or social services) that fall outside the scope of existing services offered by the provider to residents;

■ those that require the provider to offer housing or benefits of a fundamentally different nature from the type of housing or benefits provided; and/or

■ those that substantially impair the provider's ability to meet its obligations as a landlord, as defined in the lease.[175]

(C) Assessing Undue Burdens. The report also lists factors to consider when assessing whether an accommodation imposes undue burdens on the provider. These factors vary somewhat, depending on whether the housing is assisted or public. They include size of the program or property budget; availability of employees at the property; availability of surplus cash; access to replacement reserves; availability of sources of capital other than income generated by the property; feasibility of a rent increase; and the property's ability to meet govern-

ment and private lender requirements, to complete planned improvements or repairs, and to maintain full occupancy.[176]

Whether or not they provide public or assisted housing, providers of seniors' housing may wish to refer to these guidelines in drafting and implementing their own disability compliance programs. The report's suggestions for agreeing on reasonable accommodations and its examples of undue burdens and fundamental alterations to the program might prove particularly useful.

(d) Section 504

(1) Applicability

To the extent that facilities pass the stringent criteria for dwellings, public accommodations, and HUD projects as discussed above, another, older law prohibits discrimination on the basis of handicap— Section 504 of the Rehabilitation Act of 1973.[177] This law applies only to projects that receive "federal financial assistance." Nonetheless, facilities constructed solely with private monies may be subject to Section 504 if they participate in one or more federal programs. Although the issue has not been finally resolved, some courts have found that receipt of Medicare and Medicaid funds makes a facility a recipient of federal assistance within the meaning of the Rehabilitation Act and subjects it to the requirements of Section 504.[178]

(2) Prohibited Discrimination

Section 504 provides that no "otherwise qualified" handicapped individual shall be excluded from participation in, or denied the benefits of, any program that receives federal financial assistance.[179]

The plaintiffs in both HUD Section 202 discrimination cases discussed in §23.3(c) argued that the facilities' actions violated Section 504 of the Rehabilitation Act. The key to the *Brecker* court's analysis of the claim was whether the handicapped individuals were "otherwise qualified" for the facility. The Supreme Court has defined an otherwise qualified individual as "one who is able to meet all of a program's requirements in spite of his handicap."[180] The Court has also held that Section 202 facilities may restrict admissions to the elderly and the mobility impaired. Since the developmentally disabled patients were neither elderly nor mobility impaired, they did not meet the program's requirements and were therefore not otherwise qualified.[181]

In *Wagner v. Fair Acres Geriatric Center*,[182] however, a county-operated intermediate-care nursing facility was found to have violated Section 504 by denying admission to a combative, assaultive woman who was afflicted with Alzheimer's disease. The court rejected the facility's claim that the resident was not "otherwise qualified" because of her psychotic symptoms manifested by periods of uncontrolled agitation. In nursing homes, the court reasoned, all applicants seek admission because they are "handicapped" in some manner that requires continuous nursing care. Accordingly, a prospective resident's "challenging and demanding behavior" would not justify exclusion from a nursing home that received federal funds. The court held that the defendant's reasoning would permit nursing homes to be "free to 'pick and choose' among patients, accepting and admitting only the easiest patients to care for, leaving the more challenging and demanding patients with no place to turn for care."[183]

The *Wagner* court also held that a decision as to whether a person was otherwise qualified for admission was not a "medical treatment decision" immune from scrutiny under Section 504 but rather was an "administrative decision." Although several witnesses for the facility had offered testimony that the facility could not adequately care for the Alzheimer's patient, the appeals court deferred to the jury's decision that the nursing facility failed to offer any factual basis to demonstrate that admitting the patient would have changed the essential nature of the facility or imposed on it an undue burden—financial or otherwise. In the absence of such facts, the court held that there was no basis to defer to the judgment of the facility administrators. Therefore, the court held that the jury could have determined that the plaintiff should have been admitted because the nursing facility could care for her if it made reasonable accommodations.[184] In *Roe v. Housing Authority*,[185] a court similarly held that a housing authority had a duty to extend reasonable accommodations to a manic depressive, hearing-impaired tenant who had physically attacked or verbally threatened others at the facility.

Courts reviewing no-wheelchair policies have generally not been sympathetic to facilities enforcing such policies. For example, in *Weinstein v. Cherry Oaks Retirement Community*,[186] a Colorado court upheld a finding that a residential care facility violated the state's fair housing law when it required residents who used wheelchairs to transfer to ordinary chairs when they ate in the facility's common dining room. When a disabled resident complained about the facility's policy, the facility responded that wheelchairs "did not look good in the dining room," that allowing wheelchairs in the dining room violated the city's fire code, that regulations required the policy, and that allowing one wheelchair would lead to other requests for the same treatment. The court affirmed the administrative agency's finding that these reasons were a pretext for maintaining a "disability-free" atmosphere.

Likewise, in *Morgan v. Retirement Unlimited, Inc.*,[187] a jury awarded an injured plaintiff $500,000 after he fell while attempting to enter the dining room with his walker. Apparently, the retirement center required wheelchair users to leave their chairs outside the common dining room before entering the room. The court vacated the award for evidentiary reasons and the plaintiff is appealing the decision.

These cases suggest that the courts are apparently unwilling to condone dining room restrictions based purely on "aesthetic" objections to wheelchairs, although they may uphold policies based on care considerations or avoidance of disruption (see subsection (3) below).

Courts might also challenge facilities' occupancy policies if the policies have a discriminatory effect on disabled residents. For example, in *Lloyd v. Housing Authority*,[188] a court denied summary judgment to a housing authority that refused to permit a disabled resident to occupy a double-sized apartment to help accommodate her disability (by permitting her to have a live-in aide).

Furthermore, seniors' facilities that enforce no-pet policies may have to make two important accommodations when those pets are service animals trained to provide assistance to persons with disabilities. First, under the ADA, any no-pets policy must be modified to allow the use of service animals by disabled persons. In addition to assisting blind or visually impaired persons, service animals might alert hearing-impaired persons to sounds, pull wheelchairs, carry or pick up items for mobility-impaired persons, or assist mobility-impaired persons with balance. Second, even if deposits are routinely required for pets, neither a deposit nor a surcharge may be imposed on an individual with a disability as a condition of allowing a service animal to accompany the individual with the disability. However, this policy does not preclude a public accommodation from charging disabled customers for damage caused by their service animals, provided that the facility's regular practice is to charge nondisabled customers for the same types of damage (e.g., damage to furniture or carpeting).[189]

(3) Permitted Discrimination

Case law has recognized that Section 504 is not an affirmative action program for the handicapped and does not require a program sponsor to modify the essential purpose of its program or undergo financial burdens to accommodate all handicapped persons.[190] For example, in *Grubbs v. Medical Facilities of America, Inc.,*[191] nursing facilities were not required by Section 504 of the Rehabilitation Act to admit the plaintiff, a grossly overweight individual who suffered from multiple sclerosis and required subacute care. Because neither facility in question was licensed to provide subacute care, the federal court agreed that the plaintiff was not "otherwise qualified" for admission. Similarly, in *Alexander v. Pathfinder, Inc.,*[192] a district court concluded that an intermediate-care facility had properly discharged a mentally retarded man whose complex medical problems required a level of care that the facility simply was not equipped to provide.

In *Appenfelder v. Dupree St. Luke,*[193] a nursing facility was granted summary judgment upholding its policy of requiring an Alzheimer's resident who needed spoon-feeding to eat in the "dependent" dining room rather than in the main dining room. The court held that the plaintiff was not "otherwise qualified" to eat in the main dining room and that, due to the disruption involved with spoon-feeding, accommodating the patient in the "dependent" dining room was not unreasonable.

The U.S. Supreme Court has ruled that the Rehabilitation Act does not require a state to provide greater medical coverage to handicapped persons than to nonhandicapped persons, even if handicapped persons' needs may be greater.[194] Therefore, one key in analyzing if a policy that places restrictions on handicapped persons violates Section 504 is whether the individual's handicap is sufficiently program-related such that it would prevent the individual from adequately participating in a facility's program or interfere with achievement of the program's goals. Thus, for example, a facility with an included health care program whose admission criteria are based on health status may be justified in excluding an applicant requiring kidney dialysis if that treatment cannot be offered at the facility, but the same facility may not be justified in excluding a blind applicant if the handicap does not preclude participation in the program.

(4) Covered Disabilities

Regulations adopted pursuant to Section 504 of the Rehabilitation Act of 1973[195] prohibit the exclusion from participation, denial of benefits, or other discrimination against a qualified handicapped person in any activity receiving benefits from federal financial assistance.[196] A "qualified handicapped person" is one who meets the essential eligibility requirements for receipt of a program's services.[197] Regulations include in the definition of covered physical impairments hemic and lymphatic conditions that substantially limit major life activities, such as self-care, working, and breathing, and conditions in which the attitudes of others toward the conditions result in substantial limitations on major life activities.[198] For example, a person with contagious tuberculosis was deemed a handicapped person within the meaning of the act in a U.S. Supreme Court decision.[199]

In 1988, the U.S. Department of Justice defined "individuals with handicaps" to include persons with AIDS or AIDS-related complex (ARC) or persons who test seropositive.[200] The federal courts have also found that AIDS is covered by the act.[201] In *Glanz v. Vernick,*[202] a hospital was found liable under Section 504 for its physician's failure to perform surgery on an HIV-positive patient when reasonable accommodations could have been made to reduce the risk of infection. Similarly, a hospital and a physician engaged by the hospital were both held liable for discrimination under the Rehabilitation Act for the physician's refusal to admit a patient infected with HIV.[203] In contrast, in *Miller v. Spicer,*[204] a federal court found that a hospital could not be held liable for a physician's discriminatory treatment of a patient suspected to have HIV because the physician was an independent contractor.

In one decision, HUD found that a landlord did not violate the Fair Housing Act when it inquired about a tenant's HIV status.[205] In that case, the tenant was a known drug addict, the landlord used children to help clean the apartment, and evidence suggested a relatively low risk of transmission in the event a person was cut or punctured by a razor or needle hidden in the garbage. The administrative law judge noted that, although the probability of infection was low, the potential harm (death) and existence of an environment in which universal precautions were not normally practiced could make such an inquiry legitimate.

In *Kohl v. Woodhaven Learning Center,*[206] a vocational facility for the handicapped denied admission to an active carrier of hepatitis B who exhibited behavioral problems such as scratching and biting. The circuit court disagreed with the trial court's opinion that the cost of inoculating direct-contact staff did not constitute an unreasonable burden on the defendant facility, finding that the proposed inoculation plan would expose the staff to unreasonable risk.

Concern about the transmission of AIDS has led the federal Centers for Disease Control and Prevention (CDC) to develop "universal precautions" to prevent transmission of HIV or hepatitis B virus (HBV) from patients to health care workers and vice versa.[207] In addition, the U.S. Department of Labor's Occupational Safety and Health Administration (OSHA) has established regulations regarding precautions to be taken in the workplace with respect to bloodborne pathogens.[208]

A retirement facility that adheres to such standards in its health facilities and that bases employment and admissions decisions on its ability to satisfy the guidelines established by the CDC and OSHA can make a compelling argument that it has not discriminated unfairly on the basis of HIV or HBV status under the Rehabilitation Act. In fact, courts have relied on the CDC's universal precautions in setting a standard for reasonableness with respect to hiring decisions based on HIV status.[209]

Although AIDS is a disease that does not strike members of the elderly population as frequently as other age groups, it is nonetheless an issue of great concern in skilled-nursing facilities. Retirement communities with nursing facilities may find themselves the object of investigations by the U.S. Department of Health and Human Services, the Office of Civil Rights, or other groups seeking to amend written admissions policies to preclude discrimination against AIDS patients. Usually, age criteria cannot be used to screen residents in nursing facilities (see §23.2).

HUD has issued rules for the enforcement of Section 504 in programs or activities it conducts. The rules establish standards for what constitutes discrimination on the basis of disability, provide definitions of "individuals with disabilities" and "qualified individuals with disabilities," establish a complaint procedure for resolving allegations of discrimination, and incorporate additional changes to reflect implementation of the ADA.[210]

Important features of the rules include the following:

- HUD follows the Uniform Federal Accessibility Standards, except where the accessibility standards issued under the public accommodations title of the ADA require greater accessibility.
- The definition of "physical and mental impairment" has been revised to include HIV disease (symptomatic or asymptomatic).
- The term "individual with disabilities" does not include individuals currently engaging in the illegal use of drugs; however, this exclusion does not cover individuals who are erroneously regarded as engaging in such use or are no longer engaging in such use as a result of rehabilitation.
- In determining whether an individual presents a direct threat to the health or safety of others, the agency must make an individualized assessment, based on a reasonable judgment that relies on current medical knowledge or the best available objective evidence, to determine the nature, duration, and severity of the risk; the probability that the potential injury will actually occur; and whether reasonable modifications of policies, practices, or procedures will mitigate the risk. This standard codifies federal case law.[211]

(e) Due Process Issues

Occasionally, plaintiffs have sought placement or treatment on the ground that they have a constitutionally protected property interest in receiving a government benefit. In *Overton v. John Knox Tower, Inc.,*[212] the court rejected the claim of an 88-year-old woman that her Fifth Amendment due process rights had been violated when she was denied admission to a Section 202 housing project. The project's admissions committee had denied admission on the basis of evidence raising doubts about the woman's ability to live outside a nursing home. The court found that the plaintiff did not have a protected property interest or entitlement, that there was no government action, and that rejection of her application was not arbitrary because she could not show that the project had admitted someone who was incapable of living independently. In *Dempsey v. Ladd,*[213] the court held that a handicapped person in need of treatment may not avoid state-mandated criteria for placement and seek compensation from the state for treatment in the facility of his or her choice.

(f) State and Local Laws

State or local laws may provide a higher standard than that embodied in federal law. For example, in *Henson v. Department of Consumer and Regulatory Affairs,*[214] the District of Columbia Court of Appeals found that a decision to transfer a resident of a community residential facility to an intermediate-care facility was not supported by evidence sufficient to meet the "clear and convincing evidence" standard mandated by the District of Columbia code.

§23.4 Religion

The Fair Housing chapter of the Civil Rights Act of 1968 is a comprehensive statute that makes unlawful any discrimination in the sale or rental of dwellings on the basis of religion.[215] Unlike the Age Discrimination Act and the Section 504 disability discrimination provisions, the Fair Housing Act applies whether or not a particular housing facility has received federal financial assistance. Religious organizations may, however, limit sales, rentals, or occupancies of property that they operate for a noncommercial purpose to persons of the same religion unless membership in the religion is restricted on the basis of race, color, or national origin.[216]

In *United States v. Hughes Memorial Home,*[217] the federal district court outlined the following elements of this "carefully limited exception for certain religious organizations:"

- The exception is limited to religious organizations.
- Given that the exemption applies to mere occupancy, the act covers occupancies as well as the sale or rental of dwellings.
- The dwellings must be owned and operated for other than a commercial purpose.
- For the exemption to apply, the religion must not discriminate in membership on the basis of race, color, or national origin.[218]

Hughes involved an allegation that a children's home had violated the Fair Housing Act by making dwellings unavailable to black children. The court found that the exemption did not apply because the home was not a religious organization.

In *Bachman v. St. Monica's Congregation,*[219] however, the Seventh Circuit Court of Appeals determined that a Catholic parish did not violate the Fair Housing Act prohibition of discrimination on the basis of religion when it gave preference to Catholic buyers in the sale of its residential property. The court relied on the exception for religious organizations, which permits preferential treatment of individuals of the same religion in the sale of noncommercial property. The court also found that the fact that the plaintiffs were Jewish did not transform their claim into one of racial discrimination.

In *United States v. Columbus Country Club,*[220] the Third Circuit reversed the summary judgment of the district court that a private country club could restrict the availability of summer cottages to Roman Catholic club members under the Fair Housing Act exemptions applicable to religious organizations and private clubs. The circuit court rejected the club's contention that the cottages were not "dwellings" because they could not be occupied year-round. It also found that the club's affiliation with the Catholic

Church was not sufficient to conclude that the club operated "in conjunction with" the church. Finally, the club's seasonal rental of cottages was not found adequate to meet the provision of "lodgings" language contained in the private club exemption, which implies a more transient occupancy.

The courts have also held that giving preference to certain religious groups in federally assisted housing violates the due process, equal protection, and establishment of religion clauses of the U.S. Constitution. In *Otero v. New York Housing Authority*,[221] the housing authority had given preference to Jewish families in a low-income housing project because the project was conveniently located near an old and historic synagogue. The court found that the housing authority's intention to preserve cultural and other values through preferential treatment could not overcome the constitutional prohibition against government action in aid of religion.[222]

Another relevant federal statute that prohibits religious discrimination is the Hill-Burton Act, a law that provides funding for construction and modernization of hospitals, long-term-care facilities, and other medical facilities.[223] Under the act, an applicant must assure the state agency that facilities built or modernized with Hill-Burton funds will be made available without discrimination on the basis of "creed."[224] The facility must also assure the state that, with respect to professional practice privileges at the facility, it will not discriminate against professionally qualified persons on the basis of creed.[225]

HUD has investigated the advertising practices of religious-sponsored nursing homes and housing facilities. The agency claimed that references to religious names and symbols in the print media may discourage persons of other faiths from applying for admission to a facility, even when the provider states that all faiths are welcome. HUD also voiced concern that the use of religious symbols and names by homes for the aging may foster racial discrimination.[226] As a result, HUD has told facilities using religious names or symbols to include a statement that persons of all faiths are welcome. It is important to note, however, that, in certain circumstances, religious facilities may discriminate on the basis of religion.[227]

§23.5 Income Discrimination

(a) Fair Housing Laws

Landlords generally have been allowed to discriminate on the basis of wealth in determining an applicant's suitability for admission. In *Boyd v. Lefrak*,[228] a federal circuit court held that a 90 percent of rent income requirement imposed by a private landlord against prospective tenants did not violate the Fair Housing Act of 1968 or Title 42, Section 1982 of the U.S. Code, even though such a requirement may have a disparate impact on minority groups.

In *Harris v. Capital Growth Investors XIV*,[229] a state court of appeal determined that plaintiffs had a cause of action under the state's civil rights act when a landlord required prospective tenants to have gross monthly incomes at least three times the amount of their rent. However, the state's supreme court reversed, finding that landlords had a legitimate interest in minimizing defaults and could apply neutral economic criteria (without regard to race, sex, religion, etc.) to applicants. The court rejected the disparate-impact-on-women theory advanced by the two female plaintiffs and found it permissible to judge groups of applicants collectively rather than individually with respect to their ability to make rental payments.

Nonetheless, a New Jersey court ruled that a landlord with subsidized tenants could not refuse to allow other tenants to benefit from federal housing assistance. The court held that although the apartment complex had no duty to participate in the Section 8 program, it was compelled to enter into a contract for housing assistance payments with the plaintiff because it had done so with other tenants. The court found that the apartment owner breached an implied covenant of good faith to its tenants by not permitting the tenant to obtain needed federal assistance.[230]

(b) Medicaid

(1) Prohibiting or Limiting Admissions

Discrimination on the basis of wealth has created more difficult legal problems for health facilities than for providers of housing. When originally adopted, the Medicaid program was designed to guarantee patients the free choice of a health services provider ". . . who undertakes to provide him such services."[231] State Medicaid plans are required to establish reimbursement systems that attract a sufficient number of health care providers to the program.[232] Although it appears that the original legislation was designed to make provider participation voluntary, some states have attempted to require facilities enrolled in the program, particularly nursing homes, to admit all Medicaid patients who apply, or at least a sufficient number of Medicaid patients to match the percentage of such patients in the general population.[233] For example, one state has enacted a "first-come, first-served" law that prohibits discrimination based on payor source against indigent persons who apply for admission to nursing homes.[234] Other states require new applicants seeking nursing home approval to agree to admit a "reasonable percentage" of Medicaid patients.[235]

In *Linton v. Commissioner,*[236] a federal court held that regulations allowing skilled-nursing facilities to "spot" certify beds for Medicaid participation violated Title VI by disparately affecting minority Medicaid recipients, who were disproportionately poor. Subsequently, the district court outlined a remedial plan designed to eliminate the discriminatory impact of the contested regulations. The plan, upheld by the Sixth Circuit on appeal,[237] required Medicaid providers to certify all available, licensed nursing home beds within the facility and to admit residents on a first-come, first-served basis. Moreover, the state was required to prohibit involuntary transfers or discharges based on a resident's payment source and to adopt procedures for provider withdrawal from the program. In addition, the court upheld a provision requiring facilities to retain Medicaid patients after a facility withdrew from the Medicaid program in order to prevent involuntary transfers of Medicaid patients.

Similarly, the New Jersey Supreme Court, in *Matter of Healthcare Administration Board,*[238] held that a state could impose a Medicaid quota on a health care facility as a requirement of state licensure law. In Minnesota, despite constitutional objections, the state was able to eliminate discrimination between Medicaid and private-pay patients by requiring providers to lower the rate levied on private-pay patients to the Medicaid rate paid by the state ("rate equalization").[239] In New York, courts had held that a quota requirement for Medicaid patients could not be enforced unless the state agreed to reimburse facilities for Medicaid patients at the same rate the facility charged other patients.[240] More recently, however, a New York court upheld a license requirement that new nursing homes must admit 75 percent of the rate of Medicaid admissions in the county.[241]

(2) Payment Guarantees; Contributions

Outright denial of admission is not the only area of concern. Long-term-care facilities should exercise extreme caution in not linking the admission or continued stay of a Medicaid resident to a contribution, payment, or guarantee of payment beyond the rate paid by Medicaid.[242] The Social Security Act fraud and abuse provisions prohibit any facility that provides services under the Medicaid program from requiring, as a condition of a Medicaid-eligible patient's admission or continued stay in the facility, any payment for covered services that is supplemental to that paid by the Medicaid program. Violation of this requirement is a federal felony that carries with it substantial criminal sanctions of fines and imprisonment. Section 1909(d) of the Social Security Act[243] provides:

> (d) Whoever knowingly and willfully—
> (1) charges, for any services provided to a patient under a state plan approved under this subchapter, money or other consideration at a rate in excess of the rates established by the state, or
> (2) charges, solicits, accepts, or receives, in addition to any amount otherwise required to be paid under a state plan approved under this subchapter, any gift, money, donation, or other consideration (other than a charitable, religious or philanthropic contribution from an organization or from a person unrelated to the patient) (A) as a precondition of admitting a patient to a hospital, skilled nursing facility, or intermediate care facility, or (B) as a requirement for the patient's continued stay in such a facility, when the cost of the services provided therein to the patient is paid for (in whole or in part) under the state plan, shall be guilty of a felony and upon conviction thereof shall be fined not more than $25,000 or imprisoned for not more than five years, or both.

An obvious violation would occur when a facility approaches the relative of a patient who is receiving assistance for nursing services under the Medicaid program and requires that relative, under threat that the facility will otherwise discharge the patient, to pay the difference between the Medicaid rate and the facility's usual charges for care. The Social Security Act obligates the facility to accept the Medicaid payment as payment in full for the nursing services.

While a facility operator can easily avoid this obvious type of abuse, a more subtle problem historically arose under the statute. That is, if a person seeking admission into a care facility was not yet eligible for the Medicaid program but was likely in the next several years to deplete almost all of his or her assets, the facility operator might approach a son or daughter and obtain that person's agreement to pay the resident's charges for the duration of her stay at the facility (a private-pay agreement). At the time such an agreement was executed, it probably did not violate at least the letter of the Social Security Act because the resident was not yet eligible for the Medicaid program. When, however, the elderly resident did run out of funds several years later and sought a determination of eligibility under the Medicaid program, it was possible that the relative's agreement would not be considered an asset of the resident such that the resident would be eligible to enroll in the Medicaid program. At that point, if the facility sought to enforce the private-pay agreement as a condition of the resident's continued stay at the facility, that conduct could well constitute a felony violation of the fraud and abuse statute.

For many years, there was a question as to whether the facility could lawfully seek to enforce the agreement against the resident's relative without threatening eviction of the Medicaid enrollee residing at the facility. Technically, while such a practice may be permissible under a literal interpretation of the fraud and abuse statute, it was fraught with danger in light of the cases discussed below, the possible ramifications of state law, and the potential for severe penalties.

Several opinions have held that nursing facilities cannot require patients seeking admission, or their relatives, to enter into private-pay agreements as a condition of admission, even though the applicant is not yet eligible for Medicaid benefits and may or may not have been threatened with discharge. In *Glengariff Corporation v. Snook*,[244] a nursing home

that required the son of an applicant for admission to sign a contract guaranteeing payment of the full private room rate for a specified period of years was found to have violated congressional intent underlying the fraud and abuse amendments to the Social Security Act. In that case, the patient was able to apply for and be determined eligible for Medicaid even though the son had signed the private-pay agreement. The court determined that as soon as the patient became eligible for Medicaid, the private-pay agreement became unenforceable under the terms of the fraud and abuse amendments. Other states have reached similar conclusions.[245]

In 1991, commentary appearing in the *Federal Register* made it clear that 1989 federal regulations implementing the 1987 OBRA provisions for nursing facilities that participate in the Medicare or Medicaid programs prohibit a facility from requiring a third-party guarantee from any patient, including private-pay patients.[246] More specifically, private-pay agreements with relatives become unenforceable when the patient becomes Medicaid-eligible. Now that the federal government has prohibited all guarantee agreements, only non–Medicare or Medicaid-certified facilities in states without a state law prohibition have any realistic hope of receiving a payment guarantee from a third party. The former strategy of entering into agreements with relatives for payment of charges and having the agreements automatically terminate should the patient become eligible for Medicaid is no longer permissible. Interestingly, however, federal law does not prohibit a third party from voluntarily making a payment on behalf of a resident or a third-party payor such as an insurance company or continuing-care facility from making payments.[247]

Another strategy for facilities seeking to ensure that a resident will be able to pay the full charges for the duration of his or her stay is to attempt to prevent the elderly resident from becoming impoverished and thus eligible for the Medicaid program. One way to implement this strategy is to have a relative with sufficient finances give money to the applicant for residence, place the funds in trust, or purchase an annuity so that the elderly applicant will have legal or beneficial title to the funds. The resident's own funds also may be placed in trust to prevent their depletion or waste. At least one state prohibits requiring, as a condition of admission of a

Medicaid-eligible patient, a financially responsible cosigner or payment of a security deposit, but the statute does not apply, on its face, to such practices before the patient becomes eligible.[248]

Regulations governing Medicaid-certified facilities also prohibit the solicitation or acceptance of contributions as a precondition of admission, expedited admission, or continued stay in the facility.[249] Tax-exempt facility operators should be especially careful regarding solicitation of contributions from families of applicants for admission to facilities. In at least one instance, a nursing home solicited undercover "mother and son" investigators for a "contribution" as a condition of admission. The federal government prosecuted the nursing home for both Medicaid fraud and an attempt to defraud the IRS regarding the tax deductibility of the payment. (See §9.13 regarding deductibility of contributions to retirement facilities.) The law does, however, permit donations from or on behalf of residents receiving federal benefits if not tied to preferential treatment as well as donations for other residents for any reason.[250]

Given both the variation in state Medicaid eligibility criteria and nursing home licensure standards and the complexity and severity of federal provisions, a provider should consult counsel to determine, first, what lawful methods can help prevent the elderly applicant for facility admission from running out of funds and becoming dependent on the Medicaid program and, second, what types of fundraising activities can be continued without jeopardy.

§23.6 Race, Color, National Origin, Sex, and Marital Status

Title VI of the federal Civil Rights Acts[251] prohibits federally assisted programs, such as those participating in Medicare or Medicaid, from discriminating on the basis of race, color, or national origin. While retirement facilities generally do not discriminate overtly on the basis of race or color, some plaintiffs seeking access for low-income Medicaid patients have used racial discrimination theories as a means to attack Medicaid rates insufficient to pay the costs of care at many of the better-quality nursing facilities. In *Linton v. Tennessee Commissioner of Health and Environment*,[252] the state's policy of permitting distinct-part nursing facilities to decertify Medicaid beds on a "spot" basis was found to violate Title VI because of its disparate impact on minorities as a result of their higher incidence of poverty.

Title II of the Civil Rights Act prohibits discrimination on the basis of race, color, or national origin in places of "public accommodation." Public accommodations are facilities that house people for a "transient" period of time and include hotels, restaurants, theaters, or health clubs. It is unclear whether retirement communities are considered public accommodations, although, as places of long-term residency rather than transitory occupancy, they are distinguishable.[253]

The Fair Housing Act also prohibits discrimination in the sale or rental of dwellings on the basis of race, color, sex, or national origin.[254] As with discrimination on the basis of handicap or religion, the Fair Housing Act applies whether or not a housing facility is the recipient of any federal financial assistance. It also applies to places of permanent or longer-term habitation rather than to short-term accommodations.

In addition, the Hill-Burton Act, a federal law that provides for grants and loans to build or modernize hospitals and other medical facilities, incorporates the provisions of the Civil Rights Act of 1964 that prohibit discrimination on the basis of race, color, or national origin.[255]

Racial discrimination might also be alleged due to bias in advertisements placed by retirement homes. In 1994, a nonprofit advocacy group filed a suit alleging that the owner of a retirement home and the operator of continuing-care retirement communities sent a message of "racial preference" for white purchasers by running advertisements with photographs that included few if any blacks among their models. The organization also named the publishers of the advertisements as defendants in the lawsuits. The plaintiffs sought damages and an order requiring the companies to use blacks in their advertisements in proportion to the black population in the area in which the advertisement was run.[256] The plaintiffs' request was based on the fair housing regulations' creation of a presumption of fair housing compliance for advertisements that portray ethnic groups in the proportions in which they appear in the community.[257] Even though the Fair Housing Advertising Guidelines were removed from the Code of Federal Regulations as part of a streamlining effort,[258] ample case law remains on the subject of advertising that may convey racial or other unlawful preferences in housing and on the part of housing providers. Providers should ensure that photographs in advertising reasonably reflect the racial composition of the surrounding area. In addition, retirement communities should use the "Equal Housing Opportunity" slogan and logo and consider placing advertising in minority-oriented media.[259]

Some facilities may advertise themselves as identified with a particular national origin (e.g., the Swedish or Danish home). While such facilities offer a distinctive lifestyle, they normally do not restrict admission to members of the given national group. Gender bias in admissions exists, if at all, due to the high proportion of women in many facilities. Some facilities, for example, give couples an admissions preference to prevent the resident population from becoming too uniformly female. The case law on such subjects is scant.

If covered at all, matters of marital status and sexual orientation are usually the province of state antidiscrimination laws. For example, California law generally prohibits unreasonable discrimination on the basis of marital status or sexual orientation. Even though one California case recognized a property owner's religious objections as justifiable in discriminating against an unmarried heterosexual couple's purchase of housing, the state supreme court depublished the case.[260] Similarly, in *Smith v. Commission of Fair Employment & Housing,* a California appeals court held that a property owner could, on the basis of religious convictions, refuse to rent an apartment to an unmarried heterosexual couple.[261] The California Supreme Court reversed, holding that the owner's action violated the Fair Employment and Housing Act's prohibition against marital status discrimination. In addition, the court found that the First Amendment's freedom of religion protections did not exempt the landlord from complying with the act's mandate because the landlord's free exercise of religion was not infringed upon by applying a facially neutral statute that merely proscribed marital status discrimination.[262]

Race, color, national origin, sex, and marital status discrimination are issues that affect all housing, but they do not raise the unique questions for retirement communities that come with age, handicap, religion, and income distinctions. As seniors' facilities proliferate, however, these distinctions are increasingly becoming targets for all claims of discrimination.

Notes

1. Attention should also be paid to local antidiscrimination laws, which may involve emerging areas of concern not covered by federal or state provisions (such as sexual preference).

2. 42 U.S.C. §6101–6107; P.L. 94–135.

3. *See* 24 C.F.R. Part 146; 45 C.F.R. Part 91.

4. 24 C.F.R. §146.7; 45 C.F.R. §91.4.

5. *See* discussion in §23.3(d).

6. 42 U.S.C. §6103(b)(2).

7. 24 C.F.R. §146.13(e); 45 C.F.R. §91.3(b).

8. 51 *Fed. Reg.* 45,270.

9. 42 U.S.C. §6103(b)(1).

10. 24 C.F.R. §146.13(e); 45 C.F.R. §91.12(a).

11. 24 C.F.R. §146.13(e); 45 C.F.R. §91.12(b).

12. 24 C.F.R. §146.13(b); 45 C.F.R. §91.13.

13. 24 C.F.R. §146.13(d); 45 C.F.R. §91.15.

14. 51 *Fed. Reg.* 45,261–45,262.

15. Note that since the adoption of the Fair Housing Amendments Act of 1988, the ability to live independently was deemed by one court to be an impermissible criterion for admission to housing. *See* §23.3(a).

16. An interesting question existed with regard to the application of the Age Discrimination Act to the now-terminated Sections 221(d)(4) and 223(f) Retirement Service Center programs; *see* §22.2. The HUD guidelines for the program indicated that ReSCs were intended to serve the frail elderly of age 70 or over (Notice H83–58 at 3). This age restriction, however, was not contained in any statutory language, as the ReSC program was initiated by HUD on the basis of the general Section 221(d)(4) and 223(f) statutes and regulations. Nor did the age limitation appear to meet the four-part test for "necessary to the normal operation of a program," as there are many elderly under the age of 70 who are frail and in need of the services offered by ReSCs.

17. 42 U.S.C. §6103(b)(1)(B).

18. 24 C.F.R. §146.13(c) (HUD); 45 C.F.R. §91.14 (HHS).

19. For example, in *EEOC v. City of Mt. Lebanon,* 842 F.2d 1480 (3d Cir. 1988), a federal appellate court held that

a city's long-term disability plan did not discriminate on the basis of age when it continued paying salaries to disabled employees who became disabled after age 60 and used a payment schedule that decreased the duration of disability payments as the age of the onset of disability increased. The court conditioned its finding on the employer's ability to prove that the reduced benefits payable to older disabled persons were approximately equal in cost to the unreduced benefits payable to younger employees. The court elaborated that an employer may not reduce an older employee's benefits by 75 percent if it spends only 50 percent more to provide the same benefits to older workers as it provides to younger workers.

20. 24 C.F.R. §146.13(f) (HUD); 45 C.F.R. §91.17 (HHS).

21. *Ibid.*

22. "Admissions, Eligibility for Assistance, Marketing and Tenant Selection," *HUD Handbook* 4350.3, Ch. 2 (1993 ed.). *See also* McNickle, L., "Mixed Populations: A Threat to All Age-Distinct Elderly Housing," *Retirement Housing Business Report,* Oct. 1992.

23. 59 *Fed. Reg.* 17,652, Apr. 13, 1994.

24. 42 U.S.C. §§13601 *et seq.*

25. "Regulations Issued to Implement Elderly Preference Provisions," *Housing and Development Reporter Current Developments,* May 9, 1994, 831–832.

26. *Id.*

27. *Id.*

28. "HUD Rules Allow for Elderly-Only Housing," *Older Americans Report,* Apr. 22, 1994, 133–134. *See also* 59 *Fed. Reg.* 17,652, Apr. 13, 1994.

29. 42 U.S.C. §3604.

30. For example, in *United States v. Badgett,* 976 F.2d 1176 (8th Cir.), *reh'g. denied* (8th Cir. 1992), a federal court held that a policy of limiting occupancy of one-bedroom apartments to one person was discriminatory on the basis of familial status. Likewise, in *Jancik v. HUD,* 44 F.3d 553 (7th Cir. 1995), a federal court held that a landlord's advertisement for tenants that included the phrase "mature person preferred" manifested a preference based on familial status and violated the Fair Housing Act.

31. 42 U.S.C. §3607(b).

32. A trailer park was not entitled to the "older persons" exemption of Section 3607(b) when only 78.9 percent of its units were occupied by older persons. *Hooker v. Weathers,* 990 F.2d 913 (6th Cir. 1993). In *Sipio v. Township of Springfield,* 1996 U.S. Dist. LEXIS 12263 (E.D. Pa. 1996), the developers of a planned residential development unsuccessfully argued that the township had violated the Fair Housing Act by enforcing an age restriction agreed upon by the developer and the city that required at least one occupant of a residential unit to be 55 years or older or, in some cases, 50 years of age or older, and prohibited children under the age of 18 from occupying a residence. The court ruled that the age restriction met the "housing for older persons" exemption.

33. The facility will have the burden of proving that it satisfies this exemption. *See, e.g., Fallon v. Murphy,* HUDALJ No. 02–89-0202-1; *Colony Cove Associates v. Brown,* 220 Cal. App. 3d 195, 269 Cal. Rptr. 234 (2d Dist. 1990), *review denied* (1990); *Massaro v. Mainlands Section 1 & 2 Civic Ass'n.* 3 F.3d 1472 (11th Cir. 1993), *cert. denied,* 115 S. Ct. 56, 130 L. Ed. 2d 15 (1994).

34. 3 F.3d 1472 (11th Cir. 1993), *cert. denied,* 115 S. Ct. 56 (1994).

35. 42 U.S.C. §3607.

36. *See, e.g., United States v. Columbus Country Club,* 915 F.2d 877 (3d Cir. 1990), *cert. denied,* 111 S. Ct. 2797 (1991), *partial summary judgment granted,* 1992 U.S. Dist. LEXIS 11466 (E.D. Pa.), *later proceeding,* 1992 U.S. Dist. LEXIS 16438 (E.D. Pa. 1992); *United States v. Hughes Memorial Home,* 396 F. Supp. 544 (W.D. Va. 1975). *See also §23.4.*

37. 42 U.S.C. §3607.

38. *Seniors Civil Liberties Association, Inc. v. Kemp,* 965 F.2d 1030 (11th Cir. 1992).

39. 855 F. Supp. 315 (C.D. Cal. 1994).

40. *See e.g., HUD v. Mountain Side Mobile Estates* (Nos. 08–92-0010-1 and 08–92-0011-1, Secretary of HUD 7/13/93).

41. *Moutain Side Mobile Estates vs. HUD,* 56 F 3d 1243 (10, 1995).

42. 88 F.3d 739 (9th Cir. 1996).

43. 960 F.2d 975 (11th Cir.), *cert. denied,* 113 S. Ct. 376 (1992).

44. 115 S. Ct. 1776 (1995).

45. 42 U.S.C. §13601 *et seq.*

46. Notably, a federal court found that a residential community did not qualify as housing for the elderly under the act (before repeal of the significant services and facilities rule) when it provided no transportation, had no special design features for the elderly, and did not provide congregate dining, health care facilities, emergency call systems, or regular social programs. *Lanier v. Fairfield Communities, Inc.,* 776 F. Supp. 1533 (M.D. Fla. 1990).

Likewise, the U.S. Department of Justice and the state of Arizona sued a local mobile home park for illegally limiting residency to the elderly and the county in which the park was located for allowing the discrimination to occur. The complaint against the mobile home park alleged that the park provided no significant services or facilities specifically designed to meet the needs of older persons and that restricting families with children from living there was unnecessary to provide important housing opportunities to the elderly. *Arizona v. Arizona Skies Homeowners Ass'n., Inc.,* No. CIV. 93-22541 (Ariz. Super. Ct. Maricopa County 1993); *United States v. Arizona Skies Homeowners Ass'n., Inc.,* No. CIV. 94-0034-PHX-RGS (D. Ariz. 1993).

47. Proposed 24 C.F.R. §§100.305, 100.306; 59 *Fed. Reg.* 34,902, July 7, 1994.

48. In response to industry pressure, HUD withdrew the proposed rules and announced it would issue new rules in 1995 that would provide for a simple self-certification process for seniors' communities, clarify that expensive facilities and services such as medical facilities and congregate dining are not required, and provide greater weight to services provided by residents or homeowners themselves. 59 *Fed. Reg.* 64,104, Dec. 12, 1994.

49. 60 *Fed. Reg.* 43,322, Aug. 18, 1995.

50. In determining whether the facilities and services of a housing provider are *significant,* the department would apply the following criteria:

- the extent to which a facility or service can accommodate the older population of the housing facility. The capacity of each facility or service specifically designed to meet the physical or social needs of older persons will depend upon factors such as the size of the facility in relation to the scope of the service offered; the length of time during which the facility or service is made available; the frequency with which the facility or service is made available; and whether the facility or service is offered only at one location or whether there are several locations at which the facility or service is made available;
- the extent to which the facility or service will benefit older persons, given the climate and physical setting of the housing facility; and
- the extent to which the facility or service is actually usable by and regularly available to residents on a day-to-day basis. *Id.*

51. The following factors, among others, were relevant in making this determination:

- whether the owner or manager of the housing facility has endeavored to provide on its own or through some other entity significant facilities and services designed to meet the physical or social needs of older persons. Demonstrating that such services and facilities are expensive to provide is not sufficient to prove that the provision of such services is not practicable;
- the amount of rent charged, if the dwellings are rented, or the price of the dwellings, if they are offered for sale;

- geographic or other physical limitations inherent in the property that make the provision of facilities or services impractical;
- the income range of the residents of the housing facility;
- the demand for housing for older persons in the relevant geographic area;
- the vacancy rate of the housing facility; and
- the availability of other similarly priced housing for older persons in the relevant geographic area. If similarly priced housing for older persons *with significant facilities and services* is reasonably available in the relevant geographic area, then the housing facility does not meet the impracticability standard. *Id.*

52. *Marina Point, Ltd. v. Wolfson,* 30 Cal. 3d 721; 180 Cal. Rptr. 496, 640 P.2d 115 (1982). *cert. denied,* 459 U.S. 858 (1982).

53. Cal. Civ. Code §51.

54. 30 Cal. 3d at 725. In a later case, the court found that the act's reference to "business establishments" also included condominium associations and struck down a limitation on residency to persons over age 18. *O'Connor v. Village Green Owners Ass'n.,* 33 Cal. 3d 790, 191 Cal. Rptr. 320, 662 P.2d 427 (1983).

55. 30 Cal. 3d at 742-743.

56. Cal. Civ. Code §§51.2, 51.3; Section 2 of 1984 Stats., Ch. 787.

57. The California Legislative Counsel has issued an opinion that the provisions of these sections are inapplicable to licensed care facilities such as health, community care, or adult daycare health facilities. Senior Housing, Op. Cal. Leg. Counsel 24969, Jan. 11, 1986.

58. 379 So. 2d 346 (Fla. 1979).

59. 42 U.S.C. §3604(f).

60. 59 *Fed. Reg.* 33,362, 33,364, June 28, 1994.

61. 56 *Fed. Reg.* 9,472, Mar. 6, 1991; *see also* 24 C.F.R. §100.205.

62. 54 *Fed. Reg.* 3,232, Jan. 23, 1989. 24 C.F.R. §100.201. *See Casa Marie v. Superior Court,* 752 F. Supp. 1152, 1168 (D.P.R. 1990), *vacated in part and rendered in part,* 988 F.2d 252 (1st Cir. 1993), where *all* elderly residents of a retirement facility were found to be handicapped. *See also Potomac Group Home v. Montgomery County,* 823 F. Supp. 1285 (D. Md. 1993), in which the court held that elderly group home residents are "clearly handicapped" within the meaning of the Fair Housing Amendments Act. While a person currently using illegal drugs is not handicapped (42 U.S.C. §3602(h)), a *recovering* addict is, according to *United States v. Southern Management Corp.,* 955 F.2d 914 (4th Cir. 1992). *See* §23.3(d), for more discussion of the definition of a handicap.

63. 24 C.F.R. §100.202(c). *See also Secretary, HUD v. Williams,* 1991 WL 442796 (HUDALJ) (Mar. 22, 1991).

64. *Ibid.*

65. *United States v. California Mobile Home Park Management Co.,* 29 F.3d 1413 (9th Cir. 1994) (issue of fact whether guest fee waiver required for live-in medical aide); 107 F.3d 1374 (9th Cir. 1997) (plaintiff failed to show at trial that fee caused her denial of access).

66. *Shapiro v. Cadman Towers,* 51 F.3d 328 (2d Cir. 1995); *See also, Jankowski, Lee & Associates v. Cisneros,* 91 F.3d 891 (7th Cir. 1996).

67. *Roberts v. Kindercare Learning Centers,* 86 F.3d 844 (8th Cir. 1996).

68. 960 F. Supp. 259 (D. Utah 1997).

69. 748 F. Supp. 1002 (W.D.N.Y. 1990).

70. (adding 24 C.F.R. §885.610).

71. 60 *Fed. Reg.* 2,658, at 2,660, Jan. 10, 1995.

72. *See O'Neal v. Alabama Department of Public Safety,* Civ. No. 92-D-633-N (M.D. Ala. Oct. 3, 1994), in which a federal court applied the Fair Housing Amendments Act to state regulations prohibiting the treatment of certain disabling conditions *(e.g.,* severe senility) in a licensed assisted-living facility. The court found that the regulations were reasonable and essential to the regulatory agency's purpose of assuring safe care. The court further cited with approval *Johnson v. Thompson,* 971 F.2d 1487 (10th Cir. 1992), *cert. denied,* 113 S. Ct. 1255 (1993), for the proposition that when a person's handicap is the very reason he seeks a program or benefit, a claim of handicap discrimination cannot reasonably be found to lie.

73. H. Rep. 100-711 (1988), 1988 *U.S. Code Cong. & Admin. News,* 2173-2203.

74. *Baxter v. City of Belleville,* 720 F. Supp. 720 (S.D. Ill. 1989) (a hospice for AIDS patients). See also numerous residential care facility cases cited in this chapter.

75. For a survey of the federal discrimination laws and an exploration of the clash between these laws and state retirement facility licensing regimes, *see* Kaufmann, P., "Ships Crashing in the Night: Retirement Facilities and the Federal Disability Discrimination Laws," *National Academy of Elder Law Attorneys (NAELA) Quarterly,* Winter 1996, 17.

76. *See Roe v. Sugar River Mills Associates, M.B. Management Corp.,* 820 F. Supp. 636 (D. N.H. 1993) (burden on federally subsidized housing complex to prove that "no reasonable accommodation" would eliminate or acceptably minimize the safety risk posed by a mentally handicapped resident before eviction).

77. *See* Kaufman, M., "Life-Care Decorum: No Wheelchairs," *Philadelphia Inquirer,* Feb. 18, 1991.

78. *See also* Gordon, P., *Fair Housing Act, Americans with Disabilities Act: The Seniors Housing Compliance Guide* (American Seniors Housing Association, 1996) for detailed guidance on complying with disability discrimination laws in specific retirement community situations. The guide appears in §16.4.

79. Memorandum from Roberta Achtenberg, assistant secretary for Fair Housing and Equal Opportunity (FHEO), to office directors, enforcement directors, and so forth, Jan. 9, 1995.

80. 728 F. Supp. 1396 (Minn. 1990), *aff'd.* 923 F.2d 91 (8th Cir.), *reh'g. denied* (1991).

81. No. 95-1138, 1996 U.S. App. LEXIS 17406 (6th Cir. July 16, 1996).

82. *See UAW v. Johnson Controls, Inc.,* 111 S. Ct. 1196 (1991), in which a company's facially discriminatory policy of barring women employees from jobs with lead exposure intentionally discriminated against women employees. Because *Familystyle* was decided before *Johnson Controls,* the court declared that *Familystyle* had been "implicitly overruled" by the Supreme Court. *See also Alliance for the Mentally Ill v. City of Naperville,* 923 F. Supp. 1057 (N.D. Ill. 1996) (criticizing *Familystyle*).

83. *United States v. City of Taylor,* 872 F. Supp. 423 (E.D. Mich. 1995).

84. 77 F.3d 249 (8th Cir. 1996).

85. *See, e.g., United States v. Scott,* 788 F. Supp. 1555 (D. Kan. 1992); *Rhodes v. Palmetto Pathway Homes, Inc.,* 303 S.C. 308, 400 S.E.2d 484 (1991); *Broadmoor San Clemente Homeowners' Association v. Nelson,* 25 Cal. App. 4th 1, 30 Cal. Rptr. 2d 316 (1994). (Covenants prohibiting commercial activity cannot bar residential care facility for the elderly.)

86. 823 F. Supp. 1285 (D. Md. 1993).

87. 923 F. Supp. 1057 (M.D. Ill. 1996).

88. 914 F. Supp. 1555 (N.D. Ill. 1996).

89. 974 F.2d 43 (6th Cir. 1992). *See also Baggett v. Baird,* 1997 U.S. Dist. LEXIS 5825 (N.D. Ga. 1997) (ambulatory requirement for personal care home residents invalidated).

90. 46 F.3d 1491 (10th Cir. 1995).

91. 74 F.3d 941 (9th Cir. 1996). *See also Smith & Lee Associates v. City of Taylor,* 102 F.3d 781 (6th Cir. 1996).

92. 18 F.3d 802 (9th Cir. 1994), *aff'd. sub nom. City of Edmonds v. Oxford House, Inc.,* 115 S. Ct. 1776 (1995).

93. 42 U.S.C. §3607(b)(1).

94. Nos. 95-5648, 95-5666, 1996 U.S. App. LEXIS 17610 (3d Cir. July 18, 1996).

95. 924 F. Supp. 845 (S.D. Ohio 1996).

96. *Id.* at 851.

97. For a survey of several successful fair housing challenges against local zoning laws and against local application of these laws to facilities for the disabled, *see* Kaufmann, P., "The Fair Housing Zone: How to Use Fair Housing Laws to Secure Zoning Approval for Your Assisted Living Facility," *Spectrum,* Mar.-Apr. 1996, 15. *See also* §25.1, for additional zoning cases.

98. 82 F.3d 172 (7th Cir. 1996). *See also Gamble v. City of Escondido,* 104 F.3d 300 (9th Cir. 1996).

99. 84 F.3d 960 (7th Cir. 1996).

100. *Bryant Woods, Inc. v. Howard County,* 911 F. Supp. 918 (D. Md. 1996). *See also Elderhaven v. City of Lubbock,* 98 F.3d 175 (5th Cir. 1996).

101. 860 F. Supp. 1123 (S.D.W.Va. 1994).

102. Civil Action No. 95–356–A (E.D. Va. 1995), *dismissed* (May 12, 1995).

103. 849 F. Supp. 685 (D. Neb. 1994).

104. 910 F. Supp. 21 (D. Mass. 1996).

105. *See Cabrera v. Jakabovitz,* 24 F.3d 372 (2d Cir.), *cert. denied,* 115 S. Ct. 205, 130 L. Ed. 2d 135 (1994).

106. P.L. 101–336; 42 U.S.C. §12111 *et seq.*

107. 42 U.S.C. §12111(5); *see also* regulations at 56 *Fed. Reg.* 35,726, July 26, 1991; 29 C.F.R. Part 1630. Because Title I prohibits both direct and indirect employment discrimination, it is also illegal for a facility to enter into an agreement with a contractor who violates the ADA. *See* 29 C.F.R. §1630.6.

108. 42 U.S.C. §12183(a)(1).

109. "Disability" is defined in the same broad manner as "handicap" is defined under the Fair Housing Amendments Act. 42 U.S.C. §12102(2); *see also* note 64. The regulations implementing the ADA specifically state that HIV disease, whether symptomatic or asymptomatic, constitutes a physical or mental impairment. 28 C.F.R. §36.104. Temporary psychological impairments with no residual effects on the sufferer are not disabilities under the ADA, whereas permanent conditions that manifest themselves in temporary, periodic flare-ups, such as acute migraine headaches, could be deemed "disabilities." *Sanders v. Saw Arneson Products, Inc.,* No. 95-15349, 1996 U.S. App. LEXIS 19500 (9th Cir. Aug. 6, 1996).

110. 42 U.S.C. §12182(a).

111. 42 U.S.C. §12181(7); *see also* regulations at 56 *Fed. Reg.* 35,544, July 26, 1991; 28 C.F.R. Part 36, §36.104. State antidiscrimination statutes may define "public accommodations" differently than the ADA. For example, in two New York cases, the court dismissed an administrative agency's rulings against two dentists accused of discriminating against patients with HIV infection. *Schulman v. State*

Division of Human Rights, 641 N.Y.S.2d 134 (App. Div. 1996); *Lasser v. Rosa,* 634 N.Y.S.2d 188 (App. Div. 1995). Because the dentists in both cases were private practitioners who operated within private facilities on an appointment-only basis, the court concluded that their offices were not "public accommodations" under the state antidiscrimination law. *But see Abbott v. Bragdon,* 912 F. Supp. 580 (D. Me. 1995), in which a dentist's office was deemed a public accommodation under Maine's antidiscrimination law.

112. 56 *Fed. Reg.* 35,551–35,552, July 26, 1991, adding 28 C.F.R. Part 36.

113. *Id.,* at 35,552. In at least one ADA case, a district court questioned whether the public accommodation provisions of the ADA applied to residential board-and-care and personal care homes. *Wolford v. Lewis,* 860 F. Supp. 1123 (S.D.W.Va. 1994).

114. 56 *Fed. Reg.* 35,666 (28 C.F.R. Part 36, Appendix A, 60).

115. 28 C.F.R. §36.310.

116. 49 C.F.R. §37.101(d).

117. *See* notes 64 and 109 *above.*

118. *United States v. Morvant,* 894 F. Sup. 1157 (E.D. La. 1995). *See also Abbott v. Bragdon,* 912 F. Supp. 580 (D. Me. 1995); *Howe v. Hull,* 873 F. Supp. 72 (N.D. Ohio 1994) (hospital and physician are required to post signs); *Woolfolk v. Duncan,* 872 F. Supp. 1381 (E.D. Pa. 1995) (managed-care program's vicarious liability for the conduct of participating primary care physician); *Sharrow v. Bailey,* 910 F. Supp. 187 (M.D. Pa. 1995) (delay of scheduled surgery so that surgical staff could obtain protective suits).

119. 42 U.S.C. §12182(b)(1)(A).

120. 42 U.S.C. §12182(b)(1)(B) and (C).

121. The determination of what is "readily achievable" is based on the nature and cost of the modifications required, the financial resources of the facility, and the financial resources of the parent company. 42 U.S.C. §12181(9).

122. 28 C.F.R. §36.401, 402 (56 *Fed. Reg.* 35,599–35,600), and Part 36, Appendix A.

123. 42 U.S.C. §12182(b)(2)(A).

124. *Helen L. v. Di Dario,* 46 F.3d 325 (3d Cir.), *cert. denied sub nom. Pennsylvania Secretary of Public Welfare v. Idell S.,* 116 S. Ct. 64 (1995). *See also, New York v. Mid Hudson Medical Group, P.C.,* 877 F. Supp. 143 (S.D. N.Y. 1995) (refused deaf patient's request for interpretive services).

125. 909 F. Supp. 814 (D. Colo. 1995).

126. 906 F. Supp. 502 (E.D. Ark. 1995), rev'd. on other grounds.

127. 906 F. Supp. at 507.

128. A plaintiff alleging discrimination under the ADA lacks standing to sue when he or she does not show a likelihood of being subjected to further discrimination by the defendant. *Aikens v. Saint Helena Hospital,* 843 F. Supp. 1329 (N.D. Cal. 1994); *Hoepfl v. Barlow,* 906 F. Supp. 317 (E.D.Va. 1995).

129. 42 U.S.C. §12188(a), (b).

130. 42 U.S.C. §2000–a(e).

131. 42 U.S.C. §12187. The reference to "entities controlled by a religious organization" is modeled after similar provisions in Title IX of the Education Amendments of 1972. *See* H.R. No. 101–485(II), 125.

132. P.L. 101–336 §310(b)(1).

133. P.L. 101–336 §310(b)(2). The ADA is not retroactive. *Bent v. Mount Sinai Medical Center,* 882 F. Supp. 353 (S.D. N.Y. 1995).

134. 42 U.S.C. §12201(c). For a discussion of risk classification principles, *see* "Risk Classification Statement of Principles," Committee on Risk Classification of the American Academy of Actuaries, 1980. "Subterfuge" under the ADA means evasion of the purposes of the ADA, regardless of malicious intent. *See* 136 Cong. Rec. §9,697 (daily ed. July 13, 1990) (statement of Sen. Kennedy).

135. Report from the Committee on Labor and Human Resources, Rep. 101–116, Aug. 30, 1989, 84–86.

136. *See, e.g., Arizona Governing Committee for Tax Deferred Annuity & Deferred Compensation Plans v. Norris,* 463 U.S. 1073 (1983).

137. *See, e.g., Kotev v. First Colony Life Insurance Co.,* 927 F. Supp. 1316 (C.D. Cal. 1996).

138. Interim Enforcement Guidance on the Application of the Americans with Disabilities Act of 1990, 93 C.D.O.S. 4604, June 8, 1993. (For the full text of these guidelines, *see* the Volume II, §11.12A.)

139. *Id.* at §III.B.

140. *See, e.g., Henderson v. Bodine Aluminum, Inc.,* 4:95–CV–1051–CAS U.S.D.Ct. (E.D. Mo. 1995).

141. Enforcement Guide at §III.c.2.

142. *Id.*

143. 28 C.F.R. §36.301.

144. *Id.* §36.302.

145. *Id.* §36.303.

146. *Id.* §§36.304, 36.305.

147. *Id.* §36.208.

148. *Id.* §§36.307, 36.308.

149. 28 C.F.R. §36.208(c). In *Anderson v. Little League Baseball,* 794 F. Supp. 342 (D. Ariz. 1992), a federal district court in Arizona held that, where there was no indi-

cation that a Little League team had conducted such individualized assessment, the team's policy of prohibiting coaches in wheelchairs from coaching from the coaches' box was prohibited by the ADA. *See also Bombrys v. City of Toledo,* 849 F. Supp. 1210 (N.D. Ohio 1993), in which a federal court held that a blanket disqualification of individuals with insulin-dependent diabetes as candidates for police officer positions violated the ADA, the Rehabilitation Act of 1973, the due process clause of the 14th Amendment of the U.S. Constitution, and a state civil rights act.

150. 12 U.S.C. §§1701q(d)(4)(A)–(C).

151. Pub. L. No. 102–550, 106 Stat. 3672.

152. *See also United States v. Forest Dale,* 818 F. Supp. 954 (N.D. Tex. 1993), which held that Section 504 and the Fair Housing Act preclude a Section 202 housing facility from discriminating against a disabled elderly applicant for admission.

153. *See Brecker v. Queens B'nai B'rith Housing Development,* 607 F. Supp. 428 (E.D. N.Y. 1985), *aff'd.* 798 F.2d 52 (2d Cir. 1986); *Knutzen v. Nelson,* 617 F. Supp. 977 (D. Colo. 1985), *aff'd. sub nom.; Knutzen v. Eben Ezer Lutheran Housing Center,* 815 F.2d 1343 (10th Cir. 1987). For a discussion of the Section 202 program, see §22.4(a).

154. *Knutzen* essentially follows the rationale of *Brecker.*

155. *Brecker,* 798 F.2d at 55–56.

156. *Ibid.; see also Knutzen,* 617 F. Supp. at 981.

157. Civil Action No. C2–92–054 (S.D. Ohio), Consent Decree entered into on May 21, 1993.

158. In *Verville v. Elderly Housing Corp. (a/k/a Taylor Towers)* Section 504 Complaint No. 05–89–02–007–370), HUD determined that a facility did not discriminate on the basis of handicap under Section 504 when it refused to renew the lease of an elderly, mentally impaired tenant with a history of being disruptive. However, HUD found that the facility's admissions policy did discriminate against disabled persons because it required that tenants not be "mobility impaired." In *Denver Center for Independent Living v. Eaton Terrace Residences/Jeffco American Baptist Residences* Section 504 Complaint No. 08–90–02–013–370) HUD concluded that a facility violated Section 504 when an admissions staff member advised a 33-year-old disabled individual that admission to a Section 8 new construction project with Section 221(d)(3) insurance was limited to persons 55 years or older.

159. *Hackett v. Commission on Human Rights,* 1996 Conn. Super. LEXIS 1476 (Conn. Super. Ct. 1996).

160. 53 *Fed. Reg.* 20,216, June 2, 1988; 24 C.F.R. Part 8.

161. 24 C.F.R. §8.2, Appendix A.

162. 24 C.F.R. §8.4(a), (b)(1).

163. 24 C.F.R. §8.22(b).

164. *Ibid.*

165. 24 C.F.R. §8.24(a).

166. 24 C.F.R. §8.24(a)(1), (2).

167. 24 C.F.R. §8.24(b). Operators of nonpublic housing programs who undertook structural changes in facilities were required to act "as expeditiously as possible" but in any event to complete the work by July 11, 1991. 24 C.F.R. §8.24(c)(2). Where structural changes were necessary to achieve program accessibility, recipients had to develop a transition plan by January 11, 1989. 24 C.F.R. §8.24(d). HUD reported widespread noncompliance with this requirement. *See Housing and Development Reporter Current Developments,* Jan. 4, 1993, 696.

168. 53 *Fed. Reg.* 20,218–20,219.

169. 53 *Fed. Reg.* 20,219.

170. 24 C.F.R. §100.202(d) (1992).

171. *See also* McNickle, L., "Mixed Populations: A Threat to All Age-Distinct Elderly Housing," *Retirement Housing Business Report,* Oct. 1992.

172. *Public and Assisted Housing Occupancy Task Force: Report to Congress and to the Department of Housing and Urban Development,* Apr. 7, 1994 (hereafter Task Force Report).

173. Task Force Report at 1–2 to 1–5.

174. Task Force Report at 4–21 to 4–22.

175. Task Force Report at 5–2 to 5–4.

176. Task Force Report at 5–14 to 5–17.

177. 29 U.S.C. §794. The regulations implementing Section 504, like those for the Age Discrimination in Employment Act (*see* §23.2(a)), define federal financial assistance to include either the receipt of federal funds or the services of federal personnel. 45 C.F.R. §84.3. Thus, all projects that proceed under HUD involving both mortgage assistance and direct loans must comply with Section 504.

178. *See U.S. v. Baylor University Medical Center,* 564 F. Supp. 1495 (N.D. Tex. 1983), *modified, cert. denied,* 469 U.S. 1189 (1985) 736 F.2d 1039 (5th Cir. 1984); *U.S. v. University Hospital of SUNY at Stony Brook,* 575 F. Supp. 607 (E.D. N.Y. 1983), *aff'd.* 729 F.2d 144 (2nd Cir. 1984). By similar reasoning, the Age Discrimination Act may also apply to facilities constructed with private monies but that receive Medicare or Medicaid funds. *See* §23.2(a). *See also New York v. Mid Hudson Medical Group, P.C.,* 877 F. Supp. 143 (S.D. N.Y. 1995) (holding that Medicaid and Medicare reimbursements received by a clinic constituted "federal financial assistance" for purposes of the Rehabilitation Act of 1973).

179. 29 U.S.C. §794.

180. *Southeastern Community College v. Davis,* 442 U.S. 397, 406 (1979).

181. 607 F. Supp. at 435.

182. 49 F.3d 1002 (3d in. 1995).

183. 49 F.3d at 1014.

184. *See* Infante, M., "A Step Towards First Come, First Served," *Contemporary Long Term Care,* July 1995, 59–60.

185. 909 F. Supp. 814 (D. Colo. 1995).

186. 917 P.2d 336 (Colo. Ct. App. 1996).

187. No. 139189 (4th Cir. 1996).

188. 58 F.3d 398 (8th Cir. 1995).

189. *See BNA Americans with Disabilities Act Manual,* Vol. 5, Aug. 8, 1996, 90; 28 C.F.R. Part 36, Appendix B; §36.302(c).

190. 906 F. Supp. 502 (E.D. Ark. 1995), *rev'd. on other grounds,* No. 95–3680, 1996 U.S. App. LEXIS 18582 (8th Cir. July 29, 1996).

191. *Brecker, supra,* 607 F. Supp. at 438. *See also Southeastern Community College,* 442 U.S. at 410–411.

192. 879 F. Supp. 588 (W.D. Va. 1995).

193. U.S.D.C., S.D. Ohio, Oct. 25, 1995.

194. *Alexander v. Choate,* 469 U.S. 287 (1985).

195. 45 C.F.R. §84.1 *et seq.*

196. 45 C.F.R. §84.4(a).

197. 45 C.F.R. §84.3(k)(4).

198. 45 C.F.R. §84.3(j)(1) and (2).

199. *School Board of Nassau County v. Arline,* 480 U.S. 273, 107 S. Ct. 1123, 94 L. Ed. 2d 307 (1987), *reh'g. denied,* 481 U.S. 1024 (1987).

200. Justice Department Memorandum on Application of Rehabilitation Act's Section 504 to HIV-infected Persons, Daily Lab. Rep. (BNA) No. 195, D–5, Oct. 7, 1988.

201. *See, e.g., Chalk v. United States District Court,* 832 F.2d 1158 (9th Cir. 1987), *opinion issued in* 840 F.2d 701 (9th Cir. 1988).

202. 756 F. Supp. 632 (D. Mass. 1991).

203. *Howe v. Hull,* 873 F. Supp. 72 (N.D. Ohio 1994).

204. 822 F. Supp. 158 (D. Del. 1993).

205. *Secretary of HUD v. Williams,* 1991 WL 442796 (HUDALJ, Mar. 22, 1991).

206. 865 F.2d 930 (8th Cir.), *cert. denied,* 493 U.S. 892 (1989).

207. *See, e.g.,* "Public Health Service Statement on Management of Occupational Exposure to Human Immunodeficiency Virus, Including Considerations Regarding Zidovudine Postexposure Use," *Morbidity and Mortality*

Weekly Report, Vol. 39, no. RR-1, Jan. 26, 1990, 3; "Guidelines for Prevention of Transmission of Human Immunodeficiency Virus and Hepatitis B Virus to Health-Care and Public-Safety Workers," Feb. 1989; "Recommendations for Preventing Transmission of Human Immunodeficiency Virus and Hepatitis B Virus to Patients during Exposure-Prone Invasive Procedures," *Morbidity and Mortality Weekly Report,* Vol. 40, no. RR-8, July 12, 1991; "Recommendations for Prevention of HIV Transmission in Health-Care Settings," *Morbidity and Mortality Weekly Report,* Vol. 36, no. 2S, Aug. 21, 1987; "Update: Universal Precautions for Prevention of Transmission of Human Immunodeficiency Virus, Hepatitis B Virus, and Other Bloodborne Pathogens in Health-Care Settings," *Morbidity and Mortality Weekly Report,* Vol. 37, no. 24, June 24, 1988.

208. 29 C.F.R. §1910.1030.

209. *See, e.g., Chalk, v. United States District Court,* 832 F.2d 1158 (9th Cir. 1987), *opinion issued,* 840 F.2d 701 (9th Cir. 1988). *See also American Dental Ass'n. v. Martin,* 984 F.2d 823 (7th Cir. 1993), *cert. denied,* 114 S. Ct. 172 (1993), in which the Seventh Circuit denied the American Dental Association's petition for exemption from OSHA standards regarding exposure to bloodborne pathogens on the ground that OSHA was not required to establish a significant risk within the dental industry of HIV or HBV exposure in order to regulate dental practices. In the same case, the court held that the OSHA standards did not apply to work sites that were not controlled either by the employer or by a hospital, nursing home, or other entity that was itself subject to the bloodborne pathogens rule. On this basis, the court exempted from the bloodborne pathogen rules an employer of home health care workers that did not supervise its employees' work or control their work sites.

210. 24 C.F.R. Part 9.

211. *Id. See School Board of Nassau County v. Arline,* 480 U.S. 273, *reh'g. denied,* 481 U.S. 1024 (1987).

212. 720 F. Supp. 934 (N.D. Ala. 1989).

213. 840 F.2d 638 (9th Cir. 1988).

214. 560 A.2d 543 (D.C. Ct. App. 1989).

215. 42 U.S.C. §3604.

216. 42 U.S.C. §3607.

217. 396 F. Supp. 544 (W.D. Va. 1975).

218. *Id.* at 550.

219. 902 F.2d 1259 (7th Cir. 1990), *reh'g. denied* (1990).

220. 915 F.2d 877 (3d Cir. 1990), *cert. denied,* 111 S. Ct. 2797 (1991), *remanded,* 1992 WL 189403 (E.D. Pa. 1992).

221. 344 F. Supp. 737 (S.D. N.Y. 1972).

222. *Id.* at 746.

223. 42 U.S.C. §291 *et seq.*

224. 42 C.F.R. §53.112(a).

225. *Id.*

226. "AAHSA, HUD Counsel Meet on Religion Issue," *American Association of Homes for the Aging Washington Report,* Mar. 25, 1994.

227. 42 U.S.C. §3607.

228. 509 F.2d 1110 (2d Cir. 1975), *reh'g. denied,* 517 F.2d 918; *cert. denied,* 96 S. Ct. 197, 423 U.S. 896, 46 L. Ed. 2d 129.

229. 52 Cal. 3d 1142 (1991).

230. *M.T. v. Kentwood Construction Co.,* 651 A.2d 101 (N.J. Super. Ct. App. Div. 1994).

231. 42 U.S.C. §1396a(a)(23).

232. 42 C.F.R. §447.204.

233. *See generally* Gilbert, D., "Increasing Access to Long-Term Care through Medicaid Antidiscrimination Laws," *Journal of Health and Hospital Law,* Apr. 1991, 105.

234. Conn. Gen. Stat. Ann. §19(a)–533 (West), *as amended by* Public Act No. 92–231, Sec. 2 (1992). *See also* Wash. Rev. Code Ann. §74.42.055 (West 1991); Ohio Rev. Code Ann. §5111.31 (Anderson 1990).

235. *See* N.Y. Comp. Codes & Regs. tit. 10, §670.3(c)(2).

236. 1990 WL 180245 (M.D. Tenn. 1990).

237. *Linton v. Commissioner,* 65 F.3d 508 (6th Cir. 1995), *rehearing en banc denied,* 1995 U.S. App. LEXIS 30934.

238. 83 N.J. 67, 415 A.2d 1147, *cert. denied sub nom. Wayne Haven Nursing Home v. Finley,* 449 U.S. 944 (1980).

239. *Minnesota Ass'n. of Health Care Facilities, Inc. v. Minnesota Department of Public Welfare,* 742 F.2d 442 (8th Cir. 1984), *cert. denied,* 469 U.S. 1215 (1985).

240. *Blue v. Whalen,* 57 A.D.2d 240, 243 (N.Y. App. Div. 3d Dept. 1977), *appeal denied,* 43 N.Y.2d 642 (1977).

241. *New York State Health Facilities Ass'n. v. Axelrod,* 568 N.Y.S.2d 1, 569 N.E.2d 860 (1991), *reconsideration denied,* 77 N.Y.2d 990 (1991).

242. Facilities should likewise exercise care in accepting payments from hospitals under a "reserved bed agreement," whereby the facility's skilled-nursing facility sets aside a number of beds for hospital patients requiring discharge. Such a bed reservation agreement violates the Medicare laws if the beneficiary or other party is charged for covered services; Medicare beneficiaries, as a class, are discriminated against in admission; or payments are made to refer patients to the skilled-nursing facility. *Medicare Provider Reimbursement Manual (PRM),* §2105.3. *See also* §13.2(b).

243. 42 U.S.C. §1320a–7b(d).

244. 122 Misc. 2d 784, 471 N.Y.S.2d 973 (Sup. Ct. 1984).

245. Maryland's Department of Health and Mental Hygiene determined that, under the federal fraud and abuse provisions, nursing homes could not require private-pay agreements as a condition of admission of *any* person. It further found that such agreements would conflict with the patients' bill of rights, which is applicable to all patients in Medicaid-certified nursing homes, regardless of private- or public-pay status. Finally, the Maryland decision concluded that the continued use of private-pay agreements would amount to a deceptive and misleading practice under federal law in that the patient was likely to be unaware that the clause is unenforceable. *Matter of Summit Nursing Home, Medicare and Medicaid Guide* (CCH), ¶ 33,977 (1987). In Wisconsin, the attorney general issued an opinion that likewise found that private-pay agreements obtained before a patient became eligible for Medicaid violated federal law and applicable state laws, both civil and criminal. OAG 4–86, Mar. 7, 1986; *Medicare and Medicaid Guide* (CCH), ¶ 35,317. *See also* Ohio Attorney General Opinion No. 85–063, Sept. 24, 1985 *(Medicare and Medicaid Guide* (CCH), ¶ 34,988). In a 1986 opinion, the Rhode Island attorney general determined that a nursing home may not require Medicaid-eligible individuals or their families to sign private-pay agreements or to show ability to pay the private rate for a period of time before any conversion to Medicaid. The opinion found that any state laws that appeared to authorize such private-pay agreements were void pursuant to the supremacy clause of the U.S. Constitution and further found that the practice violates federal criminal law and state laws prohibiting fraud. CCH at ¶ 35,441.

246. 24 C.F.R. §483.12(d)(2); *see* commentary at 56 *Fed. Reg.* 48,841, Sept. 26, 1991; *see also* §20.3(a) regarding OBRA generally.

247. *See* 56 *Fed. Reg.* 48,841–48,842.

248. *See* California Welf. & Inst. Code §§14110.8 and 14110.9.

249. 24 C.F.R. §483.12(d)(3).

250. 56 *Fed. Reg.* 48,842.

251. 24 U.S.C. §2000d.

252. 1990 WL 180245 (M.D. Tenn. 1990).

253. A hospital was not considered to be subject to Title II in *Verhagen v. Olarte,* 1989 WL 146265 (S.D. N.Y. 1989), *reb'g. denied,* 1990 WL 41730 (S.D. N.Y. 1990). However, ADA regulations cover hospitals and may cover residential facilities with social services components. *See* §23.3(b).

254. 24 U.S.C. §3604.

255. 42 C.F.R. §53.112(c).

256. *Baltimore Neighborhoods, Inc. v. Peninsula United Methodist Homes, Inc.,* No. 94–018017 (Cir. Ct. Baltimore County, filed Jan. 18, 1994). *See also* Apperson, J., "Suits Allege Bias in Ads for Retirement Homes," *The Sun,* Jan. 20, 1994.

257. *See, e.g., former* 24 C.F.R. §109.30(b).

258. 61 *Fed. Reg.* 14,380, Apr. 1, 1996, removing 24 C.F.R. Part 109.

259. *See generally* Templer, C., "The Potholes of Fair Housing Advertising," *Spectrum,* Sept.–Oct. 1994; Gordon, P., American Seniors Housing Association, *Fair Housing Advertising: A Handbook for the Seniors Housing Industry,* 1996.

260. *Donahue v. Fair Employment and Housing Comm'n.* 1 Cal. App. 4th 387 (1991). 13 Cal. App. 4th 350 (2d Dist. 1991), *review granted,* 825 P.2d 766, 5 Cal. Rptr. 2d 781 (1992), *review dismissed and case remanded,* 859 P.2d 671, 23 Cal. Rptr. 2d 591 (1993), *republication denied,* No. 5024538, Dec. 16, 1993.

261. 30 Cal. Rptr. 2d 395 (1994), *modified and reb'g. denied,* 1994 Cal. App. LEXIS 649, *review granted* by Cal. Supreme Court, 33 Cal. Rptr. 2d 567, 880 P.2d 111 (Cal. 1994), *reprinted for tracking pending review,* 30 Cal. App. 4th 1008 (1994). The opposite result was reached in *Swanner v. Anchorage Equal Rights Comm'n.* 874 P.2d 274 (Alaska 1994).

262. 12 Cal. 4th 1143 (1996).

Friendship Heights; Chevy Chase, Maryland.

Courtesy of Marriott Senior Living Services; Bethesda, Maryland

24 Securities Registration

§24.1 In General

One of the most often overlooked subjects in the development of retirement facilities is the application of federal or state securities laws to the financial transaction between the resident and the facility operator or developer. The traditional practice of many continuing-care retirement communities of collecting deposits from prospective residents before construction of a facility and then using those monies to help finance facility development can raise securities issues that have gone largely ignored by developers, consumers, and the government. Perhaps the most significant reason for the failure to address securities matters is that continuing-care facilities have primarily been nonprofit, church-affiliated enterprises; moreover, in states where continuing care has flourished, other forms of regulation have diverted attention from the securities question.[1] With the trend toward profit-motivated developers, refundable entrance fees, memberships, and similar structures whereby a resident expects to receive a payment several years after investing money in the facility, all parties to retirement facility development need to pay close attention to the applicable securities laws.

Federal law defines a security as follows:

The term "security" means any note, stock, treasury stock, bond, debenture, evidence of indebtedness, certificate of interest or participation in any profit-sharing agreement, collateral-trust certificate, preorganization certificate or subscription, transferable share, investment contract, voting-trust certificate, certificate of deposit for a security, fractional undivided interest in oil, gas, or other mineral rights, any put, call, straddle, option, or privilege on any security, certificate of deposit, or group or index of securities (including any interest therein or based on the value thereof), or any put, call, straddle, option, or privilege entered into on a national securities exchange relating to foreign currency, or, in general, any interest or instrument commonly known as a "security," or any certificate of interest or participation in, temporary or interim certificate for, receipt for, guarantee of, or warrant or right to subscribe to or purchase, any of the foregoing.[2]

Given the extremely broad language of the statutory definition, it is theoretically possible that a refundable entrance fee contract could constitute evidence of indebtedness; a preconstruction entrance fee deposit might be classified as a preorganization certificate or subscription; a cooperative share, membership, or condominium interest could be considered a transferable share; and any residence agreement in which the purchaser has a risk of financial loss or the opportunity to realize a profit might be argued to be an investment contract.

§24.2 Application to Seniors' Housing

Federal courts interpreting the definition of securities have tended to focus on whether the investment creates an opportunity for profit. In cases of cooperatives, transferable memberships, condominium sales, or limited-partnership or stock purchase arrangements entitling a person to admission in a seniors' housing facility whereby, for example, a resident might be able to sell the interest after several years to a new resident at a profit, there is a substantial question as to whether a security is created.

However, the U.S. Supreme Court held in *United Housing Foundation, Inc. v. Forman*[3] that the sale of shares in a "limited-equity" cooperative real estate development is exempt from the federal securities act, where residents could resell shares to the cooperative at the original purchase price upon termination of occupancy. The Court found that, although that type of investment might ordinarily be characterized as a security, it presented no reasonable expectation of profit from the managerial or entrepreneurial efforts of others. The Court also noted that the promoters emphasized housing and did not seek to attract investors by the prospect of profits. Residents were found to have been attracted solely by the prospect of acquiring a place to live, and not by financial returns on investment.

Although *United Housing Foundation* may stand for an exemption from federal securities laws for all forms of housing used as a personal residence, its facts precluded any possibility of profit. At least one federal circuit court of appeals reviewed a transaction wherein cooperative tenants could sell their shares to a new lessee-purchaser at whatever profit (or loss) the market would bear. In addition, tenants could receive periodic distributions and dividends. The court found that despite the profit opportunity, the continuing requirement that tenants pay monthly fees indicated that the transaction was for housing and not for investment in a security.[4] The Tenth Circuit has also reiterated that the promotional emphasis of the developer is central in determining whether real estate sales are securities and that they are not securities when "purchasers were induced to obtain them primarily for residential purposes" and when "the benefit to the purchasers of the amenities promised . . . was largely in their own use and enjoyment."[5] The Securities and Exchange Commission (SEC) has likewise ruled that a proposal to offer retirement condominiums need not comply with registration requirements.[6] At least two federal district courts have also found that nontransferable life-care contract interests were not securities.[7]

The SEC issued a "no-action" letter to the Marriott Corporation with respect to its proposed sale to residents of stock in a life-care corporation.[8] The proposal would have required a resident to pay an initial nonrefundable entrance fee of approximately $20,000 and to purchase between $125,000 and $250,000 of Class B stock in the life-care corporation. The stock could not be pledged, encumbered, or bequeathed, except to a surviving spouse, along with the life-care unit. The resident would be required to sell the stock upon death, permanent transfer to a nursing home, or termination of the residency agreement. Any gain or loss on the sale of the stock would belong to the residents. The stock would also yield a modest dividend. Residence in the community was not to be promoted as a potentially profitable investment opportunity. The legal reasoning in the request for the no-action letter followed closely the analysis in the paragraphs above and cited many of the referenced cases.

State laws pose particular concerns with respect to securities registration of seniors' housing transactions because state statutes and the interpretations of state courts and administrative agencies may differ widely from federal standards. For example, in *Silver Hills Country Club v. Sobiesky,*[9] the California Supreme Court found that a registerable security was issued when developers planning to construct a country club solicited membership fees that were used to finance development of the facility. Members later would be able to sell their memberships at a profit, if possible. The court determined that because the investment of the prospective members was at risk, the transaction fit within the definition of a security under California law, which is almost identical to the definition in the federal statute. At the same time, though, continuing-care legislation in California exempts from treatment as securities any transactions subject to regulation as continuing-care contracts.[10] Other states, such as New York, impose extensive registration and disclosure requirements for cooperative housing offerings.[11]

As more developers enter the retirement housing field and develop creative and unusual payment structures for their facilities, the risk of application of federal or state securities laws to retirement facility transactions will increase. Although most elderly people seeking to enter a retirement facility are looking primarily for a residence and not an investment, they nevertheless may be risking substantial assets in a venture whose success depends on the development and operational abilities of others. If there are inadequate licensing laws and other protections in a particular state, government officials or consumers who have lost their investment in a failed project are likely to resort to federal or state securities laws for relief.

Notes

1. In states without continuing-care regulation, prosecutors have used securities laws to convict certain promoters of fraudulent life-care facility offerings (see §5.2).

2. 15 U.S.C. §77b(1); emphasis added.

3. 421 U.S. 837 (1975), *reh'g. denied*, 423 U.S. 884 (1975).

4. *Grenader v. Spitz,* 537 F.2d 612 (2d Cir. 1976). *cert. denied,* 429 U.S. 1009 (1976).

5. *Aldrich v. McCulloch Properties, Inc.,* 627 F.2d 1036 (10th Cir. 1980).

6. *Culverhouse et al.* (SEC 1973), '73–'74 CCH dec. ¶ 79,612.

7. *Waldo v. Central Indiana Lutheran Retirement Home* (S.D. Ind., Nov. 16, 1979) *Fed. Sec. L. Rep.* (CCH), ¶ 97,680 (1980); *Ashenback v. Covenant Living Centers-North Fed. Sec. L. Rep.* (CCH), ¶ 97,369 (1979–1980). 482 F. Supp. 1241 (E.D. Wis. 1980).

8. SEC "No Action Letter," July 21, 1987.

9. 55 Cal. 2d 811, 361 P.2d 906 (1961).

10. West's Cal. Health & Safety Code §1774.

11. *See Blue Sky Law Reports* (CCH), ¶ 42,523.

Eventide Home; Quincy, Massachusetts.

25 Local Laws

§25.1 Zoning

Local government's most direct impact on the development of seniors' housing and care facilities comes through the zoning and permit approval processes. While specific requirements vary widely from one jurisdiction to another, several common issues often present themselves.

Lack of understanding of the retirement community concept is frequently a principal concern when sponsors deal with local government bodies. Uninitiated cities or towns may erroneously view retirement centers as primarily health care institutions, thus according them the less-favored land use planning status often reserved for hospitals, nursing homes, or psychiatric facilities. Sponsors must therefore emphasize the primarily residential character of most such facilities. One author points out that the key to successful zoning approvals is early, active communication and cooperation with city planning staff and neighborhood groups. Retirement communities generally do not fit standard zoning classes but rather fall between institutional and purely residential uses. They are said to generate lower traffic volumes, parking needs, and noise levels than other residential developments. While they must accommodate staff and commercial deliveries, such demands are said to be less intensive than those associated with other comparable businesses.[1] In general, most courts consider retirement complexes to be excluded from zoning ordinances prohibiting hospitals or hotels in a given area but included in ordinance definitions permitting apartments or multifamily uses.[2]

Municipalities may, of course, restrict the development of seniors' facilities in accordance with their zoning ordinances. Nonetheless, certain limitations apply to the arbitrary use of zoning powers or ordinances that are not authorized by a state's zoning enabling act. For example, some states prohibit local restrictions on the number of unrelated individuals who may live together in a house.[3] Such regulations might have an impact on a small assisted-living or board-and-care home. Municipalities may also not be able to prevent the development of seniors' projects that are compatible with the other uses already permitted in a district.

The U.S. Supreme Court decision in *City of Cleburne v. Cleburne Living Center* is instructive in the latter regard.[4] In *Cleburne*, the city denied a conditional use permit for the operation of a group home for the mentally retarded in a zone that allowed such permits for hospitals, nursing homes, and homes for the aging. The Supreme Court found that mental retardation was not a "quasi suspect class" and did not merit special scrutiny under the Equal Protection Clause. Nonetheless, the Court, holding that the Texas statute was based solely on unsubstantiated fears of the mentally retarded, struck down the law as having no rational basis. The Court in *Cleburne* used a stricter rational basis test than it had applied in past decisions and found that group homes for the mentally retarded did not differ from those uses already permitted in the area.

It is likely that the Court would apply a similar analysis to a case involving a home for the aging. Like mental retardation, age is not a suspect classification under the Equal Protection Clause.[5] Nonetheless, facilities for senior citizens are unlikely to cause unique problems if their use is generally compatible with others in the zone. Thus, special restrictions on retirement facilities are likely to be struck down under the Cleburne rationale. A municipality probably could not prohibit a small board-and-care home in an area zoned for single-family residences or a senior citizens' complex in an area zoned for multi-family use; nor could it deny a conditional use permit to a home for the aging where hospitals were permitted, absent a convincing demonstration of special circumstances.

In *Jayber, Inc. v. Municipal Council*,[6] a New Jersey appellate court ruled that a seniors' congregate housing facility was entitled to a zoning variance over the objection of neighbors in that it promoted the general welfare and constituted an inherently beneficial use of the property even though the facility was not constructed for low-income persons. The court cited generally the need for elderly housing. Similarly, *Maull v. Community Living for the Handicapped*[7] denied an injunction against the development of a group home for eight mentally retarded persons in a subdivision with a single-family-home covenant on the basis of the Fair Housing Act and the home's single-family appearance and similar functioning as a single-family dwelling.[8]

Moreover, in *United States v. City of Taylor*,[9] the U.S. District Court held that the city had violated the Fair Housing Act in refusing to permit the operation of an adult foster care home for 12 elderly disabled persons in an area zoned for single-family residential use. The court ordered the city to provide a reasonable accommodation to the home by amending its zoning ordinance to permit the operation of the home. Finally, in *United States v. Commonwealth of Puerto Rico*,[10] the U.S. District Court granted a preliminary injunction blocking an order to close a nursing home under Puerto Rico zoning rules. The court declared that Puerto Rico must make "reasonable accommodations" under the Fair Housing Act—

in this case, waiving parking lot requirements for a nursing home when the actual use of the home would never require the amount of parking technically required by the zoning regulations.

The U.S. Supreme Court addressed a similar issue in *City of Edmonds v. Oxford House, Inc.*[11] In that case, Oxford House was cited for opening a group home for ten to 12 adult recovering alcoholics and drug addicts in an area zoned for single-family residences. The zoning law limited the number of unrelated persons permitted to live in a single-family unit to five; the law did not limit the number of related persons who could live in a unit. The Court held that while the Fair Housing Act exempts from its regulation laws that limit the number of occupants permitted in a residence in order to prevent overcrowded living quarters, the city of Edmond's zoning law does not fall within this exemption. The Court reasoned that rather than capping the total number of occupants per dwelling unit, the law merely limits the number of *unrelated* persons who may live in a dwelling. Therefore, the law is subject to scrutiny under the Fair Housing Act. (See also §23.3(a) for discussion of several zoning cases decided on the basis of the handicap discrimination provisions of the Fair Housing Act.)

On the other hand, many municipalities have enacted ordinances specifically designed to enable the development of retirement centers.[12] These ordinances may make appropriate distinctions between congregate housing, assisted-living, and continuing-care facilities, prescribing different treatment for each. They may also cover issues such as site size and coverage densities; proximity to health services, grocery stores, and other facilities; parking; kitchens; architectural details and amenities; staffing; basic services; and even resident contract terms.[13]

Zoning ordinances that provide for districts where residency is restricted to senior citizens have withstood a variety of legal challenges. Key cases in the New York and New Jersey courts have held that such ordinances are authorized by state zoning enabling acts, which permit zoning for the purpose of promoting the general welfare of the community.[14] These courts have found that communities promote the general welfare by providing for the specialized needs of the elderly that the general housing market does not adequately meet.

Courts have also rejected constitutional challenges to age-restrictive zoning on due process and equal protection grounds. The supreme court of New Jersey in the *Weymouth Township* case[15] held that housing is not a fundamental right protected by the Fourteenth Amendment[16] and that age is not a suspect classification,[17] thereby making the court's strict scrutiny of the township's zoning ordinance inappropriate. Rather, the municipality had only to show that the ordinance had a rational basis related to the public welfare, a fact already established to the court's satisfaction in its consideration of whether the ordinance was within the scope of the zoning enabling act.

Finally, courts have generally upheld age-restrictive zoning against claims that it violated general state statutes prohibiting housing discrimination on the basis of age. Although conceding facial violations of the general terms of the statutes, the courts refused to give effect to such a literal interpretation, noting that favoritism to the elderly was not among the statute's enumerated prohibited practices and citing the state's policies of encouraging construction of housing for the aging.[18] Some states have either amended their zoning statutes specifically to authorize zoning to promote housing for the elderly or have amended their antidiscrimination statutes to remove housing for the elderly from their prohibitions.[19]

The U.S. Supreme Court's decision in *Moore v. City of East Cleveland*[20] suggests one limitation on the extent of age-restrictive zoning. There, the Court held that a municipality cannot, through the enforcement of a single-family residence zoning ordinance, restrict which family members can live together. Thus, an age-restrictive zoning ordinance that operated in such a manner as to prevent family members (even extended ones) from living with one another would probably be unconstitutional.

§25.2 Assessments; Rent Controls

Retirement projects tend to raise additional special issues not present in conventional real estate developments. A major concern of local governments is that a not-for-profit project, like most health facilities, will not be listed on the tax rolls (see discussion of state tax exemptions in Chapter 10). On the other hand, retirement communities tend to have a less severe impact on local services than many other types of uses. Seniors' facilities, even if operated for profit, may therefore have legitimate grounds for asserting exemption from school district assessments or other payments that do not benefit elderly residents.

However, even if a facility is entitled to tax exemption under state or local law, the facility may often find it necessary to agree to accept local taxation or assessments "in lieu of taxes" as a condition of planning approval. These assessments may be levied by a municipality through the subdivision approval process, the issuance of building permits, or where a zoning variance, conditional use permit, or rezoning is needed from the municipality to secure development approval.

The courts have readily upheld requirements that call for developers to provide internal streets and similar improvements needed by a subdivision or facility.[21] More difficult problems have arisen where dedications of land or in-lieu fees are required for off-site streets, parks, and schools. Nonetheless, the courts have generally sustained such assessments where two conditions are met. First, the state's zoning enabling act must authorize the assessments. While such authority has frequently been implied from the statute, more and more states are enacting specific provisions that authorize contributions for off-site facilities such as parks.[22] Second, a rational nexus must exist between the burden on the community created by the development and the municipality's assessment. Such a nexus has generally been found where there is a reasonable basis for attributing increased off-site community needs to the development.[23] Thus, the development of large seniors' communities might justify an assessment for parks or public transportation (if authorized by the statute), but not in-lieu fees to support schools.

Rent controls are another form of local regulation that often uniquely affect seniors' projects. Often, licensure as a care facility may be a basis for exemption from rent controls on the ground that charges are based largely on facility service costs rather than simply on provision of housing (see §20.4(b)). In addition, rules attendant to HUD financing may result in preemption of local rent control laws (see §22.6(a)). Local rent control ordinances may also by their terms exclude retirement communities from their ambit, but such exclusions must be explicit, as courts are unlikely to imply an exclusion from the language of the ordinance.[24] For example, a city's attempt to ensure compliance with the familial status provisions of the Fair Housing Act (see §23.2) by requiring a mobile home park owner to reduce rents and decrease services after the park rescinded its adults-only status proved to be a violation of that act.[25]

Given the general absence of binding interpretive precedents and the sometimes apparently whimsical application of local ordinances to specific projects, local laws can be among the most vexing of all laws to deal with in developing a seniors' facility. Moreover, local government bodies are commonly among the first encountered in the process of development. Yet, all too often, seniors' facilities progress through the design, legal, marketing, and licensure application processes only to be halted at the local government approval level after numerous hearings. Sometimes, though, when planning approval is a problem, substantial progress in design, legal, marketing, and financial planning can aid in obtaining approval. At other times, that progress simply adds up to wasted resources.

The site selection process should carefully consider the characteristics of the local jurisdiction and its experience with other related facilities or projects. If possible, local planning approvals should be secured at the earliest possible date before other expenses mount.

Notes

1. Tanner, F.W., "Retirement Centers Are Good Neighbors," *Contemporary Long Term Care,* June 1990. *See also* "Assisted Living Residences—A Study of Traffic and Parking Implications," American Seniors Housing Association, 1997.

2. *See generally* the extensive case annotations on zoning for senior citizens' communities and elderly housing at 83 ALR 3d 1084 and 83 ALR 3d 1103. *See also* Hancock, J., ed., *Housing the Elderly,* (New Brunswick, NJ: Center for Urban Policy Research, 1987) 49–56, 95–117, regarding public policy arguments for age-segregated housing for the elderly.

3. California, New Jersey, Pennsylvania, and Michigan, among others, have struck down such restrictions on state constitutional grounds. *City of Santa Barbara v. Adam-*

son, 27 Cal. 3d 123, 153 Cal. Rptr. 507, 610 P.2d 436 (Cal. 1980); *State v. Baker,* 405 A.2d 368 (N.J. 1979); *Children's Home v. City of Easton* 417 A.2d 830 (Pa. 1980); *Charter Township v. Dinolfo,* 351 N.W.2d 831 (Mich. 1984). However, most states follow the U.S. Supreme Court's lead in *Village of Belle Terre v. Boraas,* 416 U.S. 1 (1974), which held that consideration of family relationships in zoning ordinances is appropriate under the due process clause. *See, e.g., Town of Durham v. White Enterprises,* 348 A.2d 706 (N.H. 1975); *Rademan v. City and County of Denver,* 526 P.2d 1325 (Colo. 1974). *See* §23.2(b) for more recent cases under the Fair Housing Act.

4. 471 U.S. 1002 (1985); *see also* Note, "*City of Cleburne v. Cleburne Living Center:* Rational Basis with a Bite?" 20 *U.S.F.L. Rev.* 927 (1986). In *Casa Marie v. Superior Court,* 752 F. Supp. 1152 (D. Puerto Rico 1991), *Cleburne* was applied to a zoning case involving a retirement community.

5. *Mass. Bd. of Retirement v. Murgia,* 427 U.S. 307 (1976).

6. 569 A.2d 304 (N.J. App. 1990). *cert. denied,* 584 A.2d 214 (N.J. 1990).

7. 813 S.W.2d 90 (Mo. Ct. App. 1991).

8. In *Hagenmann v. Worth,* 782 P.2d 1072 (Wash. App. 1989). However, the Washington State Court of Appeals found that a board-and-care facility for the elderly could not be operated on property subject to a restrictive covenant limiting the land use to residential and recreational purposes and prohibiting commercial uses. Although residential in character, the home was found to constitute a commercial use because it was an activity engaged in for gain, the home was depreciated as a business deduction, and nonfamily employees worked at the facility.

9. 872 F. Supp. 423 (E.D. Mich. 1995).

10. 764 F. Supp. 220 (D.P.R. 1991) *See also Martin v. Constance,* 843 F. Supp. 1321 (E.D. Mo. 1994).

11. 115 S. Ct. 1776 (1995).

12. *E.g.,* Niles, Orland Park, and Schaumberg, IL.

13. *See* Ordinance No. 1540, Orland Park, IL, June 17, 1986.

14. *See Maldini v. Ambro,* 36 N.Y.2d 481, 330 N.E.2d 403, 396 N.Y.S.2d 385, *cert. denied,* 423 U.S. 993 (1985). *Taxpayer's Assn., Inc. v. Weymouth Township, 80 N.J. 6, 364 A.2d 1016 (1976), Shepard v. Woodland Township Committee and Planning Board,* 71 N.J. 230, 364 A.2d 1005 (1976). *See also Berger v. Burns,* (N.Y. Supr. Ct., Albany, No. 7255-90 (Mar. 21, 1991), upholding an ordinance promoting development of a low-income seniors' housing development notwithstanding arguments that it was an unlawful "floating zone" and constituted "spot zoning."

15. *Taxpayer's Assn., Inc. v. Weymouth Township, 80 N.J. 6, 364 A.2d 1016 (1976).*

16. *Linsey v. Normet,* 405 U.S. 56 (1972).

17. *Murgia,* note 5.

18. *Weymouth,* note 14; 71 N.J. 285 n. 16; *see also* discussion of laws regarding age discrimination in housing, §23.2.

19. N.J. Stat. Ann. §40:55D–65g; Cal. Civ. Code §§51.2, 51.3.

20. 431 U.S. 494 (1977).

21. *See, e.g., Blevens v. City of Manchester,* 120 A.2d 121 (N.H. 1961).

22. Cal. Govt. Code §65970; Colo. Rev. Stat. §30–28–133(4)(a).

23. *Jordan v. Village of Menomonee Falls,* 137 N.W.2d 442 (Wis. 1965) *appeal dismissed,* 385 U.S. 4 (1966).

24. *Klarfeld v. Berg,* 29 Cal. 3d 893, 176 Cal. Rptr. 539, 633 P.2d 204 (1981).

25. *United States v. City of Hayward,* 36 F.3d 832 (9th Cir. 1994).

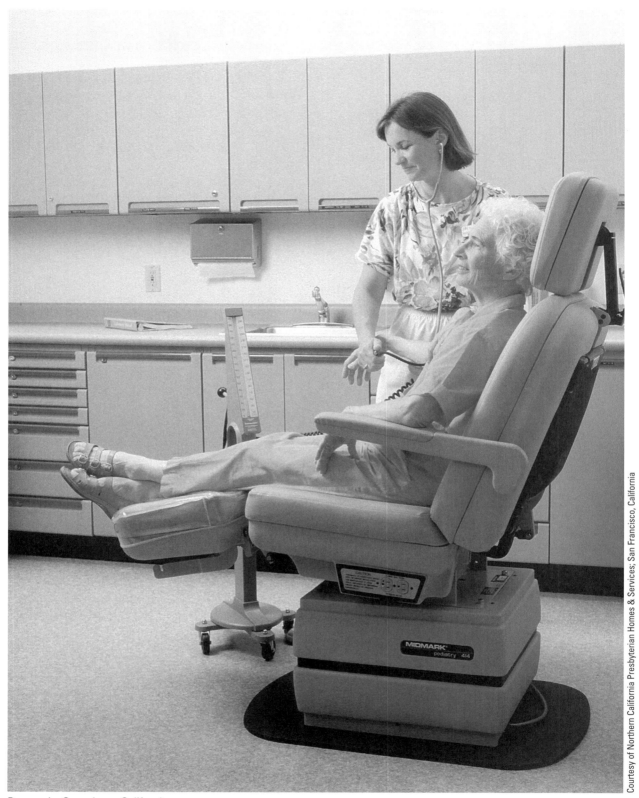

Pamapais; Greenbrae, California.

Part VIII
Financing Health Care

An elderly person approaching the retirement years should be planning for his or her financial future. Given that retired persons can no longer depend on employment income and must instead rely on the proceeds of pensions, Social Security, and earnings on investments, they often seek a living situation that provides some measure of economic stability over a long period. Although factors such as inflation and other changes in the cost of living pose some concern for anyone planning for future financial needs, a more significant concern for an elderly person is that a serious illness may strike, wipe out a lifetime's worth of savings, and force the person either to depend on subsistence-level government programs or become a burden to family or friends.

Many seniors' communities, both nonprofit and, more recently, for-profit, are seeking to help residents ensure that they will be able to maintain a consistent standard of living for the remainder of their lives by investing in a health insurance-type program early

in residents' retirement years. Some retirement community programs may take advantage of available government benefits and supplement them with private funds either pooled in an in-house reserve or used to purchase an indemnity policy; others may enroll in a health plan furnished by a third-party service provider.

For many years, the funding of care for the elderly has been one of the greatest challenges facing national policy makers. At present, retirement community plans are among the few existing methods by which long-term care for the nonpoor elderly is being funded on a group basis. The coming years will likely see substantial attention devoted to expanding residentially based health financing programs for seniors, thereby leading to federal and state incentives to encourage the development of privately funded insurance and health plans and redirecting government resources from expensive acute care to less intensive, longer-term health needs.[1]

471

Newbury Court Retirement Community; Concord, Massachusetts.

26 Government Funding Of Health Care

§26.1 In General

In 1986, health care expenditures in the United States totaled approximately $425 billion, or 10.7 percent of the gross national product.[2] In 1990 and 1991, the same expenditure reached about $750 billion and 12.2 percent of GNP.[3] By the year 2000, health care expenditures are expected to represent 15 percent of GNP.[4] While constituting only 12 percent of the population, persons 65 and over are responsible for 36 percent of all personal health care expenditures.[5] Two principal federal health financing programs, Medicare and Medicaid, account for 45 and 12 percent, respectively, of all personal health care expenditures.[6] The cost of health care for the elderly has risen dramatically over the years. In the 1980s alone, government payments to the elderly increased by 35 percent and constituted more than 25 percent of all government spending. The $50 billion spent on health care for the aging in 1981 is expected to reach $200 billion by the year 2000.[7] In 1990, researchers predicted that annual Medicare costs alone could rise to more than $200 billion by the year 2040, which is approximately triple the 1987 expenditure. By 2040, those over the age of 85 in nursing homes are predicted to reach double to triple the *total* number of nursing home patients of any age in 1990.[8]

Of the total health care expenditures for older Americans, about 42 percent goes for hospital-related charges, 20 percent each for physician and nursing home services, and the remainder for other forms of care.[9] Yet, while government pays about $58 billion of the $69 billion spent on hospital care for the elderly, it covers only $13.6 billion of the $32.8 billion expended for nursing care.[10] Of the out-of-pocket health care costs reported in 1985 to have been paid by the elderly, only 6 percent went for hospitalizations, whereas 42 percent went for nursing home services.[11] Reports for 1991 that include Medigap and other private insurance note that of out-of-pocket costs totaled 32 percent for nursing homes and 17 percent for hospitals.[12] Nursing home expenses were predicted to increase by 75 percent from 1984 to 1990, for a total expenditure of $56.3 billion.[13] Of this, it was estimated that $28.1 billion would be paid directly out of pocket by senior citizens.[14] As a percentage of income, out-of-pocket health care expenditures rose from 15 percent in 1987 to 23 percent in 1994.[15] Obviously, the need for long-term nursing care continues to be one of the greatest financial issues facing older persons today.

§26.2 Hospital Orientation of Medicare

Fundamental differences in Medicare and Medicaid eligibility criteria and program coverage help explain the disparity in government financing for the different levels of care. The Medicare program is available to, among others, all persons entitled to Social Security benefits as of the first day of the month in which they attain age 65.[16] The widely available Medicare dollars for the elderly go predominantly for hospital care (69 percent) and physicians (25 percent) while only 1 percent pays for nursing home care.[17] In 1991, Medicare paid $2.7 billion for skilled-nursing facility care, representing only 4.5 percent of the total spent on nursing home care and only slightly over 2 percent of total Medicare spending.[18] Although Medicare coverage is extensive, it by no means covers all hospital costs and is of minimal usefulness for long-term-care needs.

(a) Medicare Copayments and Deductibles for Acute Hospitalization

NOTE: The Catastrophic Health Insurance Act of 1988 substantially amended the following provisions, which were then restored when the act was repealed in 1989 (see §28.2).

Medicare covers most costs of acute care for the elderly population. Medicare Part A, available to Social Security recipients, covers 150 days of inpatient hospital services for a single episode of illness. In general, the first 60 are fully covered, subject only to the initial deductible amount ($764 for 1998). Each of the next 30 days is subject to a coinsurance payment by the patient of one-fourth of the inpatient hospital deductible ($191 for 1998). The last 60 days are subject to a daily coinsurance payment of half the inpatient deductible ($382 for 1998). The last 60 days of coverage are also limited to once-in-a-lifetime use.[19] Although deductibles and copayments rise rapidly over time, most hospital stays are, as a practical matter, of increasingly short duration[20]; however, Medigap insurance policies (see §27.1) can cover the deductibles and coinsurance payments at relatively little expense.

Medicare Part B, which is generally available to Part A recipients for a monthly premium, covers certain physician, outpatient hospital, and other charges. The permitted monthly premium for 1998 is $43.80,[21] with an annual deductible of $100 and a 20 percent copayment requirement for patients.[22] Often, however, physicians accept the 80 percent paid by Medicare as payment in full.

(b) Minimal Medicare Coverage for Long-Term Care

Most long-term nursing care is not eligible for Medicare coverage, which extends only to short-term periods of recuperation in a nursing facility begun within 30 days after an acute hospital stay of three or more days.[23] The benefits last for 100 days and trigger a patient coinsurance payment of $95.50 per day (1998 figure) after the 20th day.[24] Except in markets where nursing care is unusually expensive, Medicare's limited coverage of long-term care effectively eliminates the benefit for many typical long-term-care arrangements. Only 1 percent of the Medicare budget goes for nursing home care.[25] For a discussion of Medicare payments to skilled-nursing facilities under the Balanced Budget Act of 1997, see §28.12.

(c) Home Health Limited

Home health benefits are available under Medicare Part A or Part B for persons confined to their homes and in need of intermittent nursing care or physical or speech therapy.[26] Services can also include social services and home health aide services.[27] No patient copayments or deductibles are required. About 9 percent of Medicare benefits go to home health.[28] (See also §20.5 for a discussion of Medicare coverage problems and home health needs.)

§26.3 Medicaid: Long-Term Care for the Poor

(a) Generally

Unlike Medicare, which is available without regard to economic status, Medicaid is a federal- and state-funded program designed to benefit only the poor and near-poor.[29] All state Medicaid programs must permit enrollment of certain categorically needy persons, such as recipients of Aid to Families with Dependent Children (AFDC) or Supplemental Security Income (SSI).[30] In addition, states may elect to cover medically needy persons who have sufficient income and assets to pay for daily living expenses but not for health care. The asset limit for a single applicant's coverage is $2,000, excluding home value.[31]

Unlike Medicare, Medicaid covers nursing care without placing blanket restrictions on lengths of stay or requiring patients to absorb deductible or copayment costs. While 69 percent of Medicaid expenditures for the elderly go to nursing home costs,[32] elderly persons must first become impoverished before they can take advantage of the program (see §26.3(b)).

In 1985, the American Association of Retired Persons surveyed its members and found that nearly 80 percent of those who thought they would spend some time in a nursing facility believed that the federal government's Medicare program would pay for all or part of their stay.[33] In fact, Medicare pays for only 0.8 percent of the cost of nursing home care, whereas Medicaid pays for over 61 percent of nursing facility charges.[34] The elderly themselves or their families pay more than 48 percent of the bill, with only the remaining 1 percent covered by private insurance.[35] (See discussion of private long-term-care insurance in §27.2.)

For many middle- or upper-income elderly persons, the prospect of becoming eligible for Medicaid is not a desirable alternative. Although the eligibility criteria may vary from one state to another, the program essentially requires an elderly applicant to spend down virtually all of his or her assets and income to pay for nursing care before Medicaid picks up the bill. One study found that 63 percent of elderly persons without a spouse became poor after only 13 weeks in a nursing facility[36]; within a year, 83 percent had become impoverished. However, during the past decade, planned transfers of the assets of middle- and upper-income older persons to ensure Medicaid eligibility became a small industry, which has since been outlawed (see §26.3(b)).

Because of government's limited resources, Medicaid programs in the various states tend to pay considerably less for nursing services than facility owners charge patients who pay their own bills or are covered by private insurance. According to the American Health Care Association, a national organization of nursing home operators, government reimbursements for Medicaid patients make up only 41 percent of nursing home revenues even though Medicaid patients account for 65 percent of all nursing home

patients.[37] In facilities that cater to Medicaid patients in high percentages, the disparity between the government rate of reimbursement and the usual private-pay charges can mean that Medicaid-dependent facilities provide a lower quality of care and amenities than their non–Medicaid-dependent counterparts. Moreover, due in part to an increase in operating costs and the fixed price paid by a given state Medicaid program, many investor-owned nursing chains have experienced significant losses or declines in operating income.[38] Difficulties in covering costs of Medicaid services have persisted despite passage of the Boren Amendment, which required states to establish reasonable rates of reimbursement under the program. In 1997, Congress repealed the Boren Amendment, leaving states with broad powers to reduce Medicaid reimbursement rates (see §28.12).

(b) Eligibility of Recipients

Medicaid eligibility rules are extremely complicated such that eligibility planning requires consultation with a specialist. A Medicaid-eligible person's resources may not exceed an amount, determined by each state, generally between $1,500 and $2,000 for an individual and $2,250 for a couple, although the amounts can be as high as $3,000 for an individual. Certain assets are excluded from the resource determination, such as the applicant's home for six months after institutionalization and thereafter if occupied by the spouse or dependent children or if the patient intends to return to his or her home. Only "available" amounts are counted.[39] Funds transferred to a trust established by the applicant or his or her spouse for the benefit of the applicant are considered "available" for purposes of Medicaid eligibility.[40]

When spouses live together and neither is institutionalized, the nonapplying spouse's resources are deemed to be owned by the applicant.[41] For admissions on or after September 30, 1989, the couple's total resources are considered when one spouse is institutionalized, subject, however, to the "community spouse resource allowance." This allowance is the greater of (1) $12,000 or (2) the lesser of one-half the resources of both spouses, or $80,760 for 1998.[42] The community spouse resource allowance must be transferred to the community spouse within 90 days of the initial eligibility determination.

For purposes of Medicaid eligibility, all transfers for less-than-adequate consideration from an institutionalized applicant's resources to a nonspouse are considered part of the applicant's resources if the transfer occurs within a certain period before the eligibility determination date. Transfers of exempt property, such as a home transferred to a spouse, are not disqualifying.

Many nursing facility operators and some public policy commentators[43] believed that the eligibility rules were initially too liberal in that they allowed wealthy people to shield substantial assets from the eligibility criteria. The growth of an "elder law" attorney specialty in the 1990s has been largely a response to the demand for Medicaid transfer-of-asset planning by well-to-do elderly persons anticipating a move to nursing care.

Effective October 1, 1993,[44] Congress made several changes to the Medicaid eligibility rules to curb perceived abuses, but it also retained and even extended some protections to beneficiaries. Among other things, the rules

- extended the "look-back" period for uncompensated asset transfers from 30 months to 36 months before application for benefits and eliminated the 30-month cap on the period of ineligibility resulting from such transfers;
- retained the exemptions for transfers of assets between spouses and to a disabled child and added an exemption for trusts established for a disabled child;
- tightened requirements concerning joint ownership so that transfers between co-owners or the loss of control over funds by a co-owner's unilateral action could be considered disqualifying;
- amended existing rules concerning trusts (other than those established by will) so that the corpus of a revocable trust would be considered an available asset to the beneficiary when a trust is created by the individual or the individual's spouse;
- expanded the definition of "asset," for transfer purposes, to include income and other resources of the applicant or applicant's spouse;
- required states to establish estate recovery programs to recoup Medicaid payments from the estates of beneficiaries; and

- did *not* enact a proposed abolition of the right of nursing facility operators to inquire about the finances of an applicant for admission.

The Health Insurance Portability and Accountability Act of 1996 further[45] provides for a five-year prison term and $25,000 fine for any person who willfully disposes of assets in order to become eligible for Medicaid benefits. In 1997, Congress repealed the provisions applying criminal sanctions to applicants for benefits but left in place sanctions against those (such as lawyers) who *assist* applicants regarding asset transfers (see §28.12).

(c) Medicaid Waivers

As Medicaid costs for nursing home care continues to rise precipitously, government programs are coming under increasing pressure to cover services in noninstitutional settings. Proponents of flexibility in Medicaid programs not only argue that such care is less expensive but also point out that the care is markedly more advantageous for the individuals served.

The main mechanism that provides reimbursement for assisted-living-type services is Medicaid waivers for home- and community-based services.[46] A second waiver option for home- and community-based services for individuals 65 years of age or older[47] allows states to provide medical and social services to elderly individuals in return for which states accept an aggregate expenditure limit. Under the waiver programs, a state applies for a waiver of statutory requirements that allows it to reimburse providers of services that do not fall within the traditional Medicaid categories. Several states demonstrated successful use of this option in the 1980s, and now almost every state offers some type of waiver program that provides reimbursement for varying types of services for the aged and disabled.[48]

The types of services a state may provide under the waiver program include homemaker and health aide services, personal-care services, adult day health services, respite care, case management, and other appropriate services.[49] States may use or develop their own definitions of what constitutes appropriate services as long as such services do not extend to room and board.[50] States must provide assurances that the necessary safeguards are in place to protect the health and welfare of individuals served by the program[51] and must inform individuals of their alternatives with respect to the services and levels of care available to them.[52]

Although some of the more tentative state programs have not incorporated supportive services for assisted-living-type residences, the trend clearly is toward enhanced flexibility and creativity in structuring reimbursable care for seniors. Each year, states renew and expand waiver requests to provide more extensive services in noninstitutional settings.

Indeed, states enjoy a fair amount of flexibility in designing their programs. In particular, one of the most significant advantages of waivers is that a state may modify its Medicaid eligibility requirements.[53] In addition, a state may limit the availability of reimbursement. For example, states are not required to provide services statewide and may target a specific segment of or communities within the general population.[54] The flexibility to cap participation was an important incentive in encouraging states to take advantage of the waiver program. Today, however, most states that have experienced success with the program are expanding rather than restricting participation.[55]

Although most states are satisfied with the current program, some have found the conditions of participation onerous. States must demonstrate that services are provided to recipients who would otherwise require nursing home care and that delivering alternative care to recipients is more cost-effective than furnishing care in a nursing home.[56] Proof is based on the so-called "cold-bed" formula, which requires states to show that an actual nursing home bed would be available for the recipient. Even though such a requirement is reasonable for states with a flexible or large supply of nursing home beds, it can be a source of frustration for states with strict Certificate of Need laws or moratoriums on nursing home construction.

In view of such difficulties, Congress enacted a new program in 1990 to disengage the availability of federal funds from the above conditions of participation and thus theoretically reduce administrative burdens.[57] The "Home and Community Care" plan for "Functionally Disabled Elderly Individuals" is targeted exclusively to the senior population and limited to individuals in need of substantial assistance with two

out of three activities of daily living (toileting, transferring, and eating) as well as to victims of certain classes of Alzheimer's disease.[58] While the intent of the program is to provide a strong incentive for states to expand services to elders, critics argue that the program's serious drawbacks outweigh its advantages. Under the plan, the amount of federal funds available each year is subject to a cap, with the restricted funds apportioned among as many states as decide to apply.[59] Moreover, because states cannot restrict the number of participants in Home and Community Care, they are left vulnerable to unlimited financial liability.

By combining flexibility in program design with predictable levels of financial accountability, waivers are widely viewed as the best of the currently available options for funding nonmedical care. A study by the Intergovernmental Health Policy Project concludes that waivers are seen as a "workable and effective means of offering [home- and community-based] services to a target population with specific fiscal controls."[60] As state waiver programs become better established and more operators take advantage of their benefits, new developments and wider use are expected.

§26.4 Miscellaneous Federal Programs

Federal programs that were not necessarily designed specifically to provide care for older persons but that may contribute to the cost of care include Supplemental Security Income, Social Services Block Grants, and the Older Americans Act.[61]

(a) Supplemental Security Income

Supplemental Security Income (SSI)[62] is a federal assistance program available to aging, blind, and disabled persons whose income falls below specified levels. States may supplement federal SSI payments; in fact, about 35 states make specific payments to support persons in some type of community-based group living arrangement that provides nonmedical services such as assisted living.[63]

(b) Older Americans Act

The Older Americans Act makes grants to the states for creating supportive services for the elderly such as in-home services, home health aides, visitation, adult daycare, respite services, congregate meals, home-delivered meals, long-term-care ombudsperson programs, and senior centers.[64] State and area agencies on aging administer the grants. The appropriation from 1987 to 1993 increased from $829 million to $925 million.[65]

(c) Social Services Block Grants

The Social Services Block Grant program[66] (Title XX of the Social Security Act) provides federal grants to states for, among other things, "preventing or reducing inappropriate institutional care by providing for community-based care, home-based care, or other forms of less intensive care."[67] All states provide some form of home care services under the program, but the program stresses social services rather than health care.[68] The program is not designed for the elderly, and there are many competing demands on the comparatively moderate sums available.[69]

Notes

1. A comprehensive symposium on long-term-care financing, covering topics such as public and long-term-care insurance, home care and community-based care program design, continuing-care retirement communities, nursing home reimbursement, the politics of long-term-care financing, and public/private partnerships, appears in the Spring 1990 issue of *Generations* (American Society on Aging).

2. *HHS News,* July 29, 1986, U.S. Department of Health and Human Services, citing 1985 figures.

3. "Medicaid Costs May Reach $200 Billion," *The Spectrum,* Sept. 1991, reporting on U.S. Health and Human Services task force conclusions.

4. MacNeil, N., "Employer Mandated Health Insurance: A Solution for the Working Uninsured?" *Journal of Health and Hospital Law,* Nov. 1991, 337, citing the Pepper Commission Report.

5. "A Profile of Older Americans," American Association of Retired Persons, 1996.

6. *Aging America: Trends and Projections,* 1991 ed., U.S. Senate Special Committee on Aging, pp. 137–138; personal health care expenditures include all expenditures except research.

7. "Grays on the Go," *Time,* Feb. 22, 1988, 66, 70.

8. "Medicare Costs to Continue to Spiral," *Contemporary Long Term Care,* July 1990, 18. The study suggests that research on diseases causing long-term disabilities is the best approach to dealing with the problem.

9. *Aging America,* note 5 *above,* Table 4-13.

10. *Id.,* Table 4-14.

11. *Aging America,* 1985–1986 ed., at 106.

12. *Aging America,* note 5 *above,* Chart 4-13.

13. Kunerth, A., "Group LTC Insurance as a Marketing Tool," *Contemporary Long Term Care,* Dec. 1987, 38.

14. *Ibid.*

15. "Coming Up Short: Increasing Out-of-Pocket Health Spending by Older Americans," American Association of Retired Persons, The Urban Institute, Apr. 1994.

16. *See Medicare and Medicaid Guide* (CCH), ¶¶ 1101, 1115.

17. *Aging America,* note 5 *above,* at 107.

18. "Developments in Aging: 1992," U.S. Senate Special Committee on Aging, S. Rep. 103–40, Vol. 1, Apr. 20, 1993, 206.

19. *See generally* note 15 *above,* ¶¶ 1263, 13010.33.

20. The average hospital length of stay in 1988 was 8.9 days for those 65 and older compared with 14.2 days in 1968. *Aging America,* note 5 *above,* at 99. By 1994, it was reduced to 7.4 days. "A Profile of Older Americans," note 4 *above.*

21. *See generally* note 15 *above,* ¶¶ 13040, 13040.64.

22. Note 15, ¶¶ 13,020.

23. *Id.* at ¶ 1309.

24. *Id.* at ¶ 13,010.80.

25. *Aging America,* note 5 *above,* Chart 4-11.

26. Note 15 *above,* ¶ 1401. Under the Balanced Budget Act of 1997, between FYs 1998 and 2003, payment for home health services, other than the first 100 visits after a hospital or skilled-nursing stay, will be shifted to Part B. Pub. L. 105–33, Sec. 4611.

27. *Ibid.*

28. *See* "Basic Statistics about Home Care 1996," National Association for Home Care.

29. Note 15 *above,* at ¶ 14,010.

30. Note 15 *above,* at ¶ 14,231.

31. *See* Kapp, M., "Options for Long-Term Care Financing: A Look to the Future," *Hastings Law Journal,*

Mar. 1991, 724, citing the Pepper Commission Report. For the 30 states that had medically needy programs in 1985, eligible enrollees were permitted, on average, to have no greater than about $1,800 in resources. ICF, Inc., "Private Financing of Long Term Care: Current Methods and Resources," Phase I Final Report, U.S. Department of Health and Human Resources, 1985, at 91 (Phase II also published 1985).

32. *See Aging America*, note 5 *above*, Chart 4-12.

33. *See* Garland, S., "Nursing-Home Time Bomb Threatens an Aging Nation," *San Francisco Examiner,* Nov. 3, 1985, E-1.

34. *Aging America,* note 5 *above,* Table 4-13 (1987 figures).

35. *Id.* at 172 (1988 figures).

36. Massachusetts Blue Cross-Blue Shield Study, 1985, reported in *Congressional Quarterly,* May 31, 1986, 1,228.

37. *Older Americans Report,* June 10, 1988, 233.

38. *See* Wagner, L., "Nursing Homes Buffeted by Troubles," *Modern Health Care,* Mar. 18, 1988, 33.

39. 42 U.S.C. §1396a(a)(17).

40. 42 U.S.C. §1396a(k)(1).

41. 42 U.S.C. §1396a(a)(17)(D).

42. 42 U.S.C. §§1396r-5(c), (f)(2).

43. Kosterlitz J., "Middle-Class Medicaid," *National Journal,* Nov. 9, 1991, 2,728.

44. Omnibus Budget Reconciliation Act, H.R. 2264, Pub. L. No. 103-66, 107 Stat. 312 (amending 42 U.S.C. §§1395 and 1396p).

45. Pub. L. No. 104-191.

46. 42 U.S.C. §1396n(c); 42 C.F.R. §441.300 *et seq.*

47. 42 U.S.C. §1396n(d).

48. *HCFA Medicaid Waiver Fact Sheet,* Jan. 6, 1994.

49. 42 U.S.C. §1396n(c)(4)(B).

50. 42 U.S.C. §1396n(c)(1); 42 C.F.R. §441.310(a)(3).

51. 42 U.S.C. §1396n(c)(2)(A); 42 C.F.R. §441.302.

52. 42 U.S.C. §1396n(c)(2)(C); 42 C.F.R. §441.302(d).

53. 42 U.S.C. §1396n(c)(3).

54. 42 U.S.C. §1396n(c)(3).

55. *HCFA Fact Sheet.*

56. 42 U.S.C. §1396n(c)(2)(C) and (D).

57. *See* 42 U.S.C. §1396t.

58. 42 U.S.C. §1396t(l).

59. 42 U.S.C. §1396t(m).

60. "State Home and Community-Based Services for the Aged Under Medicaid," American Association of Retired Persons, Public Policy Institute, 1991.

61. *See* O'Shaughnessy, Price, and Griffith, "Financing and Delivery of Long-Term Care Services for the Elderly," Congressional Research Service, Feb. 24, 1987, 31-39.

62. *See* 42 U.S.C. §§1381 *et seq.*

63. O'Shaughnessy *et al.,* note 60 *above,* at 38-39.

64. *See* 42 U.S.C. §§3001 *et seq.*

65. O'Shaughnessy *et al.,* note 60 *above,* at 35. *See* "Developments in Aging: 1992," U.S. Senate Special Committee on Aging, S. Rep. 103-40, Vol. I, Apr. 20, 1993, at 208.

66. 42 U.S.C. §§1397 *et seq.*

67. 42 U.S.C. §1397(4).

68. O'Shaughnessy *et al.,* note 60 *above,* at 31-34.

69. About $2.7 billion. *Id.*

Sunlake Terrace; Las Vegas, Nevada.

27 Private Funding of Health Care

§27.1 Medigap Insurance

The many out-of-pocket copayments and deductibles chargeable to Medicare beneficiaries in connection with their hospital care[1] have led to a proliferation of so-called Medigap insurance policies designed to cover such expenses. A General Accounting Office (GAO) study that reviewed nearly 400 different policies offered by 92 commercial firms and 13 Blue Cross/Blue Shield plans represented less than half the estimated $5 billion Medigap market.[2] About two-thirds of the elderly have been said to have a Medigap policy in force.[3]

Although plentiful, Medigap insurance policies are not at all effective in filling the largest gap in Medicare coverage—the expenses of long-term care. Federal legislation[4] enacted in 1980 established minimum benefit coverage standards for Medigap policies on a nationwide basis. For inpatient hospitalizations, Medigap policies must pay the daily Medicare beneficiary copayment from the 61st through 150th day of stay, plus 90 percent of covered charges from the 151st to the 365th day.[5] The legislation did not, however, require any coverage whatsoever for nursing or home health care, even for copayments required in connection with Medicare-covered convalescent nursing care.[6] Amendments passed in 1990[7] required the National Association of Insurance Commissioners (NAIC) to adopt a uniform core benefits package and mandated that policies be guaranteed renewable and meet specified loss ratios.

In 1991, NAIC adopted a set of ten standard policies that included coverage for 20 percent of the patient's share of physician charges, a $157 per day contribution for the 61st through 90th hospital day, some coverage beyond 90 days, the $78.50 Medicare copayment for days 20 through 100 at a nursing facility, and some home care.[8]

§27.2 Long-Term-Care Insurance

(a) Historical Unavailability; Increasing Demand

In sharp contrast to the eagerness demonstrated by the Medigap market, the insurance industry was exceedingly slow (or reluctant) in the early 1980s to respond to the need for private sector initiatives to help indemnify the costs of long-term nursing care. Although only 12 policies covering a scant 50,000 persons nationwide were estimated to exist as of early 1985, predictions held that, over the next 35 years, the market would sustain a $20 billion industry.[9] In the meantime, several reasons were offered for the scarcity of policies.[10] People believed they were already covered by Medicare; the elderly were unwilling to acknowledge the eventuality of needing chronic care when they were still young enough to ensure the affordability of premiums; insurers feared overuse of services; consumers realized that Medicaid would be available in case of dire emergency; the demand for group insurance did not exist, and marketing policies on an individual basis was too costly; state regulations were too diverse, requiring a custom product to be tailored to each state; state regulations were overly broad and failed to make distinctions between long-term-care and other types of health insurance; and the product would be too expensive for most elderly persons. More recently, however, some innovations are challenging many of these assumptions (see §27.2(c)).

Recent data indicate that many insurance carriers have developed individual long-term-care insurance policies.[11] In 1988, approximately 70 different companies in the United States offered such policies; approximately 500,000 policies were in force compared with an estimated 120,000 in 1983.[12] By 1990, the number had grown to nearly 2 million policies for an increase of 29 percent (425,000 policies) over 1989.[13] The average purchase age for individual plans was 72; for group plans, 69; and for employer-sponsored plans, 43.[14] In a survey published by the Health Insurance Association of America, nearly three-quarters of respondents said they were willing and able to pay for an insurance policy that would provide long-term care[15] while 60 percent believed that the government's role should be limited to financing long-term care only for the most needy.[16]

Nevertheless, commentators have questioned the ability of long-term-care insurance to solve the problems of financing the long-term-care services needed by elderly Americans. Despite predictions that the proportion of elderly with private long-term-care insurance will increase from the 1988 level of 2 percent to a level of 30 or 40 percent in 30 years, 60 to 70 percent of the elderly will not be able to afford private coverage.[17]

Not surprisingly, the debate over whether long-term-care costs can be funded by private long-term-care insurance, as opposed to federal subsidy, continues to intensify. Some elderly advocacy groups contend that most elderly cannot afford private nursing home insurance and that companies engage in abusive sales and claims-processing practices. A study by the Families USA Foundation revealed that long-

term-care insurance policies tend to require either extremely high premiums or extremely high copayments and that, as a result, more than 80 percent of middle-aged and older Americans cannot afford to purchase long-term-care insurance.[18] On the other hand, insurance groups claim that as many as 40 percent of the elderly can afford a sufficient long-term-care policy. In any event, both parties to the debate concede that because claims will not have to be paid for another ten to 15 years, the viability of today's product cannot be fully assessed.[19]

(b) Confusing Array of Benefits

Even the few policies that had evolved by the mid-1980s tended to contain a widely divergent range of eligibility conditions and limitations on coverages. A General Accounting Office (GAO) report released in 1987 studied 33 policies offered by 25 insurers and concluded that "the lack of uniform standards and marketing requirements means consumers have little protection against substandard policies and sales abuse."[20] A 1989 House of Representatives subcommittee report went so far as to recommend a ban on private long-term-care insurance due to questionable sales tactics and marketing abuses.[21]

One 1986 review of the nine "most comprehensive" policies[22] revealed a bewilderingly broad spectrum of benefits and limitations as follows:

- skilled-nursing daily benefits from only $12 to as much as $120;
- custodial care daily benefits from as little as $10 after 20 days of skilled or intermediate care to a high of $120 after skilled care of any duration;
- home care benefits from zero to $60 per day following 30 days of nursing care;
- prior hospitalization requirements of up to three days within 14 days of nursing home admission;
- waiting periods of up to 100 days before the commencement of benefits;
- limits on total available nursing coverage from 1,000 days to five years; and
- annual premiums starting at $179 for some 55-year-olds and reaching $4,460 for some 75-year-olds.

An exhaustive survey of 53 policies conducted by *Consumer Reports* in 1988[23] disclosed an even broader array of benefits, premiums, and conditions as follows:

- monthly premiums ranging from $16.11 to $102.56;
- benefits ranging from $46 to $100 per day;
- waiting periods ranging from zero to 100 days;
- maximum benefits ranging from $730 to levels without limit; and
- variations in coverage of home care and custodial care, prior hospitalization requirements, Alzheimer's coverage, inflation adjustments, exclusion of preexisting conditions, level premium features, guaranteed renewability, and waiver of premium after the beneficiary has been admitted to a nursing home for a certain period.

The *Consumer Reports* study listed the following characteristics of a good long-term-care insurance policy:

- daily nursing home benefit of $80;
- maximum 20-day waiting period;
- four-year maximum benefit period for one stay;
- unlimited maximum benefit period for all stays;
- coverage of skilled-nursing, intermediate, and custodial care;
- commencement of coverage within no more than 30 days after a three-day hospital stay;
- coverage of home care benefits without requiring a prior nursing home or hospital stay;
- waiver of premium after the beneficiary has entered the nursing facility for a specified period;
- guaranteed renewability for life;
- express coverage of Alzheimer's disease;
- a level premium for life; and
- a company rated by Best's as A or A+.

Because of the scarcity of policies offering inflation adjustments, the report did not list built-in inflation protection as a necessary element of a good policy. It did note, however, that the major drawback of nearly every policy is its fixed benefit, especially given that the average cost of a year's nursing home stay is expected to jump from 1988's figure of $22,000 to $55,000 by the year 2018. According to a 1993 study, other drawbacks to long-term-care policies are a tendency toward excluding from enrollment people with certain conditions or illnesses, benefit restrictions limiting access to covered care, and lim-

ited periods of coverage, usually up to a maximum of four to five years.[24]

When *Consumer Reports* studied long-term-care policies again in 1991,[25] the publication's scathing cover story outlined a deteriorating situation characterized by a "dizzying array of new policies, riders, and features," a disturbing degree of agent confusion and even deceit, a fragmented regulatory scheme, record insolvencies among carriers, and rising long-term-care costs that were projected to outpace most policies' coverage limits. In one example, the article found a $200,000 shortfall in coverage when it compared the projected cost of care for a 65-year-old entering a nursing facility for four years in 2010 ($317,000) with the $80-a-day benefit provided by a no-inflation insurance policy (total $116,800).

(c) Long-Term-Care Insurance Innovations

(1) Development of Standards and Incentives

Some commentators found that the confusing array of benefits, conditions, and limitations that typified the first long-term-care insurance products were reminiscent of the Medigap market in its early days before federal legislation. As a result, these same commentators called for uniform definitions, minimum coverage standards, and other reforms.[26]

One early development designed to spur both greater uniformity among long-term-care insurance policies and expedited product development on a national scale was the adoption by the National Association of Insurance Commissioners of a mid-1980s Model Long Term Care Insurance Act. Among its other provisions, the act prohibits the following: cancellation of coverage on the grounds of age or mental or physical deterioration, a new waiting period in the event of a conversion or replacement of coverage, coverage exclusion for losses arising from preexisting illnesses when the loss occurs more than 12 months following the effective date of coverage for those 65 or over and 24 months thereafter for those under 65, mandated loss ratios, and a prior institutionalization requirement within a period of less than 14 days. At the same time, the act requires minimum disclosure standards for advertising materials.[27]

In addition, the report accompanying the model act recommends prohibiting optionally renewable policies, preserving prior institutionalization options, promoting tax credits or deductions for premiums, restricting Medicaid eligibility that results from the intentional spending down of assets, developing long-term-care riders on existing insurance products, establishing a database for pricing and loss ratio determination, and educating consumers.[28]

NAIC's model statute came under sharp criticism in the 1988 *Consumer Reports* study of long-term-care insurance policies.[29] Specifically, the study cited deficiencies related to the prior hospital or nursing home stay requirement as a condition of receiving benefits for less intensive care, the possibility of cancellation of coverage in limited circumstances, the absence of standards for the language used in long-term-care policies, the absence of express coverage of Alzheimer's disease, and the failure to require inclusion of a state insurance department telephone number for consumer inquiries about limitations on policy coverages.

The NAIC model act underwent revision, first, to prohibit the sale of policies that offer only skilled care in nursing facilities[30] and, second, to prohibit prior hospitalization provisions and the conditioning of the benefits for one level of care on the prior receipt of another level of care.[31] In 1993, NAIC added a nonforfeiture of benefits requirement that forces insurance companies to pay benefits to enrollees who stop making payments on their policies. Some groups, such as the American Association of Homes for the Aging and the Health Insurance Association of America, oppose mandated nonforfeiture on the ground that it will lead to large increases in the cost of long-term care insurance.[32]

As of February 1990, 40 states had adopted legislation based on the NAIC model statute.[33] Still, a GAO study published in 1991 found that many states had not adopted all the NAIC standards. The study further criticized the NAIC standards for failing to require uniformity in definitions and eligibility criteria, financial protections, and marketing standards. Finally, it recommended the adoption of federal standards if the states and NAIC did not act quickly.[34]

Despite the states' failure to adopt federal standards, some efforts have encouraged the use of long-term-care insurance. In his 1986 report to the president, the secretary of the U.S. Department of Health and Human Services, for example, called for a limited tax credit for long-term-care insurance premiums for persons over age 55, favorable tax treatment of long-term-care insurance reserves in parallel with the tax treatment then available for life insurance, and removal of employer restrictions on prefunding of employee long-term-care benefits.[35] It was not until 1996, however, that Congress adopted tax incentives for private funding of long-term-care costs and insurance premiums (see §28.11).[36]

That federal and state governments and national organizations and interest groups have given widespread recognition to the long-term-care insurance issue should help solve the problems of consumer confusion, disparate and overly broad state regulation, and other barriers to product development and acceptance.

(2) Group Coverages: Retirement Facility Plans, Employee Plans, HMOs, SHMOs

The heightened marketing expenses and underwriting risks associated with selling long-term-care policies on an individual basis have been perceived as an impediment to the development of long-term-care insurance products.[37] Nonetheless, different forms of group long-term-care insurance coverage have evolved in the marketplace.

By the late 1980s, a few major insurance carriers had begun to offer group long-term-care insurance policies for continuing-care communities or related retirement facility groups. As of 1988, at least 26 facilities or multiple-facility operators had purchased such policies from providers that included Aetna, Metropolitan Life, and the Provident Life and Accident Company.[38] The policies, which usually require mandatory resident participation in the program, were targeted to facilities with entrance fees, a minimum of 200 units, and nursing facilities and other services and amenities on site or nearby.[39] In addition, the insurance carriers have generally custom-designed the policies and offer full life-time coverage without prior hospitalization requirements. Although insurers charge a 10 percent annual fee and achieve profit margins of 5 to 10 percent, the facility and residents may gain certain advantages—such as rating expertise, better benefits, and possibly broader risk pools—over the self-insurance or individual policy models otherwise available.[40] Reportedly, group long-term-care insurance policies established for retirement communities typically have a higher loss ratio than individual long-term-care insurance policies. In other words, more dollars are used to pay claims than to cover costs of marketing, administration, and underwriting. Individual policies often have loss ratios as low as 50 percent, whereas group long-term-care insurance policies for retirement communities often have loss ratios of 75 percent.[41]

As of 1990, at least five insurance carriers were marketing group long-term-care insurance products to retirement communities. Some require mandatory participation for all residents, others make the program voluntary for existing residents and mandatory for new admittees, and some are voluntary for all residents. While nursing home lengths of stay average 90 days or less for more than 50 percent of patients, more than 25 percent have a length of stay in excess of one year. One commentator concludes that the older and more frail residents attracted to CCRCs generate higher premium rates for group long-term-care insurance programs than would individuals purchasing policies marketed to the population at large.[42]

Another reviewer of group long-term-care insurance plans argues that a home health care benefit may be detrimental to the long-term interests of a retirement community because it results in slow turnover of units, transformation of an independent-living facility into an assisted-living facility, difficulty in attracting new residents to the facility, and a loss of expected income from entry fees. One suggested remedy is to limit in dollars or days the annual home health benefit covered by the policy. Another suggestion calls for discouraging waiver of premium provisions. Such provisions were designed for an employed population for which health care needs would mean an unanticipated loss of income, which is not the case for a retired person. Level premium provisions (where higher-than-cost premiums in the early years build reserves to fund excess costs in later years) can be illusory when, after a two- to four-year premium guarantee period, rates may increase by a substantial margin in the next year (e.g., 25 percent).[43]

Employee group health plans have also occasionally provided some long-term-care benefits beyond the recuperative approach taken by Medicare.[44] In fact, large employers have shown significant interest in long-term-care coverage for their employees.[45]

By 1990, 81 employer group-sponsored programs were in effect, with another 51 reportedly to be added in 1991.[46] A 1991 study found that 10 percent of Fortune 500 companies had group long-term-care policies and that 76 percent planned to sponsor such policies in the next five years.[47]

Prepaid group health plans[48] traditionally have not ventured far into the long-term-care arena.[49] Some health maintenance organizations (HMOs) have, however, developed plans that specifically cater to elderly enrollees and provide some long-term-care and home health benefits.[50] In addition, the Health Care Financing Administration has conducted four demonstration projects for Social Health Maintenance Organizations (SHMOs), which offer coverage for a continuum of care, including acute and long-term care. These plans are offered on a prepaid fixed-rate basis, with service use controlled by a case management system.[51] For a discussion of managed-care plans and their impact on seniors' care facilities, see §27.4.

(3) Advantages of Senior Center Long-Term-Care Insurance

As compared to self-insurance, a seniors' facility purchase of a long-term-care insurance product in the marketplace offers an important advantage: the risk of loss may be spread over a larger population base. In fact, if the insurance carrier is careful in selecting its clientele, the result can be substantial cost savings, especially for smaller facilities. Specifically, insurance carriers can significantly reduce the cost of insurance by offering their product only to selected seniors' facilities rather than to the general public and by paying preferred benefits for health care or custodial care delivered at selected facilities where there is an incentive to control costs and manage care. Of course, the involvement of a well-respected insurance company in a retirement community's health insurance program may help promote consumer confidence and enhance marketing efforts.

From the point of view of many developers, the use of long-term-care insurance policies may also be desirable because a developer generally does not wish to engage in the business of self-insurance. Instead, by simply arranging for group coverage for the residents of the facility under development, the developer can provide many of the benefits of a continuing-care type of arrangement without directly assuming responsibility for calculating the risks of paying for future health care needs. Depending on state law, shifting the obligation to cover future health care expenses to a licensed insurance company may also have certain regulatory benefits for the retirement community. Often, states adopt laws regulating life-care or continuing-care facilities because of the self-insurance aspect of the transaction. To the extent that state requirements for reserves for continuing-care facilities are duplicated by reserve requirements imposed on the long-term-care insurance company, the burden of regulatory compliance may be passed on to the insurance carrier.

Of course, the disadvantage of contracting for group coverage is that the portion of the premium allocated by the carrier to "administration," as opposed to claims paid to beneficiaries, is often about 25 percent. Self-insurance can eliminate this out-of-pocket expense.

(4) Coordination of Benefits

One problem associated with new long-term-care insurance products is coordination with other benefits. Unlike Medigap policies, which are designed to build on a uniform base of Medicare benefits, new comprehensive long-term-care policies may provide coverages on top of a potpourri of Medicare benefits, employee health plans, retirement benefits, existing continuing-care contracts, Medigap policies, and various other less comprehensive programs of an unpredictable nature. When an individual has already invested substantial funds in such a program (e.g., a retirement benefits policy), that individual may find it necessary to purchase duplicative base coverage to obtain the desired excess long-term-care coverage. Until the market grows and more coverage options become available, it may be difficult to obtain comprehensive long-term-care coverage that is supplemental to rather than partially duplicative of coverages already in place (see also §27.4).

§27.3 Self-Insurance Methods

In addition to the options of purchasing health care insurance from a third party or enrolling in a prepaid health plan, consumers may self-insure for their fu-

ture health care needs by taking advantage of home equity conversion methods such as a contract with a continuing-care provider,[52] reverse annuity mortgages, or the funding of a Medical Savings Account.

(a) Continuing Care

Continuing-care retirement communities (CCRCs) were probably the first type of seniors' facility to respond in a significant way to the absence of government insurance for the costs of long-term health care. Many continuing-care facilities that offer nursing care as part of their overall program do not substantially increase the charges to a resident when he or she moves from residential living in an apartment unit to continuous care in the nursing facility. A facility that does not substantially increase charges based on level of care is often called a Type A CCRC (see §2.3(d)). The provision of various levels of care at a level price is made possible by a self-insurance program whereby the operator, using actuarial tables and drawing on experience in the delivery of health care, predicts the life-time costs of caring for the residents in its community and relies on a combination of entrance fees and adjustable monthly fees to finance these costs. To the extent that usual monthly fees are insufficient to cover the costs of care, the operator may reserve monies from entrance fees or other sources.

CCRCs in which residents pay entrance fees and/or monthly fees in return for housing, services, and health care have been recognized as one of the most important existing methods of privately financing long-term-care needs.[53] Except for the emerging long-term-care insurance market, continuing-care communities are in fact one of the only material forms of private long-term-care financing currently in general use and likely the most widespread group product.

CCRCs are often perceived as primarily targeted to the wealthy,[54] and indeed many such facilities do cater to the upper-income elderly. Most facilities are, however, affordable to a wide range of older people.[55] Given the growing need for and public awareness of long-term-care financing vehicles, CCRC development for middle-income groups should expand more rapidly once higher-income markets have been saturated.

As with other products, CCRCs may vary considerably in terms of the scope of benefits offered and the varying costs and means of payment.[56] Some may charge a higher monthly rate for residence in the nursing unit than for apartment living or may provide a limited number of days of care without any increase in normal periodic fees. Others may offer a full indemnity type of plan in which all needed care is provided at a uniform price charged to all residents. Various combinations of entrance fees and monthly fees and of refund, unit resale, or fee credit policies further complicate the field.

Facilities that promise future care or priority access to facilities but do not offer any significant form of risk-pooled prepayment mechanism or other insurance component may lead to consumer confusion of the type that led the federal government to regulate Medigap policies. In fact, disagreement within the industry itself is considerable with respect to the precise bounds of the continuing-care or life-care concept.[57]

Many view the self-insurance aspect of continuing-care facilities as the riskiest element of the retirement home business. Facility failures have not, however, resulted as much from the failure to predict the cost of future health care for the resident population as from excessive optimism in the developer's ability to market the project or the creation of fee mechanisms that do not allow adjustments to meet rising expenses (see Chapter 5). With careful analysis of residents' finances, verification of the statistical need for nursing home care, documentation of actuarial life expectancies of the specific resident mix, careful enumeration of the health care services that are and are not covered by the arrangement, control of health care delivery costs, use of reserve funds, and the ability to adjust fees, most continuing-care facilities are usually able to operate on a financially sound basis and to continue offering substantial health care benefits at stable, predictable rates.[58]

At present, no federal law sets forth minimum standards for CCRC benefits,[59] and even states noted for comprehensive regulation of the business do not prescribe minimum health benefits or coverages, loss ratios, eligibility criteria, or permitted levels of fees.[60] Due to the larger risk pools and greater degree of regulation inherent in the commercial insurance industry, long-term-care insurance presents an argu-

ably more secure risk than individually self-insured facilities. However, the residential community character of a CCRC introduces lifestyle and health care utilization controls not typically addressed by most health insurance policies. Thus, long-term-care insurance may be best used to enhance rather than supplant continuing-care facility programs.[61]

(b) Home Equity Conversion

CCRCs often rely on resident home sales to fund the entrance fees required on admission. However, senior citizens still in their homes may be able to tap their existing home equity to purchase a plan to fund their future health care needs both before and after moving into a seniors' housing facility. For example, a homeowner can use accrued equity to purchase home health care on a prepaid basis (sometimes called "life care at home") or to secure deferred admission to a retirement community at a time when the resident's home cannot be sold due to market conditions or because the resident is not yet ready to move.

Home equity conversion may take the form of a reverse annuity mortgage (RAM), in which the homeowner retains title to the property but uses the equity to secure a loan, the proceeds of which are paid out in monthly installments. At the end of the loan term, the principal and interest are due and may be recovered by sale of the house.[62]

A second form of home equity conversion is a sale-leaseback, in which the homeowner sells the residence to an investor, retains a life-time tenancy, and receives the purchase price in the form of monthly payments.[63] Home equity conversion also can be used in conjunction with property tax deferral programs that permit individuals to borrow money from state or local governments to pay property taxes. Most property tax deferral programs require the borrower to be at least 65 years old and have income below a stated level. The loans do not have to be repaid until the borrower dies, moves, or sells the home.[64]

The use of home equity conversion contracts is estimated to be extremely limited.[65] The types of programs described here typically provide small payments over long periods of time, whereas long-term care often requires larger payments over shorter time spans.[66] It has been observed that lines of credit secured by home equity may be more suitable for funding long-term care than traditional equity conversion programs.[67] Since passage of the Tax Reform Act of 1986, which eliminated personal interest deductions except for certain home loans, banks have begun to offer such home equity lines of credit more regularly.

In 1989, HUD launched a home equity conversion mortgage insurance demonstration project involving 50 mortgage lenders and 2,500 FHA-insured loans to homeowners over the age of 62.[68] HUD has since expanded the program to 25,000 loans.[69] Regulations [70] specified that the demonstration program must involve three types of loans. The first "tenure option" provides a fixed payment to the borrower as long as he or she lives in the home. A second "term plan" furnishes payments for a fixed period. A third "line of credit" plan allows the homeowner to draw funds on an irregular, as needed, basis. Fixed- or adjustable-rate reverse mortgages are available. Repayment is not due until the property is sold or the homeowner dies or ceases to live in the residence for 12 months by reason of illness. The lender may also require immediate payment when the property is no longer the homeowner's principal residence or the homeowner does not perform an obligation.[71] One commentator advises that a durable power of attorney should be used in conjunction with a reverse mortgage so that the borrower's attorney-in-fact may sell, refinance, or otherwise cure defaults or defend against foreclosure in the event that the borrower ceases to occupy the property or otherwise fails to perform loan covenants.[72]

Individuals considering home equity conversion to help finance long-term care should determine whether the conversion will have an effect on any government benefits that they are currently receiving or may receive in the future. Amounts received under a reverse mortgage will not affect a person's eligibility for Medicare, retirement, survivor, or disability benefits but may affect eligibility for Supplemental Security Income (SSI) and Medicaid. To prevent payments under a reverse mortgage from affecting eligibility under SSI or Medicaid, one commentator recommends the following precautions:

- Pay careful attention to federal and state resource limits when structuring the payments to the borrower.
- Schedule payments early in the month to allow as much time as possible to spend the proceeds.
- Calculate the payments to meet projected expenses with little or no carryover.

The extent to which reverse mortgages will be available in the future is unclear. One observer cited the following obstacles to the expanded availability of both lender-insured reverse mortgages and FHA-insured reverse mortgages under HUD's home equity conversion mortgage insurance demonstration project:

- State usury laws may prohibit interest and other charges required by reverse mortgages.
- Reverse mortgages may be subject to restrictions imposed by other state laws such as banking and consumer credit laws that limit the ability to make reverse mortgages; maturity date or term limitations on open-end credit agreements; adjustable-rate mortgage restrictions; and priority limits for future advances.
- Reverse mortgages may affect the borrower's government benefits.
- Interest paid by a reverse mortgage borrower is currently not tax deductible.
- State due-on-sale limitations may restrict the ability of a lender to accelerate a lender-insured reverse mortgage loan on the borrower's death.
- No secondary market exists for lender-insured reverse mortgages.[73]

(c) Medical Savings Accounts

In 1996, Congress authorized a pilot program permitting medical expense deductions for contributions to Medical Savings Accounts (see §28.11(e)). The concept was first proposed in the mid-1980s as the Individual Medical Account (IMA). Similar to an Individual Retirement Account (IRA), the IMA would permit a person to defer taxes on a portion of income deposited each year in a restricted account, the assets of which could be used only for specified medical expenses. Among the concerns with medical savings accounts is that people may not be inclined to participate in a plan at a sufficiently young age because they do not believe they will need long-term care or because they believe Medicare will pay for such care. Furthermore, the fiscal impact of the tax deferral remains unknown.[74] One study has also seriously questioned whether long-term-care savings accounts can generate adequate funds to cover long-term-care liabilities for the elderly.[75]

(d) Use of Transferable Memberships, Refunds, and Equity Loans as a Health Care Reserve

In recent years, many seniors' housing communities have developed creative methods for helping residents to, in effect, self-insure their own health care costs after admission. The traditional CCRC customarily pooled entrance fees and monthly fees on a facilitywide basis and used the funds for operating expenses as well as for general reserves for health care costs and other contingencies. With the fees typically nonrefundable, pooling made sense.

More recently, with the advent of refundable entrance fees, facilities keep separate account of entrance fee refunds or other resident resources that the resident may draw on to pay for health care costs in the facility. When memberships have resale value or ownership arrangements provide a resident with an equity interest in real estate,[76] facility operators may create a lien to secure payment of nursing charges, usual monthly fees, or health insurance premiums. While such a method of financing health care is not as precise as an actuarially planned, pooled insurance program, it can yield a substantial emergency fund that an individual in the facility may tap as a last resort before becoming dependent on government programs.

§27.4 Managed Care and Retirement Communities

(a) Generally

The skyrocketing costs of health care have led to a proliferation of methods by which the marketplace and government attempt to control the delivery of care. The primary strategy has been to gather health care consumers and providers into organizations that control the use of services and pool the risks and costs associated with providing health care. The resulting alphabet soup of acronyms for health care organizations—for example, HMOs (health maintenance organizations, discussed generally in §20.6), PSOs (provider-sponsored organizations), PPOs (preferred provider organizations), IPAs (individual practice associations), and MSOs (management services organizations)—reflects something of a revolution in the way health care is structured in the United States. Some of these organizations merely represent ways for providers to form alliances and save costs by taking advantage of economies of scale and cost sharing. Others also "manage care" by restricting the right of enrolled consumers to use services or to choose their health care providers. Providers also contract with payors to provide services for a fixed or per capita cost. The resulting economic pressures can lead not only to an emphasis on preventive care but also to undertreatment of serious health problems.

While most of the activity of managed-care organizations has involved acute care hospital and physician services, the recent growth of these organizations has begun to affect the operation of retirement communities and other providers of long-term care.

(b) Residents Enrolled in Managed-Care Organizations

Seniors' housing communities that have contracted to provide care to their residents sometimes discover that a number of residents are also enrolled in an HMO. In some cases, enrollment is a job-related benefit that was available to the resident at the time of entry into the retirement community. In other cases, the resident enrolled in an HMO to obtain a benefit not available under the retirement community contract (for example, coverage of medications). For the retirement community, a resident's current enrollment in an HMO may pose a problem. As a prerequisite to coverage of a service not offered by the retirement community (for example, Medicare hospital copayments), the HMO may require the enrollee to use only the specified providers for follow-up services that are offered by the retirement community (for example, nursing or assisted living). If the retirement community does not have a contract with the HMO to provide services to its enrolled residents,

residents may have to go elsewhere for the specified services.

The retirement community should not be particularly concerned about a resident going elsewhere for an element of care and may even welcome the arrangement if it relieves the community of its responsibility to provide that care, assuming no corresponding loss of revenues (for example, a short-term transfer out of an assisted-living unit paid for by the month). The following circumstances, however, may pose some concern for a retirement community:

- Transfer of the resident to an outside facility may result in an uncompensated vacancy (for example, of a daily-rate nursing bed).
- The HMO-contracting nursing facility may "skim" only the better-compensated Medicare nursing days and then allow the resident to return to the retirement community to receive poorly compensated Medicaid nursing care. (See §§26.2 and 26.3 regarding Medicare and Medicaid coverage of nursing care.)
- Pressured by a capitated or fixed reimbursement structure, the HMO or its contracting provider may return to the retirement community a resident who suffers from medical complications due to undertreatment or premature transfer.
- If the retirement community is itself structured like an HMO (for example, a Type A continuing-care retirement community; see §§2.3(d) and 27.3(a)), it may lose its ability to manage residents' care and to predict reimbursement levels, thereby potentially jeopardizing its fiscal soundness.

(c) Responding to Managed-Care Challenges

(1) Alliances

Whether or not existing residents are enrolled in HMOs, retirement communities must address the challenges of managed care if they are to remain a viable part of the health care delivery system and attract new residents. Regardless of the source of retirement community admissions—hospitals, nursing facilities, or workforce retirees—those sources have forged relationships with managed-care organizations that, in turn, affect the retirement community's relationship with its residents or even motivate consumers to avoid the retirement community altogether.

A major theme in response to the rapid growth of managed care is "alliances." Given that managed-care organizations deal in volume, they may not find it efficient to contract with individual retirement communities when a chain of nursing facilities can provide a one-stop contracting opportunity. Accordingly, "horizontal" alliances among retirement communities with similar services such as nursing can be formed to ensure bargaining power and promote cost efficiencies. Such alliances, however, must be carefully structured to take into consideration the following issues: antitrust law compliance (see §13.3), referral agency or other licensing requirements, Medicare antikickback law compliance (see §13.2), form of the business, insulation of members from liability, and taxation or the effect on tax-exempt status. See Volume II, §8.2A, for a shared administrative services agreement for a horizontal alliance group.

Of course, "vertical" alliances with other providers such as hospitals and nursing facilities can create an ongoing source of residents for any retirement community. In fact, mainstream health care providers have shown increasing interest in relationships with retirement communities as health care consumers are pushed to lower levels of care for economic reasons (see generally §11.2). Moreover, for a retirement community to be able to serve its own residents enrolled in a managed-care program, it may become necessary to contract with hospitals, physician groups, and others who hold provider-based managed-care contracts. See Volume II, §15.17, for a form for such an agreement.

The Balanced Budget Act of 1997 included provisions that permit health care providers, including long-term-care providers, to form vertical alliances called provider-sponsored organizations (PSOs) and to contract directly with Medicare to provide services to Medicare beneficiaries. These provisions will not go into effect until the Health Care Financing Administration issues its regulations.[77] At present, providers may participate in Medicare's managed-care program only by contracting with an HMO that has a contract with Medicare. By participating in provider-sponsored organizations, long-term-care providers may be able to gain greater access to Medicare beneficiaries, retain a larger share of the Medicare dollar, and exert stronger control over the care delivered to enrolled beneficiaries. See §28.12 for more information on the Balanced Budget Act of 1997 and provider-sponsored organizations.

(2) Responses Particular to CCRCs

Managed care uniquely affects CCRCs, which are essentially in the same business as HMOs. CCRCs control the delivery of care, charge standardized and periodic fees rather than à la carte fees, and pool economic risks among a group of consumers. The growth of HMOs not only interferes with the existing relationships between CCRCs and their residents (see §27.3(b)) but, in the view of some observers, also threatens to supplant the CCRC product altogether.[78]

The inability of CCRCs to control service delivery to their own residents has given rise to the following responses:

- writing admission contracts that prohibit or restrict resident participation in HMOs. While such an approach may be justified on the ground that the CCRC needs to be able to control care delivery in order to remain effective and financially sound, it may be difficult to sustain from a marketing perspective;
- disclaiming responsibility for HMO-covered services (see form in Volume II, §13.18A). A disclaimer is less drastic than a total prohibition, but it is difficult to allocate CCRC/HMO responsibilities and liabilities for service delivery;
- contracting with all residents' HMOs to provide services to CCRC residents. Such an arrangement is feasible only if one or a few HMOs predominate and if the retirement community commands sufficient size or clout to attract the attention of the affected HMOs; and
- enacting legislation to require HMOs to contract with CCRCs with respect to their own residents (see Volume II, §16.2). Florida took the legislative approach, and other states have proposed the necessary legislation. Nonetheless, HMOs afraid of the creep toward a broader "any willing provider" rule may object strenuously.

Notes

1. *See* §26.2(a).

2. "Medigap Insurance," GAO Report to House Subcommittee on Health, Committee on Ways and Means, Oct. 1986, at 3.

3. O'Shaughnessy, Price, and Griffith, "Financing and Delivery of Long-Term Care Services for the Elderly," Congressional Research Service, Feb. 24, 1987, 56.

4. P.L. 96–265 (Baucus Amendment); 42 U.S.C. §1395ss.

5. GAO Report, note 2 *above,* at 20.

6. *Ibid.*

7. *See* 42 U.S.C. §§1395ss(b)–(r).

8. "Ten Medigap Policies to Replace Hundreds," *Contemporary Long Term Care,* Sept. 1991, 11.

9. ICF, Inc., "Private Financing of Long Term Care: Current Methods and Resources," Phase I Final Report, U.S. Department of Health and Human Services, 1985, 12 [Phase II, also published 1985]; and *Older Americans Reports,* Mar. 20, 1987, 2.

10. *See generally* Meiners and Gollub, "Long-Term Care Insurance: The Edge of an Emerging Market," *Healthcare Financial Management,* Mar. 1984, 58; *New England Journal of Medicine,* Vol. 314, no. 11, Mar. 13, 1986, 725; ICF, Inc., note 9 *above,* at 81–105.

11. "Who Can Afford a Nursing Home?" *Consumer Reports,* May 1988, 300.

12. Wagner, L., "Nursing Homes Buffeted by Troubles," *Modern Health Care,* Mar. 18, 1988, 36. In 1989, the number of companies selling long-term-care insurance was reported to have grown by a factor of six since 1984, with 105 insurers selling 1.1 million policies per year. *Today's Nursing Home,* May 1989, 3. By 1990, the field was expected to grow to a $2 to $3 billion business. Galson, J., "Health Care Ventures Enliven Private Placement Syndications," *Real Estate Forum,* Aug. 1987, 54. The Health Insurance Association of America reported that more than 1.5 million long-term-care insurance policies were purchased as of December 1989, with 1989 sales increasing by 12 percent over 1988 figures. *Older Americans Report,* July 27, 1990, 293.

13. "Sales of LTC Insurance Policies Continue to Climb," *Contemporary Long Term Care,* Sept. 1991, 11.

14. *Ibid.*

15. "H.I.A.A. Study Notes Big Growth in LTC Insurance Policies," *Contemporary Long Term Care,* May 1989, 17.

16. *Ibid.*

17. Wagner, note 12 *above,* at 36, quoting Joshua M. Wiener of the Brookings Institution.

18. "Nursing Home Insurance Called Unaffordable," *Older Americans Report,* Feb. 5, 1993, 44.

19. Kosterlitz, J., "Debating How to Care for the Aged," *National Journal,* Mar. 31, 1990, 788.

20. "House Report Suggests Banning Private LTC Policies," *Contemporary Long Term Care,* July 1989.

21. Burda, D., "Fraud Threatens LTC Insurance Market," *Hospitals,* Oct. 4, 1987, 88.

22. *See* Topolnicki, D., "When a Nursing Home Becomes Your Poorhouse," *Money,* Mar. 1986, 175.

23. *See* note 11 *above.*

24. "Developments in Aging: 1992," U.S. Senate Special Committee on Aging, S. Rep. No. 103–40. Vol. 1, Apr. 20, 1993, 209.

25. "Gotcha! The Traps in Long Term Care Insurance: An Empty Promise to the Elderly?" *Consumer Reports,* June 1991, 425.

26. *See* remarks of Lawrence Kirsch, "Private Long Term Care Insurance: The Maturing Market," Conference Proceedings, Jan. 1987, San Antonio, Texas, at 11.

27. *See* "Long Term Care Insurance: An Industry Perspective on Market Development and Consumer Protection," National Association of Insurance Commissioners, Jan. 1987, Appendix M.

28. By 1989, 19 states had adopted the National Association of Insurance Commissioners Model Act: Arizona, Florida, Georgia, Hawaii, Idaho, Illinois, Indiana, Iowa, Kansas, Nebraska, Nevada, North Carolina, North Dakota, Oklahoma, Rhode Island, South Carolina, Tennessee, Virginia, and Wyoming. *Older Americans Report,* Jan. 27, 1989, 32. States with more stringent regulation than the NAIC model are California, Connecticut, Maine, Massachusetts, Minnesota, Washington, and Wisconsin. *Ibid.*

29. *Consumer Reports,* note 11 *above,* at 308.

30. Burda, note 21 *above.*

31. "NAIC Strengthens LTC Model Insurance Legislation," *Contemporary Long Term Care,* Feb. 1989, 15.

32. Rajecki, R., "Keeping Individuals and an Industry Afloat," *Contemporary Long Term Care,* May 1993, 33.

33. "Insurance Market Boom Ongoing," *Contemporary Long Term Care,* May 1990, 18.

34. "Long-Term Care Insurance: Risks to Consumers Should be Reduced," General Accounting Office (HRD–92-14), Dec. 26, 1991. *See also* "State Variation in the Regulation of Long-Term Care Insurance Products," American Association of Retired Persons, Jan. 1992, which reports that only 13 states complied with 80 percent or more of the NAIC standards.

35. *See* O'Shaughnessy *et al.,* note 3 *above,* at 62.

36. In Revenue Ruling 89–43, 1989–1 C.B. 213, the IRS ruled that reserves set aside for a level premium, guaranteed renewable, group long-term-care insurance policy providing indemnity benefits for an impaired individual qualifies as life insurance reserves that are eligible for a tax deduction under Internal Revenue Code Section 816(b). This ruling was seen as a needed clarification to help promote the development of long-term-care insurance policies.

37. *See* §27.2(a).

38. Diamond, L., "Private Long Term Insurance: A New Option for Life Care Communities," *Retirement Housing Report,* Apr. 1988, 2.

39. *Id.* at 3.

40. *Id.* at 4.

41. MacKenzie, R., "Evaluating Long Term Care Insurance Options for Retirement Communities," *Retirement Housing Report,* Feb. 1989, 2.

42. Kunerth, A., "Nationally Underwritten LTC Programs in CCRCs—How Good a Deal for Residents?" *Retirement Housing Report,* June 1990, 4.

43. MacKenzie, R., "Evaluating Plan Design Options," *Contemporary Long Term Care,* Apr. 1990, 56.

44. *E.g.,* Blue Cross of MI, United Auto Workers policy. *See* ICF, Phase I, note 9 *above,* at 27.

45. One 1987 survey showed that 25 percent of the benefits managers of corporations with 500 or more employees said their companies were interested in group long-term-care insurance products. Of companies with more than 2,000 employees, 45 percent were considering purchasing coverage in the next three years. Burda, D., "The Nation Looks for New Ways to Finance Care for the Aged," *Hospitals,* Sept. 20, 1987, 48. In late 1987, new contracts between the United Auto Workers and General Motors and Ford Motor Company were the first on a nationwide basis to cover long-term care for employees at the expense of the employer. "Caring for the Elderly: Public/Private Sector Responsibilities Point Way to Future Trends," *Federation of American Health Systems,* Jan.–Feb. 1988, 28.

46. "Sales of LTC Insurance Policies Continue to Climb," note 13 *above.*

47. "Employer Views on Group Long-Term Care Insurance," Washington Business Group on Health, Oct. 1991.

48. *See also* the discussion of continuing care, §27.3(a).

49. *E.g.,* the Kaiser Health Plan reportedly offers some long-term-care coverage but coordinates it closely with Medicare benefits. ICF, Phase I, note 9 *above,* at 31.

50. *E.g.,* Blue Cross of Southern California. *Id.* at 34.

51. *Id.* at 33–34. The Balanced Budget Act of 1997 extends waivers for demonstrations of SHMOs through December 31, 2000, and expands the limit on the number of persons served per site from 12,000 to 36,000. Pub. L. 105–33, Sec. 4014.

52. Although similar to a prepaid health plan, continuing-care arrangements are treated here as a self-insurance method because enrollment is usually restricted to residents of a given facility, whereas insurance is generally available on a more widespread basis. However, such distinctions are fading as insurers attempt to control care delivery systems and larger continuing-care providers spread their risks among multiple facilities.

53. *See, e.g.,* MacKenzie, "Catastrophic Illness: Private Financing of Health Care for the Elderly," *Compensation & Benefits Management,* Winter 1987, 5; ICF, Phase I, note 9 *above,* at 36–43; O'Shaughnessy *et al.,* note 3 *above,* at 64–69; and "How Continuing Care Retirement Communities Manage Services for the Elderly," U.S. General Accounting Office, Jan. 1997.

54. *See, e.g.,* O'Shaughnessy *et al.,* note 3 *above.*

55. In the late 1980s, entrance fees averaged $35,000 for one person and ranged as low as $11,000. *Ibid. See also* discussion in §2.3(d) and Chapter 21.

56. *See* discussion in §2.3(d).

57. *See* §§2.3(d), 21.1.

58. For a discussion of long-term-care screening, financing, and case management in CCRCs, see Tell, E., and M. Cohen, "Lessons in Managing Long-Term-Care Costs: Continuing Care Retirement Communities," *Generations,* Spring 1990, 55.

59. There is, however, a federal definition for purposes of qualifying for exemption from imputed interest taxation rules. *See* §6.2(b)(2).

60. *See* Chapter 21. However, escrows, reserves, refunds, lien rights, and other statutory financial protections do exist in many states.

61. *See generally* MacKenzie, note 53 *above,* and §27.2(c)(2).

62. *See* ICF, Phase II, note 9 *above,* at 17.

63. *Id.* at 21.

64. *See* Scholen, K., *"Home-Made Money, Consumer's Guide to Home Equity Conversion,"* American Association of Retired Persons, 3d ed., 1991, 12–14.

65. O'Shaughnessy *et al.,* note 3 *above,* reported only 300 to 400 contracts nationwide in 1987.

66. *See* ICF, Phase II, note 9 *above,* at 25.

67. *Id.* at 25–28.

68. *Housing the Elderly Report,* June 1989, 8.

69. *See* 12 U.S.C. §1715z–20(g).

70. 54 *Fed. Reg.* 24832 adding part 206 to Title 24, C.F.R.

71. *HUD Handbook* 4235.1 (1989).

72. Rooney, M., "Reverse Mortgages and Related Housing Issues," American Bar Association Annual Meeting, Elderly Housing Program, Aug. 7, 1990.

73. Nauts, C., "Reverse Mortgages—Backing into the '90s," *Probate & Property,* Jan.-Feb. 1994, 55.

74. *See* ICF, Phase I, note 9 *above,* at 48–49.

75. Smallwood, D., H. Simon, and B. Brody, "Questioning Long-Term Care IRAs," *Health Affairs,* Summer 1987, 132.

76. *See generally* Part III for a discussion of different resident payment and ownership structures.

77. Pub. L. 105–33, Sec. 4001.

78. *See, generally,* Scruggs, D., "The Future of Continuing Care Retirement Communities," American Association of Homes and Services for the Aging, 1995.

RiverMead Retirement Community; Peterborough, New Hampshire.

Courtesy of Tsomides Associates Architects Planners; Newton Upper Falls, Massachusetts; Photographer: Hutchins Photography; Watertown, Massachusetts

28 Health Care Reform

§28.1 In General

The problems of inadequate funding and fulfillment of the nation's health care needs, particularly those related to long-term care for the elderly, have been acknowledged and studied widely. Many proposals have been put forth, and some modest legislative changes have been made, but no plan has presented the combination of effectiveness, affordability, and consensus building that is apparently necessary to solve the identified problems. This chapter provides a selective chronology of the past decade's major proposals to reform health care. Despite intense national effort, the only significant legislative achievements have been health insurance reform in 1996 (see §28.11), and, in 1997, more managed-care choices and reimbursement cutbacks (see §28.12).

§28.2 Harvard Medicare Project

The Harvard Medicare Project used the occasion of the 20th anniversary of Medicare to study the program's successes and failures and to make suggestions for fundamental areas of change.[1] In general, the project recommended reduced reliance on beneficiary copayments and advocated increases in premiums to offset the resulting revenue loss. Copayments, the project reasoned, are unpredictable and impose the greatest burden on the sickest, whereas premiums are predictable, do not penalize the sick, and can be adjusted to income levels.

For chronic illnesses, the study recommended expanding Medicare coverage for nursing home care from its currently limited, posthospital rehabilitative approach to coverage for long-term illnesses. Coverage would be funded as it is for other Medicare benefits, but with a residential copayment from beneficiaries equal to 80 percent of Social Security benefits. The copayment would be designed to help reimburse the nonhealth care residential living expenses that make up a large part of the cost of nursing care.

The study also recommended increasing benefits for less cost-intensive outpatient health services, such as home health, establishing physician reimbursement rate schedules, requiring physicians to accept assignment of Medicare benefits as payment in full for their services, establishing target budgets for hospitals, and creating incentives for health maintenance organizations to create more programs specializing in the health care needs of the elderly.

§28.3 The Catastrophic Coverage Act

(a) The Push for a Long-Term-Care Solution

In the mid-1980s, proposals for federal legislation focused serious attention on expanding Medicare benefits to cover so-called catastrophic health care problems.[2] However, critics of proposals to revamp coverage affecting hospital care had long contended that the true health finance catastrophe for most elderly people is not the occurrence of an acute illness requiring hospitalization but rather the onset of a chronic condition requiring long-term nursing care.[3] While long-term care is almost certainly the greatest unresolved health finance problem for the elderly, its cost is potentially staggering, particularly in view of the general lack of comprehensive government or private insurance coverage. Not surprisingly, critics evidence wide disagreement as to how the nation should address the problem.[4]

Because of the considerable public and private sector attention focused on long-term-care issues, some groups declared 1988—a presidential election year—"the year of long-term care."[5] More specifically, several elderly advocacy groups undertook a national effort entitled Long-Term Care 88 to encourage all presidential candidates to establish a position on how to finance long-term care for the elderly.[6] According to Long-Term Care 88, six out of seven respondents to a nationwide survey stated that it was time to consider a government program for long-term care. Ninety-two percent of Democrats and 82 percent of Republicans were said to agree on this point.[7] At the same time, a task force of the U.S. Department of Health and Human Services recommended the financing of long-term-care costs through group insurance offered to workers before retirement.[8] Many thoughtful commentators believed that some combination of direct government benefits and tax incentives for private insurance policies would be required to solve the long-term-care problem.

(b) The Act as Adopted and Repealed

In 1988, Congress passed the Catastrophic Health Care Act, adding so-called catastrophic health protection to Medicare. After spending a year and a half to forge legislation acceptable to both the House and the Senate, Congress had crafted a law that provided a large collection of benefits at a much higher price than originally anticipated.[9] In 1989, Congress repealed the act that it had adopted only one year before, leaving intact only some low-income protections such as the spousal impoverishment rules. This embarrass-

ing reversal was the result of an outcry by higher-income elderly persons who were subject to the income-indexed premium that in 1989 ranged as high as $800 per year. In an effort to salvage some part of the 1988 act, the administration and some members of Congress attempted unsuccessfully to modify the law's premium and benefits provisions. The following summary of the 1988 act may have relevance for claims made during law's brief life, but its principal usefulness is as a guide to what reforms are politically infeasible.

(1) Medicare Benefits (repealed)
The 1988 law eliminated the "spell of illness" concept as adopted under earlier law, thereby permitting the inpatient hospital deductible to apply only once a year[10] and removing the 90-day limit on Medicare coverage for inpatient hospital care. The 1988 law provided unlimited coverage for days of inpatient hospital services[11] and eliminated all coinsurance charges required under former law.[12]

With respect to extended-care services in skilled-nursing facilities, the 1988 law eliminated the coinsurance requirement for the last 80 days of coverage, although it did impose a coinsurance requirement for the first eight days of extended-care services in a skilled-nursing facility[13] and set that coinsurance at 20 percent of the national average per diem reasonable cost for skilled-nursing facility services, which was to be approximately $20.50 per day in 1989.[14] The number of days of Medicare-covered skilled-nursing facility services increased from 100 days to 150 days per calendar year.[15] In addition, the 1998 law eliminated the three-day prior hospitalization requirement provided by the old law.[16]

Beginning January 1, 1991, Medicare would cover all prescription drugs.[17] Copayments by the elderly were to decline from 50 percent in 1991, to 40 percent in 1992, and to 20 percent thereafter.[18] After 1992, the deductible would be indexed so that approximately 16.8 percent of Medicare beneficiaries would exceed the deductible limit.[19] Once an elderly patient reached the deductible as of January 1, 1991, the patient's copayment would be 50 percent.[20]

Under the then-existing law, home health services were covered for five days a week for up to two or three weeks; the 1988 law increased that coverage to 38 consecutive days of care.[21]

(2) Medicare Premiums (repealed)

The benefits under the 1988 act were to be funded primarily by the elderly who participated in Medicare. The elderly would make payments in two forms: an increase in the federal income tax liability of all Medicare-eligible individuals (referred to as the supplemental premium); and an increase in the Part B monthly premium, which is also called the flat premium.[22] The supplemental premium was created by amending the Internal Revenue Code to impose a surcharge on all Medicare-eligible individuals' federal income tax liability.[23] The amount of the supplemental premium was to be determined by dividing the individual's federal income tax liability by $150.[24] That result was then multiplied by the supplemental premium rate for the year. Premium rates and premium limits were determined for the years through 1993 as follows:

Year	Premium Rate	Premium Limit
1989	$22.50	$ 800
1990	$27.14	$ 850
1991	$30.17	$ 900
1992	$30.55	$ 950
1993	$29.55	$1,050[25]

With respect to the flat monthly Part B premium, the former rates were to be increased by the following amounts:

Year	Amount
1989	$ 4.00
1990	$ 4.90
1991	$ 7.36
1992	$ 9.20
1993	$10.20[26]

Beginning on January 1, 1990, the law would have placed an upper limit on the amount of out-of-pocket expenses a beneficiary had to pay in cost-sharing charges per year under Part B. That limit was set at $1,370 for 1990; thereafter, the amount was to be indexed and would change from year to year.[27]

For those individuals ineligible for Medicare but who voluntarily chose to enroll, a new formula determined the amount of the Part A premium.[28]

(3) Medicare Impoverishment Issues (not repealed)

Not repealed by Congress in 1989 were those parts of the 1988 law requiring individual states to revise their standards so as to equalize resources between spouses. After an institutionalized individual has established eligibility for Medicare, the state must allow the noninstitutionalized spouse to retain a certain minimum income.[29] Further, effective September 30, 1989, a state must, when determining Medicaid eligibility for an institutionalized individual with a community spouse, total all nonexempt resources held by either spouse and divide them equally. The state must protect at least $12,000 for the community spouse but may raise the minimum as high as $60,000 (plus inflation adjustments).[30]

Effective July 1, 1988, at the time of an individual's application for Medicaid, the state must determine whether the applicant has disposed of any asset for less than fair market value within the past 30 months. If such a disposition has occurred, the state must delay Medicaid eligibility for a period sufficient to make up for the uncompensated value of the transferred resources.[31] (For a discussion of Medicaid eligibility generally, see §26.3(b).)

§28.4 Brookings Institution Long-Term-Care Finance Study

A study published by the Brookings Institution in 1988 analyzed all the methods of long-term health care financing discussed in Chapters 26 and 27 and forecast the affordability and effectiveness of each method in meeting the need for care for the next 30 to 35 years.[32] Table 28.1 illustrates the study's projections for the years 2016 to 2020 for the percentage of elderly who can afford various private insurance options, the percentage of nursing home expenditures paid for by each option, and the resulting reduction in Medicaid expenditures and patients for each option.[33] The study concluded that most private insurance methods are not affordable by the majority of elderly persons and that the most effective (e.g., continuing care) are the most costly. The following are among the problems identified with each method:

- Private long-term-care insurance—High premiums, unwillingness of employers to fund insurance, insurer's fears of overuse and inflation

Table 28.1 **Private Health Insurance Options and Their Impact**

Option	Number of Elderly Participating (percent)	Total Nursing Home Expenditures Paid by Option (percent)	Change from Base Case Medicaid Nursing Home Expenditures (percent)	Change from Number of Base Case Medicaid Nursing Home Patients (percent)
Private Insurance $30, $40, or $50 Nursing Home Benefit	45.03	11.69	−4.94	−4.52
$50 Nursing Home Benefit	25.41	7.04	−1.18	−1.37
Continuing-Care Retirement Communities	18.24	13.68	−2.60	−2.77
Social/Health Maintenance Organizations	26.32	10.30	−7.77	−5.59
Individual Medical Account	28.19	2.97	−1.25	−1.84
Home Equity Conversions	66.61	NA	2.02	2.39

leading to high deductibles, limited coverage, fixed benefits;

■ Continuing care—Reluctance of elderly to leave their homes, increased use of fee-for-service charges, restricting admission to healthy residents, rare but highly publicized financial failures;

■ Social/Health Maintenance Organizations—Limited nursing coverage, low enrollment;

■ Individual medical accounts—High levels of savings required, reduced tax advantages, possibility that loss of income to U.S. Treasury could exceed Medicaid savings; and

■ Home equity conversion—Consumer reluctance, lender fears that elderly will outlive actuarial life expectancies.

The Brookings study reviewed and found disfavor with the following public sector financing strategies: a long-term-care block grant program for states, family responsibility for relatives' long-term-care expenses, direct financial support for family caregivers, expanded home care benefits, and liberalized Medicaid benefits. The reasons for the study's disapproval of these strategies included cost, ineffectiveness, a preference for federal rather than state assumption of responsibility, and creation of a two-class system of health care benefits. Instead, the study concluded that long-term-care costs should be covered by a public insurance program that either pays for nurs-

ing and home care with significant cost sharing by patients (similar to Medicare) or pays for care in excess of a defined one- to two-year period expected to be covered by private insurance.

§28.5 Consumers Union Long-Term-Care Proposal

A 1989 report issued by the Consumers Union[34] outlined a range of proposals for solving various long-term-care problems based on several levels of proposed federal expenditure.

(a) Extra-Low-Budget Option

The report recommended a voluntary long-term-care insurance policy to be offered through Medicare. Premiums would be charged to cover all costs, and the option to buy into the system would be limited to two or three defined age points in order to reduce adverse selection. Premiums would be scaled to income, with a cap to prevent the loss of upper-income people from the system. The policy would adjust for inflation and be available to all who chose to purchase it. In the alternative, the proposal called for the U.S. Department of Health and Human Services to develop a standard long-term-care insurance policy with three to four option levels. Private insurers would compete to be franchised to market the policy on a regional basis. A third alternative called for uniform definitions for key long-term-care insurance policy terms and a restriction on variations permitted among private insurance policies. All these proposals, in the opinion of the Consumers Union, would involve minimal expenditure of federal funds.

(b) Low-Budget Option

For a federal expenditure of approximately $10 billion, the report recommended the establishment of a comprehensive home health care benefit for people of all ages, in addition to the voluntary long-term-care insurance policy for nursing home coverage.

(c) Medium-Budget Option

For $20 billion, the proposal included a voluntary insurance program, comprehensive home health care benefits, and nursing home coverage for the first six months of care, with cost sharing for people with incomes above 200 percent of the poverty level. Those who needed more than six months of nursing care would have the option of purchasing the voluntary long-term-care insurance through Medicare.

(d) High-Budget Option

For $50 billion, the proposal included comprehensive home health and nursing care benefits. Nursing benefits would begin after one or two months, with cost sharing of approximately 20 to 35 percent. No cost sharing or waiting periods would be required for people with incomes below 200 percent of the federal poverty level.

In general, the Consumers Union report seriously questioned the capability of the private sector to serve consumers adequately through private long-term-care insurance policies.

§28.6 Pepper Commission Proposal

In 1990, the Pepper Commission (U.S. Bipartisan Commission on Health Care) released its report on the nation's health care delivery and financing system,

together with recommendations for a comprehensive health care and long-term-care services program for all Americans. Of the $66 billion per year in proposed program expenditures, $42.8 billion would go to long-term-care expenses. The proposal, to be phased in over four years, would provide federally financed coverage for the first three months of nursing home services, with a 20 percent copayment for all except low-income people, who would be subsidized.

For nursing home stays beyond three months, the patient would be required to share costs subject to retention of assets equal to the following: $30,000 for individuals or $60,000 for couples, in addition to housing; a 30 percent of income housing allowance; a $100 per month personal needs allowance; and a further income allowance of up to 200 percent of the poverty level for a couple. The cost of nursing home stays would be shared by the state and federal governments. In addition, the federal government would finance a home health care program for those unable to perform three of five activities of daily living (bathing, dressing, eating, transferring, toileting). Again, the program would require a 20 percent copayment, except for subsidized low-income persons.

Private long-term-care insurance meeting federal standards would be made available to fill in gaps in coverage. The commission did not recommend how to fund its various proposals.[35]

§28.7 Congressional Proposals for the 1990s

Health care finance, including long-term care, was a major issue before Congress in the early 1990s. Proposals put forth fell into the following categories:

- employer-mandated health insurance;
- public health insurance; and
- public/private incentive programs.

(a) Employer-Mandated Health Insurance

It is estimated that of the up to 37 million Americans lacking health insurance, two-thirds to three-quarters are working people and their dependents.[36] In a Gallup California health care poll, 87 percent of respondents stated that employers should be required to provide basic health insurance to all employees.[37]

Proposals introduced in Congress would have required employers to extend basic health care coverage to employees for services such as hospital and physician services, diagnostic tests, and prenatal care —subject to various deductibles, premium-sharing responsibilities, phase-in periods, and so on.[38] An alternative was the "play or pay" approach that required employers either to purchase insurance for their employees or contribute to a state-operated insurance program.[39] These proposals generally did not address long-term-care costs and did not account for unemployed persons. Small businesses generally opposed the measures.

(b) Public Health Insurance

Congress also put forth numerous proposals for government-funded universal health insurance.[40] Proponents argued that universal coverage provided by the government is more efficient than private insurance (no profit margin or marketing expense) and is necessary to cover the unemployed, who are hardest hit by health care expenses.[41] Many of the proposals were modeled after the Canadian system, which imposes cost controls on service providers.[42]

Universal health insurance proposals raised several public policy choices, including the following:[43]

- Social (Medicare-style) insurance versus a "means-tested" (Medicaid-style) system—The arguments in favor of a social program maintain that such an approach spreads risk further, avoids adverse selection of only the sickest population, and does not force the elderly to impoverish themselves to receive care.
- Front-end ("first dollar") versus back-end ("catastrophic") coverage—The Brookings Institution approach (see §28.4) favors catastrophic coverage, with private insurance or personal resources covering upfront costs. The Pepper Commission (see §28.6) favored upfront coverage.
- Free market versus limited provider access—Cost controls, contracting with preferred providers, and similar methods may reduce costs, but they all limit consumer choice.

- Funding sources—A progressive income tax, an estate tax, and "sin," sales, or payroll tax increases are among the possible options.
- Intergenerational or age-restricted—One of the problems with the Catastrophic Health Care Act of 1988 that led to its 1989 repeal was that Medicare beneficiaries, not the population at large, paid program costs out of income-indexed supplemental premiums.

Bills calling for expansion of long-term-care benefits under Medicare also resurfaced in Congress, including proposals for upfront coverage of nursing care and increased home care and community care coverages funded from higher Social Security deductions, payroll taxes, or income taxes.[44] One 1989 survey, however, showed that most people believed the government should finance long-term care only for the most needy.[45]

(c) Public/Private Incentive Programs

To some extent, all major approaches to health care finance have involved some combination of public coverage and private financial responsibility, whether on the part of the patient, family, or employer. Some proposals, however, have been more directly designed to accomplish the public interest by encouraging individuals to save or insure for their own health care costs that are not otherwise covered by Medicare. (See §27.2(a) regarding the demand for and affordability of private long-term-care insurance.)

Congressional proposals designed to encourage private long-term-care coverage have included the following:[46]

- a tax credit for long-term-care insurance or savings accounts;
- an exclusion from gross income for retirement plan withdrawals used for long-term-care premiums;
- federal standards for long-term-care insurance policies as a prerequisite to tax preferences or other benefits (see §27.2(b) regarding industry criticism);
- Medicaid waivers for state demonstration programs permitting those with long-term-care insurance to receive Medicaid benefits without spending

down as much of their resources as they must currently spend down; and

■ an income tax exemption for life insurance benefits paid to a terminally ill person before death.

§28.8 The Clinton Health Care Reform Proposal

In early 1993, the Clinton Administration assembled a Health Reform Task Force chaired by First Lady Hillary Rodham Clinton and consisting of over 500 representatives from government, academia, and the private sector. The task force's deliberations were secret, but, on September 22, 1993, President Clinton unveiled his plan before a joint session of Congress and on, October 27, submitted a 1,300-page bill called the American Health Security Act of 1993.

(a) The Goals of Health Care Reform

Given the spiraling increases in health care costs nationally, the overall goal of the Clinton Administration's health care reform proposal was to control costs yet increase consumer access by fundamentally restructuring the entire health care system. The component objectives of the plan were to

■ provide a national minimum level of guaranteed health security, including coverage without regard to employment or health care status;

■ establish a fixed health care budget, with fixed premiums paid to providers who competitively bid to provide services to groups of consumers. Consumers would have an option to pay extra for higher-cost plans;

■ eliminate some bureaucracy by simplifying forms, limiting budget increases based on growth in personal income, and eventually folding in Medicare and Medicaid as well as the workers' compensation and automobile insurance systems;

■ increase the quality of care by shifting the orientation of enforcement from regulatory violations to "patient outcomes" and by favoring primary care and preventive services;

■ expand access to health care by promoting investment, training nonphysician workers, creating incentives for primary care physicians, and en-

couraging consumers to receive in-home and community-based care;

■ promote care in underserved areas by enhancing rural infrastructure and creating physician incentives; and

■ curb fraud and abuse by expanding coverage of antikickback rules to all providers, facilitating the use of civil monetary penalties, and prohibiting all self-referrals of medical services.

(b) Guaranteed National Benefits Package

The Health Security Act would have established a Guaranteed National Benefits Package for all lawful residents, to be phased in by January 1, 1998. Coverage would have included inpatient and outpatient hospital care, emergency services, preventive services, home health care, mental health and substance abuse services, family planning, physician services, diagnostics, rehabilitation, and other goods and services. A National Health Board would implement the plan, establish the requirements for states, control costs nationally, and make adjustments in the Guaranteed National Benefits Package.

All consumers in a given region would be required to join a single "regional health alliance," with an exception for employers with 5,000 or more employees, who could form their own corporate health alliances. States could also elect to form a "single payor" system for the entire state (i.e., one statewide health alliance). Employers would be required to pay, on behalf of their employees, approximately 80 percent of the average premium cost for the health benefits provided through the alliance.

Health plans providing the full range of guaranteed benefits would bid competitively to provide services to the regional and corporate alliances. No benefit exclusions would be allowed. Health plans could not refuse to enroll any alliance member and would have to base premiums on a "community rating" for all participants rather than on individual health care status or risk.

Participants would be entitled to choose from among high-cost (fee for service), low-cost (HMO model), or moderate-cost (PPO model) payment plans, with higher copayments and deductibles for plans offering greater choice of physicians or other providers.

(c) Medicare and Medicaid

Both Medicare and Medicaid would remain in effect during the initial years of the plan, thus making the Guaranteed National Benefits Package a program that would essentially benefit those under age 65. Yet, a new and comprehensive Medicare prescription drug benefit was to be added, with a $250 annual deductible, a 20 percent beneficiary copayment, and a $1,000 per year cap on out-of-pocket costs to beneficiaries. Part B premiums would increase in an amount sufficient to cover 25 percent of the costs of the drug benefit.

Medicaid would be expanded to provide "community-based" long-term-care services to people with severe disabilities, with services including personal care, frail elderly services, supported living, home health, and clinic and rehabilitation services. However, the scope of services (beyond assessment and care planning) and eligibility rules were to be left to state discretion. Asset limits for Medicaid beneficiaries would increase from $2,000 to $12,000.

(d) Home- and Community-Based Services

The proposal also created a new home- and community-based services benefit to be phased in by the end of 2002. The program would be available to severely disabled persons with severe cognitive difficulties or in need of assistance with three or more of the following five activities of daily living: dressing, bathing, transferring, eating, and toileting. Applicants would not be means-tested (screened according to asset or income levels) but would be subject to a sliding scale copayment obligation based on their ability to pay. States were to be granted broad flexibility to design and define the system and to include case management, respite, adult daycare, home health, rehabilitation, and homemaker services. The proposal expressly excluded room and board.

Another element of the plan called for the establishment of federal standards for long-term-care insurance. Similar to those of the National Association of Insurance Commissioners (NAIC) model, the standards would include nonforfeiture provisions and the mandatory offering of inflation protection (see §27.2(c) regarding the NAIC standards). Tax incentives, such as clarification of the availability of med-

ical deductions for premiums, would also be available to encourage the purchase of long-term-care insurance. Interestingly, the plan also specified that the insurance aspects of continuing-care retirement communities would be subject to the jurisdiction of the U.S. Department of Health and Human Services.

Finally, the proposal called for a demonstration project to integrate acute- and long-term-care services.

(e) Health Care Reform and Communities for Seniors

Of particular interest for seniors' facilities was the Health Care Task Force's apparently strong interest in home- and community-based (rather than nursing home) services as a focal point for future development. Retirement communities, particularly CCRCs, fulfill in microcosm many of the objectives of health care reform, such as managed care, a preventive or "wellness" orientation, a low-tech/nonmedical level of care, coordinated transitioning of residents between levels of care, and systemwide risk pooling of health care costs.

Unfortunately, the Health Security Act did not clearly identify the role of residential-care communities in the context of massive health alliances and comprehensive health plans oriented to the acute hospital model. Moreover, the plan failed to provide significant new incentives to encourage older persons with substantial home equity to plan for and fund their long-term-care needs as an alternative to spending down their assets and enrolling in Medicaid. The emphasis on funding home care provided yet another disincentive for people with care needs to leave their homes for seniors' communities where care, security, companionship, activities, good nutrition, and other benefits are available on a more cost-efficient and coordinated basis.

Although the focal point of the administration's overall proposal was the uninsured in need of acute medical care rather than the elderly in need of long-term care, a major health care reform proposal for the first time recognized residential models of care as an integral and desirable part of the health care continuum.

§28.9 Aftermath of the Clinton Proposal

The Clinton health care reform proposal was declared "dead on arrival" when it reached Congress. The principal objections centered on employer mandates (requiring coverage of employees' health insurance costs), the size and power of the proposed regional health alliances, the perceived threat of more government control and bureaucracy, and the program's overall cost. As alternative bills emerged in both houses of Congress, President Clinton at first threatened to veto any plan not providing universal health care coverage. In time, however, the president softened his position as the major Democratic bills to get through committee were represented as providing up to 95 percent coverage phased in over several years.

The Democratic bills, most notably the Mitchell Bill, retained employer mandates and a federally funded home- and community-based care component. Republican efforts included a proposal by Senator Dole to implement long-term-care insurance reforms, but not much else. Bipartisan groups fashioned proposals that avoided employer mandates and instead offered tax incentives that would encourage consumers to pay privately for long-term care.

Of particular interest to retirement communities was a bill[47] authored by Congressman Peterson that would have removed the 7.5 percent threshold for the tax deduction of medical expenses, when the expense was for the purchase of assisted-living or other long-term-care services or the payment of long-term-care insurance premiums (see discussion in §6.1(c)(1)); and that would have permitted homeowners to carry over gain from the sale of a prior principal residence (i.e., defer taxation), when the proceeds were used as entrance fees for admission to a qualified continuing-care retirement community (see discussion in §6.1(c)(2)).

In the end, no health reform bill succeeded in the 1993–1994 congressional session. Many observers attributed the stalemate to the highly politicized atmosphere of a midterm election year and hoped that 1995 would yield a health care reform law with broad, bipartisan support.

With the stunning Republican takeover of both houses of Congress in the November 1994 elections, the health care reform landscape underwent significant alteration. Initially, as part of their Contract with America, House Republicans were expected to introduce legislation that would call for an elder care assistance tax credit of $500 for each household member unable to perform certain activities of daily living; a medical expense deduction for qualified long-term-care expenses required by a chronically ill person in a nursing facility or retirement community; a medical expense deduction for long-term-care insurance premiums, subject to a dollar limit based upon the person's age range; long-term-care insurance benefits of up to $200 per day excluded from gross income; tax-free distributions of retirement plan holdings to purchase long-term-care insurance; and tax-free distribution of life insurance benefits for terminally ill persons.[48]

By the end of the 1995 session, Congress had introduced legislation that would have cut the growth in Medicare spending by $270 billion over seven years by

- allowing beneficiaries to enroll in "coordinated care company" plans that could limit physician choice and change copayments and deductible levels in return for added benefits;
- creating a "Medisave" alternative that would permit beneficiaries to set aside savings in an account with an early withdrawal penalty, receive a high-deductible insurance policy, and determine their own level of health care spending;
- permitting beneficiaries to elect enrollment in provider-sponsored networks covering standard Medicare benefits;
- increasing premiums for individuals with incomes over $75,000 and for couples with incomes over $150,000;
- reducing payments to providers, including a freeze on payment increases to nursing facilities; and
- limiting medical malpractice awards to $250,000 for noneconomic damages and to the greater of $250,000 or three times the economic loss for punitive damages.[49]

In addition, the proposal originally called for elimination of the OBRA nursing facility standards. Eventually, though, revisions to the proposal would have repealed only the OBRA preadmission screening requirements and added flexibility in nurse's aide training program requirements.

Republican conferees also agreed on tax reforms that would promote the purchase of long-term-care insurance by, first, excluding benefits and most employer-funded premiums from taxable income and, second, permitting penalty-free withdrawals from IRAs and 401(k) retirement plans when the proceeds were used to purchase such insurance.[50]

Congress also proposed to cut Medicaid expenditures by $182 billion over seven years while requiring the states to spend 85 percent of their 1992–1994 levels of health care expenditures on low-income persons, especially those in nursing homes. The program could be restructured from an individual "entitlement" program to a federal block grant to the states.[51]

As of year-end 1995, the federal government was deadlocked over these and other budget proposals. While the Republican-controlled Congress had agreed on most of the above proposals, the president threatened a veto. Meanwhile, Congress repeatedly tied the bill for continuing funding of government operations to the president's acceptance of cuts in the Medicare program. The result was a temporary shut-down of federal government operations and temporary compromises to extend funding—all without resolution of the underlying budget issues. In the end, Congress failed to pass any significant health care reform legislation.

§28.10 The 1995 White House Conference on Aging

After four years of delay, the decennial White House Conference on Aging, initiated in 1961, was held for the fourth time, in May 1995. Delegates from around the nation converged on Washington for four days and adopted 50 broad resolutions, including exhortations to

- preserve Social Security, Medicare, Medicaid, and the Older Americans Act;
- expand long-term-care funding, community-based services, federal involvement in gerontological

education, research of the aging process, and job opportunities for older workers;
- prevent elder abuse and crime; and
- reform the health care system.

Beyond a call for "assuming personal responsibility for the state of one's health," conference delegates showed little affinity with congressional sentiment.[52] In urging expansion of government health programs, the conference, which was credited with originating the Medicare and Medicaid programs decades ago, was a disappointing footnote to the health care reform efforts of the 1990s.

§28.11 The Health Insurance Portability and Accountability Act of 1996

In 1996, after years of attempts to reform health care, Congress passed the Health Insurance Portability and Accountability Act (HIPAA), which makes relatively modest changes in the tax treatment of health insurance, imposes some limits on health insurance companies, and establishes a pilot program for Medical Saving Accounts (MSAs). These developments may affect retirement centers by encouraging older persons to save and plan more prudently for their long-term-care needs.

(a) Long-Term-Care Insurance Benefits

Similar to the present treatment of health and accident insurance, HIPAA treats certain long-term-care insurance benefits of up to $175 per day as an exclusion from taxable income. To qualify, policies must be guaranteed renewable and must meet the other consumer protection requirements (such as those relating to preexisting health conditions and prior hospitalization) adopted in 1993 by the National Association of Insurance Commissioners (see §27.2(c)). The insurance contract cannot pay expenses that are reimbursable under Medicare, except when Medicare is the secondary payor or the contract makes per diem or other periodic payments without regard to actual expense.

A qualifying policy can provide personal care and other health-related services to a "chronically ill individual," who is defined as a person who, due to functional incapacity, is unable to perform at least two activities of daily living for a period of at least 90 days; a similarly disabled person; or a person with a severe cognitive impairment requiring substantial supervision for protection from health or safety threats.

Any person furnishing long-term-care insurance must report any paid benefits to the IRS and the recipient. The provisions pertaining to the tax treatment of long-term-care insurance benefits and expenses generally took effect on January 1, 1997.

(b) Long-Term-Care Expenses

The act provides that unreimbursed expenses for long-term care for chronically ill persons (see above) qualify for the medical expense deduction of Internal Revenue Code Section §213. These provisions expand the availability of the medical expense deduction for such care, which (at least in the case of prepaid expenses) was previously limited to facilities providing life-time care (see §6.1(c)). Premiums for qualified long-term-care insurance policies are also deductible, subject to the following annual caps based on the age of the taxpayer before the close of the tax year:

Age	Annual Premium Cap
40 or younger	$200
Over 40, but not over 50	$375
Over 50, but not over 60	$750
Over 60, but not over 70	$2,000
Over 70	$2,500

(c) Accelerated Death Benefits

Life insurance death benefits that can be paid out before the death of a terminally ill or chronically ill person may be excluded from gross income. A terminally ill individual is one who is certified by a physician to be reasonably expected to die from an illness or physical condition within 24 months. The definition of a chronically ill individual is the same as for long-term-care insurance.

Chronically ill persons may exclude from income any death benefits paid under a qualifying long-term-care insurance rider to a life insurance policy, to the extent that the proceeds are used to pay for the actual costs of long-term care and the care is not otherwise covered by insurance. Per diem or other periodic payments made without regard to expense are fully excludable, irrespective of other coverage, up to the $175 per day cap.

(d) Insurance Discrimination; Portability

Employee group health plans, including HMOs, are prohibited from discriminating in eligibility for coverage on the basis of health status, disability, claims experience, and other common underwriting considerations. Insurers may, however, decline to cover particular procedures and to limit benefits so long as they do not discriminate among similarly situated employees. Prohibited, too, are periods of exclusion from coverage for preexisting conditions beyond 12 months (18 months for late enrollees).

Subject to certain exclusion rights of insurers within the 12-month limit, employees may move to a new employer without loss of coverage. The law applies to plans effective July 1, 1997.

(e) Medical Savings Accounts

The act provides for a pilot program that permits self-employed persons and small businesses of 50 or fewer employees to defer tax on contributions to a Medical Savings Account (MSA). As with an Individual Retirement Account (IRA), contributions by an individual are tax deductible, with employer contributions generally excluded from gross income.

Distributions from an MSA for qualified medical expenses are deductible and are not subject to the 7.5 percent threshold that normally must be exceeded to deduct medical expenses (see §6.1(c)). Although distributions may not be used to purchase general health insurance, they may be used to purchase long-term-care insurance.

MSAs must be used in conjunction with "high-deductible" health insurance that has the following features:

	Minimum Deductible	Maximum Deductible	Maximum Out-of-Pocket
Individual coverage	$1,500	$2,250	$3,000
Family coverage	$3,000	$4,500	$5,000

Participation in the MSA pilot program is limited to 750,000 enrollees per year from 1997 through 2000. The program was expanded in 1997 to incorporate deposits of Medicare savings (see §28.12(a)).

§28.12 The Balanced Budget Act of 1997

On August 5, 1997, President Clinton signed into law the Balanced Budget Act of 1997. The act, which contains several provisions that affect the Medicare and Medicaid programs, is expected to produce a savings of $115 billion in Medicare expenditures and $13 billion in Medicaid expenditures over five years. Some of the major provisions affecting long-term-care facilities are discussed below.

(a) Medicare+Choice Program

The act creates a new Part C of Medicare, called the Medicare+Choice Program (MCP), which is intended to give Medicare beneficiaries more options in obtaining health care services.[53] Medicare beneficiaries may elect to participate in the MCP or to remain in the traditional fee-for-service Medicare program. Those participating in the MCP may enroll in one of the following types of plans: coordinated care plans, which include preferred provider organizations, health maintenance organizations, and provider-sponsored organizations; Medical Savings Accounts; or unrestricted fee-for-service plans.

One of the more significant changes, which will be implemented by the MCP, is the introduction of provider-sponsored organizations (PSOs). A PSO is an entity organized and operated by health care providers that can contract directly with Medicare to provide services to Medicare beneficiaries. Thus, providers, including long-term-care providers, no longer need to contract with HMOs to participate in Medi-

care managed care. The general rule is that PSOs need to be licensed by their states as insurers or health plans; however, they may obtain a three-year waiver of such licensure requirements if their license is denied for solvency reasons or is not approved within 90 days of application. PSOs also must meet federal solvency and capitalization requirements, which must be issued by April 1, 1998.

The Medical Savings Account (MSA) portion of the MCP is a demonstration program available only to the first 390,000 enrollees who elect it before December 31, 2002.[54] Under the MSA program, a Medicare beneficiary purchases a private health insurance policy with a high deductible. Medicare deposits into each beneficiary account the difference between the per capita rate that Medicare would otherwise pay and the policy's premium. The beneficiary may use funds in the account to pay for qualified medical expenses, which include the cost of long-term care or long-term-care insurance.

(b) PACE Program

The act shifts the Program of All-Inclusive Care for the Elderly (PACE) from a demonstration project to a permanent Medicare program. Under PACE, providers can contract with Medicare to provide comprehensive health care services to persons age 55 or older who require a nursing-facility level of care, reside in the program's service area, and meet many other conditions. The PACE provider receives a prospective monthly capitation payment for each of its enrollees and must furnish enrollees with all items and services covered under Medicare and Medicaid through a comprehensive, multidisciplinary team that integrates acute and long-term-care services.

(c) Skilled-Nursing Facility Reimbursement

The act changes Medicare skilled-nursing facility reimbursement from a retrospective (cost-based) system to a prospective system.[55] The prospective payment system (PPS) is in effect for cost reporting periods on or after July 1, 1998. For the first three years, skilled-nursing facilities receive a blend of the facility-specific per diem rate and the federal per diem rate as follows:

	Facility-Specific Rate	Federal Rate
Year 1	75%	25%
Year 2	50%	50%
Year 3	25%	75%

Beginning with the fourth year, facilities will receive 100 percent of their reimbursement based on the federal rate.

Generally, the facility-specific rate is to be set by projecting forward the facilities' 1995 cost reports. The federal rate will be based on an average of 1995 cost reports and will be adjusted based on a case mix weighing factor, wages, and geographic area.

(d) Repeal of the Boren Amendment

The act repeals the Boren Amendment, which required state Medicaid programs to pay hospitals, skilled-nursing facilities, and intermediate-care facilities for the mentally retarded reasonable and adequate rates to cover the costs incurred by "efficiently and economically operated facilities."[56] In its place, the act establishes a public process under which proposed rates and methodologies are published and subject to public review and comment. With repeal of the Boren Amendment, it will be more difficult for institutional providers to challenge state Medicaid rates.

§28.13 Public Policy, Long-Term Care, and Retirement Communities

Medicare provides substantial coverage for hospitalization costs, but in the more than 30 years of its existence, it has not reduced the percentage of personal income the elderly must spend on health care.[57] Moreover, while Medicare pays for expensive acute health care for elderly persons who might be able to afford to purchase insurance privately, government funding for less expensive nursing care is available only to the virtually poor. Government funding for assisted living is even less forthcoming. Although cost-based Medicare reimbursement has been largely replaced with a less generous prospective payment system, the Medicare program has created, and still continues to foster, financial incentives to care for the elderly in the more costly hospital setting, sometimes

unnecessarily. Medicaid funds likewise direct the elderly into nursing care when lower-cost, but unreimbursed, assisted living may be more appropriate.

Approaches to containment of the nation's rising health care costs can be divided into direct regulatory efforts, such as limits on government reimbursement, and market-oriented strategies, such as incentives for the creation of health maintenance organizations and other alternative delivery systems.[58] Given the substantial resources of many elderly persons, in the form of home equity, for example, some of the assumptions of financial need that underlie a pure social insurance program may no longer be applicable. Seniors' facilities such as CCRCs that encourage healthy older persons to invest their resources in plans that will cover or help defray future long-term-care costs offer a market-oriented strategy that can help relieve the government of some of its health expenditure burden.[59] The savings can provide one source of revenue for programs designed to help the financially needy. And retirement facilities, as residential communities, furnish opportunities for utilization controls, preventive health care, and use of social/psychological support mechanisms unavailable to typical health plans or long-term-care insurance programs.[60]

Only a very few federal incentives have spurred privately funded residential models for long-term care.[61] However, the new $500,000 capital gain exclusion for home sales[62] as well as the Medical Savings Account demonstration program[63] could encourage older persons to set aside funds for their future long-term health needs rather than spend down their assets to become eligible for Medicaid. Penalties for those who assist in asset transfers for those seeking to qualify financially for Medicaid should also prove helpful (see §26.3(b)). Some of the tax incentives to purchase long-term-care insurance policies are also on the right track (§28.11).

While some progress has been made, an enormous long-term-care financing problem looms. If Medicare provided some funding for chronic long-term care (as opposed to recuperative benefits), on condition that the beneficiary were also enrolled in a qualified private plan paying a substantial share of the costs, the government might help discourage unnecessary reimbursement-motivated Medicare hospitalizations. Home care may also be more efficiently provided in a retirement facility such that a loosening of Medicare's "intermittent" and "home bound" requirements may be economically justified.[64] Although providers fear regulation and regulators fear overutilization, increased Medicaid coverage of assisted-living benefits should be expanded, especially when seniors would otherwise have to reside in a more expensive setting such as a nursing facility. Any successful plan will likely be dependent on, but at the same time generate, increased consumer awareness of the general absence of long-term-care coverage.

To solve the long-term-care problem, government must create incentives for the development of privately funded managed-care models such as CCRCs, redirect government funding of care from hospitals and nursing facilities to less intensive models such as assisted-living and residential-care facilities, and encourage individuals who can do so to set aside their accumulated wealth for long-term care in a controlled setting.

Notes

1. *See New England Journal of Medicine,* Vol. 314, no. 11, Mar. 13, 1986, 722, for a summary of the findings.

2. *E.g.,* H.R. 65, 1245, 1280, 1281 (100th Congress); *See* "Panel Considers Alternatives to Bowen Plan," *Congressional Quarterly,* Mar. 7, 1987, 434.

3. *See* "Long Term Care: The True 'Catastrophe'?" *Congressional Quarterly,* May 31, 1986, 1,227; Brickfield, C., "Long Term Care Insurance: One Piece of the Puzzle," *Health Span,* June 1985, 11.

4. *See, e.g., Congressional Quarterly,* May 31, 1986, discussing federal and private sector alternatives.

5. *Hospitals,* Jan. 5, 1988, 94. For a general discussion of the concerns facing Congress, see also, Kosterlitz, J., "The Coming Crisis," *National Journal,* Aug. 6, 1988, 2,029.

6. McMorran, W., "A Pivotal Month for National LTC Insurance," *Contemporary Long Term Care,* Feb. 1988, 23.

7. *Ibid.*

8. Rosenblatt, R., "Panel Backs Nursing Home Insurance," *New York Times,* Sept. 20, 1987, 4.

9. *Older Americans Reports,* May 27, 1988, 213.

10. Pub. L. No. 100–360, §102(1).

11. *Id.,* §101(1).

12. *Id.,* §102(1).

13. *Ibid.*

14. *Ibid.*

15. *Id.,* §101(2).

16. *Id.,* §§101(1), 101(2), 104(a)(2).

17. *Id.,* §§202(a), 202(b).

18. *Ibid.* This coverage was to be effective for items dispensed on or after January 1, 1990, with deductibles set as follows:

1990	$550
1991	$600
1992	$652 *Id.,* §202(c)(1)(c).

19. *Ibid.*

20. *Id.,* §202(c)(2)(c). The U.S. Department of Health and Human Services (HHS) was not to have the authority to eliminate classes of drugs, change the method of calculating whether the deductible has been met, or alter the coinsurance levels specified in the statute. *Id.,* §202(b)(3).

21. *Id.,* §206.

22. *Id.,* §211(a).

23. An individual was not responsible for the supplemental premium unless he had been Medicare-eligible for more than six full months during that taxable year. Further, no supplemental premium was required of individuals who had an income tax liability of less than $150 for a year. *Ibid.*

24. *Ibid.*

25. Thereafter, the rate was not to increase by more than $1.50 per year. In the case of married couples where both spouses were Medicare-eligible, the limits were doubled. If only one spouse was Medicare-eligible, the tax liability on which the supplemental premium was based would be cut in half. *Ibid.*

26. *Id.,* §211(a).

27. *Id.,* §201.

28. *Id.,* §103.

29. *Id.,* §303(a).

30. *Ibid.*

31. *Id.,* §303(c).

32. Rivlin, A., and J. Wiener, *Caring for the Disabled Elderly: Who Will Pay?* (Washington, DC: The Brookings Institution, 1988).

33. *Id.* at 22.

34. Shearer, G., *Long Term Care: Analysis of Public Policy Options* (Washington, DC: Consumers Union, 1989).

35. *See Older Americans Report,* Mar. 9, 1990, 93; Bowe, J., "Recommending a New Role," *Contemporary Long Term Care,* Apr. 1990, 49.

36. MacNeil, N., "Employer Mandated Health Insurance: A Solution for the Working Uninsured?" *Journal of Health and Hospital Law,* Nov. 1991, 337.

37. *Older Americans Report,* May 12, 1989, 189.

38. MacNeil, note 36 *above,* at 339.

39. *Ibid.*

40. *See, e.g.,* Kosterlitz, J., "Radical Surgeons," *National Journal,* Apr. 27, 1991, 993, discussing several universal health care insurance proposals in Congress.

41. *Id.* at 995.

42. *Id.* at 996.

43. *See* Kapp, M., "Options for Long-Term Care Financing: A Look to the Future," *Hastings Law Journal,* Mar. 1991, 719.

44. Weissenstein, E., "Legislators Use Bills to Put Long-Term Care in Public Eye," *Modern Healthcare,* Dec. 2, 1991, 25.

45. *See* §27.2.

46. *See* Capistrant, G., "Congress Eyes Private Long-Term Care Financing," *The Spectrum,* Apr. 1991, 14.

47. H.R. 4632.

48. Special Report, Research Institute of America, Nov. 23, 1994.

49. *Aging News Alert,* Sept. 27, 1995, 5–8.

50. *Federal Taxes Weekly Alert,* Nov. 16, 1995, 475.

51. *Id.* at 8–10.

52. *See Aging Today,* July–Aug. 1995, 6.

53. Pub. L. 105–33, Sec. 4001.

54. *Id.,* Sec. 4801.

55. *Id.,* Sec. 4432.

56. *Id.,* Sec. 4711.

57. The elderly continue to spend about 15 percent of their income on health care, as before the enactment of the Medicare program. *See Aging America: Trends and Projections,* 1991 ed., U.S. Senate Special Committee on Aging, 106.

58. *See* Lundy, J., "Issue Brief: Health Care Cost Containment," Congressional Research Service, Oct. 31, 1986.

59. *See* §27.3(a).

60. *See generally,* "Seniors Housing: The Market-Driven Solution to Long-Term Care," America Seniors Housing Association, 1994.

61. Certain homes for the aging may be eligible for tax exemption (*see* §9.3), and some continuing-care facilities are eligible for an imputed interest rule exemption (*see* §6.2(b)(2)). Prepaid medical expenses for life-time care facilities are eligible for a tax deduction (*see* §6.1(c)(1)), but only to the extent they exceed 7.5 percent of adjusted gross income.

62. *See* §6.1(c)(2).

63. *See* §28.11(e).

64. *See* §20.5.

Sunrise Assisted Living; Fairfax, Virginia.

Part IX
Operations

Country Meadows of Hershey; Hershey, Pennsylvania.

29 Civil Liability for Operations

§29.1 Increased Exposure to Operational Liability

Many of the subjects discussed throughout this book can lead to liability for the seniors' housing or care facility developer or operator, for example,

- poor project planning (see Chapter 5);
- violation of tax laws (see Chapters 6–12);
- violation of employment, antitrust, or reimbursement laws (see Chapter 13);
- failure to abide by licensing or similar regulations (see Chapters 20–22 and 24); and
- unlawful discrimination (see Chapter 23).

In addition, general liability for operations of long-term-care and seniors' housing communities has emerged in the mid-1990s as a distinct issue that warrants separate treatment.

From 1987 to 1994, the mean award in negligence lawsuits against nursing homes nearly doubled, from $238,285 to $525,853, according to Jury Verdict Research, a consulting firm that tracks litigation. Furthermore, more than 20 percent of the plaintiffs in nursing facility suits were awarded damages compared with about 5 percent in other types of personal injury suits. The fast-growing specialty of elder law is one factor in this trend; many such lawyers handle nothing but cases against nursing homes and other facilities.[1]

Moreover, as an alternative to nursing care, the rise of assisted living, which is less strictly regulated than nursing care, has resulted in widespread concerns about the scope and extent of responsibility and liability assumed by retirement communities for resident care needs. Even unlicensed seniors' housing, which often serves elderly populations with health and assistance needs, is not immune from exposure.

Possible reasons for an increase in the litigation risk for long-term-care and retirement communities include

- higher-acuity residents moving to lower levels of care;
- economic pressures on the health care system;
- the blurring of lines between formerly distinct facility types or levels of care, which is the result of the emergence of home health care and other "community-based services" as an alternative to institutional care, disability discrimination laws that may weaken regulatory or provider attempts to enforce rules based on health or functional status, and public policy favoring seniors' right to choose to "age in place";
- the growth of "elder law" as a practice specialty among attorneys;
- increased enforcement activity against nursing facilities since OBRA regulations took effect in 1995;[2] and

- state elder abuse laws that provide more powerful causes of action and legal remedies for plaintiffs than traditional negligence law.

§29.2 General Rules of Civil Liability

(a) Foreseeable Harm

The general laws governing civil liability may require a seniors' community operator to do more than is specifically promised in the contract between operator and resident. For example, even if a facility's contract expressly states that no care will be provided, it is possible that the facility may be held responsible for injury or damage suffered by a resident when that resident has an unmet care need that the manager notices but does not address.

Although the scope of liability may vary substantially across states based on statutory and case law, the general rule for determining civil liability is that if harm from a retirement community operator's action or inaction is foreseeable, the operator likely has a duty to act reasonably to prevent the harm from taking place. Such duty is probably heightened because of the operator's overall control of the retirement community premises, the vulnerability and dependency of residents entrusted to the facility's care, industry customs or standards that may be applied to determine what is reasonable, and specifically applicable laws and regulations, such as licensing and construction standards. It is important to note that such a duty may extend not only to residents and others on the premises but also to an outsider (e.g., the incompetent resident who injures another while driving).

(b) Employee Conduct

Generally speaking, a property's operator is liable for the negligent acts of its employees. Therefore, even if a facility operator takes great care to screen new employees, perform background checks, conduct periodic training programs, and supervise and evaluate employees, the operator still may be liable for injuries caused by the negligent acts of its employees. Even the intentional conduct of an employee (such as resident abuse) committed in the course

of his or her duties may result in liability for the employer.

The California Supreme Court in *California Ass'n. of Health v. Department of Health Services*[3] confirmed the liability of a licensed care provider for the unauthorized and unanticipated acts of its employee, notwithstanding management's best efforts to prevent the unwanted conduct and its harmful consequences. A California statute provides a defense to civil penalties issued against a long-term health care facility licensee (based on patient injuries or endangerment) if the licensee can prove it "did what might reasonably be expected of a long-term health facility licensee, acting under similar circumstances, to comply with the regulation."[4] In 1996, the California Association of Health Facilities brought suit against the California Department of Health Services (DHS) because the DHS interpreted the statute as requiring that a facility not only prove that it acted reasonably but also that the employee who committed the violation acted reasonably. On appeal, the court concluded that the licensee must prove only that *it* acted reasonably. The court posited a situation in which a health care facility licensee did everything it could to prevent the physical abuse of residents. It conducted in-service training for its staff, ensured that staff members had good records of treating patients appropriately, and maintained procedures for monitoring potential problems and investigating actual problems. One day, a previously model staff member became frustrated with a resident and hit him. In proceedings against the licensee, the licensing agency proved a violation of a regulation prohibiting physical abuse. Under the court's interpretation of the statute, the license citation had to be dismissed. However, the state supreme court reversed, finding the licensee strictly liable for the employee's acts under the licensure statute, just as it would be in a civil negligence case.

(c) Regulatory Violations

If a regulated business violates a regulation designed to prevent injury and damage occurs as a result of the violation, the business is deemed to be "negligent per se." Consequently, the injured plaintiff need not put on evidence at trial to demonstrate actual negligence but merely must prove that the regulatory violation took place and show what damages resulted.

Licensed communities such as assisted-living, nursing, or continuing-care facilities face increased liability exposure when civil litigation is brought as a consequence of an incident that is the subject of a license deficiency or citation. The community's acceptance of a regulatory deficiency (or its payment of fines) without appeal may be construed as an admission of the regulatory violation, which can then be used against the community in a later civil case. Even if not deemed an admission of guilt, the existence of the license citation or deficiency, if admitted into evidence in a later civil trial, can be extremely damaging to the defense in a personal injury or wrongful death lawsuit.

(d) Volunteers

In 1997, Congress granted immunity from personal liability to volunteers working for nonprofit organizations. To receive immunity, the volunteer must act within the scope of the volunteer activity, be properly licensed (if applicable), and not be grossly negligent or act willfully, recklessly, or with a flagrant disregard for the rights or safety of others. Damages caused while the volunteer is operating a vehicle are not covered. Likewise, criminal or sexual conduct, a civil rights violation, or conduct while under the influence of alcohol is not covered. Volunteers working for tax-exempt nonprofit organizations under Sections 501(c)(3), (c)(4), and (c)(6) of the Internal Revenue Code are included (see Chapter 9). It is important to note also that most states grant limited protection from liability for volunteer directors of a nonprofit organization.

§29.3 Areas of Exposure

(a) Unmet Care Needs

The trend toward allowing residents to "age in place" can pose significant liability problems for seniors' housing and care facilities of all types. As residents age, they often require greater levels of care, and the question arises as to what extent the community must provide or participate in the provision of med-

ical or other care beyond its contractual or licensure requirements. This issue received national attention in 1995 in response to an incident at an assisted-living facility in Maryland, where a resident died of a cranial hemorrhage after falling and hitting her head. The accident occurred four days after a laboratory allegedly informed the facility that a blood test revealed that anticoagulants had excessively thinned the resident's blood. After an investigation of the facility by the Maryland Department of Health and Mental Hygiene, the state investigators found that the facility failed to relay the blood test results to the resident's doctor. It was speculated that four additional days' worth of anticoagulants may have contributed to the resident's death.

Although the state found other deficiencies at both the subject facility and other facilities operated by the same company, it did not find that the facility was directly responsible for the resident's death. The state did conclude, however, that the facility should have monitored the resident more closely and notified the resident's doctor of the results of the blood test. In response, the operator distinguished assisted-living facilities from nursing facilities, reportedly maintaining that assisted-living facilities are not in the business of practicing medicine and noticing changes in the condition of residents.[5]

Interestingly, a duty to provide care or to intervene when care is needed may arise even for unlicensed facilities. A seniors' housing executive survey conducted in 1995 by the American Seniors Housing Association indicated that about one-third of respondents had employees who provided residents of *unlicensed* independent-living facilities with assistance in eating, transferring from bed, incontinence, medication monitoring, bathing, and dressing on a routine or occasional basis. The same respondents overwhelmingly agreed that operators of congregate housing should periodically monitor resident well-being and summon help if an obvious medical need arises.

Even a resident's self-inflicted intentional harm can lead to retirement community liability if the resident's care needs are not met. For example, a California court ruled that a licensed residential-care facility for the elderly could potentially be held liable for a patient suicide on the theory that the facility was negligent per se.[6] In this case, a regulation required updated appraisals of residents' physical and mental conditions and notification of the residents' families and physicians when significant changes occurred. Although the facility did not provide psychological counseling services, it could be held responsible for not identifying the need for such services and helping the resident gain access to them. This opinion demonstrates that retirement communities' liability for injuries to residents may not be limited to conditions that the facility was designed to treat but may also extend to injuries that are foreseeable and arguably preventable by reasonable intervention.[7]

By contrast, an Iowa court was less sympathetic to a woman who sued a nursing home for negligence and emotional distress after her mother committed suicide at the nursing home. The trial court directed the jury to find in favor of the defendant on the emotional distress claim but refused to submit a punitive damages claim to the jury and reduced the plaintiff's $400,000 award to $100,000. An appellate court upheld the trial court's actions.[8]

(b) Confused or Combative Residents

Combative residents with Alzheimer's disease or other dementias are an obvious source of potential liability for any seniors' community. Not only may they inflict injury on other residents and staff, but they may also injure themselves in the course of their outbursts. For nursing facilities, strict OBRA rules about the use of antianxiety medications, including high standards for justifying both the use of such drugs and periodic attempts at dosage reduction, increase the difficulty in controlling such residents' agitation and combativeness, thus adding to the facility's liability exposure. Restrictions on the use of restraints also may increase the risk of falls or elopement (wandering) of residents.

Although a facility may be found liable for its failure to protect residents or others (such as visitors) from a combative resident, the resident probably will not be liable to an injured staff person. In a 1996 Wisconsin case, a nurse sued the insurer of an Alzheimer's patient after sustaining injuries when a patient knocked her down. The Wisconsin Supreme Court ruled that an individual institutionalized with a mental disability, who does not have the capacity to control or appreciate his or her conduct, cannot

be liable for injuries caused to caretakers who are employed for financial compensation.[9]

Similarly, a California nurse's aide employed by a convalescent hospital sued a patient with Alzheimer's for severe personal injuries sustained when the patient struck the plaintiff in the head several times.[10] The court denied the nurse recovery based on the doctrine of "primary assumption of risk"; that is, the court ruled that the defendant owed no legal duty to protect the plaintiff from the particular risk of harm that caused the injury because the nurse was specifically employed to care for patients with Alzheimer's. The plaintiff's duties ostensibly included dealing with and preventing violent behavior on the part of Alzheimer's patients.[11]

The rights of a staff person to recover for such an injury are therefore probably limited to workers' compensation insurance. If, like the employee, the workers' compensation carrier cannot recover against the resident, it will probably mean higher premiums for the retirement community.

(c) Private-Duty Aides

Private-duty aides represent a significant liability potential for seniors' housing and care facilities. Such aides may be licensed or unlicensed, may provide personal care services or mere household assistance, and may be spouses or relatives of a resident or employees of a home health agency. Potential security and safety problems include those of access and loitering, solicitation of business from other residents, failure to provide adequate care, accidental injury or damage caused by the aide, theft, resident abuse, and double billing of residents or third-party reimbursers.

Private-duty aides' most significant liability issues relate to adequacy of care. Those who deliver personal care services may not be competent to do so or may render care negligently. For unlicensed facilities, liability may arise if the aide's incompetence or negligent conduct is or should be obvious to the retirement community's management. For licensed facilities, the exposure is exacerbated by the fact that the aide is probably performing certain duties that the community is required to furnish under its license. In such a case, even though the resident may have the right to refuse care from the facility and instead receive it from the aide, the facility must be vigilant that the services required by regulation are actually received by the resident. In such a case, the facility may have to insist that private-duty aides report to facility staff and that the facility staff periodically perform an independent assessment of the resident's physical and mental status.[12]

§29.4 Risk Reduction

(a) Regulatory Compliance Plans

The years 1997 and 1998 have seen increased attention devoted to the development of comprehensive regulatory or "corporate" compliance plans as a means of reducing both exposure to liability and the fines and other penalties associated with federal regulatory violations. Medicare- and Medicaid-certified health care providers, who are vulnerable to claims of fraud and abuse for their billing practices, have been urged to adopt such plans as a means of better ensuring regulatory compliance. The Office of Inspector General (OIG) of the U.S. Department of Health and Human Services (HHS) issued model compliance plans for clinical laboratories in 1997 and for hospitals in early 1998. Court decisions indicate that an organization's directors may have personal liability for not having an effective regulatory compliance plan in place. Federal sentencing guidelines also indicate that the existence of such a plan can result in reduced penalties for criminal convictions. The call for adoption of such comprehensive plans has occurred in a climate of increased prosecution of regulatory violations by federal and state agencies and the advent of private "whistleblowers" (often disgruntled employees of the target defendant who stand to profit from any successful prosecution).

A regulatory compliance plan should include identification and review of all relationships with health care providers and other vendors and of the organization's policies, procedures, advertising, and other documents; creation of a detailed written compliance manual for all applicable laws; appointment of a compliance officer or committee; training of employees; and implementation of a monitoring and enforcement system.

Compliance plans should not be limited to health care reimbursement matters but should also include all applicable laws, particularly at the federal level. Areas of particular interest to senior care providers include incentive and referral arrangements with other providers (e.g., leases with home health agencies, physician or therapy contracts); overlapping payment sources and services (e.g., home health and assisted living, continuing care and Medicaid or Medicare nursing services); compliance with the Fair Housing Act and Americans with Disabilities Act; substandard care, elder abuse, and employment practices; OSHA requirements; and antitrust issues (information sharing, market division, tied products or services).

Development of a compliance plan should involve legal counsel and be brought within attorney-client privilege. In addition, use of outside counsel and financial consultants may bring objectivity, experience, and a perspective that may not be achievable by relying on personnel from within the organization.

(b) Policies for Staff and Private Aides

The adoption of policies and procedures for employed staff and private-duty aides can be useful in reducing the risk of liability for their conduct. For example, employee personnel files that contain documentation of employee qualifications, reference checks, verification of licenses, criminal record clearances, records of in-service training, performance reviews, and written acknowledgment of the employee's responsibility to honor residents' rights and to report instances of resident neglect or abuse may help reduce a facility's liability.

For private-duty aides in particular, policies that require registration, criminal record clearances, sign-in/sign-out logs, rules of conduct, insurance coverage, and reporting of changes in the resident's condition can help reduce exposure. It is also important to clarify that the private aide is not an employee of the facility. For a sample policy, see Volume II, §§15.11–15.16.

(c) Assessment and Handling of Claims

Early assessment of any incident or claim is critical to reducing potential facility liability and often should include consultation with legal counsel. For example, after receiving notice of a regulatory violation that involves allegations of physical and mental harm to one or more residents, the facility operator must determine whether to appeal the alleged violation at the administrative level as a means of avoiding any possible presumption of liability in a subsequent civil proceeding for money damages (see §29.2). Among the factors to consider in assessing the likelihood of litigation are the severity of the alleged harm to the resident; whether there is a pattern or widespread scope of the alleged conduct; the facility's overall relationship with the resident's family; the interest of the press or resident advocates or the presence of a lawyer; and the overall record of the facility. In the case of substantial possibility of subsequent civil litigation, the facility should vigorously pursue an appeal of the alleged regulatory violation.

Timing may be critical to preservation of the facility's right to appeal a regulatory violation or to respond to a claim of damages. The facility operator should immediately consult legal counsel when determining whether and how to appeal regulatory violations and whether and how to defend claims for damages. Insurance carriers should be informed of any potential claim, and the retirement community should insist that the carrier pay for a defense counsel familiar with both the industry and licensing standards. Generally, legal counsel should conduct the investigation of an incident likely to lead to litigation because many of the results may be protected by attorney-client privilege or as the attorney's work product. Liability issues involving employee conduct should be coordinated between employment counsel and defense counsel.[13]

(d) Negotiated Risk Agreements

Some leaders in the assisted-living movement have advocated the use of "negotiated risk agreements," in which residents agree to absolve facilities of the responsibility to provide certain types of care or services and to release them from liability for injury that may result as a consequence of service limitations. These provisions supposedly are intended to make available a wider variety of housing options for those who can no longer live independently. Residents who agree to such provisions arguably have more freedom to reside in lower-acuity, noninstitutional settings where they have greater autonomy

and privacy than are possible in more restricted environments such as nursing facilities. Moreover, in the case of a difficult resident (such as with a severe behavioral problem), it sometimes may be wise to enter into such an agreement in order to develop a consensus among the resident, family, physician, and facility as to the bounds of acceptable conduct and to define the steps to be taken if the resident exceeds those bounds.

Resident advocates worry, however, that such agreements may permit assisted-living facilities to retain residents whose care needs exceed what the facilities can provide or that residents may assume serious risks out of fear that they will have no desirable place to live.[14] Moreover, such agreements may be ineffective because of common law principles, such as those discussed in §29.2, or because a reviewing court may view the agreements as unenforceable contracts of adhesion. Although it is certainly prudent for the provider to involve the resident and others in care planning and for a facility's contracts to describe the limits of its service program and licensure,[15] an operator should not rely on a negotiated risk agreement to absolve it of all responsibility to intervene when necessary to prevent foreseeable harm to a resident.

Notes

1. Sullivan, J., "Long Term Care on Trial," *Contemporary Long Term Care,* Mar. 1996.

2. *See* §20.3.

3. 16 Cal. 4th 284, 940 P. 2d 323, 65 Cal. Rptr. 2d 872 (1997).

4. Cal. Health & Safety Code §1424(b), (c), (d).

5. *See* Vick, "Death Prompts MD Probe of 'Assisted Living' Facility," *Washington Post,* Jan. 9, 1995, 1.

6. Under the doctrine of negligence per se, a defendant may be presumed to be negligent if the defendant has violated a law.

7. *Klein v. BIA Hotel Corp.,* 41 Cal. App. 4th 1133, 49 Cal. Rptr. 2d 60 (1996). *See* the discussion of the negligence per se doctrine in §29.2.

8. *See Lamb v. Newton-Livingston, Inc.,* 551 N.W.2d 333 (Iowa 1996).

9. *Gould v. American Family Mutual Insurance Co.,* 198 Wis. 2d 450, 543 N.W.2d 282 (1996).

10. *Herrle v. Marshall,* 45 Cal. App. 4th 1761 (1996).

11. The court cited *Gould* and two Florida cases in support of the proposition that mentally incompetent patients should not owe a legal duty to protect caregivers from injuries suffered in attending to them. *See also Anicet v. Gant,* 580 So. 2d 273 (Fla. Dist. Ct. App. 1991); *Mujica v. Turner,* 582 So. 2d 24 (Fla. Dist. Ct. App. 1991).

12. *See also* Vol. I §20.4; Morton, A., "Camouflaging," *Contemporary Long Term Care,* July 1995, 40.

13. For a general discussion of steps to reduce liability exposure, *see* Sullivan, J., "Long Term Care on Trial," *Contemporary Long Term Care,* Mar. 1996, 38.

14. *See* Vignery, B., and Z. Dresner, "Troubling Assisted Living Facility Issues: Negotiated Risk Agreements," *Elder Law Forum,* Nov.–Dec. 1995. *See also* Bianculli, J., "How Much Risk Can You Really Negotiate?" *Contemporary Long Term Care,* Jan. 1997, 46.

15. *See* Volume II, §§4.4A and 4.4B; Richards, D., "One Way to Spell Liability Relief," *Contemporary Long Term Care,* Sept. 1996, 64.

Villa Santa Barbara; Santa Barbara, California.

Part X
Case Studies

The Fountains at La Cholla; Tucson, Arizona

David W. Parham

Franciscan Village; Lemont, Illinois

Samia Wilson

Newbury Court; Concord, Massachusetts

Adrienne Schmitz

Peninsula Regent; San Mateo, California

Steven Fader

Seasons at Redondo Beach; Redondo Beach, California

David W. Parham

The Fountains at La Cholla
Tucson, Arizona

General Description

The Fountains at La Cholla is a rental congregate housing and assisted-living community located on a scenic 15.4-acre site in the northwest suburbs of Tucson, Arizona, one of the region's fastest-growing areas. In addition to the site's aesthetic qualities, it offers quick access to 15 nearby medical facilities, including hospitals, nursing homes, and medical and dental clinics.

The Town Center, the project's primary facility, was completed in 1987 and includes 263 independent-living units. Thirteen adjacent patio homes called the Casitas opened in the early 1990s. More recently, a 62-unit assisted-living facility called the Inn opened, along with two nine-unit buildings with 34 beds for Alzheimers patients called the Gardens. Future plans call for another 17-bed Alzheimers unit and a skilled nursing facility with 60 to 80 beds.

The project is operated by Fountains Retirement Communities of Arizona, Inc. (dba the Fountains), and is owned by Fountains Retirement Properties, Inc., both fully owned subsidiaries of Fountains Affiliated Companies, Inc. While the company owns 14 communities and manages six others in six different states, the Fountains at La Cholla was the first and only project developed by the company.

At the time the Fountains was developed, there was a wave of construction of congregate housing facilities in the local area and across the nation. Many developers had turned to seniors' housing in response to declining economic prospects for other property types. This type of development, however, is unique, and it requires extensive operations and management skills. Not realizing that, many of those developers subsequently ran into difficulty. Realizing the importance of operations skills in seniors' housing, Fountains Affiliated Companies thereafter focused its efforts on acquisitions and management rather than development. The company now specializes in startups, fill-ups, and management turnarounds.

About eight other competing projects came on the market at the same time or soon after the Fountains, resulting in an overbuilt seniors' housing market in Tucson. The project has been able to maintain high occupancy rates despite the crowded market due to careful market research and planning before development, an exceptional location, high-quality management, and a focus on the moderate-income market. In addition, the general partner convinced the lender to allow the project to be self-managed and then brought staff with the necessary management and administrative skills to the project. As a result, the management operation has remained consistent, under the same development, ownership, and management team.

The Town Center building was built in Spanish colonial style. It houses the assisted-living facility, dining areas, a bank, a convenience store, and a wellness clinic.

The management at the Fountains understands that many residents shopped around at numerous other communities before deciding to move in, and it continually endeavors to understand its market and assess the level of satisfaction among residents. To that end, annual resident surveys are conducted to provide feedback and a residents council is maintained that includes 12 action committees headed by an executive committee. The project has always focused on the moderate-income market, and research indicates that the residents were sold on the project because it is perceived as good value, providing an active community life with diverse programs.

Because employee satisfaction and performance are important to the quality of management, feedback is obtained from employees as well as residents. Automated systems, including proprietary marketing, property management, and personnel software, help the community run more efficiently. Residents also participate, managing an employee holiday fund that lets them show their appreciation for outstanding employees with holiday bonuses. The level of employee satisfaction is indicated by a very low rate of turnover, which helps to provide continuity and indicates how well the company is doing in personnel management.

Assisted-living residents receive three meals per day in the community's elegant dining room.

Design

The main building, called the Town Center, houses the independent-living facility. The Spanish colonial–style building is three stories high, with a cross-shaped design to minimize the walking distance between apartments, dining areas, and other common areas. The main entrance opens onto a community club-house with a three-story main lobby that forms a large common room for activities. Amenities in the common area include a bank; hair salon; convenience store; chapel; wellness clinic; mail room; residents' art gallery; multipurpose rooms for games and arts and crafts; and assembly rooms. The dining and administrative office areas also are located off the lobby.

There are five apartment floor plans in the Town Center. Entrances to the residential units are set back along the building's carpeted corridors. Each apartment has a full kitchen, wall-to-wall carpeting and vinyl floors, smoke detectors and sprinklers, individual HVAC controls, bathroom safety bars, and an emergency monitoring system. All units feature a balcony or patio, many with private storage areas. Laundry rooms on each floor contain coin-free washers and dryers. The Town Center also includes spe-cial design features such as an energy-efficient four-pipe HVAC system; a sprinkler system, in excess of code to reduce insurance rates; "gypcrete" topping on floors to improve fire safety, energy efficiency, and sound insulation; and barrier-free access.

Exterior features include landscaping that combines greenery and Xeriscaping for water conservation. The building's footprint forms courtyards that enclose an outdoor heated pool, a spa, and a recreational area with horseshoe and shuffleboard courts.

The Inn and the Gardens, new assisted-living and Alzheimers facilities, are located adjacent to the Town Center. Previously, 45 converted independent-living units in the Town Center had served as assisted-living facilities. When the new assisted-living facility opened, those units were redesignated independent-living units. A majority of the residents then moved into the assisted-living building.

The Inn is designed for residents who require assistance with some aspects of daily living. The V-shaped building has three stories plus a basement and contains 62 apartments similar to those in the main building, all of which are wheelchair accessible. There is a three-story atrium lobby with a massive stone fireplace as a central focus. The first floor contains a library, sitting and TV rooms, a convenience store, activity rooms, administrative offices, and dining facilities. On the basement level are classrooms, adult daycare rooms, a chapel, a hair salon, a lounge, a clinic, and an exercise room with men's and women's lockers.

The Gardens is the Alzheimers facility, based both architecturally and programmatically on a European social/residential model for Alzheimers care. At present, there are two one-story, H-shaped buildings, each of which is designed to provide a secure, flexible, and activity-focused living environment for 17 residents in nine rooms. Each building has a gated entry; solarium; game and arts and crafts room; piano; country kitchen; dining area; central bathroom with shower; and laundry room. There are three half-bath floor plans and one with a full bath, and all have the same basic features as the other buildings, with the exception of kitchens. Exterior features include circular walking paths and therapeutic gardens. Future phases of the project will include a third 17-bed building for Alzheimers patients and a skilled nursing facility containing up to 80 beds.

Project Costs and Financing

Total project costs to date have been almost $18.2 million, spread over a development period of more than 13 years. The initial 9.6-acre site was bought for $1,500,000 in 1985, and the developer spent $132,000 on site improvements. Subsequent acquisition costs included $54,000 for a small parcel for the Casitas and $451,000 for a 5.2-acre site for the Inn and the Gardens. Development of the Town Center was completed in 1987 and included about $9.8 million in hard and soft development costs. Including land and site improvements, cost of the Town Center was about $43,850 per unit. The thirteen units in the Casitas were opened in 1992 and 1994 at a cost of almost $1.1 million. Phase I financing included about $3 million in developer equity,

industrial revenue bonds, and a HUD 221(d)4 loan, which was refinanced in 1996.

The most recent phase of the project, opened in March 1998, consists of the assisted-living and Alzheimers facilities, which cost about $5.2 million to construct. Including land, development costs for the Inn and the Gardens were about $70,900 per unit.

Leasing

At the opening of the Fountains in December 1987, about 60 units were leased. By mid-1990, the project had achieved 95 percent occupancy, despite the opening of several other new projects in the area during the same time period. When marketing began, there was only one competing project, but by mid-

The main lobby forms a large common area that includes a bank, a hair salon, a convenience store, a chapel, a wellness clinic, multipurpose rooms for games and arts and crafts, assembly rooms, a mail room, and a residents' art gallery.

1990, eight other competing projects in the Tucson market area were open.

Tucson is a popular destination for "snowbirds" from the colder Northern states. About 30 percent of the residents at the Fountains moved in from another state, and management has learned that almost all moved to Tucson because they have a close relative there.

The marketing program for the Fountains includes a wide variety of media, such as direct mail, television ads, open houses, newspaper inserts, and printed advertorials. The community life programs also help sell the community. As many of these activities are open to the public or guests, they serve as a form of advertising. The best marketing sources, according to management, are the residents themselves, their friends and families, and physicians who refer prospects.

Currently, the Fountains enjoys a virtually full occupancy rate of 97 percent in the Town Center and the Casitas. Forty-five of the units in the Inn

were immediately occupied at opening by residents of the Town Center occupying converted assisted-living units. This left 17 units available in the Inn for new residents, and six of those were preleased. Eleven of the 17 beds (65 percent) in the first of the two buildings in the Gardens were leased within one month, and leasing will begin in the second building when the first is full.

Rent and Services

Monthly rents for single-occupancy independent-living units are $865 for a studio, $1,075 for a standard one-bedroom, $1,375 for a deluxe one-bedroom, $1,695 for a standard two-bedroom, and $1,895 for a deluxe two-bedroom unit. Rents for the 13 separate Casitas units are $2,295 to $2,495 per month. The charge for an additional occupant is $300 per month. All rents are full service and include biweekly housekeeping, scheduled transportation, 24-hour security, utilities (except telephone and cable TV), one main meal a day (either lunch or dinner) plus free continental breakfast and Sunday dinner, an emergency call system in each unit, and free laundry facilities on each floor of each wing. Casitas units have fewer meals included.

At the Inn, the assisted-living facility, single-occupancy monthly rents are $1,985 to $2,650 for deluxe two-bedroom units. The additional occupant charge is $600 per month. Assisted living includes the same services provided in the independent-care building, plus three meals a day, activities and exercise programs, weekly housekeeping plus daily tidying and bed making, weekly linen service, five daily checks by 24-hour attendants, medication reminders and general health monitoring, and monthly barber and beauty services. The Inn also offers an extra-cost Care Plus program, which includes extended nursing consultations, in-room dining, escort and companion services, personal hygiene and grooming assistance, protective oversight, and other services.

The Gardens provides care for people with Alzheimers for a daily rate of $90 for a semiprivate room and $149 for a private room. Services provided include 24-hour staffing, three meals a day, daily housekeeping, and personal laundry and linen services. Activity-focused individual care plans are developed

---

Development Team

Owner
Fountains Retirement Properties, Inc.
Tucson, Arizona

Developer
David Freshwater
Fountains Retirement Properties, Inc.
Tucson, Arizona

Operator/Manager
Fountains Retirement Communities of Arizona, Inc.
Tucson, Arizona

Architect
Phase I: James Barg & Associates, Tucson
Casitas: James Chace, Phoenix
Assisted-living and Alzheimers facilities: Rees
   Associates, Oklahoma City

Other Team Members
Marketing director: June Hussey
Operations director: John Nighswander

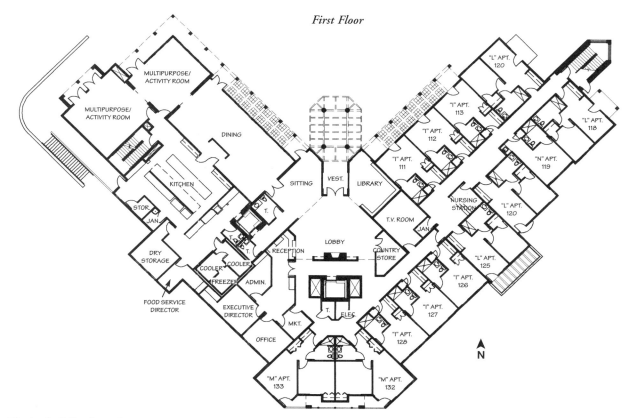

First Floor

The Inn building footprint.

for each resident. Specialized programs include assistance, as necessary, with dressing, personal hygiene, grooming, nutrition, and getting around, as well as music therapy, arts and crafts, special outings, occupational activities, and exploration. As appropriate, residents help with supervised activities such as meal preparation, table setting and clearing, and bed making, which help them maintain familiar routines and encourage self-reliance.

Promoting residents' health is a major focus of the health care program, which emphasizes preventive health care, wellness programs, and early intervention. For example, the community offers a wellness clinic staffed with registered nurses five days a week, exercise classes taught by a registered exercise physiologist, ongoing health and wellness education programs, and menus featuring heart-healthy selections and foods for diabetic residents.

Experience Gained

- Adequate advance market research and planning helped to achieve full occupancy quickly and maintain it in an overbuilt market.
- The project's success is due to its focus on the moderate-income market and delivery of good value to the residents.
- Effective management and administration depend on maintaining awareness of the level of satisfaction among both residents and employees.
- The management operation has remained consistent, under the same development, ownership, and management team.
- Automated systems, including marketing, property management, and personnel software, help the project run efficiently.

Project Data

Land Use Information

Site area: 15.4 acres

Total dwelling units planned: 276 independent living, 62 assisted living, and 27 Alzheimers units, plus a 60–80 bed skilled nursing facility

Total dwelling units completed: 276 independent living, 62 assisted living, and 18 Alzheimers units

Gross density: 23 units per acre

Off-street parking: 116 spaces

Land Use Plan[1]

Use	Acres	Percent of site
Buildings	8.1	53
Roads/paved areas	2.7	17
Common open space	4.6	30
Total	15.4	100

Residential Unit Information

Unit	Approximate size (square feet)	Number of units planned/ built	Monthly rent
Independent living			
Studio	210	3/3	$865
1 bedroom	420	54/54	1,075
1 bedroom deluxe	550	126/126	1,375
2 bedroom/1 bath	625	26/26	1,695
2 bedroom/2 bath	750	54/54	1,895
Casitas	1,250	11/11	2,295
Casitas	1,360	2/2	2,495
Assisted living	270–520	62/62	1,985–2,650
Alzheimers	320–490	27/18	90/day semiprivate, 149/day private
Skilled nursing	n/a	60–80 (beds)/0	n/a
Total		425–445/356	

Development Cost Information

Phase I

Town Center

Site acquisition	$1,500,000
Site improvements	132,000
Construction costs	8,500,000
Soft costs	1,268,000
Total	$11,400,000

Casitas

Casitas I construction (8 units)	$653,000
Casitas II site acquisition	54,000
Casitas II construction (5 units)	408,000
Total	$1,115,000

Phase II

The Inn/The Gardens

Site acquisition	$452,000
Hard and soft costs	5,221,000
Total	$5,673,000

Total development costs	**$18,188,000**

Annual Operating Expenses (1997)

Administration	$341,453
Security	44,198
Maintenance	263,659
Utilities	301,266
Housekeeping	156,285
Laundry	5,694
Transportation	54,028
Food service	1,040,301
Resident care (assisted living)	258,476
Activities	72,646
Taxes	119,133
Insurance	48,276
Management fee	319,281
Marketing	138,442
Total	$3,163,138

Financing Information

Town Center

Developer equity	$3,000,000
HUD 221(d)4	$1,086,919 (refinanced 1996)
Industrial revenue bonds	
Total	$11,400,000

Casitas

Cash	$1,115,000
Total	$1,115,000

The Inn/The Gardens

Cash	$5,673,000
Total	$5,673,000

Development Schedule

Town Center

Site purchased: 1985
Planning started: 1985
Construction started: 1986
Sales/leasing started: 1986
First move-in: December 1987
Full occupancy achieved: July 1990 (95%)

The Inn/The Gardens

Site purchased: 1995
Planning started: 1994
Construction started: April 1997
Sales/leasing started: October 1998
First move-in: March 1998

Note
1. Approximate measurements.

The Fountains at La Cholla

Franciscan Village
Lemont, Illinois

General Description

Located in Lemont, Illinois, a small town about 30 miles outside Chicago, Franciscan Village is a continuing-care retirement community (CCRC) designed to accommodate seniors as they age in place. Sponsored and managed by the Franciscan Sisters of Chicago, the 33-acre project comprises 50 single-story cottages known as coach homes, 150 independent-living apartments, and 30 assisted-living apartments known as the Village Inn. In addition, the CCRC includes the Mother Theresa Home, a 150-bed skilled-nursing facility. The Village Inn, independent-living apartments, and Mother Theresa Home are connected by a mall that provides direct access to the common areas of the campus. The mall features a convenience shop, deli, restaurant-style dining facilities, library, bank, beauty/barber shop, activity rooms, exercise facilities, and the heart of the Franciscan Village campus, the St. Francis of Assisi Chapel.

Franciscan Village and the Mother Theresa Home, Inc., thrive as a program-based CCRC in part because of the Franciscan Sisters' commitment to serving the senior community beyond simply providing long-term care. The sisters also promote through management and operations the concept of a "community of companionship and caring" in order to alleviate the trauma seniors often feel upon being uprooted as they go through various phases of their mature life. The sisters played a pivotal role in the development of Franciscan Village, ensuring that their philosophy and vision were implemented in every aspect of the project.

Site History

The history of Franciscan Village begins with the Mother Theresa Home, Inc., which before 1964 existed as a convent for the Franciscan Sisters of Chicago. In 1963, in keeping with the sisters' mission of serving the elderly, the convent was converted into a nursing home for 57 residents that served as the local intermediate-care facility for some 25 years. The new construction project included the building of a new Mother Theresa Home, increasing the number of nursing beds to 150. Upon evaluation of the site and infrastructure, the sisters determined that it would be more feasible to build a new assisted-living facility than to renovate the existing structure. It also would allow for efficiencies in operations and in use of space that were not possible in the original building.

After studying three different sites, the sisters determined that the Lemont site was most suitable. At the time the site was located just outside Lemont in unincorporated rural Cook County, occupying five acres surrounded by undeveloped green fields.

The design of Franciscan Village strives to provide a seamless transition for its residents as they move to different levels of care. The exterior of the mall, Village Inn, apartment units, and nursing facility feature red brick, colored concrete, and cream-and-yellow stucco.

The rural location would provide a country-like environment, although redevelopment would require additional land as well as a new drainage and water retention system. The existing building was left vacant with the intention of converting it into an assisted-living unit. The sisters set forth to develop their retirement facility, balancing environmental and economic concerns.

The sisters asked O'Donnell Wicklund Pigozzi and Peterson, Architects, Inc. (OWP&P) to prepare several possible concepts for the site. They decided to develop a facility for moderate-income seniors that would serve not only the sick elderly but healthy seniors as well, and from that decision came the idea of building an entire campus to house seniors throughout their mature life. The result is now a 33-acre CCRC graced with mature trees that has a small-town feel and European ambience. The park-like setting features landscaped areas throughout, as well as flowering gardens and a gazebo.

Planning and Development

Development of Franciscan Village began in 1987, at which time the CCRC concept was relatively new to the area. Being unfamiliar with the idea, the town initially resisted development; concerns included project density, public safety, use of community resources, and parking. The planning phase of the project therefore entailed a great deal of community outreach and education.

The sisters shared their vision and goals for the CCRC at an initial public meeting, and that meeting was followed by a series of informational and educational sessions that included the village planning board, architects, and county administrators. The sessions occurred regularly until construction began, by which time the concept and plans for the CCRC were well received by community residents and officials, who became quite supportive. Local community acceptance led to approval of the project by

Unlike at many CCRC developments, the nursing facility at Franciscan Village was the first phase of the project to be completed.

Design

The Franciscan Sisters selected OWP&P to design the project because of their experience in designing for aging populations. The sisters knew exactly what they wanted, and the architects helped them realize their vision. It was thus a partnership in which the sisters were involved in every step of the design, and their hands-on approach greatly influenced the look and the feel of the village.

The design was driven by program and service requirements and the need for efficient operations as well as by aesthetics. Specifically, the campus facilities were designed to look and feel like home, regardless of residents' functional capacity. In this respect, "seamless transition" of design was an important feature of the village, not only in the exterior of the facilities but in the interiors as well. The sisters wanted to ensure that there would be no disruption or trauma associated with residents' moving to a different type of dwelling.

Continuity and consistency are evident in the color scheme and materials used in development of the village. The facade of the mall, the Village Inn, the apartment units, and the Mother Theresa Home are composed of red brick, colored concrete, and cream-and-yellow stucco, while the coach homes display cream-colored vinyl siding. Most interiors feature similar color, design, and lighting throughout, using neutral finishes. The common areas such as the library and dining halls use light-toned surface treatments as well as rich solid and accented patterns. The corridors in the residential units have individual color schemes so that they can be easily distinguished from the common areas. Brighter, more intense colors are used in the acute care areas, creating contrast for the benefit of residents who may have diminished visual acuity. In addition to visual continuity, physical continuity is created by connecting all residences to the mall and chapel.

Nevertheless, the various facilities are distinct and independent; each has its own points of entry and control. The coach homes and apartments surround the mall in clusters, promoting residents' privacy while making them feel part of the community.

The design of the village takes into consideration the importance of natural light and neutral colors, privacy and common spaces. The chapel, for instance,

Cook County, which at that time had jurisdiction over unincorporated Lemont Township.

The Franciscan Sisters resolved to complete the Mother Theresa Home first because the need for a nursing facility was most acute. In this respect the development of Franciscan Village was unique. Typically housing is completed first, with the promise of a nursing facility to follow, which often never does. Also significant was the phasing of the development, which allowed the sisters and the development team to accommodate and adjust to new legislation and regulations that came into effect during construction. Phasing also allowed for continual redesign to accommodate growth and change.

While development was carried out in four individual phases, the overall process was continuous. Phase I included development of the Mother Theresa Home and the construction of some of the coach homes, which were built in clusters. In Phase II, the mall, 78 apartments, and the remainder of the coach homes were completed. Phase III saw the completion of the assisted-living units and the administrative offices of the Village Inn. The final phase included the completion of 72 additional independent apartment units.

belongs to everyone and yet to no one, but because most residents would spend a significant amount of time in their units, the decision was made to provide more private than common space. The mall features a three-story octagonal atrium finished with beige walls and white mill work that provides access to all common areas; the main dining hall, which seats 80, features large windows and French doors to provide plenty of natural light. The library, located adjacent to the atrium, is distinguished by upholstered seating, a marble fireplace, and bold-patterned wallpaper.

Marketing

The Franciscan Sisters, who had no experience in marketing, relied on their reputation and experience and on the community's trust to market Franciscan Village. While the sisters initially hired a marketing consultant, they subsequently assumed the marketing task themselves, taking their cues from potential residents and demographic trends as they continuously implement the most appropriate responses to issues and changes that affect seniors.

The sisters have created a market niche for the village by offering a variety of levels of care in rental units to middle-income seniors, most of whom cannot afford the life-care housing contracts often associated with CCRCs and assisted-living facilities. The sisters developed one of the first CCRCs in Illinois to provide rental housing to seniors at various levels of dependence in a campus setting at an affordable price.

The most successful marketing, according to the sisters, was through word of mouth. As a result of the monthly information and education sessions held throughout the planning and development process, the community gained a great deal of understanding of and trust in the sisters's mission. In addition, many of the attendees were children of seniors for whom the campus was being planned. Following the meetings potential residents and their family members exchanged information about Franciscan Village, which also was available through the print media.

The sisters greatest marketing asset is their outstanding reputation; they are well known throughout Chicago and the surrounding areas for their knowledge, dedication, and provision of quality care to

Franciscan Village features a range of life-care housing options ranging from independent-living cottages to skilled-nursing facilities, allowing residents to age in place.

seniors. Reflecting that reputation, occupancy reached 96 percent within 13 months and typically lingers at around 98 percent. In addition, the Mother Theresa Home was awarded the Illinois Governor's Award for Excellence in social programming in 1991 and also received the Theresa Dudzik Service Award in 1993 for its outstanding interdisciplinary team approach to overall resident health and well-being.

Operations and Management

Franciscan Village is composed of two separate corporations. The Mother Theresa Home, Inc., is a skilled-nursing facility regulated and licensed by the state of Illinois, while Franciscan Village operates as an independent-housing corporation. Though legally separate, they share services and facilities. The Village Mall is known as the campus "bridge," bringing management facilities and services together in one central location. The common areas throughout the mall, including the deli, dining halls, chapel, barber/beauty shop, and kitchen are shared by all residents, and the human resources department, finance de-

Development Team

Developer/Manager
Franciscan Sisters of Chicago
Lemont, Illinois

Architect
O'Donnell Wicklund Pigozzi and Peterson Architects, Inc. (OWP&P)
Chicago, Illinois

Contractor
Pepper Construction Company
Chicago, Illinois

Other Team Members
OWP&P Architects, Inc./Interior Design
Dickerson Engineering/Electrical Engineering
Brian Berg Associates/Mechanical Engineering
Branecki Virgilio & Associates/Civil Engineering
David McCullum & Associates/Landscaping

Common areas such as the main dining hall feature light-toned surface treatments, as well as rich solid and accented patterns.

partment, and administrative and residential offices located on the first level of the Village Inn serve the entire campus as well.

Sharing services and facilities has been economically feasible in most respects. The sisters consider the campus as a whole when planning and operating the facilities, while providing individual attention and care to the various segments of the resident population. Despite the dual management structure, all residents are admitted to either the village or the Mother Theresa Home. The application process is based on suitability and compatibility. All applicants are screened with respect to established health and financial parameters, a personal interview, and their desire to live in the village. A fee is required to secure a unit or dwelling on campus. While there are internal and external waiting lists for admittance to Franciscan Village and the Mother Theresa Home, priority is given to current residents who wish to move to another level of care. If no units are available, potential residents are referred to another seniors facility in the area for temporary placement. Village staff contact potential residents on the waiting list monthly.

Regardless of dwelling type, financial dealings are with Franciscan Village only; no outside sources or agencies are used. The coach homes require a monthly service fee of $911 and a 90 percent refundable entrance fee of $79,000. This entrance fee, required only for the coach homes, is among the lowest in the area. The 960-square-foot homes are single-level, with two bedrooms and two bathrooms, eat-in-kitchens, attached patios, laundries, and garages. The monthly service fee ensures that residents receive security services, home and lawn maintenance, courtesy transportation, an emergency response system, planned social events and activities, semiannual cleaning, and all utilities except telephone and cable.

The apartments include efficiencies and one- and two-bedroom units ranging in size from 468 square feet to 950 square feet. The 150 units offer individual entrances, lounge areas, on-site laundry facilities, and patios or porches on each floor. In addition, residents have direct access to the mall, the Village Inn, and the Mother Theresa Home. Monthly service fees range from $1,193 for the smallest efficiency to $2,183 for the largest two-bedroom apartment units. This fee includes the main meal each day in the dining rooms, security services, courtesy transportation, biweekly housekeeping, social events and activities, an emergency response system, maintenance, and all utilities except cable and telephone. If there is a second occupant, there is an additional monthly fee of $350. Patios and storage facilities are an additional $15 each per month.

Offering 30 private efficiencies ranging in size from 323 to 438 square feet, the Village Inn assisted-living apartments carry a monthly service fee of $2,048 to $2,213 per month depending on the size of the unit. The fee includes all the services afforded to those in the apartments, with the addition of three meals daily and a 24-hour snack service; medication reminders; access to assistance if necessary 24 hours a day, seven days a week; and weekly rather than biweekly housekeeping. There also is a $550 monthly fee assessed for any second occupant in the unit.

The Mother Theresa Home provides comprehensive, licensed care to 150 residents who are charged a daily rate that is assessed on a monthly basis. Accommodations include either a private or semiprivate furnished room, and residents receive assistance with bathing, dressing, laundry, housekeeping, and medications and constant evaluation and monitoring. Three levels of care are offered. The first level, known as sheltered care, is for seniors who need personal care and assistance in meeting their daily needs. These residents are offered a private room at

a daily rate of $100. The second level is intermediate care, which can be broken down further to three sublevels of care: light intermediate care for those who need daily monitoring, some nursing services, and minimal assistance with dressing, bathing, and diet; general intermediate care for those who need assistance with several daily activities and moderate supervision; and heavy intermediate care for seniors who depend on staff for the majority of their daily needs and who require rehabilitative services and a great deal of intervention and redirection. The daily rates for these intermediate-care units are as follows: light intermediate care, $114 per day (private room); general intermediate care, $115 a day (semiprivate room) and $127 a day (private room); and heavy intermediate care, $128 a day (semiprivate room) and $140 per day (private room). The third level of care provided is skilled care. At this level, seniors who require a licensed nurse or personnel to tend to their daily needs are offered a semiprivate or private room at a daily rate of $138 and $150, respectively. This is typically for seniors who are in a post-acute phase or experiencing recurrence of a chronic illness.

The ultimate goal of the staff at the Mother Theresa Home is to focus on the individual's capabilities rather than disabilities, and the staff provides personal care programs for residents and their families to promote their overall wellness. The administration is dedicated to providing restorative care,

Acute care areas feature brighter, more intense colors that create contrast in an area where residents may have diminished visual acuity.

activities, pastoral care, and social services while accommodating residents' dietary, nursing, and psychosocial needs. Staff do not focus on recreation but rather on "re-creation," encouraging independence and social interaction.

There is constant evaluation of residents throughout the village as they age in place. The resident services director evaluates all residents continuously to make sure that they are placed in appropriate housing and receive the correct level of care. Every level of care includes internal assessments, adequate staff and nursing, available professional experts, and close working relationships with residents' families.

Franciscan Village also has a close working relationship with the surrounding community. The sisters provide educational outreach and seminars to the local community on aging and related issues, and local college interns and nursing students gain practical experience in caring for seniors and mature adults at Franciscan Village, particularly the Village Inn and Mother Theresa Home. Other programs include a intergenerational volunteer program through which seniors, children, young adults, and adolescents are bought together for social interaction and programmed activities. Franciscan Village also operates a successful job training program in which Lemont High School students are trained to work in various areas.

Impact and Impressions

Franciscan Village has had a tremendous impact on the surrounding community and the development of CCRCs in general. With more than 400 residents, the town of Lemont views the village as important to its overall growth and requested the village to annex to the town in 1994. The village provides nearly 300 local jobs and is committed to using local vendors and services whenever possible. Its community outreach program helps educate the public on issues related to aging as well as serves as a training site for health care professionals and local high school students. Franciscan Village residents go into Lemont for shopping, services, and various activities, enhancing the economic base of the town.

Franciscan Village has been recognized in Illinois as a model for continuing-care retirement commu-

nities; other senior services providers frequently contact village staff for insight and advice. Recognized by the Retirement Research Foundation as "exemplary" in the provision of seniors services, it also provides a social model for assisted living that allows residents to remain as independent as possible for as long as possible. The sisters maintain an open-door policy to other developers and architects interested in pursuing this model of development.

The Franciscan Sisters believe that having a mission and being willing to take risks are vital to the development of CCRCs and that those traits explain their success in developing Franciscan Village. The sisters chose OWP&P as the architects for Franciscan Village because of the firm's knowledge of and commitment to the seniors market, which were essential to the success of the project and to fostering the intimate involvement of all team members in all its aspects. Also critical to success was all members' flexibility throughout the development process.

Plans for future development based on current needs and Illinois demographics include the potential for additional coach homes and the expansion of health care services to serve the village and the local community through the provision of a seniors wellness center. In addition, a greater number of residents are being admitted with some form of dementia; the sisters therefore are looking at developing specialized units within the Mother Theresa Home to serve residents with dementia, including Alzheimer's disease. Finally, the village is exploring the possibility of offering rehabilitative and sub-acute level services. The Franciscan Sisters' long-term expectations for Franciscan Village include simply serving the community and accommodating legislative and demographic changes as well as residents' needs, always remembering that the village is the place residents call home, "a community of companionship and caring."

Experience Gained

■ Issues surrounding zoning and community support of the project were most problematic. The sisters engaged in a significant community outreach and education effort to gain local support.

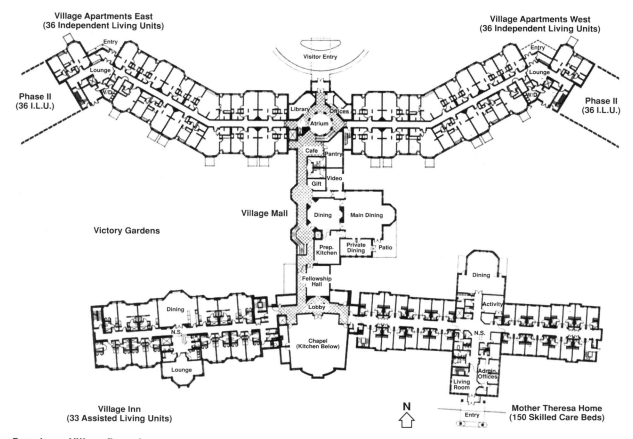

Village Apartments East
(36 Independent Living Units)

Village Apartments West
(36 Independent Living Units)

Entry

Entry

Lounge

Lounge

Phase II
(36 I.L.U.)

W/D

W/D

Phase II
(36 I.L.U.)

Visitor Entry

Library

Offices

Atrium

Cafe

Pantry

Gift

Video

Village Mall

Dining

Main Dining

Victory Gardens

Prep.
Kitchen

Private
Dining

Patio

Fellowship
Hall

Dining

Lobby

Activity

Dining

N.S.

N.S.

Chapel
(Kitchen Below)

Admin.
Offices

Lounge

Living
Room

Village Inn
(33 Assisted Living Units)

N

Entry

Mother Theresa Home
(150 Skilled Care Beds)

Franciscan Village floor plan.

■ Besides antidevelopment sentiments, several regulatory obstacles had to be overcome. When planning first began, retirement housing was considered simply another multi-unit housing project. During construction, the Americans with Disabilities Act came into effect as well as other regulations governing assisted living. Flexibility is essential in designing and developing new product types. The sisters' vision allowed for innovative design features and programming to resolve issues as they arose and for planning for future regulatory constraints.

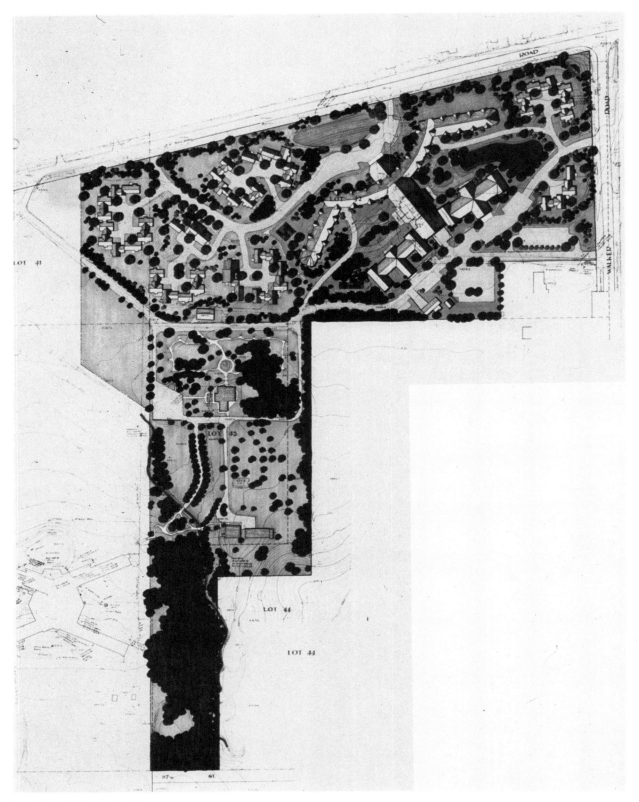

Franciscan Village site plan.

Project Data

Land Use Information

Site area: 33 acres
Total dwelling units: 380
Gross density: 11.5 units/acre
Off-street parking spaces: 270

Land Use Plan

Use	Acres	Percent of site
Buildings	4.4	13
Roads/paved areas	4.0	12
Common open space	13.6	41
Other	11.0	34
Total	33	100

Development Cost Information

Site improvement costs: $2,158,000
Construction costs: $30,036,000
Soft costs: $1,806,000
Total development cost: $34 Million

Annual Operating Expenses

Franciscan Village: $5,000,000
Mother Theresa Home, Inc.: $6,000,000

Financing Source

Tax-exempt bond: $24,125,000
Franciscan Sisters of Chicago equity contribution: $10,000,000

Development Schedule

Planning started: 1987
Construction started: 1989
Sales/leasing started: 1989

Residential Unit Information

Type	Unit size (square feet)	Number of units planned/built	Entrance fee	Monthly rent/fee
Coach homes[1]	960	62/50	$79,000	$911
Apartments[1]	468–950	200/150	0	$1,193–2,183
Apartments[2]	323–438	45/30	0	$2,048–2,213
Skilled-nursing units	–	150/150	0	Variable

Notes
1. Independent-living units.
2. Assisted-living units.

Newbury Court
Concord, Massachusetts

General Description

Newbury Court is an upscale congregate housing facility comprising 75 apartment-style suites. The six-story structure is nestled in a wooded setting on the Sudbury River in the historic town of Concord, Massachusetts, 35 minutes west of Boston. Incorporated in 1635, the town is steeped in tradition and has been home to many historic figures, including Henry David Thoreau, Nathaniel Hawthorne, Ralph Waldo Emerson, and Louisa May Alcott. Today, Concord has a population of just under 16,000 residents.

The majority of Newbury Court's 100 residents are from within a 25-mile radius of the project. Others have relocated to the area in order to be near their children. The average age of residents is about 82 and has ranged to 96. Typically, residents are 81 or 82 at the time they move in. About one-quarter of the residents are married couples, a relatively high ratio for a retirement community.

Services provided to residents of Newbury Court include housekeeping, one meal per day, local transportation, a nurse practitioner on site one-half day per week, and an extensive calendar of planned activities for residents seeking an active lifestyle. The project is part of a full lifecare campus that includes an intermediate-care facility and a nursing home.

Site History

Newbury Court is the most recent development on the 35-acre campus, which is owned and managed by the New England Deaconess Association, a non-profit, nondenominational organization that has provided health and social services for residents of the region since 1889. Other components include the 108-bed Rivercrest Nursing Home, built in 1964 and expanded at the time of Newbury Court's construction, and Chamberlin, a 58-bed intermediate-care facility built in 1969. A 12-unit, moderate-income apartment building completes the inventory of on-site residences. In addition, the Deaconess Building, the original 1913 elderly care home, remains and is currently undergoing renovation for use as residences. A nondenominational chapel and staff offices complete the development.

Emerson Hospital is conveniently located adjacent to the campus, and across the street is the Concord Country Club, of which some Newbury Court residents are members. Transportation is provided to stores, doctors' offices, and services located in the surrounding area.

The site was deeded to the New England Deaconess Association by Charles Emerson more than one hundred years ago, along with an endowment to build retirement facilities. The Deaconess association began as a means of caring for elderly people

The red brick and Georgian architectural elements of Newbury Court recall the historic buildings of Concord.

of low and moderate means residing in urban areas. The first building on the site was constructed in 1913. Today, a percentage of the nursing home residents are subsidized, either by the New England Deaconness Association or by Medicaid.

Newbury Court was developed to provide congregate housing facilities for those who no longer want to maintain their homes but do not require assisted-living services. The facility is classified as a Section 501(c)(3) nonprofit and is therefore eligible for tax-exempt status.

Planning and Design

Great care was taken in selecting the development team. The architectural firm of Tsomides Associates, specialists in senior living facilities, designed Newbury Court. The red brick and Georgian architectural elements of the facility echo the historic buildings of the area in modern form. Preservation of the site's natural woods, wetlands, and panoramic river views was essential, both for the project's success and in order to facilitate zoning approvals. Original plans called for a 100-unit cluster of apartments. The project eventually was approved for 75 units. However, according to the developer, that is not quite enough to ensure financial stability. The Reverend Guy Morrison, president of the New England Deaconess Association, believes that 90 units would be ideal. However, because of the project's location within a historic town on a site replete with wetlands, it is highly unlikely that a larger facility could have obtained approvals.

The front of the six-story building features a classical columned portico that provides a welcoming entrance. Electronic sliding doors allow easy access for handicapped residents. A generous brick terrace

The rear terrace of Newbury Court provides a panoramic view of the Sudbury River and is an ideal spot for residents to socialize during summer barbecues and other events.

to the rear of the building overlooks the river and wildlife habitat and serves as the site of summer barbecues and other events. The underground parking garage and individual storage areas are accessed with a security card. One parking space is provided for each unit at no additional cost.

On the main level of the building, large windows and a skylight bring natural light into the elegantly furnished lobby. Other spaces on this level include a library, meeting and activity rooms, a casual dining area, and a formal dining room where most residents gather for dinner. A private dining room also is available and can be reserved for parties.

Residential suites are arranged in clusters off short hallways, with recessed entryways for privacy. Elevators are located in the center of the building so that the distance to each unit is as short as possible. Newbury Court offers a total of 12 different plans, includ-

ing one-bedroom, two-bedroom, and two-bedroom-plus-den units ranging from 730 to 1,420 square feet. Each suite includes a living/dining room, a fully equipped eat-in kitchen, laundry facilities, one or two baths, a walk-in closet, a private balcony, and individual climate control. Bathroom doors swing in both directions, permitting access in case of emergency. Bedrooms and baths are equipped with a pull cord that rings the reception desk.

Operations and Services

The campus offers a full range of on-site services. Facilities include a fitness center, an automated teller machine, a hair salon, a hobby room, a guest room, a woodworking shop, and a convenience store with limited hours. The Duvall Chapel, a nondenominational place of worship, also is located on campus. There are 14 gas fireplaces throughout the Newbury Court building, including some in the top-floor units. These lend a homelike atmosphere to the interior and according to the developer are well worth the costs.

One meal per day is included in the fees; residents may choose lunch or dinner. Restaurant-quality meals are prepared by a staff chef and served by wait staff in the formal dining room. The menu offers a choice of seasonal and daily specials. Special dietary requests are honored. More casual meals also are available in a smaller café.

Housekeeping services include biweekly cleaning of units, weekly linen service, and daily cleaning of all common areas. Transportation is provided by staff drivers. Approximately two-thirds of residents have their own cars, but often they prefer to use transportation services. Recreational and cultural events and trips are offered on a regular basis. A nurse practitioner is on site for four hours per week to provide routine services such as giving flu shots and making evaluations and to assist with other medical needs.

The reception desk is staffed 24 hours per day. Staff check on residents daily by means of a simple tag system: At the entrance of each unit is a tag. If a resident has not been out of the unit, the tag will not be moved, and a staff member will know to check on the resident.

Marketing

Admission to Newbury Court is available to singles and couples aged 62 and over. Prospective residents are carefully screened for their ability to function independently. An interview with staff as well as a medical form filled out by a doctor are required to complete the assessment. In general, a wheelchair-bound person is accepted if the person is self-reliant or if the spouse can serve as caretaker. Applicants with early-stage dementia also are accepted with a spouse caretaker.

The marketing effort began in October 1991, three years before completion. Full occupancy was achieved in September 1995. A long marketing period is essential for a retirement facility since residents must make many difficult decisions and usually have to sell their homes in order to move in. The marketing program was extensive, including advertisements in local newspapers; there is an on-site sales office/information center.

The project team initially considered setting up a sales office at an in-town location rather than on site, affording greater visibility and downplaying the connection with the nursing home. But that idea was rejected. It was decided that potential residents should be able to see the actual site of their new homes and, further, that it would be an advantage rather than a disadvantage to acknowledge the on-site nursing home.

Marketing has been an ongoing process, despite a waiting list of about 100 interested applicants. Future residents are invited to the frequent events, such as teas and wine-and-cheese parties, held at Newbury Court. In addition, outsiders can rent meeting rooms, which provides additional public exposure as well as revenue. Marketing is managed by a full-time marketing director.

Even with a long waiting list, few potential residents are ready to move in immediately when a vacancy arises, and sometimes the vacant unit is not the type most desired. Flexibility is important. Often an applicant moves into a less than ideal unit and then relocates when a more suitable one becomes available.

Financing

Entrance fees range from $205,000 to $430,000, depending on the unit. A second person in a unit pays an additional $15,000. The entrance fees are 90 percent refundable to the resident or the resident's estate upon leaving. Monthly fees range from $1,432 to $2,600 for the first person in a unit; an additional $400 per month is charged for the second. Fees cover utilities, home maintenance, housekeeping and linen service, activities and services, and one meal per day.

In addition, there is a one-time fee of $1,900 per person for long-term-care insurance, plus monthly insurance fees of $363 for singles and $818 for couples. Those residents who do not qualify for long-term-care insurance due to a preexisting condition must try to obtain this insurance by other means. Long-term-care insurance covers the resident in the event of placement in the adjoining assisted-living center or nursing home. Any home health care services also are covered as needed. The entire facility —congregate housing, assisted living, and nursing home—operates under the New England Deaconess Association, providing the full scope of services of a continuing-care retirement community.

Residents of Newbury Court do not own their units but have a lifetime occupancy agreement. Because residents do not actually own their unit, property taxes are not deductible, nor is a loan for the initial fee considered a mortgage.

Joined to a preexisting nursing home, 185,000-square-foot Newbury Court is nestled among natural woods and protected wetlands.

Hutchins Photography, Inc.

Period furnishings and details, along with careful attention to lighting, create bright, comfortable common areas.

Experience Gained

- The attached nursing home is a crucial component of Newbury Court's success. Some Newbury Court residents have a spouse in the nursing home, and it is important to them to be able to visit daily. Others eventually will move into the nursing home, and the continuity provided is reassuring. That the buildings are attached by an enclosed hallway makes it easy for residents of each facility to visit. Some services, such as meals, may be shared by family members in any of the facility dining rooms.

- Residents of high-quality retirement communities tend to live longer and healthier lives than actuarial tables suggest. While this certainly speaks

well of such facilities, managers need to be aware of this when structuring their entrance fees. Infrequent unit turnover does not allow for entrance fees to be increased as often as may be expected. Similarly, existing tables and guidelines for estimating expenses are never completely accurate, since each project is unique. It takes several years of operation to be able to judge accurately the costs of utilities and other operating expenses.

- Another variable developers should be aware of is the issue of tax status. Throughout the country, local jurisdictions are seeking ways to raise additional revenue and are reexamining the tax exemptions of many facilities. Newbury Court currently is involved in a legal action with the town of Concord regarding its tax-exempt status. It is advisable to fully consider these issues at the start of development in order to determine more accurately the potential tax burden on the facility and on residents.

- It is important to maintain an adequate emergency response system. At Newbury Court a pull cord is located in each bedroom to signal the front-desk staff for assistance. Administrators believe that a "Lifeline" type of system, in which residents wear a portable call button that can be activated anywhere in the facility, would be more effective. This type of system is highly sensitive to sound and will transmit voice in both directions, so that there is full communication at all times during an emergency.

- Newbury Court's brochure and advertisements depict actual residents rather than hired actors. Concord is largely a white, upper-income community, and Newbury Court, whose residents are mostly from the local area, do not include any racial minority members. In its efforts to fight housing discrimination, a national grass-roots organization called ACORN (Association of Community Organizations for Reform Now) has targeted numerous groups, including the New England Deaconess Association, for not representing minorities in their advertising. Developers should be aware of the potential for such law suits when producing their advertising and promotional materials.

- It is important not to promise services that cannot be delivered. Originally, a physician was to main-

Development Team

Developer/Owner/Manager
New England Deaconess Association
Concord, Massachusetts

Architect
Tsomides Associates
Newton Upper Falls, Massachusetts

Planners
Hurley Associates
Concord, Massachusetts

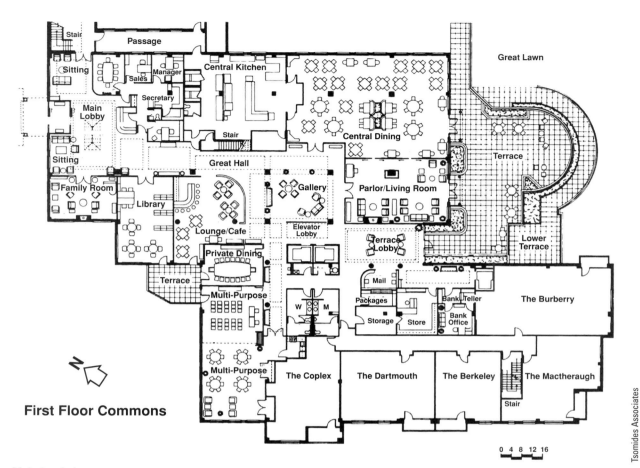

First Floor Commons

N

Main-level plan.

tain regular limited on-site office hours. As the developer was unable to find a doctor willing to make such a commitment, there is instead a nurse on site for four hours per week. While residents would like additional medical care, it is important not to furnish a higher level of medical care than deemed necessary, thus redefining the congregate housing facility as a higher-care facility.

■ Pets can provide companionship and continuity for older people, and many do not want to give them up when moving to a new home. But some residents may be too disabled to care for them, and they can prove disruptive to other residents. Newbury Court allows one cat per unit, but no dogs, as a compromise to what can be a difficult issue.

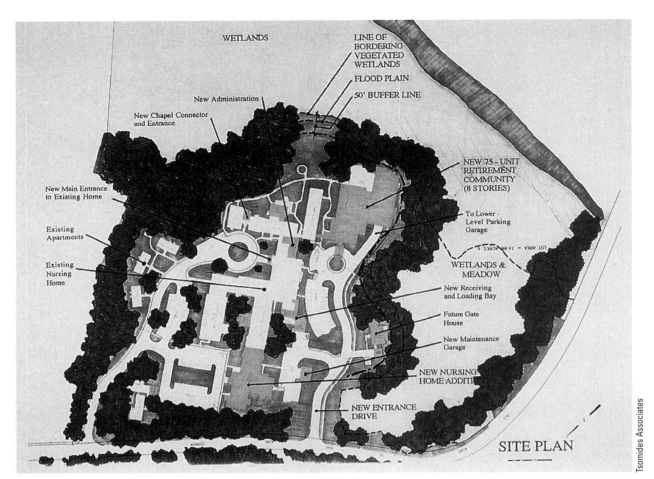

WETLANDS

LINE OF
BORDERING
VEGETATED
WETLANDS

FLOOD PLAIN

50' BUFFER LINE

New Administration

New Chapel Connector
and Entrance

NEW 75 - UNIT
RETIREMENT
COMMUNITY
(8 STORIES)

New Main Entrance
to Existing Home

To Lower -
Level Parking
Garage

Existing
Apartments

WETLANDS &
MEADOW

Existing
Nursing
Home

New Receiving
and Loading Bay

Future Gate
House

New Maintenance
Garage

NEW NURSING
HOME ADDITION

NEW ENTRANCE
DRIVE

SITE PLAN

Tsomides Associates

Site plan.

Project Data

Land Use Information

Site area: 35 acres (entire campus)
Building coverage: 1 acre
Other buildings: 3.5 acres
Roads/paved areas: 2.5 acres
Off-street parking spaces: 90
Common open space: 27 acres
Dwelling units: 75
Number of residents: 100

Residential Unit Information[1]

Unit type	Square feet	Number of units	Sales price	Monthly fees
1 bedroom	732–973	17	$205,000–$290,000	$1,432–$1,829
2 bedroom	936–1,063	47	$305,000–$370,000	$1,951–$2,332
3 bedroom/den	1,306–1,412	11	$405,000–$430,000	$2,581–$2,600

Development Cost Information

Site acquisition cost	$0
Site improvement costs	328,400
Construction costs	12,959,000
Soft costs	992,100
Total development cost	$14,279,500
Total development cost per unit	$190,393

Annual Operating Expenses (1996)

Administration	$340,400
Maintenance	469,000
Housekeeping/laundry	164,700
Food service	545,400
Activities	54,600
Depreciation	143,400
Long-term-care insurance	308,000
Corporate allocations	102,500
Total	$2,128,000

Financing Information[2]

Tax-exempt bonds Series B	$21,000,000
Tax-exempt bonds Series A	3,145,000
New England Deaconess Association	3,961,000
Total	$28,106,000

Development Schedule

Site acquisition: 1911
Planning started: 1988
Construction started: April 1992
Sales started: October 1991
First move-in: December 1994
Full occupancy: June 1996

Notes

1. Additional $15,000 entrance fee and $400 per month for second person in unit. Entrance fee is 90 percent refundable upon leaving community.
2. Financing package provided funds for construction besides the Newbury Court facility, including a connector to the chapel, a 28-bed addition to the nursing home, additions and renovations to the administrative offices, a new employee dining room, a loading dock, and a remodeled and expanded kitchen and dining room in residential care.

Peninsula Regent
San Mateo, California

General Description

The Peninsula Regent (TPR) is both a continuing-care retirement community and a luxury, high-rise condominium project. Residents purchase a membership in the community, which includes health care services and health insurance, social and recreational programs, one meal per day in the elegant dining room, weekly housekeeping, and other services. Membership also includes a condominium interest in a fully equipped one- or two-bedroom residential unit. Residents pay an initial membership fee—essentially the purchase price of the residential unit—plus a monthly fee covering the cost of Life-care Members' Association dues, homeowners association dues, health insurance, and other services.

Recalling its namesakes—the world-famous Peninsula and Regent hotels—the 207-unit Peninsula Regent was designed to provide the luxury environment and services of a first-class hotel. TPR offers its residents a variety of facilities and services—from a fitness room to a hair salon, an art studio, and club rooms—in a traditional interior with marble floors and thick plaster walls, crystal chandeliers, and wood paneling.

TPR provides a comprehensive health care program for residents that includes a wellness program, a drop-in clinic, and the services of an on-site medical director. It also maintains an assisted-living wing with 20 private rooms, a lounge, a dining room, and a nurses' station staffed 24 hours a day. If necessary, members can move temporarily from their condominium unit to the assisted-living wing, where they are served three meals a day. Skilled nursing is not provided on site at TPR, but it is covered by member health insurance policies; when required, skilled-nursing care is arranged at off-site locations. The concept, notes Peter Palmisano, marketing director for the project, is "a condominium that just happens to have a safety net."

Planning and Design

The Peninsula Regent is built on a two-acre (one square block) site at the edge of downtown San Mateo. The site is located in a mixed-use area, adjacent to a hospital, a church, multifamily housing, medical offices, and commercial uses. For seniors, the site is well located; in addition to its proximity to Mills hospital, the project is within walking distance of downtown shops, restaurants, and clubs and a library.

The ten-story (plus penthouse) structure has a cruciform floor plan arranged around a central elevator lobby. On the upper floors, the elevator lobby is circled by a ring corridor from which four radial corridors fan out to serve the units. Each corridor

Located near the edge of downtown San Mateo in a mixed-use area, the Peninsula Regent is convenient to downtown shops and restaurants and adjacent to a hospital, a church, and other commercial uses.

serves no more than seven units, thereby limiting walking distances and creating a sense of privacy for the residents.

TPR offers eight unit types—four one-bedroom models, and, defying conventional wisdom regarding life-care communities, four two-bedroom models. The market for TPR, notes Tom Callinan, principal of BAC Associates, the project developer, is affluent seniors in the San Mateo area, who made it clear in focus group discussions that they desired (and could afford) the larger spaces. The units are finished as high-end condominiums and include Corian countertops, stacked washer/dryer units, spacious closets for storage, and balconies. For security, the units are equipped with an intercom system and a pull-cord alarm in the bathroom and bedroom. With permission, the unit owner may customize the unit by removing non-load-bearing partitions.

Common facilities—including the main lobby, board room, library, dining room and kitchen, health center offices, administrative offices, and social and recreational rooms—are located on the ground floor, where the assisted-living facilities also are located. At the penthouse level are four rooms that are rented out to guests of TPR members, much like hotel rooms. A large meeting room also is located on the penthouse level, as are storage spaces that have been converted into additional administrative office space.

Outside, four individual, quarter-acre landscaped recreational spaces have been created in the areas between the wings of the building. These include a semi-enclosed pool in one quadrant, a putting green in the second, potting shed and individual planting plots in the third, and a dining terrace and fountain adjacent to the main dining room in the fourth. The site is gated and fenced and secured by a card-key entry system. Two levels of subterranean parking are provided, including one space for each dwelling unit as well as spaces for staff and guests.

Marketing and Development

For the Peninsula Regent, the marketing process and the development process were intertwined. Intensive focus group discussions went hand-in-hand

Landscaped recreational spaces have been created in the areas between the wings of the building.

with the planning and design of the project, and the design evolved considerably based on the feedback received. According to Palmisano, the developers of TPR learned many things through those sessions about the emotional and financial issues involved in retirement decisions. From the sessions came both the condominium concept—to preserve owner equity—and the hotel concept—to make the retirement lifestyle more attractive than continuing to own a single-family home. The idea of membership and participation, as in a country club, also came from the focus groups. By tying these threads together, the core idea emerged, which was that TPR would offer members "a housing choice," not a last resort.

An informal but effective system was developed to market the Peninsula Regent. Most of the marketing was by word of mouth; no advertising was done.

Development Team

Owner/Developer
BAC Associates, LP
San Francisco, California

Operator/Manager
Bay Area Senior Services, Inc.
San Mateo, California

Architect
Backen, Arrigoni, & Ross
San Francisco, California

In addition to the focus groups, small social gatherings and seminars were held to reach out to prospective buyers. "Workbooks" were created for use in these small gatherings to illustrate the lifestyle and design concepts envisioned for TPR. An advisory group of community leaders was created, which helped to establish the desired marketing position for the project. An on-site information center also was established. Through this series of contacts, prospective buyers were brought to the project and simultaneously influenced project design. The focus groups reviewed all aspects of the project, notes Palmisano, "down to the place settings."

The first 107 buyers, whose $25,000 refundable deposits allowed the project to proceed, essentially brought in the second hundred buyers, says Palmisano. They were invited to the groundbreaking and to monthly job-site lunches throughout the construction period. All 207 units were sold by completion. "We built the community while building the building," remarks Palmisano.

Financing and Ownership

The Peninsula Regent was developed and is owned on a for-profit basis by BAC Associates, a limited partnership formed for the purpose of developing TPR. BAC's general partner is the Plenesis Corporation, whose corporate executives are Thomas Callinan, Gerson Bakar, and Peter Applegate, San Francisco commercial real estate developers.

Upon completion, BAC subdivided the completed project into two parcels in order to preserve operational control by management. The first (service areas) includes the site, garage, first floor, tower elevators, and penthouse; the second (residential areas) includes all residential units on Floors 2 through 10 and the associated corridors.

BAC then leased the project to Bay Area Senior Services, Inc. (BASS), a 501(c)(3) nonprofit, public benefit, tax-exempt corporation, which in turn contracted with prospective members of the Peninsula Regent for the purchase of their units (technically a leasehold condominium interest.)

BASS is a subsidiary of Bridge Housing, Inc., an established provider of affordable housing in the Bay Area, and was established for the sole purpose of managing the Peninsula Regent on a nonprofit basis. As owner, BAC approves the hiring and firing of BASS's executive director and approves BASS's annual budget under the terms of the 40-year lease agreement.

Construction financing for TPR was difficult to obtain, according to Callinan, due to several factors: the single-purpose nature of the building; bankruptcies of similar projects; and the pioneering nature of the high-end concept. Eventually a construction loan was negotiated with Wells Fargo Financial Services based on the bank's appraisal of the building as an apartment complex. Among the loan conditions was a stipulation that 50 percent of the units had to be sold before construction began. Additional interim financing was provided from partnership equity.

Payoff of initial financing was made through the sale of memberships. Essentially, upon completion of construction, the initial residents paid membership fees (on an all cash basis) equal to the development costs for their units.

Profit to the developer/owner comes primarily through unit turnover. When an owner, or the estate of an owner, sells its membership (including leasehold condominium) to an eligible buyer, the purchase price is determined by the market. Upon sale, a transfer fee is paid, equal to 10 percent of the seller's original purchase price (akin to a broker's fee) plus 75 percent of any appreciation in value. Three-quarters of the total transfer fee is passed through to BAC, the developer/owner; BASS, the operator, retains one-quarter of the fee. BASS also receives a management fee for operating the Peninsula Regent.

The seller of the residential unit (the unit owner, heirs, or estate), in turn, obtains the return of the original equity (membership price), minus 10 percent or less of the original price (depending on the amount of unit appreciation).

Marketing and Management

Over the nearly ten years since the Peninsula Regent was completed, TPR has built a strong presence for itself in the local community, which sustains the demand for the units. TPR advertises in many Bay Area newspapers and magazines, including various seniors' guides and newspaper supplements. Beyond such name-recognition advertising, TPR's marketing department works to place articles about the project in local periodicals and hosts teas, receptions, and educational meetings on site several times a year.

The Peninsula Regent, which targets affluent seniors, offers residents luxurious indoor and outdoor spaces.

Currently, the average age of new residents is about 79. Approximately 70 percent are from the San Mateo area, and approximately 75 percent are single. Ethnically, TPR mirrors the local community; residents primarily are white, but there are a variety of ethnic and racial minorities.

New residents come predominantly from referrals by current residents. About 15 new leads come in per week, and the marketing department conducts five or six tours each week. In addition, the marketing department keeps about 400 names in its database, tracking their status and trying to match prospective residents with particular unit types as they become available. Of the eight unit types offered at TPR, the two-bedroom units have been most in demand, and the H-unit, a two-bedroom, 1,333-square-foot model, constantly has a waiting list. Currently, 11 of TPR's 207 condominium units are on the market.

The Peninsula Regent marketing department assists sellers in establishing sale prices for their units. Over the last several years, ten to 12 units have been trans- ferred each year, and so a database of sales comparables has been built up. In the first few years, price appreciation was substantial, with some units doubling in value. Since that initial surge, price appreciation has stabilized at an average of about 4 percent per year over the last several years. Generally, notes Callinan, demand for TPR units fluctuates with the state of the overall economy because it is tied to the sale of the current primary residence of prospective members.

To maintain the luxury environment and services expected at TPR, BASS employs an on-site staff of 145 (approximately 50 percent full-time and 50 percent part-time employees). BASS provides for management, maintenance, operations, and accounting. All maintenance is done in house, with the exception of landscaping and major renovations. Residents sit on a variety of committees that advise BASS on everything from seasonal plant selection to major health care issues.

One meal per day is provided to residents in the formal dining room. Residential units include fully equipped kitchens.

Master Bedroom
13' x 15'

Kitchen
11' x 12'

Dining Room
9' x 10.6'

Living Room
13' x 17'

Master Bath

Entry

Bedroom
11' x 14'

W/D

Storage

Floor Plans Subject to Change
Scale: ⁴⁄₁₆ = 1

The Peninsula Regent offers a range of floor-plan options from one-bedroom/one-bath units to two-bedroom/two-bath units that include a dramatic entryway and a spacious master suite. All units feature a private balcony.

Experience Gained

- For well-to-do seniors, the Peninsula Regent represents an attractive alternative to the standard continuing-care retirement community. Unlike the traditional CCRC, which, according to Palmisano, says "You give me your assets, I'll take care of you for life," TPR offers the prospect of equity preservation and housing choice. At the Peninsula Regent, "you can sell your membership, like at a country club," notes Palmisano.

- TPR is an interesting experiment in life-care communities. The larger issue, however, is the transferability of the TPR concept to housing for less affluent seniors. Clearly, the luxury appointments and high level of services may not be feasible in middle- to lower-income projects. But the Peninsula Regent's concept of homeownership remains intriguing and may offer lessons for life-care community design in the future.

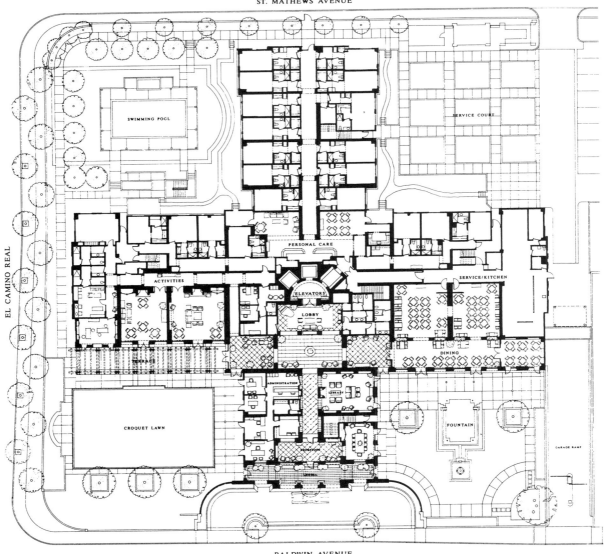

ST. MATHEWS AVENUE

SWIMMING POOL

SERVICE COURT

EL CAMINO REAL

PERSONAL CARE

ACTIVITIES

SERVICE/KITCHEN

ELEVATORS

LOBBY

DINING

TERRACE

CROQUET LAWN

ADMINISTRATION

LIBRARY

FOUNTAIN

GARAGE RAMP

RECEPTION

LOBBY

BALDWIN AVENUE

· P E N I N S U L A   R E G E N T ·
BACKEN ARRIGONI & ROSS, INC.

Project Data

Land Use Information

Site area: Two acres

Total dwelling units planned and completed: 207 plus 20 assisted living units

Gross density: 113.5 units per acre

Off-street parking spaces: 282

Land Use Plan

Use	Acres	Percent of site
Buildings	1	50
Common open space	1	50

Residential Unit Information

Unit type	Unit size (square feet)	Number of units planned/ built	Sale price	Monthly fee[1]
1 bedroom/1 bath	794	27/27	$270,000– 300,000	$1,893
1 bedroom/1 bath + den	1,000	36/36	310,000– 350,000	2,118
1 bedroom/1 bath + den	929	36/36	310,000– 350,000	2,118
1 bedroom/2 bath + den	1,110	27/27	370,000– 425,000	2,408
2 bedroom/2 bath	1,136	36/36	400,000– 440,000	2,408
2 bedroom/2 bath	1,207	9/9	410,000– 450,000	2,667
2 bedroom/2 bath	1,229	9/9	450,000– 510,000	2,667
2 bedroom/2 bath	1,333	27/27	500,000– 550,000	2,667

Note

1. As of November 1997 for a single occupant; additional person costs $1,252.

Annual Operating Expenses

Health services	$230,000
Assisted living	448,000
Health care program	1,800,000
Food services	1,254,000
Housekeeping	548,000
Laundry services	57,000
Program services	153,000
Maintenance	330,000
Grounds	60,000
Taxes, utilities, insurance	785,000
Security	87,000
Front office	116,000
Administration	430,000
General services	296,000
Marketing	180,000
Sustaining fees	326,000
Replacement reserve	367,000
Total	$7,467,000

Development Cost Information

Site acquisition cost	$6.7 million
Construction costs	30.8 million
Soft costs	18.5 million
Total	$56 million
Total cost per unit	$270,531

Financing Information

Partnership equity	$10 million
Construction loan	46 million
Total	$56 million

Development Schedule

Construction started: November 1986

Sales/leasing started: October 1986 (All units were presold.)

First move-in: November 1988

Seasons at Redondo Beach
Redondo Beach, California

General Description

Seasons at Redondo Beach is a 150-unit seniors' apartment complex on a 4.1-acre site in a historic neighborhood of Redondo Beach near shopping areas and the Pacific Ocean. The project contains one- and two-bedroom units with private balconies or patios and gated off-street parking. A community center includes a clubhouse with a common room, laundry facilities, a swimming pool, a spa, and a sundeck. The project was developed by a public/private partnership of the developer, the Redondo Beach Redevelopment Agency, and the local school district, which owns the site. The school district leased the site and the redevelopment agency provided the financing, which included a loan and tax-exempt bonds issued by the agency. Under the terms of the partnership, 30 affordable units are reserved for low-income seniors. A nonprofit corporation is the owner/operator of the project.

Site and Development Process

The project was developed on the site of the McCandless School, which the Redondo Beach Unified School District closed in 1984 because of declining enrollment. The site is located on the Pacific Coast Highway only five blocks from the beach. The school district, recognizing the site's value, hoped to groundlease it for development in order to generate income for educational programs.

In addition to the school district's economic goals, the city of Redondo Beach saw the site as an ideal location for needed affordable seniors' housing in an area with high housing costs. Besides proximity to the beach, it offers a variety of nearby shopping and dining options. The Redondo Beach Senior Club also is nearby, and the civic center and public library are just a few blocks to the north. Six nearby churches provide community services and social programs for the neighborhood. Residents have access to public transportation by way of the Wave (a dial-a-ride service) and the Metropolitan Transit Authority (MTA) bus system.

The site was zoned for retail use, and an earlier development proposal called for a mixed-use project that included retail and a congregate care facility. Although the project received its entitlements, the developer was unable to obtain financing. Subsequently, the city invited Metropolitan Development, of El Segundo, California, to submit a proposal for the site. Its proposal omitted retail uses and significantly involved the public sector in the project.

Metropolitan Development proposed forming a public/private partnership with the school district and the city redevelopment agency in order to achieve the goals of both parties. Under the partnership agreement, the redevelopment agency made an initial loan to the project in exchange for the

The community center features a large two-story recreational clubhouse with a lounge area, game tables, a wrap-around balcony, and an adjacent heated swimming pool and spa.

affordable units and a portion of the cash flow. In addition, the agency issued tax-exempt bonds to provide permanent financing. The school district entered into a 60-year ground lease for an annual payment and a portion of the cash flow. Metropolitan Development developed the project for a fee and assumed the entitlement and construction risk. Nonprofit LINC Housing of Long Beach was selected as the owner/operator and receives an asset management fee, plus a portion of the cash flow. Project planning began in 1992, and construction began in July 1996. The first move-in took place six months later, in December 1996.

The public/private partnership arrangement offers several advantages. First, the project provides income to help fund the school district's educational programs. Second, the redevelopment agency can achieve its affordable housing goals by investing public funds that will be recaptured with interest and reinvested in other projects. In addition, the public investment and tax-exempt financing allowed the developer to deliver high-quality seniors' housing in an aesthetically appealing project that enhances the surrounding historic neighborhood.

The total development cost was $11,400,000, or $76,000 per unit. The cost included a first-year ground-lease payment of $350,000 and $7,500,000 in construction costs. Soft costs totaled $2,760,000. Storm drainage and widening of Pacific Coast Highway accounted for $500,000 in off-site improvements, and on-site improvements required another $290,000.

Design

The project is located in a neighborhood of one- and two-story homes, many built in the Craftsman style, as well as small apartment and condominium buildings. In addition to its affordable seniors' housing goal, the city of Redondo Beach wanted to maintain the area's historic architectural character. The challenge was to meet the city's goals with a design that included a garden apartment community for seniors at a density of 36 units per acre in one- and two-story buildings without interior corridors and with as many ground-floor units as possible.

The project is a series of seven residential buildings composed of L-shaped units that form cruciform modules when four units are joined together. The buildings are created by combinations of the cruciform modules, and each is constructed on its own

The project, which targets independent seniors, contains one- and two-bedroom units with private balconies or patios and gated off-street parking.

pad on the site. The L-shaped unit plan allows for flexible interior layouts, reduces the scale of the buildings, creates several exterior courtyard styles, and makes every unit, in effect, a corner unit. The architectural style and scale of the buildings reflect and reinforce the character of the surrounding neighborhood.

In order to maximize the number of ground-floor units, the floor of the west half of each building was lowered by 4.5 feet. This allowed construction of 90 units at grade, and 40 are only a half-flight up, which is an important advantage in a project for seniors. The remaining 20 units are entered by a full flight of interior private stairs.

There are 130 one-bedroom, one-bath units and 20 two-bedroom, 1.5-bath units in the project. Unit sizes range from 530 to 550 square feet in the one-bedroom units and from 765 to 780 square feet in the two-bedroom units. All units are designed for independent living. Standard features include window treatments, wall-to-wall carpeting, and ceiling fans. Kitchens are equipped with a frostfree refrigerator, oven/range, double sink, dishwasher, and disposal. Some of the units have cathedral ceilings.

Development Team

Owner
LINC–Redondo Beach Seniors, Inc.
Long Beach, California

Developer
McCandless Senior Partners
Los Angeles, California

Metropolitan Development
El Segundo, California

Asset Manager
LINC Housing Corporation
Long Beach, California

Property Management
Insignia Residential Group
Irvine, California

Architect
John Cotton Architecture
Marina Del Rey, California

Other Team Members
Redevelopment Agency of the City of Redondo Beach
Redondo Beach, California

Redondo Beach Unified School District
Redondo Beach, California

The community also features a large two-story recreational clubhouse with a lounge area, game tables, a kitchen, central laundry facilities, management and administrative offices, and a wrap-around balcony. Adjacent to the clubhouse is a heated swimming pool and spa surrounded by a large sundeck.

The site includes 4.06 acres, yielding a gross density of 36 units per acre. Two parking lots on the northwest and southwest corners of the site, each of which has an electronic security gate, provide 150 parking spaces. Ground-floor units open directly outside onto a system of curvilinear sidewalks that connect all the buildings. Grass lawns, shrubbery, and flowers cover the grounds.

Leasing

The leasing plan for the project targeted the local market, both seniors already living in the area and younger people whose parents lived elsewhere. A key strategy was to tap the congregations of six nearby churches, which were a ready source of prospects. The local senior community had welcomed the project during the planning phase and supported it during the approval process. At one point, the marketing staff had developed an interest list of almost 200 persons.

Leasing began in May 1996, and the first move-in took place in December 1996, six months after construction began. By September 1997, 103 units were occupied, for an occupancy rate of 79 percent. Rents for market-rate units range from $850 to $1,150 per month, which translates into $1.30 to $1.75 per square foot, plus utilities. The 30 units set aside for low-income seniors, whose incomes are less than 50 percent of the area median, are $512 for one-bedroom and $577 for two-bedroom units.

Financing and Management

The Seasons project was completely financed through the two public agencies that entered into the partnership to develop it. The Redondo Beach Redevelopment Agency loaned the project $2.2 million in exchange for including the 30 affordable units. Twenty percent of project cash flow is allocated to

repay this loan, with interest. The redevelopment agency also issued $9.2 million in tax-exempt bonds to finance construction and provide long-term financing for the project. The Redondo Beach Unified School District entered into a 60-year ground lease on the site for $350,000 per year, plus a portion of the cash flow.

Because of the strength of the market and the type of public participation, a bank letter of credit was issued to secure the bond issue. The letter of credit allowed the bonds to be placed as variable-interest "low floaters" at a rate of about 3.5 percent. This resulted in savings on interest of about $400,000 during the construction period. The bonds will be

Ground-floor units open directly outside onto a system of curvilinear sidewalks that connect all buildings. The floor of the west half of each building was lowered by 4.5 feet to maximize the number of ground-floor units.

The L-shaped unit plan reduces the scale of the buildings, allows for several exterior courtyard styles, and makes every unit, in effect, a corner unit.

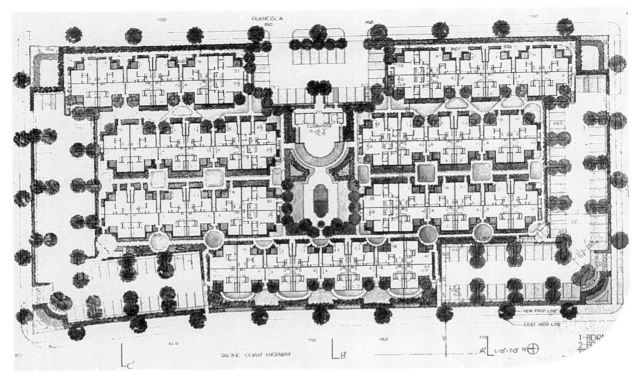

Site plan.

amortized at 7.5 percent. Because of this approach, the $9.2 million bond issue will be fully retired in approximately 12 years if short-term rates stay the same.

The project is owned and managed by LINC Housing, a nonprofit housing corporation based in Long Beach. In cooperation with the city of Redondo Beach, the project provides senior services and transportation for the residents. The project's clubhouse contains the on-site administrative and management offices and serves as the setting for an ongoing program of social activities, such as potlucks, book reviews, lectures, and theme parties.

Units are designed for independent living and include window treatments, wall-to-wall carpeting, ceiling fans, and fully equipped kitchens. Some of the units feature cathedral ceilings.

Experience Gained

■ The economic benefits of public sector financing allowed the public/private partnership to build an attractive project that enhances the surrounding neighborhood and provides high-quality seniors' housing. The L-shaped unit plan provides flexibility in interior layouts, reduces the scale of the buildings, creates a variety of exterior courtyard styles, and makes every unit a "corner unit." Because the financing plan minimized the risk for the public agencies and maximized potential income, the project is viewed as an excellent investment of public funds.

Project Data

Land Use Information

Site area: 4.06 acres
Total dwelling units planned/completed: 150 units
Gross density: 36 units per acre
Off-street parking:150 spaces

Land Use Plan

Use	Acres	Percent of Site
Buildings	1.38	34
Roads/paved areas	1.06	26
Common open space	1.62	40

Residential Unit Information

Unit type	Unit size (square feet)	Planned/ built	Monthly rent
1 bedroom/1 bath	530	74/74	$850
1 bedroom/1 bath	540	16/16	895
1 bedroom/1 bath	550	40/40	880–965
2 bedroom/1.5 bath	780	16/16	1,085–1,150
2 bedroom/1.5 bath	765	4/4	995–1,065

Development Cost Information

Site acquisition	$350,000
Site improvements	790,000[1]
Construction	$7,500,000
Soft costs	$2,760,000
Total	$11,400,000

Annual Operating Expenses[2]

Personnel	110,500
Administration	9,100
Marketing	33,500
Repairs/maintenance	9,250
Cleaning/decorating	1,500
Contract services	38,800
Professional fees	60,000
Utilities	50,500
Taxes/insurance	86,100
Total	$399,250

Financing Information

Principal amount of bonds	$9,140,000
Redevelopment agency loan	2,438,000
(Less underwriter's discount)	(182,000)
Total	$11,396,000

Development Schedule

Planning started: July 1992
Ground lease signed: May 1995
Construction started: July 1996
Sales/leasing started: May 1996
First move-in: December 1996
Full occupancy: September 1997

Notes
1. Includes $500,000 in off-site costs.
2. Year-one budget.

Appendix

Bibliography

Part I

"A Dare in the Desert: 5,500 Retirement Homes." *Business Week,* December 9, 1991, 94.

"A New Kind of Retirement Home." *Nation's Business,* January 1986, 77.

Adams, E. "Meeting the Varied Market for the Graying of America." *Professional Builder,* April 1986, 68.

Aging News Alert. March 8, 1995, 12.

Allen, J. *Investor Outlook,* Vol. 6, No. 2, 2d Quarter, Grubb & Ellis, 1986.

American Association of Homes for the Aging. *Market and Economic Feasibility Studies—Guidelines for Continuing Care Retirement Facilities.*

American Association of Homes for the Aging and Ernst & Young. *Continuing Care Retirement Communities: An Industry in Action.* Washington, D.C.: 1987, 1989.

American Association of Homes for the Aging and Ernst & Young. *Continuing Care Retirement Communities: An Industry in Action.* 1993.

American Association of Homes and Services for the Aging. *Currents,* Vol. 10, No. 7, July 1995, D.

American Association of Retired Persons. *Progress in the Housing of Older Persons.* 1997, 10.

American Association of Retired Persons. *Understanding Senior Housing for the 1990s.* Washington, D.C., 1990.

American Association of Retired Persons and Administration on Aging. *A Profile of Older Americans.* 1994.

American Association of Retired Persons and Administration on Aging. *A Profile of Older Americans.* 1996.

American Association of Retired Persons Public Policy Institute and Health Policy Center of the Urban Institute. *Coming Up Short: Increasing Out-of-Pocket Health Spending by Older Americans.* April 19, 1994.

Apgar, W. "Home Sweet Home to Stay." *Mortgage Banking,* September 1987, 70.

Assisted Living Facilities Association of America. "Fact Sheet." October 8, 1991.

"Assisted Living Interests Still Growing." *Modern Healthcare's Elder Care Business,* April 30, 1990, 16.

Baltay, M. *Long-Term Care for the Elderly and Disabled.* Congressional Budget Office, 1977.

"Before You Settle on a Retirement Community." *Business Week,* May 20, 1991, 150.

Beyer, Bulkley, and Hopkins. "A Model Act Regulating Board and Care Homes: Guidelines for States." *8 Mental and Physical Disability Law Reporter,* March-April 1984.

Bowe, J. "Chains Take on Retirement Housing." *Contemporary Long Term Care,* May 1990, 46.

Brass, K. "California Builders Find a New Market." *New York Times,* Sept. 10, 1995, 30.

Bureau of the Census. "Household Wealth and Asset Ownership, 1988." *Current Population Reports,* Series P–70, Nd. 22, December 1990.

Bureau of the Census. "Housing Arrangements of the Elderly." *Statistical Brief,* SB–2–90, January 1990.

Bureau of the Census, Edwin Byerly. "Projections of the Population of the Bureau of the Census. State Population and Household Estimates: July 1, 1989." *Current Population Reports,* Series P–25, No. 1058, March 1990.

Callahan, J. and Wallack, S. eds. *Reforming the Long Term Care System.* Lexington, MA: Lexington Books, 1981.

"Capital Crunch Restrains CCRC Development." *Modern Healthcare,* May 20, 1991, 92.

"Caring for the Elderly: Public/Private Sector Responsibilities Point Way to Future Trends." *Federation of American Health Systems Review,* January/February 1988, 28.

Carlson, J. "What the Experts Are Saying: New Developments in Retirement Housing." *Retirement Housing Report,* September 1986, 16.

Caulfield, L., and Carlucci, J. "The Adult Congregate Living Facility—A Comparison and Critical Discussion of Assistance-Oriented Facilities and an Alternative Concept for the Marketplace." *The Real Estate Appraiser and Analyst,* Fall 1985, 43.

Chellis, R., and Meister, S. "Resident Payment Mechanisms: Five Models of Retirement Communities." *Retirement Housing Report,* May 1988, 10.

Chellis, R., Seagle, J., and Seagle, B. eds. *Congregate Housing for Older People.* Lexington, MA: Lexington Books, 1982.

Clark, L., Jr. "A Dandy Retirement, If You Can Pay." *Wall Street Journal,* May 25, 1994, A-16.

The Consumers' Directory of Continuing Care Retirement Communities. 1994–1995.

Dannenfeldt, D. "Hospitals Wary about Retirement Ventures." *Modern Healthcare,* October 20, 1989, 44.

Diesenhouse, S. "Housing the Elderly Who Do Not Require Nursing Home Care." *New York Times,* January 3, 1993, 3–12.

Dine, D. "Demand for Retirement Housing Accommodates Industry Growth." *Modern Healthcare,* June 3, 1988, 56.

Dobkin, L. "AARP Releases Nationwide Housing Survey of Older Consumers." *Aging Network News,* June 1987, 5.

Dobkin, L. "The World of Retirement Housing According to AARP: Opportunities and Obstacles." *Spectrum,* January 1993, 20.

Doty, Liu, and Wiener, "An Overview of Long Term Care." *Health Care Financing Review,* Vol. 6, No. 3, Spring 1985.

Doyle, M. "Retirement Housing: Bigger Isn't Always Better." *Hospitals,* March 20, 1989.

Dwight, M. "Affluent Elderly Want to Live Where Quality Care's Readily Available." *Modern Healthcare,* April 26, 1985.

Dychtwald, K., ed. *Wellness and Health Promotion for the Elderly.* Rockville, MD: Aspen Publications, 1986.

Eden, J. "Retirement Communities Offer Something for Everyone." *Spectrum,* December 1991, 28.

"Elderly Japanese May Be Encouraged to Retire Abroad." *San Francisco Chronicle* (UPI), August 8, 1986.

Elrod, L. "Housing Alternatives for the Elderly." *Journal of Family Law,* Vol. 18, 1979–1980, 723.

Fairbanks, J. "Lifetime Care Contracts: Are Senior Citizens Putting All Their Eggs in One Basket?" *Probate and Property* (American Bar Association), March/April 1990.

Fairchild, T. "Profit or Nonprofit Retirement Housing: Is There a Difference?" *Aging Network News,* July 1986, 6.

Feldblum, C. "Home Health Care for the Elderly: Programs, Problems, and Potentials." *Harvard Journal on Legislation,* 22:193 (1985).

Gamzon, M. "Assisted Living Reigns." *Contemporary Long Term Care,* June 1993, 31.

Gamzon, M. "Buyers, Capital Sources Warm Up to Senior Housing." *Contemporary Long Term Care,* June 1994, 46.

Gamzon, M. "A Look Ahead: What Lies Down the Road for Retirement Housing." *Contemporary Long Term Care,* June 1992, 38.

Gamzon, M. "Profit Potential for Senior Housing Points Up Both Near and Long Term." *National Real Estate Investor,* February 1992, 86.

Gamzon, M. "Senior Housing Comes of Age." *Contemporary Long Term Care,* June 1995, 46.

Gamzon, M. "State of the Seniors Housing Industry: Insights for the 90's." *Multi-Housing News,* May 1990.

Gamzon, M. "28 Seniors Housing Experts Identify Affordable Solutions." *Multi-Housing News,* May 1989,

Garcia, K. "Generation Gap at Seniors' Mecca." *San Francisco Chronicle,* February 15, 1993.

Gjullin, E., and Miller, R. "An Untapped Senior Housing Market Segment." *Retirement Housing Report,* March 1989.

Graham, J. "Demand Should Foster Rapid Growth in Retirement Center Industry." *Modern Healthcare,* April 24, 1987.

"Grays on the Go." *Time,* February 22, 1988, 66.

"Growth Slows, But Continues." *Contemporary Long Term Care,* June 1990, 53.

Hancock, J., ed. *Housing the Elderly.* New Brunswick, NJ: Center for Urban Policy Research, 1987.

Harney, K. "Facilities for the Elderly Booming." *Washington Post,* March 9, 1985.

Hartman, C. "Gearing Up for Business in the '90s: Helping Companies Sell to an Aging Population." *Inc.,* June 1988 (cover story), 58.

Hoffman, C. "Seniors Housing Hit Its Prime." *Real Estate Forum.* August 1997, 52.

Holbrook, A., and Quinley, W. "Personal Care Facilities: Opportunity for Future Development." *NASLI News,* December 1987, 5.

House Select Committee on Aging. "Fraud and Abuse in Boarding Homes." June 25, 1981.

Howell, J. "Learning from Mistakes." National Association of Senior Living Industries 1987 Conference Proceedings, 29.

ICF, Inc. "Private Financing of Long Term Care: Current Methods and Resources." *Phase I Final Report,* U.S. Department of Health and Human Services, 1985.

"Insurance for the Twilight Years: Life Care Takes the Uncertainty Out of Retirement." *Time,* April 6, 1987, 53.

Jacobs and Weissart, "Long Term Care Financing and Delivery Systems." *Conference Proceedings,* Health Care Financing Administration, Washington, D.C., January 1984.

Jaffe, R. "Graying of America Assures Future for Retirement Housing." *Real Estate Forum*, August 1987, 49.

"Japan Is Turning Gray Fast." *San Francisco Examiner,* September 14, 1986, A-16.

"Japan to Export Seniors." *San Francisco Examiner,* October 26, 1986, A-23.

Jeck, A., and Carlson, J. "Retirement Housing: Exploring the Gray Area of Housing's Gray Market." *Real Estate Finance,* Winter 1986.

"Joint Forum on Elderly Housing Options." Subcommittee on Housing and Consumer Interests of the Select Committee on Aging, House of Representatives, and the Federal Council on Aging, Comm. Pub. No. 100-651, Washington, D.C., 1988.

Johnson, B. "Seniors Housing Comes of Age at NIC '96." *National Real Estate Investor,* December 1996.

Kaufman, G., and Waite, M. "Retirement Communities as a Profitable Land Use in Large Planned Communities." *Investment Properties International,* March/April 1990, 29.

Kenan, M. "Changing Needs for Long-Term: Chart Book." Washington, D.C.: American Association of Retired Persons, 1989.

Kunerth, A. "The Impact of Long-Term Care Insurance on the Marketing of Senior Living Facilities: Part III–A Model CCRC." *Retirement Housing Report,* February 1988, 9.

Kunerth, A. "LTC Group Insurance: The Catalyst in Blending CCRCs, Rental Projects." *Contemporary Long Term Care,* March 1988, 67.

Lachman, M. "Outlook for U.S. Commercial Real Estate in the 90s." *The Guarantor,* January/February 1991, 3.

Lewin, T. "How Needs, and Market, for Care Have Changed." *New York Times*, December 2, 1990, 24.

Longino, C., and Crown, W. "Older Americans: Rich or Poor?" *American Demographics,* August 1991, 48.

"LTC Business Booming for Architectural Firms." *Contemporary Long Term Care,* June 1988, 86.

Lublin, J. "Costly Retirement-Home Market Booms, Raising Concern for Aged." *Wall Street Journal,* October 22, 1986, 35.

Mariano, A. "As Old Grow Older, Housing Needs Change." *Washington Post*, September 15, 1984.

"Marriott Tells Plans to Build 150 Retirement Communities." *Modern Healthcare,* August 4, 1989, 41.

Michaux, R., and Kempner, J. "Apartments Taking on a Growth Mode." *Urban Land,* November 1995, 33.

Mollica, R. Presentation at National Investment Conference for Senior Living, October 12, 1995.

Morris, R., and Youket, P. "The Long Term Care Issues: Identifying the Problems and Potential Solutions." in *Reforming the Long Term Care System,* Callahan, J., and Wallack, S., eds. Lexington, MA: Lexington Books, 1981.

Multi-Housing News, October 1988, 59.

The Need for Personal Assistance with Everyday Activities: Recipients and Caregivers. Current Population Reports, Series P-70, No. 19. Washington, D.C.: U.S. Government Printing Office, 1990, Table B.

Nemes, J. "Retirement Centers Grow Despite Fewer Providers." *Modern Healthcare,* June 2, 1989.

Neuman, E. "Golden Years without a Care." *Insight,* January 13, 1992.

Newcomer, R., and Stone, R. "Board and Care Housing: Expansion and Improvement Needed." *Generations,* Summer 1985, 38.

O'Shaughnessy, Price, & Griffith. "Financing and Delivery of Long-Term Care Services for the Elderly." Congressional Research Service, February 24, 1987.

Older Americans Report. June 26, 1987, 6.

Older Americans Report. April 1, 1988, 138.

Older Americans Report. October 21, 1988, 415.

Otten, A. "The Oldest Old." *Wall Street Journal,* July 30, 1984.

Pallarito, K. "CCRC Industry Growth Steady." *Modern Healthcare,* May 22, 1995, 78.

Pallarito, K. "CCRCs See Slow Growth, Challenges in HMO Care." *Modern Healthcare,* May 23, 1994, 76.

Pallarito, K. "Opportunities Await in Retiree Communities." *Modern Healthcare,* May 18, 1992, 96.

Petre, P. "Marketers Mine for Gold in the Old." *Fortune,* March 31, 1986; *Professional Builder,* September 1985 and April 1986.

Prins, R. "'Seniors Housing' by Whatever Name, It's Big Business." *Real Estate Forum*, September 1994, 52, 53.

Projections of the Population of the United States, by Age, Sex, and Race: 1989 to 2010. Current Population Reports, Series P-25, No. 1053. Washington, D.C.: U.S. Government Printing Office, 1990.

Raper, A., ed. *National Continuing Care Directory.* Washington, D.C.: American Association of Homes for the Aging/American Association of Retired Persons, 1984.

"Rental Retirement Housing." The Stanger Report, September 1986, 2.

"Retirement Communities: Assessing the Liability of Alternative Health Care Guarantees." *The Journal of Long Term Care Administration,* Winter 1981, 9.

"Retirement Housing Industry Entering Consolidation Phase." *Contemporary Long Term Care,* July 1989, 65.

"Retiring with Equity in a Full-Health-Care Facility." *New York Times*, August 12, 1990.

Rivlin, A., and Wiener, J. *Caring for the Disabled Elderly: Who Will Pay?* Washington, D.C.: The Brookings Institution, 1988, 41–42, 92.

Rosenblatt and Peterson. "Life Care: Insurance against Age." *Los Angeles Times,* August 5, 1986, 6.

Schless, D. "Seniors Explosion Hasn't Yet Begun." *National Real Estate Investor,* September 1991.

Seaberry, J. "CEA Says Aged Have Attained Economic Parity." *Washington Post*, February 6, 1985.

Seip, D. "Changes in Retirement Industry Impact on Built Environment." *Contemporary Long Term Care,* March 1988, 46.

Seip, D. "1987: An Insider's Perspective on the Retirement Industry." *Contemporary Long Term Care,* December 1987, 48.

Seip, D. "1988 in Review: A Year of Refinement." *Contemporary Long Term Care,* December 1988.

Seip, D, "Retirement Communities: What to Expect during 1988." *Contemporary Long Term Care,* January 1988, 25.

Seip, D. "The Retirement Housing Industry Plainly Defined." *Contemporary Long Term Care,* November 1987, 31.

Seip, D. "Specializing in Assisted Living Facilities." *Contemporary Long Term Care,* September 1987, 34.

Seniors' Housing: A State of the Industry Report, Senior Housing Investment Advisors, Inc., and *Multi-Housing News,* 1988.

"Seniors Housing Audit." *Multi-Housing News,* September 1988, 14.

Seniors Housing Update. American Seniors Housing Association, June 1993.

The Senior Living Industry 1986. Laventhol & Horwath.

Sirrocco, A. "An Overview of the 1982 National Master Facility Inventory Survey of Nursing and Related Care Homes." *Advancedata,* National Center for Health Statistics, September 20, 1985.

"Sizing Up Life Care." *Changing Times,* May 1987, 65.

Snow, C. "Assisted Living Still a Popular Property." *Modern Healthcare,* May 26, 1997, 84.

Somers, A., and Spears, N. *The Continuing Care Retirement Community: A Significant Option for Long-Term Care?* New York: Springer Publishing Co., 1992.

"Special Report: The Future of Medicare." *New England Journal of Medicine,* Vol. 314, No. 11, March 13, 1986.

"State Laws and Programs Serving Elderly Persons and Disabled Adults." 7 *Mental Disability Law Reporter* 158, March-April 1983.

"The State of the Seniors Housing 1996." Washington, D.C.: American Seniors Housing Association, 1997.

"The State of the Seniors Housing Industry." American Seniors Housing Association and Coopers & Lybrand, 1993.

"Survey Finds Health Occupancy Acquisition Activity, Rising Rents." *Units,* July-August 1995, 35–41.

Swallow W. "Elderly Seen as Giant New Market." *Washington Post*, September 15, 1984.

Taeuber, C. "65 Plus in America." *Current Population Reports,* Bureau of the Census, Series P-23, No. 178.

Thomas, M. "Retirement Housing Industry Burgeoning." *Contemporary Long Term Care,* July 1988, 27.

Thompson, M., and Donahue, W. *Planning and Implementing Management of Congregate Housing for Older People.* Washington, D.C.: International Center for Social Gerontology, Inc., 1980.

"The Top 50 Retirement Housing Communities." *Contemporary Long Term Care,* June 1993, 35.

U.S. Department of Health and Human Services. "Catastrophic Illness Expenses." Report to the President, November 1986.

U.S. Department of Housing and Urban Development. *How Well Are We Housed, The Elderly.* 1979.

U.S. Department of Housing and Urban Development. "U.S. Housing Market Conditions." May 1995, 75.

U.S. House of Representatives. "Fraud and Abuse in Boarding Homes." Select Committee on Aging, June 25, 1981.

U.S. Senate Special Committee on Aging. *Aging America: Trends and Projections.* 1985–1986 ed., 71.

"United States, by Age, Sex, and Race: 1988 to 2080." *Current Population Reports,* Series P-25, No. 1018, January 1989.

Walbert, L. "Money & Worth." *Lear's,* October 1993, 22.

Warner, Katharine P. "Demographics and Housing." *Housing for a Maturing Population,* Washington, D.C.: Urban Land Institute, 1983.

"What's Putting New Life into 'Life Care' Communities." *Business Week,* March 3, 1986, 108.

"Who's Taking Care of Our Parents?" *Newsweek,* May 6, 1985, 61.

Wilcox, M. "Not a Place to Sit and Watch the Traffic." *Kiplinger's Personal Finance Magazine,* June 1996, 63.

Winklevoss, H. E., and Powell, A. V. *Continuing Care Retirement Communities—An Empirical, Financial, and Legal Analysis.* Pension Research Council, Wharton School, University of Pennsylvania, Richard D. Irwin, 1984.

Wood, M. "Seniors Housing, The Unconventional Real Estate Investment." *Real Estate Forum*, September 1995, 73.

Part II

An Analysis of Nationwide Absorption Rates: The Critical Element in the Feasibility of Senior Living Projects. National Association for Senior Living Industries (NASLI), March 1992.

AAHA Development Manual: A Step-by-Step Guide for Trustees and Chief Executives Undertaking Development of Non-Profit Facilities for the Elderly. American Association of Homes for the Aging, 1986.

Bernstein, H. and Peters, H. "Housing for the Elderly: A Primer for Developers." *Contemporary Long Term Care,* October 1987, 154.

Brecht, S. *Retirement Housing Markets.* New York: John Wiley, 1991.

"Building Types Study 651: Housing for the Aging." *Architectural Record.* April 1988, 98.

Capital Valuation Group and the American Seniors Housing Association (ASHA). *Seniors Absorption Study 1990 to 1996: Insights into Development and Feasibility.* Washington, D.C.: Author, 1997.

Coleman, B. "Life Care Pacts Create Woes for Some People." *AARP News Bulletin,* April 1988.

"Continuing-Care Communities for the Elderly: Potential Pitfalls and Proposed Regulation." 128 *U. Pa. L. Rev.* 900 (1980).

"Continuing Care Retirement Communities: A Promise Falling Short." 8 *George Mason Univ. L. Rev.* 47 (1985).

Curran and Brecht. "A Perspective on Risks for Lifecare Projects." *Real Estate Finance Journal,* Summer 1985, 64.

Evanson, D., and Mullen, A. *Retirement Housing Construction Finance Directory.* New York: John Wiley, 1991.

Forster, W., and Orfanon, E. "Life Care Facilities Will Struggle with Proposed Auditing Rules." *Contemporary Long Term Care,* October 1988, 42.

Gimmy, A., and Boehm, M. *Elderly Housing: A Guide to Appraisal, Market Analysis, Development and Financing.* Chicago: American Institute of Real Estate Appraisers, 1988.

Gordon, P. "What Counsel Should Know about Full Service Retirement Communities." *The Practical Real Estate Lawyer,* March 1986, 7.

Graham, J. "Retirement Centers Increasing Numbers in Effort to Accommodate Affluent Elderly." *Modern Healthcare,* June 5, 1987, 112.

John Knox Village (Lee's Summit, Missouri) news release. December 11, 1985.

Laughlin, J., and Moseley, S. *Retirement Housing: A Step-By-Step Approach.* New York: John Wiley, 1989.

Laventhol and Horwath. *The Senior Living Industry* 1986, 33.

"Life Care Communities: Promises and Problems." Senate Special Committee on Aging, 98th Cong., 1st Sess. 1983.

Los, J. "Straight Talk about Retirement Housing." *Contemporary Long Term Care,* September 1987, 120.

McMullin. "Common Financial Problems Encountered by CCRCs." *Contemporary Long Term Care,* February 1986, 50.

Moore. "Major Southern Firms Swept into Bond Default Litigation Net." *Legal Times,* October 14, 1985.

Porter, D., et al. *Housing for Seniors: Developing Successful Projects.* Washington, D.C.: Urban Land Institute, 1995.

"Predicting Successful Projects in Today's Retirement Industry." *Contemporary Long Term Care,* June 1988, 96.

Pyle. "Bank Sues over Maple Village Bonds." *Fresno Bee,* July 18, 1986, B–1.

Reiss, R. "Management Contracts: Are They Worth It?" *Contemporary Long Term Care,* March 1988, 52.

Ruchlin, H. "Continuing Care Retirement Communities: An Analysis of Financial Viability and Health Care Coverage." *The Gerontologist,* April 1988, 156.

Rudnitsky and Konrad. "Trouble in the Elysian Fields." *Forbes,* August 29, 1983, 58.

Schifrin, M. "An Expensive Free Lunch." *Forbes,* January 25, 1988, 34.

Seip, D. "Challenging Absorption in Retirement Housing." *Contemporary Long Term Care,* February 1988, 20.

Senate Special Committee on Aging. "Life Care Communities: Promises and Problems." S. Hrg. 98–276, 98th Cong., 1st Sess, 1983.

Seniors Housing, A Development and Management Handbook. Washington, D.C.: National Association of Home Builders, 1987.

"Shaky Lifecare Center Put Up for Sale." *Modern Healthcare,* November 1980, 54.

Smith. "Baptist Homes in Bankruptcy." *Detroit News,* March 19, 1977.

Steiner, J., and Kneen, J. "Senior Housing Developments Raise Legal Issues for CFOs." *Health Care Financial Management,* December 1987, 70.

Struve, K. "Turning Around Troubled Senior Housing and Health Care Projects." *Commercial Lending Review,* Spring 1992, 8.

Swallow. "Agreement Near to Resolve Life-Care Homes' Bankruptcy." *Washington Post,* October 13, 1984.

Topolnicki. "The Broken Promise of Life-Care Communities." *Money,* April 1985, 150.

U.S. General Accounting Office. "Tax Exempt Bonds: Retirement Center Bonds Were Risky and Benefited Moderate-Income Elderly." March 1991.

Wade and McMullin. "Lessons to Learn in Retirement Living." *Contemporary Long Term Care,* October 1985, 21.

Winkelvoss, H., and Powell, A. *Continuing Care Retirement Communities—An Empirical, Financial, and Legal Analysis.* Pension Research Council, Wharton School, University of Pennsylvania, Richard D. Irwin, 1984.

Zaner, L. "From Main Street to Wall Street, Seniors Housing Emerges as a Viable Real Estate Niche." *Seniors Housing* (special supp. to National Real Estate Investor) 3 (1994).

Zeisel, J., and Sloan, K. "Troubled Senior Housing Projects." American Society on Aging/American Association of Retired Persons Conference, March 1991.

Part III

AAHA Provider News. January 8, 1988.

A Complete Guide to the Tax Reform Act of 1986. Englewood Cliffs: Prentice-Hall, 1986.

American Association of Homes for the Aging and Ernst & Young. *Continuing Care Retirement Communities: An Industry in Action,* 1993.

Annot. "Self-Dealing by Condominium Developers." 73 *A.L.R.* 3d 613.

Annot. "Validity, Construction, and Application of Statutes, or of Condominium Association's Bylaws or Regulations, Restricting Sale, Transfer, or Lease of Condominium Units." 17 *A.L.R.* 4th 1247.

BNA Tax Management Portfolio. 47–4th, A–42–A–44, 1989.

CCH. *Standard Federal Tax Reports.*

"CCRC's Lease-Hold Condo Status Offers Tax Savings for Buyers." *Multi-Housing News,* March 1989, 31.

"Continuing Care Retirement Communities: An Industry in Action." American Association of Homes for the Aging and Ernst & Whinney, 1987.

DiLorenzo, V. "Restraints on Alienation in a Condominium Context: An Evaluation and Theory for Decisionmaking." *Real Property, Probate and Trust Journal,* Fall 1989.

Gallagher, R. "The Current Status of the Imputed Interest Rules." *American Association of Homes for the Aging Technical Assistance Brief,* 1992.

Gordon, P. "Taking a Closer Look at Continuing Care Condos and Co-Ops." *Retirement Housing Report,* February 1990.

Gordon, P. "Taxation of Lump Sum Admission Fees." *Retirement Housing Housing Report,* August 1990.

Gordon, P., Goldman, J., and Kaufmann, P. "Membership Formats for Retirement Facilities." *Spectrum*, November 1990, 19.

Holtz and Brecht. "Tax Reform Will Hit Retirement Housing." *Retirement Housing Report,* Vol. 1, No. 1, September 1986, 12.

Housing for Seniors: Developing Successful Projects. Washington, D.C.: Urban Land Institute, 1995.

Internal Revenue Service. *Market Segment Specialization Program Guide for Passive Activity Losses.* 1994.

Kaufmann, P. "Phantom Income of the Elderly: The IRS Clarifies the Application of the Imputed Interest Rules to Refundable Entrance Fees Paid to Retirement Communities." *California Tax Lawyer,* Fall 1995, 21–26.

Kazlow and Schrager. "Cooperative, Condominium Ownership Compared." *The National Law Journal,* June 16, 1980, 9.

National Investment Conference Lender & Investor Survey. 1994.

"Passive Activity Audit Guide Issued by IRS." *RIA Special Report,* May 5, 1994.

"Passive Activity Tax Break for Real Estate Professionals— IRS Issues Proposed Regs." *Federal Tax Coordinator 2d,* January 12, 1995, 9–11.

"Private Financing of Long Term Care: Current Methods and Resources." ICF, Inc., Phase 1, 1985, 6.

Restatement of Property. 1st, 399, 450.

"Restraints on Alienation in a Condominium Context: An Evaluation and Theory for Decision-Making." *Real Property, Probate & Trust Journal,* 24:403 (Fall 1989).

Rohan and Reskin. *Condominium Law & Practice.* New York: Bender (annual).

"The Rule of Law in Residential Associations." 99 *Harvard L. Rev.* 472 (1985).

Smith. "Syndication Topics: Rental Retirement Housing." 16 *Real Estate Review,* Winter 1987, 4.

U.S. Code Congressional and Administrative News. 99th Congress, 1st Sess., V. 2, 451–452.

U.S. Department of Health and Human Services. *A Profile of Older Americans.* American Association of Retired Persons and Administration on Aging, 1986, 1990.

Warren, Gorham, and Lamont. *Housing & Development Reporter.*

Wood, S. "A Warming Trend: Climate Right for Condo/Coop Development." *Contemporary Long Term Care,* July 1990, 48.

Part IV

AAHA Provider News. January 22, 1988, 4.

Bromley, R., and Clark, M. "Congress Looks at Overhaul of Unrelated Business Income Tax." *Hospital Law,* October 1987.

CCH. *Medicare and Medicaid Guide.*

CCH. *Standard Federal Tax Reports.*

Colvin, G. "A Guide to the New IRS Rules on Lobbying by Charities." Presented to the Tax-Exempt Organizations

Committee of the Taxation Section of the State Bar of California, October 4, 1991.

"Exempt Healthcare Guidance Is in the Works, Says IRS's Sullivan." *The Exempt Organization Tax Review,* July 1995, 18-19.

"Expect More Guidance for Health Care Entities, IRS and Treasury Officials Say." *BNA Daily Tax Report,* April 25, 1995, G-2.

Federal Tax Coordinator. August 17, 1989, 245.

Gallagher, J. "The Nonprofit Tax Climate in the Fifty States." *Association Management,* February 1988, 29.

Hopkins, B. *The Law of Tax Exempt Organizations.* 4th ed. New York: John Wiley, 1983.

Internal Revenue Service Audit Guidelines for Hospitals. Contained in Manual Transmittal 7 (10) 69-38 for Exempt Organizations Guidelines Handbook, March 27, 1992.

"IRS Issues Guidance to Expedite Charitable Housing Tax-Exemptions." *BNA Daily Tax Report,* May 2, 1995.

Kaufmann, P., and M. Curry. "IRS Proposed Guidelines Allow for Reasonable Physician Recruitment Incentives." *The Journal of Taxation,* September 1995, 162-67.

"Lawmakers, IRS Questions Nonprofit's Tax-Free Status." *AAHA Provider News,* March 1991.

Mancino, D. "The Unrelated Business Income Taxation of Nonprofit Hospitals." *The Exempt Organization Tax Review,* March 1991, 35.

Mayer, D. "Challenges to Non-Profits' Tax Exemption on the Rise." *Health Week,* February 1, 1988, 1.

"Nursing Facilities Still Threatened by 'First-Come-First-Served' Rule." *American Association of Homes and Services for the Aging Health Reform Update,* July 22, 1994.

"One Hospital Likely to Face Revocation as Result of Audits, IRS Official Says." *Bureau of National Affairs Health Law Reporter*, May 6, 1993.

"Practitioners Praise New and Improved Safe Harbor for Low-Income Housing." *The Exempt Organization Tax Review,* June 1995, 1173-1174.

Rajecki, R. "Aiming at Not-for-Profits: Congress Looks for Justification of Tax Exemptions." *Contemporary Long Term Care,* August 1991, 36.

"Senate Votes to Make 501(c)(4) Groups That Lobby Ineligible for Federal Grants." *BNA Taxation, Budget and Accounting,* July 25, 1995, G-6 to G-7.

Simpson, J., and Strum, S. "How Good a Samaritan? Federal Income Tax Exemption for Charitable Hospitals Reconsidered." *Univ. of Puget Sound L. Rev.,* Spring 1991.

Stark, P. Fortney. "The Exempt Organization Reform Act of 1993." November 22, 1993.

Sweterlitsch, M. State Tax Exemptions: Homes for the Aging. Unpublished paper, September 1986.

"Tax Aspects of Healthcare Report: The Tax Treatment of Healthcare Providers." *Congressional Research Service Report for Congress,* 1994 WL 546254, April 25, 1994.

"Tax-Exemption Threats Target Nonprofits in Several States." *AAHSA Provider News,* April 1995.

"Tax Exemptions Still Threatened." *AAHA Provider News,* May 27, 1988.

U.S. General Accounting Office. "Nonprofit Hospitals: Better Standards Needed for Tax Exemption." May 1990.

U.S. House of Representatives. Hearing on Unrelated Business Income Tax on Exempt Organizations before the Subcommittee on Oversight of the House Committee on Ways and Means, 100th Cong., 1st Sess., 1987.

Utah State Tax Commission. "Nonprofit Hospital and Nursing Home Charitable Property Tax Exemption Standards." August 22, 1990.

Part V

"A New Breed of Retirement Community." *Newsweek,* November 11, 1991, 62.

Brier, B. "Special Tax Problems of Health Care Providers." *The Exempt Organization Tax Revenue,* August/September 1989.

Bowe, J. "New Growth Opportunity: Hospitals Expand Their Continuum of Care." *Contemporary Long Term Care,* February 1992, 27.

Cohen, D. "Contracting Issues Regarding Life Care Retirement Communities." *The Medical Staff Counselor,* Summer 1988, 57.

Federal Tax Coordinator 2d. RIA, 1993, L-8133, at 34, 788A-92 to 34,789-89, citing S. Rep., Pub. L. No. 98-369, at 137-141.

"IRS Sees Need for Intermediate Sanctions for Exempt Health Organizations." *BNA Daily Tax Report,* April 27, 1995, J-1.

Lanahan, M. "Hospitals as Owners of Retirement Communities." *Contemporary Long Term Care,* April 1988, 87.

"Life Care: You Must Know More Than Health Care." *Hospitals,* May 5, 1987, 98.

McMullin, D. "Hospitals and CCRCs: A Growing Alternative." *Contemporary Long Term Care,* November 1985, 43.

Moore, J. "Hospitals and Nursing Homes Eye Housing." *Contemporary Long Term Care,* October 1991, 22.

Nemes, J. "Retirement Centers Grow Despite Fewer Providers." *Modern Healthcare,* June 2, 1989, 50.

Pallarito, K. "CCRCs See Slow Growth, Challenges in HMO Care." *Modern Healthcare,* May 23, 1994, 76.

Pallarito, K. "Slowdown Signals Transition for Retirement Centers Run by Nursing Homes, Hospitals." *Modern Healthcare,* May 21, 1990, 77.

Plantner, K. "Limited Liability Companies Are Increasingly Popular." *Taxation for Lawyers,* January/February 1992.

Research Institute of America. *Federal Tax Coordinator,* 2d ed.

Roble and Mason. "The Legal Aspects of Health Care Joint Ventures." 24 *Duquesne Law Review* 455 (1985).

Southerland, K. "Hospitals' Plans for Long-Term Care." *Contemporary Long Term Care,* October 1988, 32.

Sweeney, J., and D'Itri, J. "New Success Factors for Management Under Prospective Payment." *Topics in Health Care Financing,* Spring 1985, 10.

U.S. Department of Health and Human Services. "Special Fraud Alert on Hospital Incentives to Physicians." 1992.

U.S. Department of Health and Human Services. "Special Fraud Alert-Joint Venture Arrangements." 1984.

Part VI

AAHA *Provider News.* January 22, 1988.

AAHA *Provider News.* March 4, 1988, 3.

"A Decent Place to Live: The Report of the National Housing Task Force." March 1988, 10.

Aging News Alert. March 10, 1993, 9.

Aging News Alert. August 24, 1994, 5.

American Association of Homes for the Aging. *Housing Bulletin,* February 10,1994.

American Seniors Housing Association. *1995 Seniors Housing Industry Executive Survey.*

American Seniors Housing Association. *Seniors Housing Finance: Trends and Prospects.* 1992, 35.

California Association of Homes and Services for the Aging. *The CAHSA Report.* October 28, 1994, 6.

"Conduit Financing: A Road Map." *Multi-Housing Newsletter,* April 1993.

"Establishment Clause Analysis of Legislative and Administrative Aid to Religion." 74 *Colum. L. Rev.* 1175, 1974.

Gamzon, M. "New Program Broadens Financing Alternatives for Frail Elderly Housing." *Contemporary Long Term Care,* October 1988, 83.

Greco, M. "Mortgage-backed Securities Financing Gains Popularity." *National Real Estate Investor,* January 1993.

Housing and Development Reporter, October 11, 1993, 323. *HUD Handbook* 4571.3 REV-1.

Housing and Development Reporter. March 13, 1995, 673.

Housing and Development Reporter. April 10, 1995, 738.

Housing and Development Reporter. April 24, 1995, 673, 738, 772.

Housing and Development Reporter. August 14, 1995, 194.

Housing and Development Reporter. October 9, 1995, 321.

Housing and Development Reporter. November 20, 1995, 421.

Housing and Development Reporter. December 4, 1995, 450.

Housing and Development Reporter. 70:0011 et seq.

Housing and Development Reporter. August 8, 1988, 235.

Housing and Development Reporter. October 17, 1988, 476.

Housing and Development Reporter. July 10, 1989, 139-140.

Housing and Development Reporter. October 30, 1989, 432.

Housing and Development Reporter. August 20, 1990, 279.

Housing and Development Reporter. October 29, 1990, 501.

Housing and Development Reporter. October 14, 1991, 423.

Jarchow, S. *Real Estate Syndication.* New York: John Wiley, 1985.

Larkin, H. "Feds Take Aim at Continuing Care Tax Exemption." *Hospitals,* September 5, 1988, 106.

Older Americans Report. February 19, 1988, 75.

Older Americans Report. September 13, 1991, 355.

Older Americans Report. September 27, 1996, 316; Issues Brief, American Association of Homes and Services for the Aging, March 1998.

Schwartz, R. "HUD Coinsurance Program Hits Temporary Snag." *Contemporary Long Term Care,* July 1989.

Seip, D. "1987: An Insider's Perspective on the Retirement Industry." *Contemporary Long Term Care,* December 1987, 48.

U.S. Department of Housing and Urban Development. *Programs of HUD,* 1984,1989-1990.

U.S. General Accounting Office. *Tax Exempt Bonds.* March 1991.

U.S. House of Representatives. Tax Report Bill of 1986 (H.R. 3838). *Statement of the Managers.*

U.S. Senate Report. *Standard Federal Tax Reports* (CCH). 11,286.

Washington Report. American Association of Homes for the Aging, May 6, 1993.

Woodside, J. "Affordable Retirement Housing in a Post-HUD Era." *Spectrum,* September–October 1995, 34.

Part VII

"AAHSA, HUD Counsel Meet on Religion Issue." *Washington Report.* American Association of Homes and Services for the Aging, March 25, 1994.

"Admissions, Eligibility for Assistance, Marketing and Tenant Selection." *HUD Handbook* 4350.3, ch. 2, 1993 ed.

Aging News Alert. October 11, 1995, 15.

American Association of Homes for the Aging. *Housing Bulletin,* February 10, 1994.

American Association of Homes for the Aging. "Current Status of State Regulation of Continuing Care Retirement Communities." January 1987 and August 1991.

American Association of Homes for the Aging. Draft Policy Objective. January 16, 1992.

American Association of Homes for the Aging. "Guidelines for Regulation of Continuing Care Retirement Communities." May 1987 and 1992.

American Association of Homes for the Aging. *Housing Bulletin,* February 22, 1991, and February 6, 1992.

American Association of Homes for the Aging. "Summary of State Board and Care Requirements." *Legal Memo,* April 1989.

American Association of Homes for the Aging. "Summary of State Certificate of Need Requirements." December 1988.

American Association of Retired Persons. "Assisted Living and Its Implications for Long-Term Care." February 1995, 7-10.

American Association of Retired Persons. "The Regulation of Board and Care Homes: Results of a Survey in the Fifty States and the District of Columbia." 1993.

American Health Care Association and Murtha, Culina, Richter, & Pinney, *Assisted Living: A State-by-State Summary.* 1995.

American Seniors Housing Association. *Assisted Living Residences: A Study of Traffic and Parking Implications.* 1997.

Annot. "Validity and Construction of Contract Under Which Applicant for Admission to Home for Aged or Infirm Turns over His Property to Institution for Lifetime Care." 44 *A.L.R.* 3d 1174.

Annot. "Validity of Zoning for Senior Citizen Communities." 83 *A.L.R.* 3d 1084.

Annot. "Zoning Regulations as Applied to Homes for the Elderly." 83 *A.L.R.* 3d 1103.

Apperson, J. "Suits Allege Bias in Ads for Retirement Homes." *The Sun,* January 20, 1994.

Beyer, Bulkley, and Hopkins. "A Model Act Regulating Board and Care Homes: Guidelines for the States." *Mental and Physical Disability Law Reporter,* Vol. 8, No. 2, March–April 1984.

"Board & Care." Office of Inspector General, U.S. Department of Health & Human Services, March 1990.

"Board and Care Homes in the United States: Failure in Public Policy." U.S. Senate Special Committee on Aging, March 9, 1989.

"Board and Care: Insufficient Assurances that Residents' Needs Are Identified and Met." U.S. General Accounting Office, February 1989.

CCH. *Blue Sky Law Reports.*

CCH. *Medicare & Medicaid Guide.* ¶¶ 13,945 *et seq.*

CCH. Trade Regulation Reporter. *Contemporary Long Term Care,* August 1989, 12-13.

"Continuing Care Retirement Communities: Issues and State Regulation." 8 *St. Louis Public Law Review,* 245 (1989).

Continuing Care Retirement Facilities Working Group of the National Association of Insurance Commissioners. Draft report, July 1, 1993.

"Developments in Aging: 1992." U.S. Senate Special Committee on Aging, S. Rep. No. 103-40, Vol. 1, April 20, 1993, 206.

Dobkin, L. *The Board and Care System: A Regulatory Jungle.* Washington, D.C.: American Association of Retired Persons, 1989.

F.W. Tanner. "Retirement Centers Are Good Neighbors." *Contemporary Long Term Care,* June 1990.

Fair Housing Advertising: A Handbook for the Seniors Housing Industry. American Seniors Housing Association, 1993.

Fairbanks, J. "Lifetime Care Contracts: Are Senior Citizens Putting All Their Eggs in One Basket?" *Probate and Property,* March-April 1990.

Fox, T. *Long Term Care and Retirement Facilities.* New York: Bender, 1989.

Fox and Ritchie. "Watch Your Language: Regulators Scrutinize Resident Contracts and Advertising Materials." *Retirement Housing Report,* October 1986.

Gilbert, D. "Increasing Access to Long-Term Care through Medicaid Antidiscrimination Laws." *Journal of Health and Hospital Law,* April 1991, 105.

Gordon, P. "Are Your Resident Contracts Due for a Tune-Up?" *D&O Forum,* Summer 1995.

"Guidelines for Prevention of Transmission of Human Immunodeficiency Virus and Hepatitis B Virus to Health-Care and Public-Safety Workers." *Morbidity & Mortality Weekly Report,* February 1989.

Hancock, J., ed. *Housing the Elderly.* New Brunswick, NJ: Center for Urban Policy Research, 1987.

"Home Care at the Crossroads." *U.S. Senate Special Committee on Aging, S. Rep. 100-102, April 1988.*

Hospital Law Manual. "Health Planning." *Aspen Systems,* 1983.

Hospital Law Manual. "Health Planning." Vol. IIA, 1-5 et seq. *Aspen Systems,* 1983.

"Hospitals Travel Some Rough Ground in LTC." *Hospitals,* December 20, 1986, 70.

Housing and Development Reporter. September 21, 1987, 342.

Housing and Development Reporter. October 17, 1988, 464.

Housing and Development Reporter. October 29, 1990, 502.

"HUD Rules Allow for Elderly-Only Housing." *Older Americans Report,* April 22, 1994, 13 3–34.

Hudson, T. "Senior Surge: Are you Ready?" *Hospitals and Health Networks,* April 15, 1997.

Infante, M. "The Interpretive Guidelines: Rote, Reason or Regulation." *Contemporary Long Term Care,* July 1991, 54.

Infante, M. "A Step towards First Come, First Served." *Contemporary Long Term Care,* July 1995, 59–60.

Kaufman, M. "Life-Care Decorum: No Wheelchairs." *Philadelphia Inquirer,* February 18, 1991.

Kemper, P., Applebaum, R., and Harrigan, M. "Community Care Demonstrations: What Have We Learned?" *Health Care Financing Review,* Vol. 8, No. 4, Summer 1987, 87.

McNickle, L. "Mixed Populations: A Threat to All Age-Distinct Elderly Housing." *Retirement Housing Business Report,* October 1992.

"Medicare Costs to Continue to Spiral." *Contemporary Long Term Care,* July 1990, 18.

Medicare and Medicaid Guide.

Mental and Physical Disability Law Reporter. 8, No. 2 (March/April 1984), 157.

Modern Healthcare. August 11, 1997, 33.

Morton, A. "Camouflaging." *Contemporary Long Term Care,* July 1995, 40.

National Association for Home Care. *Basic Statistics about Home Care.* April 1986 and October 1996.

National Association of Home Care. *How to Establish a Home Health Agency: Some Preliminary Considerations.* January 1984.

Note, "*City of Cleburne v. Cleburne Living Center:* Rational Basis with a Bite?" 20 *U.S.F. L. Rev.* 927 (1986).

Ohio Attorney General Opinion No. 85-063. September 24, 1985.

Older Americans Report. February 12, 1988, 63.

Older Americans Report. December 1, 1989, 463.

Older Americans Report. June 24, 1994, 211.

Older Americans Report. July 22, 1994, 246.

"Public Health Service Statement on Management of Occupational Exposure to Human Immunodeficiency Virus, Including Considerations Regarding Zidovudine Post-exposure Use." 39 *Morbidity & Mortality Weekly Report,* No. RR–I, January 26, 1990, 3.

"Recommendations for Preventing Transmission of Human Immunodeficiency Virus and Hepatitis B Virus to Patients during Exposure-Prone Invasive Procedures." 40 *Morbidity & Mortality Weekly Report,* No. RR–8, July 12, 1991.

"Recommendations for Prevention of HIV Transmission in Health-Care Settings." 36 *Morbidity & Mortality Weekly Report,* No. 2S (August 21, 1987).

Reding, R. "Certificate of Need Review of Continuing Care Retirement Communities." *Spectrum,* April 1991, 34.

Regan, J. *Tax, Estate and Financial Planning for the Elderly.* New York: Bender, 1985.

"Regulations Issued to Implement Elderly Preference Provisions." *Housing Development Reporter Current Developments,* May 9, 1994, 831–832.

"Risk Classification Statement of Principles." *American Academy of Actuaries,* 1980.

Romano, M. "Unshackling the Elderly." *Contemporary Long Term Care,* April 1994, 37.

Schact. "Protection for the Elderly Person and His Estate: Regulating and Enforcing Life-Care Contracts." 5 *Probate Law Journal* 105 (1983).

Schwartz, R. "Home Care versus Nursing Home Costs." *Contemporary Long Term Care,* February 1988, 16.

Scott. "Home-Care Revenues Soar to $5.1 Billion via Mergers." *Modern Healthcare,* May 23, 1994, 85.

Sfekas. "Can Health Planning Survive the 1980's?" *Aging Network News,* June 1986.

Snow, C. "Home Health Heats Up." *Modern Healthcare,* August 18, 1997.

"State Laws and Programs Serving Elderly Persons and Disabled Adults." *Mental Disability Law Reporter,* Vol. 7, No. 2, March and April 1983.

"States Explore Assisted Living Licensure." 9 *American Association of Homes and Services for the Aging News,* 1994.

Stearns, L., et al. "Lessons from the Implementation of CCRC Regulations." *The Gerontologist,* Vol. 30, No. 2, 1990, 154.

Tanner, F.W. "Retirement Centers Are Good Neighbors." *Contemporary Long Term Care,* June 1990.

Templer, C. "The Potholes of Fair Housing Advertising." *Spectrum,* September–October 1994.

"Update: Universal Precautions for Prevention of Transmission of Human Immunodeficiency Virus, Hepatitis B Virus, and Other Bloodborne Pathogens in Health-Care Settings." 37 *Morbidity & Mortality Weekly Report,* No. 24, June 24, 1988.

U.S. Code, Congressional and Administrative News.

U.S. Department of Health and Human Services, *Medicaid Manual.*

U.S. Department of Health and Human Services, *Medicare Intermediary Manual.*

U.S. Department of Housing and Urban Development, Independent Agencies Appropriations Bill, 1987. H.R. Rep. No. 731, 99th Congress, 2nd Sess., at 9 (1986).

U.S Department of Housing and Urban Development, Public and Assisted Housing Occupancy Task Force. "Report to Congress and the Department of Housing and Urban Development." April 7, 1994.

U.S. Department of Justice. "Application of Rehabilitation Act's Section 504 to HIV-infected Persons." 1988.

U.S. Equal Employment Opportunity Commission. "Interim Enforcement Guidelines on the Americans with Disabilities Act of 1990." 1993.

U.S. House of Representatives. "Maximizing Support Services for the Elderly in Assisted Housing: Experiences from the Congregate Housing Services Program." Hearings before the Subcomm. on Housing and Consumer Interests of the House Select Comm. on Aging, 99th Cong., 1st Sess., 4 (1985).

Vick. "Death Prompts MD. Probe of 'Assisted Living' Facility." *Washington Post*, January 9, 1995, 1.

Ward. "Congregate Living Arrangements: The Financing Option." *Topics In Health Care Financing* 34 (Spring 1984).

Part VIII

Aging Today. July–August 1995, 6.

Aging News Alert. September 27, 1995, 5–8.

American Association of Retirement Persons. *A Profile of Older Americans.* 1996.

American Association of Retired Persons Public Policy Institute. *State Home and Community-Based Services for the Aged under Medicaid.* 1991.

American Association of Retired Persons Public Policy Institute and Health Policy Center of the Urban Institute. "Coming Up Short: Increasing Out-of-Pocket Health Spending by Older Americans." April 19, 1994.

Bowe, J. "Recommending a New Role." *Contemporary Long Term Care,* April 1990, 49.

Brickfield, C. "Long Term Care Insurance: One Piece of the Puzzle." *Health Span,* June 1985, 11.

Burda, D. "Fraud Threatens LTC Insurance Market." *Hospitals,* October 4, 1987, 88.

Burda, D. "The Nation Looks for New Ways to Finance Care for the Aged." *Hospitals,* September 20, 1987, 48.

CCH. *Medicare and Medicaid Guide. Congressional Quarterly,* May 31, 1986.

Capistrant, G. "Congress Eyes Private Long-Term Care Financing." *Spectrum,* April 1991, 14.

"Caring for the Elderly: Public/Private Sector Responsibilities Point Way to Future Trends." *Federation of American Health Systems,* January/February 1988, 28.

"Congress Takes Ball and Runs after State of the Union Punt." *Congressional Quarterly,* January 31, 1987.

Contemporary Long Term Care. April 1990, 49–56.

Contemporary Long Term Care. May 1990, 18.

"Developments in Aging: 1992." U.S. Senate Special Committee on Aging, S. Rep. No. 103–40, Vol. 1, April 20, 1993, 206.

Diamond, L. "Private Long Term Insurance: A New Option for Life Care Communities." *Retirement Housing Report,* April 1988, 2.

"Employer Views on Group Long-Term Care Insurance." *Washington Business Group on Health,* October 1991.

Federal Taxes Weekly Alert. November 16, 1995, 475.

Galston, J. "Health Care Ventures Enliven Private Placement Syndications." *Real Estate Forum,* August 1987, 54.

Garland, S. "Nursing-Home Time Bomb Threatens an Aging Nation." *San Francisco Examiner,* November 3, 1985, E-1.

"Gotcha! The Traps in Long Term Care Insurance: An Empty Promise to the Elderly?" *Consumer Reports,* June 1991, 425.

"Grays on the Go." *Time,* February 22, 1988, 66, 70.

HCFA Medicaid Waiver Fact Sheet. January 6, 1994.

"H.I.A.A. Study Notes Big Growth in LTC Insurance Policies." *Contemporary Long Term Care,* May 1989, 17.

Hospitals. January 5, 1988, 94.

"House Report Suggests Banning Private LTC Policies." *Contemporary Long Term Care,* July 1989.

Housing the Elderly Report. June 1989, 8.

"How Continuing Care Retirement Communities Manage Services for the Elderly." U.S. General Accounting Office, January 1997.

HUD Handbook. 4235.1, 1989.

ICF, Inc. "Private Financing of Long Term Care: Current Methods and Resources." Phase I Final Report, U.S. Department of Health and Human Resources, 1985, 12, 91.

"Insurance Market Boom Ongoing." *Contemporary Long Term Care,* May 1990, 18.

Kapp, M. "Options for Long-Term Care Financing: A Look to the Future." *Hastings Law Journal,* March 1991.

Kosterlitz, J. "The Coming Crisis." *National Journal,* August 6, 1988, 2029.

Kosterlitz, J. "Debating How to Care for the Aged." *National Journal,* March 31, 1990, 788.

Kosterlitz, J. "Middle-Class Medicaid." *National Journal,* November 9, 1991, 2728.

Kosterlitz, J. "Radical Surgeons." *National Journal,* April 27, 1991, 993.

Kunerth, A. "Group LTC Insurance as a Marketing Tool." *Contemporary Long Term Care,* December 1987, 38.

Kunerth, A. "Nationally Underwritten LTC Programs in CCRCs—How Good a Deal for Residents?" *Retirement Housing Report,* June 1990, 4.

Larkin, H. "Will Regulation Stifle Long-Term Care Insurance?" *Hospitals,* February 5, 1988, 76.

"Long Term Care: The True 'Catastrophe'?" *Congressional Quarterly,* May 31, 1986, 1227.

Lundy, J. "Issue Brief: Health Care Cost Containment." *Congressional Research Service,* October 31, 1986.

MacKenzie, R. "Catastrophic Illness: Private Financing of Health Care for the Elderly." *Compensation & Benefits Management,* Winter 1987, 5.

MacKenzie, R. "Evaluating Long-Term Care Insurance Options for Retirement Communities." *Retirement Housing Report,* February 1989, 2.

MacKenzie, R. "Evaluating Plan Design Options." *Contemporary Long Term Care,* April 1990.

MacNeil, N. "Employer Mandated Health Insurance: A Solution for the Working Uninsured?" *Journal of Health and Hospital Law,* November 1991.

Massachusetts Blue Cross-Blue Shield Study, 1985. Reported in *Congressional Quarterly,* May 31, 1986, 1228.

McMorran, W. "A Pivotal Month for National LTC Insurance." *Contemporary Long Term Care,* February 1988, 23.

"Medicare Costs to Continue to Spiral." *Contemporary Long Term Care,* July 1990, 18.

"Medicaid Costs May Reach $200 Billion." *Spectrum,* September 1991.

Meiners and Gollub. "Long-term Care Insurance: The Edge of an Emerging Market." *Healthcare Financial Management,* March 1984, 58.

"NAIC Strengthens LTC Model Insurance Legislation." *Contemporary Long Term Care,* February 1989, 15.

National Association for Home Care. "Basic Statistics about Home Care." 1996.

National Association of Insurance Commissioners. "Long Term Care Insurance: An Industry Perspective on Market Development and Consumer Protection" (undated (January 1987)). *National Journal,* March 31, 1990, 788.

Nauts, C. "Reverse Mortgages—Backing into the '90s." *Probate & Property,* January/February 1994, 55.

New England Journal of Medicine. Vol. 314, No. 11 (March 13, 1986) 722.

"Nursing Home Insurance Called Unaffordable." *Older Americans Report,* February 5, 1993, 44.

Older Americans Report. March 20, 1987, 2.

Older Americans Report. May 27, 1988.

Older Americans Report. June 10, 1988, 233.

Older Americans Report. January 27, 1989, 32.

Older Americans Report. May 12, 1989, 189.

Older Americans Report. March 9, 1990, 93.

Older Americans Report. April 13, 1990, 147.

Older Americans Report. July 27, 1990, 293.

"Panel Considers Alternatives to Bowen Plan." *Congressional Quarterly,* March 7, 1987, 434.

"Private Long Term Care Insurance: The Maturing Market." Conference Proceedings, January 1987, San Antonio, Texas.

Rajecki, R. "Keeping Individuals and an Industry Afloat." *Contemporary Long Term Care,* May 1993, 33.

Retirement Housing Report. June 1990, 4.

Rivlin, A., and Wiener, J. *Caring for the Disabled Elderly: Who Will Pay?* Washington, D.C.: The Brookings Institution, 1988.

Rodney, M. "Reverse Mortgages and Related Housing Issues." American Bar Association Annual Meeting, Elderly Housing Program, August 7, 1990.

Rooney, M. "Reverse Mortgages and Related Housing Issues." *American Bar Association Annual Meeting,* Elderly Housing Program, August 7, 1990.

Rosenblatt R. "Panel Backs Nursing Home Insurance." *New York Times*, September 20, 1987, 4.

"Sales of LTC Insurance Policies Continue to Climb." *Contemporary Long Term Care,* September 1991, 11.

Scholen, K. "Home-Made Money, Consumer's Guide to Home Equity Conversion." American Association of Retired Persons, 3d ed., 12–14.

Shearer, G. *Long Term Care: Analysis of Public Policy Options.* Washington D.C.: Consumers Union, January 1989.

Smallwood, D., Simon, H., and Brody, B. "Questioning Long-Term Care IRAs." *Health Affairs,* Summer 1987, 132.

"State Variation in the Regulation of Long-Term Care Insurance Products." American Association of Retired Persons, January 1992.

Tell, E., and Cohen, M. "Lessons in Managing Long-Term Care Costs: Continuing Care Retirement Facilities." *Generations,* Spring 1990, 55.

"Ten Medigap Policies to Replace Hundreds." *Contemporary Long Term Care,* September 1991, 11.

Today's Nursing Home. May 1989, 3.

Topolnicki, D. M. "When a Nursing Home Becomes Your Poorhouse." *Money,* March 1986, 175.

U.S. Department of Health and Human Services. *HHS News.* July 29, 1986.

U.S. General Accounting Office. "Long Term Care Insurance: Risks to Consumers Should Be Reduced." HRD–92–14, December 16, 1991.

U.S. General Accounting Office. "Medigap Insurance." Report to House Subcommittee on Health, Committee on Ways and Means, October 1986.

U.S. Senate Special Committee on Aging. "Aging America: Trends and Projections." 1985–1986 and 1991 eds.

U.S. Senate Special Committee on Aging. "Developments in Aging: 1992." S. Rep. 103–40, Vol. 1, April 20, 1993.

Wagner, L. "Nursing Homes Buffeted by Troubles." *Modern Health Care,* March 18, 1988, 33.

Weissenstein, E. "Legislators Use Bills to Put Long-Term Care in Public Eye." *Modern Healthcare,* December 2, 1991, 25.

"Who Can Afford a Nursing Home?" *Consumer Reports,* May 1988, 300.

Part IX

Morton, A. "Camouflaging." *Contemporary Long Term Care,* July 1995, 40.

Richards, D. "One Way to Spell Liability Relief." *Contemporary Long Term Care,* September 1996, 64.

Sullivan, J. "Long Term Care on Trial." *Contemporary Long Term Care,* March 1996.

Vick. "Death Prompts MD. Probe of 'Assisted Living' Facility." *Washington Post*, January 9, 1995, 1.

Table of Authorities*

Cases

*Some references may appear only in section's notes.

Boyd v. Lefrak, 509 F.2d 1110 (2d Cir. 1975), *reh'g. den.,* 517 F.2d 918; *cert. den.,* 96 S. Ct. 197,
  423 U.S. 896, 46 L.Ed.2d 129   23.5(a)

Brandt v. Village of Chebanse, 82 F.3d 172 (7th Cir. 1996)   23.3(a)(3)

Brecker v. Queens B'nai B'rith Housing Development, 607 F. Supp. 428 (1985) *aff'd.,* 798 F.2d 52
  (2d Cir. 1986)   23.3(a)

Broadmoore San Clemente Homeowners' Ass'n. v. Nelson, 25 Cal.App. 4th 1, 30 Cal. Rptr.
  2d 316 (1994)   23.3(a)(2)

Bryant Woods, Inc., v. Howard County, 911 F.Supp. 918 D. Md '96   23.3(a)(3)

Cabrera v. Jakabovitz, 24 F.3d 372 (2d Cir.), *cert. den.,* 115 S. Ct. 205, 130 L. Ed. 2d 135 (1994)   23.3(a)

California Ass'n. of Health Facilities v. Department of Health Servs., 16 Cal. 4th 284, 940 p. 2d 323,
  65 Cal. Rptr. 2d 872 (1997)   29.2(b)

Cambridge Co. v. East Slope Investment Corp., 672 P.2d 211 (Colo. App. 1983), *rev'd.,* 700 P.2d 537
  (Colo. 1985)   7.1(c)

Cape Retirement Community, Inc. v. Kuehle, 798 S.W.2d 201 (1990)   10.2(t)

Capital Extended Care, In re, 609 A.2d 896 (Pa. Commnw. Ct. 1992)   10.2(gg)

Care Initiatives v. Board of Review, 500 N.W.2d 14 (Iowa 1993)   10.2(m)

Casa Marie v. Superior Court, 752 F. Supp. 1152 (D.P.R. 1990), *vacated in part, rendered in part,*
  988 F.2d 252 (1st Cir. 1993)   23.3(a), 25.1

Cason v. Rochester Housing Authority, 748 F. Supp. 1002 (W.D.N.Y. 1990)   23.3(a)

Caughlin Homeowners Ass'n. v. Caughlin Club, 849 P.2d 310 (Nev. 1993)   7.1(c)(4)

Central Union Church, 624 P.2d 1346 (Hawaii 1981)   10.2(j)

Central Vt. Hosp., Inc. v. Town of Berlin, 672 A.2d 474 (Vt. 1995)   10.2(nn)

Chalk v. United States Dist. Court, 832 F.2d 1158 (9th Cir. 1987), *opinion issued,* 840 F.2d 701
  (9th Cir. 1988)   23.3(d)

Challenge Homes, Inc. v. County of Lubbock, 474 S.W.2d 746 (Tex. 1971)   10.2(ll)

Chapel Hill Residential Retirement Ctr., Inc., Appeal of, 299 S.E.2d 782 (1983), *review denied,*
  302 S.E.2d 249 (N.C. 1983)   10.2(bb)

Chapel Hill Residential Retirement Center, Inc., 299 S.E.2d 782 (1983)   10.2(bb)

Chapel View, Inc. v. Hennepin County, No. TC–5686 (Minn. Tax Court, 4th Dist., 1988)   10.2(r)

Charter Township v. Dinolfo, 351 N.W.2d 831 (Mich. 1984)   25.1

Chianese v. Culley, 397 F. Supp. 1344 (S.D. Fla. 1975)   7.1(c)

Chicago Health Serv. v. Commissioner of Revenue, 462 N.W.2d 386 (1990)   10.2(r)

Children's Home v. City of Easton, 417 A.2d 830 (Pa. 1980)   25.1

Christian Benevolent Ass'n. v. Limbach, 631 N.E.2d 1034 (Ohio 1994)   10.2.(dd)

Christian Home for the Aged, Inc. v. Tennessee Assessment Appeals Commission, 790 S.W.2d 288 (1990)   10.2(kk)

Christian Research Institute v. Dover, 5 N.J. Tax 376 (1983)   10.2(y)

Christian Retirement Homes v. Board of Equalization, 180 N.W.2d 136 (Neb. 1970)   10.2(v)

City of Cleburne v. Cleburne Living Center, 471 U.S. 1002 (1985)   25.1

City of McAllen v. Evangelical Lutheran, 518 S.W.2d 557 (Tex. 1975), *aff'd.,* 530 S.W.2d 806 (1976)   10.2(ll)

City of Oceanside v. McKenna, 215 Cal. App. 3d 1420 (1989)   7.1(c)

City of Santa Barbara v. Adamson, 27 Cal. 3d 123, 153 Cal. Rptr. 507, 610 P.2d 436 (Cal. 1980)   25.1

Intercare Health Sys., Inc. v. Cedar Grove, 11 N.J. Tax 423 (1990), *aff'd.,* 12 N.J. Tax 273 (1991), *cert. den.,* 606 A.2d 369 (N.J. 1992)
10.2(y)

James v. United States, 366 U.S. 213 (1961)
6.2(a)

Jancik v. HUD, 44 F.3d 553 (7th Cir. 1995)
23.3(b)

Jayber, Inc. v. Municipal Council, 569 A.2d 304 (N.J. App. Div. 1990), *cert. den.,* 584 A.2d 214 (N.J. 1990)
25.1

Jefferson Parish Hosp. Dist. No. 2 v. Hyde, 466 U.S. 2 (1984)
13.3

John Tennant Memorial Homes v. City of Pacific Grove, 27 Cal. App.3d 372, 103 Cal. Rptr. 215 (1972)
10.2(d)

Johnson v. Nationwide Indus., Inc., 450 F. Supp. 948 (N.D. Ill.1978), *aff'd.,* 715 F.2d 1233 (7th Cir. 1983)
7.1(c)(2)

Johnson v. Soundview Apartments, 585 F. Supp. 559; 588 F. Supp. 1381(S.D.N.Y. 1984)
22.6(d)

Johnson v. Thompson, 971 F.2d 1487 (10th Cir. 1992), *cert. den.,* 113 S. Ct. 1255 (1993)
23.3(a)

Jordan v. Village of Menomonee Falls, 137 N.W.2d 442 (Wis. 1965), *appeal dismissed,* 385 U.S. 4 (1966)
25.2

Judson Retirement Community v. Limbach, 638 N.E.2d 546 (Ohio 1994)
10.2(ee)

Judson Retirement Community v. Tracy, Ohio, Board of Tax Appeals, No. 95–T–674, June 6, 1997

Klappenbach v. Commissioner, 52 T.C.M. 437 (1986)
9.13

Klarfeld v. Berg, 29 Cal. 3d 893, 176 Cal. Rptr. 539, 633 P.2d 204 (1981)
25.2

Klein v. BIA Hotel Corp., 41 Cal. App. 4th 1133, 49 Cal. Rptr. 2d 60 (1996)
29.3(a)

Knutzen v. Eben Ezer Lutheran Housing Center, 815 F.2d 1343 (10th Cir. 1987)
23.3(c)

Knutzen v. Nelson, 617 F. Supp. 977 (D. Co. 1985)
23.3(c)

Kohl v. Woodhaven Learning Ctr., 672 F. Supp. 1226 (W.D. Mo. 1987), *rev'd. and remanded,* 865 F.2d 930 (8th Cir.), *cert. den.,* 493 U.S. 892 (1989)
23.3(d)

Kotev v. First Colony Life Ins. Co., 927 F. Supp. 1316 (C.D. Cal. 1996)
23.3(b)(5)

Ladue, City of v. Gilleo, 114 S. Ct. 2038 (1994)
7.1(b)(2)

Lamb v. Newton-Livingston, Inc., 551 N.W.2d 333 (Iowa 1996)
29.3(a)

Lanier v. Fairfield Communities, Inc., 776 F. Supp. 1533 (M.D. Fla 1990)
23.2(b)

Larkin v. Michigan Dep't. of Social Serv., No. 95–1138, 1996 U.S. App. LEXIS 17406 (6th Cir. July 16, 1996)
23.3(a)(3)

Larson v. Commissioner, 66 T.C. 159 (1976)
19.5

Lasser v. Rosa, 634 N.Y.S.2d 188 (App. Div. 1995)
23.3(b)(1)

Lewiston, City of v. Marcotte Congregate Hous., Inc., 673 A.2d 209 (Me. 1996)
10.2(o)

Lincoln Hills Dev. Corp. v. Tax Comm'rs., 521 N.E.2d 1360 (1988)
10.2(l)

Lindsey v. Normet, 405 U.S. 56 (1972)
25.1

Linton v. Commissioner, 65 F.3d 508 (6th Cir.), *reh'g. en banc den.,* 1995 U.S. App. LEXIS 30934 (6th Cir. 1995)
23.5(b)(1)

Linton v. Tennessee Comm'r. of Health & Env't., 1990 WL 180245 (M.D. Tenn. 1990)
23.6

Lowry Hospital Ass'n. v. Commissioner, 66 T.C. 850 (1976)
12.1(d)

Lloyd v. Housing Auth., 58 F.3d 398 (8th Cir. 1995)
23.3(d)(2)

Lutheran Home v. Board of Assessment, 515 A.2d 59 (Pa. 1986), *appeal denied,* 529 A.2d 1084 (Pa. 1987)
10.2(gg)

Lutheran Home at Topton v. Board of Assessment, 515 A.2d 59 (Pa. 1986)
10.2(gg)

Lutheran Social Services, East Region, 539 A.2d 895 (1988)
10.2(gg)

M.E. Schlude v. Commissioner, 372 U.S. 128 (1963), 63–1 USTC 9284
6.1(b)

M&I First Nat'l. Bank v. Episcopal Homes Management, Inc., 195 Wis. 2d 485, 536 N.W.2d 175 (1995)
21.5

	Section Number
Point East One Condominium Corp. v. Point East Developers, Inc., 348 So. 2d 32 (Fla. 1977)	7.1(c)
Potomac Group Home v. Montgomery County, 823 F. Supp. 1285 (D. Md. 1993)	23.3(a)
Presbyterian Homes v. Div. of Tax Appeals, 55 N.J. 275 (1970)	10.2(y)
Presbyterian Manor, Inc., In re, 380 P.2d 60 (Kan.1992)	10.2(n)
Proviso Ass'n. of Retarded Citizens v. Village of Westchester, 914 F. Supp. 1555 (N.D. Ill. 1996)	23.3(a)(3)
Rademan v. City and County of Denver, 526 P.2d 1325 (Colo. 1974)	25.1
Radio & Television Broadcast Technicians Local 1264 v. Broadcast Services of Mobile, Inc., 380 U.S. 255 (1965)	13.4(c)
Rains v. Belshe, 32 Cal. App. 4th 157 (1995)	20.3(a)(3)
Raintree Friends Hous., Inc., v. Indiana Dep't. of State Revenue, 1996 Ind. Tax LEXIS 16 (Ind. T.C. 1996)	10.2(l)
Raven's Cove Townhomes, Inc. v. Knuppe Dev. Co., 114 Cal. App. 3d 783 (1981)	7.1(c)(1)
Retirement Homes of Detroit v. Sylvan Township, 330 N.W.2d 682 (Mich. 1982)	10.2(q)
Retirement Ranch, Inc. v. Curry Cty. Val. Protest Bd., 546 P.2d 1199 (N. Mex. 1976), *cert. den.*, 89 N.M. 206 (1976)	10.2(z)
Rhodes v. Palmetto Pathway Homes, Inc., 303 S.C. 308, 400 S.E.2d 484 (1991)	23.3(a)(2)
Richards v. Iowa Dept. of Revenue, 414 N.W.2d 344 (1987)	10.2(m)
Richards v. Iowa Dept. of Revenue and Finance, 454 N.W.2d 573 (1990)	10.2(m)
Rigas Maja, Inc. v. Department of Revenue, 12 Or. Tax 471 (1993)	10.2(ff)
Riverview Place, Inc. v. Cass County, 448 N.W.2d 635 (1989)	10.2(cc)
Roberts v. Kindercare Learning Ctr., 86 F.3d 844 (8th Cir. 1996)	23.3(a)(1)
Roe v. District of Columbia, 842 F. Supp. 563 (D.D.C. 1993)	23.3(d)
Roe v. Housing Authority, 909 F. Supp. 814 (D. Colo. 1995)	23.3(b)(3) 23.3(d)(2)
Roe v. Sugar River Mills Assocs., M.B. Management Corp., 820 F. Supp. 636 (D.N.H. 1993)	23.3(a)
Rolla Apartments/Overall Constr. Indus., Inc. v. State Tax Comm'n., 797 S.W.2d 781 (1990)	10.2(t)
Ross v. Bank S., 885 F.2d 723 (11th Cir. 1989), *cert. den.*, 495 U.S. 905 (1990)	5.2
Ross v. Bank South, 837 F.2d 980 (11th Cir. 1988)	5.2
S.E.M. Villa II v. Kinney, 419 N.E.2d 879 (Ohio 1981)	10.2(dd)
Sanders v. Saw Arneson Prods., Inc., No. 95-15349, 1996 U.S. App. LEXIS 19500 (9th Cir. Aug. 6, 1996)	23.3(b)(1)
Sanderson v. Commissioner, 50 T.C.M. 1033 (1985)	19.5
Schoger Found. v. Commissioner, 76 T.C. 380 (1981)	9.7
School Board of Nassau County v. Arline, 480 U.S. 273, 107 S. Ct. 1123, 94 L. Ed. 2d 307, *reh'g. denied*, 481 U.S. 1024 (1987)	23.3(d)
Schulman v. State Div. of Human Rights, 641 N.Y.S.2d 134 (App. Div. 1996)	23.3(b)(1)
Secretary of HUD v. United Church Homes, Inc., Civ. No. C2-92-054 (S.D. Ohio), consent decree entered into May 21, 1993	23.3(c)
Secretary of HUD v. Williams, 1991 WL 442796 (HUDALJ March 22, 1991)	23.3(a), 23.3(d)
Sedam v. United States, 518 F.2d 242 (7th Cir. 1975)	9.13
Sehome Park Care Ctr., Inc., In re, 903 P.2d 443 (Wash. 1995)	10.2(pp)
Senior Citizens Bootheel Serv. Inc. v. Dover, 811 S.W.2d 35 (1991)	10.2(t)

	Section Number
United States v. University Hospital of SUNY at Stony Brook, 575 F. Supp. 607 (E.D.N.Y. 1983), *aff'd.,* 729 F.2d 144 (2nd Cir. 1984)	23.3(d)
United States v. W. B. Williams, 395 F.2d 508 (5th Cir. 1968), 68-1 USTC 9394	6.2(a)
Universal Church of Jesus Christ, Inc. v. Commissioner, 55 T.C.M. (CCH) 144 (1988)	9.7
University of Maryland Physicians v. Commissioner, 41 T.C.M. 732 (1981)	12.1(e)
Urbanek v. U.S., 52 A.F.T.R. 2d 83-5231, 83-1 USTC, *aff'd.,* 731 F.2d 870 (Fed. Cir. 1984)	7.1(c)
Utah County v. Intermountain Health Care, Inc., 709 P.2d (1985)	10.2(mm)
Vaughn v. U.S., 740 F.2d 941 (Fed. Cir. 1984)	12.3(b)
Verhagen v. Olarte, 1989 WL 146265 (S.D.N.Y. 1989), *reargument denied,* 1990 WL 41730 (S.D.N.Y. 1990)	23.6
Verville v. Elderly Hous. Corp., Section 504 Complaint No. 05-89-02-007-370	23.3(c)
Village North, Inc. v. State Tax Comm'n. of Missouri, 799 S.W.2d 197 (1990)	10.2(t)
Village of Belle Terre v. Boraas, 416 U.S. 1 (1974)	25.1
Wagner v. Fair Acres Geriatric Ctr., 49 F.3d 1002 (3d Cir. 1995)	23.3(d)
Waldo v. Central Indiana Lutheran Retirement Home, S.D. Ind., (Nov. 16, 1979) 1980 (CCH) Fed. Sec. L. Rep. 97,680	24.2
Weinstein v. Cherry Oaks Retirement Community, 917 P.2d 336 (Colo. Ct. App. 1996)	23.3(d)(2)
Wardwell v. Commissioner, 301 F.2d 632 (8th Cir. 1962)	9.13
Washington Athletic Club v. United States, 614 F.2d 670 (9th Cir. 1980)	7.3(b)
Westminster-Canterbury of Hampton Roads, Inc. v. City of Virginia Beach, 385 S.E.2d 561 (1989)	10.2(oo)
White Egret Condominiums v. Franklin, 379 So. 2d 346 (Fla. 1979)	23.2(c)
William K. Warren Medical Research Ctr., Inc. v. Paynes County Bd. of Equalization, 905 P.2d 824 (Okla. Ct. App. 1994)	10.2(ee)
Williams Home, Inc. v. United States, 540 F. Supp. 310 (W.D. Va., 1982)	9.11
Wolford v. Lewis, 860 F. Supp. 1123 (S.D. W.Va. 1994)	23.3(a)(3), 23(b)(1)
Woodstown Borough v. Friends Home, 12 N.J. Tax 197 (1992)	10.2(y)
Woolfolk v. Duncan, 872 F. Supp. 1381 (E.D. Pa. 1995)	23.3(b)(2)
World Family Corp. v. Commission, 81 T.C. 958 (1983)	9.12(a)
Wyndemere Retirement Community v. Department of Revenue, 654 N.E.2d 608 (Ill. App. Ct.), *reb'g. den.,* 660 N.E.2d 1282 (Ill. 1995)	10.2(k)
Yakima First Baptist Homes v. Gray, 510 P.2d 243 (Wash. 1973)	10.2(pp)
Yorgason v. County Bd. of Equalization, 714 P.2d 653 (1986)	10.2(mm)

Internal Revenue Service Rulings

Revenue Ruling	Section Number
54–430; 1954–2 C.B. 101	9.13
55–37; 1955–1 C.B. 347	6.1(c), 7.4
55–316; 1955–1 C.B. 312	7.2(b)
55–449; 1955–2 C.B. 599	9.12(a)
56–185; 1956–1 C.B. 202	9.6
58–17; 1958–1 C.B. 11	6.2(a)
58–303; 1958–1 C.B. 61	9.13
60–76; 1960–1 C.B. 296	7.2(b)
60–85; 1960–1 C.B. 181	6.1(b)
60–135; 1960–1 C.B. 298	6.1(c)
61–72; 1961–1 C.B. 188	9.4, 9.5
62–177; 1962–2 C.B. 89	7.1(c), 7.2(b)
62–178; 1962–2 C.B. 91	7.1(c), 7.2(b)
63–20; 1963–1 C.B. 24	15.6(e)
64–31; 1964–1 C.B. 300	7.1(d), 7.2(b)
64–118; 1964–1 C.B. 182	7.1(d)
64–231; 1964–2 C.B. 139	9.3(a), 9.4
66–347; 1966–2 C.B. 196	6.2(a)
67–185; 1967–1 C.B. 70	6.1(c)
67–246; 1967–2 C.B. 104	9.14
68–17; 1968–1 C.B. 247	9.5(a)
68–387; 1968–2 C.B. 112	7.2(b)
68–525; 1968–2 C.B. 112	6.1(c)
68–655; 1968–2 C.B. 213	9.5(a)
69–76; 1969–1 C.B. 56	7.2(b)
69–267; 1969–1 C.B. 160	9.12(a)
69–268; 1969–1 C.B. 160	9.12(a)
69–269; 1969–1 C.B. 160	9.12(a)
69–281; 1969–1 C.B. 155	7.1(d)
69–463; 1969–2 C.B. 131	12.1(b)
69–464; 1969–2 C.B. 132	12.1(b)
69–545; 1969–2 C.B. 117	9.6
70–535; 1970–2 C.B. 117	9.9, 12.1(d)
70–585; 1970–2 C.B. 115	9.5(a),(b)
70–607; 1970–2 C.B. 9	7.1(c),(d)
71–299; 1971–2 C.B. 218	6.1(b)
71–529; 1971–2 C.B. 234	9.9
72–102; 1972–1 C.B. 49	7.1(d)

Revenue Ruling	Section Number
72–124; 1972–1 C.B. 145	7.1(d), 7.2(c), 9.3(a),(b), 9.4, 9.5(a), 9.5(b), 9.6, 9.9, 9.12(a), 10.1, 10.2(p), 12.1(b), (e), 12.3(b), 15.4(g)
72–147; 1972–1 C.B. 147	9.5(a)
72–209; 1972–1 C.B. 148	9.6
72–266; 1972–1 C.B. 227	7.1(c)
72–369; 1972–2 C.B. 245	9.9
72–506; 1972–2 C.B. 106	9.13
73–549; 1973–2 C.B. 17	6.1(b)
74–17; 1974–1 C.B. 130	7.1(d)
74–99; 1974–1 C.B. 131	7.1(d)
74–197; 1974–1 C.B. 143	12.1(b)
74–241; 1974–1 C.B. 68	7.2(b)
74–563; 1974–2 C.B. 38	7.1(d)
74–607; 1974–2 C.B. 149	6.1(b)
75–198; 1975–1 C.B. 157	9.9
75–302; 1975–2 C.B. 86	6.1(c)
75–303; 1975–2 C.B. 87	6.2(c)
75–370; 1975–2 C.B. 25	7.1(d)
75–371; 1975–2 C.B. 52	7.1(d)
75–385; 1975–2 C.B. 205	9.9
75–494; 1975–2 C.B. 214	7.1(d)
76–106; 1976–1 C.B. 71	6.1(c)
76–244; 1976–1 C.B. 155	9.9
76–408; 1976–2 C.B. 145	9.5(a)
76–481; 1976–2 C.B. 82	6.1(c)
77–3; 1977–1 C.B. 140	9.5(a)
77–246; 1977–2 C.B. 190	9.9
77–260; 1977–2 C.B. 466	6.1(b)
78–41; 1978–1 C.B. 148	15.2
79–18; 1979–1 C.B. 194	9.3(a), 9.5(a),(b), 9.12(a)
79–137; 1979–1 C.B. 118	7.3(a)
79–222; 1979–2 C.B. 236	12.1(b)
79–300; 1979–2 C.B. 112	19.5
80–63; 1980–1 C.B. 116	7.1(d)
81–28; 1981–1 C.B. 328	9.6
81–61; 1981–1 C.B. 355	9.12(a)

Revenue Ruling	Section Number
81-62; 1981-1 C.B. 355	9.12(a)
83-51; 1983-1 C.B. 48	7.4
83-153; 1983-2 C.B. 48	9.11
83-157; 1983-2 C.B. 94	9.6
84-43; 1984-1 C.B. 27	7.1(c), (d), 7.4
85-1; 1985-1 C.B. 178	9.5(a)
85-2; 1985-1 C.B. 178	9.5(a)
85-132; 1985-2 C.B. 182	7.1(d), 7.2(d)
85-147; 1985-2 C.B. 86	7.2(b)
87-41; 1987-1 C.B. 296	13.4(a)
88-76; 1998-2 C.B. 360	12.1 (c)
90-36; 1990-1 C.B. 59	7.2(c)
93-72; 1993-34 I.R.B.	6.2(c)
94-18; 1994-13 I.R.B. 18	6.2(b)(3)
95-11; 1995-5 I.R.B. 45	6.2(b)(4), 6.2(b)(5)
Announcement 95-25; 1995-14 I.R.B. 11	9.1(b)
Announcement 95-38; 1995-20 I.R.B. 21	9.12(c)
97-13; 1997-5 I.R.B. 18	15.2
97-42; I.R.B. 1997-33	19.8
97-57; I.R.B. 1997-52	6.2(b)(4)

Revenue Procedure/Notice	Section Number
71-21; 1971-2 C.B. 549	6.1(b)
75-21; 1975-1 C.B. 715	12.3(b)
75-28; 1975-1 C.B. 752	12.3(b)
76-30; 1976-2 C.B. 647	12.3(b)
79-48; 1979-2 C.B. 529	12.3(b)
80-27; 1980-1 C.B. 677	9.7
81-71; 1981-2 C.B. 731	12.3(b)
82-14; 1982-1 C.B. 459	12.1(e), 15.2
82-15; 1982-1 C.B. 460	12.1(e), 15.2
82-26; 1982-1 C.B. 476	15.6(e)
86-23	9.7
88-120; 1988-2 C.B. 454	9.14
89-1; 1989-3 C.B. 761	7.1(c)
89-34; 1989-20 I.R.B.145	9.12(a)
89-43; 1989-1 C.B. 213	27.2(c)
89-51; 1989-36 I.R.B. 19	9.12(a)

Revenue Procedure/Notice	Section Number
90-12; 1990-8 I.R.B.	9.14
90-27; 1990-1 C.B. 514	9.14
93-17; 1993-1 C.B. 84	15.4(g)
93-19; 1993-11 I.R.B. 52	15.2, 9.14
93-23; 1993-1 C.B. 180	9.14
94-54; 1994-2 C.B. 87	19.8(a)
96-32; 1996-1 C. B. 177	9.5(a)
96-46; 1996-2 C.B. 40	19.8(a)
97-13; I.R.B. 1997-16, 4	12.1(e)
Notice 86-20	14.2(d)
Notice 89-1; 1989-2 I.R.B. 10	19.8(c)
Notice 89-6; 1989-2 I.R.B. 13	19.8(b)
Notice 90-41; 1990-26 I.R.B. 7	9.12(c)
Notice 95-15; 1995-15 I.R.B. 22	9.14

Private Letter Ruling/ Technical Advice Memorandum	Section Number
7718008	9.7
7733070	9.12(a)
7820058	12.1(b)
7823072	9.5(b)
7852009	6.1(b)
7916068	9.4
7948104	9.6
8022085	9.3(a)
8025132	9.12(c)
8030105	9.3(b)
8034068	7.2(b)
8101009	9.5(a), (b)
8111030	12.1(c)
8116121	12.1(c)
8117221	9.3(b), 9.12(c), 10.2(p)
8134021	9.12(a), (b), 12.1(d)
8138024	12.1(d)
8201072	9.12(a), 12.1(b)
8206093	12.1(b)
8221134	6.1(c)
8226146	12.1(b)
8232035	12.1(b), (d)

Private Letter Ruling/ Technical Advice Memorandum	Section Number	Private Letter Ruling/ Technical Advice Memorandum	Section Number
8243212	12.1(b)	8818041	9.12(a)
8301003	9.12(a)	8821044	12.1(c)
8303019	12.1(c)	8821062	9.12(a)
8312129	9.12(a)	8830038	9.12(a)
8326113	6.1(b), (c)	8831004	6.2(b)
8405083	9.3 (a)	8832016	9.12(a)
8417054	12.1(b)	8833038	12.1(b)
8425129	12.1(b), (e)	8835034	9.9
8427078	9.6	8836060	9.12(a)
8427105	9.6	8837022	7.3(c)
8449070	12.1(b)	8837053	9.12(a)
8502009	6.1(c)	8839073	13.4(a)
8502309	6.1(c)	8840037	13.4(a)
8506116	9.11	8845020	9.12(a)
8510068	9.6	8845049	13.4(a)
8517006	7.2(b)	8850054	9.12(a)
8521055	12.1(b)	8851030	9.13
8534089	9.6	8912042	9.12(a)
8545063	12.1(b)	8915023	13.4(a)
8616095	9.6	8920003	19.8(b)
8622017	6.2(b)	8920055	9.12(a)
8630005	6.1(c)	8921035	19.8(b)
8638052	6.2(b)	8922065	9.12(a)
8641037	6.1(c)	8925069	9.12(a)
8651027	6.1(c)	8927061	9.12(a), 12.1(b)
8715058	9.12(a)	8930023	6.1(c)
8722059	6.2(b)	8930024	6.1(c)
8722082	9.3(a), (b)	8941006	9.12(a)
8748026	6.1(c)	8941007	9.12(a)
8752008	9.12(a)	8941012	9.12(a)
8801067	9.5(b)	8941015	9.12(a)
8806017	13.4(b)	8941061	9.12(a)
8807007	9.12(a)	8941073	9.12(a)
8807049	9.12(a)	8941082	9.12(a)
8808082	9.12(a)	8941083	9.12(a)
8813024	19.8(a)	8945036	19.8(b)
8817039	12.1(b)	8946079	7.1(c)
8817051	9.12(a)	8949036	7.1(c)

Private Letter Ruling/ Technical Advice Memorandum	Section Number	Private Letter Ruling/ Technical Advice Memorandum	Section Number
8952001	6.2(b)	9438039	9.12(a)
9001036	9.3(a), (b)	9501037	9.6
9009038	9.4, 9.12(a)	9501040	9.6
9014050	9.12(a)	9517029	12.1(c)
9023091	12.1(d)	9518014	12.1(b)(1)
9026033	7.1(c)	9521001	6.2(b)(5)
9035075	7.2(b)	9540067	9.12(a)
9039011	7.3(a)	9552021	9.12(a)
9107030	9.12(a)	9607012	19.6
9114031	9.12(a)	9608006	9.12(a)
9124030	15.4(g)	9609012	9.6
9131003	6.2(b)	9615031	9.12(a)
9141011	9.13	9617053	9.12(a)
9147017	12.1(c)	9619024	9.7
9210032	9.6	9623011	9.6
9213027	9.12(a)	9729018	9.12(a)
9214031	9.3(a)	9729019	9.12(a)
9220053	9.12(a)	9729020	9.12(a)
9225041	9.3(a)	9729021	9.12(a)
9227030	15.4(g)	9729022	9.12(a)
9234042	9.12(a)	9735002	6.2(a)(2)
9235056	9.12(a)	9735047	9.6(a)
9241055	9.6, 9.12(a)	9736039	12.1
9246006	6.1(b), 6.2(a)(2)		
9247003	8.2(a)		
9252015	6.2(a), 6.2(b)(2), 6.2(b)(3)	**General Counsel Memorandum**	**Section Number**
		9.5(a)	33671
9307027	9.12(a)	37019	6.1(b)
9308034	12.1(b)	37101	9.3(a), (b)
9311034	9.5(a), 12.1(c)	37464	7.2(c)
9315020	7.1(d)	37852	12.1(b)
9315021	9.12(a), 12.1(d)	39326	12.1(c)
9318048	9.3(b), 9.9, 9.12(a)	39487	7.1(d), 9.3(b), 9.5(b), 12.1(d)(e)
9322024	19.8(a)	39735	9.6, 9.12(a)
9349032	12.1(c)	39862	9.1(B), 12.1(b), 13.2(B)
9405004	9.6, 9.12(a)		
9423001	9.13		

Federal Statutes

Internal Revenue Code Section	Section Number
25	8.3
42	8.3, 19.8(a)
42(b)	19.8(a)
42(c)(6)	19.8(a)
42(d)(2)	19.8(a)
42(e)(j), (n)	19.8
42(g)(2)(B)(iii)	19.8(b)
42(h)(3)	19.8(a)
42(h)(6)	19.8(a)
48(g)	15.2
103	12.2(b), 15.1, 15.6(d)
103(b)	15.1, 15.4(a)
105(h)	13.4(b)
108	8.3
121	7.1(d), 7.2(b)
125	13.4(b)
141(b)	12.1(e)
142(a)	12.2(b)
142(d)	12.2(b), 15.3
143	8.3
145	15.2
145(a)	12.1(e)
145(d)	15.2, 15.2(b)
146	15.3
147(b)	15.2, 15.4(b)
147(f)	15.4(c)
147(g)	15.4(d)
148(a), (c), (d), (f)	15.4(a)
148(b)	15.6(f)
149(d)	15.4(f)
163	7.1(d), 7.3(c)(3)
164	7.1(d)
168	8.2(a), 8.3
168(b), (c)	12.2(a)
168(g), (h), (j)	12.2(b)
170	9.11, 9.13, 9.14
170(b)	9.7

Internal Revenue Code Section	Section Number
183	19.5
213	28.7(h)
213(a)	6.1(c)
214(f)	10.2(d)
216(a), (b)	7.2(a), (b)
219	27.3(c)
262	7.1(d)
368(c)	12.1(d)
401	13.4(b)
410	13.4(b)
414(b)	13.4(b)
414(c), (m), (n)	13.4(b)
416	13.4(b)
416(c)(2)	13.4(b)
451(a)	6.1(b)
465(a), (b), (c)	8.2(b)
469	8.2(a)
469(c), (h), (i), (j)	8.2(a)
469(c)(1)	8.2(a)
469(c)(7)	8.2(a), 8.3
469(h)(1)	8.2(a)
482	12.1(c)
501(c)	9.14
501(c)(2)	8.3, 12.1(c)
501(c)(3)	9.1(a), 9.2(a),(b), 9.5(a), 9.6, 9.7, 9.12(a), 9.14, 9.15, 10.2(d), 10.2(h), 10.2(u), 12.1(a),(b), 12.2(b), 15.1, 15.2, 15.2(a), (b), 15.3, 15.4(f)
501(c)(4)	7.1(d), 9.1(b), 9.2(b), 9.6, 9.12(a), 9.15, 12.2(b)
501(c)(7)	7.1(d)
501(c)(25)	8.3, 12.1(c)
501(m)	9.6, 9.9, 9.12(a)
501(m)(3)	9.6, 9.12(a)
502(b)(1)	12.1(c)
505	13.4(b)

Internal Revenue Code Section	Section Number	Internal Revenue Code Section	Section Number
509(a)(1), (2), (3)	9.11	6714	8.3
511–514	9.12(a)	7701(e)(1), (5)	12.2(b)
512	8.3	7872	6.2(b)
512(B)	8.3, 9.14		

Internal Revenue Code Section	Section Number	Other U.S. Code Sections	Section Number
512(b)(1)	9.12(b), (c), 12.1(b), (d)	12 U.S.C. 1451	14.2(e)
512(b)(3)	9.12(b), 12.1(c)	12 U.S.C. 1701	22.5(a)
512(b)(4)	9.12(c)	12 U.S.C. 1701q	14.4(a), 22.4(a), (b),
512(b)(5)	12.1(d)	12 U.S.C. 1701q(d)(4)(A), (B), and (C)	23.3(c)
512(b)(13)	12.1(c), (d)	12 U.S.C. 1701q(g)(1)	22.4(a)
512(c)	9.14, 12.1(b)	12 U.S.C. 1701q(j)(6)	22.6(e)
514	8.3	12 U.S.C. 1705	22.5(b)
514(a), (b)	9.12(c)	12 U.S.C. 1715(a)	22.3
514(c)(9)	9.12(c)	12 U.S.C. 1715(b)(6)	2.3(c), 14.2(d),
528	9.12		22.3
528(b), (c), (d)	7.1(d), 9.10	12 U.S.C. 1715(w)(d)	14.2(d), 22.3
643	6.1(b)	12 U.S.C. 1715l	14.2(d)
651	6.1(b)	12 U.S.C. 1715n	14.2(d)
661	6.1(b)	12 U.S.C. 1715n(f)	14.2(d)(3a)
664	9.13	12 U.S.C. 1715w	22.3
673–675	6.1(b)	12 U.S.C. 1715w(d)	14.2(d)(3)
676	6.1(b)	12 U.S.C. 1715y	14.2(d)
816(b)	27.2(c)	12 U.S.C. 1715z–1	9.3(a)
856(h)	8.3	12 U.S.C. 1715z–20(g)	27.3(b)
1014	7.1(d)	12 U.S.C. 1717	14.2(e)
1017	8.3	12 U.S.C. 1721(g)	14.2(e)
1034	6.1(c)(2)	12 U.S.C. 17511	14.2(d)
1245(a)	12.2(a)	15 U.S.C. 1	13.3
1274(d)	6.2(b)	15 U.S.C. 2	13.3
2001	7.1(d)	15 U.S.C. 13–13c	13.3
2010	7.1(d)	15 U.S.C. 77a et seq.	19.3
2522(a), (c)	9.13	15 U.S.C. 77b(1)	24.1
3506(a)	13.4(a)	15 U.S.C. 3601–3616	7.1(c)
4940 et seq.	9.11	19 U.S.C. 151 et seq.	13.4(c)
4958	9.2(b), 9.15	29 U.S.C. 201 et seq.	13.4(c)
6033(b)(9)	9.14	29 U.S.C. 794	23.3(d)
6104(e)	9.14	42 U.S.C. 291	23.4
6110(j)(3)	6.1(b), 12.1(b)	42 U.S.C. 300e et seq.	20.6
6113	9.14	42 U.S.C. 300k et seq.	20.2(a)
6115	8.3		
6711	9.14		

Other U.S. Code Sections	Section Number
42 U.S.C. 300m-6	20.2(a)
42 U.S.C. 300n(5)	20.2(a)
42 U.S.C. 1320a-7b(d)	132(b), 235(b)
42 U.S.C. 1381 et seq.	26.4(a)
42 U.S.C. 1382e(e)	204(c)
42 U.S.C. 1395	26.3(b)
42 U.S.C. 1395cc	20.3(a)
42 U.S.C. 1395f	20.5
42 U.S.C. 1395i-3	20.3
42 U.S.C. 1395ss	27.1
42 U.S.C. 1395x(m), (n), (o)	20.5
42 U.S.C. 1396	26.3(b)
42 U.S.C. 1396(a)(10)	20.5
42 U.S.C. 1396(a)23	23.5(a)
42 U.S.C. 1396a(a)(17)	26.3(b)
42 U.S.C. 1396n(c)	26.3(c)
42 U.S.C. 1396n(c)(4)	26.3(c)
42 U.S.C. 1396n(d)	20.5, 26.3(c)
42 U.S.C. 1396p-(c)(1)	26.3(b)
42 U.S.C. 1396r	20.3(a)
42 U.S.C. 1396r(e)	20.3, 20.3(a)
42 U.S.C. 1396r-5(c), (f)(2)	26.3(b)
42 U.S.C. 1396t	26.3(c)
42 U.S.C. 1397 et seq.	26.4(c)
42 U.S.C. 1437e	2.3(b)
42 U.S.C. 1437o	14.4(d), (e)
42 U.S.C. 1452b	14.3(b)
42 U.S.C. 2000-a(e)	23.3(b)
42 U.S.C. 2000d	23.6
42 U.S.C. 3001	9.3(a), 26.4(b)
42 U.S.C. 3601-3631	7.1(c), 23.3(a)
42 U.S.C. 3604	23.2(b), 23.4, 23.6
42 U.S.C. 3604(f)	23.3(a)
42 U.S.C. 3607	23.4
42 U.S.C. 3607	23.4
42 U.S.C. 3607(a)	23.2(b)
42 U.S.C. 3607(b)(1)	23.3(a)
42 U.S.C. 5301 et seq.	14.4(c)
42 U.S.C. 5318	14.4(b)

Other U.S. Code Sections	Section Number
42 U.S.C. 5320	14.4(b)
42 U.S.C. 6101-6107	23.2(a)
42 U.S.C. 6103(b)	23.2(a)
42 U.S.C. 8001-8011	22.4(c)
42 U.S.C. 12102(2)	23.3(b)
42 U.S.C. 12111 et seq.	23.3(b)
42 U.S.C. 12181(7)	23.3(b)
42 U.S.C. 12182	23.3(b)
42 U.S.C. 12183(a)	23.3(b)
42 U.S.C. 12187	23.3(b)
42 U.S.C. 12188(a), (b)	23.3(b)
42 U.S.C. 12189(9)	23.3(b)
42 U.S.C. 12201(c)	2.3(b)
42 U.S.C. 13601 et seq.	23.2(a), 23.2(c)
42 U.S.C. 13631	22.6(e)
42 U.S.C. 13632	22.6(e)

Public Law	Section Number
P.L. 90-364	15.1
P.L. 93-383	22.4(a)
P.L. 93-641	20.2(a)
P.L. 94-566	2.3(c), 20.4(c)
P.L. 95-557	14.2(e), 22.4(e)
P.L. 96-265	27.1
P.L. 96-399	7.1(c)
P.L. 98-181	14.2(d), 22.3, 22.6(c)
P.L. 98-369	6.2(b)
P.L. 99-121	6.2(b)
P.L. 99-514	6.1(b), 8.2(a), 12.1(e), 12.2(a), (b)
P.L. 99-660	20.2(a), (b)
P.L. 100-203	20.3(a)
P.L. 100-203	9.2
P.L. 100-360	28.3(b)
P.L. 100-647	15.2
P.L. 101-336	23.3(b)
P.L. 101-508	26.2(a)

Public Law	Section Number
P.L. 101–625	14.3(b), 14.4(d), (e), 22.4(a), (c)
P.L. 102–550	2.3(c), 14.2(d), 14.2(d)(3), 14.2(d)(3a), 22.1, 22.3, 22.4(c), 23.3(c), 26.2(a)
P.L. 103–66	8.2(a), 8.3, 19.8(c), 26.2(a), 26.3(b)
P.L. 104–120	14.2(d)(7)
P.L. 104–191	26.3(b)
P.L. 105–33	15.2, 26.3(c), 27.2(c)(2), 27.3(b)
P.L 105–34	6.1(c)(2)

Federal Acts by Name	Section Number
Americans with Disabilities Act	23.3(b)(3), 23.3(b)(4), 23.3(d)(2)
Balanced Budget Act of 1997	28.12
Cranston-Gonzalez National Affordable Housing Act	14.4(a), 22.4(a)
Fair Housing Act	23.3(a)(3), 23.3(b)(3), 23.3(d)(2)
§8	19.8(b), 22.6(d), 23.3(c)
§202	22.4(c), 22.6(d), 23.2(a), 23.3
§202/8	22.5(a), 22.6(b), (c)
§213	14.2(d)
§221	22.5(a)
§221(d)(3)	14.2(d), 22.2(a), 22.6(c), (d)
§221(d)(4)	14.2(d)
§221(d)(5)	22.6(d)
§223(f)	14.2(d), 22.2(a), (b), 22.6(a)
§231	22.2(a), 22.5(a), 22.6(c), (d)

Federal Acts by Name	Section Number
§232	14.2(d), (e), 22.2(a), (b), 22.6
§236	22.5(a)
§312	14.3(b)
§515(b)	10.2(kk)
§521	10.2(kk)
Fair Housing Amendments Act of 1988	23.2(b)
Health Insurance Portability and Accountability Act of 1996	28.11
Hill-Burton Act	23.4, 23.6
Housing and Community Development Act of 1987	14.2(d)(3a)
Housing and Community Development Act of 1992	14.2(d)(3), 14.2(d)(3a), 22.1
Housing Opportunity Program Extension Act of 1996	14.2(d)(7)
Low-Income Housing Preservation and Resident Homeownership Act of 1990	14.2(d)(7)
National Labor Relations Act	13.4(c)
Older American's Act of 1965	9.3(a), 26.4(b)
Omnibus Budget Reconciliation Act of 1987	20.3(a)
Rehabilitation Act of 1973	23.3(b)(3), 23.4
Revenue Act of 1987	
§10511	9.14
§10711(a)	9.14
§10711(b)	9.14
§10712	9.14
§10713	9.14
§10714	9.14
Revenue Reconciliation Act of 1993	8.3, 9.12(c), 9.14
Social Security Act	
§1616(e)	22.3
§1909(d)	23.5(b)
Taxpayer Bill of Rights	9.2(b), 9.15

Federal Regulations

Code of Federal Regulations	Section Number	Code of Federal Regulations	Section Number
24 C.F.R. Part 109	23.6	24 C.F.R. 705	22.2(a)
24 C.F.R. Part 146	23.2(a)	24 C.F.R. 850	14.4(d)
24 C.F.R. 146.7	23.2(a)	24 C.F.R. Part 880	14.3(a), 22.4(b), 22.6(b)
24 C.F.R. 146.13	23.2(a)		
24 C.F.R. 203(a)	22.2(a)	24 C.F.R. Part 881	22.6(b)
24 C.F.R. 203.45	14.2(e)	24 C.F.R. Part 882	22.6(b)
24 C.F.R. 203.47	14.2(e)	24 C.F.R. Part 885	14.3(a), 22.4(a), (b)
24 C.F.R. 207.32a	14.2(d)	24 C.F.R. 885.610	23.3(a)
24 C.F.R. 213	14.2(d)	24 C.F.R. Part 889	14.4(a), 22.4(a)
24 C.F.R. Part 221	22.2(a)	24 C.F.R. 889.210	22.4(a)
24 C.F.R. 231	22.5(a)	24 C.F.R. Part 891, subpt. E	22.4(b)
24 C.F.R. Part 232	14.2(d)(3), 14.2(d)(3a), 22.3	24 C.F.R. 891.115	14.4(a)(2)
		24 C.F.R. 891.120(b)	22.4(a)
24 C.F.R. 232.30	14.2(d)(3)	24 C.F.R. 891.120(c)	22.4(a)
24 C.F.R. 232.32	14.2(d)(3)	24 C.F.R. 891.220	22.4(a)
24 C.F.R. 232.901 et seq.	14.2(d)(3a)	24 C.F.R. 891.505	22.4(b)
24 C.F.R. 232.902	14.2(d)(3a)	26 C.F.R. 1.103–17	15.4(e)
24 C.F.R. 232.903	14.2(d)(3a)	28 C.F.R. Part 36, App. B	23.3(d)(2)
24 C.F.R. 232.904	14.2(d)(3a)	28 C.F.R. 36, 36.104	23.3(b)
24 C.F.R. 234	14.2(d)	28 C.F.R. 36.104	23.3(b)
24 C.F.R. 236.1	22.5(b)	28 C.F.R. 36.208	23.3(b)
24 C.F.R. 246	22.6(a), (b)	28 C.F.R. 36.208(c)	23.3(b)
24 C.F.R. 246.5	22.6(a)	28 C.F.R. 36.301	23.3(b)
24 C.F.R. 246.6	22.6(a)	28 C.F.R. 36.302	23.3(b)
24 C.F.R. 246.12	22.6(a)	28 C.F.R. 36.302(c)	23.3(d)(2)
24 C.F.R. 246.21	22.6(a)	28 C.F.R. 36.303	23.3(b)
24 C.F.R. 247.3	22.6(b)	28 C.F.R. 36.304	23.3(b)
24 C.F.R. 247.4	22.6(b)	28 C.F.R. 36.305	23.3(b)
24 C.F.R. Part 248	14.2(d)	28 C.F.R. 36.307	23.3(b)
24 C.F.R. 251	14.2(d), 22.2(a)	28 C.F.R. 36.308	23.3(b)
24 C.F.R. 251.703(c)	22.2(a)	28 C.F.R. 36.310	23.3(b)
24 C.F.R. 251.704	22.2(a)	28 C.F.R. 36.310(a)(2)	23.3(b)
24 C.F.R. 252	14.2(d)	28 C.F.R. 36.401, 402	23.3(b)
24 C.F.R. 255	14.2(d)	29 C.F.R. 791.2	13.4(c)
24 C.F.R. 255.233	22.2(a), (b)	29 C.F.R. Part 1630	23.3(b)
24 C.F.R. 278	22.6(d)	29 C.F.R. 1910.1030 et seq.	23.3(d)
24 C.F.R. Part 510	14.3(b)	42 C.F.R. 52.112(a)	23.4
24 C.F.R. 570	14.4(c)	42 C.F.R. 52.112(c)	23.6
24 C.F.R. Part 700	22.4(c)	42 C.F.R. 122.412	20.2(a)
24 C.F.R. 704(d)	22.2(a)	42 C.F.R. 123.401	20.2(a)

Federal Register	Section Number
59 Fed. Reg. 22223	22.4(c)
59 Fed. Reg. 33362	23.3(a)
60 Fed. Reg. 2557	8.2(a)
60 Fed. Reg. 2658	23.3(a)(2)
60 Fed. Reg. 11831	22.6
60 Fed. Reg. 33262	20.3(a)(3)
60 Fed. Reg. 43322	23.2(c)
60 Fed. Reg. 47260	22.6(d)
60 Fed. Reg. 53126	9.14
60 Fed. Reg. 62209	9.14
60 Fed. Reg. 65660	9.7
61 Fed. Reg. 11956	14.4(a), 22.4(a)
61 Fed. Reg. 14380	23.6

State Statutes	Supp.
Alabama Code 22-21-20 et seq.	20.4(b)
Alaska Stat. 47.33.005 et seq.	20.4(b)
Alaska Stat. 47.60.030	10.2(a)
Alaska Stat. 47.60.080	10.2(a)
Ariz. Rev. Stat. Ann. 20-1801 et seq.	21.2
Ariz. Rev. Stat. Ann. 42-271(13)	10.2(c)
Ariz. Rev. Stat. Ann. 42-271 (A)(11), (12)	10.2(c)
Ark. Rev. Stat. Ann 20-10-213 et seq.	20.4(b)
Ark. Rev. Stat. Ann. 23-93-101 et seq.	21.2
Ark. Rev. Stat. Ann. 26-26-1206	10.2(b)
Cal. Civ. Code 51	23.2(d)
Cal. Civ. Code 51.2, 51.3	23.2(d), 25.1
Cal. Gov. Code 15459	15.6
Cal. Gov. Code 65970	25.2
Cal. Health & Safety Code 436 et seq.	17.4
Cal. Health & Safety Code 436.82	18.3
Cal. Health & Safety Code 1418.8	20.3(a)(3)
Cal. Health & Safety Code 1424(b)	29.2(b)
Cal. Health & Safety Code 1424(c)	29.2(b)
Cal. Health & Safety Code 1424(d)	29.2(b)
Cal. Health & Safety Code 1569.2 et seq.	20.4(b)
Cal. Health & Safety Code 1770 et seq.	21.2
Cal. Health & Safety Code 1775(b)	7.1(c)
Cal. Health & Safety Code 33335, 33760, 33760.5, 51335, 52080	15.6(f)

State Statutes	Supp.
Cal. Rev. & Tax Code 6363.6	10.2(d)
Cal. Stats. 1984, c. 1102 at 22, 1	10.2(d)
Colo. Rev. Stat. 7-80-503	12.1(c)
Colo. Rev. Stat. 12-13-101 et seq.	21.2
Colo. Rev. Stat. 25-27-101; 26-4.5-133 et seq.	20.4(b)
Colo. Rev. Stat. 30-28-133(4)(a)	25.2
Colo. Rev. Stat. 39-3-112(2)	10.2(e)
Colo. Rev. Stat. 39-3-112(2), (3)	10.2(e)
Colo. Rev. Stat. 39-3-112(3)(c)	10.2(e)
Conn. Gen. Stat. 12-81(7)	10.2(f)
Conn. Gen. Stat. 19a-490	20.4(b)
Conn. Gen. Stat. 19a-533	23.5(b)
Conn. Gen. Stat. 176-520 et seq.	21.2
Del. Rev. Code Ann. Ch. 46, 4601 et seq.	21.2
Del. Rev. Code Ann. Title 9, 8151-8156	10.2(g)
Del. Rev. Code Ann. Title 16, 1101 et seq.	20.4(b)
Fla. Stat. Ann. 196.1975	10.2(h)
Fla. Stat. Ann. 196.1975(1)	10.2(h)
Fla. Stat. Ann. 212.08(7)(m)	10.2(h)
Fla. Stat. Ann. 400.401 et seq.	20.4(b)
Fla. Stat. Ann. 651.011 et seq.	21.2
Fla. Stat. Ann. 608441	12.1(c)
Ga. Code Ann. 31-2-4 et seq.	20.4(b)
Ga. Code Ann. 33-45-1 et seq.	21.2
Hawaii Rev. Stat. 246-32(b)(2), (c)(2)	10.2(i)
Idaho Code 39-3301 et seq.	20.4(b)
Idaho Code 63-105C	10.2(j)
Idaho Code 67-2750 et seq.	21.2
Ill. Rev. Stat. Ch. 35, 200/15-65	10.2(k)
Ill. Rev. Stat. Ch. 111½, 4151-101 et seq.	20.4(b)
Ill. Rev. Stat. Ch. 210 40/1 et seq.	21.2
Ind. Code Ann. 6-1, 1-10-18.5(2)	10.2(l)
Ind. Code Ann. 6-2.1-3-20	10.2(l)
Ind. Code Ann. 24-2-4-1 et seq.	21.2
Iowa Code 135.C.1 et seq.	20.4(b)
Iowa Code 427.1(9)	10.2(m)
Iowa Code 523.D.1 et seq.	21.2
Kansas Stat. Ann. 16-1101 et seq.	21.2
Kansas Stat. Ann. 39-923 et seq.	20.4(b)
Kentucky Rev. Stat. Ann. 216B.010 et seq.	20.4(b)

State Statutes	Supp.
Louisiana Rev. Stat. 40:2151	20.4(b)
Louisiana Rev. Stat. 51:2171 et seq.	21.2
Me. Rev. Stat. Ann. Tit. 22, 7901-A et seq.	20.4(b)
Me. Rev. Stat. Ann. Tit. 24-A, 6201 et seq.	21.2
Me. Rev. Stat. Ann. Tit. 36, 652(1)(A)	10.2(o)
Md. Code Ann. Art. 70B, 7 et seq.	21.2
Md. Code Ann. 708.4 et seq.	20.4(b)
Md. Tax, Property Code Ann. 7-202	10.2(p)
Md. Tax, Property Code Ann. 7-206	10.2(p)
Md. Tax, Property Code Ann. 7-502	10.2(p)
Mass. Ann. Laws Ch. 93, 76	21.2
Mass. Ann. Laws Ch. 109, 1 et seq.	20.4(b)
Mich. Comp. Laws Ann. 211.7d	10.2(q)
Mich. Comp. Laws Ann. Title 14, Ch. 15, 20301 et seq.	20.4(b)
Mich. Comp. Laws Ann. Title 14, Ch. 130, 544.801 et seq.	21.2
Minn. Stat. Ann. 80D §§80D.01 et seq.	21.2
Minn. Stat. Ann. 272.02	10.2(r)
Minn. Stat Ann. 459, 144B.01 et seq., 157.01 et seq.	20.4(b)
Miss. Code Ann. 43-11-1	20.4(b)
Mo. Ann. Stat. 137.100(5)	10.2(t)
Mo. Ann. Stat. Title XXIV, Ch. 376, 376.900 et seq.	21.2
Mo. Rev. Stat. 198.003 et seq.	20.4(b)
Mont. Code Ann. 15-6-201(1)(e) & (o)	10.2(u)
Mont. Code Stat. Ann. 50-5-101; 50-5-225 et seq.	20.4(b)
Mont. Legis. 123 (1991), S.B. 85	10.2(u)
Neb. Rev. Stat. 71-2017	20.4(b)
Nev. Rev. Stat. 361.086	10.2(w)
Nev. Rev. Stat. 449.017 et seq.	20.4(b)
N.H. Rev. Stat Ann. 72:23	10.2(x)
N.H. Rev. Stat. Ann. 151:1 et seq.	20.4(b)
N.H. Rev. Stat. Ann. Title XXXVII, Ch. 420-D	21.2
N.J. Stat. Ann. 40:55D-65g	25.1
N.J. Stat. Ann. 52:27-330 et seq.	21.2
N.J. Stat. Ann. 54:4-3.6	10.2(w), 10.2(y)
N.M. Stat. Ann. 24-17-1 et seq.	21.2, 20.4(b)

State Statutes	Supp.
N.Y. Comp. Codes & Regs Tit. 10, 670.3(c)(2)	23.5(b)
N.Y. Public Health Law Art. 46, 4600 et seq.	21.2
N.Y. Soc. Serv. Law, 461-1 et seq.	20.4(b)
N.C. Gen. Stat. 58-64-1 et seq.	21.2
N.C. Gen. Stat. 105-275(32)	10.2(bb)
N.C. Gen. Stat. 131D-2 et seq.	20.4(b)
N.D. Cent. Code, 23-09.3-01 et seq.	20.4(b)
N.D. Cent. Code, 57-02-08.8	10.2(cc)
Ohio Legis. 30, 1993 WL 5701.13	10.2(dd)
Ohio Rev. Code 173 §173.13	21.2
Ohio Rev. Code 3721.01 et seq.	20.4(b)
Ohio Rev. Code 5709.12	10.2(dd)
Ohio Rev. Code 5709.13	10.2(dd)
Ohio Rev. Code Ann. 5111.31	23.5(b)
Okla. Stat. Tit. 63, 1-819 et seq.	20.4(b)
Okla. Stat. Tit. 68, 2887	10.2(ee)
Or. Rev. Stat. 307.130	10.2(ff)
Or. Rev. Stat. 307.166(1)	10.2(ff)
Or. Rev. Stat. 443.400 et seq.	20.4(b)
Or. Tit. 10, Ch. 101, 101.010 et seq.	21.2
Pa. Stat. Ann. Tit. 27, 5020-204(a)	10.2(gg)
Pa. Stat. Ann. Tit. 40, 3201 et seq.	21.2
Pa. Stat. Ann. Tit. 62, 211 et seq.	20.4(b)
R.I. Gen. Laws 23-17.4-1 et seq.	20.4(b)
R.I. Gen. Laws 23-59-1 et seq.	21.2
R.I. Gen. Laws 44-3-3	10.2(hh)
S.C. Code 12-37-220.A	10.2(gg)
S.C. Code 37-11-10 et seq.	21.2
S.C. Code 40-35-10 et seq., 44-7-130, 44-7-260 et seq.	20.4(b)
S.D. Cod. Laws 10-4-9.3	10.2(jj)
S.D. Cod. Laws 34-12-1.1 et seq.	20.4(b)
Tenn. Stat. 4-3-1305 et seq.	21.2
Tenn. Stat. 67-5-207	10.2(kk)
Tenn. Code 68-11-201	20.4(b)
Tex. Health & Safety Code, 247.001 et seq.	20.4(b)
Tex. Tax Code 11.18(d)	10.2(ll)
Tex. Tit. 4, 246.001 et seq.	21.2
Utah Code Ann. 26-21-1 et seq.	20.4(b)
Utah Code Ann. 48-2(b)-116	12.1(c)

State Statutes	Supp.	State Statutes	Supp.
Vt. Stat. Ann. Part 4, Ch. 151, 8001 et seq.	21.2	Wash. Rev. Code 74.42.055	23.5(b)
Vt. Stat. Ann. Tit. 32, 3802(4)	10.2(nn)	Wash. Rev. Code 82.04.4289	10.2(pp)
Vt. Stat. Ann. Tit. 32, 3832(6)	10.2(nn)	Wash. Rev. Code 84.36.040(4)	10.2(pp)
Vt. Stat. Ann. Tit. 33, 710 et seq.	20.4(b)	Wash. Rev. Code 84.36.800	10.2(pp)
Va. Stat. 13.1–1023	12.1(c)	Wash. Rev. Code 84.36.805	10.2(pp)
Va. Stat. 63.1–172 et seq.	20.4(b)	Wis. Stat. 46.03, 50.01 et seq.	20.4(b)
Va. Stat. 4900 et seq.	21.2	Wis. Stat. 70.11(4)	10.2(rr)
W. Va. Code 11–3–9	10.2(qq)	Wis. Stat. 647.01 et seq.	21.2
W. Va. Code 16-5C-1 et seq.	20.4(b)	Wyo. Stat. 35–2–901 et seq.	20.4(b)
Wash. Rev. Code 7.38 and 74.39A et seq.	20.4(b)	Wyo. Stat. 1977 39–1–201	10.2(ss)
Wash. Rev. Code 70.38.015 et seq.	21.2		

Index

Using the CD-ROM

The CD-ROM can be used on a PC that runs Windows or on a Macintosh. You will need Adobe Acrobat Reader 3.0 and a CD-ROM drive. This CD-ROM contains an index to Volume II. To use this index you will need Adobe Acrobat Reader 3.0 with Acrobat Search.

If you have Adobe Acrobat Reader 3.0 or Adobe Acrobat Reader 3.0 with Search:

1. Insert the CD-ROM into your CD-ROM drive.
2. Open the WELCOME.PDF file located on the CD-ROM. The WELCOME.PDF file contains the table of contents and other information that will link you to the various chapters and document forms included on the CD-ROM. To access chapters or document forms, click on the desired chapter or document form to view it.

If you do not have Adobe Acrobat Reader 3.0 or would like to install Adobe Acrobat Reader 3.0 with Search:

1. Insert the CD-ROM into your CD-ROM drive.
2. Open the READER folder on the CD-ROM. Open the folder for your platform and then view the README file, which provides the complete installation instructions and system requirements.

Adobe Acrobat Reader 3.0 and Adobe Acrobat Reader 3.0 with Search also are available at Adobe's Web site: www.adobe.com.